LITERATURE CONNECTIONS
TO AMERICAN HISTORY, 7-12

LITERATURE CONNECTIONS TO AMERICAN HISTORY, 7-12

RESOURCES TO ENHANCE AND ENTICE

LYNDA G. ADAMSON

1998
Libraries Unlimited, Inc.
Englewood, Colorado

For Frank

LIBRARIES UNLIMITED, INC.
P. O. Box 6633
Englewood, CO 80155-6633
1-800-237-6124
www.lu.com

Production Editor: Stephen Haenel
Bibliography Copy Editor: Aviva Rothschild
Bibliography Proofreader: Ann Marie Damian
Layout and Design: Michael Florman

Library of Congress Cataloging-in-Publication Data

Adamson, Lynda G.
    Literature connections to American history, 7-12 : resources to enhance and entice / Lynda G. Adamson.
        xii, 624 p. 19x26 cm.
        Includes bibliographical references and index.
        ISBN 1-56308-503-8
        1. United States--History--Juvenile literature--Bibliography.
    2. United States--History--Juvenile fiction--Bibliography.
    3. United States--History--CD-ROM catalogs. 4. Unites States--History--Juvenile films--Catalogs. I. Title.
    E178.3.A28 1998
    016.973--dc21   97-19560
                                                                          CIP

CONTENTS

PREFACE

Studies show that people must respond emotionally to something in order to remember it.

If readers travel with Bright Morning in O'Dell's *Sing Down the Moon* as U.S. federal troops force her and her tribe to leave their canyon home and march on the Long Walk toward Fort Sumner where they will have to live enclosed and separated from their past, or if readers stand with the thirsty Cassie Logan in Taylor's *Let the Circle Be Unbroken* when an adult tells her she cannot drink at a whites-only court house water fountain, they will wonder how some laws can favor one group over another. By becoming angry at the helpless situations in which Bright Morning and Cassie find themselves, these readers remember the time and the place of the incidents.

Their responses might lead them to read further in additional sources about the government's treatment of other groups such as immigrants. They might want to know who entered the United States through Ellis Island and what fears they had when they arrived, often unable to speak English or sick from a long sea journey in steerage class. These vicarious experiences could even help readers empathize more readily with the difficulties of contemporary refugees or the hostility of people whose families have lived in America for many decades.

If a reader becomes interested in a topic, a character, or a time period and asks for books or multimedia about them, the adult consulted needs timely retrieval capabilities. I have attempted to fulfill that need. This resource connects historical fiction, biography, history trade books, CD-ROMs, and videotapes for individual grade levels within specific time periods and geographic areas. The books, CD-ROMs, and videotapes included have received at least one favorable review, are well written, or fit a category for which few resources are available. Some of the books and videotapes are award winners, and I have listed awards won at the end of the annotations. Some of the books are out-of-print but are still available in many libraries. Reprints of them, especially award winners, regularly become available in paper or under the imprint of another publisher.

When I first began this project, it was to link "good reads" in historical fiction, biography, and history trade books. That focus has continued throughout the creation of this annotated bibliography. I did not anticipate finding as many entries as appear in this resource, but the writing in both biography and history trade books has improved. For that reason, I have listed biographies about the same person by several different authors. I have not made a choice as to which is the "best," because each has a different focus. Authors of biography as literature try to make their subjects come alive, and the authors here have achieved this goal. The annotations in the final section attempt to include different facts about the biographical subjects instead of always identifying a sometimes elusive nuance of difference among the authors' writing styles and themes.

History trade books differ from history textbooks because their authors rarely use passive voice, and they rely heavily on diaries, letters, documents, or other references that tell about the people who lived during the time. Thus, readers might more often respond to these books than to history textbooks that seem to be filled with dull dates and incident inventories. Some of the history trade books included have more illustrations than text, but they can be valuable for enticing slow or unwilling readers to look for other books. These information books bridge the gap between nonillustrated books and videotapes.

The multimedia category covers CD-ROMs and videotapes. Because videotapes are more accessible for the classroom, or even for home use, I have omitted laser discs and filmstrips. But with computer use increasing in homes and schools, I have included favorably reviewed CD-ROMs or those on specific topics that will help readers find further information. Some of the more recent CD-ROMs have stunning pictures, film clips, and other attractions that may lead a viewer to books.

Because readers become interested in a variety of topics for many different reasons, the books in the historical fiction category listed in a specific grade level may or may not contain the names of those persons in the biographies, cover the variety of time periods in the history trade titles, or fulfill the traditional definition of "historical fiction." A specific correspondence of titles seems unnecessary. Andrew Jackson may not be named in O'Dells *Sing Down the Moon*, but his decisions as President permeate the book. The same reader might want more information about other people who believed that white settlers, not Native Americans, should inhabit and control the fertile lands of the West. The book lists, along with the annotations, will reveal other resources on these subjects. Additionally, I have broadened the definition of historical fiction to include books outside the readers' memory rather than just those books whose authors are writing about time periods prior to two or more generations. Children and young adults today do not know the significance of America's role in the Persian Gulf War, and many do not understand that Bosnia is an area of the world in which people have recently repeated crimes as heinous as the Holocaust. Thus, I have included some books that might loosely be termed "historical fiction" or "contemporary realistic fiction" because they will give readers an insight into a time separate from their own.

While doing the research for this reference, I realized that it should include as many good books or videotapes published since 1990 as possible, plus some highly regarded works from prior years. I hope that adults will find most of the recommended books on library shelves or can order them from a publisher. I have tried to include a wide range of titles so that the researcher will have choices if the first title selected from the resource is not readily available. My goal is for young readers to have emotional responses to the people who have made history so that they, as future world decision-makers, can better understand themselves and the times in which they live.

Many publishers have made this resource easier to create by sending me recent books. Their generosity saved me many hours of searching. I would like to list their names, but I fear omitting even one of them. During this intensive period of work, two individuals have helped make this book possible. Elena Rodriguez at Gunston Middle School in Arlington, Virginia, allowed me to raid her library shelves for many days. Without her excellent collection, I would not have been able to easily locate many of the books that I included. The other indispensable helper was my husband, who edited the text. Additionally, Stephen Haenel as well as other members of the editorial staff at Libraries Unlimited have offered excellent advice and aid in an effort to make this resource available.

INTRODUCTION

This resource divides naturally into two main parts. The first part lists authors and titles in the categories of historical fiction, biography, collective biography, history trade book, CD-ROM, and videotape within specific time periods according to grade levels. The second part contains annotated bibliographies of titles listed in the first part: books, CD-ROMs, and videotapes. The books, videotapes, and CD-ROMs merit inclusion because they have received favorable reviews, are well written, or are one of the few titles available on a particular subject, so the annotations are descriptive rather than evaluative.

The first part is divided into chapters based on chronological time periods. In each chapter, works appropriate for a particular grade level appear under that grade-level heading in their specific category of historical fiction, biography (including collective biography), history, and multimedia (CD-ROMs and videotapes). Books are alphabetized according to author's last name so the researcher can easily locate the annotation in the second part of the resource. CD-ROMs and videotapes are alphabetized in the second section according to their titles.

Some titles in the first part appear several different times. When a title about expansion into the West is suitable for grades seven through nine, the title appears under each grade level of seven, eight, and nine in the chapter titled "The Settling of the West, Native Americans, and Sea Journeys, 1775-1916." Other titles appear in different chapters because their settings, either fiction or fact, occur in more than one place or involve more than one time period. For example, people with long lives such as Benjamin Franklin span several time periods. Benjamin Franklin functioned as a contributing citizen in the colonies, during the American Revolution, and during the infancy of the United States—three distinct and important periods in the formation of the nation.

I have based grade-level choices on recommended grade levels in review sources or publisher catalogs. In some cases, when the grade levels seemed unusually low or high, I have adjusted them after evaluating the text and the subject matter.

In the section Grades Eleven and Twelve, I have listed books marketed for adults which are suitable for and might be of interest to high school students. Books which might interest middle and high school students who have reading levels lower than seventh grade appear in *Literature Connections to American History, K-6: Resources to Enhance and Entice.* Many of the biographical and historical subjects in this book are the same, but the content is less complex.

The chapter divisions correspond as nearly as possible to general time periods in the history of America. In the late eighteenth, the nineteenth, and the early twentieth centuries, three distinct groups were functioning within the area that has become the continental United States. Pioneers began traveling to the frontier, which kept moving west as they displaced more and more Native Americans. Immigrants began coming from Asia and Europe around 1815 and moved to any area in which they thought they could succeed. The third group remained within the borders of the United States and divided into two hostile factions—those who felt that slaves should be freed and women should have equal rights (abolitionists and suffragists) and those who wanted to maintain the status quo of Anglo white male supremacy. Therefore, I have divided these groups into three parallel but separate chapters even though their concerns may have overlapped. Those settling the West might have a connection to the Civil War, but most often they were more anxious about encounters with Native Americans. Immigrants had other difficulties in facing a new culture while retaining their own traditions, and their problems have continued to the present.

The annotations include such information as author, title, publisher, price, ISBN, paper imprint, and grade levels. The book prices are accurate at printing, based on publishers' catalogs and such library buying sources as *Books in Print* and the distributor Baker and Taylor. I have made a similar attempt to include sources for books and their paper imprints, if available. The range of grade levels appears at the end of each bibliographic entry.

For easiest access to this resource, researchers should find the time period of interest in the table of contents. Grade levels under the chapter listings will tell where to locate the book and multimedia categories. In the grade-level listings, researchers should select titles. They then should refer to the appropriate section of the second part of the book.

Researchers unsure of the dates of a particular historical event might want to skim the listings for the seventh or eighth grade level since these grade levels have more entries with titles referring to historical events than the other levels. After finding the correct time period, the researcher can then refer to the appropriate grade level to see if a book or multimedia source is available. If it is not, the researcher may be able to choose an appropriate title from the next highest or lowest grade-level categories. A final resource is the index, which lists all references to a particular subject.

NORTH AMERICA BEFORE 1600

GRADE SEVEN

Historical Fiction

Anderson. *A Williamsburg Household*
Baker. *Walk the World's Rim*
Bruchac. *Children of the Longhouse*
Dorris. *Sees Behind Trees*
Garland. *Cabin 102*
Garland. *Indio*
Gates. *Journey to Center Place*
Gear. *People of the Sea*
Hooks. *The Legend of the White Doe*
James. *Sing for a Gentle Rain*
O'Dell. *The King's Fifth*
Spinka. *White Hare's Horses*
Steele. *The Magic Amulet*
Vick. *Walker of Time*
Vick. *Walker's Journey Home*

Biography

McClard. *Hiawatha and the Iroquois League*

History

Avakian. *A Historical Album of Massachusetts*
Avakian. *A Historical Album of New York*
Ayer. *The Anasazi*
Barboza. *Door of No Return: The Legend of Gorée Island*
Berrill. *Mummies, Masks, & Mourners*
Beyer. *The Totem Pole Indians of the Northwest*
Brown. *Discovery and Settlement: 1490-1700*
Capek. *Murals: Cave, Cathedral, to Street*
Civilizations of the Americas
Cocke. *A Historical Album of Virginia*
Cocke. *A Historical Album of Washington*
Colman. *Toilets, Bathtubs, Sinks, and Sewers*
Corbishley. *Secret Cities*
Cordoba. *Pre-Columbian Peoples of North America*
Cush. *Disasters That Shook the World*
Deem. *How to Make a Mummy Talk*
Hakim. *The First Americans*
Hakim. *Making Thirteen Colonies*
Jacobs. *The Tainos: The People Who Welcomed Columbus*
Karl. *America Alive: A History*
Katz. *Breaking the Chains: African-American Slave Resistance*
Katz. *Exploration to the War of 1812: 1492-1814*
La Pierre. *Native American Rock Art*
Marrin. *Empires Lost and Won: The Spanish Heritage in the Southwest*
Medearis. *Come This Far to Freedom*
Monroe. *First Houses: Native American Homes and Sacred Structures*
Palmer. *The First Passage: Blacks in the Americas, 1502-1617*
Pascoe. *Mexico and the United States: Cooperation and Conflict*
Platt. *The Smithsonian Visual Timeline of Inventions*
San Souci. *N. C. Wyeth's Pilgrims*
Sattler. *The Earliest Americans*
Sattler. *Hominids: A Look Back at Our Ancestors*
Schouweiler. *The Lost Colony of Roanoke*
Smith. *Millions and Billions of Years Ago: Dating Our Earth and Its Life*
Stones and Bones: How Archaeologists Trace Human Origins
Time-Life. *Tribes of the Southern Woodlands*
Topper. *A Historical Album of New Jersey*
Ventura. *1492: The Year of the New World*
Warburton. *The Beginning of Writing*
Warren. *Cities in the Sand: The Ancient Civilizations of the Southwest*
Whitman. *Get Up and Go: American Road Travel*
Williams. *The Age of Discovery*
Wills. *A Historical Album of California*
Wills. *A Historical Album of Florida*
Wills. *A Historical Album of Illinois*

Multimedia
CD-ROM
American History Explorer   *SkyTrip America*   *Total History*

Video
Balancing the Budget
The Chumash of California, A Docent's Story
Colonization and Settlement (1585-1763)

A History of Slavery in America
The Iroquois
Lost in Time
More Than Bows and Arrows

Native Americans: The History of a People
Pirates: Passion and Plunder
Three Worlds Meet (Origins-1620)

GRADE EIGHT

Historical Fiction
Baker. *Walk the World's Rim*
Bruchac. *Children of the Longhouse*
Dorris. *Sees Behind Trees*
Garland. *Cabin 102*

Garland. *Indio*
Gear. *People of the Sea*
James. *Sing for a Gentle Rain*
O'Dell. *The King's Fifth*
Rostkowski. *Moon Dancer*

Spinka. *White Hare's Horses*
Vick. *Walker of Time*
Vick. *Walker's Journey Home*

Biography
McClard. *Hiawatha and the Iroquois League*

Collective Biography
Anderson. *Explorers Who Found New Worlds*

History
Avakian. *A Historical Album of Massachusetts*
Avakian. *A Historical Album of New York*
Ayer. *The Anasazi*
Barboza. *Door of No Return: The Legend of Gorée Island*
Brown. *Discovery and Settlement: 1490-1700*
Capek. *Murals: Cave, Cathedral, to Street*
Civilizations of the Americas
Cocke. *A Historical Album of Virginia*
Cocke. *A Historical Album of Washington*
Colman. *Toilets, Bathtubs, Sinks, and Sewers*
Cush. *Disasters That Shook the World*
Deem. *How to Make a Mummy Talk*
Faber. *The Discoverers of America*
Hakim. *The First Americans*
Hakim. *Making Thirteen Colonies*
Jacobs. *The Tainos: The People Who Welcomed Columbus*

Karl. *America Alive: A History*
Katz. *Breaking the Chains: African-American Slave Resistance*
Katz. *Exploration to the War of 1812: 1492-1814*
Marrin. *Empires Lost and Won: The Spanish Heritage in the Southwest*
Medearis. *Come This Far to Freedom*
Monroe. *First Houses: Native American Homes and Sacred Structures*
Palmer. *The First Passage: Blacks in the Americas, 1502-1617*
Pascoe. *Mexico and the United States: Cooperation and Conflict*
Platt. *The Smithsonian Visual Timeline of Inventions*
San Souci. *N. C. Wyeth's Pilgrims*
Sattler. *The Earliest Americans*
Sattler. *Hominids: A Look Back at Our Ancestors*
Schouweiler. *The Lost Colony of Roanoke*

Smith. *Millions and Billions of Years Ago: Dating Our Earth and its Life*
Stones and Bones: How Archaeologists Trace Human Origins
Time-Life. *The European Challenge*
Time-Life. *The First Americans*
Time-Life. *Mound Builders & Cliff Dwellers*
Time-Life. *Tribes of the Southern Woodlands*
Topper. *A Historical Album of New Jersey*
Warburton. *The Beginning of Writing*
Whitman. *Get Up and Go: American Road Travel*
Williams. *The Age of Discovery*
Wills. *A Historical Album of California*
Wills. *A Historical Album of Florida*
Wills. *A Historical Album of Illinois*
Wood. *Ancient America*

Multimedia

CD-ROM

American History Explorer   *SkyTrip America*   *Total History*

Video

Balancing the Budget
The Chumash of California, A
  Docent's Story
Colonization and Settlement
  (1585-1763)

A History of Slavery in
  America
The Iroquois
Lost in Time
More Than Bows and Arrows

Native Americans: The
  History of a People
Pirates: Passion and Plunder
Three Worlds Meet
  (Origins-1620)

GRADE NINE

Historical Fiction

Baker. *Walk the World's Rim*
Garland. *Cabin 102*
Garland. *Indio*

Gear. *People of the Sea*
James. *Sing for a Gentle Rain*
O'Dell. *The King's Fifth*

Vick. *Walker of Time*
Vick. *Walker's Journey Home*

Collective Biography

Anderson. *Explorers Who*
  Found New Worlds

History

Ayer. *The Anasazi*
Barboza. *Door of No Return:*
  The Legend of Gorée Island
Capek. *Murals: Cave,*
  Cathedral, to Street
Civilizations of the Americas
Cush. *Disasters That Shook*
  the World
Davis. *Don't Know Much*
  About History
Faber. *The Discoverers of*
  America
Fernandez-Shaw. *The*
  Hispanic Presence in
  North America from 1492
  to Today
Hakim. *The First Americans*
Hakim. *Making Thirteen*
  Colonies
Jacobs. *The Tainos: The*
  People Who Welcomed
  Columbus
Katz. *Breaking the Chains:*
  African-American Slave
  Resistance

Katz. *Exploration to the War*
  of 1812: 1492-1814
Marrin. *Empires Lost and*
  Won: The Spanish
  Heritage in the Southwest
Medearis. *Come This Far to*
  Freedom
Monroe. *First Houses: Native*
  American Homes and
  Sacred Structures
Palmer. *The First Passage:*
  Blacks in the Americas,
  1502-1617
Pascoe. *Mexico and the*
  United States: Cooperation
  and Conflict
Platt. *The Smithsonian Visual*
  Timeline of Inventions
Salmoral. *America 1492:*
  Portrait of a Continent 500
  Years Ago
San Souci. *N. C. Wyeth's*
  Pilgrims
Sattler. *The Earliest*
  Americans

Schouweiler. *The Lost Colony*
  of Roanoke
Smith. *Millions and Billions*
  of Years Ago: Dating Our
  Earth and its Life
Stones and Bones: How
  Archaeologists Trace
  Human Origins
Time-Life. *The European*
  Challenge
Time-Life. *The First*
  Americans
Time-Life. *The Indians of*
  California
Time-Life. *Mound Builders &*
  Cliff Dwellers
Time-Life. *Tribes of the*
  Southern Woodlands
Warburton. *The Beginning of*
  Writing
Whitman. *Get Up and Go:*
  American Road Travel
Wood. *Ancient America*

Multimedia

CD-ROM

American History Explorer

Events That Changed the
  World

Ideas That Changed the World
Total History

Video

Balancing the Budget
The Chumash of California, A
   Docent's Story
Colonization and Settlement
   (1585-1763)

A History of Slavery in
   America
The Iroquois
Legacy
Lost in Time
More Than Bows and Arrows

Pirates: Passion and Plunder
The Search for the First
   Americans
Three Worlds Meet
   (Origins-1620)

GRADE TEN

Historical Fiction

Garland. Indio
Gear. People of the Sea

James. Sing for a Gentle Rain
O'Dell. The King's Fifth

History

Barboza. Door of No Return:
   The Legend of Gorée Island
Capek. Murals: Cave,
   Cathedral, to Street
Civilizations of the Americas
Davis. Don't Know Much
   About History
Dudley. Puritanism:
   Opposing Viewpoints
Faber. The Discoverers of
   America
Fernandez-Shaw. The
   Hispanic Presence in
   North America from 1492
   to Today
Hakim. The First Americans
Hakim. Making Thirteen
   Colonies

Katz. Breaking the Chains:
   African-American Slave
   Resistance
Katz. Exploration to the War
   of 1812: 1492-1814
Marrin. Empires Lost and
   Won: The Spanish
   Heritage in the Southwest
Palmer. The First Passage:
   Blacks in the Americas,
   1502-1617
Pascoe. Mexico and the
   United States: Cooperation
   and Conflict
Salmoral. America 1492:
   Portrait of a Continent 500
   Years Ago

San Souci. N. C. Wyeth's
   Pilgrims
Smith. Millions and Billions
   of Years Ago: Dating Our
   Earth and its Life
Time-Life. The European
   Challenge
Time-Life. The First
   Americans
Time-Life. The Indians of
   California
Time-Life. Mound Builders &
   Cliff Dwellers
Time-Life. Tribes of the
   Southern Woodlands
Warburton. The Beginning of
   Writing

Multimedia

CD-ROM

Events That Changed the
   World

Ideas That Changed the World
Total History

Video

Balancing the Budget
The Chumash of California, A
   Docent's Story
A History of Slavery in
   America

The Iroquois
Legacy
Lost in Time
More Than Bows and Arrows
Pirates: Passion and Plunder

The Search for the First
   Americans

GRADES ELEVEN AND TWELVE

Historical Fiction

Coldsmith. Runestone
McKee. Woman of the Mists

Shuler. She Who Remembers
Shuler. Voice of the Eagle

History

Capek. *Murals: Cave, Cathedral, to Street*

Civilizations of the Americas

Davis. *Don't Know Much About History*

Dudley. *Puritanism: Opposing Viewpoints*

Faber. *The Discoverers of America*

Fernandez-Shaw. *The Hispanic Presence in North America from 1492 to Today*

Hakim. *The First Americans*

Hakim. *Making Thirteen Colonies*

Paiewonsky. *Conquest of Eden, 1493-1515*

Palmer. *The First Passage: Blacks in the Americas, 1502-1617*

Salmoral. *America 1492: Portrait of a Continent 500 Years Ago*

Thomas. *Human Origin: The Search for Our Beginnings*

Time-Life. *The European Challenge*

Time-Life. *The First Americans*

Time-Life. *The Indians of California*

Time-Life. *Mound Builders & Cliff Dwellers*

Time-Life. *Tribes of the Southern Woodlands*

Wilson. *The Circumnavigators*

Multimedia

CD-ROM

Events That Changed the World

Ideas That Changed the World

Total History

Video

Balancing the Budget

The Chumash of California, A Docent's Story

A History of Slavery in America

Legacy

Lost in Time

More Than Bows and Arrows

Pirates: Passion and Plunder

The Search for the First Americans

Surviving Columbus

THE AMERICAN COLONIES, 1600-1774

GRADE SEVEN

Historical Fiction

Avi. *Encounter at Easton*
Avi. *Night Journeys*
Clapp. *Constance*
Clapp. *Witches' Children*
Clifford. *When the Great Canoes Came*
Coombs. *Sarah on Her Own*
Dillon. *The Seekers*
Duey. *Sarah Anne Hartford: Massachusetts, 1651*
Durrant. *Echohawk*
Field. *Calico Bush*
Fleischman. *Graven Images*
Fleischman. *Saturnalia*
Forbes. *Johnny Tremain*
Harrah. *My Brother, My Enemy*
Hildick. *Hester Bidgood: Invetigatrix of Evill Deedes*

Holmes. *Cross of Gold*
Holmes. *Thunder Foot 1730*
Jacobs. *James Printer: A Novel of King Philip's War*
Koller. *The Primrose Way*
Krensky. *The Printer's Apprentice*
Lasky. *Beyond the Burning Time*
Lasky. *A Journey to the New World: Diary, 1620*
Levin. *Mercy's Mill*
Luhrmann. *Only Brave Tomorrows*
Martinello. *With Domingo Leal in San Antonio 1734*
Myers. *The Glory Field*

O'Dell. *The Serpent Never Sleeps: A Novel of Jamestown and Pocahontas*
Petry. *Tituba of Salem Village*
Rawls. *Never Turn Back: Father Serra's Mission*
Richter. *The Light in the Forest*
Rinaldi. *A Break with Charity*
Speare. *Calico Captive*
Speare. *The Sign of the Beaver*
Speare. *The Witch of Blackbird Pond*
Steele. *Wayah of the Real People*
Wibberley. *John Treegate's Musket*
Wisler. *This New Land*

Biography

Brill. *John Adams*
Bruns. *George Washington*
Conle. *Benjamin Banneker: Scientist and Mathematician*
Cousins. *Ben Franklin of Old Philadelphia*
Cwiklik. *King Philip and the War with the Colonists*
de Varona. *Bernardo de Gálvez*
Diamond. *Paul Cuffe: Merchant and Abolitionist*
Diamond. *Prince Hall: Social Reformer*
Dolan. *Junípero Serra*
Dwyer. *John Adams*
Farley. *Samuel Adams: Grandfather of His Country*

Farley. *Thomas Paine: Revolutionary Author*
Feldman. *Benjamin Franklin: Scientist and Inventor*
Ford. *Paul Revere: Rider for the Revolution*
Fritz. *The Double Life of Pocahontas*
Gleiter. *Junípero Serra*
Hilton. *The World of Young George Washington*
Hilton. *The World of Young Tom Jefferson*
IlgenFritz. *Anne Hutchinson*
LaFarelle. *Bernardo de Gálvez: Hero of the American Revolution*
Lindop. *George Washington, Thomas Jefferson, and Andrew Jackson*

Looby. *Benjamin Franklin*
Nichols. *A Matter of Conscience: The Trial of Anne Hutchinson*
Osborne. *George Washington: Leader of a New Nation*
Osborne. *The Many Lives of Benjamin Franklin*
Potter. *Benjamin Franklin*
Richmond. *Phillis Wheatley*
Roman. *King Philip: Wampanoag Rebel*
Schwartz. *George Washington*
Shuter. *Charles Ball and American Slavery 1790's*
Stewart. *Benjamin Franklin*
Zeinert. *Captured by Indians: The Life of Mary Jemison*

Collective Biography

Altman. *Extraordinary Black Americans*
Brill. *Extraordinary Young People*
Faber. *Great Lives: American Government*
Jacobs. *Great Lives: World Religions*
Katz. *Proudly Red and Black: Stories of African and Native Americans*
Myers. *Now Is Your Time*
Provenson. *My Fellow Americans*
Rennert. *Female Writers*
Saxby. *The Great Deeds of Heroic Women*

History

Avakian. *A Historical Album of Massachusetts*
Avakian. *A Historical Album of New York*
Barboza. *Door of No Return: The Legend of Gorée Island*
Bernards. *Gun Control*
Beyer. *The Totem Pole Indians of the Northwest*
Brown. *Discovery and Settlement: 1490-1700*
Carnes. *Us and Them: A History of Intolerance in America*
Carter. *The Colonial Wars: Clashes in the Wilderness*
Cocke. *A Historical Album of Virginia*
Colman. *Strike: The Bitter Struggle of American Workers*
Colman. *Toilets, Bathtubs, Sinks, and Sewers*
Corbishley. *Secret Cities*
Cray. *American Datelines*
Davies. *Transport: On Land, Road and Rail*
Earle. *Home Life in Colonial Days*
Feelings. *The Middle Passage: White Ships, Black Cargo*
Fradin. *The Connecticut Colony*
Fradin. *The Delaware Colony*
Fradin. *The Georgia Colony*
Fradin. *The Maryland Colony*
Fradin. *The Massachusetts Colony*
Fradin. *The New Hampshire Colony*
Fradin. *The New Jersey Colony*
Fradin. *The New York Colony*
Fradin. *The North Carolina Colony*
Fradin. *The Pennsylvania Colony*
Fradin. *The Rhode Island Colony*
Fradin. *The South Carolina Colony*

Fradin. *The Virginia Colony*
Giblin. *Be Seated: A Book About Chairs*
Goor. *Williamsburg: Cradle of the Revolution*
Hakim. *From Colonies to Country*
Hakim. *Making Thirteen Colonies*
Hakim. *The New Nation*
Hirsch. *Taxation: Paying for Government*
Howarth. *Colonial People*
Howarth. *Colonial Places*
Karl. *America Alive: A History*
Katz. *Breaking the Chains: African-American Slave Resistance*
Katz. *Exploration to the War of 1812: 1492-1814*
Landau. *Armed America: The Status of Gun Control*
Markham. *Inventions That Changed Modern Life*
Marrin. *Empires Lost and Won: The Spanish Heritage in the Southwest*
Marrin. *The Sea Rovers: Pirates, Privateers, and Buccaneers*
Marrin. *Struggle for a Continent: The French and Indian Wars: 1690-1760*
McHugh. *Western Art 1600-1800*
McNeese. *America's Early Canals*
McNeese. *Early River Travel*
Medearis. *Come This Far to Freedom*
Meltzer. *The American Revolutionaries, 1750-1800*
Meltzer. *The Black Americans*
Monroe. *First Houses: Native American Homes and Sacred Structures*
Morley. *Clothes: For Work, Play and Display*
Mulcahy. *Diseases: Finding the Cure*

Nardo. *Braving the New World: 1619-1784*
Newton. *Gun Control: An Issue for the Nineties*
Palmer. *The First Passage: Blacks in the Americas, 1502-1617*
Pascoe. *Mexico and the United States: Cooperation and Conflict*
Phelan. *The Story of the Boston Massacre*
Platt. *Pirate*
Platt. *The Smithsonian Visual Timeline of Inventions*
Rappaport. *American Women: Their Lives in Their Words*
Salmon. *The Limits of Independence: American Women 1760-1800*
Smith. *The Arts and Sciences*
Smith. *Battles in a New Land*
Smith. *Daily Life*
Smith. *Governing and Teaching*
St. George. *Mason and Dixon's Line of Fire*
Stein. *Witches*
Steins. *A Nation Is Born: 1700-1820*
Stevens. *Colonial American Craftspeople*
Sullivan. *Children of Promise: African-American Literature and Art*
Sullivan. *Slave Ship: The Story of the Henrietta Marie*
The Americas in the Colonial Era
Time-Life. *African Americans: Voices of Triumph: Leadership*
Topper. *A Historical Album of New Jersey*
Warner. *Colonial American Homelife*
Washburne. *A Multicultural Portrait of Colonial Life*

Wheeler. *Events That Changed American History*
Whitman. *Get Up and Go: American Road Travel*

Williams. *The Age of Discovery*
Williams. *Forts and Castles*
Wills. *A Historical Album of Connecticut*

Wills. *A Historical Album of Illinois*
Zeinert. *The Salem Witchcraft Trials*

Multimedia

CD-ROM

American History Explorer
Eyewitness Encyclopedia of Science
Her Heritage: A Biographical Encyclopedia of American History

Landmark Documents in American History
Science Navigator
SkyTrip America
Stowaway! Stephen Biesty's Incredible Cross-Sections

Total History
The Way Things Work

Video

Candlemaking
Causes of Revolt
Colonial Williamsburg
Colonization and Settlement (1585-1763)
Countdown to Independence: Causes of the American Revolution
The Early Colonists
From an Eagle's Nest
Great Black Innovators
A History of Slavery in America
Jamestown

Jamestown: The Beginning
Last of the Mohicans
The Life and Times of George Washington
The Life of George Washington
The Loom
Making It Happen: Masters of Invention
The Mayflower Pilgrims
Mission Life
Missions of California: Mission Santa Barbara

Native Americans: The History of a People
Patrick Henry's Fight for Individual Rights
The Pilgrims' Story
Pirates: Passion and Plunder
Pride & Prejudice: A History of Black Culture in America
Seeds of Liberty: The Causes of the American Revolution
Spinning Wheel
Unearthing the Slave Trade

GRADE EIGHT

Historical Fiction

Avi. *Encounter at Easton*
Avi. *Night Journeys*
Clapp. *Constance*
Clapp. *Witches' Children*
Coombs. *Sarah on Her Own*
Dillon. *The Seekers*
Durrant. *Echohawk*
Field. *Calico Bush*
Fleischman. *Graven Images*
Fleischman. *Saturnalia*
Forbes. *Johnny Tremain*
Harrah. *My Brother, My Enemy*
Holmes. *Cross of Gold*
Holmes. *Thunder Foot 1730*

Jacobs. *James Printer: A Novel of King Philip's War*
Koller. *The Primrose Way*
Lasky. *Beyond the Burning Time*
Lasky. *A Journey to the New World: Diary, 1620*
Levin. *Mercy's Mill*
Luhrmann. *Only Brave Tomorrows*
Martinello. *With Domingo Leal in San Antonio 1734*
Myers. *The Glory Field*
O'Dell. *The Serpent Never Sleeps*

Petry. *Tituba of Salem Village*
Rawls. *Never Turn Back: Father Serra's Mission*
Richter. *The Light in the Forest*
Rinaldi. *A Break with Charity*
Speare. *Calico Captive*
Speare. *The Witch of Blackbird Pond*
Steele. *Wayah of the Real People*
Wibberley. *John Treegate's Musket*

Biography

Brill. *John Adams*
Bruns. *George Washington*
Conle. *Benjamin Banneker: Scientist and Mathematician*
Cousins. *Ben Franklin of Old Philadelphia*

Cwiklik. *King Philip and the War with the Colonists*
Diamond. *Paul Cuffe: Merchant and Abolitionist*
Diamond. *Prince Hall: Social Reformer*
Dolan. *Junípero Serra*

Dwyer. *John Adams*
Farley. *Samuel Adams: Grandfather of His Country*
Farley. *Thomas Paine: Revolutionary Author*
Feldman. *Benjamin Franklin: Scientist and Inventor*

Ford. *Paul Revere: Rider for the Revolution*

Fritz. *The Double Life of Pocahontas*

Hilton. *The World of Young George Washington*

Hilton. *The World of Young Tom Jefferson*

IlgenFritz. *Anne Hutchinson*

LaFarelle. *Bernardo de Gálvez: Hero of the American Revolution*

Lindop. *George Washington, Thomas Jefferson, and Andrew Jackson*

Looby. *Benjamin Franklin*

Nichols. *A Matter of Conscience: The Trial of Anne Hutchinson*

Potter. *Benjamin Franklin*

Richmond. *Phillis Wheatley*

Roman. *King Philip: Wampanoag Rebel*

Schwartz. *George Washington*

Shuter. *Charles Ball and American Slavery 1790's*

Stewart. *Benjamin Franklin*

Zeinert. *Captured by Indians: The Life of Mary Jemison*

Collective Biography

Altman. *Extraordinary Black Americans*

Brill. *Extraordinary Young People*

Faber. *Great Lives: American Government*

Katz. *Proudly Red and Black: Stories of African and Native Americans*

Myers. *Now Is Your Time*

Otfinoski. *Great Black Writers*

Provenson. *My Fellow Americans*

Rennert. *Female Writers*

Saxby. *The Great Deeds of Heroic Women*

History

Avakian. *A Historical Album of Massachusetts*

Avakian. *A Historical Album of New York*

Barboza. *Door of No Return: The Legend of Gorée Island*

Bernards. *Gun Control*

Brown. *Discovery and Settlement: 1490-1700*

Carnes. *Us and Them: A History of Intolerance in America*

Carter. *The Colonial Wars: Clashes in the Wilderness*

Cocke. *A Historical Album of Virginia*

Colman. *Strike: The Bitter Struggle of American Workers*

Colman. *Toilets, Bathtubs, Sinks, and Sewers*

Cray. *American Datelines*

Davies. *Transport: On Land, Road and Rail*

Earle. *Home Life in Colonial Days*

Feelings. *The Middle Passage: White Ships, Black Cargo*

Fradin. *The Connecticut Colony*

Fradin. *The Delaware Colony*

Fradin. *The Georgia Colony*

Fradin. *The Maryland Colony*

Fradin. *The Massachusetts Colony*

Fradin. *The New Hampshire Colony*

Fradin. *The New Jersey Colony*

Fradin. *The New York Colony*

Fradin. *The North Carolina Colony*

Fradin. *The Pennsylvania Colony*

Fradin. *The Rhode Island Colony*

Fradin. *The South Carolina Colony*

Fradin. *The Virginia Colony*

Giblin. *Be Seated: A Book About Chairs*

Goor. *Williamsburg: Cradle of the Revolution*

Hakim. *From Colonies to Country*

Hakim. *Making Thirteen Colonies*

Hakim. *The New Nation*

Hirsch. *Taxation: Paying for Government*

Howarth. *Colonial People*

Howarth. *Colonial Places*

Karl. *America Alive: A History*

Katz. *Breaking the Chains: African-American Slave Resistance*

Katz. *Exploration to the War of 1812: 1492-1814*

Landau. *Armed America: The Status of Gun Control*

Markham. *Inventions That Changed Modern Life*

Marrin. *Empires Lost and Won: The Spanish Heritage in the Southwest*

Marrin. *The Sea Rovers: Pirates, Privateers, and Buccaneers*

Marrin. *Struggle for a Continent: The French and Indian Wars: 1690-1760*

McHugh. *Western Art 1600-1800*

McNeese. *America's Early Canals*

McNeese. *Early River Travel*

Medearis. *Come This Far to Freedom*

Meltzer. *The American Revolutionaries, 1750-1800*

Meltzer. *The Black Americans*

Monroe. *First Houses: Native American Homes and Sacred Structures*

Morley. *Clothes: For Work, Play and Display*

Mulcahy. *Diseases: Finding the Cure*

Nardo. *Braving the New World: 1619-1784*

Newton. *Gun Control: An Issue for the Nineties*

Palmer. *The First Passage: Blacks in the Americas, 1502-1617*

Pascoe. *Mexico and the United States: Cooperation and Conflict*

Platt. *Pirate*

Platt. *The Smithsonian Visual Timeline of Inventions*

Rappaport. *American Women: Their Lives in Their Words*

Salmon. *The Limits of Independence: American Women 1760-1800*

Scott. *Settlers on the Eastern Shore: The British Colonies 1607-1750*
Smith. *The Arts and Sciences*
Smith. *Battles in a New Land*
Smith. *Daily Life*
Smith. *Governing and Teaching*
St. George. *Mason and Dixon's Line of Fire*
Stanley. *Women in the Military*
Stein. *Witches*
Steins. *A Nation Is Born: 1700-1820*
Stevens. *Colonial American Craftspeople*

Sullivan. *Children of Promise: African-American Literature and Art*
Sullivan. *Slave Ship: The Story of the Henrietta Marie*
The Americas in the Colonial Era
Time-Life. *African Americans: Voices of Triumph: Leadership*
Topper. *A Historical Album of New Jersey*
Warner. *Colonial American Homelife*

Washburne. *A Multicultural Portrait of Colonial Life*
Wheeler. *Events That Changed American History*
Whitman. *Get Up and Go: American Road Travel*
Williams. *The Age of Discovery*
Williams. *Forts and Castles*
Wills. *A Historical Album of Connecticut*
Wills. *A Historical Album of Illinois*
Zeinert. *The Salem Witchcraft Trials*

Multimedia

CD-ROM

American History Explorer
Eyewitness Encyclopedia of Science
Her Heritage: A Biographical Encyclopedia of American History

Landmark Documents in American History
Science Navigator
SkyTrip America
Stowaway! Stephen Biesty's Incredible Cross-Sections

Total History
The Way Things Work

Video

Candlemaking
Causes of Revolt
Colonial Williamsburg
Colonization and Settlement (1585-1763)
Countdown to Independence: Causes of the American Revolution
The Early Colonists
From an Eagle's Nest
Great Black Innovators
A History of Slavery in America
Jamestown

Jamestown: The Beginning
Last of the Mohicans
The Life and Times of George Washington
The Life of George Washington
The Loom
Making It Happen: Masters of Invention
The Mayflower Pilgrims
Mission Life
Missions of California: Mission Santa Barbara

Native Americans: The History of a People
Patrick Henry's Fight for Individual Rights
The Pilgrims' Story
Pirates: Passion and Plunder
Pride & Prejudice: A History of Black Culture in America
Seeds of Liberty: The Causes of the American Revolution
Spinning Wheel
Unearthing the Slave Trade

GRADE NINE

Historical Fiction

Avi. *Night Journeys*
Clapp. *Constance*
Clapp. *Witches' Children*
Coombs. *Sarah on Her Own*
Dillon. *The Seekers*
Fleischman. *Graven Images*
Fleischman. *Saturnalia*
Forbes. *Johnny Tremain*
Harrah. *My Brother, My Enemy*
Koller. *The Primrose Way*

Lasky. *Beyond the Burning Time*
Lasky. *A Journey to the New World: Diary, 1620*
Levin. *Mercy's Mill*
Luhrmann. *Only Brave Tomorrows*
Myers. *The Glory Field*
O'Dell. *The Serpent Never Sleeps: A Novel of Jamestown and Pocahontas*
Petry. *Tituba of Salem Village*

Rawls. *Never Turn Back: Father Serra's Mission*
Richter. *The Light in the Forest*
Rinaldi. *A Break with Charity*
Speare. *Calico Captive*
Speare. *The Witch of Blackbird Pond*
Steele. *Wayah of the Real People*
Wibberley. *John Treegate's Musket*

Biography

Brill. *John Adams*
Bruns. *George Washington*
Campion. *Mother Ann Lee: Morning Star of the Shakers*
Conle. *Benjamin Banneker: Scientist and Mathematician*
Cousins. *Ben Franklin of Old Philadelphia*
Diamond. *Paul Cuffe: Merchant and Abolitionist*
Diamond. *Prince Hall: Social Reformer*
Dolan. *Junípero Serra*
Dwyer. *John Adams*

Farley. *Samuel Adams: Grandfather of His Country*
Farley. *Thomas Paine: Revolutionary Author*
Ford. *Paul Revere: Rider for the Revolution*
Fritz. *The Double Life of Pocahontas*
Hilton. *The World of Young George Washington*
Hilton. *The World of Young Tom Jefferson*
IlgenFritz. *Anne Hutchinson*
Looby. *Benjamin Franklin*
Meltzer. *Benjamin Franklin: The New American*

Meltzer. *George Washington and the Birth of Our Nation*
Nichols. *A Matter of Conscience: The Trial of Anne Hutchinson*
Potter. *Benjamin Franklin*
Richmond. *Phillis Wheatley*
Roman. *King Philip: Wampanoag Rebel*
Schwartz. *George Washington*
Shuter. *Charles Ball and American Slavery 1790's*
Stewart. *Benjamin Franklin*
Zeinert. *Captured by Indians: The Life of Mary Jemison*

Collective Biography

Brill. *Extraordinary Young People*
Faber. *Great Lives: American Government*

Myers. *Now Is Your Time*
O'Brien. *American Political Leaders*
Otfinoski. *Great Black Writers*

Rennert. *Female Writers*
Saxby. *The Great Deeds of Heroic Women*

History

Ardley. *Music: An Illustrated Encyclopedia*
Barboza. *Door of No Return: The Legend of Gorée Island*
Bernards. *Gun Control*
Carnes. *Us and Them: A History of Intolerance in America*
Cray. *American Datelines*
Davis. *Don't Know Much About History*
Davis. *Man-Made Catastrophes*
Earle. *Home Life in Colonial Days*
Feelings. *The Middle Passage: White Ships, Black Cargo*
Fernandez-Shaw. *The Hispanic Presence in North America from 1492 to Today*
Fradin. *The Connecticut Colony*
Fradin. *The Delaware Colony*
Fradin. *The Georgia Colony*
Fradin. *The Maryland Colony*
Fradin. *The Massachusetts Colony*
Fradin. *The New Hampshire Colony*
Fradin. *The New Jersey Colony*
Fradin. *The New York Colony*
Fradin. *The North Carolina Colony*

Fradin. *The Pennsylvania Colony*
Fradin. *The Rhode Island Colony*
Fradin. *The South Carolina Colony*
Fradin. *The Virginia Colony*
Garza. *Barred from the Bar: A History of Women and the Legal Profession*
Hakim. *From Colonies to Country*
Hakim. *Making Thirteen Colonies*
Hakim. *The New Nation*
Haskins. *Black Music in America*
Hirsch. *Taxation: Paying for Government*
Jakoubek. *The Colonial Mosaic: American Women 1600-1700*
Katz. *Breaking the Chains: African-American Slave Resistance*
Katz. *Exploration to the War of 1812: 1492-1814*
Knappman. *Great American Trials*
Landau. *Armed America: The Status of Gun Control*
Markham. *Inventions That Changed Modern Life*
Marrin. *Empires Lost and Won: The Spanish Heritage in the Southwest*

Marrin. *The Sea Rovers: Pirates, Privateers, and Buccaneers*
Marrin. *Struggle for a Continent: The French and Indian Wars: 1690-1760*
McHugh. *Western Art 1600-1800*
Medearis. *Come This Far to Freedom*
Meltzer. *The American Revolutionaries, 1750-1800*
Meltzer. *The Black Americans*
Monroe. *First Houses: Native American Homes and Sacred Structures*
Mulcahy. *Diseases: Finding the Cure*
Nardo. *Braving the New World: 1619-1784*
Newton. *Gun Control: An Issue for the Nineties*
Palmer. *The First Passage: Blacks in the Americas, 1502-1617*
Pascoe. *Mexico and the United States: Cooperation and Conflict*
Pickford. *The Atlas of Shipwrecks & Treasure*
Platt. *The Smithsonian Visual Timeline of Inventions*
Rappaport. *American Women: Their Lives in Their Words*

Salmon. *The Limits of Independence: American Women 1760-1800*
Scott. *Settlers on the Eastern Shore: The British Colonies 1607-1750*
Smith. *The Arts and Sciences*
Smith. *Battles in a New Land*
Smith. *Daily Life*
Smith. *Fascinating People and Astounding Events from American History*

Smith. *Governing and Teaching*
Stanley. *Women in the Military*
Steele. *Freedom's River*
Stein. *Witches*
Stevens. *Colonial American Craftspeople*
The Americas in the Colonial Era
Time-Life. *African Americans: Voices of Triumph: Leadership*

Warner. *Colonial American Homelife*
Washburne. *A Multicultural Portrait of Colonial Life*
Wheeler. *Events That Changed American History*
Whitman. *Get Up and Go: American Road Travel*
Williams. *Forts and Castles*
Zeinert. *The Salem Witchcraft Trials*

Multimedia

CD-ROM

American History Explorer
Events That Changed the World
Her Heritage: A Biographical Encyclopedia of American History

Ideas That Changed the World
Landmark Documents in American History
Life in Colonial America
Science Navigator

Stowaway! Stephen Biesty's Incredible Cross-Sections
Total History
The Way Things Work

Video

Candlemaking
Causes of Revolt
Colonial Williamsburg
Colonization and Settlement (1585-1763)
From an Eagle's Nest
Hidden Heritage: The Roots of Black American Painting

A History of Slavery in America
Jamestown
Jamestown: The Beginning
Last of the Mohicans
The Life of George Washington
The Loom

The Mayflower Pilgrims
Mission Life
The Pilgrims' Story
Pirates: Passion and Plunder
Pride & Prejudice: A History of Black Culture in America
Spinning Wheel
Unearthing the Slave Trade

GRADE TEN

Historical Fiction

Clapp. *Constance*
Coombs. *Sarah on Her Own*
Dillon. *The Seekers*
Fleischman. *Graven Images*
Fleischman. *Saturnalia*

Koller. *The Primrose Way*
Myers. *The Glory Field*
Petry. *Tituba of Salem Village*
Richter. *The Light in the Forest*

Rinaldi. *A Break with Charity*
Wibberley. *John Treegate's Musket*

Biography

Bruns. *George Washington*
Campion. *Mother Ann Lee: Morning Star of the Shakers*
Conle. *Benjamin Banneker: Scientist and Mathematician*
Diamond. *Paul Cuffe: Merchant and Abolitionist*
Diamond. *Prince Hall: Social Reformer*

Dolan. *Junípero Serra*
Dwyer. *John Adams*
IlgenFritz. *Anne Hutchinson*
Looby. *Benjamin Franklin*
Meltzer. *Benjamin Franklin: The New American*
Meltzer. *George Washington and the Birth of Our Nation*
Richmond. *Phillis Wheatley*

Roman. *King Philip: Wampanoag Rebel*
Schwartz. *George Washington*
Seaver. *A Narrative of the Life of Mrs. Mary Jemison*
Zeinert. *Captured by Indians: The Life of Mary Jemison*

Collective Biography

Brill. *Extraordinary Young People*
Myers. *Now Is Your Time*

O'Brien. *American Political Leaders*
Otfinoski. *Great Black Writers*

Saxby. *The Great Deeds of Heroic Women*

History

Ardley. *Music: An Illustrated Encyclopedia*
Barboza. *Door of No Return: The Legend of Gorée Island*
Bernards. *Gun Control*
Carnes. *Us and Them: A History of Intolerance in America*
Cray. *American Datelines*
Davis. *Don't Know Much About History*
Davis. *Man-Made Catastrophes*
Earle. *Home Life in Colonial Days*
Evans. *Born for Liberty: A History of Women in America*
Feelings. *The Middle Passage: White Ships, Black Cargo*
Fernandez-Shaw. *The Hispanic Presence in North America from 1492 to Today*
Garza. *Barred from the Bar: A History of Women and the Legal Profession*
Hakim. *From Colonies to Country*
Hakim. *Making Thirteen Colonies*
Hakim. *The New Nation*
Haskins. *Black Music in America*

Jakoubek. *The Colonial Mosaic: American Women 1600-1700*
Katz. *Breaking the Chains: African-American Slave Resistance*
Katz. *Exploration to the War of 1812: 1492-1814*
Knappman. *Great American Trials*
Landau. *Armed America: The Status of Gun Control*
Markham. *Inventions That Changed Modern Life*
Marrin. *Empires Lost and Won: The Spanish Heritage in the Southwest*
Marrin. *The Sea Rovers: Pirates, Privateers, and Buccaneers*
McHugh. *Western Art 1600-1800*
Meltzer. *The American Revolutionaries, 1750-1800*
Meltzer. *The Black Americans*
Mulcahy. *Diseases: Finding the Cure*
Newton. *Gun Control: An Issue for the Nineties*
Palmer. *The First Passage: Blacks in the Americas, 1502-1617*
Pascoe. *Mexico and the United States: Cooperation and Conflict*

Pickford. *The Atlas of Shipwrecks & Treasure*
Rappaport. *American Women: Their Lives In Their Words*
Salmon. *The Limits of Independence: American Women 1760-1800*
Scott. *Settlers on the Eastern Shore: The British Colonies 1607-1750*
Smith. *The Arts and Sciences*
Smith. *Battles in a New Land*
Smith. *Daily Life*
Smith. *Fascinating People and Astounding Events from American History*
Smith. *Governing and Teaching*
Stanley. *Women in the Military*
Steele. *Freedom's River*
The Americas in the Colonial Era
Time-Life. *African Americans: Voices of Triumph: Leadership*
Warner. *Colonial American Homelife*
Washburne. *A Multicultural Portrait of Colonial Life*
Wheeler. *Events That Changed American History*
Zeinert. *The Salem Witchcraft Trials*

Multimedia

CD-ROM

Events That Changed the World
Her Heritage: A Biographical Encyclopedia of American History

Ideas That Changed the World
Landmark Documents in American History
Life in Colonial America
Science Navigator

Stowaway! Stephen Biesty's Incredible Cross-Sections
Total History
The Way Things Work

Video

Colonial Williamsburg
From an Eagle's Nest
Hidden Heritage: The Roots of Black American Painting
A History of Slavery in America

Last of the Mohicans
The Life of George Washington
The Mayflower Pilgrims
The Pilgrims' Story
Pirates: Passion and Plunder

Pride & Prejudice: A History of Black Culture in America
Unearthing the Slave Trade

GRADES ELEVEN AND TWELVE

Historical Fiction

Clapp. *Constance*
Dillon. *The Seekers*
Meyers. *The Dutchman*
Meyers. *Dutchman's Dilemma*

Meyers. *The High Constable*
Riefe. *For Love of Two Eagles*
Smith. *The Stratford Devil*

Wibberley. *John Treegate's Musket*
Youmans. *Catherwood*

Biography

Campion. *Mother Ann Lee: Morning Star of the Shakers*
Diamond. *Paul Cuffe: Merchant and Abolitionist*
Diamond. *Prince Hall: Social Reformer*
IlgenFritz. *Anne Hutchinson*

Meltzer. *Benjamin Franklin: The New American*
Meltzer. *George Washington and the Birth of Our Nation*
Roman. *King Philip: Wampanoag Rebel*
Schwartz. *George Washington*

Seaver. *A Narrative of the Life of Mrs. Mary Jemison*
Zeinert. *Captured by Indians: The Life of Mary Jemison*

Collective Biography

Foster. *Written by Herself: African American Women, 1746-1892*

Myers. *Now Is Your Time*
O'Brien. *American Political Leaders*

Otfinoski. *Great Black Writers*
Saxby. *The Great Deeds of Heroic Women*

History

Ardley. *Music: An Illustrated Encyclopedia*
Carnes. *Us and Them: A History of Intolerance in America*
Cray. *American Datelines*
Davidson. *Everyday Life Through the Ages*
Davis. *Don't Know Much About History*
Davis. *Man-Made Catastrophes*
Evans. *Born for Liberty: A History of Women in America*
Feelings. *The Middle Passage: White Ships, Black Cargo*
Ferguson. *Uncommon Ground: Archaeology and Colonial African America, 1650-1800*
Fernandez-Shaw. *The Hispanic Presence in North America from 1492 to Today*

Garza. *Barred from the Bar: A History of Women and the Legal Profession*
Hakim. *From Colonies to Country*
Hakim. *Making Thirteen Colonies*
Hakim. *The New Nation*
Haskins. *Black Music in America*
Jakoubek. *The Colonial Mosaic: American Women 1600-1700*
Knappman. *Great American Trials*
Meltzer. *The American Revolutionaries, 1750-1800*
Mulcahy. *Diseases: Finding the Cure*
Noble. *Bookbanning in America: Who Bans Books?*
Norton. *Founding Mothers & Fathers: Gendered Power and the Forming of American Society*

Palmer. *The First Passage: Blacks in the Americas, 1502-1617*
Perry. *Arrogant Armies*
Pickford. *The Atlas of Shipwrecks & Treasure*
Rappaport. *American Women: Their Lives in Their Words*
Salmon. *The Limits of Independence: American Women 1760-1800*
Scott. *Settlers on the Eastern Shore: The British Colonies 1607-1750*
Simpson. *The Great Dismal: A Carolinian's Swamp Memoir*
Smith. *Fascinating People and Astounding Events from American History*
Stanley. *Women in the Military*
Steele. *Freedom's River*
Time-Life. *African Americans: Voices of Triumph: Leadership*
Wheeler. *Events That Changed American History*

Multimedia

CD-ROM

Events That Changed the World
Her Heritage: A Biographical Encyclopedia of American History
Ideas That Changed the World

Landmark Documents in American History
Life in Colonial America
Science Navigator

Stowaway! Stephen Biesty's Incredible Cross-Sections
Total History
The Way Things Work

Video

The American Republic
Colonial Williamsburg
Dark Passages
From an Eagle's Nest
Hidden Heritage: The Roots
of Black American Painting

A History of Slavery in
America
Last of the Mohicans
The Life of George
Washington
The Mayflower Pilgrims

The Pilgrims' Story
Pirates: Passion and Plunder
Pride & Prejudice: A History
of Black Culture in America
Unearthing the Slave Trade

THE AMERICAN REVOLUTION, 1775-1783

GRADE SEVEN

Historical Fiction

Avi. *Captain Grey*
Avi. *The Fighting Ground*
Caudill. *Tree of Freedom*
Clapp. *I'm Deborah Sampson*
Collier. *My Brother Sam Is Dead*
DeFord. *An Enemy Among Them*
Duey. *Mary Alice Peale*
Edwards. *George Midgett's War*
Forman. *Prince Charlie's Year*
Fritz. *Early Thunder*

Gregory. *The Winter of Red Snow: Diary, 1777-1778*
Keehn. *Moon of Two Dark Horses*
Monjo. *A Namesake for Nathan*
Moore. *Distant Thunder*
O'Dell. *Sarah Bishop*
Pope. *The Sherwood Ring*
Rinaldi. *The Fifth of March*
Rinaldi. *Finishing Becca*
Rinaldi. *Hang a Thousand Trees with Ribbons*

Rinaldi. *A Ride into Morning*
Rinaldi. *The Secret of Sarah Revere*
Rinaldi. *Time Enough for Drums*
Wibberley. *Peter Treegate's War*
Wibberley. *Sea Captain from Salem*
Wibberley. *Treegate's Raiders*
Woodruff. *George Washington's Socks*

Biography

Beller. *Woman of Independence: The Life of Abigail Adams*
Bober. *Thomas Jefferson: Man on a Mountain*
Brill. *John Adams*
Bruns. *George Washington*
Bruns. *Thomas Jefferson*
Clinton. *James Madison: Fourth President*
Conle. *Benjamin Banneker: Scientist and Mathematician*
Cousins. *Ben Franklin of Old Philadelphia*
Diamond. *Paul Cuffe: Merchant and Abolitionist*
Diamond. *Prince Hall: Social Reformer*
Dwyer. *John Adams*
Farley. *Samuel Adams: Grandfather of His Country*

Farley. *Thomas Paine: Revolutionary Author*
Feldman. *Benjamin Franklin: Scientist and Inventor*
Ford. *Paul Revere: Rider for the Revolution*
Fritz. *Traitor: The Case of Benedict Arnold*
Latham. *Carry On, Mr. Bowditch*
Leavell. *James Madison*
Lindop. *George Washington, Thomas Jefferson, and Andrew Jackson*
Looby. *Benjamin Franklin*
Meltzer. *Thomas Jefferson: The Revolutionary Aristocrat*
Nardo. *Thomas Jefferson*
O'Brien. *Alexander Hamilton*
Osborne. *Abigail Adams: Women's Rights Advocate*

Osborne. *George Washington: Leader of a New Nation*
Osborne. *The Many Lives of Benjamin Franklin*
Patterson. *Thomas Jefferson*
Potter. *Benjamin Franklin*
Sandak. *The Jeffersons*
Sandak. *The John Adamses*
Sandak. *The Washingtons*
Schwartz. *George Washington*
Stefoff. *James Monroe: 5th President*
Stefoff. *John Adams: 2nd President*
Stefoff. *Thomas Jefferson: 3rd President*
Stewart. *Benjamin Franklin*
Vail. *Thomas Paine*
Zeinert. *The Memoirs of Andrew Sherburne*

Collective Biography

Altman. *Extraordinary Black Americans*
Cohen. *The Ghosts of War*
Faber. *Great Lives: American Government*

Myers. *Now Is Your Time*
Provenson. *My Fellow Americans*
Rennert. *Pioneers of Discovery*

Sheafer. *Women in America's Wars*
Wilkinson. *Generals Who Changed the World*

History

Beyer. *The Totem Pole Indians of the Northwest*
Cray. *American Datelines*
Davies. *Transport: On Land, Road and Rail*
Dolan. *The American Revolution*
Evans. *Freedom of Religion*
Evans. *Freedom of Speech*
Evans. *Freedom of the Press*
Gay. *Revolutionary War*
Hakim. *From Colonies to Country*
Hakim. *The New Nation*
Hirsch. *Taxation: Paying for Government*
Hoig. *It's the Fourth of July*
Jaffe. *Who Were the Founding Fathers?*
Karl. *America Alive: A History*
Katz. *Exploration to the War of 1812: 1492-1814*
Kirby. *Glorious Days, Dreadful Days: The Battle of Bunker Hill*
Leinwand. *Do We Need a New Constitution?*

Lukes. *The American Revolution*
Marrin. *The War for Independence*
McNeese. *America's Early Canals*
Medearis. *Come This Far to Freedom*
Meltzer. *The American Revolutionaries, 1750-1800*
Meltzer. *The Black Americans*
Meltzer. *Weapons & Warfare*
Morley. *Clothes: For Work, Play and Display*
Murphy. *Young Patriot: The American Revolution as Experienced by One Boy*
Newton. *Gun Control: An Issue for the Nineties*
Pascoe. *Freedom of Expression*
Platt. *The Smithsonian Visual Timeline of Inventions*
Rappaport. *American Women: Their Lives in Their Words*

Salmon. *The Limits of Independence: American Women 1760-1800*
Silverman. *Songs and Stories from the American Revolution*
Smith. *The Revolutionary War*
Stein. *Valley Forge*
Steins. *A Nation Is Born: 1700-1820*
Stewart. *The Revolutionary War*
Time-Life. *The Revolutionaries*
Warner. *The U.S. Marine Corps*
Wheeler. *Events That Changed American History*
Williams. *The Age of Discovery*
Zall. *Becoming American: Young People in the American Revolution*
Zell. *A Multicultural Portrait of the American Revolution*

Multimedia

CD-ROM

American History Explorer
Her Heritage: A Biographical Encyclopedia of American History

Landmark Documents in American History
SkyTrip America
Total History

Video

Abigail Adams
American Constitution: The Road to Runnymede
American Independence 1776
The American Revolution
The Battle of Yorktown: 1781
Causes of Revolt
Countdown to Independence: Causes of the American Revolution

Equality: A History of the Women's Movement in America
Give Me Liberty: Patrick Henry—Voice of the Revolution
The Life and Times of George Washington
The Life of George Washington

A New Nation (1776-1815)
Patrick Henry's Fight for Individual Rights
The Revolutionary War Series
Seeds of Liberty: The Causes of the American Revolution
Thomas Jefferson: The Pursuit of Liberty
Valley Forge: The Battle for Survival

GRADE EIGHT

Historical Fiction

Avi. *Captain Grey*
Avi. *The Fighting Ground*
Caudill. *The Far-off Land*
Caudill. *Tree of Freedom*
Clapp. *I'm Deborah Sampson*

Collier. *My Brother Sam Is Dead*
DeFord. *An Enemy Among Them*
Edwards. *George Midgett's War*

Forman. *Prince Charlie's Year*
Fritz. *Early Thunder*
Gregory. *The Winter of Red Snow: Diary, 1777-1778*

Keehn. *Moon of Two Dark
    Horses*
Moore. *Distant Thunder*
O'Dell. *Sarah Bishop*
Pope. *The Sherwood Ring*
Rinaldi. *The Fifth of March*
Rinaldi. *Finishing Becca*

Rinaldi. *Hang a Thousand
    Trees with Ribbons*
Rinaldi. *The Secret of Sarah
    Revere*
Rinaldi. *Time Enough for
    Drums*

White. *Jordan Freeman Was
    My Friend*
Wibberley. *Peter Treegate's
    War*
Wibberley. *Sea Captain from
    Salem*
Wibberley. *Treegate's Raiders*

Biography

Beller. *Woman of
    Independence: The Life of
    Abigail Adams*
Bober. *Thomas Jefferson:
    Man on a Mountain*
Brill. *John Adams*
Bruns. *George Washington*
Bruns. *Thomas Jefferson*
Clinton. *James Madison:
    Fourth President*
Conle. *Benjamin Banneker:
    Scientist and
    Mathematician*
Cousins. *Ben Franklin of Old
    Philadelphia*
Diamond. *Paul Cuffe:
    Merchant and Abolitionist*
Diamond. *Prince Hall: Social
    Reformer*
Dwyer. *John Adams*

Farley. *Samuel Adams:
    Grandfather of His Country*
Farley. *Thomas Paine:
    Revolutionary Author*
Feldman. *Benjamin Franklin:
    Scientist and Inventor*
Ford. *Paul Revere: Rider for
    the Revolution*
Fritz. *Traitor: The Case of
    Benedict Arnold*
Latham. *Carry On, Mr.
    Bowditch*
Leavell. *James Madison*
Lindop. *George Washington,
    Thomas Jefferson, and
    Andrew Jackson*
Looby. *Benjamin Franklin*
Meltzer. *Thomas Jefferson:
    The Revolutionary
    Aristocrat*

Nardo. *Thomas Jefferson*
O'Brien. *Alexander Hamilton*
Osborne. *Abigail Adams:
    Women's Rights Advocate*
Patterson. *Thomas Jefferson*
Potter. *Benjamin Franklin*
Sandak. *The Jeffersons*
Sandak. *The John Adamses*
Sandak. *The Washingtons*
Schwartz. *George Washington*
Stefoff. *James Monroe: 5th
    President*
Stefoff. *John Adams: 2nd
    President*
Stefoff. *Thomas Jefferson:
    3rd President*
Stewart. *Benjamin Franklin*
Vail. *Thomas Paine*
Zeinert. *The Memoirs of
    Andrew Sherburne*

Collective Biography

Altman. *Extraordinary Black
    Americans*
Cohen. *The Ghosts of War*
Faber. *Great Lives: American
    Government*

Myers. *Now Is Your Time*
Provenson. *My Fellow
    Americans*
Rennert. *Pioneers of
    Discovery*

Sheafer. *Women in America's
    Wars*
Wilkinson. *Generals Who
    Changed the World*

History

Cray. *American Datelines*
Davies. *Transport: On Land,
    Road and Rail*
Dolan. *The American
    Revolution*
Evans. *Freedom of Religion*
Evans. *Freedom of Speech*
Evans. *Freedom of the Press*
Gay. *Revolutionary War*
Hakim. *From Colonies to
    Country*
Hakim. *The New Nation*
Hirsch. *Taxation: Paying for
    Government*
Hoig. *It's the Fourth of July*
Jaffe. *Who Were the
    Founding Fathers?*
Karl. *America Alive: A
    History*
Katz. *Exploration to the War
    of 1812: 1492-1814*

Kirby. *Glorious Days,
    Dreadful Days: The Battle
    of Bunker Hill*
Leinwand. *Do We Need a
    New Constitution?*
Lukes. *The American
    Revolution*
Marrin. *The War for
    Independence*
McNeese. *America's Early
    Canals*
Medearis. *Come This Far to
    Freedom*
Meltzer. *The American
    Revolutionaries, 1750-1800*
Meltzer. *The Black Americans*
Meltzer. *Weapons & Warfare*
Morley. *Clothes: For Work,
    Play and Display*
Murphy. *Young Patriot: The
    American Revolution as
    Experienced by One Boy*

Newton. *Gun Control: An
    Issue for the Nineties*
Pascoe. *Freedom of
    Expression*
Pascoe. *Mexico and the
    United States: Cooperation
    and Conflict*
Platt. *The Smithsonian Visual
    Timeline of Inventions*
Rappaport. *American
    Women: Their Lives in
    Their Words*
Salmon. *The Limits of
    Independence: American
    Women 1760-1800*
Silverman. *Songs and Stories
    from the American
    Revolution*
Smith. *The Revolutionary War*
Stein. *Valley Forge*
Steins. *A Nation Is Born:
    1700-1820*

Stewart. *The Revolutionary War*
Time-Life. *The Revolutionaries*
Warner. *The U.S. Marine Corps*

Wheeler. *Events That Changed American History*
Williams. *The Age of Discovery*

Zall. *Becoming American: Young People in the American Revolution*
Zell. *A Multicultural Portrait of the American Revolution*

Multimedia

CD-ROM

American History Explorer
Her Heritage: A Biographical Encyclopedia of American History

Landmark Documents in American History
SkyTrip America
Total History

Video

Abigail Adams
American Constitution: The Road to Runnymede
American Independence 1776
The American Revolution
The Battle of Yorktown: 1781
Causes of Revolt
Countdown to Independence: Causes of the American Revolution

Equality: A History of the Women's Movement in America
Give Me Liberty: Patrick Henry—Voice of the Revolution
The Life and Times of George Washington
The Life of George Washington

A New Nation (1776-1815)
Patrick Henry's Fight For Individual Rights
The Revolutionary War Series
Seeds of Liberty: The Causes of the American Revolution
Thomas Jefferson: The Pursuit of Liberty
Valley Forge: The Battle for Survival

GRADE NINE

Historical Fiction

Avi. *Captain Grey*
Caudill. *Tree of Freedom*
Clapp. *I'm Deborah Sampson*
Collier. *My Brother Sam Is Dead*
DeFord. *An Enemy Among Them*
Edwards. *George Midgett's War*
Forman. *Prince Charlie's Year*

Fritz. *Early Thunder*
Gregory. *The Winter of Red Snow: Diary,1777-1778*
O'Dell. *Sarah Bishop*
Pope. *The Sherwood Ring*
Rinaldi. *The Fifth of March*
Rinaldi. *Finishing Becca*
Rinaldi. *Hang a Thousand Trees with Ribbons*
Rinaldi. *A Ride into Morning*

Rinaldi. *The Secret of Sarah Revere*
Rinaldi. *Time Enough for Drums*
Wibberley. *Peter Treegate's War*
Wibberley. *Sea Captain from Salem*
Wibberley. *Treegate's Raiders*

Biography

Beller. *Woman of Independence: The Life of Abigail Adams*
Bober. *Abigail Adams*
Bober. *Thomas Jefferson: Man on a Mountain*
Brill. *John Adams*
Bruns. *George Washington*
Bruns. *Thomas Jefferson*
Clinton. *James Madison: Fourth President*
Conle. *Benjamin Banneker: Scientist and Mathematician*
Cousins. *Ben Franklin of Old Philadelphia*

Diamond. *Paul Cuffe: Merchant and Abolitionist*
Diamond. *Prince Hall: Social Reforme*
Dwyer. *John Adams*
Farley. *Samuel Adams: Grandfather of His Country*
Farley. *Thomas Paine: Revolutionary Author*
Ford. *Paul Revere: Rider for the Revolution*
Fritz. *Traitor: The Case of Benedict Arnold*
Latham. *Carry On, Mr. Bowditch*
Leavell. *James Madison*

Looby. *Benjamin Franklin*
Meltzer. *Benjamin Franklin: The New American*
Meltzer. *George Washington and the Birth of Our Nation*
Meltzer. *Thomas Jefferson: The Revolutionary Aristocrat*
Meltzer. *Tom Paine: Voice of Revolution*
O'Brien. *Alexander Hamilton*
Osborne. *Abigail Adams: Women's Rights Advocate*
Patterson. *Thomas Jefferson*
Potter. *Benjamin Franklin*
Schwartz. *George Washington*

Stefoff. *James Monroe: 5th President*
Stefoff. *John Adams: 2nd President*

Stefoff. *Thomas Jefferson: 3rd President*
Stewart. *Benjamin Franklin*
Vail. *Thomas Paine*

Collective Biography

Faber. *Great Lives: American Government*
Mahoney. *Women in Espionage: A Biographical Dictionary*
Myers. *Now Is Your Time*

O'Brien. *American Political Leaders: From Colonial Times to the Present*
Rennert. *Pioneers of Discovery*

Sheafer. *Women in America's Wars*
Wilkinson. *Generals Who Changed the World*

History

Cray. *American Datelines*
Davis. *Don't Know Much About History*
Dolan. *The American Revolution*
Dudley. *The American Revolution: Opposing Viewpoints*
Dudley. *The Creation of the Constitution: Opposing Viewpoints*
Evans. *Freedom of Religion*
Evans. *Freedom of Speech*
Evans. *Freedom of the Press*
Gay. *Revolutionary War*
Hakim. *From Colonies to Country*
Hakim. *The New Nation*
Hirsch. *Taxation: Paying for Government*
Jaffe. *Who Were the Founding Fathers?*
Katz. *Exploration to the War of 1812: 1492-1814*

Leinwand. *Do We Need a New Constitution?*
Lukes. *The American Revolution*
Marrin. *The War for Independence*
Medearis. *Come This Far to Freedom*
Meltzer. *The American Revolutionaries, 1750-1800*
Meltzer. *The Black Americans*
Meltzer. *Weapons & Warfare*
Murphy. *Young Patriot: The American Revolution as Experienced by One Boy*
Newton. *Gun Control: An Issue for the Nineties*
Pascoe. *Freedom of Expression*
Pascoe. *Mexico and the United States: Cooperation and Conflict*
Platt. *The Smithsonian Visual Timeline of Inventions*

Rappaport. *American Women: Their Lives in their Words*
Salmon. *The Limits of Independence: American Women 1760-1800*
Silverman. *Songs and Stories from the American Revolution*
Smith. *Fascinating People and Astounding Events from American History*
Smith. *The Revolutionary War*
Steele. *Freedom's River*
Stewart. *The Revolutionary War*
Time-Life. *The Revolutionaries*
Wheeler. *Events That Changed American History*
Zall. *Becoming American: Young People in the American Revolution*
Zell. *A Multicultural Portrait of the American Revolution*

Multimedia

CD-ROM

American History Explorer
Events That Changed the World

Her Heritage: A Biographical Encyclopedia of American History
Ideas That Changed the World

Landmark Documents in American History
Total History

Video

Abigail Adams
American Constitution: The Road to Runnymede
American Independence 1776
The American Revolution
The Battle of Yorktown: 1781
Causes of Revolt

Equality: A History of the Women's Movement in America
Give Me Liberty: Patrick Henry—Voice of the Revolution
The Life of George Washington

A New Nation (1776-1815)
The Revolutionary War Series
Thomas Jefferson: The Pursuit of Liberty
Valley Forge: The Battle for Survival

GRADE TEN

Historical Fiction

Clapp. *I'm Deborah Sampson*
Collier. *My Brother Sam Is Dead*
Edwards. *George Midgett's War*
Forman. *Prince Charlie's Year*
O'Dell. *Sarah Bishop*

Pope. *The Sherwood Ring*
Rinaldi. *The Fifth of March*
Rinaldi. *Finishing Becca*
Rinaldi. *Hang a Thousand Trees with Ribbons*

Rinaldi. *Time Enough for Drums*
Wibberley. *Peter Treegate's War*
Wibberley. *Sea Captain from Salem*
Wibberley. *Treegate's Raiders*

Biography

Bober. *Abigail Adams*
Bober. *Thomas Jefferson: Man on a Mountain*
Bruns. *George Washington*
Bruns. *Thomas Jefferson*
Conle. *Benjamin Banneker: Scientist and Mathematician*
Diamond. *Prince Hall: Social Reformer*

Dwyer. *John Adams*
Latham. *Carry On, Mr. Bowditch*
Leavell. *James Madison*
Looby. *Benjamin Franklin*
Meltzer. *Benjamin Franklin: The New American*
Meltzer. *George Washington and the Birth of Our Nation*

Meltzer. *Tom Paine: Voice of Revolution*
O'Brien. *Alexander Hamilton*
Osborne. *Abigail Adams: Women's Rights Advocate*
Schwartz. *George Washington*
Stefoff. *John Adams: 2nd President*
Vail. *Thomas Paine*

Collective Biography

Mahoney. *Women in Espionage: A Biographical Dictionary*
Myers. *Now Is Your Time*

O'Brien. *American Political Leaders: From Colonial Times to the Present*

Wilkinson. *Generals Who Changed the World*

History

Cray. *American Datelines*
Davis. *Don't Know Much About History*
Dudley. *The American Revolution: Opposing Viewpoints*
Dudley. *The Creation of the Constitution: Opposing Viewpoints*
Evans. *Born for Liberty: A History of Women in America*
Evans. *Freedom of Religion*
Evans. *Freedom of Speech*
Evans. *Freedom of the Press*
Hakim. *From Colonies to Country*
Hakim. *The New Nation*
Jaffe. *Who Were the Founding Fathers?*
Katz. *Exploration to the War of 1812: 1492-1814*

Leinwand. *Do We Need a New Constitution?*
Lukes. *The American Revolution*
Marrin. *The War for Independence*
Meltzer. *The American Revolutionaries, 1750-1800*
Meltzer. *The Black Americans*
Meltzer. *Weapons & Warfare*
Murphy. *Young Patriot: The American Revolution as Experienced by One Boy*
Newton. *Gun Control: An Issue for the Nineties*
Pascoe. *Freedom of Expression*
Pascoe. *Mexico and the United States: Cooperation and Conflict*
Rappaport. *American Women: Their Lives in Their Words*

Salmon. *The Limits of Independence: American Women 1760-1800*
Silverman. *Songs and Stories from the American Revolution*
Smith. *Fascinating People and Astounding Events from American History*
Smith. *The Revolutionary War*
Steele. *Freedom's River*
Stewart. *The Revolutionary War*
Time-Life. *The Revolutionaries*
Wheeler. *Events That Changed American History*
Zall. *Becoming American: Young People in the American Revolution*
Zell. *A Multicultural Portrait of the American Revolution*

Multimedia

CD-ROM

Events That Changed the World
Her Heritage: A Biographical Encyclopedia of American History

Ideas That Changed the World
Landmark Documents in American History
Total History

Video

Abigail Adams
American Constitution: The
   Road to Runnymede
American Independence 1776
The Battle of Yorktown: 1781

Equality: A History of the
   Women's Movement in
   America
Give Me Liberty: Patrick
   Henry—Voice of the
   Revolution
The Life of George Washington

Paul Revere: The Midnight
   Rider
The Revolutionary War Series
Thomas Jefferson: The
   Pursuit of Liberty
Valley Forge: The Battle for
   Survival

GRADES ELEVEN AND TWELVE

Historical Fiction

Byrd. Jefferson: A Novel
Grimes. My Thomas
Meyers. The Knightsbridge
   Plot

Wibberley. Peter Treegate's
   War
Wibberley. Sea Captain from
   Salem

Wibberley. Treegate's Raiders

Biography

Bober. Abigail Adams
Bober. Thomas Jefferson:
   Man on a Mountain
Diamond. Prince Hall: Social
   Reformer

Fischer. Paul Revere's Ride
Meltzer. Benjamin Franklin:
   The New American
Meltzer. George Washington
   and the Birth of Our Nation

Meltzer. Tom Paine: Voice of
   Revolution
O'Brien. Alexander Hamilton
Schwartz. George Washington
Vail. Thomas Paine

Collective Biography

Mahoney. Women in
   Espionage: A Biographical
   Dictionary

O'Brien. American Political
   Leaders: From Colonial
   Times to the Present

History

Cray. American Datelines
Davidson. Everyday Life
   Through the Ages
Davis. Don't Know Much
   About History
Dudley. The American
   Revolution: Opposing
   Viewpoints
Dudley. The Creation of the
   Constitution: Opposing
   Viewpoints
Evans. Born for Liberty: A
   History of Women in
   America
Hakim. From Colonies to
   Country
Hakim. The New Nation

Hibbert. Redcoats and
   Rebels: The American
   Revolution Through British
   Eyes
Keegan. History of Warfare
Jaffe. Who Were the
   Founding Fathers?
Leinwand. Do We Need a
   New Constitution?
Meltzer. The American
   Revolutionaries, 1750-1800
Meltzer. Weapons & Warfare
Rappaport. American
   Women: Their Lives in
   Their Words
Salmon. The Limits of
   Independence: American
   Women 1760-1800

Shenkman. "I Love Paul
   Revere, Whether He Rode
   or Not"
Silverman. Songs and Stories
   from the American
   Revolution
Smith. Fascinating People
   and Astounding Events
   from American History
Steele. Freedom's River
Time-Life. The
   Revolutionaries
Tinling. With Women's Eyes:
   Visitors to the New World,
   1775-1918
Wheeler. Events That
   Changed American History

Multimedia

CD-ROM

Events That Changed the
   World

Her Heritage: A Biographical
   Encyclopedia of American
   History
Ideas That Changed the World

Landmark Documents in
   American History
Total History

Video

Abigail Adams
American Constitution: The Road to Runnymede
American Independence 1776
The American Revolution
The Battle of Yorktown: 1781

Equality: A History of the Women's Movement in America
Give Me Liberty: Patrick Henry—Voice of the Revolution
The Life of George Washington,

Paul Revere: The Midnight Rider
The Revolutionary War Series
Thomas Jefferson: The Pursuit of Liberty
Valley Forge: The Battle for Survival

THE EARLY UNITED STATES, 1784-1814

GRADE SEVEN

Historical Fiction

Brady. *Reluctant Hero*
Collier. *The Clock*
Curry. *Moon Window*
Fleischman.
    Coming-and-Going Men
Fleischman. *Path of the Pale*
    Horse
Fritz. *The Cabin Faced West*
Hansen. *The Captive*
Lawson. *If Pigs Could Fly*
Rinaldi. *The Second Bend in*
    the River
Rinaldi. *A Stitch in Time*
Rinaldi. *Wolf by the Ears*
Sanders. *Badman Ballad*
Whelan. *Once on This Island*
Wibberley. *The Last Battle*
Wibberley. *Leopard's Prey*
Wibberley. *Red Pawns*
Wood. *Becoming Rosemary*

Biography

Anderson. *Martha*
    Washington: First Lady of
    the Land
Beller. *Woman of*
    Independence: The Life of
    Abigail Adams
Bober. *Thomas Jefferson:*
    Man on a Mountain
Brill. *John Adams*
Bruns. *George Washington*
Bruns. *Thomas Jefferson*
Clinton. *James Madison:*
    Fourth President
Coelho. *John Quincy Adams*
Conle. *Benjamin Banneker:*
    Scientist and
    Mathematician
Cousins. *Ben Franklin of Old*
    Philadelphia
Davidson. *Dolly Madison:*
    Famous First Lady
Diamond. *Paul Cuffe:*
    Merchant and Abolitionist
Diamond. *Prince Hall: Social*
    Reformer
Dwyer. *John Adams*
Edwards. *Denmark Vesey:*
    Slave Revolt Leader
Equiano. *The Kidnapped*
    Prince: The Life of
    Olaudah Equiano
Feinberg. *John Marshall: The*
    Great Chief Justice
Feldman. *Benjamin Franklin:*
    Scientist and Inventor
Fitz-Gerald. *James Monroe:*
    Fifth President
Fitz-Gerald. *William Henry*
    Harrison: Ninth President
Fritz. *The Great Little*
    Madison
Hargrove. *Thomas Jefferson:*
    Third President
Klots. *Richard Allen:*
    Religious Leader and
    Social Activist
Latham. *Carry On, Mr.*
    Bowditch
Leavell. *James Madison*
Lindop. *George Washington,*
    Thomas Jefferson, and
    Andrew Jackson
Looby. *Benjamin Franklin*
Meltzer. *Thomas Jefferson:*
    The Revolutionary
    Aristocrat
Morris. *The Jefferson Way*
Morris. *The Washington Way*
Nardo. *Thomas Jefferson*
O'Brien. *Alexander Hamilton*
Osborne. *Abigail Adams:*
    Women's Rights Advocate
Osborne. *George*
    Washington: Leader of a
    New Nation
Osborne. *The Many Lives of*
    Benjamin Franklin
Patterson. *Thomas Jefferson*
Polikoff. *James Madison: 4th*
    President
Potter. *Benjamin Franklin*
Sandak. *The Jeffersons*
Sandak. *The John Adamses*
Sandak. *The Madisons*
Sandak. *The Washingtons*
Schwartz. *George Washington*
Stefoff. *James Monroe: 5th*
    President
Stefoff. *John Adams: 2nd*
    President
Stefoff. *Thomas Jefferson:*
    3rd President
Stewart. *Benjamin Franklin*
Vail. *Thomas Paine*
Wilson. *The Ingenious Mr.*
    Peale

Collective Biography

Allen. *As Long as the Rivers*
    Flow: The Stories of Nine
    Native Americans
Altman. *Extraordinary Black*
    Americans
Beard. *The Presidents in*
    American History
Blassingame. *The Look-It-Up*
    Book of Presidents
Cohen. *The Ghosts of War*

Dolan. *Shaping U.S. Foreign Policy: Profiles of Twelve Secretaries of State*
Faber. *Great Lives: American Government*
Glenn. *Discover America's Favorite Architects*

Katz. *Proudly Red and Black: Stories of African and Native Americans*
Myers. *Now Is Your Time*
Pascoe. *First Facts About the Presidents*
Provenson. *My Fellow Americans*

Rennert. *Pioneers of Discovery*
Rubel. *The Scholastic Encyclopedia of the Presidents*
Smith. *The Founding Presidents*
Sullivan. *Presidents at Play*

History

Bosco. *The War of 1812*
Bowler. *Trains*
Carnes. *Us and Them: A History of Intolerance in America*
Colman. *Toilets, Bathtubs, Sinks, and Sewers*
Cray. *American Datelines*
Davies. *Transport: On Land, Road and Rail*
Emert. *Top Lawyers and Their Famous Cases*
Faber. *From Sea to Sea: The Growth of the United States*
Faber. *We the People: The Story of the United States Constitution*
Feinberg. *American Political Scandals Past and Present*
Gay. *War of 1812*
Giblin. *Be Seated: A Book About Chairs*
Hakim. *From Colonies to Country*
Hakim. *The New Nation*
Hilton. *A Capital Capital City, 1790-1814*
Hirsch. *Taxation: Paying for Government*

Jaffe. *Who Were the Founding Fathers?*
Karl. *America Alive: A History*
Katz. *Exploration to the War of 1812: 1492-1814*
Kroll. *By the Dawn's Early Light: The Star-Spangled Banner*
Kronenwetter. *Covert Action*
Landau. *Armed America: The Status of Gun Control*
Lucas. *Civil Rights: The Long Struggle*
Markham. *Inventions That Changed Modern Life*
Marrin. *1812: The War Nobody Won*
McNeese. *America's Early Canals*
McNeese. *Early River Travel*
Medearis. *Come This Far to Freedom*
Meltzer. *The Black Americans*
Meltzer. *Weapons & Warfare*
Morley. *Clothes: For Work, Play and Display*
Mulcahy. *Diseases: Finding the Cure*

Pascoe. *Mexico and the United States: Cooperation and Conflict*
Patrick. *The Young Oxford Companion to the Supreme Court*
Platt. *The Smithsonian Visual Timeline of Inventions*
Rappaport. *American Women: Their Lives in Their Words*
Salmon. *The Limits of Independence: American Women 1760-1800*
Sandler. *Presidents*
Smith-Baranzini. *USKids History: The New American Nation*
St. George. *The White House: Cornerstone of a Nation*
Steins. *A Nation Is Born: 1700-1820*
Turner. *Shaker Hearts*
Warner. *The U.S. Marine Corps*
Wheeler. *Events That Changed American History*
Whitman. *Get Up and Go: American Road Travel*

Multimedia

CD-ROM

American History Explorer Campaigns, Candidates and the Presidency
Eyewitness Encyclopedia of Science

Her Heritage: A Biographical Encyclopedia of American History
Inside the White House
Landmark Documents in American History

Portraits of American Presidents
Science Navigator
SkyTrip America
Total History
The Way Things Work

Video

Abigail Adams
Choosing a President
Equality: A History of the Women's Movement in America
Fort McHenry: Preserving the Spirit of Liberty
A History of Slavery in America

The Legacy of Thomas Jefferson
The Life and Times of George Washington
The Life of George Washington
Making It Happen: Masters of Invention
Mansions of Newport

A More Perfect Union: The Three Branches of the Federal Government
Mount Vernon: Home of George Washington
Mr. Jefferson and His University
A New Nation (1776-1815)

Our Federal Government:
   The Legislative Branch
Our Federal Government:
   The Presidency

Our Federal Government:
   The Supreme Court
Patrick Henry's Fight For
   Individual Rights

Pride & Prejudice: A History
   of Black Culture in America
Reading Terminal Market
Thomas Jefferson: The
   Pursuit of Liberty

GRADE EIGHT

Historical Fiction

Brady. *Reluctant Hero*
Collier. *The Clock*
Curry. *Moon Window*
Fleischman.
   Coming-and-Going Men
Fleischman. *Path of the Pale
   Horse*

Hansen. *The Captive*
Lawson. *If Pigs Could Fly*
O'Dell. *Streams to the River,
   River to the Sea*
Rinaldi. *The Second Bend in
   the River*
Rinaldi. *A Stitch in Time*

Rinaldi. *Wolf by the Ears*
Sanders. *Badman Ballad*
Whelan. *Once on This Island*
Wibberley. *The Last Battle*
Wibberley. *Leopard's Prey*
Wibberley. *Red Pawns*
Wood. *Becoming Rosemary*

Biography

Beller. *Woman of
   Independence: The Life of
   Abigail Adams*
Bober. *Thomas Jefferson:
   Man on a Mountain*
Brill. *John Adams*
Bruns. *George Washington*
Bruns. *Thomas Jefferson*
Clinton. *James Madison:
   Fourth President*
Coelho. *John Quincy Adams*
Conle. *Benjamin Banneker:
   Scientist and
   Mathematician*
Cousins. *Ben Franklin of Old
   Philadelphia*
Diamond. *Paul Cuffe:
   Merchant and Abolitionist*
Diamond. *Prince Hall: Social
   Reformer*
Dwyer. *John Adams*
Edwards. *Denmark Vesey:
   Slave Revolt Leader*

Equiano. *The Kidnapped
   Prince: The Life of
   Olaudah Equiano*
Feinberg. *John Marshall: The
   Great Chief Justice*
Feldman. *Benjamin Franklin:
   Scientist and Inventor*
Fitz-Gerald. *James Monroe:
   Fifth President*
Fitz-Gerald. *William Henry
   Harrison: Ninth President*
Fritz. *The Great Little Madison*
Hargrove. *Thomas Jefferson:
   Third President*
Klots. *Richard Allen:
   Religious Leader and
   Social Activist*
Latham. *Carry On, Mr. Bowditch*
Leavell. *James Madison*
Lindop. *George Washington,
   Thomas Jefferson, and
   Andrew Jackson*
Looby. *Benjamin Franklin*
Meltzer. *Thomas Jefferson:
   The Revolutionary Aristocrat*

Morris. *The Jefferson Way*
Morris. *The Washington Way*
Nardo. *Thomas Jefferson*
O'Brien. *Alexander Hamilton*
Osborne. *Abigail Adams:
   Women's Rights Advocate*
Patterson. *Thomas Jefferson*
Polikoff. *James Madison: 4th
   President*
Potter. *Benjamin Franklin*
Sandak. *The Jeffersons*
Sandak. *The John Adamses*
Sandak. *The Madisons*
Sandak. *The Washingtons*
Schwartz. *George Washington*
Stefoff. *James Monroe: 5th
   President*
Stefoff. *John Adams: 2nd
   President*
Stefoff. *Thomas Jefferson:
   3rd President*
Stewart. *Benjamin Franklin*
Vail. *Thomas Paine*
Wilson. *The Ingenious Mr.
   Peale*

Collective Biography

Aaseng. *Great Justices of the
   Supreme Court*
Allen. *As Long as the Rivers
   Flow: The Stories of Nine
   Native Americans*
Altman. *Extraordinary Black
   Americans*
Beard. *The Presidents in
   American History*
Blassingame. *The Look-It-Up
   Book of Presidents*
Cohen. *The Ghosts of War*

Dolan. *Shaping U.S. Foreign
   Policy: Profiles of Twelve
   Secretaries of State*
Faber. *Great Lives: American
   Government*
Glenn. *Discover America's
   Favorite Architects*
Katz. *Proudly Red and Black:
   Stories of African and
   Native Americans*
Myers. *Now Is Your Time*
Otfinoski.
   Nineteenth-Century Writers

Pascoe. *First Facts About the
   Presidents*
Provenson. *My Fellow
   Americans*
Rennert. *Pioneers of Discovery*
Rubel. *The Scholastic
   Encyclopedia of the
   Presidents*
Smith. *The Founding
   Presidents*
Sullivan. *Presidents at Play*

History

Bosco. *The War of 1812*

Carnes. *Us and Them: A History of Intolerance in America*

Colman. *Toilets, Bathtubs, Sinks, and Sewers*

Cray. *American Datelines*

Davies. *Transport: On Land, Road and Rail*

Emert. *Top Lawyers and Their Famous Cases*

Faber. *From Sea to Sea: The Growth of the United States*

Faber. *We the People: The Story of the United States Constitution*

Feinberg. *American Political Scandals Past and Present*

Gay. *Revolutionary War*

Giblin. *Be Seated: A Book About Chairs*

Hakim. *From Colonies to Country*

Hakim. *The New Nation*

Hilton. *A Capital Capital City, 1790-1814*

Hirsch. *Taxation: Paying for Government*

Jaffe. *Who Were the Founding Fathers?*

Karl. *America Alive: A History*

Katz. *Exploration to the War of 1812: 1492-1814*

Kronenwetter. *Covert Action*

Landau. *Armed America: The Status of Gun Control*

Lucas. *Civil Rights: The Long Struggle*

Markham. *Inventions That Changed Modern Life*

Marrin. *1812: The War Nobody Won*

McNeese. *America's Early Canals*

McNeese. *Early River Travel*

Medearis. *Come This Far to Freedom*

Meltzer. *The Black Americans*

Meltzer. *Weapons & Warfare*

Morley. *Clothes: For Work, Play and Display*

Mulcahy. *Diseases: Finding the Cure*

Pascoe. *Mexico and the United States: Cooperation and Conflict*

Patrick. *The Young Oxford Companion to the Supreme Court*

Platt. *The Smithsonian Visual Timeline of Inventions*

Rappaport. *American Women: Their Lives in Their Words*

Salmon. *The Limits of Independence: American Women 1760-1800*

Sandler. *Presidents*

St. George. *The White House: Cornerstone of a Nation*

Steins. *A Nation Is Born: 1700-1820*

Turner. *Shaker Hearts*

Warner. *The U.S. Marine Corps*

Wheeler. *Events That Changed American History*

Whitman. *Get Up and Go: American Road Travel*

Multimedia

CD-ROM

American History Explorer

Campaigns, Candidates and the Presidency

Eyewitness Encyclopedia of Science

Her Heritage: A Biographical Encyclopedia of American History

Inside the White House

Landmark Documents in American History

Portraits of American Presidents

Science Navigator

SkyTrip America

Total History

The Way Things Work

Video

Abigail Adams

Choosing a President

Equality: A History of the Women's Movement in America

Fort McHenry: Preserving the Spirit of Liberty

A History of Slavery in America

The Legacy of Thomas Jefferson

The Life and Times of George Washington

The Life of George Washington

Making It Happen: Masters of Invention

Mansions of Newport

A More Perfect Union: The Three Branches of the Federal Government

Mount Vernon: Home of George Washington

Mr. Jefferson and His University

A New Nation (1776-1815)

Our Federal Government: The Legislative Branch

Our Federal Government: The Presidency

Our Federal Government: The Supreme Court

Patrick Henry's Fight For Individual Rights

Pride & Prejudice: A History of Black Culture in America

Reading Terminal Market

Thomas Jefferson: The Pursuit of Liberty

GRADE NINE

Historical Fiction

Collier. *The Clock*
Curry. *Moon Window*
Fleischman. *Coming-and-Going Men*
Fleischman. *Path of the Pale Horse*
Lawson. *If Pigs Could Fly*
Rinaldi. *A Stitch in Time*
Rinaldi. *Wolf by the Ears*
Sanders. *Badman Ballad*
Wibberley. *The Last Battle*
Wibberley. *Leopard's Prey*
Wibberley. *Red Pawns*
Wood. *Becoming Rosemary*

Biography

Beller. *Woman of Independence: The Life of Abigail Adams*
Bober. *Abigail Adams*
Bober. *Thomas Jefferson: Man on a Mountain*
Brill. *John Adams*
Bruns. *George Washington*
Bruns. *Thomas Jefferson*
Clinton. *James Madison: Fourth President*
Coelho. *John Quincy Adams*
Conle. *Benjamin Banneker: Scientist and Mathematician*
Cousins. *Ben Franklin of Old Philadelphia*
Diamond. *Paul Cuffe: Merchant and Abolitionist*
Diamond. *Prince Hall: Social Reformer*
Dwyer. *John Adams*
Edwards. *Denmark Vesey: Slave Revolt Leader*

Equiano. *The Kidnapped Prince: The Life of Olaudah Equiano*
Feinberg. *John Marshall: The Great Chief Justice*
Fitz-Gerald. *James Monroe: Fifth President*
Fitz-Gerald. *William Henry Harrison: Ninth President*
Hargrove. *Thomas Jefferson: Third President*
Klots. *Richard Allen: Religious Leader and Social Activist*
Latham. *Carry On, Mr. Bowditch*
Leavell. *James Madison*
Looby. *Benjamin Franklin*
Meltzer. *Benjamin Franklin: The New American*
Meltzer. *George Washington and the Birth of Our Nation*
Meltzer. *Thomas Jefferson: The Revolutionary Aristocrat*

Meltzer. *Tom Paine: Voice of Revolution*
Morris. *The Jefferson Way*
Morris. *The Washington Way*
O'Brien. *Alexander Hamilton*
Osborne. *Abigail Adams: Women's Rights Advocate*
Patterson. *Thomas Jefferson*
Polikoff. *James Madison: 4th President*
Potter. *Benjamin Franklin*
Schwartz. *George Washington*
Stefoff. *James Monroe: 5th President*
Stefoff. *John Adams: 2nd President*
Stefoff. *Thomas Jefferson: 3rd President*
Stewart. *Benjamin Franklin*
Vail. *Thomas Paine*
Wilson. *The Ingenious Mr. Peale*

Collective Biography

Aaseng. *Great Justices of the Supreme Court*
Anthony. *First Ladies: 1789-1961*
Beard. *The Presidents in American History*
Blassingame. *The Look-It-Up Book of Presidents*

Dolan. *Shaping U.S. Foreign Policy: Profiles of Twelve Secretaries of State*
Faber. *Great Lives: American Government*
Glenn. *Discover America's Favorite Architects*
Myers. *Now Is Your Time*

O'Brien. *American Political Leaders: From Colonial Times to the Present*
Otfinoski. *Nineteenth-Century Writers*
Rennert. *Pioneers of Discovery*
Smith. *The Founding Presidents*
Sullivan. *Presidents at Play*

History

Alderman. *In Our Defense: The Bill of Rights in Action*
Ardley. *Music: An Illustrated Encyclopedia*
Bosco. *The War of 1812*
Carnes. *Us and Them: A History of Intolerance in America*
Cray. *American Datelines*

Davis. *Don't Know Much About History*
Davis. *Man-Made Catastrophes*
Emert. *Top Lawyers and Their Famous Cases*
Faber. *From Sea to Sea: The Growth of the United States*

Faber. *We the People: The Story of the United States Constitution*
Feinberg. *American Political Scandals Past and Present*
Frost-Knappman. *Women's Suffrage in America*
Garza. *Barred from the Bar: A History of Women and the Legal Profession*

Gay. *War of 1812*
Greenblatt. *The War of 1812*
Hakim. *From Colonies to Country*
Hakim. *The New Nation*
Hilton. *A Capital Capital City, 1790-1814*
Hirsch. *Taxation: Paying for Government*
Jaffe. *Who Were the Founding Fathers?*
Katz. *Exploration to the War of 1812: 1492-1814*
Knappman. *Great American Trials*
Kronenwetter. *Covert Action*
Landau. *Armed America: The Status of Gun Control*
Markham. *Inventions That Changed Modern Life*

Marrin. *1812: The War Nobody Won*
Medearis. *Come This Far to Freedom*
Meltzer. *The Bill of Rights: How We Got It and What It Means*
Meltzer. *The Black Americans*
Meltzer. *Weapons & Warfare*
Mulcahy. *Diseases: Finding the Cure*
Nardo. *The War of 1812*
Pascoe. *Mexico and the United States: Cooperation and Conflict*
Patrick. *The Young Oxford Companion to the Supreme Court*
Platt. *The Smithsonian Visual Timeline of Inventions*

Rappaport. *American Women: Their Lives in Their Words*
Salmon. *The Limits of Independence: American Women 1760-1800*
Schreiner. *Mayday! Mayday!*
Smith. *Fascinating People and Astounding Events from American History*
St. George. *The White House: Cornerstone of a Nation*
Steele. *Freedom's River*
Wheeler. *Events That Changed American History*
Whitman. *Get Up and Go: American Road Travel*

Multimedia

CD-ROM

American History Explorer Campaigns, Candidates and the Presidency
Events That Changed the World

Her Heritage: A Biographical Encyclopedia of American History
Ideas That Changed the World
Inside the White House Landmark Documents in American History

Portraits of American Presidents
Science Navigator
Total History
The Way Things Work

Video

Abigail Adams
The American Constitution: The Ghosts of '87
Choosing a President
The Constitution of the United States
Equality: A History of the Women's Movement in America
Fort McHenry: Preserving the Spirit of Liberty

George Washington: The Man Who Wouldn't Be King
Hidden Heritage: The Roots of Black American Painting
A History of Slavery in America
The Legacy of Thomas Jefferson
The Life of George Washington
Mansions of Newport

A More Perfect Union: The Three Branches of the Federal Government
Mount Vernon: Home of George Washington
Mr. Jefferson and His University
A New Nation (1776-1815)
Pride & Prejudice: A History of Black Culture in America
Reading Terminal Market
Thomas Jefferson: The Pursuit of Liberty

GRADE TEN

Historical Fiction

Rinaldi. *A Stitch in Time*
Rinaldi. *Wolf by the Ears*

Wibberley. *The Last Battle*
Wibberley. *Leopard's Prey*

Wibberley. *Red Pawns*

Biography

Bober. *Abigail Adams*
Bober. *Thomas Jefferson: Man on a Mountain*
Bruns. *George Washington*
Bruns. *Thomas Jefferson*

Coelho. *John Quincy Adams*
Conle. *Benjamin Banneker: Scientist and Mathematician*

Diamond. *Paul Cuffe: Merchant and Abolitionist*
Diamond. *Prince Hall: Social Reformer*
Dwyer. *John Adams*

Edwards. *Denmark Vesey: Slave Revolt Leader*
Equiano. *The Kidnapped Prince: The Life of Olaudah Equiano*
Feinberg. *John Marshall: The Great Chief Justice*
Klots. *Richard Allen: Religious Leader and Social Activist*

Latham. *Carry On, Mr. Bowditch*
Leavell. *James Madison*
Looby. *Benjamin Franklin*
Meltzer. *Benjamin Franklin: The New American*
Meltzer. *George Washington and the Birth of Our Nation*
Meltzer. *Tom Paine: Voice of Revolution*

O'Brien. *Alexander Hamilton*
Osborne. *Abigail Adams: Women's Rights Advocate*
Schwartz. *George Washington*
Stefoff. *John Adams: 2nd President of the United States*
Vail. *Thomas Paine*

Collective Biography

Aaseng. *Great Justices of the Supreme Court*
Anthony. *First Ladies: 1789-1961*
Myers. *Now Is Your Time*

O'Brien. *American Political Leaders*
Otfinoski. *Nineteenth-Century Writers*

Smith. *The Founding Presidents*
Sullivan. *Presidents at Play*

History

Alderman. *In Our Defense: The Bill of Rights in Action*
Ardley. *Music: An Illustrated Encyclopedia*
Bosco. *The War of 1812*
Carnes. *Us and Them: A History of Intolerance in America*
Cray. *American Datelines*
Davis. *Don't Know Much About History*
Davis. *Man-Made Catastrophes*
Evans. *Born for Liberty: A History of Women in America*
Faber. *From Sea to Sea: The Growth of the United States*
Faber. *We the People: The Story of the United States Constitution*
Feinberg. *American Political Scandals Past and Present*
Frost-Knappman. *Women's Suffrage in America*

Garza. *Barred from the Bar: A History of Women and the Legal Profession*
Greenblatt. *The War of 1812*
Hakim. *From Colonies to Country*
Hakim. *The New Nation*
Hilton. *A Capital Capital City, 1790-1814*
Jaffe. *Who Were the Founding Fathers?*
Katz. *Exploration to the War of 1812: 1492-1814*
Knappman. *Great American Trials*
Kronenwetter. *Covert Action*
Landau. *Armed America: The Status of Gun Control*
Markham. *Inventions That Changed Modern Life*
Meltzer. *The Bill of Rights: How We Got It and What It Means*
Meltzer. *The Black Americans*
Meltzer. *Weapons & Warfare*

Mulcahy. *Diseases: Finding the Cure*
Nardo. *The War of 1812*
Pascoe. *Mexico and the United States: Cooperation and Conflict*
Patrick. *The Young Oxford Companion to the Supreme Court*
Rappaport. *American Women: Their Lives in Their Words*
Salmon. *The Limits of Independence: American Women 1760-1800*
Schreiner. *Mayday! Mayday!*
Smith. *Fascinating People and Astounding Events from American History*
Steele. *Freedom's River*
Wheeler. *Events That Changed American History*

Multimedia

CD-ROM

Campaigns, Candidates and the Presidency
Events That Changed the World
Her Heritage: A Biographical Encyclopedia of American History

Ideas That Changed the World
Inside the White House
Landmark Documents in American History
Portraits of American Presidents
Science Navigator

Total History
The Way Things Work

Video

Abigail Adams
The American Constitution: The Ghosts of '87
Choosing a President

The Constitution of the United State
Equality: A History of the Women's Movement in America

George Washington: The Man Who Wouldn't Be King
Hidden Heritage: The Roots of Black American Painting

A History of Slavery in America
The Legacy of Thomas Jefferson
The Life of George Washington

Mansions of Newport
A More Perfect Union: The Three Branches of the Federal Government
Mount Vernon: Home of George Washington

Mr. Jefferson and His University
Pride & Prejudice: A History of Black Culture in America
Thomas Jefferson: The Pursuit of Liberty

GRADES ELEVEN AND TWELVE

Historical Fiction

Brown. *Dolley: A Novel of Dolley Madison*

Roesch. *Ashana*
Wibberley. *The Last Battle*

Wibberley. *Leopard's Prey*
Wibberley. *Red Pawns*

Biography

Bober. *Abigail Adams*
Bober. *Thomas Jefferson: Man on a Mountain*
Coelho. *John Quincy Adams*
Diamond. *Paul Cuffe: Merchant and Abolitionist*
Diamond. *Prince Hall: Social Reformer*

Klots. *Richard Allen: Religious Leader and Social Activist*
McLanathan. *Gilbert Stuart*
Meltzer. *Benjamin Franklin: The New American*
Meltzer. *George Washington and the Birth of Our Nation*

Meltzer. *Tom Paine: Voice of Revolution*
O'Brien. *Alexander Hamilton*
Schwartz. *George Washington*
Vail. *Thomas Paine*

Collective Biography

Aaseng. *Great Justices of the Supreme Court*
Anthony. *First Ladies: 1789-1961*

Foster. *Written by Herself: African American Women, 1746-1892*
Myers. *Now Is Your Time*
Otfinoski. *Nineteenth-Century Writers*

O'Brien. *American Political Leaders: From Colonial Times to the Present*
Sullivan. *Presidents at Play*
Truman. *First Ladies*

History

Alderman. *In Our Defense: The Bill of Rights in Action*
Ardley. *Music: An Illustrated Encyclopedia*
Boller. *Presidential Wives: An Anecdotal History*
Carnes. *Us and Them: A History of Intolerance in America*
Cray. *American Datelines*
Davidson. *Everyday Life Through the Ages*
Davis. *Don't Know Much About History*
Davis. *Man-Made Catastrophes*
Evans. *Born for Liberty: A History of Women in America*
Faber. *From Sea to Sea: The Growth of the United States*
Faber. *We the People: The Story of the United States Constitution*
Feinberg. *American Political Scandals Past and Present*

Fogle. *Two Hundred Years: Stories of the Nation's Capital*
Frost-Knappman. *Women's Suffrage in America*
Garza. *Barred from the Bar: A History of Women and the Legal Profession*
Greenblatt. *The War of 1812*
Hakim. *From Colonies to Country*
Hakim. *The New Nation*
Hilton. *A Capital Capital City, 1790-1814*
Jaffe. *Who Were the Founding Fathers?*
Keegan. *History of Warfare*
Knappman. *Great American Trials*
Kronenwetter. *Covert Action*
Meltzer. *The Bill of Rights: How We Got It and What It Means*
Meltzer. *Weapons & Warfare*
Mulcahy. *Diseases: Finding the Cure*

Nardo. *The War of 1812*
Pascoe. *Mexico and the United States: Cooperation and Conflict*
Patrick. *The Young Oxford Companion to the Supreme Court*
Rappaport. *American Women: Their Lives in Their Words*
Salmon. *The Limits of Independence: American Women 1760-1800*
Schreiner. *Mayday! Mayday!*
Smith. *Fascinating People and Astounding Events from American History*
Steele. *Freedom's River*
Stevenson. *Life in Black and White: Family and Community in the Slave South*
Tinling. *With Women's Eyes: Visitors to the New World, 1775-1918*
Wheeler. *Events That Changed American History*

Multimedia

CD-ROM

Campaigns, Candidates and the Presidency
Events That Changed the World
Her Heritage: A Biographical Encyclopedia of American History

Ideas That Changed the World
Inside the White House
Landmark Documents in American History
Portraits of American Presidents
Science Navigator

Total History
The Way Things Work

Video

Abigail Adams
The American Constitution: The Ghosts of '87
Choosing a President
The Constitution of the United States
Dark Passages
Equality: A History of the Women's Movement in America

George Washington: The Man Who Wouldn't Be King
Hidden Heritage: The Roots of Black American Painting
A History of Slavery in America
The Legacy of Thomas Jefferson
The Life of George Washington
Mansions of Newport

A More Perfect Union: The Three Branches of the Federal Government
Mount Vernon: Home of George Washington
Mr. Jefferson and His University
Pride & Prejudice: A History of Black Culture in America
Thomas Jefferson: The Pursuit of Liberty

THE SETTLING OF THE WEST, NATIVE AMERICANS, AND SEA JOURNEYS, 1775-1916

GRADE SEVEN

Historical Fiction

Auch. *Journey to Nowhere*
Beatty. *Behave Yourself, Bethany Brant*
Beatty. *Bonanza Girl*
Beatty. *By Crumbs, It's Mine!*
Beatty. *The Coach That Never Came*
Beatty. *Hail Columbia*
Beatty. *How Many Miles to Sundown?*
Beatty. *Jonathan Down Under*
Beatty. *Just Some Weeds from the Wilderness*
Beatty. *Lacy Makes a Match*
Beatty. *A Long Way to Whiskey Creek*
Beatty. *Melinda Takes a Hand*
Beatty. *The Nickel-Plated Beauty*
Beatty. *O the Red Rose Tree*
Beatty. *Red Rock over the River*
Beatty. *Sarah and Me and the Lady from the Sea*
Beatty. *Something to Shout About* .
Beatty. *That's One Ornery Orphan*
Brenner. *On the Frontier with Mr. Audubon*
Burks. *Runs with Horses*
Burks. *Soldier Boy*
Calvert. *The Snowbird*
Conrad. *Prairie Songs*
Cushman. *The Ballad of Lucy Whipple*
DeFelice. *Weasel*
Donahue. *Straight Along a Crooked Road*
Donahue. *The Valley in Between*

Duey. *Anisett Lundberg: California, 1851*
Fleischman. *The Ghost in the Noonday Sun*
Fleischman. *Humbug Mountain*
Fleischman. *Jim Ugly*
Fleischman. *Mr. Mysterious & Co.*
Gipson. *Old Yeller*
Gregory. *Earthquake at Dawn*
Gregory. *Jenny of the Tetons*
Gregory. *Jimmy Spoon and the Pony Express*
Gregory. *The Legend of Jimmy Spoon*
Hahn. *The Gentleman Outlaw and Me—Eli: A Story of the Old West*
Highwater. *The Ceremony of Innocence*
Highwater. *Eyes of Darkness*
Highwater. *I Wear the Morning Star*
Highwater. *Legend Days*
Holmes. *Year of the Sevens 1777*
Hotze. *A Circle Unbroken*
Howard. *Out of Step with the Dancers*
Karr. *Go West, Young Women!*
Karr. *Oh, Those Harper Girls!*
Karr. *Phoebe's Folly*
Keehn. *I Am Regina*
Keith. *The Obstinate Land*
Kherdian. *Bridger: The Story of a Mountain Man*
Lasky. *Beyond the Divide*
Lawlor. *Gold in the Hills*
Lenski. *Indian Captive: The Story of Mary Jemison*

Mazzio. *Leaving Eldorado*
McCall. *Message from the Mountains*
McClung. *Hugh Glass, Mountain Man*
McClung. *The True Adventures of Grizzly Adams*
McGraw. *Moccasin Trail*
Meyer. *Where the Broken Heart Still Beats:Cynthia Ann Parker*
Moeri. *Save Queen of Sheba*
Morrow. *On to Oregon!*
Murrow. *West Against the Wind*
Myers. *The Righteous Revenge of Artemis Bonner*
Nixon. *Caught in the Act: The Orphan Quartet Two*
Nixon. *A Deadly Promise*
Nixon. *High Trail to Danger*
Nixon. *In the Face of Danger*
Nixon. *A Place to Belong*
O'Dell. *Island of the Blue Dolphins*
O'Dell. *Sing Down the Moon*
O'Dell. *Thunder Rolling in the Mountains*
O'Dell. *Zia*
Paulsen. *Call Me Francis Tucket*
Paulsen. *Mr. Tucket*
Paulsen. *Tucket's Ride*
Rawls. *Dame Shirley and the Gold Rush*
Rockwood. *Groundhog's Horse*
Sandoz. *The Horsecatcher*
Scott. *The Covered Wagon and Other Adventures*
Shura. *Kate's Book*

Shura. *Kate's House*
Steele. *The Buffalo Knife*
Steele. *Flaming Arrows*
Steele. *The Lone Hunt*
Steele. *The Man with the Silver Eyes*
Steele. *Tomahawk Border*
Steele. *Trail Through Danger*
Steele. *Wilderness Journey*
Steele. *Winter Danger*
Taylor. *Walking Up a Rainbow*
Toht. *Sodbuster*
Tunbo. *Stay Put, Robbie McAmis*
Vick. *Tag Against Time*
Wangerin. *The Crying for a Vision*

Watson. *Audacious: Ivy's Story*
Watson. *Dangerous: Savannah's Story*
Watson. *Impetuous: Mattie's Story*
Watson. *Scandalous: Eden's Story*
Watson. *Tempestuous: Opal's Story*
Weaver. *Striking Out*
Weitzman. *Thrashin' Time*
Wilder. *By the Shores of Silver Lake*
Wilder. *Farmer Boy*
Wilder. *The First Four Years*
Wilder. *Little House in the Big Woods*

Wilder. *Little House on the Prairie*
Wilder. *Little Town on the Prairie*
Wilder. *The Long Winter*
Wilder. *On the Banks of Plum Creek*
Wilder. *On the Way Home*
Wilder. *These Happy Golden Years*
Wilkes. *Little House in Brookfield*
Wilson. *Earthquake!*
Wisler. *Jericho's Journey*
Wisler. *Piper's Ferry*

Biography

Badt. *Charles Eastman: Sioux Physician and Author*
Bernotas. *Sitting Bull: Chief of the Sioux*
Black. *Sitting Bull and the Battle of the Little Bighorn*
Bland. *Osceola: Seminole Rebel*
Bland. *Pontiac: Ottawa Rebel*
Bodow. *Sitting Bull: Sioux Leader*
Bolton. *Joseph Brant: Mohawk Chief*
Bonvillain. *Black Hawk: Sac Rebel*
Bruns. *John Wesley Powell: Explorer of Grand Canyon*
Carlson. *Harriet Tubman: Call to Freedom*
Cavan. *Daniel Boone and the Opening of the Ohio Country*
Chrisman. *David Farragut*
Collins. *Pioneer Plowmaker: John Deere*
Connell. *These Lands Are Ours: Tecumseh's Fight*
Conrad. *Prairie Visions: Solomon Butcher*
Cox. *Mark Twain*
Cwiklik. *Sequoyah and the Cherokee Alphabet*
Cwiklik. *Tecumseh: Shawnee Rebel*
Dolan. *James Beckwourth: Frontiersman*
Faber. *Calamity Jane: Her Life and Her Legend*
Ferris. *Native American Doctor: The Story of Susan La Flesche Picotte*

Fitz-Gerald. *Meriwether Lewis and William Clark*
Force. *John Muir*
Foster. *David Farragut*
Fox. *Chief Joseph of the Nez Perce Indians*
Freedman. *The Life and Death of Crazy Horse*
Gaines. *John Wesley Powell and the Great Surveys of the American West*
Goldman. *Crazy Horse: War Chief of the Oglala Sioux*
Guttmacher. *Crazy Horse: Sioux War Chief*
Harris. *John Charles Frémont and the Great Western Reconnaissance*
Henry. *Everyone Wears His Name: A Biography of Levi Strauss*
Hilts. *Quanah Parker*
Holler. *Pocahontas: Powhatan Peacemaker*
Kent. *Geronimo*
Klausner. *Sequoyah's Gift*
Kroeber. *Ishi: Last of His Tribe*
Lawlor. *Daniel Boone*
Lazar. *Red Cloud: Sioux War Chief*
Ledbetter. *John Muir*
Lyttle. *Mark Twain: The Man and His Adventures*
Marrin. *Plains Warrior: Chief Quanah Parker and the Comanches*
McClung. *The True Adventures of Grizzly Adams*

Morrison. *Chief Sarah: Sarah Winnemucca's Fight for Indian Rights*
O'Rear. *Charles Goodnight: Pioneer Cowman*
Otfinoski. *Lewis and Clark: Leading America West*
Petersen. *Meriwether Lewis and William Clark*
Press. *Mark Twain*
Rappaport. *The Flight of the Red Bird*
Roop. *Capturing Nature: John James Audubon*
St. George. *Crazy Horse*
St. George. *To See With the Heart: The Life of Sitting Bull*
Sanford. *Chief Joseph: Nez Percé Warrior*
Sanford. *Crazy Horse: Sioux Warrior*
Sanford. *Geronimo: Apache Warrior*
Sanford. *Osceola: Seminole Warrior*
Sanford. *Quanah Parker: Comanche Warrior*
Sanford. *Red Cloud: Sioux Warrior*
Sanford. *Sitting Bull: Sioux Warrior*
Schwarz. *Cochise, Apache Chief*
Schwarz. *Geronimo: Apache Warrior*
Scordato. *Sarah Winnemucca*
Scott. *Chief Joseph and the Nez Percés*

Shorto. *Geronimo and the Struggle for Apache Freedom*

Shorto. *Tecumseh and the Dream of an American Indian Nation*

Shumate. *Chief Gall: Sioux War Chief*

Shumate. *Sequoyah: Inventor of the Cherokee Alphabet*

Shuter. *Parkman and the Plains Indians*

Shuter. *Sarah Royce and the American West*

Sinnott. *Zebulon Pike*

Sonneborn. *Will Rogers: Cherokee Entertainer*

Stallones. *Zebulon Pike and the Explorers of the American Southwest*

Steltenkamp. *Black Elk: Holy Man of the Oglala*

Stevenson. *Sitting Bull: Dakota Boy*

Stiles. *Jesse James*

Sufrin. *George Catlin: Painter of the Indian West*

Taylor. *Chief Joseph: Nez Perce Leader*

Warburton. *Chief Joseph*

Wilson. *Quanah Parker: Comanche Chief*

Wormser. *Pinkerton: America's First Private Eye*

Yates. *Chief Joseph*

Collective Biography

Aaseng. *You Are the General II: 1800-1899*

Allen. *As Long as the Rivers Flow: The Stories of Nine Native Americans*

Allen. *Jedediah Smith and the Mountain Men of the American West*

Anderson. *Explorers Who Found New Worlds*

Avery. *Extraordinary American Indians*

Duncan. *People of the West*

Freedman. *Indian Chiefs*

Haskins. *Against All Opposition: Black Explorers in America*

Hazell. *Heroines: Great Women Through the Ages*

Italia. *Courageous Crimefighters*

Jacobs. *Great Lives: World Religions*

Katz. *Black Women of the Old West*

Katz. *Proudly Red and Black: Stories of African and Native Americans*

Mayberry. *Business Leaders Who Built Financial Empires*

Provenson. *My Fellow Americans*

Rennert. *Pioneers of Discovery*

Sherrow. *Political Leaders and Peacemakers*

Stefoff. *Pioneers*

Streissguth. *Hoaxers & Hustlers*

Walker. *Great Figures of the Wild West*

Walker. *Spiritual Leaders*

History

Andrews. *Indians of the Plains*

Ashabranner. *A Strange and Distant Shore: Indians of the Great Plains in Exile*

Bachrach. *Custer's Last Stand*

Barr. *The American Frontier*

Bealer. *Only the Names Remain*

Bentley. *Brides, Midwives, and Widows*

Bentley. *Explorers, Trappers, and Guides*

Blake. *The Gold Rush of 1849*

Blakely. *Native Americans and the U.S. Government*

Blumberg. *Full Steam Ahead: The Race to Build a Transcontinental Railroad*

Blumberg. *The Incredible Journey of Lewis and Clark*

Bonvillain. *The Haidas: People of the Northwest Coast*

Bowler. *Trains*

Brill. *The Trail of Tears*

Burby. *The Pueblo Indians*

Carlson. *A Historical Album of Minnesota*

Carter. *The Mexican War: Manifest Destiny*

Carter. *The Spanish-American War: Imperial Ambitions*

Chu. *Going Home to Nicodemus*

Claro. *The Apache Indians*

Claro. *The Cherokee Indians*

Cocke. *A Historical Album of Washington*

Cohen. *The Alaska Purchase*

Cory. *Pueblo Indian*

Cox. *The Forgotten Heroes: The Story of the Buffalo Soldiers*

Cray. *American Datelines*

Cush. *Disasters That Shook the World*

Deem. *How to Make a Mummy Talk*

Diamond. *Smallpox and the American Indian*

Duncan. *The West: An Illustrated History for Children*

Dunn. *The Relocation of the North American Indian*

Echo-Hawk. *Battlefields and Burial Grounds*

Elish. *The Transcontinental Railroad*

Faber. *From Sea to Sea: The Growth of the United States*

Ferrell. *The Battle of the Little Bighorn in American History*

Fisher. *The Oregon Trail*

Fisher. *Tracks Across America: The Story of the American Railroad, 1825-1900*

Fleischner. *The Apaches: People of the Southwest*

Franck. *The American Way West*

Freedman. *Buffalo Hunt*

Freedman. *Cowboys of the Wild West*

Fry. *The Orphan Train*

Giblin. *Be Seated: A Book About Chairs*

Giblin. *When Plague Strikes*

Gintzler. *Cowboys*

Gintzler. *Homesteaders*

Gintzler. *Prospectors*

Golston. *Changing Woman of the Apache*

Gourley. *Hunting Neptune's Giants: American Whaling*

Granfield. *Cowboy: An Album*

Green. *Women in American Indian Society*

Greenberg. *A Pioneer Woman's Memoir*

Greenwood. *A Pioneer Sampler: A Pioneer Family in 1840*

Harvey. *Farmers and Ranchers*

Herb. *Beyond the Mississippi: Early Westward Expansion of the United States*

Herda. *Outlaws of the American West*

Hevly. *Preachers and Teachers*

Hilton. *Miners, Merchants, and Maids*

Hirsch. *Taxation: Paying for Government*

Holmas. *Apache Pass*

Humble. *Ships*

Jacobs. *War with Mexico*

Jones. *The American Indians in America*

Karl. *America Alive: A History*

Katz. *We Rode the Wind*

Katz. *The Westward Movement and Abolitionism: 1815-1850*

Kelly. *Federal Indian Policy*

Kerr. *Keeping Clean*

Ketchum. *The Gold Rush*

Klausmeier. *Cowboy*

Koslow. *The Seminole Indians*

Landau. *Cowboys*

Lavender. *Snowbound: The Tragic Story of the Donner Party*

Lucas. *The Cherokees: People of the Southeast*

Marrin. *Cowboys, Indians and Gunfighters*

Marrin. *Empires Lost and Won: The Spanish Heritage in the Southwest*

Marrin. *The Spanish-American War*

Marrin. *War Clouds in the West: Indians and Calvarymen 1860-1890*

McGrath. *The Lewis and Clark Expedition*

McNeese. *America's Early Canals*

McNeese. *America's First Railroads*

McNeese. *Clippers and Whaling Ships*

McNeese. *Conestogas and Stagecoaches*

McNeese. *Early River Travel*

McNeese. *From Trails to Turnpikes*

McNeese. *West by Steamboat*

Medearis. *Come This Far to Freedom*

Meltzer. *Gold*

Miller. *Buffalo Gals*

Miller. *The Buffalo Soldiers*

Miller. *Cowboys*

Miller. *Pioneers*

Morley. *Clothes: For Work, Play and Display*

Morris. *The Harvey Girls: The Women Who Civilized the West*

Murdoch. *Cowboy*

Murdoch. *North American Indian*

Murphy. *Across America on an Emigrant Train*

Murphy. *Across the Plains in the Donner Party*

Nirgiotis. *Erie Canal: Gateway to the West*

O'Neill. *Wounded Knee*

Platt. *Pirate*

Platt. *The Smithsonian Visual Timeline of Inventions*

Pollard. *The Nineteenth Century*

Rappaport. *American Women: Their Lives in Their Words*

Reef. *Buffalo Soldiers*

Ritchie. *Frontier Life*

Savage. *Cowboys and Cow Towns of the Wild West*

Savage. *Gold Miners of the Wild West*

Savage. *Gunfighters of the Wild West*

Savage. *Pioneering Women of the Wild West*

Savage. *Pony Express Riders of the Wild West*

Savage. *Scouts of the Wild West*

Schlissel. *Black Frontiers*

Smith. *Bridging the Continent*

Smith. *The Conquest of the West*

Smith. *Exploring the Frontier*

Smith. *A Historical Album of Kentucky*

Smith. *The Legendary Wild West*

Smith. *Native Americans of the West*

Smith. *The Riches of the West*

Steedman. *A Frontier Fort on the Oregon Trail*

Steele. *Bighorn*

Stefoff. *Children of the Westward Trail*

Stewart. *Cowboys in the Old West*

Stewart. *Where Lies Butch Cassidy?*

Swanson. *Buffalo Sunrise: The Story of a North American Giant*

Time-Life. *The Spirit World*

Time-Life. *Tribes of the Southern Woodlands*

Time-Life. *The Woman's Way*

Trimble. *The People: Indians of the American Southwest*

Turner. *Shaker Hearts*

Van Der Linde. *The Pony Express*

Van Steenwyk. *The California Gold Rush*

Van Steenwyk. *Frontier Fever—Medicine of the Pioneers*

Ventura. *Food: Its Evolution Through the Ages*

Warburton. *The Beginning of Writing*

Warburton. *Railroads: Bridging the Continents*

Wheeler. *Events That Changed American History*

Whitman. *Get Up and Go: American Road Travel*

Wills. *The Battle of Little Bighorn*

Wills. *A Historical Album of Alabama*

Wills. *A Historical Album of California*

Wills. *A Historical Album of Connecticut*

Wills. *A Historical Album of Florida*

Wills. *A Historical Album of Illinois*

Wills. *A Historical Album of Nebraska*

Wills. *A Historical Album of Oregon*

Wills. *A Historical Album of Texas*

Winslow. *Loggers and Railroad Workers*

Wormser. *The Iron Horse: How the Railroads Changed America*

Multimedia

CD-ROM

Eyewitness Encyclopedia of
  Science
Her Heritage: A Biographical
  Encyclopedia of American
  History

Landmark Documents in
  American History
One Tribe
Science Navigator
SkyTrip America

Total History
The Way Things Work
Wyatt Earp's Old West: A
  Multimedia Adventure in
  the Wild West

Video

Across the Plains
America's Great Indian
  Leaders
America's Westword
  Expansion
The Apache
As the Wind Rocks the
  Wagon: An American
  Odyssey
Birth of a Community: Jews
  and the Gold Rush
The Black West
The Buffalo Soldiers
California Gold: Stories of
  Two Women
Candlemaking
The Cherokee
The Cheyenne
The Chinook
Colonizing the American West
The Creek
The Crow
Dakota Encounters
Dancing in Moccasins
Expansionism
The Final Steps
Frontier Forts and the
  American Indian Wars in
  Texas
Ghost Trains of the Old West
The Great Age of Salmon
Great Ranches of the West
Heritage of the Black West
Herman Melville: Consider
  the Sea
A History of Native Americans

Homesteading: 70 Years on
  the Great Plains,
  1862-1932
The Huron
Indians of California
Indians of the Northwest
Indians of the Plains
Indians of the Southeast
Indians of the Southwest
Ishi, the Last Yahi
Kentucky Rifle
The Last Cowboys
The Lenape
The Lewis and Clark Trail
The Loom
Men of the Frontier
The Menominee
Mining Made the West
Mississippi Steamboats
Monument Valley: Navajo
  Homeland
More Than Bows and Arrows
Mountain Men
Mountain Wolf Woman:
  1884-1960
My Heroes Have Always
  Been Cowboys
The Narragansett
Native American Medicine
Native Americans: People of
  the Desert
Native Americans: People of
  the Forest
Native Americans: People of
  the Northwest Coast

Native Americans: People of
  the Plains
Native Americans: The
  History of a People
The Navajo
The Oregon Trail
Placer Gold
The Poet and the Rough Rider
Pony Express
The Potawatomi
Prairie Cabin: A Norwegian
  Pioneer Woman's Story
Pueblo
Railroads on the Frontier
Ranch Album
Rancho Life
Sacajawea
Secrets of Little Bighorn
The Seminole
Settlers of the West
Spinning Wheel
The Spirit of Pioneer Women
Stagecoach West
Tarawa and the Island War
This World Is Not Our Home
Through the Rockies
Totem Poles: The Stories
  They Tell
The Unsinkable Delta Queen
Westward Expansion: The
  Pioneer Challenge
Women of the West
Woodland Tribal Arts: Native
  American Arts
The Working Cowboy
The Yankton Sioux

GRADE EIGHT

Historical Fiction

Beatty. *Behave Yourself,
  Bethany Brant*
Beatty. *Bonanza Girl*
Beatty. *By Crumbs, It's Mine!*
Beatty. *The Coach That
  Never Came*
Beatty. *Hail Columbia*
Beatty. *How Many Miles to
  Sundown?*

Beatty. *Jonathan Down Under*
Beatty. *Just Some Weeds
  from the Wilderness*
Beatty. *Lacy Makes a Match*
Beatty. *Melinda Takes a Hand*
Beatty. *The Nickel-Plated
  Beauty*
Beatty. *O the Red Rose Tree*

Beatty. *Red Rock over the
  River*
Beatty. *Sarah and Me and the
  Lady from the Sea*
Beatty. *Something to Shout
  About*
Beatty. *That's One Ornery
  Orphan*

Brenner. *On the Frontier with Mr. Audubon*
Burks. *Runs with Horses*
Burks. *Soldier Boy*
Calvert. *The Snowbird*
Carter. *Borderlands*
Conrad. *Prairie Songs*
DeFelice. *Weasel*
Donahue. *Straight Along a Crooked Road*
Donahue. *The Valley in Between*
Highwater. *The Ceremony of Innocence*
Highwater. *Eyes of Darkness*
Highwater. *I Wear the Morning Star*
Highwater. *Legend Days*
Holmes. *Year of the Sevens 1777*
Hotze. *A Circle Unbroken*
Howard. *Out of Step with the Dancers*
Karr. *Oh, Those Harper Girls!*
Karr. *Phoebe's Folly*
Keehn. *I Am Regina*
Keith. *The Obstinate Land*
Kherdian. *Bridger: The Story of a Mountain Man*
Lasky. *Beyond the Divide*

Lenski. *Indian Captive: The Story of Mary Jemison*
Mazzio. *Leaving Eldorado*
McCall. *Message from the Mountains*
McClung. *Hugh Glass, Mountain Man*
McClung. *The True Adventures of Grizzly Adams*
McGraw. *Moccasin Trail*
Meyer. *Where the Broken Heart Still Beats:Cynthia Ann Parker*
Moeri. *Save Queen of Sheba*
Morrow. *On to Oregon!*
Murrow. *West Against the Wind*
Myers. *The Righteous Revenge of Artemis Bonner*
Nixon. *A Deadly Promise*
Nixon. *High Trail to Danger*
Nixon. *In the Face of Danger*
Nixon. *A Place to Belong*
O'Dell. *Island of the Blue Dolphins*
O'Dell. *Sing Down the Moon*
O'Dell. *Thunder Rolling in the Mountains*
O'Dell. *Zia*

Paulsen. *Call Me Francis Tucket*
Paulsen. *Mr. Tucket*
Paulsen. *Tucket's Ride*
Sandoz. *The Horsecatcher*
Taylor. *Walking Up a Rainbow*
Tunbo. *Stay Put, Robbie McAmis*
Vick. *Tag Against Time*
Wangerin. *The Crying for a Vision*
Watson. *Audacious: Ivy's Story*
Watson. *Dangerous: Savannah's Story*
Watson. *Impetuous: Mattie's Story*
Watson. *Scandalous: Eden's Story*
Watson. *Tempestuous: Opal's Story*
Weaver. *Farm Team*
Weaver. *Striking Out*
Wilder. *These Happy Golden Years*
Wilson. *Earthquake!*
Wisler. *Jericho's Journey*
Wisler. *Piper's Ferry*

Biography

Badt. *Charles Eastman: Sioux Physician and Author*
Bernotas. *Sitting Bull: Chief of the Sioux*
Black. *Sitting Bull and the Battle of the Little Bighorn*
Bland. *Osceola: Seminole Rebel*
Bland. *Pontiac: Ottawa Rebel*
Bodow. *Sitting Bull: Sioux Leader*
Bolton. *Joseph Brant: Mohawk Chief*
Bonvillain. *Black Hawk: Sac Rebel*
Bruns. *John Wesley Powell: Explorer of Grand Canyon*
Carlson. *Harriet Tubman: Call to Freedom*
Cavan. *Daniel Boone and the Opening of the Ohio Country*
Collins. *Pioneer Plowmaker: John Deere*
Conrad. *Prairie Visions: Solomon Butcher*
Cox. *Mark Twain*
Cwiklik. *Sequoyah and the Cherokee Alphabet*

Cwiklik. *Tecumseh: Shawnee Rebel*
Dolan. *James Beckwourth: Frontiersman*
Faber. *Calamity Jane: Her Life and Her Legend*
Ferris. *Native American Doctor: The Story of Susan La Flesche Picotte*
Fitz-Gerald. *Meriwether Lewis and William Clark*
Force. *John Muir*
Fox. *Chief Joseph of the Nez Perce Indians*
Freedman. *The Life and Death of Crazy Horse*
Gaines. *John Wesley Powell and the Great Surveys of the American West*
Goldman. *Crazy Horse: War Chief of the Oglala Sioux*
Guttmacher. *Crazy Horse: Sioux War Chief*
Harris. *John Charles Frémont and the Great Western Reconnaissance*
Henry. *Everyone Wears His Name: A Biography of Levi Strauss*

Holler. *Pocahontas: Powhatan Peacemaker*
Klausner. *Sequoyah's Gift*
Kroeber. *Ishi: Last of His Tribe*
Lawlor. *Daniel Boone*
Lawlor. *Shadow Catcher: The Life and Work of Edward S. Curtis*
Lazar. *Red Cloud: Sioux War Chief*
Ledbetter. *John Muir*
Lyttle. *Mark Twain: The Man and His Adventures*
Marrin. *Plains Warrior: Chief Quanah Parker and the Comanches*
McClung. *The True Adventures of Grizzly Adams*
Morrison. *Chief Sarah: Sarah Winnemucca's Fight for Indian Rights*
O'Rear. *Charles Goodnight: Pioneer Cowman*
Otfinoski. *Lewis and Clark: Leading America West*
Petersen. *Meriwether Lewis and William Clark*

Press. *Mark Twain*

Rappaport. *The Flight of the Red Bird*

Roop. *Capturing Nature: John James Audubon*

Schwarz. *Cochise, Apache Chief*

Schwarz. *Geronimo: Apache Warrior*

Scordato. *Sarah Winnemucca*

Scott. *Chief Joseph and the Nez Percés*

Shorto. *Geronimo and the Struggle for Apache Freedom*

Shorto. *Tecumseh and the Dream of an American Indian Nation*

Shumate. *Chief Gall: Sioux War Chief*

Shumate. *Sequoyah: Inventor of the Cherokee Alphabet*

Shuter. *Parkman and the Plains Indians*

Shuter. *Sarah Royce and the American West*

Sinnott. *Zebulon Pike*

Sonneborn. *Will Rogers: Cherokee Entertainer*

St. George. *Crazy Horse*

St. George. *To See with the Heart: The Life of Sitting Bull*

Stallones. *Zebulon Pike and the Explorers of the American Southwest*

Steltenkamp. *Black Elk: Holy Man of the Oglala*

Stiles. *Jesse James*

Sufrin. *George Catlin: Painter of the Indian West*

Taylor. *Chief Joseph: Nez Perce Leader*

Warburton. *Chief Joseph*

Wilson. *Quanah Parker: Comanche Chief*

Wormser. *Pinkerton: America's First Private Eye*

Yates. *Chief Joseph*

Collective Biography

Aaseng. *You Are the General II: 1800-1899*

Allen. *As Long as the Rivers Flow: The Stories of Nine Native Americans*

Allen. *Jedediah Smith and the Mountain Men of the American West*

Anderson. *Explorers Who Found New Worlds*

Avery. *Extraordinary American Indians*

Freedman. *Indian Chiefs*

Haskins. *Against All Opposition: Black Explorers in America*

Hazell. *Heroines: Great Women Through the Ages*

Italia. *Courageous Crimefighters*

Katz. *Black Women of the Old West*

Katz. *Proudly Red and Black: Stories of African and Native Americans*

Mayberry. *Business Leaders Who Built Financial Empires*

Provenson. *My Fellow Americans*

Rennert. *Pioneers of Discovery*

Sherrow. *Political Leaders and Peacemakers*

Stefoff. *Pioneers*

Streissguth. *Hoaxers & Hustlers*

Walker. *Great Figures of the Wild West*

Walker. *Spiritual Leaders*

History

Andrews. *Indians of the Plains*

Ashabranner. *A Strange and Distant Shore: Indians of the Great Plains in Exile*

Bachrach. *Custer's Last Stand*

Barr. *The American Frontier*

Bealer. *Only the Names Remain*

Bentley. *Brides, Midwives, and Widows*

Bentley. *Explorers, Trappers, and Guides*

Blake. *The Gold Rush of 1849*

Blakely. *Native Americans and the U.S. Government*

Blumberg. *Full Steam Ahead: The Race to Build a Transcontinental Railroad*

Blumberg. *The Incredible Journey of Lewis and Clark*

Bonvillain. *The Haidas: People of the Northwest Coast*

Brill. *The Trail of Tears*

Carlson. *A Historical Album of Minnesota*

Carter. *The Mexican War: Manifest Destiny*

Carter. *The Spanish-American War: Imperial Ambitions*

Chu. *Going Home to Nicodemus*

Cocke. *A Historical Album of Washington*

Cohen. *The Alaska Purchase*

Cox. *The Forgotten Heroes: The Story of the Buffalo Soldiers*

Cray. *American Datelines*

Cush. *Disasters That Shook the World*

Deem. *How to Make a Mummy Talk*

Diamond. *Smallpox and the American Indian*

Dunn. *The Relocation of the North American Indian*

Echo-Hawk. *Battlefields and Burial Grounds*

Elish. *The Transcontinental Railroad*

Faber. *From Sea to Sea: The Growth of the United States*

Ferrell. *The Battle of the Little Bighorn in American History*

Fisher. *The Oregon Trail*

Fisher. *Tracks Across America: The Story of the American Railroad, 1825-1900*

Fleischner. *The Apaches: People of the Southwest*

Franck. *The American Way West*

Freedman. *Buffalo Hunt*

Freedman. *Cowboys of the Wild West*

Fry. *The Orphan Train*

Giblin. *Be Seated: A Book About Chairs*

Giblin. *When Plague Strikes*

Gintzler. *Cowboys*

Gintzler. *Homesteaders*

Gintzler. *Prospectors*

Golston. *Changing Woman of the Apache*

Granfield. *Cowboy: An Album*

Green. *Women in American Indian Society*

Greenberg. *A Pioneer Woman's Memoir*

Harvey. *Farmers and Ranchers*

Herb. *Beyond the Mississippi: Early Westward Expansion of the United States*

Hevly. *Preachers and Teachers*

Hilton. *Miners, Merchants, and Maids*

Hirsch. *Taxation: Paying for Government*

Holmas. *Apache Pass*

Jacobs. *War with Mexico*

Jones. *The American Indians in America*

Karl. *America Alive: A History*

Katz. *We Rode the Wind*

Katz. *The Westward Movement and Abolitionism: 1815-1850*

Kelly. *Federal Indian Policy*

Landau. *Cowboys*

Lavender. *Snowbound: The Tragic Story of the Donner Party*

Lucas. *The Cherokees: People of the Southeast*

Marrin. *Cowboys, Indians and Gunfighters*

Marrin. *Empires Lost and Won: The Spanish Heritage in the Southwest*

Marrin. *The Spanish-American War*

Marrin. *War Clouds in the West: Indians and Calvarymen 1860-1890*

McGrath. *The Lewis and Clark Expedition*

McNeese. *America's Early Canals*

McNeese. *America's First Railroads*

McNeese. *Clippers and Whaling Ships*

McNeese. *Conestogas and Stagecoaches*

McNeese. *Early River Travel*

McNeese. *From Trails to Turnpikes*

McNeese. *West by Steamboat*

Medearis. *Come This Far to Freedom*

Meltzer. *Gold*

Miller. *Buffalo Gals*

Miller. *The Buffalo Soldiers*

Miller. *Cowboys*

Miller. *Pioneers*

Morley. *Clothes: For Work, Play and Display*

Morris. *The Harvey Girls: The Women Who Civilized the West*

Murdoch. *North American Indian*

Murphy. *Across America on an Emigrant Train*

Murphy. *Across the Plains in the Donner Party*

Platt. *Pirate*

Platt. *The Smithsonian Visual Timeline of Inventions*

Rappaport. *American Women: Their Lives in Their Words*

Reef. *Buffalo Soldiers*

Smith. *Bridging the Continent*

Smith. *The Conquest of the West*

Smith. *Exploring the Frontier*

Smith. *A Historical Album of Kentucky*

Smith. *The Legendary Wild West*

Smith. *Native Americans of the West*

Smith. *The Riches of the West*

Steedman. *A Frontier Fort on the Oregon Trail*

Steele. *Bighorn*

Stefoff. *Children of the Westward Trail*

Stewart. *Cowboys in the Old West*

Stewart. *Where Lies Butch Cassidy?*

Time-Life. *Cycles of Life*

Time-Life. *The Spirit World*

Time-Life. *Tribes of the Southern Woodlands*

Time-Life. *The Woman's Way*

Trimble. *The People: Indians of the American Southwest*

Turner. *Shaker Hearts*

Van Der Linde. *The Pony Express*

Van Steenwyk. *Frontier Fever—Medicine of the Pioneers*

Ventura. *Food: Its Evolution Through the Ages*

Warburton. *The Beginning of Writing*

Warburton. *Railroads: Bridging the Continents*

Wheeler. *Events That Changed American History*

Whitman. *Get Up and Go: American Road Travel*

Wills. *The Battle of Little Bighorn*

Wills. *A Historical Album of Alabama*

Wills. *A Historical Album of California*

Wills. *A Historical Album of Connecticut*

Wills. *A Historical Album of Florida*

Wills. *A Historical Album of Illinois*

Wills. *A Historical Album of Nebraska*

Wills. *A Historical Album of Oregon*

Wills. *A Historical Album of Texas*

Winslow. *Loggers and Railroad Workers*

Wormser. *The Iron Horse: How the Railroads Changed America*

Multimedia

CD-ROM

Eyewitness Encyclopedia of Science

Her Heritage: A Biographical Encyclopedia of American History

Landmark Documents in American History

One Tribe

Science Navigator

SkyTrip America

Total History

The Way Things Work

Wyatt Earp's Old West: A Multimedia Adventure in the Wild West

Video

Across the Plains
America's Great Indian Leaders
America's Westword Expansion
The Apache
As the Wind Rocks the Wagon: An American Odyssey
Birth of a Community: Jews and the Gold Rush
The Black West
The Buffalo Soldiers
California Gold: Stories of Two Women
Candlemaking
The Cherokee
The Cheyenne
The Chinook
Colonizing the American West
The Creek
The Crow
Dakota Encounters
Dancing in Moccasins
Expansionism
The Final Steps
Frontier Forts and the American Indian Wars in Texas
Ghost Trains of the Old West
The Great Age of Salmon
Great Ranches of the West
Heritage of the Black West
Herman Melville: Consider the Sea
A History of Native Americans

Homesteading: 70 Years on the Great Plains, 1862-1932
The Huron
Indians of California
Indians of the Northwest
Indians of the Plains
Indians of the Southeast
Indians of the Southwest
Ishi, the Last Yahi
Kentucky Rifle
The Last Cowboys
The Lenape
The Lewis and Clark Trail
The Loom
Men of the Frontier
The Menominee
Mining Made the West
Monument Valley: Navajo Homeland
More Than Bows and Arrows
Mountain Men
Mountain Wolf Woman: 1884-1960
My Heroes Have Always Been Cowboys
The Narragansett
Native American Medicine
Native Americans: People of the Desert
Native Americans: People of the Forest
Native Americans: People of the Northwest Coast
Native Americans: People of the Plains

Native Americans: The History of a People
The Navajo
The Oregon Trail
Placer Gold
The Poet and the Rough Rider
Pony Express
The Potawatomi
Prairie Cabin: A Norwegian Pioneer Woman's Story
Pueblo
Railroads on the Frontier
Ranch Album
Rancho Life
Sacajawea
Secrets of Little Bighorn
The Seminole
Settlers of the West
Spinning Wheel
The Spirit of Pioneer Women
Stagecoach West
Tarawa and the Island War
This World Is Not Our Home
Through the Rockies
Totem Poles: The Stories They Tell
The Unsinkable Delta Queen
Westward Expansion: The Pioneer Challenge
Women of the West
Woodland Tribal Arts: Native American Arts
The Working Cowboy
The Yankton Sioux

GRADE NINE

Historical Fiction

Beatty. *Behave Yourself, Bethany Brant*
Beatty. *Bonanza Girl*
Beatty. *By Crumbs, It's Mine!*
Beatty. *How Many Miles to Sundown?*
Beatty. *Jonathan Down Under*
Beatty. *Melinda Takes a Hand*
Beatty. *Sarah and Me and the Lady from the Sea*
Brenner. *On the Frontier with Mr. Audubon*
Burks. *Runs with Horses*
Burks. *Soldier Boy*
Calvert. *The Snowbird*
Conrad. *Prairie Songs*
DeFelice. *Weasel*

Donahue. *Straight Along a Crooked Road*
Donahue. *The Valley in Between*
Ferris. *Into the Wind*
Highwater. *The Ceremony of Innocence*
Highwater. *Eyes of Darkness*
Highwater. *I Wear the Morning Star*
Highwater. *Legend Days*
Hotze. *A Circle Unbroken*
Howard. *Out of Step with the Dancers*
Karr. *Oh, Those Harper Girls!*
Karr. *Phoebe's Folly*
Keith. *The Obstinate Land*

Lasky. *Beyond the Divide*
Lenski. *Indian Captive: The Story of Mary Jemison*
Mazzio. *Leaving Eldorado*
McCall. *Message from the Mountains*
McClung. *Hugh Glass, Mountain Man*
McClung. *The True Adventures of Grizzly Adams*
McGraw. *Moccasin Trail*
Meyer. *Where the Broken Heart Still Beats:Cynthia Ann Parker*
Morrow. *On to Oregon!*

Murrow. *West Against the Wind*

Myers. *The Righteous Revenge of Artemis Bonner*

Nixon. *A Deadly Promise*

Nixon. *High Trail to Danger*

Nixon. *In the Face of Danger*

Nixon. *A Place to Belong*

O'Dell. *Island of the Blue Dolphins*

O'Dell. *Sing Down the Moon*

O'Dell. *Thunder Rolling in the Mountains*

Paulsen. *Mr. Tucket*

Sandoz. *The Horsecatcher*

Taylor. *Walking Up a Rainbow*

Vick. *Tag Against Time*

Wangerin. *The Crying for a Vision*

Watson. *Audacious: Ivy's Story*

Watson. *Dangerous: Savannah's Story*

Watson. *Impetuous: Mattie's Story*

Watson. *Scandalous: Eden's Story*

Watson. *Tempestuous: Opal's Story*

Weaver. *Striking Out*

Wilson. *Earthquake!*

Biography

Badt. *Charles Eastman: Sioux Physician and Author*

Bernotas. *Sitting Bull: Chief of the Sioux*

Black. *Sitting Bull and the Battle of the Little Bighorn*

Bland. *Osceola: Seminole Rebel*

Bland. *Pontiac: Ottawa Rebel*

Bodow. *Sitting Bull: Sioux Leader*

Bolton. *Joseph Brant: Mohawk Chief*

Bonvillain. *Black Hawk: Sac Rebel*

Bruns. *John Wesley Powell*

Carlson. *Harriet Tubman: Call to Freedom*

Cavan. *Daniel Boone and the Opening of the Ohio Country*

Cox. *Mark Twain*

Cwiklik. *Tecumseh: Shawnee Rebel*

Dolan. *James Beckwourth: Frontiersman*

Faber. *Calamity Jane: Her Life and Her Legend*

Faragher. *Daniel Boone*

Force. *John Muir*

Fox. *Chief Joseph of the Nez Perce Indians*

Freedman. *The Life and Death of Crazy Horse*

Gaines. *John Wesley Powell and the Great Surveys of the American West*

Goldman. *Crazy Horse: War Chief of the Oglala Sioux*

Guttmacher. *Crazy Horse: Sioux War Chief*

Harris. *John Charles Frémont and the Great Western Reconnaissance*

Henry. *Everyone Wears His Name: A Biography of Levi Strauss*

Kroeber. *Ishi: Last of His Tribe*

Lawlor. *Shadow Catcher: The Life and Work of Edward S. Curtis*

Lazar. *Red Cloud: Sioux War Chief*

Ledbetter. *John Muir*

Lyttle. *Mark Twain: The Man and His Adventures*

Marrin. *Plains Warrior: Chief Quanah Parker and the Comanches*

Otfinoski. *Lewis and Clark: Leading America West*

Petersen. *Meriwether Lewis and William Clark*

Press. *Mark Twain*

Rappaport. *The Flight of the Red Bird*

Schwarz. *Cochise, Apache Chief*

Schwarz. *Geronimo: Apache Warrior*

Scordato. *Sarah Winnemucca*

Scott. *Chief Joseph and the Nez Percés*

Sonneborn. *Will Rogers: Cherokee Entertainer*

Steltenkamp. *Black Elk: Holy Man of the Oglala*

Stiles. *Jesse James*

Sufrin. *George Catlin: Painter of the Indian West*

Taylor. *Chief Joseph: Nez Perce Leader*

Warburton. *Chief Joseph*

Wilson. *Quanah Parker: Comanche Chief*

Wormser. *Pinkerton: America's First Private Eye*

Yates. *Chief Joseph*

Collective Biography

Aaseng. *You Are the General II: 1800-1899*

Allen. *Jedediah Smith and the Mountain Men of the American West*

Anderson. *Explorers Who Found New Worlds*

Avery. *Extraordinary American Indians*

Freedman. *Indian Chiefs*

Haskins. *Against All Opposition: Black Explorers in America*

Italia. *Courageous Crimefighters*

Katz. *The Black West*

O'Brien. *American Political Leaders: From Colonial Times to the Present*

Rennert. *Pioneers of Discovery*

Sherrow. *Political Leaders and Peacemakers*

Stefoff. *Pioneers*

Streissguth. *Hoaxers & Hustlers*

Walker. *Great Figures of the Wild West*

Walker. *Spiritual Leaders*

History

Alderman. *In Our Defense: The Bill of Rights in Action*

Ardley. *Music: An Illustrated Encyclopedia*

Bosco. *The War of 1812*

Carnes. *Us and Them: A History of Intolerance in America*

Cray. *American Datelines*

Davis. *Don't Know Much About History*

Davis. *Man-Made Catastrophes*

Emert. *Top Lawyers and Their Famous Cases*

Faber. *From Sea to Sea: The Growth of the United States*

Faber. *We the People: The Story of the United States Constitution*

Feinberg. *American Political Scandals Past and Present*

Ferrell. *The Battle of the Little Bighorn in American History*

Frost-Knappman. *Women's Suffrage in America*

Garza. *Barred from the Bar: A History of Women and the Legal Profession*

Greenblatt. *The War of 1812*

Hakim. *From Colonies to Country*

Hakim. *The New Nation*

Herb. *Beyond the Mississippi: Early Westward Expansion of the United States*

Hilton. *A Capital Capital City, 1790-1814*

Hirsch. *Taxation: Paying for Government*

Katz. *Exploration to the War of 1812: 1492-1814*

Knappman. *Great American Trials*

Kronenwetter. *Covert Action*

Landau. *Armed America: The Status of Gun Control*

Markham. *Inventions That Changed Modern Life*

Marrin. *Empires Lost and Won: The Spanish Heritage in the Southwest*

Marrin. *1812: The War Nobody Won*

Medearis. *Come This Far to Freedom*

Meltzer. *The Bill of Rights: How We Got It and What It Means*

Meltzer. *The Black Americans*

Mulcahy. *Diseases: Finding the Cure*

Nardo. *The War of 1812*

Patrick. *The Young Oxford Companion to the Supreme Court*

Platt. *The Smithsonian Visual Timeline of Inventions*

Rappaport. *American Women: Their Lives in Their Words*

Salmon. *The Limits of Independence: American Women 1760-1800*

Schreiner. *Mayday! Mayday!*

Smith. *Fascinating People and Astounding Events from American History*

St. George. *The White House: Cornerstone of a Nation*

Steele. *Freedom's River*

Wheeler. *Events That Changed American History*

Whitman. *Get Up and Go: American Road Travel*

Wormser. *The Iron Horse: How the Railroads Changed America*

Multimedia

CD-ROM

Events That Changed the World

Her Heritage: A Biographical Encyclopedia of American History

Ideas That Changed the World

Landmark Documents in American History

One Tribe

Science Navigator

Total History

The Way Things Work

Wyatt Earp's Old West: A Multimedia Adventure in the Wild West

Video

Across the Plains

Act of War: The Overthrow of the Hawaiian Nation

The American Experience: The Iron Road

America's Great Indian Leaders

America's Westword Expansion

The Apache

As the Wind Rocks the Wagon: An American Odyssey

Birth of a Community: Jews and the Gold Rush

The Black West

The Buffalo Soldiers

California Gold: Stories of Two Women

Candlemaking

The Cherokee

The Cheyenne

The Chinook

Colonizing the American West

The Creek

The Crow

Custer at Little Bighorn

Custer's Last Trooper

The Dakota Conflict

Dakota Encounters

Dancing in Moccasins

Dineh Nation: The Navajo Story

Expansionism

The Final Steps

Forever in Time: The Art of Edward S. Curtis

Frontier Forts and the American Indian Wars in Texas

Ghost Trains of the Old West

The Great Age of Salmon

Great Ranches of the West

Heritage of the Black West

Herman Melville: Consider the Sea

A History of Native Americans

Homesteading: 70 Years on the Great Plains, 1862-1932

The Huron

Ishi, the Last Yahi

Kentucky Rifle

The Last Cowboys

Last Stand at Little Big Horn

The Lenape

The Lewis and Clark Trail

The Loom

Men of the Frontier

The Menominee

Mining Made the West

Monument Valley: Navajo Homeland

More Than Bows and Arrows

Mountain Men

Mountain Wolf Woman: 1884-1960

My Heroes Have Always Been Cowboys

The Narragansett

Native American Medicine

The Navajo

The Oregon Trail

The Peyote Road

Placer Gold

The Poet and the Rough Rider
Pony Express
The Potawatomi
Prairie Cabin: A Norwegian
  Pioneer Woman's Story
Pueblo
Railroads on the Frontier
Ranch Album
Rancho Life
The Reindeer Queen: The Story
  of Alaska's Sinrock Mary
Secrets of Little Bighorn

The Seminole
Settlers of the West
Spinning Wheel
The Spirit of Pioneer Women
Stagecoach West
Strangers in Their Own Land
The Sunrise Dance
Tarawa and the Island War
Thieves of Time
This World Is Not Our Home
Through the Rockies

Totem Poles: The Stories
  They Tell
Touring America's Ghost Towns
The Unsinkable Delta Queen
Wiping the Tears of Seven
  Generations
Women of the West
Wonders of Man's Creation
Woodland Tribal Arts: Native
  American Arts
The Working Cowboy
The Yankton Sioux

GRADE TEN

Historical Fiction

Burks. *Runs with Horses*
Burks. *Soldier Boy*
Calvert. *The Snowbird*
Donahue. *Straight Along a
  Crooked Road*
Ferris. *Into the Wind*
Highwater. *The Ceremony of
  Innocence*
Highwater. *Eyes of Darkness*
Highwater. *I Wear the
  Morning Star*
Highwater. *Legend Days*

Howard. *Out of Step with the
  Dancers*
Keith. *The Obstinate Land*
Lasky. *Beyond the Divide*
Lenski. *Indian Captive: The
  Story of Mary Jemison*
McClung. *Hugh Glass,
  Mountain Man*
McGraw. *Moccasin Trail*
Murrow. *West Against the Wind*
O'Dell. *Island of the Blue
  Dolphins*
O'Dell. *Sing Down the Moon*

Sandoz. *The Horsecatcher*
Wangerin. *The Crying for a
  Vision*
Watson. *Audacious: Ivy's Story*
Watson. *Dangerous:
  Savannah's Story*
Watson. *Impetuous: Mattie's
  Story*
Watson. *Scandalous: Eden's
  Story*
Watson. *Tempestuous: Opal's
  Story*

Biography

Bernotas. *Sitting Bull: Chief
  of the Sioux*
Bland. *Osceola: Seminole
  Rebel*
Bland. *Pontiac: Ottawa Rebel*
Bolton. *Joseph Brant:
  Mohawk Chief*
Bonvillain. *Black Hawk: Sac
  Rebel*
Cavan. *Daniel Boone and the
  Opening of the Ohio
  Country*
Cwiklik. *Tecumseh: Shawnee
  Rebel*
Dolan. *James Beckwourth:
  Frontiersman*
Faragher. *Daniel Boone*

Freedman. *The Life and
  Death of Crazy Horse*
Gaines. *John Wesley Powell
  and the Great Surveys of
  the American West*
Goldman. *Crazy Horse: War
  Chief of the Oglala Sioux*
Guttmacher. *Crazy Horse:
  Sioux War Chief*
Harris. *John Charles Frémont
  and the Great Western
  Reconnaissance*
Johnson. *Cuts: Legendary
  Black Rodeo Cowboy Bill
  Pickett*
Kastner. *John James Audubon*
Kroeber. *Ishi: Last of His
  Tribe*

Lawlor. *Shadow Catcher: The
  Life and Work of Edward
  S. Curtis*
Lyttle. *Mark Twain: The Man
  and His Adventures*
Otfinoski. *Lewis and Clark:
  Leading America West*
Rappaport. *The Flight of the
  Red Bird*
Scott. *Chief Joseph and the
  Nez Percés*
St. George. *Crazy Horse*
Steltenkamp. *Black Elk: Holy
  Man of the Oglala*
Stiles. *Jesse James*
Wilson. *Quanah Parker:
  Comanche Chief*
Yates. *Chief Joseph*

Collective Biography

Avery. *Extraordinary
  American Indians*
Freedman. *Indian Chiefs*
Haskins. *Against All
  Opposition: Black
  Explorers in America*

Katz. *The Black West*
O'Brien. *American Political
  Leaders: From Colonial
  Times to the Present*
Sherrow. *Political Leaders
  and Peacemakers*

Stefoff, Rebecca. *Pioneers*
Streissguth. *Hoaxers &
  Hustlers*
Walker. *Great Figures of the
  Wild West*

History

Alderman. *In Our Defense: The Bill of Rights in Action*
Ardley. *Music: An Illustrated Encyclopedia*
Bosco. *The War of 1812*
Carnes. *Us and Them: A History of Intolerance in America*
Cray. *American Datelines*
Davis. *Don't Know Much About History*
Davis. *Man-Made Catastrophes*
Evans. *Born for Liberty: A History of Women in America*
Faber. *From Sea to Sea: The Growth of the United States*
Faber. *We the People: The Story of the United States Constitution*
Feinberg. *American Political Scandals Past and Present*
Frost-Knappman. *Women's Suffrage in America*

Garza. *Barred from the Bar: A History of Women and the Legal Profession*
Greenblatt. *The War of 1812*
Hakim. *From Colonies to Country*
Hakim. *The New Nation*
Herb. *Beyond the Mississippi: Early Westward Expansion of the United States*
Hilton. *A Capital Capital City, 1790-1814*
Jones. *The American Frontier: Opposing Viewpoints*
Katz. *Exploration to the War of 1812: 1492-1814*
Knappman. *Great American Trials*
Kronenwetter. *Covert Action*
Landau. *Armed America: The Status of Gun Control*
Markham. *Inventions That Changed Modern Life*
Marrin. *Empires Lost and Won: The Spanish Heritage in the Southwest*

Meltzer. *The Bill of Rights: How We Got It and What It Means*
Meltzer. *The Black Americans*
Mulcahy. *Diseases: Finding the Cure*
Nardo. *The War of 1812*
Patrick. *The Young Oxford Companion to the Supreme Court*
Rappaport. *American Women: Their Lives in Their Words*
Salmon. *The Limits of Independence: American Women 1760-1800*
Schreiner. *Mayday! Mayday!*
Smith. *Fascinating People and Astounding Events from American History*
Steele. *Freedom's River*
Wheeler. *Events That Changed American History*
Wormser. *The Iron Horse: How the Railroads Changed America*

Multimedia

CD-ROM

Events That Changed the World
Her Heritage: A Biographical Encyclopedia of American History
Ideas That Changed the World
Landmark Documents in American History
One Tribe
Science Navigator
Total History
The Way Things Work
Wyatt Earp's Old West: A Multimedia Adventure in the Wild West

Video

Act of War: The Overthrow of the Hawaiian Nation
The American Experience: The Iron Road
America's Great Indian Leaders
The Apache
As the Wind Rocks the Wagon: An American Odyssey
The Birth of a Community: Jews and the Gold Rush Buffalo Soldiers
California Gold: Stories of Two Women
The Cherokee
The Cheyenne
The Chinook
Colonizing the American West
The Creek
The Crow
Custer at Little Bighorn

Custer's Last Trooper
The Dakota Conflict
Dakota Encounters
Dancing in Moccasins
Dineh Nation: The Navajo Story
Forever in Time: The Art of Edward S. Curtis
Frontier Forts and the American Indian Wars in Texas
Ghost Trains of the Old West
The Great Age of Salmon
Great Ranches of the West
Herman Melville: Consider the Sea
A History of Native Americans
Homesteading: 70 Years on the Great Plains, 1862-1932
The Huron
Ishi, the Last Yahi

The Last Cowboys
Last Stand at Little Big Horn
The Lenape
The Lewis and Clark Trail
Monument Valley: Navajo Homeland
More Than Bows and Arrows
Mountain Wolf Woman: 1884-1960
My Heroes Have Always Been Cowboys
The Narragansett
Native American Medicine
The Navajo
The Oregon Trail
The Peyote Road
The Poet and the Rough Rider
Pony Express
The Potawatomi
Prairie Cabin: A Norwegian Pioneer Woman's Story
Pueblo

Ranch Album
The Reindeer Queen: The
Story of Alaska's Sinrock
Mary
Secrets of Little Bighorn
The Seminole
The Spirit of Pioneer Women

Strangers in Their Own Land
The Sunrise Dance
Tarawa and the Island War
Thieves of Time
This World Is Not Our Home
Touring America's Ghost
Towns

The Unsinkable Delta Queen
Wiping the Tears of Seven
Generations
Wonders of Man's Creation
The Working Cowboy
The Yankton Sioux

GRADES ELEVEN AND TWELVE

Historical Fiction

Blakely. *Shortgrass Song*
Cotton. *Powder River*
Cotton. *While Angels Dance*
Cummings. *The Indian
Fighter's Return*
Eidson. *St. Agnes's Stand*
Ferris. *Into the Wind*
Galvin. *The Meadow*
Graham. *Runaway*
Harmon. *Colorado Ransom*
Highwater. *The Ceremony of
Innocence*

Highwater. *I Wear the
Morning Star*
Highwater. *Legend Days*
Holland. *The Bear Flag*
Holland. *Pacific Street*
Howard. *Out of Step with the
Dancers*
Jones. *Elkhorn Tavern*
Jones. *Gone the Dreams and
Dancing*
Jones. *Roman*
Jones. *The Search for
Temperance Moon*

Jones. *Winding Stair*
McMurtry. *Lonesome Dove*
Michener. *Centennial*
Osborn. *Between Earth and
Sky*
Turner. *Third Girl from the
Left*
Watson. *Justice*
Williamson. *Heart of the West*
Windle. *True Women*
Zelazny. *Wilderness*
Zimmer. *Cottonwood Station*
Zimmer. *Dust and Glory*

Biography

Ambrose. *Undaunted
Courage*
Cavan. *Daniel Boone and the
Opening of the Ohio
Country*
Derr. *The Frontiersman:
Davy Crockett*
Faragher. *Daniel Boone*
Freedman. *The Life and
Death of Crazy Horse*
Gaines. *John Wesley Powell
and the Great Surveys of
the American West*

Goldman. *Crazy Horse: War
Chief of the Oglala Sioux*
Harris. *John Charles Frémont
and the Great Western
Reconnaissance*
Johnson. *Cuts: Legendary
Black Rodeo Cowboy Bill
Pickett*
Kastner. *John James Audubon*
Kroeber. *Ishi: Last of His
Tribe*
Lyttle. *Mark Twain: The Man
and His Adventures*

Sherrow. *Political Leaders
and Peacemakers*
St. George. *Crazy Horse*
Steltenkamp. *Black Elk: Holy
Man of the Oglala*
Stiles. *Jesse James*
Wert. *Custer: The
Controversial Life of
George Armstrong Custer*
Yates. *Chief Joseph*

Collective Biography

Avery. *Extraordinary
American Indians*
Freedman. *Indian Chiefs*
Haskins. *Against all
Opposition: Black
Explorers in America*
Katz. *The Black West*

McCullough. *Brave
Companions: Portraits in
History*
O'Brien. *American Political
Leaders: From Colonial
Times to the Present*
Stefoff. *Pioneers*

Streissguth. *Hoaxers &
Hustlers*
Walker. *Great Figures of the
Wild West*

History

Alderman. *In Our Defense:
The Bill of Rights in Action*
Ardley. *Music: An Illustrated
Encyclopedia*
Carnes. *Us and Them: A
History of Intolerance in
America*
Cray. *American Datelines*

Dary. *Seeking Pleasure in the
Old West*
Davidson. *Everyday Life
Through the Ages*
Davis. *Don't Know Much
About History*
Davis. *Man-Made
Catastrophes*

Ehle. *Trail of Tears: The Rise
and Fall of the Cherokee
Nation*
Evans. *Born for Liberty: A
History of Women in
America*
Faber. *From Sea to Sea: The
Growth of the United States*

Faber. *We the People: The Story of the United States Constitution*

Feinberg. *American Political Scandals Past and Present*

Frost-Knappman. *Women's Suffrage in America*

Garza. *Barred from the Bar: A History of Women and the Legal Profession*

Greenblatt. *The War of 1812*

Hakim. *From Colonies to Country*

Hakim. *The New Nation*

Hauptman. *Between Two Fires: American Indians in the Civil War*

Hilton. *A Capital Capital City, 1790-1814*

Jones. *The American Frontier: Opposing Viewpoints*

Knappman. *Great American Trials*

Kronenwetter. *Covert Action*

Meltzer. *The Bill of Rights: How We Got It and What It Means*

Milner. *The Oxford History of the American West*

Mulcahy. *Diseases: Finding the Cure*

Nardo. *The War of 1812*

Patrick. *The Young Oxford Companion to the Supreme Court*

Peters. *Seven Trails West*

Rappaport. *American Women: Their Lives in Their Words*

Reader's Digest. *America's Fascinating Indian Heritage*

Salmon. *The Limits of Independence: American Women 1760-1800*

Schlissel. *Far from Home: Families of the Westward Journey*

Schreiner. *Mayday! Mayday!*

Smith. *Fascinating People and Astounding Events from American History*

Steele. *Freedom's River*

Tinling. *With Women's Eyes: Visitors to the New World, 1775-1918*

Trimble. *Talking with the Clay: The Art of Pueblo Pottery*

Wheeler. *Events That Changed American History*

Young. *Nothing to Do but Stay: My Pioneer Mother*

Multimedia

CD-ROM

Events That Changed the World

Her Heritage: A Biographical Encyclopedia of American History

Ideas That Changed the World

Landmark Documents in American History

One Tribe

Science Navigator

Total History

The Way Things Work

Wyatt Earp's Old West: A Multimedia Adventure in the Wild West

Video

Act of War: The Overthrow of the Hawaiian Nation

The American Experience: The Iron Road

America's Great Indian Leaders

America's Westword Expansion

As the Wind Rocks the Wagon: An American Odyssey

Birth of a Community: Jews and the Gold Rush

The Buffalo Soldiers

California Gold: Stories of Two Women

Colonizing the American West

Custer at Little Bighorn

Custer's Last Trooper

The Dakota Conflict

Dakota Encounters

Dancing in Moccasins

Dineh Nation: The Navajo Story

Forever in Time: The Art of Edward S. Curtis

Ghost Trains of the Old West

The Great Age of Salmon

Great Ranches of the West

Herman Melville: Consider the Sea

Homesteading: 70 Years on the Great Plains, 1862-1932

Ishi, the Last Yahi

The Last Cowboys

Last Stand at Little Big Horn

Monument Valley: Navajo Homeland

More Than Bows and Arrows

Mountain Wolf Woman: 1884-1960

My Heroes Have Always Been Cowboys

Native American Medicine

The Oregon Trail

The Peyote Road

The Poet and the Rough Rider

Ranch Album

The Reindeer Queen: The Story of Alaska's Sinrock Mary

Secrets of Little Bighorn

The Spirit of Pioneer Women

Strangers in Their Own Land

The Sunrise Dance

Tarawa and the Island War

Thieves of Time

This World Is Not Our Home

Touring America's Ghost Towns

Wiping the Tears of Seven Generations

Wonders of Man's Creation

The Working Cowboy

IMMIGRANTS AND MULTICULTURAL HERITAGES,
1814 TO THE PRESENT

GRADE SEVEN

Historical Fiction

Angell. *One-Way to Ansonia*
Conlon-McKenna. *Wildflower Girl*
Howard. *Sister*
Lasky. *The Night Journey*
Levitin. *Annie's Promise*
Levitin. *Silver Days*
Lord. *In the Year of the Boar and Jackie Robinson*
Lord. *The Luck of Z.A.P. and Zoe*
Lord. *Today's Special: Z.A.P. and Zoe*
Lord. *Z.A.P., Zoe, & the Musketeers*
Marvin. *A Bride for Anna's Papa*
Morpurgo. *Twist of Gold*
Nixon. *Land of Dreams*
Nixon. *Land of Hope*
Nixon. *Land of Promise*
Pellowski. *First Farm in the Valley: Anna's Story*
Sherman. *Independence Avenue*
Uchida. *Samurai of Gold Hill*
Vogt. *A Race for Land*
Wallace. *Buffalo Gal*
Winter. *Klara's New World*
Yep. *Dragon's Gate*
Yep. *Dragonwings*

Biography

Altman. *Cesar Chavez*
Codye. *Luis W. Alvarez*
Codye. *Vilma Martinez*
Collins. *Farmworker's Friend: Cesar Chavez*
Conord. *Cesar Chavez: Union Leader*
de Ruiz. *To Fly with the Swallows: A Story of Old California*
Gonzales. *Cesar Chavez: Leader for Migrant Farm Workers*
Holmes. *Cesar Chavez: Farm Worker Activist*
Rodriguez. *Cesar Chavez*
Sonder. *The Tenement Writer: An Immigrant's Story*
Uchida. *The Invisible Thread*

Collective Biography

Glenn. *Discover America's Favorite Architects*
Jacobs. *World Government*
Mayberry. *Business Leaders Who Built Financial Empires*
Pile. *Women Business Leaders*
Provenson. *My Fellow Americans*

History

Altman. *Migrant Farm Workers: The Temporary People*
Anderson. *Immigration*
Ashabranner. *An Ancient Heritage: The Arab-American Minority*
Ashabranner. *Dark Harvest: Migrant Farmworkers*
Bandon. *Asian Indian Americans*
Bandon. *Chinese Americans*
Bandon. *Dominican Americans*
Bandon. *Filipino Americans*
Bandon. *Korean Americans*
Bandon. *Mexican Americans*
Bandon. *Vietnamese Americans*
Bandon. *West Indian Americans*
Bar-Lev. *Jewish Americans Struggle for Equality*
Bial. *Shaker Home*
Bolick. *Shaker Villages*
Bratman. *Becoming a Citizen: Adopting a New Home*
Caroli. *Immigrants Who Returned Home*
Catalano. *The Mexican Americans*
Cavan. *The Irish-American Experience*
Cozic. *Civil Liberties*
Daley. *The Chinese Americans*
de Ruiz. *La Causa: The Migrant Farmworkers' Story*
Di Franco. *The Italian Americans*

Fisher. *Ellis Island: Gateway to the New World*

Freedman. *Kids at Work: Lewis Hine Against Child Labor*

Goldish. *Immigration: How Should It Be Controlled?*

Greenberg. *Newcomers to America*

Halliburton. *The West Indian-American Experience*

Hamanaka. *The Journey: Japanese Americans, Racism, and Renewal*

Hoobler. *The Chinese American Family Album*

Hoobler. *The Irish American Family Album*

Hoobler. *The Italian American Family Album*

Hoobler. *The Japanese American Family Album*

Hoobler. *The Jewish American Family Album*

Johnson. *The Irish in America*

Katz. *Minorities Today*

Kitano. *The Japanese Americans*

Koral. *An Album of War Refugees*

Kroll. *Ellis Island*

Kuropas. *Ukrainians in America*

Langley. *Religion*

Lawlor. *I Was Dreaming to Come to America*

Leathers. *The Japanese in America*

Lehrer. *The Korean Americans*

Magocsi. *The Russian Americans*

Mendez. *Cubans in America*

Muggamin. *The Jewish Americans*

Pascoe. *Mexico and the United States: Cooperation and Conflict*

Pinchot. *The Mexicans in America*

San Souci. *N. C. Wyeth's Pilgrims*

Sandler. *Immigrants*

Sawyer. *Refugees: Seeking a Safe Haven*

Saxon-Ford. *The Czech Americans*

Seymour-Jones. *Refugees*

Sherrow. *The Triangle Factory Fire*

Sinnott. *Chinese Railroad Workers*

Sinnott. *Extraordinary Asian Pacific Americans*

Stanley. *Big Annie of Calumet*

Takaki. *The Chinese in Nineteenth Century America*

Takaki. *Democracy and Race*

Takaki. *Ethnic Islands*

Takaki. *From the Land of Morning Calm*

Takaki. *India in the West*

Takaki. *Issei and Nisei*

Takaki. *Raising Cane*

Takaki. *Spacious Dreams*

Takaki. *Strangers at the Gates Again*

Uschan. *A Multicultural Portrait of World War I*

Williams. *The Amish*

Williams. *The Mormons*

Wormser. *American Islam: Growing Up Muslim in America*

Multimedia

CD-ROM

Eyewitness Encyclopedia of Science

Her Heritage: A Biographical Encyclopedia of American History

One Tribe

Religions of the World

Science Navigator

SkyTrip America

Total History

The Way Things Work

Video

American Fever

The Amish

Arab Americans

Cesar Chavez

Charles Garry: Street Fighter in the Courtroom

Freedom in Diversity

From East to West: The Asian-American Experience

German Americans

Greek Americans

Immigration and Cultural Change

The Immigration Experience

Irish Americans

Italian Americans

Japanese Americans

Jewish Americans

Korean Americans

Latino Art and Culture in the United States

Luisa Capetillo: Passion for Justice

One World, Many Worlds: Hispanic Diversity in the United States

Polish Americans

Prejudice: Monster Within

Public Sculpture: America's Legacy

Puerto Ricans

The San Patricios: The Tragic Story of the St. Patrick's Battalion

The Shakers

Ziveli: Medicine for the Heart

GRADE EIGHT

Historical Fiction

Angell. *One-Way to Ansonia*
Lasky. *The Night Journey*
Levitin. *Annie's Promise*
Levitin. *Silver Days*
Morpurgo. *Twist of Gold*

Nixon. *Land of Dreams*
Nixon. *Land of Hope*
Nixon. *Land of Promise*
Sherman. *Independence Avenue*

Uchida. *Samurai of Gold Hill*
Wallace. *Buffalo Gal*
Yep. *Dragon's Gate*
Yep. *Dragonwings*
Yep. *Mountain Light*

Biography

Altman. *Cesar Chavez*
de Ruiz. *To Fly with the Swallows: A Story of Old California*

Gonzales. *Cesar Chavez: Leader for Migrant Farm Workers*
Holmes. *Cesar Chavez: Farm Worker Activist*

Rodriguez. *Cesar Chavez*
Sonder. *The Tenement Writer: An Immigrant's Story*
Uchida. *The Invisible Thread*

Collective Biography

Glenn. *Discover America's Favorite Architects*
Jacobs. *World Government*

Mayberry. *Business Leaders Who Built Financial Empires*

Pile. *Women Business Leaders*
Provenson. *My Fellow Americans*

History

Altman. *Migrant Farm Workers: The Temporary People*
Anderson. *Immigration*
Ashabranner. *An Ancient Heritage: The Arab-American Minority*
Ashabranner. *Dark Harvest: Migrant Farmworkers*
Bandon. *Asian Indian Americans*
Bandon. *Chinese Americans*
Bandon. *Dominican Americans*
Bandon. *Filipino Americans*
Bandon. *Korean Americans*
Bandon. *Mexican Americans*
Bandon. *Vietnamese Americans*
Bandon. *West Indian Americans*
Bar-Lev. *Jewish Americans Struggle for Equality*
Bial. *Shaker Home*
Bolick. *Shaker Villages*
Bratman. *Becoming a Citizen: Adopting a New Home*
Caroli. *Immigrants Who Returned Home*
Catalano. *The Mexican Americans*
Cozic. *Civil Liberties*
Di Franco. *The Italian Americans*

Freedman. *Kids at Work: Lewis Hine Against Child Labor*
Garza. *Latinas: Hispanic Women in the United States*
Goldish. *Immigration: How Should It Be Controlled?*
Greenberg. *Newcomers to America*
Halliburton. *The West Indian-American Experience*
Hamanaka. *The Journey: Japanese Americans, Racism, and Renewal*
Hoobler. *The Chinese American Family Album*
Hoobler. *The Irish American Family Album*
Hoobler. *The Italian American Family Album*
Hoobler. *The Japanese American Family Album*
Hoobler. *The Jewish American Family Album*
Johnson. *The Irish in America*
Katz. *Minorities Today*
Kitano. *The Japanese Americans*
Koral. *An Album of War Refugees*
Kuropas. *Ukrainians in America*
Lawlor. *I Was Dreaming to Come to America*

Leathers. *The Japanese in America*
Lehrer. *The Korean Americans*
Magocsi. *The Russian Americans*
Mendez. *Cubans in America*
Muggamin. *The Jewish Americans*
Pascoe. *Mexico and the United States: Cooperation and Conflict*
Pinchot. *The Mexicans in America*
San Souci. *N. C. Wyeth's Pilgrims*
Sandler. *Immigrants*
Sawyer. *Refugees: Seeking a Safe Haven*
Saxon-Ford. *The Czech Americans*
Sherrow. *The Triangle Factory Fire*
Sinnott. *Chinese Railroad Workers*
Sinnott. *Extraordinary Asian Pacific Americans*
Stanley. *Big Annie of Calumet*
Takaki. *The Chinese in Nineteenth Century America*
Takaki. *Democracy and Race*
Takaki. *Ethnic Islands*
Takaki. *From the Land of Morning Calm*

Takaki. *India in the West*
Takaki. *Issei and Nisei*
Takaki. *Raising Cane*
Takaki. *Spacious Dreams*

Takaki. *Strangers at the Gates Again*
Uschan. *A Multicultural Portrait of World War I*
Williams. *The Amish*

Williams. *The Mormons*
Wormser. *American Islam: Growing Up Muslim in America*

Multimedia

CD-ROM

Eyewitness Encyclopedia of Science
Famous American Speeches: 1850 to the Present

Her Heritage: A Biographical Encyclopedia of American History
One Tribe
Religions of the World

Science Navigator
SkyTrip America
Total History
The Way Things Work

Video

American Fever
The Amish
Arab Americans
Cesar Chavez
Charles Garry: Street Fighter in the Courtroom
Freedom in Diversity
From East to West: The Asian-American Experience
German Americans
Greek Americans
Immigration and Cultural Change

The Immigration Experience
Irish Americans
Italian Americans
Japanese Americans
Jewish Americans
Korean Americans
Latino Art and Culture in the United States
Luisa Capetillo: Passion for Justice
One World, Many Worlds: Hispanic Diversity in the United States

Polish Americans
Prejudice: Monster Within
Public Sculpture: America's Legacy
Puerto Ricans
The San Patricios: The Tragic Story of the St. Patrick's Battalion
The Shakers
Ziveli: Medicine for the Heart

GRADE NINE

Historical Fiction

Lasky. *The Night Journey*
Morpurgo. *Twist of Gold*
Nixon. *Land of Dreams*

Nixon. *Land of Hope*
Nixon. *Land of Promise*
Wallace. *Buffalo Gal*

Yep. *Dragonwings*

Biography

Altman. *Cesar Chavez*
de Ruiz. *To Fly with the Swallows: A Story of Old California*

Gonzales. *Cesar Chavez: Leader for Migrant Farm Workers*
Holmes. *Cesar Chavez: Farm Worker Activist*

Rodriguez. *Cesar Chavez*
Sonder. *The Tenement Writer: An Immigrant's Story*

Collective Biography

Glenn. *Discover America's Favorite Architects*

Jacobs. *World Government*
Pile. *Women Business Leaders*

History

Alvarez. *The Official Baseball Hall of Fame Answer Book*
Anderson. *Battles That Changed the Modern World*
Archer. *Rage in the Streets: Mob Violence in America*
Basinger. *American Cinema: One Hundred Years of Filmmaking*

Beckett. *The Story of Painting*
Bernards. *Gun Control*
Bortz. *Catastrophe! Great Engineering Failure—and Success*
Bremness. *Herbs*
Brown. *Christianity*
Calabro. *Zap! A Brief History of Television*

Capek. *Artistic Trickery: The Tradition of the Trompe L'oeil Art*
Capek. *Murals: Cave, Cathedral, to Street*
Carnegy. *The 1980s*
Carnes. *Us and Them: A History of Intolerance in America*

Chafe. *The Road to Equality: American Women Since 1962*

Cohen. *America: Then and Now*

Collier. *Jazz, the American Theme Song*

Colman. *Women in Society: United States*

Cozic. *Civil Liberties*

Cozic. *Israel: Opposing Viewpoints*

Cray. *American Datelines*

Cush. *Disasters That Shook the World*

Davies. *Transport: On Land, Road and Rail*

Davis. *Don't Know Much About History*

Davis. *Man-Made Catastrophes*

Emert. *Top Lawyers and Their Famous Cases*

Evans. *Freedom of Religion*

Evans. *Freedom of Speech*

Evans. *Freedom of the Press*

Faber. *We the People: The Story of the United States Constitution*

Fradin. *Medicine: Yesterday, Today, and Tomorrow*

Garfunkel. *On Wings of Joy: The Story of Ballet*

Giblin. *When Plague Strikes*

Gold. *Roberts v. U.S. Jaycees*

Golston. *Changing Woman of the Apache*

Green. *Women in American Indian Society*

Greenberg. *The Painter's Eye: Learning to Look at Contemporary American Art*

Greene. *Child Labor: Then and Now*

Hakim. *All the People*

Haskins. *Black Music in America*

Herald. *The 1970s*

Hill. *Our Century: 1970-1980*

Hirsch. *Taxation: Paying for Government*

Hull. *Breaking Free*

Jacobs. *Search for Peace: The United Nations*

Jenkins. *Nicaragua and the United States: Years of Conflict*

Katz. *The Great Society to the Reagan Era: 1964-1990*

Kelley. *Into the Fire: African Americans Since 1970*

Kelly. *Election Day: An American Holiday, an American History*

Kelly. *Federal Indian Policy*

King. *The Gulf War*

Knappman. *Great American Trials*

Knappman. *Great American Trials: From Salem Witchcraft to Rodney King*

Kronenwetter. *Capital Punishment*

Kronenwetter. *United They Hate: White Supremacist Groups in America*

Kronenwetter. *The War Against Terrorism*

Lackmann. *Same Time. . . Same Station: An A-Z Guide to Radio*

Landau. *Armed America: The Status of Gun Control*

Landau. *The White Power Movement: America's Racist Hate Groups*

Lang. *Extremist Groups in America*

Langone. *Spreading Poison: A Book About Racism and Prejudice*

Lawson. *Famous Presidential Scandals*

Leiner. *First Children: Growing Up in the White House*

Leinwand. *Do We Need a New Constitution?*

Levi. *Cowboys of the Sky*

Macy. *Winning Ways: A Photohistory of American Women in Sports*

Markham. *Inventions That Changed Modern Life*

May. *Pushing the Limits: American Women 1940-1961*

Medearis. *Come This Far to Freedom*

Meltzer. *The Black Americans*

Mizell. *Think About Racism*

Mulcahy. *Diseases: Finding the Cure*

Newton. *Gun Control: An Issue for the Nineties*

Pascoe. *Freedom of Expression*

Pascoe. *Mexico and the United States: Cooperation and Conflict*

Patrick. *The Young Oxford Companion to the Supreme Court*

Patterson. *The Oxford 50th Anniversary Book of the United Nations*

Perl. *From Top Hats to Baseball Caps, from Bustles to Blue Jeans*

Philip. *Singing America: Poèms That Define a Nation*

Pietrusza. *The End of the Cold War*

Platt. *The Smithsonian Visual Timeline of Inventions*

Potter. *African-American Firsts*

Rappaport. *American Women: Their Lives in Their Words*

Ride. *To Space and Back*

Ritchie. *Please Stand By: A Prehistory of Television*

Ross. *The United Nations*

Senna. *The Black Press and the Struggle of Civil Rights*

Sifakis. *Hoaxes and Scams: A Compendium of Deceptions, Ruses, and Swindles*

Smith. *Fascinating People and Astounding Events from American History*

Spangenburg. *The History of Science from the 1946 to the 1990s*

Spangenburg. *Opening the Space Frontier: Space Exploration*

St. George. *The White House: Cornerstone of a Nation*

Steele. *Freedom's River*

Stefoff. *The American Environmental Movement*

Stones and Bones: How Archaeologists Trace Human Origins

Suter. *Our Century: 1980-1990*

Tames. *The 1980s*

Tchudi. *Lock and Key*

Time-Life. *African Americans: Voices of Triumph: Leadership*

Wakin. *How TV Changed America's Mind*

Wakin. *Photos That Made U.S. History: Cold War Era to Space Age*

Walker. *Hand, Heart, and Mind*
Warburton. *Railroads: Bridging the Continents*
Wekesser. *The Death Penalty: Opposing Viewpoints*

Wekesser. *Feminism: Opposing Viewpoints*
Wheeler. *Events That Changed American History*
Whitman. *Get Up and Go: American Road Travel*
Wilkinson. *Building*

Williams. *The Amish*
Williams. *The Mormons*
Woods. *Affirmative Action*

Multimedia

CD-ROM

Events That Changed the World
Famous American Speeches: 1850 to the Present
Her Heritage: A Biographical Encyclopedia of American History

Ideas That Changed the World
One Tribe
Our Times: The Multimedia Encyclopedia of the Twentieth Century
Religions of the World
Science Navigator

Total History
The Way Things Work

Video

Adelante Mujeres
American Fever
The Amish
Arab Americans
Cesar Chavez
Charles Garry: Street Fighter in the Courtroom
German Americans
God Bless America and Poland Too
Greek Americans
Home from the Eastern Sea

Immigration and Cultural Change
Irish Americans
Italian Americans
Japanese Americans
Jewish Americans
Korean Americans
Latino Art and Culture in the United States
Luisa Capetillo: Passion for Justice
Polish Americans

Prejudice: Monster Within
Public Sculpture: America's Legacy
Puerto Ricans
The San Patricios: The Tragic Story of the St. Patrick's Battalion
The Shakers
West of Hester Street
Ziveli: Medicine for the Heart

GRADE TEN

Historical Fiction

Nixon. *Land of Dreams*
Nixon. *Land of Hope*
Nixon. *Land of Promise*

Pascoe. *Mexico and the United States: Cooperation and Conflict*

Williams. *The Amish*
Williams. *The Mormons*

Biography

Altman. *Cesar Chavez*
Lord. *Legacies: A Chinese Mosaic*

Ortiz Cofer. *Silent Dancing: A Puero Rican Childhood*
Rodriguez. *Cesar Chavez*

Collective Biography

Jacobs. *World Government*

History

Altman. *Migrant Farm Workers: The Temporary People*
Aparicio. *Latino Voices*
Ashabranner. *An Ancient Heritage: The Arab-American Minority*
Bar-Lev. *Jewish Americans Struggle for Equality*

Caroli. *Immigrants Who Returned Home*
Cox. *The Challenge of Immigration*
Cozic. *Civil Liberties*
Evans. *Born for Liberty: A History of Women in America*
Fernandez-Shaw. *The Hispanic Presence in*

North America from 1492 to Today
Fox. *The Unknown Internment: Relocation of Italian-Americans During World War II*
Freedman. *Kids at Work: Lewis Hine Against Child Labor*

Garza. *Latinas: Hispanic Women in the United States*
Greenberg. *Newcomers to America*
Hamanaka. *The Journey: Japanese Americans, Racism, and Renewal*
Hoobler. *The Chinese American Family Album*
Hoobler. *The Irish American Family Album*
Hoobler. *The Italian American Family Album*
Hoobler. *The Japanese American Family Album*

Katz. *Minorities Today*
San Souci. *N. C. Wyeth's Pilgrims*
Sawyer. *Refugees: Seeking a Safe Haven*
Sinnott. *Extraordinary Asian Pacific Americans*
Smith. *The Frugal Gourmet on our Immigrant Ancestors*
Takaki. *The Chinese in Nineteenth Century America*
Takaki. *Democracy and Race*
Takaki. *Ethnic Islands*

Takaki. *From the Land of Morning Calm*
Takaki. *India in the West*
Takaki. *Issei and Nisei*
Takaki. *Raising Cane*
Takaki. *Spacious Dreams*
Takaki. *Strangers at the Gates Again*
Uschan. *A Multicultural Portrait of World War I*
Wormser. *American Islam: Growing Up Muslim in America*

Multimedia

CD-ROM

Events That Changed the World
Famous American Speeches: 1850 to the Present
Her Heritage: A Biographical Encyclopedia of American History

Ideas That Changed the World
One Tribe
Our Times: The Multimedia Encyclopedia of the Twentieth Century
Religions of the World
Science Navigator

Total History
The Way Things Work

Video

Adelante Mujeres
American Fever
The Amish
Arab Americans
Cesar Chavez
Charles Garry: Street Fighter in the Courtroom
German Americans
God Bless America and Poland Too
Greek Americans

Home from the Eastern Sea
Irish Americans
Italian Americans
Japanese Americans
Jewish Americans
Korean Americans
Latino Art and Culture in the United States
Luisa Capetillo: Passion for Justice
Polish Americans

Public Sculpture: America's Legacy
Puerto Ricans
The San Patricios: The Tragic Story of the St. Patrick's Battalion
The Shakers
West of Hester Street
Ziveli: Medicine for the Heart

GRADES ELEVEN AND TWELVE

Biography

Lord. *Legacies: A Chinese Mosaic*

Ortiz Cofer. *Silent Dancing: A Puerto Rican Childhood*

Smith. *Women Who Write*

Collective Biography

History

Altman. *Migrant Farm Workers: The Temporary People*
Aparicio. *Latino Voices*
Chan. *Asian Americans: An Interpretive History*
Cox. *The Challenge of Immigration*
Cozic. *Civil Liberties*

Daniels. *Coming to America: A History of Immigration and Ethnicity in American Life*
Evans. *Born for Liberty: A History of Women in America*
Fernandez-Shaw. *The Hispanic Presence in*

North America from 1492 to Today
Fox. *The Unknown Internment: Relocation of Italian-Americans During World War II*
Garza. *Latinas: Hispanic Women in the United States*

Hamanaka. *The Journey: Japanese Americans, Racism, and Renewal*

Hoobler. *The Chinese American Family Album*

Hoobler. *The Irish American Family Album*

Hoobler. *The Italian American Family Album*

Kessler. *Stubborn Twig: Three Generations in the*

Life of a Japanese American Family

Krause. *Grandmothers, Mothers, and Daughters: Ethnic American Women*

Lacey. *The Essential Immigrant*

Mangione. *La Storia: Five Centuries of the Italian-American Experience*

Pascoe. *Mexico and the United States: Cooperation and Conflict*

Sinnott. *Extraordinary Asian Pacific Americans*

Smith. *The Frugal Gourmet on our Immigrant Ancestors*

Takaki. *Democracy and Race*

Takaki. *A Different Mirror: The Making of Multicultural America*

Multimedia

CD-ROM

Events That Changed the World

Famous American Speeches: 1850 to the Present

Her Heritage: A Biographical Encyclopedia of American History

Ideas That Changed the World

One Tribe

Our Times: The Multimedia Encyclopedia of the Twentieth Century

Religions of the World

Science Navigator

Total History

The Way Things Work

Video

Adelante Mujeres

American Fever

Cesar Chavez

God Bless America and Poland Too

Home from the Eastern Sea

Latino Art and Culture in the United States

Luisa Capetillo: Passion for Justice

Public Sculpture: America's Legacy

The San Patricios: The Tragic Story of the St. Patrick's Battalion

The Shakers

West of Hester Street

Ziveli: Medicine for the Heart

SLAVERY, ABOLITIONISTS, AND WOMEN'S RIGHTS, 1814-1865

GRADE SEVEN

Historical Fiction

Avi. *Beyond the Western Sea, Book Two: Lord Kirkle's Money*
Avi. *The Man Who Was Poe*
Avi. *Something's Upstairs: A Tale of Ghosts*
Avi. *The True Confessions of Charlotte Doyle*
Beatty. *Jayhawker*
Blos. *Brothers of the Heart, 1837-38*
DeFelice. *The Apprenticeship of Lucas Whitaker*
Duff. *Radical Red*
Fleischman. *The Borning Room*
Fox. *The Slave Dancer*
Fritz. *Brady*
Gaeddert. *Breaking Free*
Guccione. *Come Morning*
Hamilton. *The House of Dies Drear*
Lampman. *White Captives*
Lasky. *True North: A Novel of the Underground Railroad*
Levin. *Mercy's Mill*
Lyons. *Letters from a Slave Girl*
Nixon. *A Family Apart*
Paterson. *Jip: His Story*
Paterson. *Lyddie*
Paulsen. *Nightjohn*
Rinaldi. *The Blue Door*
Rosen. *A School for Pompey Walker*
Rosenburg. *William Parker*
Ruby. *Steal Away Home*
Sauerwein. *The Way Home*
Smucker. *Runaway to Freedom*
Stone. *Autumn of the Royal Tar*
Tate. *The Secret of Gumbo Grove*
Turner. *Running for Our Lives*
Walter. *Second Daughter*

Biography

Bennett. *Stonewall Jackson: Lee's Greatest Lieutenant*
Bentley. *"Dear Friend": Thomas Garrett and William Still*
Bisson. *Nat Turner: Slave Revolt Leader*
Borzendowski. *John Russwurm*
Brown. *Elizabeth Blackwell: Physician*
Brown. *Franklin Pierce: 14th President of the United States*
Brown. *Robert E. Lee*
Bruns. *Abraham Lincoln*
Bryant. *Lucretia Mott: A Guiding Light*
Burke. *Louisa May Alcott*
Burleigh. *A Man Named Thoreau*
Carlson. *Harriet Tubman: Call to Freedom*
Casey. *Millard Fillmore: Thirteenth President*
Clinton. *Benjamin Harrison: Twenty-Third President*
Coelho. *John Quincy Adams*
Coil. *Harriet Beecher Stowe*
Collins. *Zachary Taylor: 12th President of the United States*
Colver. *Abraham Lincoln: For the People*
Connell. *They Shall Be Heard: Susan B. Anthony and Elizabeth Cady Stanton*
Cullen-DuPont. *Elizabeth Cady Stanton and Women's Liberty*
Davidson. *Dolly Madison: Famous First Lady*
Douglass. *Escape from Slavery: The Boyhood of Frederick Douglass*
Dubowski. *Andrew Johnson: Rebuilding the Union*
Durwood. *John C. Calhoun*
Edwards. *Denmark Vesey: Slave Revolt Leader*
Ellis. *Martin Van Buren: 8th President of the United States*
Falkof. *John Tyler: 10th President of the United States*
Feinberg. *John Marshall: The Great Chief Justice*
Fitz-Gerald. *James Monroe: Fifth President*
Fitz-Gerald. *William Henry Harrison: Ninth President*
Freedman. *Lincoln: A Photobiography*
Freedman. *Roger Taney: The Dred Scott Legacy*
Fritz. *The Great Little Madison*
Fritz. *Harriet Beecher Stowe and the Beecher Preachers*
Fritz. *Stonewall*
Gehre. *Susan B. Anthony*
Graham. *John Brown: A Cry for Freedom*
Greenblatt. *James K. Polk*

Hamilton. *Anthony Burns: The Defeat and Triumph of a Fugitive Slave*
Hargrove. *Abraham Lincoln: Sixteenth President*
Hargrove. *Martin Van Buren: Eighth President*
Hilto. *The World of Young Andrew Jackson*
Jakoubek. *Harriet Beecher Stowe*
Johnston. *Harriet: The Life and World of Harriet Beecher Stowe*
Kendall. *Susan B. Anthony*
Kent. *Andrew Johnson: Seventeenth President*
Kent. *Zachary Taylor: Twelfth President*
Kerby. *Robert E. Lee*
Klots. *Richard Allen: Religious Leader and Social Activist*
Krass. *Sojourner Truth: Antislavery Activist*
Law. *Milliard Fillmore: 13th President of the United States*
Leavell. *James Madison*
LeVert. *Edgar Allan Poe: Mournful and Never Ending Remembrance*
Lillegard. *James K. Polk: Eleventh President*
Lillegard. *John Tyler: Tenth President*
Lindop. *George Washington, Thomas Jefferson, and Andrew Jackson*

Collective Biography

Altman. *Extraordinary Black Americans*
Beard. *The Presidents in American History*
Blassingame. *The Look-It-Up Book of Presidents*
Dolan. *Shaping U.S. Foreign Policy: Profiles of Twelve Secretaries of State*
Faber. *Great Lives: American Government*
Hazell. *Heroines: Great Women Through the Ages*
Jacobs. *Great Lives: Human Rights*

Lindop. *James K. Polk, Abraham Lincoln, Theodore Roosevelt*
Loewen. *Poe: A Biography*
Marrin. *Virginia's General: Robert E. Lee*
Marston. *Isaac Johnson: From Slave to Stonecutter*
McClard. *Harriet Tubman: Slavery and the Underground Railroad*
McKissack. *Frederick Douglass: The Black Lion*
McKissack. *Sojourner Truth: Ain't I a Woman?*
Meltzer. *Andrew Jackson and His America*
Meltzer. *Frederick Douglass: In His Own Words*
Meltzer. *Lincoln in His Own Words*
Miller. *Henry David Thoreau: A Man for All Seasons*
Morris. *The Lincoln Way*
Neimark. *A Deaf Child Listened: Thomas Gallaudet*
Osinski. *Andrew Jackson: Seventh President*
Peterson. *Henry Clay: Leader in Congress*
Pflueger. *Stonewall Jackson*
Potter. *John Brown: Militant Abolitionist*
Randolph. *Woodrow Wilson: President*
Reef. *Henry David Thoreau: A Neighbor to Nature*

Katz. *Proudly Red and Black: Stories of African and Native Americans*
Lindop. *Presidents by Accident*
Lyons. *Keeping Secrets: The Girlhood Diaries of Seven Women Writers*
McKissack. *Rebels Against Slavery: American Slave Revolts*
Morin. *Women Who Reformed Politics*
Myers. *Now Is Your Time*

Reef. *Walt Whitman*
Robinet. *If You Please, President Lincoln*
Rosen. *A Fire in Her Bones: Mary Lyon*
Russell. *Frederick Douglass: Abolitionist Editor*
Ryan. *Louisa May Alcott: Her Girlhood Diary*
Sandak. *The Jacksons*
Sandak. *The Lincolns*
Sandburg. *Abe Lincoln Grows Up*
Schleichert. *The Life of Dorothea Dix*
Schleichert. *The Life of Elizabeth Blackwell*
Scott. *John Brown of Harper's Ferry*
Sproule. *Abraham Lincoln*
Stefoff. *Abraham Lincoln: 16th President*
Stefoff. *Andrew Jackson: 7th President*
Stefoff. *Herman Melville*
Stefoff. *William Henry Harrison: 9th President*
Stevens. *Chester Arthur: 21st President*
Tilton. *Clara Barton*
Trump. *Lincoln's Little Girl: A True Story*
Viola. *Andrew Jackson*
Weisberg. *Susan B. Anthony*
Wilson. *The Ingenious Mr. Peale*
Yates. *Prudence Crandall: Woman of Courage*

Pascoe. *First Facts About the Presidents*
Provenson. *My Fellow Americans*
Rennert. *Pioneers of Discovery*
Rubel. *The Scholastic Encyclopedia of the Presidents*
Smith. *Presidents of a Young Republic*
Sullivan. *Black Artists in Photography, 1840-1940*
Sullivan. *Presidents at Play*

History

Archer. *Breaking Barriers: The Feminist Movement*

Barboza. *Door of No Return: The Legend of Gorée Island*

Barrett. *Harpers Ferry: John Brown's Raid*

Bial. *The Underground Railroad*

Black. *Battle of the Atlantic*

Blockson. *The Underground Railroad*

Bowler. *Trains*

Carnes. *Us and Them: A History of Intolerance in America*

Colman. *Strike: The Bitter Struggle of American Workers*

Colman. *Toilets, Bathtubs, Sinks, and Sewers*

Colman. *Women in Society: United States*

Connell. *Tales from the Underground Railroad*

Cosner. *The Underground Railroad*

Cray. *American Datelines*

Davies. *Transport: On Land, Road and Rail*

Emert. *Top Lawyers and Their Famous Cases*

Feelings. *The Middle Passage: White Ships, Black Cargo*

Feinberg. *American Political Scandals Past and Present*

Fisher. *Tracks Across America: The Story of the American Railroad, 1825-1900*

Fradin. *Medicine: Yesterday, Today, and Tomorrow*

Frank. *The Birth of Black America: The Age of Discovery and the Slave Trade*

Giblin. *Be Seated: A Book About Chairs*

Gorrell. *North Star to Freedom: The Story of the Underground Railroad*

Hakim. *Liberty for All?*

Hamilton. *Many Thousand Gone: African Americans*

Haskins. *Get On Board: The Story of the Underground Railroad*

Herda. *The Dred Scott Case*

Hirsch. *Taxation: Paying for Government*

Jones. *The President Has Been Shot*

Karl. *America Alive: A History*

Katz. *Breaking the Chains: African-American Slave Resistance*

Katz. *The Westward Movement and Abolitionism: 1815-1850*

Landau. *Armed America: The Status of Gun Control*

Leiner. *First Children: Growing Up in the White House*

Lucas. *Civil Rights: The Long Struggle*

Macy. *Winning Ways: A Photohistory of American Women in Sports*

Markham. *Inventions That Changed Modern Life*

McKissack. *A Long Hard Journey: The Story of the Pullman Porter*

McNeese. *America's Early Canals*

McNeese. *America's First Railroads*

Medearis. *Come This Far to Freedom*

Meltzer. *The Black Americans*

Meltzer. *Cheap Raw Material*

Morley. *Clothes: For Work, Play and Display*

Mulcahy. *Diseases: Finding the Cure*

Patrick. *The Young Oxford Companion to the Supreme Court*

Paulson. *Days of Sorrow; Years of Glory*

Philip. *Singing America: Poems That Define a Nation*

Platt. *The Smithsonian Visual Timeline of Inventions*

Pleasant. *Kirsten's Cookbook*

Pollard. *The Nineteenth Century*

Rappaport. *American Women: Their Lives in Their Words*

Rogers. *The Antislavery Movement*

Sagan. *Women's Suffrage*

Sandler. *Presidents*

Sigerman. *An Unfinished Battle: American Women 1848-1865*

St. George. *The White House: Cornerstone of a Nation*

Stepto. *Our Song, Our Toil: The Story of American Slavery as Told by Slaves*

Sullivan. *Children of Promise: African-American Literature and Art*

Taylor. *Black Abolitionists and Freedom Fighters*

Toynton. *Growing Up in America: 1830-1860*

Ventura. *Clothing*

Ventura. *Food: Its Evolution Through the Ages*

Walter. *Mississippi Challenge*

Wheeler. *Events That Changed American History*

White. *Let My People Go: African Americans 1804-1860*

Whitman. *Get Up and Go: American Road Travel*

Wormser. *The Iron Horse: How the Railroads Changed America*

Young. *Testaments of Courage: Selections from Men's Slave Narratives*

Multimedia

CD-ROM

American History Explorer

Campaigns, Candidates and the Presidency

Eyewitness Encyclopedia of Science

Her Heritage: A Biographical Encyclopedia of American History

Landmark Documents in American History

Portraits of American Presidents

Science Navigator

SkyTrip America

Total History

The Way Things Work

Video

Abraham Lincoln
African Americans
Black Is My Color: The
  African American
  Experience
Blind Tom
Causes of the Civil War
Daring to Dream
Democracy and Reform
Edgar Allan Poe: Architect of
  Dreams
Equality: A History of the
  Women's Movement in
  America
Frederick Douglass

Frederick Douglass: When
  the Lion Wrote History
Harriet Tubman
A History of Slavery in
  America
The Life and Times of
  Abraham Lincoln
Lighthouses of New England
Lincoln: A Photobiography
Lucretia Mott
Mansions of Newport
Mt. Clare: Cradle of the
  American Dream
Old Sturbridge Village:
  Growing Up in New
  England

Presenting Mr. Frederick
  Douglass
Pride & Prejudice: A History
  of Black Culture in America
Raisin' Cane
Reading Terminal Market
The Sellin' of Jamie Thomas
Slavery and Freedom
Slavery and the Road to
  Freedom
Sojourner Truth
Susan B. Anthony
Susan B. Anthony Story
Unearthing the Slave Trade

GRADE EIGHT

Historical Fiction

Avi. *Beyond the Western Sea,
  Book Two: Lord Kirkle's
  Money*
Avi. *The Man Who Was Poe*
Avi. *The True Confessions of
  Charlotte Doyle*
Beatty. *Jayhawker*
Blos. *Brothers of the Heart,
  1837-38*
DeFelice. *The Apprenticeship
  of Lucas Whitaker*
Duff. *Radical Red*

Fleischman. *The Borning
  Room*
Fox. *The Slave Dancer*
Gaeddert. *Breaking Free*
Lampman. *White Captives*
Lasky. *True North: A Novel
  of the Underground
  Railroad*
Levin. *Mercy's Mill*
Lyons. *Letters from a Slave
  Girl*
Paterson. *Jip: His Story*
Paterson. *Lyddie*

Paulsen. *Nightjohn*
Rinaldi. *The Blue Door*
Ruby. *Steal Away Home*
Sauerwein. *The Way Home*
Smucker. *Runaway to
  Freedom*
Stone. *Autumn of the Royal
  Tar*
Tate. *The Secret of Gumbo
  Grove*
Turner. *Running for Our Lives*
Walter. *Second Daughter*

Biography

Bennett. *Stonewall Jackson:
  Lee's Greatest Lieutenant*
Bentley. *"Dear Friend":
  Thomas Garrett and
  William Still*
Bentley. *Harriet Tubman*
Bisson. *Nat Turner: Slave
  Revolt Leader*
Borzendowski. *John
  Russwurm*
Brown. *Elizabeth Blackwell:
  Physician*
Brown. *Franklin Pierce: 14th
  President*
Brown. *Robert E. Lee*
Bruns. *Abraham Lincoln*
Bryant. *Lucretia Mott: A
  Guiding Light*
Burke. *Louisa May Alcott*
Carlson. *Harriet Tubman:
  Call to Freedom*

Casey. *Millard Fillmore:
  Thirteenth President*
Clinton. *Benjamin Harrison:
  Twenty-Third President*
Coelho. *John Quincy Adams*
Coil. *Harriet Beecher Stowe*
Collins. *Zachary Taylor: 12th
  President*
Cullen-DuPont. *Elizabeth
  Cady Stanton and
  Women's Liberty*
Douglass. *Escape from
  Slavery: The Boyhood of
  Frederick Douglass*
Dubowski. *Andrew Johnson:
  Rebuilding the Union*
Durwood. *John C. Calhoun*
Edwards. *Denmark Vesey:
  Slave Revolt Leader*
Ellis. *Martin Van Buren: 8th
  President*

Falkof. *John Tyler: 10th
  President of the United
  States*
Feinberg. *John Marshall: The
  Great Chief Justice*
Fitz-Gerald. *James Monroe:
  Fifth President*
Fitz-Gerald. *William Henry
  Harrison: Ninth President*
Freedman. *Lincoln: A
  Photobiography*
Freedman. *Roger Taney: The
  Dred Scott Legacy*
Fritz. *The Great Little
  Madison*
Fritz. *Harriet Beecher Stowe
  and the Beecher Preachers*
Fritz. *Stonewall*
Gehre. *Susan B. Anthony*
Graham. *John Brown: A Cry
  for Freedom*
Greenblatt. *James K. Polk*

Hamilton. *Anthony Burns:
The Defeat and Triumph of
a Fugitive Slave*

Hargrove. *Abraham Lincoln:
Sixteenth President*

Hargrove. *Martin Van Buren:
Eighth President*

Hilto. *The World of Young
Andrew Jackson*

Jakoubek. *Harriet Beecher
Stowe*

Johnston. *Harriet: The Life
and World of Harriet
Beecher Stowe*

Kendall. *Susan B. Anthony*

Kent. *Andrew Johnson:
Seventeenth President*

Kent. *Zachary Taylor:
Twelfth President*

Kerby. *Robert E. Lee*

Klots. *Richard Allen:
Religious Leader and
Social Activist*

Krass. *Sojourner Truth:
Antislavery Activist*

Law. *Milliard Fillmore: 13th
President*

Leavell. *James Madison*

LeVert. *Edgar Allan Poe:
Mournful and Never
Ending Remembrance*

Lillegard. *James K. Polk:
Eleventh President*

Lillegard. *John Tyler: Tenth
President*

Lindop. *George Washington,
Thomas Jefferson, and
Andrew Jackson*

Lindop. *James K. Polk,
Abraham Lincoln,
Theodore Roosevelt*

Loewen. *Poe: A Biography*

Marrin. *Virginia's General:
Robert E. Lee*

McClard. *Harriet Tubman:
Slavery and the
Underground Railroad*

McKissack. *Sojourner Truth:
Ain't I a Woman?*

Meltzer. *Andrew Jackson and
His America*

Meltzer. *Frederick Douglass:
In His Own Words*

Meltzer. *Lincoln in His Own
Words*

Miller. *Henry David
Thoreau: A Man for All
Seasons*

Morris. *The Lincoln Way*

Neimark. *A Deaf Child
Listened: Thomas
Gallaudet*

Osinski. *Andrew Jackson:
Seventh President*

Pflueger. *Stonewall Jackson*

Potter. *John Brown: Militant
Abolitionist*

Randolph. *Woodrow Wilson:
President*

Reef. *Henry David Thoreau:
A Neighbor to Nature*

Reef. *Walt Whitman*

Robinet. *If You Please,
President Lincoln*

Rosen. *A Fire in Her Bones:
Mary Lyon*

Russell. *Frederick Douglass:
Abolitionist Editor*

Ryan. *Louisa May Alcott:
Her Girlhood Diary*

Sandak. *The Jacksons*

Sandak. *The Lincolns*

Sandburg. *Abe Lincoln Grows
Up*

Scott. *John Brown of
Harper's Ferry*

Sproule. *Abraham Lincoln*

Stefoff. *Abraham Lincoln:
16th President*

Stefoff. *Andrew Jackson: 7th
President*

Stefoff. *Herman Melville*

Stefoff. *William Henry
Harrison: 9th President*

Stevens. *Chester Arthur: 21st
President*

Tilton. *Clara Barton*

Trump. *Lincoln's Little Girl:
A True Story*

Viola. *Andrew Jackson*

Weisberg. *Susan B. Anthony*

Yates. *Prudence Crandall:
Woman of Courage*

Collective Biography

Aaseng. *Great Justices of the
Supreme Court*

Altman. *Extraordinary Black
Americans*

Beard. *The Presidents in
American History*

Blassingame. *The Look-It-Up
Book of Presidents*

Dolan. *Shaping U.S. Foreign
Policy: Twelve Secretaries
of State*

Faber. *Great Lives: American
Government*

Hazell. *Heroines: Great
Women Through the Ages*

Katz. *Proudly Red and Black:
Stories of African and
Native Americans*

Lindop. *Presidents by
Accident*

Lyons. *Keeping Secrets: The
Girlhood Diaries of Seven
Women Writers*

McKissack. *Rebels Against
Slavery: American Slave
Revolts*

Morin. *Women Who
Reformed Politics*

Myers. *Now Is Your Time*

Otfinoski.
Nineteenth-Century Writers

Pascoe. *First Facts About the
Presidents*

Provenson. *My Fellow
Americans*

Rennert. *Pioneers of
Discovery*

Rubel. *The Scholastic
Encyclopedia of the
Presidents*

Smith. *Presidents of a Young
Republic*

Sullivan. *Black Artists in
Photography, 1840-1940*

Sullivan. *Presidents at Play*

History

Archer. *Breaking Barriers:
The Feminist Movement*

Barboza. *Door of No Return:
The Legend of Gorée Island*

Barrett. *Harpers Ferry: John
Brown's Raid*

Bial. *The Underground
Railroad*

Black. *Battle of the Atlantic*

Blockson. *The Underground
Railroad*

Carnes. *Us and Them: A
History of Intolerance in
America*

Colman. *Strike: The Bitter
Struggle of American
Workers*

Colman. *Toilets, Bathtubs, Sinks, and Sewers*

Colman. *Women in Society: United States*

Cosner. *The Underground Railroad*

Cray. *American Datelines*

Davies. *Transport: On Land, Road and Rail*

Emert. *Top Lawyers and Their Famous Cases*

Feelings. *The Middle Passage: White Ships, Black Cargo*

Feinberg. *American Political Scandals Past and Present*

Fisher. *Tracks Across America: The Story of the American Railroad, 1825-1900*

Fradin. *Medicine: Yesterday, Today, and Tomorrow*

Frank. *The Birth of Black America: The Age of Discovery and the Slave Trade*

Giblin. *Be Seated: A Book About Chairs*

Gorrell. *North Star to Freedom: The Story of the Underground Railroad.*

Hakim. *Liberty for All?*

Hamilton. *Many Thousand Gone: African Americans*

Haskins. *Get on Board: The Story of the Underground Railroad*

Herda. *The Dred Scott Case*

Hirsch. *Taxation: Paying for Government*

Jones. *The President Has Been Shot*

Karl. *America Alive: A History*

Katz. *Breaking the Chains: African-American Slave Resistance*

Katz. *The Westward Movement and Abolitionism: 1815-1850*

Landau. *Armed America: The Status of Gun Control*

Leiner. *First Children: Growing Up in the White House*

Lucas. *Civil Rights: The Long Struggle*

Macy. *Winning Ways: A Photohistory of American Women in Sports*

Markham. *Inventions That Changed Modern Life*

McKissack. *A Long Hard Journey: The Story of the Pullman Porter*

McNeese. *America's Early Canals*

McNeese. *America's First Railroads*

Medearis. *Come This Far to Freedom*

Meltzer. *The Black Americans*

Meltzer. *Cheap Raw Material*

Morley. *Clothes: For Work, Play and Display*

Mulcahy. *Diseases: Finding the Cure*

Patrick. *The Young Oxford Companion to the Supreme Court*

Paulson. *Days of Sorrow; Years of Glory*

Philip. *Singing America: Poems That Define a Nation*

Platt. *The Smithsonian Visual Timeline of Inventions*

Rappaport. *American Women: Their Lives in Their Words*

Rogers. *The Antislavery Movement*

Sagan. *Women's Suffrage*

Sandler. *Presidents*

Sigerman. *An Unfinished Battle: American Women 1848-1865*

St. George. *The White House: Cornerstone of a Nation*

Stepto. *Our Song, Our Toil: The Story of American Slavery as Told by Slaves*

Sullivan. *Children of Promise: African-American Literature and Art*

Taylor. *Black Abolitionists and Freedom Fighters*

Toynton. *Growing Up in America: 1830-1860*

Ventura. *Clothing*

Ventura. *Food: Its Evolution Through the Ages*

Walter. *Mississippi Challenge*

Wekesser. *The Death Penalty: Opposing Viewpoints*

Wheeler. *Events That Changed American History*

White. *Let My People Go: African Americans 1804-1860*

Whitman. *Get Up and Go: American Road Travel*

Wormser. *The Iron Horse: How the Railroads Changed America*

Young. *Testaments of Courage: Selections from Men's Slave Narratives*

Multimedia

CD-ROM

American History Explorer

Campaigns, Candidates and the Presidency

Eyewitness Encyclopedia of Science

Famous American Speeches: 1850 to the Present

Her Heritage: A Biographical Encyclopedia of American History

Landmark Documents in American History

Portraits of American Presidents

Science Navigator

SkyTrip America

Total History

The Way Things Work

Video

Abraham Lincoln

African Americans

Black Is My Color: The African American Experience

Blind Tom

Causes of the Civil War

Daring to Dream

Democracy and Reform

Edgar Allan Poe: Architect of Dreams

Equality: A History of the Women's Movement in America

Frederick Douglass
Frederick Douglass: When
   the Lion Wrote History
Harriet Tubman
A History of Slavery in
   America
The Life and Times of
   Abraham Lincoln
Lighthouses of New England
Lincoln: A Photobiography
Lucretia Mott

Mansions of Newport
Mt. Clare: Cradle of the
   American Dream
Old Sturbridge Village:
   Growing Up in New
   England
Presenting Mr. Frederick
   Douglass
Pride & Prejudice: A History
   of Black Culture in America
Raisin' Cane

Reading Terminal Market
Slavery and Freedom
Slavery and the Road to
   Freedom
Sojourner Truth
Susan B. Anthony
Susan B. Anthony Story
Unearthing the Slave Trade

GRADE NINE

Historical Fiction

Avi. *Beyond the Western Sea,
   Book Two: Lord Kirkle's
   Money*
Beatty. *Jayhawker*
Blos. *Brothers of the Heart,
   1837-38*
DeFelice. *The Apprenticeship
   of Lucas Whitaker*
Farr. *I Never Came to You in
   White: A Novel*

Fleischman. *The Borning
   Room*
Lampman. *White Captives*
Lasky. *True North: A Novel
   of the Underground
   Railroad*
Levin. *Mercy's Mill*
Lyons. *Letters from a Slave
   Girl*
Paterson. *Jip: His Story*

Paterson. *Lyddie*
Paulsen. *Nightjohn*
Rinaldi. *The Blue Door*
Sauerwein. *The Way Home*
Tate. *The Secret of Gumbo
   Grove*
Walter. *Second Daughter*

Biography

Anderson. *Edgar Allan Poe:
   A Mystery*
Bentley. *"Dear Friend":
   Thomas Garrett and
   William Still*
Bentley. *Harriet Tubman*
Bisson. *Nat Turner: Slave
   Revolt Leader*
Borzendowski. *John
   Russwurm*
Brown. *Franklin Pierce: 14th
   President*
Brown. *Robert E. Lee*
Bruns. *Abraham Lincoln*
Bryant. *Lucretia Mott: A
   Guiding Light*
Burke. *Louisa May Alcott*
Carlson. *Harriet Tubman:
   Call to Freedom*
Casey. *Millard Fillmore:
   Thirteenth President*
Clinton. *Benjamin Harrison:
   Twenty-Third President*
Coelho. *John Quincy Adams*
Coil. *Harriet Beecher Stowe*
Collins. *Zachary Taylor: 12th
   President*
Cullen-DuPont. *Elizabeth
   Cady Stanton and
   Women's Liberty*
Durwood. *John C. Calhoun*

Edwards. *Denmark Vesey:
   Slave Revolt Leader*
Ellis. *Martin Van Buren: 8th
   President*
Falkof. *John Tyler: 10th
   President*
Feinberg. *John Marshall: The
   Great Chief Justice*
Fitz-Gerald. *James Monroe:
   Fifth President*
Fitz-Gerald. *William Henry
   Harrison: Ninth President*
Freedman. *Lincoln: A
   Photobiography*
Freedman. *Roger Taney: The
   Dred Scott Legacy*
Fritz. *Stonewall*
Gehre. *Susan B. Anthony*
Graham. *John Brown: A Cry
   for Freedom*
Greenblatt. *James K. Polk*
Hamilton. *Anthony Burns:
   The Defeat and Triumph of
   a Fugitive Slave*
Hargrove. *Abraham Lincoln:
   Sixteenth President*
Hargrove. *Martin Van Buren:
   Eighth President*
Jakoubek. *Harriet Beecher
   Stowe*

Johnston. *Harriet: The Life
   and World of Harriet
   Beecher Stowe*
Kendall. *Susan B. Anthony*
Kent. *Andrew Johnson:
   Seventeenth President*
Kent. *Zachary Taylor:
   Twelfth President*
Kerby. *Robert E. Lee*
Klots. *Richard Allen:
   Religious Leader and
   Social Activist*
Krass. *Sojourner Truth:
   Antislavery Activist*
Law. *Milliard Fillmore: 13th
   President of the United
   States*
Leavell. *James Madison*
LeVert. *Edgar Allan Poe:
   Mournful and Never
   Ending Remembrance*
Lillegard. *James K. Polk:
   Eleventh President*
Lillegard. *John Tyler: Tenth
   President*
Loewen. *Poe: A Biography*
Loewen. *Walt Whitman*
Marrin. *Virginia's General:
   Robert E. Lee*

McClard. *Harriet Tubman: Slavery and the Underground Railroad*

Meigs. *Invincible Louisa*

Meltzer. *Andrew Jackson and His America*

Meltzer. *Frederick Douglass: In His Own Words*

Meltzer. *Lincoln in His Own Words*

Meltzer. *Theodore Roosevelt and His America*

Miller. *Henry David Thoreau: A Man for All Seasons*

Morris. *The Lincoln Way*

Neimark. *A Deaf Child Listened: Thomas Gallaudet*

Osinski. *Andrew Jackson: Seventh President*

Pflueger. *Stonewall Jackson*

Potter. *John Brown: Militant Abolitionist*

Randolph. *Woodrow Wilson: President*

Reef. *Walt Whitman*

Robinet. *If You Please, President Lincoln*

Russell. *Frederick Douglass: Abolitionist Editor*

Scott. *John Brown of Harper's Ferry*

Sproule. *Abraham Lincoln*

Stefoff. *Abraham Lincoln: 16th President*

Stefoff. *Andrew Jackson: 7th President*

Stefoff. *Herman Melville*

Stevens. *Chester Arthur: 21st President*

Tilton. *Clara Barton*

Viola. *Andrew Jackson*

Yates. *Prudence Crandall: Woman of Courage*

Collective Biography

Aaseng. *Great Justices of the Supreme Court*

Anthony. *First Ladies: 1789-1961*

Beard. *The Presidents in American History*

Blassingame. *The Look-It-Up Book of Presidents*

Dolan. *Shaping U.S. Foreign Policy: Twelve Secretaries of State*

Faber. *Great Lives: American Government*

Lindop. *Presidents by Accident*

Lyons. *Keeping Secrets: The Girlhood Diaries of Seven Women Writers*

Morin. *Women Who Reformed Politics*

Myers. *Now Is Your Time*

O'Brien. *American Political Leaders*

Otfinoski. *Nineteenth-Century Writers*

Rennert. *Pioneers of Discovery*

Smith. *Presidents of a Young Republic*

Sullivan. *Presidents at Play*

History

Archer. *Breaking Barriers: The Feminist Movement*

Ardley. *Music: An Illustrated Encyclopedia*

Awmiller. *This House on Fire: The Story of the Blues*

Barboza. *Door of No Return: The Legend of Gorée Island*

Black. *Battle of the Atlantic*

Blockson. *The Underground Railroad*

Carnes. *Us and Them: A History of Intolerance in America*

Colman. *Women in Society: United States*

Cosner. *The Underground Railroad*

Cray. *American Datelines*

Dale. *Early Railways*

Davis. *Don't Know Much About History*

Davis. *Man-Made Catastrophes*

Dudley. *Slavery: Opposing Viewpoints*

Emert. *Top Lawyers and Their Famous Cases*

Feelings. *The Middle Passage: White Ships, Black Cargo*

Feinberg. *American Political Scandals Past and Present*

Fradin. *Medicine: Yesterday, Today, and Tomorrow*

Frost-Knappman. *Women's Suffrage in America*

Garza. *Barred from the Bar: A History of Women and the Legal Profession*

Goldberg. *Breaking New Ground: American Women 1800-1848*

Hakim. *Liberty for All?*

Hamilton. *Many Thousand Gone: African Americans*

Haskins. *Get on Board: The Story of the Underground Railroad*

Herda. *The Dred Scott Case*

Hirsch. *Taxation: Paying for Government*

Jenkins. *Nicaragua and the United States: Years of Conflict*

Jones. *The President Has Been Shot*

Katz. *Breaking the Chains: African-American Slave Resistance*

Katz. *The Westward Movement and Abolitionism: 1815-1850*

Kelly. *Election Day: An American Holiday, an American History*

Knappman. *Great American Trials*

Landau. *Armed America: The Status of Gun Control*

Leiner. *First Children: Growing Up in the White House*

Macy. *Winning Ways: A Photohistory of American Women in Sports*

Markham. *Inventions That Changed Modern Life*

McKissack. *A Long Hard Journey: The Story of the Pullman Porter*

Medearis. *Come This Far to Freedom*

Meltzer. *The Black Americans*

Meltzer. *Cheap Raw Material*

Mulcahy. *Diseases: Finding the Cure*

Patrick. *The Young Oxford Companion to the Supreme Court*

Paulson. *Days of Sorrow; Years of Glory*

Philip. *Singing America: Poems That Define a Nation*

Platt. *The Smithsonian Visual Timeline of Inventions*

Rappaport. *American Women: Their Lives in Their Words*

Rogers. *The Antislavery Movement*

Sagan. *Women's Suffrage*

Schreiner. *Mayday! Mayday!*

Sigerman. *An Unfinished Battle: American Women 1848-1865*

Smith. *Fascinating People and Astounding Events from American History*

Spangenburg. *The History of Science in the Nineteenth Century*

St. George. *The White House: Cornerstone of a Nation*

Steele. *Freedom's River*

Stepto. *Our Song, Our Toil: The Story of American Slavery as Told by Slaves*

Sullivan. *Black Artists in Photography, 1840-1940*

Taylor. *Black Abolitionists and Freedom Fighters*

Toynton. *Growing Up in America: 1830-1860*

Walter. *Mississippi Challenge*

Wekesser. *The Death Penalty: Opposing Viewpoints*

Wekesser. *Feminism: Opposing Viewpoints*

Wheeler. *Events That Changed American History*

White. *Let My People Go: African Americans 1804-1860*

Whitman. *Get Up and Go: American Road Travel*

Wormser. *The Iron Horse: How the Railroads Changed America*

Young. *Testaments of Courage: Selections from Men's Slave Narratives*

Multimedia

CD-ROM

American History Explorer

Campaigns, Candidates and the Presidency

Events That Changed the World

Famous American Speeches: 1850 to the Present

Her Heritage: A Biographical Encyclopedia of American History

A House Divided: The Lincoln-Douglas Debates

Ideas That Changed the World

Landmark Documents in American History

Portraits of American Presidents

Science Navigator

Total History

The Way Things Work

Video

African Americans

Blind Tom

Causes of the Civil War

Daring to Dream

Democracy and Reform

Dreams of Equality

Edgar Allan Poe: Architect of Dreams

Equality: A History of the Women's Movement in America

Frederick Douglass

Frederick Douglass: When the Lion Wrote History

Harriet Tubman

Hidden Heritage: The Roots of Black American Painting

A History of Slavery in America

The Life and Times of Abraham Lincoln

Lighthouses of New England

Lincoln: A Photobiography

Living Portraits of Historic Women: Of All the Nerve

Lucretia Mott

Mansions of Newport

Mt. Clare: Cradle of the American Dream

The Orphan Trains

Presenting Mr. Frederick Douglass

Pride & Prejudice: A History of Black Culture in America

Race to Freedom: The Story of the Underground Railroad

Raisin' Cane

Reading Terminal Market

Slavery and Freedom

Slavery and the Road to Freedom

Sojourner Truth

Susan B. Anthony

Susan B. Anthony Story

Unearthing the Slave Trade

GRADE TEN

Historical Fiction

Blos. *Brothers of the Heart, 1837-38*

Farr. *I Never Came to You in White: A Novel*

Fleischman. *The Borning Room*

Lampman. *White Captives*

Lyons. *Letters from a Slave Girl*

Rinaldi. *The Blue Door*

Sauerwein. *The Way Home*

Biography

Anderson. *Edgar Allan Poe: A Mystery*
Bentley. *Harriet Tubman*
Bisson. *Nat Turner: Slave Revolt Leader*
Borzendowski. *John Russwurm*
Brown. *Robert E. Lee*
Bruns. *Abraham Lincoln*
Bryant. *Lucretia Mott: A Guiding Light*
Burke. *Louisa May Alcott*
Coelho. *John Quincy Adams*
Coil. *Harriet Beecher Stowe*
Cullen-DuPont. *Elizabeth Cady Stanton and Women's Liberty*
Edwards. *Denmark Vesey: Slave Revolt Leader*
Feinberg. *John Marshall: The Great Chief Justice*
Freedman. *Lincoln: A Photobiography*
Freedman. *Roger Taney: The Dred Scott Legacy*

Hamilton. *Anthony Burns: The Defeat and Triumph of a Fugitive Slave*
Jakoubek. *Harriet Beecher Stowe*
Klots. *Richard Allen: Religious Leader and Social Activist*
Krass. *Sojourner Truth: Antislavery Activist*
Kunhardt. *Lincoln: An Illustrated Biography*
Leavell. *James Madison*
LeVert. *Edgar Allan Poe: Mournful and Never Ending Remembrance*
Loewen. *Poe: A Biography*
Loewen. *Walt Whitman*
Marrin. *Virginia's General: Robert E. Lee*
Meigs. *Invincible Louisa*
Meltzer. *Andrew Jackson and His America*
Meltzer. *Frederick Douglass: In His Own Words*

Meltzer. *Lincoln in His Own Words*
Meltzer. *Theodore Roosevelt and His America*
Miller. *Henry David Thoreau: A Man for All Seasons*
Morris. *The Lincoln Way*
Neimark. *A Deaf Child Listened: Thomas Gallaudet*
Reef. *Walt Whitman*
Robinet. *If You Please, President Lincoln*
Russell. *Frederick Douglass: Abolitionist Editor*
Silverman. *Edgar A. Poe*
Stefoff. *Herman Melville*
Sterling. *Ahead of Her Time: Abby Kelley*
Tilton. *Clara Barton*
Viola. *Andrew Jackson*
Yates. *Prudence Crandall: Woman of Courage*

Collective Biography

Aaseng. *Great Justices of the Supreme Court*
Anthony. *First Ladies: 1789-1961*
Lindop. *Presidents by Accident*

Lyons. *Keeping Secrets: The Girlhood Diaries of Seven Women Writers*
Morin. *Women Who Reformed Politics*
Myers. *Now Is Your Time*

O'Brien. *American Political Leaders: From Colonial Times to the Present*
Otfinoski. *Nineteenth-Century Writers*
Sullivan. *Presidents at Play*

History

Archer. *Breaking Barriers: The Feminist Movement*
Ardley. *Music: An Illustrated Encyclopedia*
Awmiller. *This House on Fire: The Story of the Blues*
Barboza. *Door of No Return: The Legend of Gorée Island*
Blockson. *The Underground Railroad*
Carnes. *Us and Them: A History of Intolerance in America*
Colman. *Women in Society: United States*
Cray. *American Datelines*
Dale. *Early Railways*
Davis. *Don't Know Much About History*
Davis. *Man-Made Catastrophes*
Dudley. *Slavery: Opposing Viewpoints*

Evans. *Born for Liberty: A History of Women in America*
Feelings. *The Middle Passage: White Ships, Black Cargo*
Feinberg. *American Political Scandals Past and Present*
Fradin. *Medicine: Yesterday, Today, and Tomorrow*
Frost-Knappman. *Women's Suffrage in America*
Garza. *Barred from the Bar: A History of Women and the Legal Profession*
Goldberg. *Breaking New Ground: American Women 1800-1848*
Hakim. *Liberty for All?*
Haskins. *Get on Board: The Story of the Underground Railroad*
Jenkins. *Nicaragua and the United States: Years of Conflict*

Katz. *Breaking the Chains: African-American Slave Resistance*
Katz. *The Westward Movement and Abolitionism: 1815-1850*
Kelly. *Election Day: An American Holiday, an American History*
Knappman. *Great American Trials*
Landau. *Armed America: The Status of Gun Control*
Macy. *Winning Ways: A Photohistory of American Women in Sports*
Markham. *Inventions That Changed Modern Life*
McKissack. *A Long Hard Journey: The Story of the Pullman Porter*
Meltzer. *The Black Americans*
Mulcahy. *Diseases: Finding the Cure*

Patrick. *The Young Oxford Companion to the Supreme Court*

Philip. *Singing America: Poems That Define a Nation*

Rappaport. *American Women: Their Lives in Their Words*

Rogers. *The Antislavery Movement*

Sagan. *Women's Suffrage*

Schreiner. *Mayday! Mayday!*

Sigerman. *An Unfinished Battle: American Women 1848-1865*

Smith. *Fascinating People and Astounding Events from American History*

Spangenburg. *The History of Science in the Nineteenth Century*

Steele. *Freedom's River*

Walter. *Mississippi Challenge*

Wekesser. *The Death Penalty: Opposing Viewpoints*

Wekesser. *Feminism: Opposing Viewpoints*

Wheeler. *Events That Changed American History*

White. *Let My People Go: African Americans 1804-1860*

Wormser. *The Iron Horse: How the Railroads Changed America*

Young. *Testaments of Courage: Selections from Men's Slave Narratives*

Multimedia

CD-ROM

Campaigns, Candidates and the Presidency

Events That Changed the World

Famous American Speeches: 1850 to the Present

Her Heritage: A Biographical Encyclopedia of American History

A House Divided: The Lincoln-Douglas Debates

Ideas That Changed the World

Landmark Documents in American History

Portraits of American Presidents

Science Navigator

Total History

The Way Things Work

Video

African Americans

Daring to Dream

Dreams of Equality

Edgar Allan Poe: Architect of Dreams

Equality: A History of the Women's Movement in America

Frederick Douglass

Frederick Douglass: When the Lion Wrote History

Harriet Tubman

Hidden Heritage: The Roots of Black American Painting

A History of Slavery in America

The Life and Times of Abraham Lincoln

Lighthouses of New England

Living Portraits of Historic Women: Of All the Nerve

Lucretia Mott

Mansions of Newport

Mt. Clare: Cradle of the American Dream

The Orphan Trains

Pride & Prejudice: A History of Black Culture in America

Race to Freedom: The Story of the Underground Railroad

Raisin' Cane

Slavery and the Road to Freedom

Sojourner Truth

Susan B. Anthony

Unearthing the Slave Trade

GRADES ELEVEN AND TWELVE

Historical Fiction

Cliff. *Free Enterprise*

Farr. *I Never Came to You in White: A Novel*

Olds. *Raising Holy Hell*

Waniek. *The Homeplace*

Biography

Anderson. *Edgar Allan Poe: A Mystery*

Bentley. *Harriet Tubman*

Coelho. *John Quincy Adams*

Coil. *Harriet Beecher Stowe*

Collins. *Shattered Dreams: The Story of Mary Todd Lincoln*

Cullen-DuPont. *Elizabeth Cady Stanton and Women's Liberty*

Faber. *Printer's Devil to Publisher: Adolph S. Ochs of the New York Times*

Freedman. *Lincoln: A Photobiography*

Hamilton. *Anthony Burns: The Defeat and Triumph of a Fugitive Slave*

Klots. *Richard Allen: Religious Leader and Social Activist*

Kunhardt. *Lincoln: An Illustrated Biography*

Loewen. *Walt Whitman*

McLanathan. *Gilbert Stuart*

Meigs. *Invincible Louisa*

Meltzer. *Frederick Douglass: In His Own Words*

Meltzer. *Lincoln in His Own Words*

Meltzer. *Theodore Roosevelt and His America*

Morris. *The Lincoln Way*
Neimark. *A Deaf Child Listened: Thomas Gallaudet*
Robinet. *If You Please, President Lincoln*

Collective Biography

Aaseng. *Great Justices of the Supreme Court*
Anthony. *First Ladies: 1789-1961*
Foster. *Written by Herself: African American Women, 1746-1892*

Sherr. *Failure Is Impossible: Susan B. Anthony*
Silverman. *Edgar A. Poe*
Stefoff. *Herman Melville*
Sterling. *Ahead of Her Time: Abby Kelley*

Lindop. *Presidents by Accident*
Lyons. *Keeping Secrets: The Girlhood Diaries of Seven Women Writers*

Viola. *Andrew Jackson*
Yates. *Prudence Crandall: Woman of Courage*

O'Brien. *American Political Leaders: From Colonial Times to the Present*
Otfinoski. *Nineteenth-Century Writers*
Truman. *First Ladies*

History

Ardley. *Music: An Illustrated Encyclopedia*
Awmiller. *This House on Fire: The Story of the Blues*
Boller. *Presidential Wives: An Anecdotal History*
Carnes. *Us and Them: A History of Intolerance in America*
Colman. *Women in Society: United States*
Cray. *American Datelines*
Dale. *Early Railways*
Davidson. *Everyday Life Through the Ages*
Davis. *Don't Know Much About History*
Davis. *Man-Made Catastrophes*
Dublin. *Farm to Factory: Women's Letters, 1830-1860*
Dublin. *Transforming Women's Work: New England Lives*
Dudley. *Slavery: Opposing Viewpoints*
Evans. *Born for Liberty: A History of Women in America*
Feelings. *The Middle Passage: White Ships, Black Cargo*
Feinberg. *American Political Scandals Past and Present*
Fogle. *Two Hundred Years: Stories of the Nation's Capital*
Frost-Knappman. *Women's Suffrage in America*

Garza. *Barred from the Bar: A History of Women and the Legal Profession*
Goldberg. *Breaking New Ground: American Women 1800-1848*
Hakim. *Liberty for All?*
Hanmer. *Taking a Stand Against Sexism and Sex Discrimination*
Jenkins. *Nicaragua and the United States: Years of Conflict*
Kelly. *Election Day: An American Holiday, an American History*
Knappman. *Great American Trials*
McLaurin. *Celia, a Slave*
McLynn. *Famous Trials: Cases That Made History*
Melder. *Hail to the Candidate: Presidential Campaigns*
Mulcahy. *Diseases: Finding the Cure*
Patrick. *The Young Oxford Companion to the Supreme Court*
Philip. *Singing America: Poems That Define a Nation*
Rappaport. *American Women: Their Lives in Their Words*
Rogers. *The Antislavery Movement*
Sagan. *Women's Suffrage*
Sante. *Low Life: Lures and Snares of Old New York*
Schreiner. *Mayday! Mayday!*

Sigerman. *An Unfinished Battle: American Women 1848-1865*
Smith. *Fascinating People and Astounding Events from American History*
Spangenburg. *The History of Science in the Nineteenth Century*
Steele. *Freedom's River*
Stevenson. *Life in Black and White: Family and Community in the Slave South*
Thoreau. *Walden: An Annotated Edition*
Tinling. *With Women's Eyes: Visitors to the New World, 1775-1918*
Vlach. *Back of the Big House*
Wallace. *The Long, Bitter Trail: Andrew Jackson and the Indians*
Walter. *Mississippi Challenge*
Wekesser. *The Death Penalty: Opposing Viewpoints*
Wekesser. *Feminism: Opposing Viewpoints*
Wheeler. *Events That Changed American History*
Wheeler. *A Rising Thunder: From Lincoln's Election to the Battle of Bull Run*
White. *Let My People Go: African Americans 1804-1860*
Young. *Testaments of Courage: Selections from Men's Slave Narratives*

Multimedia ————————————————————————————————

CD-ROM

*Campaigns, Candidates and
the Presidency*
*Events That Changed the
World*
*Famous American Speeches:
1850 to the Present*

*Her Heritage: A Biographical
Encyclopedia of American
History*
*A House Divided: The
Lincoln-Douglas Debates*
Ideas That Changed the World

*Landmark Documents in
American History*
*Portraits of American
Presidents*
Science Navigator
Total History
The Way Things Work

Video

Daring to Dream
Dark Passages
Dreams of Equality
*Edgar Allan Poe: Architect of
Dreams*
*Equality: A History of the
Women's Movement in
America*
Frederick Douglass
*Frederick Douglass: When
the Lion Wrote History*
Harriet Tubman

*Hidden Heritage: The Roots
of Black American Painting*
*A History of Slavery in
America*
*The Life and Times of
Abraham Lincoln*
Lighthouses of New England
*Living Portraits of Historic
Women: Of All the Nerve*
Lucretia Mott
Mansions of Newport
*Mt. Clare: Cradle of the
American Dream*

The Orphan Trains
*Pride & Prejudice: A History
of Black Culture in America*
*Race to Freedom: The Story
of the Underground
Railroad*
Raisin' Cane
*Slavery and the Road to
Freedom*
Sojourner Truth
Susan B. Anthony
Unearthing the Slave Trade

THE CIVIL WAR, 1861-1865

GRADE SEVEN

Historical Fiction

Armstrong. *The Dreams of Mairhe Mehan: A Novel of the Civil War*
Beatty. *Blue Stars Watching*
Beatty. *Charley Skedaddle*
Beatty. *Eben Tyne, Powdermonkey*
Beatty. *Turn Homeward, Hannalee*
Beatty. *Wait for Me, Watch for Me, Eula Bee*
Beatty. *Who Comes with Cannons?*
Blos. *A Gathering of Days: A New England Girl's Journal, 1830-32*
Clapp. *The Tamarack Tree*
Climo. *A Month of Seven Days*
Collier. *With Every Drop of Blood*

Denenberg. *When Will This Cruel War Be Over? Diary, 1864*
Donahue. *An Island Far from Home*
Duey. *Emma Eileen Grove: Mississippi, 1865*
Fleischman. *Bull Run*
Forman. *Becca's Story*
Forrester. *Sound the Jubilee*
Hansen. *Out from This Place*
Hansen. *Which Way Freedom?*
Holland. *Behind the Lines*
Houston. *Mountain Valor*
Hunt. *Across Five Aprils*
Kassem. *Listen for Rachel*
Keith. *Rifles for Watie*
Lyon. *Here and Now*
Myers. *The Glory Field*
Nixon. *A Dangerous Promise*

Nixon. *Keeping Secrets*
Perez. *The Slopes of War*
Polacco. *Pink and Say*
Reeder. *Across the Lines*
Reeder. *Shades of Gray*
Rinaldi. *In My Father's House*
Rinaldi. *The Last Silk Dress*
Shore. *The Sacred Moon Tree, 1861-1865*
Shura. *Gentle Annie: The True Story of a Civil War Nurse*
Steele. *The Perilous Road*
Wisler. *The Drummer of Vicksburg*
Wisler. *Mr. Lincoln's Drummer*
Wisler. *Red Cap*

Biography

Brown. *Elizabeth Blackwell: Physician*
Brown. *Robert E. Lee*
Bruns. *Abraham Lincoln*
Burchard. *Charlotte Forten: A Black Teacher in the Civil War*
Burke. *Louisa May Alcott*
Carlson. *Harriet Tubman: Call to Freedom*
Casey. *Millard Fillmore: Thirteenth President*
Claflin. *Sojourner Truth and the Struggle for Freedom*
Clinton. *Benjamin Harrison: Twenty-Third President*
Coil. *Harriet Beecher Stowe*
Colver. *Abraham Lincoln: For the People*

Connell. *They Shall Be Heard: Susan B. Anthony and Elizabeth Cady Stanton*
Cooper. *From Slave to Civil War Hero: Robert Small*
Cullen-DuPont. *Elizabeth Cady Stanton and Women's Liberty*
Dubowski. *Andrew Johnson: Rebuilding the Union*
Dubowski. *Clara Barton: Healing the Wounds*
Dubowski. *Robert E. Lee*
Freedman. *Lincoln: A Photobiography*
Fritz. *Harriet Beecher Stowe and the Beecher Preachers*
Gay. *Emma Goldman*
Gehre. *Susan B. Anthony*
Hamilton. *Clara Barton*

Hargrove. *Abraham Lincoln: Sixteenth President*
Jakoubek. *Harriet Beecher Stowe*
Johnston. *Harriet: The Life and World of Harriet Beecher Stowe*
Kendall. *Susan B. Anthony*
Kent. *Andrew Johnson: Seventeenth President*
Kerby. *Robert E. Lee*
King. *Jefferson Davis*
Krass. *Sojourner Truth: Antislavery Activist*
Lindop. *James K. Polk, Abraham Lincoln, Theodore Roosevelt*
Marrin. *Unconditional Surrender*
Marrin. *Virginia's General: Robert E. Lee*

Marston. *Isaac Johnson: From Slave to Stonecutter*

McClard. *Harriet Tubman: Slavery and the Underground Railroad*

McHale. *Dr. Samuel Mudd and the Lincoln Assassination*

McKissack. *Frederick Douglass: The Black Lion*

McKissack. *Sojourner Truth: Ain't I a Woman?*

Meltzer. *Frederick Douglass: In His Own Words*

Meltzer. *Lincoln in His Own Words*

Morris. *The Lincoln Way*

O'Brien. *Ulysses S. Grant*

O'Neal. *The Assassination of Abraham Lincoln*

Peterson. *Henry Clay: Leader in Congress*

Pflueger. *Stonewall Jackson: Confederate General*

Potter. *Jefferson Davis: Confederate President*

Randolph. *Woodrow Wilson: President*

Reef. *Walt Whitman*

Rickarby. *Ulysses S. Grant*

Robinet. *If You Please, President Lincoln*

Russell. *Frederick Douglass: Abolitionist Editor*

Ryan. *Louisa May Alcott: Her Girlhood Diary*

Sandak. *The Lincolns*

Shorto. *Abraham Lincoln: To Preserve the Union*

Shorto. *David Farragut and the Great Naval Blockade*

Sproule. *Abraham Lincoln*

Stefoff. *Abraham Lincoln: 16th President*

Stevens. *Frank Thompson: Her Civil War Story*

Sullivan. *Matthew Brady: His Life and Photographs*

Tilton. *Clara Barton*

Trump. *Lincoln's Little Girl: A True Story*

Weidhorn. *Robert E. Lee*

Weisberg. *Susan B. Anthony*

Whitelaw. *William Tecumseh Sherman*

Zeinert. *Elizabeth Van Lew: Southern Belle, Union Spy*

Collective Biography

Aaseng. *You Are the General II: 1800-1899*

Altman. *Extraordinary Black Americans*

Beard. *The Presidents in American History*

Blassingame. *The Look-It-Up Book of Presidents*

Faber. *Great Lives: American Government*

Lindop. *Presidents by Accident*

Lyons. *Keeping Secrets: The Girlhood Diaries of Seven Women Writers*

Myers. *Now Is Your Time*

Pascoe. *First Facts About the Presidents*

Provenson. *My Fellow Americans*

Rennert. *Pioneers of Discovery*

Rubel. *The Scholastic Encyclopedia of the Presidents*

Sheafer. *Women in America's Wars*

Smith. *President of a Divided Nation*

Sullivan. *Black Artists in Photography, 1840-1940*

Sullivan. *Presidents at Play*

Wilkinson. *Generals Who Changed the World*

History

Anderson. *Battles That Changed the Modern World*

Ashabranner. *A Memorial for Mr. Lincoln*

Beller. *Cadets at War: The Battle of New Market*

Beller. *To Hold This Ground: Gettysburg*

Biel. *The Civil War*

Bolotin. *For Home and Country: A Civil War Scrapbook*

Chang. *A Separate Battle: Women and the Civil War*

Colman. *Spies! Women in the Civil War*

Corrick. *The Battle of Gettysburg*

Cosner. *War Nurses*

Cox. *Undying Glory*

Cray. *American Datelines*

Currie. *Music in the Civil War*

Czech. *Snapshot: America Discovers the Camera*

Damon. *When the Cruel War Is Over: The Civil War Home Front*

Davies. *Transport: On Land, Road and Rail*

Fisher. *Tracks Across America: The Story of the American Railroad, 1825-1900*

Fradin. *Medicine: Yesterday, Today, and Tomorrow*

Gay. *Civil War*

Hakim. *War Terrible War*

Hansen. *Between Two Fires: Black Soldiers in the Civil War*

Hirsch. *Taxation: Paying for Government*

Jones. *The President Has Been Shot*

Kantor. *Gettysburg*

Karl. *America Alive: A History*

Katz. *Breaking the Chains: African-American Slave Resistance*

Katz. *The Civil War to the Last Frontier: 1850-1880s*

Kent. *The Battle of Chancellorsville*

Kent. *The Battle of Shiloh*

Kent. *The Story of the Battle of Bull Run*

Kent. *The Story of the Surrender at Yorktown*

Leiner. *First Children: Growing Up in the White House*

McKissack. *A Long Hard Journey: The Story of the Pullman Porter*

Medearis. *Come This Far to Freedom*

Meltzer. *The Black Americans*

Meltzer. *Voices from the Civil War*

Meltzer. *Weapons & Warfare*

Mettger. *Till Victory Is Won: Black Soldiers in the Civil War*

Morley. *Clothes: For Work, Play and Display*

Murphy. *The Boys' War*

Murphy. *The Long Road to Gettysburg*

Patrick. *The Young Oxford Companion to the Supreme Court*

Philip. *Singing America: Poems That Define a Nation*

Piggins. *A Multicultural Portrait of the Civil War*

Platt. *The Smithsonian Visual Timeline of Inventions*

Pleasant Company. *Addy's Cook Book 1864*

Pollard. *The Nineteenth Century*

Rappaport. *American Women: Their Lives in their Words*

Ray. *Behind the Blue and the Gray: The Soldier's Life in the Civil War*

Ray. *A Nation Torn: The Story of How the Civil War Began*

Reef. *Civil War Soldiers*

Sandler. *Presidents*

Sigerman. *Laborers for Liberty: American Women 1865-1890*

Smith. *Behind the Lines*

Smith. *1863: The Crucial Year*

Smith. *The First Battles*

Smith. *One Nation Again*

Smith. *Prelude to War*

Smith. *The Road to Appomattox*

St. George. *The White House: Cornerstone of a Nation*

Steins. *The Nation Divides: The Civil War, 1820-1880*

Sullivan. *Children of Promise: African-American Literature and Art*

Wakin. *Photos That Made U.S. History: Civil War to the Atomic Age*

Walter. *Mississippi Challenge*

Warner. *The U.S. Marine Corps*

Weiner. *The Civil War*

Wheeler. *Events That Changed American History*

Williams. *Forts and Castles*

Wormser. *The Iron Horse: How the Railroads Changed America*

Young. *The Emancipation Proclamation*

Multimedia

CD-ROM

American History Explorer

Campaigns, Candidates and the Presidency

Landmark Documents in American History

Portraits of American Presidents

SkyTrip America

Total History

The Way Things Work

Video

Abraham Lincoln

African Americans

Black Is My Color: The African American Experience

Causes of the Civil War

Civil War Trains

Clara Barton Emily Dickinson

Daring to Dream

Elizabeth Cady Stanton and Susan B. Anthony

Farming in America: A History

Frederick Douglass

Frederick Douglass: When the Lion Wrote History

Gettysburg

The Great Campaigns of the Civil War

Harriet Tubman

The Life and Times of Abraham Lincoln

Lincoln: A Photobiography

Lucretia Mott

Mt. Clare: Cradle of the American Dream

Presenting Mr. Frederick Douglass

The Rebel Slave

Susan B. Anthony

Susan B. Anthony Story

GRADE EIGHT

Historical Fiction

Armstrong. *The Dreams of Mairhe Mehan: A Novel of the Civil War.*

Beatty. *Blue Stars Watching*

Beatty. *Charley Skedaddle*

Beatty. *Eben Tyne, Powdermonkey*

Beatty. *Turn Homeward, Hannalee*

Beatty. *Wait for Me, Watch for Me, Eula Bee*

Beatty. *Who Comes with Cannons?*

Clapp. *The Tamarack Tree*

Collier. *With Every Drop of Blood*

Denenberg. *When Will This Cruel War Be Over? Diary, 1864*

Fleischman. *Bull Run*

Forman. *Becca's Story*

Forrester. *Sound the Jubilee*

Hansen. *Out from This Place*

Holland. *Behind the Lines*

Houston. *Mountain Valor*

Hunt. *Across Five Aprils*

Kassem. *Listen for Rachel*

Keith. *Rifles for Watie*

Myers. *The Glory Field*

Nixon. *A Dangerous Promise*
Nixon. *Keeping Secrets*
Perez. *The Slopes of War*
Polacco. *Pink and Say*
Rinaldi. *In My Father's House*

Rinaldi. *The Last Silk Dress*
Shore. *The Sacred Moon Tree, 1861-1865*
Wisler. *The Drummer of Vicksburg*

Wisler. *Mr. Lincoln's Drummer*
Wisler. *Red Cap*

Biography

Bentley. *Harriet Tubman*
Brown. *Elizabeth Blackwell: Physician*
Brown. *Robert E. Lee*
Bruns. *Abraham Lincoln*
Burchard. *Charlotte Forten: A Black Teacher in the Civil War*
Burke. *Louisa May Alcott*
Carlson. *Harriet Tubman: Call to Freedom*
Casey. *Millard Fillmore: Thirteenth President*
Claflin. *Sojourner Truth and the Struggle for Freedom*
Clinton. *Benjamin Harrison: Twenty-Third President*
Coil. *Harriet Beecher Stowe*
Cooper. *From Slave to Civil War Hero: Robert Small*
Cullen-DuPont. *Elizabeth Cady Stanton and Women's Liberty*
Dubowski. *Andrew Johnson: Rebuilding the Union*
Dubowski. *Clara Barton: Healing The Wounds*
Dubowski. *Robert E. Lee*
Freedman. *Lincoln: A Photobiography*
Fritz. *Harriet Beecher Stowe and the Beecher Preachers*
Gay. *Emma Goldman*
Gehre. *Susan B. Anthony*
Hamilton. *Clara Barton*
Hargrove. *Abraham Lincoln: Sixteenth President*

Jakoubek. *Harriet Beecher Stowe*
Johnston. *Harriet: The Life and World of Harriet Beecher Stowe*
Kendall. *Susan B. Anthony*
Kent. *Andrew Johnson: Seventeenth President*
Kerby. *Robert E. Lee*
King. *Jefferson Davis*
Krass. *Sojourner Truth: Antislavery Activist*
Lindop. *James K. Polk, Abraham Lincoln, Theodore Roosevelt*
Marrin. *Unconditional Surrender*
Marrin. *Virginia's General: Robert E. Lee*
McClard. *Harriet Tubman: Slavery and the Underground Railroad*
McHale. *Dr. Samuel Mudd and the Lincoln Assassination*
McKissack. *Sojourner Truth: Ain't I a Woman?*
Meltzer. *Frederick Douglass: In His Own Words*
Meltzer. *Lincoln in His Own Words*
Morris. *The Lincoln Way*
O'Brien. *Ulysses S. Grant*
O'Neal. *The Assassination of Abraham Lincoln*
Pflueger. *Stonewall Jackson: Confederated General*

Potter. *Jefferson Davis: Confederate President*
Randolph. *Woodrow Wilson: President*
Reef. *Walt Whitman*
Rickarby. *Ulysses S. Grant*
Robinet. *If You Please, President Lincoln*
Russell. *Frederick Douglass: Abolitionist Editor*
Ryan. *Louisa May Alcott: Her Girlhood Diary*
Sandak. *The Lincolns*
Shorto. *Abraham Lincoln: To Preserve the Union*
Shorto. *David Farragut and the Great Naval Blockade*
Sproule. *Abraham Lincoln*
Stefoff. *Abraham Lincoln: 16th President*
Stevens. *Frank Thompson: Her Civil War Story*
Sullivan. *Matthew Brady: His Life and Photographs*
Tilton. *Clara Barton*
Trump. *Lincoln's Little Girl: A True Story*
Weidhorn. *Robert E. Lee*
Weisberg. *Susan B. Anthony*
Whitelaw. *William Tecumseh Sherman*
Zeinert. *Elizabeth Van Lew: Southern Belle, Union Spy*

Collective Biography

Aaseng. *You Are the General II: 1800-1899*
Altman. *Extraordinary Black Americans*
Beard. *The Presidents in American History*
Blassingame. *The Look-It-Up Book of Presidents*
Faber. *Great Lives: American Government*
Lindop. *Presidents by Accident*

Lyons. *Keeping Secrets: The Girlhood Diaries of Seven Women Writers*
Myers. *Now Is Your Time*
Pascoe. *First Facts About the Presidents*
Provenson. *My Fellow Americans*
Rennert. *Pioneers of Discovery*

Rubel. *The Scholastic Encyclopedia of the Presidents*
Sheafer. *Women in America's Wars*
Smith. *President of a Divided Nation*
Sullivan. *Black Artists in Photography, 1840-1940*
Sullivan. *Presidents at Play*
Wilkinson. *Generals Who Changed the World*

History

Anderson. *Battles That Changed the Modern World*

Ashabranner. *A Memorial for Mr. Lincoln*

Beller. *Cadets at War: The Battle of New Market*

Beller. *To Hold This Ground: Gettysburg*

Biel. *The Civil War*

Bolotin. *For Home and Country: A Civil War Scrapbook*

Chang. *A Separate Battle: Women and the Civil War*

Colman. *Spies! Women in the Civil War*

Corrick. *The Battle of Gettysburg*

Cosner. *War Nurses*

Cox. *Undying Glory*

Cray. *American Datelines*

Currie. *Music in the Civil War*

Czech. *Snapshot: America Discovers the Camera*

Damon. *When the Cruel War Is Over: The Civil War Home Front*

Davies. *Transport: On Land, Road and Rail*

Fisher. *Tracks Across America: The Story of the American Railroad, 1825-1900*

Fleming. *Band of Brothers: West Point in the Civil War*

Fradin. *Medicine: Yesterday, Today, and Tomorrow*

Frankel. *Break Those Chains at Last: African Americans 1860-1880*

Gay. *Civil War*

Hakim. *War Terrible War*

Hansen. *Between Two Fires: Black Soldiers in the Civil War*

Hirsch. *Taxation: Paying for Government*

Jones. *The President Has Been Shot*

Kantor. *Gettysburg*

Karl. *America Alive: A History*

Katz. *Breaking the Chains: African-American Slave Resistance*

Katz. *The Civil War to the Last Frontier: 1850-1880s*

Leiner. *First Children: Growing Up in the White House*

McKissack. *A Long Hard Journey: The Story of the Pullman Porter*

Medearis. *Come This Far to Freedom*

Meltzer. *The Black Americans*

Meltzer. *Voices from the Civil War*

Meltzer. *Weapons & Warfare*

Mettger. *Till Victory Is Won: Black Soldiers in the Civil War*

Morley. *Clothes: For Work, Play and Display*

Murphy. *The Boys' War*

Murphy. *The Long Road to Gettysburg*

Patrick. *The Young Oxford Companion to the Supreme Court*

Philip. *Singing America: Poems That Define a Nation*

Piggins. *A Multicultural Portrait of the Civil War*

Platt. *The Smithsonian Visual Timeline of Inventions*

Rappaport. *American Women: Their Lives in Their Words*

Ray. *Behind the Blue and the Gray: The Soldier's Life in the Civil War*

Ray. *A Nation Torn: The Story of How the Civil War Began*

Reef. *Civil War Soldiers*

Sandler. *Presidents*

Sigerman. *Laborers for Liberty: American Women 1865-1890*

Smith. *Behind the Lines*

Smith. *1863: The Crucial Year*

Smith. *The First Battles*

Smith. *One Nation Again*

Smith. *Prelude to War*

Smith. *The Road to Appomattox*

St. George. *The White House: Cornerstone of a Nation*

Stanley. *Women in the Military*

Steins. *The Nation Divides: The Civil War, 1820-1880*

Sullivan. *Children of Promise: African-American Literature and Art*

Wakin. *Photos That Made U.S. History: Civil War to the Atomic Age*

Walter. *Mississippi Challenge*

Warner. *The U.S. Marine Corps*

Weiner. *The Civil War*

Wheeler. *Events That Changed American History*

Williams. *Forts and Castles*

Wormser. *The Iron Horse: How the Railroads Changed America*

Young. *The Emancipation Proclamation*

Multimedia

CD-ROM

American History Explorer Campaigns, Candidates and the Presidency

Famous American Speeches: 1850 to the Present

Landmark Documents in American History

Portraits of American Presidents

SkyTrip America

Total History

The Way Things Work

Video

Abraham Lincoln

African Americans

Black Is My Color: The African American Experience

Causes of the Civil War

The Civil War, Episode 1: The Cause—1861

The Civil War, Episode 2: A Very Bloody Affair—1862

The Civil War, Episode 3: Forever Free—1862
The Civil War, Episode 4: Simply Murder—1863
The Civil War, Episode 5: The Universe Of Battle—1863
The Civil War, Episode 6: Valley of the Shadow of Death—1864
The Civil War, Episode 7: Most Hallowed Ground—1864
The Civil War, Episode 8: War Is All Hell—1865

The Civil War, Episode 9: The Better Angels of Our Nature—1865
Civil War Trains
Clara Barton Emily Dickinson Daring to Dream
Elizabeth Cady Stanton and Susan B. Anthony
Farming in America: A History
Frederick Douglass
Frederick Douglass: When the Lion Wrote History
Gettysburg

The Great Campaigns of the Civil War
Harriet Tubman
The Life and Times of Abraham Lincoln
Lincoln: A Photobiography
Lucretia Mott
Mt. Clare: Cradle of the American Dream
Presenting Mr. Frederick Douglass
The Rebel Slave
Susan B. Anthony
Susan B. Anthony Story

GRADE NINE

Historical Fiction

Armstrong. *The Dreams of Mairhe Mehan: A Novel of the Civil War.*
Beatty. *Blue Stars Watching*
Beatty. *Charley Skedaddle*
Beatty. *Eben Tyne, Powdermonkey*
Beatty. *Turn Homeward, Hannalee*
Beatty. *Wait for Me, Watch for Me, Eula Bee*

Beatty. *Who Comes with Cannons?*
Clapp. *The Tamarack Tree*
Collier. *With Every Drop of Blood*
Denenberg. *When Will This Cruel War Be Over? Diary, 1864*
Fleischman. *Bull Run*
Forman. *Becca's Story*
Forrester. *Sound the Jubilee*
Hansen. *Out From This Place*

Holland. *Behind the Lines*
Hunt. *Across Five Aprils*
Kassem. *Listen for Rachel*
Keith. *Rifles for Watie*
Myers. *The Glory Field*
Perez. *The Slopes of War*
Rinaldi. *In My Father's House*
Rinaldi. *The Last Silk Dress*
Shore. *The Sacred Moon Tree, 1861-1865*
Wisler. *Red Cap*

Biography

Bentley. *Harriet Tubman*
Brown. *Robert E. Lee*
Bruns. *Abraham Lincoln*
Burke. *Louisa May Alcott*
Carlson. *Harriet Tubman: Call to Freedom*
Casey. *Millard Fillmore: Thirteenth President*
Clinton. *Benjamin Harrison: Twenty-Third President*
Coil. *Harriet Beecher Stowe*
Cullen-DuPont. *Elizabeth Cady Stanton and Women's Liberty*
Dubowski. *Clara Barton: Healing the Wounds*
Dubowski. *Robert E. Lee*
Freedman. *Lincoln: A Photobiography*
Gay. *Emma Goldman*
Gehre. *Susan B. Anthony*
Hamilton. *Clara Barton*
Hargrove. *Abraham Lincoln: Sixteenth President*

Jakoubek. *Harriet Beecher Stowe*
Johnston. *Harriet: The Life and World of Harriet Beecher Stowe*
Kendall. *Susan B. Anthony*
Kent. *Andrew Johnson: Seventeenth President*
Kerby. *Robert E. Lee*
King. *Jefferson Davis*
Krass. *Sojourner Truth: Antislavery Activist*
Loewen. *Walt Whitman*
Marrin. *Unconditional Surrender*
Marrin. *Virginia's General: Robert E. Lee*
McClard. *Harriet Tubman: Slavery and the Underground Railroad*
McHale. *Dr. Samuel Mudd and the Lincoln Assassination*
Meigs. *Invincible Louisa*

Meltzer. *Frederick Douglass: In His Own Words*
Meltzer. *Lincoln in His Own Words*
Morris. *The Lincoln Way*
O'Brien. *Ulysses S. Grant*
O'Neal. *The Assassination of Abraham Lincoln*
Pflueger. *Stonewall Jackson: Confederate General*
Potter. *Jefferson Davis: Confederate President*
Randolph. *Woodrow Wilson: President*
Reef. *Walt Whitman*
Rickarby. *Ulysses S. Grant*
Robinet. *If You Please, President Lincoln*
Russell. *Frederick Douglass: Abolitionist Editor*
Shorto. *Abraham Lincoln: To Preserve the Union*
Shorto. *David Farragut and the Great Naval Blockade*
Sproule. *Abraham Lincoln*

Stefoff. *Abraham Lincoln: 16th President*

Stevens. *Frank Thompson: Her Civil War Story*

Collective Biography

Aaseng. *You Are the General II: 1800-1899*

Anthony. *First Ladies: 1789-1961*

Beard. *The Presidents in American History*

Blassingame. *The Look-It-Up Book of Presidents*

Faber. *Great Lives: American Government*

Lindop. *Presidents by Accident*

Sullivan. *Matthew Brady: His Life and Photographs*

Tilton. *Clara Barton*

Weidhorn. *Robert E. Lee*

Lyons. *Keeping Secrets: The Girlhood Diaries of Seven Women Writers*

Mahoney. *Women in Espionage: A Biographical Dictionary*

Myers. *Now Is Your Time*

O'Brien. *American Political Leaders*

Rennert. *Pioneers of Discovery*

Whitelaw. *William Tecumseh Sherman*

Zeinert. *Elizabeth Van Lew: Southern Belle, Union Spy*

Sheafer. *Women in America's Wars*

Smith. *President of a Divided Nation*

Sullivan. *Black Artists in Photography, 1840-1940*

Sullivan. *Presidents at Play*

Wilkinson. *Generals Who Changed the World*

History

Anderson. *Battles That Changed the Modern World*

Ashabranner. *A Memorial for Mr. Lincoln*

Beller. *Cadets at War: The Battle of New Market*

Beller. *To Hold This Ground: Gettysburg*

Cohen. *America: Then and Now*

Corrick. *The Battle of Gettysburg*

Cosner. *War Nurses*

Cox. *Undying Glory*

Cray. *American Datelines*

Currie. *Music in the Civil War*

Czech. *Snapshot: America Discovers the Camera*

Dale. *Early Railways*

Damon. *When the Cruel War Is Over: The Civil War Home Front*

Davis. *Don't Know Much About History*

Dudley. *The Civil War: Opposing Viewpoints*

Fleming. *Band of Brothers: West Point in the Civil War*

Fradin. *Medicine: Yesterday, Today, and Tomorrow*

Frankel. *Break Those Chains at Last: African Americans 1860-1880*

Frost-Knappman. *Women's Suffrage in America*

Gay. *Civil War*

Hakim. *War Terrible War*

Hansen. *Between Two Fires: Black Soldiers in the Civil War*

Hirsch. *Taxation: Paying for Government*

Jones. *The President Has Been Shot*

Kantor. *Gettysburg*

Katcher. *The Civil War Source Book*

Katz. *Breaking the Chains: African-American Slave Resistance*

Katz. *The Civil War to the Last Frontier: 1850-1880s*

Kirchberger. *The Civil War and Reconstruction*

Knappman. *Great American Trials*

Leiner. *First Children: Growing Up in the White House*

McKissack. *A Long Hard Journey: The Story of the Pullman Porter*

McPherson. *Images of the Civil War*

McPherson. *Marching Toward Freedom: Blacks 1861-1865*

Medearis. *Come This Far to Freedom*

Meltzer. *The Black Americans*

Meltzer. *Voices from the Civil War*

Meltzer. *Weapons & Warfare*

Mettger. *Till Victory Is Won: Black Soldiers in the Civil War*

Murphy. *The Boys' War*

Murphy. *The Long Road to Gettysburg*

Patrick. *The Young Oxford Companion to the Supreme Court*

Philip. *Singing America: Poems That Define a Nation*

Piggins. *A Multicultural Portrait of the Civil War*

Platt. *The Smithsonian Visual Timeline of Inventions*

Rappaport. *American Women: Their Lives in Their Words*

Ray. *Behind the Blue and the Gray: The Soldier's Life in the Civil War*

Reef. *Civil War Soldiers*

Schreiner. *Mayday! Mayday!*

Sigerman. *Laborers for Liberty: American Women 1865-1890*

Smith. *Behind the Lines*

Smith. *1863: The Crucial Year*

Smith. *Fascinating People and Astounding Events from American History*

Smith. *The First Battles*

Smith. *One Nation Again*

Smith. *Prelude to War*

Smith. *The Road to Appomattox*

St. George. *The White House: Cornerstone of a Nation*

Stanley. *Women in the Military*

Steele. *Freedom's River*

Wakin. *Photos That Made U.S. History: Civil War to the Atomic Age*

Walter. *Mississippi Challenge*

Wheeler. *Events That Changed American History*

Williams. *Forts and Castles*

Wormser. *The Iron Horse: How the Railroads Changed America*

Young. *The Emancipation Proclamation*

Multimedia

CD-ROM

American History Explorer
Campaigns, Candidates and
the Presidency
Events That Changed the
World

Famous American Speeches:
1850 to the Present
Ideas That Changed the World
Landmark Documents in
American History

Portraits of American
Presidents
Total History
The Way Things Work

Video

African Americans
America at War: The
Undersea Stranglers
Causes of the Civil War
The Civil War
The Civil War, Episode 1:
The Cause—1861
The Civil War, Episode 2: A
Very Bloody Affair—1862
The Civil War, Episode 3:
Forever Free—1862
The Civil War, Episode 4:
Simply Murder—1863
The Civil War, Episode 5:
The Universe of
Battle—1863
The Civil War, Episode 6:
Valley of the Shadow of
Death—1864

The Civil War, Episode 7:
Most Hallowed
Ground—1864
The Civil War, Episode 8:
War Is All Hell—1865
The Civil War, Episode 9:
The Better Angels of Our
Nature—1865
Civil War Trains
Clara Barton
Daring to Dream
Farming in America: A
History
Frederick Douglass
Frederick Douglass: When
the Lion Wrote History
Gettysburg
The Great Campaigns of the
Civil War

Harriet Tubman
The Life and Times of
Abraham Lincoln
Lincoln: A Photobiography
The Lottery: Who Fights Our
Wars?
Lucretia Mott
Mt. Clare: Cradle of the
American Dream
Presenting Mr. Frederick
Douglass
Smithsonian's Great Battles
of the Civil War
Susan B. Anthony
Susan B. Anthony Story

GRADE TEN

Historical Fiction

Fleischman. Bull Run
Forman. Becca's Story
Holland. Behind the Lines

Hunt. Across Five Aprils
Keith. Rifles for Watie
Myers. The Glory Field

Rinaldi. The Last Silk Dress
Shore. The Sacred Moon
Tree, 1861-1865

Biography

Bentley. Harriet Tubman
Brown. Robert E. Lee
Bruns. Abraham Lincoln
Burke. Louisa May Alcott
Coil. Harriet Beecher Stowe
Cullen-DuPont. Elizabeth
Cady Stanton and
Women's Liberty
Freedman. Lincoln: A
Photobiography
Gay. Emma Goldman
Hamilton. Clara Barton
Jakoubek. Harriet Beecher
Stowe
King. Jefferson Davis

Krass. Sojourner Truth:
Antislavery Activist
Kunhardt. Lincoln: An
Illustrated Biography
Loewen. Walt Whitman
Marrin. Unconditional
Surrender
Marrin. Virginia's General:
Robert E. Lee
Meigs. Invincible Louisa
Meltzer. Frederick Douglass:
In His Own Words
Meltzer. Lincoln in His Own
Words
Morris. The Lincoln Way

O'Brien. Ulysses S. Grant
Reef. Walt Whitman
Robinet. If You Please,
President Lincoln
Russell. Frederick Douglass:
Abolitionist Editor
St. George. Dear Dr. Bell. . .
Your Friend, Helen Keller
Sullivan. Matthew Brady: His
Life and Photographs
Tilton. Clara Barton
Weidhorn. Robert E. Lee
Whitelaw. William Tecumseh
Sherman

Collective Biography

Anthony. First Ladies:
1789-1961
Lindop. Presidents by
Accident

Lyons. Keeping Secrets: The
Girlhood Diaries of Seven
Women Writers

Mahoney. Women in
Espionage: A Biographical
Dictionary
Myers. Now Is Your Time

O'Brien. *American Political Leaders: From Colonial Times to the Present*

Sullivan. *Black Artists in Photography, 1840-1940*

Sullivan. *Presidents at Play*

Wilkinson. *Generals Who Changed the World*

History

Anderson. *Battles That Changed the Modern World*

Beller. *Cadets at War: The Battle of New Market*

Beller. *To Hold This Ground: Gettysburg*

Cohen. *America: Then and Now*

Cox. *Undying Glory*

Cray. *American Datelines*

Currie. *Music in the Civil War*

Dale. *Early Railways*

Davis. *Don't Know Much About History*

Denney. *Civil War Prisons & Escapes: A Day-by-Day Chronicle*

Dudley. *The Civil War: Opposing Viewpoints*

Evans. *Born for Liberty: A History of Women in America*

Fleming. *Band of Brothers: West Point in the Civil War*

Fradin. *Medicine: Yesterday, Today, and Tomorrow*

Frankel. *Break Those Chains at Last: African Americans 1860-1880*

Frost-Knappman. *Women's Suffrage in America*

Hakim. *War Terrible War*

Hansen. *Between Two Fires: Black Soldiers in the Civil War*

Kantor. *Gettysburg*

Katcher. *The Civil War Source Book*

Katz. *Breaking the Chains: African-American Slave Resistance*

Katz. *The Civil War to the Last Frontier: 1850-1880s*

Kirchberger. *The Civil War and Reconstruction*

Knappman. *Great American Trials*

McKissack. *A Long Hard Journey: The Story of the Pullman Porter*

McPherson. *Images of the Civil War*

McPherson. *Marching Toward Freedom: Blacks 1861-1865*

Meltzer. *The Black Americans*

Meltzer. *Voices from the Civil War*

Meltzer. *Weapons & Warfare*

Murphy. *The Boys' War*

Murphy. *The Long Road to Gettysburg*

Patrick. *The Young Oxford Companion to the Supreme Court*

Philip. *Singing America: Poems That Define a Nation*

Piggins. *A Multicultural Portrait of the Civil War*

Rappaport. *American Women: Their Lives in Their Words*

Ray. *Behind the Blue and the Gray: The Soldier's Life in the Civil War*

Reef. *Civil War Soldiers*

Schreiner. *Mayday! Mayday!*

Sigerman. *Laborers for Liberty: American Women 1865-1890*

Smith. *Behind the Lines*

Smith. *1863: The Crucial Year*

Smith. *Fascinating People and Astounding Events from American History*

Smith. *The First Battles*

Smith. *One Nation Again*

Smith. *Prelude to War*

Smith. *The Road to Appomattox*

Stanley. *Women in the Military*

Steele. *Freedom's River*

Wakin. *Photos That Made U.S. History: Civil War to the Atomic Age*

Walter. *Mississippi Challenge*

Wheeler. *Events That Changed American History*

Wormser. *The Iron Horse: How the Railroads Changed America*

Young. *The Emancipation Proclamation*

Multimedia

CD-ROM

Campaigns, Candidates and the Presidency

Events That Changed the World

Famous American Speeches: 1850 to the Present

Ideas That Changed the World

Landmark Documents in American History

Portraits of American Presidents

Total History

The Way Things Work

Video

African Americans

America at War: The Undersea Stranglers

The Civil War

The Civil War, Episode 1: The Cause—1861

The Civil War, Episode 2: A Very Bloody Affair—1862

The Civil War, Episode 3: Forever Free—1862

The Civil War, Episode 4: Simply Murder—1863

The Civil War, Episode 5: The Universe of Battle—1863

The Civil War, Episode 6: Valley of the Shadow of Death—1864

The Civil War, Episode 7: Most Hallowed Ground—1864

The Civil War, Episode 8: War Is All Hell—1865

The Civil War, Episode 9: The Better Angels of Our Nature—1865

Civil War Trains

Clara Barton

Daring to Dream
Farming in America: A
  History
Frederick Douglass
Frederick Douglass: When
  the Lion Wrote History
Gettysburg

The Great Campaigns of the
  Civil War
Harriet Tubman
The Life and Times of
  Abraham Lincoln
The Lottery: Who Fights Our
  Wars?

Lucretia Mott
Mt. Clare: Cradle of the
  American Dream
Smithsonian's Great Battles
  of the Civil War
Susan B. Anthony

GRADES ELEVEN AND TWELVE

Historical Fiction

Coyle. *Look Away*
Jones. *The Barefoot Brigade*
Jones. *The Fifth Conspiracy*

Jones. *Hard Road to
  Gettysburg*
Meriwether. *Fragments of the
  Ark*

Mitchell. *Gone with the Wind*
Schultz. *Glory Enough for
  All: The Battle of the Crater*
Shaara. *The Killer Angels*

Biography

Bentley. *Harriet Tubman*
Coil. *Harriet Beecher Stowe*
Collins. *Shattered Dreams:
  The Story of Mary Todd
  Lincoln*
Cullen-DuPont. *Elizabeth
  Cady Stanton and
  Women's Liberty*
Faber. *Printer's Devil to
  Publisher: Adolph S. Ochs
  of the New York Times*
Fischer. *Paul Revere's Ride*

Freedman. *Lincoln: A
  Photobiography*
Gay. *Emma Goldman*
King. *Jefferson Davis*
Kunhardt. *Lincoln: An
  Illustrated Biography*
Loewen. *Walt Whitman*
Marrin. *Unconditional
  Surrender*
Meigs. *Invincible Louisa*
Meltzer. *Frederick Douglass:
  In His Own Words*

Meltzer. *Lincoln in His Own
  Words*
Morris. *The Lincoln Way*
Robinet. *If You Please,
  President Lincoln*
Sherr. *Failure Is Impossible:
  Susan B. Anthony*
Weidhorn. *Robert E. Lee*
Wert. *Custer: The
  Controversial Life of
  George Armstrong Custer*

Collective Biography

Anthony. *First Ladies:
  1789-1961*
Foster. *Written by Herself:
  African American Women,
  1746-1892*
Lindop. *Presidents by
  Accident*

Lyons. *Keeping Secrets: The
  Girlhood Diaries of Seven
  Women Writers*
Mahoney. *Women in
  Espionage: A Biographical
  Dictionary*

O'Brien. *American Political
  Leaders: From Colonial
  Times to the Present*
Sears. *Lincoln's Generals*
Truman. *First Ladies*

History

Beller. *Cadets at War: The
  Battle of New Market*
Beller. *To Hold This Ground:
  Gettysburg*
Boller. *Presidential Wives:
  An Anecdotal History*
Cohen. *America: Then and
  Now*
Cox. *Undying Glory*
Cray. *American Datelines*
Currie. *Music in the Civil War*
Dale. *Early Railways*
Damon. *When the Cruel War
  Is Over: The Civil War
  Home Front*
Davidson. *Everyday Life
  Through the Ages*

Davis. *Don't Know Much
  About History*
Denney. *Civil War Prisons &
  Escapes: A Day-by-Day
  Chronicle*
Dudley. *The Civil War:
  Opposing Viewpoints*
Evans. *Born for Liberty: A
  History of Women in
  America*
Fleming. *Band of Brothers:
  West Point in the Civil War*
Fogle. *Two Hundred Years:
  Stories of the Nation's
  Capital*
Fradin. *Medicine: Yesterday,
  Today, and Tomorrow*

Frankel. *Break Those Chains
  at Last: African Americans
  1860-1880*
Frost-Knappman. *Women's
  Suffrage in America*
Guernsey. *Harper's Pictorial
  History of the Civil War*
Hakim. *War Terrible War*
Hansen. *Between Two Fires:
  Black Soldiers in the Civil
  War*
Hauptman. *Between Two
  Fires: American Indians in
  the Civil War*
Katcher. *The Civil War
  Source Book*
Keegan. *History of Warfare*

Kennett. *Marching Through Georgia: Sherman's Campaign*

Kirchberger. *The Civil War and Reconstruction*

Knappman. *Great American Trials*

Leckie. *None Died in Vain: The Saga of the American Civil War*

Marius. *The Columbia Book of Civil War Poetry*

McPherson. *Abraham Lincoln and the Second American Revolution*

McPherson. *Battle Cry of Freedom: The Civil War Era*

McPherson. *Images of the Civil War*

McPherson. *Marching Toward Freedom: Blacks 1861-1865*

McPherson. *What They Fought For, 1861-1865*

McPherson. *Why the Confederacy Lost*

Meltzer. *Voices from the Civil War*

Meltzer. *Weapons & Warfare*

Patrick. *The Young Oxford Companion to the Supreme Court*

Philip. *Singing America: Poems That Define a Nation*

Rappaport. *American Women: Their Lives in Their Words*

Reck. *A. Lincoln: His Last 24 Hours*

Ripple. *Dancing Along the Deadline: The Andersonville Memoir*

Schreiner. *Mayday! Mayday!*

Schultz. *Month of the Freezing Moon: The Sand Creek Massacre, November 1864*

Sigerman. *Laborers for Liberty: American Women 1865-1890*

Smith. *Fascinating People and Astounding Events from American History*

Stanley. *Women in the Military*

Steele. *Freedom's River*

Tinling. *With Women's Eyes: Visitors to the New World, 1775-1918*

Walter. *Mississippi Challenge*

Ward. *The Civil War: An Illustrated History*

Wheeler. *Events That Changed American History*

Wheeler. *Lee's Terrible Swift Sword: From Antietam to Chancellorsville*

Wheeler. *On Fields of Fury: From the Wilderness to the Crater*

Wheeler. *Sword over Richmond: McClellan's Peninsula Campaign*

Wheeler. *Witness to Appomattox*

Wheeler. *Witness to Gettysburg*

Multimedia

CD-ROM

Campaigns, Candidates and the Presidency

Events That Changed the World

Famous American Speeches: 1850 to the Present

Ideas That Changed the World

Landmark Documents in American History

Portraits of American Presidents

Total History

The Way Things Work

Video

America at War: The Undersea Stranglers

The Civil War

The Civil War, Episode 1: The Cause—1861

The Civil War, Episode 2: A Very Bloody Affair—1862

The Civil War, Episode 3: Forever Free—1862

The Civil War, Episode 4: Simply Murder—1863

The Civil War, Episode 5: The Universe of Battle—1863

The Civil War, Episode 6: Valley of the Shadow of Death—1864

The Civil War, Episode 7: Most Hallowed Ground—1864

The Civil War, Episode 8: War Is All Hell—1865

The Civil War, Episode 9: The Better Angels of Our Nature—1865

Civil War Trains

Clara Barton

Daring to Dream

Frederick Douglass

Frederick Douglass: When the Lion Wrote History

The Great Campaigns of the Civil War

Harriet Tubman

The Life and Times of Abraham Lincoln

The Lottery: Who Fights Our Wars?

Lucretia Mott

Mt. Clare: Cradle of the American Dream

Smithsonian's Great Battles of the Civil War

Susan B. Anthony

RECONSTRUCTION, THE PROGRESSIVE ERA, AND THE EARLY TWENTIETH CENTURY, 1866-1916

GRADE SEVEN

Historical Fiction

Alexander. *The Philadelphia Adventure*
Avi. *Punch with Judy*
Beatty. *Be Ever Hopeful, Hannalee*
Beatty. *Eight Mules from Monterey*
Bethancourt. *The Tommorow Connection*
Calvert. *Bigger*
Clark. *Nellie Bishop*
Collier. *My Crooked Family*
Conrad. *My Daniel*
Cross. *The Great American Elephant Chase*
DeFelice. *Lostman's River*
Dexter. *Mazemaker*
Edmonds. *Bert Breen's Barn*
Emerson. *Julia's Mending*
Garland. *The Last Rainmaker*
Griffin. *Switching Well*
Hamm. *Bunkhouse Journal*
Hill. *The Banjo Player*
Holmes. *For Bread 1893*
Hooks. *A Flight of Dazzle Angels*
Hoppe. *Dream Spinner*

Howard. *Edith Herself*
Hurmence. *Dixie in the Big Pasture*
Irwin. *I Be Somebody*
Karr. *Gideon and the Mummy Professor*
Karr. *It Ain't Always Easy*
Kirkpatrick. *Keeping the Good Light*
Lenski. *Strawberry Girl*
Leonard. *Saving Damaris*
Lowell. *I Am Lavina Cumming*
McCall. *Better Than a Brother*
Meyer. *Gideon's People*
Nelson. *Devil Storm*
Neufeld. *Gaps in Stone Walls*
Nixon. *Circle of Love*
Oke. *The Bluebird and the Sparrow*
Paulsen. *The Winter Room*
Peck. *Voices After Midnight*
Pendergraft. *Hear the Wind Blow*
Perez. *Breaker*
Pfeffer. *Justice for Emily*
Pfeffer. *Nobody's Daughter*

Phillips. *A Haunted Year*
Rappaport. *Trouble at the Mines*
Riskind. *Apple Is My Sign*
Roberts. *Jo and the Bandit*
Robinet. *Mississippi Chariot*
Rodowsky. *Fitchett's Folly*
Ross. *The Bet's On, Lizzie Bingman!*
Rossiter. *Moxie*
Rostkowski. *After the Dancing Days*
Sauerwein. *The Way Home*
Savage. *To Race a Dream*
Sebestyen. *Words by Heart*
Snyder. and *Condors Danced*
Stolz. *Cezanne Pinto: A Memoir*
Terris. *Nell's Quilt*
Todd. *Squaring Off*
Townsend. *The Ghost Flyers*
Van Raven. *Harpoon Island*
Winter. *The Christmas Tree Ship*
Wisler. *Mustang Flats*
Wyman. *Red Sky at Morning*
Yarbro. *Floating Illusions*

Biography

Adair. *Thomas Alva Edison: Inventing the Electric Age*
Adler. *Our Golda: The Story of Golda Meir*
Andronik. *Prince of Humbugs: A Life of P. T. Barnum*
Archbold. *Deep-Sea Explorer: Robert Ballard*
Ayer. *Lewis Latimer: Creating Bright Ideas*

Beneduce. *A Weekend with Winslow Homer*
Berman. *James McNeill Whistler*
Bernotas. *Jim Thorpe: Sac and Fox Athlete*
Berry. *Emily Dickinson*
Bowman. *Andrew Carnegie: Steel Tycoon*
Brown. *Belva Lockwood Wins Her Case*

Brown. *Chester Arthur: Twenty-First President*
Brown. *Elizabeth Blackwell: Physician*
Brown. *James Garfield: 20th President of the United States*
Brown. *Robert E. Lee*
Bundles. *Madam C. J. Walker*
Buranelli. *Thomas Alva Edison*

Burchard. *Charlotte Forten: A Black Teacher in the Civil War*

Burke. *Louisa May Alcott*

Cain. *Mary Cassatt*

Canadeo. *Warren G. Harding*

Carlson. *Harriet Tubman: Call to Freedom*

Casey. *Millard Fillmore: Thirteenth President*

Casey. *William H. Taft: Twenty-Seventh President*

Charleston. *Peary Reaches the North Pole*

Clinton. *Benjamin Harrison: Twenty-Third President*

Collins. *William McKinley: 25th President of the United States*

Connell. *They Shall Be Heard: Susan B. Anthony and Elizabeth Cady Stanton*

Cooper. *From Slave to Civil War Hero: Robert Small*

Cullen-DuPont. *Elizabeth Cady Stanton and Women's Liberty*

Davis. *Frank Lloyd Wright: Maverick Architect*

Dominy. *Katherine Dunham: Dancer and Choreographer*

Driemen. *Clarence Darrow*

Dubowski. *Andrew Johnson: Rebuilding the Union*

Dubowski. *Clara Barton: Healing the Wounds*

Dubowski. *Robert E. Lee*

Dwyer. *Robert Peary and the Quest for the North Pole*

Ehrlich. *Nelly Bly: Journalist*

Falkof. *William H. Taft*

Fleming. *P. T. Barnum*

Freedman. *The Wright Brothers: How They Invented the Airplane*

Fritz. *Bully for You, Teddy Roosevelt*

Fritz. *Harriet Beecher Stowe and the Beecher Preachers*

Gehre. *Susan B. Anthony*

Gentry. *Paul Laurence Dunbar: Poet*

Gilman. *Matthew Henson: Explorer*

Gormley. *Maria Mitchell: The Soul of an Astronomer*

Greene. *Thomas Alva Edison: Bringer of Light*

Hamilton. *Clara Barton*

Hawxhurst. *Mother Jones: Labor Crusader*

Haynes. *Ida B. Wells*

Horton. *Mother Jones*

Hovde. *Jane Addams*

Jakoubek. *Harriet Beecher Stowe*

Johnston. *Harriet: The Life and World of Harriet Beecher Stowe*

Kaye. *The Life of Daniel Hale Williams*

Keller. *The Story of My Life*

Kendall. *Susan B. Anthony*

Kent. *Andrew Johnson: Seventeenth President*

Kent. *Calvin Coolidge: Thirtieth President*

Kent. *Dorothy Day: Friend to the Forgotten*

Kent. *Grover Cleveland: Twenty-Second and Twenty-Fourth President*

Kent. *Rutherford B. Hayes: Nineteenth President*

Kent. *Theodore Roosevelt: Twenty-Sixth President*

Kent. *Ulysses S. Grant: Eighteenth President*

Kent. *William McKinley: Twenty-Fifth President*

Kerby. *Robert E. Lee*

Kittredge. *Jane Addams*

Klots. *Ida Wells-Barnett: Civil Rights Leader*

Kozodoy. *Isadora Duncan: Dancer*

Kraft. *Mother Jones: One Woman's Fight for Labor*

Krass. *Sojourner Truth: Antislavery Activist*

Leavell. *Woodrow Wilson*

Lefer. *Emma Lazarus*

Levinson. *I Lift My Lamp: Emma Lazarus and the Statue of Liberty*

Lillegard. *James Garfield: Twentieth President*

Lindop. *James K. Polk, Abraham Lincoln, Theodore Roosevelt*

Lipsyte. *Jim Thorpe: Twentieth-Century Jock*

Lipsyte. *Joe Louis: A Champ for All America*

Malone. *Will Rogers: Cowboy Philosopher*

Markham. *Helen Keller*

Markham. *Theodore Roosevelt*

Marrin. *Unconditional Surrender*

Marrin. *Virginia's General: Robert E. Lee*

Marston. *Isaac Johnson: From Slave to Stonecutter*

McClard. *Harriet Tubman: Slavery and the Underground Railroad*

McKissack. *Frederick Douglass: The Black Lion*

McKissack. *Sojourner Truth: Ain't I a Woman?*

McPherson. *Peace and Bread: Jane Addams*

Meltzer. *Frederick Douglass: In His Own Words*

Meyer. *Mary Cassatt*

Mintz. *Thomas Edison: Inventing the Future*

Muhlberger. *What Makes a Cassatt a Cassatt?*

Nardo. *Jim Thorpe*

Nicholson. *Georgia O'Keeffe*

Nicholson. *Helen Keller: Humanitarian*

Norman. *Lewis Latimer: Scientist*

O'Brien. *Ulysses S. Grant*

Olsen. *Emily Dickinson: Poet*

Parker. *Thomas Edison and Electricity*

Parker. *The Wright Brothers and Aviation*

Pasachoff. *Alexander Graham Bell*

Pfeifer. *Henry O. Flipper*

Plain. *Mary Cassatt: An Artist's Life*

Ravage. *George Westinghouse*

Reef. *Walt Whitman*

Rickarby. *Ulysses S. Grant*

Russell. *Frederick Douglass: Abolitionist Editor*

Ryan. *Louisa May Alcott: Her Girlhood Diary*

Sandak. *The Tafts*

Sandak. *The Theodore Roosevelts*

Sandak. *The Wilsons*

Sandomir. *Isadora Duncan: Revolutionary Dancer*

Schleichert. *The Life of Dorothea Dix*

Schleichert. *The Life of Elizabeth Blackwell*

Schroeder. *Booker T. Washington*

Schroeder. *Jack London*

Simon. *Franklin Pierce*

Sonneborn. *Will Rogers: Cherokee Entertainer*

St. George. *Dear Dr. Bell. . . Your Friend, Helen Keller*

Stafford. *W. E. B. Dubois: Scholar and Activist*
Stefoff. *Herman Melville*
Stefoff. *Theodore Roosevelt: 26th President*
Stevens. *Andrew Johnson: 17th President*
Stevens. *Benjamin Harrison: 23rd President*

Sufrin. *Stephen Crane*
Thompson. *Charles Chesnutt*
Tilton. *Clara Barton*
Tolbert-Rouchaleau. *James Weldon Johnson: Author*
Turner. *Lewis Howard Latimer*
Van Steenwyk. *Ida B. Wells-Barnett*

Waldstreicher. *Emma Goldman*
Weidhorn. *Robert E. Lee*
Weisberg. *Susan B. Anthony*
Whitelaw. *Theodore Roosevelt Takes Charge*
Whitelaw. *William Tecumseh Sherman*
Woog. *Harry Houdini*

Collective Biography

Aaseng. *America's Third-Party Presidential Candidates*
Aaseng. *Close Calls*
Aaseng. *From Rags to Riches*
Altman. *Extraordinary Black Americans*
Beard. *The Presidents in American History*
Blassingame. *The Look-It-Up Book of Presidents*
Blue. *People of Peace*
Camp. *American Astronomers: Searchers and Wonderers*
Cush. *Artists Who Created Great Works*
Cush. *Women Who Achieved Greatness*
Dolan. *Shaping U.S. Foreign Policy: Twelve Secretaries of State*
Faber. *Great Lives: American Government*
Fireside. *Is There a Woman in the House. . . or Senate?*
Fradin. *We Have Conquered Pain: The Discovery of Anesthesia*
Glubok. *Great Lives: Painting*
Jacobs. *Great Lives: Human Rights*

Katz. *Proudly Red and Black: Stories of African and Native Americans*
Krull. *Lives of the Artists: Masterpieces, Messes*
Krull. *Lives of the Musicians: Good Times, Bad Times*
Krull. *Lives of the Writers: Comedies, Tragedies*
Lindop. *Presidents by Accident*
Lyons. *Keeping Secrets: The Girlhood Diaries of Seven Women Writers*
Mayberry. *Business Leaders Who Built Financial Empires*
Mayberry. *Leaders Who Changed the 20th Century*
Mayo. *Smithsonian Book of the First Ladies*
Morin. *Women Chosen for Public Office*
Morin. *Women Who Reformed Politics*
Myers. *Now Is Your Time*
Pascoe. *First Facts About the Presidents*
Plowden. *Famous Firsts of Black Women*
Provenson. *My Fellow Americans*

Rennert. *Book of Firsts: Leaders of America*
Rennert. *Pioneers of Discovery*
Rubel. *The Scholastic Encyclopedia of the Presidents*
Schraff. *American Heroes of Exploration and Flight*
Schraff. *Women of Peace: Nobel Peace Prize Winners*
Sills. *Visions: Stories About Women Artists*
Smith. *Presidents of a Growing Country*
Streissguth. *Hatemongers and Demagogues*
Streissguth. *Hoaxers & Hustlers*
Sullivan. *Black Artists in Photography, 1840-1940*
Sullivan. *Presidents at Play*
Vare. *Women Inventors and Their Discoveries*
Veglahn. *Women Scientists*
Whitelaw. *They Wrote Their Own Headlines*
Yount. *Black Scientists*

History

Altman. *The Pullman Strike of 1894*
Anderson. *Battles That Changed the Modern World*
Archer. *Breaking Barriers: The Feminist Movement*
Ballard. *Exploring the Titanic*
Bartoletti. *Growing Up in Coal Country*
Berliner. *Aviation: Reaching for the Sky*
Branch. *The Water Brought Us: The Story of the Gullah-Speaking People*
Brashler. *The Story of the Negro League Baseball*

Brown. *The Struggle to Grow (1880-1913)*
Carlin. *Jazz*
Carnes. *Us and Them: A History of Intolerance in America*
Colman. *Strike: The Bitter Struggle of American Workers*
Colman. *Toilets, Bathtubs, Sinks, and Sewers*
Colman. *Women in Society: United States*
Cooper. *Bound for the Promised Land: The Great Black Migration*

Cosner. *War Nurses*
Cray. *American Datelines*
Cush. *Disasters That Shook the World*
Czech. *Snapshot: America Discovers the Camera*
Dash. *We Shall Not Be Moved: The Women's Factory Strike of 1909*
Davies. *Transport: On Land, Road and Rail*
Dolan. *Panama and the United States: Their Canal, Their Stormy Years*
Emert. *Top Lawyers and Their Famous Cases*

Feinberg. *American Political Scandals Past and Present*

Ferrell. *The U.S. Air Force*

Fradin. *Medicine: Yesterday, Today, and Tomorrow*

Freedman. *Kids at Work: Lewis Hine Against Child Labor*

Fry. *The Orphan Train*

Garfunkel. *On Wings of Joy: The Story of Ballet*

Gay. *Spanish American War*

Giblin. *Be Seated: A Book About Chairs*

Gilbert. *Deadball: Major League Baseball Before Babe Ruth*

Greene. *Child Labor: Then and Now*

Greene. *Our Century: 1900-1910*

Gutman. *World Series Classics*

Hakim. *An Age of Extremes*

Hakim. *Reconstruction and Reform*

Herald. *The 1920s*

Hirsch. *Taxation: Paying for Government*

Hoig. *It's the Fourth of July*

Jones. *The President Has Been Shot*

Karl. *America Alive: A History*

Katz. *The Civil War to the Last Frontier: 1850-1880s*

Katz. *The Great Migrations: 1880s-1912*

Landau. *Armed America: The Status of Gun Control*

Landau. *The White Power Movement: America's Racist Hate Groups*

Langone. *Spreading Poison: A Book About Racism and Prejudice*

Lawrence. *The Great Migration*

Leiner. *First Children: Growing Up in the White House*

Leuzzi. *Urban Life*

Levinson. *Turn of the Century*

Libreatore. *Our Century: 1910-1920*

Lucas. *Civil Rights: The Long Struggle*

Macy. *Winning Ways: A Photohistory of American Women in Sports*

Markham. *Inventions That Changed Modern Life*

Mason. *Peary and Amundsen: Race to the Poles*

Maurer. *Airborne: The Search for the Secret of Flight*

McKissack. *A Long Hard Journey: The Story of the Pullman Porter*

Medearis. *Come This Far to Freedom*

Meltzer. *The Black Americans*

Meltzer. *Cheap Raw Material*

Mettger. *Reconstruction: America After the Civil War*

Mizell. *Think About Racism*

Monceaux. *Jazz: My Music, My People*

Morley. *Clothes: For Work, Play and Display*

Mulcahy. *Diseases: Finding the Cure*

Murphy. *Across America on an Emigrant Train*

Murphy. *The Great Fire*

Patrick. *The Young Oxford Companion to the Supreme Court*

Philip. *Singing America: Poems That Define a Nation*

Platt. *The Smithsonian Visual Timeline of Inventions*

Pleasant. *Samantha's Cookbook*

Pollard. *The Nineteenth Century*

Pollard. *The Red Cross and the Red Crescent*

Press. *A Multicultural Portrait of Professional Sports*

Rappaport. *American Women: Their Lives in Their Words*

Rappaport. *The Lizzie Borden Trial*

Sagan. *Women's Suffrage*

Sandler. *Presidents*

Scott. *Funny Papers: Behind the Scenes of the Comics*

Sherrow. *The Triangle Factory Fire*

Sigerman. *Laborers for Liberty: American Women 1865-1890*

Smith. *New Paths to Power: American Women 1890-1920*

St. George. *Panama Canal: Gateway to the World*

St. George. *The White House: Cornerstone of a Nation*

Stacey. *The Titanic*

Sullivan. *Children of Promise: African-American Literature and Art*

Time-Life. *African Americans: Voices of Triumph: Leadership*

Time-Life. *This Fabulous Century: 1870-1900, Prelude*

Time-Life. *This Fabulous Century: 1900-1910*

Time-Life. *This Fabulous Century: 1910-1920*

Ventura. *Clothing*

Ventura. *Food: Its Evolution Through the Ages*

Wakin. *Photos That Made U.S. History: Civil War to the Atomic Age*

Walker. *Hand, Heart, and Mind*

Walter. *Mississippi Challenge*

Warburton. *The Chicago Fire*

Warner. *The U.S. Marine Corps*

Wheeler. *Events That Changed American History*

Whitman. *Get Up and Go: American Road Travel*

Whitman. *This Land Is Your Land*

Wormser. *Hoboes: Wandering in America 1870-1940*

Yepsen. *City Trains: America's Cities by Rail*

Multimedia

CD-ROM

Air and Space Smithsonian Dreams of Flight

American History Explorer

Campaigns, Candidates and the Presidency

Daring to Fly!
Exploring the Titanic
Eyewitness Encyclopedia of
  Science
Her Heritage: A Biographical
  Encyclopedia of American
  History

History Through Art: 20th
  Century
Landmark Documents in
  American History
Portraits of American
  Presidents
Science Navigator

SkyTrip America
Time Almanac of the 20th
  Century
Total History
The Way Things Work

Video

African Americans
Alexander Graham Bell
Alice Paul: We Were Arrested
  of Course!
All Aboard for Philadelphia!
American Consumerism
  (1890-1930)
The Atlantic Coast of
  Winslow Homer
Barnum's Big Top
Black Is My Color: The
  African American
  Experience
Booker T. Washington
Clara Barton
Daring to Dream
Elizabeth Cady Stanton and
  Susan B. Anthony
Emily Dickinson
Emily Dickinson: A Certain
  Slant of Light
Equality: A History of the
  Women's Movement in
  America
The Era of Segregation: A
  Personal
Farming in America: A
  History
Frederick Douglass

Frederick Douglass: When
  the Lion Wrote History
Gandy Dancers
Great Black Innovators
Great Black Women
Harriet Tubman
Helen Keller
Houdini:The Great Escape
Industrialization and
  Urbanization (1870-1910)
Jane Addams
Lucretia Mott
Madam C. J. Walker
Making It Happen: Masters
  of Invention
Mansions of Newport
Mary McLeod Bethune
Michigan Avenue: From
  Museums to the
  Magnificent Mile
A Nation in Turmoil
The Poet and the Rough Rider
Presenting Mr. Frederick
  Douglass
Pride & Prejudice: A History
  of Black Culture in America
Progressive Movement
Public Sculpture: America's
  Legacy

Reading Terminal Market
Reconstruction and
  Segregation (1870-1910)
Samuel Morse: The Telegraph
Sojourner Truth
Susan B. Anthony
Susan B. Anthony Story
This House of Power: The
  Church in
  African-American
  Experience
Thomas Alva Edison
Thomas Edison: Electric Light
Tragedy to Triumph: An
  Adventure with Helen
  Keller
Traveling in Style:
  Automobiles and Trolleys
Traveling in Style: Trains,
  Riverboats, and Planes
U.S. and the World
  (1865-1917)
Votes for Women?! The 1913
  U.S. Senate Testimony
Women in Rural America
The Wright Brothers: How
  They Invented the Airplane

GRADE EIGHT

Historical Fiction

Alexander. *The Philadelphia*
  Adventure
Beatty. *Be Ever Hopeful,*
  Hannalee
Bethancourt. *The Tommorow*
  Connection
Calvert. *Bigger*
Clark. *Nellie Bishop*
Collier. *My Crooked Family*
Conrad. *My Daniel*
Cross. *The Great American*
  Elephant Chase
DeFelice. *Lostman's River*
Edmonds. *Bert Breen's Barn*
Garland. *The Last Rainmaker*
Griffin. *Switching Well*

Hamm. *Bunkhouse Journal*
Hill. *The Banjo Player*
Holmes. *For Bread 1893*
Hooks. *A Flight of Dazzle*
  Angels
Hoppe. *Dream Spinner*
Hurmence. *Tancy*
Irwin. *I Be Somebody*
Karr. *Gideon and the Mummy*
  Professor
Karr. *It Ain't Always Easy*
Kirkpatrick. *Keeping the*
  Good Light
Lenski. *Strawberry Girl*
Meyer. *Gideon's People*
Nelson. *Devil Storm*

Neufeld. *Gaps in Stone Walls*
Nixon. *Circle of Love*
Oke. *The Bluebird and the*
  Sparrow
Paulsen. *The Winter Room*
Peck. *Voices After Midnight*
Pendergraft. *Hear the Wind*
  Blow
Perez. *Breaker*
Phillips. *A Haunted Year*
Riskind. *Apple Is My Sign*
Rodowsky. *Fitchett's Folly*
Ross. *The Bet's On, Lizzie*
  Bingman!
Rossiter. *Moxie*

Rostkowski. *After the Dancing Days*
Sauerwein. *The Way Home*
Savage. *To Race a Dream*
Sebestyen. *Words by Heart*
Skurzynski. *The Tempering*

Stolz. *Cezanne Pinto: A Memoir*
Terris. *Nell's Quilt*
Todd. *Squaring Off*
Townsend. *The Ghost Flyers*
Van Raven. *Harpoon Island*

Winter. *The Christmas Tree Ship*
Wisler. *Mustang Flats*
Yarbro. *Floating Illusions*

Biography

Adler. *Our Golda: The Story of Golda Meir*
Andronik. *Prince of Humbugs: A Life of P. T. Barnum*
Archbold. *Deep-Sea Explorer: Robert Ballard*
Ayer. *Lewis Latimer: Creating Bright Ideas*
Beneduce. *A Weekend with Winslow Homer*
Bentley. *Harriet Tubman*
Berman. *James McNeill Whistler*
Bernotas. *Jim Thorpe: Sac and Fox Athlete*
Berry. *Emily Dickinson*
Boulton. *Frank Lloyd Wright: Architect*
Bowman. *Andrew Carnegie: Steel Tycoon*
Brown. *Chester Arthur: Twenty-First President*
Brown. *Elizabeth Blackwell: Physician*
Brown. *James Garfield: 20th President of the United States*
Brown. *Robert E. Lee*
Bundles. *Madam C. J. Walker*
Burchard. *Charlotte Forten: A Black Teacher in the Civil War*
Burke. *Louisa May Alcott*
Cain. *Mary Cassatt*
Canadeo. *Warren G. Harding*
Carlson. *Harriet Tubman: Call to Freedom*
Casey. *Millard Fillmore: Thirteenth President*
Casey. *William H. Taft: Twenty-Seventh President*
Clinton. *Benjamin Harrison: Twenty-Third President*
Collins. *William McKinley: 25th President*
Cooper. *From Slave to Civil War Hero: Robert Small*
Cullen-DuPont. *Elizabeth Cady Stanton and Women's Liberty*
Davis. *Frank Lloyd Wright: Maverick Architect*

Dominy. *Katherine Dunham: Dancer and Choreographer*
Driemen. *Clarence Darrow*
Dubowski. *Andrew Johnson: Rebuilding the Union*
Dubowski. *Clara Barton: Healing the Wounds*
Dubowski. *Robert E. Lee*
Dwyer. *Robert Peary and the Quest for the North Pole*
Ehrlich. *Nelly Bly: Journalist*
Falkof. *William H. Taft*
Fleming. *P. T. Barnum*
Freedman. *The Wright Brothers: How They Invented the Airplane*
Fritz. *Bully for You, Teddy Roosevelt*
Fritz. *Harriet Beecher Stowe and the Beecher Preachers*
Gehre. *Susan B. Anthony*
Gentry. *Paul Laurence Dunbar: Poet*
Gilman. *Matthew Henson: Explorer*
Gormley. *Maria Mitchell: The Soul of an Astronomer*
Greene. *Thomas Alva Edison: Bringer of Light*
Hamilton. *Clara Barton*
Hawxhurst. *Mother Jones: Labor Crusader*
Haynes. *Ida B. Wells*
Horton. *Mother Jones*
Hovde. *Jane Addams*
Jakoubek. *Harriet Beecher Stowe*
Johnston. *Harriet: The Life and World of Harriet Beecher Stowe*
Kaye. *The Life of Daniel Hale Williams*
Keller. *The Story of My Life*
Kendall. *Susan B. Anthony*
Kent. *Andrew Johnson: Seventeenth President*
Kent. *Calvin Coolidge: Thirtieth President*
Kent. *Dorothy Day: Friend to the Forgotten*
Kent. *Grover Cleveland: Twenty-Second and Twenty-Fourth President*

Kent. *Rutherford B. Hayes: Nineteenth President*
Kent. *Theodore Roosevelt: Twenty-Sixth President*
Kent. *Ulysses S. Grant: Eighteenth President*
Kent. *William McKinley: Twenty-Fifth President*
Kerby. *Robert E. Lee*
Klots. *Ida Wells-Barnett: Civil Rights Leader*
Kozodoy. *Isadora Duncan: Dancer*
Kraft. *Mother Jones: One Woman's Fight for Labor*
Krass. *Sojourner Truth: Antislavery Activist*
Leavell. *Woodrow Wilson*
Lefer. *Emma Lazarus*
Levinson. *I Lift My Lamp: Emma Lazarus and the Statue of Liberty*
Lillegard. *James Garfield: Twentieth President*
Lindop. *James K. Polk, Abraham Lincoln, Theodore Roosevelt*
Lipsyte. *Joe Louis: A Champ for All America*
Malone. *Will Rogers: Cowboy Philosopher*
Markham. *Helen Keller*
Markham. *Theodore Roosevelt*
Marrin. *Unconditional Surrender*
Marrin. *Virginia's General: Robert E. Lee*
McClard. *Harriet Tubman: Slavery and the Underground Railroad*
McKissack. *Sojourner Truth: Ain't I A Woman?*
Meltzer. *Frederick Douglass: In His Own Words*
Meyer. *Mary Cassatt*
Mintz. *Thomas Edison: Inventing the Future*
Muhlberger. *What Makes a Cassatt a Cassatt?*
Nardo. *Jim Thorpe*
Nicholson. *Georgia O'Keeffe*
Nicholson. *Helen Keller: Humanitarian*

Norman. *Lewis Latimer: Scientist*

O'Brien. *Ulysses S. Grant*

Olsen. *Emily Dickinson: Poet*

Parker. *Thomas Edison and Electricity*

Pasachoff. *Alexander Graham Bell*

Plain. *Mary Cassatt: An Artist's Life*

Ravage. *George Westinghouse*

Reef. *Walt Whitman*

Rickarby. *Ulysses S. Grant*

Russell. *Frederick Douglass: Abolitionist Editor*

Ryan. *Louisa May Alcott: Her Girlhood Diary*

Sandak. *The Tafts*

Sandak. *The Theodore Roosevelts*

Sandak. *The Wilsons*

Sandomir. *Isadora Duncan: Revolutionary Dancer*

Schroeder. *Booker T. Washington*

Schroeder. *Jack London*

Simon. *Franklin Pierce*

Sonneborn. *Will Rogers: Cherokee Entertainer*

St. George. *Dear Dr. Bell. . . Your Friend, Helen Keller*

Stafford. *W. E. B. Dubois: Scholar and Activist*

Stefoff. *Herman Melville*

Stefoff. *Theodore Roosevelt: 26th President*

Stevens. *Andrew Johnson: 17th President*

Stevens. *Benjamin Harrison: 23rd President*

Sufrin. *Stephen Crane*

Thompson. *Charles Chesnutt*

Tilton. *Clara Barton*

Tolbert-Rouchaleau. *James Weldon Johnson: Author*

Turner. *Lewis Howard Latimer*

Van Steenwyk. *Ida B. Wells-Barnett*

Waldstreicher. *Emma Goldman*

Weidhorn. *Robert E. Lee*

Weisberg. *Susan B. Anthony*

Whitelaw. *Theodore Roosevelt Takes Charge*

Whitelaw. *William Tecumseh Sherman*

Woog. *Harry Houdini*

Collective Biography

Aaseng. *America's Third-Party Presidential Candidates*

Aaseng. *Close Calls*

Aaseng. *Great Justices of the Supreme Court*

Aaseng. *Twentieth-Century Inventors*

Aaseng. *You Are the President*

Altman. *Extraordinary Black Americans*

Beard. *The Presidents in American History*

Blassingame. *The Look-It-Up Book of Presidents*

Blue. *People of Peace*

Camp. *American Astronomers: Searchers and Wonderers*

Cush. *Artists Who Created Great Works*

Cush. *Women Who Achieved Greatness*

Dolan. *Shaping U.S. Foreign Policy: Profiles of Twelve Secretaries of State*

Faber. *Great Lives: American Government*

Fireside. *Is There a Woman in the House. . . or Senate?*

Fradin. *We Have Conquered Pain: The Discovery of Anesthesia*

Glubok. *Great Lives: Painting*

Jones. *Big Star Fallin' Mama*

Katz. *Proudly Red and Black: Stories of African and Native Americans*

Krull. *Lives of the Artists: Masterpieces, Messes*

Krull. *Lives of the Musicians: Good Times, Bad Times*

Krull. *Lives of the Writers: Comedies, Tragedies*

Lindop. *Presidents by Accident*

Lyons. *Keeping Secrets: The Girlhood Diaries of Seven Women Writers*

Mayberry. *Business Leaders Who Built Financial Empires*

Mayberry. *Leaders Who Changed the 20th Century*

Mayo. *Smithsonian Book of the First Ladies*

Morin. *Women Chosen for Public Office*

Morin. *Women Who Reformed Politics*

Myers. *Now Is Your Time*

Otfinoski. *Nineteenth-Century Writers*

Pascoe. *First Facts About the Presidents*

Plowden. *Famous Firsts of Black Women*

Provenson. *My Fellow Americans*

Rennert. *Book of Firsts: Leaders of America*

Rennert. *Pioneers of Discovery*

Rubel. *The Scholastic Encyclopedia of the Presidents*

Schraff. *American Heroes of Exploration and Flight*

Schraff. *Women of Peace: Nobel Peace Prize Winners*

Sills. *Visions: Stories About Women Artists*

Smith. *Presidents of a Growing Country*

Streissguth. *Hatemongers and Demagogues*

Streissguth. *Hoaxers & Hustlers*

Sullivan. *Black Artists in Photography, 1840-1940*

Sullivan. *Presidents at Play*

Veglahn. *Women Scientists*

Whitelaw. *They Wrote Their Own Headlines*

Yount. *Black Scientists*

History

Altman. *The Pullman Strike of 1894*

Anderson. *Battles That Changed the Modern World*

Archer. *Breaking Barriers: The Feminist Movement*

Bartoletti. *Growing Up in Coal Country*

Berliner. *Aviation: Reaching for the Sky*

Branch. *The Water Brought Us: The Story of the Gullah-Speaking People*

Brashler. *The Story of the Negro League Baseball*

Brown. *The Struggle to Grow (1880-1913)*

Carlin. *Jazz*

Carnes. *Us and Them: A History of Intolerance in America*

Colman. *Strike: The Bitter Struggle of American Workers*

Colman. *Toilets, Bathtubs, Sinks, and Sewers*

Colman. *Women in Society: United States*

Cooper. *Bound for the Promised Land: The Great Black Migration*

Cosner. *War Nurses*

Cray. *American Datelines*

Cush. *Disasters That Shook the World*

Czech. *Snapshot: America Discovers the Camera*

Dash. *We Shall Not Be Moved: The Women's Factory Strike of 1909*

Davies. *Transport: On Land, Road and Rail*

Dolan. *Panama and the United States: Their Canal, Their Stormy Years*

Emert. *Top Lawyers and Their Famous Cases*

Feinberg. *American Political Scandals Past and Present*

Ferrell. *The U.S. Air Force*

Fradin. *Medicine: Yesterday, Today, and Tomorrow*

Frankel. *Break Those Chains at Last: African Americans 1860-1880*

Freedman. *Kids at Work: Lewis Hine Against Child Labor*

Fry. *The Orphan Train*

Garfunkel. *On Wings of Joy: The Story of Ballet*

Gay. *Spanish American War*

Giblin. *Be Seated: A Book About Chairs*

Gilbert. *Deadball: Major League Baseball Before Babe Ruth*

Greene. *Child Labor: Then and Now*

Greene. *Our Century: 1900-1910*

Gutman. *World Series Classics*

Hakim. *An Age of Extremes*

Hakim. *Reconstruction and Reform*

Herald. *The 1920s*

Hirsch. *Taxation: Paying for Government*

Hoig. *It's the Fourth of July*

Jones. *The President Has Been Shot*

Karl. *America Alive: A History*

Katz. *The Civil War to the Last Frontier: 1850-1880s*

Katz. *The Great Migrations: 1880s-1912*

Kronenwetter. *United They Hate: White Supremacist Groups in America*

Landau. *Armed America: The Status of Gun Control*

Landau. *The White Power Movement: America's Racist Hate Groups*

Langone. *Spreading Poison: A Book About Racism and Prejudice*

Lawson. *Famous Presidential Scandals*

Leiner. *First Children: Growing Up in the White House*

Leuzzi. *Urban Life*

Levinson. *Turn of the Century*

Libreatore. *Our Century: 1910-1920*

Lucas. *Civil Rights: The Long Struggle*

Macy. *Winning Ways: A Photohistory of American Women in Sports*

Markham. *Inventions That Changed Modern Life*

Mason. *Peary and Amundsen: Race to the Poles*

Maurer. *Airborne: The Search for the Secret of Flight*

McKissack. *A Long Hard Journey: The Story of the Pullman Porter*

Medearis. *Come This Far to Freedom*

Meltzer. *The Black Americans*

Meltzer. *Cheap Raw Material*

Mettger. *Reconstruction: America After the Civil War*

Mizell. *Think About Racism*

Monceaux. *Jazz: My Music, My People*

Morin. *Inpeaching the President*

Morley. *Clothes: For Work, Play and Display*

Mulcahy. *Diseases: Finding the Cure*

Murphy. *Across America on an Emigrant Train*

Murphy. *The Great Fire*

Patrick. *The Young Oxford Companion to the Supreme Court*

Philip. *Singing America: Poems That Define a Nation*

Platt. *The Smithsonian Visual Timeline of Inventions*

Pollard. *The Red Cross and the Red Crescent*

Press. *A Multicultural Portrait of Professional Sports*

Rappaport. *American Women: Their Lives in Their Words*

Rappaport. *The Lizzie Borden Trial*

Sagan. *Women's Suffrage*

Sandler. *Presidents*

Scott. *Funny Papers: Behind the Scenes of the Comics*

Senna. *The Black Press and the Struggle of Civil Rights*

Sherrow. *The Triangle Factory Fire*

Sigerman. *Laborers for Liberty: American Women 1865-1890*

Smith. *New Paths to Power: American Women 1890-1920*

St. George. *Panama Canal: Gateway to the World*

St. George. *The White House: Cornerstone of a Nation*

Sullivan. *Children of
    Promise:
    African-American
    Literature and Art*
Time-Life. *African
    Americans: Voices of
    Triumph: Leadership*
Time-Life. *This Fabulous
    Century: 1870-1900,
    Prelude*
Time-Life. *This Fabulous
    Century: 1900-1910*

Time-Life. *This Fabulous
    Century: 1910-1920*
Ventura. *Clothing*
Ventura. *Food: Its Evolution
    Through the Ages*
Wakin. *Photos That Made
    U.S. History: Civil War to
    the Atomic Age*
Walker. *Hand, Heart, and
    Mind*
Walter. *Mississippi Challenge*
Warner. *The U.S. Marine
    Corps*

Wheeler. *Events That
    Changed American History*
Whitman. *Get Up and Go:
    American Road Travel*
Whitman. *This Land Is Your
    Land*
Wormser. *Hoboes:
    Wandering in America
    1870-1940*
Yepsen. *City Trains:
    America's Cities by Rail*

Multimedia

CD-ROM

*Air and Space Smithsonian
    Dreams of Flight*
American History Explorer
*Campaigns, Candidates and
    the Presidency*
Daring to Fly!
Exploring the Titanic
*Eyewitness Encyclopedia of
    Science*

*Famous American Speeches:
    1850 to the Present*
*Her Heritage: A Biographical
    Encyclopedia of American
    History*
*History Through Art: 20th
    Century*
*Landmark Documents in
    American History*

*Portraits of American
    Presidents*
Science Navigator
SkyTrip America
*Time Almanac of the 20th
    Century*
Total History
The Way Things Work

Video

African Americans
Alexander Graham Bell
*Alice Paul: We Were Arrested
    of Course!*
All Aboard for Philadelphia!
*American Consumerism
    (1890-1930)*
*The Atlantic Coast of
    Winslow Homer*
Barnum's Big Top
*Black Is My Color: The
    African American
    Experience*
Booker T. Washington
Clara Barton
Daring to Dream
*Elizabeth Cady Stanton and
    Susan B. Anthony*
Emily Dickinson
*Emily Dickinson: A Certain
    Slant of Light*
*Equality: A History of the
    Women's Movement in
    America*
*The Era of Segregation: A
    Personal Perspective*
*Farming in America: A
    History*
Frederick Douglass

*Frederick Douglass: When
    the Lion Wrote History*
Gandy Dancers
Great Black Innovators
Great Black Women
Harriet Tubman
Helen Keller
Houdini:The Great Escape
*Industrialization and
    Urbanization (1870-1910)*
Jane Addams
Lucretia Mott
Madam C. J. Walker
*Making It Happen: Masters
    of Invention*
Mansions of Newport
Mary McLeod Bethune
*Michigan Avenue: From
    Museums to the
    Magnificent Mile*
A Nation in Turmoil
The Poet and the Rough Rider
*Presenting Mr. Frederick
    Douglass*
*Pride & Prejudice: A History
    of Black Culture in America*
Progressive Movement
*Public Sculpture: America's
    Legacy*

Reading Terminal Market
*Reconstruction and
    Segregation (1870-1910)*
Samuel Morse: The Telegraph
Sojourner Truth
Susan B. Anthony
Susan B. Anthony Story
*This House of Power: The
    Church in
    African-American
    Experience*
Thomas Alva Edison
Thomas Edison: Electric Light
*Tragedy to Triumph: An
    Adventure with Helen
    Keller*
*Traveling in Style:
    Automobiles and Trolleys*
*Traveling in Style: Trains,
    Riverboats, and Planes*
*U.S. and the World
    (1865-1917)*
*Votes for Women?! The 1913
    U.S. Senate Testimony*
Women in Rural America
*The Wright Brothers: How
    They Invented the Airplane*

GRADE NINE

Historical Fiction

Alexander. *The Philadelphia Adventure*
Beatty. *Be Ever Hopeful, Hannalee*
Bethancourt. *The Tommorow Connection*
Clark. *Nellie Bishop*
Collier. *My Crooked Family*
Conrad. *My Daniel*
Edmonds. *Bert Breen's Barn*
Garland. *The Last Rainmaker*
Hamm. *Bunkhouse Journal*
Hooks. *A Flight of Dazzle Angels*
Hoppe. *Dream Spinner*
Hurmence. *Tancy*
Kirkpatrick. *Keeping the Good Light*
Lenski. *Strawberry Girl*
Meyer. *Gideon's People*
Oke. *The Bluebird and the Sparrow*
Pendergraft. *Hear the Wind Blow*
Perez. *Breaker*
Riskind. *Apple Is My Sign*
Ross. *The Bet's On, Lizzie Bingman!*
Rossiter. *Moxie*
Rostkowski. *After the Dancing Days*
Sauerwein. *The Way Home*
Savage. *To Race a Dream*
Stolz. *Cezanne Pinto: A Memoir*
Terris. *Nell's Quilt*
Todd. *Squaring Off*
Van Raven. *Harpoon Island*
Winter. *The Christmas Tree Ship*
Wisler. *Mustang Flats*

Biography

Abramson. *Hero in Disgrace: Frederick A. Cook*
Andronik. *Prince of Humbugs: A Life of P. T. Barnum*
Archbold. *Deep-Sea Explorer: Robert Ballard*
Bentley. *Harriet Tubman*
Berman. *James McNeill Whistler*
Berry. *Emily Dickinson*
Boulton. *Frank Lloyd Wright: Architect: An Illustrated Biography*
Bowman. *Andrew Carnegie: Steel Tycoon*
Brown. *Chester Arthur: Twenty-First President*
Brown. *James Garfield: 20th President of the United States*
Brown. *Robert E. Lee*
Bundles. *Madam C. J. Walker*
Burke. *Louisa May Alcott*
Cain. *Mary Cassatt*
Carlson. *Harriet Tubman: Call to Freedom*
Casey. *Millard Fillmore: Thirteenth President*
Casey. *William H. Taft: Twenty-Seventh President*
Clinton. *Benjamin Harrison: Twenty-Third President*
Collins. *William McKinley: 25th President of the United States*
Cullen-DuPont. *Elizabeth Cady Stanton and Women's Liberty*
Davis. *Frank Lloyd Wright: Maverick Architect*
Dominy. *Katherine Dunham: Dancer and Choreographer*
Driemen. *Clarence Darrow*
Dubowski. *Clara Barton: Healing the Wounds*
Dubowski. *Robert E. Lee*
Dwyer. *Robert Peary and the Quest for the North Pole*
Ehrlich. *Nelly Bly: Journalist*
Falkof. *William H. Taft*
Fleming. *P. T. Barnum*
Fritz. *Bully for You, Teddy Roosevelt*
Gehre. *Susan B. Anthony*
Gentry. *Paul Laurence Dunbar: Poet*
Gilman. *Matthew Henson: Explorer*
Hamilton. *Clara Barton*
Hawxhurst. *Mother Jones: Labor Crusader*
Haynes. *Ida B. Wells*
Horton. *Mother Jones*
Hovde. *Jane Addams*
Jakoubek. *Harriet Beecher Stowe*
Johnston. *Harriet: The Life and World of Harriet Beecher Stowe*
Kaye. *The Life of Daniel Hale Williams*
Keller. *The Story of My Life*
Kendall. *Susan B. Anthony*
Kent. *Andrew Johnson: Seventeenth President*
Kent. *Calvin Coolidge: Thirtieth President*
Kent. *Dorothy Day: Friend to the Forgotten*
Kent. *Grover Cleveland: Twenty-Second and Twenty-Fourth President*
Kent. *Theodore Roosevelt: Twenty-Sixth President*
Kent. *Ulysses S. Grant: Eighteenth President*
Kerby. *Robert E. Lee*
Klots. *Ida Wells-Barnett: Civil Rights Leader*
Kozodoy. *Isadora Duncan: Dancer*
Kraft. *Mother Jones: One Woman's Fight for Labor*
Krass. *Sojourner Truth: Antislavery Activist*
Leavell. *Woodrow Wilson*
Lefer. *Emma Lazarus*
Levinson. *I Lift My Lamp: Emma Lazarus and the Statue of Liberty*
Lillegard. *James Garfield: Twentieth President*
Lipsyte. *Joe Louis: A Champ for all America*
Loewen. *Walt Whitman*
Malone. *Will Rogers: Cowboy Philosopher*
Markham. *Theodore Roosevelt*
Marrin. *Unconditional Surrender*
Marrin. *Virginia's General: Robert E. Lee*
McClard. *Harriet Tubman: Slavery and the Underground Railroad*
Meigs. *Invincible Louisa*

Meltzer. *Frederick Douglass: In His Own Words*

Muhlberger. *What Makes a Cassatt a Cassatt?*

Nardo. *Jim Thorpe*

Nicholson. *Georgia O'Keeffe*

Nicholson. *Helen Keller: Humanitarian*

Norman. *Lewis Latimer: Scientist*

O'Brien. *Ulysses S. Grant*

Olsen. *Emily Dickinson: Poet*

Pasachoff. *Alexander Graham Bell*

Plain. *Mary Cassatt: An Artist's Life*

Reef. *Walt Whitman*

Rickarby. *Ulysses S. Grant*

Russell. *Frederick Douglass: Abolitionist Editor*

Sandomir. *Isadora Duncan: Revolutionary Dancer*

Schroeder. *Booker T. Washington*

Schroeder. *Jack London*

Simon. *Franklin Pierce*

Sonneborn. *Will Rogers: Cherokee Entertainer*

Stefoff. *Herman Melville*

Stefoff. *Theodore Roosevelt: 26th President*

Stevens. *Andrew Johnson: 17th President*

Stevens. *Benjamin Harrison: 23rd President*

Sufrin. *Stephen Crane*

Thompson. *Charles Chesnutt*

Tilton. *Clara Barton*

Tolbert-Rouchaleau. *James Weldon Johnson: Author*

Turner. *Lewis Howard Latimer*

Van Steenwyk. *Ida B. Wells-Barnett*

Waldstreicher. *Emma Goldman*

Weidhorn. *Robert E. Lee*

Whitelaw. *Theodore Roosevelt Takes Charge*

Whitelaw. *William Tecumseh Sherman*

Woog. *Harry Houdini*

Worth. *Edith Wharton*

Collective Biography

Aaseng. *America's Third-Party Presidential Candidates*

Aaseng. *Close Calls*

Aaseng. *Great Justices of the Supreme Court*

Aaseng. *Twentieth-Century Inventors*

Aaseng. *You Are the President*

Anthony. *First Ladies: 1789-1961*

Beard. *The Presidents in American History*

Blassingame. *The Look-It-Up Book of Presidents*

Camp. *American Astronomers: Searchers and Wonderers*

Cush. *Artists Who Created Great Works*

Cush. *Women Who Achieved Greatness*

Dolan. *Shaping U.S. Foreign Policy: Twelve Secretaries of State*

Faber. *Great Lives: American Government*

Fradin. *We Have Conquered Pain: The Discovery of Anesthesia*

Glubok. *Great Lives: Painting*

Jones. *Big Star Fallin' Mama*

Lindop. *Presidents by Accident*

Lyons. *Keeping Secrets: The Girlhood Diaries of Seven Women Writers*

Mayberry. *Leaders Who Changed the 20th Century*

Mayo. *Smithsonian Book of the First Ladies*

Morin. *Women Chosen for Public Office*

Morin. *Women Who Reformed Politics*

Myers. *Now Is Your Time*

O'Brien. *American Political Leaders*

Otfinoski. *Nineteenth-Century Writers*

Plowden. *Famous Firsts of Black Women*

Rennert. *Book of Firsts: Leaders of America*

Rennert. *Pioneers of Discovery*

Schraff. *American Heroes of Exploration and Flight*

Schraff. *Women of Peace: Nobel Peace Prize Winners*

Smith. *Presidents of a Growing Country*

Streissguth. *Hatemongers and Demagogues*

Streissguth. *Hoaxers & Hustlers*

Sullivan. *Black Artists in Photography, 1840-1940*

Sullivan. *Presidents at Play*

Veglahn. *Women Scientists*

Whitelaw. *They Wrote Their Own Headlines*

Yount. *Black Scientists*

History

Alderman. *In Our Defense: The Bill of Rights in Action*

American Women in the Progressive Era: 1900-1920

Anderson. *Battles That Changed the Modern World*

Archer. *Breaking Barriers: The Feminist Movement*

Ardley. *Music: An Illustrated Encyclopedia*

Awmiller. *This House on Fire: The Story of the Blues*

Aymar. *Men in the Air: The Best Flight Stories of All Time*

Basinger. *American Cinema: One Hundred Years of Filmmaking*

Beckett. *The Story of Painting*

Berliner. *Aviation: Reaching for the Sky*

Branch. *The Water Brought Us: The Story of the Gullah-Speaking People*

Brashler. *The Story of the Negro League Baseball*

Carlin. *Jazz*

Carnes. *Us and Them: A History of Intolerance in America*

Cohen. *America: Then and Now*

Collier. *Jazz, the American Theme Song*

Colman. *Women in Society: United States*

Cooper. *Bound for the Promised Land: The Great Black Migration*

Cosner. *War Nurses*

Cray. *American Datelines*

Cush. *Disasters That Shook the World*

Czech. *Snapshot: America Discovers the Camera*

Dale. *Early Cars*

Dale. *Early Railways*

Dash. *We Shall Not Be Moved: The Women's Factory Strike of 1909*

Davis. *Don't Know Much About History*

Davis. *Man-Made Catastrophes*

Dolan. *Panama and the United States: Their Canal, Their Stormy Years*

Emert. *Top Lawyers and Their Famous Cases*

Ewing. *Women in Uniform Through the Centuries*

Feinberg. *American Political Scandals Past and Present*

Fradin. *Medicine: Yesterday, Today, and Tomorrow*

Frankel. *Break Those Chains at Last: African Americans 1860-1880*

Freedman. *Kids at Work: Lewis Hine Against Child Labor*

Frost-Knappman. *Women's Suffrage in America*

Garfunkel. *On Wings of Joy: The Story of Ballet*

Garza. *Barred from the Bar: A History of Women and the Legal Profession*

Gay. *Spanish American War*

Gilbert. *Deadball: Major League Baseball Before Babe Ruth*

Greene. *Child Labor: Then and Now*

Greene. *Our Century: 1900-1910*

Hakim. *An Age of Extremes*

Hakim. *Reconstruction and Reform*

Haskins. *Black Music in America*

Herald. *The 1920s*

Hirsch. *Taxation: Paying for Government*

Jones. *The President Has Been Shot*

Katz. *The Civil War to the Last Frontier: 1850-1880s*

Katz. *The Great Migrations: 1880s-1912*

Kirchberger. *The Civil War and Reconstruction*

Knappman. *Great American Trials*

Kronenwetter. *United They Hate: White Supremacist Groups in America*

Landau. *Armed America: The Status of Gun Control*

Landau. *The White Power Movement: America's Racist Hate Groups*

Langone. *Spreading Poison: A Book About Racism and Prejudice*

Lawson. *Famous Presidential Scandals*

Leiner. *First Children: Growing Up in the White House*

Leuzzi. *Urban Life*

Levinson. *Turn of the Century*

Libreatore. *Our Century: 1910-1920*

Macy. *Winning Ways: A Photohistory of American Women in Sports*

Markham. *Inventions That Changed Modern Life*

McKissack. *A Long Hard Journey: The Story of the Pullman Porter*

Medearis. *Come This Far to Freedom*

Meltzer. *The Black Americans*

Meltzer. *Cheap Raw Material*

Mettger. *Reconstruction: America After the Civil War*

Mizell. *Think About Racism*

Monceaux. *Jazz: My Music, My People*

Morin. *Impeaching the President*

Mulcahy. *Diseases: Finding the Cure*

Patrick. *The Young Oxford Companion to the Supreme Court*

Philip. *Singing America: Poems That Define a Nation*

Platt. *The Smithsonian Visual Timeline of Inventions*

Potter. *African-American Firsts*

Press. *A Multicultural Portrait of Professional Sports*

Rappaport. *American Women: Their Lives in Their Words*

Rappaport. *The Lizzie Borden Trial*

Sagan. *Women's Suffrage*

Schreiner. *Mayday! Mayday!*

Senna. *The Black Press and the Struggle of Civil Rights*

Sigerman. *Laborers for Liberty: American Women 1865-1890*

Smith. *Fascinating People and Astounding Events from American History*

Smith. *New Paths to Power: American Women 1890-1920*

Spangenburg. *The History of Science from 1895 to 1945*

Spangenburg. *The History of Science in the Nineteenth Century*

St. George. *Panama Canal: Gateway to the World*

St. George. *The White House: Cornerstone of a Nation*

Stalcup. *Reconstruction*

Steele. *Freedom's River*

Time-Life. *African Americans: Voices of Triumph: Leadership*

Time-Life. *This Fabulous Century: 1870-1900, Prelude*

Time-Life. *This Fabulous Century: 1900-1910*

Time-Life. *This Fabulous Century: 1910-1920*

Wakin. *Photos That Made U.S. History: Civil War to the Atomic Age*

Walker. *Hand, Heart, and Mind*

Walter. *Mississippi Challenge*

Wheeler. *Events That Changed American History*

Whitman. *Get Up and Go: American Road Travel*

Whitman. *This Land Is Your Land*

Wormser. *Hoboes: Wandering in America 1870-1940*

Multimedia

CD-ROM

Air and Space Smithsonian Dreams of Flight
American History Explorer
Campaigns, Candidates and the Presidency
Daring to Fly!
Events That Changed the World
Famous American Speeches: 1850 to the Present

Her Heritage: A Biographical Encyclopedia of American History
History Through Art: 20th Century
Ideas That Changed the World
Landmark Documents in American History

Our Times: The Multimedia Encyclopedia of the Twentieth Century
Portraits of American Presidents
Science Navigator
Time Almanac of the 20th Century
Total History
The Way Things Work

Video

African Americans
Alexander Graham Bell
Alice Paul: We Were Arrested of Course!
All Aboard for Philadelphia!
American Consumerism (1890-1930)
The American Experience: Insanity on Trial
The Atlantic Coast of Winslow Homer
Barnum's Big Top
Booker T. Washington
Buffalo Soldiers: Black Soldiers in the Frontier Army
Clara Barton
Daring to Dream
Dreams of Equality
Emily Dickinson
Emily Dickinson: A Certain Slant of Light
Equality: A History of the Women's Movement in America
The Era of Segregation: A Personal Perspective
Farming in America: A History
Frederick Douglass
Frederick Douglass: When the Lion Wrote History
Gandy Dancers

Great Black Women
Harriet Tubman
Helen Keller
Houdini:The Great Escape
Hull House: The House That Jane Built
Ida B. Wells—A Passion for Justice
In Times Past: Traveling in Style
Industrialization and Urbanization (1870-1910)
Jane Addams
Land and Landscape: Views of America's History and Culture
Living Portraits of Historic Women: Of All the Nerve
Lucretia Mott
Madam C. J. Walker
Mansions of Newport
Mary McLeod Bethune
Michigan Avenue: From Museums to the Magnificent Mile
A Nation in Turmoil
Nikola Tesla: The Genius Who Lit the World
The Poet and the Rough Rider
Presenting Mr. Frederick Douglass
Pride & Prejudice: A History of Black Culture in America

Progressive Movement
Public Sculpture: America's Legacy
Reading Terminal Market
Reconstruction and Segregation (1870-1910)
Samuel Morse: The Telegraph
Sojourner Truth
Susan B. Anthony
Susan B. Anthony Story
This House of Power: The Church in African-American Experience
Thomas Alva Edison
Thomas Edison: Electric Light
Tragedy to Triumph: An Adventure with Helen Keller
Traveling in Style: Automobiles and Trolleys
Traveling in Style: Trains, Riverboats, and Planes
U.S. and the World (1865-1917)
Votes for Women?! The 1913 U.S. Senate Testimony
Women in Rural America
Wonders of Man's Creation
The Wright Brothers: How They Invented the Airplane
The Wright Stuff: Invention of Airplanes

GRADE TEN

Historical Fiction

Clark. Nellie Bishop
Edmonds. Bert Breen's Barn
Garland. The Last Rainmaker
Hamm. Bunkhouse Journal
Hooks. A Flight of Dazzle Angels

Hoppe. Dream Spinner
Hurmence. Tancy
Meyer. Gideon's People
Oke. The Bluebird and the Sparrow
Sauerwein. The Way Home

Savage. To Race a Dream
Todd. Squaring Off
Van Raven. Harpoon Island

Biography

Abramson. *Hero in Disgrace: Frederick A. Cook*
Archbold. *Deep-Sea Explorer: Robert Ballard*
Bentley. *Harriet Tubman*
Berman. *James McNeill Whistler*
Berry. *Emily Dickinson*
Boulton. *Frank Lloyd Wright: Architect: An Illustrated Biography*
Bowman. *Andrew Carnegie: Steel Tycoon*
Brown. *Robert E. Lee*
Bundles. *Madam C. J. Walker*
Burke. *Louisa May Alcott*
Cain. *Mary Cassatt*
Cullen-DuPont. *Elizabeth Cady Stanton and Women's Liberty*
Davis. *Frank Lloyd Wright: Maverick Architect*
Dominy. *Katherine Dunham: Dancer and Choreographer*
Driemen. *Clarence Darrow*
Dwyer. *Robert Peary and the Quest for the North Pole*
Ehrlich. *Nelly Bly: Journalist*

Gentry. *Paul Laurence Dunbar: Poet*
Gilman. *Matthew Henson: Explorer*
Hamilton. *Clara Barton*
Hawxhurst. *Mother Jones: Labor Crusader*
Hovde. *Jane Addams*
Jakoubek. *Harriet Beecher Stowe*
Keller. *The Story of My Life*
Klots. *Ida Wells-Barnett: Civil Rights Leader*
Kozodoy. *Isadora Duncan: Dancer*
Krass. *Sojourner Truth: Antislavery Activist*
Leavell. *Woodrow Wilson*
Lefer. *Emma Lazarus*
Loewen. *Walt Whitman*
Markham. *Theodore Roosevelt*
Marrin. *Unconditional Surrender*
Marrin. *Virginia's General: Robert E. Lee*
Meigs. *Invincible Louisa*
Meltzer. *Frederick Douglass: In His Own Words*
Nardo. *Jim Thorpe*

Nicholson. *Georgia O'Keeffe*
Nicholson. *Helen Keller: Humanitarian*
Norman. *Lewis Latimer: Scientist*
O'Brien. *Ulysses S. Grant*
Olsen. *Emily Dickinson: Poet*
Plain. *Mary Cassatt: An Artist's Life*
Reef. *Walt Whitman*
Russell. *Frederick Douglass: Abolitionist Editor*
Stefoff. *Herman Melville*
Sufrin. *Stephen Crane*
Thompson. *Charles Chesnutt*
Tilton. *Clara Barton*
Tolbert-Rouchaleau. *James Weldon Johnson: Author*
Van Steenwyk. *Ida B. Wells-Barnett*
Waldstreicher. *Emma Goldman*
Weidhorn. *Robert E. Lee*
Whitelaw. *Theodore Roosevelt Takes Charge*
Whitelaw. *William Tecumseh Sherman*
Woog. *Harry Houdini*
Worth. *Edith Wharton*

Collective Biography

Aaseng. *America's Third-Party Presidential Candidates*
Aaseng. *Great Justices of the Supreme Court*
Aaseng. *Twentieth-Century Inventors*
Aaseng. *You Are the President*
Anthony. *First Ladies: 1789-1961*
Jones. *Big Star Fallin' Mama*
Lindop. *Presidents by Accident*

Lyons. *Keeping Secrets: The Girlhood Diaries of Seven Women Writers*
Mayberry. *Leaders Who Changed the 20th Century*
Morin. *Women Chosen for Public Office*
Morin. *Women Who Reformed Politics*
Myers. *Now Is Your Time*
O'Brien. *American Political Leaders: From Colonial Times to the Present*

Otfinoski. *Nineteenth-Century Writers*
Streissguth. *Hatemongers and Demagogues*
Streissguth. *Hoaxers & Hustlers*
Sullivan. *Presidents at Play*
Whitelaw. *They Wrote Their Own Headlines*
Yount. *Black Scientists*

History

Alderman. *In Our Defense: The Bill of Rights in Action*
American Women in the Progressive Era: 1900-1920
Anderson. *Battles That Changed the Modern World*
Archer. *Breaking Barriers: The Feminist Movement*
Ardley. *Music: An Illustrated Encyclopedia*
Awmiller. *This House on Fire: The Story of the Blues*

Aymar. *Men in the Air: The Best Flight Stories of All Time*
Basinger. *American Cinema: One Hundred Years of Filmmaking*
Beckett. *The Story of Painting*
Berliner. *Aviation: Reaching for the Sky*
Carlin. *Jazz*
Carnes. *Us and Them: A History of Intolerance in America*

Cohen. *America: Then and Now*
Collier. *Jazz, the American Theme Song*
Colman. *Women in Society: United States*
Cray. *American Datelines*
Dale. *Early Cars*
Dale. *Early Railways*
Davis. *Don't Know Much About History*
Davis. *Man-Made Catastrophes*

Evans. *Born for Liberty: A History of Women in America*

Ewing. *Women in Uniform Through the Centuries*

Feinberg. *American Political Scandals Past and Present*

Fradin. *Medicine: Yesterday, Today, and Tomorrow*

Frankel. *Break Those Chains at Last: African Americans 1860-1880*

Freedman. *Kids at Work: Lewis Hine Against Child Labor*

Frost-Knappman. *Women's Suffrage in America*

Garfunkel. *On Wings of Joy: The Story of Ballet*

Garza. *Barred from the Bar: A History of Women and the Legal Profession*

Gilbert. *Deadball: Major League Baseball Before Babe Ruth*

Greene. *Child Labor: Then and Now*

Greene. *Our Century: 1900-1910*

Hakim. *An Age of Extremes*

Hakim. *Reconstruction and Reform*

Haskins. *Black Music in America*

Herald. *The 1920s*

Katz. *The Civil War to the Last Frontier: 1850-1880s*

Katz. *The Great Migrations: 1880s-1912*

Kirchberger. *The Civil War and Reconstruction*

Knappman. *Great American Trials*

Kronenwetter. *United They Hate: White Supremacist Groups in America*

Landau. *Armed America: The Status of Gun Control*

Landau. *The White Power Movement: America's Racist Hate Groups*

Langone. *Spreading Poison: A Book About Racism and Prejudice*

Lawson. *Famous Presidential Scandals*

Levinson. *Turn of the Century*

Libreatore. *Our Century: 1910-1920*

Macy. *Winning Ways: A Photohistory of American Women in Sports*

Markham. *Inventions That Changed Modern Life*

McKissack. *A Long Hard Journey: The Story of the Pullman Porter*

Meltzer. *The Black Americans*

Mizell. *Think About Racism*

Monceaux. *Jazz: My Music, My People*

Morin. *Impeaching the President*

Mulcahy. *Diseases: Finding the Cure*

Patrick. *The Young Oxford Companion to the Supreme Court*

Philip. *Singing America: Poems That Define a Nation*

Potter. *African-American Firsts*

Press. *A Multicultural Portrait of Professional Sports*

Rappaport. *American Women: Their Lives in Their Words*

Rappaport. *The Lizzie Borden Trial*

Sagan. *Women's Suffrage*

Schreiner. *Mayday! Mayday!*

Senna. *The Black Press and the Struggle of Civil Rights*

Sigerman. *Laborers for Liberty: American Women 1865-1890*

Smith. *Fascinating People and Astounding Events from American History*

Smith. *New Paths to Power: American Women 1890-1920*

Spangenburg. *The History of Science from 1895 to 1945*

Spangenburg. *The History of Science in the Nineteenth Century*

Stalcup. *Reconstruction*

Steele. *Freedom's River*

Time-Life. *African Americans: Voices of Triumph: Leadership*

Time-Life. *This Fabulous Century: 1870-1900, Prelude*

Time-Life. *This Fabulous Century: 1900-1910*

Time-Life. *This Fabulous Century: 1910-1920*

Wakin. *Photos That Made U.S. History: Civil War to the Atomic Age*

Walter. *Mississippi Challenge*

Wheeler. *Events That Changed American History*

Wormser. *Hoboes: Wandering in America 1870-1940*

Multimedia

CD-ROM

Air and Space Smithsonian Dreams of Flight

Campaigns, Candidates and the Presidency

Daring to Fly!

Events That Changed the World

Famous American Speeches: 1850 to the Present

Her Heritage: A Biographical Encyclopedia of American History

History Through Art: 20th Century

Ideas That Changed the World

Landmark Documents in American History

Our Times: The Multimedia Encyclopedia of the Twentieth Century

Portraits of American Presidents

Science Navigator

Time Almanac of the 20th Century

Total History

The Way Things Work

Video

African Americans
Alice Paul: We Were Arrested
of Course!
All Aboard for Philadelphia!
The American Experience:
Insanity on Trial
The Atlantic Coast of
Winslow Homer
Barnum's Big Top
Booker T. Washington
Buffalo Soldiers: Black
Soldiers in the Frontier
Army
Clara Barton
Daring to Dream
Dreams of Equality
Emily Dickinson
Emily Dickinson: A Certain
Slant of Light
Equality: A History of the
Women's Movement in
America
The Era of Segregation: A
Personal Perspective
Farming in America: A
History
Frederick Douglass

Frederick Douglass: When
the Lion Wrote History
Gandy Dancers
Great Black Women
Harriet Tubman
Helen Keller
Houdini: The Great Escape
Hull House: The House That
Jane Built
Ida B. Wells—A Passion for
Justice
In Times Past: Traveling in
Style
Jane Addams
Land and Landscape: Views
of America's History and
Culture
Living Portraits of Historic
Women: Of All the Nerve
Lucretia Mott
Madam C. J. Walker
Mansions of Newport
Michigan Avenue: From
Museums to the
Magnificent Mile
Midnight Ramble

Nikola Tesla: The Genius
Who Lit the World
The Poet and the Rough Rider
Pride & Prejudice: A History
of Black Culture in America
Public Sculpture: America's
Legacy
Sojourner Truth
Susan B. Anthony
This House of Power: The
Church in
African-American
Experience
Tragedy to Triumph: An
Adventure with Helen
Keller
Traveling in Style:
Automobiles and Trolleys
Traveling in Style: Trains,
Riverboats, and Planes
Votes for Women?! The 1913
U.S. Senate Testimony
Women in Rural America
Wonders of Man's Creation
The Wright Stuff: Invention of
Airplanes

GRADES ELEVEN AND TWELVE

Historical Fiction

Bass. *Maiden Voyage*
Boyle. *The Road to Wellville*
Brewer. *No Justice*
Bristol. *Legacy*
Brown. *Crossing over Jordan*
Doctorow. *Ragtime*

Doctorow. *The Waterworks*
Hamm. *Bunkhouse Journal*
Jones. *Come Winter*
Jones. *Remember Santiago*
Lee. *The Serpent's Gift*
Mason. *Feather Crowns*

Matthiessen. *Killing Mister
Watson*
Mitchell. *Trial of the Innocent*
Stephens. *Stories from the
Old Squire's Farm*
Waniek. *The Homeplace*

Biography

Abramson. *Hero in Disgrace:
Frederick A. Cook*
Bentley. *Harriet Tubman*
Berlin. *King of Ragtime:
Scott Joplin and His Era*
Berman. *James McNeill
Whistler*
Boulton. *Frank Lloyd Wright:
Architect: An Illustrated
Biography*
Bowman. *Andrew Carnegie:
Steel Tycoon*
Collins. *Shattered Dreams:
The Story of Mary Todd
Lincoln*

Cullen-DuPont. *Elizabeth
Cady Stanton and
Women's Liberty*
Dominy. *Katherine Dunham:
Dancer and Choreographer*
Driemen. *Clarence Darrow*
Dwyer. *Robert Peary and the
Quest for the North Pole*
Ehrlich. *Nelly Bly: Journalist*
Faber. *Printer's Devil to
Publisher: Adolph S. Ochs
of the New York Times*
Keller. *The Story of My Life*
Leavell. *Woodrow Wilson*
Lefer. *Emma Lazarus*
Loewen. *Walt Whitman*

Marrin. *Unconditional
Surrender*
Meigs. *Invincible Louisa*
Meltzer. *Frederick Douglass:
In His Own Words*
Meyers. *Robert Frost: A
Biography*
Norman. *Lewis Latimer:
Scientist*
Sherr. *Failure Is Impossible:
Susan B. Anthony*
Stefoff. *Herman Melville*
Sufrin. *Stephen Crane*
Thompson. *Charles Chesnutt*
Tolbert-Rouchaleau. *James
Weldon Johnson: Author*

Waldstreicher. *Emma Goldman*
Weidhorn. *Robert E. Lee*

Wert. *Custer: The Controversial Life of George Armstrong Custer*

Whitelaw. *Theodore Roosevelt Takes Charge*
Whyte. *Rising Above It*
Worth. *Edith Wharton*

Collective Biography

Aaseng. *Great Justices of the Supreme Court*
Aaseng. *Twentieth-Century Inventors*
Aaseng. *You Are the President*
Anthony. *First Ladies: 1789-1961*
Foster. *Written by Herself: African American Women, 1746-1892*
Jones. *Big Star Fallin' Mama*
Lindop. *Presidents by Accident*

Lyons. *Keeping Secrets: The Girlhood Diaries of Seven Women Writers*
Mayberry. *Leaders Who Changed the 20th Century*
McCullough. *Brave Companions: Portraits in History*
Morin. *Women Chosen for Public Office*
O'Brien. *American Political Leaders: From Colonial Times to the Present*

Otfinoski. *Nineteenth-Century Writers*
Streissguth. *Hatemongers and Demagogues*
Streissguth. *Hoaxers & Hustlers*
Terkel. *Giants of Jazz*
Truman. *First Ladies*
Wills. *Certain Trumpets: The Call of Leaders*
Yount. *Black Scientists*

History

Alderman. *In Our Defense: The Bill of Rights in Action*
American Women in the Progressive Era: 1900-1920
Ardley. *Music: An Illustrated Encyclopedia*
Awmiller. *This House on Fire: The Story of the Blues*
Aymar. *Men in the Air: The Best Flight Stories of All Time*
Basinger. *American Cinema: One Hundred Years of Filmmaking*
Beckett. *The Story of Painting*
Berliner. *Aviation: Reaching for the Sky*
Black. *In the Shadow of Polio: A Personal and Social History*
Boller. *Presidential Wives: An Anecdotal History*
Busby. *Daughters of Africa: An International Anthology*
Carlin. *Jazz*
Carnes. *Us and Them: A History of Intolerance in America*
Clark. *America's Gilded Age*
Cohen. *America: Then and Now*
Cole. *Perspective*
Collier. *Jazz, the American Theme Song*
Colman. *Women in Society: United States*
Cray. *American Datelines*
Dale. *Early Cars*
Dale. *Early Railways*

Davidson. *Everyday Life Through the Ages*
Davis. *Don't Know Much About History*
Davis. *Man-Made Catastrophes*
Evans. *Born for Liberty: A History of Women in America*
Ewing. *Women in Uniform Through the Centuries*
Feinberg. *American Political Scandals Past and Present*
Fogle. *Two Hundred Years: Stories of the Nation's Capital*
Frankel. *Break Those Chains at Last: African Americans 1860-1880*
Frost-Knappman. *Women's Suffrage in America*
Garfunkel. *On Wings of Joy: The Story of Ballet*
Garza. *Barred from the Bar: A History of Women and the Legal Profession*
Gilbert. *Deadball: Major League Baseball Before Babe Ruth*
Hakim. *An Age of Extremes*
Hakim. *Reconstruction and Reform*
Hanmer. *Taking a Stand Against Sexism and Sex Discrimination*
Haskins. *Black Music in America*
Kirchberger. *The Civil War and Reconstruction*

Knappman. *Great American Trials*
Kronenwetter. *United They Hate: White Supremacist Groups in America*
Landau. *The White Power Movement: America's Racist Hate Groups*
Langone. *Spreading Poison: A Book About Racism and Prejudice*
Lawson. *Famous Presidential Scandals*
Levinson. *Turn of the Century*
Marling. *George Washington Slept Here, 1876-1986*
Melder. *Hail to the Candidate: Presidential Campaigns*
Monceaux. *Jazz: My Music, My People*
Morin. *Impeaching the President*
Mulcahy. *Diseases: Finding the Cure*
Patrick. *The Young Oxford Companion to the Supreme Court*
Peterson. *Cages to Jump Shots: Pro Basketball's Early Years*
Philip. *Singing America: Poems That Define a Nation*
Potter. *African-American Firsts*
Press. *A Multicultural Portrait of Professional Sports*

Rappaport. *American Women: Their Lives in Their Words*
Rappaport. *The Lizzie Borden Trial*
Sagan. *Women's Suffrage*
Sante. *Low Life: Lures and Snares of Old New York*
Schreiner. *Mayday! Mayday!*
Senna. *The Black Press and the Struggle of Civil Rights*
Sigerman. *Laborers for Liberty: American Women 1865-1890*

Smith. *Fascinating People and Astounding Events from American History*
Smith. *New Paths to Power: American Women 1890-1920*
Spangenburg. *The History of Science from 1895 to 1945*
Spangenburg. *The History of Science in the Nineteenth Century*
Stalcup. *Reconstruction*
Steele. *Freedom's River*
Time-Life. *African Americans: Voices of Triumph: Leadership*

Time-Life. *This Fabulous Century: 1870-1900, Prelude*
Time-Life. *This Fabulous Century: 1900-1910*
Time-Life. *This Fabulous Century: 1910-1920*
Tinling. *With Women's Eyes: Visitors to the New World, 1775-1918*
Walter. *Mississippi Challenge*
Wheeler. *Events That Changed American History*
Wilson. *The Circumnavigators*

Multimedia

CD-ROM

Air and Space Smithsonian Dreams of Flight
Campaigns, Candidates and the Presidency
Daring to Fly!
Events That Changed the World
Famous American Speeches: 1850 to the Present

Her Heritage: A Biographical Encyclopedia of American History
History Through Art: 20th Century
Ideas That Changed the World
Landmark Documents in American History

Our Times: The Multimedia Encyclopedia of the Twentieth Century
Portraits of American Presidents
Science Navigator
Time Almanac of the 20th Century
Total History
The Way Things Work

Video

African Americans
Alice Paul: We Were Arrested of Course!
All Aboard for Philadelphia!
The American Experience: Insanity on Trial
The Atlantic Coast of Winslow Homer
Barnum's Big Top
Booker T. Washington
Buffalo Soldiers: Black Soldiers in the Frontier Army
Clara Barton
Daring to Dream
Dreams of Equality
Emily Dickinson
Emily Dickinson: A Certain Slant of Light
Equality: A History of the Women's Movement in America
The Era of Segregation: A Personal Perspective
Farming in America: A History
Frederick Douglass

Frederick Douglass: When the Lion Wrote History
Gandy Dancers
Great Black Women
Harriet Tubman
Helen Keller
Houdini: The Great Escape
Hull House: The House That Jane Built
Ida B. Wells—A Passion For Justice
In Times Past: Traveling in Style
Jane Addams
Land and Landscape: Views of America's History and Culture
Living Portraits of Historic Women: Of All the Nerve
Lucretia Mott
Madam C. J. Walker
Mansions of Newport
Michigan Avenue: From Museums to the Magnificent Mile
Midnight Ramble
A New Public

Nikola Tesla: The Genius Who Lit the World
The Poet and the Rough Rider
Pride & Prejudice: A History of Black Culture in America
Public Sculpture: America's Legacy
Sojourner Truth
Susan B. Anthony
This House of Power: The Church in African-American Experience
Tragedy to Triumph: An Adventure with Helen Keller
Traveling in Style: Automobiles and Trolleys
Traveling in Style: Trains, Riverboats, and Planes
Votes for Women?! The 1913 U.S. Senate Testimony
Women in Rural America
Wonders of Man's Creation
The Wright Stuff: Invention of Airplanes

WORLD WAR I AND THE DEPRESSION, 1917-1941

Historical Fiction

Ames. *Grandpa Jake and the Grand Christmas*
Amoss. *The Mockingbird Song*
Armstrong. *Sounder*
Armstrong. *Steal Away*
Avi. *Shadrach's Crossing*
Beatty. *Billy Bedamned, Long Gone By*
Buechner. *The Wizard's Tide: A Story*
Cochrane. *Purely Rosie Pearl*
Collier. *The Jazz Kid*
Corbin. *Me and the End of the World*
Crew. *Fire on the Wind*
Crofford. *A Place to Belong*
Cuneo. *Anne Is Elegant*
Ducey. *The Bittersweet Time*
Ferry. *One More Time!*
Fowler. *The Last Innocent Summer*
Froelich. *Reasons to Stay*
Greene. *Dotty's Suitcase*
Hesse. *A Time of Angels*

Hooks. *Circle of Fire*
Horvath. *The Happy Yellow Car*
Houston. *Littlejim's Dreams*
Karr. *The Cave*
Karr. *In the Kaiser's Clutch*
Kinsey-Warnock. *The Night the Bells Rang*
Koller. *Nothing to Fear*
Lehrman. *The Store That Mama Built*
Lyon. *Borrowed Children*
Mazer. *Cave Under the City*
McKenzie. *Under the Bridge*
Meyer. *White Lilacs*
Mills. *What About Annie?*
Myers. *Fire in the Hills*
Myers. *The Glory Field*
Myers. *Red-Dirt Jessie*
Myers. *Spotting the Leopard*
Olsen. *The View from the Pighouse Roof*
Pendergraft. *As Far as Mill Springs*
Reeder. *Moonshiner's Son*

Ross. *The Dancing Tree*
Ross. *Hillbilly Choir*
Sebestyen. *Far from Home*
Skurzynski. *Good-bye, Billy Radish*
Snyder. *Cat Running*
Taylor. *Let the Circle Be Unbroken*
Taylor. *Mississippi Bridge*
Taylor. *Roll of Thunder, Hear My Cry*
Taylor. *The Well: David's Story*
Thesman. *The Ornament Tree*
Thesman. *Rachel Chance*
Uchida. *A Jar of Dreams*
Van Raven. *A Time of Troubles*
Voight. *Tree by Leaf*
Whelan. *That Wild Berries Should Grow*
Whittaker. *Angels of the Swamp*
Yep. *The Star Fisher*

Biography

Adair. *George Washington Carver: Botanist*
Adair. *Thomas Alva Edison: Inventing the Electric Age*
Adler. *Our Golda: The Story of Golda Meir*
Aldred. *Thurgood Marshall: Supreme Court Justice*
Anderson. *Aldo Leopold: American Ecologist*
Anderson. *Thomas Edison*
Andryszewski. *The Amazing Life of Moe Berg*
Appel. *Joe Dimaggio*
Ayer. *Lewis Latimer: Creating Bright Ideas*
Bachrach. *Margaret Sanger*

Barr. *Malcolm X*
Berke. *Babe Ruth*
Berkow. *Hank Greenberg: Hall-of-Fame Slugger*
Bernotas. *Jim Thorpe: Sac and Fox Athlete*
Berry. *Georgia O'Keeffe: Painter*
Berry. *Gordon Parks*
Berry. *Langston Hughes*
Buranelli. *Thomas Alva Edison*
Butts. *May Chinn: The Best Medicine*
Cain. *Louise Nevelson: Sculptor*
Canadeo. *Warren G. Harding*

Casey. *William H. Taft: Twenty-Seventh President*
Castiglia. *Margaret Mead*
Chadwick. *Amelia Earhart: Aviation Pioneer*
Chadwick. *Anne Morrow Lindbergh: Pilot and Poet*
Clinton. *Herbert Hoover: Thirty-First President*
Collier. *Duke Ellington*
Collier. *Louis Armstrong: An American Success Story*
Collins. *Charles Lindbergh: Hero Pilot*
Collins. *Woodrow Wilson: 28th President of the United States*

Colman. *Fannie Lou Hamer and the Fight for the Vote*

Colman. *A Woman Unafraid: Frances Perkins*

Daffron. *Margaret Bourke-White: Photographer*

Dallard. *Ella Baker: A Leader Behind the Scenes*

Darby. *Douglas MacArthur*

Darby. *Dwight D. Eisenhower*

Davies. *Malcolm X*

Davis. *Frank Lloyd Wright: Maverick Architect*

Denenberg. *An American Hero: The True Story of Charles A. Lindbergh*

Denenberg. *The True Story of J. Edgar Hoover*

Devane. *Franklin Delano Roosevelt: President*

Dominy. *Katherine Dunham: Dancer and Choreographer*

Driemen. *Atomic Dawn: A Biography of Robert Oppenheimer*

Driemen. *Clarence Darrow*

Duggleb. *Artist in Overalls: Grant Wood*

Dunlap. *Aldo Leopold: Living with the Land*

Erlich. *Paul Robeson: Singer and Actor*

Falkof. *William H. Taft*

Farley. *Robert H. Goddard*

Ferris. *What I Had Was Singing: Marian Anderson*

Frankl. *Charlie Parker: Musician*

Fraser. *Walter White: Civil Rights Leader*

Frazier. *William Randolph Hearst: Press Baron*

Freedman. *Eleanor Roosevelt: A Life of Discovery*

Freedman. *Franklin Delano Roosevelt*

Freedman. *Louis Brandeis: The People's Justice*

Garfunkel. *Letter to the World: The Life and Dances of Martha Graham*

Gay. *Emma Goldman*

Gentry. *Jesse Owens: Champion Athlete*

Gourse. *Dizzy Gillespie and the Birth of Bebop*

Gray. *George Washington Carver*

Greenblatt. *Franklin D. Roosevelt*

Greene. *Thomas Alva Edison: Bringer of Light*

Halasa. *Elijah Muhammad: Religious Leader*

Halasa. *Mary McLeod Bethune: Educator*

Hanley. *Philip Randolph*

Hart. *Up in the Air: Bessie Coleman*

Haskins. *Thurgood Marshall: A Life for Justice*

Haynes. *Ida B. Wells*

Heiligman. *Barbara McClintock: Alone in Her Field*

Herda. *Thurgood Marshall: Civil Rights Champion*

Israel. *Franklin Delano Roosevelt*

Ito. *John Steinbeck*

Jakoubek. *Joe Louis: Heavyweight Champion*

James. *Julia Morgan: Architect*

Kallen. *Thurgood Marshall: A Dream of Justice for All*

Kaye. *The Life of Alexander Fleming*

Kaye. *The Life of Benjamin Spock*

Kaye. *The Life of Daniel Hale Williams*

Kaye. *The Life of Florence Sabin*

Keller. *Margaret Bourke-White: A Photographer's Life*

Keller. *The Story of My Life*

Kent. *Calvin Coolidge: Thirtieth President*

Kittredge. *Barbara McClintock*

Kittredge. *Helen Hayes: Actress*

Kittredge. *Jane Addams*

Kliment. *Billie Holiday: Singer*

Kliment. *Count Basie: Bandleader and Musician*

Kliment. *Ella Fitzgerald: Singer*

Klots. *Ida Wells-Barnett: Civil Rights Leader*

Kozodoy. *Isadora Duncan: Dancer*

Kronstadt. *Florence Sabin: Medical Researcher*

La Farge. *Pearl Buck*

Larsen. *Amelia Earhart: Missing, Declared Dead*

Larsen. *Paul Robeson: Hero Before His Time*

Lauber. *Lost Star: The Story of Amelia Earhart*

Lawler. *Marcus Garvey: Black Nationalist Leader*

Lazo. *Eleanor Roosevelt*

Leavell. *Woodrow Wilson*

Leder. *Amelia Earhart: Opposing Viewpoints*

Liles. *Sam and the Speaker's Chair*

Lindop. *Woodrow Wilson, Franklin D. Roosevelt, Harry S. Truman*

Lipsyte. *Jim Thorpe: Twentieth-Century Jock*

Lipsyte. *Joe Louis: A Champ for All America*

Lynn. *Babe Didrikson Zaharias*

Lyons. *Sorrow's Kitchen: Zora Neale Hurston*

Lyons. *Starting Home: Horace Pippin, Painter*

Macht. *Lou Gehrig*

Mahone-Lonesome. *Charles R. Drew*

Malone. *Will Rogers: Cowboy Philosopher*

Markham. *Helen Keller*

McDonough. *Frank Lloyd Wright*

McPherson. *Peace and Bread: Jane Addams*

McPherson. *TV's Forgotten Hero: Philo Farnsworth*

Mintz. *Thomas Edison: Inventing the Future*

Morey. *Amelia Earhart*

Morris. *The FDR Way*

Murphy. *Frank Lloyd Wright*

Myers. *Malcolm X: By Any Means Necessary*

Nardo. *Franklin D. Roosevelt*

Nardo. *Jim Thorpe*

Nicholson. *Babe Ruth: Sultan of Swat*

Nicholson. *Georgia O'Keeffe*

Nicholson. *Helen Keller: Humanitarian*

O'Connor. *The Soldier's Voice: Ernie Pyle*

Osofsky. *Free to Dream: Langston Hughes*

Palmer. *Lena Horne: Entertainer*

Parker. *Thomas Edison and Electricity*

Patterson. *A. Philip Randolph*
Patterson. *Marian Anderson*
Pfeifer. *Henry O. Flipper*
Polikoff. *Herbert C. Hoover*
Potter. *Buckminster Fuller*
Pratt. *Martha Graham*
Probosz. *Martha Graham*
Randolph. *Amelia Earhart*
Randolph. *Charles Lindbergh*
Randolph. *Woodrow Wilson:
   President*
Ravage. *Rachel Carson,
   Gentle Crusader*
Reef. *John Steinbeck*
Rogers. *George Washington
   Carver*
Rubin. *Frank Lloyd Wright*
Rummel. *Langston Hughes*
Sandak. *The Franklin
   Roosevelts*
Sandak. *The Wilsons*
Schroeder. *Josephine Baker*
Schuman. *Eleanor Roosevelt*
Scott. *Jackie Robinson*
Shapiro. *Charles Drew:
   Founder of the Blood Bank*

Sherrow. *Linus Pauling*
Shore. *Amelia Earhart:
   Aviator*
Sloate. *Amelia Earhart*
Sonneborn. *Will Rogers:
   Cherokee Entertainer*
St. George. *Dear Dr. Bell. . .
   Your Friend, Helen Keller*
Stafford. *W. E. B. Dubois:
   Scholar and Activist*
Stevens. *Calvin Coolidge:
   30th President*
Stine. *The Story of Malcolm
   X, Civil Rights Leader*
Streissguth. *Rocket Man:
   Robert Goddard*
Talmadge. *The Life of
   Charles Drew*
Tanenhaus. *Louis Armstrong:
   Musician*
Tedards. *Marian Anderson:
   Singer*
Tessitore. *The Hunt and the
   Feast: A Life of Ernest
   Hemingway*
Thompson. *Charles Chesnutt*

Thorleifson. *Ethel Barrymore*
Tilton. *Margaret Mead*
Tolbert-Rouchaleau. *James
   Weldon Johnson: Author*
Toor. *Eleanor Roosevelt*
Van Steenwyk. *Ida B.
   Wells-Barnett*
Wade. *Warren G. Harding:
   Twenty-Ninth President*
Waldstreicher. *Emma
   Goldman*
Weidhorn. *Jackie Robinson*
Weisbrot. *Father Divine:
   Religious Leader*
Whitelaw. *Grace Hopper*
Whitelaw. *Margaret Sanger*
Whitelaw. *Mr. Civil Rights:
   The Story of Thurgood
   Marshall*
Witcover. *Zora Neale Hurston*
Woog. *Louis Armstrong*
Wright. *A. Philip Randolph*
Yannuzzi. *Zora Neale
   Hurston: Southern
   Storyteller*
Ziesk. *Margaret Mead*

Collective Biography

Aaseng. *America's
   Third-Party Presidential
   Candidates*
Aaseng. *Close Calls: From
   the Brink of Ruin to
   Business Success*
Aaseng. *From Rags to Riches*
Aaseng. *True Champions*
Aaseng. *You Are the General*
Altman. *Extraordinary Black
   Americans*
Anderson. *Explorers Who
   Found New Worlds*
Beard. *The Presidents in
   American History*
Blassingame. *The Look-It-Up
   Book of Presidents*
Blue. *People of Peace*
Brill. *Extraordinary Young
   People*
Camp. *American
   Astronomers: Searchers
   and Wonderers*
Cush. *Artists Who Created
   Great Works*
Cush. *Women Who Achieved
   Greatness*
Dolan. *Shaping U.S. Foreign
   Policy: Profiles of Twelve
   Secretaries of State*
Faber. *Great Lives: American
   Government*

Fireside. *Is There a Woman in
   the House. . . or Senate?*
Fradin. *We Have Conquered
   Pain: The Discovery of
   Anesthesia*
Glenn. *Discover America's
   Favorite Architects*
Glubok. *Great Lives: Painting*
Haskins. *Against All
   Opposition: Black
   Explorers in America*
Haskins. *Black Eagles:
   African Americans in
   Aviation*
Haskins. *The Harlem
   Renaissance*
Hazell. *Heroines: Great
   Women Through the Ages*
Jacobs. *Great Lives: Human
   Rights*
Katz. *Proudly Red and Black:
   Stories of African and
   Native Americans*
Krull. *Lives of the Artists:
   Masterpieces, Messes*
Krull. *Lives of the Athletes*
Krull. *Lives of the Musicians:
   Good Times, Bad Times*
Krull. *Lives of the Writers:
   Comedies, Tragedies*
Lindop. *Presidents by
   Accident*

Lyons. *Keeping Secrets: The
   Girlhood Diaries of Seven
   Women Writers*
Mayberry. *Business Leaders
   Who Built Financial
   Empires*
Morin. *Women Chosen for
   Public Office*
Morin. *Women of the U.S.
   Congress*
Morin. *Women Who
   Reformed Politics*
Myers. *Now Is Your Time*
Pascoe. *First Facts About the
   Presidents*
Pile. *Top Entrepreneurs and
   Their Businesses*
Plowden. *Famous Firsts of
   Black Women*
Provenson. *My Fellow
   Americans*
Rennert. *Book of Firsts:
   Leaders of America*
Rennert. *Civil Rights Leaders*
Rennert. *Female Writers*
Rennert. *Jazz Stars*
Rennert. *Pioneers of
   Discovery*
Rubel. *The Scholastic
   Encyclopedia of the
   Presidents*
Schraff. *American Heroes of
   Exploration and Flight*

Sheafer. *Women in America's Wars*

Streissguth. *Hatemongers and Demagogues*

Streissguth. *Hoaxers & Hustlers*

Sullivan. *Black Artists in Photography, 1840-1940*

Sullivan. *Presidents at Play*

Vare. *Women Inventors and Their Discoveries*

Veglahn. *Women Scientists*

Weitzman. *Great Lives: Human Culture*

Whitelaw. *They Wrote Their Own Headlines*

Wilkinson. *People Who Changed the World*

Wolf. *Focus: Five Women Photographers*

Yount. *Black Scientists*

Yount. *Women Aviators*

History

Aaseng. *You Are the Senator*

Andryszewski. *The Dust Bowl*

Ashabranner. *A Memorial for Mr. Lincoln*

Bosco. *World War I*

Bowler. *Trains*

Brashler. *The Story of the Negro League Baseball*

Brown. *Conflict in Europe and the Great Depression (1914-1940)*

Calabro. *Zap!: A Brief History of Television*

Carlin. *Jazz*

Carnes. *Us and Them: A History of Intolerance in America*

Clare. *First World War*

Colman. *Strike: The Bitter Struggle of American Workers*

Colman. *Toilets, Bathtubs, Sinks, and Sewers*

Colman. *Women in Society: United States*

Cooper. *Bound for the Promised Land: The Great Black Migration*

Cooper. *Hell Fighters: African American Soldiers in World War I*

Cooper. *Playing America's Game: Negro League Baseball*

Cosner. *War Nurses*

Costantino. *The 1930's*

Cray. *American Datelines*

Davies. *Transport: On Land, Road and Rail*

Dolan. *America in World War I*

Emert. *Top Lawyers and Their Famous Cases*

Farrell. *The Great Depression*

Farris. *The Dust Bowl*

Feinberg. *American Political Scandals Past and Present*

Ferrell. *The U.S. Air Force*

Finkelstein. *Sounds in the Air: The Golden Age of Radio*

Fradin. *Medicine: Yesterday, Today, and Tomorrow*

Gardner. *The Forgotten Players: The Story of Black Baseball in America*

Garfunkel. *On Wings of Joy: The Story of Ballet*

Gay. *World War I*

Giblin. *Be Seated: A Book About Chairs*

Gilbert. *Deadball: Major League Baseball Before Babe Ruth*

Gilbert. *The Soaring Twenties: Babe Ruth and the Home-Run Decade*

Granfield. *In Flanders Fields*

Greene. *Child Labor: Then and Now*

Gutman. *World Series Classics*

Hakim. *An Age of Extremes*

Hakim. *War, Peace, and All That Jazz*

Herald. *The 1920s*

Hill. *Our Century: 1920-1930*

Hintz. *Farewell, John Barleycorn: Prohibition in the United States*

Hirsch. *Taxation: Paying for Government*

Humble. *Ships*

Karl. *America Alive: A History*

Katz. *The New Freedom to the New Deal: 1913-1939*

Kent. *World War I*

Kronenwetter. *Covert Action*

Landau. *Armed America: The Status of Gun Control*

Landau. *The White Power Movement: America's Racist Hate Groups*

Langone. *Spreading Poison: A Book About Racism and Prejudice*

Lawrence. *The Great Migration*

Leiner. *First Children: Growing Up in the White House*

Leuzzi. *Urban Life*

Levi. *Cowboys of the Sky*

Libreatore. *Our Century: 1910-1920*

Macy. *Winning Ways: A Photohistory of American Women in Sports*

Markham. *Inventions That Changed Modern Life*

McKissack. *Black Diamond*

McKissack. *A Long Hard Journey: The Story of the Pullman Porter*

Medearis. *Come This Far to Freedom*

Meltzer. *The Black Americans*

Meltzer. *Brother Can You Spare a Dime?*

Meltzer. *Cheap Raw Material*

Meltzer. *Weapons & Warfare*

Migneco. *The Crash of 1929*

Mizell. *Think About Racism*

Monceaux. *Jazz: My Music, My People*

Morley. *Clothes: For Work, Play and Display*

Mulcahy. *Diseases: Finding the Cure*

Naden. *The U.S. Coast Guard*

Norrell. *We Want Jobs!*

Owen. *Our Century: 1930-1940*

Patrick. *The Young Oxford Companion to the Supreme Court*

Philip. *Singing America: Poems That Define a Nation*

Platt. *The Smithsonian Visual Timeline of Inventions*

Press. *A Multicultural Portrait of Professional Sports*

Rappaport. *American Women: Their Lives in Their Words*

Rappaport. *The Sacco-Vanzetti Trial*

Sagan. *Women's Suffrage*

Sandler. *Presidents*

Schraff. *The Great Depression and the New Deal*

Scott. *Funny Papers: Behind the Scenes of the Comics*

Smith. *New Paths to Power: American Women 1890-1920*

St. George. *The White House: Cornerstone of a Nation*

Stanley. *Big Annie of Calumet*

Stanley. *Children of the Dust Bowl*

Stewart. *World War I*

Sullivan. *Children of Promise: African-American Literature and Art*

Tames. *The 1930s*

Tanaka. *The Disaster of the Hindenburg*

Tessendorf. *Wings Around the World: The American World Flight of 1924*

Time-Life. *African Americans: Voices of Triumph: Leadership*

Time-Life. *This Fabulous Century: 1910-1920*

Time-Life. *This Fabulous Century: 1920-1930*

Time-Life. *This Fabulous Century: 1930-1940*

Uschan. *A Multicultural Portrait of World War I*

Ventura. *Clothing*

Ventura. *Food: Its Evolution Through the Ages*

Wakin. *Photos That Made U.S. History: Civil War to the Atomic Age*

Walker. *Hand, Heart, and Mind*

Walter. *Mississippi Challenge*

Warner. *The U.S. Marine Corps*

Warren. *Orphan Train Rider: One Boy's True Story*

Wheeler. *Events That Changed American History*

Whitman. *Get Up and Go: American Road Travel*

Whitman. *This Land Is Your Land*

Whitman. *V Is for Victory*

Wormser. *Hoboes: Wandering in America 1870-1940*

Yepsen. *City Trains: America's Cities by Rail*

Multimedia

CD-ROM

Air and Space Smithsonian Dreams of Flight

Campaigns, Candidates and the Presidency

Daring to Fly!

Eyewitness Encyclopedia of Science

Her Heritage: A Biographical Encyclopedia of American History

History Through Art: 20th Century

Landmark Documents in American History

Portraits of American Presidents

Science Navigator

SkyTrip America

Time Almanac of the 20th Century

Total History

Voices of the 30s

The Way Things Work

Video

African Americans

Alice Paul: We Were Arrested of Course!

Amelia Earhart

American Consumerism (1890-1930)

Barnum's Big Top

Black Is My Color: The African American Experience

Daring to Dream

Elijah Muhammad

Equality: A History of the Women's Movement in America

The Era of Segregation: A Personal Perspective

Frank Lloyd Wright: An American Original

Franklin D. Roosevelt

Frontier Buildings

George Washington Carver

George Washington Carver: A Man of Vision

Great Black Innovators

Great Black Women

The Great Depression and the New Deal

Helen Keller

A History of the Civil Rights Movement

In Times Past: Radio Days

Jackie Robinson

Jane Addams

Jesse Owens

Langston Hughes

Lighthouses of New England

Making It Happen: Masters of Invention

Malcolm X

Marcus Garvey

Marian Anderson

Mary McLeod Bethune

Matthew Henson

Michigan Avenue: From Museums to the Magnificent Mile

Mt. Clare: Cradle of the American Dream

Organizing America: The History of Trade Unions

Pride & Prejudice: A History of Black Culture in America

Public Sculpture: America's Legacy

The Real Stories of Al Capone, John Dillinger, Bonnie and Clyde

Riding the Rails

The Sky's the Limit

Sojourner Truth

The Southwest of Georgia O'Keeffe

This House of Power: The Church in African-American Experience

Thomas Alva Edison

Thomas Edison: Electric Light

Thurgood Marshall

Tragedy to Triumph: An Adventure with Helen Keller

Traveling in Style: Automobiles and Trolleys

Traveling in Style: Trains, Riverboats, and Planes

Tsiolkovski: The Space Age

W. E. B. DuBois

Women in Rural America

Women with Wings

World War I

GRADE EIGHT

Historical Fiction

Armstrong. *Sounder*
Armstrong. *Steal Away*
Avi. *Shadrach's Crossing*
Beatty. *Billy Bedamned, Long Gone By*
Buechner. *The Wizard's Tide: A Story*
Collier. *The Jazz Kid*
Corbin. *Me and the End of the World*
Crew. *Fire on the Wind*
Cuneo. *Anne Is Elegant*
Ducey. *The Bittersweet Time*
Ferry. *One More Time!*
Fowler. *The Last Innocent Summer*

Froelich. *Reasons to Stay*
Hesse. *A Time of Angels*
Hooks. *Circle of Fire*
Karr. *In the Kaiser's Clutch*
Mazer. *Cave Under the City*
Meyer. *White Lilacs*
Mills. *What About Annie?*
Myers. *Fire in the Hills*
Myers. *The Glory Field*
Myers. *Red-Dirt Jessie*
Myers. *Spotting the Leopard*
Pendergraft. *As Far as Mill Springs*
Ross. *The Dancing Tree*
Sebestyen. *Far from Home*

Skurzynski. *Good-bye, Billy Radish*
Snyder. *Cat Running*
Taylor. *Let the Circle Be Unbroken*
Taylor. *Roll of Thunder, Hear My Cry*
Thesman. *The Ornament Tree*
Thesman. *Rachel Chance*
Van Raven. *A Time of Troubles*
Whittaker. *Angels of the Swamp*
Yep. *The Star Fisher*

Biography

Adair. *George Washington Carver: Botanist*
Adair. *Thomas Alva Edison: Inventing the Electric Age*
Adler. *Our Golda: The Story of Golda Meir*
Aldred. *Thurgood Marshall: Supreme Court Justice*
Anderson. *Aldo Leopold: American Ecologist*
Anderson. *Thomas Edison*
Andryszewski. *The Amazing Life of Moe Berg*
Appel. *Joe Dimaggio*
Ayer. *Lewis Latimer: Creating Bright Ideas*
Bachrach. *Margaret Sanger*
Barr. *Malcolm X*
Berke. *Babe Ruth*
Bernotas. *Jim Thorpe: Sac and Fox Athlete*
Berry. *Georgia O'Keeffe: Painter*
Berry. *Gordon Parks*
Berry. *Langston Hughes*
Boulton. *Frank Lloyd Wright: Architect: An Illustrated Biography*
Brown. *Malcolm X: His Life and Legacy*
Butts. *May Chinn: The Best Medicine*
Cain. *Louise Nevelson: Sculptor*
Canadeo. *Warren G. Harding*
Casey. *William H. Taft: Twenty-Seventh President*
Castiglia. *Margaret Mead*

Chadwick. *Amelia Earhart: Aviation Pioneer*
Chadwick. *Anne Morrow Lindbergh: Pilot and Poet*
Clinton. *Herbert Hoover: Thirty-First President*
Collier. *Duke Ellington*
Collier. *Louis Armstrong: An American Success Story*
Collins. *Woodrow Wilson: 28th President*
Daffron. *Margaret Bourke-White: Photographer*
Dallard. *Ella Baker: A Leader Behind the Scenes*
Darby. *Douglas MacArthur*
Darby. *Dwight D. Eisenhower*
Davies. *Malcolm X*
Davis. *Frank Lloyd Wright: Maverick Architect*
Denenberg. *An American Hero: The True Story of Charles A. Lindbergh*
Denenberg. *The True Story of J. Edgar Hoover*
Devane. *Franklin Delano Roosevelt: President*
Dominy. *Katherine Dunham: Dancer and Choreographer*
Driemen. *Atomic Dawn: A Biography of Robert Oppenheimer*
Driemen. *Clarence Darrow*
Erlich. *Paul Robeson: Singer and Actor*
Falkof. *William H. Taft*
Farley. *Robert H. Goddard*

Frankl. *Charlie Parker: Musician*
Fraser. *Walter White: Civil Rights Leader*
Frazier. *William Randolph Hearst: Press Baron*
Freedman. *Eleanor Roosevelt: A Life of Discovery*
Freedman. *Franklin Delano Roosevelt*
Freedman. *Louis Brandeis: The People's Justice*
Garfunkel. *Letter to the World: The Life and Dances of Martha Graham*
Gay. *Emma Goldman*
Gentry. *Jesse Owens: Champion Athlete*
Gourse. *Dizzy Gillespie and the Birth of Bebop*
Gray. *George Washington Carver*
Greenblatt. *Franklin D. Roosevelt*
Greene. *Thomas Alva Edison: Bringer of Light*
Halasa. *Elijah Muhammad: Religious Leader*
Halasa. *Mary McLeod Bethune: Educator*
Hanley. *Philip Randolph*
Haskins. *Thurgood Marshall: A Life for Justice*
Haynes. *Ida B. Wells*
Herda. *Thurgood Marshall: Civil Rights Champion*

Israel. *Franklin Delano Roosevelt*

Ito. *John Steinbeck*

Jakoubek. *Joe Louis: Heavyweight Champion*

James. *Julia Morgan: Architect*

Kallen. *Thurgood Marshall: A Dream of Justice for All*

Kaye. *The Life of Daniel Hale Williams*

Keller. *Margaret Bourke-White: A Photographer's Life*

Keller. *The Story of My Life*

Kent. *Calvin Coolidge: Thirtieth President*

Kittredge. *Barbara McClintock*

Kittredge. *Helen Hayes: Actress*

Kliment. *Billie Holiday: Singer*

Kliment. *Count Basie: Bandleader and Musician*

Kliment. *Ella Fitzgerald: Singer*

Klots. *Ida Wells-Barnett: Civil Rights Leader*

Kozodoy. *Isadora Duncan: Dancer*

Kronstadt. *Florence Sabin: Medical Researcher*

La Farge. *Pearl Buck*

Larsen. *Amelia Earhart: Missing, Declared Dead*

Larsen. *Franklin D. Roosevelt*

Larsen. *Paul Robeson: Hero Before His Time*

Lauber. *Lost Star: The Story of Amelia Earhart*

Lawler. *Marcus Garvey: Black Nationalist Leader*

Lazo. *Eleanor Roosevelt*

Leavell. *Woodrow Wilson*

Leder. *Amelia Earhart: Opposing Viewpoints*

Liles. *Sam and the Speaker's Chair*

Lindop. *Woodrow Wilson, Franklin D. Roosevelt, Harry S. Truman*

Lipsyte. *Joe Louis: A Champ for All America*

Lynn. *Babe Didrikson Zaharias*

Lyons. *Sorrow's Kitchen: Zora Neale Hurston*

Macht. *Lou Gehrig*

Mahone-Lonesome. *Charles R. Drew*

Malone. *Will Rogers: Cowboy Philosopher*

Markham. *Helen Keller*

McDonough. *Frank Lloyd Wright*

Mintz. *Thomas Edison: Inventing the Future*

Morey. *Amelia Earhart*

Morris. *The FDR Way*

Murphy. *Frank Lloyd Wright*

Myers. *Malcolm X: By Any Means Necessary*

Nardo. *Franklin D. Roosevelt*

Nardo. *Jim Thorpe*

Nicholson. *Babe Ruth: Sultan of Swat*

Nicholson. *Georgia O'Keeffe*

Nicholson. *Helen Keller: Humanitarian*

Osofsky. *Free to Dream: Langston Hughes*

Palmer. *Lena Horne: Entertainer*

Parker. *Thomas Edison and Electricity*

Patterson. *A. Philip Randolph*

Patterson. *Marian Anderson*

Polikoff. *Herbert C. Hoover*

Potter. *Buckminster Fuller*

Pratt. *Martha Graham*

Probosz. *Martha Graham*

Randolph. *Amelia Earhart*

Randolph. *Charles Lindbergh*

Randolph. *Woodrow Wilson: President*

Ravage. *Rachel Carson, Gentle Crusader*

Reef. *John Steinbeck*

Rubin. *Frank Lloyd Wright*

Rummel. *Langston Hughes*

St. George. *Dear Dr. Bell. . . Your Friend, Helen Keller*

Sandak. *The Franklin Roosevelts*

Sandak. *The Wilsons*

Schroeder. *Josephine Baker*

Schuman. *Eleanor Roosevelt*

Scott. *Jackie Robinson*

Shapiro. *Charles Drew: Founder of the Blood Bank*

Sherrow. *Linus Pauling*

Shore. *Amelia Earhart: Aviator*

Sloate. *Amelia Earhart*

Sonneborn. *Will Rogers: Cherokee Entertainer*

St. George. *Dear Dr. Bell. . . Your Friend, Helen Keller*

Stafford. *W. E. B. Dubois: Scholar and Activist*

Stevens. *Calvin Coolidge: 30th President*

Talmadge. *The Life of Charles Drew*

Tanenhaus. *Louis Armstrong: Musician*

Tedards. *Marian Anderson: Singer*

Tessitore. *The Hunt and the Feast: A Life of Ernest Hemingway*

Thompson. *Charles Chesnutt*

Thorleifson. *Ethel Barrymore*

Tilton. *Margaret Mead*

Tolbert-Rouchaleau. *James Weldon Johnson: Author*

Toor. *Eleanor Roosevelt*

Van Steenwyk. *Ida B. Wells-Barnett*

Wade. *Warren G. Harding: Twenty-Ninth President*

Waldstreicher. *Emma Goldman*

Weidhorn. *Jackie Robinson*

Weisbrot. *Father Divine: Religious Leader*

Whitelaw. *Grace Hopper*

Whitelaw. *Margaret Sanger*

Whitelaw. *Mr. Civil Rights: The Story of Thurgood Marshall*

Witcover. *Zora Neale Hurston*

Woog. *Louis Armstrong*

Wright. *A. Philip Randolph*

Yannuzzi. *Zora Neale Hurston: Southern Storyteller*

Ziesk. *Margaret Mead*

Collective Biography

Aaseng. *America's Third-Party Presidential Candidates*

Aaseng. *Close Calls: From the Brink of Ruin to Business Success*

Aaseng. *Great Justices of the Supreme Court*

Aaseng. *True Champions*

Aaseng. *Twentieth-Century Inventors*

Aaseng. *You Are the General*

Aaseng. *You Are the President*

Altman. *Extraordinary Black Americans*

Anderson. *Explorers Who Found New Worlds*

Beard. *The Presidents in American History*

Blassingame. *The Look-It-Up Book of Presidents*

Blue. *People of Peace*

Brill. *Extraordinary Young People*

Camp. *American Astronomers: Searchers and Wonderers*

Cush. *Artists Who Created Great Works*

Cush. *Women Who Achieved Greatness*

Dolan. *Shaping U.S. Foreign Policy: Profiles of Twelve Secretaries of State*

Faber. *Great Lives: American Government*

Fireside. *Is There a Woman in the House. . . or Senate?*

Fradin. *We Have Conquered Pain: The Discovery of Anesthesia*

Glenn. *Discover America's Favorite Architects*

Glubok. *Great Lives: Painting*

Haskins. *Against All Opposition: Black Explorers in America*

Haskins. *Black Eagles: African Americans in Aviation*

Haskins. *The Harlem Renaissance*

Hazell. *Heroines: Great Women Through the Ages*

Jones. *Big Star Fallin' Mama*

Katz. *The New Freedom to the New Deal: 1913-1939*

Krull. *Lives of the Artists: Masterpieces, Messes*

Krull. *Lives of the Musicians: Good Times, Bad Times*

Krull. *Lives of the Writers: Comedies, Tragedies*

Lindop. *Presidents by Accident*

Lyons. *Keeping Secrets: The Girlhood Diaries of Seven Women Writers*

Mayberry. *Business Leaders Who Built Financial Empires*

Mayberry. *Leaders Who Changed the 20th Century*

Morin. *Women Chosen for Public Office*

Morin. *Women Who Reformed Politics*

Myers. *Now Is Your Time*

Otfinoski. *Great Black Writers*

Otfinoski. *Nineteenth-Century Writers*

Pascoe. *First Facts About the Presidents*

Plowden. *Famous Firsts of Black Women*

Provenson. *My Fellow Americans*

Rennert. *Book of Firsts: Leaders of America*

Rennert. *Civil Rights Leaders*

Rennert. *Female Writers*

Rennert. *Jazz Stars*

Rennert. *Pioneers of Discovery*

Rubel. *The Scholastic Encyclopedia of the Presidents*

Schraff. *American Heroes of Exploration and Flight*

Sheafer. *Women in America's Wars*

Streissguth. *Hatemongers and Demagogues*

Streissguth. *Hoaxers & Hustlers*

Sullivan. *Black Artists in Photography, 1840-1940*

Sullivan. *Presidents at Play*

Veglahn. *Women Scientists*

Weitzman. *Great Lives: Human Culture*

Whitelaw. *They Wrote Their Own Headlines*

Wilkinson. *People Who Changed the World*

Wolf. *Focus: Five Women Photographers*

Yount. *Black Scientists*

Yount. *Women Aviators*

History

Aaseng. *You Are the Senator*

Ashabranner. *A Memorial for Mr. Lincoln*

Bosco. *World War I*

Brashler. *The Story of the Negro League Baseball*

Brown. *Conflict in Europe and the Great Depression (1914-1940)*

Calabro. *Zap!: A Brief History of Television*

Carlin. *Jazz*

Carnes. *Us and Them: A History of Intolerance in America*

Clare. *First World War*

Colman. *Strike: The Bitter Struggle of American Workers*

Colman. *Toilets, Bathtubs, Sinks, and Sewers*

Colman. *Women in Society: United States*

Cooper. *Bound for the Promised Land: The Great Black Migration*

Cooper. *Hell Fighters: African American Soldiers in World War I*

Cooper. *Playing America's Game: Negro League Baseball*

Cosner. *War Nurses*

Costantino. *The 1930's*

Cray. *American Datelines*

Davies. *Transport: On Land, Road and Rail*

Dolan. *America in World War I*

Emert. *Top Lawyers and Their Famous Cases*

Farrell. *The Great Depression*

Feinberg. *American Political Scandals Past and Present*

Ferrell. *The U.S. Air Force*

Finkelstein. *Sounds in the Air: The Golden Age of Radio*

Fradin. *Medicine: Yesterday, Today, and Tomorrow*

Gardner. *The Forgotten Players: The Story of Black Baseball in America*

Garfunkel. *On Wings of Joy: The Story of Ballet*

Gay. *World War I*

Giblin. *Be Seated: A Book About Chairs*

Gilbert. *Deadball: Major League Baseball Before Babe Ruth*

Gilbert. *The Soaring Twenties: Babe Ruth and the Home-Run Decade*

Granfield. *In Flanders Fields*

Greene. *Child Labor: Then and Now*

Gutman. *World Series Classics*

Hakim. *An Age of Extremes*

Hakim. *War, Peace, and All That Jazz*

Herald. *The 1920s*

Hill. *Our Century: 1920-1930*

Hintz. *Farewell, John Barleycorn: Prohibition in the United States*

Hirsch. *Taxation: Paying for Government*

Jantzen. *Hooray for Peace, Hurrah for War: The US During World War I*

Karl. *America Alive: A History*

Katz. *The New Freedom to the New Deal: 1913-1939*

Kent. *World War I*

Kronenwetter. *Covert Action*

Kronenwetter. *United They Hate: White Supremacist Groups in America*

Landau. *Armed America: The Status of Gun Control*

Landau. *The White Power Movement: America's Racist Hate Groups*

Langone. *Spreading Poison: A Book About Racism and Prejudice*

Lawson. *Famous Presidential Scandals*

Leiner. *First Children: Growing Up in the White House*

Leuzzi. *Urban Life*

Levi. *Cowboys of the Sky*

Libreatore. *Our Century: 1910-1920*

Macy. *Winning Ways: A Photohistory of American Women in Sports*

Markham. *Inventions That Changed Modern Life*

McKissack. *Black Diamond*

McKissack. *A Long Hard Journey: The Story of the Pullman Porter*

Medearis. *Come This Far to Freedom*

Meltzer. *The Black Americans*

Meltzer. *Brother Can You Spare A Dime?*

Meltzer. *Cheap Raw Material*

Meltzer. *Weapons & Warfare*

Mizell. *Think About Racism*

Monceaux. *Jazz: My Music, My People*

Morley. *Clothes: For Work, Play and Display*

Mulcahy. *Diseases: Finding the Cure*

Naden. *The U.S. Coast Guard*

Norrell. *We Want Jobs!*

Owen. *Our Century: 1930-1940*

Patrick. *The Young Oxford Companion to the Supreme Court*

Philip. *Singing America: Poems That Define a Nation*

Platt. *The Smithsonian Visual Timeline of Inventions*

Press. *A Multicultural Portrait of Professional Sports*

Rappaport. *American Women: Their Lives in Their Words*

Rappaport. *The Sacco-Vanzetti Trial*

Sagan. *Women's Suffrage*

Sandler. *Presidents*

Schraff. *The Great Depression and the New Deal*

Scott. *Funny Papers: Behind the Scenes of the Comics*

Senna. *The Black Press and the Struggle of Civil Rights*

Smith. *New Paths to Power: American Women 1890-1920*

St. George. *The White House: Cornerstone of a Nation*

Stanley. *Big Annie of Calumet*

Stanley. *Children of the Dust Bowl*

Stanley. *Women in the Military*

Stewart. *World War I*

Sullivan. *Children of Promise: African-American Literature and Art*

Tames. *The 1930s*

Tanaka. *The Disaster of the Hindenburg*

Tessendorf. *Wings Around the World: The American World Flight of 1924*

Time-Life. *African Americans: Voices of Triumph: Leadership*

Time-Life. *This Fabulous Century: 1910-1920*

Time-Life. *This Fabulous Century: 1920-1930*

Time-Life. *This Fabulous Century: 1930-1940*

Uschan. *A Multicultural Portrait of World War I*

Ventura. *Clothing*

Ventura. *Food: Its Evolution Through the Ages*

Wakin. *Photos That Made U.S. History: Civil War to the Atomic Age*

Walker. *Hand, Heart, and Mind*

Walter. *Mississippi Challenge*

Warner. *The U.S. Marine Corps*

Wekesser. *The Death Penalty: Opposing Viewpoints*

Wheeler. *Events That Changed American History*

Whitman. *Get Up and Go: American Road Travel*

Whitman. *This Land Is Your Land*

Whitman. *V Is for Victory*

Wormser. *Hoboes: Wandering in America 1870-1940*

Yepsen. *City Trains: America's Cities by Rail*

Multimedia

CD-ROM

Air and Space Smithsonian Dreams of Flight

Campaigns, Candidates and the Presidency

Daring to Fly!

Eyewitness Encyclopedia of Science

Famous American Speeches: 1850 to the Present

Her Heritage: A Biographical Encyclopedia of American History

History Through Art: 20th Century

Landmark Documents in American History

Portraits of American Presidents

Science Navigator

SkyTrip America

Time Almanac of the 20th Century

Total History

Voices of the 30s

The Way Things Work

Video

African Americans
Alice Paul: We Were Arrested
of Course!
Amelia Earhart
American Consumerism
(1890-1930)
Arsenal of Democracy
Barnum's Big Top
Black Is My Color: The
African American
Experience
Daring to Dream
Elijah Muhammad
Equality: A History of the
Women's Movement in
America
The Era of Segregation: A
Personal Perspective
Frank Lloyd Wright: An
American Original
Franklin D. Roosevelt
Frontier Buildings
George Washington Carver
George Washington Carver:
A Man of Vision
Great Black Innovators
Great Black Women
The Great Depression and the
New Deal
Helen Keller

A History of the Civil Rights
Movement
In Times Past: Radio Days
Jackie Robinson
Jane Addams
Jesse Owens
A Job at Ford's
Langston Hughes
Lighthouses of New England
Making It Happen: Masters
of Invention
Malcolm X
Marcus Garvey
Marian Anderson
Mary McLeod Bethune
Matthew Henson
Mean Things Happening
Michigan Avenue: From
Museums to the
Magnificent Mile
Mt. Clare: Cradle of the
American Dream
New Deal, New York
1914-1918: World War I
Organizing America: The
History of Trade Unions
Pride & Prejudice: A History
of Black Culture in America
Public Sculpture: America's
Legacy

The Real Stories of Al
Capone, John Dillinger,
Bonnie and Clyde
Riding the Rails
The Sky's the Limit
Sojourner Truth
The Southwest of Georgia
O'Keeffe
This House of Power: The
Church in
African-American
Experience
Thomas Alva Edison
Thomas Edison: Electric Light
Thurgood Marshall
To Be Somebody
Tragedy to Triumph: An
Adventure with Helen
Keller
Traveling in Style:
Automobiles and Trolleys
Traveling in Style: Trains,
Riverboats, and Planes
Tsiolkovski: The Space Age
W. E. B. DuBois
Women in Rural America
Women with Wings
World War I

GRADE NINE

Historical Fiction

Armstrong. *Sounder*
Armstrong. *Steal Away*
Avi. *Shadrach's Crossing*
Buechner. *The Wizard's Tide:
A Story*
Collier. *The Jazz Kid*
Corbin. *Me and the End of
the World*
Crew. *Fire on the Wind*
Ferry. *One More Time!*
Fowler. *The Last Innocent
Summer*

Froelich. *Reasons to Stay*
Hooks. *Circle of Fire*
Meyer. *White Lilacs*
Mills. *What About Annie?*
Myers. *Fire in the Hills*
Myers. *The Glory Field*
Myers. *Red-Dirt Jessie*
Pendergraft. *As Far as Mill
Springs*
Ross. *The Dancing Tree*
Sebestyen. *Far from Home*

Skurzynski. *Good-bye, Billy
Radish*
Taylor. *Let the Circle Be
Unbroken*
Taylor. *Roll of Thunder, Hear
My Cry*
Thesman. *Rachel Chance*
Van Raven. *A Time of
Troubles*
Yep. *The Star Fisher*

Biography

Adair. *George Washington
Carver: Botanist*
Adair. *Thomas Alva Edison:
Inventing the Electric Age*
Aldred. *Thurgood Marshall:
Supreme Court Justice*
Anderson. *Aldo Leopold:
American Ecologist*
Anderson. *Thomas Edison*

Appel. *Joe Dimaggio*
Bachrach. *Margaret Sanger*
Barr. *Malcolm X*
Berke. *Babe Ruth*
Berry. *Georgia O'Keeffe:
Painter*
Berry. *Gordon Parks*
Berry. *Langston Hughes*

Bober. *A Restless Spirit:
Robert Frost*
Boulton. *Frank Lloyd Wright:
Architect: An Illustrated
Biography*
Brown. *Louis Armstrong:
Swinging, Singing Satchmo*
Brown. *Malcolm X: His Life
and Legacy*

Cain. *Louise Nevelson: Sculptor*

Casey. *William H. Taft: Twenty-Seventh President*

Castiglia. *Margaret Mead*

Chadwick. *Amelia Earhart: Aviation Pioneer*

Chadwick. *Anne Morrow Lindbergh: Pilot and Poet*

Chalberg. *Emma Goldman: American Individualist*

Clinton. *Herbert Hoover: Thirty-First President*

Coil. *Robert Hutchings Goddard*

Collier. *Duke Ellington*

Collier. *Louis Armstrong: An American Success Story*

Collins. *Woodrow Wilson: 28th President*

Daffron. *Margaret Bourke-White: Photographer*

Dallard. *Ella Baker: A Leader Behind the Scenes*

Darby. *Douglas MacArthur*

Darby. *Dwight D. Eisenhower*

Davies. *Malcolm X*

Davis. *Frank Lloyd Wright: Maverick Architect*

Denenberg. *An American Hero: The True Story of Charles A. Lindbergh*

Denenberg. *The True Story of J. Edgar Hoover*

Devane. *Franklin Delano Roosevelt: President*

Dominy. *Katherine Dunham: Dancer and Choreographer*

Driemen. *Clarence Darrow*

Erlich. *Paul Robeson: Singer and Actor*

Falkof. *William H. Taft*

Farley. *Robert H. Goddard*

Frankl. *Charlie Parker: Musician*

Fraser. *Walter White: Civil Rights Leader*

Frazier. *William Randolph Hearst: Press Baron*

Freedman. *Eleanor Roosevelt: A Life of Discovery*

Garfunkel. *Letter to the World: The Life and Dances of Martha Graham*

Gay. *Emma Goldman*

Gentry. *Jesse Owens: Champion Athlete*

Gish. *An Actor's Life for Me!*

Gourse. *Dizzy Gillespie and the Birth of Bebop*

Graham. *Franklin D. Roosevelt*

Gray. *George Washington Carver*

Greenberg. *Hank Greenberg: The Story of My Life*

Greenblatt. *Franklin D. Roosevelt*

Halasa. *Elijah Muhammad: Religious Leader*

Halasa. *Mary McLeod Bethune: Educator*

Hanley. *Philip Randolph*

Haskins. *Thurgood Marshall: A Life for Justice*

Haynes. *Ida B. Wells*

Herda. *Earl Warren: Chief Justice for Social Change*

Herda. *Thurgood Marshall: Civil Rights Champion*

Israel. *Franklin Delano Roosevelt*

Ito. *John Steinbeck*

Jakoubek. *Joe Louis: Heavyweight Champion*

James. *Julia Morgan: Architect*

Kallen. *Thurgood Marshall: A Dream of Justice for All*

Kaye. *The Life of Daniel Hale Williams*

Keller. *Margaret Bourke-White: A Photographer's Life*

Keller. *The Story of My Life*

Kent. *Calvin Coolidge: Thirtieth President*

Kittredge. *Barbara McClintock*

Kittredge. *Helen Hayes: Actress*

Kliment. *Billie Holiday: Singer*

Kliment. *Count Basie: Bandleader and Musician*

Kliment. *Ella Fitzgerald: Singer*

Klots. *Ida Wells-Barnett: Civil Rights Leader*

Kozodoy. *Isadora Duncan: Dancer*

Kronstadt. *Florence Sabin: Medical Researcher*

La Farge. *Pearl Buck*

Larsen. *Franklin D. Roosevelt*

Larsen. *Paul Robeson: Hero Before His Time*

Lawler. *Marcus Garvey: Black Nationalist Leader*

Leavell. *Woodrow Wilson*

Leder. *Amelia Earhart: Opposing Viewpoints*

Liles. *Sam and the Speaker's Chair*

Lipsyte. *Joe Louis: A Champ for All America*

Lynn. *Babe Didrikson Zaharias*

Lyons. *Sorrow's Kitchen: Zora Neale Hurston*

Macht. *Lou Gehrig*

Mack-Williams. *Malcom X*

Mahone-Lonesome. *Charles R. Drew*

Malone. *Will Rogers: Cowboy Philosopher*

McDonough. *Frank Lloyd Wright*

McKissack. *W. E. B. DuBois*

Morey. *Amelia Earhart*

Morris. *The FDR Way*

Murphy. *Frank Lloyd Wright*

Myers. *Malcolm X: By Any Means Necessary*

Nardo. *Franklin D. Roosevelt*

Nardo. *Jim Thorpe*

Nicholson. *Babe Ruth: Sultan of Swat*

Nicholson. *Georgia O'Keeffe*

Nicholson. *Helen Keller: Humanitarian*

Osofsky. *Free to Dream: Langston Hughes*

Palmer. *Lena Horne: Entertainer*

Patterson. *A. Philip Randolph*

Patterson. *Marian Anderson*

Polikoff. *Herbert C. Hoover*

Potter. *Buckminster Fuller*

Pratt. *Martha Graham*

Probosz. *Martha Graham*

Randolph. *Charles Lindbergh*

Randolph. *Woodrow Wilson: President*

Reef. *John Steinbeck*

Rubin. *Frank Lloyd Wright*

Rummel. *Langston Hughes*

Schroeder. *Josephine Baker*

Schuman. *Eleanor Roosevelt*

Scott. *Jackie Robinson*

Sonneborn. *Will Rogers: Cherokee Entertainer*

St. George. *Dear Dr. Bell. . . Your Friend, Helen Keller*

Stevens. *Calvin Coolidge: 30th President*

Sullivan. *Black Artists in Photography, 1840-1940*

Tanenhaus. *Louis Armstrong: Musician*

Tedards. *Marian Anderson: Singer*

Tessitore. *The Hunt and the Feast : A Life of Ernest Hemingway*

Thompson. *Charles Chesnutt*

Thorleifson. *Ethel Barrymore*

Tilton. *Margaret Mead*

Tolbert-Rouchaleau. *James Weldon Johnson: Author*

Toor. *Eleanor Roosevelt*

Van Steenwyk. *Ida B. Wells-Barnett*

Wade. *Warren G. Harding: Twenty-Ninth President*

Waldstreicher. *Emma Goldman*

Weidhorn. *Jackie Robinson*

Weisbrot. *Father Divine: Religious Leader*

Whitelaw. *Margaret Sanger*

Whitelaw. *Mr. Civil Rights: The Story of Thurgood Marshall*

Witcover. *Zora Neale Hurston*

Woog. *Louis Armstrong*

Worth. *Edith Wharton*

Wright. *A. Philip Randolph*

Yannuzzi. *Zora Neale Hurston: Southern Storyteller*

Ziesk. *Margaret Mead*

Collective Biography

Aaseng. *America's Third-Party Presidential Candidates*

Aaseng. *Close Calls: From the Brink of Ruin to Business Success*

Aaseng. *Great Justices of the Supreme Court*

Aaseng. *True Champions*

Aaseng. *Twentieth-Century Inventors*

Aaseng. *You Are the General*

Aaseng. *You Are the President*

Anderson. *Explorers Who Found New Worlds*

Anthony. *First Ladies: 1789-1961*

Beard. *The Presidents in American History*

Blassingame. *The Look-It-Up Book of Presidents*

Brill. *Extraordinary Young People*

Camp. *American Astronomers: Searchers and Wonderers*

Cush. *Artists Who Created Great Works*

Cush. *Women Who Achieved Greatness*

Dolan. *Shaping U.S. Foreign Policy: Twelve Secretaries of State*

Faber. *Great Lives: American Government*

Fradin. *We Have Conquered Pain: The Discovery of Anesthesia*

Glenn. *Discover America's Favorite Architects*

Glubok. *Great Lives: Painting*

Haskins. *Against All Opposition: Black Explorers in America*

Jones. *Big Star Fallin' Mama*

Landrum. *Profiles of Female Genius: Thirteen Creative Women*

Landrum. *Profiles of Genius: Thirteen Creative Men*

Lindop. *Presidents by Accident*

Lomask. *Great Lives: Exploration*

Lyons. *Keeping Secrets: The Girlhood Diaries of Seven Women Writers*

Mahoney. *Women in Espionage: A Biographical Dictionary*

Mayberry. *Leaders Who Changed the 20th Century*

Morin. *Women Chosen for Public Office*

Morin. *Women Who Reformed Politics*

Myers. *Now Is Your Time*

O'Brien. *American Political Leaders*

Otfinoski. *Great Black Writers*

Otfinoski. *Nineteenth-Century Writers*

Plowden. *Famous Firsts of Black Women*

Rennert. *Book of Firsts: Leaders of America*

Rennert. *Civil Rights Leaders*

Rennert. *Female Writers*

Rennert. *Pioneers of Discovery*

Schraff. *American Heroes of Exploration and Flight*

Sheafer. *Women in America's Wars*

Streissguth. *Hatemongers and Demagogues*

Streissguth. *Hoaxers & Hustlers*

Sullivan. *Presidents at Play*

Veglahn. *Women Scientists*

Weitzman. *Great Lives: Human Culture*

Weitzman. *Great Lives: Theater*

Whitelaw. *They Wrote Their Own Headlines*

Wilkinson. *People Who Changed the World*

Wolf. *Focus: Five Women Photographers*

Yount. *Black Scientists*

Yount. *Women Aviators*

History

Aaseng. *You Are the Senator*

Alderman. *In Our Defense: The Bill of Rights in Action*

Ardley. *Music: An Illustrated Encyclopedia*

Ashabranner. *A Memorial for Mr. Lincoln*

Awmiller. *This House on Fire: The Story of the Blues*

Aymar. *Men in the Air: The Best Flight Stories of All Time*

Basinger. *American Cinema: One Hundred Years of Filmmaking*

Bosco. *World War I*

Brashler. *The Story of the Negro League Baseball*

Brown. *Conflict in Europe and the Great Depression (1914-1940)*

Calabro. *Zap!: A Brief History of Television*

Carlin. *Jazz*

Carnes. *Us and Them: A History of Intolerance in America*

Cohen. *America: Then and Now*

Collier. *Jazz, the American Theme Song*
Colman. *Women in Society: United States*
Cooper. *Bound for the Promised Land: The Great Black Migration*
Cooper. *Hell Fighters: African American Soldiers in World War I*
Cosner. *War Nurses*
Costantino. *The 1930's*
Cray. *American Datelines*
Dale. *Early Cars*
Davis. *Don't Know Much About History*
Davis. *Man-Made Catastrophes*
Deutsch. *From Ballots to Breadlines: American Women 1920-1940*
Dolan. *America in World War I*
Emert. *Top Lawyers and Their Famous Cases*
Ewing. *Women in Uniform Through the Centuries*
Farrell. *The Great Depression*
Feinberg. *American Political Scandals Past and Present*
Finkelstein. *Sounds in the Air: The Golden Age of Radio*
Fradin. *Medicine: Yesterday, Today, and Tomorrow*
Frost. *The Mexican Revolution*
Frost-Knappman. *Women's Suffrage in America*
Garfunkel. *On Wings of Joy: The Story of Ballet*
Garza. *Barred from the Bar: A History of Women and the Legal Profession*
Gay. *World War I*
Gilbert. *Deadball: Major League Baseball Before Babe Ruth*
Gilbert. *The Soaring Twenties: Babe Ruth and the Home-Run Decade*
Granfield. *In Flanders Fields*
Greene. *Child Labor: Then and Now*
Hakim. *An Age of Extremes*
Hakim. *War, Peace, and All That Jazz*
Haskins. *Black Music in America*
Herald. *The 1920s*
Hill. *Our Century: 1920-1930*

Hintz. *Farewell, John Barleycorn: Prohibition in the United States*
Hirsch. *Taxation: Paying for Government*
Jantzen. *Hooray for Peace, Hurrah for War: The US During World War I*
Katz. *The New Freedom to the New Deal: 1913-1939*
Kent. *World War I*
Kirchberger. *The First World War*
Knappman. *Great American Trials*
Kronenwetter. *Covert Action*
Kronenwetter. *United They Hate: White Supremacist Groups in America*
Lackmann. *Same Time. . . Same Station: An A-Z Guide to Radio*
Landau. *Armed America: The Status of Gun Control*
Landau. *The White Power Movement: America's Racist Hate Groups*
Langone. *Spreading Poison: A Book About Racism and Prejudice*
Lawson. *Famous Presidential Scandals*
Leiner. *First Children: Growing Up in the White House*
Leuzzi. *Urban Life*
Levi. *Cowboys of the Sky*
Libreatore. *Our Century: 1910-1920*
Macy. *Winning Ways: A Photohistory of American Women in Sports*
Markham. *Inventions That Changed Modern Life*
McGowen. *The Great Monkey Trial: Science vs. Fundamentalism*
McKissack. *Black Diamond*
McKissack. *A Long Hard Journey: The Story of the Pullman Porter*
Medearis. *Come This Far to Freedom*
Meltzer. *The Black Americans*
Meltzer. *Brother Can You Spare a Dime?*
Meltzer. *Cheap Raw Material*
Meltzer. *Weapons & Warfare*
Mizell. *Think About Racism*
Monceaux. *Jazz: My Music, My People*

Mulcahy. *Diseases: Finding the Cure*
Owen. *Our Century: 1930-1940*
Patrick. *The Young Oxford Companion to the Supreme Court*
Philip. *Singing America: Poems That Define A Nation*
Platt. *The Smithsonian Visual Timeline of Inventions*
Pollack. *Women on the Hill: A History of Women in Congress*
Potter. *African-American Firsts*
Press. *A Multicultural Portrait of Professional Sports*
Rappaport. *American Women: Their Lives in Their Words*
Rappaport. *The Sacco-Vanzetti Trial*
Ritchie. *Please Stand By: A Prehistory of Television*
Sagan. *Women's Suffrage*
Schneider. *Into the Breach: American Women Overseas in World War I*
Schraff. *The Great Depression and the New Deal*
Schreiner. *Mayday! Mayday!*
Senna. *The Black Press and the Struggle of Civil Rights*
Smith. *Fascinating People and Astounding Events from American History*
Smith. *New Paths to Power: American Women 1890-1920*
Spangenburg. *The History of Science from 1895 to 1945*
St. George. *The White House: Cornerstone of a Nation*
Stanley. *Children of the Dust Bowl*
Stanley. *Women in the Military*
Steele. *Freedom's River*
Stewart. *World War I*
Tames. *The 1930s*
Tanaka. *The Disaster of the Hindenburg*
Time-Life. *African Americans: Voices of Triumph: Leadership*
Time-Life. *This Fabulous Century: 1910-1920*

Time-Life. *This Fabulous Century: 1920-1930*
Time-Life. *This Fabulous Century: 1930-1940*
Uschan. *A Multicultural Portrait of World War I*
Wakin. *Photos That Made U.S. History: Civil War to the Atomic Age*

Walker. *Hand, Heart, and Mind*
Walter. *Mississippi Challenge*
Wekesser. *Feminism: Opposing Viewpoints*
Wekesser. *The Death Penalty: Opposing Viewpoints*
Wheeler. *Events That Changed American History*

Whitman. *Get Up and Go: American Road Travel*
Whitman. *This Land Is Your Land*
Whitman. *V Is for Victory*
Wormser. *Hoboes: Wandering in America 1870-1940*

Multimedia

CD-ROM

Air and Space Smithsonian Dreams of Flight
Campaigns, Candidates and the Presidency
Daring to Fly!
Events That Changed the World
Famous American Speeches: 1850 to the Present

Her Heritage: A Biographical Encyclopedia of American History
History Through Art: 20th Century
Ideas That Changed the World
Landmark Documents in American History
Our Times: The Multimedia Encyclopedia of the Twentieth Century

Portraits of American Presidents
Science Navigator
Time Almanac of the 20th Century
Total History
Voices of the 30s
The Way Things Work

Video

Aces: A Story of the First Air War
African Americans
Alice Paul: We Were Arrested of Course!
Amelia Earhart
America at War: The Undersea Stranglers
America in the Thirties: Depression and Optimism
American Consumerism (1890-1930)
The American Experience: Amelia Earhart
The American Experience: Lindbergh
Arsenal of Democracy
Barnum's Big Top
Borderlines
The Crash of 1929
Daring to Dream
Elijah Muhammad
Equality: A History of the Women's Movement in America
The Era of Segregation: A Personal Perspective
Forever Activists: Veterans of the Abraham Lincoln Brigade
Forever in Time: The Art of Edward S. Curtis
Frank Lloyd Wright: An American Original
Franklin D. Roosevelt

Frontier Buildings
George Washington Carver
George Washington Carver: A Man of Vision
Great Black Women
The Great Depression and the New Deal
Helen Keller
A History of the Civil Rights Movement
Ida B. Wells—A Passion for Justice
In Times Past: Radio Days
In Times Past: Traveling in Style
Jackie Robinson
Jane Addams
Jesse Owens
A Job at Ford's
Land and Landscape: Views of America's History and Culture
Langston Hughes
Lighthouses of New England
Living Portraits of Historic Women: Of All the Nerve
The Lottery: Who Fights Our Wars?
Malcolm X
Marcus Garvey
Marian Anderson
Mary McLeod Bethune
Matthew Henson
Mean Things Happening

Michigan Avenue: From Museums to the Magnificent Mile
Mt. Clare: Cradle of the American Dream
New Deal, New York
1914-1918: World War I
Organizing America: The History of Trade Unions
Pride & Prejudice: A History of Black Culture in America
Public Sculpture: America's Legacy
The Real Stories of Al Capone, John Dillinger, Bonnie and Clyde
Riding the Rails
The Sky's the Limit
Sojourner Truth
The Southwest of Georgia O'Keeffe
Submarine: Steel Boats, Iron Men
This House of Power: The Church in African-American Experience
Thomas Alva Edison
Thomas Edison: Electric Light
Thurgood Marshall
To Be Somebody
Tragedy to Triumph: An Adventure with Helen Keller

Traveling in Style: Automobiles and Trolleys
Traveling in Style: Trains, Riverboats, and Planes

Tsiolkovski: The Space Age
The 20's: From Illusion to Disillusion
W. E. B. Du Bois

Women in Rural America
Women with Wings
World War I

GRADE TEN

Historical Fiction

Buechner. *The Wizard's Tide: A Story*
Ferry. *One More Time!*
Froelich. *Reasons to Stay*
Meyer. *White Lilacs*

Myers. *Fire in the Hills*
Myers. *The Glory Field*
Skurzynski. *Good-bye, Billy Radish*

Taylor. *Let the Circle Be Unbroken*
Van Raven. *A Time of Troubles*

Biography

Adair. *George Washington Carver: Botanist*
Adair. *Thomas Alva Edison: Inventing the Electric Age*
Aldred. *Thurgood Marshall: Supreme Court Justice*
Bachrach. *Margaret Sanger*
Barr. *Malcolm X*
Berry. *Georgia O'Keeffe: Painter*
Berry. *Gordon Parks*
Bober. *A Restless Spirit: Robert Frost*
Boulton. *Frank Lloyd Wright: Architect: An Illustrated Biography*
Brown. *Louis Armstrong: Swinging, Singing Satchmo*
Brown. *Malcolm X: His Life and Legacy*
Cain. *Louise Nevelson: Sculptor*
Chalberg. *Emma Goldman: American Individualist*
Coil. *Robert Hutchings Goddard*
Daffron. *Margaret Bourke-White: Photographer*
Darby. *Douglas MacArthur*
Davies. *Malcolm X*
Davis. *Frank Lloyd Wright: Maverick Architect*
Denenberg. *An American Hero: The True Story of Charles A. Lindbergh*
Denenberg. *The True Story of J. Edgar Hoover*
Dominy. *Katherine Dunham: Dancer and Choreographer*
Driemen. *Clarence Darrow*
Erlich. *Paul Robeson: Singer and Actor*

Frankl. *Charlie Parker: Musician*
Frazier. *William Randolph Hearst: Press Baron*
Freedman. *Eleanor Roosevelt: A Life of Discovery*
Garfunkel. *Letter to the World: The Life and Dances of Martha Graham*
Gay. *Emma Goldman*
Gentry. *Jesse Owens: Champion Athlete*
Gish. *An Actor's Life for Me!*
Graham. *Franklin D. Roosevelt*
Greenberg. *Hank Greenberg: The Story of My Life*
Halasa. *Elijah Muhammad: Religious Leader*
Halasa. *Mary McLeod Bethune: Educator*
Hanley. *Philip Randolph*
Haskins. *Thurgood Marshall: A Life for Justice*
Herda. *Earl Warren: Chief Justice for Social Change*
Herda. *Thurgood Marshall: Civil Rights Champion*
Israel. *Franklin Delano Roosevelt*
Ito. *John Steinbeck*
Jakoubek. *Joe Louis: Heavyweight Champion*
James. *Julia Morgan: Architect*
Keller. *The Story of My Life*
Kittredge. *Barbara McClintock*
Kittredge. *Helen Hayes: Actress*
Kliment. *Billie Holiday: Singer*

Kliment. *Count Basie: Bandleader and Musician*
Kliment. *Ella Fitzgerald: Singer*
Klots. *Ida Wells-Barnett: Civil Rights Leader*
Kozodoy. *Isadora Duncan: Dancer*
Kremer. *George Washington Carver: In His Own Words*
Kronstadt. *Florence Sabin: Medical Researcher*
La Farge. *Pearl Buck*
Larsen. *Franklin D. Roosevelt*
Lawler. *Marcus Garvey: Black Nationalist Leader*
Leavell. *Woodrow Wilson*
Lewis. *W. E. B. DuBois*
Liles. *Sam and the Speaker's Chair*
Lynn. *Babe Didrikson Zaharias*
Lyons. *Sorrow's Kitchen: Zora Neale Hurston*
Mack-Williams. *Malcom X*
Mahone-Lonesome. *Charles R. Drew*
Marable. *W. E. B. DuBois*
McDonough. *Frank Lloyd Wright*
McKissack. *W. E. B. DuBois*
Morris. *The FDR Way*
Myers. *Malcolm X: By Any Means Necessary*
Nardo. *Franklin D. Roosevelt*
Nardo. *Jim Thorpe*
Nicholson. *Georgia O'Keeffe*
Nicholson. *Helen Keller: Humanitarian*
Owens. *Jesse: The Man Who Outran Hitler*
Palmer. *Lena Horne: Entertainer*

Patterson. *A. Philip Randolph*
Patterson. *Marian Anderson*
Pratt. *Martha Graham*
Randolph. *Charles Lindbergh*
Reef. *John Steinbeck*
Robinson. *Iron Horse: Lou Gehrig in His Time*
Rodgers. *Beyond the Barrier: Byrd's First Expedition*
Rummel. *Langston Hughes*
Tedards. *Marian Anderson: Singer*

Tessitore. *The Hunt and the Feast: A Life of Ernest Hemingway*
Thompson. *Charles Chesnutt*
Thorleifson. *Ethel Barrymore*
Tilton. *Margaret Mead*
Tolbert-Rouchaleau. *James Weldon Johnson: Author*
Toor. *Eleanor Roosevelt*
Van Steenwyk. *Ida B. Wells-Barnett*

Waldstreicher. *Emma Goldman*
Weidhorn. *Jackie Robinson*
Weisbrot. *Father Divine: Religious Leader*
Whitelaw. *Margaret Sanger*
Witcover. *Zora Neale Hurston*
Worth. *Edith Wharton*
Yagoda. *Will Rogers: A Biography*
Ziesk. *Margaret Mead*

Collective Biography

Aaseng. *America's Third-Party Presidential Candidates*
Aaseng. *Great Justices of the Supreme Court*
Aaseng. *Twentieth-Century Inventors*
Aaseng. *You Are the President*
Anthony. *First Ladies: 1789-1961*
Brill. *Extraordinary Young People*
Haskins. *Against All Opposition: Black Explorers in America*
Jones. *Big Star Fallin' Mama*
Landrum. *Profiles of Female Genius: Thirteen Creative Women*

Landrum. *Profiles of Genius: Thirteen Creative Men*
Lindop. *Presidents by Accident*
Lomask. *Great Lives: Exploration*
Lyons. *Keeping Secrets: The Girlhood Diaries of Seven Women Writers*
Mahoney. *Women in Espionage: A Biographical Dictionary*
Mayberry. *Leaders Who Changed the 20th Century*
Morin. *Women Chosen for Public Office*
Morin. *Women Who Reformed Politics*
Myers. *Now Is Your Time*

O'Brien. *American Political Leaders*
Otfinoski. *Great Black Writers*
Otfinoski. *Nineteenth-Century Writers*
Streissguth. *Hatemongers and Demagogues*
Streissguth. *Hoaxers & Hustlers*
Sullivan. *Presidents at Play*
Weitzman. *Great Lives: Theater*
Whitelaw. *They Wrote Their Own Headlines*
Wilkinson. *People Who Changed the World*
Wolf. *Focus: Five Women Photographers*
Yount. *Black Scientists*
Yount. *Women Aviators*

History

Aaseng. *You Are the Senator*
Alderman. *In Our Defense: The Bill of Rights in Action*
Ardley. *Music: An Illustrated Encyclopedia*
Awmiller. *This House on Fire: The Story of the Blues*
Aymar. *Men in the Air: The Best Flight Stories of All Time*
Basinger. *American Cinema: One Hundred Years of Filmmaking*
Bosco. *World War I*
Calabro. *Zap!: A Brief History of Television*
Carlin. *Jazz*
Carnes. *Us and Them: A History of Intolerance in America*
Cohen. *America: Then and Now*
Collier. *Jazz, the American Theme Song*

Colman. *Women in Society: United States*
Cooper. *Hell Fighters: African American Soldiers in World War I*
Costantino. *The 1930's*
Cray. *American Datelines*
Dale. *Early Cars*
Davis. *Don't Know Much About History*
Davis. *Man-Made Catastrophes*
Deutsch. *From Ballots to Breadlines: American Women 1920-1940*
Evans. *Born for Liberty: A History of Women in America*
Ewing. *Women in Uniform Through the Centuries*
Farrell. *The Great Depression*
Feinberg. *American Political Scandals Past and Present*

Finkelstein. *Sounds in the Air: The Golden Age of Radio*
Fradin. *Medicine: Yesterday, Today, and Tomorrow*
Frost. *The Mexican Revolution*
Frost-Knappman. *Women's Suffrage in America*
Garfunkel. *On Wings of Joy: The Story of Ballet*
Garza. *Barred from the Bar: A History of Women and the Legal Profession*
Gilbert. *Deadball: Major League Baseball Before Babe Ruth*
Gilbert. *The Soaring Twenties: Babe Ruth and the Home-Run Decade*
Granfield. *In Flanders Fields*
Greene. *Child Labor: Then and Now*
Hakim. *An Age of Extremes*
Hakim. *War, Peace, and All That Jazz*

Haskins. *Black Music in America*

Herald. *The 1920s*

Hill. *Our Century: 1920-1930*

Hintz. *Farewell, John Barleycorn: Prohibition in the United States*

Jantzen. *Hooray for Peace, Hurrah for War: The U.S. During World War I*

Katz. *The New Freedom to the New Deal: 1913-1939*

Kirchberger. *The First World War*

Knappman. *Great American Trials*

Kronenwetter. *Covert Action*

Kronenwetter. *United They Hate: White Supremacist Groups in America*

Lackmann. *Same Time. . . Same Station: An A-Z Guide to Radio*

Landau. *Armed America: The Status of Gun Control*

Landau. *The White Power Movement: America's Racist Hate Groups*

Langone. *Spreading Poison: A Book About Racism and Prejudice*

Lawson. *Famous Presidential Scandals*

Libreatore. *Our Century: 1910-1920*

Macy. *Winning Ways: A Photohistory of American Women in Sports*

Markham. *Inventions That Changed Modern Life*

McGowen. *The Great Monkey Trial: Science vs. Fundamentalism*

McKissack. *A Long Hard Journey: The Story of the Pullman Porter*

Meltzer. *The Black Americans*

Meltzer. *Brother Can You Spare a Dime?*

Meltzer. *Weapons & Warfare*

Mizell. *Think About Racism*

Monceaux. *Jazz: My Music, My People*

Mulcahy. *Diseases: Finding the Cure*

Owen. *Our Century: 1930-1940*

Patrick. *The Young Oxford Companion to the Supreme Court*

Philip. *Singing America: Poems That Define a Nation*

Pollack. *Women on the Hill: A History of Women in Congress*

Potter. *African-American Firsts*

Press. *A Multicultural Portrait of Professional Sports*

Rappaport. *American Women: Their Lives in Their Words*

Rappaport. *The Sacco-Vanzetti Trial*

Ritchie. *Please Stand By: A Prehistory of Television*

Sagan. *Women's Suffrage*

Schneider. *Into the Breach: American Women Overseas in World War I*

Schraff. *The Great Depression and the New Deal*

Schreiner. *Mayday! Mayday!*

Senna. *The Black Press and the Struggle of Civil Rights*

Smith. *Fascinating People and Astounding Events from American History*

Smith. *New Paths to Power: American Women 1890-1920*

Spangenburg. *The History of Science from 1895 to 1945*

Stanley. *Children of the Dust Bowl*

Stanley. *Women in the Military*

Steele. *Freedom's River*

Stewart. *World War I*

Time-Life. *African Americans: Voices of Triumph: Leadership*

Time-Life. *This Fabulous Century: 1910-1920*

Time-Life. *This Fabulous Century: 1920-1930*

Time-Life. *This Fabulous Century: 1930-1940*

Uschan. *A Multicultural Portrait of World War I*

Wakin. *Photos That Made U.S. History: Civil War to the Atomic Age*

Walter. *Mississippi Challenge*

Wekesser. *The Death Penalty: Opposing Viewpoints*

Wekesser. *Feminism: Opposing Viewpoints*

Wheeler. *Events That Changed American History*

Wormser. *Hoboes: Wandering in America 1870-1940*

Multimedia

CD-ROM

Air and Space Smithsonian Dreams of Flight

Campaigns, Candidates and the Presidency

Daring to Fly!

Events That Changed the World

Famous American Speeches: 1850 to the Present

Her Heritage: A Biographical Encyclopedia of American History

History Through Art: 20th Century

Ideas That Changed the World

Landmark Documents in American History

Our Times: The Multimedia Encyclopedia of the Twentieth Century

Portraits of American Presidents

Science Navigator

Time Almanac of the 20th Century

Total History

Voices of the 30s

The Way Things Work

Video

Aces: A Story of the First Air War
African Americans
Alice Paul: We Were Arrested of Course!
Amelia Earhart
America at War: The Undersea Stranglers
America in the Thirties: Depression and Optimism
The American Experience: Amelia Earhart
The American Experience: Lindbergh
Arsenal of Democracy
Barnum's Big Top
Borderlines
The Crash of 1929
Daring to Dream
Elijah Muhammad
Equality: A History of the Women's Movement in America
The Era of Segregation: A Personal Perspective
FDR
Forever Activists: Veterans of the Abraham Lincoln Brigade
Forever in Time: The Art of Edward S. Curtis
Frank Lloyd Wright: An American Original
Franklin D. Roosevelt
George Washington Carver

Great Black Women
Helen Keller
A History of the Civil Rights Movement
Ida B. Wells—A Passion for Justice
In Times Past: Radio Days
In Times Past: Traveling in Style
Jane Addams
A Job at Ford's
Land and Landscape: Views of America's History and Culture
Langston Hughes
Lighthouses of New England
Living Portraits of Historic Women: Of All the Nerve
The Lottery: Who Fights Our Wars?
Malcolm X
Marcus Garvey
Marian Anderson
Mean Things Happening
Michigan Avenue: From Museums to the Magnificent Mile
Midnight Ramble
Mt. Clare: Cradle of the American Dream
New Deal, New York
1914-1918: World War I
1929-1941: The Great Depression

Organizing America: The History of Trade Unions
Pride & Prejudice: A History of Black Culture in America
Public Sculpture: America's Legacy
The Real Stories of Al Capone, John Dillinger, Bonnie and Clyde
Riding the Rails
The Sky's the Limit
Sojourner Truth
The Southwest of Georgia O'Keeffe
Submarine: Steel Boats, Iron Men
This House of Power: The Church in African-American Experience
Thurgood Marshall
To Be Somebody
Tragedy to Triumph: An Adventure with Helen Keller
Traveling in Style: Automobiles and Trolleys
Traveling in Style: Trains, Riverboats, and Planes
The 20's: From Illusion to Disillusion
W. E. B. DuBois
Women in Rural America
Women with Wings

GRADES ELEVEN AND TWELVE

Historical Fiction

Boyne. *Eagles at War*
Boyne. *Trophy for Eagles*
De Haven. *Derby Dugan's Depression Funnies*
Deford. *Love and Infamy*
Doctorow. *Ragtime*

Doctorow. *World's Fair*
Ferry. *One More Time!*
Harris. *The Longest Winter*
Hogan. *Mean Spirit*
Jakes. *Homeland*
Jones. *Weedy Rough*

Mendelsohn. *I Was Amelia Earhart*
Taylor. *Let the Circle Be Unbroken*
Tilghman. *Mason's Retreat*

Biography

Adair. *Thomas Alva Edison: Inventing the Electric Age*
Bachrach. *Margaret Sanger*
Bober. *A Restless Spirit: Robert Frost*
Boulton. *Frank Lloyd Wright: Architect: An Illustrated Biography*
Bragg. *Soaring Above Setbacks: The*

Autobiography of Janet Harmon Bragg
Brown. *Louis Armstrong: Swinging, Singing Satchmo*
Brown. *Malcolm X: His Life and Legacy*
Chalberg. *Emma Goldman: American Individualist*
Coil. *Robert Hutchings Goddard*

Darby. *Douglas MacArthur*
Davies. *Malcolm X*
Denenberg. *An American Hero: The True Story of Charles A. Lindbergh*
Denenberg. *The True Story of J. Edgar Hoover*
Dominy. *Katherine Dunham: Dancer and Choreographer*
Driemen. *Clarence Darrow*

Dyson. *Making Malcolm: The Myth and Meaning of Malcolm X*

Erlich. *Paul Robeson: Singer and Actor*

Faber. *Printer's Devil to Publisher: Adolph S. Ochs of The New York Times*

Freedman. *Eleanor Roosevelt: A Life of Discovery*

Gay. *Emma Goldman*

Gish. *An Actor's Life for Me!*

Graham. *Franklin D. Roosevelt*

Greenberg. *Hank Greenberg: The Story of My Life*

Halasa. *Elijah Muhammad: Religious Leader*

Herda. *Earl Warren: Chief Justice for Social Change*

James. *Julia Morgan: Architect*

Keller. *The Story of My Life*

Kittredge. *Barbara McClintock*

Kittredge. *Helen Hayes: Actress*

Kliment. *Billie Holiday: Singer*

Kliment. *Count Basie: Bandleader and Musician*

Kliment. *Ella Fitzgerald: Singer*

Kremer. *George Washington Carver: In His Own Words*

Kronstadt. *Florence Sabin: Medical Researcher*

La Farge. *Pearl Buck*

Larsen. *Franklin D. Roosevelt*

Lawler. *Marcus Garvey: Black Nationalist Leader*

Leavell. *Woodrow Wilson*

Lewis. *W. E. B. DuBois*

Liles. *Sam and the Speaker's Chair*

Lynn. *Babe Didrikson Zaharias*

Lyons. *Sorrow's Kitchen: Zora Neale Hurston*

Mack-Williams. *Malcom X*

Mahone-Lonesome. *Charles R. Drew*

Marable. *W. E. B. DuBois*

McKissack. *W. E. B. DuBois*

Meyers. *Robert Frost: A Biography*

Morris. *The FDR Way*

Owens. *Jesse: The Man Who Outran Hitler*

Palmer. *Lena Horne: Entertainer*

Partridge. *Dorothea Lange: A Visual Life*

Powers. *Secrecy and Power: The Life of J. Edgar Hoover*

Randolph. *Charles Lindbergh*

Reef. *John Steinbeck*

Robinson. *Iron Horse: Lou Gehrig in His Time*

Rodgers. *Beyond the Barrier: Byrd's First Expedition*

Rummel. *Langston Hughes*

Tessitore. *The Hunt and the Feast: A Life of Ernest Hemingway*

Thompson. *Charles Chesnutt*

Thorleifson. *Ethel Barrymore*

Tolbert-Rouchaleau. *James Weldon Johnson: Author*

Waldstreicher. *Emma Goldman*

Weisbrot. *Father Divine: Religious Leader*

Whitelaw. *Margaret Sanger*

Worth. *Edith Wharton*

Yagoda. *Will Rogers: A Biography*

Collective Biography

Aaseng. *Great Justices of the Supreme Court*

Aaseng. *Twentieth-Century Inventors*

Aaseng. *You Are the President*

Anthony. *First Ladies: 1789-1961*

Conway. *Written by Herself—Autobiographies of American Women*

Jones. *Big Star Fallin' Mama*

Landrum. *Profiles of Female Genius: Thirteen Creative Women*

Landrum. *Profiles of Genius: Thirteen Creative Men*

Lindop. *Presidents by Accident*

Lomask. *Great Lives: Exploration*

Lyons. *Keeping Secrets: The Girlhood Diaries of Seven Women Writers*

Mahoney. *Women in Espionage: A Biographical Dictionary*

Mayberry. *Leaders Who Changed the 20th Century*

Morin. *Women Chosen for Public Office*

O'Brien. *American Political Leaders*

Otfinoski. *Great Black Writers*

Otfinoski. *Nineteenth-Century Writers*

Streissguth. *Hatemongers and Demagogues*

Streissguth. *Hoaxers & Hustlers*

Terkel. *Giants of Jazz*

Truman. *First Ladies*

Weitzman. *Great Lives: Theater*

Wolf. *Focus: Five Women Photographers*

Yount. *Black Scientists*

Yount. *Women Aviators*

History

Aaseng. *You Are the Senator*

Alderman. *In Our Defense: The Bill of Rights in Action*

Ardley. *Music: An Illustrated Encyclopedia*

Awmiller. *This House on Fire: The Story of the Blues*

Aymar. *Men in the Air: The Best Flight Stories of All Time*

Basinger. *American Cinema: One Hundred Years of Filmmaking*

Black. *In the Shadow of Polio: A Personal and Social History*

Boller. *Presidential Wives: An Anecdotal History*

Bosco. *World War I*

Busby. *Daughters of Africa: An International Anthology*

Calabro. *Zap!: A Brief History of Television*

Carlin. *Jazz*

Carnes. *Us and Them: A History of Intolerance in America*

Cohen. *America: Then and Now*

Collier. *Jazz, the American Theme Song*

Colman. *Women in Society: United States*

Cooper . *Hell Fighters: African American Soldiers in World War I*

Cray. *American Datelines*

Dale. *Early Cars*

Davidson. *Everyday Life Through the Ages*

Davis. *Don't Know Much About History*

Davis. *Man-Made Catastrophes*

Deutsch. *From Ballots to Breadlines: American Women 1920-1940*

Evans. *Born for Liberty: A History of Women in America*

Ewing. *Women in Uniform Through the Centuries*

Farrell. *The Great Depression*

Feinberg. *American Political Scandals Past and Present*

Finkelstein. *Sounds in the Air: The Golden Age of Radio*

Frost. *The Mexican Revolution*

Frost-Knappman. *Women's Suffrage in America*

Garfunkel. *On Wings of Joy: The Story of Ballet*

Garza. *Barred from the Bar: A History of Women and the Legal Profession*

Gilbert. *Deadball: Major League Baseball Before Babe Ruth*

Gilbert. *The Soaring Twenties: Babe Ruth and the Home-Run Decade*

Hakim. *An Age of Extremes*

Hakim. *War, Peace, and All That Jazz*

Hanmer. *Taking a Stand Against Sexism and Sex Discrimination*

Hansen. *Gentlemen Volunteers: American Ambulance Drivers*

Haskins. *Black Music in America*

Hintz. *Farewell, John Barleycorn: Prohibition in the United States*

Jantzen. *Hooray for Peace, Hurrah for War: The US During World War I*

Keegan. *History of Warfare*

Kirchberger. *The First World War*

Knappman. *Great American Trials*

Kronenwetter. *Covert Action*

Kronenwetter. *United They Hate: White Supremacist Groups in America*

Lackmann. *Same Time. . . Same Station: An A-Z Guide to Radio*

Landau. *The White Power Movement: America's Racist Hate Groups*

Langone. *Spreading Poison: A Book About Racism and Prejudice*

Lawson. *Famous Presidential Scandals*

Marling. *George Washington Slept Here, 1876-1986*

McGowen. *The Great Monkey Trial: Science vs. Fundamentalism*

McKissack. *A Long Hard Journey: The Story of the Pullman Porter*

McLynn. *Famous Trials: Cases That Made History*

Melder. *Hail to the Candidate: Presidential Campaigns*

Meltzer. *Brother Can You Spare a Dime?*

Meltzer. *Weapons & Warfare*

Monceaux. *Jazz: My Music, My People*

Mulcahy. *Diseases: Finding the Cure*

Patrick. *The Young Oxford Companion to the Supreme Court*

Peterson. *Cages to Jump Shots: Pro Basketball's Early Years*

Philip. *Singing America: Poems That Define a Nation*

Pollack. *Women on the Hill: A History of Women in Congress*

Potter. *African-American Firsts*

Press. *A Multicultural Portrait of Professional Sports*

Rappaport. *American Women: Their Lives in Their Words*

Rappaport. *The Sacco-Vanzetti Trial*

Riley. *The Biographical Encyclopedia of Negro Baseball Leagues*

Ritchie. *Please Stand By: A Prehistory of Television*

Sagan. *Women's Suffrage*

Schneider. *Into the Breach: American Women Overseas in World War I*

Schreiner. *Mayday! Mayday!*

Senna. *The Black Press and the Struggle of Civil Rights*

Smith. *Fascinating People and Astounding Events from American History*

Smith. *New Paths to Power: American Women 1890-1920*

Spangenburg. *The History of Science from 1895 to 1945*

Stanley. *Women in the Military*

Steele. *Freedom's River*

Time-Life. *African Americans: Voices of Triumph: Leadership*

Time-Life. *This Fabulous Century: 1910-1920*

Time-Life. *This Fabulous Century: 1920-1930*

Time-Life. *This Fabulous Century: 1930-1940*

Walter. *Mississippi Challenge*

Wekesser. *The Death Penalty: Opposing Viewpoints*

Wekesser. *Feminism: Opposing Viewpoints*

Wheeler. *Events That Changed American History*

Fogle. *Two Hundred Years: Stories of the Nation's Capital*

Ward. *Closest Companion: Franklin Roosevelt and Margaret Suckley*

Watkins. *The Great Depression: American in the 1930s*

Multimedia

CD-ROM

Air and Space Smithsonian
    Dreams of Flight
Campaigns, Candidates and
    the Presidency
Daring to Fly!
Events That Changed the
    World
Famous American Speeches:
    1850 to the Present

Her Heritage: A Biographical
    Encyclopedia of American
    History
History Through Art: 20th
    Century
Ideas That Changed the World
Landmark Documents in
    American History
Our Times: The Multimedia
    Encyclopedia of the
    Twentieth Century

Portraits of American
    Presidents
Science Navigator
Time Almanac of the 20th
    Century
Total History
Voices of the 30s
The Way Things Work

Video

Aces: A Story of the First Air
    War
Alice Paul: We Were Arrested
    of Course!
Amelia Earhart
America at War: The
    Undersea Stranglers
America in the Thirties:
    Depression and Optimism
The American Experience:
    Amelia Earhart
The American Experience:
    Lindbergh
Arsenal of Democracy
Borderlines
The Crash of 1929
Daring to Dream
Elijah Muhammad
Equality: A History of the
    Women's Movement in
    America
The Era of Segregation: A
    Personal Perspective
FDR
Forever Activists: Veterans of
    the Abraham Lincoln
    Brigade
Forever in Time: The Art of
    Edward S. Curtis
Frank Lloyd Wright: An
    American Original
Franklin D. Roosevelt
George Washington Carver

Great Black Women
Helen Keller
A History of the Civil Rights
    Movement
Ida B. Wells—A Passion for
    Justice
In Times Past: Radio Days
In Times Past: Traveling in
    Style
Jane Addams
A Job at Ford's
Land and Landscape: Views
    of America's History and
    Culture
Langston Hughes
Lighthouses of New England
Living Portraits of Historic
    Women: Of All the Nerve
The Lottery: Who Fights Our
    Wars?
Malcolm X
Marcus Garvey
Marian Anderson
Mean Things Happening
Michigan Avenue: From
    Museums to the
    Magnificent Mile
Midnight Ramble
Mt. Clare: Cradle of the
    American Dream
New Deal, New York
1914-1918: World War I

1929-1941: The Great
    Depression
Organizing America: The
    History of Trade Unions
Pride & Prejudice: A History
    of Black Culture in America
Public Sculpture: America's
    Legacy
The Real Stories of Al
    Capone, John Dillinger,
    Bonnie and Clyde
Riding the Rails
Sojourner Truth
The Southwest of Georgia
    O'Keeffe
Submarine: Steel Boats, Iron
    Men
This House of Power: The
    Church in
    African-American
    Experience
Thurgood Marshall
To Be Somebody
Traveling in Style:
    Automobiles and Trolleys
Traveling in Style: Trains,
    Riverboats, and Planes
The 20's: From Illusion to
    Disillusion
W. E. B. DuBois
Women in Rural America
Women with Wings

WORLD WAR II, 1941-1945

GRADE SEVEN

Historical Fiction

Avi. *"Who Was That Masked Man, Anyway?"*
Banks. *Under the Shadow of Wings*
Barrie. *Lone Star*
Bauer. *Rain of Fire*
Bethancourt. *The Tommorow Connection*
Branscum. *Old Blue Tilley*
Cormier. *Other Bells for Us to Ring*
Cutler. *My Wartime Summers*
Ferry. *One More Time!*
Ford. *The Most Wonderful Movie in the World*
Giff. *Lily's Crossing*
Green. *The War at Home*
Greene. *Summer of My German Soldier*
Hahn. *Following My Own Footsteps*
Hahn. *Stepping on the Cracks*
Herman. *A Summer on Thirteenth Street*
Hotze. *Summer Endings*
Kudlinski. *Pearl Harbor Is Burning!*
Lisle. *Sirens and Spies*
Manley. *She Flew No Flags*
Murphy. *Gold Star Sister*
Oughton. *The War in Georgia*
Paterson. *Jacob Have I Loved*
Platt. *Honor Bright*
Poynter. *A Time Too Swift*
Rabinowitz. *Bethie*
Rinaldi. *Keep Smiling Through*
Ross. *Harper & Moon*
Rylant. *I Had Seen Castles*
Salisbury. *Under the Blood-Red Sun*
Savin. *The Moon Bridge*
Taylor. *The Bomb*
Taylor. *The Cay*
Taylor. *Timothy of the Cay*
Thesman. *Molly Donnelly*
Uchida. *Journey to Topaz*
Vick. *Tag Against Time*
Willis. *A Place to Claim as Home*
Willis. *Out of the Storm*
Wunderli. *The Blue Between the Clouds*

Biography

Aldred. *Thurgood Marshall: Supreme Court Justice*
Andryszewski. *The Amazing Life of Moe Berg*
Bachrach. *Margaret Sanger*
Barr. *Malcolm X*
Berkow. *Hank Greenberg: Hall-of-Fame Slugger*
Berry. *Georgia O'Keeffe: Painter*
Berry. *Gordon Parks*
Berry. *Langston Hughes*
Billings. *Grace Hopper: Navy Admiral and Computer Pioneer*
Butts. *May Chinn: The Best Medicine*
Cain. *Louise Nevelson: Sculptor*
Cannon. *Dwight David Eisenhower: War Hero and President*
Castiglia. *Margaret Mead*
Chin. *When Justice Failed: The Fred Korematsu Story*
Collier. *Duke Ellington*
Collier. *Louis Armstrong: An American Success Story*
Collins. *Harry S. Truman*
Colman. *Fannie Lou Hamer and the Fight for the Vote*
Colman. *A Woman Unafraid: The Achievements of Frances Perkins*
Cross. *Roosevelt and the Americans at War*
Daffron. *Margaret Bourke-White: Photographer*
Dallard. *Ella Baker: A Leader Behind the Scenes*
Darby. *Douglas MacArthur*
Darby. *Dwight D. Eisenhower*
Davies. *Malcolm X*
Davis. *Frank Lloyd Wright: Maverick Architect*
Deitch. *Dwight D. Eisenhower*
Denenberg. *The True Story of J. Edgar Hoover*
Devane. *Franklin Delano Roosevelt: President*
Dominy. *Katherine Dunham: Dancer and Choreographer*
Driemen. *Atomic Dawn: A Biography of Robert Oppenheimer*
Ellis. *Dwight D. Eisenhower*
Erlich. *Paul Robeson: Singer and Actor*
Farley. *Robert H. Goddard*
Ferris. *What I Had Was Singing: Marian Anderson*
Fleming. *Harry S. Truman*
Frankl. *Charlie Parker: Musician*
Fraser. *Walter White: Civil Rights Leader*
Freedman. *Eleanor Roosevelt: A Life of Discovery*

Freedman. *Franklin Delano Roosevelt*

Garfunkel. *Letter to the World: The Life and Dances of Martha Graham*

Gentry. *Jesse Owens: Champion Athlete*

Gourse. *Dizzy Gillespie and the Birth of Bebop*

Greenblatt. *Franklin D. Roosevelt*

Halasa. *Elijah Muhammad: Religious Leader*

Halasa. *Mary McLeod Bethune: Educator*

Hanley. *Philip Randolph*

Hargrove. *Dwight D. Eisenhower*

Hargrove. *Harry S. Truman: Thirty-Third President*

Haskins. *Thurgood Marshall: A Life for Justice*

Heiligman. *Barbara McClintock: Alone in Her Field*

Herda. *Thurgood Marshall: Civil Rights Champion*

Israel. *Franklin Delano Roosevelt*

Ito. *John Steinbeck*

Jakoubek. *Adam Clayton Powell, Jr.*

Jakoubek. *Joe Louis: Heavyweight Champion*

James. *Julia Morgan: Architect*

Kallen. *Thurgood Marshall: A Dream of Justice for All*

Kaye. *The Life of Alexander Fleming*

Kaye. *The Life of Benjamin Spock*

Kaye. *The Life of Florence Sabin*

Keller. *Margaret Bourke-White: A Photographer's Life*

Keller. *The Story of My Life*

Kittredge. *Barbara McClintock*

Kittredge. *Helen Hayes: Actress*

Kliment. *Count Basie: Bandleader and Musician*

Kliment. *Ella Fitzgerald: Singer*

Kronstadt. *Florence Sabin: Medical Researcher*

La Farge. *Pearl Buck*

Larsen. *Paul Robeson: Hero Before His Time*

Lazo. *Eleanor Roosevelt*

Leavell. *Harry S. Truman*

Liles. *Sam and the Speaker's Chair*

Lindop. *Dwight D. Eisenhower*

Lindop. *Woodrow Wilson, Franklin D. Roosevelt, Harry S. Truman*

Lubetkin. *George Marshall*

Lynn. *Babe Didrikson Zaharias*

Lyons. *Sorrow's Kitchen: Zora Neale Hurston*

Mahone-Lonesome. *Charles R. Drew*

Markham. *Helen Keller*

McDonough. *Frank Lloyd Wright*

McPherson. *TV's Forgotten Hero: Philo Farnsworth*

Morris. *The FDR Way*

Morris. *The Truman Way*

Murphy. *Frank Lloyd Wright*

Myers. *Malcolm X: By Any Means Necessary*

Nardo. *Franklin D. Roosevelt*

Nicholson. *Georgia O'Keeffe*

Nicholson. *Helen Keller: Humanitarian*

O'Connor. *The Soldier's Voice: Ernie Pyle*

Osofsky. *Free to Dream: Langston Hughes*

Palmer. *Lena Horne: Entertainer*

Patterson. *A. Philip Randolph*

Patterson. *Marian Anderson*

Peifer. *Soldier of Destiny: A Biography of George Patton*

Potter. *Buckminster Fuller*

Pratt. *Martha Graham*

Probosz. *Martha Graham*

Ravage. *Rachel Carson, Gentle Crusader*

Reef. *John Steinbeck*

Rubin. *Frank Lloyd Wright*

Rummel. *Langston Hughes*

Rummel. *Robert Oppenheimer: Dark Prince*

Sandak. *The Franklin Roosevelts*

Sandak. *The Trumans*

Sandberg. *Dwight D. Eisenhower*

Saunders. *George C. Marshall: A General for Peace*

Schuman. *Eleanor Roosevelt*

Schuman. *Elie Wiesel*

Schuman. *Martin Luther King, Jr.*

Scott. *Jackie Robinson*

Shapiro. *Charles Drew: Founder of the Blood Bank*

Sherrow. *Linus Pauling*

St. George. *Dear Dr. Bell. . . Your Friend, Helen Keller*

Stine. *The Story of Malcolm X, Civil Rights Leader*

Streissguth. *Rocket Man: Robert Goddard*

Talmadge. *The Life of Charles Drew*

Tanenhaus. *Louis Armstrong: Musician*

Tedards. *Marian Anderson: Singer*

Tessitore. *The Hunt and the Feast: A Life of Ernest Hemingway*

Thorleifson. *Ethel Barrymore*

Tilton. *Margaret Mead*

Toor. *Eleanor Roosevelt*

Weidhorn. *Jackie Robinson*

Weisbrot. *Father Divine: Religious Leader*

Whitelaw. *Grace Hopper*

Whitelaw. *Margaret Sanger*

Whitelaw. *Mr. Civil Rights: The Story of Thurgood Marshall*

Witcover. *Zora Neale Hurston*

Woog. *Louis Armstrong*

Wright. *A. Philip Randolph*

Wyman. *Ella Fitzgerald: Jazz Singer Supreme*

Yannuzzi. *Zora Neale Hurston: Southern Storyteller*

Ziesk. *Margaret Mead*

Collective Biography

Aaseng. *Navajo Code Talkers*

Aaseng. *You Are the General*

Altman. *Extraordinary Black Americans*

Beard. *The Presidents in American History*

Blassingame. *The Look-It-Up Book of Presidents*

Blue. *People of Peace*

Cohen. *Prophets of Doom*

Cush. *Artists Who Created Great Works*

Cush. *Women Who Achieved Greatness*

Dolan. *Shaping U.S. Foreign Policy: Twelve Secretaries of State*

Faber. *Great Lives: American Government*

Fireside. *Is There a Woman in the House. . . or Senate?*

Haskins. *Black Eagles: African Americans in Aviation*

Italia. *Courageous Crimefighters*

Jacobs. *Great Lives: Human Rights*

Krull. *Lives of the Athletes*

Lindop. *Presidents by Accident*

Mayberry. *Business Leaders Who Built Financial Empires*

Morin. *Women Chosen for Public Office*

Morin. *Women Who Reformed Politics*

Myers. *Now Is Your Time*

Pascoe. *First Facts About the Presidents*

Plowden. *Famous Firsts of Black Women*

Provenson. *My Fellow Americans*

Rennert. *Book of Firsts: Leaders of America*

Rennert. *Civil Rights Leaders*

Rennert. *Female Writers*

Rennert. *Jazz Stars*

Rennert. *Pioneers of Discovery*

Rubel. *The Scholastic Encyclopedia of the Presidents*

Saunders. *George C. Marshall: A General for Peace*

Sheafer. *Women in America's Wars*

Streissguth. *Hatemongers and Demagogues*

Streissguth. *Hoaxers & Hustlers*

Sullivan. *Presidents at Play*

Veglahn. *Women Scientists*

Weitzman. *Great Lives: Human Culture*

Whitelaw. *They Wrote Their Own Headlines*

Wilkinson. *Generals Who Changed the World*

Wolf. *Focus: Five Women Photographers*

Yount. *Black Scientists*

Yount. *Women Aviators*

History

Anderson. *Battles That Changed the Modern World*

Baker. *The 1940s*

Black. *America Prepares for War*

Black. *Bataan and Corregidor*

Black. *Battle of the Atlantic*

Black. *Battle of the Bulge*

Black. *D-Day*

Black. *Desert Warfare*

Black. *Flattops at War*

Black. *Guadalcanal*

Black. *Hiroshima and the Atomic Bomb*

Black. *Invasion of Italy*

Black. *Island Hopping in the Pacific*

Black. *Iwo Jima and Okinawa*

Black. *Jungle Warfare*

Black. *Pearl Harbor!*

Black. *Victory in Europe*

Black. *War Behind the Lines*

Bowler. *Trains*

Brashler. *The Story of the Negro League Baseball*

Calabro. *Zap!: A Brief History of Television*

Carlin. *Jazz*

Colman. *Rosie the Riveter*

Colman. *Women in Society: United States*

Cooper. *Playing America's Game: Negro League Baseball*

Cosner. *War Nurses*

Cray. *American Datelines*

Cross. *Children and War*

Cross. *Technology of War*

Davies. *Transport: On Land, Road and Rail*

Davis. *Behind Barbed Wire*

Devaney. *America Goes to War: 1941*

Devaney. *America on the Attack: 1943*

Devaney. *America Storms the Beaches: 1944*

Devaney. *America Triumphs: 1945*

Dolan. *America in World War II: 1941*

Dolan. *America in World War II: 1942*

Dolan. *America in World War II: 1943*

Dolan. *America in World War II: 1944*

Dolan. *America in World War II: 1945*

Dunnahoo. *Pearl Harbor: America Enters the War*

Ferrell. *The U.S. Air Force*

Finkelstein. *Sounds in the Air: The Golden Age of Radio*

Fradin. *Medicine: Yesterday, Today, and Tomorrow*

Gardner. *The Forgotten Players: The Story of Black Baseball in America*

Gay. *World War II*

Greenberg. *Letters from a World War II GI*

Hakim. *War, Peace, and All That Jazz*

Hamanaka. *On the Wings of Peace*

Harris. *The Tuskegee Airmen: Black Heroes of World War II*

Helmer. *Belles of the Ballpark*

Hill. *Our Century: 1940-1950*

Hirsch. *Taxation: Paying for Government*

Humble. *Ships*

Humble. *A World War Two Submarine*

Isserman. *World War II*

Karl. *America Alive: A History*

Katz. *World War II to the New Frontier: 1940-1963*

Kronenwetter. *Covert Action*

Krull. *V Is for Victory: America Remembers World War II*

Langone. *Spreading Poison: A Book About Racism and Prejudice*

Levine. *A Fence Away from Freedom: Japanese Americans and World War II*

Macy. *A Whole New Ballgame: All-American Girls Professional Baseball League*

Macy. *Winning Ways: A Photohistory of American Women in Sports*

Marrin. *The Airman's War: World War II in the Sky*

Marrin. *OVERLORD: D-Day and the Invasion of Europe*

Marrin. *The Secret Armies: Spies, Counterspies, and Saboteurs*

Marrin. *Victory in the Pacific*

May. *Pushing the Limits: American Women 1940-1961*

McKissack. *Black Diamond*

McKissack. *A Long Hard Journey: The Story of the Pullman Porter*

McKissack. *Red-Tail Angels: Tuskegee Airmen of World War II*

Medearis. *Come This Far to Freedom*

Meltzer. *The Black Americans*

Meltzer. *Weapons & Warfare*

Mizell. *Think About Racism*

Morley. *Clothes: For Work, Play and Display*

Naden. *The U.S. Coast Guard*

Nicholson. *Pearl Harbor Child*

O'Neal. *President Truman and the Atomic Bomb*

Patrick. *The Young Oxford Companion to the Supreme Court*

Philip. *Singing America: Poems That Define a Nation*

Pietrusza. *The Invasion of Normandy*

Platt. *The Smithsonian Visual Timeline of Inventions*

Press. *A Multicultural Portrait of Professional Sports*

Rappaport. *American Women: Their Lives in Their Words*

Rice. *The Battle of Midway*

Rogers. *The Secret War: Espionage in World War II*

Stanley. *I Am an American: A True Story of Japanese Internment*

Stein. *World War II in Europe: America Goes to War*

Stein. *World War II in the Pacific: "Remember Pearl Harbor"*

Steins. *The Allies Against the Axis: World War II (1940-1950)*

Taylor. *Air Raid-Pearl Harbor: The Story of December 7, 1941*

Time-Life. *African Americans: Voices of Triumph: Leadership*

Time-Life. *This Fabulous Century: 1940-1950*

Tunnell. *The Children of Topaz*

Vail. *World War II: The War in Europe*

Walter. *Mississippi Challenge*

Warner. *The U.S. Marine Corps*

Wheeler. *Events That Changed American History*

Whitman. *Uncle Sam Wants You!*

Young. *Hiroshima: Fifty Years of Debate*

Multimedia

CD-ROM

Air and Space Smithsonian Dreams of Flight

Critical Mass: America's Race to Build the Atomic Bomb

Daring to Fly!

Eyewitness Encyclopedia of Science

Her Heritage: A Biographical Encyclopedia of American History

Landmark Documents in American History

Lest We Forget: A History of the Holocaust

Portraits of American Presidents

Science Navigator

SkyTrip America

Time Almanac of the 20th Century

Total History

The Way Things Work

World War II, Global Conflict

Video

African Americans

Airmen of World War II

Anzio and the Italian Campaign

The Battle of the Bulge and the Drive to the Rhine

D-Day and the Battle for France

D-Day Omaha Beach

Daring to Dream

The Eagle Triumphant

Elijah Muhammad

The Era of Segregation: A Personal Perspective

The Fighting Marines

Frank Lloyd Wright: An American Original

Franklin D. Roosevelt

From the Home Front to the Front Lines

Genbaku Shi: Killed by the Atomic Bomb

General Douglas MacArthur

Guadalcanal and the Pacific Counterattack

Helen Keller

Hiroshima Maiden

Iwo Jima, Okinawa and the Push on Japan

Jackie Robinson

Jesse Owens

Langston Hughes

Malcolm X

Marian Anderson

The Merchant Marine

More Than Bows and Arrows

Mt. Clare: Cradle of the American Dream

Navajo Code Talkers: The Epic Story

North Africa and the Global War

Oregon's Historic Covered Bridges

Pearl Harbor to Midway

Prejudice: Monster Within

Pride & Prejudice: A History of Black Culture in America

The Rails to Hell . . . and Back

Remembering Pearl Harbor

Riding the Rails

The Southwest of Georgia O'Keeffe

Thurgood Marshall

A Time Remembered

Tragedy to Triumph: An Adventure with Helen Keller

Tuskegee Airmen
W. E. B. DuBois
Women with Wings

GRADE EIGHT

Historical Fiction

Banks. *Under the Shadow of Wings*
Barrie. *Lone Star*
Bauer. *Rain of Fire*
Bethancourt. *The Tommorow Connection*
Cooney. *Both Sides of Time*
Cooney. *Out of Time*
Cutler. *My Wartime Summers*
Ferry. *One More Time!*
Green. *The War at Home*

Greene. *Summer of My German Soldier*
Hahn. *Following My Own Footsteps*
Lisle. *Sirens and Spies*
Manley. *She Flew No Flags*
Murphy. *Gold Star Sister*
Oughton. *The War in Georgia*
Paterson. *Jacob Have I Loved*
Platt. *Honor Bright*
Poynter. *A Time Too Swift*
Rabinowitz. *Bethie*

Ross. *Harper & Moon*
Rylant. *I Had Seen Castles*
Salisbury. *Under the Blood-Red Sun*
Taylor. *The Bomb*
Taylor. *The Cay*
Taylor. *Timothy of the Cay*
Thesman. *Molly Donnelly*
Uchida. *Journey to Topaz*
Vick. *Tag Against Time*
Wunderli. *The Blue Between the Clouds*

Biography

Aldred. *Thurgood Marshall: Supreme Court Justice*
Andryszewski. *The Amazing Life of Moe Berg*
Bachrach. *Margaret Sanger*
Barr. *Malcolm X*
Berry. *Gordon Parks*
Berry. *Langston Hughes*
Billings. *Grace Hopper: Navy Admiral and Computer Pioneer*
Boulton. *Frank Lloyd Wright: Architect: An Illustrated Biography*
Brown. *Malcolm X: His Life and Legacy*
Butts. *May Chinn: The Best Medicine*
Cain. *Louise Nevelson: Sculptor*
Cannon. *Dwight David Eisenhower: War Hero and President*
Castiglia. *Margaret Mead*
Collier. *Duke Ellington*
Collier. *Louis Armstrong: An American Success Story*
Cross. *Roosevelt and the Americans at War*
Daffron. *Margaret Bourke-White: Photographer*
Dallard. *Ella Baker: A Leader Behind the Scenes*
Darby. *Douglas MacArthur*
Darby. *Dwight D. Eisenhower*
Davies. *Malcolm X*

Davis. *Frank Lloyd Wright: Maverick Architect*
Deitch. *Dwight D. Eisenhower*
Denenberg. *The True Story of J. Edgar Hoover*
Devane. *Franklin Delano Roosevelt: President*
Dominy. *Katherine Dunham: Dancer and Choreographer*
Driemen. *Atomic Dawn: A Biography of Robert Oppenheimer*
Ellis. *Dwight D. Eisenhower*
Erlich. *Paul Robeson: Singer and Actor*
Farley. *Robert H. Goddard*
Fleming. *Harry S. Truman*
Frankl. *Charlie Parker: Musician*
Fraser. *Walter White: Civil Rights Leader*
Freedman. *Eleanor Roosevelt: A Life of Discovery*
Freedman. *Franklin Delano Roosevelt*
Garfunkel. *Letter to the World: The Life and Dances of Martha Graham*
Gentry. *Jesse Owens: Champion Athlete*
Gourse. *Dizzy Gillespie and the Birth of Bebop*
Greenblatt. *Franklin D. Roosevelt*
Halasa. *Elijah Muhammad: Religious Leader*

Halasa. *Mary McLeod Bethune: Educator*
Hanley. *Philip Randolph*
Hargrove. *Dwight D. Eisenhower*
Hargrove. *Harry S. Truman: Thirty-Third President*
Haskins. *Thurgood Marshall: A Life for Justice*
Herda. *Thurgood Marshall: Civil Rights Champion*
Israel. *Franklin Delano Roosevelt*
Ito. *John Steinbeck*
Jakoubek. *Adam Clayton Powell, Jr.*
Jakoubek. *Joe Louis: Heavyweight Champion*
James. *Julia Morgan: Architect*
Kallen. *Thurgood Marshall: A Dream of Justice for All*
Keller. *Margaret Bourke-White: A Photographer's Life*
Keller. *The Story of My Life*
Kittredge. *Barbara McClintock*
Kittredge. *Helen Hayes: Actress*
Kliment. *Count Basie: Bandleader and Musician*
Kliment. *Ella Fitzgerald: Singer*
Kronstadt. *Florence Sabin: Medical Researcher*
La Farge. *Pearl Buck*

Larsen. *Franklin D. Roosevelt*
Larsen. *Paul Robeson: Hero Before His Time*
Lazo. *Eleanor Roosevelt*
Leavell. *Harry S. Truman*
Liles. *Sam and the Speaker's Chair*
Lindop. *Dwight D. Eisenhower*
Lindop. *Woodrow Wilson, Franklin D. Roosevelt, Harry S. Truman*
Lubetkin. *George Marshall*
Lynn. *Babe Didrikson Zaharias*
Lyons. *Sorrow's Kitchen: Zora Neale Hurston*
Mahone-Lonesome. *Charles R*
Markham. *Helen Keller*
McDonough. *Frank Lloyd Wright*
Morris. *The FDR Way*
Morris. *The Truman Way*
Murphy. *Frank Lloyd Wright*
Myers. *Malcolm X: By Any Means Necessary*
Nardo. *Franklin D. Roosevelt*
Nicholson. *Georgia O'Keeffe*
Nicholson. *Helen Keller: Humanitarian*

Osofsky. *Free to Dream: Langston Hughes*
Palmer. *Lena Horne: Entertainer*
Patterson. *A. Philip Randolph*
Patterson. *Marian Anderson*
Peifer. *Soldier of Destiny: A Biography of George Patton*
Potter. *Buckminster Fuller*
Pratt. *Martha Graham*
Probosz. *Martha Graham*
Ravage. *Rachel Carson, Gentle Crusader*
Reef. *John Steinbeck*
Rubin. *Frank Lloyd Wright*
Rummel. *Langston Hughes*
Rummel. *Robert Oppenheimer: Dark Prince*
Sandak. *The Franklin Roosevelts*
Sandak. *The Trumans*
Sandberg. *Dwight D. Eisenhower*
Schuman. *Martin Luther King, Jr.*
Shapiro. *Charles Drew: Founder of the Blood Bank*
Sherrow. *Linus Pauling*
St. George. *Dear Dr. Bell. . . Your Friend, Helen Keller*

Talmadge. *The Life of Charles Drew*
Tanenhaus. *Louis Armstrong: Musician*
Tedards. *Marian Anderson: Singer*
Tessitore. *The Hunt and the Feast: A Life of Ernest Hemingway*
Thorleifson. *Ethel Barrymore*
Tilton. *Margaret Mead*
Toor. *Eleanor Roosevelt*
Weidhorn. *Jackie Robinson*
Weisbrot. *Father Divine: Religious Leader*
Whitelaw. *Grace Hopper*
Whitelaw. *Margaret Sanger*
Whitelaw. *Mr. Civil Rights: The Story of Thurgood Marshall*
Witcover. *Zora Neale Hurston*
Woog. *Louis Armstrong*
Wright. *A. Philip Randolph*
Wyman. *Ella Fitzgerald: Jazz Singer Supreme*
Yannuzzi. *Zora Neale Hurston: Southern Storyteller*
Ziesk. *Margaret Mead*

Collective Biography

Aaseng. *Great Justices of the Supreme Court*
Aaseng. *Navajo Code Talkers*
Aaseng. *Twentieth-Century Inventors*
Aaseng. *You Are the General*
Aaseng. *You Are the President*
Altman. *Extraordinary Black Americans*
Beard. *The Presidents in American History*
Blassingame. *The Look-It-Up Book of Presidents*
Blue. *People of Peace*
Cohen. *Prophets of Doom*
Cush. *Artists Who Created Great Works*
Cush. *Women Who Achieved Greatness*
Dolan. *Shaping U.S. Foreign Policy: Twelve Secretaries of State*
Faber. *Great Lives: American Government*
Fireside. *Is There a Woman in the House. . . or Senate?*

Haskins. *Black Eagles: African Americans in Aviation*
Italia. *Courageous Crimefighters*
Jones. *Big Star Fallin' Mama*
Lindop. *Presidents by Accident*
Mayberry. *Business Leaders Who Built Financial Empires*
Mayberry. *Leaders Who Changed the 20th Century*
Morin. *Women Chosen for Public Office*
Morin. *Women Who Reformed Politics*
Myers. *Now Is Your Time*
Oleksy. *Military Leaders of World War II*
Otfinoski. *Great Black Writers*
Pascoe. *First Facts About the Presidents*
Plowden. *Famous Firsts of Black Women*
Provenson. *My Fellow Americans*

Rennert. *Book of Firsts: Leaders of America*
Rennert. *Civil Rights Leaders*
Rennert. *Female Writers*
Rennert. *Jazz Stars*
Rennert. *Pioneers of Discovery*
Rubel. *The Scholastic Encyclopedia of the Presidents*
Sheafer. *Women in America's Wars*
Streissguth. *Hatemongers and Demagogues*
Streissguth. *Hoaxers & Hustlers*
Sullivan. *Presidents at Play*
Veglahn. *Women Scientists*
Weitzman. *Great Lives: Human Culture*
Whitelaw. *They Wrote Their Own Headlines*
Wilkinson. *Generals Who Changed the World*
Wolf. *Focus: Five Women Photographers*
Yount. *Black Scientists*
Yount. *Women Aviators*

History

Anderson. *Battles That Changed the Modern World*

Bachrach. *Pearl Harbor: Opposing Viewpoints*

Black. *America Prepares for War*

Black. *Bataan and Corregidor*

Black. *Battle of the Atlantic*

Black. *Battle of the Bulge*

Black. *D-Day*

Black. *Desert Warfare*

Black. *Flattops at War*

Black. *Guadalcanal*

Black. *Hiroshima and the Atomic Bomb*

Black. *Invasion of Italy*

Black. *Island Hopping in the Pacific*

Black. *Iwo Jima and Okinawa*

Black. *Jungle Warfare*

Baker. *The 1940s*

Black. *Pearl Harbor!*

Black. *Victory in Europe*

Black. *War Behind the Lines*

Brashler. *The Story of the Negro League Baseball*

Calabro. *Zap!: A Brief History of Television*

Carlin. *Jazz*

Colman. *Rosie the Riveter*

Colman. *Women in Society: United States*

Cooper. *Playing America's Game: Negro League Baseball*

Cosner. *War Nurses*

Cray. *American Datelines*

Davies. *Transport: On Land, Road and Rail*

Davis. *Behind Barbed Wire*

Devaney. *America Goes to War: 1941*

Devaney. *America on the Attack: 1943*

Devaney. *America Storms the Beaches: 1944*

Devaney. *America Triumphs: 1945*

Dunnahoo. *Pearl Harbor: America Enters the War*

Ferrell. *The U.S. Air Force*

Finkelstein. *Sounds in the Air: The Golden Age of Radio*

Fradin. *Medicine: Yesterday, Today, and Tomorrow*

Gardner. *The Forgotten Players: The Story of Black Baseball in America*

Gay. *World War II*

Greenberg. *Letters From a World War II GI*

Hakim. *War, Peace, and All That Jazz*

Hamanaka. *On the Wings of Peace*

Harris. *The Tuskegee Airmen: Black Heroes of World War II*

Helmer. *Belles of the Ballpark*

Hill. *Our Century: 1940-1950*

Hirsch. *Taxation: Paying for Government*

Isserman. *World War II*

Karl. *America Alive: A History*

Katz. *World War II to the New Frontier: 1940-1963*

Kronenwetter. *Covert Action*

Krull. *V Is for Victory: America Remembers World War II*

Langone. *Spreading Poison: A Book About Racism and Prejudice*

Levine. *A Fence Away from Freedom: Japanese Americans and World War II*

Macy. *A Whole New Ballgame: All-American Girls Professional Baseball League*

Macy. *Winning Ways: A Photohistory of American Women in Sports*

Marrin. *The Airman's War: World War II in the Sky*

Marrin. *OVERLORD: D-Day and the Invasion of Europe*

Marrin. *The Secret Armies: Spies, Counterspies, and Saboteurs*

Marrin. *Victory in the Pacific*

May. *Pushing the Limits: American Women 1940-1961*

McKissack. *Black Diamond*

McKissack. *A Long Hard Journey: The Story of the Pullman Porter*

McKissack. *Red-Tail Angels: Tuskegee Airmen of World War II*

Medearis. *Come This Far to Freedom*

Meltzer. *The Black Americans*

Meltzer. *Weapons & Warfare*

Mizell. *Think About Racism*

Morley. *Clothes: For Work, Play and Display*

Naden. *The U.S. Coast Guard*

Nicholson. *Pearl Harbor Child*

O'Neal. *President Truman and the Atomic Bomb*

Patrick. *The Young Oxford Companion to the Supreme Court*

Philip. *Singing America: Poems That Define a Nation*

Pietrusza. *The Invasion of Normandy*

Platt. *The Smithsonian Visual Timeline of Inventions*

Press. *A Multicultural Portrait of Professional Sports*

Rappaport. *American Women: Their Lives in Their Words*

Rice. *The Battle of Midway*

Rogers. *The Secret War: Espionage in World War II*

Stanley. *I Am an American: A True Story of Japanese Internment*

Stanley. *Women in the Military*

Stein. *World War II in Europe: America Goes to War*

Stein. *World War II in the Pacific: "Remember Pearl Harbor"*

Steins. *The Allies Against the Axis: World War II (1940-1950)*

Taylor. *Air Raid-Pearl Harbor: The Story of December 7, 1941*

Time-Life. *African Americans: Voices of Triumph: Leadership*

Time-Life. *This Fabulous Century: 1940-1950*

Vail. *World War II: The War in Europe*

Walter. *Mississippi Challenge*

Warner. *The U.S. Marine Corps*

Wheeler. *Events That Changed American History*

Whitman. *Uncle Sam Wants You!*

Young. *Hiroshima: Fifty Years of Debate*

Multimedia

CD-ROM

Air and Space Smithsonian Dreams of Flight

Critical Mass: America's Race to Build the Atomic Bomb

Daring to Fly!

Eyewitness Encyclopedia of Science

Famous American Speeches: 1850 to the Present

Her Heritage: A Biographical Encyclopedia of American History

Landmark Documents in American History

Lest We Forget: A History of the Holocaust

Portraits of American Presidents

Science Navigator

SkyTrip America

Time Almanac of the 20th Century

Total History

The Way Things Work

World War II, Global Conflict

Video

African Americans

Airmen of World War II

Anzio and the Italian Campaign

The Battle of the Bulge and the Drive to the Rhine

Daring to Dream

D-Day and the Battle for France

D-Day Omaha Beach

The Eagle Triumphant

Elijah Muhammad

The Era of Segregation: A Personal Perspective

The Fighting Marines

Frank Lloyd Wright: An American Original

Franklin D. Roosevelt

From the Home Front to the Front Lines

Genbaku Shi: Killed by the Atomic Bomb

General Douglas MacArthur

Guadalcanal and the Pacific Counterattack

Helen Keller

Hiroshima Maiden

Iwo Jima, Okinawa and the Push on Japan

Jackie Robinson

Jesse Owens

Langston Hughes

Malcolm X

Marian Anderson

The Merchant Marine

More Than Bows and Arrows

Mt. Clare: Cradle of the American Dream

Navajo Code Talkers: The Epic Story

1945-1989: The Cold War

North Africa and the Global War

Oregon's Historic Covered Bridges

Pearl Harbor to Midway

Prejudice: Monster Within

Pride & Prejudice: A History of Black Culture in America

The Rails to Hell . . . and Back

Remembering Pearl Harbor

Riding the Rails

The Southwest of Georgia O'Keeffe

Thurgood Marshall

A Time Remembered

Tragedy to Triumph: An Adventure with Helen Keller

Tuskegee Airmen

W. E. B. DuBois

Women with Wings

GRADE NINE

Historical Fiction

Bethancourt. The Tommorow Connection

Cooney. Both Sides of Time

Cooney. Out of Time

Ferry. One More Time!

Greene. Summer of My German Soldier

Lisle. Sirens and Spies

Murphy. Gold Star Sister

Paterson. Jacob Have I Loved

Platt. Honor Bright

Poynter. A Time Too Swift

Rabinowitz. Bethie

Rylant. I Had Seen Castles

Taylor. The Bomb

Taylor. The Cay

Taylor. The Road to Memphis

Thesman. Molly Donnelly

Vick. Tag Against Time

Wunderli. The Blue Between the Clouds

Biography

Aldred. Thurgood Marshall: Supreme Court Justice

Bachrach. Margaret Sanger

Barr. Malcolm X

Berry. Gordon Parks

Berry. Langston Hughes

Billings. Grace Hopper: Navy Admiral and Computer Pioneer

Bober. A Restless Spirit: Robert Frost

Boulton. Frank Lloyd Wright: Architect: An Illustrated Biography

Brown. Louis Armstrong: Swinging, Singing Satchmo

Brown. Malcolm X: His Life and Legacy

Cain. Louise Nevelson: Sculptor

Cannon. Dwight David Eisenhower: War Hero and President

Castiglia. Margaret Mead

Collier. Duke Ellington

Collier. Louis Armstrong: An American Success Story

Daffron. Margaret Bourke-White: Photographer

Dallard. *Ella Baker: A Leader Behind the Scenes*
Darby. *Douglas MacArthur*
Darby. *Dwight D. Eisenhower*
Davies. *Malcolm X*
Davis. *Frank Lloyd Wright: Maverick Architect*
Deitch. *Dwight D. Eisenhower*
Denenberg. *The True Story of J. Edgar Hoover*
Devane. *Franklin Delano Roosevelt: President*
Dominy. *Katherine Dunham: Dancer and Choreographer*
Ellis. *Dwight D. Eisenhower*
Erlich. *Paul Robeson: Singer and Actor*
Farley. *Robert H. Goddard*
Feinberg. *Harry S. Truman*
Fleming. *Harry S. Truman*
Frankl. *Charlie Parker: Musician*
Fraser. *Walter White: Civil Rights Leader*
Freedman. *Eleanor Roosevelt: A Life of Discovery*
Garfunkel. *Letter to the World: The Life and Dances of Martha Graham*
Gentry. *Jesse Owens: Champion Athlete*
Gourse. *Dizzy Gillespie and the Birth of Bebop*
Graham. *Franklin D. Roosevelt*
Greenberg. *Hank Greenberg: The Story of My Life*
Greenblatt. *Franklin D. Roosevelt*
Halasa. *Elijah Muhammad: Religious Leader*
Halasa. *Mary McLeod Bethune: Educator*
Hanley. *Philip Randolph*
Hargrove. *Dwight D. Eisenhower*
Haskins. *Thurgood Marshall: A Life for Justice*
Herda. *Earl Warren: Chief Justice for Social Change*
Herda. *Thurgood Marshall: Civil Rights Champion*

Israel. *Franklin Delano Roosevelt*
Ito. *John Steinbeck*
Jakoubek. *Adam Clayton Powell, Jr.*
Jakoubek. *Joe Louis: Heavyweight Champion*
James. *Julia Morgan: Architect*
Kallen. *Thurgood Marshall: A Dream of Justice for All*
Keller. *Margaret Bourke-White: A Photographer's Life*
Keller. *The Story of My Life*
Kittredge. *Barbara McClintock*
Kittredge. *Helen Hayes: Actress*
Kliment. *Count Basie: Bandleader and Musician*
Kliment. *Ella Fitzgerald: Singer*
Kronstadt. *Florence Sabin: Medical Researcher*
La Farge. *Pearl Buck*
Larsen. *Franklin D. Roosevelt*
Larsen. *Paul Robeson: Hero Before His Time*
Leavell. *Harry S. Truman*
Liles. *Sam and the Speaker's Chair*
Lubetkin. *George Marshall*
Lynn. *Babe Didrikson Zaharias*
Lyons. *Sorrow's Kitchen: Zora Neale Hurston*
Mack-Williams. *Malcom X*
Mahone-Lonesome. *Charles R. Drew*
McDonough. *Frank Lloyd Wright*
McKissack. *W. E. B. DuBois*
Morris. *The FDR Way*
Morris. *The Truman Way*
Murphy. *Frank Lloyd Wright*
Myers. *Malcolm X: By Any Means Necessary*
Nardo. *Franklin D. Roosevelt*
Nicholson. *Georgia O'Keeffe*
Nicholson. *Helen Keller: Humanitarian*

Osofsky. *Free to Dream: Langston Hughes*
Palmer. *Lena Horne: Entertainer*
Patterson. *A. Philip Randolph*
Patterson. *Marian Anderson*
Paulsen. *Eastern Sun, Winter Moon*
Peifer. *Soldier of Destiny: A Biography of George Patton*
Potter. *Buckminster Fuller*
Pratt. *Martha Graham*
Probosz. *Martha Graham*
Reef. *John Steinbeck*
Rubin. *Frank Lloyd Wright*
Rummel. *Langston Hughes*
Rummel. *Robert Oppenheimer: Dark Prince*
Sandberg. *Dwight D. Eisenhower*
Saunders. *George C. Marshall: A General for Peace*
Schuman. *Eleanor Roosevelt*
Schuman. *Elie Wiesel*
Scott. *Jackie Robinson*
St. George. *Dear Dr. Bell. . . Your Friend, Helen Keller*
Tanenhaus. *Louis Armstrong: Musician*
Tedards. *Marian Anderson: Singer*
Thorleifson. *Ethel Barrymore*
Tilton. *Margaret Mead*
Toor. *Eleanor Roosevelt*
Weidhorn. *Jackie Robinson*
Weisbrot. *Father Divine: Religious Leader*
Whitelaw. *Margaret Sanger*
Whitelaw. *Mr. Civil Rights: The Story of Thurgood Marshall*
Witcover. *Zora Neale Hurston*
Woog. *Louis Armstrong*
Wright. *A. Philip Randolph*
Wyman. *Ella Fitzgerald: Jazz Singer Supreme*
Yannuzzi. *Zora Neale Hurston: Southern Storyteller*
Ziesk. *Margaret Mead*

Collective Biography

Aaseng. *Great Justices of the Supreme Court*
Aaseng. *Navajo Code Talkers*
Aaseng. *Twentieth-Century Inventors*
Aaseng. *You Are the General*

Aaseng. *You Are the President*
Anthony. *First Ladies: 1789-1961*
Beard. *The Presidents in American History*

Blassingame. *The Look-It-Up Book of Presidents*
Cohen. *Prophets of Doom*
Cush. *Artists Who Created Great Works*

Cush. *Women Who Achieved Greatness*

Dolan. *Shaping U.S. Foreign Policy: Twelve Secretaries of State*

Faber. *Great Lives: American Government*

Italia. *Courageous Crimefighters*

Jones. *Big Star Fallin' Mama*

Landrum. *Profiles of Female Genius: Thirteen Creative Women*

Landrum. *Profiles of Genius: Thirteen Creative Men*

Lindop. *Presidents by Accident*

Mahoney. *Women in Espionage: A Biographical Dictionary*

Mayberry. *Leaders Who Changed the 20th Century*

Morin. *Women Chosen for Public Office*

Morin. *Women Who Reformed Politics*

Myers. *Now Is Your Time*

O'Brien. *American Political Leaders*

Oleksy. *Military Leaders of World War II*

Otfinoski. *Great Black Writers*

Plowden. *Famous Firsts of Black Women*

Rennert. *Book of Firsts: Leaders of America*

Rennert. *Civil Rights Leaders*

Rennert. *Female Writers*

Rennert. *Pioneers of Discovery*

Sheafer. *Women in America's Wars*

Streissguth. *Hatemongers and Demagogues*

Streissguth. *Hoaxers & Hustlers*

Sullivan. *Presidents at Play*

Veglahn. *Women Scientists*

Weitzman. *Great Lives: Human Culture*

Whitelaw. *They Wrote Their Own Headlines*

Wilkinson. *Generals Who Changed the World*

Wolf. *Focus: Five Women Photographers*

Yount. *Black Scientists*

Yount. *Women Aviators*

History

Anderson. *Battles That Changed the Modern World*

Ardley. *Music: An Illustrated Encyclopedia*

Astor. *Operation Iceberg: Okinawa in World War II*

Baker. *The 1940s*

Black. *Battle of the Atlantic*

Black. *Battle of the Bulge*

Black. *D-Day*

Black. *Desert Warfare*

Black. *Flattops at War*

Black. *Guadalcanal*

Black. *Hiroshima and the Atomic Bomb*

Black. *Invasion of Italy*

Black. *Island Hopping in the Pacific*

Black. *Iwo Jima and Okinawa*

Black. *Jungle Warfare*

Black. *Victory in Europe*

Black. *War Behind the Lines*

Brashler. *The Story of the Negro League Baseball*

Calabro. *Zap!: A Brief History of Television*

Carlin. *Jazz*

Childers. *Wings of Morning: World War II*

Cohen. *America: Then and Now*

Collier. *Jazz, the American Theme Song*

Colman. *Rosie the Riveter*

Colman. *Women in Society: United States*

Cosner. *War Nurses*

Cray. *American Datelines*

Davis. *Behind Barbed Wire*

Davis. *Don't Know Much About History*

Devaney. *America Goes to War: 1941*

Devaney. *America on the Attack: 1943*

Devaney. *America Storms the Beaches: 1944*

Devaney. *America Triumphs: 1945*

Douglas. *The World War, 1939-1945: The Cartoonists' Vision*

Dunnahoo. *Pearl Harbor: America Enters the War*

Ewing. *Women in Uniform Through the Centuries*

Finkelstein. *Sounds in the Air: The Golden Age of Radio*

Fox. *The Unknown Internment: Relocation of Italian-Americans During World War II*

Fradin. *Medicine: Yesterday, Today, and Tomorrow*

Garza. *Barred from the Bar: A History of Women and the Legal Profession*

Gay. *World War II*

Gray. *Chronicle of the First World War—Vol I: 1914-1916*

Greenberg. *Letters From a World War II GI*

Hakim. *War, Peace, and All That Jazz*

Hamanaka. *On the Wings of Peace*

Harris. *The Tuskegee Airmen: Black Heroes of World War II*

Helmer. *Belles of the Ballpark*

Hill. *Our Century: 1940-1950*

Hirsch. *Taxation: Paying for Government*

Isserman. *World War II*

Katz. *World War II to the New Frontier: 1940-1963*

Knappman. *Great American Trials: From Salem Witchcraft to Rodney King*

Kronenwetter. *Covert Action*

Lackmann. *Same Time. . . Same Station: An A-Z Guide to Radio*

Langone. *Spreading Poison: A Book About Racism and Prejudice*

Levine. *A Fence Away from Freedom: Japanese Americans and World War II*

Macy. *A Whole New Ballgame: All-American Girls Professional Baseball League*

Macy. *Winning Ways: A Photohistory of American Women in Sports*

Marrin. *The Airman's War: World War II in the Sky*

Marrin. *OVERLORD: D-Day and the Invasion of Europe*

Marrin. *The Secret Armies: Spies, Counterspies, and Saboteurs*

Marrin. *Victory in the Pacific*

May. *Pushing the Limits: American Women 1940-1961*
McKissack. *Black Diamond*
McKissack. *A Long Hard Journey: The Story of the Pullman Porter*
McKissack. *Red-Tail Angels: Tuskegee Airmen of World War II*
Medearis. *Come This Far to Freedom*
Meltzer. *The Black Americans*
Meltzer. *Weapons & Warfare*
Mizell. *Think About Racism*
Nardo. *World War II: The War in the Pacific*
O'Neal. *President Truman and the Atomic Bomb*
Patrick. *The Young Oxford Companion to the Supreme Court*
Philip. *Singing America: Poems That Define a Nation*

Pickford. *The Atlas of Shipwrecks & Treasure*
Pietrusza. *The Invasion of Normandy*
Pimlott. *The Elite: The Special Forces of the World*
Platt. *The Smithsonian Visual Timeline of Inventions*
Potter. *African-American Firsts*
Press. *A Multicultural Portrait of Professional Sports*
Rappaport. *American Women: Their Lives in Their Words*
Rice. *The Battle of Midway*
Rogers. *The Secret War: Espionage in World War II*
Schreiner. *Mayday! Mayday!*
Smith. *Fascinating People and Astounding Events from American History*
Spangenburg. *The History of Science from 1895 to 1945*

Stanley. *I Am an American: A True Story of Japanese Internment*
Stanley. *Women in the Military*
Steele. *Freedom's River*
Stein. *World War II in Europe: America Goes to War*
Stein. *World War II in the Pacific: "Remember Pearl Harbor"*
Time-Life. *African Americans: Voices of Triumph: Leadership*
Time-Life. *This Fabulous Century: 1940-1950*
Vail. *World War II: The War in Europe*
Walter. *Mississippi Challenge*
Wheeler. *Events That Changed American History*
Whitman. *Uncle Sam Wants You!*
Young. *Hiroshima: Fifty Years of Debate*

Multimedia

CD-ROM

Air and Space Smithsonian Dreams of Flight
Critical Mass: America's Race to Build the Atomic Bomb
Daring to Fly!
Events That Changed the World
Famous American Speeches: 1850 to the Present

Her Heritage: A Biographical Encyclopedia of American History
Ideas That Changed the World
Landmark Documents in American History
Lest We Forget: A History of the Holocaust
Our Times: The Multimedia Encyclopedia of the Twentieth Century

Portraits of American Presidents
Science Navigator
Time Almanac of the 20th Century
Total History
The Way Things Work
World War II, Global Conflict

Video

African Americans
Airmen of World War II
America at War: The Undersea Stranglers
Anzio and the Italian Campaign
The Battle of the Bulge and the Drive to the Rhine
D-Day and the Battle for France
D-Day Omaha Beach
Daring to Dream
Dateline: 1943 Europe
The Eagle Triumphant
Elijah Muhammad
The Era of Segregation: A Personal Perspective
A Family Gathering
The Fighting Marines

Frank Lloyd Wright: An American Original
Franklin D. Roosevelt
From the Home Front to the Front Lines
Genbaku Shi: Killed by the Atomic Bomb
General Douglas MacArthur
Guadalcanal and the Pacific Counterattack
Harry S. Truman
Helen Keller
Hiroshima Maiden
Iwo Jima, Okinawa and the Push on Japan
Jackie Robinson
Jesse Owens

Land and Landscape: Views of America's History and Culture
Langston Hughes
The Lottery: Who Fights Our Wars?
Lucky Ones: Allied Airmen and Buchenwald
Malcolm X
The Malcolm X: Make It Plain
Marian Anderson
The Merchant Marine
More Than Bows and Arrows
Mt. Clare: Cradle of the American Dream
Navajo Code Talkers: The Epic Story
Nightfighters
1945-1989: The Cold War

North Africa and the Global
War
Oregon's Historic Covered
Bridges
Patton, A Genius for War
Pearl Harbor to Midway
Prejudice: Monster Within
Pride & Prejudice: A History
of Black Culture in America
The Rails to Hell . . . and Back

Remembering Pearl Harbor
Riding the Rails
The Second World War
The Southwest of Georgia
O'Keeffe
Submarine: Steel Boats, Iron
Men
Thurgood Marshall
A Time Remembered

Tragedy to Triumph: An
Adventure with Helen
Keller
Tuskegee Airmen
U.S.A. vs. Tokyo Rose
USS Arizona: The Life and
Death of a Lady
W. E. B. DuBois
Women with Wings
World War Two

GRADE TEN

Historical Fiction

Cooney. *Both Sides of Time*
Cooney. *Out of Time*
Ferry. *One More Time!*
Levoy. *Alan and Naomi*

Paterson. *Jacob Have I Loved*
Platt. *Honor Bright*
Rabinowitz. *Bethie*
Rylant. *I Had Seen Castles*

Taylor. *The Bomb*
Taylor. *The Road to Memphis*

Biography

Aldred. *Thurgood Marshall:
Supreme Court Justice*
Bachrach. *Margaret Sanger*
Barr. *Malcolm X*
Berry. *Gordon Parks*
Billings. *Grace Hopper: Navy
Admiral and Computer
Pioneer*
Bober. *A Restless Spirit:
Robert Frost*
Boulton. *Frank Lloyd Wright:
Architect: An Illustrated
Biography*
Brown. *Louis Armstrong:
Swinging, Singing Satchmo*
Brown. *Malcolm X: His Life
and Legacy*
Cain. *Louise Nevelson:
Sculptor*
Cannon. *Dwight David
Eisenhower: War Hero and
President*
Daffron. *Margaret
Bourke-White:
Photographer*
Darby. *Douglas MacArthur*
Davies. *Malcolm X*
Davis. *Frank Lloyd Wright:
Maverick Architect*
Deitch. *Dwight D. Eisenhower*
Denenberg. *The True Story of
J. Edgar Hoover*
Dominy. *Katherine Dunham:
Dancer and Choreographer*
Erlich. *Paul Robeson: Singer
and Actor*
Feinberg. *Harry S. Truman*
Fleming. *Harry S. Truman*

Frankl. *Charlie Parker:
Musician*
Freedman. *Eleanor
Roosevelt: A Life of
Discovery*
Garfunkel. *Letter to the
World: The Life and
Dances of Martha Graham*
Gentry. *Jesse Owens:
Champion Athlete*
Graham. *Franklin D.
Roosevelt*
Greenberg. *Hank Greenberg:
The Story of My Life*
Halasa. *Elijah Muhammad:
Religious Leader*
Halasa. *Mary McLeod
Bethune: Educator*
Hanley. *Philip Randolph*
Haskins. *Thurgood Marshall:
A Life for Justice*
Herda. *Earl Warren: Chief
Justice for Social Change*
Herda. *Thurgood Marshall:
Civil Rights Champion*
Howe. *The Hunt for Tokyo
Rose*
Israel. *Franklin Delano
Roosevelt*
Ito. *John Steinbeck*
Jakoubek. *Adam Clayton
Powell, Jr.*
Jakoubek. *Joe Louis:
Heavyweight Champion*
James. *Julia Morgan:
Architect*
Keller. *The Story of My Life*

Kittredge. *Barbara
McClintock*
Kittredge. *Helen Hayes:
Actress*
Kliment. *Count Basie:
Bandleader and Musician*
Kliment. *Ella Fitzgerald:
Singer*
Kronstadt. *Florence Sabin:
Medical Researcher*
La Farge. *Pearl Buck*
Larsen. *Franklin D. Roosevelt*
Leavell. *Harry S. Truman*
Lewis. *W. E. B. DuBois*
Liles. *Sam and the Speaker's
Chair*
Lubetkin. *George Marshall*
Lynn. *Babe Didrikson
Zaharias*
Lyons. *Sorrow's Kitchen:
Zora Neale Hurston*
Mack-Williams. *Malcom X*
Mahone-Lonesome. *Charles
R. Drew*
Marable. *W. E. B. DuBois*
McDonough. *Frank Lloyd
Wright*
McKissack. *W. E. B. DuBois*
Morris. *The FDR Way*
Myers. *Malcolm X: By Any
Means Necessary*
Nardo. *Franklin D. Roosevelt*
Nicholson. *Georgia O'Keeffe*
Nicholson. *Helen Keller:
Humanitarian*
Owens. *Jesse: The Man Who
Outran Hitler*

Palmer. *Lena Horne: Entertainer*
Patterson. *A. Philip Randolph*
Patterson. *Marian Anderson*
Paulsen. *Eastern Sun, Winter Moon*
Pratt. *Martha Graham*
Reef. *John Steinbeck*
Robinson. *I Never Had It Made: An Autobiography*
Rummel. *Langston Hughes*
Rummel. *Robert Oppenheimer: Dark Prince*

Sandberg. *Dwight D. Eisenhower*
Saunders. *George C. Marshall: A General for Peace*
Schuman. *Eleanor Roosevelt*
Schuman. *Elie Wiesel*
Scott. *Jackie Robinson*
Tedards. *Marian Anderson: Singer*
Tessitore. *The Hunt and the Feast: A Life of Ernest Hemingway*

Thorleifson. *Ethel Barrymore*
Tilton. *Margaret Mead*
Toor. *Eleanor Roosevelt*
Weidhorn. *Jackie Robinson*
Weisbrot. *Father Divine: Religious Leader*
Whitelaw. *Margaret Sanger*
Witcover. *Zora Neale Hurston*
Wyman. *Ella Fitzgerald: Jazz Singer Supreme*
Ziesk. *Margaret Mead*

Collective Biography

Aaseng. *Great Justices of the Supreme Court*
Aaseng. *Twentieth-Century Inventors*
Aaseng. *You Are the President*
Anthony. *First Ladies: 1789-1961*
Jones. *Big Star Fallin' Mama*
Landrum. *Profiles of Female Genius: Thirteen Creative Women*
Landrum. *Profiles of Genius: Thirteen Creative Men*
Lindop. *Presidents by Accident*

Mahoney. *Women in Espionage: A Biographical Dictionary*
Mayberry. *Leaders Who Changed the 20th Century*
Morin. *Women Chosen for Public Office*
Morin. *Women Who Reformed Politics*
Myers. *Now Is Your Time*
O'Brien. *American Political Leaders*
Oleksy. *Military Leaders of World War II*
Otfinoski. *Great Black Writers*

Streissguth. *Hatemongers and Demagogues*
Streissguth. *Hoaxers & Hustlers*
Sullivan. *Presidents at Play*
Whitelaw. *They Wrote Their Own Headlines*
Wilkinson. *Generals Who Changed the World*
Wolf. *Focus: Five Women Photographers*
Yount. *Black Scientists*
Yount. *Women Aviators*

History

Anderson. *Battles That Changed the Modern World*
Ardley. *Music: An Illustrated Encyclopedia*
Astor. *Operation Iceberg: Okinawa in World War II*
Baker. *The 1940s*
Beyer. *The Manhattan Project: America Makes the First Atomic Bomb*
Black. *D-Day*
Black. *Desert Warfare*
Black. *Flattops at War*
Black. *Guadalcanal*
Black. *Hiroshima and the Atomic Bomb*
Black. *Invasion of Italy*
Black. *Island Hopping in the Pacific*
Black. *Iwo Jima and Okinawa*
Black. *Jungle Warfare*
Black. *Victory in Europe*
Black. *War Behind the Lines*
Calabro. *Zap!: A Brief History of Television*
Carlin. *Jazz*
Childers. *Wings of Morning: World War II*

Cohen. *America: Then and Now*
Collier. *Jazz, the American Theme Song*
Colman. *Women in Society: United States*
Cray. *American Datelines*
Davis. *Behind Barbed Wire*
Davis. *Don't Know Much About History*
Devaney. *America Goes to War: 1941*
Devaney. *America on the Attack: 1943*
Devaney. *America Storms the Beaches: 1944*
Devaney. *America Triumphs: 1945*
Douglas. *The World War, 1939-1945: The Cartoonists' Vision*
Dunnahoo. *Pearl Harbor: America Enters the War*
Evans. *Born for Liberty: A History of Women in America*
Ewing. *Women in Uniform Through the Centuries*

Finkelstein. *Sounds in the Air: The Golden Age of Radio*
Fox. *The Unknown Internment: Relocation of Italian-Americans During World War II*
Fradin. *Medicine: Yesterday, Today, and Tomorrow*
Garza. *Barred from the Bar: A History of Women and the Legal Profession*
Gray. *Chronicle of the First World War—Vol I: 1914-1916*
Greenberg. *Letters From a World War II GI*
Hakim. *War, Peace, and All That Jazz*
Hamanaka. *On the Wings of Peace*
Harris. *The Tuskegee Airmen: Black Heroes of World War II*
Hill. *Our Century: 1940-1950*
Isserman. *World War II*
Katz. *World War II to the New Frontier: 1940-1963*

Knappman. *Great American Trials: From Salem Witchcraft to Rodney King*
Kronenwetter. *Covert Action*
Lackmann. *Same Time. . . Same Station: An A-Z Guide to Radio*
Langone. *Spreading Poison: A Book About Racism and Prejudice*
Levine. *A Fence Away from Freedom: Japanese Americans and World War II*
Macy. *Winning Ways: A Photohistory of American Women in Sports*
Marrin. *OVERLORD: D-Day and the Invasion of Europe*
Marrin. *The Secret Armies: Spies, Counterspies, and Saboteurs*
Marrin. *Victory in the Pacific*
May. *Pushing the Limits: American Women 1940-1961*
McKissack. *A Long Hard Journey: The Story of the Pullman Porter*

Meltzer. *The Black Americans*
Meltzer. *Weapons & Warfare*
Mizell. *Think About Racism*
Nardo. *World War II: The War in the Pacific*
Patrick. *The Young Oxford Companion to the Supreme Court*
Philip. *Singing America: Poems That Define a Nation*
Pickford. *The Atlas of Shipwrecks & Treasure*
Pimlott. *The Elite: The Special Forces of the World*
Potter. *African-American Firsts*
Press. *A Multicultural Portrait of Professional Sports*
Rappaport. *American Women: Their Lives in Their Words*
Rice. *The Battle of Midway*
Rogers. *The Secret War: Espionage in World War II*
Schreiner. *Mayday! Mayday!*

Smith. *Fascinating People and Astounding Events from American History*
Spangenburg. *The History of Science from 1895 to 1945*
Stanley. *I Am an American: A True Story of Japanese Internment*
Stanley. *Women in the Military*
Steele. *Freedom's River*
Stein. *World War II in Europe: America Goes to War*
Stein. *World War II in the Pacific: "Remember Pearl Harbor"*
Time-Life. *African Americans: Voices of Triumph: Leadership*
Time-Life. *This Fabulous Century: 1940-1950*
Vail. *World War II: The War in Europe*
Walter. *Mississippi Challenge*
Wheeler. *Events That Changed American History*
Young. *Hiroshima: Fifty Years of Debate*

Multimedia

CD-ROM

Air and Space Smithsonian Dreams of Flight
Critical Mass: America's Race to Build the Atomic Bomb
Daring to Fly!
Events That Changed the World
Famous American Speeches: 1850 to the Present

Her Heritage: A Biographical Encyclopedia of American History
Ideas That Changed the World
Landmark Documents in American History
Lest We Forget: A History of the Holocaust
Normandy: The Great Crusade

Our Times: The Multimedia Encyclopedia of the Twentieth Century
Portraits of American Presidents
Science Navigator
Time Almanac of the 20th Century
Total History
The Way Things Work
World War II, Global Conflict

Video

African Americans
Airmen of World War II
America at War: The Undersea Stranglers
Anzio and the Italian Campaign
The Battle of the Bulge and the Drive to the Rhine
Dateline: 1943 Europe
D-Day and the Battle for France
D-Day Omaha Beach
D-Day + 50 . . . Normandy
Daring to Dream
The Eagle Triumphant
Elijah Muhammad

The Era of Segregation: A Personal Perspective
A Family Gathering
FDR
The Fighting Marines
Frank Lloyd Wright: An American Original
Franklin D. Roosevelt
From the Home Front to the Front Lines
Genbaku Shi: Killed by the Atomic Bomb
General Douglas MacArthur
Guadalcanal and the Pacific Counterattack
Harry S. Truman

Helen Keller
Hiroshima: Why the Bomb Was Dropped
Hiroshima Maiden
Iwo Jima, Okinawa and the Push on Japan
Jackie Robinson
Land and Landscape: Views of America's History and Culture
Langston Hughes
The Lottery: Who Fights Our Wars?
The Lucky Ones: Allied Airmen and Buchenwald
Malcolm X

Malcolm X: Make It Plain
Marian Anderson
The Merchant Marine
More Than Bows and Arrows
Mt. Clare: Cradle of the
  American Dream
Navajo Code Talkers: The
  Epic Story
Nightfighters
1945-1989: The Cold War
North Africa and the Global
  War
Oregon's Historic Covered
  Bridges

Patton, A Genius for War
Pearl Harbor to Midway
Pride & Prejudice: A History
  of Black Culture in America
The Rails to Hell . . . and Back
Remembering Pearl Harbor
Riding the Rails
The Second World War
The Southwest of Georgia
  O'Keeffe
Submarine: Steel Boats, Iron
  Men
Thurgood Marshall
A Time Remembered

Tragedy to Triumph: An
  Adventure with Helen
  Keller
Tuskegee Airmen
U.S.A. vs. Tokyo Rose
USS Arizona: The Life and
  Death of a Lady
W. E. B. DuBois
Women with Wings
World War Two

GRADES ELEVEN AND TWELVE

Historical Fiction

Boyne. *Air Force Eagles*
Boyne. *Eagles at War*
Bunkley. *Wild Embers*
Ferry. *One More Time!*

Glasco. *Slow Through Eden*
Greenberg. *No Reck'ning
Made*
Levoy. *Alan and Naomi*

Rylant. *I Had Seen Castles*
Taylor. *The Road to Memphis*

Biography

Bachrach. *Margaret Sanger*
Barr. *Malcolm X*
Beschloss. *Eisenhower: A
Centennial Life*
Billings. *Grace Hopper: Navy
Admiral and Computer
Pioneer*
Bober. *A Restless Spirit:
Robert Frost*
Boulton. *Frank Lloyd Wright:
Architect: An Illustrated
Biography*
Bragg. *Soaring Above
Setbacks: The
Autobiography of Janet
Harmon Bragg*
Brown. *Louis Armstrong:
Swinging, Singing Satchmo*
Brown. *Malcolm X: His Life
and Legacy*
Darby. *Douglas MacArthur*
Davies. *Malcolm X*
Deitch. *Dwight D. Eisenhower*
Denenberg. *The True Story of
J. Edgar Hoover*
Dominy. *Katherine Dunham:
Dancer and Choreographer*
Dyson. *Making Malcolm: The
Myth and Meaning of
Malcolm X*
Erlich. *Paul Robeson: Singer
and Actor*

Feinberg. *Harry S. Truman*
Freedman. *Eleanor
Roosevelt: A Life of
Discovery*
Graham. *Franklin D.
Roosevelt*
Greenberg. *Hank Greenberg:
The Story of My Life*
Halasa. *Elijah Muhammad:
Religious Leader*
Herda. *Earl Warren: Chief
Justice for Social Change*
Howe. *The Hunt for Tokyo
Rose*
Jakoubek. *Adam Clayton
Powell, Jr.*
James. *Julia Morgan:
Architect*
Keller. *The Story of My Life*
Kittredge. *Barbara
McClintock*
Kittredge. *Helen Hayes:
Actress*
Kliment. *Count Basie:
Bandleader and Musician*
Kliment. *Ella Fitzgerald:
Singer*
Kronstadt. *Florence Sabin:
Medical Researcher*
La Farge. *Pearl Buck*
Larsen. *Franklin D. Roosevelt*
Lewis. *W. E. B. DuBois*

Liles. *Sam and the Speaker's
Chair*
Lubetkin. *George Marshall*
Lynn. *Babe Didrikson
Zaharias*
Lyons. *Sorrow's Kitchen:
Zora Neale Hurston*
Mack-Williams. *Malcom X*
Mahone-Lonesome. *Charles
R. Drew*
Marable. *W. E. B. DuBois*
McCullough. *Truman*
McKissack. *W. E. B. DuBois*
Meyers. *Robert Frost: A
Biography*
Morris. *The FDR Way*
Owens. *Jesse: The Man Who
Outran Hitler*
Palmer. *Lena Horne:
Entertainer*
Partridge. *Dorothea Lange: A
Visual Life*
Paulsen. *Eastern Sun, Winter
Moon*
Phelps. *Chappie: Daniel
James, Jr*
Powers. *Secrecy and Power:
The Life of J. Edgar Hoover*
Raymer. *Descent into
Darkness: Pearl Harbor,
1941*
Reef. *John Steinbeck*

Robinson. *I Never Had It Made: An Autobiography*

Rummel. *Langston Hughes*

Rummel. *Robert Oppenheimer: Dark Prince*

Saunders. *George C. Marshall: A General for Peace*

Schultz. *Hero of Bataan: The Story of General Jonathan M. Wainwright*

Tessitore. *The Hunt and the Feast: A Life of Ernest Hemingway*

Thorleifson. *Ethel Barrymore*

Weisbrot. *Father Divine: Religious Leader*

Whitelaw. *Margaret Sanger*

Collective Biography

Aaseng. *Great Justices of the Supreme Court*

Aaseng. *Twentieth-Century Inventors*

Aaseng. *You Are the President*

Anthony. *First Ladies: 1789-1961*

Jones. *Big Star Fallin' Mama*

Landrum. *Profiles of Female Genius: Thirteen Creative Women*

Landrum. *Profiles of Genius: Thirteen Creative Men*

Lindop. *Presidents by Accident*

Mahoney. *Women in Espionage: A Biographical Dictionary*

Mayberry. *Leaders Who Changed the 20th Century*

McCullough. *Brave Companions: Portraits in History*

Morin. *Women Chosen for Public Office*

O'Brien. *American Political Leaders: From Colonial Times to the Present*

Oleksy. *Military Leaders of World War II*

Otfinoski. *Great Black Writers*

Streissguth. *Hatemongers and Demagogues*

Streissguth. *Hoaxers & Hustlers*

Truman. *First Ladies*

Wills. *Certain Trumpets: The Call of Leaders*

Wolf. *Focus: Five Women Photographers*

Yount. *Black Scientists*

Yount. *Women Aviators*

History

Ardley. *Music: An Illustrated Encyclopedia*

Astor. *Operation Iceberg: Okinawa in World War II*

Baker. *The 1940s*

Beyer. *The Manhattan Project: America Makes the First Atomic Bomb*

Black. *In the Shadow of Polio: A Personal and Social History*

Boller. *Presidential Wives: An Anecdotal History*

Brimner. *Voices from the Camps: Internment of Japanese Americans During World War II*

Burgess. *The Longest Tunnel: The True Story of World War II's Great Escape*

Calabro. *Zap!: A Brief History of Television*

Carlin. *Jazz*

Childers. *Wings of Morning: World War II*

Cohen. *America: Then and Now*

Collier. *Jazz, the American Theme Song*

Colman. *Women in Society: United States*

Cray. *American Datelines*

Daniels. *Prisoners Without Trial: Japanese-Americans In World War II*

Davidson. *Everyday Life Through the Ages*

Davis. *Behind Barbed Wire*

Davis. *Don't Know Much About History*

Devaney. *America Goes to War: 1941*

Devaney. *America on the Attack: 1943*

Devaney. *America Storms the Beaches: 1944*

Devaney. *America Triumphs: 1945*

Douglas. *The World War, 1939-1945: The Cartoonists' Vision*

Dunnahoo. *Pearl Harbor: America Enters the War*

Evans. *Born for Liberty: A History of Women in America*

Ewing. *Women in Uniform Through the Centuries*

Finkelstein. *Sounds in the Air: The Golden Age of Radio*

Fogle. *Two Hundred Years: Stories of the Nation's Capital*

Fox. *The Unknown Internment: Relocation of Italian-Americans During World War II*

Garza. *Barred from the Bar: A History of Women and the Legal Profession*

Gilbert. *They Also Served: Baseball and the Home Front 1941-1945*

Gray. *Chronicle of the First World War—Vol I: 1914-1916*

Greenberg. *Letters From a World War II GI*

Hakim. *War, Peace, and All That Jazz*

Isserman. *World War II*

Keegan. *History of Warfare*

Kelly. *Proudly We Served: The Men of the USS Mason*

Knappman. *Great American Trials*

Kronenwetter. *Covert Action*

Lackmann. *Same Time. . . Same Station: An A-Z Guide to Radio*

Langone. *Spreading Poison: A Book About Racism and Prejudice*

Leckie. *Okinawa: The Last Battle of World War II*

Marling. *Iwo Jima: Monuments, Memories, and the American Hero*

Marrin. *The Secret Armies: Spies, Counterspies, and Saboteurs*

May. *Pushing the Limits: American Women 1940-1961*
Melder. *Hail to the Candidate: Presidential Campaigns*
Meltzer. *Weapons & Warfare*
Miller. *Nothing Less Than Victory: The Oral History of D-Day*
Nardo. *World War II: The War in the Pacific*
Okihiro. *Whispered Silences: Japanese Americans and World War II*
Patrick. *The Young Oxford Companion to the Supreme Court*
Philip. *Singing America: Poems That Define a Nation*
Pickford. *The Atlas of Shipwrecks & Treasure*

Pimlott. *The Elite: The Special Forces of the World*
Potter. *African-American Firsts*
Press. *A Multicultural Portrait of Professional Sports*
Rappaport. *American Women: Their Lives in Their Words*
Riley. *The Biographical Encyclopedia of Negro Baseball Leagues*
Rogers. *The Secret War: Espionage in World War II*
Schreiner. *Mayday! Mayday!*
Schultz. *The Maverick War: Chennault and the Flying Tigers*
Smith. *Fascinating People and Astounding Events from American History*

Spangenburg. *The History of Science from 1895 to 1945*
Stanley. *Women in the Military*
Steele. *Freedom's River*
Takaki. *Hiroshima: Why America Dropped the Atomic Bomb*
Terkel. *The Good War*
Time-Life. *African Americans: Voices of Triumph: Leadership*
Time-Life. *This Fabulous Century: 1940-1950*
Voss. *Reporting the War: The Journalistic Coverage of World War II*
Walter. *Mississippi Challenge*
Ward. *Closest Companion: Franklin Roosevelt and Margaret Suckley*
Wheeler. *Events That Changed American History*

Multimedia

CD-ROM

Air and Space Smithsonian Dreams of Flight
Critical Mass: America's Race to Build the Atomic Bomb
Daring to Fly!
Events That Changed the World
Famous American Speeches: 1850 to the Present

Her Heritage: A Biographical Encyclopedia of American History
Ideas That Changed the World
Landmark Documents in American History
Lest We Forget: A History of the Holocaust
Normandy: The Great Crusade

Our Times: The Multimedia Encyclopedia of the Twentieth Century
Portraits of American Presidents
Science Navigator
Time Almanac of the 20th Century
Total History
The Way Things Work
World War II, Global Conflict

Video

Airmen of World War II
America at War: The Undersea Stranglers
Anzio and the Italian Campaign
The Battle of the Bulge and the Drive to the Rhine
Daring to Dream
Dateline: 1943 Europe
D-Day and the Battle for France
D-Day Omaha Beach
D-Day + 50. . .Normandy
Elijah Muhammad
The Era of Segregation: A Personal Perspective
A Family Gathering
FDR
The Fighting Marines

Frank Lloyd Wright: An American Original
Franklin D. Roosevelt
From the Home Front to the Front Lines
Genbaku Shi: Killed by the Atomic Bomb
General Douglas MacArthur
Guadalcanal and the Pacific Counterattack
Harry S. Truman
Helen Keller
Hiroshima: Why the Bomb Was Dropped
Hiroshima Maiden
Iwo Jima, Okinawa and the Push on Japan
Jackie Robinson

Land and Landscape: Views of America's History and Culture
Langston Hughes
The Lottery: Who Fights Our Wars?
The Lucky Ones: Allied Airmen and Buchenwald
Malcolm X
Malcolm X: Make It Plain
Marian Anderson
The Merchant Marine
More Than Bows and Arrows
Mt. Clare: Cradle of the American Dream
Navajo Code Talkers: The Epic Story
Nightfighters
1945-1989: The Cold War

THE MID-TWENTIETH CENTURY, 1946-1975

Historical Fiction

Barnes. *Promise Me the Moon*
Bellairs. *The Drum, the Doll, and the Zombie*
Belton. *Ernestine and Amanda*
Bennett. *The Moon Stops Here*
Bolden. *Just Family*
Boutis. *Looking Out*
Brooks. *The Moves Make the Man*
Brooks. *Naked in Winter*
Calvert. *The Hour of the Wolf*
Cameron. *The Court of the Stone Children*
Cohen. *The Ghost of Elvis*
Cleaver. *Dust of the Earth*
Cole. *The Final Tide*
Cormier. *Tunes for Bears to Dance To*
Curtis. *The Watsons Go to Birmingham—1963*
Dixon, Jeanne. *The Tempered Wind*
Freeman. *The Cuckoo's Child*
Fromm. *Monkey Tag*
Greene. *Morning Is a Long Time Coming*
Hall. *Halsey's Pride*
Hausman. *Night Flight*
Herman. *Millie Cooper, Take a Chance*
Herman. *Millie Cooper, 3B*

High. *The Summer of the Great Divide*
Hite. *It's Nothing to a Mountain*
Hotze. *Acquainted with the Night*
Irwin. *Kim/Kimi*
Johnston. *Hero of Lesser Causes*
Jones. *Long Time Passing*
Kinsey-Warnock. *The Canada Geese Quilt*
Lelchuk. *On Home Ground*
Levin. *Fire in the Wind*
Levinson. *Your Friend, Natalie Popper*
Lyon. *Red Rover, Red Rover*
Marino. *The Day That Elvis Came to Town*
Marino. *For the Love of Pete*
Martin. *Night Riding*
Moore. *Freedom Songs*
Myers. *Rosie's Tiger*
Nelson. *and One for All*
Nelson. *Mayfield Crossing*
Oughton. *Music from a Place Called Half Moon*
Paulsen. *The Cookcamp*
Paulsen. *Harris and Me: A Summer Remembered*
Paulsen. *The Rifle*

Pendergraft. *Brushy Mountain*
Pennebaker. *Don't Think Twice*
Qualey. *Come in from the Cold*
Qualey. *Everybody's Daughter*
Rosofsky. *Miriam*
Rostkowski. *The Best of Friends*
Rumbaut. *Dove Dream*
Salisbury. *Blue Skin of the Sea*
Slepian. *Risk n' Roses*
Smothers. *Down in the Piney Woods*
Steiner. *Tessa*
Strauch. *Hey You, Sister Rose*
Strickland. *The Hand of the Necromancer*
Talbert. *The Purple Heart*
Uchida. *The Best Bad Thing*
Uchida. *The Happiest Ending*
Uchida. *Journey Home*
Von Ahnen. *Heart of Naosaqua*
White. *Belle Prater's Boy*
White. *Come Next Spring*
White. *The Road Home*
White. *Sweet Creek Holler*
Wyss. *A Stranger Here*
Young. *Learning by Heart*

Biography

Aldred. *Thurgood Marshall: Supreme Court Justice*
Anderson. *Jackie Kennedy Onassis*
Ashabranner. *The Times of My Life: A Memoir*
Ayers. *Chuck Yeager: Fighter Pilot*
Bachrach. *Margaret Sanger*

Baldwin. *DNA Pioneer: James Watson and the Double Helix*
Barnes. *Samuel Goldwyn*
Barr. *Malcolm X*
Barr. *Richard Nixon*
Berkow. *Hank Greenberg: Hall-of-Fame Slugger*
Bernstein. *Judith Resnick: Challenger Astronaut*

Berry. *Georgia O'Keeffe: Painter*
Berry. *Gordon Parks*
Berry. *Langston Hughes*
Billings. *Grace Hopper: Navy Admiral and Computer Pioneer*
Bishop. *Ralph Ellison: Author*
Blau. *Betty Friedan: Feminist*
Blue. *Barbara Jordan: Politician*

Bredeson. *Jonas Salk: Discoverer of the Polio Vaccine*

Brown. *Romare Bearden: Artist*

Butts. *May Chinn: The Best Medicine*

Cain. *Louise Nevelson: Sculptor*

Cannon. *Dwight David Eisenhower: War Hero and President*

Castiglia. *Margaret Mead*

Celsi. *Ralph Nader: The Consumer Revolution*

Chin. *When Justice Failed: The Fred Korematsu Story*

Cohen. *Joseph McCarthy*

Cole. *John F. Kennedy*

Cole. *John Glenn: Astronaut and Senator*

Collier. *Duke Ellington*

Collier. *Louis Armstrong: An American Success Story*

Collins. *Gerald R. Ford*

Collins. *Harry S. Truman*

Colman. *Fannie Lou Hamer and the Fight for the Vote*

Colman. *A Woman Unafraid: The Achievements of Frances Perkins*

Conord. *John Lennon*

Curson. *Jonas Salk*

Daffron. *Margaret Bourke-White: Photographer*

Dallard. *Ella Baker: A Leader Behind the Scenes*

Darby. *Douglas MacArthur*

Darby. *Dwight D. Eisenhower*

Darby. *Martin Luther King, Jr.*

Davies. *Malcolm X*

Davis. *Frank Lloyd Wright: Maverick Architect*

Deitch. *Dwight D. Eisenhower*

Denenberg. *John Fitzgerald Kennedy: America's 35th President*

Denenberg. *The True Story of J. Edgar Hoover*

Diamond. *Jackie Robinson*

Ellis. *Dwight D. Eisenhower*

Erlich. *Paul Robeson: Singer and Actor*

Falkof. *John F. Kennedy*

Falkof. *Lyndon B. Johnson*

Ferris. *What I Had Was Singing: Marian Anderson*

Fleming. *Harry S. Truman*

Frankl. *Charlie Parker: Musician*

Fraser. *Walter White: Civil Rights Leader*

Freedman. *Dian Fossey: Befriending the Gorillas*

Freedman. *Eleanor Roosevelt: A Life of Discovery*

Friese. *Rosa Parks: The Movement Organizes*

Garfunkel. *Letter to the World: Martha Graham*

Gentry. *Dizzy Gillespie: Musician*

Gentry. *Jesse Owens: Champion Athlete*

Gherman. *E. B. White: Some Writer!*

Gonzales. *Alex Haley: Author of Roots*

Gottfried. *Alan Turing: The Architect of the Computer Age*

Gourse. *Billie Holiday: The Tragedy and Triumph of Lady Day*

Gourse. *Dizzy Gillespie and the Birth of Bebop*

Greenberg. *The Buck Stops Here: Harry Truman*

Halasa. *Elijah Muhammad: Religious Leader*

Halasa. *Mary McLeod Bethune: Educator*

Hanley. *Philip Randolph*

Hargrove. *Dwight D. Eisenhower*

Hargrove. *Harry S. Truman: Thirty-Third President*

Hargrove. *Lyndon B. Johnson: Thirty-sixth President*

Harrison. *A Ripple of Hope: The Life of Robert F. Kennedy*

Harrison. *A Twilight Struggle: The Life of John Fitzgerald Kennedy*

Haskins. *I Have a Dream: The Life and Words of Martin Luther King, Jr*

Haskins. *Thurgood Marshall: A Life for Justice*

Heiligman. *Barbara McClintock: Alone in Her Field*

Henry. *Betty Friedan: Fighter for Women's Rights*

Henry. *Coretta Scott King: Keeper of the Dream*

Herda. *Thurgood Marshall: Civil Rights Champion*

Hudson. *The Will and the Way: Paul R. Williams*

Hull. *Rosa Parks: Civil Rights Leader*

Ito. *John Steinbeck*

Jakoubek. *Adam Clayton Powell, Jr.*

Jakoubek. *Joe Louis: Heavyweight Champion*

Jakoubek. *Martin Luther King, Jr.*

James. *Julia Morgan: Architect*

Jezer. *Rachel Carson: Biologist and Author*

Johnson. *Ted Williams*

Kallen. *Martin Luther King: A Man and His Dream*

Kallen. *Thurgood Marshall: A Dream of Justice for All*

Kaye. *The Life of Alexander Fleming*

Kaye. *The Life of Benjamin Spock*

Kaye. *The Life of Florence Sabin*

Kaye. *Lyndon B. Johnson*

Keller. *Margaret Bourke-White: A Photographer's Life*

Keller. *The Story of My Life*

Kent. *John F. Kennedy: Thirty-Fifth President*

King. *My Life with Martin Luther King, Jr*

Kittredge. *Barbara McClintock*

Kittredge. *Helen Hayes: Actress*

Kliment. *Count Basie: Bandleader and Musician*

Kliment. *Ella Fitzgerald: Singer*

Krohn. *Elvis Presley: The King*

Kronstadt. *Florence Sabin: Medical Researcher*

La Farge. *Pearl Buck*

Lansche. *Stan "The Man" Musial: Born to Be a Ballplayer*

Larsen. *Paul Robeson: Hero Before His Time*

Larsen. *Richard Nixon: Rise and Fall of a President*

Lazo. *Eleanor Roosevelt*

Leavell. *Harry S. Truman*

Liles. *Sam and the Speaker's Chair*

Lillegard. *Richard Nixon: Thirty-Seventh President*
Lindop. *Richard M. Nixon, Jimmy Carter, Ronald Reagan*
Lindop. *Woodrow Wilson, Franklin D. Roosevelt, Harry S. Truman*
Loewen. *Elvis*
Lubetkin. *George Marshall*
Lynn. *Babe Didrikson Zaharias*
Lyons. *Clare Boothe Luce*
Lyons. *Painting Dreams: Minnie Evans*
Lyons. *Sorrow's Kitchen: Zora Neale Hurston*
Markham. *Helen Keller*
McDonough. *Frank Lloyd Wright*
McPherson. *TV's Forgotten Hero: Philo Farnsworth*
Meltzer. *Betty Friedan: A Voice for Women's Rights*
Meryman. *Andrew Wyeth*
Mills. *John F. Kennedy*
Morris. *The Truman Way*
Murphy. *Frank Lloyd Wright*
Myers. *Malcolm X: By Any Means Necessary*
Myers. *A Place Called Heartbreak: A Story of Vietnam*
Nicholson. *Georgia O'Keeffe*
Nicholson. *Helen Keller: Humanitarian*
Oneal. *Grandma Moses: Painter of Rural America*
Osofsky. *Free to Dream: Langston Hughes*
Palmer. *Lena Horne: Entertainer*
Patrick. *Coretta Scott King*
Patterson. *A. Philip Randolph*
Patterson. *Marian Anderson*
Patterson. *Martin Luther King and the Montgomery Bus Boycott*
Peduzzi. *Ralph Nader*
Petrillo. *Robert F. Kennedy*
Pietrusza. *John F. Kennedy*
Pollack. *Shirley Chisholm*

Potter. *Buckminster Fuller*
Pratt. *Martha Graham*
Presnal. *Rachel Carson*
Probosz. *Martha Graham*
Randall. *John F. Kennedy*
Ravage. *Rachel Carson, Gentle Crusader*
Reef. *John Steinbeck*
Reef. *Ralph David Abernathy*
Richman. *James E. Carter*
Rosset. *James Baldwin: Author*
Rowland. *Martin Luther King, Jr*
Rubel. *Elvis Presley: The Rise of Rock and Roll*
Rubel. *Fannie Lou Hamer*
Rubin. *Frank Lloyd Wright*
Rummel. *Langston Hughes*
Rummel. *Robert Oppenheimer: Dark Prince*
Sandak. *The Eisenhowers*
Sandak. *The Lyndon Johnsons*
Sandak. *The Nixons*
Sandak. *The Trumans*
Sandberg. *Dwight D. Eisenhower*
Saunders. *George C. Marshall: A General for Peace*
Sawyer. *Marjory Stoneman Douglas*
Schroeder. *Josephine Baker*
Schuman. *Eleanor Roosevelt*
Schuman. *Elie Wiesel*
Scott. *Jackie Robinson*
Shapiro. *Charles Drew: Founder of the Blood Bank*
Sherrow. *Linus Pauling*
Shirley. *Satchel Paige*
Shuker. *Elizabeth Arden*
Sklansky. *James Farmer*
Smith. *Coming out Right: Jacqueline Cochran*
Speaker-Yuan. *Agnes de Mille: Choreographer*
St. George. *Dear Dr. Bell. . . Your Friend, Helen Keller*
Stafford. *W. E. B. DuBois: Scholar and Activist*
Stefoff. *Richard M. Nixon*

Stine. *The Story Of Malcolm X, Civil Rights Leader*
Stwertka. *Duke Ellington: A Life of Music*
Talmadge. *The Life of Charles Drew*
Tanenhaus. *Louis Armstrong: Musician*
Taylor-Boyd. *Betty Friedan*
Tedards. *Marian Anderson: Singer*
Tessitore. *The Hunt and the Feast: A Life of Ernest Hemingway*
Thorleifson. *Ethel Barrymore*
Tilton. *Margaret Mead*
Tingum. *E. B. White*
Tomlinson. *Jonas Salk*
Toor. *Eleanor Roosevelt*
Urban. *Richard Wright: Author*
Wade. *James Carter: Thirty-Ninth President*
Wadsworth. *Rachel Carson: Voice for the Earth*
Walker. *Pride of Puerto Rico: The Life of Roberto Clemente*
Weidhorn. *Jackie Robinson*
Weisbrot. *Father Divine: Religious Leader*
Whitelaw. *Grace Hopper*
Whitelaw. *Margaret Sanger*
Whitelaw. *Mr. Civil Rights: The Story of Thurgood Marshall*
Williams. *Patrick Desjarlait*
Witcover. *Zora Neale Hurston*
Wolfe. *Mahalia Jackson: Gospel Singer*
Woog. *Duke Ellington*
Woog. *Louis Armstrong*
Wright. *A. Philip Randolph*
Wright. *John Lennon*
Wyman. *Ella Fitzgerald: Jazz Singer Supreme*
Yannuzzi. *Zora Neale Hurston: Southern Storyteller*
Yates. *Woodie Guthrie: American Balladeer*
Ziesk. *Margaret Mead*

Collective Biography

Aaseng. *America's Third-Party Presidential Candidates*
Aaseng. *Close Calls: From the Brink of Ruin to Business Success*
Aaseng. *From Rags to Riches*

Aaseng. *Genetics: Unlocking the Secrets of Life*
Aaseng. *True Champions: Great Athletes and Their Off-the-Field Heroics*

Allen. *Black Women Leaders of the Civil Rights Movement*
Altman. *Extraordinary Black Americans*
Beard. *The Presidents in American History*

Blassingame. *The Look-It-Up Book of Presidents*
Blue. *People of Peace*
Brill. *Extraordinary Young People*
Camp. *American Astronomers: Searchers and Wonderers*
Cohen. *Prophets of Doom*
Cush. *Artists Who Created Great Works*
Cush. *Women Who Achieved Greatness*
Dolan. *Shaping U.S. Foreign Policy: Profiles of Twelve Secretaries of State*
Faber. *Great Lives: American Government*
Fireside. *Is There a Woman in the House. . . or Senate?*
Glenn. *Discover America's Favorite Architects*
Glubok. *Great Lives: Painting*
Haskins. *Against All Opposition: Black Explorers in America*
Haskins. *Black Eagles: African Americans in Aviation*
Italia. *Courageous Crimefighters*
Jacobs. *Great Lives: Human Rights*
Jacobs. *Great Lives: World Religions*
Krull. *Lives of the Artists: Masterpieces, Messes*

Krull. *Lives of the Athletes*
Krull. *Lives of the Musicians: Good Times, Bad Times*
Krull. *Lives of the Writers: Comedies, Tragedies*
Lindop. *Presidents by Accident*
Mayberry. *Business Leaders Who Built Financial Empires*
Mayberry. *Leaders Who Changed the 20th Century*
Morin. *Women Chosen for Public Office*
Morin. *Women of the U.S. Congress*
Morin. *Women Who Reformed Politics*
Myers. *Now Is Your Time*
Pascoe. *First Facts About the Presidents*
Pile. *Top Entrepreneurs and Their Businesses*
Pile. *Women Business Leaders*
Plowden. *Famous Firsts of Black Women*
Provenson. *My Fellow Americans*
Rennert. *Book of Firsts: Leaders of America*
Rennert. *Civil Rights Leaders*
Rennert. *Female Writers*
Rennert. *Jazz Stars*
Rennert. *Pioneers of Discovery*
Rochelle. *Witnesses to Freedom: Young People*

Who Fought for Civil Rights
Rubel. *The Scholastic Encyclopedia of the Presidents*
Schraff. *American Heroes of Exploration and Flight*
Smith. *Presidents in a Time of Change*
Streissguth. *Hatemongers and Demagogues*
Streissguth. *Hoaxers & Hustlers*
Sullivan. *Presidents at Play*
Taylor. *Black Civil Rights Champions*
Vare. *Women Inventors and Their Discoveries*
Veglahn. *Women Scientists*
Weitzman. *Great Lives: Human Culture*
Whitelaw. *They Wrote Their Own Headlines*
Wilkinson. *People Who Changed the World*
Wilkinson. *Statesmen Who Changed the World*
Wolf. *Focus: Five Women Photographers*
Young. *Cy Young Award Winners*
Yount. *Black Scientists*
Yount. *Women Aviators*

History

Aaseng. *You Are the Senator*
Aaseng. *You Are the Corporate Executive*
Alvarez. *The Official Baseball Hall of Fame Answer Book*
Anderson. *Battles That Changed the Modern World*
Archer. *Breaking Barriers: The Feminist Movement*
Ashabranner. *Always to Remember: Vietnam Veteran's Memorial*
Bachrach. *The Korean War*
Baker. *The 1940s*
Baker. *The 1950s*
Bortz. *Catastrophe! Great Engineering Failure—and Success*
Bowler. *Trains*
Brown. *The Nation in Turmoil: 1960-1973*

Calabro. *Zap! A Brief History of Television*
Carlin. *Jazz*
Carlin. *Rock and Roll: 1955-1970*
Carnes. *Us and Them: A History of Intolerance in America*
Clements. *An Illustrated History of the World*
Colman. *Strike: The Bitter Struggle of American Workers*
Colman. *Toilets, Bathtubs, Sinks, and Sewers*
Colman. *Women in Society: United States*
Connikie. *The 1960s*
Cosner. *War Nurses*
Cozic. *Israel: Opposing Viewpoints*
Cray. *American Datelines*

Cross. *Aftermath of War*
Davies. *Transport: On Land, Road and Rail*
Detzer. *An Asian Tragedy: America and Vietnam*
Dudley. *Engel v. Vitale*
Dudley. *Gideon v. Wainwright*
Dudley. *The Vietnam War: Opposing Viewpoints*
Emert. *Top Lawyers and Their Famous Cases*
Faber. *From Sea to Sea: The Growth of the United States*
Feinberg. *American Political Scandals Past and Present*
Feinberg. *Watergate: Scandal in the White House*
Ferrell. *The U.S. Air Force*
Finkelstein. *Thirteen Days! The Cuban Missile Crisis*
Fireside. *Brown v. Board of Education*

Fradin. *Medicine: Yesterday, Today, and Tomorrow*

Gardner. *The Forgotten Players: The Story of Black Baseball in America*

Garfunkel. *On Wings of Joy: The Story of Ballet*

Garrett. *The Seventies*

Gay. *Korean War*

Gay. *Vietnam War*

Giblin. *Be Seated: A Book About Chairs*

Gibson. *The War in Vietnam*

Gold. *Board of Education v. Pico*

Gold. *In Re Gault (1967)*

Gold. *Miranda v. Arizona*

Gold. *Roe v. Wade*

Gutman. *World Series Classics*

Haas. *Engel v. Vitale*

Hakim. *All the People*

Haskins. *Freedom Rides*

Heater. *The Cold War*

Helmer. *Belles of the Ballpark*

Herald. *The 1970s*

Herda. *Furman v. Georgia*

Herda. *Roe v. Wade*

Herda. *United States v. Nixon*

Hill. *Our Century: 1940-1950*

Hill. *Our Century: 1970-1980*

Hirsch. *Taxation: Paying for Government*

Humble. *Ships*

Isserman. *The Korean War: America at War*

Jacobs. *Search for Peace: The United Nations*

Jones. *Our Century: 1950-1960*

Jones. *The President Has Been Shot*

Karl. *America Alive: A History*

Katz. *The Great Society to the Reagan Era: 1964-1990*

Katz. *World War II to the New Frontier: 1940-1963*

Kelso. *Days of Courage: The Little Rock Story*

Kelso. *Walking for Freedom: The Montgomery Bus Boycott*

Kerr. *Keeping Clean*

Kort. *The Cold War*

Kronenwetter. *Covert Action*

Kronenwetter. *The War Against Terrorism*

Landau. *Armed America: The Status of Gun Control*

Landau. *The White Power Movement: America's Racist Hate Groups*

Lane. *Our Century: 1960-1970*

Langone. *Spreading Poison: A Book About Racism and Prejudice*

Leiner. *First Children: Growing Up in the White House*

Levi. *Cowboys of the Sky*

Levine. *Freedom's Children*

Lucas. *Civil Rights: The Long Struggle*

Macy. *A Whole New Ballgame: All-American Girls Professional Baseball League*

Macy. *Winning Ways: A Photohistory of American Women in Sports*

Markham. *Inventions That Changed Modern Life*

May. *Pushing the Limits: American Women 1940-1961*

McKissack. *Black Diamond*

McKissack. *A Long Hard Journey: The Story of the Pullman Porter*

Medearis. *Come This Far to Freedom*

Meltzer. *The Black Americans*

Meltzer. *Weapons & Warfare*

Mizell. *Think About Racism*

Morley. *Clothes: For Work, Play and Display*

Mulcahy. *Diseases: Finding the Cure*

Naden. *The U.S. Coast Guard*

O'Neill. *Little Rock: The Desegregation of Central High*

Patrick. *The Young Oxford Companion to the Supreme Court*

Patterson. *The Oxford 50th Anniversary Book of the United Nations*

Philip. *Singing America: Poems That Define a Nation*

Platt. *The Smithsonian Visual Timeline of Inventions*

Powledge. *We Shall Overcome: Heroes of the Civil Rights Movement*

Press. *A Multicultural Portrait of Professional Sports*

Rappaport. *The Alger Hiss Trial*

Rappaport. *American Women: Their Lives in Their Words*

Rappaport. *Tinker vs. Des Moines*

Riley. *Miranda v. Arizona*

Ross. *The United Nations*

Sandler. *Presidents*

Scott. *Funny Papers: Behind the Scenes of the Comics*

Sherrow. *Gideon v. Wainwright*

Sherrow. *Separation of Church and State*

Siegel. *Murder on the Highway: The Viola Luizzo Story*

Siegel. *The Year They Walked: Rosa Parks and the Montgomery Bus Boycott*

Smith. *The Korean War*

St. George. *The White House: Cornerstone of a Nation*

Stamper. *Save the Everglades*

Stefoff. *The American Environmental Movement*

Stein. *The Korean War*

Steins. *The Postwar Years: 1950-1959*

Sullivan. *Children of Promise: African-American Literature and Art*

Sullivan. *The Day We Walked on the Moon: A Photo History*

Sullivan. *Slave Ship: The Story of the Henrietta Marie*

Super. *Vietnam War Soldiers*

Tames. *The 1950s*

Time-Life. *African Americans: Voices of Triumph: Leadership*

Time-Life. *This Fabulous Century: 1940-1950*

Time-Life. *This Fabulous Century: 1950-1960*

Time-Life. *This Fabulous Century: 1960-1970*

Tompkins. *Roe v. Wade: The Fight over Life and Liberty*

Ventura. *Clothing*

Ventura. *Food: Its Evolution Through the Ages*

Waggoner. *The Assassination of President Kennedy*

Wakin. *How TV Changed America's Mind*

Wakin. *Photos That Made U.S. History: Cold War Era to Space Age*

Walker. *Hand, Heart, and Mind*

Walter. *Mississippi Challenge*

Warburton. *Railroads: Bridging the Continents*

Warner. *The U.S. Marine Corps*

Weisbrot. *Marching Toward Freedom: 1957-1965*

Westerfeld. *The Berlin Airlift*

Wheeler. *Events That Changed American History*

Whitman. *Get Up and Go: American Road Travel*

Whitman. *This Land Is Your Land*

Wice. *Miranda v. Arizona*

Wormser. *Three Faces of Vietnam*

Wright. *A Multicultural Portrait of the War in Vietnam*

Yepsen. *City Trains: America's Cities by Rail*

Multimedia

CD-ROM

Air and Space Smithsonian Dreams of Flight

Apollo Interactive: The Complete Insider's Guide

Beyond the Wall: Stories Behind Vietnan Wall

Campaigns, Candidates and the Presidency

Daring to Fly!

Eyewitness Encyclopedia of Science

Her Heritage: A Biographical Encyclopedia of American History

History Through Art: 20th Century

Landmark Documents in American History

Portraits of American Presidents

Science Navigator

SkyTrip America

Time Almanac of the 20th Century

Total History

The War in Vietnam

The Way Things Work

Video

African Americans

All the Unsung Heroes: The Vietnam Veterans Memorial

Barnum's Big Top

Black Is My Color: The African American Experience

Changing Faces of Our Land: Once Upon a Time on the Farm

The Cold War

Daring to Dream

Dr. Ethel Allen: Minuses into Pluses

Dr. Martin Luther King, Jr

Elijah Muhammad

The Era of Segregation: A Personal Perspective

Eyes on the Prize II: The Time Has Come, 1964-1966

Farming in America: A History

Freedom and Justice

From the Bay of Pigs to the Brink

Great Black Innovators

Great Black Women

Helen Keller

A History of the Civil Rights Movement

In the Land of Jim Crow: Fighting for Civil Rights

Jackie Robinson

Jesse Owens

Langston Hughes

Making It Happen: Masters of Invention

Malcolm X

Marian Anderson

Martin Luther King, Jr

Mississippi America

Murder in Mississippi: The Price for Freedom

Organizing America: The History of Trade Unions

Post War U.S.A.

Prejudice: Monster Within

Pride & Prejudice: A History of Black Culture in America

Public Sculpture: America's Legacy

Riding the Rails

Roberto Clemente

Roe v. Wade: The Debate Continues

The Southwest of Georgia O'Keeffe

Super Chief: The Life and Legacy of Earl Warren

This House of Power: The Church in African-American Experience

Thurgood Marshall

The Times and Dreams of Martin Luther King, Jr

Tragedy to Triumph: An Adventure with Helen Keller

Vietnam: A Case Study for Critical Thinking

W. E. B. DuBois

Wilma Rudolph

Women with Wings

GRADE EIGHT

Historical Fiction

Barnes. *Promise Me the Moon*

Bennett. *The Moon Stops Here*

Boutis. *Looking Out*

Brooks. *The Moves Make the Man*

Brooks. *Naked in Winter*

Calvert. *The Hour of the Wolf*

Cameron. *The Court of the Stone Children*

Cleaver. *Dust of the Earth*

Cole. *The Final Tide*

Cormier. *Tunes for Bears to Dance To*

Curtis. *The Watsons Go to Birmingham—1963*

Dixon, Jeanne. *The Tempered Wind*

Freeman. *The Cuckoo's Child*

Greene. *Morning Is a Long Time Coming*

Hall. *Halsey's Pride*

Hausman. *Night Flight*

Hite. *It's Nothing to a Mountain*

Hotze. *Acquainted with the Night*

Irwin. *Kim/Kimi*

Johnston. *Hero of Lesser Causes*

Jones. *Long Time Passing*

Lyon. *Red Rover, Red Rover*

Marino. *The Day That Elvis Came to Town*

Marino. *For the Love of Pete*

Martin. *Night Riding*

Moore. *Freedom Songs*

Nelson. and *One for All*

Neumann. *Playing a Virginia Moon*

Oughton. *Music from a Place Called Half Moon*

Paulsen. *The Cookcamp*

Paulsen. *Harris and Me: A Summer Remembered*

Paulsen. *The Rifle*

Pennebaker. *Don't Think Twice*

Qualey. *Come in from the Cold*

Qualey. *Everybody's Daughter*

Rosofsky. *Miriam*

Rostkowski. *The Best of Friends*

Rumbaut. *Dove Dream*

Slepian. *Risk n' Roses*

Smothers. *Down in the Piney Woods*

Steiner. *Tessa*

Strickland *The Hand of the Necromancer*

Talbert. *The Purple Heart*

Uchida. *Journey Home*

Von Ahnen. *Heart of Naosaqua*

White. *Belle Prater's Boy*

White. *Come Next Spring*

White. *The Road Home*

White. *Sweet Creek Holler*

Wyss. *A Stranger Here*

Biography

Aldred. *Thurgood Marshall: Supreme Court Justice*

Anderson. *Jackie Kennedy Onassis*

Ayers. *Chuck Yeager: Fighter Pilot*

Bachrach. *Margaret Sanger*

Baldwin. *DNA Pioneer: James Watson and the Double Helix*

Barnes. *Samuel Goldwyn*

Barr. *Malcolm X*

Barr. *Richard Nixon*

Berry. *Gordon Parks*

Berry. *Langston Hughes*

Billings. *Grace Hopper: Navy Admiral and Computer Pioneer*

Bishop. *Ralph Ellison: Author*

Blau. *Betty Friedan: Feminist*

Blue. *Barbara Jordan: Politician*

Boulton. *Frank Lloyd Wright: Architect: An Illustrated Biography*

Bredeson. *Jonas Salk: Discoverer of the Polio Vaccine*

Brown. *Malcolm X: His Life and Legacy*

Brown. *Romare Bearden: Artist*

Butts. *May Chinn: The Best Medicine*

Cain. *Louise Nevelson: Sculptor*

Cannon. *Dwight David Eisenhower: War Hero and President*

Castiglia. *Margaret Mead*

Celsi. *Ralph Nader: The Consumer Revolution*

Cohen. *Joseph McCarthy*

Cole. *John F. Kennedy*

Cole. *John Glenn: Astronaut and Senator*

Collier. *Duke Ellington*

Collier. *Louis Armstrong: An American Success Story*

Collins. *Gerald R. Ford*

Conord. *John Lennon*

Curson. *Jonas Salk*

Daffron. *Margaret Bourke-White: Photographer*

Dallard. *Ella Baker: A Leader Behind the Scenes*

Darby. *Douglas MacArthur*

Darby. *Dwight D. Eisenhower*

Darby. *Martin Luther King, Jr.*

Davies. *Malcolm X*

Davis. *Frank Lloyd Wright: Maverick Architect*

Deitch. *Dwight D. Eisenhower*

Denenberg. *John Fitzgerald Kennedy: America's 35th President*

Denenberg. *The True Story of J. Edgar Hoover*

Diamond. *Jackie Robinson*

Ellis. *Dwight D. Eisenhower*

Erlich. *Paul Robeson: Singer and Actor*

Falkof. *John F. Kennedy*

Falkof. *Lyndon B. Johnson*

Fleming. *Harry S. Truman*

Frankl. *Charlie Parker: Musician*

Fraser. *Walter White: Civil Rights Leader*

Freedman. *Dian Fossey: Befriending the Gorillas*

Freedman. *Eleanor Roosevelt: A Life of Discovery*

Friese. *Rosa Parks: The Movement Organizes*

Garfunkel. *Letter to the World: Martha Graham*

Gentry. *Dizzy Gillespie: Musician*

Gentry. *Jesse Owens: Champion Athlete*

Gherman. *E. B. White: Some Writer!*

Gonzales. *Alex Haley: Author of Roots*

Gottfried. *Alan Turing: The Architect of the Computer Age*

Gourse. *Billie Holiday: The Tragedy and Triumph of Lady Day*

Gourse. *Dizzy Gillespie and the Birth of Bebop*

Greenberg. *The Buck Stops Here: Harry Truman*

Halasa. *Elijah Muhammad: Religious Leader*

Halasa. *Mary McLeod Bethune: Educator*

Hanley. *Philip Randolph*

Hargrove. *Dwight D. Eisenhower*

Hargrove. *Harry S. Truman: Thirty-Third President*

Tessitore. *The Hunt and the Feast: A Life of Ernest Hemingway*
Thorleifson. *Ethel Barrymore*
Tilton. *Margaret Mead*
Tingum. *E. B. White*
Tomlinson. *Jonas Salk*
Toor. *Eleanor Roosevelt*
Urban. *Richard Wright: Author*
Wade. *James Carter: Thirty-Ninth President*
Wadsworth. *Rachel Carson: Voice for the Earth*

Weidhorn. *Jackie Robinson*
Weisbrot. *Father Divine: Religious Leader*
Whitelaw. *Grace Hopper*
Whitelaw. *Margaret Sanger*
Whitelaw. *Mr. Civil Rights: The Story of Thurgood Marshall*
Williams. *Patrick Desjarlait*
Witcover. *Zora Neale Hurston*
Wolfe. *Mahalia Jackson: Gospel Singer*
Woog. *Duke Ellington*
Woog. *Louis Armstrong*

Wright. *A. Philip Randolph*
Wright. *John Lennon*
Wyman. *Ella Fitzgerald: Jazz Singer Supreme*
Yannuzzi. *Zora Neale Hurston: Southern Storyteller*
Yates. *Woodie Guthrie: American Balladeer*
Ziesk. *Margaret Mead*

Collective Biography

Aaseng. *America's Third-Party Presidential Candidates*
Aaseng. *Close Calls: From the Brink of Ruin to Business Success*
Aaseng. *Genetics: Unlocking the Secrets of Life*
Aaseng. *Great Justices of the Supreme Court*
Aaseng. *True Champions: Great Athletes and Their Off-the-Field Heroics*
Aaseng. *Twentieth-Century Inventors*
Aaseng. *You Are the President*
Allen. *Black Women Leaders of the Civil Rights Movement*
Altman. *Extraordinary Black Americans*
Beard. *The Presidents in American History*
Blassingame. *The Look-It-Up Book of Presidents*
Blue. *People of Peace*
Brill. *Extraordinary Young People*
Camp. *American Astronomers: Searchers and Wonderers*
Cohen. *Prophets of Doom*
Cush. *Artists Who Created Great Works*
Cush. *Women Who Achieved Greatness*
Dolan. *Shaping U.S. Foreign Policy: Twelve Secretaries of State*
Faber. *Great Lives: American Government*

Fireside. *Is There a Woman in the House. . . or Senate?*
Glenn. *Discover America's Favorite Architects*
Glubok. *Great Lives: Painting*
Haskins. *Against All Opposition: Black Explorers in America*
Haskins. *Black Eagles: African Americans in Aviation*
Italia. *Courageous Crimefighters*
Jones. *Big Star Fallin' Mama*
Krull. *Lives of the Artists: Masterpieces, Messes*
Krull. *Lives of the Musicians: Good Times, Bad Times*
Krull. *Lives of the Writers: Comedies, Tragedies*
Lindop. *Presidents by Accident*
Mayberry. *Business Leaders Who Built Financial Empires*
Mayberry. *Leaders Who Changed the 20th Century*
Morin. *Women Chosen for Public Office*
Morin. *Women Who Reformed Politics*
Myers. *Now Is Your Time*
Otfinoski. *Great Black Writers*
Pascoe. *First Facts About the Presidents*
Pile. *Women Business Leaders*
Plowden. *Famous Firsts of Black Women*
Provenson. *My Fellow Americans*

Rennert. *Book of Firsts: Leaders of America*
Rennert. *Civil Rights Leaders*
Rennert. *Female Writers*
Rennert. *Jazz Stars*
Rennert. *Pioneers of Discovery*
Rochelle. *Witnesses to Freedom: Young People Who Fought for Civil Rights*
Rubel. *The Scholastic Encyclopedia of the Presidents*
Schraff. *American Heroes of Exploration and Flight*
Smith. *Presidents in a Time of Change*
Streissguth. *Hatemongers and Demagogues*
Streissguth. *Hoaxers & Hustlers*
Sullivan. *Presidents at Play*
Taylor. *Black Civil Rights Champions*
Veglahn. *Women Scientists*
Weitzman. *Great Lives: Human Culture*
Whitelaw. *They Wrote Their Own Headlines*
Wilkinson. *People Who Changed the World*
Wilkinson. *Statesmen Who Changed the World*
Wolf. *Focus: Five Women Photographers*
Young. *Cy Young Award Winners*
Yount. *Black Scientists*
Yount. *Women Aviators*

History

Aaseng. *You Are the Senator*

Aaseng. *You Are the Corporate Executive*

Alvarez. *The Official Baseball Hall of Fame Answer Book*

Anderson. *Battles That Changed the Modern World*

Archer. *Breaking Barriers: The Feminist Movement*

Bachrach. *The Korean War*

Baker. *The 1940s*

Baker. *The 1950s*

Bortz. *Catastrophe! Great Engineering Failure—and Success*

Brown. *The Nation in Turmoil: 1960-1973*

Calabro. *Zap! A Brief History of Television*

Carlin. *Jazz*

Carlin. *Rock and Roll: 1955-1970*

Carnes. *Us and Them: A History of Intolerance in America*

Clements. *An Illustrated History of the World*

Colman. *Strike: The Bitter Struggle of American Workers*

Colman. *Toilets, Bathtubs, Sinks, and Sewers*

Colman. *Women in Society: United States*

Connikie. *The 1960s*

Cosner. *War Nurses*

Cozic. *Israel: Opposing Viewpoints*

Cray. *American Datelines*

Davies. *Transport: On Land, Road and Rail*

Denenberg. *Voices from Vietnam*

Detzer. *An Asian Tragedy: America and Vietnam*

Dudley. *Engel v. Vitale*

Dudley. *Gideon v. Wainwright*

Dudley. *The Vietnam War: Opposing Viewpoints*

Emert. *Top Lawyers and Their Famous Cases*

Faber. *From Sea to Sea: The Growth of the United States*

Feinberg. *American Political Scandals Past and Present*

Feinberg. *Watergate: Scandal in the White House*

Ferrell. *The U.S. Air Force*

Finkelstein. *Thirteen Days! The Cuban Missle Crisis*

Fireside. *Brown v. Board of Education*

Fradin. *Medicine: Yesterday, Today, and Tomorrow*

Gardner. *The Forgotten Players: The Story of Black Baseball in America*

Garfunkel. *On Wings of Joy: The Story of Ballet*

Gay. *Korean War*

Gay. *Vietnam War*

Giblin. *Be Seated: A Book About Chairs*

Gibson. *The War in Vietnam*

Gold. *Board of Education v. Pico*

Gold. *In Re Gault (1967)*

Gold. *Miranda v. Arizona*

Gold. *Roe v. Wade*

Gutman. *World Series Classics*

Haas. *Engel v. Vitale*

Hakim. *All the People*

Haskins. *Freedom Rides*

Heater. *The Cold War*

Helmer. *Belles of the Ballpark*

Herald. *The 1970s*

Herda. *Furman v. Georgia*

Herda. *Roe v. Wade*

Herda. *United States v. Nixon*

Hill. *Our Century: 1940-1950*

Hill. *Our Century: 1970-1980*

Hirsch. *Taxation: Paying for Government*

Isserman. *The Korean War: America at War*

Jacobs. *Search for Peace: The United Nations*

Jones. *Our Century: 1950-1960*

Jones. *The President Has Been Shot*

Karl. *America Alive: A History*

Katz. *The Great Society to the Reagan Era: 1964-1990*

Katz. *World War II to the New Frontier: 1940-1963*

Kelley. *Into the Fire: African Americans Since 1970*

Kilian. *What Was Watergate*

Kort. *The Cold War*

Kronenwetter. *Covert Action*

Kronenwetter. *United They Hate: White Supremacist Groups in America*

Kronenwetter. *The War Against Terrorism*

Landau. *Armed America: The Status of Gun Control*

Landau. *The White Power Movement: America's Racist Hate Groups*

Lane. *Our Century: 1960-1970*

Langone. *Spreading Poison: A Book About Racism and Prejudice*

Lawson. *Famous Presidential Scandals*

Leiner. *First Children: Growing Up in the White House*

Levi. *Cowboys of the Sky*

Levine. *Freedom's Children*

Lucas. *Civil Rights: The Long Struggle*

Macy. *A Whole New Ballgame: All-American Girls Professional Baseball League*

Macy. *Winning Ways: A Photohistory of American Women in Sports*

Markham. *Inventions That Changed Modern Life*

May. *Pushing the Limits: American Women 1940-1961*

McKissack. *Black Diamond*

McKissack. *A Long Hard Journey: The Story of the Pullman Porter*

Medearis. *Come This Far to Freedom*

Meltzer. *The Black Americans*

Meltzer. *Weapons & Warfare*

Mizell. *Think About Racism*

Morin. *Impeaching the President*

Morley. *Clothes: For Work, Play and Display*

Mulcahy. *Diseases: Finding the Cure*

Naden. *The U.S. Coast Guard*

O'Neill. *Little Rock: The Desegregation of Central High*

Patrick. *The Young Oxford Companion to the Supreme Court*

Patterson. *The Oxford 50th Anniversary Book of the United Nations*

Philip. *Singing America: Poems That Define a Nation*

Platt. *The Smithsonian Visual Timeline of Inventions*
Powledge. *We Shall Overcome: Heroes of the Civil Rights Movement*
Press. *A Multicultural Portrait of Professional Sports*
Rappaport. *The Alger Hiss Trial*
Rappaport. *American Women: Their Lives in Their Words*
Rappaport. *Tinker vs. Des Moines*
Riley. *Miranda v. Arizona*
Ross. *The United Nations*
Sandler. *Presidents*
Scott. *Funny Papers: Behind the Scenes of the Comics*
Senna. *The Black Press and the Struggle of Civil Rights*
Sherrow. *Gideon v. Wainwright*
Sherrow. *Separation of Church and State*
Siegel. *Murder on the Highway: The Viola Luizzo Story*
Smith. *The Korean War*
St. George. *The White House: Cornerstone of a Nation*
Stamper. *Save the Everglades*

Stanley. *Women in the Military*
Stefoff. *The American Environmental Movement*
Stein. *The Korean War*
Steins. *The Postwar Years: 1950-1959*
Stevens. *The Case of Roe v. Wade*
Sullivan. *Children of Promise: African-American Literature and Art*
Sullivan. *Slave Ship: The Story of the Henrietta Marie*
Sullivan. *The Day We Walked on the Moon: A Photo History*
Tames. *The 1950s*
Time-Life. *African Americans: Voices of Triumph: Leadership*
Time-Life. *This Fabulous Century: 1940-1950*
Time-Life. *This Fabulous Century: 1950-1960*
Time-Life. *This Fabulous Century: 1960-1970*
Tompkins. *Roe v. Wade: The Fight over Life and Liberty*
Ventura. *Clothing*
Ventura. *Food: Its Evolution Through the Ages*

Waggoner. *The Assassination of President Kennedy*
Wakin. *How TV Changed America's Mind*
Wakin. *Photos That Made U.S. History: Cold War Era to Space Age*
Walker. *Hand, Heart, and Mind*
Walter. *Mississippi Challenge*
Warburton. *Railroads: Bridging the Continents*
Warner. *The U.S. Marine Corps*
Weisbrot. *Marching Toward Freedom: 1957-1965*
Wekesser. *The Death Penalty: Opposing Viewpoints*
Westerfeld. *The Berlin Airlift*
Wheeler. *Events That Changed American History*
Whitman. *Get Up and Go: American Road Travel*
Whitman. *This Land Is Your Land*
Wice. *Miranda v. Arizona*
Wormser. *Three Faces of Vietnam*
Wright. *A Multicultural Portrait of the War in Vietnam*
Yepsen. *City Trains: America's Cities by Rail*

Multimedia

CD-ROM

Air and Space Smithsonian Dreams of Flight
Apollo Interactive: The Complete Insider's Guide
Beyond the Wall: Stories Behind Vietnam Wall
Campaigns, Candidates and the Presidency
Daring to Fly!
Eyewitness Encyclopedia of Science

Famous American Speeches: 1850 to the Present
Her Heritage: A Biographical Encyclopedia of American History
History Through Art: 20th Century
Landmark Documents in American History
Portraits of American Presidents

Science Navigator
SkyTrip America
Time Almanac of the 20th Century
Total History
The War in Vietnam
The Way Things Work

Video

African Americans
All the Unsung Heroes: The Vietnam Veterans Memorial
Barnum's Big Top
Black Is My Color: The African American Experience
Changing Faces of Our Land: Once Upon a Time on the Farm
The Cold War

Daring to Dream
Dr. Ethel Allen: Minuses into Pluses
Dr. Martin Luther King, Jr.
Elijah Muhammad
The Era of Segregation: A Personal
Eyes on the Prize II: The Time Has Come, 1964-1966
Farming in America: A History

Freedom and Justice
From the Bay of Pigs to the Brink
Great Black Innovators
Great Black Women
Helen Keller
A History of the Civil Rights Movement
In the Land of Jim Crow: Fighting for Civil Rights
Jackie Robinson

Jesse Owens
Langston Hughes
Making It Happen: Masters of Invention
Malcolm X
Marian Anderson
Martin Luther King, Jr.
Martin Luther King, Jr. and the Civil Rights Movement
Mississippi America
Murder in Mississippi: The Price for Freedom
1945-1989: The Cold War
Organizing America: The History of Trade Unions
Post War U.S.A.
Prejudice: Monster Within

Pride & Prejudice: A History of Black Culture in America
Public Sculpture: America's Legacy
Riding the Rails
Roberto Clemente
Roe v. Wade: The Debate Continues
The Southwest of Georgia O'Keeffe
Super Chief: The Life and Legacy of Earl Warren
The Torch Has Been Passed: A History of the Early 60's
This House of Power: The Church in

African-American Experience
Thurgood Marshall
The Times and Dreams of Martin Luther King, Jr.
The Torch Has Been Passed: A History of the Early '60s
Tragedy to Triumph: An Adventure with Helen Keller
Vietnam: A Case Study for Critical Thinking
W. E. B. DuBois
Wilma Rudolph
Women with Wings

GRADE NINE

Historical Fiction

Bennett. *The Moon Stops Here*
Boutis. *Looking Out*
Brooks. *The Moves Make the Man*
Brooks. *Naked in Winter*
Calvert. *The Hour of the Wolf*
Cormier. *Tunes for Bears to Dance To*
Dixon. *The Tempered Wind*
Frank. *Cooder Cutlas*
Freeman. *The Cuckoo's Child*
Greene. *Morning Is a Long Time Coming*
Hall. *Halsey's Pride*
Hite. *It's Nothing to a Mountain*
Hotze. *Acquainted with the Night*

Iida. *Middle Son: A Novel*
Irwin. *Kim/Kimi*
Jones. *Long Time Passing*
Lyon. *Red Rover, Red Rover*
Marino. *The Day That Elvis Came to Town*
Marino. *For the Love of Pete*
Moore. *Freedom Songs*
Nelson. and *One for All*
Neumann. *Playing a Virginia Moon*
Oughton. *Music from a Place Called Half Moon*
Paulsen. *The Rifle*
Pennebaker. *Don't Think Twice*
Qualey. *Come in from the Cold*

Qualey. *Everybody's Daughter*
Rosofsky. *Miriam*
Rostkowski. *The Best of Friends*
Roth-Hano. *Safe Harbors*
Rumbaut. *Dove Dream*
Slepian. *Risk n' Roses*
Smothers. *Down in the Piney Woods*
Steiner. *Tessa*
Uchida. *Journey Home*
White. *The Road Home*
Wyss. *A Stranger Here*

Biography

Aldred. *Thurgood Marshall: Supreme Court Justice*
Anderson. *Jackie Kennedy Onassis*
Ayers. *Chuck Yeager: Fighter Pilot*
Bachrach. *Margaret Sanger*
Baldwin. *DNA Pioneer: James Watson and the Double Helix*
Barnes. *Samuel Goldwyn*
Barr. *Malcolm X*
Berry. *Gordon Parks*
Berry. *Langston Hughes*
Billings. *Grace Hopper: Navy Admiral and Computer Pioneer*

Bishop. *Ralph Ellison: Author*
Blau. *Betty Friedan: Feminist*
Blue. *Barbara Jordan: Politician*
Bober. *A Restless Spirit: Robert Frost*
Boulton. *Frank Lloyd Wright: Architect: An Illustrated Biography*
Bredeson. *Jonas Salk: Discoverer of the Polio Vaccine*
Brown. *Louis Armstrong: Swinging, Singing Satchmo*
Brown. *Malcolm X: His Life and Legacy*

Brown. *Romare Bearden: Artist*
Cain. *Louise Nevelson: Sculptor*
Cannon. *Dwight David Eisenhower: War Hero and President*
Castiglia. *Margaret Mead*
Celsi. *Ralph Nader: The Consumer Revolution*
Cohen. *Joseph McCarthy*
Cohen. *The Life of Hubert Humphrey: Undefeated*
Cole. *John F. Kennedy*
Collier. *Duke Ellington*
Collier. *Louis Armstrong: An American Success Story*

Collins. *Gerald R. Ford*

Conord. *John Lennon*

Curson. *Jonas Salk*

Daffron. *Margaret Bourke-White: Photographer*

Dallard. *Ella Baker: A Leader Behind the Scenes*

Darby. *Douglas MacArthur*

Darby. *Dwight D. Eisenhower*

Darby. *Martin Luther King, Jr.*

Davies. *Malcolm X*

Davis. *Frank Lloyd Wright: Maverick Architect*

Deitch. *Dwight D. Eisenhower*

Denenberg. *John Fitzgerald Kennedy: America's 35th President*

Denenberg. *The True Story of J. Edgar Hoover*

Diamond. *Jackie Robinson*

Ellis. *Dwight D. Eisenhower*

Erlich. *Paul Robeson: Singer and Actor*

Eskow. *Lyndon Baines Johnson*

Falkof. *John F. Kennedy*

Falkof. *Lyndon B. Johnson*

Feinberg. *Harry S. Truman*

Fleming. *Harry S. Truman*

Frankl. *Charlie Parker: Musician*

Fraser. *Walter White: Civil Rights Leader*

Freedman. *Eleanor Roosevelt: A Life of Discovery*

Friese. *Rosa Parks: The Movement Organizes*

Garfunkel. *Letter to the World: Martha Graham*

Gentry. *Dizzy Gillespie: Musician*

Gentry. *Jesse Owens: Champion Athlete*

Gherman. *E. B. White: Some Writer!*

Gonzales. *Alex Haley: Author of Roots*

Gottfried. *Alan Turing: The Architect of the Computer Age*

Gourse. *Billie Holiday: The Tragedy and Triumph of Lady Day*

Gourse. *Dizzy Gillespie and the Birth of Bebop*

Greenberg. *The Buck Stops Here: Harry Truman*

Guthrie. *Bound for Glory*

Halasa. *Elijah Muhammad: Religious Leader*

Halasa. *Mary McLeod Bethune: Educator*

Hanley. *Philip Randolph*

Hargrove. *Dwight D. Eisenhower*

Hargrove. *Harry S. Truman: Thirty-Third President*

Hargrove. *Lyndon B. Johnson: Thirty-sixth President*

Harrison. *A Ripple of Hope: The Life of Robert F. Kennedy*

Harrison. *A Twilight Struggle: The Life of John Fitzgerald Kennedy*

Haskins. *I Have a Dream: The Life and Words of Martin Luther King, Jr.*

Haskins. *Thurgood Marshall: A Life for Justice*

Henry. *Coretta Scott King: Keeper of the Dream*

Herda. *Earl Warren: Chief Justice for Social Change*

Herda. *Thurgood Marshall: Civil Rights Champion*

Hudson. *The Will and the Way: Paul R. Williams*

Hull. *Rosa Parks: Civil Rights Leader*

Ito. *John Steinbeck*

Jakoubek. *Adam Clayton Powell, Jr.*

Jakoubek. *Joe Louis: Heavyweight Champion*

Jakoubek. *Martin Luther King, Jr.*

James. *Julia Morgan: Architect*

Jezer. *Rachel Carson: Biologist and Author*

Johnson. *Ted Williams*

Kallen. *Martin Luther King: A Man and His Dream*

Kallen. *Thurgood Marshall: A Dream of Justice for All*

Kaye. *Lyndon B. Johnson*

Keller. *Margaret Bourke-White: A Photographer's Life*

Keller. *The Story of My Life*

Kenan. *James Baldwin*

Kent. *John F. Kennedy: Thirty-Fifth President*

King. *My Life with Martin Luther King, Jr.*

Kittredge. *Barbara McClintock*

Kittredge. *Helen Hayes: Actress*

Kliment. *Count Basie: Bandleader and Musician*

Kliment. *Ella Fitzgerald: Singer*

Kronstadt. *Florence Sabin: Medical Researcher*

La Farge. *Pearl Buck*

Lansche. *Stan "The Man" Musial: Born to Be a Ballplayer*

Larsen. *Paul Robeson: Hero Before His Time*

Larsen. *Richard Nixon: Rise and Fall of a President*

Leavell. *Harry S. Truman*

Liles. *Sam and the Speaker's Chair*

Lillegard. *Richard Nixon: Thirty-Seventh President*

Lubetkin. *George Marshall*

Lynn. *Babe Didrikson Zaharias*

Lyons. *Clare Boothe Luce*

Lyons. *Sorrow's Kitchen: Zora Neale Hurston*

Mack-Williams. *Malcom X*

McDonough. *Frank Lloyd Wright*

McKissack. *W. E. B. DuBois*

Meltzer. *Starting from Home: A Writer's Beginnings*

Meryman. *Andrew Wyeth*

Mills. *John F. Kennedy*

Morris. *The Truman Way*

Murphy. *Frank Lloyd Wright*

Myers. *Malcolm X: By Any Means Necessary*

Myers. *A Place Called Heartbreak: A Story of Vietnam*

Newton. *Linus Pauling: Scientist and Advocate*

Nicholson. *Georgia O'Keeffe*

Nicholson. *Helen Keller: Humanitarian*

Oneal. *Grandma Moses: Painter of Rural America*

Osofsky. *Free to Dream: Langston Hughes*

Palmer. *Lena Horne: Entertainer*

Parks. *Quiet Strength*

Patrick. *Coretta Scott King*

Patterson. *A. Philip Randolph*

Patterson. *Marian Anderson*

Patterson. *Martin Luther King and the Montgomery Bus Boycott*

Peduzzi. *Ralph Nader*

Petrillo. *Robert F. Kennedy*
Pietrusza. *John F. Kennedy*
Pollack. *Shirley Chisholm*
Potter. *Buckminster Fuller*
Pratt. *Martha Graham*
Presnal. *Rachel Carson*
Probosz. *Martha Graham*
Randall. *John F. Kennedy*
Reef. *John Steinbeck*
Reef. *Ralph David Abernathy*
Richman. *James E. Carter*
Rosset. *James Baldwin: Author*
Rowland. *Martin Luther King, Jr.*
Rubel. *Elvis Presley: The Rise of Rock and Roll*
Rubel. *Fannie Lou Hamer*
Rubin. *Frank Lloyd Wright*
Rummel. *Langston Hughes*
Rummel. *Robert Oppenheimer: Dark Prince*
Sandberg. *Dwight D. Eisenhower*
Saunders. *George C. Marshall: A General for Peace*
Schroeder. *Josephine Baker*

Schuman. *Eleanor Roosevelt*
Schuman. *Elie Wiesel*
Scott. *Jackie Robinson*
Shirley. *Satchel Paige*
Shuker. *Elizabeth Arden*
Sklansky. *James Farmer*
Speaker-Yuan. *Agnes de Mille: Choreographer*
St. George. *Dear Dr. Bell. . . Your Friend, Helen Keller*
Stefoff. *Richard M. Nixon*
Stwertka. *Duke Ellington: A Life of Music*
Tanenhaus. *Louis Armstrong: Musician*
Taylor-Boyd. *Betty Friedan*
Tedards. *Marian Anderson: Singer*
Tessitore. *The Hunt and the Feast: A Life of Ernest Hemingway*
Thorleifson. *Ethel Barrymore*
Tilton. *Margaret Mead*
Tingum. *E. B. White*
Tomlinson. *Jonas Salk*
Toor. *Eleanor Roosevelt*
Urban. *Richard Wright: Author*

Wade. *James Carter: Thirty-Ninth President*
Wadsworth. *Rachel Carson: Voice for the Earth*
Weidhorn. *Jackie Robinson*
Weisbrot. *Father Divine: Religious Leader*
Whitelaw. *Margaret Sanger*
Whitelaw. *Mr. Civil Rights: The Story of Thurgood Marshall*
Williams. *Patrick Desjarlait*
Witcover. *Zora Neale Hurston*
Wolfe. *Mahalia Jackson: Gospel Singer*
Woog. *Duke Ellington*
Woog. *Louis Armstrong*
Wright. *A. Philip Randolph*
Wright. *John Lennon*
Wyman. *Ella Fitzgerald: Jazz Singer Supreme*
Yannuzzi. *Zora Neale Hurston: Southern Storyteller*
Yates. *Woodie Guthrie: American Balladeer*
Ziesk. *Margaret Mead*

Collective Biography

Aaseng. *America's Third-Party Presidential Candidates*
Aaseng. *Close Calls: From the Brink of Ruin to Business Success*
Aaseng. *Genetics: Unlocking the Secrets of Life*
Aaseng. *Great Justices of the Supreme Court*
Aaseng. *True Champions: Great Athletes and Their Off-the-Field Heroics*
Aaseng. *Twentieth-Century Inventors*
Aaseng. *You Are the President*
Allen. *Black Women Leaders of the Civil Rights Movement*
Anthony. *First Ladies: 1789-1961*
Beard. *The Presidents in American History*
Blassingame. *The Look-It-Up Book of Presidents*
Borklund. *Military Leaders Since World War II*
Brill. *Extraordinary Young People*

Camp. *American Astronomers: Searchers and Wonderers*
Cohen. *Prophets of Doom*
Cush. *Artists Who Created Great Works*
Cush. *Women Who Achieved Greatness*
Dolan. *Shaping U.S. Foreign Policy: Twelve Secretaries of State*
Faber. *Great Lives: American Government*
Glenn. *Discover America's Favorite Architects*
Glubok. *Great Lives: Painting*
Haskins. *Against All Opposition: Black Explorers in America*
Italia. *Courageous Crimefighters*
Jones. *Big Star Fallin' Mama*
Landrum. *Profiles of Female Genius: Thirteen Creative Women*
Landrum. *Profiles of Genius: Thirteen Creative Men*
Lindop. *Presidents by Accident*
Mayberry. *Leaders Who Changed the 20th Century*

Morin. *Women Chosen for Public Office*
Morin. *Women Who Reformed Politics*
Myers. *Now Is Your Time*
O'Brien. *American Political Leaders: From Colonial Times to the Present*
Otfinoski. *Great Black Writers*
Phelps. *They Had a Dream: The Story of African-American Astronauts*
Pile. *Women Business Leaders*
Plowden. *Famous Firsts of Black Women*
Rennert. *Book of Firsts: Leaders of America*
Rennert. *Civil Rights Leaders*
Rennert. *Female Writers*
Rennert. *Pioneers of Discovery*
Schraff. *American Heroes of Exploration and Flight*
Sherrow. *James Watson & Francis Crick: Decoding the Secrets of DNA*
Smith. *Presidents in a Time of Change*
Streissguth. *Hatemongers and Demagogues*

Streissguth. *Hoaxers &
  Hustlers*
Sullivan. *Presidents at Play*
Taylor. *Black Civil Rights
  Champions*
Veglahn. *Women Scientists*
Weitzman. *Great Lives:
  Human Culture*

Weitzman. *Great Lives:
  Theater*
Whitelaw. *They Wrote Their
  Own Headlines*
Wilkinson. *People Who
  Changed the World*
Wilkinson. *Statesmen Who
  Changed the World*

Wolf. *Focus: Five Women
  Photographers*
Yount. *Black Scientists*
Yount. *Women Aviators*

History

Aaseng. *You Are the
  Corporate Executive*
Aaseng. *You Are the Senator*
Alderman. *In Our Defense:
  The Bill of Rights in Action*
Alvarez. *The Official
  Baseball Hall of Fame
  Answer Book*
Anderson. *Battles That
  Changed the Modern World*
Archer. *Breaking Barriers:
  The Feminist Movement*
Ardley. *Music: An Illustrated
  Encyclopedia*
Ashton. *The Cold War*
Bachrach. *The Korean War*
Baker. *The 1940s*
Baker. *The 1950s*
Balaban. *Remembering
  Heaven's Face: A Moral
  Witness in Vietnam*
Basinger. *American Cinema:
  One Hundred Years of
  Filmmaking*
Beckett. *The Story of Painting*
Bortz. *Catastrophe! Great
  Engineering Failure—and
  Success*
Brown. *The Nation in
  Turmoil: 1960-1973*
Burns. *Social Movements of
  the 1960s*
Calabro. *Zap! A Brief History
  of Television*
Carlin. *Jazz*
Carlin. *Rock and Roll:
  1955-1970*
Carnes. *Us and Them: A
  History of Intolerance in
  America*
Chafe. *The Road to Equality:
  American Women Since
  1962*
Cohen. *America: Then and
  Now*
Collier. *Jazz, the American
  Theme Song*
Colman. *Women in Society:
  United States*
Connikie. *The 1960s*
Cosner. *War Nurses*

Cozic. *Israel: Opposing
  Viewpoints*
Cray. *American Datelines*
Davis. *Don't Know Much
  About History*
Davis. *Man-Made
  Catastrophes*
De Benedetti. *An American
  Ordeal: The Antiwar
  Movement of the Vietnam
  Era*
Detzer. *An Asian Tragedy:
  America and Vietnam*
Dudley. *The Cold War:
  Opposing Viewpoints*
Dudley. *Engel v. Vitale*
Dudley. *Gideon v. Wainwright*
Dudley. *The Vietnam War:
  Opposing Viewpoints*
Emert. *Top Lawyers and
  Their Famous Cases*
Faber. *From Sea to Sea: The
  Growth of the United States*
Feinberg. *American Political
  Scandals Past and Present*
Feinberg. *Watergate: Scandal
  in the White House*
Finkelstein. *Thirteen Days!
  The Cuban Missle Crisis*
Fireside. *Brown v. Board of
  Education*
Fradin. *Medicine: Yesterday,
  Today, and Tomorrow*
Gay. *Korean War*
Gay. *Vietnam War*
Garfunkel. *On Wings of Joy:
  The Story of Ballet*
Garza. *Barred from the Bar:
  A History of Women and
  the Legal Profession*
Gold. *Board of Education v.
  Pico*
Gold. *In Re Gault (1967)*
Gold. *Miranda v. Arizona*
Gold. *Roe v. Wade*
Greenberg. *The Painter's
  Eye: Learning to Look at
  Contemporary American
  Art*
Haas. *Engel v. Vitale*

Hakim. *All the People*
Haskins. *Black Music in
  America*
Haskins. *Freedom Rides*
Heater. *The Cold War*
Helmer. *Belles of the Ballpark*
Herald. *The 1970s*
Herda. *Furman v. Georgia*
Herda. *Roe v. Wade*
Herda. *United States v. Nixon*
Hill. *Our Century: 1940-1950*
Hill. *Our Century: 1970-1980*
Hirsch. *Taxation: Paying for
  Government*
Isserman. *The Korean War:
  America at War*
Jacobs. *Search for Peace:
  The United Nations*
Jenkins. *Nicaragua and the
  United States: Years of
  Conflict*
Jones. *Our Century:
  1950-1960*
Jones. *The President Has
  Been Shot*
Katz. *The Great Society to the
  Reagan Era: 1964-1990*
Katz. *World War II to the
  New Frontier: 1940-1963*
Kelley. *Into the Fire: African
  Americans Since 1970*
Kilian. *What Was Watergate*
Knappman. *Great American
  Trials: From Salem
  Witchcraft to Rodney King*
Kort. *The Cold War*
Kronenwetter. *Covert Action*
Kronenwetter. *United They
  Hate: White Supremacist
  Groups in America*
Kronenwetter. *The War
  Against Terrorism*
Lackmann. *Same Time. . .
  Same Station: An A-Z
  Guide to Radio*
Landau. *Armed America: The
  Status of Gun Control*
Landau. *The White Power
  Movement: America's
  Racist Hate Groups*

Lane. *Our Century: 1960-1970*

Langone. *Spreading Poison: A Book About Racism and Prejudice*

Lawson. *Famous Presidential Scandals*

Leiner. *First Children: Growing Up in the White House*

Levi. *Cowboys of the Sky*

Levine. *Freedom's Children*

Macy. *A Whole New Ballgame: All-American Girls Professional Baseball League*

Macy. *Winning Ways: A Photohistory of American Women in Sports*

Markham. *Inventions That Changed Modern Life*

Marrin. *America and Vietnam: The Elephant and the Tiger*

May. *Pushing the Limits: American Women 1940-1961*

McKissack. *Black Diamond*

McKissack. *A Long Hard Journey: The Story of the Pullman Porter*

Medearis. *Come This Far to Freedom*

Meltzer. *The Black Americans*

Meltzer. *Weapons & Warfare*

Mizell. *Think About Racism*

Morin. *Impeaching the President*

Mulcahy. *Diseases: Finding the Cure*

Patrick. *The Young Oxford Companion to the Supreme Court*

Patterson. *The Oxford 50th Anniversary Book of the United Nations*

Philip. *Singing America: Poems That Define a Nation*

Pimlott. *The Elite: The Special Forces of the World*

Platt. *The Smithsonian Visual Timeline of Inventions*

Potter. *African-American Firsts*

Powledge. *We Shall Overcome: Heroes of the Civil Rights Movement*

Press. *A Multicultural Portrait of Professional Sports*

Rappaport. *The Alger Hiss Trial*

Rappaport. *American Women: Their Lives in Their Words*

Rappaport. *Tinker vs. Des Moines*

Reinberg. *In the Field: The Language of the Vietnam War*

Riley. *Miranda v. Arizona*

Ritchie. *Please Stand By: A Prehistory of Television*

Ross. *The United Nations*

Schreiner. *Mayday! Mayday!*

Senna. *The Black Press and the Struggle of Civil Rights*

Sherrow. *Gideon v. Wainwright*

Sherrow. *Separation of Church and State*

Siegel. *Murder on the Highway: The Viola Luizzo Story*

Smith. *Fascinating People and Astounding Events from American History*

Spangenburg. *The History of Science from the 1946 to the 1990s*

Spangenburg. *Opening the Space Frontier: Space Exploration*

St. George. *The White House: Cornerstone of a Nation*

Stamper. *Save the Everglades*

Stanley. *Women in the Military*

Steele. *Freedom's River*

Stefoff. *The American Environmental Movement*

Stein. *The Korean War*

Stevens. *The Case of Roe v. Wade*

Sullivan. *The Day We Walked on the Moon: A Photo History*

Summers. *Korean War Almanac*

Tames. *The 1950s*

Time-Life. *African Americans: Voices of Triumph: Leadership*

Time-Life. *This Fabulous Century: 1940-1950*

Time-Life. *This Fabulous Century: 1950-1960*

Time-Life. *This Fabulous Century: 1960-1970*

Tompkins. *Roe v. Wade: The Fight over Life and Liberty*

Waggoner. *The Assassination of President Kennedy*

Wakin. *How TV Changed America's Mind*

Wakin. *Photos That Made U.S. History: Cold War Era to Space Age*

Walker. *Hand, Heart, and Mind*

Walter. *Mississippi Challenge*

Warburton. *Railroads: Bridging the Continents*

Warren. *Cold War*

Weisbrot. *Marching Toward Freedom: 1957-1965*

Wekesser. *The Death Penalty: Opposing Viewpoints*

Wekesser. *Feminism: Opposing Viewpoints*

Westerfeld. *The Berlin Airlift*

Wheeler. *Events That Changed American History*

Whitman. *Get Up and Go: American Road Travel*

Whitman. *This Land Is Your Land*

Wice. *Miranda v. Arizona*

Wormser. *Three Faces of Vietnam*

Wright. *A Multicultural Portrait of the War in Vietnam*

Multimedia

CD-ROM

Air and Space Smithsonian Dreams of Flight

Apollo Interactive: The Complete Insider's Guide

Beyond the Wall: Stories Behind Vietnan Wall

Campaigns, Candidates and the Presidency

Daring to Fly!

Events That Changed the World

Eyewitness Encyclopedia of Science

*Famous American Speeches:
1850 to the Present*
*Her Heritage: A Biographical
Encyclopedia of American
History*
*History Through Art: 20th
Century*
Ideas That Changed the World

*Landmark Documents in
American History*
*Our Times: The Multimedia
Encyclopedia of the
Twentieth Century*
*Portraits of American
Presidents*
Science Navigator

SkyTrip America
*Time Almanac of the 20th
Century*
Total History
The War in Vietnam
The Way Things Work

Video

African Americans
*All the Unsung Heroes: The
Vietnam Veterans Memorial*
*America's Relations with
Eastern Europe*
Barnum's Big Top
*Breaking Barriers: Women
and the Role of the United
Nations*
*Building the American
Dream: Levittown, NY*
*Changing Faces of Our
Land: Once Upon a Time
on the Farm*
The Cold War
Daring to Dream
*Disobeying Orders: GI
Resistance to the Vietnam
War*
*Dr. Ethel Allen: Minuses into
Pluses*
Dr. Martin Luther King, Jr.
Elijah Muhammad
*The Era of Segregation: A
Personal Perspective*
*Eyes on the Prize II: A Nation
of Law?*
*Eyes on the Prize II: Ain't
Gonna Shufle No More
(1964-1972)*
*Eyes on the Prize II: Power!
(1967-1968)*
*Eyes on the Prize II:The
Promised Land
(1967-1968)*
*Eyes on the Prize II: The
Time Has Come, 1964-1966*
The Fabulous Sixties
*Farming in America: A
History*
*Fateful Decade: From Little
Rock to the Civil Rights Bill*

Freedom and Justice
Freedom Train
*From the Bay of Pigs to the
Brink*
Goin' to Chicago
Great Black Women
Harry S. Truman
Heart of the Warrior
Helen Keller
*A History of the Civil Rights
Movement*
*In the Land of Jim Crow:
Fighting for Civil Rights*
Jackie Robinson
Jesse Owens
*JFK: The Age of the Kennedy
Presidency*
JFK: The Death of a President
JFK: The Early Years
*John Fitzgerald Kennedy's
Lost Pathway to Peace*
Kontum Diary
*Land and Landscape: Views
of America's History and
Culture*
Langston Hughes
*The Lottery: Who Fights Our
Wars?*
Malcolm X
Malcolm X: Make It Plain
Marian Anderson
Martin Luther King, Jr.
*Martin Luther King, Jr. and
the Civil Rights Movement*
Mississippi America
*Murder in Mississippi: The
Price for Freedom*
*New York the Way It Was:
The Old Neighborhood*
*New York the Way It Was:
Wish You Were Here*
1945-1989: The Cold War

Nixon
*No Time for Tears—Vietnam:
The Women Who Served*
*Organizing America: The
History of Trade Unions*
Post War U.S.A.
Prejudice: Monster Within
*Pride & Prejudice: A History
of Black Culture in America*
*Public Sculpture: America's
Legacy*
Riding the Rails
Roberto Clemente
*Roe v. Wade: The Debate
Continues*
The Satellite Sky
The Sensational Seventies
*The Southwest of Georgia
O'Keeffe*
*Spy in the Sky: Story of U2
Spy Plane*
*Super Chief: The Life and
Legacy of Earl Warren*
*This House of Power: The
Church in
African-American
Experience*
Thurgood Marshall
*The Torch Has Been Passed:
A History of the Early '60s*
*Tragedy to Triumph: An
Adventure with Helen
Keller*
*Vietnam: A Case Study for
Critical Thinking*
Vietnam: After the Fire
*We Shall Overcome: The
Song That Moved a Nation*
W. E. B. DuBois
Wilma Rudolph
Women with Wings

GRADE TEN

Historical Fiction

Bennett. *The Moon Stops Here*
Brooks. *The Moves Make the Man*
Brooks. *Naked in Winter*
Calvert. *The Hour of the Wolf*
Dixon, Jeanne. *The Tempered Wind*
Frank. *Cooder Cutlas*
Greene. *Morning Is a Long Time Coming*

Iida. *Middle Son: A Novel*
Irwin. *Kim/Kimi*
Jones. *Long Time Passing*
Moore. *Freedom Songs*
Neumann. *Playing a Virginia Moon*
Paulsen. *The Rifle*
Pennebaker. *Don't Think Twice*

Qualey. *Come in from the Cold*
Qualey. *Everybody's Daughter*
Rosofsky. *Miriam*
Rostkowski. *The Best of Friends*
Roth-Hano. *Safe Harbors*
Rumbaut. *Dove Dream*
White. *The Road Home*

Biography

Aldred. *Thurgood Marshall: Supreme Court Justice*
Bachrach. *Margaret Sanger*
Baldwin. *DNA Pioneer: James Watson and the Double Helix*
Barnes. *Samuel Goldwyn*
Barr. *Malcolm X*
Berry. *Gordon Parks*
Billings. *Grace Hopper: Navy Admiral and Computer Pioneer*
Bishop. *Ralph Ellison: Author*
Blau. *Betty Friedan: Feminist*
Blue. *Barbara Jordan: Politician*
Bober. *A Restless Spirit: Robert Frost*
Boulton. *Frank Lloyd Wright: Architect: An Illustrated Biography*
Brown. *Louis Armstrong: Swinging, Singing Satchmo*
Brown. *Malcolm X: His Life and Legacy*
Brown. *Romare Bearden: Artist*
Cain. *Louise Nevelson: Sculptor*
Cannon. *Dwight David Eisenhower: War Hero and President*
Celsi. *Ralph Nader: The Consumer Revolution*
Cohen. *Joseph McCarthy*
Cohen. *The Life of Hubert Humphrey: Undefeated*
Conord. *John Lennon*
Daffron. *Margaret Bourke-White: Photographer*
Darby. *Douglas MacArthur*
Davies. *Malcolm X*

Davis. *Frank Lloyd Wright: Maverick Architect*
Deitch. *Dwight D. Eisenhower*
Denenberg. *The True Story of J. Edgar Hoover*
Diamond. *Jackie Robinson*
Erlich. *Paul Robeson: Singer and Actor*
Eskow. *Lyndon Baines Johnson*
Feinberg. *Harry S. Truman*
Fleming. *Harry S. Truman*
Frankl. *Charlie Parker: Musician*
Freedman. *Eleanor Roosevelt: A Life of Discovery*
Garfunkel. *Letter to the World: Martha Graham*
Gentry. *Dizzy Gillespie: Musician*
Gentry. *Jesse Owens: Champion Athlete*
Gonzales. *Alex Haley: Author of Roots*
Gottfried. *Alan Turing: The Architect of the Computer Age*
Gourse. *Billie Holiday: The Tragedy and Triumph of Lady Day*
Greenberg. *The Buck Stops Here: Harry Truman*
Guthrie. *Bound for Glory*
Halasa. *Elijah Muhammad: Religious Leader*
Halasa. *Mary McLeod Bethune: Educator*
Hanley. *Philip Randolph*
Haskins. *I Have a Dream: The Life and Words of Martin Luther King, Jr.*
Haskins. *Thurgood Marshall: A Life for Justice*

Herda. *Earl Warren: Chief Justice for Social Change*
Herda. *Thurgood Marshall: Civil Rights Champion*
Hudson. *The Will and the Way: Paul R. Williams*
Hull. *Rosa Parks: Civil Rights Leader*
Ito. *John Steinbeck*
Jakoubek. *Adam Clayton Powell, Jr.*
Jakoubek. *Joe Louis: Heavyweight Champion*
Jakoubek. *Martin Luther King, Jr.*
James. *Julia Morgan: Architect*
Jezer. *Rachel Carson: Biologist and Author*
Johnson. *Ted Williams*
Kallen. *Martin Luther King: A Man and His Dream*
Kaye. *Lyndon B. Johnson*
Keller. *The Story of My Life*
Kenan. *James Baldwin*
King. *My Life with Martin Luther King, Jr.*
Kittredge. *Barbara McClintock*
Kittredge. *Helen Hayes: Actress*
Kliment. *Count Basie: Bandleader and Musician*
Kliment. *Ella Fitzgerald: Singer*
Kronstadt. *Florence Sabin: Medical Researcher*
La Farge. *Pearl Buck*
Lansche. *Stan "The Man" Musial: Born to Be a Ballplayer*
Leavell. *Harry S. Truman*
Lewis. *W. E. B. DuBois*

Liles. *Sam and the Speaker's Chair*
Lubetkin. *George Marshall*
Lynn. *Babe Didrikson Zaharias*
Lyons. *Clare Boothe Luce*
Lyons. *Sorrow's Kitchen: Zora Neale Hurston*
Mack-Williams. *Malcom X*
Manchester. *The Death of a President, November 20-November 25, 1963*
Manchester. *One Brief Shining Moment: Remembering Kennedy*
Marable. *W. E. B. DuBois*
McDonough. *Frank Lloyd Wright*
McKissack. *W. E. B. DuBois*
Meltzer. *Starting from Home: A Writer's Beginnings*
Mills. *John F. Kennedy*
Myers. *Malcolm X: By Any Means Necessary*
Newton. *Linus Pauling: Scientist and Advocate*
Nicholson. *Georgia O'Keeffe*

Nicholson. *Helen Keller: Humanitarian*
Owens. *Jesse: The Man Who Outran Hitler*
Palmer. *Lena Horne: Entertainer*
Parks. *Quiet Strength*
Patterson. *A. Philip Randolph*
Patterson. *Marian Anderson*
Petrillo. *Robert F. Kennedy*
Pietrusza. *John F. Kennedy*
Pollack. *Shirley Chisholm*
Pratt. *Martha Graham*
Randall. *John F. Kennedy*
Reef. *John Steinbeck*
Reef. *Ralph David Abernathy*
Robinson. *I Never Had It Made: An Autobiography*
Rosset. *James Baldwin: Author*
Rummel. *Langston Hughes*
Rummel. *Robert Oppenheimer: Dark Prince*
Sandberg. *Dwight D. Eisenhower*
Saunders. *George C. Marshall: A General for Peace*

Shuker. *Elizabeth Arden*
Stwertka. *Duke Ellington: A Life of Music*
Tedards. *Marian Anderson: Singer*
Tessitore. *The Hunt and the Feast: A Life of Ernest Hemingway*
Thorleifson. *Ethel Barrymore*
Tilton. *Margaret Mead*
Toor. *Eleanor Roosevelt*
Urban. *Richard Wright: Author*
Weidhorn. *Jackie Robinson*
Weisbrot. *Father Divine: Religious Leader*
Whitelaw. *Margaret Sanger*
Williams. *Patrick Desjarlait*
Witcover. *Zora Neale Hurston*
Woog. *Duke Ellington*
Wright. *John Lennon*
Wyman. *Ella Fitzgerald: Jazz Singer Supreme*
Yates. *Woodie Guthrie: American Balladeer*
Ziesk. *Margaret Mead*

Collective Biography

Aaseng. *America's Third-Party Presidential Candidates*
Aaseng. *Great Justices of the Supreme Court*
Aaseng. *Twentieth-Century Inventors*
Aaseng. *You Are the President*
Allen. *Black Women Leaders of the Civil Rights Movement*
Anthony. *First Ladies: 1789-1961*
Borklund. *Military Leaders Since World War II*
Brill. *Extraordinary Young People*
Haskins. *Against All Opposition: Black Explorers in America*
Jones. *Big Star Fallin' Mama*

Landrum. *Profiles of Female Genius: Thirteen Creative Women*
Landrum. *Profiles of Genius: Thirteen Creative Men*
Lindop. *Presidents by Accident*
Mayberry. *Leaders Who Changed the 20th Century*
Morin. *Women Chosen for Public Office*
Morin. *Women Who Reformed Politics*
Myers. *Now Is Your Time*
O'Brien. *American Political Leaders*
Otfinoski. *Great Black Writers*
Phelps. *They Had a Dream*
Sherrow. *James Watson & Francis Crick*

Streissguth. *Hatemongers and Demagogues*
Streissguth. *Hoaxers & Hustlers*
Sullivan. *Presidents at Play*
Taylor. *Black Civil Rights Champions*
Weitzman. *Great Lives: Theater*
Whitelaw. *They Wrote Their Own Headlines*
Wilkinson. *People Who Changed the World*
Wilkinson. *Statesmen Who Changed the World*
Wolf. *Focus: Five Women Photographers*
Yount. *Black Scientists*
Yount. *Women Aviators*

History

Aaseng. *You Are the Senator*
Aaseng. *You Are the Corporate Executive*
Alderman. *In Our Defense: The Bill of Rights in Action*
Alvarez. *The Official Baseball Hall of Fame Answer Book*

Anderson. *Battles That Changed the Modern World*
Archer. *Breaking Barriers: The Feminist Movement*
Ardley. *Music: An Illustrated Encyclopedia*
Ashton. *The Cold War*
Bachrach. *The Korean War*

Baker. *The 1940s*
Baker. *The 1950s*
Balaban. *Remembering Heaven's Face: A Moral Witness in Vietnam*
Basinger. *American Cinema: One Hundred Years of Filmmaking*

Beckett. *The Story of Painting*

Burns. *Social Movements of the 1960s*

Calabro. *Zap! A Brief History of Television*

Carlin. *Jazz*

Carlin. *Rock and Roll: 1955-1970*

Carnes. *Us and Them: A History of Intolerance in America*

Chafe. *The Road to Equality: American Women Since 1962*

Cohen. *America: Then and Now*

Collier. *Jazz, the American Theme Song*

Colman. *Women in Society: United States*

Connikie. *The 1960s*

Cozic. *Israel: Opposing Viewpoints*

Cray. *American Datelines*

Davis. *Don't Know Much About History*

Davis. *Man-Made Catastrophes*

De Benedetti. *An American Ordeal: The Antiwar Movement of the Vietnam Era*

Dudley. *The Cold War: Opposing Viewpoints*

Dudley. *Engel v. Vitale*

Dudley. *Gideon v. Wainwright*

Dudley. *The Vietnam War: Opposing Viewpoints*

Evans. *Born for Liberty: A History of Women in America*

Faber. *From Sea to Sea: The Growth of the United States*

Feinberg. *American Political Scandals Past and Present*

Feinberg. *Watergate: Scandal in the White House*

Finkelstein. *Thirteen Days! The Cuban Missle Crisis*

Fradin. *Medicine: Yesterday, Today, and Tomorrow*

Garfunkel. *On Wings of Joy: The Story of Ballet*

Garza. *Barred from the Bar: A History of Women and the Legal Profession*

Gold. *Board of Education v. Pico*

Gold. *In Re Gault (1967)*

Gold. *Miranda v. Arizona*

Gold. *Roe v. Wade*

Greenberg. *The Painter's Eye: Learning to Look at Contemporary American Art*

Hakim. *All the People*

Haskins. *Black Music in America*

Heater. *The Cold War*

Herald. *The 1970s*

Hill. *Our Century: 1940-1950*

Hill. *Our Century: 1970-1980*

Isserman. *The Korean War: America at War*

Jacobs. *Search for Peace: The United Nations*

Jenkins. *Nicaragua and the United States: Years of Conflict*

Jones. *Our Century: 1950-1960*

Katz. *The Great Society to the Reagan Era: 1964-1990*

Katz. *World War II to the New Frontier: 1940-1963*

Kelley. *Into the Fire: African Americans Since 1970*

Kilian. *What Was Watergate*

Knappman. *Great American Trials: From Salem Witchcraft to Rodney King*

Kort. *The Cold War*

Kronenwetter. *Covert Action*

Kronenwetter. *United They Hate: White Supremacist Groups in America*

Kronenwetter. *The War Against Terrorism*

Lackmann. *Same Time. . . Same Station: An A-Z Guide to Radio*

Landau. *Armed America: The Status of Gun Control*

Landau. *The White Power Movement: America's Racist Hate Groups*

Lane. *Our Century: 1960-1970*

Langone. *Spreading Poison: A Book About Racism and Prejudice*

Lawson. *Famous Presidential Scandals*

Levine. *Freedom's Children*

Macy. *Winning Ways: A Photohistory of American Women in Sports*

Markham. *Inventions That Changed Modern Life*

Marrin. *America and Vietnam: The Elephant and the Tiger*

May. *Pushing the Limits: American Women 1940-1961*

McKissack. *A Long Hard Journey: The Story of the Pullman Porter*

Meltzer. *The American Promise: Voices of a Changing Nation 1945-Present*

Meltzer. *The Black Americans*

Meltzer. *Weapons & Warfare*

Mizell. *Think About Racism*

Morin. *Impeaching the President*

Mulcahy. *Diseases: Finding the Cure*

Patrick. *The Young Oxford Companion to the Supreme Court*

Patterson. *The Oxford 50th Anniversary Book of the United Nations*

Philip. *Singing America: Poems That Define a Nation*

Pimlott. *The Elite: The Special Forces of the World*

Potter. *African-American Firsts*

Powledge. *We Shall Overcome: Heroes of the Civil Rights Movement*

Press. *A Multicultural Portrait of Professional Sports*

Rappaport. *The Alger Hiss Trial*

Rappaport. *American Women: Their Lives in Their Words*

Rappaport. *Tinker vs. Des Moines*

Reinberg. *In the Field: The Language of the Vietnam War*

Riley. *Miranda v. Arizona*

Ritchie. *Please Stand By: A Prehistory of Television*

Ross. *The United Nations*

Safer. *Flashbacks: On Returning to Vietnam*

Schreiner. *Mayday! Mayday!*

Senna. *The Black Press and the Struggle of Civil Rights*

Sherrow. *Gideon v. Wainwright*

Sherrow. *Separation of Church and State*

Siegel. *Murder on the Highway: The Viola Luizzo Story*

Smith. *Fascinating People and Astounding Events from American History*

Spangenburg. *The History of Science from the 1946 to the 1990s*

Spangenburg. *Opening the Space Frontier: Space Exploration*

Stanley. *Women in the Military*

Steele. *Freedom's River*

Stefoff. *The American Environmental Movement*

Stevens. *The Case of Roe v. Wade*

Sullivan. *The Day We Walked on the Moon: A Photo History*

Summers. *Korean War Almanac*

Time-Life. *African Americans: Voices of Triumph: Leadership*

Time-Life. *This Fabulous Century: 1940-1950*

Time-Life. *This Fabulous Century: 1950-1960*

Time-Life. *This Fabulous Century: 1960-1970*

Tompkins. *Roe v. Wade: The Fight over Life and Liberty*

Waggoner. *The Assassination of President Kennedy*

Wakin. *How TV Changed America's Mind*

Wakin. *Photos That Made U.S. History: Cold War Era to Space Age*

Walter. *Mississippi Challenge*

Warren. *Cold War*

Wekesser. *The Death Penalty: Opposing Viewpoints*

Wekesser. *Feminism: Opposing Viewpoints*

Westerfeld. *The Berlin Airlift*

Wheeler. *Events That Changed American History*

Wice. *Miranda v. Arizona*

Wormser. *Three Faces of Vietnam*

Wright. *A Multicultural Portrait of the War in Vietnam*

Multimedia

CD-ROM

Air and Space Smithsonian Dreams of Flight

Apollo Interactive: The Complete Insider's Guide

Beyond the Wall: Stories Behind Vietnan Wall

Campaigns, Candidates and the Presidency

Daring to Fly!

Events That Changed the World

Eyewitness Encyclopedia of Science

Famous American Speeches: 1850 to the Present

Her Heritage: A Biographical Encyclopedia of American History

History Through Art: 20th Century

Ideas That Changed the World

Landmark Documents in American History

Our Times: The Multimedia Encyclopedia of the Twentieth Century

Portraits of American Presidents

Science Navigator

SkyTrip America

The War in Vietnam

Time Almanac of the 20th Century

Total History

The Way Things Work

Video

African Americans

All the Unsung Heroes: The Vietnam Veterans Memorial

America's Relations with Eastern Europe

Are We Winning Mommy? America and the Cold War

Barnum's Big Top

Breaking Barriers: Women and the Role of the United Nations

Building the American Dream: Levittown, NY

Changing Faces of Our Land: Once Upon a Time on the Farm

The Cold War

Daley: The Last Boss

Daring to Dream

Disobeying Orders: GI Resistance to the Vietnam War

Dr. Ethel Allen: Minuses into Pluses

Dr. Martin Luther King, Jr.

Elijah Muhammad

The Era of Segregation: A Personal Perspective

Eyes on the Prize II: A Nation of Law?

Eyes on the Prize II: Ain't Gonna Shufle No More (1964-1972)

Eyes on the Prize II: Power! (1967-1968)

Eyes on the Prize II:The Promised Land (1967-1968)

Eyes on the Prize II: The Time Has Come, 1964-1966

The Fabulous Sixties

Farming in America: A History

Fateful Decade: From Little Rock to the Civil Rights Bill

Freedom and Justice

Freedom Train

From the Bay of Pigs to the Brink

Goin' to Chicago

Great Black Women

Harry S. Truman

Heart of the Warrior

Helen Keller

A History of the Civil Rights Movement

In the Land of Jim Crow: Fighting for Civil Rights

Jackie Robinson

JFK: The Age of the Kennedy Presidency

JFK: The Death of a President

JFK: The Early Years

John Fitzgerald Kennedy's Lost Pathway to Peace

Kontum Diary

Korea/Vietnam

Land and Landscape: Views of America's History and Culture
Langston Hughes
The Lottery: Who Fights Our Wars?
Malcolm X
Malcolm X: Make It Plain
Marian Anderson
Martin Luther King, Jr.
Martin Luther King, Jr. and the Civil Rights Movement
Mississippi America
Murder in Mississippi: The Price for Freedom
New York the Way It Was: The Old Neighborhood
New York the Way It Was: Wish You Were Here
1945-1989: The Cold War
Nixon

No Time for Tears—Vietnam: The Women Who Served
Organizing America: The History of Trade Unions
Pride & Prejudice: A History of Black Culture in America
Public Sculpture: America's Legacy
Riding the Rails
Roberto Clemente
Roe v. Wade: The Debate Continues
The Satellite Sky
The Sensational Seventies
The Southwest of Georgia O'Keeffe
Spy in the Sky: Story of U2 Spy Plane
Super Chief: The Life and Legacy of Earl Warren

This House of Power: The Church in African-American Experience
Thurgood Marshall
The Torch Has Been Passed: A History of the Early '60s
Tragedy to Triumph: An Adventure with Helen Keller
Vietnam: A Case Study for Critical Thinking
Vietnam: After the Fire
W. E. B. DuBois
We Shall Overcome: The Song That Moved a Nation
Wilma Rudolph
Women with Wings
As Seen By Both Sides: American and Vietnamese Artists Look at the War

GRADES ELEVEN AND TWELVE

Historical Fiction

Boyne. *Air Force Eagles*
Carey. *The Other Family*
Cole. *A Killing in Quail County*
de Hartog. *The Lamb's War*
Ducker. *Lead Us Not into Penn Station*
Erhart. *Augusta Cotton*
Filene. *Home and Away*
Frank. *Cooder Cutlas*
Greenberg. *No Reck'ning Made*

Greene. *Morning Is a Long Time Coming*
Haley. *Roots*
Iida. *Middle Son: A Novel*
Jones. *Long Time Passing*
Kadohata. *The Floating World*
Learmon. *Unheard Melodies*
Mickle. *The Queen of October*
Mosley. *A Little Yellow Dog*
Nash. *Bigmama Didn't Shop at Woolworth's*
Palmer. *The Karma Charmer*

Pennebaker. *Don't Think Twice*
Qualey. *Everybody's Daughter*
Roth-Hano. *Safe Harbors*
Tracy. *What Do Cowboys Like?*
Volk. *Montana Women*
White. *The Road Home*
Yount. *Thief of Dreams*

Biography

Alvarez. *Chained Eagle*
Bachrach. *Margaret Sanger*
Baldwin. *DNA Pioneer: James Watson and the Double Helix*
Beschloss. *Eisenhower: A Centennial Life*
Billings. *Grace Hopper: Navy Admiral and Computer Pioneer*
Bober. *A Restless Spirit: Robert Frost*
Boulton. *Frank Lloyd Wright: Architect: An Illustrated Biography*
Bragg. *Soaring Above Setbacks: The Autobiography of Janet Harmon Bragg*

Brown. *Louis Armstrong: Swinging, Singing Satchmo*
Brown. *Malcolm X: His Life and Legacy*
Cohen. *Joseph McCarthy*
Cohen. *The Life of Hubert Humphrey: Undefeated*
Conord. *John Lennon*
Darby. *Douglas MacArthur*
Davies. *Malcolm X*
Davis. *Benjamin O. Davis*
Deitch. *Dwight D. Eisenhower*
Denenberg. *The True Story of J. Edgar Hoover*
Dyson. *Making Malcolm: The Myth and Meaning of Malcolm X*
Erlich. *Paul Robeson: Singer and Actor*

Eskow. *Lyndon Baines Johnson*
Feinberg. *Harry S. Truman*
Fleming. *Harry S. Truman*
Freedman. *Eleanor Roosevelt: A Life of Discovery*
Gentry. *Dizzy Gillespie: Musician*
Gottfried. *Alan Turing: The Architect of the Computer Age*
Gourse. *Billie Holiday: The Tragedy and Triumph of Lady Day*
Guthrie. *Bound for Glory*
Halasa. *Elijah Muhammad: Religious Leader*

Herda. *Earl Warren: Chief Justice for Social Change*
Humphrey. *The Education of a Public Man: My Life and Politics*
Hunt. *JFK for a New Generation*
Jakoubek. *Adam Clayton Powell, Jr.*
James. *Julia Morgan: Architect*
Keller. *The Story of My Life*
Kenan. *James Baldwin*
King. *My Life with Martin Luther King, Jr.*
Kittredge. *Barbara McClintock*
Kittredge. *Helen Hayes: Actress*
Kliment. *Count Basie: Bandleader and Musician*
Kliment. *Ella Fitzgerald: Singer*
Kronstadt. *Florence Sabin: Medical Researcher*
La Farge. *Pearl Buck*
Lewis. *W. E. B. DuBois*
Liles. *Sam and the Speaker's Chair*

Lubetkin. *George Marshall*
Lynn. *Babe Didrikson Zaharias*
Lyons. *Clare Boothe Luce*
Lyons. *Sorrow's Kitchen: Zora Neale Hurston*
Mack-Williams. *Malcom X*
Manchester. *The Death of a President, November 20-November 25, 1963*
Manchester. *One Brief Shining Moment: Remembering Kennedy*
Marable. *W. E. B. DuBois*
McCullough. *Truman*
McKissack. *W. E. B. DuBois*
Meltzer. *Starting from Home: A Writer's Beginnings*
Meyers. *Robert Frost: A Biography*
Moates. *A Bridge of Childhood: Truman Capote's Southern Years*
Newton. *Linus Pauling: Scientist and Advocate*
O'Neil. *I Was Right on Time*
Owens. *Jesse: The Man Who Outran Hitler*

Palmer. *Lena Horne: Entertainer*
Parks. *Quiet Strength*
Partridge. *Dorothea Lange: A Visual Life*
Petrillo. *Robert F. Kennedy*
Pietrusza. *John F. Kennedy*
Phelps. *Chappie: Daniel James, Jr.*
Powers. *Secrecy and Power: The Life of J. Edgar Hoover*
Reef. *John Steinbeck*
Robinson. *I Never Had It Made: An Autobiography*
Rosset. *James Baldwin: Author*
Rummel. *Langston Hughes*
Rummel. *Robert Oppenheimer: Dark Prince*
Tessitore. *The Hunt and the Feast: A Life of Ernest Hemingway*
Thorleifson. *Ethel Barrymore*
Weisbrot. *Father Divine: Religious Leader*
Whitelaw. *Margaret Sanger*
Wright. *John Lennon*

Collective Biography

Aaseng. *Great Justices of the Supreme Court*
Aaseng. *Twentieth-Century Inventors*
Aaseng. *You Are the President*
Allen. *Black Women Leaders of the Civil Rights Movement*
Anthony. *First Ladies: 1789-1961*
Borklund. *Military Leaders Since World War II*
Conway. *Written by Herself—Autobiographies of American Women*
Jones. *Big Star Fallin' Mama*

Landrum. *Profiles of Female Genius: Thirteen Creative Women*
Landrum. *Profiles of Genius: Thirteen Creative Men*
Lindop. *Presidents by Accident*
Mayberry. *Leaders Who Changed the 20th Century*
McCullough. *Brave Companions: Portraits in History*
Morin. *Women Chosen for Public Office*
O'Brien. *American Political Leaders*
Otfinoski. *Great Black Writers*
Phelps. *They Had a Dream*

Reaves. *Oliphant's Presidents: Twenty-five Years of Caricature*
Sherrow. *James Watson & Francis Crick*
Streissguth. *Hatemongers and Demagogues*
Streissguth. *Hoaxers & Hustlers*
Truman. *First Ladies*
Weitzman. *Great Lives: Theater*
Wills. *Certain Trumpets: The Call of Leaders*
Wolf. *Focus: Five Women Photographers*
Yount. *Black Scientists*
Yount. *Women Aviators*

History

Alderman. *In Our Defense: The Bill of Rights in Action*
Ardley. *Music: An Illustrated Encyclopedia*
Ashton. *The Cold War*
Bachrach. *The Korean War*
Baker. *The 1940s*
Baker. *The 1950s*

Balaban. *Remembering Heaven's Face: A Moral Witness in Vietnam*
Basinger. *American Cinema: One Hundred Years of Filmmaking*
Beckett. *The Story of Painting*
Black. *In the Shadow of Polio: A Personal and Social History*

Boller. *Presidential Wives: An Anecdotal History*
Brady. *The Coldest War: A Memoir of Korea*
Burns. *Social Movements of the 1960s*
Busby. *Daughters of Africa: An International Anthology*
Calabro. *Zap! A Brief History of Television*

Carlin. *Jazz*

Carlin. *Rock and Roll: 1955-1970*

Carnes. *Us and Them: A History of Intolerance in America*

Chafe. *The Road to Equality: American Women Since 1962*

Cohen. *America: Then and Now*

Cole. *Perspective*

Collier. *Jazz, the American Theme Song*

Colman. *Women in Society: United States*

Cozic. *Israel: Opposing Viewpoints*

Cray. *American Datelines*

Davidson. *Everyday Life Through the Ages*

Davis. *Don't Know Much About History*

Davis. *Man-Made Catastrophes*

De Benedetti. *An American Ordeal: The Antiwar Movement of the Vietnam Era*

Dudley. *The Cold War: Opposing Viewpoints*

Dudley. *The Vietnam War: Opposing Viewpoints*

Engelmann. *Tears Before the Rain: The Fall of South Vietnam*

Evans. *Born for Liberty: A History of Women in America*

Faber. *From Sea to Sea: The Growth of the United States*

Feinberg. *American Political Scandals Past and Present*

Feinberg. *Watergate: Scandal in the White House*

Finkelstein. *Thirteen Days! The Cuban Missle Crisis*

Fogle. *Two Hundred Years: Stories of the Nation's Capital*

Fradin. *Medicine: Yesterday, Today, and Tomorrow*

Garfunkel. *On Wings of Joy: The Story of Ballet*

Garza. *Barred from the Bar: A History of Women and the Legal Profession*

Gold. *Board of Education v. Pico*

Gold. *In Re Gault (1967)*

Gold. *Miranda v. Arizona*

Gold. *Roe v. Wade*

Greenberg. *The Painter's Eye: Learning to Look at Contemporary American Art*

Hakim. *All the People*

Hampton. *Voices of Freedom: An Oral History of the Civil Rights Movement*

Hanmer. *Taking a Stand Against Sexism and Sex Discrimination*

Harris. *Diamond: Baseball Writings*

Haskins. *Black Music in America*

Heater. *The Cold War*

Isserman. *The Korean War: America at War*

Jacobs. *Search for Peace: The United Nations*

Jenkins. *Nicaragua and the United States: Years of Conflict*

Keegan. *History of Warfare*

Kelley. *Into the Fire: African Americans Since 1970*

Kilian. *What Was Watergate*

Knappman. *Great American Trials*

Kronenwetter. *Covert Action*

Kronenwetter. *United They Hate: White Supremacist Groups in America*

Landau. *The White Power Movement: America's Racist Hate Groups*

Langone. *Spreading Poison: A Book About Racism and Prejudice*

Lawson. *Famous Presidential Scandals*

Levine. *Freedom's Children*

Marling. *George Washington Slept Here, 1876-1986*

Marrin. *America and Vietnam: The Elephant and the Tiger*

May. *Pushing the Limits: American Women 1940-1961*

Melder. *Hail to the Candidate: Presidential Campaigns*

Meltzer. *The American Promise: Voices of a Changing Nation 1945-Present*

Meltzer. *Weapons & Warfare*

Morin. *Impeaching the President*

Mulcahy. *Diseases: Finding the Cure*

Okihiro. *Whispered Silences: Japanese Americans and World War II*

Patrick. *The Young Oxford Companion to the Supreme Court*

Patterson. *The Oxford 50th Anniversary Book of the United Nations*

Philip. *Singing America: Poems That Define a Nation*

Pimlott. *The Elite: The Special Forces of the World*

Posner. *Case Closed: Lee Harvey Oswald and the Assassination of JFK*

Potter. *African-American Firsts*

Press. *A Multicultural Portrait of Professional Sports*

Prochnau. *Once upon a Distant War*

Rappaport. *The Alger Hiss Trial*

Rappaport. *American Women: Their Lives in Their Words*

Rappaport. *Tinker vs. Des Moines*

Reinberg. *In the Field: The Language of the Vietnam War*

Riley. *The Biographical Encyclopedia of Negro Baseball Leagues*

Ritchie. *Please Stand By: A Prehistory of Television*

Safer. *Flashbacks: On Returning to Vietnam*

Schreiner. *Mayday! Mayday!*

Senna. *The Black Press and the Struggle of Civil Rights*

Siegel. *Murder on the Highway: The Viola Luizzo Story*

Smith. *Fascinating People and Astounding Events from American History*

Spangenburg. *The History of Science from the 1946 to the 1990s*

Spangenburg. *Opening the Space Frontier: Space Exploration*

Stanley. *Women in the Military*

Steele. *Freedom's River*

Stern. *Sixties People*
Stevens.*The Case of Roe v. Wade*
Sullivan. *The Day We Walked on the Moon: A Photo History*
Summers. *Korean War Almanac*
Time-Life. *African Americans: Voices of Triumph: Leadership*
Time-Life. *This Fabulous Century: 1940-1950*

Time-Life. *This Fabulous Century: 1950-1960*
Time-Life. *This Fabulous Century: 1960-1970*
Tompkins. *Roe v. Wade: The Fight over Life and Liberty*
Walter. *Mississippi Challenge*
Warren. *Cold War*
Weisbrot. *Freedom Bound: A History of America's Civil Rights Movement*

Wekesser. *The Death Penalty: Opposing Viewpoints*
Wekesser. *Feminism: Opposing Viewpoints*
Westerfeld. *The Berlin Airlift*
Wheeler. *Events That Changed American History*
Wice. *Miranda v. Arizona*
Wormser. *Three Faces of Vietnam*

Multimedia

CD-ROM

Air and Space Smithsonian Dreams of Flight
Apollo Interactive: The Complete Insider's Guide
Beyond the Wall: Stories Behind Vietnan Wall
Campaigns, Candidates and the Presidency
Daring to Fly!
Events That Changed the World

Eyewitness Encyclopedia of Science
Famous American Speeches: 1850 to the Present
Her Heritage: A Biographical Encyclopedia of American History
History Through Art: 20th Century
Ideas That Changed the World
Landmark Documents in American History

Our Times: The Multimedia Encyclopedia of the Twentieth Century
Portraits of American Presidents
Science Navigator
SkyTrip America
Time Almanac of the 20th Century
Total History
The War in Vietnam
The Way Things Work

Video

All the Unsung Heroes: The Vietnam Veterans Memorial
America's Relations with Eastern Europe
Are We Winning Mommy? America and the Cold War
As Seen By Both Sides: American and Vietnamese Artists Look at the War
Breaking Barriers: Women and the Role of the United Nations
Brother Minister: The Assassination of Malcolm X
Building the American Dream: Levittown, NY
Changing Faces of Our Land: Once Upon a Time on the Farm
The Cold War
Daley: The Last Boss
Daring to Dream
Disobeying Orders: GI Resistance to the Vietnam War
Dr. Ethel Allen: Minuses into Pluses
Dr. Martin Luther King, Jr.
Elijah Muhammad
The Era of Segregation: A Personal Perspective

Eyes on the Prize II: A Nation of Law?
Eyes on the Prize II: Ain't Gonna Shufle No More (1964-1972)
Eyes on the Prize II: Power! (1967-1968)
Eyes on the Prize II:The Promised Land (1967-1968)
Eyes on the Prize II: The Time Has Come, 1964-1966
The Fabulous Sixties
Fateful Decade: From Little Rock to the Civil Rights Bill
Freedom and Justice
Freedom Train
From Danger to Dignity: The Fight for Safe Abortion
From the Bay of Pigs to the Brink
Goin' to Chicago
Great Black Women
Harry S. Truman
Heart of the Warrior
Helen Keller
A History of the Civil Rights Movement
In the Land of Jim Crow: Fighting for Civil Rights
Jackie Robinson

JFK: The Age of the Kennedy Presidency
JFK: The Death of a President
JFK: The Early Years
John Fitzgerald Kennedy's Lost Pathway to Peace
Kontum Diary
Korea/Vietnam
Land and Landscape: Views of America's History and Culture
Langston Hughes
The Lottery: Who Fights Our Wars?
Malcolm X
Malcolm X: Make It Plain
Marian Anderson
Martin Luther King, Jr.
Martin Luther King, Jr. and the Civil Rights Movement
Mississippi America
Murder in Mississippi: The Price for Freedom
New York the Way It Was: The Old Neighborhood
New York the Way It Was: Wish You Were Here
1945-1989: The Cold War
Nixon
Nixon—Man and President

SINCE 1975

GRADE SEVEN

Historical Fiction

Cannon. *Begin the World Again*

Choi. *Gathering of Pearls*

Biography

Aldred. *Thurgood Marshall: Supreme Court Justice*

Anderson. *Jackie Kennedy Onassis*

Archbold. *Deep-Sea Explorer: Robert Ballard*

Ashabranner. *The Times of My Life: A Memoir*

Bishop. *Ralph Ellison: Author*

Blau. *Betty Friedan: Feminist*

Blue. *Barbara Jordan: Politician*

Bredeson. *Jonas Salk: Discoverer of the Polio Vaccine*

Brown. *Romare Bearden: Artist*

Butts. *May Chinn: The Best Medicine*

Cain. *Louise Nevelson: Sculptor*

Celsi. *Ralph Nader: The Consumer Revolution*

Cleary. *A Girl from Yamhill: A Memoir*

Cleary. *My Own Two Feet*

Cole. *John Glenn: Astronaut and Senator*

Conord. *John Lennon*

Curson. *Jonas Salk*

Dolan. *Susan Butcher and the Iditarod Trail*

Ferris. *What I Had Was Singing: Marian Anderson*

Glassman. *Mikhail Baryshnikov*

Glassman. *Wilma Mankiller: Chief of the Cherokee Nation*

Gonzales. *Alex Haley: Author of Roots*

Fleischman. *The Abracadabra Kid: A Writer's Life*

Haskins. *Thurgood Marshall: A Life for Justice*

Heiss. *Barbara Bush*

Henry. *Betty Friedan: Fighter for Women's Rights*

Henry. *Coretta Scott King: Keeper of the Dream*

Herda. *Thurgood Marshall: Civil Rights Champion*

Johnson. *Stokely Carmichael: The Story of Black Power*

Kallen. *Thurgood Marshall: A Dream of Justice for All*

Kent. *George Bush: Forty-First President*

Kent. *Ronald Reagan: Fortieth President*

Kittredge. *Barbara McClintock*

Kittredge. *Helen Hayes: Actress*

Kliment. *Ella Fitzgerald: Singer*

Larsen. *Ronald Reagan*

Lazo. *Wilma Mankiller*

Lewis-Ferguson. *Alvin Ailey, Jr.: A Life in Dance*

Lyons. *Clare Boothe Luce*

Malone. *Maya Lin: Architect and Artist*

Meltzer. *Betty Friedan: A Voice for Women's Rights*

Meryman. *Andrew Wyeth*

Morris. *The Reagan Way*

Palmer. *Lena Horne: Entertainer*

Patrick. *Coretta Scott King*

Patterson. *Marian Anderson*

Paulsen. *Woodsong*

Peduzzi. *Ralph Nader*

Pemberton. *George Bush*

Pollack. *Shirley Chisholm*

Probosz. *Martha Graham*

Reef. *Ralph David Abernathy*

Richman. *James E. Carter*

Robbins. *Ronald W. Reagan*

Rosset. *James Baldwin: Author*

Sandak. *The Reagans*

Sawyer. *Marjory Stoneman Douglas*

Scheader. *Shirley Chisholm*

Schuman. *Elie Wiesel*

Schwartzberg. *Ronald Reagan*

Schwarz. *Wilma Mankiller*

Selfridge. *John F. Kennedy: Courage in Crisis*

Sherrow. *Linus Pauling*

Sipiera. *Gerald Ford: Thirty-Eighth President*

Slavin. *Jimmy Carter*

Speaker-Yuan. *Agnes de Mille: Choreographer*

Stefoff. *George H. Bush*

Sullivan. *George Bush*

Sullivan. *Ronald Reagan*

Super. *Daniel "Chappie" James*

Taylor-Boyd. *Betty Friedan*

Tedards. *Marian Anderson: Singer*

Tomlinson. *Jonas Salk*

Wade. *James Carter: Thirty-Ninth President*

Wadsworth. *Susan Butcher: Sled Dog Racer*

Whitelaw. *Mr. Civil Rights: The Story of Thurgood Marshall*

Wright. *Arthur Ashe*

Wright. *John Lennon*

Wyman. *Ella Fitzgerald: Jazz Singer Supreme*

Yannuzzi. *Wilma Mankiller: Leader of the Cherokee Nation*

Collective Biography

Aaseng. *America's Third-Party Presidential Candidates*

Aaseng. *Close Calls: From the Brink of Ruin to Business Success*

Aaseng. *From Rags to Riches*

Aaseng. *Genetics: Unlocking the Secrets of Life*

Aaseng. *True Champions: Great Athletes and Their Off-the-Field Heroics*

Altman. *Extraordinary Black Americans*

Beard. *The Presidents in American History*

Blassingame. *The Look-It-Up Book of Presidents*

Blue. *People of Peace*

Brill. *Extraordinary Young People*

Burns. *Black Stars in Orbit: NASA's African American Astronauts*

Camp. *American Astronomers: Searchers and Wonderers*

Cush. *Artists Who Created Great Works*

Cush. *Women Who Achieved Greatness*

Dolan. *Shaping U.S. Foreign Policy: Profiles of Twelve Secretaries of State*

Faber. *Great Lives: American Government*

Fireside. *Is There a Woman in the House. . . or Senate?*

Glenn. *Discover America's Favorite Architects*

Glubok. *Great Lives: Painting*

Haskins. *Against All Opposition: Black Explorers in America*

Haskins. *Black Eagles: African Americans in Aviation*

Krull. *Lives of the Athletes*

Krull. *Lives of the Writers: Comedies, Tragedies*

Mayberry. *Business Leaders Who Built Financial Empires*

Mayberry. *Leaders Who Changed the 20th Century*

Morin. *Women Chosen for Public Office*

Morin. *Women of the U.S. Congress*

Morin. *Women Who Reformed Politics*

Myers. *Now Is Your Time*

Pascoe. *First Facts About the Presidents*

Pile. *Top Entrepreneurs and Their Businesses*

Pile. *Women Business Leaders*

Plowden. *Famous Firsts of Black Women*

Provenson. *My Fellow Americans*

Rennert. *Book of Firsts: Leaders of America*

Rennert. *Jazz Stars*

Rennert. *Pioneers of Discovery*

Rubel. *The Scholastic Encyclopedia of the Presidents*

Sills. *Inspirations: Stories About Women Artists*

Sills. *Visions: Stories About Women Artists*

Streissguth. *Hatemongers and Demagogues*

Streissguth. *Hoaxers & Hustlers*

Sullivan. *Presidents at Play*

Veglahn. *Women Scientists*

Whitelaw. *They Wrote Their Own Headlines*

Young. *Cy Young Award Winners*

Yount. *Women Aviators*

History

Aaseng. *You Are the Senator*

Aaseng. *You Are the Corporate Executive*

Alvarez. *The Official Baseball Hall of Fame Answer Book*

Anderson. *Battles That Changed the Modern World*

Ashabranner. *Always to Remember: Vietnam Veteran's Memorial*

Avakian. *A Historical Album of Massachusetts*

Avakian. *A Historical Album of New York*

Ballard. *Exploring the Titanic*

Bernards. *Gun Control*

Biel. *The Challenger*

Bortz. *Catastrophe!: Great Engineering Failure—and Success*

Bowler. *Trains*

Burke. *Food and Fasting*

Calabro. *Zap!: A Brief History of Television*

Capek. *Artistic Trickery: The Tradition of the Trompe L'oeil Art*

Capek. *Murals: Cave, Cathedral, to Street*

Carlson. *A Historical Album of Minnesota*

Carnegy. *The 1980s*

Carnes. *Us and Them: A History of Intolerance in America*

Clements. *An Illustrated History of the World*

Cocke. *A Historical Album of Virginia*

Cocke. *A Historical Album of Washington*

Colman. *Toilets, Bathtubs, Sinks, and Sewers*

Colman. *Women in Society: United States*

Compton. *Marriage Customs*

Cozic. *Civil Liberties*

Cozic. *Israel: Opposing Viewpoints*

Cray. *American Datelines*

Cush. *Disasters That Shook the World*

Davies. *Transport: On Land, Road and Rail*

Emert. *Top Lawyers and Their Famous Cases*

Evans. *Freedom of Religion*

Multimedia

CD-ROM

Air and Space Smithsonian
   Dreams of Flight
Beyond the Wall: Stories
   Behind Vietnan Wall
Campaigns, Candidates and
   the Presidency
Daring to Fly!
Exploring the Titanic
Eyewitness Encyclopedia of
   Science

Her Heritage: A Biographical
   Encyclopedia of American
   History
History Through Art: 20th
   Century
Inside the White House
Landmark Documents in
   American History
Portraits of American
   Presidents

Religions of the World
Science Navigator
SkyTrip America
Time Almanac of the 20th
   Century
Total History
The Way Things Work

Video

African Americans
All the Unsung Heroes: The
   Vietnam Veterans Memorial
America's Political Parties:
   The Republican Party
Barnum's Big Top
Changing Faces of Our
   Land: Once Upon a Time
   on the Farm
Choosing a President
Great Black Innovators
Great Black Women
History in the Making: The
   1980's Series

Judaism: The Religion of the
   People
Making It Happen: Masters
   of Invention
Marian Anderson
A More Perfect Union: The
   Three Branches of the
   Federal Government
Our Federal Government:
   The Legislative Branch
Our Federal Government:
   The Presidency
Our Federal Government:
   The Supreme Court

Pride & Prejudice: A History
   of Black Culture in America
The Role of the First Lady
Sisters and Friends
This House of Power: The
   Church in
   African-American
   Experience
Thurgood Marshall
Western Europe: Our Legacy
Wilma Rudolph
Women with Wings

GRADE EIGHT

Historical Fiction

Cannon. *Begin the World
   Again*

Choi. *Gathering of Pearls*

Biography

Aldred. *Thurgood Marshall:
   Supreme Court Justice*
Anderson. *Jackie Kennedy
   Onassis*
Archbold. *Deep-Sea
   Explorer: Robert Ballard*
Bishop. *Ralph Ellison: Author*
Blau. *Betty Friedan: Feminist*
Blue. *Barbara Jordan:
   Politician*
Bredeson. *Jonas Salk:
   Discoverer of the Polio
   Vaccine*
Brown. *Romare Bearden:
   Artist*
Butts. *May Chinn: The Best
   Medicine*
Cain. *Louise Nevelson:
   Sculptor*
Celsi. *Ralph Nader: The
   Consumer Revolution*

Chin. *When Justice Failed:
   The Fred Korematsu Story*
Cleary. *A Girl from Yamhill:
   A Memoir*
Cleary. *My Own Two Feet*
Cole. *John Glenn: Astronaut
   and Senator*
Conord. *John Lennon*
Curson. *Jonas Salk*
Dolan. *Susan Butcher and the
   Iditarod Trail*
Fleischman. *The
   Abracadabra Kid: A
   Writer's Life*
Glassman. *Mikhail
   Baryshnikov*
Glassman. *Wilma Mankiller:
   Chief of the Cherokee
   Nation*
Gonzales. *Alex Haley: Author
   of Roots*

Haskins. *Thurgood Marshall:
   A Life for Justice*
Heiss. *Barbara Bush*
Henry. *Coretta Scott King:
   Keeper of the Dream*
Herda. *Thurgood Marshall:
   Civil Rights Champion*
Johnson. *Stokely Carmichael:
   The Story of Black Power*
Kallen. *Thurgood Marshall:
   A Dream of Justice for All*
Kent. *George Bush:
   Forty-First President*
Kent. *Ronald Reagan:
   Fortieth President*
Kittredge. *Barbara
   McClintock*
Kittredge. *Helen Hayes:
   Actress*
Kliment. *Ella Fitzgerald:
   Singer*
Larsen. *Ronald Reagan*

Lazo. *Wilma Mankiller*
Lyons. *Clare Boothe Luce*
Malone. *Maya Lin: Architect and Artist*
Meltzer. *Betty Friedan: A Voice for Women's Rights*
Meryman. *Andrew Wyeth*
Morris. *The Reagan Way*
Palmer. *Lena Horne: Entertainer*
Patrick. *Coretta Scott King*
Patterson. *Marian Anderson*
Paulsen. *Woodsong*
Peduzzi. *Ralph Nader*
Pollack. *Shirley Chisholm*
Probosz. *Martha Graham*
Reef. *Ralph David Abernathy*
Richman. *James E. Carter*
Robbins. *Ronald W. Reagan*
Rosset. *James Baldwin: Author*

Sandak. *The Reagans*
Sawyer. *Marjory Stoneman Douglas*
Scheader. *Shirley Chisholm: Teacher and Congresswoman*
Schuman. *Elie Wiesel*
Schwartzberg. *Ronald Reagan*
Schwarz. *Wilma Mankiller*
Selfridge. *John F. Kennedy: Courage in Crisis*
Sherrow. *Linus Pauling*
Sipiera. *Gerald Ford: Thirty-Eighth President*
Slavin. *Jimmy Carter*
Speaker-Yuan. *Agnes de Mille: Choreographer*
Stefoff. *George H. Bush*
Sullivan. *George Bush*
Sullivan. *Ronald Reagan*

Super. *Daniel "Chappie" James*
Taylor-Boyd. *Betty Friedan*
Tedards. *Marian Anderson: Singer*
Tomlinson. *Jonas Salk*
Wade. *James Carter: Thirty-Ninth President*
Wadsworth. *Susan Butcher: Sled Dog Racer*
Whitelaw. *Mr. Civil Rights: The Story of Thurgood Marshall*
Wright. *John Lennon*
Wyman. *Ella Fitzgerald: Jazz Singer Supreme*
Yannuzzi. *Wilma Mankiller: Leader of the Cherokee Nation*

Collective Biography

Aaseng. *America's Third-Party Presidential Candidates*
Aaseng. *Close Calls: From the Brink of Ruin to Business Success*
Aaseng. *Genetics: Unlocking the Secrets of Life*
Aaseng. *Great Justices of the Supreme Court*
Aaseng. *True Champions: Great Athletes and Their Off-the-Field Heroics*
Aaseng. *Twentieth-Century Inventors*
Altman. *Extraordinary Black Americans*
Beard. *The Presidents in American History*
Blassingame. *The Look-It-Up Book of Presidents*
Blue. *People of Peace*
Brill. *Extraordinary Young People*
Burns. *Black Stars in Orbit: NASA's African American Astronauts*
Camp. *American Astronomers: Searchers and Wonderers*
Cush. *Artists Who Created Great Works*

Cush. *Women Who Achieved Greatness*
Dolan. *Shaping U.S. Foreign Policy: Twelve Secretaries of State*
Faber. *Great Lives: American Government*
Fireside. *Is There a Woman in the House. . . or Senate?*
Glenn. *Discover America's Favorite Architects*
Glubok. *Great Lives: Painting*
Haskins. *Against All Opposition: Black Explorers in America*
Haskins. *Black Eagles: African Americans in Aviation*
Jones. *Big Star Fallin' Mama*
Krull. *Lives of the Writers: Comedies, Tragedies*
Matthews. *Power Brokers*
Mayberry. *Business Leaders Who Built Financial Empires*
Mayberry. *Leaders Who Changed the 20th Century*
Morin. *Women Chosen for Public Office*
Morin. *Women Who Reformed Politics*
Myers. *Now Is Your Time*

Otfinoski. *Great Black Writers*
Pascoe. *First Facts About the Presidents*
Pile. *Women Business Leaders*
Plowden. *Famous Firsts of Black Women*
Provenson. *My Fellow Americans*
Rennert. *Book of Firsts: Leaders of America*
Rennert. *Jazz Stars*
Rennert. *Pioneers of Discovery*
Rubel. *The Scholastic Encyclopedia of the Presidents*
Sills. *Inspirations: Stories About Women Artists*
Sills. *Visions: Stories About Women Artists*
Streissguth. *Hatemongers and Demagogues*
Streissguth. *Hoaxers & Hustlers*
Sullivan. *Presidents at Play*
Veglahn. *Women Scientists*
Whitelaw. *They Wrote Their Own Headlines*
Young. *Cy Young Award Winners*
Yount. *Women Aviators*

History

Aaseng. *You Are the Senator*
Aaseng. *You Are the Corporate Executive*

Alvarez. *The Official Baseball Hall of Fame Answer Book*

Anderson. *Battles That Changed the Modern World*
Avakian. *A Historical Album of Massachusetts*

Avakian. *A Historical Album of New York*

Bernards. *Gun Control*

Biel. *The Challenger*

Bortz. *Catastrophe!: Great Engineering Failure—and Success*

Burke. *Food and Fasting*

Calabro. *Zap!: A Brief History of Television*

Capek. *Artistic Trickery: The Tradition of the Trompe L'oeil Art*

Capek. *Murals: Cave, Cathedral, to Street*

Carlson. *A Historical Album of Minnesota*

Carnegy. *The 1980s*

Carnes. *Us and Them: A History of Intolerance in America*

Clements. *An Illustrated History of the World*

Cocke. *A Historical Album of Virginia*

Cocke. *A Historical Album of Washington*

Colman. *Toilets, Bathtubs, Sinks, and Sewers*

Colman. *Women in Society: United States*

Compton. *Marriage Customs*

Cozic. *Civil Liberties*

Cozic. *Israel: Opposing Viewpoints*

Cray. *American Datelines*

Cush. *Disasters That Shook the World*

Davies. *Transport: On Land, Road and Rail*

Emert. *Top Lawyers and Their Famous Cases*

Evans. *Freedom of Religion*

Evans. *Freedom of Speech*

Evans. *Freedom of the Press*

Faber. *We the People: The Story of the United States Constitution*

Fradin. *Medicine: Yesterday, Today, and Tomorrow*

Garfunkel. *On Wings of Joy: The Story of Ballet*

Gay. *Persian Gulf War*

Giblin. *When Plague Strikes*

Gold. *Roberts V. U.S. Jaycees*

Golston. *Changing Woman of the Apache*

Green. *Women in American Indian Society*

Greene. *Child Labor: Then and Now*

Hakim. *All the People*

Herald. *The 1970s*

Hill. *Our Century: 1970-1980*

Hirsch. *Taxation: Paying for Government*

Hoig. *It's the Fourth of July*

Hull. *Breaking Free*

Jacobs. *Search for Peace: The United Nations*

Jones. *The President Has Been Shot*

Karl. *America Alive: A History*

Katz. *The Great Society to the Reagan Era: 1964-1990*

Kelley. *Into the Fire: African Americans Since 1970*

Kelly. *Federal Indian Policy*

Kimmel. *Bar Mitzvah: A Jewish Boy's Coming of Age*

King. *The Gulf War*

Kronenwetter. *United They Hate: White Supremacist Groups in America*

Kronenwetter. *The War Against Terrorism*

Landau. *Armed America: The Status of Gun Control*

Landau. *The White Power Movement: America's Racist Hate Groups*

Lang. *Extremist Groups in America*

Langone. *Spreading Poison: A Book About Racism and Prejudice*

Lawlor. *Where Will This Shoe Take You?*

Lawson. *Famous Presidential Scandals*

Leiner. *First Children: Growing Up in the White House*

Leinwand. *Do We Need a New Constitution?*

Levi. *Cowboys of the Sky*

Lucas. *Civil Rights: The Long Struggle*

Macy. *Winning Ways: A Photohistory of American Women in Sports*

Markham. *Inventions That Changed Modern Life*

May. *Pushing the Limits: American Women 1940-1961*

Medearis. *Come This Far to Freedom*

Meltzer. *The Black Americans*

Mizell. *Think About Racism*

Morley. *Clothes: For Work, Play and Display*

Mulcahy. *Diseases: Finding the Cure*

Nash. *The Baseball Hall of Shame*

Newton. *Gun Control: An Issue for the Nineties*

Pascoe. *Freedom of Expression*

Patrick. *The Young Oxford Companion to the Supreme Court*

Patterson. *The Oxford 50th Anniversary Book of the United Nations*

Perl. *From Top Hats to Baseball Caps, from Bustles to Blue Jeans*

Philip. *Singing America: Poems That Define a Nation*

Pietrusza. *The End of the Cold War*

Platt. *The Smithsonian Visual Timeline of Inventions*

Prior. *Initiation Customs*

Prior. *Pilgrimages and Journeys*

Rappaport. *American Women: Their Lives in Their Words*

Richardson. *Inside the Metropolitan Museum*

Ride. *To Space and Back*

Ross. *The United Nations*

Rowland-Warne. *Costume*

Rushton. *Birth Customs*

Rushton. *Death Customs*

Scott. *Funny Papers: Behind the Scenes of the Comics*

Senna. *The Black Press and the Struggle of Civil Rights*

Sifakis. *Hoaxes and Scams: A Compendium of Deceptions, Ruses, and Swindles*

St. George. *The White House: Cornerstone of a Nation*

Stefoff. *The American Environmental Movement*

Stein. *The Iran Hostage Crisis*

Stevens.*The Case of Roe V. Wade*

Stones and Bones: How Archaeologists Trace Human Origins

Sullivan. *Children of Promise: African-American Literature and Art*

Suter. *Our Century: 1980-1990*
Tames. *The 1980s*
Tchudi. *Lock and Key*
Time-Life. *African Americans: Voices of Triumph: Leadership*
Topper. *A Historical Album of New Jersey*
Turvey. *Inventions: Inventors and Ingenious Ideas*
Wakin. *How TV Changed America's Mind*
Wakin. *Photos That Made U.S. History: Cold War Era to Space Age*

Walker. *Hand, Heart, and Mind*
Warburton. *Railroads: Bridging the Continents*
Wekesser. *The Death Penalty: Opposing Viewpoints*
Wheeler. *Events That Changed American History*
Whitman. *Get Up and Go: American Road Travel*
Wilkinson. *Building*
Wills. *A Historical Album of Alabama*
Wills. *A Historical Album of California*

Wills. *A Historical Album of Connecticut*
Wills. *A Historical Album of Florida*
Wills. *A Historical Album of Illinois*
Wills. *A Historical Album of Nebraska*
Wills. *A Historical Album of Oregon*
Wills. *A Historical Album of Texas*
Woods. *Affirmative Action*
Yepsen. *City Trains: America's Cities by Rail*

Multimedia

CD-ROM

Air and Space Smithsonian Dreams of Flight
Beyond the Wall: Stories Behind Vietnam Wall
Campaigns, Candidates and the Presidency
Daring to Fly!
Exploring the Titanic
Eyewitness Encyclopedia of Science

Famous American Speeches: 1850 to the Present
Her Heritage: A Biographical Encyclopedia of American History
History Through Art: 20th Century
Inside the White House
Landmark Documents in American History

Portraits of American Presidents
Religions of the World
Science Navigator
SkyTrip America
Time Almanac of the 20th Century
Total History
The Way Things Work

Video

African Americans
All the Unsung Heroes: The Vietnam Veterans Memorial
America's Political Parties: The Republican Party
Barnum's Big Top
Changing Faces of Our Land: Once Upon a Time on the Farm
Choosing a President
Great Black Innovators
Great Black Women
History in the Making: The 1980's Series

Judaism: The Religion of the People
Making It Happen: Masters of Invention
Marian Anderson
A More Perfect Union: The Three Branches of the Federal Government
Our Federal Government: The Legislative Branch
Our Federal Government: The Presidency
Our Federal Government: The Supreme Court

Pride & Prejudice: A History of Black Culture in America
The Role of the First Lady
Sisters and Friends
This House of Power: The Church in African-American Experience
Thurgood Marshall
Wilma Rudolph
Women with Wings

GRADE NINE

Historical Fiction

Cannon. *Begin the World Again*

Choi. *Gathering of Pearls*
Iida. *Middle Son: A Novel*

Biography

Aldred. *Thurgood Marshall: Supreme Court Justice*
Anderson. *Jackie Kennedy Onassis*

Archbold. *Deep-Sea Explorer: Robert Ballard*
Bishop. *Ralph Ellison: Author*
Blau. *Betty Friedan: Feminist*

Blue. *Barbara Jordan: Politician*
Bredeson. *Jonas Salk: Discoverer of the Polio Vaccine*

Brown. *Romare Bearden: Artist*

Cain. *Louise Nevelson: Sculptor*

Celsi. *Ralph Nader: The Consumer Revolution*

Cleary. *A Girl from Yamhill: A Memoir*

Cleary. *My Own Two Feet*

Conord. *John Lennon*

Curson. *Jonas Salk*

Ferguson. *Alvin Ailey, Jr.: A Life in Dance*

Fleischman. *The Abracadabra Kid: A Writer's Life*

Glassman. *Mikhail Baryshnikov*

Gonzales. *Alex Haley: Author of Roots*

Haskins. *Thurgood Marshall: A Life for Justice*

Heiss. *Barbara Bush*

Henry. *Coretta Scott King: Keeper of the Dream*

Herda. *Thurgood Marshall: Civil Rights Champion*

Johnson. *Stokely Carmichael: The Story of Black Power*

Kallen. *Thurgood Marshall: A Dream of Justice for All*

Kenan. *James Baldwin*

Kent. *George Bush: Forty-First President*

Kent. *Ronald Reagan: Fortieth President*

Kittredge. *Barbara McClintock*

Kittredge. *Helen Hayes: Actress*

Kliment. *Ella Fitzgerald: Singer*

Larsen. *Ronald Reagan*

Lyons. *Clare Boothe Luce*

Malone. *Maya Lin: Architect and Artist*

Meltzer. *Starting from Home: A Writer's Beginnings*

Meryman. *Andrew Wyeth*

Morris. *The Reagan Way*

Newton. *Linus Pauling: Scientist and Advocate*

Palmer. *Lena Horne: Entertainer*

Patrick. *Coretta Scott King*

Patterson. *Marian Anderson*

Paulsen. *Woodsong*

Peduzzi. *Ralph Nader*

Pollack. *Shirley Chisholm*

Probosz. *Martha Graham*

Reef. *Ralph David Abernathy*

Richman. *James E. Carter*

Robbins. *Ronald W. Reagan*

Rosset. *James Baldwin: Author*

Scheader. *Shirley Chisholm: Teacher and Congresswoman*

Schuman. *Elie Wiesel*

Schwartzberg. *Ronald Reagan*

Schwarz. *Wilma Mankiller*

Selfridge. *John F. Kennedy: Courage in Crisis*

Sipiera. *Gerald Ford: Thirty-Eighth President*

Slavin. *Jimmy Carter*

Speaker-Yuan. *Agnes de Mille: Choreographer*

Stefoff. *George H. Bush*

Sullivan. *George Bush*

Sullivan. *Ronald Reagan*

Super. *Daniel "Chappie" James*

Taylor-Boyd. *Betty Friedan*

Tedards. *Marian Anderson: Singer*

Tomlinson. *Jonas Salk*

Wade. *James Carter: Thirty-Ninth President*

Wadsworth. *Susan Butcher: Sled Dog Racer*

Whitelaw. *Mr. Civil Rights: The Story of Thurgood Marshall*

Wright. *John Lennon*

Wyman. *Ella Fitzgerald: Jazz Singer Supreme*

Collective Biography

Aaseng. *America's Third-Party Presidential Candidates*

Aaseng. *Close Calls: From the Brink of Ruin to Business Success*

Aaseng. *Genetics: Unlocking the Secrets of Life*

Aaseng. *Great Justices of the Supreme Court*

Aaseng. *True Champions: Great Athletes and Their Off-the-Field Heroics*

Aaseng. *Twentieth-Century Inventors*

Beard. *The Presidents in American History*

Blassingame. *The Look-It-Up Book of Presidents*

Borklund. *Military Leaders Since World War II*

Brill. *Extraordinary Young People*

Burns. *Black Stars in Orbit: NASA's African American Astronauts*

Camp. *American Astronomers: Searchers and Wonderers*

Cush. *Artists Who Created Great Works*

Cush. *Women Who Achieved Greatness*

Dolan. *Shaping U.S. Foreign Policy: Profiles of Twelve Secretaries of State*

Faber. *Great Lives: American Government*

Glenn. *Discover America's Favorite Architects*

Glubok. *Great Lives: Painting*

Haskins. *Against All Opposition: Black Explorers in America*

Jones. *Big Star Fallin' Mama*

Landrum. *Profiles of Female Genius: Thirteen Creative Women*

Landrum. *Profiles of Genius: Thirteen Creative Men*

Mahoney. *Women in Espionage: A Biographical Dictionary*

Matthews. *Power Brokers*

Mayberry. *Leaders Who Changed the 20th Century*

Morin. *Women Chosen for Public Office*

Morin. *Women Who Reformed Politics*

Myers. *Now Is Your Time*

O'Brien. *American Political Leaders: From Colonial Times to the Present*

Otfinoski. *Great Black Writers*

Phelps. *They Had a Dream: The Story of African-American Astronauts*

Pile. *Women Business Leaders*

Plowden. *Famous Firsts of Black Women*

Rennert. *Book of Firsts: Leaders of America*

Rennert. *Pioneers of Discovery*

Streissguth. *Hatemongers and Demagogues*
Streissguth. *Hoaxers & Hustlers*

Sullivan. *Presidents at Play*
Veglahn. *Women Scientists*
Weitzman. *Great Lives: Theater*

Whitelaw. *They Wrote Their Own Headlines*
Yount. *Women Aviators*

History

Aaseng. *You Are the Senator*
Aaseng. *You Are the Corporate Executive*
Alvarez. *The Official Baseball Hall of Fame Answer Book*
Anderson. *Battles That Changed the Modern World*
Archer. *Rage in the Streets: Mob Violence in America*
Basinger. *American Cinema: One Hundred Years of Filmmaking*
Beckett. *The Story of Painting*
Bernards. *Gun Control*
Bortz. *Catastrophe!: Great Engineering Failure—and Success*
Bremness. *Herbs*
Brown. *Christianity*
Calabro. *Zap!: A Brief History of Television*
Capek. *Artistic Trickery: The Tradition of the Trompe L'oeil Art*
Capek. *Murals: Cave, Cathedral, to Street*
Carnegy. *The 1980s*
Carnes. *Us and Them: A History of Intolerance in America*
Chafe. *The Road to Equality: American Women Since 1962*
Cohen. *America: Then and Now*
Collier. *Jazz, the American Theme Song*
Colman. *Women in Society: United States*
Cozic. *Civil Liberties*
Cozic. *Israel: Opposing Viewpoints*
Cray. *American Datelines*
Cush. *Disasters That Shook the World*
Davis. *Don't Know Much About History*
Davis. *Man-Made Catastrophes*
Emert. *Top Lawyers and Their Famous Cases*
Evans. *Freedom of Religion*
Evans. *Freedom of Speech*
Evans. *Freedom of the Press*

Faber. *We the People: The Story of the United States Constitution*
Fradin. *Medicine: Yesterday, Today, and Tomorrow*
Garfunkel. *On Wings of Joy: The Story of Ballet*
Gay. *Persian Gulf War*
Giblin. *When Plague Strikes*
Gold. *Roberts V. U.S. Jaycees*
Golston. *Changing Woman of the Apache*
Green. *Women in American Indian Society*
Greenberg. *The Painter's Eye: Learning to Look at Contemporary American Art*
Greene. *Child Labor: Then and Now*
Hakim. *All the People*
Haskins. *Black Music in America*
Herald. *The 1970s*
Hill. *Our Century: 1970-1980*
Hirsch. *Taxation: Paying for Government*
Hull. *Breaking Free*
Jacobs. *Search for Peace: The United Nations*
Jenkins. *Nicaragua and the United States: Years of Conflict*
Jones. *The President Has Been Shot*
Katz. *The Great Society to the Reagan Era: 1964-1990*
Kelley. *Into the Fire: African Americans Since 1970*
Kelly. *Election Day: An American Holiday, an American History*
Kelly. *Federal Indian Policy*
King. *The Gulf War*
Knappman. *Great American Trials*
Kronenwetter. *Capital Punishment*
Kronenwetter. *United They Hate: White Supremacist Groups in America*
Kronenwetter. *The War Against Terrorism*

Lackmann. *Same Time. . . Same Station: An A-Z Guide to Radio*
Landau. *Armed America: The Status of Gun Control*
Landau. *The White Power Movement: America's Racist Hate Groups*
Lang. *Extremist Groups in America*
Langone. *Spreading Poison: A Book About Racism and Prejudice*
Lawson. *Famous Presidential Scandals*
Leiner. *First Children: Growing Up in the White House*
Leinwand. *Do We Need a New Constitution?*
Levi. *Cowboys of the Sky*
Macy. *Winning Ways: A Photohistory of American Women in Sports*
Markham. *Inventions That Changed Modern Life*
May. *Pushing the Limits: American Women 1940-1961*
Medearis. *Come This Far to Freedom*
Meltzer. *The Black Americans*
Mizell. *Think About Racism*
Mulcahy. *Diseases: Finding the Cure*
Newton. *Gun Control: An Issue for the Nineties*
Pascoe. *Freedom of Expression*
Patrick. *The Young Oxford Companion to the Supreme Court*
Patterson. *The Oxford 50th Anniversary Book of the United Nations*
Perl. *From Top Hats to Baseball Caps, from Bustles to Blue Jeans*
Philip. *Singing America: Poems That Define a Nation*
Pietrusza. *The End of the Cold War*
Platt. *The Smithsonian Visual Timeline of Inventions*

Pollack. *Women on the Hill: A History of Women in Congress*

Potter. *African-American Firsts*

Rappaport. *American Women: Their Lives in Their Words*

Ride. *To Space and Back*

Ritchie. *Please Stand By: A Prehistory of Television*

Ross. *The United Nations*

Senna. *The Black Press and the Struggle of Civil Rights*

Sifakis. *Hoaxes and Scams: A Compendium of Deceptions, Ruses, and Swindles*

Smith. *Fascinating People and Astounding Events from American History*

Spangenburg. *The History of Science from 1946 to the 1990s*

Spangenburg. *Opening the Space Frontier: Space Exploration*

St. George. *The White House: Cornerstone of a Nation*

Steele. *Freedom's River*

Stefoff. *The American Environmental Movement*

Stevens.*The Case of Roe V. Wade*

Stones and Bones: How Archaeologists Trace Human Origins

Suter. *Our Century: 1980-1990*

Tames. *The 1980s*

Tchudi. *Lock and Key*

Time-Life. *African Americans: Voices of Triumph: Leadership*

Wakin. *How TV Changed America's Mind*

Wakin. *Photos That Made U.S. History: Cold War Era to Space Age*

Walker. *Hand, Heart, and Mind*

Warburton. *Railroads: Bridging the Continents*

Warren. *Cold War*

Wekesser. *The Death Penalty: Opposing Viewpoints*

Wekesser. *Feminism: Opposing Viewpoints*

Wheeler. *Events That Changed American History*

Whitman. *Get Up and Go: American Road Travel*

Wilkinson. *Building*

Woods. *Affirmative Action*

Multimedia

CD-ROM

Air and Space Smithsonian Dreams of Flight

Beyond the Wall: Stories Behind Vietnam Wall

Campaigns, Candidates and the Presidency

Daring to Fly!

Events That Changed the World

Famous American Speeches: 1850 to the Present

Her Heritage: A Biographical Encyclopedia of American History

History Through Art: 20th Century

Ideas That Changed the World

Inside the White House

Landmark Documents in American History

Our Times: The Multimedia Encyclopedia of the Twentieth Century

Portraits of American Presidents

Religions of the World

Science Navigator

Time Almanac of the 20th Century

Total History

The Way Things Work

Video

African Americans

African Americans Tell Their Story

All the Unsung Heroes: The Vietnam Veterans Memorial

America's Political Parties: The Republican Party

America's Relations with Eastern Europe

Barnum's Big Top

Bill of Rights Today: The 4th Amendment

Changing Faces of Our Land: Once Upon a Time on the Farm

Choosing a President

Eyes on the Prize II: Back to the Movement, (1979-mid 1980s)

Great Black Women

History in the Making: The 1980's Series

Judaism: The Religion of the People

Marian Anderson

A More Perfect Union: The Three Branches of the Federal Government

The Peyote Road

Pride & Prejudice: A History of Black Culture in America

The Role of the First Lady

The Sensational Seventies

Sisters and Friends

The Sunrise Dance

This House of Power: The Church in African-American Experience

Thurgood Marshall

Who Owns History?

Wilma Rudolph

Women: First and Foremost

Women with Wings

GRADE TEN

Historical Fiction

Cannon. *Begin the World Again*

Choi. *Gathering of Pearls*
Iida. *Middle Son: A Novel*

Biography

Aldred. *Thurgood Marshall: Supreme Court Justice*
Archbold. *Deep-Sea Explorer: Robert Ballard*
Bishop. *Ralph Ellison: Author*
Blau. *Betty Friedan: Feminist*
Blue. *Barbara Jordan: Politician*
Brown. *Romare Bearden: Artist*
Cain. *Louise Nevelson: Sculptor*
Celsi. *Ralph Nader: The Consumer Revolution*
Cleary. *A Girl from Yamhill: A Memoir*
Cleary. *My Own Two Feet*
Conord. *John Lennon*
Ferguson. *Alvin Ailey, Jr.: A Life in Dance*

Fleischman. *The Abracadabra Kid: A Writer's Life*
Gallen. *Bill Clinton as They Know Him*
Gonzales. *Alex Haley: Author of Roots*
Haskins. *Thurgood Marshall: A Life for Justice*
Heiss. *Barbara Bush*
Herda. *Thurgood Marshall: Civil Rights Champion*
Johnson. *Stokely Carmichael: The Story of Black Power*
Kenan. *James Baldwin*
Kittredge. *Barbara McClintock*
Kittredge. *Helen Hayes: Actress*
Kliment. *Ella Fitzgerald: Singer*
Larsen. *Ronald Reagan*

Lyons. *Clare Boothe Luce*
Malone. *Maya Lin: Architect and Artist*
Meltzer. *Starting from Home: A Writer's Beginnings*
Newton. *Linus Pauling: Scientist and Advocate*
Palmer. *Lena Horne: Entertainer*
Patterson. *Marian Anderson*
Pollack. *Shirley Chisholm*
Reef. *Ralph David Abernathy*
Rosset. *James Baldwin: Author*
Schuman. *Elie Wiesel*
Sullivan. *George Bush*
Tedards. *Marian Anderson: Singer*
Wright. *John Lennon*
Wyman. *Ella Fitzgerald: Jazz Singer Supreme*

Collective Biography

Aaseng. *America's Third-Party Presidential Candidates*
Aaseng. *Great Justices of the Supreme Court*
Aaseng. *Twentieth-Century Inventors*
Borklund. *Military Leaders Since World War II*
Brill. *Extraordinary Young People*
Haskins. *Against All Opposition: Black Explorers in America*
Jones. *Big Star Fallin' Mama*
Landrum. *Profiles of Female Genius: Thirteen Creative Women*

Landrum. *Profiles of Genius: Thirteen Creative Men*
Mahoney. *Women in Espionage: A Biographical Dictionary*
Matthews. *Power Brokers*
Mayberry. *Leaders Who Changed the 20th Century*
Morin. *Women Chosen for Public Office*
Morin. *Women Who Reformed Politics*
Myers. *Now Is Your Time*
O'Brien. *American Political Leaders: From Colonial Times to the Present*
Otfinoski. *Great Black Writers*

Phelps. *They Had a Dream: The Story of African-American Astronauts*
Streissguth. *Hatemongers and Demagogues*
Streissguth. *Hoaxers & Hustlers*
Sullivan. *Presidents at Play*
Weitzman. *Great Lives: Theater*
Whitelaw. *They Wrote Their Own Headlines*
Yount. *Women Aviators*

History

Aaseng. *You Are the Corporate Executive*
Aaseng. *You Are the Senator*
Alvarez. *The Official Baseball Hall of Fame Answer Book*
Anderson. *Battles That Changed the Modern World*

Archer. *Rage in the Streets: Mob Violence in America*
Basinger. *American Cinema: One Hundred Years of Filmmaking*
Beckett. *The Story of Painting*
Bernards. *Gun Control*

Bremness. *Herbs* Brown. *Christianity*
Calabro. *Zap!: A Brief History of Television*
Capek. *Artistic Trickery: The Tradition of the Trompe L'oeil Art*

Capek. *Murals: Cave, Cathedral, to Street*

Carnegy. *The 1980s*

Carnes. *Us and Them: A History of Intolerance in America*

Chafe. *The Road to Equality: American Women Since 1962*

Cohen. *America: Then and Now*

Collier. *Jazz, the American Theme Song*

Colman. *Women in Society: United States*

Cozic. *Civil Liberties*

Cozic. *Israel: Opposing Viewpoints*

Cray. *American Datelines*

Davis. *Don't Know Much About History*

Davis. *Man-Made Catastrophes*

Evans. *Born for Liberty: A History of Women in America*

Evans. *Freedom of Religion*

Evans. *Freedom of Speech*

Evans. *Freedom of the Press*

Faber. *We the People: The Story of the United States Constitution*

Fradin. *Medicine: Yesterday, Today, and Tomorrow*

Garfunkel. *On Wings of Joy: The Story of Ballet*

Gold. *Roberts V. U.S. Jaycees*

Golston. *Changing Woman of the Apache*

Green. *Women in American Indian Society*

Greenberg. *The Painter's Eye: Learning to Look at Contemporary American Art*

Greene. *Child Labor: Then and Now*

Hakim. *All the People*

Haskins. *Black Music in America*

Herald. *The 1970s*

Hill. *Our Century: 1970-1980*

Jacobs. *Search for Peace: The United Nations*

Jenkins. *Nicaragua and the United States: Years of Conflict*

Katz. *The Great Society to the Reagan Era: 1964-1990*

Kelley. *Into the Fire: African Americans Since 1970*

Kelly. *Election Day: An American Holiday, an American History*

Kelly. *Federal Indian Policy*

King. *The Gulf War*

Knappman. *Great American Trials*

Kronenwetter. *Capital Punishment*

Kronenwetter. *United They Hate: White Supremacist Groups in America*

Kronenwetter. *The War Against Terrorism*

Lackmann. *Same Time. . . Same Station: An A-Z Guide to Radio*

Landau. *Armed America: The Status of Gun Control*

Landau. *The White Power Movement: America's Racist Hate Groups*

Lang. *Extremist Groups in America*

Langone. *Spreading Poison: A Book About Racism and Prejudice*

Lawson. *Famous Presidential Scandals*

Leinwand. *Do We Need a New Constitution?*

Macy. *Winning Ways: A Photohistory of American Women in Sports*

Markham. *Inventions That Changed Modern Life*

May. *Pushing the Limits: American Women 1940-1961*

Meltzer. *The American Promise: Voices of a Changing Nation 1945-Present*

Meltzer. *The Black Americans*

Mizell. *Think About Racism*

Mulcahy. *Diseases: Finding the Cure*

Newton. *Gun Control: An Issue for the Nineties*

Pascoe. *Freedom of Expression*

Patrick. *The Young Oxford Companion to the Supreme Court*

Patterson. *The Oxford 50th Anniversary Book of the United Nations*

Philip. *Singing America: Poems That Define a Nation*

Pollack. *Women on the Hill A History of Women in Congress*

Potter. *African-American Firsts*

Rappaport. *American Women: Their Lives in Their Words*

Ritchie. *Please Stand By: A Prehistory of Television*

Ross. *The United Nations*

Senna. *The Black Press and the Struggle of Civil Rights*

Sherr. *Susan B. Anthony Slept Here*

Sifakis. *Hoaxes and Scams: A Compendium of Deceptions, Ruses, and Swindles*

Smith. *Fascinating People and Astounding Events from American History*

Spangenburg. *Opening the Space Frontier: Space Exploration*

Spangenburg. *The History of Science from 1946 to the 1990s*

Steele. *Freedom's River*

Steele. *Riots*

Stefoff. *The American Environmental Movement*

Stevens. *The Case of Roe V. Wade*

Suter. *Our Century: 1980-1990*

Tchudi. *Lock and Key*

Time-Life. *African Americans: Voices of Triumph: Leadership*

Wakin. *How TV Changed America's Mind*

Wakin. *Photos That Made U.S. History: Cold War Era to Space Age*

Warren. *Cold War*

Wekesser. *The Death Penalty: Opposing Viewpoints*

Wekesser. *Feminism: Opposing Viewpoints*

Wheeler. *Events That Changed American History*

Wilkinson. *Building*

Woods. *Affirmative Action*

Multimedia

CD-ROM

Air and Space Smithsonian Dreams of Flight
Beyond the Wall: Stories Behind Vietnan Wall
Campaigns, Candidates and the Presidency
Daring to Fly!
Events That Changed the World
Famous American Speeches: 1850 to the Present

Her Heritage: A Biographical Encyclopedia of American History
History Through Art: 20th Century
Ideas That Changed the World
Inside the White House
Landmark Documents in American History

Our Times: The Multimedia Encyclopedia of the Twentieth Century
Portraits of American Presidents
Religions of the World
Science Navigator
Time Almanac of the 20th Century
Total History
The Way Things Work

Video

African Americans
African Americans Tell Their Story
All the Unsung Heroes: The Vietnam Veterans Memorial
America's Political Parties: The Republican Party
America's Relations with Eastern Europe
Are We Winning Mommy? America and the Cold War
Barnum's Big Top
Bill of Rights Today: The 4th Amendment
Changing Faces of Our Land: Once Upon a Time on the Farm

Choosing a President
Eyes on the Prize II: Back to the Movement, (1979-mid 1980s)
Eyes on the Prize II: The Keys to the Kingdom (1974-1980)
Great Black Women
The Gulf War, Parts 1 and 2
History in the Making: The 1980's Series
Judaism: The Religion of the People
Marian Anderson
A More Perfect Union: The Three Branches of the Federal Government

The Peyote Road
Pride & Prejudice: A History of Black Culture in America
The Role of the First Lady
The Sensational Seventies
Sisters and Friends
The Sunrise Dance
This House of Power: The Church in African-American Experience
Thurgood Marshall
Who Owns History?
Wilma Rudolph
Women: First and Foremost
Women with Wings

GRADES ELEVEN AND TWELVE

Historical Fiction

Berent. *Eagle Station*
Berent. *Phantom Leader*
Berent. *Rolling Thunder*

Berent. *Steel Tiger*
Bingham. *Matron of Honor*
Bingham. *Small Victories*

Choi. *Gathering of Pearls*
Iida. *Middle Son: A Novel*

Biography

Anderson. *Den of Lions: Memoirs of Seven Years*
Cleary. *A Girl from Yamhill: A Memoir*
Cleary. *My Own Two Feet*
Conord. *John Lennon*
Crowley. *Nixon Off the Record*
Ferguson. *Alvin Ailey, Jr.: A Life in Dance*
Gallen. *Bill Clinton as They Know Him*

Hunter-Gault. *In My Place*
Johnson. *Stokely Carmichael: The Story of Black Power*
Kenan. *James Baldwin*
Kittredge. *Barbara McClintock*
Kittredge. *Helen Hayes: Actress*
Kliment. *Ella Fitzgerald: Singer*
Lyons. *Clare Boothe Luce*

Meltzer. *Starting from Home: A Writer's Beginnings*
Newton. *Linus Pauling: Scientist and Advocate*
Palmer. *Lena Horne: Entertainer*
Rosset. *James Baldwin: Author*
Wright. *John Lennon*

Collective Biography

Aaseng. *Great Justices of the Supreme Court*

Aaseng. *Twentieth-Century Inventors*

Bell-Scott. *Life Notes: Personal Writings of Contemporary Black Women*

Boorstin. *The Creators: A History of Heroes of the Imagination*

Borklund. *Military Leaders Since World War II*

Conway. *Written by Herself—Autobiographies of American Women*

Jones. *Big Star Fallin' Mama*

Landrum. *Profiles of Female Genius: Thirteen Creative Women*

Landrum. *Profiles of Genius: Thirteen Creative Men*

Mahoney. *Women in Espionage: A Biographical Dictionary*

Matthews. *Power Brokers*

Mayberry. *Leaders Who Changed the 20th Century*

Morin. *Women Chosen for Public Office*

O'Brien. *American Political Leaders*

Otfinoski. *Great Black Writers*

Phelps. *They Had a Dream*

Reaves. *Oliphant's Presidents: Twenty-five Years of Caricature*

Sifakis. *Encyclopedia of Assassinations*

Smith. *Women Who Write*

Streissguth. *Hatemongers and Demagogues*

Streissguth. *Hoaxers & Hustlers*

Truman. *First Ladies*

Weitzman. *Great Lives: Theater*

Wills. *Certain Trumpets: The Call of Leaders*

Yount. *Women Aviators*

History

Aaseng. *You Are the Corporate Executive*

Aaseng. *You Are the Senator*

Archer. *Rage in the Streets: Mob Violence in America*

Basinger. *American Cinema: One Hundred Years of Filmmaking*

Beckett. *The Story of Painting*

Boller. *Presidential Wives: An Anecdotal History*

Bremness. *Herbs*

Brown. *Christianity*

Busby. *Daughters of Africa: An International Anthology*

Calabro. *Zap!: A Brief History of Television*

Capek. *Artistic Trickery: The Tradition of the Trompe L'oeil Art*

Capek. *Murals: Cave, Cathedral, to Street*

Carnes. *Us and Them: A History of Intolerance in America*

Chafe. *The Road to Equality: American Women Since 1962*

Cohen. *America: Then and Now*

Cole. *Perspective*

Collier. *Jazz, the American Theme Song*

Colman. *Women in Society: United States*

Cozic. *Civil Liberties*

Cozic. *Israel: Opposing Viewpoints*

Cray. *American Datelines*

Davidson. *Everyday Life Through the Ages*

Davis. *Don't Know Much About History*

Davis. *Man-Made Catastrophes*

Evans. *Born for Liberty: A History of Women in America*

Faber. *We the People: The Story of the United States Constitution*

Fogle. *Two Hundred Years: Stories of the Nation's Capital*

Garfunkel. *On Wings of Joy: The Story of Ballet*

Gold. *Roberts V. U.S. Jaycees*

Green. *Women in American Indian Society*

Greenberg. *The Painter's Eye: Learning to Look at Contemporary American Art*

Hakim. *All the People*

Hampton. *Voices of Freedom: An Oral History of the Civil Rights Movement*

Hanmer. *Taking a Stand Against Sexism and Sex Discrimination*

Harris. *Diamond: Baseball Writings*

Haskins. *Black Music in America*

Jacobs. *Search for Peace: The United Nations*

Jenkins. *Nicaragua and the United States: Years of Conflict*

Kelley. *Into the Fire: African Americans Since 1970*

Kelly. *Election Day: An American Holiday, an American History*

Kelly. *Federal Indian Policy*

Knappman. *Great American Trials*

Kronenwetter. *Capital Punishment*

Kronenwetter. *United They Hate: White Supremacist Groups in America*

Lackmann. *Same Time... Same Station: An A-Z Guide to Radio*

Landau. *The White Power Movement: America's Racist Hate Groups*

Lang. *Extremist Groups in America*

Langone. *Spreading Poison: A Book About Racism and Prejudice*

Lawson. *Famous Presidential Scandals*

Leinwand. *Do We Need a New Constitution?*

Marling. *George Washington Slept Here, 1876-1986*

May. *Pushing the Limits: American Women 1940-1961*

Melder. *Hail to the Candidate: Presidential Campaigns*

Meltzer. *The American Promise: Voices of a Changing Nation 1945-Present*

Mulcahy. *Diseases: Finding the Cure*

Noble. *Bookbanning in America: Who Bans Books?*

Partnow. *The New Quotable Woman*

Patrick. *The Young Oxford Companion to the Supreme Court*

Patterson. *The Oxford 50th Anniversary Book of the United Nations*

Philip. *Singing America: Poems That Define a Nation*

Pollack. *Women on the Hill: A History of Women in Congress*

Potter. *African-American Firsts*

Rappaport. *American Women: Their Lives in Their Words*

Ritchie. *Please Stand By: A Prehistory of Television*

Schimmel. *Mystery of Numbers*

Senna. *The Black Press and the Struggle of Civil Rights*

Sherr. *Susan B. Anthony Slept Here*

Sifakis. *Hoaxes and Scams: A Compendium of Deceptions, Ruses, and Swindles*

Simpson. *The Great Dismal: A Carolinian's Swamp Memoir*

Smith. *Fascinating People and Astounding Events from American History*

Spangenburg. *The History of Science from 1946 to the 1990s*

Spangenburg. *Opening the Space Frontier: Space Exploration*

Steele. *Freedom's River*

Steele. *Riots*

Stevens. *The Case of Roe V. Wade*

Terkel. *The Great Divide: Second Thoughts on the American Dream*

Time-Life. *African Americans: Voices of Triumph: Leadership*

Warren. *Cold War*

Wekesser. *The Death Penalty: Opposing Viewpoints*

Wekesser. *Feminism: Opposing Viewpoints*

Wheeler. *Events That Changed American History*

Wilkinson. *Building*

Multimedia

CD-ROM

Air and Space Smithsonian Dreams of Flight

Beyond the Wall: Stories Behind Vietnan Wall

Campaigns, Candidates and the Presidency

Daring to Fly!

Events That Changed the World

Famous American Speeches: 1850 to the Present

Her Heritage: A Biographical Encyclopedia of American History

History Through Art: 20th Century

Ideas That Changed the World

Inside the White House

Landmark Documents in American History

Our Times: The Multimedia Encyclopedia of the Twentieth Century

Portraits of American Presidents

Religions of the World

Science Navigator

Time Almanac of the 20th Century

Total History

The Way Things Work

Video

African Americans Tell Their Story

All the Unsung Heroes: The Vietnam Veterans Memorial

America in Asia

America's Political Parties: The Republican Party

America's Relations with Eastern Europe

Are We Winning Mommy? America and the Cold War

Bill of Rights Today: The 4th Amendment

Changing Faces of Our Land: Once Upon a Time on the Farm

Choosing a President

The Cold War

Eyes on the Prize II: Back to the Movement, (1979-mid 1980s)

Eyes on the Prize II: The Keys to the Kingdom (1974-1980)

From Danger to Dignity: The Fight for Safe Abortion

Frontline: The Gulf War

Great Black Women

The Gulf War, Parts 1 and 2

History in the Making: The 1980's Series

Judaism: The Religion of the People

Marian Anderson

A More Perfect Union: The Three Branches of the Federal Government

The Peyote Road

Pride & Prejudice: A History of Black Culture in America

The Role of the First Lady

The Sensational Seventies

Sisters and Friends

The Sunrise Dance

The Technological Revolution

This House of Power: The Church in African-American Experience

Thurgood Marshall

Toward the Future

Who Owns History?

Wilma Rudolph

Women: First and Foremost

Women with Wings

BOOKS: AN ANNOTATED BIBLIOGRAPHY

A

1. Aaseng, Nathan. **America's Third-Party Presidential Candidates**. Minneapolis, MN: Oliver Press, 1995. 160p. $14.95. ISBN 1-881508-19-6. (Profiles). 7-10

In the United States, a third-party candidate runs for office outside the Democrat or Republican parties. In this century, eight candidates have offered voters another choice and run for office against the odds. The candidates discussed are Theodore Roosevelt (1858-1919), Eugene V. Debs (1855-1926), Robert M. La Follette (1855-1925), Henry A. Wallace (1888-1965), Strom Thurmond (b. 1902), George Wallace (b. 1919), John Anderson (b. 1922), and Ross Perot (b. 1930). U.S. Presidential Election Results, Bibliography, and Index.

2. Aaseng, Nathan. **Twentieth-Century Inventors**. New York: Facts on File, 1991. 132p. $17.95. ISBN 0-8160-2485-5. (American Profiles). 8-12

Ten twentieth-century inventors created such things as plastics, airplanes, rockets, lasers, televisions, and pacemakers. Aaseng places the Wright brothers, Robert Goddard, Gordon Gould, Leo Baekeland, Vladimir Zworykin, Ernest Lawrence, Chester Carlson, and William Shockley in the times they worked by showing political, social, and economic influences on their lives. Bibliography and Index.

3. Aaseng, Nathan. **You Are the Corporate Executive**. Minneapolis, MN: Oliver Press, 1997. 160p. $17.95. ISBN 1-881508-35-8. (Great Decisions). 7 up

Aaseng presents several decisions corporate executives made and offers options for readers to take before revealing the executives' choices. The situations described are Parker's ballpoint pen breakthrough in 1945; DuPont's leather look-alike in 1963; Boeing's large aircraft in 1966; Sony's VCR static in 1974; Johnson & Johnson's product that killed in 1982; Osborne computers' growing pains in 1982; Harley-Davidson's decisions regarding Honda competition in 1982; and the Coca-Cola conflict when New Coke failed in 1985. Source Notes, Bibliography, and Index.

4. Aaseng, Nathan. **You Are the General**. Minneapolis, MN: Oliver Press, 1994. 160p. $14.95. ISBN 1-881508-11-0. (Great Decisions). 6 up

The text presents the decisions that several twentieth-century generals had to make in the middle of battle. Readers can decide what they would do in the same situation. What they decide will help them understand those who had to make real and life-threatening decisions in the past. Generals include those from the Kaiser's army in August 1914, the German Reich in the summer of 1940, the Imperial Japanese Navy in June 1942, the Allied Forces in June 1944, the United Nations Forces in July 1950, the Vietnamese Communist Forces in July 1967, and the Coalition Forces of Operation Desert Storm in February 1991. Source Notes, Bibliography, and Index.

5. Aaseng, Nathan. **You Are the General II: 1800-1899**. Minneapolis, MN: Oliver Press, 1995. 160p. $14.95. ISBN 1-881508-25-0. (Great Decisions). 6 up

Battles are carefully created patterns of military strategy to gain territory, erode an enemy army's morale, and win a broader war. The text presents eight battles and the generals who fought them. The battles are the British Army at New Orleans in 1815, the Prussian Army at Waterloo in 1815, the U.S. Army in Mexico in August of 1847, the Allied Army in Crimea in September 1854, the Army of Northern Virginia at Chancellorsville in May 1863, the U.S. Army at Little Bighorn in June 1876, and the Boer Army in Natal in December 1899. Source Notes, Bibliography, and Index.

6. Aaseng, Nathan. **You Are the President**. Minneapolis, MN: Oliver Press, 1994. 160p. $14.95. ISBN 1-881508-10-2. (Great Decisions). 8 up

The text presents eight problems of U.S. Presidents, suggests several solutions, asks what the reader would do, and then tells what the President did. The situations and Presidents are Theodore Roosevelt and the Pennsylvania Coal Strike in 1902; Woodrow Wilson and the Covenant of the League of Nations in 1919;

179

Franklin Delano Roosevelt and whether to join Great Britain in World War II during 1940; Harry Truman and dropping the atomic bomb on Japan to end World War II in 1945; Dwight Eisenhower and the race riot that stemmed from integration in Little Rock during 1957; John F. Kennedy and what to do about missiles in Cuba in 1962; Lyndon Johnson and decisions about Southeast Asia and Vietnam in 1965; and Richard Nixon and the Watergate burglary in 1972. Source Notes, Bibliography, and Index.

7. Aaseng, Nathan. **You Are the Senator**. Minneapolis, MN: Oliver Press, 1997. 160p. $17.95. ISBN 1-881508-36-6. (Great Decisions). 7 up

U.S. senators make serious decisions that have far-reaching consequences. Aaseng presents several of these and offers options for readers to take before revealing the Senate's choice. The decisions include Prohibition in 1917; Social Security in 1935; labor strikes in 1947; public discrimination in 1964; direct election of the President in 1970; war powers in 1973; balancing the budget in 1985; and gun control in 1993. Source Notes, Bibliography, and Index.

8. Abramson, Howard S. **Hero in Disgrace: The True Discoverer of the North Pole, Frederick A. Cook**. New York: Paragon House, 1991. 250p. $21.95. ISBN 1-55778-322-5. YA

According to Abramson, Frederick A. Cook (1865-1940), an American physician and explorer who once worked with Robert Peary, reached the North Pole before Peary. Peary's influential friends may have destroyed Cook's reputation so that Peary could get credit for reaching one of the last frontiers on Earth. Historians now know that Peary did not reach the Pole and that he knew he was several hundred miles away. Still, he gets credit, and Cook, the real discoverer of the North Pole, does not. Bibliography and Index.

9. Adair, Gene. **George Washington Carver: Botanist**. New York: Chelsea House, 1989. 110p. $18.95; $7.95pa. ISBN 1-55546-577-3; 0-7910-0234-9pa. (Black Americans of Achievement). 7-10

Adair notes most of Carver's achievements, but he balances his view with the perspective that Carver thought he deserved more consideration from Booker T. Washington at Tuskegee Institute. After Washington's death, Carver was freed from the administrative work that he hated, and his research on the peanut led to his international fame. He tried to help people in need, especially farmers whose crops did not grow well. Carver must also be commended for his painting as well as his botanical achievements, because one of his works was chosen to represent Iowa at the 1893 Chicago Exposition celebrating the 400 years since Columbus's arrival. Chronology, Further Reading, and Index.

10. Adair, Gene. **Thomas Alva Edison: Inventing the Electric Age**. New York: Oxford University Press, 1996. 141p. $20. ISBN 0-19-508799-2. (Oxford Scientists). 7 up

Thomas Alva Edison (1847-1931) changed the world with the invention of the electric light, but he had many other inventions credited to him. The text looks at these achievements as well as Edison's use of animals in his laboratory for experimentation. Drawings of his inventions and photographs complement the text. Chronology, Further Reading, and Index.

11. Adler, David A. **Our Golda: The Story of Golda Meir**. Donna Ruff, illustrator. New York: Viking, 1984. 52p. $4.99pa. ISBN 0-14-032104-7pa. 3-7

Golda Meir (1898-1978) lived in Kiev, Russia, outside the Pale of Settlement where only skilled Jews, like her carpenter father, were allowed. At five, Golda had to return to the Pale when her father left for America. In Pinsk, amid the Cossacks and pogroms, they heard talk of a Jewish homeland. Meir's family went to Milwaukee to join her father, and she left for Denver to live with her sister before she and her husband went to Palestine in the 1920s. Meir spoke to crowds about Jewish causes from the time she was 11, and during the rest of her life she led others in the fight for Israel. In 1956, she became the Foreign Minister, and then Prime Minister in 1969. Before her death in 1978, she met with Anwar Sadat in one of many attempts to find peace between the Arabs and the Jews.

12. Alderman, Ellen, and Caroline Kennedy. **In Our Defense: The Bill of Rights in Action**. New York: Morrow, 1991. 430p. $22.95. ISBN 0-688-07801-X. New York: Avon, 1992. 430p. $12.50pa. ISBN 0-380-71720-4pa. YA

Alderman and Kennedy present 19 vignettes of people who have used the Bill of Rights, the first 10 amendments added to the Constitution of the United States in 1791, to protect themselves. For example, Native Americans have protested the development of public land that they believe is sacred; those against them have invoked the First Amendment. The authors show how individuals have carefully thought about these freedoms and how the courts have tried to interpret the laws fairly. Both sides of legal arguments are presented. Endnotes, Bibliography, and Index.

13.　Aldred, Lisa. **Thurgood Marshall: Supreme Court Justice**. New York: Chelsea House, 1990. 127p. $18.95; $7.95pa. ISBN 1-55546-601-X; 0-7910-0245-4pa. (Black Americans of Achievement). 7-10

Clear explanations of the contributions Thurgood Marshall made to the country with his hard work for groups such as the NAACP reveal him as an intelligent and compassionate man. He successfully argued the Brown vs. Board of Education of Topeka, Kansas, case in front of the Supreme Court in 1953 to get equal school opportunities for all races. His work at Howard Law School and his ability to overcome the scarcity of clients for his Baltimore practice during the Depression prepared him for arguing in front of the Court. Aldred explains the federal judicial system so that Marshall's achievements from 1904 to 1975 seem even more impressive as he became a federal judge, then the Solicitor General of the United States, and finally Supreme Court justice, the first Black man appointed. Chronology, Further Reading, and Index.

14.　Alexander, Lloyd. **The Philadelphia Adventure**. New York: Dutton, 1990. 150p. $12.95. ISBN 0-525-44564-1. 6-9

Before the 1876 Centennial Exposition in Philadelphia, the President calls Vesper Holly and asks her to help stop an expected kidnapping. Don Pedro, a Brazilian leader in town, has brought his children, and someone has threatened them. Vesper and her friends find the children and reach the convention hall just in time to defuse dynamite set to explode.

15.　Allen, John Logan. **Jedediah Smith and the Mountain Men of the American West**. New York: Chelsea House, 1991. 120p. $19.95. ISBN 0-7910-1301-4. (World Explorers). 5 up

Among the men who were called mountain men were John Colter, George Drouillard, Andrew Henry, Edward Rose, Wilson Price Hunt, Robert Stuart, Jim Bridger, Thomas "Peg Leg" Smith, "old" Hugh Glass, James Ohio Pattie, Kit Carson, and Joseph Walker. When Jedediah Smith went on an expedition to Santa Fe in 1831, a band of Comanche Indians killed him. Photographs and reproductions enhance the text. Chronology, Further Reading, and Index.

16.　Allen, Paula Gunn, and Patricia Clark Smith. **As Long as the Rivers Flow: The Stories of Nine Native Americans**. New York: Scholastic, 1996. 328p. $15.95. ISBN 0-590-47869-9. 5-8

This collective biography covers nine Native Americans who lived from the seventeenth century to the present. From a variety of professions, they include Geronimo (1829-1909), Will Rogers (1879-1935), Maria Tallchief, Wilma Mankiller (b. 1945), Michael Naranjo (b. 1944), and Louise Erdich (b. 1954). Photographs, Bibliography, and Index.

17.　Allen, Zita. **Black Women Leaders of the Civil Rights Movement**. New York: Franklin Watts, 1996. 128p. $22.70. ISBN 0-531-11271-3. (African-American Experience). 6 up

Included here are women whose efforts are often overlooked in texts devoted to the contributions of men in the Civil Rights movement. These women participated in the desegregation of schools, buses, lunch counters, and other facilities and represented sharecroppers, students, domestics, teachers, and college professors. Some of them are nationally known such as Charlayne Hunter Gault and Marian Wright Edelman. Photographs, Notes, and Index.

18.　Altman, Linda. **Migrant Farm Workers: The Temporary People**. New York: Franklin Watts, 1994. 112p. $20.60. ISBN 0-531-13033-9. (Impact Book). 7 up

Firsthand accounts from migrant workers reveal people who have been abused by cruel hiring practices and poor working conditions. During the 1930s, thousands of farm families were displaced, and Mexican workers came across the border in search of any jobs available. Not until the work of Cesar Chavez did life begin to change for them. Source Notes, For Further Reading, and Index.

19.　Altman, Linda. **The Pullman Strike of 1894: Turning Point for American Labor**. Brookfield, CT: Millbrook Press, 1994. 63p. $15.40. ISBN 1-56294-346-4. 5-8

In 1894, Pullman Palace Car announced pay cuts for everyone, but did not lower prices in the company store where employees shopped. The company continued to pay dividends to stockholders, and workers decided to strike because of the unfair practices. The strike began on May 11, 1894, and by the end of June it had become a historical event. In addition to discussing the strike and the major figures involved, Altman also examines the beginning of industrialization in the nation and the people who made the most money from it. Chronology, Further Reading, Sources, and Index.

20.　Altman, Linda Jacobs. **Cesar Chavez**. San Diego, CA: Lucent, 1996. 112p. $16.95. ISBN 1-56006-071-9. (The Importance Of). 7 up

Cesar Chavez (1927-1993) never finished high school, but his work to help migrant farmworkers who had no other advocates is his legacy to the country. He served in the navy, became the national director for the Community Service Organization, started the National Farm Workers Association, led the strike against grape growers, and fasted for nonviolence in 1968, 1972, and 1988. In 1990, he signed an agreement with the Mexican government allowing Mexican farmworkers in the United States to provide medical benefits to their families in Mexico. Notes, For Further Reading, Additional Works Consulted, and Index.

21.   Altman, Susan. **Extraordinary Black Americans: From Colonial to Contemporary Times**. Chicago: Childrens Press, 1989. 240p. $33.80; $15.95pa. ISBN 0-516-00581-2; 0-516-40851-0pa. 4 up

From the slave Estevanico, who helped guide the first expedition through the American Southwest on its way to the Seven Cities of Cibola, to Jesse Jackson and Toni Morrison, these vignettes pinpoint the contributions of 85 Black Americans. Short essays introduce the historical periods and topics—slave uprisings, Black Seminoles, the Underground Railroad, the Emancipation Proclamation, Black Civil War soldiers, Reconstruction, the Little Rock Nine, sit-ins, Freedom Riders, the 1963 march on Washington, the Black Power movement, and the "I Have a Dream" speech. Bibliography and Index.

22.   Alvarez, Everett, Jr., and Anthony S. Pitch. **Chained Eagle**. 1989. New York: Dell, 1991. 354p. $4.95pa. ISBN 0-440-20747-9pa. YA

After being a prisoner of war in Vietnam from 1964 until 1972, Alvarez returned to the United States to find that his wife had not waited for him and to a family that had had to cope with his imprisonment from afar. He received awards as a hero and put his life back together, which included meeting a woman with whom he fell in love and married. His autobiography gives insight about the character values necessary for survival through intense adversity. It also shows that one can succeed even though one may have to change one's original expectations.

23.   Alvarez, Mark. **The Official Baseball Hall of Fame Answer Book**. New York: Simon & Schuster, 1989. 96p. $6.95pa. ISBN 0-671-67377-7pa. 3 up

In his answers to 76 questions on baseball, Alvarez tells anecdotes about each situation, sometimes dispelling myths, sometimes offering suggestions on how to shape the statistics. Questions on hitters, runners, types of pitches, the "Black Sox," ballparks, crowds, uniforms, plays, and other topics reveal baseball facts.

24.   Ambrose, Stephen E. **Undaunted Courage: Meriwether Lewis, Thomas Jefferson, and the Opening of the American West**. New York: Simon & Schuster, 1996. 511p. $27.50. ISBN 0-684-81107-3. YA

Meriwether Lewis (1774-1809) was an intensely curious naturalist. He also had the ability to clearly record what he observed. Thomas Jefferson asked him to lead a search for a water route between the Mississippi and the Pacific. The text looks at his life while additionally considering Lewis's partners, William Clark and Sacagawea, plus Thomas Jefferson's decisions to buy the Louisiana Territory and to have someone map it. It also includes the adventure of the expedition, which lasted from 1803 to 1806. Bibliography, Notes, and Index. *School Library Journal Best Book.*

25.   **The Americas in the Colonial Era**. Remo Berselli, illustrator. Austin, TX: Raintree/Steck-Vaughn, 1993. 82p. $17.97. ISBN 0-8114-3326-9. (History of the World). 7 up

This overview uses informative illustrations and clear maps to complement the text. The two-page spreads begin with the pre-Columbian civilizations' encounters with European explorers and continues through the American Revolution. Topics refer to the discovery of America; the explorers who came afterward; Native Americans; Spanish colonization; the Portuguese, French, and Dutch in America; Creoles; and other aspects of the civilizations. Glossary and Index.

26.   Ames, Mildred. **Grandpa Jake and the Grand Christmas**. New York: Scribner's, 1990. 96p. $12.95. ISBN 0-684-19241-1. 4-7

After her mother dies, Lizzie, 12, worries about her father finding work during the Depression, about the rising costs of her ballet lessons, and about she and her sister and father having to go to Aunt Mary Margaret's home for Christmas. Their aunt gives them hand-me-downs and thinks they should be grateful. Then Lizzie's Grandpa Jake, a man she has never known, arrives unexpectedly, saying they will have the best Christmas ever, with cookies and presents. Grandpa Jake does make cookies, but he leaves before Christmas without fulfilling all of his promises. His influence, however, encourages Lizzie to tell her father that she and her sister prefer a Christmas at home with only the three of them. *School Library Journal Best Book.*

27.   Amoss, Berthe. **The Mockingbird Song**. New York: HarperCollins, 1988. 123p. $12.95. ISBN 0-06-020062-6. 5-7

Lindy, 11, mourns for her mother, who deserted her in the 1930s, and takes out her frustration on her stepmother Millie. When Millie becomes pregnant, Lindy goes to live with her neighbor, Miss Ellie, who is confined to a wheelchair. When the baby arrives prematurely, Millie stays weak, and Lindy goes to the house after school to help her. Miss Ellie reveals why she never married. She helps Lindy realize that her mother did not leave because of anything Lindy did, and Lindy begins to adjust to her new family.

28.   Anderson, Catherine Corley. **Jackie Kennedy Onassis**. Minneapolis, MN: Lerner, 1995. 88p. $18.95; $6.95pa. ISBN 0-8225-2885-1; 0-8225-9714-4pa. 4-9

Jacqueline Kennedy Onassis (1929-1994) grew up in wealthy New England society, where she learned to be an excellent horsewoman. Then she attended Vassar and studied in France at the Sorbonne. She became fluent in French, Italian, and Spanish. She spent her senior year at George Washington University in Washington, D.C. After graduation, she became an Inquiring Reporter for the *Washington Times-Herald* (much to her mother's dismay). She met John Fitzgerald Kennedy, a congressman, and they married. She became the First Lady of the United States when he became President. His assassination in 1963 made her a widow with a son and daughter, John and Caroline. In 1968, she married Aristotle Onassis, a Greek shipping magnate. When he died in 1975, her inheritance guaranteed financial comfort. As an editor at Viking and Doubleday, she became close friends with Maurice Tempelsman. Always in the public eye but disliking scrutiny, she persevered. Perhaps she remembered her mother's warning to remount the horse as soon as she fell. Epilogue.

29.   Anderson, Catherine Corley. **John F. Kennedy: Young People's President**. Minneapolis, MN: Lerner, 1991. 144p. $22.95. ISBN 0-8225-4904-2. 5-7

John Fitzgerald Kennedy (1917-1963) served as President of the United States from 1961 to 1963, when he was assassinated in Dallas. He was lively and witty, and the text shows these attributes. Bibliography and Index.

30.   Anderson, Dale. **Battles That Changed the Modern World**. Austin, TX: Raintree/Steck-Vaughn, 1994. 48p. $15.96. ISBN 0-8114-4928-9. (20 Events Series). 6 up

Since the beginning of the nineteenth century, 20 battles have had a great impact on the world. In two-page spreads, Anderson presents the important aspects of these battles. They are Waterloo (1812), Antietam (1862), Gettysburg (1863), Sedan (1870), Little Bighorn (1875), Tsushima Strait (1905), the Marne (1914), Guernica (1937), Nanking (1937), Britain (1940), El Alamein (1942), Midway (1942), Stalingrad (1941-1943), Normandy (1944), the Chinese Civil War (1947-1949), Inchon (1950), Dien Bien Phu (1954), the Six-Day War (1967), the Tet Offensive (1968), and Desert Storm (1991). Glossary, Suggested Readings, and Index.

31.   Anderson, Dale. **Explorers Who Found New Worlds**. Austin, TX: Raintree/Steck-Vaughn, 1994. 48p. $15.96. ISBN 0-8114-4931-9. (20 Events Series). 6 up

Anderson identifies 20 explorers who have found places that changed the lives of people throughout the world and presents profiles of them in two-page spreads. The explorers discussed here start with Marco Polo (Venice) in the thirteenth century. In the fifteenth century, Christopher Columbus (Portugal) and Vasco da Gama (Portugal) set forth. Their work continued in the sixteenth century with Vasco Nuñez de Balboa (Spain), Ferdinand Magellan (Portugal), Francisco Vasquez de Coronado (Spain), and Jacques Cartier (France). In the seventeenth century, Henry Hudson (England), Louis Jolliet and Jacques Marquette (France), and René-Robert Cavelier, Sieur de La Salle (France) explored North America. The eighteenth-century explorers were Vitus Bering (Denmark), James Cook (England), and Alexander Mackenzie (Scotland). The nineteenth century began with Americans Meriwether Lewis and William Clark, and continued with David Livingstone (Scotland), Richard Francis Burton and John Hanning Speke (England), John McDouall Stuart (Scotland and Australia), Sven Hedin (Sweden), and Robert Peary (America). The twentieth century boasts Roald Amundsen (Norway). Glossary, Suggested Readings, and Index.

32.   Anderson, Joan. **A Williamsburg Household**. George Ancona, photographs. New York: Clarion, 1988. 48p. $15.95; $5.95pa. ISBN 0-89919-516-4; 0-395-54791-1pa. 3-7

In the Williamsburg of 1770, Rippon and his family are slaves in different families. Although they have difficult lives, they enjoy doing errands in town because they have a chance to see each other. Photographs from the Williamsburg living history museum complement the text.

33.   Anderson, Kelly. **Thomas Edison**. San Diego, CA: Lucent, 1994. 112p. $16.95. ISBN 1-56006-041-7. (The Importance Of). 6-9

Thomas Edison (1847-1931) is perhaps the most famous inventor who ever lived. He was not a scientist, which probably hindered him, but he was very logical in his approach to problems and willing to experiment endlessly. He also hired people who had the expertise he lacked. Newspapers early in his career referred to him as the "Wizard of Menlo Park" (the New Jersey town where he lived). The age of Edison covers the invention of the telegraph in the mid-1800s to the mid-1900s when he died. His phonograph and electric light are only two of his 1,093 patents. Notes, For Further Reading, Additional Works Consulted, and Index.

34.   Anderson, Kelly C. **Immigration**. San Diego, CA: Lucent, 1993. 112p. $16.95. ISBN 1-56006-140-5. (Overview). 4-8

The text discusses the difficulties for immigrants trying to adjust to life in America. Problems of illegal immigration, being refugees, and border disputes often complicate their lives as well. They also have to decide to accept either the "salad bowl" or the "melting pot" attitude toward assimilation into American culture.

35.   Anderson, LaVere. **Martha Washington: First Lady of the Land**. Cary, illustrator. New York: Chelsea Juniors, 1991. 80p. $14.95. ISBN 0-7910-1452-5. (Discovery). 3-7

After a childhood in Virginia, marriage, and the death of that husband, Martha Dandridge Custis (1731-1802) met George Washington and married him in 1759. Their marriage spanned the American Revolution and his presidency.

36.   Anderson, LaVere. **Mary Todd Lincoln: President's Wife**. Cary, illustrator. New York: Chelsea Juniors, 1991. 80p. $14.95. ISBN 0-7910-1415-0. (Discovery). 3-7

Mary Todd Lincoln (1818-1882) grew up in a Kentucky family that helped runaway slaves. After Lincoln started courting her and they married, he gave her a ring with "Love is Eternal" engraved on it; she wore it until she died. After she and Lincoln moved into the White House, she faced several family tragedies. One son died from pneumonia, her husband was assassinated, and another son died at 18 after she had left Washington. The text gives an overview of her life.

37.   Anderson, Madelyn Klein. **Edgar Allan Poe: A Mystery**. New York: Franklin Watts, 1993. 158p. $14.40. ISBN 0-531-13012-6. (Impact Biography). 9-12

Edgar Allan Poe (1809-1849) was the "father of the detective story" and probably of science fiction. He told various stories about himself that few could verify. He said that he was the grandson of Benedict Arnold, that he went to Russia, and that he fought in the Greek revolution. Critics have accused him of plagiarism and gossiped that he died of alcoholism when he might have had a brain disorder. The text examines these and other "mysteries" about Poe. Chronology of Compositions, Source Notes, Bibliography, and Index.

38.   Anderson, Terry A. **Den of Lions: Memoirs of Seven Years**. New York: Crown, 1993. 349p. $25. ISBN 0-517-59301-7. YA

Terry Anderson, chief Middle East correspondent for the Associated Press, endured seven years of captivity in Beirut, Lebanon. Before he was captured, he fell in love with a Lebanese Maronite Catholic, and his life changed. Poems in the text show his spiritual regeneration and complement his recollection of the time spent in the company of "hamsters," the unkempt youths who carried weapons throughout Beirut and who treated him as an unclean animal. The account of his life begins with 1985 and focuses on his years without freedom. Index.

39.   Anderson, William. **Laura Ingalls Wilder: A Biography**. New York: HarperCollins, 1992. 240p. $16; $5.95pa. ISBN 0-06-020113-4; 0-06-446103-3pa. 4-7

Laura Ingalls Wilder (1867-1957) wrote books about her own life. In this biography, Anderson divides the chapter headings into the time periods that relate to her fiction. Wilder and her pioneer family lived in Indian territory, Plum Creek, Burr Oak, and Dakota Territory. She was a prairie girl who married and lived with her own family in Big Red Apple, on Rocky Ridge Farm, and in Gem City of the Ozarks. Her family encouraged her to write the stories that she told so vividly, and she won many awards for them. Index.

40.   Andrews, Elaine. **Indians of the Plains**. New York: Facts on File, 1992. 96p. $21.95. ISBN 0-8160-2387-5. (First Americans). 6 up

The text presents the history of the Plains Indians, their way of life, their rituals, and the changes they have endured. The tribes known as the Plains Indians include the farmer-hunter tribes of the Arikara, Kansa, Mandan, Osage, Pawnee, and Wichita. The hunters are the Arapaho, Assiniboin, Blackfoot, Cheyenne, Comanche, Crow, Kiowa, and Sioux. Photographs enhance the text. Index.

41.   Andronik, Catherine M. **Prince of Humbugs: A Life of P. T. Barnum**. New York: Atheneum, 1994. 136p. $15.95. ISBN 0-689-31796-4. 6-9

Phineas Taylor Barnum (1810-1891) had as many setbacks as he had successes, but he discovered that people would pay to see George Washington's nurse, who claimed to be 160 years old. He promoted Tom Thumb and Jenny Lind and showcased Jumbo the elephant. In later life, he met circus owner James A. Bailey, and with him brought to Americans "The Greatest Show on Earth." Notes, For More Information, and Index.

42.   Andryszewski, Tricia. **The Amazing Life of Moe Berg: Catcher, Scholar, Spy**. Brookfield, CT: Millbrook Press, 1996. 127p. $16.40. ISBN 1-56294-610-2. 5-8

Moe Berg, an intellectual trained in linguistics at Princeton with a law degree from Columbia, played professional baseball for 20 years on a variety of teams. He was not a particularly effective batter or runner, but he was an excellent catcher. In World War II, he became a spy for the OSS. He traveled throughout Latin America and Europe making propaganda speeches in Japanese because he had gone to Japan before the war as a baseball player and knew the language. The text looks at the life of this unusual man. Photographs, Notes, and Index.

43. Andryszewski, Tricia. **The Dust Bowl: Disaster in the Plains**. Brookfield, CT: Millbrook Press, 1993. 64p. $15.90; $5.95pa. ISBN 1-56294-272-7; 1-56294-747-8pa. (Spotlight on American History). 5-7

The text presents the 1930s drought that turned the Great Plains into a "dust bowl." Both human and natural forces caused this disaster. The lack of rain coupled with the Great Depression led to enormous economic and emotional loss. Bibliography and Index.

44. Angell, Judie. **One-Way to Ansonia**. New York: Bradbury, 1985. 183p. $11.95. ISBN 0-02-705860-3. 5-8

Rose, 11, and her siblings arrive at Ellis Island in 1893 after escaping from Russian pogroms to meet their father and his new wife. When Rose chooses to add the effort of night school to her long days of work, she surprises her family, but she realizes that she must work to escape the poverty of a New York tenement life.

45. Anthony, Carl Sferrazza. **First Ladies: The Saga of the Presidents' Wives and Their Power**. New York: Morrow, 1990. 685p. $30; $15pa. ISBN 0-688-07704-8; 0-688-12575-1pa. YA

Each First Lady up to Jackie Kennedy appears in this collective biography. Anthony believes that this role has given the women who filled it a unique opportunity to be political and social powers separate from those of the sitting Presidents, their husbands. He discusses these powers as he tells what each woman accomplished. Bibliography and Index.

46. Aparicio, Frances, ed. **Latino Voices**. Brookfield, CT: Millbrook Press, 1994. 144p. $17.40. ISBN 1-56294-388-X. (Writers of America). YA

Aparicio says that "Latino" or "Latina" best describes the diversity of people in the United States who come from cultures where Spanish is the native language. In 1990, the census identified more than 22 million Latinos. In trying to give a voice to Latinos, Aparicio incorporates personal true-life narratives, poetry, and fiction in this anthology to show the past as it was and how it influences the present. She groups the works under the themes of immigrating, homes, families, faiths, work, language and identity, and race and racial discrimination. Further Reading and Index.

47. Appel, Marty. **Joe DiMaggio**. New York: Chelsea House, 1990. 64p. $14.95; $4.95pa. ISBN 0-7910-1183-6; 0-7910-1198-4pa. (Baseball Legends). 6-9

In addition to information about DiMaggio, son of an Italian immigrant, Appel presents a brief history of baseball on the West Coast. DiMaggio's fame began in 1933, when he had a 61-game hitting streak for his San Francisco team. In 1936, DiMaggio left for New York and the Yankees, the team of Babe Ruth and Lou Gehrig. His record there astounded baseball fans, and he played consistently until injuries sidelined him. Appel includes photographs of DiMaggio with his family and his ex-wife, Marilyn Monroe. Statistics, Chronology, Further Reading, and Index.

48. Applegate, Katherine. **Benjamin O. Davis, Jr., and Colin L. Powell: The Story of Two American Generals**. Minneapolis, MN: Gareth Stevens, 1995. 112p. $13.95. ISBN 0-8368-1380-4. (Famous Lives). 3 up

As the first Black cadet at the U.S. Military Academy at West Point, no one would speak to Benjamin O. Davis (b. 1912) for a while. But in 1941, he became the commander of the first all-Black Air Corps, and in 1967 he became the commander of the 13th Air Force. Following him is Colin L. Powell (b. 1937). Powell joined the ROTC at the City University of New York and from there went into service in Vietnam. His rise through the army ranks led him to become Chairman of the Joint Chiefs of Staff, America's highest military office. Photographs included. For Further Study and Index.

49. Archbold, Rick. **Deep-Sea Explorer: The Story of Robert Ballard, Discoverer of the Titanic**. New York: Scholastic, 1994. 144p. $13.95. ISBN 0-590-47232-1. 5-10

Growing up on the Pacific Coast in California gave Bob Ballard (b. 1942) a love for the sea. This influence, along with the fact that his sister was unable to talk (although she was otherwise normal), made Ballard realize that he must use his full faculties to improve the world. Intrigued with submarines through reading Jules Verne, he won an internship before his senior year in high school with the Scripps Institution of Oceanography. After setbacks, he attended graduate school and eventually had his first dive in a submersible in 1969 in Woods Hole, Massachusetts. Diving led to his 1986 discovery of the *Titanic*, wrecked in 1912. Since then he has run electronic educational programs to share with people his knowledge of what exists below sea level. Epilogue, Glossary, and Index.

50. Archer, Jules. **Breaking Barriers: The Feminist Movement from Susan B. Anthony to Margaret Sanger to Betty Friedan**. New York: Viking, 1991. 207p. $14.95; $5.99pa. ISBN 0-670-83104-2; 0-14-037968-1pa. 7 up

The text explores the American feminist movement by looking at the lives and works of Susan B. Anthony (1820-1906), Margaret Sanger (1883-1966), and Betty Friedan (b. 1921). Anthony fought for suffrage; Sanger fought for birth control rights; and Friedan founded the National Organization for Women. Each woman worked for social change in the face of enormous hostility, not only from men but also from other women. Quotes from the works of these women and interviews with Friedan let the trio speak for themselves. Bibliography and Index.

51. Archer, Jules. **Rage in the Streets: Mob Violence in America**. Lydia J. Hess, illustrator. San Diego, CA: Browndeer Press, Harcourt Brace, 1994. 174p. $16.95. ISBN 0-15-277691-5. YA

Archer traces the history of mob violence in the United States from the Revolutionary War to the 1992 riots in Los Angeles. He sees that people tend to form mobs when specific things occur. They may think that court decisions are unfair, perceive others as intolerant, see racial prejudice, fear losing their jobs, observe police turn violent, think taxes are excessive, disagree on going to war, or feel despair. They may also be part of a group that reacts violently to sports, rock concerts, or other such events. Bibliography, Recommended Reading, and Index.

52. Ardley, Neil. **Music: An Illustrated Encyclopedia**. New York: Facts on File, 1986. 192p. $18.95. ISBN 0-8160-1542-0. YA

In this comprehensive overview, a reader can find an answer to almost any general, and some detailed, questions about music. A collection of articles presents all types of instruments, kinds of music, performers, and specific works. A brief look at music in Japan, Indonesia, Australia, Africa, Europe, and North, South, and Central America helps the reader see the cultural differences in music. A history of music presents Egypt, Greece, Rome, and Asia. Additionally, material covers how artists and technicians make various types of recordings. Annotated Bibliography of "Music Makers" and Index.

53. Arginteanu, Judy. **The Movies of Alfred Hitchcock**. Minneapolis, MN: Lerner, 1994. 80p. $9.50. ISBN 0-8225-1642-X. 5-9

Alfred Hitchcock (1899-1980) made some of the scariest movies of the twentieth century. Knowing about the man and his movies gives insight into his decisions. He saw suspense as something that the audience must feel while the character seems to be unaware that anything might be wrong, and he used this situation in unexpected ways. The movies discussed here are *The 39 Steps*, *The Lady Vanishes*, *Shadow of a Doubt*, *Strangers on a Train*, *Vertigo*, *North by Northwest*, *Psycho*, and *The Birds*. For Further Reading and Index.

54. Armstrong, Jennifer. **The Dreams of Mairhe Mehan: A Novel of the Civil War**. New York: Knopf, 1996. 119p. $18. ISBN 0-679-88152-2. 6 up

Living in Washington, D.C., during the Civil War, Mairhe watches her brother Mike go off to fight and her Da lose his mind. She tries to make enough lace to buy Mike's place in the army. Mairhe meets Walt Whitman while he nurses the soldiers, and he encourages her. *Bulletin Blue Ribbon Book*.

55. Armstrong, Jennifer. **Steal Away**. New York: Orchard, 1992. 207p. $14.95. ISBN 0-531-05983-9. 6-9

Mary, 13, describes her 1896 trip from New York to Toronto with her grandmother. In Toronto, she meets Bethlehem Reid, Gran's friend since 1855, with whom Gran fled Virginia and her uncle's home as a young orphan. Beth had been given to Gran as her own slave, and although Beth would not normally trust a white person, she had gone with Gran because Gran said that she hated slavery. Beth, a retired teacher, tells Mary the story of their journey north.

56. Armstrong, William O. **Sounder**. New York: HarperCollins, 1969. 128p. $14.95; $2.25pa. ISBN 0-06-020143-6; 0-06-447153-5pa. 5 up

During the Depression, a Black boy's father steals a ham to feed his starving family. A white man accuses him, and he goes to jail. The boy has to work to support his family, but in his searches for his father, a man he meets teaches him to read. The dog Sounder is the only one in the story to have a name, and he waits faithfully for his master's return just as Argus, the dog of Odysseus, waited. When the father returns, Sounder dies peacefully. *Newbery Award, Lewis Carroll Shelf Award, American Library Association Notable Children's Books of 1940-1970, Horn Book Fanfare Honor List, School Library Journal "Best of the Best" Children's Books 1966-1978, New York Times Outstanding Children's Book*, and *Publishers Weekly Select Children's Books*.

57. Ashabranner, Brent. **Always to Remember: The Story of the Vietnam Veteran's Memorial**. New York: Putnam, 1988. 40p. $14.95. ISBN 0-399-22031-3. New York: Scholastic, 1992. 40p. $2.95pa. ISBN 0-590-44590-1pa. 4-7

Although supposedly a tribute to the Vietnam Memorial in Washington, D.C., this book covers background about the war, including its inception and that it was the longest war in American history. Of the Americans who served—2.5 million men and 8,000 women—58,000 were killed and more than 300,000 wounded with 74,000 more having more than 50 percent disabilities. From the war's beginning in 1966 until its end in 1975, it cost 140 billion dollars. Some 7,500 people went to prison rather than serve, and more than 425,000 deserted. One man, Jan Scruggs, became obsessed with the creation of a memorial, and oversaw its construction, based on Maya Lin's design, by Veterans Day, 1982. Photographs of the memorial and the memorabilia left at the wall accent the power of this place for almost everyone who stands before it. Facts, Bibliography, and Index.

58.   Ashabranner, Brent. **An Ancient Heritage: The Arab-American Minority**. Paul S. Conklin, photographer. New York: HarperCollins, 1991. 148p. $14.89. ISBN 0-06-020049-9. 5 up

In the text, Ashabranner interviews many young people who were either born in the United States or immigrated because of troubles in their countries. Christians, Muslims, and Jews are represented. But regardless of their current status, they bring the traditions of their cultures into this country and have to balance the old with the new as they face the future. Bibliography and Index.

59.   Ashabranner, Brent. **Dark Harvest: Migrant Farmworkers in America**. Paul Conklin, illustrator. 1985. Hamden, CT: Linnet, Shoe String Press, 1993. 114p. $18.50. ISBN 0-208-02391-7. 5 up

Invisible workers, or migrants, drive around America following the crops, living inside shacks within huge farms where members of the surrounding communities rarely see them. Close to 1 million probably work the fields, but they remain uncounted and unrepresented by government officials. The large crops of California, Texas, and Florida seem to attract the largest number of migrants, whose median income for a family of six was $4,000 in 1982 while the average American family income was $22,000. Additionally, child labor laws do not apply to those who work with their families on these farms. The concern of teachers who periodically encounter these children helps the workers feel appreciated, but the teachers alone cannot change the system.

60.   Ashabranner, Brent. **A Memorial for Mr. Lincoln**. Jennifer Ashabranner, photographs. New York: Putnam, 1992. 113p. $15.95. ISBN 0-399-22273-1. 5 up

On Memorial Day, 1922, President Warren G. Harding dedicated the Lincoln Memorial. At the ceremony, gray-clad Confederate veterans sat with blue-clad Union veterans in the place of honor. Henry Bacon, an architect, spent much of his life trying to design the memorial, and Daniel Chester French, a sculptor with little formal training, created the extraordinary statue of Lincoln. The text looks at Lincoln's contribution to the union and the great care that the monument's creators took to make an appropriate memorial for this man. Bibliography and Index.

61.   Ashabranner, Brent K. **A Strange and Distant Shore: Indians of the Great Plains in Exile**. New York: Cobblehill, 1996. 54p. $16.99. ISBN 0-525-65201-9. 5-8

In 1875, the Red River War led to the imprisonment of 72 Indians of the Great Plains in St. Augustine, Florida, for three years. Their "jailer," Captain Richard Henry Pratt, realized that they deserved deference instead of disdain, and his attitude led to their freedom. However, he thought they should assimilate themselves rather than retain their culture. They refused. Bibliography and Index.

62.   Ashabranner, Brent. **The Times of My Life: A Memoir**. New York: Cobblehill, 1990. 114p. $14.95. ISBN 0-525-65047-4. 4-7

Some of the main issues of the twentieth century come to life in this autobiography. Ashabranner's Oklahoma boyhood during the Depression, his opportunities to write in college, his World War II navy service, and his experiences in Africa and India as a Peace Corps official show his humanitarian interests. Ashabranner also discusses the roles of U.S. Presidents in aiding the development of less-fortunate countries. Bibliography and Index.

63.   Ashton, S. R. **The Cold War**. London: Batsford, 1990. 64p. $19.95. ISBN 0-7134-5817-8. (Living Through History). 9 up

The Cold War had real personalities behind it who made the decisions for the countries involved. The people discussed here make this book as much a collective biography as a history of the time period. Those who were influential at the beginning of the Cold War are the American George Frost Kennan (b. 1904) and the Russian Andrei Zhdanov (1896-1948) for Stalin. In Eastern Europe, Stanislaw Mikolajczyk (1901-1966) fled Poland in 1947. Two significant Czechoslovakians were Eduard Bene (1884-1948) and Jan Masaryk (1886-1948). The Yugoslavian Milovan Djilas (b. 1911) also participated. In Germany, Lucius D. Clay (1897-1978) was the American general in Berlin who dealt with Konrad Adenauer (1876-1967) and Walter Ulbricht (1893-1973). The American Robert Julius Oppenheimer (1904-1967) and Klaus Fuchs (1911-1988), who left Germany for England, worked on the atomic bomb. During the Cuban crisis, Russian Nikita Sergeyevich Khrushchev (1894-1971), Cuban Fidel Castro (b. 1927), and American John Fitzgerald Kennedy (1917-1963) were the important figures. Photographs enhance the text. Date List, Books for Further Reading, and Index.

64.   Astor, Gerald. **Operation Iceberg: The Invasion and Conquest of Okinawa in World War II**. New York: Donald I. Fine, 1995. 480p. $24.95. ISBN 1-55611-425-7. New York: Dell, 1996. 480p. $5.99pa. ISBN 0-440-22178-1pa. YA

This account of Okinawa is an oral history. After presenting the background of the battle, Astor reports the responses of witnesses on opposing sides to give a balanced view. Okinawa was an especially complex fight, with an invasion, a land battle, an air battle, and a sea battle. Photographs complement the text. Index.

65. Atkin, S. Beth. **Voices from the Fields**. Boston: Joy Street; Little, Brown, 1993. 96p. $16.95. ISBN 0-316-05633-2. 6 up.

The twentieth-century hardships of Mexican laborers and migrant workers in the United States appear here in the words of children who have endured them. Their poems and first-person narratives, coupled with photographs, give insight into their fears and hopes. Suggested reading.

66. Auch, Mary Jane. **Journey to Nowhere**. New York: Henry Holt, 1997. 224p. $15.95. ISBN 0-8050-4922-3. 4-7

In 1815, Remembrance "Mem," 11, moves with her family from Hartford, Connecticut, to the wilderness of western New York State. On the journey, she becomes separated from her family members, and after finding them, almost loses them again. In addition to terrain, they must fight bears, wolves, and mountain lions before settling in the new community.

67. Avakian, Monique. **A Historical Album of Massachusetts**. Brookfield, CT: Millbrook Press, 1994. 64p. $16.40; $6.95pa. ISBN 1-56294-481-9; 1-56294-762-1pa. (Historical Album). 4-8

The text presents the land of Massachusetts before it became a state, beginning with Native American civilizations and continuing through exploration and settlement. Early statehood developments and issues and the role of large cities in the state's livelihood lead to the present day. Prints, maps, and photographs illustrate the text. Gazetteer: Quick Facts, Key Events, Personalities, and Index.

68. Avakian, Monique, and Carter Smith III. **A Historical Album of New York**. Brookfield, CT: Millbrook Press, 1994. 64p. $16.40; $6.95pa. ISBN 1-56294-005-8; 1-56294-758-3pa. (Historical Album). 4-8

The text presents the land of New York before it became a state, beginning with Native American civilizations and continuing through exploration and settlement. Early statehood developments and issues and the role of large cities in the state's livelihood lead to the present day. Prints, maps, and photographs illustrate the text. Gazetteer: Quick Facts, Key Events, Personalities, and Index.

69. Avery, Susan, and Linda Skinner. **Extraordinary American Indians**. Chicago: Childrens Press, 1992. 252p. $33.80; $15.95pa. ISBN 0-516-00583-9; 0-516-40583-7pa. 7 up

The text includes brief biographies of 60 Native Americans, beginning with Pope (c. 1632), a San Juan Pueblo resistance leader, and ending with contemporary Americans who have established themselves as professionals and protectors of their people. Biographees include Pontia, Nancy Ward, Joseph Brant, Red Jacket, Tecumseh, Sequoyah, Sacagawea, Seathl, Osceola, Ely Samuel Parker, Geronimo, Sitting Bull, Chief Joseph, Crazy Horse, Sarah Winnemucca, the La Flesche family, Charles Alexander Eastman, Wovoka, Ishi, Black Elk, Gertrude Simmons Bonnin, Will Rogers, Jim Thorpe, the Delorias, and Frank Fools Crow. For Further Reading and Index.

70. Avi. **Beyond the Western Sea, Book Two: Lord Kirkle's Money**. New York: Jackson, Orchard, 1996. 380p. $18.95. ISBN 0-531-09520-7. 5-8

Patrick and his sister, Maura O'Connell, sail with their friends, Mr. Horatio Drabble and Laurence Kirkle, on the *Robert Peel* from England to Boston in 1851. They all go to Lowell, Massachusetts, where they discover that the O'Connell father has died. The characters must endure prejudice and hardship, but they eventually overcome the evil forces that would ruin their lives.

71. Avi. **Captain Grey**. 1977. New York: Beech Tree, Morrow, 1993. 160p. $15; $3.95pa. ISBN 0-688-12233-7; 0-688-12234-5pa. 5-9

When Kevin and Cathleen Cartwright meet Captain Grey during a journey from Philadelphia to New Jersey in 1783, Captain Grey and his men kill their father and convince Kevin that his sister is also dead. Captain Grey starves Kevin long enough so that the boy does as he wants, which includes helping his men kill a crew and sink a ship in the name of helping America defeat the British. With Grey's trust, Kevin begins to roam the island on which Grey is quartered and discovers his sister hiding in a cave. They plan an escape, aided by a schooner crew coming to get revenge on Grey for his evil deeds. Kevin understands but does not condone Grey, who has turned inhumane after the death of his wife and son.

72. Avi. **Encounter at Easton**. 1980. New York: Beech Tree, Morrow, 1994. 144p. $14; $4.95pa. ISBN 0-688-05295-9; 0-688-05296-7pa. 5 up

A sequel to *Night Journeys*, *Encounter at Easton* presents the story of Elizabeth Mawes and Robert Linnly through the first-person narratives of Robert and Nathaniel Hill, the man hired to find Elizabeth. Not until Mad Moll tries to save Elizabeth and Robert finds out that Hill has papers in his saddlebag to capture Elizabeth does Robert realize that he must fear Hill. The ensuing flight and discovery cause one death and one improvement of fortune even though both young people have done nothing for which they should suffer.

73.   Avi. **The Fighting Ground**. Ellen Thompson, illustrator. New York: HarperCollins, 1984. 160p. $14.89; $4.50pa. ISBN 0-397-32074-4; 0-06-440185-5pa. 4 up

Jonathan, 11, spends a day fighting Hessians in 1778 near Trenton, New Jersey. After Hessians capture him, they shelter him in a deserted farmhouse where he sees a young boy hiding near his dead parents. Thinking the Hessians have killed the couple, Jonathan escapes to the group he had joined earlier in the day. He finds that they, not the Hessians, had killed the couple because they were Tories. When Jonathan leads the same group to the Hessians, they are pleased to kill them too. *American Library Association Notable Books for Children*, *American Library Association Recommended Books for Reluctant Young Adult Readers*, *Horn Book Fanfare Honor List*, *New York Public Library Books for the Teen Age*, and *Lesbian and Gay Children's/YA Award*.

74.   Avi. **The Man Who Was Poe**. New York: Orchard, 1989. 208p. $13.95. ISBN 0-531-08433-7. New York: Flare, 1991. 208p. $4.50pa. ISBN 0-380-71192-3pa. 4-8

In 1848, Edmund, 11, must find his sister, who disappears soon after his aunt. He must search Providence, Rhode Island, to find her. He meets a man who helps him look, but the man seems to think Edmund's difficulties are part of a story he is writing. When Edmund finds his mother, who has been gone for the past year, and his sister, who is sailing away in a boat, the man, Edgar Allan Poe, finally seems to understand that the situation is real.

75.   Avi. **Night Journeys**. 1979. New York: Beech Tree, Morrow, 1994. 160p. $14; $4.95pa. ISBN 0-688-05298-3; 0-688-13628-1pa. 5 up

In this novel, two bondservants escape from their master in 1767. When Peter York, an orphan of 12, discovers them, he has to decide whether to help them or to turn them in to the authorities and claim the reward money near Trenton, New Jersey. Because he had once been an avid searcher, his realization that he had befriended the bound girl while searching for her makes him wonder if a person has the right to sell another person. His Quaker guardian will not advise him, but because the guardian is also a justice of the peace, he cannot legally tell Peter to hide them. Peter's decision, however, pleases the Quaker. *Scott O'Dell Award for Historical Fiction*.

76.   Avi. **Punch with Judy**. New York: Bradbury, 1993. 167p. $14.95. ISBN 0-02-707755-1. New York: Avon, 1994. 167p. $3.99pa. ISBN 0-380-72253-4pa. 4-7

In 1870, when Punch is eight, the owner of a traveling medicine show sees him trying to earn bits of money by dancing for anyone who will watch. He lets Punch accompany the troop. They play to rural audiences, but soon they see that humor is the only thing that continues to entertain a hardworking but poor group of people. Punch has to accept the change in fortunes, but someone from the show helps him.

77.   Avi. **Shadrach's Crossing**. New York: Pantheon, 1983. 192p. $10.99. ISBN 0-394-95816-0. 5 up

Shadrach and his parents are bystanders cowed by bullies in a Prohibition smuggling operation on their island in 1932. The Depression forces many of the residents to help the smugglers because they need the money. When Shadrach begins talking to a man whom he hopes will reveal the operation to the government, he makes a risky decision.

78.   Avi. **Something's Upstairs: A Tale of Ghosts**. New York: Orchard, 1988. 120p. $14.95. ISBN 0-531-05782-8. New York: Flare, 1990. 120p. $4.50pa. ISBN 0-380-70853-1pa. 4-7

In this historical fantasy, Kenny's family moves to Providence, Rhode Island, and live in a house built in 1792. When Kenny sees a bloodstain on the floor of his bedroom closet, he is surprised to see a figure rising out of it. He helps the spirit of the dead slave, murdered in 1800, to uncover his killer. They must change memory before they can escape the past.

79.   Avi. **The True Confessions of Charlotte Doyle**. New York: Orchard, 1990. 215p. $15.95. ISBN 0-531-05893-X. New York: Avon, 1992. 215p. $4.50pa. ISBN 0-380-71475-2pa. 5-8

When Charlotte is 13 in 1832, she sails from England on the *Seahawk* to Rhode Island, where her family awaits her. As she is the only passenger on board, guilty crew members blame her for a murder she did not commit. She eventually realizes her plight and escapes it. But when she reaches her family, they cannot know what she has endured. They continue to treat her like a child and a female who must be confined to the home according to social norms—two conditions she can no longer accept. She runs away from them, back to sea. *Newbery Honor Book*, *Boston Globe-Horn Book Award*, *Golden Kite Award*, and *Judy Lopez Memorial Award*.

80.   Avi. **"Who Was That Masked Man, Anyway?"** New York: Orchard, 1992. 142p. $14.95. ISBN 0-531-08607-0. New York: Camelot, 1994. 142p. $3.99pa. ISBN 0-380-72113-9pa. 3-7

During World War II, Frankie, 11, prefers to pretend he is part of the radio programs to which he listens, such as *The Lone Ranger*, rather than do his homework. But when his brother returns home from war wounded, the war becomes more real to Frankie. Then his teacher's boyfriend is killed abroad. Drawing on his knowledge of plot from his favorite radio shows, Frankie creates a scheme through which his brother and teacher may meet. They do meet, but not as Frankie has imagined.

81. Awmiller, Craig. **This House on Fire: The Story of the Blues**. New York: Franklin Watts, 1996. 160p. $22; $8pa. ISBN 0-531-11253-5; 0-531-15797-0pa. (The African-American Experience). YA

According to Awmiller, the blues reflects life as it is. He gives a thorough history of this music, starting with its origins from African American slaves and including technical aspects of its creation. Among those discussed as the creators and developers of this genre are the country blues greats such as Charley Patton, "Blind" Lemon Jefferson, and Robert Johnson; those who introduced urban blues, such as Louis Armstrong, "Ma" Rainey, and Bessie Smith; singers Billie Holiday, Muddy Waters, and Sam "Lightnin'" Hopkins; and contemporary blues performers such as Robert Cray, B. B. King, and Buddy Guy. Further Reading, Notes, and Index.

82. Ayer, Eleanor H. **The Anasazi**. New York: Walker, 1993. 124p. $14.95. ISBN 0-8027-8184-5. 6-9

In covering the development of the Anasazi civilization, from the prehistoric Basket Makers approximately 14,000 years ago to the Pueblo peoples, Ayer describes archaeologists' finds in architecture and artifacts and what they reveal. Possible explanations of daily life also appear. Bibliography and Index.

83. Ayer, Eleanor H. **Lewis Latimer: Creating Bright Ideas**. Austin, TX: Raintree/Steck-Vaughn, 1997. 112p. $18.98. ISBN 0-8172-4407-7. (Innovative Minds). 7-8

As a self-educated son of former slaves, Lewis Howard Latimer (1848-1928) overcame poverty and racism to become an inventor. When he worked for Maxim's U.S. Electric Lighting Company, he learned a lot about electricity. He used his knowledge to find a long-lasting and inexpensive filament for lightbulbs. When he realized that placing the filament material inside of a cardboard envelope allowed it to burn longer, he had discovered the key that other inventors including Thomas Edison had failed to find. Glossary, Further Reading, Sources, and Index.

84. Ayers, Carter M. **Chuck Yeager: Fighter Pilot**. Minneapolis, MN: Lerner, 1988. 48p. $15.95. ISBN 0-8225-0483-9. (Achievers). 4-9

On October 14, 1947, when he was 24, Chuck Yeager (b. 1925) became the first person to fly faster than the speed of sound. He had already earned medals for bravery during World War II. Afterward, he spent a long career as a test pilot while the space program developed. He received both a Congressional Medal of Honor and the Presidential Medal of Freedom.

85. Aymar, Brandt, ed. **Men in the Air: The Best Flight Stories of All Time from Greek Mythology to the Space Age**. New York: Crown, 1990. 557p. $24.95; $12.99pa. ISBN 0-517-57403-9; 0-517-14656-8pa. YA

Both fiction and nonfiction, these stories give insight into the hardships accompanying the humans who have risked their lives to fly. Diary entries from Leonardo da Vinci, the Wright brothers, Louis Blériot, Charles Lindbergh, Eddie Rickenbacher, Amelia Earhart, and others complement the fictional accounts of danger coupled with daring, inherent in the desire to fly.

Begin here

B

86. Bachrach, Deborah. **Custer's Last Stand: Opposing Viewpoints**. San Diego, CA: Greenhaven, 1990. 111p. $16.95. ISBN 0-89908-077-4. (Great Mysteries—Opposing Viewpoints). 7-12

On June 25, 1876, while other Americans were preparing to celebrate the country's centennial, George Armstrong Custer was fighting the Sioux Indians under Sitting Bull and Crazy Horse. He lost. In five chapters, Bachrach presents the opposing concepts that historians who researched this battle have posited. Rhetorical questions introduce opposing viewpoints on five topics that could have affected the battle's outcome—Custer, Custer's officers, the Indians' superior tactics, weapons used, and the intelligence. For Further Exploration and Index.

87. Bachrach, Deborah. **The Korean War**. San Diego, CA: Lucent, 1991. 96p. $16.95. ISBN 1-56006-409-9. (America's Wars). 7 up

The text looks at the Korean War, which lasted from 1950 to 1953, and explains how America was involved; it also discusses the war's events and legacy.

88. Bachrach, Deborah. **Margaret Sanger**. San Diego, CA: Lucent, 1993. 112p. $16.95. ISBN 1-56006-032-8. (The Importance Of). 7-12

Margaret Sanger (1879-1966) sacrificed her personal life and health so that she could actively campaign for safe and legal birth control in the United States and abroad. Bibliography and Index.

89. Bachrach, Deborah. **Pearl Harbor: Opposing Viewpoints**. San Diego, CA: Greenhaven, 1989. 112p. $16.95. ISBN 0-89908-059-6. (Great Mysteries—Opposing Viewpoints). 8 up

Since the Japanese bombed Pearl Harbor in 1941, several questions have arisen about the attack and events leading up to it. Among the questions discussed in this text, with arguments for both sides, are whether Japanese-American negotiations were sincere, whether the attack was a surprise, whether America's generals were responsible for the tragedy at Pearl Harbor, whether incompetent navy officers caused Pearl Harbor, or whether the withholding of secret information caused the tragedy. For Further Exploration, Bibliography, and Index.

90. Badt, Karin Luisa. **Charles Eastman: Sioux Physician and Author**. New York: Chelsea House, 1995. 112p. $18.95. ISBN 0-7910-2048-7. (North American Indians of Achievement). 5 up

In 1858, Hadakah was born and raised as a Santee Sioux who learned about white society in South Dakota's schools. After winning at lacrosse when a teenager, he earned his adult name, Ohiyesa, "The Winner." When he went to live with his father, he took yet a third name, Charles Eastman. He became a graduate of Dartmouth College and of medical school. He was on the scene at Wounded Knee when the U.S. Army attacked the Sioux, and he gave equal help to Native Americans and white soldiers. He then worked as an educator, fought against corruption in the government's Indian services, began the Young Men's Christian Association for Indian youths, started a summer camp for white children to learn about Indians, gave lectures to mixed audiences, and held government jobs to help relations. Thus, he was a civil rights activist and a believer in a multicultural approach to life. Photographs and reproductions enhance the text. Chronology, Further Reading, and Index.

91. Baker, Betty. **The Dunderhead War**. New York: HarperCollins, 1967. $12.89. ISBN 0-06-020328-5. 6-9

When Quince Heffendorf's mother's little brother, Uncle Fritz, arrives in Independence, Missouri, from Germany, he shows that he likes order. He dislikes people shooting their guns in the air and calls them "dunderheads and donkeys." When Quince and Uncle Fritz leave for Santa Fe in 1846, Uncle Fritz's sense of order prevails. He helps the wagon train guard against sheep rustlers, and he aids the army's trades with the Indians. Eventually Quince learns to appreciate Fritz.

92. Baker, Betty. **The Spirit Is Willing**. New York: Macmillan, 1974. $12.95. ISBN 0-02-708270-9. 4-7

Bored and oppressed by the summer heat in their almost-deserted mining town in 1885, Carrie and Portia have a seance. Through happenstance and design, they get responses from a mummy, which makes them think that they are communicating with the netherworld. Others, also bored, are fascinated with the results and willing to believe anything.

93. Baker, Betty. **Walk the World's Rim**. New York: HarperCollins, 1965. 192p. $14.89. ISBN 0-06-020381-1. 5-9

Of 600 men who sailed from Cuba to Florida in 1527, only four survived. One, the black slave Esteban, encourages a young Indian, Chako, to go with him to Mexico. While their leaders petition for money to go to the seven cities of Cíbola, they wait separately in Tenochtitlán. Chako is disturbed that Esteban has not come to tell him what will happen. When Cortez tells Chako to feed his horse, he finds Esteban confined to the stables. Although taught not to respect slaves, Chako soon realizes that he respects Esteban's character despite his social class. When the Cíbolans murder Esteban, Chako dejectedly returns to his Florida home, having lost his friend.

94. Baker, Patricia. **The 1940s**. New York: Facts on File, 1992. 64p. $18.95. ISBN 0-8160-2470-7. (Fashions of a Decade). 7 up

At the beginning of the 1940s, women wore padded shoulders and narrow waistlines, while men's clothing lines fell in an inverted triangle from the shoulders to the waist. Fabric head scarves began to replace hats during the decade. As British and Parisian designers worried about war, American designers began to challenge them. The 1940s was the time of the Zoot-suiters, spivs, and zazous. Other chapters look at men's uniforms in the war and at home during peacetime, Hollywood fashions, and the new look at the end of the decade. Glossary, Reading List, Time Chart, and Index.

95. Baker, Patricia. **The 1950s**. New York: Facts on File, 1991. 64p. $18.95. ISBN 0-8160-2468-5. (Fashions of a Decade). 7 up

In the 1950s, fashion became "ultramodern." The text looks at the fashion changes in this decade, such as Peter Pan collars and synthetic fibers, with many illustrations. Among the personalities of the time were Marilyn Monroe and Elvis Presley. Glossary, Time Line, Reading List, Bibliography, and Index.

96. Balaban, John. **Remembering Heaven's Face: A Moral Witness in Vietnam**. New York: Poseidon Press, 1991. 334p. $21.95; $11pa. ISBN 0-671-69065-5; 0-671-77969-9pa. YA

Balaban, a conscientious objector during the Vietnam War, traveled to Vietnam during the war to work for the International Voluntary Services. In 1971, he returned to collect traditional songs. He kept notebooks for 20 years as a duty, but refused to open them because "their contents [were] unbearable." In 1989, he went to North Vietnam; afterward, he returned to open the notebooks and to relate the terrible things that happened.

97. Baldwin, Joyce. **DNA Pioneer: James Watson and the Double Helix**. New York: Walker, 1994. 136p. $14.95. ISBN 0-8027-8297-3. 7 up

In 1962, James Watson (b. 1928) received notice that he and two others had won the Nobel Prize for Medicine for their discovery of the double-helix secret of DNA, deoxyribonucleic acid. His work during the previous 11 years had helped him figure out the method that cells used to copy themselves. Throughout high school and college, he found that he could do biology rather than liberal arts. At the University of Chicago, which he began attending at age 15, he pursued this interest. When he went to England, he heard his first lecture on DNA in 1951, and he began working on it with Francis Crick. Since he won the prize, he has continued his research on genetics, helping to map the location of the 100,000 human genes and learning the instructions that build an organism. He currently directs the Cold Spring Harbor Laboratory for cancer research. Glossary, For Further Reading, Other References, and Index.

98. Ballard, Robert D. **Exploring the Titanic**. Ken Marschall, illustrator. New York: Madison, Scholastic, 1988. 96p. $14.95; $6.95pa. ISBN 0-590-41953-6; 0-590-41952-8pa. 4-7

Dr. Robert Ballard became fascinated with the story of the *Titanic*. When the tiny submarine *Alvin*'s tether was extended to 13,000 feet, Ballard realized that he could reach the wreck two and one-half miles under the sea. In July 1986, he saw the ship that had last been above the water on April 14, 1912. On that night, only 705 of the 1,500 people on board the magnificent ship reached the safety of a rescue vessel, the *Carpathia*, after an iceberg tore through the hull. Ballard returned to the *Titanic* eight times, going inside and reliving the scene based on what he had read or heard from survivors of that doomed voyage. Further Reading, Glossary, and *Titanic* Timeline. *American Library Association Best Books for Young Adults*, *School Library Journal Best Book*, and *Horn Book Fanfare Honor List*.

99. Bandon, Alexandra. **Asian Indian Americans**. New York: New Discovery, Silver Burdett, 1994. 112p. $14.95. ISBN 0-02-768144-0. (Footsteps to America). 5-8

Bandon examines the lives of Asian Indian Americans after they began to arrive in America around 1965. For them to leave their country was a major decision; therefore, Bandon tries to identify what in the history of the country would have precipitated such a move. Using personal narratives as a basis, she shows what the journey to America was like, what life in America has been like for those who came, the prejudice they faced, and the opportunities they found. For Further Reading and Index.

100. Bandon, Alexandra. **Chinese Americans**. New York: New Discovery, Silver Burdett, 1994. 112p. $14.95. ISBN 0-02-768149-1. (Footsteps to America). 5-8

Bandon examines the lives of Chinese Americans. For them to leave their country was a major decision; therefore, Bandon tries to identify what in the history of the country would have precipitated such a move. Using personal narratives as a basis, she shows what the journey to America was like, what life in America has been like for those who came, the prejudice they faced, and the opportunities they found. For Further Reading and Index.

101. Bandon, Alexandra. **Dominican Americans**. New York: New Discovery, Silver Burdett, 1994. 112p. $14.95. ISBN 0-02-768152-1. (Footsteps to America). 5-8

Bandon examines the lives of Dominican Americans after they began to arrive in America around 1965. For them to leave their country was a major decision, so Bandon tries to identify what in the history of their country would have precipitated such a move. Using personal narratives as a basis, she shows what the journey to America was like, what life in America has been like for those who came, the prejudice they faced, and the opportunities they found. For Further Reading and Index.

102. Bandon, Alexandra. **Filipino Americans**. New York: New Discovery, Silver Burdett, 1993. 112p. $14.95. ISBN 0-02-768143-2. (Footsteps to America). 5-8

Bandon examines the lives of Filipino Americans. For them to leave their country was a major decision; therefore, Bandon tries to identify what in the history of their country would have precipitated such a move. Using personal narratives as a basis, she shows what the journey to America was like, what life in America has been like for those who came, the prejudice they faced, and the opportunities they found. For Further Reading and Index.

103. Bandon, Alexandra. **Korean Americans**. New York: New Discovery, Silver Burdett, 1994. 111p. $14.95. ISBN 0-02-768147-5. (Footsteps to America). 5-8

Bandon examines the lives of Korean Americans. For them to leave their country was a major decision; therefore, Bandon tries to identify what in the history of their country would have precipitated such a move. Using personal narratives as a basis, she shows what the journey to America was like, what life in America has been like for those who came, the prejudice they faced, and the opportunities they found. For Further Reading and Index.

104. Bandon, Alexandra. **Mexican Americans**. New York: New Discovery, Silver Burdett, 1993. 110p. $14.95. ISBN 0-02-768412-4. (Footsteps to America). 5-8

Bandon examines the lives of Mexican Americans. For them to leave their country was a major decision; therefore, Bandon tries to identify what in the history of their country would have precipitated such a move. Using personal narratives as a basis, she shows what the journey to America was like, what life in America has been like for those who came, the prejudice they faced, and the opportunities they found. For Further Reading and Index.

105. Bandon, Alexandra. **Vietnamese Americans**. New York: New Discovery, Silver Burdett, 1994. 112p. $14.95. ISBN 0-02-768146-7. (Footsteps to America). 5-8

Bandon examines the lives of Vietnamese Americans. For them to leave their country was a major decision; therefore, Bandon tries to identify what in the history of their country would have precipitated such a move. Using personal narratives as a basis, she shows what the journey to America was like, what life in America has been like for those who came, the prejudice they faced, and the opportunities they found. For Further Reading and Index.

106. Bandon, Alexandra. **West Indian Americans**. New York: New Discovery, Silver Burdett, 1994. 112p. $14.95. ISBN 0-02-768148-3. (Footsteps to America). 5-8

In this text, Bandon examines the lives of West Indian Americans. For them to decide to leave their country was a major decision; therefore, Bandon tries to identify what in the history of their country would have precipitated such a move. Using personal narratives as a basis, she shows what the journey to America was like, what life in America has been like for those who have come, the prejudices they faced, and the opportunities they found. For Further Reading and Index.

107. Banks, Sara Harrell. **Under the Shadow of Wings**. Chris Sheban, illustrator. New York: Simon & Schuster, Atheneum, 1997. 160p. $16. ISBN 0-689-81207-8. 4-8

Tattnall, 11, lives in the South near the end of World War II. She takes care of her cousin Obie, 16, who is developmentally disabled. She decides that she no longer wants this responsibility, but when Obie tragically dies, she has to cope with her feelings of relief and of intense grief at a major loss in her life.

108. Bar-Lev, Geoffrey, and Joyce Sakkal. **Jewish Americans Struggle for Equality**. Vero Beach, FL: Rourke, 1992. 103p. $16.95. ISBN 0-86593-182-8. (Discrimination). 7-10

The text relates the historical roots of anti-Semitism throughout the world, including the United States. It discusses the immigration of Jews to America and the discrimination they have faced. Additional topics are America's refusal to interfere with the Holocaust and Zionism and the state of Israel. Photographs, charts, and drawings highlight the text. Bibliography, Time Line, Media Materials, and Index.

109. Barboza, Steven. **Door of No Return: The Legend of Gorée Island**. New York: Cobblehill, Dutton, 1994. 42p. $14.99. ISBN 0-525-65188-8. 5 up

As early as 1433, Africans captured other Africans and sold them to Portuguese traders. They assembled the captured slaves on Gorée Island, two miles west of Dakar, Senegal. According to records in Lisbon, 3,589 slaves arrived there between 1486 and 1493. In 1619, a Dutch ship sailed into Jamestown, Virginia, with 20 slaves. Many Africans also owned slaves, and by the late 1800s slaves comprised two-thirds of many African societies. On Gorée, the wealthy kept slave houses. Anne Pepin, a *signare* who acted as the wife of the French governor of Senegal (although unmarried to him), had more than 35 slaves. The island today is a place of pilgrimage for Americans wanting to see where their ancestors started their long journey to servitude. Index.

110. Barnes, Jeremy. **Samuel Goldwyn**. Englewood Cliffs, NJ: Silver Burdett, 1988. 128p. $10.95. ISBN 0-382-09586-3. (American Dream). 7-10

Samuel Goldwyn (1882-1974) immigrated to the United States from Poland, expecting to become a glove maker. He worked in a glove factory in New York State for several years while attending lectures and plays and studying English. He admired the salesmen who congregated in the local hotel and convinced his boss to let him try to sell gloves. He lured a bulk buyer, and his life changed. Eventually he and a friend moved to New York City and begin investing in plays. When he saw a cheap nickelodeon in 1911, he knew they should move to the movies. His success in movies is well documented in the text, which looks at his career and discusses his ventures. Bibliography and Index.

111. Barnes, Joyce Annette. **Promise Me the Moon**. New York: Dial Press 1997. 176p. $14.99. ISBN 0-8037-1798-9. 5-8

Annie from *The Baby Grand, the Moon in July, and Me* is 13 in 1972 and having problems in eighth grade. She is losing her boyfriend and her best friend at the same time she is having trouble in her Enriched Science class. She wants to become an astronaut, and she thinks that attending one of Ohio's best high schools will help her. But she worries about being accepted and whether she really wants the added academic pressure.

112. Barr, Roger. **The American Frontier**. San Diego, CA: Lucent, 1995. 111p. $16.95. ISBN 1-56006-282-7. (World History). 6-9

By focusing on concerns such as Manifest Destiny and the treatment of Native Americans, the text gives a view of westward expansion in the 1800s. Quotes from primary sources allow those on all sides of the debates to state their cases. The last chapter explains the significance of the time period to American history and development of the nation. Bibliography, Chronology, Further Reading, Notes, and Index.

113. Barr, Roger. **Malcolm X**. San Diego, CA: Lucent, 1994. 112p. $16.95. ISBN 1-56006-044-1. (The Importance Of). 7 up

Born Malcolm Little (1925-1965), Malcolm took the name "X" after joining the Nation of Islam. His name changed again after he took a *hajj* to Mecca; his tombstone reads " El-Hajj Malik El-Shabazz." Malcolm's occupations included hustler, pimp, thief, drug dealer, railroad worker, and waiter. At 20, he was arrested and sent to prison. There a man taught him that foul language is less powerful than informed, quiet speech. Malcolm educated himself carefully so that after his release he was able to help Elijah Muhammad lead the Nation of Islam. He started his own group, Muslim Mosque, Inc., when he broke with Muhammad but expected to be killed after someone firebombed his house. An assassin's bullet hit him in 1965. Notes, For Further Reading, Works Consulted, and Index.

114. Barr, Roger. **Richard Nixon**. San Diego, CA: Lucent, 1992. 112p. $16.95. ISBN 1-56006-035-2. (The Importance Of). 5-8

Richard Milhaus Nixon (1913-1994) won his second term in the White House by a landslide. Two years later, he had to resign in ignominy because of his implication in the burglary of the Democratic National Party office at the Watergate Hotel. While in office, he improved relations with China and the Soviet Union. However, his less-favorable moments in office seem to be his legacy. Notes, For Further Reading, Works Consulted, and Index.

115. Barrett, Katherine, and Richard Greene. **The Man Behind the Magic: The Story of Walt Disney**. New York: Viking, 1990. 208p. $18.99. ISBN 0-670-82259-0. 6 up

Walt Disney (1901-1966) grew up on a Missouri farm and built an animation empire through his vision and his willingness to try new ideas. He was determined to make the Disney studio work, and his brother Roy helped support his efforts. In the early years, artists left the studio, taking ideas with them. Making enough money to pay those who stayed was difficult, but Disney eventually built an empire that continues after his death. Index.

116.   Barrett, Tracy. **Harpers Ferry: The Story of John Brown's Raid**. Brookfield, CT: Millbrook Press, 1993. 64p. $15.90; $5.95pa. ISBN 1-56294-380-4; 1-56294-745-1pa. 5-8

John Brown led a raid on the U.S. arsenal at Harpers Ferry, West Virginia, in 1859. Although very religious, he believed that he had to use force, if necessary, to end slavery. His raid failed, and he was hung. Chronology, Further Reading, Bibliography, and Index.

117.   Barrie, Barbara. **Lone Star**. New York: Delacorte, 1990. 182p. $13.95. ISBN 0-385-30156-1. 5-8

In 1944, 10-year-old Jane and her family move from Chicago to Corpus Christi, Texas, after her father is convicted of defrauding insurance customers. Lacking the support of her Jewish family and friends in Chicago, she decides that she would like a Christmas tree. Her grandfather discovers the tiny tree in her bedroom at the same time the family hears of the Nazi concentration camps. He is furious that she has not been true to her Jewish heritage. But she has to cope with her brother's threats to join the army, her parents' bickering, her grandfather's prejudices against Gentiles, and her teacher's prejudice against Yankees. And she wants her new friend's approval.

118.   Bartoletti, Susan C. **Growing Up in Coal Country**. Boston: Houghton Mifflin, 1996. 112p. $15.95. ISBN 0-395-77847-6. 5-8

Oral history, archival documents, and black-and-white photographs help to re-create life in a mining town in northeastern Pennsylvania at the beginning of the twentieth century. Among the hostile aspects were the difficult working conditions, the squalor, and the poverty that children had to endure in such situations. Not until unions and child labor laws did the families begin to escape their plights. Bibliography and Index.

119.   Basinger, Jeanine. **American Cinema: One Hundred Years of Filmmaking**. New York: Rizzoli, 1994. 300p. $50. ISBN 0-8478-1814-4. 6 up

This survey of the American cinema covers filmmaking from 1894, when Thomas Edison first photographed a man sneezing, to current-day full-length features. The text corresponds to the PBS series on American cinema. Among the varied topics included are technical tricks, the movie star, screwball comedy, *film noire*, and the rise and fall of the major studio system. Photographs, Bibliography, and Index.

120.   Bass, Cynthia. **Maiden Voyage**. New York: Villard, 1996. 257p. $23. ISBN 0-679-43034-2. YA

As a first-class passenger on the *Titanic*, Sumner, 13, is returning from visiting his bohemian father in London. His Bostonian family of abolitionists and suffragists has prepared him to encounter a suffragist who inducts him into manhood. His friendship with an older man he meets once on board the ship helps him behave as he should when the accident occurs.

121.   Bass, Cynthia. **Sherman's March**. New York: Villard, 1994. 228p. $21. ISBN 0-679-43033-4. New York: Bantam, 1995. 228p. $11.95pa. ISBN 0-553-37547-4pa. YA

In the fall of 1864, General William Tecumseh Sherman decided to move 60,000 soldiers from Atlanta toward the sea 300 miles away. During the journey, they looted supplies, burned farms, and emancipated slaves. Bass uses three points of view to tell the story: General Sherman, a Union soldier, and a young Southern widow. They create a picture of the Civil War as the Confederates became less effective and the North more determined.

122.   Bauer, Marian. **Rain of Fire**. New York: Clarion, 1983. 160p. $10.95. ISBN 0-89919-190-8. 4-8

Steve, 12, does not understand why his brother has returned from World War II a different person, one who will not discuss his experiences. An older bully calls Steve's brother a "Jap lover." Steve starts lying, and when his brother finally intervenes in the fight that results, he tells Steve about the horror of Hiroshima and how he hates knowing that he killed people. *Jane Addams Children's Book Award*.

123.   Bealer, Alex W. **Only the Names Remain: The Cherokees and the Trail of Tears**. Kristina Rodanas, illustrator. Boston: Little, Brown, 1972, 1996. 96p. $15.95; $4.95pa. ISBN 0-316-08518-9; 0-316-08519-7pa. 6 up

On a forced march from Georgia to Oklahoma in 1837 and 1838, thousands of Cherokee Indians died. The text looks at the U.S. government's treatment of them as the troops took the Cherokees from their homes during mealtime and demanded that they leave their possessions, including land the Cherokees rightfully owned. Bibliography and Index.

124.   Beard, Charles, and Detlev Vagts. **The Presidents in American History**. New York: Julian Messner, 1981. 240p. $14.98. ISBN 0-671-44026-8. 6-10

Brief vignettes on each President of the United States give insight on their backgrounds, achievements, and personalities. Three pages of text per man give a clear understanding of his integrity (or lack thereof) and the behaviors he exhibited in the highest office one can win in America. One wonders how some of the men ever got elected. Biographical Digest.

125. Beatty, Patricia. **Be Ever Hopeful, Hannalee**. New York, Morrow, 1988. 208p. $15. ISBN 0-688-07502-9. Mahwah, NJ: Troll, 1990. 208p. $3.95pa. ISBN 0-8176-2259-5pa. 5-9

After the Civil War ends in this sequel to *Turn Homeward, Hannalee*, Hannalee, now 13, and her mother and two brothers move to Atlanta. Because Hannah's brother has only one arm, he has difficulty finding work, and she is too young to work. In desperation, he almost becomes involved with criminals. People accuse him of misconduct, but he never does anything wrong. Their life finally becomes better after a difficult period.

126. Beatty, Patricia. **Behave Yourself, Bethany Brant**. New York: Morrow, 1986. 172p. $15. ISBN 0-688-05923-6. 5-9

In 1898, when she is 11, Bethany goes to live with relatives while her father becomes a circuit rider minister in Texas. Her mother died when she was born, and she worries about her father. Tempted to spend money on a fortune-teller, she does, but feels guilty. When someone gambles away her father's money to build a new church, she swallows her guilt and gambles again to win it back. Her seemingly righteous cousin understands her decision and supports it.

127. Beatty, Patricia. **Billy Bedamned, Long Gone By**. New York: Morrow, 1977. 223p. $9.95. ISBN 0-688-22101-7. 5-8

In 1929, Merle and her brother and grandmother travel from Pasadena to New Orleans with her mother driving. When they stop at the family home in MacRae, Texas, Merle is never sure which of the family stories her two great uncles tell are actually true.

128. Beatty, Patricia. **Blue Stars Watching**. New York: Morrow, 1969. 191p. $7.95. ISBN 0-688-21110-0. 5-9

When Will finds Rab, a hired hand, dead, his father tells him that Confederates have killed Rab because he has been running an Underground Railway station. In 1861, Will and his sister find safety with relatives in San Francisco. He gets a job at the newspaper so that he can find out about his father's Maryland Union army unit. What he hears from his former schoolteacher-turned-spy is that his relatives are supporting the Confederates from San Francisco by stuffing gold into dolls that are then transported via the Panama Canal to the Confederacy. Their detective work gives grounds for the government to stop the ship for piracy.

129. Beatty, Patricia. **Bonanza Girl**. 1968. New York: Beech Tree, Morrow, 1993. 224p. $4.95pa. ISBN 0-688-12280-9pa. 5 up

Ann, her widowed mother, and brother go to Idaho Territory in 1884. Although planning to open a school, her mother meets Helga Storkersen, who convinces her to open a tent restaurant for the miners in the town and a second one in the claim area of a silver mine. To get money to hire a preacher and open a church, the two collect money in the saloons.

130. Beatty, Patricia. **By Crumbs, It's Mine!** New York: Morrow, 1976. 254p. $7.25. ISBN 0-688-22062-2. 5-9

Damaris, an independent female of 13 in 1882, and her aunt take a traveling hotel, a cardboard building capable of being erected anywhere, and run it while her mother is ill and her father mines for gold. Among their customers are Chinese and Irish railroad workers. When Damaris realizes that her mother looks weaker every day, she persuades an Apache working at the hotel to accompany her on a five-day journey to retrieve her father.

131. Beatty, Patricia. **Charley Skedaddle**. New York: Morrow, 1987. 192p. $15. ISBN 0-688-06687-9. Mahwah, NJ: Troll, 1988. 192p. $4.95pa. ISBN 0-8167-1317-0pa. 5-9

When Charley's sister decides to marry an older man whom he dislikes, he stows away on a ship, leaving New York in 1864. He finds himself in the South with Union soldiers and becomes a drummer boy. So much death sickens him, especially because his brother was killed at Gettysburg. He runs away a second time into the mountains. There he meets a woman, once a member of the Underground Railway, and bravely helps her when she needs it. *Scott O'Dell Award for Historical Fiction.*

132. Beatty, Patricia. **The Coach That Never Came**. New York: Morrow, 1985. 164p. $11.95. ISBN 0-688-05477-3. 5-8

When Paul, 13, visits his grandmother in Colorado during the summer, his investigation of a gaudy belt buckle in the shape of a heart reveals information about his family. He discovers that an outlaw in the family ambushed a stagecoach in 1873, and after he killed the passengers, Ute Indians killed him for desecrating their sacred cave.

133. Beatty, Patricia, and Phillip Robbins. **Eben Tyne, Powdermonkey**. New York: Morrow, 1990. 227p. $12.95. ISBN 0-688-08884-8. 5-9

In 1862, during the Civil War, Eben obtains a job as a powdermonkey on a ship, the *Merrimack*, which sails from Norfolk, Virginia. Then Union forces capture it. He has to decide if he will join the Northern forces and try to stop Confederate pirates, or stay a prisoner for the duration of the war. He decides to help the North even though he has no way of knowing if he made the correct decision.

134. Beatty, Patricia. **Eight Mules from Monterey**. New York: Morrow, 1982. 224p. $15; $4.95pa. ISBN 0-688-01047-4; 0-688-12281-7pa. 4-7

When Fayette's widowed mother graduates from library school and begins a job taking books into the mountains of Monterey, California, Fayette and her brother go with her. They have a variety of experiences, but most important, they learn that they can survive together without a man's help. Her mother can safely reject the proposal of a man whom none of them like.

135. Beatty, Patricia. **Hail Columbia**. New York: Morrow, 1970. 251p. $12.88. ISBN 0-688-31371-X. 4-8

When Louisa's widowed Aunt Columbia comes from Philadelphia to Washington State in 1893, Louisa is delighted to find an aunt who graduated from Oberlin, uses her maiden name, and advertises her support of suffragettes Susan B. Anthony and Elizabeth Cady Stanton. Louisa's father refuses to speak with Columbia, but she befriends the town's Finnish immigrants, congratulating them on their contribution of poetic meter from the Finnish *Kalevala* to Longfellow's *Hiawatha*. She teaches English to the Chinese workers and cleans the bars of Swill Town as a temperance worker. Then she succeeds in having her brother nominated and elected mayor. He realizes her value and starts speaking to her when she announces plans to return to Philadelphia.

136. Beatty, Patricia. **How Many Miles to Sundown?** New York: Morrow, 1974. 222p. $6.95. ISBN 0-688-20102-4. 5-9

Beulah, 13, travels with two boys across New Mexico and Arizona in 1881, searching for the town of Sundown. They have a variety of adventures, and in them, Beulah tries to do the best thing for the group.

137. Beatty, Patricia. **Jayhawker**. New York: Morrow, 1991. 214p. $13.95. ISBN 0-688-09850-9. 5 up

When Lije is 12, his father goes with the abolitionist John Brown in 1858 on a raid from Kansas into Missouri against slave owners. The slave owners kill father, and in his stead, Lije becomes a Jayhawker spy, someone who tries to find other slave owners or "bushwackers" in Missouri after the Civil War begins. Lije has to fight and is wounded before he reunites with his mother and sweetheart in Kansas. *School Library Journal Best Book.*

138. Beatty, Patricia. **Jonathan Down Under**. New York: Morrow, 1982. 219p. $10.25. ISBN 0-688-01467-4. 5-9

Jonathan Cole's father, crazy for gold in 1851, goes to Australia after little success in California and takes Jonathan with him. After Jonathan recovers from "sandy blight," a disease during which he stayed inside for several months and had his eyes scraped daily to keep him from going blind, he hears that his father's partner has left with their gold. Then a mine cave-in kills his father. Jonathan begins working for an Irish woman who has come to Australia to escape the potato famine, but she soon dies. When he helps others find gold, they give him money to return home because he is interested in neither gold nor Australia.

139. Beatty, Patricia. **Just Some Weeds from the Wilderness**. New York: Morrow, 1978. 254p. $10.75. ISBN 0-688-22137-8. 4-8

In 1874, 13-year-old Lucinda helps her aunt make a tonic from plants so that she can sell it in Oregon. Her uncle disapproves, but her aunt's proceeds lead him to change his mind. She must tell him about the project because as a woman, she cannot enter a bank to deposit her money.

140. Beatty, Patricia. **Lacy Makes a Match**. New York: Morrow, 1979. 222p. $13. ISBN 0-688-22183-1. 4-8

Tired of keeping house for her brothers in 1893 after her mother's death, Lacy decides that she will find mates for them. She tries various tactics, including writing letters to women advertising in lovelorn columns, but eventually succeeds in an unexpected way. In one episode, she visits San Francisco, and the electric lights in the Palace Hotel's Palm Court, electric trolleys, telephone, dental laughing gas, and seven-story buildings amaze her.

141. Beatty, Patricia. **A Long Way to Whiskey Creek**. New York: Morrow, 1971. 224p. $7.75. ISBN 0-688-31427-9. 5-7

In 1879, Parker, an orphan, has to travel 400 miles to retrieve his brother's body. Another orphan, Nate, accompanies him on the journey. They argue about Confederates and Yankees, and Nate tries to teach Parker to read, but Parker does not think that a horse breaker needs to know. After several adventures, a former criminal helps them, encouraging Nate to teach them both to read.

142. Beatty, Patricia. **Melinda Takes a Hand**. New York: Morrow, 1983. 197p. $10.25. ISBN 0-688-02422-X. 5-9

When Sarah Jane and her fiancé Edgar have a misunderstanding in 1893, Sarah Jane's sister Melinda helps to reunite them. Sarah Jane misreads Edgar's letter to say "lonely," and she refuses to see him while the sisters stay in the Colorado town where she has gone to marry him. Among the people in town are Melinda's Jewish friend Esther, who wants to be a rabbi, and two remittance men paid to remain away from England; they are having the family castle shipped to them, piece by piece. When Melinda lets Edgar know about the "lonely," he rushes to explain that he had written "lovely."

143.   Beatty, Patricia. **The Nickel-Plated Beauty**. 1964. New York: Beech Tree, Morrow, 1993. 272p. $4.95pa. ISBN 0-688-12279-5pa. 5 up

In Washington Territory during 1886, Hester decides that she and her siblings should work digging clams, picking berries, and gathering oysters so that they can buy their mother a stove. Hester also works at her aunt's hotel. Although they are poor, they learn that pooling their resources allows them to do much more than if they plan separately.

144.   Beatty, Patricia. **O the Red Rose Tree**. 1972. New York: Beech Tree, Morrow, 1994. 222p. $4.95pa. ISBN 0-688-13627-3pa. 4-8

Lonely old Mrs. Hankinson wants pieces of red material to build a quilt that she has designed. Amanda and four other girls, with almost no money, manage to find the materials. The articles they commandeer are a chest protector, flotsam, a doll dress, a union suit, gift dress material, and a petticoat. These contribute to the seven roses in the pattern. The girls have to finish the quilt when Mrs. Hankinson becomes ill, and she notes that their ingenuity means more than the final effort.

145.   Beatty, Patricia. **Red Rock over the River**. New York: Morrow, 1973. 253p. $7.50. ISBN 0-688-20065-6. 4-8

Dorcas befriends Hattie when she comes to Fort Yuma, Arizona, in 1881. They do "good works" by going to the local prison where they write letters for the tubercular prisoners. After Hattie loads one of the prisoners on a hot-air balloon owned by a traveling circus and rushes him away, Dorcas finds that he is Hattie's half-brother whom she is trying to keep from dying in prison. He dies from a lack of oxygen, they crash, and Hattie disappears in the desert while Dorcas returns to her boring home.

146.   Beatty, Patricia. **Sarah and Me and the Lady from the Sea**. New York: Morrow, 1989. 182p. $11.95; $4.95pa. ISBN 0-688-08045-6; 0-688-13626-5pa. 5 up

When Marcella is 12, an 1894 flood destroys her father's dry goods store in Portland, Oregon. Her formerly wealthy family has to move to their summer beach home and learn everyday survival without servants to pamper them. At first they think themselves better than the peninsula residents, but they soon learn that they have no skills and must depend on the locals for advice. They learn to clean and cook and find that such simple knowledge gives them a feeling of independence and achievement that they did not have before.

147.   Beatty, Patricia. **Something to Shout About**. New York: Morrow, 1976. 254p. $6.95. ISBN 0-688-22078-9. 4-8

In 1875, Hope Foster's family moves from Oregon to Idaho Territory to manage the Whole Shebang Store. When the new schoolteacher arrives, he is shocked to see that the school is a former chicken coop and that the mayor plans to build a town hall and a jail before improving the school. The teacher, however, is a woman masquerading as a man so she can have the job. She convinces the women in town to collect money in the saloons for a prefabricated school. Her persistence helps improve the situation for the women and children after several unexpected situations are resolved.

148.   Beatty, Patricia. **That's One Ornery Orphan**. New York: Morrow, 1980. 222p. $11.75. ISBN 0-688-22227-7. 4-8

After her grandfather dies in 1889, Hallie has to go to an orphan asylum in Texas. She tries to adjust to three sets of foster parents but makes mistakes that cause each of them to take her back to the asylum. She finally goes to live with a family she has tried to avoid because they are farmers. What she finds is unexpected pleasure in their baby and their horses.

149.   Beatty, Patricia. **Turn Homeward, Hannalee**. New York: Morrow, 1984. 208p. $15. ISBN 0-688-03871-9. Mahwah, NJ: Troll, 1991. 208p. $3.95pa. ISBN 0-8167-2260-9pa. 5-9

In 1864, the Yankees accuse Hannalee and her brother of treason and export them from Georgia to Indiana. They have to work, but Hannalee pretends to be male and escapes. She finds her brother and uses her mill wages to pay for train tickets to Nashville. On their long journey home, they go through a horrible battle, but a peddler helps them traverse the last segment. Their brother returns, unlike their father, but missing one arm. The family survives the war, but barely.

150.   Beatty, Patricia. **Wait for Me, Watch for Me, Eula Bee**. 1978. New York: Beech Tree, Morrow, 1990. 221p. $3.95pa. ISBN 0-688-10077-5pa. 5-9

In 1861, Comanches kill the family of and capture three-year-old Eula Bee and her brother Lewtie. Lewtie's bravery earns him the privilege of herding horses, and with a horse, he escapes. He and a neighbor whose two children are missing go to search for them and Eula Bee. Yankee soldiers thwart their rescue by stampeding the Comanche-Kiowa camp just as they arrive. Lewtie eventually finds Eula Bee, but she shows no recognition, having adapted to her Indian mother. Months later, she calls him by name, having overcome her shock.

151. Beatty, Patricia. **Who Comes with Cannons?** New York: Morrow, 1992. 192p. $14. ISBN 0-688-11028-2. 5-9

Twelve-year-old Truth travels from Indiana in 1861 to stay with her North Carolina relatives. They, like her, are Quakers who hate slavery. Truth is surprised to discover that her uncle is hiding a runaway slave, but she is relieved to know that she can work for freedom in a peaceable way while the horrible war continues around them.

152. Beckett, Wendy. **The Story of Painting**. New York: Dorling Kindersley, 1994. 400p. $39.95. ISBN 1-56458-615-4. YA

This book is an overview of western painting from the Lascaux cave painters to the present, with the main emphasis on the last 800 years. The material is chronological, with chapters grouped according to trends or movements. Each chapter contains leaders of the period, their most famous works, information about the artists' lives, and the political, religious, and social influences on their work. Index.

153. Bell-Scott, Patricia, ed. **Life Notes: Personal Writings of Contemporary Black Women**. New York: Norton, 1994. 429p. $25; $12pa. ISBN 0-393-03593-X; 0-393-31206-2pa. YA

This collective "biography" presents journal entries of 50 Black women written as prose, poetry, letters, or meditations. The women are divorced, married, single mothers, disabled, educators, artists, lesbians, students, activists, and unemployed. They come from America, Africa, and Europe. They write about childhood, abuse, love, work, self-identity, racial prejudice, politics, and creating one's place in society. Their three common threads are that they are women, that they are Black, and that they are honest. What they have to say gives insight into the human condition. Index.

154. Bellairs, John. **The Drum, the Doll, and the Zombie**. New York: Dial, 1994. 123p. $14.99. ISBN 0-8037-1462-9. 4-7

During the mid-1950s, the folklore professor Dr. Coote goes to a party with 12-year-old Johnny Dixon, his friend Fergie, and Professor Childermass. Dr. Coote quiets the party when he tells what he learned on a recent visit to New Orleans. To accentuate his story, he beats on a drum as he tells about voodoo cults in Haiti and the Caribbean. The beats start a chain of events that releases a zombie. A woman and her grandson come to kill Dr. Coote and to make the others into zombies, but their little bit of knowledge helps them resist.

155. Beller, Susan Provost. **Cadets at War: The True Story of Teenage Heroism at the Battle of New Market**. White Hall, VA: Shoe Tree Press, 1991. 95p. $9.95. ISBN 1-55870-196-6. 7 up

In 1864, cadets at the Virginia Military Institute fought in the Battle of New Market. Their contribution helped the South as it tried to win the Civil War. Sources for Research and Index.

156. Beller, Susan Provost. **To Hold This Ground: A Desperate Battle at Gettysburg**. New York: Margaret K. McElderry, 1995. 95p. $15. ISBN 0-689-50621-X. 7 up

On July 2, 1863, Colonel Joshua Lawrence Chamberlain, a rhetoric professor from Bowdoin College, met Colonel William Calvin Oates in Gettysburg, Pennsylvania, on Little Round Top. They fought their own battle while the larger conflict raged around them. Beller tells the story of their battle and their lives, forged from different backgrounds. Photographs and maps highlight the text. Bibliography and Index.

157. Beller, Susan Provost. **Woman of Independence: The Life of Abigail Adams**. White Hall, VA: Shoe Tree Press, 1992. 128p. $5.95pa. ISBN 1-55870-237-7pa. 6-9

Abigail Adams (1735-1826) was a woman of strong will and character who played the roles of wife, mother, teacher, correspondent, and First Lady when her husband John Adams was elected President of the United States. She faced public dismay as well as approval for her willingness to say what she thought. Bibliography and Index.

158. Belton, Sandra. **Ernestine and Amanda**. New York: Simon & Schuster, 1996. 160p. $16. ISBN 0-689-80848-8. 4-7

In the 1950s, Ernestine and Amanda, both 10, live in the same community. They become more and more irritated with each other as they meet at piano lessons, in church, at the Delta Sigma Theta Jabberwock, and at a party. When Ernestine steals Amanda's best friend, their tempers increase. Because they are so much alike, their hostility eventually turns into friendship.

159. Beneduce, Ann Keay. **A Weekend with Winslow Homer**. New York: Rizzoli, 1993. 64p. $19.95; $9.95pa. ISBN 0-8478-1622-2; 0-8478-1919-1pa. (Weekend With). 5-8

With reproductions of his works, Winslow Homer (1836-1910) talks about his paintings and how the events in his life influenced the subjects he chose to paint.

160. Bennett, Barbara J. **Stonewall Jackson: Lee's Greatest Lieutenant**. Englewood Cliffs, NJ: Silver Burdett, 1991. 135p. $12.95; $8.95pa. ISBN 0-382-09939-7; 0-382-24048-0pa. (The History of the Civil War). 5 up
Thomas Jackson (1824-1863) was always serious and shy. Students made fun of his stodginess when he was a teacher at the Virginia Military Institute. When the Civil War began, however, he had had experience in the Mexican War and knew that two important preparations for battle were scouting and flanking (not meet the enemy directly). He showed his brilliance in battle with daring maneuvers and his refusal to allow anyone to contradict him. General Barnard Bee gave him his nickname by saying "There is Jackson standing like a stone wall." He died at Chancellorsville. Epilogue, Time Table, Selected Sources, Suggested Reading, and Index.

161. Bennett, James Gordon. **The Moon Stops Here**. New York: Doubleday, 1994. 356p. $21. ISBN 0-385-47095-9. YA
Fourteen-year-old Teddy, his mother, his sister Cora, and his aunt travel from Massachusetts to California in 1969 so they can join his father, stationed in Taiwan. In first person, Teddy tells about their journey, including Cora's intelligence, his mother's concerns, his aunt's interest in Elvis and her ability to draw stares from men, and his epilepsy. The women all have different expectations from the trip, and he has to keep them focused on their journey as they experience the events of the summer when the first man walked on the moon.

162. Bentley, Judith. **Brides, Midwives, and Widows**. New York: Twenty-First Century Books, 1995. 96p. $16.98. ISBN 0-8050-2994-X. (Settling the West). 5-8
The scarcity of women in the West during the nineteenth century gave them an exalted status in such places as San Francisco. The lively text, replete with photographs and drawings, looks at their roles through marriages of convenience, falling in love and marrying, as midwives for other women, as neighbors, and as women on their own. Source Notes, Further Reading, and Index.

163. Bentley, Judith. **"Dear Friend": Thomas Garrett and William Still, Collaborators on the Underground Railroad**. New York: Cobblehill, 1997. 128p. $15.99. ISBN 0-525-65156-X. 5-9
Two men who helped slaves escape on the Underground Railroad were a white Quaker, Thomas Garrett, from the slave state of Delaware, and a free Black, William Still, of Philadelphia. Garrett was the chief operator on the eastern line and led slaves across the dangerous Mason-Dixon line. William Still met his passengers and helped them to resettle in the North or continue their journeys to Canada. The basis of the text is their correspondence, which reveals their work and their friendship. Black-and-white photographs enhance the text. Notes and Index.

164. Bentley, Judith. **Explorers, Trappers, and Guides**. New York: Twenty-First Century Books, 1995. 96p. $16.98. ISBN 0-8050-2995-8. (Settling the West). 5-8
The importance of explorers, trappers, and guides for settling the West cannot be underestimated. The explorers found the places, the trappers used the natural resources to feed and cloth the settlers, and the guides helped the settlers find new land. The lively text with photographs and drawings looks at their roles. Source Notes, Further Reading, and Index.

165. Bentley, Judith. **Harriet Tubman**. New York: Franklin Watts, 1990. 144p. $13.90. ISBN 0-531-10948-8. (Impact Biography). 8-12
In the first half of the nineteenth century, approximately 1,538,000 persons were enslaved in the United States. Bentley's well-documented text relates that Harriet Tubman was originally named Araminta "Minty" Ross, but she became Harriet when a teenager. She married John Tubman, a free man, but left him when she ran away to Philadelphia, and he remarried. She worked hard, doing things that men normally did, and other masters hired her. The scar on her forehead, obtained when an overseer threw a brick at a fleeing slave and mistakenly hit her, caused her to seem slow and unattractive. People ignored her more, which allowed her to think and plan without attracting too much attention. While she was growing up, she heard about Haitians leading a slave revolt and American slaves Gabriel Prosser, Denmark Vesey, and Nat Turner leading others. She knew William Henry Seward, Fredrick Douglass, and John Brown well. Her premonitions indicated that Brown would die, as he did when he tried to help the slaves escape at Harper's Ferry. Tubman believed that Brown, not Lincoln, was the true emancipator. Source Notes, For Further Reading, Bibliography, and Index.

166. Berent, Mark. **Eagle Station**. New York: Putnam, 1992. 396p. $22.95. ISBN 0-399-13722-X. New York: Jove, 1993. 396p. $5.99pa. ISBN 0-515-11208-9pa. YA
Air force pilots continue their work in 1968 Vietnam as they protect Eagle Station and its radar in this sequel to *Rolling Thunder, Steel Tiger,* and *Phantom Leader*. Finally, one person makes contact with the prisoners in Hanoi to let them know that the government is working on their release. However, not all Americans sympathize with their difficulties during the war.

167. Berent, Mark. **Phantom Leader**. New York: Putnam, 1991. 414p. $21.95. ISBN 0-399-13603-7. New York: Jove, 1992. 414p. $5.99pa. ISBN 0-515-10785-9pa. YA

When the Viet Cong down Flak's plane in 1967, they imprison him in Hanoi. The Tet Offensive leads to more captures, and other pilots join Flak in prison. When a pilot helps him escape, the French return him to the Viet Cong. Flak realizes that those thought to be friends may be enemies and vice versa.

168. Berent, Mark. **Rolling Thunder**. New York: Putnam, 1989. 382p. $15.95. ISBN 0-399-13439-5. New York: Jove, 1989. 382p. $5.99pa. ISBN 0-515-10190-7pa. YA

In 1965, three air force pilots do their job in Vietnam by participating in the bombing raids and by trying to escape death. They instead have to face the deaths of friends. When they return to the United States, they have to face hostile hippies who oppose the war in Vietnam and splatter red dye on their bodies.

169. Berent, Mark. **Steel Tiger**. New York: Putnam, 1990. 399p. $19.95. ISBN 0-399-13538-3. New York: Jove, 1994. 399p. $5.99pa. ISBN 0-515-10467-1pa. YA

Air force officers from *Rolling Thunder* meet in Vietnam in 1967. When the Viet Cong later catch Bannister, a Russian pilot helps him escape, but the pilot dies in an ensuing battle. The other pilots have to deal with a variety of wartime situations, not all of them military.

170. Berke, Art. **Babe Ruth**. New York: Franklin Watts, 1988. 112p. $13.90. ISBN 0-531-10472-9. (Impact Biography). 7-9

George Herman (Babe) Ruth (1895-1948) was one of the most important baseball players in the history of the game. He was the only player who could draw 30,000 people to batting practice, and he always behaved pleasantly and kindly to his fans. They adored him even though he had many failings such as eating, drinking, and carousing too much. He had enthusiasm and talent, scoring 714 home runs with a .342 lifetime batting average and a .671 winning percentage as a pitcher. His legend as the "Bambino" continues even though others have broken his records. Further Reading and Index.

171. Berkow, Ira. **Hank Greenberg: Hall-of-Fame Slugger**. Philadelphia: Jewish Publication Society, 1991. 108p. $12.95. ISBN 0-8276-0376-2. (JPS Young Biography). 3-7

Hank Greenberg (1911-1986) played baseball during the time the Nazis were killing Jews throughout Europe. He wanted to be the greatest Jewish baseball player, but the prejudice he experienced led him to establish a friendship with the first Black baseball player, Jackie Robinson. Greenberg hit the grand slam home run that won the pennant for the Tigers in 1945. In 1956, he became the first Jewish member of the Baseball Hall of Fame. The text looks at his life and his career in baseball.

172. Berlin, Edward A. **King of Ragtime: Scott Joplin and His Era**. New York: Oxford University Press, 1994. 334p. $25; $14.95pa. ISBN 0-19-508739-9; 0-19-510108-1pa. YA

Scott Joplin (1868-1917) told his wife that 25 years after he died, people would recognize his contribution to music. His assessment was correct. He dreamed of artistic greatness, and, born in the first postslavery generation, he believed that hard work, education, and self-improvement could help one overcome the obstacles of class, background, and race. By the time he was 27, he had published two songs, each showing a knowledge of composition. He continued to work and create in a style called "ragtime," which meant that the beat was syncopated and "ragged." Not until the 1940s and later was his ability recognized and ragtime accepted in concert halls. Photographs, Notes, Bibliography, and Index.

173. Berliner, Don. **Aviation: Reaching for the Sky**. Minneapolis, MN: Oliver Press, 1997. 144p. $17.95. ISBN 1-881508-33-1. (Innovators). 7 up

People have been trying to fly for centuries. Berliner traces the accomplishments of men who, since the eighteenth century, actually built a device that stayed aloft. They include the Montgolfier brothers and the hot-air balloon (1783); Henri Giffard and the dirigible (1852); Otto Lilienthal and the glider (1891); Samuel Pierpont Langley and the *Aerodrome* (1896); the Wright brothers and their airplane (1903); Glenn Curtiss and the seaplane (1908); and Igor Sikorsky and the helicopter (1911). Photographs highlight the text. Important Events in Aviation History, Bibliography, and Index.

174. Berman, Avis. **James McNeill Whistler**. New York: Harry N. Abrams, 1993. 92p. $13.95. ISBN 0-8109-3376-4. (First Impressions). 7-12

James McNeill Whistler (1834-1903), best known for the portrait of his mother, had a flamboyant personality. He also had an innovative painting style and used unique printmaking techniques that added to his reputation as an artist. He wanted his art to create a mood or emotion, and the text shows this as well as his connection to the times in which he lived. Explanations of his painting methods and reproductions of his works highlight the text. List of Illustrations and Index.

175. Bernards, Neal. **Gun Control**. San Diego, CA: Lucent, 1992. 96p. $11.95. ISBN 1-56006-127-8. (Overview). 7 up

This text discusses the importance of the gun in American history and culture. It continues to the present issue of gun control both in other countries and the United States, where many people think they have a constitutional right to bear arms. Bibliography and Index.

176. Bernotas, Bob. **Jim Thorpe: Sac and Fox Athlete**. New York: Chelsea House, 1992. 110p. $18.95. $7.95pa. ISBN 0-7910-1722-2; 0-7910-1695-1pa. (North American Indians of Achievement). 5 up

Jim Thorpe (1887-1953) was both an Olympic champion and an All-American football player. He attended the Carlisle Indian School in Carlisle, Pennsylvania, after leaving Oklahoma and the farm. He continued to work for Indian rights and remains the concept of a true champion, an Indian hero. Photographs complement the text. Chronology, Further Reading, and Index.

177. Bernotas, Bob. **Sitting Bull: Chief of the Sioux**. New York: Chelsea House, 1992. 111p. $18.95; $7.95pa. ISBN 0-7910-1703-6; 0-7910-1968-3pa. (North American Indians of Achievement). 5 up

As chief of the Sioux Indians, Sitting Bull (1834?-1890) led his warriors against Custer in the Battle of Little Bighorn. The author shows Sitting Bull as a military strategist and statesman. Black-and-white photographs supplement the text. Further Reading, Glossary, and Index.

178. Bernstein, Joanne, and Rose Blue with Alan Jay Gerber. **Judith Resnick: Challenger Astronaut**. New York: Lodestar, Dutton, 1990. 144p. $14.95. ISBN 0-525-67305-9. 5-7

In the first and last chapters, where the authors discuss the explosion of the *Challenger* space shuttle, they use present tense that intensifies the immediacy of the tragedy. The remainder of the book follows Resnick's life chronologically until January 28, 1986. Throughout her life, from her religious and academic education through her Ph.D. in engineering, her intelligence and perseverance show. Resnick was an especially private person; therefore, reasons for her divorce and her response to her parents' difficulties are unknown. Suggested Reading and Index.

179. Berrill, Margaret. **Mummies, Masks, & Mourners**. Chris Molan, illustrator. New York: Lodestar, Dutton, 1990. 48p. $14.95. ISBN 0-525-67282-6. (Time Detectives). 4-7

The "grave goods" that archaeologists find buried with the dead often reveal something about the culture and its burial customs. Berrill presents an unusual group of "finds." First are two Stone Age excavations: Çatal Hüyük in Turkey, found in 1958, and Haddenham, near Ely in England, the oldest wooden building ever discovered. From investigations of the pyramids in Egypt come mummies searching for the Field of Reeds. Recent excavations reveal Sumerians in 2500 BC. Other places excavated include the Siberian Altai horsemen from 400 BC; the Lindow Man, who died 2,000 years ago and was recently discovered in a peat bog; the Lady Dai from the Han Dynasty in China, buried 2,100 years previously; Roman memorials in Ephesus; Basket Makers in the American Southwest at Four Corners; Hopewell mounds in the Ohio/Tennessee area; Viking Ship burials; Qilakitsoq of the Inuits, buried in 1475 and found in Greenland; and the Kalabar Ijaw funeral screens from Africa. Fact boxes give additional information about each burial place and its culture. Drawings and photographs, one of a piece of 2,000-year-old preserved tattooed skin, augment the text. Glossary and Index.

180. Berry, Michael. **Georgia O'Keeffe: Painter**. New York: Chelsea House, 1988. 110p. $18.95; $7.95pa. ISBN 1-55546-673-7; 0-7910-0420-1pa. (American Women of Achievement). 5 up

As one of the first to express a woman's viewpoint in her painting, Georgia O'Keeffe (1887-1986) was a pioneer of modern art. She used beautiful flowers, scenes from the deserts, and cityscapes as her main subjects. Alfred Steiglitz "discovered" her, brought her to New York, and convinced her to marry him. Her independence continued, however, and after his death, she lived mainly in New Mexico, continuing to use the colors of the desert in her paintings. Photographs and reproductions enhance the text. Chronology, Further Reading, and Index.

181. Berry, S. L. **Emily Dickinson**. Stermer Dugald, illustrator. Mankato, MI: Creative Education, 1994. 45p. $17.95. ISBN 0-88682-609-8. (Voices in Poetry). 5 up

Emily Dickinson (1830-1886) lived in Amherst, Massachusetts, and rarely left her home. Her most innovative poetry about the world around her, written in the nineteenth century, rivals the best poetry composed before or since. Bibliography and Index.

182. Berry, S. L. **Langston Hughes**. Mankato, MN: Creative Education, 1994. 44p. $17.95. ISBN 0-88682-616-0. (Voices in Poetry). 5 up

This biography of Langston Hughes (1902-1967) shows a versatile poet who spent his career writing about the experiences of African Americans in their dialects. He went to Columbia, lived in Harlem, and flirted with socialism. Bibliography and Index.

183. Berry, Skip. **Gordon Parks**. New York: Chelsea House, 1990. 111p. $18.95. ISBN 1-55546-604-4. (Black Americans of Achievement). 6 up

As a poor young man in Kansas, Gordon Parks (b. 1912) worked as a pianist and a semipro basketball player. In 1937, he saw photographs of life in the Depression, and he knew that he could express his feelings about deprivation and racial discrimination with a camera. He won a fellowship to study and gained a position on the *Life* magazine staff in 1949. He wrote books, composed musical scores, directed films, and showed that one can overcome limited opportunities by using one's talents. Photographs enhance the text. Chronology, Further Reading, and Index.

184. Beschloss, Michael R. **Eisenhower: A Centennial Life**. New York: HarperCollins, 1990. 253p. $29.95. ISBN 0-06-016418-2. YA

Dwight Eisenhower, 10 years old in 1900, beat on a tree in anger until his fists bled because he was not allowed to accompany his older brothers on Halloween. His mother pointed out that the tree remained unimpressed. He never forgot and tried never to hate anyone and to forget those who maligned and abused him rather than to retaliate. Born of poor parents with integrity, he became a university president, a lawyer, a druggist, a banker, a businessperson, and a general in the army who became President of the United States. Photographs of Eisenhower at events and with other world leaders, coupled with the anecdotal text, make this not only a biography of Eisenhower but also a history of the twentieth century until Eisenhower's death in 1969. Source Notes and Index.

185. Bethancourt, T. Ernesto. **The Tomorrow Connection**. New York: Holiday House, 1984. 134p. $10.95. ISBN 0-8234-0543-5. 6-9

When Richie and Mattie, both 18, travel through time to 1906, they stop in 1942 and 1912. In their attempts to find the gate that will take them back to the future, they meet Houdini. After they tell him about all of his tricks, even the ones not yet invented in 1906, he has them travel with him to San Francisco, where they finally find the key to return them to the future and their lives as the first Black President of the United States and an important historian.

186. Beyer, Don E. **The Manhattan Project: America Makes the First Atomic Bomb**. New York: Franklin Watts, 1991. 112p. $21.10. ISBN 0-531-11008-7. (Twentieth Century American History Book). 10 up

This work discusses the development of the project in which scientists created the first atomic bomb, and the bomb's devastating effects. Bibliography and Index.

187. Beyer, Don E. **The Totem Pole Indians of the Northwest**. New York: Franklin Watts, 1989. 64p. $19.90; $5.95pa. ISBN 0-531-10750-7; 0-531-15607-9pa. (A First Book). 4-7

Archaeological digs in the ruins of Ozette, a Makah village buried in a mudslide more than 500 years ago along the coast of Washington State, reveal some of the habits of the seven groups who have lived along the coasts of Canada and Alaska for the last 10,000 years. These groups include the Coast Salish, Nootka, Kwakiutl, Bella Coola, Haida, Tsimshian, and Tlingit (easy pronunciation guides in the text). Totem poles, some more than 80 feet high, marked their existence. Photographs emphasize the importance of carvings not only for the totem but also for masks, spirit figures, canoes, body decorations, and homes (Big-Houses). The people also had slaves, either captured or purchased, and leaders held *potlatches* (celebrations for gift giving), some taking years to plan. White explorer Juan de Fuca arrived in 1592, and Captain James Cook came in 1777-1779 and wrote about the natives in his log. Other whites came later, bringing disease and change. Further Reading and Index.

188. Bial, Raymond. **Shaker Home**. Boston: Houghton Mifflin, 1994. 37p. $15.95. ISBN 0-395-64047-4. 3-8

Although 6,000 Shakers lived in the United States during the Civil War, none survive today. Seven Shakers, or Shaking Quakers, came with Mother Ann Lee to the American colonies and Watervliet, New York, in 1774 after they were persecuted in England. The text presents their history and beliefs with accompanying photographs. Further Reading.

189. Bial, Raymond. **The Underground Railroad**. Boston: Houghton Mifflin, 1995. 48p. $14.95. ISBN 0-395-69937-1. 4-8

Before he tells the story of the Underground Railroad in the nineteenth century, Bial gives a chronology of the antislavery movement starting in 1775. Among the artifacts telling people where to find stations on the railroad were signal lamps in upper windows, false-bottomed wagons, and hand-dug tunnels lit with lanterns. Photographs of people and of memorabilia augment the verbal history of the abolitionists. Further Reading. *Notable Children's Trade Books in the Field of Social Studies.*

190. Biel, Timothy L. **The Challenger**. San Diego, CA: Lucent, 1991. 64p. $12.95. ISBN 1-56006-013-1. (World Disasters). 5-8

On January 28, 1986, the *Challenger* space shuttle disintegrated almost immediately after it lifted off from the launch pad. Investigation showed that the O-ring seals were faulty. Among those who died was a schoolteacher who had won the right to be the first teacher in space, Christa McAuliffe. The text documents the tragedy, which was deeply shocking after the previous successes of the space program. Photographs enhance the text. Bibliography and Index.

191. Biel, Timothy L. **The Civil War**. San Diego, CA: Lucent, 1991. 144p. $16.95. ISBN 1-56006-404-8. (America's Wars). 5-8

The text looks at the Civil War (1861-1865) in terms of its political, cultural, and military aspects and how it divided the Union. Bibliography and Index.

192. Billings, Charlene W. **Grace Hopper: Navy Admiral and Computer Pioneer**. Springfield, NJ: Enslow, 128p. $17.95. ISBN 0-89490-194-X. 7-12

Retired as a rear admiral at 79 in 1986 aboard the USS *Constitution*, Grace Murray Hopper refused to accept the words "We've always done it this way." Her story is also the history of computers because she helped create and standardize the COBOL programming language. After graduating from Vassar and receiving a Ph.D. in mathematics from Yale, she joined the navy during World War II in 1943. Her first assignment as an ensign was to Harvard, where the Mark I, perhaps the first genuine computer, was located. She and colleagues worked on the Mark II in 1945. Once it stopped; she found a dead moth inside, removed it, and reported that she had "debugged" it, thus originating the term for fixing computer programs. Hopper's anecdotes when teaching help explain computer jargon, including her illustration of nanosecond as a piece of wire 11 5/8" long. Her many achievements appear in a lengthy résumé at the end of the text; also included is a brief explanation of COBOL. Further Reading and Index.

193. Bingham, Sallie. **Matron of Honor**. Cambridge, MA: Zoland, 1994. 186p. $19.95; $10.95pa. ISBN 0-944072-38-0; 0-944072-63-1pa. YA

Apple prepares for her wedding in 1970. On the day before the ceremony, her sister Cory returns home, leaving a loveless marriage. Her arrival upsets everyone, especially her mother, and disrupts Apple's plans. The points of view of the family members, the maid, and April's fiancé show the many family forces at play during this southern wedding.

194. Bingham, Sallie. **Small Victories**. Cambridge, MA: Zoland, 1992. 298p. $20.95; $9.95pa. ISBN 0-944072-20-8; 0-944072-25-9pa. YA

In 1958, Tom leaves college after his aunt in a small North Carolina town writes him about his grandparents' lives and deaths. He learns about Louise and her sister Shelby, who has fits, and finds out that his father did not tell him the truth about the family. Louise needs him to change his father's mind about committing Shelby to a hospital because Louise needs her to have meaning in her life. Tom needs to find out what he must do about his own life.

195. Biracree, Tom. **Althea Gibson**. New York: Chelsea House, 1988. 109p. $18.95; $7.95pa. ISBN 1-55546-654-0; 0-7910-0434-1pa. (American Women of Achievement). 5 up

Never playing tennis until she was 14, South Carolina–born Althea Gibson, daughter of sharecroppers, became the first Black woman to play in the U.S. tennis championships at age 23 in 1950; she almost won. A scathing letter to the tournament officials from Alice Marble, the woman's champion throughout the 1930s, shamed them into letting Gibson play. Gibson became a world champion in the late 1950s but retired in 1958 because she needed money. She played professional golf, but only when she began work as a recreational department director did she feel satisfied; she was able to help others as she had been helped throughout her life. Chronology, Further Reading, and Index.

196. Biracree, Tom. **Grandma Moses: Painter**. New York: Chelsea House, 1989. 112p. $18.95. ISBN 1-55546-670-2. (American Women of Achievement). 5 up

Anna Mary Moses (1860-1961) started working at 12, married at 17, and moved from New York to Virginia, where she milked cows and raised five children. In 1905, the family returned to New York State. After her husband died in 1927, she began painting. In 1938, an amateur art collector saw her work in a drugstore, and by 1945, museums across the country were exhibiting the work of this primitive painter. She remained unassuming despite media attention and demands for original paintings from her adoring fans. Photographs and reproductions enhance the text. Chronology, Further Reading, and Index.

197.   Biracree, Tom. **Wilma Rudolph: Champion Athlete**. New York: Chelsea House, 1987. 112p. $18.95; $7.95pa. ISBN 1-55546-675-3; 0-7910-0217-9pa. (American Women of Achievement). 5 up

Crippled by polio at the age of four, Wilma Rudolph (b. 1940) improved from walking with a leg brace to running in the 1960 Rome Olympics, where she won three gold medals. People called her the "Tennessee Tornado," the fastest woman on Earth. Later in life she established the Wilma Rudolph Foundation to help young athletes overcome odds to be successful. Photographs enhance the text. Chronology, Further Reading, and Index.

198.   Bishop, Jack. **Ralph Ellison: Author**. New York: Chelsea House, 1988. 110p. $18.95. ISBN 1-55546-585-4. (Black Americans of Achievement). 5 up

Although he won a scholarship to study music at Tuskegee Institute, Ralph Ellison (1914-1994) became a writer instead. He wrote one book on which his literary merit stands, *Invisible Man*. Afterward, he wrote shorter pieces, but he was mainly a spokesman for the importance of individual excellence and Black culture. Photographs enhance the text. Chronology, Further Reading, and Index.

199.   Bisson, Terry. **Nat Turner: Slave Revolt Leader**. New York: Chelsea House, 1988. 112p. $18.95; $7.95pa. ISBN 1-55546-613-3; 0-7910-0214-4pa. (Black Americans of Achievement). 5 up

Nat Turner (1800-1831) was a fiery preacher and a militant leader whose slave uprising struck a blow against slavery 30 years before the Civil War began. He had mystical visions and began to preach in local churches when he was not in the fields. In 1831, he began his revolt, and the men who were with him left people dead in their wake as they fought against the slave system. They dispelled the myth that slaves were content with their lives. Photographs and engravings enhance the text. Chronology, Further Reading, and Index.

200.   Black, Kathryn. **In the Shadow of Polio: A Personal and Social History**. New York: Addison-Wesley, 1996. 288p. $23. ISBN 0-201-40739-6. YA

Although the disease polio had been known for almost 3,000 years, not until the end of the eighteenth century did physicians make a connection between the symptoms of fever, headache, stiffness, and sore throat with the death or paralysis of a previously healthy child. In 1887, a Stockholm pediatrician reported 44 cases, and from that time, the number grew, especially in more developed and sanitary nations, where an immunity to a virus carried in fecal material no longer existed. In the United States in 1916, 29,000 got polio, and 6,000 died. Kathryn Black's mother contracted polio in 1954, at age 29, two months after the first inoculations with the Salk vaccine. Because she contracted both kinds of polio simultaneously, she almost died in an iron lung within 24 hours but held on for two years as a quadriplegic. Black believes that the American attitude that one can overcome anything damaged her family during this most difficult time, because neither they nor her mother could defeat the disease. Index.

201.   Black, Shelia. **Sitting Bull and the Battle of the Little Bighorn**. Ed Lee, illustrator. Englewood Cliffs, NJ: Silver Burdett, 1989. 123p. $12.95. ISBN 0-382-09572-3. (Biography of American Indians). 5-8

Known for the Battle of Little Bighorn where he defeated Custer, Sitting Bull (1834?-1890) escaped to Canada but was offered amnesty when he returned in 1881 to live on a reservation. In 1890, friends tried to rescue him, and someone (supposedly shooting at someone else) killed him. The Sioux, instead of rising against the whites, embraced Ghost Dancing. Bibliography and Index.

202.   Black, Wallace B., and Jean F. Blashfield. **America Prepares for War**. New York: Crestwood House, 1991. 48p. $12.95. ISBN 0-89686-554-1. (World War II 50th Anniversary). 5-8

The text describes the military preparations that occurred before the United States actually entered World War II in 1941 and the other ways in which the country was already unofficially involved in the war. Black-and-white photographs supplement the text. Glossary and Index.

203.   Black, Wallace B., and Jean F. Blashfield. **Bataan and Corregidor**. New York: Crestwood House, 1991. 48p. $12.95. ISBN 0-89686-557-6. (World War II 50th Anniversary). 5 up

After the attack on Pearl Harbor, the Japanese went to the Philippines. Japanese air attacks led the United States to use Corregidor in Manila Bay as the command post while Bataan, part of the island of Luzon across from Manila, was the stronghold for troops to hold off the invading Japanese. The Battle of Bataan under General MacArthur failed, and on April 9, 1942, the Allies surrendered it to the Japanese. Then Corregidor was surrendered on May 6, 1942. Black-and-white photographs supplement the text. Glossary and Index.

204.   Black, Wallace B., and Jean F. Blashfield. **Battle of the Atlantic**. New York: Crestwood House, 1991. 48p. $12.95. ISBN 0-89686-558-4. (World War II 50th Anniversary). 4-9

This account of the Battle of the Atlantic tells of the struggle that the Allied forces had in trying to keep the North Atlantic free of German U-boats, or submarines, during World War II. On September 3, 1939, when the Germans torpedoed the *Athenia*, a British ocean liner with 1,300 passengers, they claimed that they thought it was an armed merchant ship. Photos and diagrams show the blitzkrieg at sea. U-boats and bombers, along with convoys to Russia, appeared before the U.S. Navy joined the battle, and the Allies fought back. Although U-boats were discovered off the coast of New York, antisubmarine warfare helped control them. Black-and-white photographs augment the text. Closer Look at German U-Boats and Allied Ships and Planes, Glossary, and Index.

205. Black, Wallace B., and Jean F. Blashfield. **Battle of the Bulge**. New York: Crestwood House, 1992. 48p. $12.95. ISBN 0-89686-568-1. (World War II 50th Anniversary). 4-9

The road to Ardennes started in 1944. The Watch on the Rhine was Hitler's plan to divide the American and British attack before the Battle of the Bulge, December 16, 1944. He failed, but with Bastogne under siege, the German commander asked for an Allied surrender. The Allied commander, McAuliffe, replied, "Nuts!" On December 26, General Patton broke through the German lines and stopped the siege. Nordwind and Bodenplatte were two plans of the German offense that failed, and the Germans withdrew by January 22, 1945. The Bridge at Remagen was where the Allies crossed into German territory on March 7, 1945. Black-and-white photographs highlight the text. Glossary and Index.

206. Black, Wallace B., and Jean F. Blashfield. **D-Day**. New York: Crestwood House, 1992. 48p. $12.95. ISBN 0-89686-566-6. (World War II 50th Anniversary). 5 up

In planning for D-Day, the Allies decided to invade the Normandy beaches to retake France. Operation Neptune called for naval operations to land on the Normandy beaches while protected from the air by the Allied forces. The Germans delayed in their pursuit, and the June 6, 1944, Allied invasion was successful. Black-and-white photographs supplement the text. Glossary and Index.

207. Black, Wallace B., and Jean F. Blashfield. **Desert Warfare**. New York: Crestwood House, 1992. 48p. $12.95. ISBN 0-89686-561-4. (World War II 50th Anniversary). 5 up

Italy had a disaster in Africa when the British took control of East Africa in February 1941. The German army came to rescue Italians with General Rommel, the Desert Fox, in charge. The British retreated to El Alamein, 240 miles from Egypt, but General Montgomery took charge and defeated Rommel. The Allied Operation Torch invasion led to the race for Tunis. Next was the Battle of Kasserine Pass, which was won because the Germans could not agree on the best plan of attack. The resources of the Allies helped them win. Victory at Hill 609 prepared the way for the May 13, 1943, invasion of Italy. Black-and-white photographs supplement the text. Glossary and Index.

208. Black, Wallace B., and Jean F. Blashfield. **Flattops at War**. New York: Crestwood House, 1992. 48p. $12.95. ISBN 0-89686-559-2. (World War II 50th Anniversary). 5 up

After Pearl Harbor, the Battle of Coral Sea took place in February 1942. The Battle of Midway followed in June 1942. In these battles, the flattops (aircraft carriers) were most important. They continued to escort U-boats and participated in the Marianas "Turkey Shoot," June 19-21, 1944. Photographs of the war with flattops and planes of the U.S. Navy correlate with the text. Glossary and Index.

209. Black, Wallace B., and Jean F. Blashfield. **Guadalcanal**. New York: Crestwood House, 1992. 48p. $12.95. ISBN 0-89686-560-6. (World War II 50th Anniversary). 5 up

The Japanese attacked Midway Island on June 4, 1942. Following the attack, the Allies decided to invade Guadalcanal in August. Land battles ensued, as did sea battles, culminating with the Battle of the Solomon Islands on November 12, 1942. The Air Force helped, and the Japanese finally withdrew from Guadalcanal in February 1943. Black-and-white photographs augment the text. Index.

210. Black, Wallace B., and Jean F. Blashfield. **Hiroshima and the Atomic Bomb**. New York: Crestwood House, 1993. 48p. $12.95. ISBN 0-89686-571-1. (World War II 50th Anniversary). 5 up

In 1939, the Manhattan Project in Los Alamos and uranium manufacturing at Oak Ridge, Tennessee, simultaneously allowed the creation of the atomic bomb. After Iwo Jima and Okinawa, the Allies firebombed Tokyo in March 1945. Although the Japanese were starving, they kept fighting. The Enola Gay dropped "Little Boy," the first atomic bomb ordered by President Truman, on August 6, 1945, at 8:16 AM. After the second bomb ("Fat Man") was dropped on Nagasaki three days later, Japan surrendered. Black-and-white photographs supplement the text. Glossary and Index.

211. Black, Wallace B., and Jean F. Blashfield. **Invasion of Italy**. New York: Crestwood House, 1992. 48p. $12.95. ISBN 0-89686-565-7. (World War II 50th Anniversary). 5 up

In 1943, Operation Husky marked the invasion of Sicily to gain control of the Mediterranean Sea. The Allied forces landed there on July 10, 1943, under British Field Marshal Sir Harold Alexander, and Italy surrendered on September 1. Then the Allies invaded southern Italy. The Italian fleet surrendered, and the Germans retreated toward Rome. The Allies became temporarily trapped at Anzio because of misunderstandings and delays. The Battle for Monte Cassino occurred in late 1944, and Rome finally fell on June 4, 1944. The Germans made their new line 150 miles north of Rome before they surrendered Italy on April 29, 1945, after Mussolini's assassination. Black-and-white photographs augment the text. Glossary and Index.

212. Black, Wallace B., and Jean F. Blashfield. **Island Hopping in the Pacific**. New York: Crestwood House, 1992. 48p. $12.95. ISBN 0-89686-567-3. (World War II 50th Anniversary). 5 up

Japan threatened Australia in 1942, and the first encounter with naval forces occurred at the Battle of the Coral Sea. The strategy of island-hopping began from Guadalcanal and Papua, New Guinea. The Japanese had Rabaul, a fortress on the island of New Britain, that the Allies decided to capture after taking the Solomons and New Guinea. In 1944, the Allies' target date for retaking Philippines and Formosa (Taiwan) was February 1945, but they succeeded by June 1944. General MacArthur returned to the Philippines in October 1944 and plotted to take Iwo Jima. Black-and-white photographs augment the text. Glossary and Index.

213. Black, Wallace B., and Jean F. Blashfield. **Iwo Jima and Okinawa**. New York: Crestwood House, 1993. 48p. $12.95. ISBN 0-89686-569-X. (World War II 50th Anniversary). 5 up

The battles of Coral Sea and Midway occurred in 1945 before the Marines began landing on Iwo Jima beaches. They captured Mount Suribachi on February 23, 1945. Then they continued until victory on June 20 with Operation Iceberg. The Allied forces needed Okinawa for a base from which to launch other attacks on the Japanese. Black-and-white photographs highlight the text. Glossary and Index.

214. Black, Wallace B., and Jean F. Blashfield. **Jungle Warfare**. New York: Crestwood House, 1992. 48p. $12.95. ISBN 0-89686-563-0. (World War II 50th Anniversary). 5 up

In January 1942, Japan invaded Burma. The Allied commanders Vinegar Joe Stillwell, Chiang Kai-Shek, and Claire Chennault of the Flying Tigers in France disagreed about approaches to the difficult jungle terrain. Then Wingate's Chindit Raiders, British guerrilla forces, completed daring missions so that Wingate earned the label of "half genius and half mad." Merrill's Marauders were America's jungle fighters. Also in this area were the U.S. Air Force and the OSS, forerunner of the CIA. The last campaigns in the China-India-Burma area occurred in 1945. Black-and-white photographs supplement the text. Glossary and Index.

215. Black, Wallace B., and Jean F. Blashfield. **Pearl Harbor!** New York: Crestwood House, 1991. 48p. $12.95. ISBN 0-89686-555-X. (World War II 50th Anniversary). 5-8

In 1941, when the Japanese bombed the Pacific fleet at Pearl Harbor, America was ill-prepared for combat but still declared war on Japan. This account discusses the Japanese strategy and tactics and why the American forces were surprised by the attack. Black-and-white photographs complement the text. Glossary and Index.

216. Black, Wallace B., and Jean F. Blashfield. **Victory in Europe**. New York: Crestwood House, 1992. 48p. $12.95. ISBN 0-89686-570-3. (World War II 50th Anniversary). 5 up

The text gives an overview of World War II in Europe, the trek eastward from the Rhine, the Russian thousand-mile front, Germany surrounded, the Battle of Berlin in 1945, and the unconditional German surrender on May 7, 1945. The book also covers the Holocaust, starting with *Kristallnacht* (Crystal Night), as it looks at the cost of the war to all. Capsule biographies of Allied leaders end the information. Black-and-white photographs supplement the text. Glossary and Index.

217. Black, Wallace B., and Jean F. Blashfield. **War Behind the Lines**. New York: Crestwood House, 1992. 48p. $12.95. ISBN 0-89686-564-9. (World War II 50th Anniversary). 5 up

During World War II, battles behind the lines helped win the war. The text looks at the British Secret Services, the OSS of the Americans, the organization of the Resistance against the Nazis, the *Maquis* or Resistance heroes, women and the underground war, the Resistance in Norway, *Chetniks* (Yugoslavians) and Partisans (Communists against Hitler in other countries), and Russian Partisans. Heroes of the Resistance include Major General William Donovan, Marshal Tito, and General Charles de Gaulle. Glossary and Index.

218. Blake, Arthur, and Pamela Dailey. **The Gold Rush of 1849: Staking a Claim in California**. Brookfield, CT: Millbrook Press, 1995. 64p. $15.90. ISBN 1-56294-483-5. (Spotlight on American History). 5-8

James Marshall, a carpenter, found gold in front of a sawmill belonging to John Sutter on January 24, 1848. His discovery led to the beginning of the gold rush as people scurried to the spot. They came by sea and by land from everywhere. The text looks at this migration and the camps set up to house the people, the ways they dug for the gold, the ways they spent their leisure time, and the results of their quests for wealth. Chronology, Further Reading, Bibliography, and Index.

219. Blakely, Martha. **Native Americans and the U.S. Government**. New York: Chelsea House, 1995. 59p. $14.95. ISBN 0-7910-2475-X. (Junior Library of American Indians). 5-9

The U.S. government has made policies that have affected the lives of Native Americans throughout the history of the nation. The government took possession of Indian lands and placed the Indians on reservations. The General Allotment Act of 1887, the Dawes Act, divided the reservations into individual allotments of land assigned to families, which conflicted with tribal concepts of land ownership. The text looks at some of the questions that the government asked before it made decisions as well as at the Bureau of Indian Affairs, a government organization that has tried to change some of the past mistakes while simultaneously making new ones. Glossary, Chronology, and Index.

220.   Blakely, Mike. **Shortgrass Song**. New York: Forge, 1994. 432p. $23.95. ISBN 0-312-85541-9. YA

Before the Civil War, the Holcomb family moves to the West, and a runaway slave searches for them. On Pikes Peak, an Arapaho Indian tells him where they are, and he begins to work on their farm. Caleb, the son, grows up, and his relationship with the former slave helps him decide that he will sing and tell stories as a way to help people have more to their lives than work. The family's saga is also a story of the times through its involvement with slavery, Indian wars, and the Civil War.

221.   Bland, Celia. **Osceola: Seminole Rebel**. New York: Chelsea House, 1993. 110p. $18.95. ISBN 0-7910-1716-8. (North American Indians of Achievement). 5 up

Osceola's (1804-1838) resistance against the U.S. Army for seven years in Florida during the Second Seminole War showed his intelligence, his courage, and his strength of purpose. When he was 10, he fled to Florida from Alabama with his family because the government wanted the land. When the government declared that the Seminoles had to leave Florida, Osceola persuaded the Seminoles to resist, and they foiled the government. Engravings and reproductions enhance the text. Chronology, Further Reading, and Index.

222.   Bland, Celia. **Pontiac: Ottawa Rebel**. New York: Chelsea House, 1994. 110p. $18.95; $7.95pa. ISBN 0-7910-1717-6; 0-7910-2043-6pa. (North American Indians of Achievement). 5 up

In 1763, Pontiac (1725-1769) led one of the smartest campaigns that a Native American had ever waged against the whites up to that time. His people and the French fur traders together had tried to defend their lands from the British. The British declared victory in 1760 but broke their treaty terms in 1762. Pontiac inspired nearly 18 tribes to fight against them, and for six months, the Indians and the French struggled against the British for the land between the Great Lakes and the Ohio Valley. Although the Indians lost, they showed their strength. Photographs and engravings enhance the text. Chronology, Further Reading, and Index.

223.   Blassingame, Wyatt. **The Look-It-Up Book of Presidents**. New York: Random House, 1990. 159p. $7.99pa. ISBN 0-679-80358-0pa. 6-9

Short biographies of two to four pages and portraits or photographs give insight into the characters of each man who led the United States, from George Washington through George Bush. Presidents at a Glance and Index.

224.   Blau, Justine. **Betty Friedan: Feminist**. New York: Chelsea House, 1990. 102p. $18.95. ISBN 1-55546-653-2. (American Women of Achievement). 5 up

Elizabeth Naomi Goldstein (b. 1921) graduated near the top of her class in Smith College and won a prestigious research fellowship. Then she went to New York with her new husband to raise a family. The emptiness of being at home without intellectual stimulation led her to write *The Feminine Mystique* (1963), about men denying women the chance to perform meaningful work. Her book spurred the creation of the National Organization for Women (NOW), and she became its first president. As a senior citizen, she transferred her concerns to America's treatment of the aged. She talks about taboo subjects that force people to examine what they really think. Photographs enhance the text. Chronology, Further Reading, and Index.

225.   Blockson, Charles. **The Underground Railroad**. New York: Prentice Hall, 1987. 307p. $18.95. ISBN 0-13-935743-2. 7-10

Even though slaves wanted to be free, the question arises as to what kind of courage a person must have to escape from slavery when, if captured, the person would likely be tortured and perhaps killed. The text looks at the stories of more than 50 slaves, arranged by state, who escaped via the Underground Railroad in their attempts to find freedom. The slaves came from the Deep South as well as the Middle Atlantic on their long journey toward Canada. Bibliography, Suggested Readings, and Index.

226.   Blos, Joan. **Brothers of the Heart: A Story of the Old Northwest, 1837-38**. New York: Scribner's, 1985. 176p. $14.95. ISBN 0-684-18452-4. 6 up

In a flashback while celebrating his 50th wedding anniversary, Shem remembers the one year that he lived away from Millfield, Michigan. His legs crippled, Shem needed to go to Detroit to find work. He kept accounts so well that his employer asked him to go on a fur expedition to keep records. When in trouble, the other men had to leave him in the woods, but they did not return as promised. An old woman, abandoned by her tribe to die, found him and taught him how to survive the Canadian winter. In turn, he befriended her and buried her when she died. His story, told by those who knew of her secrecy, made him a hero and a worthy mate for the woman he had always loved.

227.   Blos, Joan. **A Gathering of Days: A New England Girl's Journal, 1830-32**. New York: Scribner's, 1979. 144p. $14. ISBN 0-684-16340-3. New York: Aladdin, 1990. 144p. $3.95pa. ISBN 0-689-71419-Xpa. 4-7

Catherine keeps a journal of her 14th year, 1830-1832, during which a friend dies; another departs for the Lowell, Massachusetts, factories; her father remarries; she gives one of her deceased mother's quilts to a runaway slave hiding in the woods; and she leaves home to tend someone else's child. She sends a letter and the journal to her great-granddaughter during her own 14th year in 1899. Her great granddaughter asks questions, and in a second letter, Catherine responds. The story reveals the time and life in New England. *Newbery Medal*.

228.   Blue, Rose, and Corinne Naden. **Barbara Jordan: Politician**. New York: Chelsea House, 1991. 110p. $18.85. ISBN 0-7910-1131-3. (Black Americans of Achievement). 5 up

Barbara Jordan (1936-1996), native of one of the poorest Black neighborhoods in Texas, became the South's first Black U.S. congresswoman. She went to school and established a law firm in Houston before she started campaigning for state office. In Congress, she helped investigate Watergate, and in 1976 she gave the keynote address at the Democratic National Convention. She retired to become a professor and to cope with a neurological disease that confined her to a wheelchair, but she always displayed intelligence and compassion toward her country. Photographs enhance the text. Chronology, Further Reading, and Index.

229.   Blue, Rose, and Corrine Naden. **People of Peace**. Brookfield, CT: Millbrook Press, 1994. 80p. $18.90. ISBN 1-56294-409-6. 5-8

Because some people refused to compromise with the status quo and instead worked for peace, they made the world better than before. Some of these people won the Nobel Peace Prize for their efforts, but they have all saved lives. The people presented here are Andrew Carnegie (United States, 1835-1919), Jane Addams (United States, 1860-1935), Woodrow Wilson (United States, 1856-1924), Mohandas Gandhi (India, 1869-1948), Ralph Bunche (United States, 1904-1971), Dag Hammarskjöld (Sweden, 1905-1961), Jimmy Carter (United States, b. 1924), Desmond Tutu (South Africa, b. 1931), Oscar Arias Sanchez (Costa Rica, b. 1941), Betty Williams (Northern Ireland, b. 1943), and Mairead Corrigan Maguire (Northern Ireland, b. 1944). Conclusion, For Further Reading, and Index.

230.   Blumberg, Rhoda. **Full Steam Ahead: The Race to Build a Transcontinental Railroad**. Washington, DC: National Geographic, 1996. 160p. $18.95. ISBN 0-7922-2715-8. 5-8

The text tells the story of the transcontinental railroad from its inception to its finish. What it emphasizes is the fact that the railroad ever succeeded with the political intrigues, dishonesty from a variety of people, furious Native Americans, snowdrifts, and other hazards to overcome. The text covers all of these problems and others, along with the successes that made the venture become reality. Photographs, Notes, Bibliography, and Index.

231.   Blumberg, Rhoda. **The Incredible Journey of Lewis and Clark**. New York: Lothrop, Lee & Shepard, 1987. 144p. $18; $9.95pa. ISBN 0-688-06512-0; 0-688-14421-7pa. 4-10

Blumberg's scholarly and interesting background is complemented with photographs of documents and clear maps. Blumberg traces the Lewis and Clark expedition from its inception by Thomas Jefferson through its successful end. Jefferson, fearing that the British would settle the West and spurred on by Alex MacKenzie's reports of its wealth, requested that Congress fund a secret expedition. He asked for only a small amount of money so that Congress would agree, and selected his personal secretary, Lewis, 28, to head the group. Lewis chose a former military colleague, Clark, to join him as the map maker. They departed on August 31, 1803, from St. Louis, and returned on September 23, 1806. For the first time, those in the East became aware of the Yankton, Sioux, Teton Sioux, Arikara, Mandan, Crow, Hidatsa, Shoshoni, Nez Percé, Flathead, Blackfeet, Walla Walla, Wanapam, Clatsop, and Chinook Indian tribes plus 25 others. The expedition found 122 animals and 178 plants new to science. Aftermath, Notes, Bibliography, and Index.

232.   Bober, Natalie S. **Abigail Adams: Witness to a Revolution**. New York: Atheneum, 1995. 248p. $17. ISBN 0-689-31760-3. YA

As wife of one President and mother of another, Abigail Adams (1744-1818) was a force in her own right. She wrote extraordinary letters to her friends and family, and she watched the Battle of Bunker Hill from a hill near her home while soldiers marched by her door. This proximity allowed her to write firsthand of the war's progress to her husband as he and other leaders tried to create the new government in Philadelphia. She also documented the experiences of women who had to manage their families and homes while their husbands were away. Bober uses these letters to create a vivid picture of Abigail Adams. Notes, Bibliography, and Index. *American Library Association Best Books for Young Adults* and *Boston Globe-Horn Book Award*.

233.   Bober, Natalie S. **A Restless Spirit: The Story of Robert Frost**. New York: Henry Holt, 1991. 197p. $19.95. ISBN 0-8050-1672-4. YA

Robert Frost (1874-1963) once said "When I was young, I was so interested in baseball that my family was afraid I'd waste my life and be a pitcher. Later, they were afraid I'd waste my life and be a poet. They were right." By 15, he had written and published his first poem, but Frost had difficulty supporting his family. He did not publish his first book of poems until he was 40, at the encouragement of Ezra Pound. He spoke with an American voice rather than an English one, and he made important contributions to the lives of many through his conversational tone. The text includes the full version of some of the poems discussed; chapter headings are lines from poems. Important Dates, Source Guide, Bibliography, Poetry Index, and Subject Index.

234. Bober, Natalie S. **Thomas Jefferson: Man on a Mountain**. New York: Atheneum, 1988. 274p. $15.95. ISBN 0-689-31154-0. New York: Aladdin, 1993. 274p. $6.95pa. ISBN 0-02-041797-7pa. 7 up

Bober presents Thomas Jefferson (1743-1826) as a student afraid to go to class when he had not done his lessons, a young man studying in Williamsburg, a husband, a father, and a public servant. Bober tries to relate the man and his career to the time in which he lived. She sees him as both prophet and statesman who never lost faith in the dignity of the common man. He was curious about everything and willing to say "I don't know" while turning to books to research the answers. Chapter Notes, Bibliography, and Index.

235. Bodow, Steven. **Sitting Bull: Sioux Leader**. Austin, TX: Raintree/Steck-Vaughn, 1994. 128p. $16.98. ISBN 0-8114-2328-X. (American Troublemakers). 6 up

Returns Again's son was born in 1831 into the Hunkpapa Sioux tribe but did not earn the name Sitting Bull until 1845. Throughout his life, he helped his people, eventually becoming their chief and medicine man. He worked to maintain the rights of Native Americans and encouraged the Sioux so that they defeated George Custer at the Battle of Little Bighorn in 1876. Although he took his people into Canada, lack of food forced them to return. The U.S. Army captured Sitting Bull and killed him in 1890. Maps, Photographs, Key Dates, Glossary, Places to Visit, Bibliography and Recommended Readings, and Index.

236. Bolden, Tonya. **Just Family**. New York: Cobblehill, 1996. 152p. $14.99. ISBN 0-525-65192-6. 4-7

Beryl, 10, and her older sister Randy are close friends as they grow up in the 1960s in a stable Harlem home with loving parents. Beryl discovers that Randy's father is different from hers and that Randy was born out of wedlock. That Randy knows this secret but never mentioned it before disturbs Beryl. Not until they attend a family reunion in South Carolina does Beryl begin to understand that family love and support are more important than people measuring up to others' criteria.

237. Bolick, Nancy O'Keefe, and Sally G. Randolph. **Shaker Villages**. Laura LoTurco, illustrator. New York: Walker, 1993. 79p. $13.85. ISBN 0-8027-8209-4. 4-8

After the Shakers came to America, they developed 19 communities. The sect was unusual because it kept the sexes separated and preached celibacy. While they thrived, the Shakers had their villages well organized. The text presents the architecture, industry, life, and worship of the Shakers. Time Line of Shaker History and Index.

238. Boller, Paul F., Jr. **Presidential Wives: An Anecdotal History**. New York: Oxford University Press, 1988. 533p. $27.50; $11.95pa. ISBN 0-19-503763-4; 0-19-505976-Xpa. YA

The text looks at all of the First Ladies, even those who died before their husbands became President, from Martha Washington through Nancy Reagan. Dolley Madison took snuff, Mary Todd Lincoln disliked many in her husband's cabinet, and Eleanor Roosevelt complained to her husband that she would have no identity while he was President. Lady Byrd Johnson told her daughters to read about Sudan and to not drink the wine before a state dinner with Sudanese leaders. This diverse group of women has had much influence on the history of the United States. Notes and Index.

239. Bolotin, Norman, and Angela Herb. **For Home and Country: A Civil War Scrapbook**. New York: Lodestar, Dutton, 1995. 98p. $16.99. ISBN 0-525-67495-0. (Young Readers History of the Civil War). 5 up

Sidebar text complements well-labeled photographs and reproductions showing aspects of the Civil War. Among the topics covered are outfitting the troops, the rigors of the war, food, coping, destruction of the armies as they marched, the sick and wounded, prisoners of war, news of the war, photographing the war, trying to escape boredom, and marching home at the end. Glossary and Bibliography.

240. Bolton, Jonathan, and Claire Wilson. **Joseph Brant: Mohawk Chief**. New York: Chelsea House, 1992. 112p. $18.95. ISBN 0-7910-1709-5. (North American Indians of Achievement). 5 up

As a member of two worlds, Joseph Brant (1743-1807) used his knowledge to help his country. He was a Thayendanega as a boy, reared as a Mohawk, and schooled by the British, where he gained praise for his mastery of English and understanding of European customs. He chose to be a missionary but had to abandon his plans when the American Revolution broke out. In 1775, he went on a diplomatic mission to England, and George III hosted a dinner in his honor. After England's defeat, Brant moved to Canada and tried to keep the whites from seizing Native American lands. His negotiations were so important that George Washington solicited his help. Photographs enhance the text. Chronology, Further Reading, and Index.

241. Bonvillain, Nancy. **Black Hawk: Sac Rebel**. New York: Chelsea House, 1994. 110p. $18.95 ISBN 0-7910-1711-7. (North American Indians of Achievement). 5 up

Black Hawk (1767-1838) grew up in the Indian village of Saukenuk, now called Rock Island, Illinois. He learned to hunt, trade, and lead his people in battle so that he earned the rank of war chief. When the United States tried to get Sac and Fox Indians to give up their homelands, Black Hawk defied them by leading, at age 65, a protest of more than 2,000 people against the government order. Although the movement began in peace, the military drove them into retreat. They lost the Black Hawk war, but he offered a model of wisdom and idealism. Reproductions enhance the text. Chronology, Further Reading, and Index.

242. Bonvillain, Nancy. **The Haidas: People of the Northwest Coast**. Brookfield, CT: Millbrook Press, 1994. 64p. $15.90. ISBN 1-56294-491-6. (Native Americans). 5-8

The Haida ancestors settled on the Queen Charlotte Islands in British Columbia, Canada, c. 1000. Many died in Alaska after 1750 from smallpox. Part of their culture was the celebration of potlatches and ceremonial dances that Canada outlawed in 1884. In the twentieth century, the Haidas joined with the Tlingits to file a land claim against the United States in Alaska, which they won. As they have become integrated into Alaskan and Canadian life, they have tried to preserve their identity through their traditions and artifacts. Important Dates, Glossary, Bibliography, and Index.

243. Bonvillain, Nancy. **Hiawatha: Founder of the Iroquois Confederacy**. New York: Chelsea House, 1992. 120p. $18.95; $7.95. ISBN 0-7910-1707-9; 0-7910-1693-5pa. (North American Indians of Achievement). 5 up

In his attempt to create peace more than 500 years ago, Hiawatha was first thwarted by his enemy Thadodaho, an Onondaga chief. Probably Thadodaho killed Hiawatha's three daughters, but Hiawatha continued his pursuit of peace with the help of the Huron Indian, Deganawida. They convinced the Onondaga, Mohawk, Oneida, Cayuga, and Seneca nations to stop their conflicts and to create a common rule so that they would not destroy each other. Drawings and reproductions highlight the text. Chronology, Further Reading, and Index.

244. Boorstin, Daniel J. **The Creators: A History of Heroes of the Imagination**. New York: Random House, 1992. 811p. $30. ISBN 0-394-54395-5. New York: Vintage, 1993. 811p. $17pa. ISBN 0-679-74375-8pa. YA

This sequel to *The Discoverers* (1984) investigates people who have accomplished something new in the arts. Most of the chapters are essays within themselves, but their themes connect. Boorstin covers an enormous range of information, from ancient history to the present and across countries, as he examines what being creative means. Annotated Chapter Bibliographies and Index.

245. Borklund, Carl W. **Military Leaders Since World War II**. New York: Facts on File, 1992. 130p. $17.95. ISBN 0-8160-2606-8. (American Profile). 9 up

The careers of 11 modern American military figures in the U.S. Army and Navy, including Colin Powell, William Westmoreland, Edward Rowny, and James Abrahamson, appear here. Bibliography and Index.

246. Bortz, Fred. **Catastrophe! Great Engineering Failure—and Success**. New York: W. H. Freeman, 1995. 80p. $19.95; $13.95pa. ISBN 0-7167-6538-1; 0-7167-6539-Xpa. (Scientific American's Mystery of Science). 5-9

Six engineering debacles have changed the lives of people who experienced them and lived as well as the families of those who died. The six discussed in the text are the collapse of the Kansas City Hyatt skywalk in 1980; the Tacoma Narrows Bridge in 1940; the crash of Eastern Airlines Flight 401 in Florida in 1972; the U.S. Space Shuttle *Challenger* disaster in 1986; nuclear power plant accidents (Three-Mile Island in 1979 and Chernobyl in 1986); and "The Great Northeast Blackout" of 1965. By explaining the science behind each disaster, the text shows how inadequate planning caused the problems and how engineers have corrected them. Photographs and Index.

247. Borzendowski, Janice. **John Russwurm**. New York: Chelsea House, 1989. 110p. $18.95. ISBN 1-55545-610-9. (Black Americans of Achievement). 5 up

John Russwurm (1799-1851), son of a wealthy Jamaican landowner, came to America when he was 13. He attended private schools and was one of the first Black Americans to earn a college degree (Bowdoin College). He was a journalist and publisher who helped found *Freedom's Journal*, through which he attacked slavery and promoted Black pride. He also helped establish the Maryland Colony in Liberia, Africa, for former slaves to govern themselves. There he supervised the school system and started a newspaper before becoming the governor. Engravings and reproductions enhance the text. Chronology, Further Reading, and Index.

248. Bosco, Peter I. **The War of 1812**. Brookfield, CT: Millbrook Press, 1991. 128p. $18.90. ISBN 1-56294-004-X. 7 up

The War of 1812, an armed conflict between the United States and Great Britain, began partially because the United States wanted neutral shipping rights during the Franco-British hostilities. The British began impressment of sailors and confiscation of U.S. ships. In the West, American frontiersmen and the British clashed when the British claimed to own some of the land. The text discusses these problems and the resulting naval battles, beginning with the Battle of Tippecanoe in 1811 and continuing through 1815. Bibliography and Index.

249. Bosco, Peter. **World War I**. New York: Facts on File, 1991. 124p. $17.95. ISBN 0-8160-2460-X. (America at War). 7-12

Before World War I, the United States had established a policy of isolationism. Bosco tells why America changed its policy to enter World War I and discusses military logistics, political maneuvering, and the terrors of battle. He focuses on several conflicts such as Belleau Wood and the Argonne. Bibliography and Index.

250. Boulton, Alexander O. **Frank Lloyd Wright: Architect: An Illustrated Biography**. New York: Rizzoli, 1993. 128p. $24.95. ISBN 0-8478-1683-4. 8 up

With reproductions of drawings and color photographs of his buildings, the text presents the life and work of Frank Lloyd Wright (1867-1959). His arrogant personality invited scandal, and he refused to build anything without placing it in its social order. Direct quotes from Wright help reveal his attitudes and show why he is one of the most important architects in the twentieth century. Chronology, Glossary, Annotated Bibliography, and Index.

251. Boutis, Victoria. **Looking Out**. New York: Four Winds, 1988. 139p. $11.95. ISBN 0-02-711830-4. 6-9

In 1953, Ellen, 12, wants to be an ordinary girl like those in her class, but she hides a secret: Her parents are Communists. She fears that her parents will go to jail and be executed like the Rosenbergs for giving the Russians secrets about the atomic bomb. But she also resents her parents' attitude that Communism is more important to them than she is. She knows she can never be the average person she wants to be. *Jane Addams Children's Book Award.*

252. Bowler, Mike. **Trains**. Steve Herridge, Paul Higgens, and Martin Woodward, illustrators. Austin, TX: Raintree/Steck-Vaughn, 1995. 32p. $13.98. ISBN 0-8114-6192-0. (Pointers). 3-7

The first locomotive ran along tracks in 1804. Two-page spreads of text and illustration present the history of trains. Topics and trains discussed are early railroads (c. 1825), the first inter-city railroad (1829), American locomotives (mid-nineteenth century), long-distance express trains (c. 1900), express steam trains, the largest steam engine, long-distance diesels, diesel-electric trains, high-speed diesels, subways, and the fastest trains currently in use. Glossary and Index.

253. Bowman, John S. **Andrew Carnegie: Steel Tycoon**. Englewood Cliffs, NJ: Silver Burdett, 1989. 128p. $7.95. ISBN 0-382-09582-0. (The American Dream.) 7 up

Since his birth in Dumferline, Scotland, Andrew Carnegie (1835-1919) admired the integrity and the loyalty of the Scottish heroes William Wallace and Robert Bruce. At 13, however, he and his family decided to emigrate to Pittsburgh because they could no longer live on the falling income of a damask weaver competing with the new factories. Through teaching himself how to interpret telegraph messages, and sheer luck, Carnegie landed a series of jobs that earned him enough money to begin investing in Pullman sleeping cars, steel bridges, land with oil, iron mills, and steel factories from which he made millions. He was the first to set up a foundation in order to distribute his wealth to others, especially the Carnegie libraries, begun initially in Dumferline, before his death. Bibliography and Index.

254. Boyle, T. Coraghessan. **The Road to Wellville**. New York: Viking, 1993. 476p. $16. ISBN 0-670-83766-0. New York: Penguin, 1994. 476p. $10.95pa. ISBN 0-14-016718-8pa. YA

In 1907, cereal rivals J. H. Kellogg and C. W. Post live in Battle Creek, Michigan. This novel tells the story of the wealthy clientele who visit Kellogg's sanitarium to cure themselves of spiritual and physical problems caused by meat eating and sexual activity. The three points of view are those of a patient at the clinic, a scoundrel businessman, and Kellogg. As they interact, they reveal some of the cruelty and silliness in which humans engage when they are trying to help themselves or to be near those who make them feel they belong to a higher class of people.

255. Boyne, Walter J. **Air Force Eagles**. New York: Crown, 1992. 455p. $20. ISBN 0-517-57609-0. YA

John Marshall, in *Eagles at War*, wants to be the first Black American ace during both World War II and the Korean War, but another pilot steals his "kills." Stateside, a second pilot, Riley, meets a German woman from *Trophy for Eagles* who has left her husband in Berlin; Riley marries her. Marshall returns home and goes with Riley to Little Rock in 1957, where they rescue Riley's wife from her ex-husband, who has come to America and kidnapped her. At the same time, the Ku Klux Klan and its army begins an assault on the town's Black community.

256. Boyne, Walter J. **Eagles at War**. New York: Crown, 1991. 392p. $20. ISBN 0-517-57610-4. YA

Frank Bandfield, from *Trophy for Eagles*, and Hadley Roget start to work on a plan for an Allied attack from the air when they realize the Americans will become directly involved in World War II. They compete with Bruno Hafner, the German Bandfield shot down over Guernica, as he builds Hitler's jet fighters using slave labor in underground facilities. A help to the American cause is a woman who despises Joseph Goebbels but becomes his mistress so she can learn about the military tactics that the Germans plan to use against the Allies.

257. Boyne, Walter J. **Trophy for Eagles**. New York: Crown, 1989. 455p. $20. ISBN 0-517-57276-1. YA

Frank Bandfield prepares to compete in the race from New York to Paris in 1927, but an arsonist destroys his plane, allowing Charles Lindbergh to win. Bandfield knows that Hafner, a German pilot, is responsible for the deed, and the two begin a rivalry that lasts until Bandfield shoots down Hafner over Guernica in 1937 during the Spanish Civil War.

258. Brady, James. **The Coldest War: A Memoir of Korea**. New York: Orion, Crown, 1990. 248p. $19.95. ISBN 0-517-57690-2. New York: Pocket Books, 1995. 248p. $6.50pa. ISBN 0-671-72525-4pa. YA

In a highly personal memoir, Brady discusses his participation in the war, which began in 1950 with North Korea's trespass of the 38th Parallel. The war ended in 1953 after 54,000 Americans had been killed. Brady suggests that Korea was the last campaign of World War II and the first battle of Vietnam. He was 23 during his year in Korea, and he carefully details his experience. Index.

259. Brady, Philip. **Reluctant Hero: A Snowy Road to Salem in 1802**. New York: Walker, 1990. 159p. $16.95. ISBN 0-8027-6972-1. (Walker American History). 6-8

Cutting Favour, 13, has to travel from New Hampshire to Salem, Massachusetts, in snowy weather to sell furs and shingles so his family will have money for food. He has to defend a girl from a bully and then elude his new enemy, and he has to protect the money that he makes with his shrewd salesmanship and his ability to carve wood. By the time he returns home, he has been reluctantly successful in several ways.

260. Bragg, Janet Harmon, and Marjorie M. Kriz. **Soaring Above Setbacks: The Autobiography of Janet Harmon Bragg: African American Aviator**. Washington, DC: Smithsonian, 1996. 120p. $19.95. ISBN 1-56098-458-9. (Smithsonian History of Aviation Series). YA

Janet Harmon Bragg received her Registered Nurse degree from Spelman Seminary in 1929, but the conditions in Georgia were so deplorable for Black nurses that she went to Chicago and became the night supervisor at Wilson Hospital. She continued to take medical and scientific courses and became a health inspector for an insurance company. During her leisure time, she learned to fly and in 1942 became the first Black woman to earn a commercial pilot's license. During her life, she also helped Ethiopian foreign students, and the king invited her to Ethopia to visit as his guest. Her life shows a woman who refused to be limited by her society's preconceptions.

261. Branch, Muriel Miller. **The Water Brought Us: The Story of the Gullah-Speaking People**. New York: Cobblehill, Dutton, 1995. 106p. $16.99. ISBN 0-525-65185-3. 5 up

Off the coast of South Carolina are 35 Sea Islands where the Gullah, descendants of slaves who stayed after the Emancipation, have become landowners, farmers, teachers, nurses, and other leaders in the community. The origin of their language traces to the castles and forts along the West African coast, where captured Africans awaited transport to the West Indies and America to be sold into slavery. The text presents their history through slavery, their religious traditions, and their language. Bibliography and Index.

262. Branscum, Robbie. **Old Blue Tilley**. New York: Macmillan, 1991. 96p. $11.95. ISBN 0-02-711931-9. 5-7

Hambone, a 14-year-old orphan, lives alone until he joins a circuit-riding preacher, Old Blue. He travels with Old Blue through the Ozarks as World War II begins in 1941. After a revival meeting, Old Blue's influence helps Hambone realize that he must assert himself by demanding his inheritance from his uncles and by returning to revive the family farm.

263. Brashler, William. **The Story of the Negro League Baseball**. New York: Ticknor & Fields, 1994. 166p. $15.95. ISBN 0-395-67169-8. 6 up

From 1890 to 1947, major league baseball was not an option for Black and Latino players. They formed their own leagues and teams such as the Black Yankees, the Homestead Grays, and the Kansas City Monarchs. Their wool uniforms and night lights were new, but they could not go into restaurants or hotels because of Jim Crow segregation laws. The text tells their stories. Box Score, Bibliography, and Index.

264. Bratman, Fred. **Becoming a Citizen: Adopting a New Home**. Austin, TX: Raintree/Steck-Vaughn, 1993. 48p. $15.49; $6.64pa. ISBN 0-8114-7354-6; 0-8114-5582-3pa. (Good Citizenship). 4-9

The text looks at the origins of citizenship as it discusses immigration, illegal aliens, and political asylum. Citizenship has been important throughout history. In America, citizenship began when immigrants arrived on the Mayflower in 1620. Four waves of immigrants have come to this country. The first wave occurred during the 1700s with many indentured servants. The second wave, mostly Germans and Irish, lasted from 1820 until 1870. In 1881, the third wave began and lasted for 40 years when 23 million arrived. The fourth wave began in 1965. Because of all these new people, learning the requirements for citizenship has been important. Photographs highlight the text. Further Reading, Glossary, and Index.

265. Bredeson, Carmen. **Jonas Salk: Discoverer of the Polio Vaccine**. Springfield, NJ: Enslow, 1993. 112p. $17.95. ISBN 0-89490-415-9. (People to Know). 5-9

Jonas Salk (b. 1914) found a vaccine to stop polio. At first people were leery of the serum, but desperate individuals were willing to try anything to avoid the horror of this disease, which damaged the cells of the brain and the spinal cord, leaving its sufferers paralyzed. Salk has also worked with other viruses such as HIV and influenza. His goal has always been the prevention of disease rather than fame. The text looks at his life and accomplishments. Chronology, Notes, Further Reading, and Index.

266. Bremness, Lesley. **Herbs**. New York: Dorling Kindersley, 1994. 304p. $17.95pa. ISBN 1-56458-496-8pa. (Eyewitness Handbooks). YA

Although not a history book, the text is an excellent reference for the types of herbs that people have used throughout history as cures or for other reasons. For example, belladonna dilates the eye pupils, "an effect once thought by Italian women to look seductive," but it is poisonous. Glossary and Index.

267. Brenner, Barbara. **On the Frontier with Mr. Audubon**. New York: Coward, McCann, & Geoghegan, 1977. 96p. $6.95. ISBN 0-698-20385-2. 6-9

Joseph Mason travels down the Ohio and Mississippi Rivers and through the swamplands of Louisiana with John James Audubon (1785-1851) for 18 months. He sketches 50 of the 435 plates that Audubon later includes in his book but for which he does not give Mason credit. Mason is surprised and angered, but by the time the book is published, he has established himself as a portrait painter in Philadelphia and no longer needs Audubon's approval or acknowledgment.

268. Brewer, James D. **No Justice**. New York: Walker, 1996. 246p. $21.95. ISBN 0-8027-3283-6. YA

During Reconstruction along the Mississippi River, Salina Tyner, who entertains men on riverboats, Luke Williamson, a riverboat owner and operator who once fought for the Union, and Masey Baldrige, an alcoholic Confederate, unite to find missing army Gatling guns and to solve a murder. What they discover is that these two situations are part of a plot to murder the President of the United States.

269. Brill, Marlene Targ. **Extraordinary Young People**. Chicago: Childrens Press, 1996. 212p. $35; $15.95pa. ISBN 0-516-00587-1; 0-516-26044-8pa. (Extraordinary People). 7 up

Not all people have waited until adulthood to show their talents. The text looks at more than 50 children and adolescents who have accomplished something during their young lives. Some of those included are Genghis Khan, Joan of Arc, John Stuart Mill, Phillis Wheatley, Wolfgang Amadeus Mozart, Rachel Carson, Maria Callas, S. E. Hinton, Wayne Gretzky, Pelé, and Maria Tallchief. More recent figures profiled include Wang Yani, Savion Glover, Tiger Woods, Midori, Nawruose Nur, and Ryan White. Additional essays cover engaging groups of young people who also made a mark on society. Photographs and reproductions highlight the text. Further Reading, Glossary, and Index.

270. Brill, Marlene Targ. **John Adams**. Chicago: Childrens Press, 1986. 100p. $17.27. ISBN 0-516-01384-X. (Encyclopedia of Presidents). 4-9

John Adams (1735-1826) was the second president of the United States. He grew up in Braintree, Massachusetts, and trained to be a lawyer. After becoming involved in the rebellion against the English and taxation, he served abroad in Paris because he wanted to leave public life. Then he became the President because he was encouraged by his wife to do what needed to be done for the new country. Chronology and Index.

271. Brill, Marlene Targ. **The Trail of Tears: The Cherokee Journey from Home**. Brookfield, CT: Millbrook Press, 1995. 64p. $15.90. ISBN 1-56294-486-X. (Spotlight on American History). 6-9

When the U.S. government removed Cherokees from their homes, people who once had plantations, animals, slaves, and gristmills were made to leave without taking anything with them. The Cherokees under John Ross were the last group forced to walk to Oklahoma from their lands in Georgia and North and South Carolina. Georgia passed the Indian Code in 1829 that abolished all Cherokee rights, and in 1830 Congress passed the Indian Removal Bill. In 1831, the government decided not to recognize the Cherokee as a separate nation. In 1838 and 1839, the Cherokee removal began, and the long road to Oklahoma became known as the Trail of Tears. Although the government promised to furnish supplies, the contractors delivered rancid meat and grain filled with weevils. Merchants charged inflated prices along the way, and farmers charged tolls for crossing their lands. Chronology, Further Reading, and Bibliography.

272. Brimner, Larry. **Voices from the Camps: Internment of Japanese Americans During World War II**. New York: Franklin Watts, 1994. 110p. $21.10. ISBN 0-531-11179-2. 9 up

After the Japanese bombed Pearl Harbor on December 7, 1941, President Franklin Roosevelt signed an executive order calling for the roundup and forced relocation of 110,000 persons of Japanese ancestry (two-thirds of them American citizens). This action caused many owners of small businesses to sell their livelihoods at cut-rate prices. Children spent their formative years inside barbed wire, and many families were separated until the end of the war. Brimner posits that these things happened because of racism. Neither the Italians nor the Germans in the United States endured the same treatment even though the United States declared war against Italy and Germany within a matter of days after Pearl Harbor. Glossary, Selected Bibliography, and Index.

273.   Bristol, Leigh. **Legacy**. New York: Warner, 1993. 345p. $4.99pa. ISBN 0-446-35081-9pa. YA

Laurel Sinclair, a member of Charleston, South Carolina's society in 1886, gives Seth Tait an entrance into the closed group. Seth knows that Laurel has a treasure although she does not yet know about it. He romances and marries her in attempt to steal it.

274.   Brooks, Bruce. **The Moves Make the Man**. New York: HarperCollins, 1984. 280p. $15.89; $4.50pa. ISBN 0-06-020698-5; 0-06-440564-8pa. 7 up

Jerome and Bix practice their basketball moves in the 1960s. Bix wants Jerome to go with him to see his mother in a Duke hospital mental ward in Durham, North Carolina. When the waiter in the restaurant where they stop refuses to serve Jerome, who is Black, Bix cannot cope with the discrimination toward his friend. Bix disappears even though he has always said that he hates "fakes" who make an ultimate "move." Jerome has to accept Bix's disappearance and continue to cope as the only Black in his white high school. *Newbery Honor, American Library Association Notable Books for Children, American Library Association Best of the Best Book 1966-1992, Boston Globe-Horn Book Award*, and *School Library Journal Best Book.*

275.   Brooks, Jerome. **Naked in Winter**. New York: Orchard, 1990. 182p. $14.95. ISBN 0-531-08466-3. 7 up

As the 1950s begin when Jake is 15, his father buys a house in an area removed from Jake's neighborhood and school. Jake continues going to the old school, but his friendships weaken, and he dislikes the new location. His mother is also angry, and she accuses his father of having an affair before she arrived from Poland. When Jake becomes an unwitting accomplice to his brother's infidelity, he is upset. Then he falls in love and has to make sense of that new emotion. His father, however, becomes ill, and he realizes that both he and his mother love his father deeply.

276.   Brown, Charnan. **Chester A. Arthur: Twenty-First President of the United States**. Chicago: Childrens Press, 1989. 110p. $19.80. ISBN 0-516-01369-6. (Encyclopedia of Presidents). 4-9

Chester A. Arthur (1829-1886) became President when James Garfield was assassinated. He had been appointed to the vice presidency in order to appease the New York City faction under Conkling and his Stalwart branch of the party. Additionally, Garfield's assassin stated that he was a Stalwart, and he wanted Arthur to be President. Garfield was neither the best nor the worst President in office. The text looks at this man and his life. Chronology of American History and Index.

277.   Brown, Drollene P. **Belva Lockwood Wins Her Case**. James Watling, illustrator. Morton Grove, IL: Albert Whitman, 1987. 64p. $11.95. ISBN 0-8075-0630-3. 3-7

Belva Lockwood (1830-1917) was a teacher, a suffragette, a lawyer, and a peace activist. She became the first woman to practice law before the Supreme Court. Additionally, she ran for President of the United States in 1884 and 1888. Afterword and Sources.

278.   Brown, Fern G. **Franklin Pierce: 14th President of the United States**. Ada, OK: Garrett Educational, 1989. 122p. $17.26. ISBN 0-944483-25-9. (Presidents of the United States). 5-9

As a trial lawyer from New Hampshire, Franklin Pierce (1804-1869) had great success. He was able to deliver his inauguration address from memory. He served in the presidency as the North and the South became increasingly bitter. During his administration, his minister to Mexico negotiated the Gadsden Purchase, buying the land now known as New Mexico and Arizona and completing the current map of the United States. Some of Pierce's secret plans to buy Cuba or take it by force made him undesirable, and he did not run for a second term. Bibliography and Index.

279.   Brown, Fern G. **James A. Garfield: 20th President of the United States**. Ada, OK: Garrett Educational, 1990. 124p. $17.26. ISBN 0-944483-63-1. (Presidents of the United States). 5-9

His father dead when he was young, James A. Garfield (1831-1881) had to help his mother, and children taunted him for being poor and having no father. He left home to study but missed his mother. He returned, however, but soon left again to go to sea. Illness thwarted that career, and he spent his last two years of college at Williams, where his interest in the Republican Party began. He served in Congress and was elected President, but his presidency lasted only four months before Charles Julius Guiteau assassinated him. Bibliography and Index.

280. Brown, Gene. **Conflict in Europe and the Great Depression: World War I (1914-1940)**. New York: Twenty-First Century Books, 1994. 64p. $15.98. ISBN 0-8050-2585-5. (First Person America). 5-9

Brown posits that the period between World Wars I and II was when modern America was born. He discusses the rugged individualism that characterized many Americans at the time, but the government became a major force in everyday lives during and after the Great Depression of the 1930s. Most Americans were moving to cities, and mass media was growing in importance. From a nation of ballplayers and performers, Americans became watchers. Among people presented are John Reed, Gordon Parks, Al Capone, Marcus Garvey, and Lillian Gish. Photographs enhance the text. Timeline, For Further Reading, and Index.

281. Brown, Gene. **Discovery and Settlement: Europe Meets the "New World," 1490-1700**. New York: Twenty-First Century Books, 1993. 64p. $15.95. ISBN 0-8050-2574-X. (First Person America). 5-8

With primary source materials and illustrations, the text presents the discovery and settlement of America and daily life in the colonies, including the experiences of Native Americans, African Americans, and women. Bibliography and Index.

282. Brown, Gene. **The Nation in Turmoil: Civil Rights and the Vietnam War (1960-1973)**. New York: Twenty-First Century Books, 1994. 64p. $15.98. ISBN 0-8050-2588-X. (First Person America). 5-9

At the beginning of the 1960s, America had a new, young President, John F. Kennedy, who gave idealistic college students the Peace Corps. Integration began to be a reality. But the assassination of Kennedy in 1963 changed the mood of the country. The Cuban Missile Crisis, the Vietnam War, and the assassinations of Robert Kennedy and Martin Luther King, Jr. changed the nation again. Riots shook the cities. In the early 1970s, social changes for women and homosexuals gained momentum while the Arab nations imposed an oil embargo. Then Richard Nixon compromised the presidency and resigned in 1972. Photographs enhance the text. Timeline, For Further Reading, and Index.

283. Brown, Gene. **The Struggle to Grow: Expansionism and Industrialization (1880-1913)**. New York: Twenty-First Century Books, 1993. 64p. $15.95. ISBN 0-8050-2584-7. (First Person America). 5-8

The text uses letters, poems, broadsides, speeches, lyrics, and newspaper articles to present life on the western frontier as it began to urbanize and to absorb immigrants. It also faced social reformers who disapproved of western lifestyles, and contemporary technology that changed the modes of work. Bibliography and Index.

284. Brown, Jordan. **Elizabeth Blackwell: Physician**. New York: Chelsea House, 1989. 110p. $18.95. ISBN 1-55546-642-7. (American Women of Achievement). 5 up

Elizabeth Blackwell (1821-1910) decided to become a doctor after a brief stint as a teacher. Twenty-eight medical schools rejected her before New York State's Geneva College said "yes," and she began her practice in 1851. She lost an eye from disease, which prevented her from becoming a surgeon. Instead, she opened a clinic for poor women and children in 1857; established America's first visiting nurse service; managed the Union's Civil War nursing corps; and, in 1868, founded the Women's Medical College of the New York infirmary, the first medical school in the world for women. Photographs and reproductions enhance the text. Chronology, Further Reading, and Index.

285. Brown, Kevin. **Malcolm X: His Life and Legacy**. Brookfield, CT: Millbrook Press, 1995. 112p. $19.90; $9.95pa. ISBN 1-56294-500-9; 1-56294-890-3pa. 8 up

As a celebration of the 30 years since Malcolm X was assassinated, Brown has written another view of Malcolm X based on his *Autobiography* and on current writers' assessments of his achievements. The text is part biographical essay of Malcolm X and his life and part historical analysis of the place the Nation of Islam has in the Civil Rights movement. Photographs complement the text. Chronology, Bibliography, Notes, and Index.

286. Brown, Kevin. **Romare Bearden: Artist**. New York: Chelsea House, 1995. 112p. $18.95. ISBN 0-7910-1119-4. (Black Americans of Achievement). 5 up

Romare Bearden (1911-1987), a North Carolinian, wanted "to redefine the image of man" in terms of his experience as an African American. He knew Countee Cullen and Paul Robeson during the Harlem Renaissance and played semiprofessional baseball. He graduated from New York University in 1935 with a degree in mathematics, but he wanted to be an artist. He took a chance and became an art historian, teacher, author, curator, and gallery founder as well as a member by election of the National Institute of Arts and Letters. He also received the National Medal of Arts. Photographs and reproductions enhance the text. Chronology, Further Reading, and Index.

287. Brown, Linda Beatrice. **Crossing over Jordan**. New York: Ballantine, 1995. 290p. $22; $11pa. ISBN 0-345-37857-1; 0-245-40231-6pa. YA

Story Temple, 96, recalls her life. Intertwined with it are four generations of African American women in her family, beginning in 1876. As a child, she used to dust the living room, which was only opened for company, and wonder about the faces in the family photograph album. As their stories come to light, the novel investigates the lingering damage of slavery, sexism, and racism. Story also reflects on her own life, controlled by a father who abused her and her mother.

288. Brown, Marion Marsh. **Sacagawea: Indian Interpreter to Lewis and Clark**. Chicago: Childrens Press, 1988. 119p. $17.27. ISBN 0-516-03262-3. (People of Distinction). 4 up

After being captured by an enemy tribe, the Hidatsas, Sacagawea (1786?-1812) had to leave her peaceful Shoshone home. She married a French fur trader who went with Lewis and Clark on their famous journey to survey the Louisiana Purchase. Sacagawea and their child accompanied him. She acted as translator for the expedition, which was a basis for its success. Time Line and Index.

289. Brown, Rita Mae. **Dolley: A Novel of Dolley Madison in Love and War**. New York: Bantam, 1994. 382p. $22.95; $6.50pa. ISBN 0-553-08890-4; 0-553-56949-Xpa. YA

In 1814, Dolley Madison, as First Lady, observes her Washington, D.C., world while her husband James copes with dissension among his cabinet members. Daniel Webster, who disapproves of the prominent political position of Virginia, supports the Federalists instead of Madison. Brown alternates narration with excerpts from Dolley's fictional diary to tell who Dolley is and what she thinks. Other chapters present a historical overview of the times, including the War of 1812.

290. Brown, Sanford. **Louis Armstrong: Swinging, Singing Satchmo**. New York: Franklin Watts, 1993. 124p. $22.10; $6.95pa. ISBN 0-531-13028-2; 0-531-15680-Xpa. (Impact Biography). YA

Louis Armstrong (1900-1971) helped create the uniquely American music called jazz that grew out of the Black experience in America, beginning in New Orleans. The text looks at the musical forms that make jazz, from African music to slave work songs to blues and ragtime. Armstrong's story shows America during the twentieth century, when he traveled across the country as a known star who had to suffer segregation. He also traveled around the world as an international figure and ambassador for the United States. Photographs augment the text. Glossary, Further Reading, and Index.

291. Brown, Stephen F. **Christianity**. New York: Facts on File, 1991. 128p. $17.95. ISBN 0-8160-2441-3. (World Religions). YA

The text includes a detailed overview of the origin of Christianity and follows with its history. It notes the branches and basic beliefs of Christian groups as well as their organizational structures. Rites and passages such as baptism, marriage, and confirmation help formulate the impact of Christianity and its place in the modern world as its most widespread religion. For Further Reading, Glossary, and Index.

292. Brown, Warren. **Robert E. Lee**. New York: Chelsea House, 1992. 111p. $18.95; $7.95pa. ISBN 1-55546814-4; 0-7910-0698-0pa. (World Leaders Past and Present). 5 up

Robert E. Lee (1807-1870), long recognized as the most important Confederate general in the Civil War, not only commanded the discipline of his army but also gained its love and respect. Bibliography and Index.

293. Bruchac, Joseph. **Children of the Longhouse**. New York: Dial Press, 1996. 150p. $14.99. ISBN 0-8037-1793-8. 5-8

When a small group of Mohawk adolescents decide to raid their peaceful neighbors, the Amen:taks, to gain glory as warriors, Ohkwa'ri, 11, tells the tribal council. Grabber, the leader of the group, wants revenge, and he plots when he can harm Ohkwa'ri. When the two boys find themselves on opposite sides during a game of Tekwaarathon (similar to lacrosse), Ohkwa'ri has to defend his life. Fortunately, family, including Ohkwa'ri's twin sister, Otsi:stia, and neighbors want to protect Ohkwa'ri, and they contrive ways to help him. The story includes information about Mohawk habits such as communal sleeping, name giving, government, family relationships, and the matrilineal hierarchy.

294. Bruns, Roger. **Abraham Lincoln**. New York: Chelsea House, 1986. 128p. $18.95; $7.95pa. ISBN 0-87754-597-9; 0-7910-0649-2pa. (World Leaders Past and Present). 5 up

Almost entirely self-educated, Abraham Lincoln (1809-1865) read for the law and became a lawyer in 1837. In 1856, he joined the Republican Party and ran for Congress against Stephen Douglas. Although he lost, he established himself as a campaigner of great integrity and intelligence. His skill as an orator and his humor got him the presidential nomination in 1860. He issued the Emancipation Proclamation in 1863, abolishing slavery and promising freedom to slaves in southern states. He confronted issues and tried to solve them. Photographs, engravings, and reproductions enhance the text. Chronology, Further Reading, and Index.

295. Bruns, Roger. **George Washington**. New York: Chelsea House, 1987. 116p. $18.95; $7.95pa. ISBN 0-87754-584-7; 0-7910-0668-9pa. (World Leaders Past and Present). 5 up

George Washington (1732-1799) valued his private life and tried to keep it that way. Trained as a surveyor, he became a military officer, a representative in Virginia's legislature, and a delegate to the nation's First Continental Congress. People saw him as a leader, and he had to become one even though he did not want the glory. He had administrative skill and sometimes an explosive temper. Engravings enhance the text. Chronology, Further Reading, and Index.

296.   Bruns, Roger. **John Wesley Powell: Explorer of the Grand Canyon**. New York: Enslow, 1997. 128p. $18.95. ISBN 0-89490-783-2. (Historical American Biographies). 6-9

John Wesley Powell (1834-1902) was the first explorer of the Grand Canyon. The biography looks at his impact on American history as it examines his life. Fact boxes and maps augment the text. Notes, Glossary, Further Reading, and Indexes.

297.   Bruns, Roger. **Thomas Jefferson**. New York: Chelsea House, 1986. 112p. $18.95; $7.95pa. ISBN 0-87754-583-9; 0-7910-0644-1pa. (World Leaders Past and Present). 5 up

Thomas Jefferson (1743-1826) wrote the Declaration of Independence for the colonies when he was only 33 years old, using language to make all men equal before the law. He then became, in succession, the minister to France, the Secretary of State, and the President. His ideas still inspire students of political science; his diplomacy is a guide to the modern statesperson; and his name is still linked to the concept of an ideal republic. Photographs and reproductions enhance the text. Chronology, Further Reading, and Index.

298.   Bryant, Jennifer Fisher. **Lucretia Mott: A Guiding Light**. Grand Rapids, MI: William B. Eerdman, 1995. 182p. $15; $8pa. ISBN 0-8028-5115-0; 0-8028-5098-7pa. (Women of Spirit). 7 up

Lucretia Mott (1793-1880) was a Quaker minister, abolitionist, and women's rights activist. In 1840, when she tried to attend an antislavery convention in England, the men would not let her enter the hall because of her sex. She and Elizabeth Cady Stanton organized the first U.S. women's rights convention at Seneca Falls, New York, in 1848. Further Reading and Index.

299.   Buechner, Frederick. **The Wizard's Tide: A Story**. 1990. New York: G. K. Hall, 1991. 104p. $19.95. ISBN 0-8161-5142-3. YA

Teddy, 11, has to face the loss of his pleasant home life during the Depression, when a subway train kills his father. Instead of visiting their father's wealthy New York family, he, his mother, and his sister go to live with his mother's family in Pittsburgh, where they have to learn to cope with their unexpected predicament.

300.   Bundles, A'Lelia, and Perry Bundles. **Madam C. J. Walker: Entrepreneur**. New York: Chelsea House, 1989. 112p. $18.95; $7.95pa. ISBN 1-55546-615-X; 0-7910-0251-9pa. (Black Americans of Achievement). 5 up

As the daughter of former slaves, Madam C. J. Walker (1867-1919) became America's first Black female millionaire. She was widowed at 20 and worked as a laundress for 20 years afterward. In 1905, she invented a hair care product for Black women and began to sell it door-to-door. When it became successful, she started her own company. With her money, she made contributions to Black schools, orphanages, and civil rights organizations. She campaigned for the rights of Black war veterans and for federal antilynching legislation while insisting that Blacks had to defend themselves. Photographs enhance the text. Chronology, Further Reading, and Index.

301.   Bunin, Sherry. **Dear Great American Writers School**. Boston: Houghton Mifflin, 1995. 176p. $14.95. ISBN 0-395-71645-4. 7-10

Bobby Lee (a girl), 14 in 1944, has taken several correspondence courses, but her latest is a writing course to help her make enough money to get out of Twin Branch, Kentucky. Bobby Lee's letters to the school and its replies that she owes $10 show her first love interest and her curiosity about other people's lives. She relates her surprise when an older girl gets a crush on the same boy that she likes; she watches her friend's mother who, in her depression, chooses to stay in bed; and she wants to know about a Jewish girl in town. She is naive but refreshing as she investigates her world.

302.   Bunkley, Anita. **Wild Embers**. New York: Dutton, 1995. 386p. $21.95. ISBN 0-525-93753-6. YA

During World War II, African American nurse Janelle Roy works in a prestigious private practice in Ohio, but when a wealthy woman in her care dies, she needs a lawyer. A white civil rights lawyer helps her, and she leaves for Tuskegee, Alabama, to get work where the Black fighter pilots are training. She meets a pilot with a secret he is reluctant to share, and her brother in the army kills a man. She again needs the lawyer, who is in love with her, and they save others who are unemployed as well as themselves.

303.   Buranelli, Vincent. **Thomas Alva Edison**. Englewood Cliffs, NJ: Silver Burdett, 1989. 133p. $13.98. ISBN 0-382-09522-7. (Pioneers in Change). 5-7

When asked when he planned to retire, Thomas Alva Edison (1847-1931) said "the day before the funeral." He did continue working, with more than 1,000 inventions to his credit, including the electric light, the phonograph, and the motion picture. The text looks at his life and work. Important Dates, Bibliography, and Index.

304.   Burby, Liza N. **The Pueblo Indians**. New York: Chelsea House, 1994. 79p. $14.95; $6.95pa. ISBN 0-7910-1669-2; 0-7910-2485-7pa. (Junior Library of American Indians). 3-7

The text presents the interaction of the Pueblo with Europeans as the Europeans came into the American Southwest. An essay on Pueblo architecture and photographs illustrate the text. Glossary and Index.

305.   Burchard, Peter. **Charlotte Forten: A Black Teacher in the Civil War**. New York: Crown, 1995. 106p. $16. ISBN 0-517-59242-8. 5-8

A child in a prominent Philadelphia family, Charlotte Forten (1837-1914) grew up as the United States was moving toward the Civil War. She saw the uproar surrounding the arrest of the fugitive slave Anthony Burns in Boston and the results of the war from South Carolina's Sea Islands, where she worked as a teacher and nurse. Her uncle's farm was a stop on the Underground Railroad; her grandfather had been a leading abolitionist; and her aunt had championed the rights of both women and Blacks. Charlotte was friendly with William Lloyd Garrison, John Greenleaf Whittier, and, later, Frederick Douglass when she moved to Washington, D.C. She also knew Harriet Tubman and Robert Gould Shaw, the commander of the first Black regiment. She showed that Black women could live full lives even in adversity. Bibliography and Index.

306.   Burgess, Alan. **The Longest Tunnel: The True Story of World War II's Great Escape**. New York: Grove Weidenfeld, 1990. 288p. $19.95. ISBN 1-55584-033-7. YA

In March 1944, 76 Allied prisoners of war crawled through a tunnel nicknamed "Harry" that they had dug underneath the prison at Sagan, Stalag Luft III. Only three survived after the Gestapo caught the others and murdered them without trial—acts against the Geneva Convention. By interviewing the three who survived and checking documents, Burgess reveals a stark saga of World War II. Index.

307.   Burke, Deirdre. **Food and Fasting**. New York: Thomson Learning, 1993. 32p. $13.95. ISBN 1-56847-034-7. (Comparing Religions). 4-8

Six major religions—Buddhism, Christianity, Hinduism, Judaism, Islam, and Sikhism—have rules about what some foods mean and which foods they may eat. The text looks at what they eat, how they eat it, what and when they cannot eat, what foods appear at religious festivals, and what foods (e.g., bread and wine) appear in places of worship. Photographs enhance the information. Glossary, Books to Read, and Index.

308.   Burke, Kathleen. **Louisa May Alcott**. New York: Chelsea House, 1988. 109p. $18.95. ISBN 1-55546-637-0. (American Women of Achievement). 5 up

Louisa May Alcott (1832-1888) created a new genre of fiction when she authored *Little Women*. She began writing early to help support her family, and she continued throughout her life. She also developed a commitment to helping all needy people and volunteered as a nurse during the Civil War. In later life, she became active in the women's suffrage movement. Photographs and reproductions enhance the text. Chronology, Further Reading, and Index.

309.   Burks, Brian. **Runs with Horses**. San Diego, CA: Harcourt Brace, 1995. 118p. $11; $5pa. ISBN 0-15-200264-2; 0-15-200994-9pa. 7 up

At 16 in 1886, Runs with Horses has been training to become a man in the eyes of his Chiricahua Apache tribe and looks forward to completing his last two raids. He has learned to travel great distances without water and to hunt. His father has taught him that when the people need food, he must kill his enemy and steal the food. But as a member of the last free band of Apaches still resisting the U.S. Army, he finds himself in limbo because Geronimo decides to surrender before Runs with Horses has finished making his raids. He becomes part of a greatly weakened group. Bibliography.

310.   Burks, Brian. **Soldier Boy**. San Diego, CA: Harcourt Brace, 1997. 160p. $12. ISBN 0-15-201219-2. 7-10

In the nineteenth century, Johnny "the Kid" McBane refuses to lose a fixed fight and has to leave Chicago. When he goes to an army recruiter's office, he does not know how old he is, being the son of a prostitute. When he joins the cavalry, he finds the questions even more difficult. He does not understand why he is killing other people.

311.   Burleigh, Robert. **A Man Named Thoreau**. Lloyd Bloom, illustrator. New York: Atheneum, 1985. 48p. $15. ISBN 0-689-31122-2. 3 up

As Burleigh describes Henry Thoreau's (1817-1862) response to the world when he lived at Walden Pond for two years after graduating from Harvard, he uses Thoreau's own words from his book, *Walden Pond*, rather than creating unnecessary dialogue. The accompanying illustrations are almost surreal in their attempt to capture the concept of the "oneness" with nature that Thoreau sought and tried to practice. Thoreau's attempt to keep life simple runs counter to contemporary practices. Important Dates and Bibliography.

312.   Burns, Khephra, and William Miles. **Black Stars in Orbit: NASA's African American Astronauts**. San Diego, CA: Gulliver, Harcourt Brace, 1995. 72p. $18.95; $8.95pa. ISBN 0-15-200432-7; 0-15-200276-6pa. 6 up

African Americans have been an important part of the Air Force since the inception of the Black Eagles, fighter pilots in World War II. Although others were accepted into the astronaut program, the first African American who ventured into space was Guion S. Bluford, Jr., in 1983. He was followed by others such as Ron McNair, Fred Gregory, and the first African American woman, Dr. Mae C. Jemison. These and others appear in the text with complementary photographs. Index. *Notable Children's Trade Books in the Field of Social Studies*.

313. Burns, Stewart. **Social Movements of the 1960s**. Boston: Twayne, 1990. 215p. $25.95; $15.95pa. ISBN 0-8057-9737-8; 0-8057-9738-6pa. YA

Facts and anecdotes enliven this well-documented look at the 1960s. Burns discusses the Black freedom movement in the Deep South (mid-1950s to 1960s) and comments about the Black Power movement that developed in the northern cities. He looks at the New Left student-led movement, the closely connected anti–Vietnam War sentiment, and the counterculture. He sees the feminist movement as originating in the Black and New Left groups before it reached its height in the mid-1970s. Thus, these social movements were important historical attempts to make profound social and personal changes. Notes and References, Selected Bibliography, and Index.

314. Busby, Margaret. **Daughters of Africa: An International Anthology of Words and Writing by Women of African Descent from Ancient Egypt to the Present**. New York: Random House, 1992. 1089p. $35. ISBN 0-679-41634-X. New York: Ballantine, 1994. 1089p. $19.95pa. ISBN 0-345-38268-4pa. YA

In this anthology appear the works of 200 Black women writing over four centuries from Africa, North America, the Caribbean, Latin America, Europe, and Asia. They have written in many genres including autobiography, memoirs, oral history, letters, diaries, short stories, novels (experimental, historical, science fiction), poetry, drama, humor, nonfiction (political, feminist, anthropological), journalism, speeches, essays, and folklore. This collection allows Black women to speak for themselves, and they all speak with different voices. Biographical Headnotes, Bibliography, Further Reading, and Index.

315. Butts, Ellen R., and Joyce R. Schwartz. **May Chinn: The Best Medicine**. Janet Hamlin, illustrator. New York: W. H. Freeman, 1995. 48p. $14.95; $4.95pa. ISBN 0-7167-6589-6; 0-7167-6590-Xpa. (Science Superstars). 4-8

May Chinn (1896-1980) was part African American, part Native American, and part Caucasian, although she called herself a "Negro." Even though her father believed she should marry, her mother wanted her to go to college and had secretly saved money from her jobs so that she could pay some of the tuition. Chinn loved music and played the piano beautifully, but she decided to change her major to science after successfully completing science courses. She played piano for Paul Robeson and was accepted into medical school based on an interview in which she talked about him with the interviewer. In 1926, she became the first African American woman to graduate from Bellevue Medical College. She developed a family clinic in Harlem and then began working at the Strang Clinics, trying to find out more about cancer. Index, Glossary, and Further Reading.

316. Byrd, Max. **Jefferson: A Novel**. New York: Bantam, 1993. 424p. $22.95; $5.99pa. ISBN 0-553-09470-X; 0-553-56867-1pa. YA

In 1784, Thomas Jefferson's young secretary in Paris tries to figure out his employer. Jefferson and his enigmatic ways baffle the man as he observes Jefferson dealing with the French, debating with his American colleagues, and becoming friends with married women. The secretary does his best to understand Jefferson, but all he can do is report what he sees.

C

317. Cain, Michael. **Louise Nevelson: Sculptor**. New York: Chelsea House, 1989. 109p. $18.95. ISBN 155546-671-0. (American Women of Achievement). 5 up

Louise Berliawsky Nevelson (1899-1988) immigrated with her Russian family to the United States. She married a wealthy man as soon as she graduated from high school, moved to New York, had a child, and nine years later divorced her husband. The rest of her life she devoted to her sculpture. Her "environments" define her style: scrap lumber assembled and painted black or huge steel sculptures. She also produced paintings, lithographs, and works in ceramics, Plexiglas, and aluminum. She refused to be categorized, and lived and created in the way she preferred. Photographs of her work enhance the text. Chronology, Further Reading, and Index.

318. Cain, Michael. **Mary Cassatt**. New York: Chelsea House, 1989. 112p. $18.95. ISBN 1-55546-647-8. (American Women of Achievement). 5 up

Mary Cassatt (1844-1926), an Impressionist painter, was one of her era's finest artists. She went to Europe in 1866, where she developed her bold brushwork and bright palette. Japanese prints inspired her, and she liked to paint portraits of mothers and children. Photographs and reproductions enhance the text. Chronology, Further Reading, and Index.

319. Calabro, Marian. **Zap! A Brief History of Television**. New York: Four Winds, 1992. 208p. $15.95. ISBN 0-02-716242-7. 7-12

The term *television* was in use by 1900 although the first experimental television station was not opened by NBC until 1930. Now one in every six people throughout the world owns a television set. The text looks at the history of television through its shows, programming, advertisers, public and cable stations, international connections, and detractors. It also suggests possibilities for the future of television. Appendices, Select Bibliography, Suggestions for Young Readers, and Index.

320. Calvert, Patricia. **Bigger**. New York: Atheneum, 1994. 144p. $14.95. ISBN 0-684-19685-9. 5-8

Tyler, 12, hears that his father has gone to Mexico after the end of the Civil War instead of returning to his Missouri family. With the help of his Uncle Matt, Tyler goes to look for him, and on the way, makes friends with a mistreated dog that Tyler names Bigger. After he finds his father, he realizes that his father is not what he expected. Tyler returns and Bigger dies, but Tyler begins to understand things that lessen the pain a little.

321. Calvert, Patricia. **The Hour of the Wolf**. New York: Scribner's, 1983. 147p. $12.95. ISBN 0-684-17961-X. 7 up

Jake's father sends him to Alaska after he attempts suicide. Jake has never lived up to his father's expectations and has difficulty coping with the life his father planned in Minnesota. In Alaska, he meets Danny, an Athabascan Indian, and becomes friends with him. Danny asks him to help in the Last Great Race, the Iditarod, a dogsled trek from Anchorage to Nome of more than 1,000 miles. After Danny accidentally dies, Jake succeeds in memory of his friend.

322. Calvert, Patricia. **The Snowbird**. 1980. New York: Atheneum, 1989. 160p. $16. ISBN 0-684-19120-2. 7 up

After her parents die in an arsonist's fire, Willie takes her brother from Tennessee to Dakota Territory to stay with an aunt and uncle. Failed crops and a baby's death incite her aunt to leave, and a beloved schoolteacher departs soon after. Feeling rejected, Willie surprises herself when she refuses to marry a Finnish immigrant because she understands that she, like her aunt, will not easily adjust to marriage and children. The loveliness of the silver filly that they name Snowbird symbolizes Willie's dreams.

323. Cameron, Eleanor. **The Court of the Stone Children**. 1973. Magnolia, MA: Peter Smith, 1983. 208p. $18.05. ISBN 0-8446-6757-9. New York: Puffin, 1992. $4.99pa. ISBN 0-14-034289-3pa. 4 up

Nina wants to become a museum curator because she finds solace in San Francisco's French Museum, a place where Chagall's painting *Time Is a River Without Banks* greets her. In this historical fantasy, Nina meets Dominique, a figure in an early-nineteenth-century painting. Dominique says that she dreamed about Nina as a girl and wants Nina to help her find out what happened to her father. Nina solves the puzzle by guessing about a painting and shows Dominique that her father was innocent of charges made against him by Napoleon's army. *American Book Award*.

324. Camp, Carole Ann. **American Astronomers: Searchers and Wonderers**. Springfield, NJ: Enslow, 1996. 104p. $17.95. ISBN 0-89490-631-3. (Collective Biographies). 6-9

The text profiles five men and five women who have contributed to the advancement of American astronomy. Included in the profiles are information about their lives, beginning with an exciting event and a brief overview of history to show why their particular contribution was important. Among those included are Maria Mitchell (1818-1889) and the late Carl Sagan. Notes and Index.

325. Campion, Nardi Reeder. **Mother Ann Lee: Morning Star of the Shakers**. Hanover, NH: University Press of New England, 1990. 180p. $13.95pa. ISBN 0-87451-527-0pa. 9 up

Ann Lee (1736-1784) founded one of the most successful communal living environments in the world with the Shaker community. She believed that she was the second coming of Christ; her followers believed that she was the Word of God made manifest. She preached in the streets (women were not allowed in the pulpit) and led evangelical services in Manchester, England (where people publicly confessed sin, spoke in tongues, and danced ecstatically) until she was put in jail. After marriage, she used her own name instead of her husband's in a time when women were merely a husband's property. Then she founded the United Society of Believers in Christ's Second Appearing—the Shakers. She took her group on a 59-day voyage to the colonies, and during the American Revolution she preached nonresistance. Few facts about her life remain, but she became a leader for many who wanted to escape from competition, materialism, sexism, and self-gratification. People spoke of her blue eyes and inner beauty, but no likeness remains of her. Bibliography and Index.

326. Canadeo, Anne. **Warren G. Harding: 29th President of the United States**. Ada, OK: Garrett Educational, 1990. 128p. $17.26. ISBN 0-944483-64-X. (Presidents of the United States). 5-8

Before he became President, Warren G. Harding (1865-1923) taught school, read law, worked in insurance and for a newspaper, and lost his first political race for county auditor. He won election to the Ohio state senate and then served as lieutenant governor of Ohio. After he became chairman of the Republican National Convention and a U.S. senator from Ohio, he won the nomination for the presidency after many ballots. In 1923, he died in office. After his death, scandals and convictions showed that some of his friends had been receiving bribes. Bibliography and Index.

327. Cannon, Bettie. **Begin the World Again**. New York: Scribner's, 1991. 181p. $13.95. ISBN 0-684-19292-6. 7-10

In 1979, Lake, 16, has grown up in various communes, and she likes the "family" at Barataria Farm although she would prefer privacy and a job. When Sundog, a happy transient, arrives, she becomes enamored of him, but he is both a thief and a liar. Then Lake's mother leaves to try a singing career. Baffled, Lake goes to live with her grandmother, a woman who has her own complex personality. Her wisdom guides Lake to understand herself and her mother better.

328. Cannon, Marian G. **Dwight David Eisenhower: War Hero and President**. New York: Franklin Watts, 1990. 160p. $22.10. ISBN 0-531-10915-1. (Impact Biography). 7 up

Interesting and informative background about decisions made during World War II make this book an introduction to military strategy with accompanying photographs and maps. Eisenhower (1890-1969) once said that at five years old, when he finally gained authority over the barnyard geese by brandishing a shortened broom handle, he learned that he should never "negotiate with an adversary except from a position of strength!" In this authentic biography, the reader finds that the family was very poor but that Eisenhower's mother taught her sons both Bible and music lessons to round out their education. Lack of money led Eisenhower to test for an appointment to a service academy, and he got into West Point, but his pacifist parents were distressed that he had joined the military. In his class was Omar Bradley. Early in his career, Eisenhower met George Patton and wrote articles on the role of tanks in combat that were considered radical in 1920. After the war, Eisenhower was so stunned with what he saw inside a concentration camp that he commanded reporters to tell about the horror so that humanity would never repeat it. He was briefly president of Columbia University but left to command NATO (North Atlantic Treaty Organization) and then ran for President of the United States in 1952. His term covered the beginnings of the Civil Rights movement, a visit with Khrushchev, the U-2 affair when the Soviets discovered that the Americans had been spying in order to prevent another world war, and other difficult events. Source Notes, Bibliography, and Index.

329. Capek, Michael. **Artistic Trickery: The Tradition of the Trompe L'Oeil Art**. Minneapolis, MN: Lerner, 1995. Unpaged. $21.50. ISBN 0-8225-2064-8. (Art Beyond Borders). 5 up

An enjoyable type of art is *trompe l'oeil*, paintings that confuse the eye so that the viewer sees a scene that doesn't really exist. *Trompe l'oeil* is not realism because realism tries to represent objects truthfully; *trompe l'oeil* is a visual game. The text looks at several contemporary artists who make *trompe l'oeil* paintings and the subjects that have intrigued these artists through the years. These themes include damaged goods, money and stamps, food, people, animals and bugs, slates and letter racks, doors, landscapes, and murals. The earliest illustration comes from 1475, and other illustrations cover each century since. Glossary and Index. *IRA Children's Choices*.

330. Capek, Michael. **Murals: Cave, Cathedral, to Street**. Minneapolis, MN: Lerner, 1996. 72p. $17.21. ISBN 0-8225-2065-6. (American Pastfinder). 5 up

The text looks at murals, huge drawings that decorate caves, walls, ceilings, and the sides of buildings. In an unusual order, the text looks at contemporary murals first and goes backward in history; the last chapter examines cave paintings. Among the topics are contemporary community murals, historical murals in the United States, Mexican murals, Italian Renaissance murals, early Christian murals, murals of ancient Rome and Egypt, and cave paintings. Glossary, For Further Reading, and Index.

331.   Carey, Jacqueline. **The Other Family**. New York: Random House, 1996. 207p. $22. ISBN 0-394-57639-X. YA

Joan, 14, and her brother stay with their depressed father after their mother leaves in 1966. Two years later, they go to see her in Manhattan. Their mother talks only about the success of her sister's family and how wonderful she, her husband, and her two daughters are. In a series of July 4th meetings over the next several years, Joan shows her mother how wrong she is when they find drugs, infidelity, and attempted suicide in her sister's family.

332.   Carlin, Richard. **Jazz**. New York: Facts on File, 1991. 142p. $17.95. ISBN 0-8160-2229-1. (World of Music). 7 up

The history of jazz since its beginning in the late nineteenth century and its cultural roots appear in this text. Carlin continues with New Orleans jazz; George Gershwin and the spread of jazz to all social classes; big band jazz; jazz piano in the 1930s and 1940s; singers; bebop musicians such as Charlie Parker, Dizzy Gillespie, and Thelonius Monk; jazz in transition during the 1960s; and jazz today, including the followers of Miles Davis. Glossary and Index.

333.   Carlin, Richard. **Rock and Roll: 1955-1970**. New York: Facts on File, 1988. 114p. $17.95. ISBN 0-8160-1383-7. 7 up

The text looks at the roots of rock and roll in American folk singing and jazz before exploring its earliest form, rhythm and blues. Some of the early solo performers were Chuck Berry, Little Richard, and Jerry Lee Lewis, with Elvis Presley soon afterward. Other subjects include teen idols, Motown and soul, the British invasion of the Beatles and the Rolling Stones, the American rock scene of the 1960s, and groups such as the Who and the Doors. A postscript discusses Woodstock. Glossary and Index.

334.   Carlson, Jeffrey D. **A Historical Album of Minnesota**. Brookfield, CT: Millbrook Press, 1994. 64p. $16.40; $6.95pa. ISBN 1-56294-006-6; 1-56294-757-5pa. (Historical Album). 4-8

The text presents the land of Minnesota before it became a state, beginning with Native American civilizations and continuing through exploration and settlement. Early statehood developments and issues and the role of large cities in the state's livelihood lead to the present day. Prints, maps, and photographs illustrate the text. Gazetteer: Quick Facts, Key Events, Personalities, and Index.

335.   Carlson, Judy. **Harriet Tubman: Call to Freedom**. New York: Fawcett, 1989. 118p. $4.99pa. ISBN 0-449-90376-1pa. (Great Lives). 5-9

This fictional biography begins with Harriet running for freedom around the age of 20. Then it returns to the beginning of Harriet's life and recounts most of the known facts about her life, although no notes indicate sources. One point on which Carlson elaborates is that Tubman was lonely in Philadelphia, and when she found out about the Philadelphia Vigilance Committee, she was probably very happy to have support when she returned to the South to free other slaves, including all of her family except a sister and her two children. Carlson says that slavery began in the early 1500s on the East Coast, with 15 million to 100 million slaves being transported from Africa. Other Books to Read.

336.   Carnegy, Vicky. **The 1980s**. New York: Facts on File, 1991. 64p. $18.95. ISBN 0-8160-2471-5. (Fashions of a Decade). 7 up

In the 1980s, fashion reflected politics, events, and international culture. The text looks at the fashion trends from ripped jeans, Lagerfeld, Lauren, Armani, and others, with accompanying illustrations. Pop stars and athletes influenced much of the buying. Glossary, Time Line, Reading List, Bibliography, and Index.

337.   Carnes, Jim. **Us and Them: A History of Intolerance in America**. Herbert Tauss, illustrator. New York: Oxford University Press, 1996. 132p. $22. ISBN 0-19-510378-5. 7 up

Prejudice has been a part of the history of America since the English came in the 1600s. The text looks at 14 incidents spread throughout the life of the country, including the banishment of Mary Dyer because she was a Quaker, the destruction of the African American town of Rosewood in Florida, and the drowning of a gay man in Maine. Further Reading and Index.

338.   Caroli, Betty Boyd. **Immigrants Who Returned Home**. New York: Chelsea House, 1990. 118p. $18.95. ISBN 0-87754-864-1. (Peoples of North America). 7-10

Caroli reviews the eight nationalities of immigrants who have come to America since the British arrived in the early 1600s and tells why many of them came but did not remain. The Irish began coming in the 1820s, but their numbers peaked during the potato famine in the 1840s and 1850s. Although the Swedes came in the 1630s to Delaware, they began arriving more rapidly during the 1840s. The Opium War from 1830 to 1842, when the English defeated the Chinese, and the Taiping Rebellion from 1851 to 1864 caused a great migration from China. Not until Perry entered Japan in 1853 did the Japanese begin to break out of their isolation and start traveling. By 1880, the persecution of Jews in Russia, with the Pale of Settlement and the pogroms, led to mass immigration. The Greeks had their peak year of immigration in 1907. The Italians who came in the late nineteenth century were generally from southern Italy, and many of them returned. In immigration, the family always seemed to suffer because of the enormous distance separating them, even with extra money sent or brought home. Color photographs enhance the text. Further Reading and Index.

339.   Cart, Michael. **My Father's Scar: A Novel**. New York: Simon & Schuster, 1996. 203p. $16. ISBN 0-689-80749-X. 8 up

Andy, a college freshman, grows up in the 1960s in a small town. His father, an alcoholic former football player, wears a scar as a badge of honor from his playing days and dislikes Andy's love of reading. Andy's Uncle Charles encourages him to find pleasure in his differences. What Andy realizes from his former experiences as he faces college life is that he is gay.

340.   Carter, Alden R. **The Colonial Wars: Clashes in the Wilderness**. New York: Franklin Watts, 1992. 63p. $12.40. ISBN 0-531-20079-5. (First Books). 4-8

With a general focus on the military and political strategies, the text gives the history of the Colonial Wars, also called the French and Indian Wars, which gave the British control of North America. These four wars were King William's War, 1689-1697; Queen Anne's War, 1702-1713; King George's War, 1744-1748; and the French and Indian War, 1755-1763. Bibliography and Index.

341.   Carter, Alden R. **The Mexican War: Manifest Destiny**. New York: Franklin Watts, 1992. 63p. $12.40. ISBN 0-531-20081-7. (First Books). 4-8

With a general focus on military and political strategies, the text gives the history of the Mexican War, which lasted from 1846 to 1848. It discusses events, personalities, and the aftermath of the war as well. Reproductions enhance the text. Bibliography and Index.

342.   Carter, Alden R. **The Spanish-American War: Imperial Ambitions**. New York: Franklin Watts, 1992. 64p. $12.40. ISBN 0-531-20078-7. (First Books). 4-8

The text tells of the 10-week war in 1898 between the United States and Spain over the liberation of Cuba. Theodore Roosevelt and his Rough Riders gained stature when the fight ended the Spanish colonial empire, and other countries recognized the United States as a world power. Bibliography and Index.

343.   Carter, Peter. **Borderlands**. New York: Farrar, Straus & Giroux, 1990. 424p. $17; $4.95pa. ISBN 0-374-30895-0; 0-374-40883-1pa. YA

In 1871, when Ben is 13, his mother dies. He and his 17-year-old brother join cattle herders on the Texas trail to Abilene, Kansas. Gamblers murder his brother after they arrive in Kansas, and someone else kills the murderer. Ben becomes involved in business and does well until the New York City financier underwriting his ventures goes bankrupt. Ben goes north to kill buffalo on the Plains, a job that he finds distasteful because it destroys the buffalo, but it supports him well. His relationships and situations reflect life in the Midwest during the early 1900s.

344.   Casey, Jane Clark. **Millard Fillmore: Thirteenth President of the United States**. Chicago: Childrens Press, 1988. 100p. $19.80. ISBN 0-516-01353-X. (Encyclopedia of Presidents). 4-9

Most people have forgotten Millard Fillmore (1800-1874), a self-made man who tried to leave public office four different times. He was devoted to the Union and hated the Republican Party. He was opposed to slavery, but because the Fugitive Slave Act passed while he was in office, those who opposed slavery began to hate him. He always tried to support what he believed in, but he also had to negotiate to get the best result for the weak and unprotected. Chronology of American History and Index.

345.   Casey, Jane Clark. **William H. Taft: Twenty-Seventh President of the United States**. Chicago: Childrens Press, 1989. 100p. $19.80. ISBN 0-516-01366-1. (Encyclopedia of Presidents). 4-9

As President, William Taft (1857-1930) was unlucky, but he followed his lonely stint in that office with teaching at Yale and a coveted position on the Supreme Court. His mother realized that he wanted to go on the Court rather than be President, but his wife and sons pushed him to the presidency. His last years were devoted to the Court. Chronology and Index.

346.   Castiglia, Julie. **Margaret Mead**. Englewood Cliffs, NJ: Silver Burdett, 1989. 137p. $13.95. ISBN 0-382-09525-1. (Pioneers in Change). 5-9

Margaret Mead (1901-1978), innovator, ethnologist, wife, mother, and friend, balanced her career with the other aspects of her life. Her grandmother taught her about the value of the past. Because her father set up extensions of a university, her family moved often, and the artifacts that she had from her grandmother were the few permanent fixtures in her life. Her parents, both highly educated, allowed her to come and go from school as she pleased, thinking that school was not the most important activity for her. Later, in college, she studied psychology, but she met Ruth Benedict and Franz Boas, anthropologists, who influenced her selection of anthropology as a career. The text continues with the important contributions she made to the way people perceive themselves in their societies. Important Dates, Bibliography, and Index.

347.   Catalano, Julie. **The Mexican Americans**. New York: Chelsea House, 1995. 102p. $19.95; $8.95pa. ISBN 0-7910-3359-7; 0-7910-3381-3pa. (The Immigrant Experience). 5 up

When Mexico ceded territory to the United States in 1848, nearly 75,000 Mexicans claimed citizenship. Immigrants have crossed the border since that time, taking jobs as farmhands, ranchers, railroaders, and miners. During the World Wars they moved north and to the Midwest where skilled jobs were available. Among the Mexicans best known for contributing to American life is Cesar Chavez, who gained rights for migrant workers. The text, with accompanying photographs, tells about their history and their contribution to American culture. Further Reading and Index.

348.   Caudill, Rebecca. **The Far-Off Land**. New York: Viking, 1964. 287p. $4.95. ISBN 0-670-30774-2. YA

In 1780, Ketty leaves Salem, North Carolina, with her brother for French Lick, Indiana. As a Moravian, she believes that all people are equal, including the Indians. As they travel down a river, she helps a sick Indian on shore. Her action most likely saves her group because Indians murder others traveling at the same time. She helps the children learn to read and write while refusing to burden anyone, including her sister-in-law, who sees her as merely another mouth to feed. She meets a young man whom she marries when they arrive, and they adopt a child orphaned on the journey. Her kindness to others shows that she is an asset rather than a liability.

349.   Caudill, Rebecca. **Tree of Freedom**. Dorothy Bayley, illustrator. 1949. New York: Viking, 1988. 284p. $17.50; $5.99pa. ISBN 0-8446-6401-4; 0-14-032908-0pa. 5-9

To escape taxes in the North Carolina colony in 1780, Stephanie Venable's father takes his family to Kentucky. Because he allows the children to bring only one of their favorite items, Stephanie takes an apple seed from a tree her great-grandmother transported from France. She plants the seed and names the resulting seedling "Tree of Freedom." Others try to take their land, and Stephanie's brother decides to become a lawyer in order to protect people like his father, who cannot read and write. He and Stephanie leave for Williamsburg to further their education. *Newbery Honor Book* and *New York Herald Tribune Award*.

350.   Cavan, Seamus. **Daniel Boone and the Opening of the Ohio Country**. New York: Chelsea House, 1990. 111p. $19.95. ISBN 0-7910-1309-X. (World Explorers). 5 up

The story of Daniel Boone (1734-1820) is the story of the settlement along the western frontier of the American colonies and later the states. His family always moved, and he continued the tradition by going to Kentucky after he fought with the British in the losing battle at Monongahela. He married Rebecca in 1756 when both were young. She and 10 children (later seven after Indians killed three) endured his long absences from home while exploring, until her death at 73. Boone earned and lost money enough times so that he lived both an extravagant life and a frugal one as he moved westward to St. Louis and then further west. Not until his mid-eighties did he begin to lose strength, and he died at 86. Paintings, drawings, photographs, and maps clarify the history of the times. Further Reading, Chronology, and Index.

351.   Cavan, Seamus. **The Irish-American Experience**. Brookfield, CT: Millbrook Press, 1993. 64p. $14.90. ISBN 1-56294-218-2. 5-7

The text presents the history of Ireland with an emphasis on the last two centuries, when the Irish suffered the potato famine, and many had to leave Ireland in order to survive. Among the topics included are the Irish at sea on the way to America, tenement life in America, and the way that men started to take leadership roles in politics. Photographs, Bibliography, Notes, and Index. *Child Study Association Children's Books of the Year*.

352.   Celsi, Teresa. **Ralph Nader: The Consumer Revolution**. Brookfield, CT: Millbrook Press, 1991. 101p. $15.90; $5.95pa. ISBN 1-56294-044-9;1-56294-834-2pa. 7 up

Ralph Nader upset the business world in 1965 when his book, *Unsafe at Any Speed*, told the American public that General Motors' Chevrolet Corvair was a dangerous car. He raised an individual voice against a corporation and won. As a lawyer, Nader has continued to police the market and to try to protect consumers against greedy corporations. Notes, Suggested Reading, and Index.

353.   Chadwick, Roxane. **Amelia Earhart: Aviation Pioneer**. Minneapolis, MN: Lerner, 1987. 56p. $15.95; $4.95pa. ISBN 0-8225-0484-7; 0-8225-9515-Xpa. (The Achievers). 4-9

Because Amelia Earhart (1897-1937) was the daughter of parents who allowed her to do things that girls normally did not do, she refused to be limited. Her childhood prepared her to become a female aviator capable of breaking records. For a woman, she flew the highest, the fastest, and the farthest. She crossed the Atlantic as the first female passenger and as the first woman solo pilot. She disappeared while she was trying to fly around the world at the equator. *Outstanding Science Trade Book*.

354. Chadwick, Roxane. **Anne Morrow Lindbergh: Pilot and Poet**. Minneapolis, MN: Lerner, 1987. 56p. $4.95pa. ISBN 0-8225-9516-8pa. 4-9

Anne Morrow Lindbergh (1906-) married Charles Lindbergh after he became the first pilot to fly nonstop across the Atlantic. A shy daughter of a wealthy family, she loved to write and excelled in English at Smith College. After she met Charles Lindbergh and flew for the first time, she read all that she could about aviation. They courted and even married in secret before the press began to follow them everywhere. She continued to write throughout their life together as she raised their family on two continents.

355. Chafe, William. **The Road to Equality: American Women Since 1962**. New York: Oxford University Press, 1994. 144p. $15. ISBN 0-19-508325-3. (The Young Oxford History of Women in the United States). 9 up

Since 1962, women have had a major change in their lives. The publication of Betty Friedan's *Feminine Mystique* caused a rebirth of feminism. The Equal Rights Amendment did not succeed, but it had much support. Those women who have influenced the times on both sides of the "women" question include Bella Abzug, Hillary Rodham Clinton, Rosa Parks, Phyllis Schlafly, and Shirley Chisholm. Chronology, Further Reading, and Index.

356. Chalberg, John. **Emma Goldman: American Individualist**. New York: HarperCollins, 1991. 196p. $15.95pa. ISBN 1-886746-36-2pa. (Library of American Biography). YA

Emma Goldman (1869-1940) left her parents as a young girl to immigrate to the United States and began a life in which she spoke against everything that she questioned. She criticized capitalism, weak reformists, marriage and family life, suffrage, temperance, sexuality, birth control, all types of totalitarianism, and all forms of democracy. Her anarchist views kept her from joining any group because she rarely agreed with their complete platforms. She suffered imprisonment for her beliefs but refused to stay quiet. Source Notes and Index.

357. Chan, Sucheng. **Asian Americans: An Interpretive History**. Boston: Twayne, 1991. 242p. $24.95; $12.95pa. ISBN 0-8057-8426-8; 0-8057-8426-8pa. (Immigrant Heritage of America). YA

Chan shows that Asian Americans faced discrimination even while they contributed to the growth of the United States by working and supporting themselves since their arrival in the 1840s. She then compares their experience to that of European immigrants. She believes that wars and foreign policy changes in the U.S. government have controlled the way people have responded to Asian Americans. The main detail covers Southeast Asians who have arrived since 1965. Chronology, Bibliography, and Index.

358. Chang, Ina. **A Separate Battle: Women and the Civil War**. New York: Lodestar, 1991. 103p. $15.95. ISBN 0-525-67365-2. (Young Readers' History of the Civil War). 5-8

Through primary source materials like letters and diaries, Chang shows the women who rolled bandages, nursed the injured, fought disguised as men, or tried to protect their homes. Some of the well-known figures she presents are Clara Barton, Harriet Tubman, and Belle Boyd. Maps, photographs, and reproductions complement the text. Bibliography and Index.

359. Charbonneau, Eileen. **Honor to the Hills**. New York: Tor, 1996. 192p. $18.95. ISBN 0-312-86094-3. 6-9

Lily, 16, granddaughter of Asher Woods from *The Ghosts of Stony Clove*, follows the family tradition of falling in love with society's outcasts. When Hugh Delaney arrives from Ireland with a letter of introduction to the family, Lily is immediately attracted. Hugh, however, does not know the local family politics or understand the racial tensions arising under the new Fugitive Slave Laws of 1850, and he becomes friends with a member of the prejudiced Chase family. Other carryovers from the two prior novels, as well as the attempt of Woods family members to help their Black neighbors, appear here.

360. Charleston, Gordon. **Peary Reaches the North Pole**. New York: Dillon Press, Macmillan, 1993. 32p. $13.95. ISBN 0-87518-535-5. (Great Twentieth Century Expeditions). 4-7

In 13 two-page discussions, the text describes Admiral Peary's attempts to reach the North Pole in the early twentieth century. Because his claim of reaching it first in 1909 has been disputed, the text discusses this aspect of his exploration. Maps and photographs enhance the text. Further Reading, Glossary, and Index.

361. Childers, Thomas. **Wings of Morning: The Story of the Last American Bomber Shot Down over Germany in World War II**. Boston: Addison-Wesley, 1995. 276p. $23; $12pa. ISBN 0-201-48310-6; 0-201-40722-1pa. YA

In World War II, Childers's uncle was one of the 10 (two survived) who never returned from the Black Cat, the last American bomber shot down in Germany. By using letters and interviews, including the German villagers who lived near the crash, he has investigated and found that ground flak may have led the bomber off course on what turned out to be an unnecessary mission. The two who survived may or may not have been tortured. One may have died because a parachute opened too close to the ground; another may have been trapped inside the plane. In addition to the story of the crash, information about the tension and interminable waiting between flights is also provided. Index. *American Library Association Best Books for Young Adults*.

362.   Chin, Steven A. **When Justice Failed: The Fred Korematsu Story**. David Tamura, illustrator. Austin, TX: Raintree/Steck-Vaughn, 1993. 105p. $15.49; $5.95pa. ISBN 0-8114-7236-1; 0-8114-8076-3pa. (Stories of America—Personal Challenge). 5-9

In 1967, Karen Korematsu listened to her friend give a report on World War II about a man who had challenged the U.S. government's decision to intern Americans of Japanese descent. What she heard was the story of her father, Fred Korematsu, who had decided that the edict was unfair. The American Civil Liberties Union represented Korematsu and took his case to the Supreme Court, where it failed. In 1982, it was discovered that at least two studies of Japanese Americans before the war had concluded that they were not a threat to U.S. security. Because this information was not initially revealed to the courts, a new review reversed the earlier decision. Afterword and Notes.

363.   Choi, Sook Nyul. **Gathering of Pearls**. Boston: Houghton Mifflin, 1994. 163p. $13.95. ISBN 0-395-67437-9. 7-12

Sookan leaves Seoul, Korea, for New York City, very concerned about her first year of school in a foreign country. She must simultaneously learn a new language and a new culture in the sequel to *Year of Impossible Goodbyes* and *Echoes of the White Giraffe*. Her sister's responses to her letters berate her changes from her old attitudes. Sookan feels guilty for her thoughts, but her college friend suggests that Sookan not let her sister run her life. But when Sookan receives news of her mother's death, she grieves and knows that she must continue her own strand of "pearls."

364.   Chrisman, Abbott. **David Farragut**. Francis Balistreri, illustrator. Austin, TX: Raintree/Steck-Vaughn, 1993. 32p. $13.98; $5.95pa. ISBN 0-8172-2904-3; 0-8114-6754-6pa. (Hispanic Stories). 4-7

Born in Tennessee in 1801 to a Spanish father and an American mother, David Farragut's father allowed him to be adopted after David's mother died. At 10, Farragut left to sail around Cape Horn, trying to capture British ships. At 12, he was made commander of one of the captured ships. He continued to sail, and in 1862 he took charge of a Union fleet in the Gulf of Mexico supposed to gain control of the Mississippi River. In his fight for Mobile (which he won), he yelled "Damn the torpedoes! Full speed ahead!" For his efforts, he became the first admiral in the U.S. Navy. He died in 1870. Glossary. English and Spanish text.

365.   Chu, Daniel, and Bill Shaw. **Going Home to Nicodemus: The Story of an African American Frontier Town and the Pioneers Who Settled It**. New York: Julian Messner, 1995. 96p. $14.95; $5.95pa. ISBN 0-671-88723-8; 0-671-88722-0pa. 5-9

In 1877, African American pioneers dug a community out of the Great Plains in Kansas called Nicodemus. But as the railroads bypassed it and the storms rushed through it, Nicodemus became less prosperous and lost population in the 1930s. Some people returned because they missed its charm, and the text gives the history of the settlers who lived there and those who left. Chronology, Bibliography, and Index. *Notable Children's Trade Books in the Field of Social Studies.*

366.   **Civilizations of the Americas**. Francis Balistreri, illustrator. Austin, TX: Raintree/Steck-Vaughn, 1992. 80p. $17.97. ISBN 0-8172-3306-7. (History of the World). 7 up

This overview uses informative illustrations and clear maps to complement the information about North America, Mesoamerica, and South America. Two-page discussions present North America's cultures of the West and Northwest coast, ancient peoples, Anasazi, Great Plains, Mississippi people, Arctic, and people of the Subarctic. In Mesoamerica appear the Teotihuacan, Toltecs, Aztecs, Olmecs, Zapotecs, Mixtecs, Maya and Chichén Itzá, and Veracruz. In South America, discussions concern the Andean civilization, Incas, Caribbean, Amazon basin, Brazil, Chaco, Pampa, Uruguay, Chile, Patagonia, and Tierra del Fuego. Glossary and Index.

367.   Claflin, Edward Beecher. **Sojourner Truth and the Struggle for Freedom**. Jada Rowland, illustrator. Hauppauge, NY: Barron's, 1989. 153p. $15. ISBN 0-8120-3919-X. 6 up

After being freed from slavery in 1827, Sojourner Truth (1797-1883) worked to help others find a better life. In her later years, people lined up to hear her speak. She had earned respect because of her years of traveling alone preaching freedom and equality. Glossary, References, and Index.

368.   Clapp, Patricia. **Constance: A Story of Early Plymouth**. 1968. Magnolia, MA: Peter Smith, 1993. 256p. $18. ISBN 0-8446-6647-5. New York: Beech Tree, Morrow, 1991. 256p. $4.95pa. ISBN 0-688-10976-4pa. 7 up

After she arrives in America on the *Mayflower* in 1620, Constance, 15, keeps a journal of her experiences. She tells of the 52 people who died soon after they arrived and of her friendship with Samoset's daughter cultivated through sign language. She knows Priscilla, who tries to get John Alden to ask her to marry him, and, like the others in the colony, is surprised when the Indian Massasoit comes to Thanksgiving dinner and brings 90 uninvited guests. She observes the difficulties that people have with each other and has to decide between the attentions of two men before she marries. The doubts she expresses in her diary are those that all young people share. *American Book Award Finalist.*

369. Clapp, Patricia. **I'm Deborah Sampson: A Soldier in the War of the Revolution**. New York: Morrow, 1977. 176p. $6.75. ISBN 0-688-71799-X. 7 up

In 1765, Deborah's penniless mother binds her to the Thomas family for eight years. At 60, Deborah recalls her experiences, beginning with her falling in love with the family son Robbie before he went to fight in the Revolution. After five years, when Deborah is 20, the British kill Robbie. Deborah enlists in his place, keeping her sex secret. She remembers the ways that she kept her secret from others, including pulling bullets from her thigh and shoulder with a knife. She remains successful until after the war ends.

370. Clapp, Patricia. **The Tamarack Tree: A Novel of the Siege of Vicksburg**. New York: Morrow, 1986. 224p. $15. ISBN 0-688-02852-7. New York: Viking, 1988. 256p. $3.99pa. ISBN 0-14-032406-2pa. 5-9

As a British girl living in Vicksburg, Mississippi, during the Civil War, Rosemary, 14, matures as the battles come closer and people starve during the siege of Vicksburg. That she likes people who own slaves when she hates the idea of owning another human surprises her, and that her brother is involved with the Underground Railroad relieves her. She helps during the difficult times but returns to England after the siege ends in 1863, where she waits for her Union soldier love while her brother attends medical school.

371. Clapp, Patricia. **Witches' Children**. 1982. Magnolia, MA: Peter Smith, 1992. $18.25. ISBN 0-8446-6572-X. New York: Penguin, 1987. $4.99pa. ISBN 0-14-032407-0pa. 5-9

In Salem, Massachusetts, during 1692, Mary Warren, a bound girl, visits friends freely and meets Tituba, slave to the Parris family, who reads Tarot cards and palms. Tituba refuses to tell Abigail, 11, what she sees in her future, because Abigail wants excitement of any kind. After several meetings of the 10 friends, they begin having visions and proclaiming that women in the town are trying to "possess" them like witches. Their accusations make them the center of attention, but they begin the destruction of lives perpetrated by trials in Salem and judgments of death on innocent people. As she reflects on the situation 15 years later, Mary regrets her role in this dastardly affair. *American Library Association Best Books for Young Adults* and *Jefferson Cup*.

372. Clare, John D. **First World War**. San Diego, CA: Gulliver, Harcourt Brace, 1995. 64p. $16.95. ISBN 0-15-200087-9. (Living History). 5-8

Both real and reenactment photographs augment the text, giving an overview of World War I from its beginning, when Archduke Ferdinand and his wife Sophie were murdered in Sarajevo on June 28, 1914, until its end, on November 11, 1918. The text establishes a sense of the war by discussing why men joined the armed forces, life in the trenches, the use of gas and tanks, the fight from the air and the sea, shortages that occurred, women in the war, and the Treaty of Versailles in 1919. A concluding essay explores the ways that people today benefit from knowing what happened during that time. Index. *Notable Children's Trade Books in the Field of Social Studies*.

373. Clark, Clara Gillow. **Nellie Bishop**. Honesdale, PA: Boyds Mills Press, 1996. 128p. $14.95. ISBN 1-56397-491-6. 7 up

On the day in 1886 that 13-year-old Nellie finishes common school in her Pennsylvania canal town, her mother dresses her in adult clothing and sends her to the local dance hall to find a husband. Her other three sisters met men that way, and her Irish mother had gotten the men to pay for the privilege of marrying her daughters. Nellie knows that whatever money she can get from marriage or a job will go for her parents' drinking and gambling. She also wants to save her brother from the canal gangs. When Jefferson Martin wins her from her father in a poker game, her situation begins to change.

374. Clark, Judith Freeman. **America's Gilded Age**. New York: Facts on File, 1992. 272p. $45. ISBN 0-8160-2246-1. (Eyewitness History). YA

Primary sources including memoirs, diaries, and official documents relate the history of the United States from the end of the Civil War to 1898. Arranged chronologically in segments of two years with accompanying illustrations, the text shows what people were experiencing during Reconstruction in both the North and the South. Each section begins with a chronology that keeps the events in their proper perspective. In the appendix are official documents such as the Civil Rights Act of 1866, Supreme Court decisions, and socioeconomic graphs. Bibliography and Index.

375. Claro, Nicole. **The Apache Indians**. New York: Chelsea House, 1992. 71p. $14.95; $6.95pa. ISBN 0-7910-1656-0; 0-7910-1946-2pa. (Junior Library of American Indians). 3-7

The text examines the history, culture, and future prospects of the Apache Indians, with illustrations complementing the text. Glossary, Chronology, and Index.

376. Claro, Nicole. **The Cherokee Indians**. New York: Chelsea House, 1992. 79p. $14.95; $6.95pa. ISBN 0-7910-1652-8; 0-7910-2030-4pa. (Junior Library of American Indians). 3-7

After beginning with the Cherokee legend of creation, the text gives the history of the Cherokees. The chapters cover their way of life, their exile during the Trail of Tears in 1838 when they were marched from southern states to Oklahoma, their artistic work, their life in the West, and their current concerns. Photographs and reproductions enhance the text. Glossary, Chronology, and Index.

377.   Cleary, Beverly. **A Girl from Yamhill: A Memoir**. New York: Morrow, 1988. 279p. $19.95. ISBN 0-688-07800-1. 7 up

Because her grandparents had pioneered to Oregon in 1843, Cleary was born there in 1916. She relates her experiences, mainly with best friends and teachers, as she grew up in a loving home. The only child, she and her parents experienced the tribulations of the Depression after moving from Yamhill to Portland. Because her family had no extra money, she was able to attend college only because her aunt invited her to California to live with her family while she attended a free junior college. Her departure on this venture ends the recounting of her early life.

378.   Cleary, Beverly. **My Own Two Feet**. New York: Morrow, 1995. 261p. $15. ISBN 0-688-14267-2. 7 up

In the second volume of her autobiography, Beverly Cleary tells of leaving home to attend college in California, where she worked in a student cooperative house, studied English and French, and met Clarence Cleary. After college, she became a librarian and came into contact with children from all economic and social levels. When children asked her where books were about youngsters who made scooters out of apple boxes, she began to write a "Henry" story. She submitted her first book to Morrow, and it was accepted with reservations and revisions. After both were removed, Cleary began her writing career.

379.   Cleaver, Vera, and Bill Cleaver. **Dust of the Earth**. New York: Lippincott, 1975. 160p. $13.95. ISBN 0-397-31650-X. 6-8

When Fern's mother inherits a house in South Dakota in the 1950s, the family moves there. Expecting much more than a house and a flock of sheep, they have to readjust their lives to their new environment. They learn that working as a group helps them become more productive than when they function as individuals.

380.   Clements, Gillian, author/illustrator. **An Illustrated History of the World: How We Got to Where We Are**. New York: Farrar, Straus & Giroux, 1992. 62p. $16. ISBN 0-374-33258-4. 6-8

In cartoons, Clements presents single and double-spread segments that cover the events in a period of world history, beginning with theories about the origin of the universe. She continues into the 1970s and ends with a timeline noting different epochs of history. Chronology.

381.   Cliff, Michelle. **Free Enterprise**. New York: Dutton, 1993. 213p. $19. ISBN 0-525-93704-8. New York: Plume, 1994. 213p. $9.95pa. ISBN 0-452-27222-3pa. YA

Two characters—Mary Ellen Pleasant, a real woman, and Annie Christmas, a fictional one from Jamaica—become friends and abolitionists. Narratives and letters tell about Pleasant supplying the $30,000 that John Brown needs to buy rifles for the raid at Harpers Ferry in 1859. When Brown fails, both Christmas and Pleasant flee. Pleasant goes to New England and then to San Francisco, where she opens a hotel and staffs it with runaway slaves, while Christmas hides in a Mississippi leper colony. Their courageous contributions to the abolitionist cause create an intriguing story.

382.   Clifford, Mary. **When the Great Canoes Came**. Joyce Haynes, illustrator. Gretna, LA: Pelican, 1993. 144p. $12.95. ISBN 0-88289-926-0. 4-7

The old members of the Pamunkey tribe tell the young ones about the arrival of the English settlers in Jamestown, Virginia. The promise of trinkets and English clothes lure the young members of the tribe to Jamestown before the queen can even finish telling the story. Lost Owl is angry at their defection, and he must learn to cope with it. But the tribe no longer has peace after the death of Pocahontas in England, because her father no longer seems particularly interested in tribal affairs. Bibliography.

383.   Climo, Shirley. **A Month of Seven Days**. New York: HarperCollins, 1987. 152p. $13.89. ISBN 0-690-04656-1. 5-7

Zoe, 12, stays with her younger brother and pregnant mother while her father serves in the Confederate army in Georgia during 1864. A Yankee captain and his men take over the house and demand services, including cooking. Zoe puts up with what she must, but she devises schemes to frighten the superstitious captain. Although the soldiers leave within a week, she learns that not all Yankees are despicable.

384.   Clinton, Susan. **Benjamin Harrison: Twenty-Third President of the United States**. Chicago: Childrens Press, 1989. 100p. $19.80. ISBN 0-516-01370-X. (Encyclopedia of Presidents). 4-9

Benjamin Harrison (1833-1901) fought in the Civil War against Confederates and Copperheads (Northern members of the American Democratic Party who opposed Abraham Lincoln and wanted to compromise with the South). When he became President, he helped change the Monroe Doctrine so that future territorial and trade expansion could occur. After he left the presidency, people still respected him, and he became a senior statesman. Photos, Reproductions, Chronology of American History, and Index.

385. Clinton, Susan. **Herbert Hoover: Thirty-First President of the United States**. Chicago: Childrens Press, 1988. 100p. $19.80. ISBN 0-516-41355-4. (Encyclopedia of Presidents). 4-9

Herbert Hoover (1874-1964), a mining engineer graduated from Stanford, had experience managing mining properties in Australia and China, and he became a millionaire by age 40. At the beginning of World War I in 1914, his responsibility was to organize and assist the return of thousands of Americans stranded in Europe. He became the President just before the Depression began, and his policies, although misrepresented, caused some people to vote for Franklin Roosevelt instead of him when he ran for a second term. Photographs, Chronology of American History, and Index.

386. Clinton, Susan. **James Madison: Fourth President of the United States**. Chicago: Childrens Press, 1986. 100p. $19.80. ISBN 0-516-01382-3. (Encyclopedia of Presidents). 4-9

As Father of the Constitution, James Madison (1751-1836) had a major influence on the structure of government in the new nation. Son of a Virginia planter, he was well educated and believed that people should have freedom of religion in a complete separation of church and state. He went to the Constitutional Convention, served as Secretary of State under Thomas Jefferson, and was President during the War of 1812. Chronology of American History and Index.

387. Cochrane, Patricia A. **Purely Rosie Pearl**. New York: Delacorte, 1996. 135p. $14.95. ISBN 0-385-32193-7. 4-7

Rosie, 12, and her family have steady jobs as migrant fruit pickers on the West Coast during 1936, while the rest of the country still fights the Depression. She looks forward to seeing old friends as the family makes the circuit, but she also meets a new girl whose well-educated family has had to join the migrant workers because no other jobs are available. A hiring boss makes advances toward Rosie, and her sister loses her first child when the hospital will not accept her without a cash payment. The strawberry farm owner admires Rosie's family's hard work, and he asks her father to replace the hiring boss. This change in fortunes makes the family's future look brighter.

388. Cocke, William. **A Historical Album of Virginia**. Brookfield, CT: Millbrook Press, 1994. 64p. $16.40; $6.95pa. ISBN 1-56294-596-3; 1-56294-856-3pa. (Historical Album). 4-8

The text presents the land of Virginia before it became a state, beginning with Native American civilizations and continuing through exploration and settlement. Early statehood developments and issues, and the role of large cities in the state's livelihood, lead to the present day. Prints, maps, and photographs illustrate the text. Gazetteer: Quick Facts, Key Events, Personalities, and Index.

389. Cocke, William. **A Historical Album of Washington**. Brookfield, CT: Millbrook Press, 1994. 64p. $16.40; $6.95pa. ISBN 1-56294-508-4; 1-56294-851-2pa. (Historical Album). 4-8

The text presents the land of Washington before it became a state, beginning with Native American civilizations and continuing through exploration and settlement. Early statehood developments and issues, and the role of large cities in the state's livelihood, lead to the present day. Prints, maps, and photographs illustrate the text. Gazetteer: Quick Facts, Key Events, Personalities, and Index.

390. Codye, Corinn. **Luis W. Alvarez**. Bob Masheris, illustrator. Austin, TX: Raintree/Steck-Vaughn, 1993. 32p. $13.98; $5.95pa. ISBN 0-8114-8467-X; 0-8114-6750-3pa. (Hispanic Stories). 4-7

Luis Alvarez (1911-1988) grew up in California, where he started his scientific career as a youngster by building a radio. He became especially interested in physics, and when the atom bomb fell on Hiroshima in 1945, he and a team of men flew around the area to measure its impact. Later, he and colleagues built a hydrogen bubble chamber in which they discovered many new atomic particles. His work won him the Nobel Prize in Physics in 1968. A new interest in his later life was geology. He and his son studied rocks and hypothesized that a meteor crashing into the Earth had destroyed the dinosaurs because they identified iridium that would not otherwise have been found in Earth's rocks. Glossary.

391. Codye, Corinn. **Vilma Martinez**. Susi Kilgore, illustrator. Austin, TX: Raintree/Steck-Vaughn, 1993. 32p. $13.98; $5.95pa. ISBN 0-8172-3382-2; 0-8114-6762-7pa. (Hispanic Stories). 4-7

Vilma Martinez (b. 1943) grew up speaking Spanish in her Texas home, and teachers always discouraged her from attending the best public high school and college. She disproved their theories by graduating from law school. During her career, she worked with the Mexican-American Legal Defense Fund (MALDEF) to gain voting rights for Mexican Americans and to demand that schools provide young students a bilingual education when they had only heard Spanish at home. Glossary.

392.   Coelho, Tony. **John Quincy Adams**. New York: Chelsea House, 1990. 112p. $18.95. ISBN 1-55546-802-0. (World Leaders Past and Present). 5 up

John Quincy Adams (1767-1848), son of John and Abigail Adams, witnessed the American Revolution and his father's involvement in the creation of the nation. He went with his father to Europe, where he was educated, and began his political career in 1794, when George Washington appointed him ambassador to the Netherlands. He served in a number of roles until he defeated Andrew Jackson for President in 1824. After his term ended, he served in the House of Representatives and tried to get the right of petition and a restriction on slavery in the West during his tenure. He was independent and a defender of democratic ideals. Reproductions enhance the text. Further Reading, Chronology, and Index.

393.   Cohen, Daniel. **The Life of Hubert Humphrey: Undefeated**. Minneapolis, MN: Lerner, 1978. 520p. $25. ISBN 0-8225-9953-8. YA

Hubert Humphrey (1911-1978), born in South Dakota, grew up during the Depression. He had to work and could not take time to attend college until he was 28. Although he lost political battles such as the vice presidential nomination in 1956, the presidential nomination in 1960, the presidential election to Nixon in 1968, and the Senate majority leadership in 1976, he was a warm human being whom people liked. Anecdotes about Humphrey and his friends and people he knew in politics show his real personality. Photographs, Notes, and Index.

394.   Cohen, Daniel. **The Alaska Purchase**. Brookfield, CT: Millbrook Press, 1996. 64p. $15.90. ISBN 1-56294-528-9. (Spotlight on American History). 4-8

In 1867, the United States bought from Russia the land that became the 49th state, Alaska. The text looks at the events from 1728 through 1864 that led to the completion of the purchase. Other topics cover the discovery of Alaska, the sea-otter trade, the land of Alaska under Russian rule, the American takeover of the land, and what happened to Alaska after its purchase. Primary sources help to tell Alaska's story along with photographs and reproductions. Chronology, Bibliography, Further Reading, and Index.

395.   Cohen, Daniel. **The Ghost of Elvis: And Other Celebrity Spirits**. New York: Putnam, 1994. 100p. $14.95. ISBN 0-399-22611-7. 3-7

The text entertains with selections about the various speculations that exist concerning the ghosts of Elvis, Edgar Allan Poe, and other celebrities.

396.   Cohen, Daniel. **The Ghosts of War**. New York: Putnam, 1990. 95p. $13.95. ISBN 0-399-22200-6. New York: Minstrel, 1993. 95p. $2.99pa. ISBN 0-671-74086-5pa. 5-8

Reports of ghosts near battlefields have occurred in all times. The text recounts samurai ghosts from 1180 to 1185, the angel of Mons in 1914, a Polish mercenary of the Revolutionary War, Steven Decatur's ghost after 1820 in Washington, D.C., and Lieutenant Muir in Canada in 1812. Other ghosts also appear in these 13 ghost tales, which Cohen says are "true" to the people who related them. Whether the stories can be verified is perhaps not as important as the concepts of realism and the history they impart.

397.   Cohen, Daniel. **Joseph McCarthy: The Misuse of Political Power**. Brookfield, CT: Millbrook Press, 1996. 128p. $16.90. ISBN 1-56294-917-9. 7 up

Joseph McCarthy (1908-1957) bullied and intimidated many powerful Americans after World War II. Cohen looks at his life and his tactics and how those around him in Congress disliked his approach but could not stop him until he attacked the U.S. Army. The analysis of McCarthy's life and his times gives insight into this bleak period of history.

398.   Cohen, Daniel. **Prophets of Doom**. Brookfield, CT: Millbrook Press, 1992. 144p. $15.90. ISBN 1-56294-068-6. 6-9

Taking a skeptical view that anyone can accurately predict the future, the text covers the Millerites, Jehovah's Witnesses, the Greek oracles, the Cumaean Sybil, Mother Shipton, the Bible, Nostradamus, and Edgar Cayce. By noting various prophecies and their failures, Cohen supports his thesis. Bibliography and Index.

399.   Cohen, Daniel. **Real Vampires**. New York: Cobblehill, Dutton, 1995. 114p. $13.99. ISBN 0-525-65189-6. 6-8

Among the vampires Cohen presents are vampires in various time periods throughout the world. He includes a German vampire from the early eighteenth century, Hungarian vampires in 1715 and 1725, Chinese and Russian vampires from varied centuries, and England since the twelfth century, including nineteenth-century vampires in Oxford and at Highgate. Selected Bibliography.

400.   Cohen, David, ed. **America: Then and Now**. New York: HarperCollins, 1992. 232p. $40. ISBN 0-06-250176-3. YA

The text compares scenes from the beginning of photography, approximately 150 years ago, to the present and gives a sense of the history spanning those years. A Civil War soldier is contrasted to the contemporary soldier, a man sits on top of a span of the Empire State Building while he helps construct it, and a Henry Ford assembly line in 1913 is compared to today. There are photographs of New York, Philadelphia, and Los Angeles before tall buildings made them unrecognizable. The photographs, as the author says, capture a moment in time that stays as long as the paper lasts. Selected Bibliography.

401.   Coil, Suzanne M. **Harriet Beecher Stowe**. New York: Franklin Watts, 1993. 173p. $22.10. ISBN 0-531-13006-1. 7 up

Distressed by the role of slavery in 1850, Harriet Beecher Stowe (1811-1896) began to write *Uncle Tom's Cabin* and published it in 1852. It outraged Southern readers and provoked the North to fight against slavery. The text looks at Stowe and the difficult times in which she lived. Notes, Bibliography, and Index.

402.   Coil, Suzanne M. **Robert Hutchings Goddard: Pioneer of Rocketry and Space Flight**. New York: Facts on File, 1991. 134p. $17.95. ISBN 0-8160-2591-6. (Makers of Modern Science). YA

Robert Goddard (1882-1945), often in ill health as a youngster, still worked on experiments and registered 214 patents. His vision of flying to different worlds led him to work on rockets and the possibility of jet engines after the Wright brothers made their first flight. Among his ideas that became realities were a rocket reaching the moon in 1912, multistage rockets in 1914, the basic idea of the bazooka in 1918, a rocket motor using liquid propellants from 1920 to 1925, a liquid-fuel rocket in 1926, a scientific payload (camera and barometer) in rocket flight in 1929, and a rocket that traveled faster than the speed of sound in 1935. Glossary, Further Reading, and Index.

403.   Coldsmith, Don. **Runestone**. New York: Bantam, 1995. 489p. $21.95; $5.99pa. ISBN 0-553-09643-5; 0-553-57280-6pa. YA

Because blond, blue-eyed Native Americans live in Oklahoma today, Coldsmith speculates who might have been their forefathers and mothers in this fictional work. The protagonist, Nils Thorsson, a Viking shipmaster, lands in Newfoundland, Canada, and begins exploring the continent. He and his friend have problems that they cannot solve without the help of Odin, a Native American. The two become assimilated into Odin's tribe and father offspring. Their exciting story may or may not answer the original question.

404.   Cole, Alison. **Perspective**. New York: Dorling Kindersley, 1992. 64p. $16.95. ISBN 1-56458-068-7. (Eyewitness Art). 12 up

In 27 minichapters, Cole gives a guide to the theory and techniques of perspective, from its beginnings in the Renaissance in the thirteenth century to pop art and its flatness in the twentieth. Chronology, Glossary, and Index.

405.   Cole, Jameson. **A Killing in Quail County**. New York: St. Martin's Press, 1996. 306p. $22.95. ISBN 0-312-13996-9. YA

In the 1950s, Mark, 15, looks forward to a lazy summer in Bob White, Oklahoma. Instead, his visiting female cousin, TJ, a tomboy, changes the pace. After a series of incidents, including a murder, Mark has to decide what he will reveal and to whom.

406.   Cole, Michael D. **John F. Kennedy: President of the New Frontier**. Springfield, NJ: Enslow, 1996. 128p. $17.95. ISBN 0-89490-693-3. (People to Know). 7-9

The text looks at the role that John F. Kennedy (1917-1963) played in giving the country hope. It looks at his childhood, participation in the war, political record, and the events of his administration, including the Bay of Pigs, the Berlin and Cuban Missile Crisis, the space race, and the Civil Rights Bill. It also notes that his family worked on creating the image of a Kennedy even though his own marriage was faulty. Chronology, Further Reading, Notes, and Index.

407.   Cole, Michael D. **John Glenn: Astronaut and Senator**. Springfield, NJ: Enslow, 1993. 104p. $17.95. ISBN 0-89490-413-2. (People to Know). 5-8

In February 1962, John Glenn (b. 1921) rocketed into space to become the first American to orbit the Earth in a space capsule. The text chronicles Glenn's family background, influences on his life, and his military career as a pilot and astronaut. He eventually became a U.S. senator from Ohio. Notes, Glossary, Further Reading, and Index.

408.   Cole, Norma. **The Final Tide**. New York: Macmillan, 1990. 153p. $14.95. ISBN 0-689-50510-8. 5 up

Geneva, 14, has to make her grandmother leave her rural Kentucky home in 1948 when the government decides to build a lake where the house sits. Geneva figures out how to coerce her grandmother into moving into town rather than die in the old home as she has promised she will.

409.   Collier, Christopher, and James Collier. **My Brother Sam Is Dead**. New York: Simon & Schuster, 1974. 224p. $16. ISBN 0-02-722980-7. New York: Scholastic, 1989. 240p. $3.99pa. ISBN 0-590-33694-0pa. 7 up

In a flashback, Timmy Meeker remembers the horrors of war, wondering if similar results could have been obtained without fighting. He recalls the year 1775, when his brother Sam left college to become a rebel in Captain Benedict Arnold's forces. Timmy saw the British kill a friend whose Tory family supported the British, and his father, also a Tory, died on a British prison ship. To keep soldiers from stealing cattle, Sam encouraged his mother to kill them and hide the beef in the snow. She delayed, and when Sam tried to save the cattle from thieves, the thieves are captured and blame him. Their commander refused to listen to evidence and executed Sam as an example for the other men that anyone who stole cattle would die. *Newbery Honor Book* and *Phoenix Honor Book*.

410.   Collier, Christopher, and James Collier. **The Winter Hero**. 1978. New York: Scholastic, 1985. 153p. $3.50pa. ISBN 0-590-42604-4pa. 9 up

After the Revolutionary War, increased taxes force people to borrow money for necessities. While Justin lives with his sister and her husband, the sheriff comes to claim their oxen in payment of a debt. A neighbor, Shay, suggests that Justin work for the man to pay off the debt while spying on the man and his friends to see what they know about a rebellion that Shay and others are planning. The debtors keep their accusers from entering court and obtaining judgments to confiscate property, but someone fires a gun. Justin's brother Peter is sentenced to hang but gains a reprieve at the last moment. Because Justin tries to save Peter, people think he is a hero. He knows, however, that he has done nothing heroic and that war is capricious. People did not win freedom in the Revolutionary War; they had to keep demanding further rights.

411.   Collier, James Lincoln. **Duke Ellington**. New York: Macmillan, 1991. 144p. $12.95. ISBN 0-02-722985-8. 5-9

Duke Ellington (1899-1974) often told his mother that he was going to be great. He did become one of the major figures in twentieth-century American music, with some people thinking that he was "America's most important composer." Ellington taught himself to play piano and compose music, ignoring many rules of composition to develop jazz. His self-respect and refusal to clown helped destroy the stereotypical image of the Black entertainer. The text presents his life and analyzes some of his major compositions. For Further Study and Index.

412.   Collier, James Lincoln. **The Jazz Kid**. New York: Henry Holt, 1994. 216p. $15.95. ISBN 0-8050-2821-8. 6-9

When Paulie Horvath is 12 in 1922, he hears two bands playing during a parade and decides he wants to play in one of them. His father is against music, wanting Paulie to follow him in the plumbing business. One day Paulie helps his father fix pipes in a jazz club, and when he hears a cornet solo, he knows that he must learn to play. He defies his parents to learn jazz and gets into trouble with organized crime, but his parents decide, in the end, to bargain with him. If he does well in school, they will support his decision to become a musician.

413.   Collier, James Lincoln. **Jazz, the American Theme Song**. New York: Oxford University Press, 1993. 326p. $25; $12.95pa. ISBN 0-19-507943-4; 0-19-509635-5pa. YA

Collier traces the history of jazz and its relationship to race and popular culture. He believes that Sidney Bechet and his soprano saxophone, rather than Louis Armstrong, turned jazz into a soloist's forum. He also looks at the evolution of jazz from a popular music to a type of music studied in university music departments. Index.

414.   Collier, James Lincoln. **Louis Armstrong: An American Success Story**. New York: Macmillan, 1985. 165p. $5.95pa. ISBN 0-02-042555-4pa. 5-9

Born in abject poverty in a New Orleans shack with no toilet or running water, Louis Armstrong (1900-1971) became one of the greatest jazz musicians who ever lived. As a youngster, he sang on street corners for pennies, and after reform school, he played cornet. By hanging around musicians when he was a teenager, he learned by watching, and they eventually asked him to join their jam sessions. From these experiences, his career blossomed until he became America's ambassador for peace. Index.

415.   Collier, James Lincoln. **My Crooked Family**. New York: Simon & Schuster, 1991. 181p. $15. ISBN 0-671-74224-8. 5-9

Roger, 13, and his little sister almost starve while their parents drink in 1910. When a man offers Roger a job, he decides that he prefers buying food to stealing it. However, he soon becomes involved in a robbery and finds that his father has also been a thief. When the gang asks him to join, Roger's mother begs him not to do it, but he indicates that he might.

416. Collier, James Lincoln, and Christopher Collier. **The Bloody Country**. New York: Four Winds, 1976. 192p. $13.95. ISBN 0-02-722960-2. New York: Scholastic, 1989. 180p. $3.25pa. ISBN 0-590-43126-9pa. 9 up

Indians scalp Ben's mother and brother-in-law, and the new government claims his father's mill. Ben cannot understand why his father still refuses to return to Connecticut from the Wyoming Valley of Pennsylvania in 1782. When Ben sees the freed slave Joe in the woods enjoying his new status, he begins to comprehend his father's need to stay and be free from working for others.

417. Collier, James Lincoln, and Christopher Collier. **The Clock**. Kelly Maddox, illustrator. New York: Delacorte, 1992. 162p. $15. ISBN 0-385-30037-9. 6-9

Annie, 15 in 1810, goes to work in a textile mill when her Connecticut family needs money. The overseer propositions her, and because she has heard that he is stealing from the mill owner, she rebuffs his advance and tells him that she will investigate him. The overseer in turn has her friend with a mangled foot climb on a frozen waterwheel to free it from the ice; he dies when it turns before he is prepared for movement. Annie's father sacrifices her desire to be a teacher for quick money.

418. Collier, James Lincoln, and Christopher Collier. **With Every Drop of Blood: A Novel of the Civil War**. New York: Delacorte, 1994. 233p. $15.95. ISBN 0-385-32028-0. 6-9

Johnny, 12, breaks his promise to his dying father by leaving his Virginia family to carry supplies to Rebel troops. An ex-slave, Cush, captures him. Johnny goes against his breeding and becomes friends with Cush, although Johnny takes advantage of the situation by teaching Cush to read incorrectly at first so that the Gettysburg address will reflect Confederate ideals. But when Rebels capture Cush, Johnny risks his life to find him. He rescues him just as Lee and Grant begin their talks at Appomattox.

419. Collins, David R. **Charles Lindbergh: Hero Pilot**. New York: Chelsea Juniors, 1991. 80p. $14.95. ISBN 0-7910-1417-7. (Discovery Biography). 3-7

Charles Lindbergh saw his first plane when he was eight years old. He decided then that he would fly. And he did. He became the first pilot to fly solo across the Atlantic Ocean between New York and Paris in 1927.

420. Collins, David R. **Farmworker's Friend: The Story of Cesar Chavez**. Minneapolis, MN: Carolrhoda, 1996. 80p. $14.96. ISBN 0-87614-982-4. (Trailblazers). 4-7

Cesar Chavez (1927-1993) was himself a migrant worker with other members of his family. When he saw the overwork and the underpay of migrant workers, he became an activist to make life better for the others. He helped to build a union for farmworkers and continued to fight for their rights throughout his life. Important Dates.

421. Collins, David R. **Gerald R. Ford: 38th President of the United States**. Ada, OK: Garrett Educational, 1990. 120p. $17.26. ISBN 0-944483-65-8. (Presidents of the United States). 5-9

Gerald Ford's (b. 1913) youth prepared him for some of the difficulties of being President of the United States after Richard Nixon resigned in 1974. Among the anecdotes included in the text is one about Ford's visit to North Carolina to see a football game at the invitation of a rear admiral. They flew into the airport, but the pilot discovered he was on the wrong runway, something he could not determine beforehand during a severe storm. He landed as quickly as possible and rushed everyone out of the plane. The plane exploded from the impact with the runway as soon as all had escaped. This event and Ford's experiences as a football player, a law student, and congressman shaped his approach to the presidency and his later life. Bibliography and Index.

422. Collins, David R. **Grover Cleveland: 22nd and 24th President of the United States**. Ada, OK: Garrett Educational, 1988. 119p. $17.26. ISBN 0-944483-01-1. (Presidents of the United States). 5-9

Grover Cleveland (1837-1908) served two separate and distinct terms as President. After his first term, Benjamin Harrison defeated him. Then he was reelected in the next election. During his presidency, he was honest to a fault but stubborn. He believed that public office was a "public trust," and he spent his life trying to fulfill that belief. He fought battles over the tariff system and suggested that Americans were too protectionist. He also helped to establish the gold standard. Bibliography and Index.

423. Collins, David R. **Harry S. Truman: People's President**. Paul Frame, illustrator. New York: Chelsea Juniors, 1991. 80p. $14.95. ISBN 0-7910-1421-5. (Discovery). 3-7

This biography of Harry S. Truman (1884-1972) begins with his childhood at eight, when his father crawled on the roof to get the children up to learn that Grover Cleveland, their candidate, had won the election. It continues with Truman's life and his rise to the presidency at the death of Franklin Delano Roosevelt.

424. Collins, David R. **Pioneer Plowmaker: The Story of John Deere**. Steve Michaels, illustrator. Minneapolis, MN: Carolrhoda, 1990. 63p. $9.95. ISBN 0-87614-424-5. (Creative Minds). 4-8

Not only is this a biography of John Deere, but it is also a history of the events and influences of the early 1800s. John Deere worked hard and produced one of the first self-scouring plows. Later, he refused to put his name on an implement that was not worthy of it. Customers could always be confident that his products were of the highest quality. Bibliography.

425. Collins, David R. **Shattered Dreams: The Story of Mary Todd Lincoln**. Greensboro, NC: Morgan Reynolds, 1994. 128p. $17.95. ISBN 1-884846-07-2. YA

This biography of Mary Todd Lincoln (1818-1882) begins with the trial toward the end of her life, in which her son requested that she be declared legally insane. She had continued to spend excessively and frivolously and had thought that people were following her. Robert felt that he had to protect her from herself, so he had to have her committed. Mary Todd Lincoln went from Kentucky as a girl to become the wife of Abraham Lincoln; the mother of sons, two of whom died before 20; and a maligned First Lady during the Civil War years. The text examines her life. Chronology, Bibliography, and Index.

426. Collins, David R. **William McKinley: 25th President of the United States**. Ada, OK: Garrett Educational, 1990. 120p. $17.26. ISBN 0-944483-55-0. (Presidents of the United States). 5-9

William McKinley (1843-1901) served in the Union army during the Civil War before he attended law school. The text begins with his assassination in Buffalo at a World's Fair gathering that his assistants had discouraged him from attending. There, a young man in the reception line uncovered a gun and shot him. McKinley died not from the shot but from the gangrene that set in after the operation to remove the bullet. About him Grover Cleveland said, "All our people loved their dead President. His kindly nature and lovable traits of character, his amiable consideration for all about him will long live. . . ." His assassin, Leon Czolgosz, was convicted in one day and was electrocuted one month later. McKinley's passion for others continued even as he lay dying, but he sometimes lacked strength of leadership during his presidency. Bibliography and Index.

427. Collins, David R. **Woodrow Wilson: 28th President of the United States**. Ada, OK: Garrett Educational, 1989. 120p. $17.26. ISBN 0-9444483-18-6. (Presidents of the United States). 5-9

Woodrow Wilson (1856-1924) was President for eight years. After World War I, he introduced the Fourteen Points for World Peace and worked tirelessly to establish the League of Nations, but senators in Congress voted against it. In 1920, his efforts won him the Nobel Peace Prize. At the time, he had the highest educational degrees of any man to be President and worked with people to try to get his ideas passed. He was a trained lawyer, a professor, a history scholar, and an orator. Bibliography and Index.

428. Collins, David R. **Zachary Taylor: 12th President of the United States**. Ada, OK: Garrett Educational, 1989. 121p. $17.26. ISBN 0-944483-27-8. (Presidents of the United States). 5-9

Zachary Taylor (1784-1850), nicknamed "Old Rough and Ready," never lost a battle. He became President because people hoped that a good general would still be as good a President as George Washington had been. Taylor, however, died after 16 months in office, so no one was ever sure. During his tenure, he could not offer a resolution of the slavery issue, but he owned slaves. The Galphin Claim scandal tainted his honor even though he had nothing to do with it. He did not choose subordinates well. Bibliography and Index.

429. Colman, Penny. **Rosie the Riveter: Women Working on the Home Front in World War II**. New York: Crown, 1995. 120p. $16. ISBN 0-517-59790-X. 5-9

Colman introduces World War II with the story of a woman who had saved for many years for a trip to Europe. She went in 1939 but had difficulty getting home. Although the child (now an adult) who overheard the story did not quite understand, she gathered that the woman's delayed return related to someone named Hitler and a war. Because men had to leave to fight the war, the importance of women and their work during World War II led to the nickname "Rosie the Riveter." Chapters include getting ready for the war and the opportunities for women, the concern during the war that led women to try all kinds of jobs, the final years of the war, and the loss of these jobs to the men when they returned from the war. What women did not lose was the knowledge that they could do well in the workplace. Photographs, Chronology, Bibliography, and Index. *Bulletin Blue Ribbon Book, American Library Association Notable Books for Children*, and *American Library Association Best Books for Young Adults*.

430. Colman, Penny. **Spies! Women in the Civil War**. Cincinnati, OH: Betterway, 1992. 96p. $6.95pa. ISBN 1-55870-267-9pa. 6-8

Many women took part in the Civil War, some of them serving as spies for the North and South. They include Belle "The Siren of the Shenandoah" Boyd, Elizabeth "Crazy Bet" Van Lew, and Harriet Tubman. Chronology, Further Reading, and Index.

431. Colman, Penny. **Strike: The Bitter Struggle of American Workers from Colonial Times to the Present**. Brookfield, CT: Millbrook Press, 1995. 80p. $16.90. ISBN 1-56294-459-2. 5-8

Worker struggles in the United States began before the colonies became states. When the Industrial Revolution started, the nature of work changed, but laws did not control the workplace. Children began working in factories instead of farms, and immigrants joined them. With poor working conditions, strikes offered the only chance of improvement. The text includes the strikes in 1677 by the carters; in 1768 by the tailors; in 1834 and 1859 by female factory workers in Lowell, Massachusetts; in 1867 by the Chinese railroad workers; the Great Uprising of 1877; Haymarket in 1885 for an eight-hour day; the Homestead strike in 1892; and the Pullman strike the following year. In the 1900s, the New York factory workers went on strike in 1910; in 1936, there was a General Motors strike; the migrant workers in California struck during the 1960s; and in 1973, the Harlan, Kentucky, coal miners went on strike. Important Dates, Find Out More, and Index.

432. Colman, Penny. **Toilets, Bathtubs, Sinks, and Sewers: A History of the Bathroom**. New York: Atheneum, 1994. 70p. $14.95. ISBN 0-689-31894-4. 5-8

The text looks at various civilizations, from ancient Mesopotamia through the Middle Ages and the Renaissance to contemporary America, and how they have solved waste removal, sanitation, and water management. Such sources as archaeological finds and letters have given insight into the methods of handling these plumbing problems. Bibliography and Index.

433. Colman, Penny. **A Woman Unafraid: The Achievements of Frances Perkins**. New York: Atheneum, 1993. 128p. $14.95. ISBN 0-689-31853-7. 5-8

Frances Perkins (1880-1965) was the first woman in the United States cabinet and the creator of important reforms and social legislation. She became involved in social causes, and after moving to Philadelphia, she worked to keep young women from being exploited. When she witnessed the Triangle Shirtwaist Company fire in Greenwich Village, where 146 workers lost their lives, she wanted to improve conditions for all workers. Franklin Roosevelt appointed her Secretary of Labor during the Great Depression. She helped establish safer working conditions, fairer wages, reasonable working hours, unemployment insurance, and Social Security. Chronology, Notes, Bibliography, and Index.

434. Colman, Penny. **Women in Society: United States of America**. New York: Marshall Cavendish, 1994. 128p. $21.95. ISBN 1-85435-560-0. (Women in Society). 7-12

After introducing the women of the United States through the story of the bravery of Harriet Tubman, a woman responsible for saving the lives of more than 300 slaves, the author discusses the roles of women in the United States by weaving together historical and contemporary practices. She presents the expectations imposed upon the rural and urban, the religious and secular, and the poor and wealthy. The chapters cover milestones, women in society, what being a woman means in the culture, and the life of a woman from birth to old age. Short biographies of Dorothea Lynde Dix (1802-1887); Mary Harris "Mother" Jones (1830?-1930); Madam C. J. Walker (1867-1919); Eleanor Roosevelt (1884-1962); Helen Keller (1880-1968); and Dolores Huerta, activist for migrant workers (b. 1930), show what women have done. Photographs complement the text. Women Firsts, Glossary, Further Reading, and Index.

435. Colver, Anne. **Abraham Lincoln: For the People**. New York: Chelsea Juniors, 1992. 80p. $14.95. ISBN 0-7910-01414-2. (Discovery Biography). 3-7

This biography of Abraham Lincoln (1809-1865) begins with the story of Lincoln as a boy falling off a log into a stream one Sunday and making his friend swear that he would not tell. Lincoln engineered falling off the log so that he could go swimming without breaking the Sabbath. His friend did not tell the story until after Lincoln's death. Lincoln's religious background and the things he read led him to become the President of the United States. The text ends with his funeral train going across the country back to Springfield. He was thoughtful and just.

436. Compton, Anita. **Marriage Customs**. New York: Thomson Learning, 1993. 32p. $13.95. ISBN 1-56847-033-9. (Comparing Religions). 4-8

Six major religions—Buddhism, Christianity, Hinduism, Judaism, Islam, and Sikhism—have specific ceremonies for marriage. Some have signed contracts and ways of affirming the promises connected to the marriage. In all, marriage has its basis in the family's life. Photographs enhance the information. Glossary, Books to Read, and Index.

437. Conley, Kevin. **Benjamin Banneker: Scientist and Mathematician**. New York: Chelsea House, 1989. 109p. $18.95. ISBN 1-55546-573-0. (Black Americans of Achievement). 5 up

Benjamin Banneker (1751-1806), a free Black man whose grandmother had been an indentured servant and his grandfather her slave, taught himself astronomy with the help of books and a telescope that George Ellicott, a Quaker, loaned to him. His talents in mathematics surfaced early. When he was 21, he decided to build a clock, although he had never seen one. His clock fascinated his Maryland community, and it kept correct time for his entire life. In 1792, he helped Ellicott survey the land on which the District of Columbia now stands, and he published his first almanac, with calculations from his study of the stars. His achievements earned him the title of America's first Black man of science. Chronology, Further Reading, and Index.

438. Conlon-McKenna, Marita. **Wildflower Girl**. New York: Holiday House, 1992. 173p. $14.95. ISBN 0-8234-0988-0. 5-7

In this sequel to *Under the Hawthorn Tree*, Peggy, the youngest in her family at 13, decides to leave Ireland and her siblings to go to America. After suffering through 40 days in steerage class on a ship crossing the Atlantic, she reaches Boston. She first works for an alcoholic who beats her. She finds another position with a wealthy family where the work is hard but fair. Her relationship with her fellow workers makes her feel as if she has some family around her again.

439. Connell, Kate. **Tales from the Underground Railroad**. Debbe Heller, illustrator. Austin, TX: Raintree/Steck-Vaughn, 1993. 68p. $14.95; $4.95pa. ISBN 0-8114-7223-X; 0-8114-8063-1pa. (Stories of America—Against All Odds). 4-7

The Underground Railroad was a major force in getting slaves away from cruel masters to freedom. It worked because many whites were willing to risk themselves for something they knew was right. They learned to be crafty and inventive with their methods of getting slaves or even free Blacks away from the unscrupulous slave owners. The stories of William Minnis, Harriet Eglin and Charlotte Giles, and William Still appear in this book. Epilogue.

440. Connell, Kate. **These Lands Are Ours: Tecumseh's Fight for the Old Northwest**. Jan Naimo Jones, illustrator. Austin, TX: Raintree/Steck-Vaughn, 1993. 96p. $15.49; $4.95pa. ISBN 0-8114-7227-2; 0-8114-8067-4pa. (Stories of America—Stand Up and Be Counted). 4-8

When white settlers and the U.S. government began to take Indian lands, one of the leaders who emerged to help his people was Tecumseh (1768-1813). He was a warrior and orator of the Shawnee tribe who united a confederacy of Indians to save the Indian lands. At the Battle of Tippecanoe in 1811, the Long Knives (government soldiers) under Governor William Henry Harrison defeated the Indians. Tecumseh was furious at the setback and blamed his brother for the defeat while he had been trying to talk to other tribes. With Tecumseh's death in 1813 while fighting for the British against Harrison, the Indians lost their organizer. Epilogue, Afterword, and Notes.

441. Connell, Kate. **They Shall Be Heard: Susan B. Anthony & Elizabeth Cady Stanton**. Barbara Kiwak, illustrator. Austin, TX: Raintree/Steck-Vaughn, 1993. 85p. $15.49; $4.95pa. ISBN 0-8114-7228-0; 0-8114-8068-2pa. (Stories of America—Stand Up and Be Counted). 4-8

Susan B. Anthony (1820-1906) and Elizabeth Cady Stanton (1815-1902) both worked ceaselessly for women's rights. These two women met in 1851 in Seneca Falls, New York, at an antislavery meeting; they were introduced by Amanda Bloomer. Because Stanton was older, Anthony always called her Mrs. Stanton, and Stanton called her Susan. Their dedication to equality for women laid the ground for the passage in 1920 of the constitutional amendment allowing women to vote. Unfortunately, neither woman lived to see the day, but without their work, it might not have existed. Epilogue, Afterword, and Notes.

442. Connikie, Yvonne. **The 1960s**. New York: Facts on File, 1991. 64p. $18.95. ISBN 0-8160-2470-7. (Fashions of a Decade). 7 up

In the 1960s, the youth culture became important, so a new generation of designers started to fulfill the expectations of this new clientele. More freedom in styles developed. Some of them were cocktail dresses and beehive hairdos, the Beatnik generation, the Beatles, Motown, mods and minis, the Space Age, an ethnic look, a psychedelic explosion, and flower power. Glossary, Reading List, Time Chart, and Index.

443. Conord, Bruce W. **Cesar Chavez: Union Leader**. New York: Chelsea House, 1992. 79p. $14.95. ISBN 0-7910-1739-7. (Junior World Biographies). 4-7

Cesar Chavez's life is tied to the history of the United Farm Workers, which he founded to help migrant workers gain rights in their jobs. Black-and-white photographs enhance the text. Further Reading, Glossary, and Index.

444. Conord, Bruce W. **John Lennon**. New York: Chelsea House, 1994. 127p. $18.95; $7.95pa. ISBN 0-7910-1739-7; 0-7910-1740-0pa. (Pop Culture Legends). 5 up

One of the Beatles, rock music's most famous group, John Lennon (1940-1980) was murdered outside of his New York apartment building. In addition to information about his life, the text includes a discography. Bibliography and Index.

445. Conrad, Pam. **My Daniel**. New York: HarperCollins, 1989. 137p. $13.95; $4.50pa. ISBN 0-06-021313-2; 0-06-440309-2pa. 5 up

Ellie's grandmother Julia tells her of being 12 around 1910 and finding dinosaur bones on their Nebraska farm with her brother Daniel. Their father had hoped for such luck because he needed the money that the bones would bring to save the farm. Ellie hears the story as they visit the Natural History Museum in New York, where the dinosaurs are on display. After Julia and Daniel made their find, lightning struck Daniel, and Julia's life changed. Looking at the bones in the museum momentarily brings him back to her. *Notable Children's Trade Books in the Field of Social Studies, American Library Association Best Books for Young Adults, Booklist Children's Editors Choices, IRA Teachers' Choices, Silver Spur Award for Best Juvenile Fiction, New York Public Library Children's Books*, and *New York Public Library Books for the Teen Age*.

446. Conrad, Pam. **Pedro's Journal: A Voyage with Christopher Columbus**. Peter Koeppen, illustrator. Honesdale, PA: Caroline House, 1991. 81p. $13.95. ISBN 1-878093-17-7. New York: Scholastic, 1992. 81p. $2.95pa. ISBN 0-590-46206-7pa. 3-7

Pedro accompanies Christopher Columbus on the *Santa Maria* in 1492 because he can read and write. He records the crew's frustration, Columbus's responses to events, their encounters with natives, and the fierceness of storms on their return to Spain.

447. Conrad, Pam. **Prairie Songs**. Darryl Zudeck, illustrator. New York: HarperCollins, 1985. 167p. $14.89; $4.50pa. ISBN 0-06-021337-X; 0-06-440206-1pa. 5 up

Louisa loves the books that the doctor and his wife bring with them to Nebraska, especially the one with Tennyson's poem, "The Eagle." The wife lets her enjoy the books, but after her newborn dies, the wife can no longer cope with the loneliness of the prairie. Louisa and her family continue to adjust while mourning the losses. *Boston Globe Award, Golden Kite Honor Book, Western Heritage Award, American Library Association Best Books for Young Adults, Booklist Best of the 80s, Judy Lopez Children's Book Award, New York Public Library Books for the Teen Age, Society of Midland Authors Award*, and *Golden Spur Award*.

448. Conrad, Pam. **Prairie Visions: The Life and Times of Solomon Butcher**. Solomon Butcher, photographer. New York: HarperCollins, 1991. 85p. $17; $9.95pa. ISBN 0-06-021373-6; 0-06-446135-1pa. 4-8

Solomon Butcher (1856-1927) wanted to capture the lives of the pioneers in Custer County, Nebraska, by recording their tales in writing and by capturing their images in photographs. He shows winds, locusts, outlaws, children, grand pianos in sod houses, Black homesteaders, and the vast sky. Photographs and text reveal his life and the scenes around him. Bibliography. *Notable Children's Trade Books in the Field of Social Studies, Orbis Pictus Award Honor Book*, and *New York Public Library Books for the Teen Age*.

449. Conway, Jill K., ed. **Written by Herself—Autobiographies of American Women: An Anthology**. 1992. New York: Vintage, 1996. 672p. $16pa. ISBN 0-679-73633-6pa. YA

In this collective autobiography are four categories for narratives of 25 women with major achievements, including Marian Anderson, Maya Angelou, Zora Neale Hurston, Margaret Bourke-White, Maxine Hong Kingston, Margaret Mead, Margaret Sanger, and Gloria Steinem. The categories are "My Story Ends with Freedom," for African American women; "Research Is a Passion with Me: Women Scientists and Physicians"; "Arts and Letters"; and "Pioneers and Reformers." The works show their hopes and dreams and their failures as well as their successes. Bibliography.

450. Coombs, Karen M. **Sarah on Her Own**. New York: Avon, 1996. 216p. $3.99pa. ISBN 0-380-78275-8pa. (American Dreams). 7-10

In 1620, Sarah Douglas hates having to sail from England to Virginia and decides that she will do whatever is necessary to return. She makes friends with Anne who has come on the voyage to find a husband. Anne succeeds, and Sarah actually enjoys the new country where she tutors the children and plants tobacco on her own land. But when Native Americans attack and kill people who live around the fort at Martin's Hundred, she decides that she will leave again. The novel recreates the difficult lives of these intrepid settlers.

451. Cooney, Caroline B. **Both Sides of Time**. New York: Delacorte, 1995. 210p. $10.95pa. ISBN 0-385-32174-0pa. 8-10

Annie Lockwood thinks that she is in the wrong century because her handsome boyfriend has no romantic ideas. She has the ability to be a century changer, and she goes to 1895, where young girls wear gowns and have maids to help them dress. She falls in love in that century, too, but not being able to fulfill her role causes pain for her and the woman who expects to marry the man whom she loves. Annie cannot accept the passive role of women in that century either and must leave it and the romance.

452. Cooney, Caroline B. **Out of Time**. New York: Delacorte, 1996. 210p. $10.95pa. ISBN 0-385-32226-7pa. 8-10

In *Both Sides of Time*, Annie makes the decision to leave the 1890s and her love for Strat to return to the present. When she goes on a school trip to New York City, she ends up in the 1890s again. Strat is in an insane asylum because he talked about her, and his sister knows that Annie is the only person who can rescue him. Strat's 1890s girlfriend is in a tuberculosis sanitarium. With difficulty, Annie retrieves Strat, but Harriett dies in his arms. Annie comes back to the present, but another sequel is promised.

453. Cooper, Michael L. **Bound for the Promised Land: The Great Black Migration**. New York: Lodestar, 1995. 86p. $15.99. ISBN 0-525-674476-4. 5-9

In the early twentieth century, the lure of industrial jobs and the distaste for Jim Crow laws in the South led many Blacks to migrate to the North. The text looks at the discrimination they faced, the new politics and social class, the building of Black communities in Harlem, Black-owned businesses, and cultural achievements. Not all Blacks approved migration; Booker T. Washington discouraged it. W. E. B. Du Bois openly opposed Marcus Garvey. This movement in the United States occurred against a backdrop of World War I and the Depression as well as immigration from Haiti. Photographs, Bibliography, Reading List, and Index. *Notable Children's Trade Books in the Field of Social Studies*.

454. Cooper, Michael L. **From Slave to Civil War Hero: The Life and Times of Robert Smalls**. New York: Lodestar, 1994. 73p. $13.99. ISBN 0-525-67489-6. 5-8

Robert Smalls (1839-1915) became the first slave to be a widely known hero during and after the Civil War. Smalls piloted the cotton steamer Planter past Confederate forts in Charleston harbor and joined the Union forces. After fighting for the Union, he became a spokesperson for the rights of the newly freed slaves. He served in the South Carolina legislature, and then he was elected to the U.S. Congress. His service was cut short when, after Reconstruction ended, others accused him of taking a bribe, and he was convicted. But no one is certain if he did or not. He still fought for the rights of those who had gained them with the Union victory. Glossary, Chronology, and Index.

455. Cooper, Michael L. **Hell Fighters: African American Soldiers in World War I**. New York: Lodestar, 1997. 67p. $16.99. ISBN 0-525-67534-5. 7 up

In 1916, the mostly Black Fifteenth New York Voluntary Infantry of the National Guard formed to fight in the Great War of 1914-1918. It served in France and returned to a triumphal parade in New York City. The men had difficulty securing supplies and uniforms, and only when General John J. Pershing requested that they fight under a French command were they renamed the 369th Regiment of the U.S. Army. They earned the nickname "Hell Fighters" from a Harlem newspaper. Their story helps to flesh out the contribution of Black men to the security of the country. Further Reading and Index.

456. Cooper, Michael L. **Playing America's Game: The Story of Negro League Baseball**. New York: Lodestar, 1993. 96p. $15.99. ISBN 0-525-674071-1. 5 up

By World War II, Negro League baseball rivaled major league baseball in popularity and ability to attract fans. The East-West All-Star Classic game that began in 1933 in Chicago was always a sellout, with such stars as Andrew "Rube" Foster, John Henry Lloyd, and James "Cool Papa" Bell playing in it. The main teams of the Kansas City Monarchs and the American Giants thrived until the major leagues started hiring minority baseball players. Photographs complement the text. Further Reading, Glossary, and Index.

457. Coote, Roger. **The First Voyage Around the World**. Tony Smith, illustrator. New York: Bookwright, Franklin Watts, 1990. 32p. $17. ISBN 0-531-18302-5. (Great Journeys). 4-7

Because Charles I of Spain wanted to capture some of the spice trade, he agreed to finance the Portuguese Magellan's attempt to sail west to the Spice Islands and the Philippines in 1519. Magellan faced a mutiny when he was at first unable to find a passage through South America, but he quelled it. Then he did find the opening, and he and his men eventually saw land and the Philippines in 1521. Upon his arrival, Magellan became the first man to sail around the world. His zeal to convert the islanders to Christianity did not thrill them, and they murdered him. Only 18 of the 277 men who had left Spain with him in 1519 returned with their bounty in 1522. Photographs of maps and appropriate paintings highlight the text. Glossary, Books to Read, and Index.

458. Corbin, William. **Me and the End of the World**. New York: Simon & Schuster, 1991. 222p. $15. ISBN 0-671-74223-X. 5-9

When Tim, 13, hears that the end of the world will arrive on May 1, 1928, he wants to complete four things just in case the news is true. He wants to fight a bully, to kiss a girl, to make amends to a neighbor for not defending him against a racial slur, and to hitch sled rides on a dangerous new route. As he sets out to accomplish his goals, he realizes at the end of the year that he no longer needs to risk danger in childish ways.

459. Corbishley, Mike. **Secret Cities**. Roger Walker, illustrator. New York: Lodestar, 1989. 47p. $14.95. ISBN 0-525-67275-3. (Time Detectives). 4-7

Covering a span of 8,000 years, the text speculates about the lives in cities that have been excavated or restored. The cities covered (with approximate dates) are Skara Brae in Scotland (3000 BC), Biskupin in Poland (750 BC), Jorvik in England (AD 800), Çatal Hüyük in Turkey (6500 BC), the Pyramid of Khufu in Egypt (2700 BC), Knossos in Greece (1500 BC), Pompeii and Herculaneum in Italy (AD 100), Mohenjo-Daro in China (AD 1400), Great Zimbabwe in Zimbabwe (AD 1400), Ch'in Shi-huang-ti in China (200 BC), Mesa Verde in the United States (AD 1200), Machu Picchu in Peru (AD 1400), and Williamsburg in the United States (AD 1800). Glossary and Index.

460. Corcoran, Barbara. **The Sky Is Falling**. New York: Atheneum, 1988. 185p. $13.95. ISBN 0-689-31388-8. 7-9

The family must go their separate ways in 1931 to cope with the effects of the Depression. Annah's father goes to Chicago to search for work after losing his job; her mother goes to Florida to live with her parents; and her brother has to drop out of college. Staying with her Aunt Edna in rural New Hampshire, Annah is an outsider who makes friends with another newcomer, Dodie. Annah discovers that Dodie's stepfather abuses her and that Dodie protects her blind brother from him and her alcoholic mother. Concerned for Dodie, Annah wants her to live with a former servant in Annah's house while Annah stays with her aunt, whom she has begun to understand much better.

461. Cordoba, Maria. **Pre-Columbian Peoples of North America**. Chicago: Childrens Press, 1994. 34p. $20. ISBN 0-516-08393-7. (The World Heritage). 4-7

Photographs clearly augment the text in this discussion of the people who lived in North America before Columbus arrived. The main sites presented in Canada are Bison Cliff, where bison jumped; Anthony Island, where the Haida Indians built totem poles; and L'Anse aux Meadows National Historic Park, which holds definitive proof that the Vikings settled in America before Columbus. Two sites in the United States are Mesa Verde National Park, home to the Anasazi nearly 700 years ago, and Cahokia Mounds Historic Site, where remains of mounds that denoted the Mississippian culture are found. Glossary and Index.

462. Cormier, Robert. **Other Bells for Us to Ring**. New York: Delacorte, 1990. 137p. $15. ISBN 0-385-30245-2. New York: Yearling, 1992. 137p. $3.99pa. ISBN 0-440-40717-6pa. 4-7

When Darcy is 11, she and her parents move to the Frenchtown section of Monument, Massachusetts. Her father enlists to fight in World War II, and he is reported missing. The Irish Catholic girl with whom Darcy has become friends introduces Darcy to a nun who helps Darcy understand her own fears and find her religious identity.

463. Cormier, Robert. **Tunes for Bears to Dance To**. New York: Delacorte, 1992. 101p. $15. ISBN 0-385-30818-3. New York: Laurel, 1994. 101p. $3.99pa. ISBN 0-440-21903-5pa. 5 up

Henry, 11, works for a grocer in the new place that he and his mother and father move to after World War II. His parents wanted to leave their old home so that they could forget the pain of his brother's accidental death the previous year. The grocer wants to damage a wood carving created by a Holocaust survivor, and Henry almost becomes an unwitting accomplice before he understands the grocer's motive for offering him a large reward if he will perform the deed.

464. Corrick, James A. **The Battle of Gettysburg**. San Diego, CA: Lucent, 1996. 111p. $26.59. ISBN 1-56006-451-X. (Battles of the Civil War). 6 up

The text looks at what both Confederates and the Union soldiers experienced in the summer of 1863 before the Battle of Gettysburg took place in July. It also explains why a battle in a small Pennsylvania town had such an influence on the war. A chronological day-by-day re-creation of the battle appears as well as sidebars with biographical profiles and practical information, such as a soldier's daily rations. Bibliography, Chronology, Further Reading, and Index.

465. Cory, Steven. **Pueblo Indian**. Richard Erickson, illustrator. Minneapolis, MN: Lerner, 1996. 48p. $14.96. ISBN 0-8225-2976-9. (American Pastfinder). 4-7

Not until 1888 did two cowboys rounding up cattle discover the stone houses and towers built along the side of a massive cliff in southwestern Colorado. They found skeletons, pots, an ax, and other things that people who were leaving in a hurry might have forgotten. They had discovered the cliff dwellings of the Anasazi in Mesa Verde that had not been inhabited for nearly 600 years. The text looks at the history of this culture, their world, how a pueblo would have been built, clothes, lifestyle, food, medicine, and other pieces of information that archaeologists have been able to fit together about the Anasazi. Index.

466.   Cosner, Shaaron. **The Underground Railroad**. New York: Franklin Watts, 1991. 128p. $19.70. ISBN 0-531-12505-X. (Venture). 6 up

The text gives a thorough background on the workings of the Underground Railroad since its beginning, when Quakers in 1794 encouraged one of George Washington's slaves to escape. A discussion of the economic and social reasons for slavery's long history accompanies capsule biographies of various agents of the railroad, including John Fairfield, John Brown, Laura Haviland, William McKeever, Frederick Douglass, and Harriet Tubman. Reproductions highlight the text. Glossary, Further Reading, and Index.

467.   Cosner, Shaaron. **War Nurses**. New York: Walker, 1988. 106p. $16.95. ISBN 0-8027-6826-1. 5-9

The text includes chapters on war nurses and their activities in the Civil War, the Crimean War, the Spanish-American War, World Wars I and II, the Korean War, and the Vietnam War. Letters and stories about the various personalities, among them Clara Barton and Florence Nightingale, show what the nurses had to face in their quest to help the wounded. Among the other topics included are a brief history of war weapons, the wounds from each, and the medical developments that evolved from these types of wounds. These nurses were clearly war veterans, a status for which nurses have had to petition. Index.

468.   Costantino, Maria. **The 1930s**. New York: Facts on File, 1992. 64p. $18.95. ISBN 0-8160-2466-9. (Fashions of a Decade). 7 up

Chapters in this book on fashion in the 1930s look at dancing in the Depression, Hollywood, art deco, new materials such as rayon, halter necks and bias cuts, Schiaparelli and the surrealists, health and fitness, and the sweaters and trousers that appeared in *Vogue* magazine toward the end of the decade. Glossary, Reading List, Time Chart, and Index.

469.   Cotton, Ralph W. **Powder River: A Jeston Nash Adventure**. New York: St. Martin's Press, 1995. 325p. $22.95; $5.50pa. ISBN 0-312-13146-1; 0-312-95593-6pa. YA

Jeston Nash and Jack Smith decide to steal horses and take them up Powder River, where they can sell them to the army. Their plan becomes more complex than they imagined when they have to outrun bounty hunters, steal the army's payroll, confront Chief Red Cloud of the Oglala Sioux, and have Indians kidnap them. While the army searches for them, they rescue two inebriated cowboys. These and other adventures fill the novel.

470.   Cotton, Ralph W. **While Angels Dance: The Life and Times of Jeston Nash**. New York: St. Martin's Press, 1994. 327p. $21.95. ISBN 0-312-11098-7. YA

Jeston Nash kills a Yankee soldier and goes to Missouri, where he joins his cousins, Frank and Jesse James. He rides with them during the Civil War and later with the James-Younger gang. Eventually he and his friend Quiet Jack Smith find themselves unexpectedly saved from a life of crime. Jeston made promises to his love Jeanine that he would not kill the man who killed his daughter, and because someone else does it for him, he can remain true to his word.

471.   Cousins, Margaret. **Ben Franklin of Old Philadelphia**. 1952. New York: Random House, 1981. 153p. $4.95pa. ISBN 0-394-84928-0pa. (Landmark). 7-9

The titles of the chapters in this biography of Benjamin Franklin (1706-1790) give an overview of his life. They are "Water Baby," "Schoolboy," "Apprentice," "Runaway," "Printer," "Good Citizen," "Inventor," "Statesman," "Patriot," "Ambassador," "Friend," and "American." Although the first topics are in chronological order, the text emphasizes that Franklin's most important activity was making friends. He loved company and talking and always tried to surround himself with children when his own were somewhere else or after they were grown. A list of the important contributions he made as an American show the value of his life to the history of the country. Index.

472.   Cox, Clinton. **The Forgotten Heroes: The Story of the Buffalo Soldiers**. New York: Scholastic, 1993. 180p. $14.95. ISBN 0-590-45121-9. 7-12

After the Civil War, Black cavalrymen went west when the government recruited them to protect settlers, carry the mail, and fight against Native Americans led by men like Geronimo. These African Americans enlisted because they had few choices after the war, and they wanted their freedom. Ironically, however, their goal was to take freedom from another group, the Native Americans. Cox uses personal accounts to tell an important piece of American history. Bibliography and Index.

473.   Cox, Clinton. **Undying Glory**. New York: Scholastic, 1991. 167p. $14.95. ISBN 0-590-44170-1. 7-12

In 1863, the all-Black Massachusetts Fifty-fourth Regiment was formed to fight in the Civil War. The text looks at the story of these men through primary and secondary sources, including commentary by such people as Clara Barton, Charlotte Forten, Frederick Douglass, and Abraham Lincoln. These soldiers from 22 states fought for less pay than their white peers, faced severe prejudice, and often were not allowed to fight in battles. They also had terrible fears of becoming prisoners of war in the South. Bibliography and Index.

474. Cox, Vic. **The Challenge of Immigration**. Springfield, NJ: Enslow, 1995. 128p. $17.95. ISBN 0-89490-628-3. (Multicultural Issues). 9 up

Immigration has been an issue throughout the history of the American colonies and the United States. The text gives a brief history of immigration and then discusses the concerns that accompany the decision to allow immigrants into the country, including laws, jobs, social services, assimilation, education, and crime. Glossary, Further Reading, and Index.

475. Coyle, Harold. **Look Away: A Novel**. New York: Simon & Schuster, 1996. 495p. $24. ISBN 0-684-80392-5. New York: Pocket Books, 1996. 495p. $6.99pa. ISBN 0-671-52819-Xpa. YA

The tyrannical New Jersey businessman father of brothers James and Kevin Bannon uses the excuse of the death of a girl they both love to send them off to different boarding schools. James goes to Virginia Military Academy, and Kevin goes to a Northern college. During the Civil War, they find themselves reunited at Gettysburg on different sides of the confrontation. Their story mirrors that of so many who endured this time in American history.

476. Cozic, Charles, ed. **Civil Liberties: Opposing Viewpoints**. San Diego, CA: Greenhaven, 1994. 240p. $19.95. ISBN 1-56510-057-3. (Opposing Viewpoints). 7 up

One of the major topics of discussion in the United States is how much privacy an individual should have. Some advocate extensive privacy, some limited. In short essays both pro and con written by public figures, the text examines different viewpoints toward various historical and contemporary positions on aspects of civil liberty. Privacy relates to abortion, to rape victim identity, and to monitoring an employee's activities. For freedom of expression, the concerns cover hate speech, pornography, and government subsidy for art that some people consider offensive. The role of the government in protecting the expression of religious beliefs and whether the church and state should be separate raise other issues. A final concern is the legal protection given to children, homosexuals, and minorities. For Further Discussion, Organizations to Contact, Bibliography of Books, and Index.

477. Cozic, Charles P. **Israel: Opposing Viewpoints**. San Diego, CA: Greenhaven, 1994. 288p. $19.95; $14.44pa. ISBN 1-56510-133-2; 1-56510-132-4pa. (Opposing Viewpoints). 7-12

The text looks at the questions that people have asked about the Palestinians and the Jewish state of Israel through the years since the British sanctioned the country of Israel in 1945. The focus covers both sides of six questions. Topics question whether Jews need a homeland, whether Israel needs Zionism, the prospects for Arab-Israeli peace, Palestinian rights violations, Israel giving up some of its land for peace, and U.S. support of Israel. Editorial commentary gives background for essays so that they can be seen in their original context. Such personages as the Zionist founder Theodore Herzl and Sami Hadawi, the Palestinian scholar, speak within the pages of the text. Bibliography, Chronology, and Index.

478. Cray, Ed, and Jonathan Kotler **American Datelines**. New York: Facts on File, 1990. 382p. $27.95. ISBN 8160-2033-7. YA

The text gives direct reports from newspapers for dates throughout the history of America. The various views show exactly what people were reading on the afternoon of or the morning after an event occurred. It begins in 1704 with reporting of pirates off the coast of Rhode Island and ends with the *Valdez* oil spill in Alaska in 1989. Other topics covered are the events leading to and through the American Revolution, the Alamo, the westward movement, the Civil War, the Haymarket Riot, book banning in Boston, Kitty Hawk and the Wright brothers, World Wars I and II, the Korean War, the Vietnam War, and Nixon's resignation. The present tense news reports give a sense of being in the times. Index.

479. Crew, Linda. **Fire on the Wind**. New York: Delacorte, 1995. 198p. $14.95. ISBN 0-385-32185-6. 6-9

In August 1933, Storie, 13, worries about the smoke that she smells; she is also concerned for her father and the young logger Flynn, who have left the Blue Star logging camp to fight fires in other areas of Oregon. Storie gives a sense of the everyday lives of those who lived in the camp, especially the women who wait endlessly.

480. Crofford, Emily. **A Place to Belong**. Minneapolis, MN: Carolrhoda, 1994. 152p. $14.95. ISBN 0-87614-808-9. 5-7

Talmadge, a seventh grader, has to move with his family from Tennessee to Mississippi and then to Arkansas in 1935, where his father hopes to find work during the Depression. With a club foot, Talmadge has always been an outsider, but he has reached a higher level of education than either of his parents. He plans to continue, but both his mother and brother think that he leaves the work to them, while his sisters and father support him. When the youngest child contracts polio, they are quarantined and later leave for Memphis and the hope of a better economic situation.

481. Cross, Gillian. **The Great American Elephant Chase**. New York: Holiday House, 1993. 193p. $14.95. ISBN 0-8234-1016-1. 5-8

Tad, an orphan of 15 in the nineteenth century, has his life change when he hides in a rail car cage, and the train leaves the station before he emerges. His companion in the car is an elephant. He travels with Khush and his mistress Cissie after the death of her father up the Mississippi, on the Ohio, and across the prairie. They are trying to escape people who claim to be Khush's new owners. When someone tries to steal the elephant, it will not leave Tad. They continue their travels west to Nebraska, where Cissie hopes to find sanctuary.

482. Cross, Robin. **Children and War**. New York: Thomson Learning, 1994. 48p. $14.95. ISBN 1-56847-180-7. (World War II). 5-7

By using the experiences of young people during the war, Cross presents a view of World War II. His subjects include a Polish boy imprisoned by Soviet police, a French girl who fought the Resistance, a messenger boy in Britain during bombing attacks, a child from Hiroshima, and an American who had no direct contact except through newsreels. Further Reading, Glossary, and Index.

483. Cross, Robin. **Roosevelt and the Americans at War**. New York: Gloucester, Franklin Watts, 1990. 62p. $11.90. ISBN 0-531-17254-6. (World War II Biographies). 4-8

This text presents an overview of the life of Franklin Delano Roosevelt (1882-1945) and a closer look at his military leadership during World War II before his death. Colored maps of the campaigns and historical photographs complement the text. Bibliography, Chronology, Glossary, and Index.

484. Cross, Robin. **Technology of War**. New York: Thomson Learning, 1994. 48p. $14.95. ISBN 1-56847-177-7. (World War II). 5-7

Many weapons used in World War II had been introduced in World War I, with the submarine almost winning both wars for Germany. Between 1918 and 1939, radio communications improved, and the civil aviation industry expanded. Cathode ray tubes appeared, vital for radar screens, and research into the nature of the atom progressed. In 1936-1939, the Soviet Union, Germany, and Japan tested their new weapons, fighter planes, dive bombers, and tanks. The ultimate weapon became the atom bomb that the Americans developed. Glossary, Books to Read, Chronology, and Index.

485. Crowley, Monica. **Nixon Off the Record**. New York: Random House, 1996. 231p. $23. ISBN 0-679-45681-3. YA

Crowley worked for former President Nixon during the years 1990-1994. The man she saw in her personal contact was vastly different from the man known to history. She tells an unexpected story in this text. Index.

486. Cullen-DuPont, Kathryn. **Elizabeth Cady Stanton and Women's Liberty**. New York: Facts on File, 1992. 133p. $16.95. ISBN 0-8160-2413-8. (Makers of America). 6-12

The text uses excerpts from Elizabeth Cady Stanton's (1815-1902) writings and letters that reveal a woman who wanted equality for all. Further Reading and Index.

487. Cummings, Jack. **The Indian Fighter's Return**. New York: Walker, 1993. 177p. $19.95. ISBN 0-8027-1268-1. YA

In Owyhee County, Idaho, in 1892, Jon Seaver loses the election for sheriff because Ella Gordon, an activist, campaigns against him and the government's treatment of Indians. An Indian soon abducts her, and the sheriff asks Seaver to save her. Among the ensuing difficulties are militant Indians and the arrival of bank robbers with a bounty hunter on their trail. The two protagonists have to flee, but they have to undergo a series of near-captures and escapes before they get to like each other.

488. Cuneo, Mary Louise. **Anne Is Elegant**. New York: HarperCollins, 1993. 167p. $14.89. ISBN 0-06-022993-4. 5-8

Anna, 12, suffers during 1935 in Chicago over the death of her infant brother. Her father buries his grief in work, and her mother keeps reminding her of painful memories. Her Aunt Maria and her budding love for a boy at school help her to heal, but not until the death of a relative at Christmas does everyone understand what the others have been thinking.

489. Currie, Stephen. **Music in the Civil War**. Cincinnati, OH: Betterway, 1992. 111p. $8.95. ISBN 1-55870-263-6. 5 up

Music reflected the responses of all people to their political passions, whether from the North or South. This history presents the music used to rally the troops during the Civil War and to keep them fighting, and that sung at home. In addition to actual scores are biographies of some of the better-known composers of the time, such as Julia Ward Howe, who wrote "The Battle Hymn of the Republic," and Patrick Gilmore, composer of "When Johnny Comes Marching Home." Bibliography and Index.

490. Curry, Jane Louise. **Moon Window**. New York: Margaret K. McElderry, 1996. 192p. $16. ISBN 0-689-80945-X. 5-9

JoEllen Briggs goes to stay with an elderly cousin living in a small New Hampshire castle called Winterbloom while her mother enjoys her honeymoon with her new husband. JoEllen climbs through a round window in a turret on the top floor of the castle and finds herself in a different time. When she sees 1809, she forgets her irritation at her mother and begins to solve the mystery of Winterbloom.

491. Curson, Marjorie N. **Jonas Salk**. Englewood Cliffs, NJ: Silver Burdett, 1990. 137p. $13.95. ISBN 0-382-09966-4. (Pioneers in Change). 5-9

In 1914, under Franklin D. Roosevelt, the March of Dimes drives began and netted money for medical research on polio and other viral diseases. For Jonas Salk, who once thought of becoming a lawyer, such money eventually came to his laboratories and supported his new research. Much of the book presents the process of vaccine development, from the discoveries of Semmelweis in Austria and Louis Pasteur in France during the mid-eighteenth century, through the testing and approval of the Salk vaccine, and then the Sabin vaccine, for polio. The balanced account enumerates the successes and failures in this long procedure. Important Dates, Bibliography, and Index.

492. Curtis, Christopher Paul. **The Watsons Go to Birmingham—1963**. New York: Delacorte, 1995. 210p. $14.95. ISBN 0-385-32175-9. 5-8

Kenny, 10, narrates the story of his family living in Flint, Michigan. When his older brother Byron needs more discipline, his parents take him to his grandmother's in Birmingham, Alabama. Their trip south gets them to Birmingham before a bomb explodes in the church. Kenny thinks his sister may be one of the four children killed. Although she is not, he experiences the fear that she might be a victim, so the Civil Rights movement affects him personally. *Bulletin Blue Ribbon Book, Bank Street College's Children's Book Award, Newbery Honor, Coretta Scott King Honor Book, American Library Association Notable Books for Children, American Library Association Best Books for Young Adults,* and *Horn Book Fanfare Honor List.*

493. Cush, Cathie. **Artists Who Created Great Works**. Austin, TX: Raintree/Steck-Vaughn, 1995. 48p. $15.96. ISBN 0-8114-4993-5. (20 Events Series). 6 up

In two-page spreads, Cush creates a minihistory of art by presenting profiles on 20 artists spanning from Leonardo Da Vinci (Italy, 1452-1519) to Salvadore Dali (Spain, 1904-1989). Photographs of famous paintings accompany the text. Other artists included are Albrecht Dürer (Germany, 1471-1528), Michelangelo Buonarroti (Italy, 1475-1564), Gian Lorenzo Bernini (Italy, 1598-1680), Rembrandt van Rijn (Netherlands, 1606-1669), Christopher Wren (England, 1632-1723), Francisco Goya (Spain, 1746-1828), Joseph M. W. Turner (England, 1775-1851), Eugène Delacroix (France, 1798-1863), Auguste Rodin (France, 1840-1917), Claude Monet (France, 1840-1926), Henri Matisse (France, 1869-1954), Pablo Picasso (Spain, 1881-1973), Diego Rivera (Mexico, 1886-1957), Ludwig Mies van der Rohe (Germany, 1886-1969), Georgia O'Keeffe (United States, 1887-1986), Alexander Calder (United States, 1898-1976), Henry Moore (England, 1898-1986), and Ansel Adams (United States, 1902-1984). Glossary, Suggested Readings, and Index.

494. Cush, Cathie. **Disasters That Shook the World**. Austin, TX: Raintree/Steck-Vaughn, 1994. 48p. $15.96. ISBN 0-8114-4929-7. (20 Events Series). 6 up

Some of the major changes in perception that have occurred in the world have come as a result of a disaster. In two-page spreads, Cush discusses 20 situations that were never expected to happen. They are the explosion of Vesuvius (AD 79 in Pompeii, Italy), the Black Death (fourteenth-century Europe), the destruction of the Native Americans (fifteenth through nineteenth centuries), the Great London Fire (1666), the Irish Potato Famine (1845-1849), the Great Chicago Fire (1871), Krakatoa's eruption (Indonesia, 1883), the San Francisco earthquake (1906), the *Titanic* sinking (1912), the world flu epidemic (1917-1919), the Bangladesh cyclone (1970), famine in Ethiopia and Somalia (1984-1985; 1992), the AIDS epidemic (1980s), the Bhopal chemical disaster (India, 1984), the *Challenger* explosion (United States, 1986), the Chernobyl nuclear meltdown (Russia, 1986), the Exxon *Valdez* oil spill (1989), the death of the Aral Sea (between Kazakhstan and Uzbekistan, 1960-1990), the Gulf War oil disaster (Kuwait, 1991), and hurricanes Andrew (Atlantic, 1992) and Iniki (Hawaii, 1992). Glossary, Suggested Readings, and Index.

495. Cush, Cathie. **Women Who Achieved Greatness**. Austin, TX: Raintree/Steck-Vaughn, 1995. 48p. $15.96. ISBN 0-8114-4938-6. (20 Events Series). 6 up

Women have achieved greatness in a variety of ways, and some, though not all, have received recognition for it. In two-page spreads, Cush profiles some of these women. The women included are Maria Montessori (Italy, 1870-1952), Helen Keller (1880-1968) and Annie Sullivan (d. 1936), Eleanor Roosevelt (1884-1962), Amelia Earhart (1899-1937), Golda Meir (Israel, 1898-1978), Margaret Mead (1901-1978), Barbara McClintock (1902-1992), Marian Anderson (1900-1993), Margaret Bourke-White (1906-1971), Rachel Carson (1907-1964), Mother Teresa (Albania and India, 1910-1997), Indira Gandhi (India, 1917-1984), Katharine Meyer Graham

(b. 1917), Maya Angelou (b. 1928), Violeta Chamorro (Nicaragua, b. 1929), Jane Goodall (England, b. 1934), Barbara Jordan (1936-1996), Aung San Suu Kyi (Burma, b. 1944), Wilma Mankiller (b. 1945), and Oprah Winfrey (b. 1954). Glossary, Suggested Readings, and Index.

496. Cushman, Karen. **The Ballad of Lucy Whipple**. New York: Clarion, 1996. 210p. $14.95. ISBN 0-395-72806-1. 5-7

In Lucky Diggins, California, Lucy (California Morning Whipple) and her mother run a boardinghouse in a huge tent. She wants to return home to New England where people are civilized, but she has to earn the money for the journey. She writes letters to her relatives describing the horrors of the place, but after three years, during which her brother dies and her mother remarries, she grows used to the people and decides that California is her real home. *School Library Journal Best Book.*

497. Cutler, Jane. **My Wartime Summers**. New York: Farrar, Straus & Giroux, 1994. 153p. $15. ISBN 0-374-35111-2. 5-8

While her Uncle Bob is away fighting in Europe during World War II, Ellen finishes the sixth, seventh, and eighth grades from 1942 to 1945. She thinks that she changes a lot, but she does not change as much as Uncle Bob. When he returns, her best friends' parents, who are Jewish, want to know if he saw anyone from the concentration camps. Someone else asks how he survived when so many did not. He seems to wonder the same thing and leaves with an army friend to tell another buddy's wife about his death. Ellen understands that all changes are not visible.

498. Cwiklik, Robert. **King Philip and the War with the Colonists**. Robert L. Smith, illustrator. Englewood Cliffs, NJ: Silver Burdett, 1989. 144p. $12.98. ISBN 0-382-09573-1. (Biography of the American Indians). 5-8

King Philip (Metacum) took the leadership of his tribe of Wampanoag Indians when his father Massasoit died. He tried to keep the treaties that his father had made with the English, but they continued to encroach on tribal lands. Finally, his people would not tolerate the situation, and King Philip had to fight. King Philip's war started in 1675, but he and many in his tribe lost their lives, and the colonists drove the remainder into northern New England. Suggested Reading.

499. Cwiklik, Robert. **Sequoyah and the Cherokee Alphabet**. T. Lewis, illustrator. Englewood Cliffs, NJ: Silver Burdett, 1989. 123p. $12.95; $7.95pa. ISBN 0-382-09570-7; 0-382-09759-9pa. (Biography of American Indians). 5-8

Sequoyah (1773?-1843) lived as a Cherokee concerned that his people would lose their culture and adapt all the ways of the white settlers. His father was white, possibly a wealthy man named Nathanial Gist who was George Washington's friend, or possibly a drunkard known as George Gist. Gist left Sequoyah's mother before Sequoyah was born. Sequoyah overcame a disability by developing his artistic talents and by creating a written language for the Cherokees based on syllables. The text looks at his life and his development of the language. Suggested Reading.

500. Cwiklik, Robert. **Tecumseh: Shawnee Rebel**. New York: Chelsea House, 1993. 110p. $18.95. ISBN 0-7910-1721-4. (North American Indians of Achievement). 5 up

Tecumseh (1768-1813) declared that Indians owned their land and that no individual could legally sell or buy any of it. He campaigned for a national confederation, and his movement was beginning to work when the British declared war on the United States in 1812. He sided with the British, recruiting warriors from Old Northwest tribes, and won battles. But the British betrayed him, as the American whites had. He was a diplomat, fighter, revolutionary, military genius, and idealist. Engravings enhance the text. Chronology, Further Reading, and Index.

501. Czech, Ken. **Snapshot: America Discovers the Camera**. Minneapolis, MN: Lerner, 1996. 88p. $18.95. ISBN 0-8225-1736-1. (People's History). 5 up

Photography, invented in France in 1839, has been a force in American society since its arrival in the country. Matthew Brady realized that pictures of the Civil War would make him money, and George Eastman began selling lightweight cameras in 1888 for amateurs. Other developments in photography have led to television, movies, and unusual art styles. Photographs complement the text. Bibliography and Index.

D

502.	Daffron, Carolyn. **Margaret Bourke-White: Photographer**. New York: Chelsea House, 1988. 110p. $18.95; $7.95pa. ISBN 1-55546-644-3; 0-7910-0411-2pa. (American Women of Achievement). 5 up

Margaret Bourke-White (1904-1971) photographed architecture and showed the beauty in industry. Her later photojournalistic work showed the horrors of the Deep South, Nazi concentration camps, and South African apartheid. As she grew up, she saw her amateur photographer father take, develop, and enlarge prints, and she decided to become a professional photographer. After college, she joined *Fortune* magazine and went to the Soviet Union, where she became the first Westerner to photograph Soviet industry. In World War II, she joined *Life* magazine and became the first female war correspondent. She covered the arrival of American bombers in England, went on a mission, and photographed General Patton and his troops as they marched through Germany. Her independent lifestyle set her apart as well. Her photographs augment the text. Chronology, Further Reading, and Index.

503.	Dale, Rodney. **Early Cars**. New York: Oxford University Press, 1994. 64p. $18; $10.95pa. ISBN 0-19-521002-6; 0-19-521006-9pa. (Discoveries & Inventions). 9 up

From early self-moving carriages through cars on the road, the text discusses steam omnibuses, the engines and chassis of cars, the Nuremberg carriage in 1649, and steam carriages in the eighteenth and early nineteenth centuries. Pioneers and their contributions include Walter Hancock (1749-1852), Sir Goldsworthy Gurney (1793-1875), Otto and Langen's "free piston" engine in 1866, Dr. Rudolf Diesel's engine in the late nineteenth century, Dunlop's pneumatic bicycle tires, and Wankel's rotary engine in the mid-1950s. Names important for private cars are Lenoir, Marcus, Delamare-Deboutteville, Hammel, and Carl Benz (around 1885). Daimler, Butler, Peugeot and Panhard, John Knight, and Lanchester and Austin were also working around that time. Henry Ford's first car appeared in 1896 while the Renault brothers were experimenting in France. Rolls tells the story of the first cars while diagrams and photographs reinforce the text. Chronology, Further Reading, and Index.

504.	Dale, Rodney. **Early Railways**. New York: Oxford University Press, 1994. 64p. $18; $10.95pa. ISBN 0-19-521003-4; 0-19-521007-7pa. (Discoveries & Inventions). 9 up

The world's first railway station opened in Stockton, England, in 1825, after George Stephenson and others had worked to build steam engines and devise rails on which the trains could run. The originators did not foresee that the railway would entice people who had never traveled to use them, and they replaced many coaches in the process. The text traces development in England and the United States, using diagrams, drawings, and photographs to illustrate salient points. Chronology, Further Reading, and Index.

505.	Daley, William. **The Chinese Americans**. New York: Chelsea House, 1995. 93p. $19.95; $8.95pa. ISBN 0-710-3357-0; 0-7910-3379-1pa. (The Peoples of North America). 4-7

The immigration of Chinese into the United States began to rise when the first Opium War between China and England (1839-1842) gave Hong Kong to England in the Treaty of Nanking and opened four other Chinese ports. The corrupt Manchu (Ch'ing Dynasty) rulers imposed higher taxes, causing the people to revolt in 1850 under the leadership of Hung Hsiu-ch'uan, a convert to Christianity, in the Taiping "Great Peace" Rebellion. But the Taipings were defeated in 1864. A second Opium War fought at the same time, from 1856 to 1860, caused even more turmoil. By 1848, only seven Chinese were recorded as living in San Francisco, but by 1851 the gold rush had attracted 25,000. The Chinese immigrants were prevented from voting, holding public office, and practicing certain trades. For these reasons, they started laundries and worked to build the railroads across the United States. Immigration laws tightened in 1882, keeping out many women who had stayed behind to look after their husbands' parents. In the twentieth century, other problems in China caused emigration. Sun Yat-Sen ruled from 1866 to 1925, when the Japanese began to trouble the Chinese. In 1949, Mao Zedong declared victory over Chiang and established his brand of Communism. Chinese Americans developed the Bing cherry and were the first to hatch eggs with artificial heat. They have cultural depth through their religions—Confucianism, Taoism, and Buddhism—and their artists and inventors, such as Wang, Yo-Yo Ma, Maya Lin, Maxine Hong Kingston, Lawrence Yep, and David Hwang. Selected References and Index.

506.	Dallard, Shyrlee. **Ella Baker: A Leader Behind the Scenes**. Englewood Cliffs, NJ: Silver Burdett, 1990. 130p. $12.95; $7.95pa. ISBN 0-382-09931-1; 0-382-24066-9pa. (History of the Civil Rights Movement). 6-9

As a key person who helped to form the SNCC (Student Nonviolent Coordinating Committee), Ella Baker (1903-1986) always stayed out of the limelight. A film about her was titled *Fundi*, which is Swahili for someone who gives unselfishly to others; Baker did spend her life trying to help others. Dallard recounts the life of a sharecropper who graduated first in her class. She went to New York during the Harlem Renaissance and lived through the Depression, the WPA, and lynching. In New York, Baker began working for the NAACP (National Association for the Advancement of Colored People), and continued to do so after the Civil Rights Act passed in 1964 by supporting Nelson Mandela and his bid to stop apartheid in South Africa. Civil Rights Timeline, Suggested Reading, Sources, and Index.

507. Damon, Duane. **When the Cruel War Is Over: The Civil War Home Front**. Minneapolis, MN: Lerner, 1996. 88p. $14.21. ISBN 0-8225-1731-0. (People's History). 5 up

A group of people who suffered as much in the Civil War as the soldiers were the civilians who waited at home, lonely and often overworked. The text looks at backyards as battlefields; factory workers; nurses; the professions of writer, photographer, sketch artist, and musician; women and children who managed farms; and the African Americans who waited to be free. Bibliography and Index.

508. Daniels, Roger. **Coming to America: A History of Immigration and Ethnicity in American Life**. New York: HarperCollins, 1991. 450p. $15. ISBN 0-06-092100-5. YA

Immigrants have come to North America since the first Europeans arrived after Columbus. The text presents a comprehensive look at immigration through the years from England, France, and Spain; the African slaves; the arrivals from Ireland, Germany, and Eastern Europe during the beginnings of industrialization; and immigrants from Latin America and Asia in the twentieth century. Bibliography and Index.

509. Daniels, Roger. **Prisoners Without Trial: Japanese Americans in World War II**. New York: Hill and Wang, 1994. 146p. $7.95pa. ISBN 0-8090-1553-6pa. (A Critical Issue). YA

The U.S. government took nearly 120,000 Japanese Americans from their homes during the spring and early summer of 1942 and incarcerated them in concentration camps because they or their parents had been born in Japan. Daniels believes that the internment was the result of racism toward Asians that had started with their arrival in America. Statistics support the author's thesis as he discusses the background for a roundup of Asians from 1850 to 1841; the politics of incarceration in 1941 and 1942; the Asians' return to freedom during 1942 to 1946; and rehabilitation and redress from 1943 until 1990. Additionally, the author thinks such a situation, fueled by racists, could happen again. An Essay in Photographs, Suggestions for Further Reading, Appendix, and Index.

510. Darby, Jean. **Douglas MacArthur**. Minneapolis, MN: Lerner, 1989. 112p. $22.95. ISBN 0-8225-4901-8. 5 up

Douglas MacArthur (1880-1964) led a soldier's life, graduating from West Point and serving in major wars during the early twentieth century. When the Japanese defeated him in the Philippines in 1942, he said "I shall return." He did return in 1944 when he stopped their advances. He is best known for defeating the Japanese and then helping them establish a democracy. Appendix, Glossary, For Further Reading, and Index.

511. Darby, Jean. **Dwight D. Eisenhower: A Man Called Ike**. Minneapolis, MN: Lerner, 1989. 112p. $21.50. ISBN 0-8225-4900-X. 5 up

Complemented with photographs, this text on the life of Dwight David Eisenhower (1890-1969) covers the main aspects of his youth in Abilene, Kansas, and his attendance at West Point. He excelled in his military career, rising to commander of the Allied forces in Europe. He came back to the United States after the war as a hero and was elected to the presidency. He endured heartaches but rose to his responsibilities. Appendix, Glossary, For Further Reading, and Index.

512. Darby, Jean. **Martin Luther King, Jr.** Minneapolis, MN: Lerner, 1990. 144p. $14.95; $6.95pa. ISBN 0-382-09931-1; 0-382-24066-9pa. 5-9

This fictional biography is almost a history of the Civil Rights movement in its look at Martin Luther King, Jr.'s life, from his Atlanta birth in 1929 until his assassination in 1964. Using examples to emphasize the situation, Darby shows segregation in the South as opposed to the North, how Gandhi influenced King, Rosa Parks's confrontation in Montgomery, the bus boycott, Woolworth's lunch counter sit-in in 1960, James Meredith's enrollment in the University of Mississippi, and the "I Have a Dream" speech in the 1963 march on Washington. Darby also recounts the events in Memphis leading up to the moment when James Earl Ray allegedly shot King. Glossary, Further Reading, Index.

513. Dary, David. **Seeking Pleasure in the Old West**. New York: Knopf, 1995. 352p. $30. ISBN 0-394-56178-3. YA

Diaries, period newspapers, recollections, and photographs show the Old West as a place where people did many different things besides shoot each other. The main civilization began when mail and telegraph service on the railroad became regular. The text looks at this social history of the Old West to show how it evolved into the twentieth century. Bibliography, Notes, and Index.

514. Dash, Joan. **We Shall Not Be Moved: The Women's Factory Strike of 1909**. New York: Scholastic, 1996. 176p. $15.95. ISBN 0-590-48409-5. 5-9

In 1909, female teenager factory workers between the ages of 16 and 18, mostly unskilled, united with college girls and older women with extra money to strike against the bundle system manufacturing shirtwaists. The text posits that these alliances were what allowed even the limited success of this strike and looks at the process that led to 30,000 laborers jeopardizing their futures by refusing to accept the status quo. Photographs, Bibliography, and Index.

515.   Davidson, Mary R. **Dolly Madison: Famous First Lady**. New York: Chelsea Juniors, 1992. 80p. $14.95. ISBN 0-7910-1446-0. (Discovery Biography). 3-7

Dolley Madison (1768-1849) and her family were Quakers, and her first marriage to John Todd in Philadelphia was a sedate Quaker wedding. After he died of yellow fever, James Madison began courting her, and she married him. When she became Mrs. James Madison, the wedding was a huge party instead of a quiet Quaker event. She became the nation's hostess for Thomas Jefferson and the First Lady who saved artifacts from the White House when the British burned Washington during the War of 1812. She and her husband spent their later years at Montpelier.

516.   Davidson, Michael Worth, ed. **Everyday Life Through the Ages**. Pleasantville, NY: Reader's Digest, 1992. 384p. $30. ISBN 0-276-42035-7. YA

The text, divided into three parts that cover ancient worlds, old worlds and new worlds, and the modern world, looks at different peoples throughout 30,000 years of history and how they lived their days. Russian peasants, Venetian merchants, English coal miners, and Australian aborigines appear. Also included are insights on Viking housekeeping, being a slave on a tobacco plantation, and how the Medicis treated people who lived in Florence. The illustrations try to show what words cannot say in this social history. An "A-Z of Everyday Things" mentions 100 inventions such as adhesive, beds, birth control, silk, and yokes. Index.

517.   Davies, Eryl. **Transport: On Land, Road and Rail**. New York: Franklin Watts, 1992. 47p. $7.95pa. ISBN 0-531-15741-5pa. (Timelines). 5-8

Illustrations interspersed with text show a history of transport. The text covers the first wheels, Roman roads, ancient China, Vikings, Medieval Europe, animal power, coaches, steam pioneers, the railroad age, pedal power, the first motorcycles, automobiles, underground trains, streetcars, delivery modes, racing cars, and the future in transportation. Timeline, Glossary, and Index.

518.   Davies, Mark. **Malcolm X: Another Side of the Movement**. Glenn Wolff, illustrator. Englewood Cliffs, NJ: Silver Burdett, 1990. 130p. $12.95; $7.95pa. ISBN 0-382-09925-7; 0-382-09925-7pa. (History of the Civil Rights Movement). 5-12

Malcolm Little (1925-1965) took the name Malcolm X after he joined the Nation of Islam. It symbolized his real African name, which he would never know, rather than the white man's name of "Little." He went to prison for seven years after hustling and selling drugs in Boston and New York. In prison, he educated himself so that he was prepared to lead people in the fight against racial discrimination. He saw white people as the devil over which Black people had to gain power. Throughout his career, he spoke loudly about his beliefs. After he returned from a visit to Mecca, he was assassinated. Timetable, Suggested Reading, Sources, and Index.

519.   Davis, Benjamin O., Jr. **Benjamin O. Davis, Jr., American: An Autobiography**. Washington, DC: Smithsonian Institute, 1991. 442p. $29.95. ISBN 0-87474-742-2. YA

Benjamin O. Davis, Jr. (b. 1912) went to West Point and decided that he would become an officer even though official military policy noted that Blacks were inferior. He and his wife faced discrimination in both military and civilian life even though he rose to the rank of lieutenant general in the U.S. Air Force by 1965. He believed in excellence and that Blacks could overcome racism through their achievements. His leadership qualities propelled him to the top. He does not belittle the organization in which he served, nor does he make hostile comments. He tries to show the facts as they were. Index.

520.   Davis, Daniel. **Behind Barbed Wire**. New York: Dutton, 1982. 166p. $12.95. ISBN 0-525-26320-9. 7 up

When the Japanese bombed Pearl Harbor on December 7, 1941, many lives changed in ways highly unexpected. Japanese Americans became victims of their former country when President Roosevelt signed Executive Order 9066 to inter more than 120,000 Japanese Americans behind barbed wire in case they might be a danger to the United States. The text recounts their experiences through these four years including the information that some of them did not want to leave the camps in 1945 because they had nothing to return to after the United States took away their homes and their livelihoods. Selected Bibliography and Index.

521.   Davis, Donald. **Thirteen Miles from Suncrest**. Little Rock, AR: August House, 1994. 253p. $19.95. ISBN 0-87483-379-5. YA

On his 10th birthday in 1910, Med McGee receives a journal from his father. He records in it regularly for the next three years until a horse throws his father, who dies. During the three years, Med discusses his everyday North Carolina activities such as going to school, sowing flax seed, and butchering hogs, and uncommon events such as the maiming of his brother, the murder of a schoolmate, and the public hanging of a neighbor. He inserts events of the times that his father reads aloud to the family every week from the Nashville newspaper.

522. Davis, Frances A. **Frank Lloyd Wright: Maverick Architect**. Minneapolis, MN: Lerner, 1996. 128p. $22.95. ISBN 0-8225-4953-0. 5 up

Frank Lloyd Wright (1867-1959) wanted to create a distinctly American architecture. He experimented with shapes and materials as he developed the Prairie style. Sometimes insufferable, but always dedicated, Wright's designs integrated all aspects of topography and structure. Because he was also interested in finding less-expensive ways to build innovative homes, he developed the "Usonian" partially prefabricated method. Photographs, Bibliography, and Index.

523. Davis, Kenneth C. **Don't Know Much About History: Everything You Need to Know About American History but Never Learned**. 1990. New York: Bantam, 1992. 462p. $16.99. ISBN 0-553-47103-1. YA

Davis asks more than 150 chronologically arranged questions about American history since 1492 and briefly answers them. One question asks "What was the bonus army?" Answer: In 1932, 25,000 World War I veterans marched in Washington to obtain bonuses promised them, and General MacArthur and Major Patton led an assault against them. More than 100 marchers were killed. Selected Readings and Index.

524. Davis, Lee Allyn. **Man-Made Catastrophes: From the Burning of Rome to the Lockerbie Crash**. New York: Facts on File, 1993. 352p. $40. ISBN 0-8160-2035-3. YA

The text covers 284 incidents caused by humans. The various situations include railway disasters, space disasters, fires, explosions, air crashes, terrorism, riots, nuclear accidents, and maritime disasters. Bibliography and Index.

525. De Benedetti, Charles, and Charles Chatfield. **An American Ordeal: The Antiwar Movement of the Vietnam Era**. Syracuse, NY: Syracuse University Press, 1990. 495p. $17.95pa. ISBN 0-8156-0245-6pa. YA

De Benedetti divides the period of the Vietnam War into four parts: 1955-1963, 1963-1965, 1965-1970, and 1970-1975. After the war in Indochina began, it spread to America, and with the war grew a massive antiwar sentiment that challenged cultural norms such as scientific objectivity, religious beliefs, white male dominance, adult standards, acceptance of poverty, the Cold War mission, and consensus. This scholarly book discusses the revaluation of these norms and asserts that the antiwar movement was more about America than Vietnam. Notes, Bibliography, and Index.

526. de Hartog, Jan. **The Lamb's War**. New York: HarperCollins, 1979. 461p. $13.95. ISBN 0-06-010995-5. New York: Fawcett, 1982. 461p. $3.95pa. ISBN 0-449-20019-1pa. YA

Laura, 15, goes to Schwalbenbach death camp, where Nazis have imprisoned her Dutch father for trying to save Jewish babies. An officer, irked by her father, ties him up and rapes Laura in front of him. Her father's rage and ensuing death haunt Laura after she survives the camp, marries an American for entrance into the United States, goes to medical school, and attempts to save the babies in the Southwest. She becomes increasingly fat as she tries to live with the intense guilt that she feels over her father's death.

527. De Haven, Tom. **Derby Dugan's Depression Funnies: A Novel**. New York: Metropolitan, 1996. 290p. $23. ISBN 0-8050-4445-0. YA

Two men, orphaned as youngsters, create the Derby Dugan comic strip in the 1930s. They treat the strip like their child, and although very different, they disagree only on Dugan's age. The story reveals the Depression years and two people who make something of their lives.

528. de Ruiz, Dana Catharine. **To Fly with the Swallows: A Story of Old California**. Debbe Heller, illustrator. Austin, TX: Raintree/Steck-Vaughn, 1993. 53p. $15.49; $5.95pa. ISBN 0-8114-7234-5; 0-8114-8074-7pa. (Stories of America—Personal Challenge). 5-9

In 1806, Concha, 15, lived with her family in San Francisco, where her father was commander of the presidio defending Spain's New World empire on the northern border of Alta California. Nikolai Petrovich Rezanov arrived from St. Petersburg requesting supplies for his ship. He stayed long enough for Concha and him to want to marry, but Rezanov was not Catholic. He left, as requested, to get the permission of the czar, the King of Spain, and the pope in Italy. Concha waited, but after five years she received word of his death. She never married but spent her life dedicated to Saint Francis and helping those who needed her in childbirth, sickness, and death. At 60, she became California's first nun in Santa Catalina. Epilogue, Afterword, and Notes.

529. de Ruiz, Dana Catharine, and Richard Larios. **La Causa: The Migrant Farmworkers' Story**. Rudy Gutierrez, illustrator. Austin, TX: Raintree/Steck-Vaughn, 1993. 92p. $15.49; $5.95pa. ISBN 0-8114-7231-0; 0-8114-8071-2pa. (Stories of America—Stand Up and Be Counted). 4-7

When a young boy in 1940, Cesar Chavez watched his father, a worker who had left his home to find work, faithfully fulfill a contract as he had promised, but remain unpaid when the contractor disappeared. Dolores Huerta watched workers, desperate to help their families survive, try to pay their rent. The two met and began fighting the inequity between workers and owners in the fields of California. Their efforts, including a nonviolent strike, finally led to the formation of the United Farm Workers in 1966. However, that was only the beginning of their work to preserve dignity and hope in this quest. Epilogue, Afterword, and Notes.

530.   de Varona, Frank. **Bernardo de Gálvez**. Tom Redman, illustrator. Austin, TX: Raintree/Steck-Vaughn, 1993. 32p. $13.98; $5.95pa. ISBN 0-8172-3379-2; 0-8114-6756-2pa. (Hispanic Stories). 4-7

As a Spanish soldier, Bernardo de Gálvez (1746-1786) was assigned first to duty in Mexico, where he fought the Apaches, and then the Louisiana Territory, where he fought France. He ordered the British to leave the territory and gave Americans freedom to use it. His greatest victory was in Pensacola (now Florida) in 1781, when he defeated the British. Glossary. English and Spanish text.

531.   Deem, James M. **How to Make a Mummy Talk**. True Kelley, illustrator. Boston: Houghton Mifflin, 1995. 184p. $14.95. ISBN 0-395-62427-4. 4-8

Entertaining illustrations and boxed questions guide the reader through this text about mummies. With the premise that mummies "talk" through what archaeologists discover about them, Deem explores fact and myth about how mummies were and are made, what mummies "say," and where to find them. Some of the more famous mummies discussed are the 5,000-year-old Iceman of Europe; Elmer McCurdy, an Oklahoma outlaw; mummies from California; a Bigfoot mummy from Minnesota; and an Egyptian mummy. Bibliography and Index.

532.   DeFelice, Cynthia. **The Apprenticeship of Lucas Whitaker**. New York: Farrar, Straus & Giroux, 1996. 160p. $15. ISBN 0-374-34669-0. 5 up

After Lucas Whitaker's mother dies in 1849, he hears that he could have saved her from her fatal tuberculosis by exhuming a deceased relative, removing the heart, and burning it so that his mother could have breathed the smoke. Distressed that he did not know in time, he goes to Southwick, Connecticut, and becomes an apprentice to the local physician who is also a dentist, apothecary, undertaker, and barber. When he looks through a microscope for the first time, he learns the difference between superstition and science, and that he cannot blame himself for his mother's death. *School Library Journal Best Book*.

533.   DeFelice, Cynthia. **Lostman's River**. New York: Macmillan, 1994. 160p. $14.95. ISBN 0-02-726466-1. 5-8

In 1900, 13-year-old Tyler's father runs away from New York to the Florida Everglades when he thinks he will be charged with a murder he did not commit. In 1906, after "plumers" (men who illegally kill native birds for their feathers) kill a man who pretends that he collects for a museum, and Tyler is almost lost in the swamps, Tyler's father decides to stop fleeing from something that he did not do.

534.   DeFelice, Cynthia. **Weasel**. New York: Macmillan, 1990. 119p. $15. ISBN 0-02-726457-2. New York: Camelot, 1991. 119p. $3.99pa. ISBN 0-380-71358-6pa. 5 up

When Ezra arrives at 11-year-old Nathan's cabin in 1839, he shows Nathan his dead mother's locket and then leads him to his father, almost dead from gangrene. Nathan and his sister hear their father's story about Weasel, the man who has wounded his father, killed his mother, and caused Ezra intense emotional pain. Nathan has to cope with his feelings of hatred after he has his own encounter with Weasel.

535.   DeFord, Deborah H., and Harry S. Stout. **An Enemy Among Them**. Boston: Houghton Mifflin, 1987. 203p. $13.95. ISBN 0-395-44239-7. 6-9

Margaret's brother is wounded in 1776, and when she goes to the hospital to tend him, she also helps an enemy Hessian. Christian, the Hessian, begins working for Margaret's father on the family farm instead of going to prison, and as Margaret begins to fall in love with him, she finds out that he wounded her brother. Christian, however, becomes a believer in the Patriot cause, and Margaret's German-American family begins to accept him.

536.   Deford, Frank. **Love and Infamy**. New York: Viking, 1993. 516p. $5.99. ISBN 0-670-82995-1. YA

Cotton Drake grows up in Japan after World War I with his missionary parents and makes friends with Kiyoshi. As adults, Cotton becomes a missionary, and Kiyoshi works in Honolulu in an international shipping firm. There Admiral Yamamoto recruits Kiyoshi as an intelligence officer, and he finds that the admiral is planning to bomb Pearl Harbor without informing the Imperial Army beforehand. He tells Cotton, and Cotton tries to convince American officials of the plan. Some of the historical accuracy in this story must be questioned, but it shows the Japanese culture and perceptions of work, honor, sex, religion, family, and duty, which are valuable assets in a story featuring believable characters.

537.   Deitch, Kenneth M., and JoAnne B. Weisman. **Dwight D. Eisenhower: Man of Many Hats**. Jay Connolly, illustrator. Lowell, MA: Discovery Enterprises, 1990. 48p. $17.95. ISBN 1-878668-02-1. (Picture-Book Biography). 5-12

Although the illustrations are interesting and representative of Dwight David Eisenhower's life (1890-1969), the text is more difficult than the pictures imply. Among the hats that Eisenhower wore throughout his life are high school sports enthusiast, West Point cadet, general in the army, recipient of honorary degrees, president, and golfer. No table of contents or index.

538. Deltenre, Chantal, and Martine Noblet. **The United States**. Maureen Walker, translator. Hauppauge, NY: Barron's, 1994. 77p. $11.95; $6.95pa. ISBN 0-8120-6428-3; 0-8120-1867-2pa. (Tintin's Travel Diaries). 5 up

The text asks 30 questions about the United States covering a variety of topics, such as what the American flag means, why the country is called "America," who discovered it, how did American Indians live, what was the conquest of the West, the causes of the Civil War, and who was Al Capone. Illustrations and photographs complement the simple text on the left side of the page and the more thorough and scholarly answer on the right side of the page. Glossary, Chronological Chart, Map, Bibliography, and Index.

539. Demos, John. **The Tried and the True: Native American Women Confronting Colonization**. New York: Oxford University Press, 1995. 111p. $22. ISBN 0-19-508142-0. (The Young Oxford History of Women in the United States). 9 up

Native American women had to cope with the change in their lives as much as the men. The text looks at their struggles before and after the Europeans arrived and began to colonize North America. Chronology, Bibliography, Further Reading, and Index. *Notable Children's Trade Books in the Field of Social Studies.*

540. Denenberg, Barry. **An American Hero: The True Story of Charles A. Lindbergh**. New York: Scholastic, 1996. 255p. $16.95. ISBN 0-590-46923-1. 7-12

By using quotes from Charles Lindbergh's own writing, Denenberg tells the story of the Lone Eagle (1902-1974). He divides Lindbergh's life into two segments, "Ascent" and "Descent," with the apex coming before the kidnapping and death of Lindbergh's son and his and his wife's campaign to keep America out of World War II by blaming the war on the British, the Jews, and Roosevelt's administration rather than the Nazis. Photographs, Notes, Bibliography, and Index.

541. Denenberg, Barry. **John Fitzgerald Kennedy: America's 35th President**. New York: Scholastic, 1988. 112p. $3.25pa. ISBN 0-590-41344-9pa. 5-9

John F. (Fitzgerald) Kennedy (1917-1963) was America's 35th President. The text follows him from his childhood until his assassination in Dallas, covering the memorable events of his presidency.

542. Denenberg, Barry. **The True Story of J. Edgar Hoover and the FBI**. New York: Scholastic, 1993. 202p. $13.95; $5.99pa. ISBN 0-590-43168-4; 0-590-44157-4pa. 7 up

J. Edgar Hoover (1895-1972) led the Federal Bureau of Investigation from 1924 until 1972. The text looks at his background and his commitment to hard work. At the same time, it examines his personal arrogance, snobbery, and desire for power. Some of the FBI's most famous cases show that Hoover liked to prosecute kidnappers, bank robbers, and murderers rather than members of organized crime or violators of civil rights. He saw himself above the law, a place that offered its own kind of corruption. Photographs, Bibliography, Timeline, and Index.

543. Denenberg, Barry. **Voices from Vietnam**. New York: Scholastic, 1995. 251p. $16.95. ISBN 0-590-44267-8. 8 up

From the mid-1800s until after World War II, the French controlled Vietnam, exploiting its people and its resources. In May 1954, Ho Chi Minh's Communists defeated the French, who had been supported by Americans fearful of Communist control of the area. Americans began to support Diem, and the war that ended with the final offensive of the North Vietnamese in 1975 began in earnest. Denenberg uses direct quotes by persons involved in all aspects of the war in telling what the war was about and what it did. His story makes the reasons for and results of war in Vietnam understandable. *American Library Association Best Books for Young Adults* and *American Library Association Booklist Editors' Choices.*

544. Denenberg, Barry. **When Will This Cruel War Be Over? The Diary of Emma Simpson, Gordonsville, Virginia, 1864**. New York: Scholastic, 1996. 157p. $9.95. ISBN 0-590-22862-5. (Dear America, 1). 5-9

Emma begins her journal on December 23, 1863, and ends it on December 25, 1864. Her family fights for the Confederacy during the Civil War, and they all endure terrible hardships and several deaths from the battle and from illness. At the end of the year, she recounts her sadness and wonders if the waste could possibly be worth the pain of the war. An epilogue gives information about her later life.

545. Denney, Robert E. **Civil War Prisons & Escapes: A Day-by-Day Chronicle**. New York: Sterling, 1994. 399p. $19.95pa. ISBN 0-8069-0415-1pa. YA

In a day-by-day, year-by-year format from May 1, 1861, until November 10, 1865, the text visits Andersonville, Elmira, and Salisbury as well as other Civil War prisons to see what the prisoners of war endured. With information gleaned from official war records, letters, and newspapers, Denney tells about prison breakouts such as those by John Ranson, who escaped from three Confederate prisons, and the one that anonymous troops achieved by digging tunnels so that federal officers could crawl out of Richmond's Libby Prison. More prisoners of war died in the Civil War than in all other U.S. wars combined, and the text tells about many of them as well as those who survived. Appendices, Bibliography, and Index.

546. Derr, Mark. **The Frontiersman: The Real Life and the Many Legends of Davy Crockett**. New York: Morrow, 1993. 304p. $23. ISBN 0-688-09656-5. YA

Among the labels that Derr has found in records on Davy Crockett (1786-1836) are those of drunkard, gambler, womanizer, illiterate, bear hunter, controversial politician, and hero of the Alamo. Forced to begin work at 12 as a teamster, Davy Crockett married at 19 and became a Tennessee tenant farmer. He served in the War of 1812 and after becoming a widower, married a woman with money. He went to Congress in 1827 and broke with Andrew Jackson when Jackson's people refused land reforms and tried to remove Indians east of the Mississippi. He seems to have been a man of wit and intelligence, disinterested in Congress or soldiering. Notes, Biographical Note, and Index.

547. Detzer, David. **An Asian Tragedy: America and Vietnam**. Brookfield, CT: Millbrook Press, 1992. 160p. $16.90. ISBN 1-56294-066-X. 7-9

By using "tragedy" in the title, the author shows the view of the Vietnam War from 1961 to 1975 presented in the text. In chronological order, the text details many decisions that caused difficulties for both Americans and Vietnamese after war was declared. Not too many could be called heroes in this conflict. Bibliography and Index.

548. Deutsch, Sarah Jane. **From Ballots to Breadlines: American Women 1920-1940**. New York: Oxford University Press, 1994. $15. ISBN 0-19-508015-7. (The Young Oxford History of Women in the United States). 9 up

Between the two world wars, women gained the right to vote. Among the advantages they found were new types of jobs in such professions as aviation and film. They entered public life and asserted themselves in various ways. Among the women presented are Amelia Earhart, Bette Davis, Margaret Mead, Georgia O'Keeffe, and Eleanor Roosevelt. Chronology, Further Reading, and Index.

549. Devaney, John. **America Goes to War: 1941**. New York: Walker, 1991. 188p. $16.95. ISBN 0-8027-6979-9. (World War II). 7 up

Starting with a prologue that details 1940, the text then goes month-by-month through the events in 1941 that led to the United States entering World War II on December 7, 1941. For Further Reading and Index.

550. Devaney, John. **America on the Attack: 1943**. New York: Walker, 1992. 224p. $18.85. ISBN 0-8027-8194-2. (World War II). 7 up

The beginning of 1943 was a humiliating defeat for Eisenhower at Kasserine Pass in Tunisia, but his forces returned to drive Rommel back. Patton helped contain the Germans and Italians along the beaches of the Mediterranean. In England, bombers flew to Dresden and Hamburg. In Stalingrad, Germans surrendered. Hitler stopped the Soviets but began to stall so that by 1943's end, Russians had pushed the Germans out of most of the Soviet Union. The text looks at the entire year of the war in detail. For Further Reading and Index.

551. Devaney, John. **America Storms the Beaches: 1944**. New York: Walker, 1993. 201p. $17.95. ISBN 0-8027-8244-2. (World War II). 7 up

Fighter planes and battleships filled the Pacific theater as 1944 began. Allied troops broke Germans in Italy and worked their way toward Central Europe. Eisenhower sent invading troops into Normandy in June. Original source materials help show this year of the war, including the Japanese kamikaze pilots and a failed assassination attempt on Hitler. For Further Reading and Index.

552. Devaney. John. **America Triumphs: 1945**. New York: Walker, 1995. 199p. $18.95. ISBN 0-8027-8347-3. 7 up

In his prologue, Devaney briefly summarizes the progression of World War II from its beginning in 1939 through 1944. The text, beginning on January 1, 1945, presents accounts from individuals as they face different battles, including Iwo Jima and Okinawa. Their comments show the motivations and the philosophical forces driving their choices to fight for their countries. He presents Eisenhower's first encounter with a German death camp as well as the ceremonies when the Japanese surrendered to General Douglas MacArthur. He includes photographs and biographical sketches of Chiang Kai-shek, Winston Churchill, Charles de Gaulle, Dwight Eisenhower, Emperor Hirohito, Adolf Hitler, Douglas MacArthur, George C. Marshall, Erwin Rommel, Franklin Delano Roosevelt, Josef Stalin, Hideki Tojo, and Harry S. Truman. Important Dates, Maps, For Further Reading, and Index.

553. Devaney, John. **Franklin Delano Roosevelt: President**. New York: Walker, 1987. 188p. $12.95. ISBN 0-8027-6713-3. 5-9

Franklin D. Roosevelt (1882-1945) accompanied his father to see Grover Cleveland and heard his father refuse an ambassadorship. Cleveland supposedly said to the five-year-old Franklin, "I am making a strange wish for you. It is that you may never be president of the United States." Cleveland's wish did not come true, and for the leadership that Roosevelt gave during his four terms as President, America can only be grateful. Roosevelt was able to give the country hope during the Great Depression and World War II. Photographs and Index.

554.	Dexter, Catherine. **Mazemaker**. New York: Morrow, 1989. 202p. $11.95. ISBN 0-688-07383-2. 5-7

Winnie, 12, thinks she sees a cat fade into a maze in the schoolyard, and she tries to see if she can do the same. She succeeds and finds herself in 1889 instead of 1989. She wants to return, but while she tries to find someone to help her, she observes the era's people and their superstitions. She decides to follow the cat, and she returns to 1989 to search for William, the mazemaker who disappeared into the future while she was caught in the past. When she finds him, she tells him he is welcome at home.

555.	Di Franco, J. Philip. **The Italian Americans**. New York: Chelsea House, 1988. 94p. $18.95; $7.95pa. ISBN 0-87754-886-2; 0-7910-0268-3pa. (Peoples of North America). 5 up

Although this book professes to discuss only Italian Americans, it recounts a brief history of Italy through its revolutions and the Italian unification movement, *Risorgimento*, led by Guiseppe Mazzini, G. Garibaldi, and Camillo Benso di Cavour. In the nineteenth century, however, the greed of the wealthy led to a difficult life for many southern Italians. The northern Italians emigrated first, with the southern Italians following them. The peak immigration years were 1900 to 1914, when more than 2 million Italians arrived in the United States. Not all of them remained, but by 1980, 12 million Italians had settled in the United States. Among those who influenced American life was Filippo Mazzei, a physician philosopher whom Thomas Jefferson translated and whose words closely resembled the Bill of Rights. In 1832, Lorenzo de Ponte brought opera to America. Wine growers from Italy established the Swiss Colony winery, and fruit growers began the Del Monte company. Famous Italian Americans include Fiorello La Guardia, Geraldine Ferraro, Mario Cuomo, Mother Cabrini (America's first saint), Joe DiMaggio, Mario Lanza, Frank Sinatra, Marconi, Fermi, Toscanini, Anne Bancroft, and Lee Iacocca. Selected References and Index.

556.	Diamond, Arthur. **Jackie Robinson**. San Diego, CA: Lucent, 1992. 112p. $16.95. ISBN 1-56006-029-8. (The Importance Of). 7 up

The text looks at Jackie Robinson (1919-1972) during his early life and his time in the army, in baseball, and as a businessman afterward. When at bat for the second time in the first game Robinson played in the majors, he hit a home run that drove in two other runs. The picture of a white man shaking his hand was the first one ever taken of a white congratulating a Black baseball player. Notes, For Further Reading, Works Consulted, and Index.

557.	Diamond, Arthur. **Paul Cuffe: Merchant and Abolitionist**. New York: Chelsea House, 1989. 109p. $18.95. ISBN 1-55546-579-X. (Black Americans of Achievement). 5 up

When townspeople would not join him in supporting a school, Paul Cuffe, free Black in Westport, Massachusetts, built one on his own land with his own money so that his seven children could get an education without having to travel to a neighboring town. He accepted the children of the townspeople in the school. Cuffe was born in 1759 on an island off the coast of Massachusetts to a Native American mother and an Ashanti father captured by slave traders at 10. His father worked for and won his freedom. Paul Cuffe fell in love with the sea and shipping and, after working aboard several frigates, realized that the only way he could avoid sailing into ports where people abused slaves was to form his own business with his own ship. He and his brother began running the British blockade in 1779. Because he was not allowed to vote, Cuffe protested taxation, and by 1783 he was absolved of most tax, and Massachusetts was the first state to forbid slavery. Cuffe realized that one could fight and defeat unfair laws. With aid and blessings from fellow Quakers, Cuffe decided to investigate creating a colony in Africa for slaves where they could be educated. In Sierra Leone he met many obstacles and many people, including members of the Muslim Mandingo tribe who wanted to continue slave trading. Although unable to start colonization before his death in 1817, Cuffe tried to help other American Blacks eventually do so. Chronology, Further Reading, and Index.

558.	Diamond, Arthur. **Prince Hall: Social Reformer**. New York: Chelsea House, 1991. 102p. $18.95. ISBN 1-55546-588-9. (Black Americans of Achievement). 5 up

Prince Hall (1735-1807) was the first organizer of Blacks in American history. He was shipped to Boston when 14 and witnessed the early stages of the American Revolution while he was a slave. He became free in 1770 but realized that a free Black had little more freedom than a slave. He became a member of the Order of the Free and Accepted Masons in 1775 and established his own branch for Blacks called the African Lodge. He united other Blacks, and they campaigned for the Continental army to accept slaves as soldiers. They worked to end the slave trade in Massachusetts, and they petitioned for Blacks to be educated, with Hall turning his home into the first school for Blacks in Boston. Reproductions enhance the text. Chronology, Further Reading, and Index.

559.	Diamond, Arthur. **Smallpox and the American Indian**. San Diego, CA: Lucent, 1991. 64p. $16.95. ISBN 1-56006-018-2. (World Disasters). 5-8

Between 1836 and 1840, smallpox extinguished several Native American tribes. They possessed no natural immunity to the disease and distrusted the white man's medicine. It was one of the ways that the Native Americans began to disappear from the continent. The text looks at the situation and its effect. Glossary, Further Reading, and Index.

560. Dillon, Eilís. **The Seekers**. New York: Scribner's, 1986. 136p. $12.95. ISBN 0-684-18595-4. 7 up

In 1632, Edward and his family leave England for Plymouth, Massachusetts, when his fiancée's father decides that he and his daughter Rebecca are resettling. In their new home, they all try to adjust to the religious zealots, the illnesses, and the hard work in the area. Edward and Rebecca decide that they prefer to live in England, so they return home.

561. Dixon, Jeanne. **The Tempered Wind**. New York: Atheneum, 1987. 207p. $14.95. ISBN 0-689-31339-X. 7-10

Gabriella, a 17-year-old dwarf, has lived with her aunts since being orphaned at 13. In 1948, she decides to go to Montana to work. After she falls in love with a minister, her health improves, but he tries to use her disability as an enticement for people to come to his revival meetings for healing.

562. Doctorow, E. L. **Ragtime**. 1975. New York: Modern Library, 1994. 352p. $15.50. ISBN 0-679-60088-4. New York: Plume, 1996. 352p. $9.95pa. ISBN 0-452-27570-9pa. YA

The story looks at the lives of three men during 1910 to 1917: a white upper-middle-class flag manufacturer, a Jewish immigrant silhouette artist, and a Black jazz pianist. Families of the three men meet each other in a variety of situations, with the flag maker's family looking after the pianist's girlfriend and child, and the starving Jewish artist marrying the flag maker's wife after the flag maker drowns when the *Titanic* sinks. The police shoot the pianist's girlfriend, and the pianist becomes a revolutionary. Their diverse situations give an overview of life throughout the strata of American society before and during World War I.

563. Doctorow, E. L. **The Waterworks**. New York: Random House, 1994. 253p. $23. ISBN 0-394-58754-5. New York: Signet, 1995. 253p. $6.99pa. ISBN 0-451-18563-3pa. YA

The freelance favorite of newspaper editor McIlvaine, Martin Pemberton, claims that he has seen his dead father on a horse-drawn omnibus in New York during 1871 and then disappears. McIlvaine obtains help from the only honest policeman in New York during the Tweed Ring era, and the two eventually discover that a doctor is trying to prolong the lives of several men wealthy enough to pay him as much as he demands. McIlvaine tells an honest story of a dishonest time filled with scientific and political fraud.

564. Doctorow, E. L. **World's Fair**. 1985. New York: Peter Smith, 1994. 384p. $22. ISBN 0-8446-6696-3. New York: Plume, 1996. 384p. $10.95pa. ISBN 0-452-27572-5pa. YA

When Edgar, nine, wins an honorable mention for an essay he writes sponsored by the 1939 World's Fair, his family receives free tickets to the event. As an adult, Edgar remembers the day and his life at that time when he enjoyed listening to the radio, visiting stores, watching serials in the movies, and seeing the circus clown balancing on the high wire. Edgar buries a time capsule with his momentoes, but at the last minute he keeps his ventriloquism book because he needs to continue to practice. Although the day at the fair was not one of family harmony, Edgar's memories soften the pain.

565. Dolan, Edward F. **America in World War I**. Brookfield, CT: Millbrook Press, 1996. 96p. $19.90. ISBN 1-56294-522-X. 6-9

The text introduces World War I and emphasizes the participation of the United States. Boxed essays include titles such as "American Women Go to War," "At War on the Home Front," "The War in the Air," and "Weapons of World War I." The book also presents brief biographical profiles of participants who later played important roles in World War II. Photographs, Maps, Bibliography, and Index.

566. Dolan. Edward F. **America in World War II: 1941**. Brookfield, CT: Millbrook Press, 1991. 72p. $16.40; $6.95pa. ISBN 1-878841-05-X; 1-87884-181-5pa. 4-8

America entered World War II on December 8, 1941, after Japanese planes bombed six U.S. military installations on the Hawaiian island of Oahu at Pearl Harbor. Other places bombed were the Philippine Island bases, Wake, Guam, and Midway. Then Japan's allies, Germany and Italy, declared war on the United States, and the country answered with a return declaration. Great Britain, already at war with Italy and Germany, declared war on Japan. In the closing weeks of 1941, Japanese troops captured the islands of Wake and Guam and invaded the Philippines. Photographs and maps expand the text. Bibliography and Index.

567. Dolan. Edward F. **America in World War II: 1942**. Brookfield, CT: Millbrook Press, 1991. 72p. $15.90. ISBN 1-56294-007-4. 5-8

In early 1942, Japan won control of the Philippine Islands. In June, however, the United States won a victory at the island of Midway, deep in the North Pacific. In the next months, two major campaigns began, one by the Army under General Douglas MacArthur, and the other under the Navy's Admiral Chester W. Nimitz. On the European front, America began to participate in the war in North Africa. A joint invasion of U.S. and British troops on the north coast of Africa began to drive the Germans out of Morocco, Algeria, and Tunisia. Photographs and maps expand the text. Bibliography and Index.

568.   Dolan, Edward F. **America in World War II: 1943**. Brookfield, CT: Millbrook Press, 1992. 64p. $15.90; $6.95pa. ISBN 1-56294-113-5; 1-87884-162-9pa. 4-7

This volume begins with Operation Torch, which extended from Morocco to Algeria, and finally gave the Allies a victory in May 1943. A campaign in Sicily began in July (Operation Husky), with success achieved in August. In the Pacific, MacArthur controlled the battles of New Guinea and the Solomon Islands, which had continued since 1942. Nimitz fought at Makin and Tarawa. During the year, those remaining on the mainland wanted news of the battles while they rationed food and continued war production. Roosevelt and Churchill met several times to discuss strategy. Capsule highlights of the generals include Eisenhower, Rommel, Patton, Harold Alexander, Mussolini, Mark W. Clark, MacArthur, and Nimitz. Bibliography and Index.

569.   Dolan. Edward F. **America in World War II: 1944**. Brookfield, CT: Millbrook Press, 1993. 72p. $16.40. ISBN 1-56294-221-2. 5-8

Admiral Nimitz spent the first nine months of 1944 capturing islands on his way to Japan. He sent his ships to support MacArthur's attempts on the Philippines. In October 1944, they stormed ashore on the island of Leyte, then in December on Mindoro. At the end of the year, the general was preparing to invade Luzon, home of the Philippines' capital city Manila. Nimitz continued toward Japan with his ships. In Europe, on June 6, more than 5,300 ships landed on the beaches at Normandy, France. General Eisenhower and the troops drove back the German defenders. In August, other Allied troops landed on the southern coast of France, and they spread east to the German border and north into Belgium, Luxembourg, and Holland. In December, in the snow, Hitler sent a massive force of German troops against U.S. forces stationed along the Belgium and Luxembourg borders. He wanted to separate the U.S. troops from the British forces in the Battle of the Bulge; he failed. Bibliography and Index.

570.   Dolan, Edward F. **America in World War II: 1945**. Brookfield, CT: Millbrook Press, 1994. 72p. $16.40. ISBN 1-56294-320-0. 4-7

In early 1945, U.S. troops stopped the German attack on the borders of Luxembourg and Belgium. General Dwight Eisenhower returned to his plan to reach the Rhine River in Germany. In April, the Germans fought back, and the Allies suffered heavy casualties. The fighting ended with German defeat on May 5. But the real shock was the horror of finding the extermination camps. In January in the Pacific, General Douglas MacArthur landed on Luzon in the Philippines and began his attempt to recapture Manila. In July, the fighting there ended. Far to the north, Admiral Chester Nimitz had invaded Iwo Jima and Okinawa. By July 3, the U.S. had captured both places. On August 6, 1945, the *Enola Gay* dropped an atom bomb on Hiroshima, and on August 9, another dropped on Nagasaki. With those terrible explosions the war ended in the Pacific; the Japanese formally surrendered on September 2, 1945. Photographs and maps expand the text. Bibliography and Index.

571.   Dolan, Edward F. **The American Revolution: How We Fought the War of Independence**. Brookfield, CT: Millbrook Press, 1995. 110p. $19.90. ISBN 1-56294-521-1. 6-9

The text looks at the American Revolution through battles in chronological order, beginning with Lexington and Concord. It covers all the places, people, and situations pertinent to the war, supplemented with maps and reproductions. Sidebars include information on figures such as Betsy Ross and Benedict Arnold. Bibliography and Index. *Notable Children's Trade Books in the Field of Social Studies.*

572.   Dolan, Edward F. **Panama and the United States: Their Canal, Their Stormy Years**. New York: Franklin Watts 1990. 160p. $19.86. ISBN 0-531-110911-9. 5 up

When Columbus arrived in what is now Panama on his fourth voyage in 1503, probably 750,000 people, from the Cuna tribe and others, lived there. But Balboa arrived first, in 1501. Not until 1513 did Balboa cross Panama to see the great body of water on the other side, the Pacific. Balboa realized that a waterway would make the journey much easier; thus, the idea of a canal began very early in Panama's recorded history. From 1799 to 1804, Alexander von Humbolt surveyed the area and found nine reasonable routes to cut across land to the Pacific. Because of battles, treaties, and misfortune, the United States was not free to complete the canal until the beginning of the twentieth century. The man who made it most possible was William Crawford Gorgas; he discovered that mosquitoes caused malaria and yellow fever and saved the lives of many workers. On August 15, 1913, the canal opened. A further series of treaties and disagreements between Panama and the United States have peppered the canal's history. Finally, Torrijos made an agreement with President Carter to take possession of the canal on December 31, 1999. Panama's new ruler at Torrijos's death, Noriega, did nothing to further good relationships. Photographs show the progress of the canal's construction. Source Notes, Bibliography, and Index.

573.   Dolan, Edward F., and Margaret Scariano. **Shaping U.S. Foreign Policy: Profiles of Twelve Secretaries of State**. New York: Franklin Watts, 1996. 128p. $22. ISBN 0-531-11264-0. (Democracy in Action). 7-9

Each chapter of the book begins with a brief biographical introduction to one of the 12 secretaries of state and describes the importance of that person to changing the size of the United States or changing its relationship to another country or countries. The men covered range from James Madison and his arrangement to buy the Louisiana Territory from France to Henry Kissinger, who dealt with China. Through this information, the authors show how the policy in the United States has changed from land acquisition to concerns about peace to containing Communism. Bibliography, Notes, and Index.

574.   Dolan, Ellen. **Susan Butcher and the Iditarod Trail**. New York: Walker, 1993. 103p. $15.85. ISBN 0-8027-8211-6. 5-8

Of all the sports events in the world, the Iditarod race in Alaska is considered the hardest. It officially began as a yearly event in 1973. It covers more than 1,000 miles in the snow with the racer using 7 to 20 mushers (dogs) to pull a sleigh along the trail. The value of racing mushers became clear in 1925 when the "black death" broke out in Nome, Alaska. Children infected with diphtheria needed medicine, but the closest medicine during the winter was 25 days away. By using teams of sled dogs and drivers, the medicine reached Nome in five days, seven and one-half hours. From this event, the idea of the race evolved until it became reality in 1973. Susan Butcher and her mushers have won the race four times. Appendices and Index.

575.   Dolan, Sean. **James Beckwourth: Frontiersman**. New York: Chelsea House, 1992. 118p. $18.95. ISBN 0-7910-1120-8. (Black Americans of Achievement). 5 up

As the only son of a white plantation master and a slave, James Beckwourth (1798-1866) was legally a slave himself, but his father never treated him as one. He went with his father to Missouri in 1810 and went to school in St. Louis. After training to become a blacksmith, he decided to become a fur trapper and mountain man. His story includes his fighting the Seminoles in Florida, serving in the U.S. Army in Colorado, and becoming a Crow Indian war chief. He had many experiences with diverse people. Photographs and reproductions enhance the text. Chronology, Further Reading, and Index.

576.   Dolan, Sean. **Junípero Serra**. New York: Chelsea House, 1991. 110p. $18.95; $7.95pa. ISBN 0-7910-1255-7; 0-7910-1282-4pa. (Hispanics of Achievement). 5 up

Miguel José Serra (1713-1784), born in Majorca, began his religious training at 15. He became a Franciscan and in 1748 left his home and family to become a missionary in the New World. He served the Spanish missions built by the conquerors trying to convert Indians to Catholicism by either persuasion or force. In 1769, he joined the expeditions exploring California and established the string of missions that still stand today from San Diego to San Francisco. In 1988, the church began the process of making him a saint, although Native Americans accuse him of trying to destroy their culture. Engravings and reproductions enhance the text. Chronology, Further Reading, and Index.

577.   Dominy, Jeannine. **Katherine Dunham: Dancer and Choreographer**. New York: Chelsea House, 1992. 111p. $18.95. ISBN 0-7910-1123-2. (Black Americans of Achievement). 5 up

As a teenager, Katherine Dunham (1909-) realized that she wanted to dance. She saw links between modern American dances and ancient tribal dances in Africa that won her an anthropology fellowship to the Caribbean to observe dance. Afterward, she formed a touring company to introduce dance to everyone. In 1945, she opened her own school in New York that trained Black performers. In 1962, she moved to East St. Louis, Illinois, and opened the Performance Arts Training Center to give opportunities to the city's youth. She has had a full life of giving to her community as a performer, choreographer, teacher, and scholar. Photographs and reproductions enhance the text. Chronology, Further Reading, and Index.

578.   Donahue, John. **An Island Far from Home**. Minneapolis, MN: Carolrhoda, 1995. 179p. $14.96. ISBN 0-87614-859-3. (Adventures in Time). 4-7

A button emblazoned with an "A" found in an attic begins the story. In Tilton, Massachusetts, in 1864, when Joshua Loring is 12, he hopes he might be able to join the army to fight against the enemy who killed his father. His Uncle Robert, a civilian lawyer and a wartime deputy commander of a fort called George's Island, tries to convince him that war is terrible. Uncle Robert gets Joshua to write to John, a young rebel soldier imprisoned on George's Island. Joshua quickly understands that John is very much like him, and when he suggests that his class write to this prisoner of war, he loses his friends. *Notable Children's Trade Books in the Field of Social Studies*, *IRA Children's Book Award*, and *Society of School Librarians Outstanding Book*.

579.   Donahue, Marilyn Cram. **Straight Along a Crooked Road**. New York: Walker, 1985. 188p. $14.95. ISBN 0-8027-6585-8. 7 up

In 1850, Luanna's father decides that the family will leave their Vermont home for California. Their trip takes two years because they stop for the winter. Along the way, Luanna, 14, hears that her best friend has died from typhoid. Then her brother dies on the trail. When Luanna falls in love, the pain of her loss remains, but she has new hope.

580. Donahue, Marilyn Cram. **The Valley in Between**. New York: Walker, 1987. 227p. $15.85. ISBN 0-8027-6745-1. 5 up

Emmie, 13 in 1857, likes to take off her shoes and get her feet muddy. People chastise her for this behavior, but other tensions in her California town divert attention from her. The Mormons must return to Utah, someone discovers gold, the Indians begin attacking, and notice that a civil war may begin overshadows all. Emmie likes being part of the events, including having the handsome Tad appreciate her.

581. Dorris, Michael. **Sees Behind Trees**. New York: Hyperion, 1996. 96p. $14.95. ISBN 0-7868-0224-3. 4-8

In pre-Colonial America, Walnut has myopia and knows that he can never see well enough to become the kind of hunter admired by his tribe. His mother suggests that he "look with his ears." Because of his ability to "see" what the others cannot, the tribe chooses him to accompany the village elder, Gray Fire, on a journey to find the land of water. He fulfills this role by passing his universal and age-old tests of manhood. *School Library Journal Best Book.*

582. Douglas, Roy. **The World War, 1939-1945: The Cartoonists' Vision**. New York: Routledge, 1990. 300p. $16.95pa. ISBN 0-415-07141-0pa. YA

The political cartoon encapsulates the mood of a group of people in history and reveals how subtle propaganda can be. A page of commentary and perspective accompanies each of these political cartoons collected from World War II. Included are cartoons that show how the war appeared to people in different nations and to diverse groups within those nations. Many are British; some are Italian and French; a few are German or Russian; and none are Japanese.

583. Douglass, Frederick. **Escape from Slavery: The Boyhood of Frederick Douglass in His Own Words**. Michael McCurdy, ed. New York: Knopf, 1994. 63p. $15. ISBN 0-679-84652-2. 5-8

More than 150 years ago, Frederick Douglass (1817-1895) escaped from slavery. During his boyhood, he was separated from his family, he learned to read, and he endured harsh treatment from cruel masters. McCurdy has taken excerpts from Douglass's longer book to make his experiences accessible to younger readers. Bibliography.

584. Driemen, J. E. **Atomic Dawn: A Biography of Robert Oppenheimer**. New York: Dillon Press, 1988. 160p. $13.95. ISBN 0-87518-397-2. (People in Focus). 5 up

As a physicist, Robert Oppenheimer (1904-1967) knew the danger associated with the announcement that the Germans had learned how to split uranium and could possibly create an atomic bomb. When the military approached him about the practicality of making a bomb in World War II, he knew the answers. The security check on his past revealed his flirtation with the Communist Party, so the government did not want him to head the Los Alamos, New Mexico, research laboratory, but he was the best person for the job. He succeeded in building the bombs that destroyed Hiroshima and Nagasaki in 1945. Afterward, anti-Communist sentiment in the United States, and the ability of the Soviet Union to create nuclear weapons so quickly after the first were detonated, led to an accusation that Oppenheimer had spied for the Soviet Union. He was cleared of the charges, however, and he advocated treaties against the bomb. Bibliography and Index.

585. Driemen, John E. **Clarence Darrow**. New York: Chelsea House, 1992. 112p. $18.95. ISBN 0-7910-1624-2. (Library of Biography). 5 up

As one of America's most famous lawyers, Clarence Darrow (1857-1938) represented the defense in the 1925 Scopes Monkey trial. He had a special sympathy for the oppressed because his own parents had been ostracized for their liberal ideals. He defended miners in Pennsylvania, workers whose lives were being ruined for profit, Blacks, pacifists, socialists, and any others whose personal freedom was threatened. He also became one of America's humanitarians. The text tells his story with complementary photographs. Further Reading, Chronology, and Index.

586. Dublin, Thomas, ed. **Farm to Factory: Women's Letters, 1830-1860**. New York: Columbia University Press, 1993. 217p. $35; $15pa. ISBN 0-231-08156-1; 0-231-08157-Xpa. YA

When girls went to factories and mills to work during the nineteenth century, they wrote letters home to tell about their situations. The text uses their letters to describe their economic situations, motivation in their work, friends, social lives, and concerns about their friends and family back home. The educational level of these women was not particularly high, but in the nineteenth century they were normal rather than exceptions. Index.

587. Dublin, Thomas. **Transforming Women's Work: New England Lives in the Industrial Revolution**. Ithaca, NY: Cornell University Press, 1995. 324p. $39.95; $15.95pa. ISBN 0-8014-2844-0; 0-8014-8090-6pa. YA

Although the reading may be slow at times, the information about women and their work at the end of the nineteenth century gives insight into their economic conditions. Wage work and industrialization allowed women to do "outwork" at home; find employment in the Lowell, Massachusetts, textile mills; make shoes in Lynn, Massachusetts; become garment workers; or teach in New Hampshire. Dublin believes that this economic shift caused more female dependence than before because entire families moved to the city and demanded that their daughters stay at home rather than make their own money. Bibliography and Index.

588. Dubowski, Cathy East. **Andrew Johnson: Rebuilding the Union**. Englewood Cliffs, NJ: Silver Burdett, 1991. 126p. $12.95. ISBN 0-382-09945-1. (History of the Civil War). 5 up

At the beginning of the Civil War, Andrew Johnson (1808-1875) declared that he was a "Union man." The Northerners were delighted, but his Tennessee neighbors thought him a traitor. Although born into poverty, he rose in politics because he believed in the working man. After becoming President at Lincoln's assassination, he became involved in postwar politics and had to endure an impeachment trial. He was acquitted, and then he was elected to the U.S. Senate. Timetable, Suggested Reading, Selected Sources, and Index.

589. Dubowski, Cathy East. **Clara Barton: Healing the Wounds**. Kimberly Bulcken Root, illustrator. Englewood Cliffs, NJ: Silver Burdett, 1991. 133p. $12.95. ISBN 0-382-09940-0. (History of the Civil War). 6-9

Although she began her teaching career in a one-room schoolhouse, Clara Barton (1821-1912) became the head of nursing operations during the Civil War. She convinced surgeons that they needed clean and orderly field hospitals. After the war, she went to Europe to see the emergency help available there, and later established the American Red Cross. She also led a fight for women's suffrage. Timetable, Suggested Reading, Selected Sources, and Index.

590. Dubowski, Cathy East. **Robert E. Lee and the Rise of the South**. Kimberly Bulcken Root, illustrator. Englewood Cliffs, NJ: Silver Burdett, 1991. 133p. $12.95. ISBN 0-382-09942-7. (History of the Civil War). 6-9

Lincoln offered Robert E. Lee (1807-1870) the command of the Union armies on the same day that Lee heard that Virginia had seceded from the Union. He decided to fight for his state, and he led the Army of Northern Virginia from one brilliant campaign to another against better-equipped enemies. He served with honor although what he saw made him sad. Timetable, Suggested Readings, Sources, and Index.

591. Ducey, Jean Sparks. **The Bittersweet Time**. Grand Rapids, MI: William B. Eerdman, 1995. 115p. $13; $6pa. ISBN 0-8028-5096-0; 0-8028-5113-4pa. 5-8

In October 1929, when she is 14, Jane Hartley's life changes. Her father loses his job, and she can no longer have an allowance. In this first-person novel in diary form, she discusses her love for writing and her chance to work for Mr. Walz in his new bookstore. He encourages her to read, and she discovers that she learns more by reading as many different books as possible than she learns in school. He offers her a full-time job, so she quits school to take it because her salary will keep her mother from having to go out of town to work, as her father has had to do. By March 1930, all have jobs in the area, but they must continue to pay their bills. Jane prepares to send more manuscripts to magazines.

592. Ducker, Bruce. **Lead Us Not into Penn Station**. Sag Harbor, NY: Permanent Press, 1994. 224p. $22. ISBN 1-877946-36-2. YA

Danny Meadoff, 16 in 1955, becomes a Fuller Brush salesman in his Brooklyn neighborhood, hoping to aid his family's meager finances. He subcontracts some of his work, and his subcontractors gamble the customers' down payments at the track, a situation that mirrors his father's problems. In the background are his parents' concern about polio, the rumor that the Dodgers are going to leave town, and the saxophone player on the corner who must be diabetic because of all the hypodermic needles lying around. Danny comes of age this summer as he sees his best friend's father run away with his secretary and has to protect his own father from a loan shark.

593. Dudley, Mark. **Brown v. Board of Education (1954): School Desegregation**. New York: Twenty-First Century Books, 1994. 96p. $15.98. ISBN 0-8050-3657-1. 6 up

In May 1954, the Supreme Court announced a unanimous decision that the segregation of public schools was unconstitutional. In the early 1950s, five separate but related cases filed by Black families said that separate schools were not lawful, especially since the Black schools were vastly inferior to the white ones. This decision ended more than a century of state-sanctioned discrimination against Black students. Photographs complement the text. Source Notes, Glossary, Further Reading, and Index.

594. Dudley, Mark. **United States v. Nixon (1974): Presidential Powers**. New York: Twenty-First Century Books, 1994. 96p. $15.98. ISBN 0-8050-3658-X. (Supreme Court Decisions). 6 up

In 1968, Richard Nixon became the 37th President of the United States. On June 17, 1972, the Watergate break-in occurred. In November, Nixon was reelected President. Then in January, with the beginning of the Watergate trial, the situation began to change. During 1973, events kept pointing to the President's involvement in the break-in. In October, the Vice President, Spiro Agnew, had to resign, and Nixon appointed Gerald Ford to be Vice President. In July 1974, the Supreme Court ruled that Nixon must turn over tapes made from his office to the investigators of the break-in. His involvement in the obstruction of justice became clear. He resigned on August 9, 1974. Source Notes, Glossary, Further Reading, and Index.

595. Dudley, Mark E. **Engel v. Vitale (1962): Religion and the Schools**. New York: Twenty-First Century Books, 1995. 96p. $15.98. ISBN 0-8050-3916-3. (Supreme Court Decisions). 7-10

The United States tried to establish in the Constitution that Americans would have the right to choice in religion. During revolutionary times, towns or churches operated most schools, and when public schools became the norm, they were unprepared to acknowledge different religions. When a parent complained that some student religions were not allowed, the Supreme Court heard the case. On June 25, 1962, it officially stated that schools could not have prayers because sometimes they violated the rights of those who were excluded from the prayer because of their religion. Source Notes, Glossary, Further Reading, and Index.

596. Dudley, Mark E. **Gideon v. Wainwright (1963): Right to Counsel**. New York: Twenty-First Century Books, 1995. 96p. $15.98. ISBN 0-8050-3914-7. (Supreme Court Decisions). 7-10

In 1963, Gideon, a poor middle-aged man, felt that he had been unfairly convicted of a crime because he could not afford an attorney. Wainwright, represented by the state of Florida, his employer, said that defendants were entitled to free legal counsel only in specific circumstances. On March 18, 1963, the court agreed with Gideon that anyone accused of a felony has the right to an attorney. The text looks at the ideas and arguments behind this case. Source Notes, Further Reading, Glossary, and Index.

597. Dudley, William, ed. **The American Revolution: Opposing Viewpoints**. San Diego, CA: Greenhaven, 1992. 287p. $19.95. ISBN 1-56510-011-5. (Opposing Viewpoints). 9 up

The support in the text for each side of the questions debated about the American Revolution come from people who lived during the times. Among the topics are whether the British Parliament has a right to tax, if the Parliament is abusing rights of the colonists, if blame for the Boston Massacre should lie with the colonists or with the British, and whether Americans should resist the tea tax. In debates over independence, subjects include whether the colonists should change policies toward Great Britain, if they should trade, or if independence or reconciliation is desirable. War discussions wonder if war against the British is justified, if the revolutionary cause has a chance, and how Loyalists should be treated. After the war, people debated natural rights, the government model, and whether the war was a social revolution. Chronology, Annotated Bibliography, For Discussion, and Index.

598. Dudley, William, ed. **The Civil War: Opposing Viewpoints**. San Diego, CA: Greenhaven, 1995. 310p. $19.95. ISBN 1-56510-224-X. (Opposing Viewpoints). 9 up

Theological, ideological, political, economic, geographical, and social conflicts led to the Civil War from 1861 to 1865, when 620,000 soldiers and unknown numbers of civilians died. Both sides fought for political liberty, equality, and self-government, but the causes of the war were secession and slavery. In short essays both pro and con written by public figures living during the Civil War, the text examines different viewpoints toward aspects of the conflict. Some felt that the Union must be preserved; others did not. Some thought the South had a right to secede and a right to own slaves. Then people wondered if individual states could make the choice to secede and if any could justify the decision. Still others wondered if the war was necessary for preservation of the Union. Debates raged in the North and South during the war over the importance of Manassas, the type of strategy to adopt, the value of the Emancipation Proclamation, and Lincoln's right to act in time of war. Concerns arose about the role of Black soldiers fighting for the North or being enlisted, or what would happen if the South captured them. After the war were questions as to the appropriateness of peace negotiations, Sherman's tactics, and whether the South should surrender. A final discussion from hindsight poses the question as to who freed the slaves—they themselves or Lincoln. For Discussion, Chronology, Annotated Bibliography, and Index.

599. Dudley, William, ed. **The Cold War: Opposing Viewpoints**. San Diego, CA: Greenhaven, 1992. 312p. $19.95. ISBN 1-56510-009-3. (Opposing Viewpoints). 9 up

From 1945 to 1990, the United States was part of the Cold War with the Soviet Union and other Communist states. This text discusses this political stance, the conflict, and what happened as a result. Annotated Bibliography and Index.

600. Dudley, William, ed. **The Creation of the Constitution: Opposing Viewpoints**. San Diego, CA: Greenhaven, 1995. 312p. $19.95. ISBN 1-56510-220-7. (Opposing Viewpoints). 9 up

One of the tenets present after the American Revolution was that authority comes from the consent of the governed. Debates during 1786-1788 concerned the creation of the Constitution. In short essays both pro and con written by public figures living during the time the Constitution was created, the text examines different viewpoints toward its contents. People debated the need for the Articles of Confederation, the role of the national government in relation to that of the states, and the effect of Shay's Rebellion. Others wanted to know if the Convention had the authority to establish a national government and decide its organization or just to revise the Articles of Confederation. Questions about a new government included what size it should be, what would be the role of checks and balances, how would the individual be represented, and where would the slave trade fit. A serious decision was whether the President should be one person or a committee. As for ratification, should it be a compromise or would it benefit only the elite, and was the Bill of Rights necessary for ratification. A hindsight question asks if the Constitution was created by the genius of its framers or the genius of the American people. Appendices, For Discussion, Chronology, Annotated Bibliography, and Index.

601. Dudley, William, ed. **Slavery: Opposing Viewpoints**. San Diego, CA: Greenhaven, 1992. 310p. $19.95. ISBN 1-56510-013-1. (American History). 9 up

The text looks at the living conditions and the treatment of slaves during the early years of America. It examines the arguments that people used both for and against this practice, the government's actual role in decisions about slavery, what the government's role should have been, and the importance of resistance and abolitionism. Bibliography and Index.

602. Dudley, William. **The Vietnam War: Opposing Viewpoints**. San Diego, CA: Greenhaven, 1990. 240p. $19.95. ISBN 0-89908-478-8. (Opposing Viewpoints). 7 up

The text includes essays by people involved in the Vietnam conflict, from 1945 to the present, that give differing viewpoints on five topics. The topics include why the United States became involved in Vietnam, why U.S. policy failed in Vietnam, the legacies of Vietnam, how the Vietnam War affected its veterans, and what U.S. policy toward Indochina should be. Chronology, Annotated Bibliography, and Index.

603. Dudley, William, and Teresa Dudley, eds. **Puritanism: Opposing Viewpoints**. San Diego, CA: Greenhaven, 1994. 307p. $19.95. ISBN 1-56510-081-6. (Opposing Viewpoints). 10 up

In the 1670s, the followers of Increase Mather believed that the Puritan experiment had lost its way because the people were more interested in money than religion. On the other hand, proponents of John Leverett and William Hubbard thought a middle ground was possible and that Mather's followers were spiritually arrogant. In short essays both pro and con written by public figures living during Puritan times, the text examines different viewpoints that existed in the colonies. Points covered are Puritan vision, the religious dissent in Roger Williams and the Antinomians, the tolerance level of the Puritans, the restrictions on immigrants, who should be allowed to hold political leadership, the place of economics, the establishment of laws, the relationship with Native Americans, the Puritan views toward witches, the Great Awakening, and the place of religious zealotry. A final assessment examines if Puritanism as a model for the world could work. For Discussion, Chronology, Annotated Bibliography, and Index.

604. Duey, Kathleen. **Anisett Lundberg: California, 1851**. New York: Aladdin, 1996. 144p. $3.99pa. ISBN 0-689-80386-9pa. (American Diaries, 3). 5-7

When Anisett finds a piece of gold where she and her mother serve gold diggers their food in California, she wonders whom she should tell. Her father is dead, and her mother, with no friends, only wants to return to the East. Anisett carelessly tells what she has found, and she jeopardizes her family's safety. In two days, the family identifies their friends, including a Chinese man; knows that they can start digging their own gold; and will have money to establish a place like their father wanted.

605. Duey, Kathleen. **Emma Eileen Grove: Mississippi, 1865**. New York: Aladdin, 1996. 144p. $3.99pa. ISBN 0-689-80385-0pa. (American Diaries, 2). 5-7

While Emma, her sister, and her brother travel from Mississippi to St. Louis, 10 days after Lincoln was shot in 1865, they are on a steamboat with horrible Yankees. Emma is concerned because she has not heard from her father. The boilers on the boat burst, and the boat catches fire near Memphis. A Yankee who helps Emma get to safety dies, and she begins to realize that even enemies can be kind. She and her brother decide to send the Yankee's family one of their last two pieces of gold.

606. Duey, Kathleen. **Mary Alice Peale**. New York: Aladdin, 1996. 144p. $3.99pa. ISBN 0-689-80387-7pa. (American Diaries, 4). 3-7

Mary Alice Peale lives in Philadelphia during 1777. While her Loyalist father entertains British officers at a dance, her brother, a rebel soldier fighting for the Colonies' freedom, lies wounded outside in their garden shed. She must find a way to help her brother without letting her father know. She records the difficulties of the year in her diary and the outcome that she helps to instrument.

607.   Duey, Kathleen. **Sarah Anne Hartford: Massachusetts, 1651**. New York: Aladdin, 1996. 144p. $3.99pa. ISBN 0-689-80384-2pa. (American Diaries, 1). 5-7

Sarah, 15, knows that merriment on the Sabbath in Massachusetts in 1650 is a punishable offense. She and her friend Elizabeth play in the snow, but people think that she is Elizabeth's brother Roger because she is wearing his coat. When the town officials announce public punishment for the two, Elizabeth must decide if she will confess that they should punish her instead of Roger. One of Sarah's main concerns is the woman her father is planning to marry—a person who warns Sarah that Elizabeth is a bad influence. Fortunately, her father realizes his mistake.

608.   Duffy, James. **Radical Red**. New York: Scribner's, 1993. 152p. $13.95. ISBN 0-684-19533-X. 5-8

Connor, 12, hears Susan B. Anthony's pleas for women to have the right to vote. Connor starts wearing a ribbon called a "radical red" in 1849 during the suffragette appeal in Albany, New York, at the state's constitutional convention to adopt universal suffrage. Connor and her mother are swayed by Aunt Susan's idea, but Connor's father, a policeman, thinks suffragettes are troublemakers. The family argues, but Connor and her mother decide to continue their support of the cause.

609.   Duggleby, John. **Artist in Overalls: The Life of Grant Wood**. New York: Chronicle, 1996. 57p. $15.95. ISBN 0-8118-1242-1. 4-7

One of the best-known American paintings is Grant Wood's *American Gothic*. The text looks at Grant Wood's life (1892-1942). He grew up in Iowa as a shy but stubborn boy; was educated in Minneapolis, Chicago, and Paris; and returned to Iowa, where he taught high school to support himself. He saw irony in the discrepancy between the romantic ideals of and realistic situations in American life, and he translated these concepts into his paintings. Included are reproductions of his paintings.

610.   Duggleby, John. **Impossible Quests**. Allan Eitzen, illustrator. New York: Crestwood House, 1990. 48p. $10.95. ISBN 0-89686-509-6. (Incredible History). 4 up

Various quests have attempted to prove the existence of Bigfoot in the Pacific Northwest of the United States and Canada, the Loch Ness Monster in Scotland, Noah's Ark in Turkey, Atlantis in the Mediterranean, and the lost continent of gold in the South Pacific. The text discusses these quests and illustrates them with black-and-white drawings. Bibliography and Index.

611.   Duncan, Dayton. **People of the West**. Boston: Little, Brown, 1996. 144p. $19.95; $10.95pa. ISBN 0-316-19627-4; 0-316-19633-9pa. 3-7

The text introduces 15 ordinary people who faced extraordinary circumstances in the West. They include people who lived there before the settlers from Europe arrived, the first white woman to cross the Continental Divide, one of the Chinese men who helped to build the railroad, an inhabitant of a prairie sod house, a gold prospector, and a Native American who faced the difficulty of keeping tribal traditions while adopting the ways of the white man. They are Sweet Medicine, Cabeza de Vaca, Kit Carson, Narcissa, Walt Whitman, Mariano Guadalupe Vallejo, William Swain, "John Chinaman," Teddy Blue Abbott, Uriah and Mattie Oblinger, Chief Joseph, Emmeline Wells, Pap Singleton, Buffalo Bird Woman, and Wolf Chief. Black-and-White Photographs, Principal Sources, and Index. *Notable Children's Trade Books in the Field of Social Sciences.*

612.   Duncan, Dayton. **The West: An Illustrated History for Children**. Boston: Little, Brown, 1996. 144p. $19.95; $10.95pa. ISBN 0-316-19628-2; 0-316-19632-0pa. 3-7

The text looks at the West, a land that for thousands of generations belonged to the Native Americans. When explorers began arriving from other countries in the sixteenth century, they began to take over the lands. But the Americans from the eastern coast were the ones who incorporated the land into their nation. Personal stories from the people who took over the land give its history, mainly from the early nineteenth through the twentieth centuries. Black-and-White Photographs, Principal Sources, and Index. *Notable Children's Trade Books in the Field of Social Sciences* and *New York Public Library Books for the Teen Age.*

613.   Dunlap, Julie. **Aldo Leopold: Living with the Land**. Antonio Castro, illustrator. New York: Twenty-First Century Books, 1993. 80p. $14.98. ISBN 0-8050-2501-4. (Earth Keepers). 4-7

As a young boy, Aldo Leopold (1886-1948) loved the land. When he went to prep school and had to give a speech, he said that people were using the forests too rapidly. He continued this concern as he attended and graduated from Yale's school of forestry. Not until he was older was he able to develop his own farmland in a way that would restore it. He saw when young that land was worth more than its ability to provide crops or lumber. He became concerned about soil conservation, ecology, and game management, and taught others what to do. Glossary and Index.

614.   Dunn, John. **The Relocation of the North American Indian**. San Diego, CA: Lucent, 1995. 128p. $16.95. ISBN 1-56006-240-1. (World History Series). 6-9

When Europeans arrived in the New World, more than 300 separate tribes speaking as many languages already thrived there—most in the Pacific coastal area, the Southwest, and east of the Mississippi. Some tribes were nomadic, some were sedentary farmers, but each tribe tended to live in a group with a tribal elder serving an advisory capacity. The disagreements that transpired between the whites and Native Americans began a dispossession that lasted 400 years and reduced the lands occupied by Native Americans to 2.3 percent of the continent. This disturbing history of the relationship between whites and the Native Americans uses works written during the periods related, the research of recognized scholars, and other relevant sources. An abbreviated litany of displacement begins when the Puritans overcame the Pequots in 1637, while the English fought and finally defeated the Powhatans in 1646. The Wampanoags lost in 1676. By 1794, Indians had ceded parts of Ohio and Indiana. In 1811, Tecumseh's confederacy was smashed, Jackson defeated the Creeks in 1814 and won Alabama, and the Seminoles had to cede most of west Florida in 1823. From 1835 to 1843, Osceola led a Seminole uprising. In 1838, the Cherokees were expelled from Georgia to walk the Trail of Tears. In 1859, gold seekers in California used guns to force the Osage tribe from its lands. From 1863 to 1868, the Navajos tried to protect themselves, but they lost, and the army marched them off their lands and onto reservations. Custer massacred the Cheyenne in 1868. In 1871, Congress ceased to recognize the tribes as individual nations. Then in 1876, Custer fought the Sioux at Little Bighorn and lost. But in 1890, the U.S. Army massacred the Sioux at Wounded Knee. Not until 1924 did Native Americans earn the right to vote in their own country. Notes, For Further Reading, Additional Works Consulted, and Index.

615.   Dunnahoo, Terry. **Pearl Harbor: America Enters the War**. New York: Franklin Watts, 1991. 112p. $21.10. ISBN 0-531-11010-9. (Twentieth Century American History). 7-12

Dunnahoo discusses the Japanese attack on Pearl Harbor at Oahu, Hawaii, on December 7, 1941. He gives background about the buildup of the Japanese military, the move of America's Pacific fleet to Hawaii, and the relationship between the United States and Japan before the attack. Dunnahoo focuses on the politics and the diplomacy of the situation rather than on the military aspect. Bibliography and Index.

616.   Durrant, Lynda. **Echohawk**. New York: Clarion, 1996. 190p. $14.95. ISBN 0-395-74430-X. 6-8

Mohicans raid four-year-old Jonathan's home in 1738 and carry him off after killing his family. He becomes Echohawk, member of a Mohawk family. Other members of the tribe, however, do not accept him. He has little interest in pursuing his relatives, and after he vaguely remembers the circumstances about his parents, he decides to stay with his Mohawk father and help him protect their land.

617.   Durwood, Thomas A. **John C. Calhoun and the Roots of the Civil War**. Englewood Cliffs, NJ: Silver Burdett, 1991. 160p. $12.95. ISBN 0-382-09936-2. (History of the Civil War). 5 up

John C. Calhoun (1782-1850), a South Carolinian senator, argued for the South's interest in slavery and helped keep it intact while he served in the U.S. Congress. The text looks at his life and the effect of his determination to keep the institution of slavery. Suggested Reading, Selected Sources, and Index.

618.   Dwyer, Christopher. **Robert Peary and the Quest for the North Pole**. New York: Chelsea House, 1992. 110p. $19.95. ISBN 0-7910-1316-2. (World Explorers). 5 up

Many people competed with Robert Peary (1856-1920) to become the first to reach the North Pole. Those explorers included Frederick Albert Cook, Elisha Kent Kane, Charles Francis Hall, Edward Parry, Fridtjof Nansen, and Adolphus Greely. They risked starvation, frostbite, scurvy, and various other maladies to reach their goal, but Peary sacrificed 23 years, his health, his money, some of his toes, and probably his sanity before he claimed the North Pole as his discovery in 1909. Photographs and reproductions enhance the text. Chronology, Further Reading, and Index.

619.   Dwyer, Frank. **John Adams**. New York: Chelsea House, 1989. 112p. $18.95; $7.95pa. ISBN 1-55546-801-2; 0-7910-0608-5pa. (World Leaders Past and Present). 5 up

Reproductions highlight the text that tells the story of John Adams, second President of the United States (1735-1826). The chapters note his childhood in Braintree, Massachusetts, and continue through his life. He became a major figure in the creation of the United States and an unlikely diplomat who feared for his life as he crossed the ocean to Paris. Further Reading, Chronology, and Index.

620.   Dyson, Michael Eric. **Making Malcolm: The Myth and Meaning of Malcolm X**. New York: Oxford University Press, 1995. 215p. $19.95; $10.95pa. ISBN 0-19-509235-X; 0-19-510285-1pa. YA

Dyson has examined almost every important biography of Malcolm X as well as popular movements that could be associated with him, such as modern movies about young Black males, to assess the influence of his life. He thinks of Malcolm as a "public moralist" who hated white racism and the temptations for Blacks to accommodate whites in order to be accepted. Malcolm had many failings, including continued repression of Black women and an ideological narrowness, but his influence continues through movies and music. Bibliography and Index.

E

621.   Earle, Alice. **Home Life in Colonial Days**. 1898. New York: Corner House, 1991. 470p. $29.95. ISBN 0-87918-063-8. Stockbridge, MA: Berkshire House, 1993. 470p. $14.95pa. ISBN 0-936399-28-8pa. 5 up

A thorough and well-documented text reveals the daily life of the settlers from the time they arrived in the early 1600s, when some had to live in caves, until they had lovely gardens surrounding permanent homes. Chapter topics include kitchens and serving meals, foods, making clothes and their styles, occupations, travel, transportation, overnight accommodations at taverns, Sunday activities, and neighborliness. Index.

622.   Echo-Hawk, Roger C., and Walter R. Echo-Hawk. **Battlefields and Burial Grounds: The Indian Struggle to Protect Ancestral Graves in the United States**. Minneapolis, MN: Lerner, 1994. 80p. $19.95. ISBN 0-8225-2663-8. 7 up

In the late 1800s and early 1900s, archaeologists dug up Native American remains almost at will, showing a lack of respect for the dead and for the living who wanted their ancestors properly buried. The Pawnee tribe, now living in Oklahoma, has spent time trying to retrieve the remains of their tribal members and rebury them. The history of the tribe is typical of the problems that Native Americans have had with the lack of government support for their traditions. Photographs complement the text. Notes and Index. *New York Public Library Books for the Teen Age, Notable Children's Trade Books in the Field of Social Studies, Carter G. Woodson Outstanding Merit*, and *Society of School Librarians International Best*.

623.   Edmonds, Walter. **Bert Breen's Barn**. 1975. Syracuse, NY: Syracuse University Press, 1991. $9.95pa. ISBN 0-8156-0255-3pa. YA

At 13 in 1910, Tom decides that he wants to buy the Breen barn from Bert's widow so that he will have a shelter for cows he plans to raise. He works and concludes the deal with her, but after her death, others tear down her house and plow up the yard looking for Bert's money, thought to be hidden somewhere in the vicinity. Tom gets his barn, and before he moves it, he realizes that the money is hidden in the unusual floor construction. He has to recover it before the others tear down his purchase. *National Book Award* and *Christopher Medal*.

624.   Edwards, Lillie J. **Denmark Vesey: Slave Revolt Leader**. New York: Chelsea House, 1990. 108p. $18.95. ISBN 1-55546-614-1. (Black Americans of Achievement). 5 up

Denmark Vesey (1767-1822), sold into slavery at 14, served as captain on voyages across the Atlantic, during which he saw the horrors of the slave trade. He started living in Charleston, South Carolina, in 1783, with an owner who permitted him to hire himself out as a carpenter. In 1799, he won a huge amount of money in a lottery and was able to buy his freedom. Then he began to try to liberate others from slavery. He read about the slave revolt in St. Dominique in 1804 and started to organize a similar uprising. In 1822, the Charleston militia crushed the uprising just before it was to begin. Although he did not succeed, his attempt frightened slave owners. Photographs and engravings enhance the text. Chronology, Further Reading, and Index.

625.   Edwards, Sally. **George Midgett's War**. New York: Atheneum, 1985. 138p. $12.95. ISBN 0-684-18315-3. 7-10

George, 14, lives in Ocrakoke on the Outer Banks of the North Carolina colony in 1777. British soldiers murder a mute woman who lives nearby, and the war comes to his neighborhood. George and his father take the salt that the woman had hidden (and for which she was killed) on a journey via land and sea to Valley Forge, Pennsylvania. They realize that their own troops need the salt as well as other supplies. They risk their lives to protect the colonies.

626.   Ehle, John. **Trail of Tears: The Rise and Fall of the Cherokee Nation**. New York: Anchor, Doubleday, 1988. 424p. $30. ISBN 0-385-23953-X. YA

In 1838, the U.S. government began a forced removal of the Cherokee Nation from their lands in Georgia, North Carolina, and South Carolina, where they had lived for generations, because white settlers wanted their land. Andrew Jackson was in the White House, and he had fought against Indians. When someone discovered gold in north Georgia where they lived, he supported the removal act authorizing federal troops to round up Indians and their Black slaves and move them by riverboat, wagon, horseback, and foot across the Mississippi to Oklahoma. The graves stretching along the route now mark the Trail of Tears. Bibliography and Index.

627.   Ehrlich, Elizabeth. **Nelly Bly: Journalist**. New York: Chelsea House, 1989. 111p. $18.95. ISBN 1-55546-643-5. (American Women of Achievement). 5 up

As the most celebrated reporter of her day, Nelly Bly (1885-1922), born Elizabeth Cochran, was prosperous. After being educated at home, she moved to Pittsburgh where she discovered that she, as a female, could not be a journalist. In 1885, however, she wrote a rebuttal to an editorial about women working and won a job. She visited prisons and slums and became a factory worker so that she could write her stories. In 1887, she moved to New York and revealed the horror of an insane asylum. She wrote about political corruption, the defenseless, and outdated traditions before she married and became a businesswoman. Later she returned to journalism. In 1890, she made a record-breaking trip around the globe. Photographs and reproductions enhance the text. Chronology, Further Reading, and Index.

628. Eidson, Tom. **St. Agnes's Stand**. New York: St. Martin's Press, 1994. 192p. $19.95. ISBN 0-399-13915-X. New York: Berkley, 1994. 192p. $4.99pa. ISBN 0-425-14396-1pa. YA

In the desert of New Mexico during July 1858, Nat Swanson meets Sister Agnes, 76, as he is running from Texas cowboys. Apaches have trapped Sister Agnes and two other nuns along with seven orphans. Sister Agnes thinks God has sent Nat to save them, and he feels obligated to fulfill her expectations. Nat has to outwit the Apache warrior Locan, who thinks that everyone's fate lies with water. And in the unexpected ending, everyone's does.

629. Elish, Dan. **The Transcontinental Railroad: Triumph of a Dream**. Brookfield, CT: Millbrook Press, 1994. 64p. $15.90; $5.95pa. ISBN 1-56294-746-X; 1-56294-337-5pa. (Spotlight on American History). 5-8

When the president and the vice president of the Central Pacific Railroad tried to drive in the last spike on the railroad to mark its official beginning in 1869, they both missed. They had to ask one of the Irish or Chinese workers to do the job for them. With this inability to drive one spike, they showed the value of the workers who had toiled unceasingly to finish the transcontinental railroad. The text, with photographs and prints, traces the progress of this major accomplishment from its groundbreaking in 1863 to its completion in 1869. Chronology, Further Reading, Bibliography, and Index.

630. Ellis, Rafaela. **Dwight D. Eisenhower: 34th President of the United States**. Ada, OK: Garrett Educational, 1989. 122p. $17.26. ISBN 0-944483-13-5. (Presidents of the United States). 5-9

The great-great-great-grandson of a German immigrant, Dwight David Eisenhower (1890-1969) rose from a life of poverty and love in dusty Abilene, Kansas, to go to West Point, achieve the highest military rank during World War II in Europe, and become President of the United States. The text relates information about his childhood and his career, including the Suez crisis, civil rights and Little Rock, the race in space, Khrushchev, and the U-2 affair. Photographs and reproductions enhance the text. Bibliography and Index.

631. Ellis, Rafaela. **Martin Van Buren: 8th President of the United States**. Ada, OK: Garrett Educational, 1989. 118p. $17.26. ISBN 0-944483-12-7. (Presidents of the United States). 5-9

Martin Van Buren (1782-1862) read law in New York State before becoming the attorney general of New York and then going to the Senate. He returned to New York as governor, and Andrew Jackson chose him to be Vice President. Van Buren became President after Jackson. During his time in office, the first major depression in the United States kept him from being reelected. Called the "Fox of Kinderhook" and "Little Magician," he knew how to manipulate events behind closed doors, but he could not end the economic problems. Bibliography and Index.

632. Emerson, Kathy Lynn. **Julia's Mending**. New York: Orchard, Franklin Watts, 1987. 136p. $11.95. ISBN 0-531-08319-5. 5-7

Julia, 12, does not want to stay with her country relatives in 1887 while her parents are missionaries in China. Her condescending attitude alienates her cousins, and when Julia breaks her leg, she cannot leave. While she is less mobile, she has to start talking to the family. When she realizes that the baby took the journal in which she had written nasty comments about everyone, she begins to adjust and make friends. Afterward, they work together to rescue a classmate.

633. Emert, Phyllis Raybin. **Top Lawyers and Their Famous Cases**. Minneapolis, MN: Oliver Press, 1996. 160p. $14.95. ISBN 1-881508-31-5. (Profiles). 5 up

Lawyers have always used the law and courts to make social, political, and economic change in the United States. The text presents some of these lawyers and their famous cases. They include Andrew Hamilton (1676?-1741) and the freedom to write the truth, John Adams (1735-1826) and the importance of justice, Abraham Lincoln (1809-1865) and the chance of equality for all, Belva Lockwood (1830-1917) and rights for Cherokees, Clarence Darrow (1857-1938) and support of society's outcasts, Robert H. Jackson (1892-1954) and his term as an international prosecutor of World War II Nazi criminals, Joseph Welch (1890-1960) as a legal folk hero during the McCarthy era, and Morris Dees (b. 1936) fighting against prejudice and hatred. Bibliography and Index.

634. Engelmann, Larry. **Tears Before the Rain: An Oral History of the Fall of South Vietnam**. New York: Oxford University Press, 1990. 375p. $22.95. ISBN 0-19-505386-9. YA

Engelmann gathered this collection of powerful stories from people in 1985 about the ending of the Vietnam War, 10 years after North Vietnam took over South Vietnam and Saigon was renamed Ho Chi Ming City. In each section of the book is a series of firsthand stories. The topics discussed with Americans are the last flight from

Danang, orphans, congressional delegations, the American Embassy, the Central Intelligence Agency, the Defense Attaché Office, the joint military team, the Military Sealift Command, marines, POWs, the media, civilians, and the presidency. Those topics that Engelmann covered with the Vietnamese he interviewed are the military, civilians, children, and victors. A final part looks at the Bui Doi (dust of the earth) and the Vietnamese as a whole. Glossary of Abbreviations and Acronyms and Index.

635. Equiano, Olaudah. **The Kidnapped Prince: The Life of Olaudah Equiano**. Ann Cameron, adapter. New York: Knopf, 1995. 133p. $16. ISBN 0-679-85619-6. 7-10

When prince Odaudah Equiano was a young boy, slavers captured him and took him from his home. He realized that knowledge might save him and learned to box, to cut hair, to navigate a ship, to ride a horse, to load a gun, to do accounts, to trade in order to buy his freedom, and, most important, to read and to write. He survived to write his story. He wanted to show that those who said that the lives of slaves were happy were wrong; these people were only interested in protecting their economic welfare. His book became a best-seller soon after its publication in 1789. Eight editions were published within three years in England and America.

636. Erhart, Margaret. **Augusta Cotton**. Cambridge, MA: Zoland, 1992. 289p. $19.95. ISBN 0-944072-21-6. YA

Augusta and her new friend Helen in the sixth grade are shocked to hear of the death of John F. Kennedy in 1963. Augusta finds that Helen questions life, and when Helen contracts lupus, Augusta is further surprised to find that the disease is serious. While visiting Helen when she is ill, Augusta learns enough about Helen and Helen's family to expand her vision beyond her limited Jewish-Protestant-French background.

637. Erlich, Scott. **Paul Robeson: Singer and Actor**. New York: Chelsea House, 1988. 110p. $18.95; $7.95pa. ISBN 1-55546-608-7; 0-7910-0206-3pa. (Black Americans of Achievement). 5 up

As an athlete and scholar, Paul Robeson (1890-1976) graduated first in his college class before becoming a lawyer. His fame rested, however, in his acting and singing abilities. Noted for his dignified portrayals of Black characters, including Othello, he had a beautiful voice with which he popularized "Ol' Man River." He spoke for the poor and the oppressed and condemned racial injustice. The government punished him for sympathizing with Communist ideals and blacklisted him during the Red Scare of the 1950s. He spent much of his later life in the Soviet Union. Photographs enhance the text. Chronology, Further Reading, and Index.

638. Eskow, Dennis. **Lyndon Baines Johnson**. New York: Franklin Watts, 1993. 160p. $13.90. ISBN 0-531-13019-3. (Impact Biography). 9-12

Lyndon Johnson (1908-1973) was a complex man whose involvement in the Vietnam War caused people to downgrade his contribution to the presidency. At the same time that he was sending troops abroad, he was approving important civil rights legislation that changed lives for many African Americans. Eskow notes that he once met Johnson, and in that brief meeting, Johnson was able to show through eye contact that he cared about humans. Eskow tries to reveal this complicated man based on primary sources and interviews. Notes, Bibliography, and Index.

639. Evans, J. Edward. **Freedom of Religion**. Minneapolis, MN: Lerner, 1990. 88p. $9.50. ISBN 0-8225-1754-X. 7-10

The First Amendment of the Constitution of the United States declares that church and state shall be separate. Many challenges to this law have occurred, including the right to sanctuary, saluting the flag, taxation of church income and property, conscientious objectors, Sunday business closings, the teaching of evolution and creationism, school prayer, and religious fraud. The text looks at these situations and cases that have threatened religious tolerance. Bibliography and Index.

640. Evans, J. Edward. **Freedom of Speech**. Minneapolis, MN: Lerner, 1990. 72p. $9.50. ISBN 0-8225-1753-1. 7 up

In this interesting history of the concept of free speech, Evans begins with the Athenians killing Socrates because he asked too many questions. His values, however, prevailed, as did those of Galileo in Italy, who suffered for saying the world was round. Printing presses led government and church officials to impose censorship throughout the sixteenth and seventeenth centuries because seditious libel supposedly hurt rulers. A big debate on free speech in the United States occurred in 1798 when Federalists passed the Sedition Act. As soon as Jefferson became President, he repealed the act and freed those who had been imprisoned under it. Another Sedition Act in 1918 decreed that people could not speak against the government about World War I and the draft. Then in 1919, the Supreme Court became involved. The Court heard cases and established that a "clear and present danger" must be apparent before speech may be silenced. The Fourteenth Amendment protected people under both state and federal laws. Appendix with the Bill of Rights, For Further Reading, Important Words, and Index.

641. Evans, J. Edward. **Freedom of the Press**. Minneapolis, MN: Lerner, 1990. 72p. $9.95. ISBN 0-8225-1753-1. 7-10

From the development of the Gutenberg printing press around 1436 through the Pentagon Papers release in 1971, the text traces the history of the concept of freedom of speech by discussing how the Supreme Court has interpreted this constitutional amendment and why the issue is controversial. Illustrations add to the information. Bibliography and Index.

642. Evans, Sara M. **Born for Liberty: A History of Women in America**. New York: Free Press, 1989. 386p. $24.95; $18.95pa. ISBN 0-02-902990-2; 0-02-903090-1pa. YA

This text is divided into chapters according to time periods in women's history, beginning with the colonization of America to the present. Notes, Further Reading, and Index.

643. Evert, Jodi, ed. **Addy's Cook Book: A Peek at Dining in the Past with Meals You Can Cook Today**. Middleton, WI: Pleasant, 1994. 44p. $7.95pa. ISBN 1-56247-123-6pa. (American Girls Pastimes). 4-8

Illustrations and text cover cooking in the Civil War and kitchens in the 1860s after Addy and her family escaped from slavery in the South. Menus and recipes for breakfast, dinner, and favorite foods appear.

644. Ewing, Elizabeth. **Women in Uniform Through the Centuries**. Totowa, NJ: Rowman and Littlefield, 1975. 160p. $21.50. ISBN 0-87471-690-X. YA

Photographs and drawings help emphasize the points that Ewing makes about uniforms, be they for military service or for a religious convent. Within the topics, she uses a historical approach to show how clothing has revealed status. The topics are service and servitude, women in a man's world, Florence Nightingale and the start of a modern age, youth, the time in war, developments between the wars, new looks for traditional uniforms, and women out of uniform. Bibliography and Index.

F

645.   Faber, Doris. **Calamity Jane: Her Life and Her Legend**. Boston: Houghton Mifflin, 1992. 62p. $14.95. ISBN 0-395-56396-8. 5-9

Martha Jane Cannary (1852-1903), later known as Calamity Jane, became so large a legend that no one is sure what she did. She was a heroine of the Old West, a sharpshooter, a scout for General Custer, and the bride of Wild Bill Hickok. Or perhaps she was not. Faber tries to decide who she was from the most reliable sources available. Photographs, Sources, and Index.

646.   Faber, Doris. **Printer's Devil to Publisher: Adolph S. Ochs of the New York Times**. New York: Black Dome Press, 1996. 192p. $12.95pa. ISBN 1-883789-09-5pa. YA

Adolph Ochs bought the *New York Times* and, through his character and accomplishment, made it into the paper that it has become. The text tells about this man and his honor as well as his concern for family along with his role in the newspaper. It also recounts the paper's coverage of such events as the *Titanic* sinking and Peary's journey to the North Pole.

647.   Faber, Doris, and Harold Faber. **Great Lives: American Government**. New York: Scribner's, 1988. 278p. $22.95. ISBN 0-684-18521-0. 5-9

Short biographical profiles of 36 individuals who made important contributions to public office and contributed to the development of the United States throughout its history appear here. Included are presidents, judges, and leaders in Congress: John Adams (1735-1826), Benjamin Franklin (1706-1790), Albert Gallatin (1761-1849), Alexander Hamilton (1755-1804), Thomas Jefferson (1743-1826), James Madison (1751-1836), John Marshall (1755-1835), James Monroe (1758-1831), George Washington (1732-1799), John Quincy Adams (1767-1848), John Calhoun (1782-1850), Samuel Houston (1792-1863), Henry Clay (1777-1852), Andrew Jackson (1767-1845), James Polk (1795-1845), Daniel Webster (1782-1852), William Jennings Bryan (1860-1925), Jefferson Davis (1808-1889), Robert La Follette (1855-1925), Abraham Lincoln (1809-1865), Justin Morrill (1810-1898), Jeannette Rankin (1880-1973), Theodore Roosevelt (1858-1919), Woodrow Wilson (1856-1924), Dwight David Eisenhower (1890-1969), Oliver Wendell Holmes (1841-1935), George Marshall (1880-1959), Eleanor Roosevelt (1884-1962), Franklin Delano Roosevelt (1882-1945), Margaret Chase Smith (1897-1994), Robert Taft (1889-1953), Harry Truman (1884-1972), Thurgood Marshall (1908-1993), Richard Nixon (1913-1994), and George Norris (1861-1944). Bibliography, Chronology, and Index.

648.   Faber, Doris, and Harold Faber. **We the People: The Story of the United States Constitution**. New York: Scribner's, 1987. 244p. $15.95. ISBN 0-684-18753-1. 7 up

The story of the Constitution begins with its establishment in 1787 and its changes since the Constitutional Convention. The Bill of Rights became part of it in 1791 and other amendments were added through the years until the 26th in 1971, when 18-year-olds were given the right to vote. Anecdotes highlight the various stages of this important document. Text of the Constitution, Bibliography, Notes, and Index.

649.   Faber, Harold. **The Discoverers of America**. New York: Scribner's, 1992. 290p. $17.95. ISBN 0-684-19217-9. 8-12

The text chronicles the discoverers of America, from the Native Americans who probably crossed the Bering Strait after the last Ice Age, through Leif Ericksson and the Vikings and the major European explorers, including Vespucci, De Soto, and La Salle. It concludes with Bering's discovery of Alaska and Sir James Cook's voyage to Hawaii. Bibliography and Index.

650.   Faber, Harold. **From Sea to Sea: The Growth of the United States**. New York: Scribner's, 1992. 246p. $15.95. ISBN 0-684-19442-2. 7 up

The original 13 colonies grew through a series of steps until the nation covered the land between the Atlantic and Pacific Oceans. The text looks at the negotiating and the deals that allowed the United States to make the appropriate purchases. When Napoleon decided to sell the entire Louisiana Territory, the country doubled in size. Then the old Northwest Territory, the Republic of Texas, the opening of the Oregon Territory, California, and the Southwest increased the width of the country. Finally, the purchase of Alaska and the annexation of Hawaii completed the additions. Anecdotes enliven the stories about each of these changes in the country. Bibliography and Index.

651.   Fahrmann, Willi. **The Long Journey of Lukas B.** Anthea Bell, translator. New York: Bradbury, 1985. 280p. $12.95. ISBN 0-02-734330-8. 8 up

Luke goes with his grandfather to America in 1870, where his grandfather plans to earn money using his carpentry skills, which will pay for his home in Germany. Luke wants to search for his father who left home several years before. He never finds his father, but his father leaves Luke 60 paintings of high quality to sell as an inheritance. Luke sells so many of them on board ship that he returns to Germany with enough money to purchase a shop. Luke realizes that his father had to leave home so that he could do the only thing he wanted—paint.

652.   Falkof, Lucille. **John F. Kennedy: 35th President of the United States**. Ada, OK: Garrett Educational, 1988. 120p. $17.26. ISBN 0-944483-03-8. (Presidents of the United States). 5-9
   The text begins with John F. Kennedy's experience on PT 109 in the Solomon Islands during World War II; he saved a man after the Japanese sank his ship. It continues with his education at Harvard (a family tradition) and his winning the Pulitzer Prize for his book *Profiles in Courage* in 1957. After he became the youngest President, he faced the Cuban Missile Crisis in 1962 and delivered a memorable speech in Berlin in June 1963 where he said, "Ich bin ein Berliner." In July 1963, the nuclear test ban treaty was concluded. Kennedy (b. 1917) was assassinated on November 22 of the same year. Bibliography and Index.

653.   Falkof, Lucille. **John Tyler: 10th President of the United States**. Ada, OK: Garrett Educational, 1990. 122p. $17.26. ISBN 0-9444483-60-7. (Presidents of the United States). 5-9
   After running with William Henry Harrison on the "Tippecanoe and Tyler, Too" campaign slogan, John Tyler (1790-1862) became Vice President. What he did not expect was that Harrison would die in office. Tyler became a reluctant President, but he did his job honestly, an unhappy proposition for many in Congress. He did not receive credit for saving the annexation of Texas to the Union; instead he was criticized. After he left office, he was only summoned once to Washington for advice. He wanted to return to public office but was never asked. He died before the Union divided because of the Civil War. Bibliography and Index.

654.   Falkof, Lucille. **Lyndon B. Johnson: 36th President of the United States**. Ada, OK: Garrett Educational, 1989. 120p. $17.26. ISBN 0-944483-20-8. (Presidents of the United States). 5-9
   Lyndon B. Johnson (1908-1973) grew up in Texas and was elected to the House of Representatives from that state in 1937. He then went to the Senate and served as both minority and majority leader. He became the Vice President and then the President when John F. Kennedy was assassinated in 1963. He won his own election in 1964. He served in Washington during World War II and the Korean War, and was President during the Vietnam War. The text looks closely at his life and his family. Bibliography and Index.

655.   Falkof, Lucille. **William H. Taft: 27th President of the United States**. Ada, OK: Garrett Educational, 1990. 124p. $17.26. ISBN 0-944483-56-9. (Presidents of the United States). 5-9
   William Taft (1857-1930) gained experience as a young lawyer trying to clean up immoral law practices. Juries thwarted him, but he gained respect from those who realized the type of work that he completed. He served in Benjamin Harrison's and Theodore Roosevelt's administrations before becoming President. As President, he was unable to get a federal budget established and was not reelected, but he did make good appointments to the Supreme Court. After his presidency, he became a professor at Yale, and then he became the Chief Justice of the United States Supreme Court. Bibliography and Index.

656.   Faragher, John Mark. **Daniel Boone: The Life and Legend of an American Pioneer**. New York: Henry Holt, 1992. 429p. $27.50. ISBN 0-8050-1603-1. YA
   Daniel Boone (1734-1820), a man of many contrasts, seems to have deserved the legends that have risen from his life. Faragher uses primary sources as well as the memories of Boone's descendants over a century after the incidents occurred. He also traces the legends about Boone in literature and culture. Boone was often away from home even though he had 10 children. He preferred to be alone but helped settlers find their way west. He seemed to like Native Americans even when he was removing them from their homes. And even though he did not like established systems, he served in the militia. These and many of Boone's other traits appear in the text. Chronology and Index.

657.   Farley, Karin Clafford. **Robert H. Goddard**. Englewood Cliffs, NJ: Silver Burdett, 1991. 138p. $13.95; $6.95pa. ISBN 0-382-24171-1; 0-382-24177-0pa. (Pioneers in Change). 5-9
   One day when a teenager, Robert Goddard (1882-1945) climbed into a tree and started looking at the sky. Influenced by the H. G. Wells story *The War of the Worlds*, he thought about traveling to places such as Mars, and his life changed. His scientific experiments began to focus on a way for that travel to occur. He studied electricity and physics in school and began to experiment with rockets in 1914, when he obtained two patents on his work. Later he began to develop weapons for the U.S. Army. He designed the forerunner of the jet engine for airplanes and began the development of jet-assisted takeoff engines for the U.S. Navy before his death. He and his heirs (on his behalf) filed 214 patents. Bibliography and Index.

658. Farley, Karin Clafford. **Samuel Adams: Grandfather of His Country**. Austin, TX: Raintree/Steck-Vaughn, 1994. 128p. $16.98. ISBN 0-8114-2379-4. (American Troublemakers). 6 up

Samuel Adams (1722-1803) believed, as John Locke espoused, that everyone is entitled to the natural rights of life, liberty, and property. Although he failed in several careers, he found his life's mission in politics and trying to free the colonies from unfair British rule. He led the Boston Tea Party, became a member of the Continental Congress, and signed the Declaration of Independence. Maps, Photographs, Key Dates, Glossary, Places to Visit, Bibliography and Recommended Readings, and Index.

659. Farley, Karin Clafford. **Thomas Paine: Revolutionary Author**. Austin, TX: Raintree/Steck-Vaughn, 1994. 128p. $16.98. ISBN 0-8114-2329-8. (American Troublemakers). 6 up

Thomas Paine (1737-1809) led a motley career. Born in England, he came to America where he published *Common Sense* and other works. He tried to get money from the French for the Continental army, but both England and France accused him of various crimes, and he was imprisoned briefly for wanting to save the life of Louis XVI. His writing and political philosophy, which showed his ideas of liberty and equality, helped to foment both the American and French Revolutions. Photographs, Key Dates, Glossary, Places to Visit, Bibliography and Recommended Readings, and Index.

660. Farr, Judith. **I Never Came to You in White: A Novel**. Boston: Houghton Mifflin, 1996. 225p. $21.95. ISBN 0-395-78840-4. YA

This novel uses Dickinson's letters as a basis for telling her story. Many of the letters focus on Dickinson's difficult year during 1847-1848 at Mary Lyon's Female Seminary (later Mount Holyoke College). The character of Dickinson emerges as an intelligent and lively young girl for whom the school is a damper and a strong force on her future choices. The surrounding details show women's education at the time as well as the effect of the religious revival psyche of the period.

661. Farrell, Jacqueline. **The Great Depression**. San Diego, CA: Lucent, 1996. 96p. $14.95. ISBN 1-56006-276-2. (The Importance Of). 7 up

The text covers the history of the Depression beginning before the American stock market crash in 1929. The Treaty of Versailles in 1919 demanded reparations from countries, and in 1927, some American banks failed because of bad investments and low prices for agricultural produce. The chapters look at these roots of the Depression; Herbert Hoover and Franklin D. Roosevelt (Presidents during the time); the first 100 days of the Depression; Roosevelt's "New Deal"; the debate as to whether to have recovery or reform; the spread of the Depression around the world; and the legacy of the Depression. Photographs and boxed topics augment the text. Notes, For Further Reading, Works Consulted, and Index.

662. Farris, John. **The Dust Bowl**. Maurie Manning, illustrator. New York: Lucent, 1990. 64p. $19.93. ISBN 1-56006-005-0. (World Disasters). 5-7

The text re-creates life on the southern Great Plains during the early 1900s, when farmers and sharecroppers tried to live off the land. The drought of the 1930s and the devastating dust storms that ensued ruined homes and farms. Drawings augment the discussion of why the Dust Bowl happened, how people survived it, and its effects. Glossary, Further Reading, and Index.

663. Faust, Drew Gilpin. **Mothers of Invention: Women of the Slaveholding South in the American Civil War**. Chapel Hill, NC: University of North Carolina Press, 1996. 326p. $29.95. ISBN 0-8078-2255-8. YA

Using the diaries, letters, and memoirs of more than 500 Confederate women, Faust delineates the ways in which the Civil War changed the identities of the women. Many white women had been raised on plantations where white men supported them financially and Black slaves did the work, giving them leisure time and a chance to write. But the end of the Civil War changed their "world order" because they had to learn how to do managerial chores such as buying food and ordering clothes. They did not like the changes, but they had no choice. Their attitudes and adjustments appear in the words that they themselves wrote.

664. Feelings, Tom, author/illustrator. **The Middle Passage: White Ships, Black Cargo**. New York: Dial Press, 1995. 80p. $40. ISBN 0-8037-1804-7. 7 up

Feelings describes his search for his African past, and John Henrik Clarke's overview of the slave trade follows it. A series of illustrations depicts the events that people forced into slavery had to endure. The strong, truthful scenes include capture, transport on land and sea, rape, murder, life on shipboard, and rats gnawing on a dead body. *Bulletin Blue Ribbon Book, American Library Association Notable Books for Children, American Library Association Best Books for Young Adults*, and *Coretta Scott King Illustrator Award*.

665.   Feinberg, Barbara Silberdick. **American Political Scandals Past and Present**. New York: Franklin Watts, 1992. 160p. $13.40. ISBN 0-531-11126-1. 7-10

Scandals have been prevalent in American political history since the beginning of the country. They have included election fraud, abuse of power, graft, violent disagreement, sexual relationships, and other types of personal misconduct. The text examines these situations of political corruption with a balanced view. Bibliography and Index.

666.   Feinberg, Barbara Silberdick. **Harry S. Truman**. New York: Franklin Watts, 1994. 144p. $13.90. ISBN 0-531-13036-3. (Impact). YA

Harry S. Truman (1884-1972) was the ninth Vice President to become President after a sitting President died in office, and he had to take the job near the end of World War II. He decided to drop an atomic bomb on Japan, and he reorganized American defenses after the war so that the Soviets could not expand. He supported the reconstruction of postwar Western Europe, ordered the Berlin Airlift, sent troops to South Korea, joined the North Atlantic Treaty Organization, and started international aid programs while he was in office. The text also looks at other aspects of his life. Notes, Glossary, Bibliography, and Index.

667.   Feinberg, Barbara Silberdick. **John Marshall: The Great Chief Justice**. Springfield, NJ: Enslow, 1995. 112p. $17.95. ISBN 0-89490-559-7. (Justices of the Supreme Court). 7-10

With little formal schooling or training as a lawyer, John Marshall became known as the "Great Chief Justice." He served for 34 years after his appointment in 1801 and showed his support for a strong federal government. He created "judicial review" in which the court had the right to declare laws as unconstitutional. He protected the rights of property owners and encouraged expansion of trade and commerce. Many of his decisions shaped the laws in effect today. The text looks at his personal and professional accomplishments. Chronology, Notes, Further Reading, and Index.

668.   Feinberg, Barbara Silberdick. **Watergate: Scandal in the White House**. New York: Franklin Watts, 1990. 144p. $21.10. ISBN 0-531-10963-1. (Twentieth Century American History). 7-12

From 1972 to 1974, the United States was embroiled in the Watergate affair. Feinberg discusses the attempted burglary of the Democratic National Committee's offices in the Watergate apartment complex and the Republican "lookout" across the street in the Howard Johnson's motel. She also details the grand jury investigation over which Sam Ervin presided and its ethical and constitutional dilemmas, impeachment proceedings concerning President Richard Nixon, Nixon's resignation, and its aftermath. Quotes from meeting transcripts and Nixon's tapes also appear. Bibliography and Index.

669.   Feldman, Eve B. **Benjamin Franklin: Scientist and Inventor**. New York: Franklin Watts, 1990. 64p. $19.90. ISBN 0-531-10867-8. (First Books). 5-8

The text about Benjamin Franklin (1706-1790) emphasizes his ideas and inventions before and after he discovered electricity with his kite experiment. They include the lightning rod, the Franklin stove, the harmonica, bifocals, writing tables, and public libraries. Experiments You Can Do with Electricity, Glossary, For Further Reading, and Index.

670.   Ferguson, Julinda Lewis. **Alvin Ailey, Jr.: A Life in Dance**. New York: Walker, 1994. 84p. $14.95. ISBN 0-8027-8241-8. YA

Alvin Ailey (1931-1989) saw people dancing when he was a child and knew that he wanted to be a dancer. He also became a choreographer who helped bring all levels of people to the ballet regardless of class or race. His African American heritage grounded his creations and excited his audiences. Bibliography and Index.

671.   Ferguson, Leland. **Uncommon Ground: Archaeology and Colonial African America, 1650-1800**. Washington, DC: Smithsonian Institution Press, 1992. 240p. $14.95pa. ISBN 1-56098-059-1pa. YA

The text discusses the contribution, heretofore unexplored, that Africa, through plantation slaves in South Carolina, made to the American colonial culture. Ferguson looks at Colono-ware, earthenware designed and used by slaves and Indians, as well as architecture, religion, food, and other aspects of the plantation society to show the traces of African heritage that appear. Africa had a much larger role than white historians have acknowledged in the creation of America, and this heritage is what permitted the plantation society to function. Bibliography and Index.

672.   Fernandez-Shaw, Carlos M. **The Hispanic Presence in North America from 1492 to Today**. New York: Facts on File, 1991. 376p. $45. ISBN 0-8160-2133-3. YA

The text shows the influence of Hispanics in North America since Spanish discovery and exploration, and in the first part, their contributions in such fields as the arts and law. The rest of the book, arranged by region, presents the Spanish presence including towns with Spanish names, historical sites, and any other Spanish association in the area. Holidays, periodicals, and radio and television stations also appear. Bibliography and Index.

673. Ferrell, Nancy Warren. **The Battle of the Little Bighorn in American History**. Springfield, NJ: Enslow, 1996. 128p. $18.95. ISBN 0-89490-768-9. 5-9

After relating background information about events and people prior to the Battle of Little Bighorn in June 1876, Ferrell then recounts the combat and its aftermath through the massacre at Wounded Knee in 1890. Her balanced reporting presents several sides of the conflict and introduces figures such as Red Cloud, Sitting Bull, and Crazy Horse. Index.

674. Ferrell, Nancy Warren. **The U.S. Air Force**. Minneapolis, MN: Lerner, 1990. 72p. $22.95. ISBN 0-8225-1433-8. 4-8

Air Force history begins in 1910, when Benjamin Foulois and Henry "Hap" Arnold became interested in flying after the Wright brothers achieved their successes. In 1915, Fokker designed a timing device to keep bullets from hitting airplane propellers as they were shot through them, and the airplane became an important part of World War I. In the United States, Eddie Rickenbacker gained fame for his "aces." In 1935, the first B-17, or "Flying Fortress," was tested, and by mid-1941 aviation production in the United States was the world's largest industry. Because of the importance of the airplane, the Air Force gained equal status with the Army and the Navy in 1947. Its first major effort was the Berlin Airlift in 1948, followed by Korea and Vietnam. Concluding sections discuss how to join the Air Force, information about the Air Force Academy, and the major commands of the Air Force. Appendix and Index.

675. Ferris, Jean. **Into the Wind**. New York: Avon, 1996. 184p. $3.99pa. ISBN 0-380-78198-0pa. (American Dreams). 9 up

In 1814, Rosie's father dies in a barroom fight before the bar explodes in fire. A sea captain rescues her, and Rosie, at 17, finds herself on a ship going to fight the British navy. Her adventures on board highlight the times.

676. Ferris, Jeri. **Native American Doctor: The Story of Susan La Flesche Picotte**. Minneapolis, MN: Carolrhoda, 1991. 88p. $19.95; $6.95pa. ISBN 0-87614-443-1; 0-87614-548-9pa. 5-8

Susan La Flesche (1865-1915) of the Omaha tribe went East for her education, and after high school, received a scholarship to Hampton Institute in Virginia. There she met a woman doctor, and she decided that she wanted to be a doctor herself. After medical school, she returned to help her people, although she had a recurring illness that began when she took long train rides between her home and Pennsylvania. She found that she had many roles in her relationship with her people; she was doctor, teacher, nurse, financial and legal advisor, translator, and fighter against alcohol. Before she died, she helped raise money so that the Omaha people could have their own hospital. Notes, Bibliography, and Index.

677. Ferris, Jeri. **What I Had Was Singing: The Story of Marian Anderson**. Minneapolis, MN: Carolrhoda, 1994. 96p. $19.95; $6.95pa. ISBN 0-87614-818-6; 0-87614-634-5pa. (Trailblazers). 4-7

Marian Anderson (1897-1993) was one of the twentieth century's greatest singers. She had to overcome prejudice against her race to show that she was one of the best. Ironically, Europeans accepted her long before her own country did; in 1955, she finally became the first African American to sing at the Metropolitan Opera House. The text looks at her life and what she achieved. Legacy, Bibliography, and Index. *Notable Children's Trade Books in the Field of Social Studies* and *Carter G. Woodson Award*.

678. Ferry, Charles. **One More Time!** Boston: Houghton Mifflin, 1985. 171p. $1.98. ISBN 0-395-36692-5. 7 up

Skeets graduates from Julliard and joins an orchestra. When the Japanese bomb Pearl Harbor in 1941, the band has risen to become one of the two top bands in the nation. The grueling tour schedule causes some of the band members to quarrel, but during their last performance before the members go off to war, their music together is almost perfect.

679. Field, Rachel. **Calico Bush**. Allen Lewis, illustrator. 1931. New York: Macmillan, 1987. 224p. $16. ISBN 0-02-734610-2. New York: Yearling, 1990. 224p. $4.50pa. ISBN 0-440-40368-5pa. 4-8

In 1740, Marguerite and her grandmother arrive in the American colonies from France. Her grandmother dies soon after, and she becomes bound to a family leaving Massachusetts to go to a northern seacoast town. When they arrive, they discover that Indians think the land on which they will live is sacred, and they have burned down the house. Marguerite misses the celebration of Christmas and has to use her ingenuity to solve various problems. With the help of an old Scottish woman who knows about herbs, she copes with her changed situation. *Newbery Honor Book*.

680. Filene, Peter. **Home and Away**. Cambridge, MA: Zoland, 1992. 332p. $19.95. ISBN 0-944072-22-4. YA

Murray, 16, lives in New York in 1951 with his Jewish parents. He decides to write his junior paper about his parents after his father refuses to sign a non-Communist loyalty oath at work. His father goes to California to start a new project for his company, but Murray realizes that part of the separation is his parents' problems with each other. He has to understand them and his mother's false accusations about his father while trying to cope with dating. What he likes best are Brooklyn Dodgers games because they give him a sense of stability.

681.   Finkelstein, Norman H. **Sounds in the Air: The Golden Age of Radio**. New York: Scribner's, 1993. 144p. $14.95. ISBN 0-684-19271-3. 7 up

By examining the effects of the medium of radio in the 1930s and 1940s, Finkelstein shows how it began to change society as families gathered around the radio set to hear Franklin Delano Roosevelt deliver his fireside chats and to learn that World War II had started.

682.   Finkelstein, Norman H. **Thirteen Days! Ninety Miles: The Cuban Missile Crisis**. New York: Julian Messner, 1994. 101p. $15. ISBN 0-671-86622-2. 7 up

Using information recently declassified, Finkelstein tells the story of the events that led to the discovery that the Soviet Union had placed missiles in Cuba and John F. Kennedy's resulting blockade of the country. Because communication was much less rapid at that time, tension developed that could have led to a nuclear war. Finkelstein recreates that tension. Bibliography and Index.

683.   Fireside, Bryna J. **Is There a Woman in the House . . . or Senate?** Morton Grove, IL: Albert Whitman, 1994. 144p. $14.95. ISBN 0-8075-3662-8. 4-8

After looking at how Congress works, Fireside highlights some of the women who have served Congress in the Senate and in the House of Representatives. The women are Jeannette Rankin, first woman in Congress (1880-1973); Margaret Chase Smith, congresswoman and senator from Maine (1897-1994); Shirley Chisholm, African American representative (b. 1924); Bella Abzug, congresswoman (b. 1920); Barbara Jordan, congresswoman (1936-1995); Patricia Schroeder, Colorado congresswoman (b. 1940); Millicent Fenwick, congresswoman (b. 1910); Barbara Mikulski, congresswoman and senator (b. 1936); Nancy Kassebaum, senator (b. 1932); and Geraldine Ferraro, congresswoman (b. 1935). Selected Bibliography and Index.

684.   Fireside, Harvey, and Sarah Betsy Fuller. **Brown v. Board of Education: Equal Schooling for All**. Springfield, NJ: Enslow, 1994. 128p. $17.95. ISBN 0-89490-469-8. (Landmark Supreme Court Cases). 6-9

This Supreme Court case occurred in 1954 because Oliver Brown's eight-year-old daughter could not go to a school reserved for white children. He sued, saying that the schools for white and Black were unequal. The text looks at the ideas and arguments behind this case as well as the people who brought it to court. Notes, Glossary, Further Reading, and Index.

685.   Fischer, David Hackett. **Paul Revere's Ride**. New York: Oxford University Press, 1994. 445p. $30; $15.95pa. ISBN 0-19-508847-6; 0-19-509831-5pa. YA

As Fischer looks at the events that occurred between September 1, 1774, and April 19, 1775, he declares that Paul Revere did not ride alone on April 19, 1775. According to Fischer, that fact does not diminish the role that Revere played at the beginning of the Revolutionary War. He and many others had planned carefully what would be needed to resist the British. Revere fulfilled his role in this plan when he and others rode to give the warning. In essence, the militia of New England grouped almost spontaneously to fight against the British as they marched on Concord, and this action is what made the situation become a revolution. Index.

686.   Fisher, Leonard Everett. **Ellis Island: Gateway to the New World**. New York: Holiday House, 1986. 64p. $15.95. ISBN 0-8234-0612-1. 3-7

Between 1892 and 1954, 15 million immigrants were processed at Ellis Island. After World War I, immigrants had to read and write in one language before they would be admitted. But fewer than 300,000 were denied admittance during the entire life of Ellis Island. Before 1892, individual states had admitted immigrants, but so many people began to come to the United States that the immigration process had to be turned over to the federal government. After World War II, Ellis Island was no longer needed, but it was restored during the late 1980s as a historical landmark. Photographs of immigrants underscore the importance of this place to those who were seeking safety. Index.

687.   Fisher, Leonard Everett. **The Oregon Trail**. New York: Holiday House, 1990. 64p. $14.95. ISBN 0-8234-0833-7. 5-9

Stunning photographs of the trail, along with maps and paintings by Albert Bierstadt and A. J. Miller, highlight the story of 300,000 people who braved terrible conditions to reach the Willamette Valley of Oregon, mainly during the 1840s and 1850s. These people wanted to find jobs; claim "free" land; gain wealth in timber, fur, fish, and ore; have an adventure; convert the heathens; escape the claustrophobia of the East; or improve their health. They called the worst conditions "seeing the elephant," and some, who did not want to go north to Wyoming where a flat "bridge" over the Rocky Mountains had been located, went south and suffered, like the Donners in 1846. They also fought Native Americans, who were furious at the pioneers for killing the buffalo. Fewer people took the journey after the Civil War began. Index.

688.   Fisher, Leonard Everett. **Tracks Across America: The Story of the American Railroad, 1825-1900**. New York: Holiday House, 1992. 192p. $17.95. ISBN 0-8234-0945-7. 5 up

The text discusses the first railroads, the railroads going west, their effect during the Civil War, the first transcontinental railroad and Native American resistance, the robbers versus the owners, those who worked on the railroad, the disasters, and the progress in building different types of cars. Photographs supplement the text. Bibliography and Index.

689.   Fitz-Gerald, Christine A. **Meriwether Lewis and William Clark**. Chicago: Childrens Press, 1991. 128p. $28.20. ISBN 0-516-03061-2. (World's Great Explorers). 5-8

The text begins with Lewis and Clark in the Pacific Northwest in 1805, where they have been wet for two weeks but are soon rewarded with their first view of the Pacific Ocean. The topics covered are the reasons for the journey, the plans and preparations, the Mississippi River, Fort Mandan, the High Plains, across the Rockies and beyond, their homeward journey, and the paths they took when they returned. Photographs, Timeline, Glossary, Bibliography, and Index.

690.   Fitz-Gerald, Christine Maloney. **James Monroe: Fifth President of the United States**. Chicago: Childrens Press, 1987. 100p. $19.80. ISBN 0-516-01383-1. (Encyclopedia of Presidents). 4-9

James Monroe (1758-1831) was a careful and honest President, but he was not brilliant. He seemed old-fashioned in 1823 while his new country was changing. The tin can had been introduced, the Erie Canal would soon open, horse racing was common, and football had arrived on American campuses. Because he was concerned that foreign countries would invade South America, he proposed to Congress that the United States must go to war with any foreign country that came to North or South America; that no foreign nation could claim any more land in the Western Hemisphere; and that the United States, in turn, would stay out of European wars. Although Congress did not see the value of this plan, European countries were annoyed that the small United States was telling them what to do. Not for 100 years, until World War I, did the United States fight abroad. Chronology of American History and Index.

691.   Fitz-Gerald, Christine Maloney. **William Henry Harrison: Ninth President of the United States**. Chicago: Childrens Press, 1987. 100p. $19.80. ISBN 0-516-01392-0. (Encyclopedia of Presidents). 4-9

In 1836, the Whig Party misrepresented their candidate William Henry Harrison (1773-1841), claiming that he was born in a log cabin. He was actually a member of a wealthy Virginia family. They told him to be quiet, and he added to his reputation, gained during his military career (his subordinates had called him "General Mum"), for saying little. In 1840, the party ran him for President with a southern Democrat, John Tyler, and used the slogan "Tippecanoe and Tyler, Too" to signify Harrison's defeat of the Shawnee in 1811. He served in Congress from Ohio before he became President, but after one month in office, he died of pneumonia. His most important decision was the appointment of Daniel Webster as Secretary of State. Photographs, Chronology of American History, and Index.

692.   Fleischman, Paul. **The Borning Room**. New York: HarperCollins, 1991. 112p. $13.95. ISBN 0-06-023762-7. 6 up

The room in the house set aside for having babies and for laying out the dead is the one that Georgina enters and exits from the time she is born in 1851 until she dies. As her death approaches, she remembers the times in the room when she was nine and when she had her first child at 19. Each story she remembers tells something more about her Ohio family of abolitionists who worry about runaway slaves, the siege of Vicksburg, chloroform, and electricity. *Bulletin Blue Ribbon Book, American Library Association Notable Books for Children, American Library Association Best Books for Young Adults, Horn Book Fanfare Honor List, School Library Journal Best Book, Booklist Books for Young Editors' Choices, IRA Teachers' Choices, Notable Children's Trade Books in the Field of Social Studies, NCTE Notable Trade Books in the Language Arts, Golden Kite Award Honor, Publishers Weekly Year's Best Books*, and *New York Public Library Books for the Teen Age*.

693.   Fleischman, Paul. **Bull Run**. New York: HarperCollins, 1993. 104p. $14.95; $4.95pa. ISBN 0-06-021446-5; 0-06-440588-5pa. 5 up

At the beginning of the Civil War, 10 people on each side begin their participation. They all meet at the First Battle of Bull Run in 1861. Their views of the war as they start and finish the battle are very different. A photographer tells of capturing the expressions of men not expecting to be alive the next evening; another character thinks of a depressed woman who has considered suicide. Other characters are slaves, soldiers, and citizens from North and South who seem to be mere observers until the battle begins. *Scott O'Dell Award for Historical Fiction, American Library Association Notable Books for Young Children, American Library Association Best Books for Young Adults, Horn Book Fanfare Honor List, School Library Journal Best Book, Notable Children's Trade Books in the Field of Social Studies, Booklist Books for Youth Editors' Choices, IRA Teachers' Choices, Publishers Weekly Year's Best Books*, and *New York Public Library Books for the Teen Age*.

694. Fleischman, Paul. **Coming-and-Going Men**. Randy Gaul, illustrator. New York: HarperCollins, 1985. 147p. $12.95. ISBN 0-06-021883-5. 6 up

In 1800, four traveling men pass through New Canaan, Vermont: Mr. Cyrus Snype, silhouette cutter; Mr. Hamby, ballad and broadside seller; Simeon Fyfe and his son, who hate heroes but exhibit a panorama of the life of Washington; and Jonathan Wardell, a peddler with dyes and a book. Each man either finds himself transformed or changes someone in the town during that unusual year.

695. Fleischman, Paul. **Graven Images**. Andrew Glass, illustrator. New York: HarperCollins, 1982. 85p. $14.89. ISBN 0-06-021907-6. 6 up

Graven images influence three people in the eighteenth century: a binnacle boy, an apprentice, and a sculptor. In one story, a poisoner who killed an entire ship's crew lives with his secret. In a second, an apprentice finally attracts the girl whom he has admired from afar. In the third, a sculptor attempts to carve a ghost's image on a marble statue. *Newbery Honor Book, American Library Association Notable Books for Children*, and *School Library Journal Best Book*.

696. Fleischman, Paul. **Path of the Pale Horse**. New York: HarperCollins, 1983. 160p. $13.89. ISBN 0-06-021905-X. 6 up

After Lep Nye's sister goes to live in Philadelphia during 1793 with an old family friend and does not contact the family, Lep goes to search for her. People throughout the city are dying from yellow fever, and Lep worries about her health as he discovers several frauds that the family friend has made. He finds not only her but himself as he pledges to dedicate his life to medicine in hope of saving people from disease.

697. Fleischman, Paul. **Saturnalia**. New York: HarperCollins, 1990. 128p. $14.95; $3.95pa. ISBN 0-06-021912-2; 0-06-447089-Xpa. 7 up

In 1681, when Baggot visits Mr. Currie, the printer, and questions William, Mr. Currie's 14-year-old Indian apprentice, he is annoyed because William knows all of the answers. Baggot suspects that the Curries may engage in a celebration far more terrible than Christmas—Saturnalia. William and a group of masters and servants people the two worlds of Boston; as Saturnalia nears, they all seem to reverse their roles. William wants to preserve the history of his Narragansett past and knows that he can only do it by using his intelligence. He finally finds a great-uncle and a cousin, two of the slaves whom he helps to rescue. *Bulletin Blue Ribbon Book, American Library Association Notable Books for Children, Horn Book Fanfare Honor List, School Library Journal Best Book, Booklist Books for Young Editors' Choices, IRA Teachers' Choices, Notable Children's Trade Books in the Field of Social Studies, NCTE Notable Trade Books in the Language Arts, Boston Globe-Horn Book Award, Publishers Weekly "Critic's Choice,"* and *New York Public Library Books for the Teen Age*.

698. Fleischman, Paul. **Townsend's Warbler**. New York: HarperCollins, 1992. 52p. $12.89. ISBN 0-06-021875-4. 3-7

In 1834, John Townsend (1809-1851) began a journey across the United States. He faced starvation, sandstorms, and Indian war parties, but he also found a bird that no scientist had ever seen. This black-and-yellow-striped warbler became Townsend's warbler. The text tells of his experience with complementary pictures from the times.

699. Fleischman, Sid. **The Abracadabra Kid: A Writer's Life**. New York: Greenwillow, 1996. 198p. $16. ISBN 0-688-14859-X. 6-10

Trained as a magician as well as a writer, Fleischman tells the story of his life in the style of his fiction, with anecdotes and action. He learned to write after his World War II service, when he worked on scripts for John Wayne movies, and he gives tips for writing well. He also reveals his sense of humor with self-deprecating commentary appropriate for the content.

700. Fleischman, Sid. **The Ghost in the Noonday Sun**. Peter Sis, illustrator. 1965. New York: Greenwillow, 1989. 144p. $16. ISBN 0-688-08410-9. New York: Scholastic, 1995. 144p. $3.50pa. ISBN 0-590-43662-7pa. 4-7

On Oliver Finch's 12th birthday, he awaits his father's arrival from a three-year whaling voyage. Instead, another captain kidnaps Oliver, takes him on a voyage, and tells him to find the ghost hoarding the gold. He and a sailor eventually foil the captain by hitting him on the head, making him think he is dead and that they are ghosts he sees. They escape the ship with food instead of booty, and another ship rescues them.

701. Fleischman, Sid. **Humbug Mountain**. 1978. Eric Von Schmidt, illustrator. Boston: Little, Brown, 1988. 149p. $4.95pa. ISBN 0-316-28613-3pa. 3-7

At 13, Willy goes with his family to find Sunrise, the town on the Missouri River started by his grandfather. They find it, but the river has receded, and boats can no longer stop there. To get people to visit, Willy and his father publish a newspaper containing enticing stories about the area. The family works together on unusual schemes to rejuvenate the town. *Boston Globe-Horn Book Award*.

702.   Fleischman, Sid. **Jim Ugly**. Marcia Sewall, illustrator. New York: Greenwillow, 1992. 130p. $15. ISBN 0-688-10886-5. New York: Yearling, 1994. 130p. $3.99pa. ISBN 0-440-40803-2pa. 4-7

Jake, 12, begins his story at his father's 1894 burial in the Old West when he tries to get his father's dog, Jim Ugly, to follow him. The uninterested dog leads Jake instead. He shows Jake that his father is still alive but hiding from someone who wants to kill him for diamonds that Jake's father does not have. Jim helps Jake and his father escape the villains and encourages a romance between Jake's father and a lovely actress.

703.   Fleischman, Sid. **Mr. Mysterious & Co.** Eric Von Schmidt, illustrator. Boston: Little, Brown, 1962. 152p. $14.95; $4.95pa. ISBN 0-316-28578-1; 0-316-28614-1pa. 4-7

In 1884, Paul and Jane accompany their father, Mr. Mysterious, as he travels across the West in a wagon performing a magic show. They have various encounters and problems, but they have fun. When they decide to stake a homestead, a man comes to tell Mr. Mysterious that he is building a local theater.

704.   Fleischner, Jennifer. **The Apaches: People of the Southwest**. Brookfield, CT: Millbrook Press, 1994. 64p. $15.90. ISBN 1-56294-464-9. (Native Americans). 5-8

On September 4, 1886, the final surrender of the Apaches occurred when Geronimo agreed to the terms of U.S. General Miles. The Apaches migrated from Canada to the southwestern United States in the thirteenth and fourteenth centuries. They raided Spanish and Mexican settlements and fought the Mexicans in the Mexican War. Since then, the Apaches had to fight the U.S. government as they attempted to keep their traditions alive. Glossary, Bibliography, and Index.

705.   Fleming, Alice. **P. T. Barnum: The World's Greatest Showman**. New York: Walker, 1993. 160p. $14.95. ISBN 0-8027-8234-5. 6-9

P. T. Barnum (1810-1891) may be linked to the circus, but his life shows that he was actually a promoter. He promoted oddities, exhibits (some of them scams), and himself. He introduced America to Jumbo the elephant, the soprano Jenny Lind, and General Tom Thumb. But most important, he entertained the public, which is what it wanted. For Further Reading and Index.

706.   Fleming, Thomas. **Band of Brothers: West Point in the Civil War**. New York: Walker, 1988. 144p. $14.85. ISBN 0-8027-6740-0. (Walker's American History). 8 up

When the Civil War broke out, even West Point became divided between those who supported the North and those who supported the South. George Custer from Ohio cheered against Thomas Lafayette Rosser from Texas. Other cadets who trained at the academy and fought in the Civil War, sometimes against each other, included Jefferson Davis, Wade Hampton Gibbes (who fired the first shot at Fort Sumter in 1861), Morris Schaff, Pierre G. T. Beauregard, Tully McCrae, Fitzhugh Lee, Richard S. "Dick" Ewell, "Pete" Longstreet, Simon Bolivar Buckner, Thomas J. "Stonewall" Jackson, George Pickett, Braxton Bragg, George H. Thomas, Winfield Scott Hancock, Lewis Armistread, John Pemberton, Powell Hill, James "Birdseye" McPherson, James Washington, Ulysses S. Grant, and Robert E. Lee. The text, with reproductions and photographs, looks at their relationships. Bibliography and Index.

707.   Fleming, Thomas. **Harry S. Truman, President**. New York: Walker, 1993. 144p. $14.98. ISBN 0-8027-8267-1. (Presidential Biography). 7-10

The text focuses on Harry Truman's two terms in the presidency as the 33rd President by looking at his honesty, his fairness, and his loyalty as well as his stubbornness and occasional temper tantrums. The book tells little about his childhood or early career. It ends with the difficulties of getting Adlai Stevenson elected as the Democratic presidential candidate and the impossibility of getting him elected to office. Background about the times during which Truman (1884-1972) served give a firm historical base to the text. Photographs, Further Reading, and Index.

708.   Fogle, Jean. **Two Hundred Years: Stories of the Nation's Capital**. Edward Fogle, illustrator. Arlington, VA: Vandamere Press, 1991. 184p. $14.95. ISBN 0-918339-16-2. YA

On July 17, 1790, Congress voted on the Residence Act, which said that it would begin meeting in a new federal capital city in December 1800. The new city became Washington, D.C., but every step of its location and construction proved problematic. The text looks at this history of Washington, from the disagreements between the designer and the commissioners chosen to oversee the work, to the present, when taxes collected cannot cover expenses. People closely involved with its developmental history include Dolley Madison, Davey Burnes, Marcia Burnes Van Ness, Daniel Carroll, Samuel Blodgett, Boss Shepherd, Frederick Douglass, Christian Heurich, the Lansburghs, and Duncan Phillips. Notes and Index.

709.   Forbes, Esther. **Johnny Tremain**. Lynd Ward, illustrator. 1943. Magnolia, MA: Peter Smith, 1992. 272p. $19.75. ISBN 0-8446-6600-9. New York: Dell, 1995. $4.99pa. ISBN 0-440-44250-8pa. 5 up

Johnny is very proud of the beautiful silver designs he created during his apprenticeship and brags about his talents to the other apprentices. When he decides to work on Sunday to complete an order for John Hancock, he breaks the law. He suffers for this decision by burning his hand so severely that he can no longer work in silver. As the American Revolution begins, a friend interests him in the Whig causes, and he starts to help the movement toward independence in any way that he can. *Newbery Medal*.

710.   Force, Eden. **John Muir**. Englewood Cliffs, NJ: Silver Burdett, 1990. 144p. $13.95. ISBN 0-382-09965-6. (Pioneers in Change). 5-9

As a boy, John Muir (1838-1914) lived in Scotland before his father decided to immigrate to America. In America, he rose at 1 AM every morning to work on his inventions because his father said he could spend time in the morning before chores on the farm doing what he wanted. He invented a sawmill, a waterwheel, locks for the doors, a thermometer, a barometer, and many clocks, including an "early rising" machine. As he began to see the beauty of the world, his focus changed to understanding the relationship of humans to nature. His experiences led him to write Theodore Roosevelt, pleading for him to save the land while he could. Roosevelt met him in Yosemite and realized that John Muir knew the value of conservation. Important Dates, Bibliography, and Index.

711.   Ford, Barbara. **Howard Carter: Searching for King Tut**. Janet Hamlin, illustrator. New York: Freeman, 1995. 63p. $14.95. ISBN 0-7167-6587-X. (Science Superstars). 4-8

Howard Carter (1873-1939) assisted others at the excavation at Tell el-Amarna in Egypt in the 1890s. In 1922, in the Valley of the Tombs of the Kings in Luxor, Egypt, he and George Herbert discovered the tomb of Tutankhamen, a pharaoh who reigned in the fourteenth century BC. Because it was untouched by grave robbers or other archaeologists, it held numerous treasures that Carter cataloged for 10 years. He also discovered the tombs of the pharaoh Thutmose IV and Queen Hatshepsut. Afterword, Index, Glossary, and Further Reading.

712.   Ford, Barbara. **The Most Wonderful Movie in the World**. New York: Dutton, 1996. 160p. $14.99. ISBN 0-525-45455-1. 5-7

In 1941, Moira, 11, wants to see *Gone with the Wind*, the film of her favorite book. The Catholic Legion of Decency says that Catholics are not to see it, so she cannot go to the movie without going against her religion—and her parents. When she mentions it to a young priest, he suggests that she consult her conscience. She has to decide what to do about both her conscience and going to the movie.

713.   Ford, Barbara. **Paul Revere: Rider for the Revolution**. New York: Enslow, 1997. 128p. $18.95. ISBN 0-89490-779-4. (Historical American Biographies). 6-9

Paul Revere (1735-1818) had a reputation as the one who made a midnight ride, but he had a wider involvement with the seeds of the American Revolution than most histories discuss. This biography looks at his impact on American history as it examines his life. Fact boxes and maps augment the text. Notes, Glossary, Further Reading, and Index.

714.   Forman, James D. **Becca's Story**. New York: Atheneum, 1992. 180p. $15. ISBN 0-684-19332-9. 7 up

Becca, 15, has two boyfriends in 1860, but the Civil War erupts, and both go away to fight with Michigan's Seventh Regiment. Her true love does not return from Gettysburg, and Becca has to recover from this loss before she faces the rest of her life with her second choice.

715.   Forman, James D. **Cow Neck Rebels**. New York: Farrar, Straus & Giroux, 1969. $3.95. ISBN 0-374-31617-1. YA

Bruce, 16, loves Rachel, but knows that his brother has the right as the oldest to ask her to marry him instead. When the American Revolution begins, their lives change because Rachel's father is a Tory, supportive of the British, and Bruce's family hates the British because of the Scots' defeat at the 1746 Battle of Culloden. Bruce finds himself sneaking back to land from his boat to burn Tory wheat fields so that the British will starve.

716.   Forman, James D. **Prince Charlie's Year**. New York: Scribner's, 1991. 136p. $12.95. ISBN 0-684-19242-X. 7-10

As Colin Macdonald prepares for a 1780 battle against the English in North Carolina, he remembers the last battle he fought against the English in 1745. He was 14 at Culloden, Scotland, when he fought for Prince Charlie. After defeat, the British took him prisoner and transported him to America, where he was bound out for seven years. After his love, Peggy, joined him, he survived. The story recounts the 1745 Jacobite rebellion and the clan system that supported a man who could not win the fight.

717.   Forrester, Sandra. **Sound the Jubilee**. New York: Lodestar, 1995. 184p. $15.99. ISBN 0-525-67486-1. 6-9

In 1861, Maddie, 11, accompanies her mistress, who broke the law by teaching her to read, to the Outer Banks of North Carolina to escape the war. Thinking that she has lost her chance to escape, Maddie is surprised when Union soldiers turn Roanoke Island into a place for runaway slaves. Her family escapes, but they face more hardships. Maddie helps teach the children but is delighted when the Yankees send a real teacher to the island. She is even more pleased when the teacher asks her to help with the younger children. The family strives for a better life, eventually leaving the island when they hear rumors of former owners returning to claim their land. *Notable Children's Trade Books in the Field of Social Studies*.

718.   Foster, Frances Smith. **Written by Herself: Literary Production by African American Women, 1746-1892**. Bloomington, IN: Indiana University Press, 1993. 206p. $13.95pa. ISBN 0-253-20786-Xpa. YA

Included in this collection are writings from African American women between 1746 and 1892 who have, according to Foster, either been misrepresented or misunderstood. The women she has chosen are Maria W. Steward, Phillis Wheatley, Anna Julia Cooper, Lucy Terry Price, Jarena Lee, Harriet Jacobs, Elizabeth Keckley, Frances Ellen Watkins Harper, and Octavia Victoria Rogers Albert. Foster notes that these women had strategies to "write into history" so that they would not be lost. They were sophisticated and self-aware writers who critiqued the society in which they lived. Index.

719.   Foster, Leila Merrell. **David Glasgow Farragut: Courageous Navy Commander**. Chicago: Childrens Press, 1991. 107p. $19.30. ISBN 0-516-03273-9. (People of Distinction). 4 up

Born in Tennessee in 1801, David Farragut moved to New Orleans, where he went to live with a commander after his mother died. He became a midshipman on the *Essex* at the age of 9 or 10 and never left the U.S. Navy. He helped during the War of 1812 and made his major contributions during the Civil War, when he won two sea battles against the Confederacy, including the capture of Mobile, Alabama. His famous response "Damn the torpedoes! Full speed ahead" still resounds in Navy lore. For his efforts, he was awarded the rank of admiral, the first in the history of the U.S. Navy. Glossary and Index.

720.   Fowler, Zinita. **The Last Innocent Summer**. Forth Worth, TX: Texas Christian University, 1990. 145p. $11.95pa. ISBN 0-87565-045-7pa. 6-9

When Skeeter is 10 in the summer of 1931, she learns that not everything is within the control of her family when two young girls in Harris, Texas, are murdered. The following scandal and trial surprise her, but understanding the motivations of self-centered, uncaring people is more difficult to accept.

721.   Fox, Mary Virginia. **Chief Joseph of the Nez Perce Indians: Champion of Liberty**. Chicago: Childrens Press, 1992. 111p. $19.30. ISBN 0-516-03275-5. (People of Distinction). 5-9

Chief Joseph (1840-1904) tried to keep peace among the different bands of his tribe, the Nimipu, or Nez Percé, but he was unable to stop one man from killing white settlers as retribution for another white man's murder of his father. This act started the serious war between the tribe and the American army in 1877. Chief Joseph could not save all of his people, and they were relocated in Oklahoma. He tried throughout his life to regain the land in Oregon where they had lived for centuries, but he could not. Time Line and Index.

722.   Fox, Paula. **The Slave Dancer**. Eros Keith, illustrator. New York: Simon & Schuster, 1973. 192p. $16. ISBN 0-02-735560-8. New York: Dell, 1996. 192p. $4.50pa. ISBN 0-440-96132-7pa. 5-8

In 1840, Jessie, 14, serves unwillingly on a ship for four months as a fife player after slavers capture him in New Orleans. He sees Black African *cabocieros* sell their own people to the slavers, and he has to play while the slaves dance to exercise as the ship returns home. When the ship wrecks, he and one of the slaves survive. They wash ashore, and a Black man guides them north. As an adult, Jessie cannot listen to music because of the horror of his experience. *Newbery Medal*.

723.   Fox, Stephen. **The Unknown Internment: An Oral History of the Relocation of Italian-Americans During World War II**. Boston: Twain, G. K. Hall, 1990. 223p. $25.95; $15.95pa. ISBN 0-8057-9108-6; 0-8057-9125-6pa. (Oral History Series). YA

In 1942, the American government decided to relocate certain nonnaturalized German and Italian Americans living on the coast of California to 150 miles inland. Very little information about this process exists, but interviews with survivors tell the story of how native-born Americans betrayed themselves and their professed values. In the chapters, Fox presents several areas of discussion and several themes that manifested during his interviews. These included the assimilation of the Italian Americans, how fascism related (or did not relate) to the Italian community, the government order to evacuate Italians from California coastal areas, the impact of the restrictions, the pitting of neighbor against neighbor and the defense of the Italian Americans by some neighbors, the government's reversal of the policy, the selective individual internment program (to refrain from removing such people as Joe DiMaggio's father) and a vindictive general, and final reflections on this historical event. Notes and References, Selected Bibliography, and Index.

724. Fradin, Dennis B. **The Connecticut Colony**. Chicago: Childrens Press, 1990. 159p. $24.70. ISBN 0-516-00393-3. 5-9

The Connecticut colony grew from 1638 to 1675. It faced and thwarted problems from 1675 to 1689. Following this were the colonial wars from 1689 to 1750. Capsule biographies of John Winthrop, Jr., Israel Putnam, Nathan Hale, Jonathan Trumbull and his family, Benedict Arnold, Joseph Plumb Martin, and Roger Sherman appear in the text. Prints and photographs supplement the text. Time Line and Index.

725. Fradin, Dennis B. **The Delaware Colony**. Chicago: Childrens Press, 1992. 159p. $24.70. ISBN 0-516-00398-4. 5-9

Delaware was under Swedish rule from 1638 to 1655, Dutch rule from 1655 to 1664, and English rule from 1664 to 1704. From 1705 to 1760, it grew until the Revolutionary War period. People with capsule biographies in the text are Henry Hudson, Peter Minuit, Johan Printz, William Penn, Caesar Rodney, Thomas McKean, and John Dickinson. Prints and photographs highlight the information. Time Line and Index.

726. Fradin, Dennis B. **The Georgia Colony**. Chicago: Childrens Press, 1990. 159p. $24.70. ISBN 0-516-00392-5. 5-9

The text covers the founding of the Georgia colony and its life through the early 1760s. With prints and photographs as illustration, the information also includes brief biographies of Tomochichi, James Oglethorpe, Mary Musgrove, George Whitefield, Henry Ellis, and Button Gwinnett. Time Line and Index.

727. Fradin, Dennis B. **The Maryland Colony**. Chicago: Childrens Press, 1990. 159p. $24.70. ISBN 0-516-00394-1. 5-9

From 1634 to 1689, Maryland was an area growing in population. It was a royal colony from 1689 to 1715 and a proprietary colony during 1715-1760. Prints and photographs complement the history. The capsule biographies include George Calvert, Cecil Calvert, Margaret Brent, Thomas Cresap, Charles Carroll, Benjamin Banneker, Charles Willson Peale, and James McHenry. Time Line and Index.

728. Fradin, Dennis B. **The Massachusetts Colony**. Chicago: Childrens Press, 1986. 159p. $24.70. ISBN 0-516-00386-0. 5-9

From the time of the first settlements, life in the Massachusetts colony was important for the birth of the United States. There are capsule biographies of Squanto, Massasoit, William Bradford, Anne Bradstreet, Cotton Mather, Phillis Wheatley, Samuel Adams, Paul Revere, John Hancock, and John Adams. Prints and photographs complement the text. Time Line and Index.

729. Fradin, Dennis B. **The New Hampshire Colony**. Chicago: Childrens Press, 1988. 159p. $24.70. ISBN 0-516-00388-7. 5-9

In telling of the early life in New Hampshire through colonial times, the text gives background history and brief biographies of Passaconaway, Eleazar Wheelock, Robert Rogers, the Johnson family of Charlestown, Benning Wentworth, John Wentworth, John Stark, and John Sullivan. Prints and photographs reveal the era. Time Line and Index.

730. Fradin, Dennis B. **The New Jersey Colony**. Chicago: Childrens Press, 1991. 159p. $24.70. ISBN 0-516-00395-X. 5-9

The English took over the colony of New Jersey between 1664 and 1702. For the years before the Revolutionary War began, 1702-1760, it stayed a royal colony. The work has capsule biographies of Lewis Morris, Patience Lovell Wright, William Franklin, Reverend John Witherspoon, Francis Hopkinson, Molly Pitcher, and William Livingston. Prints, photographs, and text. Time Line and Index.

731. Fradin, Dennis B. **The New York Colony**. Chicago: Childrens Press, 1988. 159p. $24.70. ISBN 0-516-00389-5. 5-9

Early New York colony was colonized by the Dutch until the English took over. Brief biographies of Hiawatha, Henry Hudson, Peter Minuit, Peter Stuyvesant, Captain William Kidd, Joseph Brant, Margaret Corbin, John Jay, and Alexander Hamilton show New York before the Revolutionary War. Prints and photographs highlight the text, which covers the history of the times. Time Line and Index.

732. Fradin, Dennis B. **The North Carolina Colony**. Chicago: Childrens Press, 1991. 159p. $24.70. ISBN 0-516-00396-8. 5-9

Prints, photographs, and text introduce the history of the North Carolina colony. Topics include the Native Americans who lived there when the Roanoke colony was established in 1585 (and later disappeared); the westward expansion from 1705 to 1760; the revolutionary aspects of 1764-1783; and the Declaration of Independence. Capsule biographies include Sir Walter Raleigh, Sir John White, John Lawson, Blackbeard, Daniel Boone, Cornelius Harnett, James Iredell, and Richard Dobbs Spaight. Time Line and Index.

733.   Fradin, Dennis B. **The Pennsylvania Colony**. Chicago: Childrens Press, 1988. 159p. $24.70. ISBN 0-516-00390-9. 5-9

From the first colonists, the Pennsylvania area began to grow from 1684 to 1750. Also included is the life in Pennsylvania from 1750 to 1754. Capsule biographies and accompanying prints and photographs give a sense of William Penn, Benjamin Franklin, John Dickinson, Robert Morriss, Haym Salomon, Betsy Ross, James Wilson, and Gouverneur Morris. Time Line and Index.

734.   Fradin, Dennis B. **The Rhode Island Colony**. Chicago: Childrens Press, 1989. 159p. $24.70. ISBN 0-516-00391-7. 5-9

The early years of the Rhode Island colony lasted from 1636 to 1660. During 1700-1756, important events involved planters, pirates, slaves, and ships. Afterward came the Revolutionary War. Brief biographies of Roger Williams, Anne Marbury Hutchinson, King Philip Metacomet, Stephen Hopkins, Esek Hopkins, Abraham Whipple, and Nathanael Greene reveal their contributions to the state. Prints and photographs highlight various aspects. Time Line and Index.

735.   Fradin, Dennis B. **The South Carolina Colony**. Chicago: Childrens Press, 1992. 159p. $24.70. ISBN 0-516-00397-6. 5-9

The early period in South Carolina lasted from 1680 to 1729, the golden age from 1730 to the 1760s, and the revolutionary period after that. Biographical capsules of Dr. Henry Woodward, Blackbeard, Eliza Lucas Pinckney, Dr. Alexander Garden, Henry Laurens, John Laurens, Christopher Gadsden, and Francis Marion have accompanying prints and photographs. Time Line and Index.

736.   Fradin, Dennis B. **The Virginia Colony**. Chicago: Childrens Press, 1986. 159p. $24.70. ISBN 0-516-00387-9. 5-9

Jamestown, Virginia's first settlement, had its years of turmoil and growth from 1609 to the mid-1700s, prior to the revolutionary period. Accented with prints and photographs are the history and brief biographies of Powhatan, John Smith, Pocahontas, John Rolfe, George Washington, Patrick Henry, Thomas Jefferson, and Henry "Light-Horse Harry" Lee. Time Line and Index.

737.   Fradin, Dennis Brindell. **Medicine: Yesterday, Today, and Tomorrow**. Chicago: Childrens Press, 1989. 222p. $26.60. ISBN 0-516-00538-3. 7-10

The text gives an overview of the history of medicine. Among the topics covered in part 1 on "Yesterday" are ancient medicine, the Middle Ages, the Renaissance, the seventeenth and eighteenth centuries, the glorious nineteenth century, and from 1900 to the present. In the part on "Today," the text looks at the human body, why and how things go wrong, and modern medicine. Among the topics in "Tomorrow" are cancer, cardiovascular disease, transplants and artificial organs, genetic engineering, and better life for the elderly. Glossary, Bibliography, and Index.

738.   Fradin, Dennis Brindell. **We Have Conquered Pain: The Discovery of Anesthesia**. New York: Margaret K. McElderry, 1996. 148p. $16. ISBN 0-689-50587-6. 6-9

The text looks at the four nineteenth-century men who claimed to popularize nitrous oxide and ether as ways of curbing pain through anesthetics. It shows the rivalries and the human greed and jealousy that have continually marred medical advances as it examines the claims of these men: Crawford Long, Horace Wells, William Morton, and Charles Jackson. Photographs, Bibliography, and Index.

739.   Franck, Irene M., and David M. Brownstone. **The American Way West**. New York: Facts on File, 1990. 120p. $17.95. ISBN 0-8160-1880-4. (Trade and Travel Routes). 7 up

As people went west in America, they took routes that had been established through the years by Native Americans, trappers, or cattle. The text looks at these trade routes. Included are the Mohawk Trail, running from Albany to the eastern end of Lake Erie; the trans-Appalachian routes carrying travelers through these mountains into the Mississippi Basin; the Mississippi River, carrier of crops, livestock, and people for a 2,000-mile stretch; the Santa Fe Trail and the Chicuahua Trail, former footpaths; and the Oregon and California Trails through prairies and high plains, mountains, deserts, and whitewater. Maps and Index.

740.   Frank, Andrew. **The Birth of Black America: The Age of Discovery and the Slave Trade**. New York: Chelsea House, 1996. 111p. $19.95; $8.95pa. ISBN 0-7910-2257-9; 0-7910-2683-3pa. (Milestones in Black American History). 6-8

The text covers the history of slavery in the United States. It relates the beginning of slave usage in North America, the slave trade across the Atlantic, the middle passage, and what happened when the slaves arrived. Primary source accounts from people who endured the horror make this a powerful resource. Chronology, Further Reading, and Index.

741.   Frank, Elizabeth Bales. **Cooder Cutlas**. New York: Harper, 1987. 311p. $13.95. ISBN 0-06-021860-6. 9 up

Cooder has two reasons to mourn at 23: the deaths of his girlfriend and his rock band. In 1975, he wanders from place to place and joins another group on the Jersey shore while working in a garage. He does fall in love again but almost loses her until he takes time to reassess his values.

742.   Frankel, Noralee. **Break Those Chains at Last: African Americans 1860-1880**. New York: Oxford University Press, 1996. 143p. $21. ISBN 0-19-508798-4. (The Young Oxford History of African Americans). 8 up

Primary sources as well as general histories are the basis for this history of the politics, social and economic conditions, and culture of Blacks in America. Frankel uses interviews done in the 1930s with former slaves, Reconstruction Era pension examiners' interviews with Black Civil War widows, and Freedmen's Bureau records to support the assertions in the text. Photographs, posters, prints, letters, and additional artwork complement the text. Chronology, Further Reading, and Index.

743.   Frankl, Ron. **Charlie Parker: Musician**. New York: Chelsea House, 1993. 127p. $18.95. ISBN 0-7910-1134-8. (Black Americans of Achievement). 6 up

Charlie Parker (1920-1955) perfected the musical style known as bebop. He grew up in Kansas City, learning to play the saxophone and joining a band when only 14. He then went to New York in 1942 and began to work out bebop's complex approach to harmony and rhythm. He found that its freedom allowed him to stress improvisation rather than melody. He was able to invent new variations of songs each time he played. He had begun shooting heroin at 17, and his dependency on drugs and alcohol marred his later life. Photographs enhance the text. Further Reading, Glossary, and Index.

744.   Fraser, Jane. **Walter White: Civil Rights Leader**. New York: Chelsea House, 1991. 111p. $18.95. ISBN 1-55546-617-6. (Black Americans of Achievement). 6-9

Walter White (1893-1955) served as the director of the National Association for the Advancement of Colored People (NAACP) from 1931 to 1955. He risked his life to personally investigate 41 lynchings and eight race riots. The organization, under his leadership, began to overcome segregated housing, education, employment, military service, and public facilities. White also wrote several books. Photographs enhance the text. Chronology, Further Reading, and Index.

745.   Frazier, Nancy. **William Randolph Hearst: Press Baron**. Englewood Cliffs, NJ: Silver Burdett, 1989. 128p. $10.95. ISBN 0-382-09585-5. (The American Dream). 7-10

When the movie *Citizen Kane* was released in the 1940s, many people knew it was a fictionalized account of the life of William Randolph Hearst (1863-1951). Among the holdings that Hearst acquired during his life were newspapers and news syndicates, apartment buildings, paper mills, forests, and grocery stores. The text looks at his life and tries to make sense of the enigma, a man so wealthy that he could not also be great. Bibliography and Index.

746.   Freedman, Russell. **Buffalo Hunt**. New York: Holiday House, 1988. 52p. $16.95. ISBN 0-8234-0702-0. 5-8

Freedman's introduction presents Native American lore about the buffalo and the importance of this animal to the Indians. Information covers the preparation for a hunt, techniques for approaching the herd, the attack, and the stripping of the dead buffalo. He concludes by noting that repeating rifles, railroad sports, and bounty hunters depleted the herds and, along with them, the food, clothing, and livelihoods that the buffalo provided for many Native Americans. Photographs and reproductions embellish the text. Bibliography and Index. *Booklist Starred Review, Bulletin Blue Ribbon Book, Horn Book Fanfare Honor List, Kirkus Pointer Review, Publishers Weekly Starred Review*, and *School Library Journal Best Book*.

747.   Freedman, Russell. **Cowboys of the Wild West**. New York: Clarion, 1985. 103p. $15.95; $7.95pa. ISBN 0-89919-301-3; 0-395-54800-4pa. 6-8

The cowboy trade began in Mexico during the sixteenth century, when the Spanish brought the first domesticated horses and cattle to North America. *Vaqueros*, barefoot Indian cow herders, were the first to work with these animals, and to keep them together, they used *la riata*, or the lariat. After the Civil War, men went to Texas, where the animals roamed free, and began rounding them up. The meat-packing industry in Chicago needed meat, and the men wanted the money, so they rode the herds to Kansas railroad towns for shipment to Chicago and Kansas City. The typical cowboy was rarely older than 30 because the long days and hard work tired even the strongest. Their clothes had to survive all weather conditions and protect them from thorns. Hats and bandannas were useful in a variety of ways, including as tourniquets for snakebite. Movie and television stereotypes ignore the difficulty of the job and the fact that most cowboys were either Black or Mexican. Bibliography.

748.   Freedman, Russell. **Eleanor Roosevelt: A Life of Discovery**. New York: Clarion, 1993. 198p. $17.95. ISBN 0-89919-862-7. 6-12

"If anyone were to ask me what I want out of life I would say—the opportunity to do something useful, for in no other way, I am convinced, can true happiness be attained." Eleanor Roosevelt (1884-1962), who considered herself an "ugly duckling," showed her values with that statement. As a young girl, she was very serious and reserved. She had to change when she began to travel extensively and to go where her wheelchair-bound husband could not. After his death, she was an American delegate to the United Nations, and Harry Truman called her the "First Lady of the World." Photographs, Books About and by Eleanor Roosevelt, and Index. *Newbery Honor Book* and *Bulletin Blue Ribbon Book*.

749.   Freedman, Russell. **Franklin Delano Roosevelt**. New York: Clarion, 1990. 200p. $16.95; $7.95pa. ISBN 0-89919-379-X; 0-395-62978-0pa. 5-8

Born in 1882 to a wealthy family, Franklin Delano Roosevelt (1882-1945) became a philatelist, naturalist, and photographer before he entered Harvard. His father's death while he was a freshman freed his mother to come to Boston and live near him. At Harvard, Roosevelt was happiest working on the *Crimson*. After graduation, he married Eleanor Roosevelt. He became the Secretary of the Navy during World War I, and his idea to mine the North Sea to stop German U-boats proved successful. Verdun and the 500,000 who died there horrified him, and he wanted to join the army, but the war ended too soon. Eleanor found out by 1920 that he had been unfaithful, and they began an emotional estrangement that probably lasted throughout their marriage. But in 1921, when polio struck Franklin, their lives changed. Eleanor encouraged and supported his continued public life, although his mother did not. His illness helped him understand the difficulties of people who found themselves in situations through no fault of their own. Roosevelt became President in 1932, during the height of the Depression, and his New Deal program, including the Works Progress Administration, helped save the country. The first part of his term is known as the "Hundred Days." During his fourth term, and near the end of World War II, his strength waned, and he died in 1945 at Warm Springs, Georgia. Places to Visit, FDR Photo Album, Books About FDR, and Index. *Bulletin Blue Ribbon Book*.

750.   Freedman, Russell. **Indian Chiefs**. New York: Holiday House, 1987. 151p. $15.95. ISBN 0-8234-0625-1. 7 up

The Native Americans during the nineteenth century faced a long line of broken treaties and stolen lands. These biographies show strong leaders who tried to help their people in the face of disappointment. Included are Red Cloud, Satanta, Quanah Parker, Washakie, Joseph, and Sitting Bull. They all worked during the lifetime of Sitting Bull, who became the Sioux chief in the 1860s but was murdered two weeks before the Wounded Knee massacre in 1890. Photographs, Bibliography, and Index. *Booklist Starred Review, Bulletin Blue Ribbon Book, Horn Book Fanfare Honor List, Kirkus Pointer Review, Publishers Weekly Starred Review, Notable Children's Trade Books in the Field of Social Studies*, and *School Library Journal Best Book*.

751.   Freedman, Russell. **Kids at Work: Lewis Hine and the Crusade Against Child Labor**. Lewis Hine, photographer. New York: Clarion, 1994. 104p. $16.95. ISBN 0-395-58703-4. 5 up

Lewis Wickes Hine (1874-1940) photographed thousands of working children before World War I. In 1911, more than 2 million American children under 16 were a regular part of the workforce, many working 12 or more hours a day, six days a week, in hazardous conditions for pitiful wages. Hine risked his life to get his photos because no employer wanted pictures of their underage workers. Hine had learned photography to offer his students an after-school activity, but when he spent time at Ellis Island photographing immigrants, giving them the grace and dignity they deserved, he became a master photographer. His photos led the National Child Labor Committee to fight for and gain stronger laws against child labor. Hine, however, died in poverty, unable to get funding for his projects and finally having to sell all that he owned. But his pictures are part of America's memory. Declaration of Dependence, Child Labor Then and Now, Bibliography, and Index. *Orbis Pictus Honor Book* and *Jane Addams Children's Book Award*.

752.   Freedman, Russell. **The Life and Death of Crazy Horse**. Amos Bad Heart Bull, illustrator. New York: Holiday House, 1996. 166p. $19.95. ISBN 0-8234-1219-9. 7 up

Crazy Horse (1849?-1877), the Oglala Sioux warrior, went of his own volition to a reservation and surrendered his arms to the U.S. military after the Battle of the Little Bighorn. There he met an unwarranted death. The text looks at his life as a member of his tribe in a time when the whites encroached upon their land and eventually took control of it. Amos Bad Heart Bull, the tribal historian during Crazy Horse's life, made drawings that show peacetime activities as well as concepts of raids among tribes; reproductions of those drawings augment the text. Chronology, Bibliography, and Index. *Bulletin Blue Ribbon Book*.

753.   Freedman, Russell. **Lincoln: A Photobiography**. New York: Clarion, 1987. 150p. $16.95; $7.95pa. ISBN 0-89919-380-3; 0-395-51848-2pa. 6 up

Abraham Lincoln (1809-1865) had wit and good humor that attracted crowds as much as his height did. He began his career as a country lawyer, courted and married Mary Todd, and had a difficult presidency in the White House trying to oversee the Civil War. Freedman uses photographs and prints to illustrate his text about Lincoln's life. *Newbery Medal.*

754.   Freedman, Russell. **The Wright Brothers: How They Invented the Airplane**. New York: Holiday House, 1990. 129p. $18.95. ISBN 0-8234-0875-2. 4-8

The two Wright brothers, Wilbur (1867) and Orville (1871), were extraordinarily close until Wilbur died of typhoid in 1912. Their first flight in 1904 for one minute and 36 seconds caused Amos Root to say, ". . . like [Columbus] . . . these two brothers have probably not even a faint glimpse of what their discovery is going to bring to the children of men." Their repeatedly longer flights attracted attention from other experimenters like the German Lilienthal, Langley, and Chanute. By 1905, they could stay in the air more than 30 minutes. In 1908, although the French were suspicious of their plane and considered themselves the aviation leaders, Wilbur went to France to help. He awed them with his plane's grace and reported to Orville that Blériot was ecstatic. Blériot flew across the English Channel in 1909. Orville began to make demonstration flights at Fort Meyer, Virginia. After their achievements, they received a hero's welcome when they returned home to Dayton, Ohio. At Wilbur's death, Orville seemed to lose interest in the air. Now wealthy, he spent his time tinkering with all types of mechanical things, including the toys of his nieces and nephews, until his own death in 1948. When *Apollo II* landed on the moon, Neil Armstrong carried a piece of the cotton wing from the 1903 flight that started it all. Places to Visit, For Further Reading, and Index. *Booklist Starred Review, Bulletin Blue Ribbon Book, Horn Book Fanfare Honor List, Kirkus Pointer Review, Notable Children's Trade Books in the Field of Social Studies*, and *School Library Journal Best Book*.

755.   Freedman, Suzanne. **Dian Fossey: Befriending the Gorillas**. Austin, TX: Raintree/Steck-Vaughn, 1997. 112p. $18.98. ISBN 0-8172-4405-0. (Innovative Minds). 7-8

After a difficult childhood and graduation from college, Dian Fossey (1932-1985) heard Dr. Lewis Leakey lecture, and she decided to go to Africa to do research on mountain gorillas. She always lacked necessary funding but she continued to work with the wild apes until she became an authority on them. Part of her work was opposing the poachers who killed the beautiful animals for bounty, and she left Rwanda for a while to continue her graduate studies at Cambridge in England. But after her Ph.D., she returned to the country to continue her research and fight against poachers. Someone murdered her in 1985. Although an American graduate student was charged, more likely Rwandans who wanted her gone killed her. Glossary, Further Reading, Sources, and Index.

756.   Freedman, Suzanne. **Louis Brandeis: The People's Justice**. Springfield, NJ: Enslow, 1996. 104p. $18.95. ISBN 0-89490-678-X. (Justices of the Supreme Court). 5-8

Louis Brandeis (1856-1941) was the first Jew to serve on the Supreme Court. Woodrow Wilson nominated him in 1916. Brandeis was also the first progressive justice, a social reformer. The text looks at his life and his contributions to the Court. Bibliography, Glossary, Notes, and Index.

757.   Freedman, Suzanne. **Roger Taney: The Dred Scott Legacy**. Springfield, NJ: Enslow, 1995. 112p. $17.95. ISBN 0-89490-560-0. (Justices of the Supreme Court). 7-10

Roger Brooke Taney (1777-1864) became the fifth chief justice of the Supreme Court on March 28, 1836, and remained for 28 years. He put the law of the Constitution above everything, even if it offended his moral judgment. He was opposed to slavery, but he saw the Constitution as supporting slavery, and he had to make a pro-slavery decision in the Dred Scott Case. The Court said that Dred Scott was not a citizen of the United States, that slaves were property, and that the Constitution upheld the right for a citizen to own property. This decision in 1857 was another step toward the Civil War. Chronology, Notes, Glossary, Further Reading, and Index.

758.   Freeman, Suzanne T. **The Cuckoo's Child**. New York: Greenwillow, 1996. 256p. $15. ISBN 0-688-14290-7. 6-9

In 1962, Mia wants to leave Beirut, and after her parents disappear on a sailing trip, she goes to stay with her mother's sister in Ionia, Tennessee. She finds that the town has little tolerance for outsiders, and although she tries to adjust, she has difficulty fitting into their mold. She misses her parents, who have not been found; dislikes her aunt's married boyfriend; and hates attending the summer Bible school. She had dreamed of living in America while still in Beirut, but she realizes that what she really wants is a home where she feels comfortable.

759.   Friese, Kai Jabir. **Rosa Parks: The Movement Organizes**. Eric Velasquez, illustrator. Englewood Cliffs, NJ: Silver Burdett, 1990. 130p. $12.95. ISBN 0-382-09927-3. (History of the Civil Rights Movement). 6-9

Rosa Parks (b. 1913) is the woman who refused to move to the back of the Montgomery, Alabama, bus. This refusal started the bus boycott in 1956, which lasted more than a year. She paid for her decision by being arrested, but her sacrifice allowed others to sit as she did without anyone forcing them to move. Timetable, Suggested Reading, Sources, and Index.

760. Fritz, Jean. **Brady**. Lynd Ward, illustrator. 1960. New York: Penguin, 1987. 223p. $13.95. ISBN 0-14-032258-2. 4-7

Brady accidentally finds an Underground Railway site in 1836 and runs home to tell his parents. They tell him he is wrong and should not make such foolish claims. When his father is injured in a fire, Brady takes slaves to another station along the Railway without telling his father. When his father becomes aware of Brady's deed, he acknowledges his approval by writing in the family Bible that Brady has done a man's job.

761. Fritz, Jean. **Bully for You, Teddy Roosevelt**. Mike Wimmer, illustrator. New York: Putnam, 1990. 127p. $20.95. ISBN 0-399-21769-X. 5-9

Theodore Roosevelt (1858-1919) described things that he especially liked as "Bully!" Among the activities he pursued were studying birds, shooting lions, roping steers, writing books, exploring South American rivers, and battling in Cuba. He fought corruption and worked for peace, winning the Nobel Peace Prize. He met with John Muir, saw the beauty of America, and used his presidential power to preserve it. Notes, Bibliography, and Index.

762. Fritz, Jean. **The Cabin Faced West**. Feodor Rojankovsky, illustrator. New York: Coward-McCann, 1958. 124p. $14.95. ISBN 0-698-20016-0. New York: Puffin, Penguin, 1987. 124p. $4.99pa. ISBN 0-14-032256-6pa. 4-7

Ann and her family move from Gettysburg in 1784 to the wilderness frontier of Pennsylvania. She misses her friends, so her mother tells her that they will take time off from all their work when an occasion for a party arises. One evening a stranger comes to visit, and they have a wonderful party. When the guest leaves, she is happy that she lives on Hamilton Hill. Their guest was George Washington.

763. Fritz, Jean. **China Homecoming**. New York: Putnam, 1985. 144p. $16.95. ISBN 0-399-21182-9. 5 up

As an adult, Fritz wanted to return to China, the place where she was born and lived for the first 10 years of her life. The Chinese government finally permitted her visit, and she describes the changes as well as the constancy that is Chinese life in the 1980s, after Mao's Cultural Revolution. Her ability to speak Chinese gave her insights during the continued Communist rule to which most Westerners are not privileged. Notes from the Author, Brief Outline of Chinese History, and Bibliography.

764. Fritz, Jean. **The Double Life of Pocahontas**. Ed Young, illustrator. New York: Putnam, 1983. 96p. $14.95. ISBN 0-399-21016-4. New York: Viking, 1987. 96p. $3.99pa. ISBN 0-14-032257-4pa. 6-9

In this story of Pocahontas (d. 1617), Fritz shows that all was not happy in the colony where Pocahontas met the English settlers. When she sponsored John Smith, she was probably taking a traditional role in the tribe to support someone who wanted to be accepted in the group. She was later probably kidnapped and had to stay with the English. Then she married John Rolfe and went with him to England. In England, she saw John Smith after a year because he neglected to see her sooner even though she had saved his life. Notes, Bibliography, and Index.

765. Fritz, Jean. **Early Thunder**. Lynd Ward, illustrator. 1967. New York: Penguin, 1987. 256p. $4.99pa. ISBN 0-14-032259-0pa. 5-9

When he is 14 in 1775 and living in the American colonies, Daniel West supports the British king. But when fellow Tories throw stones into a judge's window while the man lies dying of smallpox, he becomes infuriated. He begins to change his allegiance when he sees people he respects support the Rebel cause.

766. Fritz, Jean. **The Great Little Madison**. New York: Putnam, 1989. 159p. $15.95. ISBN 0-399-21768-1. 5-8

James Madison (1751-1836) was always committed to the unity of the United States, but his weak voice and small stature kept him from speaking effectively. He clashed with Patrick Henry, had a romance with and married the young widow Dolley Payne Todd, and was friends with Thomas Jefferson. He made important intellectual contributions to the beginning of the nation. Notes, Bibliography, and Index.

767. Fritz, Jean. **Harriet Beecher Stowe and the Beecher Preachers**. New York: Putnam, 1994. 144p. $15.95. ISBN 0-399-22666-4. 4-8

Harriet Beecher Stowe (1811-1896) strongly opposed slavery but did not know what to do to get rid of it. Her sister-in-law encouraged her to do what she did best—write. In 1852, *Uncle Tom's Cabin* was published, and Stowe became an instant celebrity. Her father was the most renowned preacher in America, and because he wanted more preachers in the family, he had seven children. He expected little from his girls, but Harriet was probably the most successful of his children because she became known in Europe as well as the United States. People in England crowded the streets to see her. She was a nineteenth-century wife, mother, and daughter who said that "writing is my element." Photographs, Bibliography, and Index.

768.   Fritz, Jean. **Homesick: My Own Story**. Margot Tomes, illustrator. New York: Putnam, 1982. 160p. $15.95. ISBN 0-399-20933-6. New York: Dell, 1985. 160p. $4.99pa. ISBN 0-440-43683-4pa. 3-7

Born in China, Jean Fritz did not come to America until she was 10. During the last two years that she and her parents were in Hankow, China, the conflict between Chiang Kai-shek (Sun Yat-sen's successor) and Mao Tse-tung was beginning. The autobiographical story must be cataloged as fiction because Fritz admits that she told her story as a storyteller rather than as an autobiographer. Therefore, the reader lives with a child who first meets adult problems such as the death of another child, the divorce of a friend's parents, and a war in which her servant friends are being hurt by enemies and by families turned Communist. Background of Chinese History, 1913-1927.

769.   Fritz, Jean. **Stonewall**. Stephen Gammell, illustrator. New York: Putnam, 1979. 160p. $15.95. ISBN 0-399-20698-1. New York: Viking, 1989. 160p. $4.99pa. ISBN 0-14-032937-4pa. 3-9

Tom Jackson (1824-1863) saw his mother work in menial jobs because his father had frittered away the family money and died. After her death, when Tom was seven, he determined that he would make something of his life. His rules for life were to tell the truth, not to break promises, and to do what he planned. After living with an uncle, Tom's break came when he had a chance to go to West Point even though he was not well educated. He graduated, became a hero in the Mexican war, taught at Virginia Military Institute, and fought for the South in the Civil War, where he earned the name "Stonewall." Strong religious convictions and strict rules governed his life until he died of pneumonia after one of his soldiers accidentally shot him in the arm. Bibliography.

770.   Fritz, Jean. **Traitor: The Case of Benedict Arnold**. New York: Putnam, 1981. 192p. $16.95. ISBN 0-399-20834-8. New York: Viking, 1989. 192p. $4.99pa. ISBN 0-14-032940-4pa. 5-9

Using the metaphor of wheels that turn without going anywhere, Fritz recounts the life of Benedict Arnold (1741-1801), a boy whose alcoholic father led him to think that if one could display wealth, then one would be happy and respected by others. Every aspect of Arnold's life seemed based on this premise. His final compromise with truth was to "sell" the new United States to the British by surrendering West Point, which he commanded by the grace of his friend, George Washington. This act of treason, discovered before it was concluded, only brought him exile to England and unhappiness. His name is not even carved on his tombstone. Bibliography and Index.

771.   Froelich, Margaret. **Reasons to Stay**. Boston: Houghton Mifflin, 1986. 181p. $12.95. ISBN 0-395-41068-1. 7-10

In 1906, Babe takes her two siblings to her friend's grandparents' house after her mother dies to escape her dishonest stepfather. When she finally locates her own grandparents, she realizes that they will never accept her into their family.

772.   Fromm, Peter. **Monkey Tag**. New York: Scholastic, 1994. 336p. $14.95. ISBN 0-590-46525-2. 5-7

While Eli and Thad, both 12 in 1970, play monkey tag on the bleachers, Thad falls and hurts himself enough to have to go through rehabilitation. As twins, he and Eli are close, and not even their parents' protective attitude toward Thad can keep them apart. Eli helps Thad until he begins to walk again, but Eli can only question his Catholic faith through this trauma. Eli finds no answers to his questions, and he has not yet made his decision about the church when the novel ends.

773.   Frost, Mary Pierce, and Susan E. Keegan. **The Mexican Revolution**. San Diego, CA: Lucent, 1996. 128p. $16.95. ISBN 1-56006-292-4. (World History). 9 up

The text details the Mexican revolution in chronological order from the beginning in 1910 through the 1930s when it was resolved. Archival photographs enhance the text and give a sense of the times and the places. Bibliography, Further Reading, Notes, and Index.

774.   Frost-Knappman, Elizabeth, and Kathryn Cullen-DuPont. **Women's Suffrage in America: An Eyewitness History**. New York: Facts on File, 1992. 452p. $45. ISBN 0-8160-2309-3. (Eyewitness History). YA

The women's suffrage movement in the United States lasted from 1800 to 1920. The text presents 14 essays that are excerpts from primary source material, including letters, speeches, court decisions, memoirs, newspapers, and petitions. Topics covered include abolition, temperance, women's war work, women of color, and the women's labor movement. Appendices, Bibliography, and Index.

775.   Fry, Annette R. **The Orphan Train**. New York: New Discovery, 1994. 96p. $14.95. ISBN 0-02-735721-X. (American Event). 4-8

Unwanted children have always been a concern of society. In the nineteenth century the Children's Aid Society placed orphaned, poor, and abandoned children from New York and Boston in western homes after taking them across the country on a train. Photographs enhance the text about these children, who traveled away from what they knew to unknown homes and futures. Further Reading and Index.

G

776. Gaeddert, Louann. **Breaking Free**. New York: Atheneum, 1994. 144p. $14.95. ISBN 0-689-31883-9. 5-8

Richard's uncle has no use for either school or music, Richard's two loves. His uncle also owns slaves. Richard walks 10 miles a day to school. He teaches a slave girl to read, which allows her and her father to escape, and soon Richard makes a contact that leads to his own departure.

777. Gaines, Anne. **John Wesley Powell and the Great Surveys of the American West**. New York: Chelsea House, 1992. 136p. $19.95. ISBN 0-7910-1318-9. (World Explorers). 5 up

In 1865, after the Civil War, the Homestead Act and the transcontinental railroad made settlement of the West a priority for many even though much of the land was only superficially mapped. People wanted to know if oil, gold, silver, copper, or iron was under the ground. Between 1867 and 1879, four men led surveys of the West. They were Clarence King, George Wheeler, Ferdinand Hayden, and John Wesley Powell (1834-1902), the one-armed explorer of the Grand Canyon. These surveys mapped and photographed the West from the Sierra Nevadas to the Missouri River and from Yellowstone to the Mexican border. Photographs enhance the text. Chronology, Further Reading, and Index.

778. Gallen, David. **Bill Clinton as They Know Him**. New York: Gallen, 1994. 287p. $19.95. ISBN 09636477-2-5. YA

Interviews with people who have known Bill Clinton through the years give different views of the man sitting as the 42nd President of the United States. He is intelligent though arrogant at times and has a bad temper. But he has also shown interest in improving education and incorporating more minorities and women into his governments, both as governor of Arkansas and as President. Among the scenes are Clinton singing Elvis Presley songs along his paper route and of him being a compulsive eater. Index.

779. Galvin, James. **The Meadow**. New York: Henry Holt, 1992. 230p. $19.95; $12pa. ISBN 0-8050-1684-8; 0-8050-2703-3pa. YA

The text tells the story of a meadow in Sheep Creek, Wyoming, next to Colorado's border. Galvin describes every aspect of the meadow, including the people who have lived there in the past 100 years. He gives insight into the natural world of the area as well as the human.

780. Gardner, Robert, and Dennis Shortelle. **The Forgotten Players: The Story of Black Baseball in America**. New York: Walker, 1993. 120p. $13.85. ISBN 0-8027-8248-5. 5 up

Noting how America shortchanged its Black baseball players in the late nineteenth and early twentieth centuries, the text gives a history of this maltreatment. Among the Negro League teams were the Detroit Stars, the Indianapolis ABCs, the Kansas City Monarchs, and the Chicago American Giants; they played thousands of ballgames for sellout crowds. The topics include an overview of early baseball, Rube Foster and the Negro National League, Gus Greenlee and a new Negro League, life in the leagues, barnstorming with them, and the integration of baseball with Jackie Robinson. Notes, Bibliography, and Index.

781. Garfunkel, Trudy. **Letter to the World: The Life and Dances of Martha Graham**. Boston: Little, Brown, 1995. 92p. $16.95. ISBN 0-316-30413-1. 6 up

Growing up in Pennsylvania and California, Martha Graham (1894-1991) did not know that she wanted to dance until she was 16. The text gives information about the various influences on her life, including Ruth St. Denis, Erick Hawkins, Paul Taylor, and Merce Cunningham. Among the 200 dances she choreographed and performed with her unique principles of movement are "Letter to the World," "Frontier," and "Appalachian Spring." Photographs, Bibliography, and Index.

782. Garfunkel, Trudy. **On Wings of Joy: The Story of Ballet from the 16th Century to Today**. Boston: Little, Brown, 1994. 194p. $18.95. ISBN 0-316-30412-3. 6 up

Ballet began more than 400 years ago in the courts of Europe. In the seventeenth century, the English masque and the five positions of classical ballet were established. Although some changes occurred in the eighteenth century, Jean-Georges Noverre (1727-1810), the father of modern ballet, was the theorist of the times. Dancers received training commensurate with their body types. In the nineteenth century, Romanticism and Romantic ballet began. Famous dancers included Marie Taglioni, Jules Perrot, Carlotta Grisi, and Carlotta Brianza. During the twentieth century, modern dance arrived. Still, famous dancers preferred classical ballet. Names that dominate this century are Pavlova and Balanchine. Coda, Glossary, Bibliography, and Index.

783. Garland, Sherry. **Cabin 102**. San Diego, CA: Harcourt Brace, 1995. 243p. $11; $5pa. ISBN 0-15-238631-9; 0-15-200662-1pa. 5-9

Although set in the present, this historical fantasy couples the contemporary Dusty, 12, with Tahni, an Arawak Indian girl who is in the cabin next door to Dusty's on a cruise ship. Through a series of inquiries and situations where people think he is crazy, Dusty finds out that Tahni drowned when the Spanish galleon *Estrella Vespertina* capsized in 1511. Now she is trying to return to her island of Bogati. With her story comes historical background on the Spanish conquest in the Caribbean and the end of the Arawak Indians.

784. Garland, Sherry. **Indio**. San Diego, CA: Harcourt Brace, 1995. 291p. $11; $5pa. ISBN 0-15-38631-9; 0-15-200021-6pa. 6-10

When Ipa-tah-chi is 10 in the early sixteenth century, Apache raiders take her brother prisoner and kill her grandmother. When she is older and getting married, Spanish soldiers arrive in her Jumano pueblo near the Rio Grande and capture her and her cousin and take them to work in the Mexican silver mines. Her cousin is raped, and when the man who raped her is murdered, the man's brother blames Ipa because she is an *indio*. A kind Spanish soldier with whom she has fallen in love helps her escape. She returns to her village, waits for the soldier to summon her to Mexico City, and looks after her dead cousin's baby. *American Library Association Best Books for Young Adults* and *American Bookseller Pick of the Lists*.

785. Garland, Sherry. **The Last Rainmaker**. San Diego, CA: Harcourt Brace, 1997. 336p. $12; $6pa. ISBN 0-15-200649-4; 0-15-200652-4pa. 5-10

Caroline, 13, has lived in a small Missouri River town not knowing the identity of her mother. One relative tells Caroline, who has her mother's dark eyes and hair and olive skin, that her mother was Italian royalty, and another says that she was a wicked gypsy. When her beloved grandmother dies, she escapes the jealousy of her father and great-aunt by running away to join Shawnee Sam's Wild West Extravaganza. Two Indians in the show, one old and one young, help Caroline find her mother's and her own identity.

786. Gates, Viola R. **Journey to Center Place**. Boulder, CO: Roberts Rinehart, 1996. 144p. $10.95pa. ISBN 1-57098-061-6pa. 3-7

Neekah, 12, must leave her home in Salapa, Colorado, after months without rain, so the family can find water in their world of AD 1250. They go to Center Place, the Anasazi center of the universe, in Chaco Canyon, New Mexico. The family follows the Anasazi road system that leads to Center Place and joins others who have faced the same dangers and hardships.

787. Garza, Hedda. **Barred from the Bar: A History of Women and the Legal Profession**. New York: Franklin Watts, 1996. 224p. $22; $9pa. ISBN 0-531-11265-9; 0-531-15795-4pa. (Women Then-Women Now). 9 up

In the text, Garza covers the history of women's involvement with law in America since colonial times. She presents many firsts along the way, such as the first woman admitted to the bar and the first African American woman lawyer. She shows the larger forces that unite these women into an underpaid group because of the prejudices still covertly working in the system. One woman, Esther McQuigg Morris, jailed her husband in 1870 when he complained to her court about her being the first woman judge in the United States. Photographs, Further Reading, Endnotes, and Index.

788. Garza, Hedda. **Latinas: Hispanic Women in the United States**. New York: Franklin Watts, 1994. 192p. $14.84. ISBN 0-531-11186-5. (Hispanic Experience in the Americas). 8 up

The text gives an overview of Latina history from Spanish colonization to the present by focusing on women's political and economic oppression. Among the persons featured are Lucy Parsons and Luisa Morena, Latina activists. A variety of topics includes information on women's rights as presented at Seneca Falls in 1848, the overthrow of Porfirio Diaz in 1911, and the mischaracterization of Latinas in American media. Photographs and Index.

789. Gates, Viola R. **Journey to Center Place**. Boulder, CO: Roberts Rinehart, 1996. 144p. $10.95pa. ISBN 1-57098-061-6pa. 3-7

Neekah, 12, must leave her home in Salapa, Colorado, after months without rain, so the family can find water in their world of AD 1250. They go to Center Place, the Anasazi center of the universe, in Chaco Canyon, New Mexico. The family follows the Anasazi road system that leads to Center Place and joins others who have faced the same dangers and hardships.

790. Gay, Kathlyn. **Spanish American War**. New York: Twenty-First Century Books, 1995. 64p. $15.98. ISBN 0-8050-2847-1. (Voices from the Past). 7-9

Letters, diaries, and newspaper accounts give an overview of the causes, the battles, and the results of the Spanish American War, which the Americans fought in 1898 against Spain. Photographs, Maps, Further Reading, Notes, and Index.

791. Gay, Kathlyn, and Martin Gay. **Civil War**. New York: Twenty-First Century Books, 1995. 64p. $15.98. ISBN 0-8050-2845-5. (Voices from the Past). 7-9

Letters, diaries, and newspaper accounts give an overview of the American Civil War, which lasted from 1861 to 1865. Photographs, Maps, Further Reading, Notes, and Index.

792. Gay, Kathlyn, and Martin Gay. **Korean War**. New York: Twenty-First Century Books, 1996. 64p. $15.98. ISBN 0-8050-4100-1. (Voices from the Past). 7-9

Letters, diaries, and newspaper accounts give an overview of the Korean War, in which America fought for South Korea as part of United Nations troops from 1950 to 1953. Photographs, Maps, Further Reading, Notes, and Index.

793. Gay, Kathlyn, and Martin Gay. **Persian Gulf War**. New York: Twenty-First Century Books, 1996. 64p. $15.98. ISBN 0-8050-4102-8. (Voices from the Past). 7-9

Letters, diaries, and newspaper accounts give an overview of the Persian Gulf War, in which the United States fought to help Kuwait and Saudi Arabia overcome aggression by Saddam Hussein of Iraq in January and February 1991. Photographs, Maps, Further Reading, Notes, and Index.

794. Gay, Kathlyn, and Martin Gay. **Revolutionary War**. New York: Twenty-First Century Books, 1995. 64p. $15.98. ISBN 0-8050-2844-7. (Voices from the Past). 7-9

Letters, diaries, and newspaper accounts give an overview of the causes, the battles, and the results of the war that the American colonies fought against the British between 1775 and 1783. Photographs, Maps, Further Reading, Notes, and Index.

795. Gay, Kathlyn, and Martin Gay. **Vietnam War**. New York: Twenty-First Century Books, 1996. 64p. $15.98. ISBN 0-8050-4101-X. (Voices from the Past). 7-9

Letters, diaries, and newspaper accounts give an overview of the Vietnam War. The United States became involved in 1961 to fight against Communism in Southeast Asia. The war lasted until 1975. Photographs, Maps, Further Reading, Notes, and Index.

796. Gay, Kathlyn, and Martin Gay. **War of 1812**. New York: Twenty-First Century Books, 1995. 64p. $15.98. ISBN 0-8050-2846-3. (Voices from the Past). 7-9

Letters, diaries, and newspaper accounts give an overview of the causes, the battles, and the results of the War of 1812, the second war that the Americans fought against the British. Photographs, Maps, Further Reading, Notes, and Index.

797. Gay, Kathlyn, and Martin Gay. **World War I**. New York: Twenty-First Century Books, 1995. 64p. $15.98. ISBN 0-8050-2848-X. (Voices from the Past). 7-9

Letters, diaries, and newspaper accounts give an overview of World War I, which the Americans entered in 1917 and fought until its end in 1918. Photographs, Maps, Further Reading, Notes, and Index.

798. Gay, Kathlyn, and Martin Gay. **World War II**. New York: Twenty-First Century Books, 1995. 64p. $15.98. ISBN 0-8050-2849-8. (Voices from the Past). 7-9

Letters, diaries, and newspaper accounts give an overview of World War II, which the Americans entered in 1941 and fought until its end in 1945. Photographs, Maps, Further Reading, Notes, and Index.

799. Gay, Martin, and Kathlyn Gay. **Emma Goldman**. San Diego, CA: Lucent, 1997. 128p. $19.95. ISBN 1-56006-024-7. (The Importance Of). 7 up

Emma Goldman (1869-1940), oppressed and abused during her childhood, became an anarchist who despised tyranny of any kind. She immigrated to the United States in 1885 when she was 16 after her father tried to marry her to someone she hated. When she saw the conditions in the United States, she involved herself in the labor movement. The text follows these aspects of her life as well as her time in Russia during the Revolution and after. Bibliography, Chronology, Further Reading, and Index.

800. Gear, W. Michael, and Kathleen O'Neal Gear. **People of the Sea**. 1993. New York: Tor Books, 1995. 425p. $6.99pa. ISBN 0-8125-0745-2pa. YA

While he is trying to find out where the mammoth on which his people depend for food and clothing have gone, Suncatcher falls in love with a woman whose demented husband is hunting her. He also has to compete with a rival from another tribe who wants his position as healer. His problems of 12,000 years ago mirror those of humans in any age.

801.   Gehret, Jeanne. **Susan B. Anthony: And Justice for All**. Fairport, NY: Verbal Images, 1994. 120p. $14.95; $6.95pa. ISBN 0-9625136-9-5; 09625136-8-7pa. 6-9

Susan B. Anthony (1820-1906) spent her adult life working for human rights. Among the things she did was "kidnap" an abused woman from her husband, talk to angry mobs, break laws she considered unfair, and gather 400,000 signatures on a petition asking Congress to outlaw slavery. Although she worked 50 years for women's suffrage, it did not happen until 14 years after she died. But without her work, it might have been longer. Glossary, Important Events, Selections for Young Readers, Further Reading, and Index.

802.   Gentry, Tony. **Dizzy Gillespie: Musician**. New York: Chelsea House, 1991. 112p. $18.95; $7.95pa. ISBN 0-7910-1127-5; 0-7910-1152-6pa. (Black Americans of Achievement). 5 up

John Birks Gillespie (b. 1917) began playing the trumpet when he was 12. In South Carolina, people began asking him to join them on stage, and he became a swing band member soon after, where he earned the name "Dizzy" for his energy. He developed his own approach to harmony and rhythm and, along with several other musicians, created bebop. In 1945, he began his own band, and two years later, he introduced Afro-Cuban rhythms. Photographs and reproductions enhance the text. Chronology, Further Reading, and Index.

803.   Gentry, Tony. **Jesse Owens: Champion Athlete**. New York: Chelsea House, 1990. 111p. $18.95; $7.95pa. ISBN 1-55546-603-6; 0-7910-0247-0pa. (Black Americans of Achievement). 5 up

Gentry first recounts Owens's experience at the 1936 Olympics in Berlin, when Hitler spurned him as non-Aryan while the crowds loved his fluid running style. Then Gentry turns to Owens's childhood in the South and in Cleveland, where he met his future wife and the Irish coach who encouraged him. After breaking track records, Owens (1913-1980) met Olympic gold medal winner Charlie Paddock and decided that he wanted to become an Olympian himself. In Berlin, Owens became good friends with his chief competitor in the long jump, Luz Long. The two seemed to bring out the best in each other as they exchanged jump after jump before Owens finally won the gold and Long the silver. Photographs, Chronology, Further Reading, and Index.

804.   Gentry, Tony. **Paul Laurence Dunbar: Poet**. New York: Chelsea House, 1989. 112p. $18.95; $7.95pa. ISBN 1-55546-583-8; 0-7910-0223-3pa. (Black Americans of Achievement). 5 up

Paul Laurence Dunbar (1872-1906) was the first Black American to gain international recognition as a poet. As the only Black to graduate from his Dayton, Ohio, high school, he could not get a job because of his color, though he'd been a top student, and he had no money for college. He worked as an elevator operator and wrote poetry on the side. He was able to publish two collections, and his third collection, published when he was 24, established his reputation. In his work, which also includes essays and novels, he suggested that humor can exist in all lives, even the most difficult. Photographs and reproductions enhance the text. Chronology, Further Reading, and Index.

805.   Gherman, Beverly. **E. B. White: Some Writer!** New York: Atheneum, 1992. 136p. $13.95. ISBN 0-689-31672-0. 6 up

E. B. White (1899-1985), author of *Charlotte's Web*, *Stuart Little*, and *The Trumpet of the Swan*, said that Stuart came to him in a dream, but that Charlotte did not. White had lived in Maine for five years on a farm with a barn, and he knew the behavior of spiders, geese, rats, and pigs. With this experience, he created the realities of life within his fantasy world. He also wrote for adults by editing William Strunk's older work to create the definitive style manual for writers. White was shy and hated to speak in public as a young man, but he was also someone who enjoyed adventure, his wife, and his family. Photographs, Notes, Bibliography, and Index.

806.   Giblin, James. **Be Seated: A Book About Chairs**. New York: HarperCollins, 1993. 136p. $15. ISBN 0-06-021537-2. 4-8

The text gives a history of chairs beginning with the three-legged stools and chairs of the Egyptians, which were mortise- and tenon-joined. It includes the thrones of kings such as Solomon and the *klismos* of the Greeks with their curved lines. Giblin also discusses the Sheridan chair and the Shaker rocker. The chair becomes a part of social custom, art, and politics in the society that uses it. Bibliography, Notes, and Index.

807.   Giblin, James. **When Plague Strikes: The Black Death, Smallpox, AIDS**. New York: HarperCollins, 1995. 212p. $14.95. ISBN 0-06-025854-3. 5-9

Three major plagues have hit the known world in the past 1,000 years: the Black Death, smallpox, and AIDS. They have killed millions of people and have left social, economic, and political havoc. Although each plague has helped to increase knowledge about the human body, each new one must be researched and tested for a cure. The text first recounts the Plague of Athens that struck in the summer of 430 BC. Those who lived had terrible scars or lost their eyesight or their memory. Today no one is sure what the disease might have been, although typhus, smallpox, and the bubonic plague are candidates. The sure thing is that doctors did not know how to treat it. Giblin continues with information about the three plagues that have ravaged the world since. Source Notes, Bibliography, and Index. *American Library Association Best Books for Young Adults*, *Notable Children's Trade Books in the Field of Social Studies*, and *American Library Association Notable Books for Children*.

808.   Gibson, Michael. **The War in Vietnam**. New York: Bookwright Press, Franklin Watts, 1992. 63p. $19.14. ISBN 0-531-18408-0. (Witness History). 5-8

The text traces the history of Vietnam from 1887 until the French left in 1954. It discusses the United States's entry into the conflict after it began in 1961 and the country's exit before the fighting ended in 1975, as well as the current situation within the country. Black-and-white and a few color photographs highlight the text. Chronology, Glossary, and Index.

809.   Giff, Patricia R. **Lily's Crossing**. New York: Delacorte, 1997. 176p. $14.95. ISBN 0-385-32142-2. 5-7

Lily looks forward to the summer at the family home in Far Rockaway, but after she arrives, she finds that her best friend in the summer is moving away. The only playmate around is Albert, a Hungarian boy who left Europe to escape World War II. When Lily hears that her father is going to Europe as an engineer to help clean up, she is fearful that he will not return. Lily dislikes Albert at first, but she soon realizes that he has his own fears, and the two become friends.

810.   Gilbert, Bill. **They Also Served: Baseball and the Home Front 1941-1945**. New York: Crown, 1992. 276p. $20. ISBN 0-517-58522-7. YA

During the war years of 1941-1945, major league baseball continued although many of the great players served abroad. More night games were scheduled, and teams used Hispanic players to fill in the holes left by the players in the military. Some careers were merely interrupted; others were stopped completely. The text tells about many of them. Index.

811.   Gilbert, Thomas. **Deadball: Major League Baseball Before Babe Ruth**. New York: Franklin Watts, 1996. 176p. $22. ISBN 0-531-11262-4. (The American Game). 7 up

The text recounts major league baseball, its notable teams and stars, from 1900 to 1919 when pitchers' earned-run averages were below 2.0 and the hitters who reached double digits were the league leaders. At this time, pitchers dominated the game. Many statistics, scores, and names may be overwhelming, but their accuracy gives them a place in history. Bibliography and Index.

812.   Gilbert, Thomas. **The Soaring Twenties: Babe Ruth and the Home-Run Decade**. New York: Franklin Watts, 1996. 160p. $22.70. ISBN 0-531-11279-9. 7 up

With statistics and a myriad of details, the text covers the decade of the 1920s in baseball. Gilbert discusses the many scandals and cover-ups of the period and asks why some of them were exposed while others remained hidden. This thorough look at baseball will satisfy baseball fanatics. Photographs, Bibliography, Notes, and Index.

813.   Gilman, Michael. **Matthew Henson: Explorer**. New York: Chelsea House, 1988. 112p. $18.95; $7.95pa. ISBN 1-55546-590-0; 0-7910-1158-5pa. (Black Americans of Achievement). 5 up

Matthew Henson (1886-1955) gained a chance to explore when Robert Peary walked into the hat shop where he was working and told his boss that he wanted someone to go with him to Nicaragua while he searched for a place to build a passage between the Atlantic and Pacific Oceans. The shop owner suggested his employee. Henson had traveled to major ports in his life, but as a Black in America, he had had no opportunity to continue his sailing career. Henson went with Peary to Nicaragua and then to the area of the North Pole several times before he became one of the first men to reach the Pole itself in 1909. Photographs enhance the text. Chronology, Further Reading, and Index.

814.   Gintzler, A. S. **Cowboys**. Santa Fe, NM: John Muir, 1994. 46p. $12.95. ISBN 1-56261-152-6. (Rough and Ready). 5-9

Most cowboys lived during the nineteenth century. In two-page spreads complemented with photographs, maps, and prints, Gintzler discusses topics that reveal a cowboy's life. They include the plains, roundups, cattle drives, skills, gear, horses, Texas longhorns, cow towns, the workday, law and order, Indians, famous cowboys, working cowgirls, Black cowboys, the *vaquero*, the rodeo trail, cowboy songs and poetry, range wars, and the cowboy of today. Index.

815.   Gintzler, A. S. **Homesteaders**. Santa Fe, NM: John Muir, 1994. 46p. $12.95. ISBN 1-56261-154-2. (Rough and Ready). 5-9

Homesteaders made their homes in the Great Plains, a grassland in the middle of the United States once called the "Great American Desert." They moved to this area during the nineteenth century and changed the face of the land. In two-page spreads complemented with photographs, maps, and prints, Gintzler discusses the topics that describe the homesteader's life. They include the trails they took, waterways, who they were, houses, farming, hardships, native peoples they met, range wars, law and disorder, frontier towns, African American homesteaders, women on the plains, day-to-day living, homestead diaries and letters, songs of the sodbusters, games and celebrations, traveling salesmen and entertainers, commerce, and plains ecology. Index.

816. Gintzler, A. S. **Prospectors**. Santa Fe, NM: John Muir, 1994. 46p. $12.95. ISBN 1-56261-153-4. (Rough and Ready). 5-9

The United States won California from Mexico in a war that lasted from 1846 to 1848. In 1848, John Marshall found gold on the American River in northern California on John Sutter's land. Although they agreed to keep the information a secret, someone heard, and the gold rush started. In two-page spreads complemented with photographs, maps, and prints, Gintzler describes the prospector's life. She looks at gold fever, routes to the gold, gold seekers, life in the diggings, the geology of gold, tools, hard-rock mining, dangers, mining towns, law and disorder, Indians, mule trains and muleteers, songs of the Forty-Niners, the miners' own words, tall tales, bonanza kings and paupers, ghost towns, mining and the environment, and prospecting today. Index.

817. Gipson, Fred. **Old Yeller**. 1956. Cutchogue, NY: Buccaneer, 1995. 184p. $15.95. ISBN 0-8996-6906-9. New York: HarperCollins, 1990. 184p. $4.50pa. ISBN 0-06-440382-3pa. 4-7

When Travis is 14 during the 1860s, his father departs for Florida and leaves him in charge of the Texas family homestead. When an old dog arrives, his brother and mother want to keep it, calling it "Old Yeller." Although Travis does not want the dog, Old Yeller saves him from wild hogs. However, a wild wolf bites Old Yeller, and Travis must kill him because he develops hydrophobia (rabies) after the bite. *Newbery Honor Book* and *American Library Association Notable Children's Books of 1940-1970*.

818. Gish, Lillian, and Selma G. Lanes. **An Actor's Life for Me!** Patricia Henderson Lincoln, illustrator. New York: Viking Kestrel, 1987. 74p. $15. ISBN 0-670-80416-9. YA

Lillian Gish (1893-1993) tells the story of her young life that she spent performing in the American theater. She says that she tried to make herself believe that she liked traveling on trains while others were in bed. She also disliked separation from her sister and her mother, who played in another troupe. As she began to grow taller, she learned to dance so she could still be hired. Eventually she and her family were reunited in California, where they had enough money to stop traveling.

819. Glasco, Gordon. **Slow Through Eden**. New York: Poseidon, 1992. 259p. $23. ISBN 0-671-62305-2. YA

Katherine and David, both physicists, start to develop the atomic bomb in Berlin during World War II. David, however, is Jewish, and they know they must escape as soon as possible to London. But in London, a Russian spy kills David. Katherine takes their son and goes to New York, where she begins another life by joining the team working on the Manhattan Project, a bomb for the United States.

820. Glassman, Bruce. **Mikhail Baryshnikov**. Englewood Cliffs, NJ: Silver Burdett, 1991. 128p. $14.95. ISBN 0-382-09907-9. (Genius: Artist and Process). 7-9

In 1966, Mikhail Baryshnikov (b. 1948) stunned his viewers with his dancing, and he quickly became a star in the Kirov Ballet. His unique talent and technique, developed after he had seen his first ballet at the age of six, led him to defect from the Soviet Union in 1974. In the United States, he has continued to dance and to choreograph, believing that the dance can say what he thinks. Photographs highlight the text. Chronology, Glossary, Bibliography, and Index.

821. Glassman, Bruce. **Wilma Mankiller: Chief of the Cherokee Nation**. New York: Blackbirch Press, Rosen, 1992. 64p. $14.95. ISBN 0-8239-1208-6. (Library of Famous Women). 4-8

The text begins with the point that Hollywood's idea of Indians is unrelated to reality. Wilma Mankiller (b. 1945) neither rides a horse to work nor wears stripes on her face. She is intensely interested in her people and furthering the education of all children, not just Native Americans. The text looks at her life and the events that led her to become the head of her tribe. Glossary, For Further Reading, and Index.

822. Glenn, Patricia Brown. **Discover America's Favorite Architects**. Joe Stites, illustrator. New York: Preservation, 1996. 118p. $19.95pa. ISBN 0-471-14354-5pa. 6-9

The text presents short biographies of 10 architects, arranged in chronological order according to their birth. They are Thomas Jefferson (1743-1826), Frederick Law Olmsted (1822-1903), Henry Hobson Richardson (1838-1886), Louis Henri Sullivan (1856-1924), Frank Lloyd Wright (1867-1959), Julia Morgan (1872-1957), Ludwig Mies van der Rohe (1886-1969), Paul R. Williams (1884-1980), Philip Johnson (b. 1906), and I. M. Pei (b. 1917). Although some of these architects are not American by birth, their designs grace American cities. Each segment presents the architect's background, training, and major accomplishments. Photographs, Bibliography, Glossary, and Index.

823. Glubok, Shirley. **Great Lives: Painting**. New York: Scribner's, 1994. 238p. $24.95. ISBN 0-684-19052-4. (Great Lives). 5-9

Places where they live and experiences they have influence the subjects that artists choose to paint. Biographical profiles of 23 major painters appear in the text: Mary Cassatt, American (1844-1926); Marc Chagall, Russian (1887-1985); Frederick E. Church, American (1826-1900); Jacques-Louis David, French (1748-1825); Edgar Degas, French (1834-1917); Albrecht Dürer, German (1471-1528); Thomas Gainsborough, English

(1727-1788); Paul Gaugin, French (1848-1903); El Greco, Greek (1541-1614); Winslow Homer, American (1836-1910); Leonardo da Vinci, Italian (1452-1519); Michelangelo, Italian (1475-1564); Claude Monet, French (1840-1926); Georgia O'Keeffe, American (1889-1986); Pablo Picasso, Spanish (1881-1973); Rembrandt van Rijn, Dutch (1606-1669); Diego Rivera, Mexican (1886-1957); Peter Paul Rubens, Flemish (1577-1640); Titian, Venetian (?-1576); Vincent van Gogh, Dutch (1853-1890); Diego de Veláquez, Spanish (1599-1660); Johannes Vermeer, Dutch (1632-1675); and James McNeill Whistler, American (1834-1903). Further Reading and Index.

824. Gold, John C. **Board of Education v. Pico (1982): Book Banning**. New York: Twenty-First Century Books, 1994. 93p. $15.98. ISBN 0-8050-3660-1. (Supreme Court Decisions). 7 up

Books have been banned since Plato wanted to expunge sections from Homer in 387 BC, and Thomas Bowdler "bowdlerized" Shakespeare by cutting out passages he thought unsuitable for young people. In 1928, a group in Boston managed to have more than 100 books banned there, but when the undercover vigilantism disturbed some, the group began to lose power. After World War II, more book censorship occurred. Finally, the Supreme Court ruled that no school board had the power to remove books from libraries, because those actions made them censors. Source Notes, Glossary, Further Reading, and Index.

825. Gold, Susan Dudley. **In Re Gault (1967)**. New York: Twenty-First Century Books, 1995. 96p. $15.98. ISBN 0-8050-3917-1. (Supreme Court Decisions). 7 up

When the first juvenile court was established in Chicago during 1899, it was to rehabilitate children rather than to punish them. Some judges sent children to reform institutions for minor offenses because laws did not exist to protect the children. When Gerald Gault, 15, went to an Arizona reform school in 1964 for six years because he made one obscene telephone call, civil rights advocates took his case to court. As an adult, he would have received a small fine and perhaps a maximum sentence of two months in jail. In 1967, the Supreme Court ruled that the Constitution applied to children, and they were entitled to fair treatment. Because of this decision, lawyers represent many more children than before. Source Notes, Glossary, Further Reading, and Index.

826. Gold, Susan Dudley. **Miranda v. Arizona (1966)**. New York: Twenty-First Century Books, 1995. 96p. $15.98. ISBN 0-8050-3915-5. (Supreme Court Decisions). 7 up

The text covers the circumstances of a case when a man named Miranda was convicted based on information he unwittingly gave to the police. His subsequent appeal reached the Supreme Court. In 1966, the Supreme Court ruled that the police must warn a suspect that he or she has the right to remain silent. The text also comments on the effects of this decision. Source Notes, Glossary, Further Reading, and Index.

827. Gold, Susan Dudley. **Roberts v. U.S. Jaycees (1984)**. New York: Twenty-First Century Books, 1995. 96p. $15.98. ISBN 0-8050-4238-5. (Supreme Court Decisions). 7 up

In 1984, Roberts challenged the rules of the Jaycee organization in the United States that women could not be admitted to its ranks. The case continued through appeals until it reached the Supreme Court. The ruling was that denying women membership based on sex was illegal. The text looks at the decision and its effects. Source Notes, Glossary, Further Reading, and Index.

828. Gold, Susan Dudley. **Roe v. Wade (1973): Abortion**. New York: Twenty-First Century Books, 1994. 96p. $15.98. ISBN 0-8050-3659-8. (Supreme Court Decisions). 7 up

In 1973, the Supreme Court ruled that a woman has the constitutional right to abort a pregnancy, with states having the right to ban an abortion during the last three months of the pregnancy. Rather than ending a problem, the ruling has continued the battle between those who believe a woman has fewer rights than a fetus and those who think a woman should have control over her own body. Source Notes, Glossary, Further Reading, and Index.

829. Goldberg, Michael. **Breaking New Ground: American Women 1800-1848**. New York: Oxford University Press, 1994. 144p. $15. ISBN 0-19-508202-8. (The Young Oxford History of Women in the United States). 9 up

During the first half of the nineteenth century, women had few rights, but they began to make their voices heard. Among the topics covered are the growth of the nation, courtship and marriage customs, what people considered "women's work," educational opportunities for women, abolitionist activities, religious interests, and women such as Lucy Wright and Mother Seton. Chronology, Further Reading, and Index.

830. Goldish, Meish. **Immigration: How Should It Be Controlled?** New York: Twenty-First Century Books, 1994. 64p. $15.98. ISBN 0-8050-3182-0. (Issues of Our Time). 5-8

Immigration problems began as early as 1620, when the colonists wondered who should be allowed to come to the new land. These concerns continue as people grapple with the needs of foreigners who want better lives for themselves and their children and think they can have them in the United States. Citizens wonder if their taxes should pay for health care and education for people who cannot support themselves. Laws have changed through the years, but still people enter the country illegally, willing to gamble for a chance to come to America. The text discusses these problems and posits possible solutions. Glossary, For Further Reading, Source Notes, and Index.

831.   Goldman, Martin S. **Crazy Horse: War Chief of the Oglala Sioux**. New York: Franklin Watts, 1996. 208p. $22. ISBN 0-531-11258-6. (American Indian Experience). 6 up

Goldman posits that the image of Crazy Horse divides into two, the one that Native Americans have of him and the one that whites have. He tries to re-create both of these men through careful documentation. He also discusses the decline of the Sioux through this loner thought to be very strange, a good friend, a brave warrior, or a cruel conqueror. Goldman includes cultural information and biographical sketches of people who knew Crazy Horse, the man who became war chief of the Oglalas at 23 and whom the Shirt Wearers, or ruling council, cast out in the end. Bibliography and Index.

832.   Golston, Sydele E. **Changing Woman of the Apache: Women's Lives in Past and Present**. New York: Franklin Watts, 1996. 144p. $22. ISBN 0-531-11255-1. (American Indian Experience). 7-10

The text looks at the roles of women in the Apache tribe, both historical and contemporary. Among the rituals presented are the Sunrise Dance, a four-day maturation rite; childhood; young womanhood; adulthood; and old age. The women killed enemy warriors captured in battle by chopping them up. Photographs highlight the text. Index.

833.   Gonzales, Doreen. **Alex Haley: Author of *Roots***. Springfield, NJ: Enslow, 1994. 128p. $17.95. ISBN 0-89490-573-2. (People to Know). 7-10

Alex Haley (1921-1992) did not go to Africa until 1967. He had attended college, enlisted in and retired from the U.S. Coast Guard, and been a published writer for 17 years. Not until 1976 was *Roots* published and presented to the public via television. As a child, Haley loved reading and enjoyed his grandparents' stories of family history. His research on *Roots* lasted 12 years, and scholars questioned its authenticity, but it introduced all Americans to a heritage not widely known. Chronology, Chapter Notes, Further Reading, and Index.

834.   Gonzales, Doreen. **Cesar Chavez: Leader for Migrant Farm Workers**. Springfield, NJ: Enslow, 1996. 128p. $17.95. ISBN 0-89490-760-3. (Hispanic Biographies). 5-9

Cesar Chavez (1927-1993) helped establish the United Farm Workers Union so that migrant workers would have better working conditions and more rights. As the union became established and the workers more satisfied, the union began to lose members because Chavez hesitated to delegate responsibility to other people. Chronology, Further Reading, Notes, and Index.

835.   Goor, Ron, and Nancy Goor. **Williamsburg: Cradle of the Revolution**. New York: Atheneum, 1994. 90p. $15.95. ISBN 0-689-31795-6. 4-8

Williamsburg was an important part of the nation's life during the years preceding the American Revolution; Virginia's leaders gathered there. The text uses photographs of modern-day Williamsburg and its living history museum to show what life during that time was like for the people who lived and worked there, including the slaves. Bibliography and Index.

836.   Gormley, Beatrice. **Maria Mitchell: The Soul of an Astronomer**. Grand Rapids, MI: William B. Eerdman, 1995. 123p. $15; $8pa. ISBN 0-8028-5116-9; 0-8028-5099-5pa. (Women of Spirit). 4-8

Maria Mitchell (1818-1889) grew up in a Nantucket, Massachusetts, Quaker community that did not allow women to study mathematics. However, Mitchell's father, an amateur astronomer, decided to teach her both mathematics and what he knew about astronomy. Mitchell believed that women should refuse to follow authority if they did not agree with it. Only then would they be able to accomplish the things they were capable of. Mitchell was the first female professional astronomer in the United States and the first woman elected to the American Academy of Arts and Sciences; she also became Vassar's professor of astronomy. Additionally, she discovered Comet Mitchell and won a gold medal for it. Sources, Further Reading, and Index.

837.   Gorrell, Gena K. **North Star to Freedom: The Story of the Underground Railroad**. New York: Delacorte, 1997. 168p. $17.95. ISBN 0-385-32319-0. 6-8

The focus of this book, unlike other texts on the Underground Railroad, is Canada. Many of the slaves who took the railroad ended their journey in Canada with the help of abolitionists and Quakers along the way. Individual accounts from slaves who settled in Canada add new insights about this ordeal of American history. Reproductions, Bibliography, Further Reading, Notes, and Index.

838. Gottfried, Ted. **Alan Turing: The Architect of the Computer Age**. New York: Franklin Watts, 1996. 144p. $22.70. ISBN 0-531-11287-X. (Impact Biography). 7-12

This biography examines various aspects of Alan Turing's life other than the code breaking for which he gained renown. He was a pioneer of computational theory and a homosexual who suffered severely for his sexuality. Gottfried explains some of his mathematical achievements and both the political and social aspects of Turing's life. Photographs, Notes, Further Reading, and Index.

839. Gourley, Catherine. **Hunting Neptune's Giants: True Stories of American Whaling**. Brookfield, CT: Millbrook Press, 1995. 94p. $19.90. ISBN 1-56294-534-3. 4-7

Writings from whalers and some of their wives give an idea of life and work aboard an American whaling ship in the nineteenth century. Details of the hunting, harpooning, and processing help one understand the value of whales in their lives. Who went whaling and why gives additional insight into these people. The text relates the story of George H. Newton's 1880 traveling whale show, when citizens could smell the show coming in the spring and did not need newspaper advertisements. Photographs, prints, and paintings highlight the text. Bibliography, Further Reading, and Index.

840. Gourse, Leslie. **Billie Holiday: The Tragedy and Triumph of Lady Day**. New York: Franklin Watts, 1995. 128p. $13.90. ISBN 0-531-11248-9. (Impact Biography). 7 up

Billie Holiday (1915-1959), born Eleanor Fagan, had a life filled with abuse, neglect, and betrayal. Yet she was able to sing the blues and to create interpretations in her songs that connected to her listeners. This text examines her life as a part of those performers who were working, as she was, in a segregated world. Photographs, Selected Bibliography, Selected Discography, and Index.

841. Gourse, Leslie. **Dizzy Gillespie and the Birth of Bebop**. New York: Atheneum, 1994. 150p. $14.95. ISBN 0-689-31869-3. 5-9

When he was 10, Dizzy Gillespie (b. 1917) was the last child to arrive in the instrument room when he first joined the school band. The only instrument left was the slide trombone. He was delighted with it, and his career began. As an adult, he contributed greatly to jazz music with new rhythms, harmonic color, and a style called bebop. Suggested Listening, Bibliography, and Index.

842. Graham, Heather. **Runaway**. New York: Delacorte, 1994. 445p. $18.95; $5.99pa. ISBN 0-385-31264-4; 0-440-21688-5pa. YA

In 1835, while Tara tries to escape an accusation of murder, Jarrett wins her in a poker game, and they marry. He happens to be a wealthy plantation owner who supports the Indians, but when war breaks out, she has difficulty coping. With this backdrop, they have to learn to communicate with each other and to accept each other's qualities.

843. Graham, Lorenz. **John Brown: A Cry for Freedom**. New York: Crowell, HarperCollins, 1980. 180p. $12.89. ISBN 0-690-04024-5. 6 up

In 1859, John Brown (1800-1859) and his friends took direct action to end slavery, which some think was the real beginning of the Civil War. Regardless, he was hanged for his actions. As the son of strongly religious parents who believed that humans should never be attached to things, Brown became a fighter against slavery and injustice. He was a friend of Frederick Douglass and Harriet Tubman and a supporter of the Jayhawkers, people who fought against Kansas becoming a slave state. Books for Further Reading and Index.

844. Graham, Otis L., Jr., and Meghan Robinson Wander, eds. **Franklin D. Roosevelt: His Life and Times: An Encyclopedic View**. Boston: G. K. Hall, 1985. 483p. $45. ISBN 0-8161-8667-7. YA

This view of Franklin D. Roosevelt (1882-1945) presents 321 topics that cover his life. The text was written by 125 prize-winning biographers, historians, and political scientists. Index.

845. Granfield, Linda. **Cowboy: An Album**. New York: Ticknor & Fields, 1994. 96p. $18.95. ISBN 0-395-68430-7. 5-10

Photographs, engravings, and drawings illustrate this five-part look at cowboys. The parts are the historical cowboy, the roundup, the closing of the West, the building of the cowboy myth, and cowboys today. More specific topics discussed include the cowboy's uniform, the long drive, the end of the cattle boom, cowboys and their circuses, and the new generation of cowboys. Other Books and Index.

846. Granfield, Linda. **In Flanders Fields: The Story of the Poem by John McCrae**. Janet Wilson, illustrator. New York: Doubleday, 1996. Unpaged. $15.95. ISBN 0-385-32228-3. 5 up

Using the poem "In Flanders Fields" as a base, the text discusses the poem, gives an overview of World War I, and briefly capsulizes the life of the Canadian poet, John McCrae. Sketches, photographs, and memorabilia add to the illustrations.

847.   Gray, James. **George Washington Carver**. Englewood Cliffs, NJ: Silver Burdett, 1991. 138p. $13.98. ISBN 0-382-09964-8. (Pioneers in Change). 5-9

Son of slaves, George Washington Carver (c. 1864-1943) earned educational degrees from Iowa State. While teaching at Tuskegee Institute after graduating, his research showed the value of crop rotation and the benefits of peanuts and soybeans as soil-enriching. The text presents his life. Photographs, Important Dates, Bibliography, and Index.

848.   Gray, Randal, and Christopher Argyle. **Chronicle of the First World War—Vol. I: 1914-1916**. New York: Facts on File, 1991. 420p. $45. ISBN 0-8160-2139-2. YA

To give the day-by-day events of World War I in its first two years, the text uses two-page spreads in parallel columns with the headings, "Western Front," "Eastern Front," "Southern Front," "Turkish Front," "African Operations," "Sea War," "Air War," "International Events," and "Home Fronts." Statistical tables tell of troops engaged, losses, aircraft, ships, and other pertinent information. The "Home Fronts" column helps the reader connect national events and attitudes with battles happening in other places. Glossary, Bibliography, and Index.

849.   Green, Connie Jordan. **The War at Home**. New York: Macmillan, 1989. 137p. $12.95. ISBN 0-689-50470-5. 6-8

In 1945, Mattie, 13, and her family move to Oak Ridge, Tennessee, where her father has a job working on a secret project for the government. Then her cousin Virgil, 12, comes to stay with them. At first, she resents his presence because he announces that boys are much better than girls at a lot of different things. He leaves, but when she learns that his father has abused him by making him work in adult jobs after his mother died, she is glad he returns. After the atom bomb drops in World War II, people in Oak Ridge find out that they had been making parts of the bomb.

850.   Green, Rayna. **Women in American Indian Society**. New York: Chelsea House, 1992. 111p. $19.95; $8.95pa. ISBN 1-55546-734-2; 0-7910-0401-5pa. (Indians of North America). 5 up

Women have long had a role of leadership in the Native American community. This text, a social history, looks at the Native American female after the arrival of the Europeans, on the reservation, and in contemporary society. It focuses on the average woman and her contributions to her people. Photographs and drawings enhance the text. Further Reading, Glossary, and Index.

851.   Greenberg, Hank, and Ira Berkow. **Hank Greenberg: The Story of My Life**. New York: Times Books, 1989. 311p. $19.95. ISBN 0-81291-741-3. YA

Hank Greenberg (1911-1986) was one of the first Jewish baseball players and the first Jewish player to be elected to the Baseball Hall of Fame. He played in the major leagues from 1933 to 1947, first with the Detroit Tigers and then with the Pittsburgh Pirates. Although he spent five years in the military, he still hit 331 home runs and came within two home runs of Babe Ruth's season record of 60. In 1945, his grand slam in the ninth inning on the last day of the season won the pennant for the Tigers. As great as he was in the ballpark, he still had bad days, and he tells about both in this autobiography. Opposing teams and others yelled anti-Semitic slurs at him daily; his unflappable attitude served as a model for Jackie Robinson when that man started playing major league baseball. Index.

852.   Greenberg, Jan. **The Painter's Eye: Learning to Look at Contemporary American Art**. New York: Delacorte, 1990. 96p. $22.50. ISBN 0-385-30319-X. YA

In this text, Greenberg presents contemporary paintings and discusses their styles, media, and artists. Abstract expressionism, color field painting, post-painterly abstraction, minimalism, geometric abstraction, pop art, superrealism, op art, and new imagism are the schools discussed. The artists whose works appear are Willem de Kooning, Sam Francis, Robert Motherwell, Jackson Pollock, Mark Rothko, Helen Frankenthaler, Morris Louis, Ellsworth Kelly, Frank Stella, Jasper Johns, Roy Lichtenstein, Robert Rauschenberg, James Rosenquist, Wayne Thiebaud, Andy Warhol, Tom Wesselmann, Audrey Flack, Richard Anuszkiewicz, Jennifer Bartlett, Jean-Michel Basquiat, and Donald Sultan. Artists' Biographies, Glossary, Bibliography, and Index. *Bulletin Blue Ribbon Book*.

853.   Greenberg, Joanne. **No Reck'ning Made**. New York: Henry Holt, 1993. 384p. $23; $12.95pa. ISBN 0-8050-2579-0; 0-8050-3849-3pa. YA

When Clara Coleman is nine in Colorado before World War II, her mother dies in childbirth. Since Clara has to live with a father who verbally abuses her, her one outlet is school. She wants to be a teacher, and she luckily finds a job in a one-room schoolhouse in a tiny hamlet. After World War II, the town grows, and she becomes the administrator who has to deal with newcomers who want to change things.

854. Greenberg, Judith E., and Helen Carey McKeever. **Letters from a World War II GI**. New York: Franklin Watts, 1995. 144p. $13.93. ISBN 0-531-11212-8. (In Their Own Words). 7 up

During World War II, Keith Winston sent letters to his wife that show the way one enlistee felt about the war. Because his letters were subject to censorship, he could not discuss the war itself. He shows the rumors, misinformation, and changes in orders to which enlisted personnel were subject. He gives a different view of the war and one that shows how unsettling army life could be. Photographs and drawings highlight the text. Epilogue, For Further Reading, and Index.

855. Greenberg, Judith E., and Helen Carey McKeever. **A Pioneer Woman's Memoir**. New York: Franklin Watts, 1995. 160p. $13.93. ISBN 0-531-11211-X. 7 up

In April 1864, Arabella Clemens Fulton began her migration to the West in the Great National Adventure. She traveled from Missouri as one of 300,000 men, women, and children in 75,000 wagons who went on the Oregon Trail between the 1840s and the 1860s. She recorded her experiences, and they give much insight into this difficult journey. She believed that women should claim the credit for the settling and civilizing of the Northwest because they faced dangers and prepared food, cared for children, and soothed the men. Among the incidents noted in the chapter headings are the beginning of the journey, being lost on the prairie, crossing rivers and plains, Mormons, Fort Boise, getting married, creating a home in the wilderness, and how communities grew. Photographs and drawings highlight the text. Epilogue, For Further Reading, and Index.

856. Greenberg, Morrie. **The Buck Stops Here: A Biography of Harry Truman**. New York: Dillon Press, 1989. 127p. $13.95. ISBN 0-87518-394-8. 7-10

When Franklin Roosevelt died, Eleanor Roosevelt was the one who told Harry S. Truman (1884-1972). He asked if he could do anything for her, and she replied that he was the one who needed help because he had just inherited the trouble. And as he had become President during World War II, he had. The text looks at his life and his presidency. Appendix, Selected Bibliography, and Index.

857. Greenblatt, Miriam. **Franklin D. Roosevelt: 32nd President of the United States**. Ada, OK: Garrett Educational, 1988. 120p. $17.26. ISBN 0-9444483-06-2. (Presidents of the United States). 5-9

Franklin D. Roosevelt (1882-1945) attended Harvard and Columbia Law School before marrying his cousin Eleanor. He served in New York State government, as the Assistant Secretary of the Navy, and as President of the United States for four terms. He established the New Deal to overcome the Great Depression and declared war on Japan in 1941. Bibliography and Index.

858. Greenblatt, Miriam. **James K. Polk: 11th President of the United States**. Ada, OK: Garrett Educational, 1988. 120p. $17.26. ISBN 0-944483-04-6. (Presidents of the United States). 5-9

James K. Polk (1795-1849) graduated from the University of North Carolina and became a lawyer in Tennessee. He served in the House of Representatives and became the Speaker. He was also governor of Tennessee. The text begins with the operation he had at 17 for gallstones before anesthetics or antiseptics were discovered; luckily, he survived. He continued to show through his life that he could achieve things even though odds were against him, including being elected President. He died of poor health within months after leaving the White House. Bibliography and Index.

859. Greenblatt, Miriam. **The War of 1812**. New York: Facts on File, 1994. 124p. $17.95. ISBN 0-8160-2879-6. (America at War). YA

In 1812, the United States again battled Great Britain. Great Britain's continuing war with France caught the United States when Great Britain blockaded its ports and pressed its young sailors into British service. Illustrations and maps give a sense of place, while text shows what life was like for the average soldier and what types of weapons helped the United States win this war. Recommended Reading and Index.

860. Greene, Bette. **Morning Is a Long Time Coming**. 1978. New York: Laurel, 1993. $3.99pa. ISBN 0-440-21893-4pa. 7 up

The sequel to *Summer of My German Soldier* shows Patty after graduating from high school. She uses her gift money to travel to Europe even though her father cuts her out of his will to show his disapproval and says the Jewish prayers of the dead for her. She has a love interest in Paris, and she spends time searching for the mother of her German soldier.

861. Greene, Bette. **Summer of My German Soldier**. 1973. New York: Laurel, 1994. 224p. $4.99pa. ISBN 0-440-21892-6pa. 7 up

Patty, 12 in Arkansas during the summer of 1944, is bored without school to divert her. She discovers a German prisoner of war who has escaped. She feeds him and gives him clothing, but the military finds him and kills him. The Federal Bureau of Investigation learns that Patty has helped him, and at her trial, with the support of her family's Black maid but not her parents, she receives reform school as a sentence. Her caring values contrast to her materialistic parents. *Golden Kite Award* and *National Book Award* finalist.

862. Greene, Constance C. **Dotty's Suitcase**. 1980. New York: Puffin, 1991. 147p. $3.95pa. ISBN 0-14-034882-4pa. 3-7

In 1934, during the Depression, Dotty, 12, wants a suitcase because she thinks it will make her feel like she is going somewhere. She finds one on the side of the road that, unknown to her, bank robbers threw out of their car while running from a heist. She and Jud, eight, with whom she is walking, get a ride to a town where her best friend has moved. Although Dotty has felt sorry for herself because she must stay at home alone while her older sisters work, she realizes that she has a good life. She gives the money in the suitcase to her best friend, who lost everything when her father died.

863. Greene, Laura Offenhartz. **Child Labor: Then and Now**. New York: Franklin Watts, 1992. 144p. $20.60. ISBN 0-531-13008-8. (Impact). 5-10

Ever since the British, with their chimney sweeps in the 1700s, and the Industrial Revolution, with children working in factories, child labor has been a serious problem. In the early twentieth century, Lewis Hine photographed children, especially immigrants, working in the terrible conditions of mines, mills, factories, sweatshops, and farms. A change in the laws has helped the United States, but child labor still exists in countries from which America gets many goods. Engravings enhance the text. Selected Bibliography and Index.

864. Greenwood, Barbara. **A Pioneer Sampler: The Daily Life of a Pioneer Family in 1840**. Heather Collins, illustrator. New York: Ticknor & Fields, 1995. 240p. $18.95. ISBN 0-395-71540-7. 5-8

The text introduces the Robertsons, a pioneer family on a backwoods farm in 1840. Among the chores they must complete during the year are making maple syrup, planting crops, and shearing sheep. They attend a backwoods school, visit a country store, build a house, and go to a barn dance. They have to cook their food, churn their butter, slaughter hogs, and operate a grist mill. They also have to tell time by looking at the sun, and they have no one to tell them the next day's weather. Glossary and Index. *Notable Children's Trade Books in the Field of Social Studies*.

865. Gregory, Kristiana. **Earthquake at Dawn**. San Diego, CA: Harcourt Brace, 1992. 192p. $15.95; $3.95pa. ISBN 0-15-200446-7; 0-15-200099-2pa. (Great Episodes). 3-7

In 1906, Daisy, 15, and Edith Irvine, a photographer, plan a journey around the world. On the day of their departure, a devastating earthquake shakes San Francisco, the city where they plan to disembark. Instead of traveling, they help others construct tents and rescue people during the aftershocks. When they return to Edith's home, they have both real and mental photographs of the severe damage suffered throughout the city. *American Library Association Best Books for Young Adults*, *Notable Children's Trade Books in the Field of Social Studies*, and *New York Public Library Books for the Teen Age*.

866. Gregory, Kristiana. **Jenny of the Tetons**. San Diego, CA: Harcourt Brace, 1989. 120p. $13.95. ISBN 0-15-200480-7. 5-7

Carrie, 15 in 1875, refuses to have any dealings with Indians because they killed her family in a raid. "Beaver Dick," a trapper, befriends her, but his wife is a Shoshone. Jenny and her children remain friendly toward Carrie until she adjusts to the idea that not all Indians can be equated with the ones who destroyed her family. *Golden Kite Award*.

867. Gregory, Kristiana. **Jimmy Spoon and the Pony Express**. New York: Scholastic, 1994. 117p. $13.95. ISBN 0-590-46577-5. 5-7

Based on the true exploits of Elijah Nicholas Wilson is this story of Jimmy Spoon, a 17-year-old bored with working in his father's store after living with the Shoshoni (*The Legend of Jimmy Spoon*). In 1860, he sees an advertisement for an expert rider not more than 18 who is willing to risk death daily. The lure of adventure attracts him; he applies and is hired immediately for the Pony Express. However, he still remembers a beautiful Shoshoni girl, Nahanee, and after a year passes he goes to find her and his Shoshoni family. Glossary and Bibliography.

868. Gregory, Kristiana. **The Legend of Jimmy Spoon**. San Diego, CA: Harcourt Brace, 1990. 164p. $15.95; $6pa. ISBN 0-15-200506-4; 0-15-243812-2pa. (Great Episodes). 3-7

Bored with working in his father's store in the Mormon stronghold of Utah in 1854, Jimmy, 12, agrees to go with two Shoshoni boys to their home when they promise to give him a horse. He does not realize that they expect him to live with the tribe until he proves his manhood and earns the horse. He stays, and he eventually earns enough respect so that whether he leaves or stays becomes his own decision.

869. Gregory, Kristiana. **The Winter of Red Snow: The Diary of Abigail Jane Stewart, Valley Forge, Pennsylvania, 1777-1778**. New York: Scholastic, 1996. 170p. $9.95. ISBN 0-590-22653-3. (Dear America, 2). 5-9

As Abigail looks out her window on December 19, 1777, she sees soldiers and runs outside with her family to cheer. The soldiers are "quiet and thin," and she sees that their bare feet leave footprints in the snow. Her journal covers the days from December 1, 1777, until July 4, 1778, when everyone is sure that the newly trained soldiers under George Washington will be able to defeat the British in the American Revolution. An epilogue gives information about Abby after her journal ends.

870.   Grey, Edward. **The Eighties**. Austin, TX: Raintree/Steck-Vaughn, 1990. 48p. $22.80. ISBN 0-8114-4215-2. (Decades). 5-7

Among the disasters of this decade of the 1980s were famine, war, a space tragedy, a nuclear accident, and the AIDS virus. But the world also became safer as superpowers came closer together in their philosophical outlook. It marked the beginning of global communication when in 1985, more than 1.5 billion people in 160 countries watched the Live Aid charity concert. The text looks at the music, clothes, media, leisure, youth culture, and styles of the time against a backdrop of major historical, political, and technological events. Glossary, Further Reading, and Index.

871.   Griffin, Peni. **Switching Well**. New York: Margaret K. McElderry, 1993. 218p. $15.95. ISBN 0-689-50581-7. 5-8

Each girl, Ada and Amber, wishes that she lived in another time. Both shift their 12-year-old selves to another century. Ada moves from 1891 to 1991, and Amber goes from 1991 to 1891. Their change comes inside a well. The busy life of San Antonio shocks Ada, where she is almost accosted by a child molester, and the prejudice and lack of opportunity of 100 years earlier distresses Amber. She is disturbed that the deaf are considered no different than the retarded and that Christians have more rights than Jews. An African American girl helps them return to their times after an unexpected inheritance.

872.   Grimes, Roberta. **My Thomas: A Novel of Martha Jefferson's Life**. New York: Doubleday, 1993. 320p. $20. ISBN 0-385-42399-3. YA

Before 1772 and Thomas Jefferson, Martha Skelton had decided not to remarry after her first husband died although she was only 22. She changed her mind when she met the young lawyer and legislator Jefferson. In her journal as recounted here, she records their life together until she dies in childbirth nine years later. An afterword tells that Jefferson left Monticello for 10 years after her death because of the pain of her loss associated with the place.

873.   Grosser, Morton. **The Fabulous Fifty**. New York: Atheneum, 1990. 233p. $13.95. ISBN 0-689-31656-9. 7-9

Solon, a Greek American of 15 who wants to go to the World Series in 1921, concocts a plan with the members of his club so that they can win the newspaper prize of a trip to the games. They collect enough newspaper coupons for their group to win, but only one can go. Another of the group pretends that he is one of the 49 other winners until they arrive in New York for the Giants vs. Yankee games. Their New York adventures entertain the reader.

874.   Guccione, Leslie Davis. **Come Morning**. Minneapolis, MN: Carolrhoda, 1995. 120p. $14.96. ISBN 0-87614-892-5. (Adventures in Time). 4-7

Freedom Newcastle, 12 in the 1850s, cuts willows on his free Black father's farm for the Delaware Du-Pont company to buy and make into charcoal. What he really wants is to help his father at night because he knows his father and the Quaker neighbors work for the Underground Railroad. He gets his chance sooner than expected when slavers from the South capture his father, thinking that he has helped other slaves. His father proves his free status, but their home is burned. Freedom, however, delivers the "cargo" to Moses (Harriet Tubman) before the slavers find them. *Society of School Librarians International Outstanding Book*.

875.   Guernsey, Alfred H., and Henry M. Alden. **Harper's Pictorial History of the Civil War**. New York: Random House, Gramercy, 1996. 836p. $39.99. ISBN 0-517-18334-X. YA

Primary source materials first collected in 1869 fill this work. Throughout, the details of military, political, and social issues of the Civil War era provide an understanding of the times. Illustrations, Maps, and Index.

876.   Gurasich, Marj. **Letters to Oma: A Young German Girl's Account of Her First Year in Texas, 1847**. Barbara Mathews Whitehead, illustrator. Fort Worth, TX: Texas Christian, 1989. 161p. $9.95. ISBN 0-87565-037-6pa. 7-9

When her freethinking father becomes endangered for his ideas in Germany, Christina's family immigrates to Texas in 1847 when she is 15. She writes letters to her grandmother Oma about her experiences on an overcrowded ship over the Atlantic, killing a panther, her sister's birth, and her mother's subsequent death. Before Tina left Germany, her grandmother had given her a clock that symbolized to her the tradition in the family. However, on the day her sister is kidnapped, Tina relinquishes the clock in payment for her life. She understands in a different way what tradition may mean. *Western Heritage Award*.

877.   Guthrie, Woody. **Bound for Glory**. 1943. New York: Plume, Penguin, 1983. 320p. $12pa. ISBN 0-452-26445-6pa. YA

Woody Guthrie (1912-1967), composer and singer of such songs as "This Land Is Your Land" and "I Ain't Dead Yet," came of age in the Oklahoma dust bowl where he heard the blues and ballad singing. Some consider him a national folk poet who was able to convey complex ideas in his songs so that they seemed simple. This autobiography gives his view of life through the Depression and two world wars as he refused to accept those who thought money more important than understanding the real meaning of life. He died of Huntington's chorea, a progressive degeneration of the nervous system.

878.   Gutman, Dan. **World Series Classics**. New York: Viking, 1994. 240p. $14.99. ISBN 0-670-85286-4. 6-8

Five World Series competitions have been considered the best in history. Gutman discusses each one in detail, with summaries, baseball trivia, and box scores for each. The series examined are that of 1912, when the New York Giants played the Boston Red Sox; 1924, when the Washington Senators played the New York Giants; 1947, when the New York Yankees played the Brooklyn Dodgers; 1975, when the Boston Red Sox played the Cincinnati Reds; and 1991, when the Atlanta Braves played the Minnesota Twins. Index.

879.   Guttmacher, Peter. **Crazy Horse: Sioux War Chief**. New York: Chelsea House, 1994. 120p. $18.85. ISBN 0-7910-1712-5. (North American Indians of Achievement). 5 up

Crazy Horse (1841-1877), born in Bear Butte, South Dakota, went through the rites of passage of his people and had a powerful vision that led him to try to save them many times. After his renowned victory over Custer, he tried to preserve their freedom, but was unsuccessful in the end. Photographs and reproductions enhance the text. Chronology, Further Reading, and Index.

H

880.   Haas, Carol. **Engel v. Vitale: Separation of Church and State**. Springfield, NJ: Enslow, 1994. 128p. $17.95. ISBN 0-89490-461-2. (Landmark Supreme Court Cases). 6-9

This Supreme Court case occurred in 1962, when Stephen Engel and other parents complained that prayer in public school violated the constitutional rights of nonbelievers. William Vitale believed that prayer was an important aspect of moral and spiritual training in schools. On June 25, 1962, the Supreme Court declared that prayer in school was unconstitutional. The separation of church and state continues to be challenged. The text looks at the ideas and arguments behind this case as well as the people who brought it to court. Notes, Glossary, Further Reading, and Index.

881.   Hahn, Mary Downing. **Following My Own Footsteps**. New York: Clarion, 1996. 190p. $13.95. ISBN 0-395-76477-7. 5-8

Gordy (from *Stepping on the Cracks*) goes with his mother to his grandmother's when they finally leave his abusive father during World War II. He becomes friends with the boy next door, William, whose polio has changed his life. When Gordy's brother returns from the front, he dispels Gordy's romantic ideas of war and intimates that their brother Stuart, who deserted and went to the mental ward of a veteran's hospital, might have been the only sane person around. Gordy has to digest this information, deal with his father's behavior, and decide his own values as he passes through puberty.

882.   Hahn, Mary Downing. **The Gentleman Outlaw and Me—Eli: A Story of the Old West**. New York: Clarion, 1996. 212p. $14.95. ISBN 0-395-73083-X. 4-7

Eliza, 12 in 1887, runs away from cruel relatives to Tinville, Colorado, where she looks for her missing father. After a tramp approaches her, she disguises herself as a boy. She meets Calvin, 18, who calls himself the "Gentleman Outlaw." He also goes to Tinville in search of the sheriff who shot his father in the back. Calvin, however, has no idea how to do things, and Eliza has to take charge of their adventures.

883.   Hahn, Mary Downing. **Stepping on the Cracks**. New York: Clarion, 1991. 216p. $13.95. ISBN 0-395-58507-4. 4-7

Elizabeth and her friend Margaret spend time riding bicycles and trying to avoid Gordy, a bully who annoys them in College Hill, Maryland, during 1944. When they follow him through the woods, they find that he is protecting a brother who has run away from the army because his abusive father will beat him if he returns home. They hear the brother coughing and decide that they must help. When Margaret's family receives word of the death of her brother, who had been fighting abroad, they have to cope with the ethical problems of helping a deserter. *Bulletin Blue Ribbon Book, Scott O'Dell Award for Historical Fiction, Joan G. Sugarman Children's Book Award, American Library Association Notable Books for Children*, and *School Library Journal Best Book*.

884.   Hakim, Joy. **An Age of Extremes**. New York: Oxford University Press, 1993. 160p. $14.95; $9.95pa. ISBN 0-19-509513-8; 0-19-507760-1pa. (A History of US, Book 8). 6 up

Filled with photographs, prints, sidebars, boxed text, and running commentary, this story of the United States at the beginning of the twentieth century up to 1917 and World War I is lively, entertaining, and informative. Hakim covers all aspects of society and all cultures in her text. Chronology of Events, More Books to Read, and Index.

885.   Hakim, Joy. **All the People**. New York: Oxford University Press, 1994. 160p. $14.95; $9.95pa. ISBN 0-19-509515-4; 0-19-507762-8pa. (A History of US, Book 10). 6 up

Filled with photographs, prints, sidebars, boxed text, and running commentary, this story of the United States after World War II ended in 1945 is lively, entertaining, and informative. Hakim covers all aspects of society and all cultures in her text. Chronology of Events, More Books to Read, and Index.

886.   Hakim, Joy. **The First Americans**. New York: Oxford University Press, 1993. 160p. $14.95; $9.95pa. ISBN 0-19-509506-5; 0-19-507746-6pa. (A History of US, Book 1). 6 up

This story of the Americas and their inhabitants from the earliest times until the arrival of the first Europeans is lively and entertaining as well as informative. The book is filled with photographs, prints, sidebars, boxed text, and running commentary. Hakim covers all aspects of society and all cultures in her text. Chronology of Events, More Books to Read, and Index.

887.   Hakim, Joy. **From Colonies to Country**. New York: Oxford University Press, 1993. 192p. $14.95; $9.95pa. ISBN 0-19-509508-1; 0-19-507750-4pa. (A History of US, Book 3). 6 up

Filled with photographs, prints, sidebars, boxed text, and running commentary, this is the story of the colonies, beginning with the French and Indian War around 1755 and proceeding through the Constitutional Convention in 1787. The book is lively and entertaining as well as informative. Hakim covers all aspects of society and all cultures in her text. Chronology of Events, More Books to Read, and Index.

888.   Hakim, Joy. **Liberty for All?** New York: Oxford University Press, 1993. 160p. $14.95; $9.95pa. ISBN 0-19-509510-3; 0-19-507754-7pa. (A History of US, Book 5). 6 up

This lively, informative book covers the United States during the period of growth from 1848 until it began to disintegrate at the beginning of the Civil War in 1861. It is filled with photographs, prints, sidebars, boxed text, and running commentary. Hakim covers all aspects of society and all cultures in her text, as well as such figures as Jedediah Smith, Emily Dickinson, John James Audubon, and Sojourner Truth. Chronology of Events, More Books to Read, and Index.

889.   Hakim, Joy. **Making Thirteen Colonies**. New York: Oxford University Press, 1993. 160p. $14.95; $9.95pa. ISBN 0-19-509507-3; 0-19-507748-2pa. (A History of US, Book 2). 6 up

Filled with photographs, prints, sidebars, boxed text, and running commentary, this entertaining, informative story covers the colonization of the New World through the mid-eighteenth century until the French and Indian War around 1755. Hakim covers all aspects of society and all cultures in her text. Chronology of Events, More Books to Read, and Index.

890.   Hakim, Joy. **The New Nation**. New York: Oxford University Press, 1994. 176p. $14.95; $9.95pa. ISBN 0-19-509509-X; 0-19-507752-0pa. (A History of US, Book 4). 6 up

Filled with photographs, prints, sidebars, boxed text, and running commentary, this lively story of the newly formed United States from 1787 to 1848 is both entertaining and informative. Hakim covers all aspects of society and all cultures in her text. Chronology of Events, More Books to Read, and Index.

891.   Hakim, Joy. **Reconstruction and Reform**. New York: Oxford University Press, 1994. 192p; $14.95. 160p. $9.95pa. ISBN 0-19-509512-X; 0-19-507758-Xpa. (A History of US, Book 7). 6 up

Filled with photographs, prints, sidebars, boxed text, and running commentary, this story of Reconstruction after the Civil War and ensuing reform from 1865 to 1898 is lively and entertaining as well as informative. Hakim covers all aspects of society and all cultures in her text. Chronology of Events, More Books to Read, and Index.

892.   Hakim, Joy. **War, Peace, and All That Jazz**. New York: Oxford University Press, 1994. 192p. $14.95; $9.95pa. ISBN 0-19-509514-6; 0-19-507762-8pa. (A History of US, Book 9). 6 up

Filled with photographs, prints, sidebars, boxed text, and running commentary, this story of the United States from 1918 through World War II is lively and entertaining as well as informative. Hakim covers all aspects of society and all cultures in her text. Chronology of Events, More Books to Read, and Index.

893.   Hakim, Joy. **War Terrible War**. New York: Oxford University Press, 1994. 192p. $14.95; $9.95pa. ISBN 0-19-507755-5; 0-19-507756-3pa. (A History of US, Book 6). 6 up

Filled with photographs, prints, sidebars, boxed text, and running commentary, this story of the Civil War years shows the war's horror but is lively and entertaining as well. Hakim covers all aspects of society and all cultures in her text. Chronology of Events, More Books to Read, and Index.

894.   Halasa, Malu. **Elijah Muhammad: Religious Leader**. New York: Chelsea House, 1990. 110p. $18.95; $7.95pa. ISBN 1-55546-602-8; 0-7910-0246-2pa. (Black Americans of Achievement). 5 up

When a young boy, Elijah Poole (1897-1975) was forbidden to go into the woods on the way home from school. One day he did. He saw a man from his church lynched by a group of white men, and he never forgot the horror. He moved to the North, where he had to go on relief during the Depression before he could find a job to support his family. He was interested in Marcus Garvey's Black Nationalism and Ali's Moorish Temple of America. But when he heard Fard talk about his Nation of Islam, Elijah in turn eloquently proclaimed the values of Islam to the Black community. He became Elijah Muhammad, the father of the Black Muslims. Chronology, Further Reading, and Index.

895.   Halasa, Malu. **Mary McLeod Bethune: Educator**. New York: Chelsea House, 1989. 112p. $18.95; $7.95pa. ISBN 1-55546-574-9; 0-7910-0225-Xpa. (Black Americans of Achievement). 5 up

Awarded scholarships to schools in North Carolina and Chicago, Mary McLeod Bethune (1875-1955) returned to the South to become a teacher. She settled in Daytona Beach, Florida, and established a school for Black girls. She campaigned constantly to raise funds and saw the school merger with Cookman Institute, over which she presided for 40 years. She also fought for equal education for Blacks by leading the National Association of Colored Women and the National Council of Negro Women. Photographs and reproductions enhance the text. Chronology, Further Reading, and Index.

896.   Haley, Alex. **Roots**. New York: Doubleday, 1976. $25; $6.99pa. ISBN 0-385-03787-2; 0-440-17464-3pa. YA

In this book, Alex Haley traces the background of an African American whose ancestor was transported to America as a slave. He finds his African home and his position as tribal royalty. Index.

897.   Hall, Donald. **Old Home Day**. Emily Arnold McCully, illustrator. San Diego, CA: Browndeer, Harcourt Brace, 1996. Unpaged. $16. ISBN 0-15-276896-3. 2 up

When people in the nineteenth century came to an area where Ice Age water had melted and formed ponds, they called the area Blackwater Pond. A village began, and then the railroad came, and finally a general store. The people began to prosper, but many moved away. In 1899, the governor of New Hampshire decided that people could celebrate "Old Home Day" on the last weekend in August, 100 years after Enoch Boswell had built the first cabin. Each year families come back to the town to see each other, and now the town has revitalized as a place where people have built homes that they visit in the summer.

898.   Hall, Lynn. **Halsey's Pride**. New York: Scribner's, 1990. 119p. $12.95. ISBN 0-684-19155-5. 6-9

March Halsey remembers when she was 13 and living with her father in Illinois during 1955. Her father spends all his money on a dog kennel, hoping that his prize collie Pride will earn enough money as a stud to support the kennel. March spends her days hiding her epilepsy from her classmates and helping her father. But she also has to keep the kennel running after Pride's offspring die of torsion (being twisted), and Pride cannot support the investment. As she grows older, she begins breeding her own dogs.

899.   Halliburton, Warren. **The West Indian-American Experience**. Brookfield, CT: Millbrook Press, 1994. 64p. $16.40. ISBN 1-56294-340-5. (Coming to America). 4-8

European settlers eradicated the Arawaks, original inhabitants of the Caribbean, but traces of the culture remain. In the centuries after Columbus, many of the inhabitants died from diseases or became slaves to their conquerors. Between 1640 and 1713 more than seven slave revolts occurred in the British islands. In 1760, Tacky's Rebellion broke out in Jamaica, and in 1831 another revolt led to the abolishment of slavers in 1833. More recent inhabitants of the islands have immigrated to the United States, looking for economic opportunities. They found them, along with racial discrimination, unlike any they had experienced in the West Indies. Between 1952 and the 1960s, few islanders were admitted to the country, but after that the laws changed. More About West Indian Americans and Index.

900.   Hamanaka, Shelia, author/illustrator. **The Journey: Japanese Americans, Racism, and Renewal**. New York: Orchard, Franklin Watts, 1990. 39p. $19.99; $8.95pa. ISBN 0-531-08449-3; 0-531-07060-3pa. 4 up

Hamanaka painted a five-panel mural, 8x25-feet, in which she depicted Japanese American history. Lured to America by its wealth, the first Japanese immigrants (Issei) worked as "stoop laborers," picking vegetables, and fishing. They and the second generation (Nisei) faced intense prejudice, and during World War II, after the Japanese bombed Pearl Harbor, many lost everything when the U.S. government interred them in 10 camps. After the war, they eventually won reparations of $20,000 each, but many had already died, some by fighting for America against the Germans and the Japanese in the war. The author's family endured this indignity.

901.   Hamanaka, Shelia. **On the Wings of Peace: Writers and Illustrators Speak Out for Peace, in Memory of Hiroshima and Nagasaki**. New York: Clarion, 1995. 144p. $21.95. ISBN 0-395-72619-0. 4 up

In commemoration of the bombing of Hiroshima and Nagasaki in 1945, 60 writers and illustrators agreed to have portions of old or new work published in a book. The diverse entries and pictures provide insight into how this event affected people from different parts of the world and in Japan. Bibliography. *Notable Children's Trade Books in the Field of Social Studies.*

902.   Hamilton, Leni. **Clara Barton**. New York: Chelsea House, 1988. 112p. $18.95. ISBN 1-55546-641-9. (American Women of Achievement). 5 up

Clara Barton (1821-1912) founded the American Red Cross, an organization that helped victims during both wartime and peacetime. She was initially a teacher who helped set up New Jersey's first public school. Then she moved to Washington, D.C., and became the only female employee of the federal government. During the Civil War, she organized the distribution of supplies for solders and traveled to the battlefields to make sure that soldiers received nursing care. In 1869, after the war, she went to Europe, where she received the Cross of Imperial Russia and the Iron Cross of Germany for her work. Photographs and reproductions enhance the text. Chronology, Further Reading, and Index.

903.   Hamilton, Virginia. **Anthony Burns: The Defeat and Triumph of a Fugitive Slave**. New York: Knopf, 1988. 195p. $12.99; $3.99pa. ISBN 0-394-98185-5; 0-679-83997-6pa. 5 up

When he escaped to Boston in 1854, Anthony Burns was 20. But his former owner located him and held him under the Fugitive Slave Act. Burns, however, had many abolitionist friends, and Richard Dana, a superb lawyer, decided to defend him without charge. This case incited Boston, and many rioted, but Burns gained freedom. His health, however, had declined, and he died at age 28. Fugitive Slave Act, Bibliography, and Index.

904.   Hamilton, Virginia. **The House of Dies Drear**. Eros Keith, illustrator. New York: Macmillan, 1968. 247p. $17; $3.95pa. ISBN 0-02-742500-2; 0-02-043520-7pa. 5-7

Thomas and his family move into a house once owned by the wealthy abolitionist Dies Drear when his father takes a job teaching at an Ohio college. Drear had helped more than 40,000 slaves pass through the Underground Railway before he and two slaves were murdered. Strange things happen around the house. Thomas and his father investigate the tunnels and secret entrances even though the hostile caretaker Pluto tries to thwart their efforts. *Edgar Allen Poe Award*.

905.   Hamilton, Virginia. **Many Thousand Gone: African Americans from Slavery to Freedom**. Leo and Diane Dillon, illustrators. New York: Knopf, 1993. 151p. $16. ISBN 0-394-82873-9. 4-9

Divided into three main parts, the text covers slavery in America, the runaways of the nineteenth century, and the exodus to freedom. Among the topics and people are the Quaker protests, Jenny Slew, Elizabeth Freeman, the Gabriel Prosser uprising, Josiah Henson, Nat Turner, Underground Railroad, Anthony Burns, Alexander Ross, Henry Box Brown (who mailed himself to liberty), Jackson (who came north dressed as his wife's maid), Eliza (who inspired *Uncle Tom's Cabin* as she crossed the frozen Ohio), and the tide of freedom. Bibliography and Index.

906.   Hamm, Diane Johnston. **Bunkhouse Journal**. New York: Atheneum, Scribner's, 1990. 89p. $13.95. ISBN 0-684-19206-3. 7 up

In 1911, Sandy leaves Denver after his alcoholic father embarrasses him in front of others to go to Wyoming and live with his cousin and her husband. He writes in his journal about his father and feels responsible for his death, but people he meets help him better understand his emotions and that he cannot know about his parents' private relationship. He decides to return to Denver for at least one year of college. *Western Heritage Award*.

907.   Hampton, Henry, Steve Fayer, and Sarah Flynn, comps. **Voices of Freedom: An Oral History of the Civil Rights Movement from the 1950s Through the 1980s**. New York: Bantam, 1990. 692p. $18.95pa. ISBN 0-553-35235-6pa. YA

As a companion to the public television series *Eyes on the Prize*, the text contains excerpts from interviews recorded while the series was in production. In chronological order, the 31 chapters cover the history of civil rights, beginning with the 1955 Emmett Till lynching and ending with the controversy over affirmative action. Among the topics are Selma, Birmingham, the Detroit riots of 1967, Attica, the Black Panthers, Andrew Young, Stokely Carmichael, and others. The text complements the series but also stands on its own. Bibliography and Index.

908.   Hanley, Sally. **A. Philip Randolph**. New York: Chelsea House, 1989. 110p. $18.95; $7.95pa. ISBN 1-55546-607-9; 0-7910-0222-5pa. (Black Americans of Achievement). 5 up

A. (Asa) Philip Randolph (1889-1979) organized the Brotherhood of Sleeping Car Porters in 1925, which acted as the labor union for Pullman car porters. He was also a member of the Fair Employment Practices Committee in World War II. As a leading opponent of segregation in the armed forces and of racial discrimination in organized labor, he was appointed in 1955 as a vice president of the American Federation of Labor and Congress of Industrial Organizations. He also directed the March on Washington for Jobs and Freedom in 1963, at which Martin Luther King delivered his "I Have a Dream" speech. Bibliography and Index.

909.   Hanmer, Trudy J. **Taking a Stand Against Sexism and Sex Discrimination**. New York: Franklin Watts, 1990. 142p. $13.40. ISBN 0-531-10962-3. (Taking a Stand). 9 up

The text looks at the history of American feminism by showing the struggles that women have undergone for their rights. It indicates that basic reasons for the movement include economic independence and freedom from oppression. Among those leaders presented with capsule biographies are Elizabeth Cady Stanton and Sojourner Truth. Notes, Bibliography, and Index.

910.   Hansen, Arlen J. **Gentlemen Volunteers: The Story of the American Ambulance Drivers in the Great War: August 1914-September 1918**. New York: Arcade, 1996. 254p. $27.95. ISBN 1-55970-313-X. YA

In World War I, Americans, mainly from Ivy League schools, went to Flanders to drive ambulances. There they took the "Lizzies," or ambulances, through mud and fire while they transported the wounded. Although most of them returned, their experiences gave them a sense of comaraderie that they could not retain at home. Index.

911.   Hansen, Joyce. **Between Two Fires: Black Soldiers in the Civil War**. New York: Franklin Watts, 1993. 160p. $21.40; $6.95pa. ISBN 0-531-11151-2; 0-531-15676-1pa. (African-American Experience). 7 up

In the Civil War, Black soldiers fought for the Union. The text, taken from primary sources, including letters, speeches, and battle accounts, covers their recruitment and training as well as their struggles. Even though eager to join the fight against the South, Black soldiers had difficulty being accepted into the army, and once they were, officers often denied them health care, equal pay, and status. Photographs and engravings from the period show the strain of these men as they fought for something in which they believed. Bibliography and Index.

912.   Hansen, Joyce. **The Captive**. New York: Scholastic, 1994. 195p. $13.95; $3.50pa. ISBN 0-590-41625-1; 0-590-41624-3pa. 5-8

Slavers capture Kofi, 12, when a family servant betrays him, and take him from his African home to America in 1788. There he works for a New England family of somber Puritans. Then he meets Paul Cuffe, an African American shipbuilder who wants to take Africans back to their homeland. He becomes a first mate on Cuffe's ship, which gives him a chance to go home. *Coretta Scott King Honor* and *Notable Children's Trade Books in the Field of Social Studies.*

913.   Hansen, Joyce. **Out from This Place**. New York: Walker, 1988. 135p. $13.95. ISBN 0-8027-6817-2. 6-9

This sequel to *Which Way Freedom?* shows Easter at 14, the girl that Obi left behind, as she tries to escape from a Charleston, South Carolina, plantation and to remain free. She joins people recently emancipated from Sea Island, fighting for the land that the government refuses to grant although it had been promised to them. Easter continues her search for Obi and decides that she will go north to begin training as a teacher, after encouragement from another teacher who has watched her work with children. Easter hopes to find Obi there.

914.   Hansen, Joyce. **Which Way Freedom?** New York: Walker, 1986. 120p. $13.95. ISBN 0-8027-6623-4. New York: Camelot, 1992. $3.99pa. ISBN 0-380-71408-6pa. 4-7

After hearing that they will be sold, Obi and Easter escape from the plantation where they are slaves in 1861. Confederate soldiers stop them, but Obi escapes to the South Carolina coastal islands. There he joins Union troops and meets a "colored Yankee" who begins teaching him to read. At the end of the war, Obi is wounded but alive, and he starts searching for Easter and the little boy Easter stayed on the plantation to save.

915.   Hargrove, Jim. **Abraham Lincoln: Sixteenth President of the United States**. Chicago: Childrens Press, 1988. 100p. $19.80. ISBN 0-516-01359-9. (Encyclopedia of Presidents). 4-9

As a young man, Abraham Lincoln (1809-1865) prepared himself to face his role as the sixteenth President. The text begins with Lincoln reading a humorous Artemis Ward story to his cabinet before he told the members about the Emancipation Proclamation. When they did not laugh, he admonished them for not realizing the importance of a balanced approach to life. Everything could not be serious, or they would not survive. After reviewing Lincoln's youth and young adulthood, the text ends with his assassination on Good Friday. Chronology of American History and Index.

916.   Hargrove, Jim. **Dwight D. Eisenhower: Thirty-Fourth President of the United States**. Chicago: Childrens Press, 1987. 100p. $19.80. ISBN 0-516-01389-0. (Encyclopedia of Presidents). 4-9

Starting with Dwight David Eisenhower's (1890-1969) achievement on D-Day as the Supreme Commander of Allied Forces in Europe, the text recounts his life as a young boy in Abilene, Kansas, his career at West Point, and his role as the 34th President of the United States. Chronology of American History and Index.

917.   Hargrove, Jim. **Harry S. Truman: Thirty-Third President of the United States**. Chicago: Childrens Press, 1987. 100p. $19.80. ISBN 0-516-01388-2. (Encyclopedia of Presidents). 4-9

Harry S. Truman (1884-1972) became President in 1945 when Franklin Roosevelt died. Within five months, he had to decide if the country should use the atomic bomb on Japan. As soon as the war ended, he had to make decisions about the best way to thwart the Soviet Union and to simultaneously help the weakened Western European countries. The text looks at his life and the decisions he made in the Senate and as President. Chronology of American History and Index.

918.   Hargrove, Jim. **Lyndon B. Johnson: Thirty-Sixth President of the United States**. Chicago: Childrens Press, 1987. 100p. $19.80. ISBN 0-516-01396-3. (Encyclopedia of Presidents). 4-9

Beginning with Lyndon B. Johnson's (1908-1973) transfer to the presidency at the death of John F. Kennedy in 1963, the text then gives an overview of his life, from serving Texas to leading the United States during his days in Washington. Chronology of American History and Index.

919.   Hargrove, Jim. **Martin Van Buren: Eighth President of the United States**. Chicago: Childrens Press, 1987. 100p. $19.80. ISBN 0-516-01391-2. (Encyclopedia of Presidents). 4-9

Martin Van Buren (1782-1862) became President a few months after Andrew Jackson declared that all land in the West had to be purchased with gold or silver rather than paper money. Banks would no longer make easy loans, and times became hard. A few months after Van Buren took office, America entered its first great depression, called the Panic of 1837. It lasted for five years, throughout his administration. Although lacking in education, Van Buren was a skilled political organizer and earned the names "Red Fox" and "Little Magician." However, the depression was a problem he could not solve. Chronology of American History and Index.

920.   Hargrove, Jim. **Thomas Jefferson: Third President of the United States**. Chicago: Childrens Press, 1986. 100p. $19.80. ISBN 0-516-01385-8. (Encyclopedia of Presidents). 4-9

These six chapters about Thomas Jefferson (1743-1826) cover his childhood in colonial Virginia, his participation in the change of American government from colony to country, the difficulty of forming a democracy, his role as the third President, and his return to Monticello. Chronology of American History and Index.

921.   Harmon, Susan. **Colorado Ransom**. New York: Walker, 1992. 169p. $19.95. ISBN 0-8027-4125-8. YA

Forrest Bates hires a drifter named Shannon to help him work his gold mine in 1872, but the woman to whom Forrest has proposed dislikes Shannon. When someone murders Forrest, she suspects Shannon. She writes to Forrest's nephew and heir to warn him about the problem, and he comes to settle the situation. Although she falls in love with the nephew, she refuses to marry him immediately.

922.   Harrah, Madge. **My Brother, My Enemy**. Sheldon Greenberg, illustrator. New York: Simon & Schuster, 1997. 144p. $16. ISBN 0-689-80968-9. 5-9

After Robert Bradford finds his home burning and his family massacred by the Susquehannocks around 1675, he sees an arrow that tells him his blood brother Naokan is involved in the destruction. When Nathaniel Bacon, a plantation owner, organizes a band to protect their land, Robert volunteers, vowing to avenge his family's deaths. When he finds, however, that Bacon also wants to sever ties with the English, his affiliation becomes more complicated.

923.   Harris, Edward D. **John Charles Frémont and the Great Western Reconnaissance**. New York: Chelsea House, 1990. 112p. $18.95. ISBN 0-7910-1312-X. (World Explorers). 5 up

As a self-educated man, son of a mother not married to his father, John Charles Frémont (1813-1890) investigated whatever interested him. He led five exploratory surveys of the American West to find out about the area's suitability for settlement. He was a presidential candidate, scientist, explorer, governor, land baron, railroad magnate, Indian fighter, senator, and author. From the regions he explored came 13 states. Photographs and drawings enhance the text. Further Reading, Glossary, and Index.

924.   Harris, Jacqueline L. **The Tuskegee Airmen: Black Heroes of World War II**. Englewood Cliffs, NJ: Silver Burdett, 1996. 144p. $13.95; $7.95pa. ISBN 0-382-39215-9; 0-382-39217-5pa. 6 up

In addition to telling about the Tuskegee Airmen, Harris tells about race relations in the mid-twentieth century of the United States. Testimonies from individuals and journal entries form a background to the training of this all-Black squadron and its leader, Benjamin O. Davis, as they prepared for fighting in World War II. Their courage and success contradicts the military's unjustified prior treatment of them.

925.   Harris, Julie. **The Longest Winter**. New York: St. Martin's Press, 1996. 306p. $23.95. ISBN 0-312-13115-1. YA

In 1926, 24-year-old John Robert Shaw's plane crashes in the Aleutians. When he wakes up, he finds himself with one arm amputated, a scarred face, and a useless leg. He stays on the island for 17 years, marrying two of the local chief's daughters, raising his two children, and gathering shellfish. In 1943, the American Army comes to evacuate the island, and one of the soldiers tries to rape his 11-year-old daughter. Afterward, John returns to his hometown in Georgia but decides that he must move to Alaska where he can cope with the culture.

926.   Harris, Mark. **Diamond: Baseball Writings of Mark Harris**. New York: Donald I. Fine, 1994. 289p. $13.95pa. ISBN 1-55611-431-1pa. YA

This collection of essays offers history, anecdote, and wisdom. They provide a cerebral view of baseball on such topics as Pete Rose, Bart Giamatti, Japanese baseball, and sandlot balls. He sees baseball as a microcosm of life, and he gives details as to how the game has paralleled the social changes in America to prove his points. He loves baseball, and he wants the reader to love it too. Index.

927.   Harrison, Barbara, and Daniel Terris. **A Ripple of Hope: The Life of Robert F. Kennedy**. New York: Lodestar, 1997. 144p. $16.99. ISBN 0-525-67506-X. 5-9

The authors researched a documentary for Home Box Office cable television and used recorded interviews, photographs, newspaper clippings, and films as a basis for this story of a man who worked to help his country. Robert F. Kennedy (1925-1968) served his brother John F. Kennedy as attorney general, and after JFK's assassination, decided to run for President himself. The book looks at the life of this man, arrogant to some, but committed to those less fortunate.

928.   Harrison, Barbara, and Daniel Terris. **A Twilight Struggle: The Life of John Fitzgerald Kennedy**. New York: Lothrop, Lee & Shepard, 1992. 159p. $18. ISBN 0-688-08830-9. 7-9

Born into luxury and possessed of a charismatic personality, John F. Kennedy (1917-1963) had weaknesses as well as the strengths that inspired Americans. The competition in his family led him to form close friendships with others. He was slow to follow the Civil Rights movement although he intervened at the University of Mississippi. While stopping possible nuclear disaster in Cuba, he became further mired in Vietnam. Yet he always tried for social progress. The chapters begin with lines from Robert Frost's poem "Birches." Bibliography, Chronology, Notes, and Index.

929.   Hart, Philip S. **Up in the Air: The Story of Bessie Coleman**. Minneapolis, MN: Carolrhoda, 1996. 80p. $14.96. ISBN 0-87614-949-2. (Trailblazers). 4-7

Bessie Coleman (1896-1926), a Black woman growing up in the South in the early 1900s, had to stay at home to watch her sister while her mother worked, but she planned to make something of her life. In 1920, she became the first African American woman to fly an airplane, and built a career as a barnstorming pilot in the 1920s. She did not live long enough to open a school for Black aviators, but she became an inspiration to many who followed her into new and risky occupations. Notes, Bibliography, and Index.

930.   Harvey, Brett. **Farmers and Ranchers**. New York: Twenty-First Century Books, 1995. 96p. $16.98. ISBN 0-8050-2999-0. (Settling the West). 5-8

Farmers and ranchers took advantage of the wide expanses of land in the West and went there to settle. The text, enhanced with photographs and drawings, looks at their roles. Source Notes, Further Reading, and Index.

931.   Haskins, James. **Black Music in America**. New York: Crowell, 1987. 197p. $12.95. ISBN 0-690-04460-7. YA

The text looks at the history of Black music and the people who made it. It begins with slave music brought from Africa. The first age of American Black music was ragtime and blues with Scott Joplin, W. C. Handy, and James Reese Europe. The second age was jazz, and its stars were Buddy Bolden, Jelly Roll Morton, Ma Rainey, and Louis Armstrong. During the Black Renaissance from 1920 to 1940, performers included Duke Ellington, Billie Holiday, and William Grant Still. In the 1940s, during World War II, Charlie "Yardbird" Parker, Nat "King" Cole, and Mahalia Jackson shared their talents. Rhythm, blues, and arias came to the fore in the 1950s with Bo Diddley, Miles Davis, and Leontyne Price. Soul music of the 1960s featured James Brown, Motown, and Aretha Franklin. Others are still developing new variations on music. Bibliography and Index.

932.   Haskins, James. **Freedom Rides: Journey for Justice**. New York: Hyperion, 1995. 99p. $14.95. ISBN 0-7868-0048-8. 6-9

When the Supreme Court declared in 1960 that segregation of waiting rooms and rest rooms in bus and train stations was unconstitutional, people in parts of the South continued to ignore the law. In 1961, a group of Blacks and whites decided to take a bus ride through the South to test *Boynton v. Virginia*. They survived 700 miles through Virginia, but as they entered Alabama, they faced burning and beating. Haskins gives background history, starting with the 1947 Journey of Reconciliation, the *Brown v. Board of Education* decision, and the Montgomery Bus Boycott of 1955. Bibliography and Index.

933.   Haskins, James. **The Harlem Renaissance**. Brookfield, CT: Millbrook Press, 1996. 192p. $21.90. ISBN 1-56294-565-3. 5-8

After background on the Harlem Renaissance, Haskins discusses the various groups of people who contributed to it in separate chapters. Among them are performing artists, writers, and fine artists. Individuals include Langston Hughes, Jean Toomer, Jessie Fauset, Countee Cullen, Aaron Douglas, Palmer Hayden, Augusta Savage, Josephine Baker, Duke Ellington, and Bill Robinson. Endnotes, Bibliography, and Index.

934.   Haskins, James. **Thurgood Marshall: A Life for Justice**. New York: Henry Holt, 1992. 163p. $14.95; $7.95pa. ISBN 0-8050-2095-0; 0-8050-4256-3pa. 6 up

Among the activities in which Thurgood Marshall (1908-1993) participated in order to promote racial equality were quietly desegregating a movie theater, challenging the laws that Blacks were "separate but equal," and arguing for the rights of all. This biography looks at his background and his career. Bibliography and Index.

935.   Haskins, Jim. **Against All Opposition: Black Explorers in America**. New York: Walker, 1992. 86p. $13.95. ISBN 0-8027-8137-3. 7 up

Among the important explorations completed by Blacks in America were Estevanico and the Seven Cities of Gold (early sixteenth century); Jean Baptiste Point du Sable (c. 1750-1818) and the founding of Chicago; York (Clark's slave) with the Lewis and Clark expedition; James P. Beckwourth (1798-1867) and the mountains; Matthew Henson (1866-1955) and the Arctic; Guion Stewart Bluford, Jr. (b. 1942) in space; and Ronald McNair (1950-1986) as part of the *Challenger* disaster. Bibliography and Index.

936.   Haskins, Jim. **Black Eagles: African Americans in Aviation**. New York: Scholastic, 1995. 196p. $14.95. ISBN 0-590-45912-0. 5-8

Eugene Bullard, an African American, went to France in World War I and received highest honors flying for the French. Then Bessie Coleman, an African American woman, received her pilot's license in France. By 1921, Hubert Fauntleroy Julian had arrived in New York City and become known as the Black Eagle. Many others gained fame for their achievements as Black flyers through the twentieth century and into the Space Age, with Dr. Mae C. Jemison as the first African American woman in space. Bibliography, Chronology, and Index. *Notable Children's Trade Books in the Field of Social Studies.*

937.   Haskins, Jim. **Get on Board: The Story of the Underground Railroad**. New York: Scholastic, 1993. 160p. $13.95. ISBN 0-590-45418-8. 7-10

Among the stories showing the Underground Railroad at work is that of Eliza, the slave who crossed the Ohio River on ice floes. She reached Canada safely with her child, and the Quaker couple who helped them through Indiana came to visit. Haskins also tells of the white carpenter who helped mail Henry Brown to freedom, but he was unsuccessful with two other slaves and was imprisoned. He mentions Ellen Craft, a slave with light skin who posed as a planter traveling with her slave on board a steamer—actually her husband. The accounts show that African Americans as well as whites helped to free many who would never have been successful alone. Timeline, Bibliography, and Index.

938.   Haskins, Jim. **I Have a Dream: The Life and Words of Martin Luther King, Jr.** Brookfield, CT: Millbrook Press, 1993. 111p. $19.90; $8.95pa. ISBN 1-56294-087-2; 1-56294-837-7pa. 7 up

The text covers the life of Martin Luther King, Jr. (1929-1968) using as chapter titles quotes from King and others. Among the quotes are "You are as good as anyone"; "An inner urge"; "My feet is real tired, but my soul is rested," in reference to Montgomery; "The way of nonviolence"; "Now is the time," in Birmingham; "Fire hoses, snarling dogs and even death"; and "Free at last." Photographs, Important Events, Sources, Other Books, Bibliography, and Index. *IRA-CBC Children's Choices, Notable Children's Trade Books in the Field of Social Studies,* and *New York Public Library Books for the Teen Age.*

939.   Hauptman, Laurence M. **Between Two Fires: American Indians in the Civil War**. New York: Free Press, 1995. 350p. $25; $13pa. ISBN 0-02-914180-X; 0-684-82668-2pa. YA

More than 20,000 Native Americans served in the Civil War, some as commissioned officers. The text looks at their stories. Among them was Ely S. Parker, an aide to General Grant, who drew up the articles of Lee's surrender. As a Seneca, he later became the Commissioner of Indian Affairs. His brother also served. Some of the last troops to surrender to the federal army were Confederate Cherokee units. The service of these men, however, did not free them from attempted assimilation after the war's end. Bibliography and Index.

940.   Hausman, Gerald. **Night Flight**. New York: Philomel, 1996. 133p. $15.95. ISBN 0-399-22758-X. 5-8

Jeff Hausman and Max Maeder, both 12 in rural New Jersey during 1957, expect to have fun with their dogs during the summer. On their first camp-out, their dogs are fatally poisoned along with several other neighborhood dogs. Max insists that immigrant Jews have killed them, and Jeff does not want to admit that he is half Jewish. He knows that he must confront Max, a decision made more difficult because Max's father, a German immigrant, admires Hitler and keeps his photograph on his desk. As they investigate the mysterious poisonings further, their leads point to Max's father.

941.   Hawxhurst, Joan C. **Mother Jones: Labor Crusader**. Austin, TX: Raintree/Steck-Vaughn, 1994. 128p. $16.98. ISBN 0-8114-2327-1. (American Troublemakers). 6 up

Mother Jones, born Mary Harris (1843?-1930), was once called "the most dangerous woman in America." She lost her husband and her four children to a yellow fever epidemic in 1867, and the Chicago Fire of 1871 destroyed her home and her business. She spent the rest of her life organizing coal miners, Mexican revolutionaries, brewery workers, and textile mill laborers. She helped improve their lives by getting them to demand their rights from callous employers. Maps, Photographs, Key Dates, Glossary, Places to Visit, Bibliography and Recommended Readings, and Index.

942.   Haynes, Richard M. **Ida B. Wells: Antilynching Crusader**. Austin, TX: Raintree/Steck-Vaughn, 1994. 128p. $16.98. ISBN 0-8114-2326-3. (American Troublemakers). 6 up

Among the labels for Ida B. Wells (1862-1931) are journalist, educator, suffragist, and militant civil rights leader. Her voice was loudest to expose lynching so that its horror became known throughout the world. At 16, she became a teacher to support her family. When she verbally denounced the inferior education available to Black children, she was fired. In 1910, she helped found the NAACP. Maps, Photographs, Key Dates, Glossary, Places to Visit, Bibliography and Recommended Readings, and Index.

943.   Hays, Scott. **Racism**. Freeport, NY: Marshall Cavendish, 1994. 96p. $14.95. ISBN 1-85435-615-1. (Life Issues). 8-12

Examples of racist incidents and definitions of stereotypes clarify the kinds of situations in which children and young adults can unexpectedly find themselves. The examples indicate that racism is a learned response and can be unlearned. But problematic throughout society is the infiltration of hate groups that have tried to undermine relationships and cause people to hurt each other. A brief history of civil rights advocates, quotes by various leaders, and photographs enhance the text. Glossary and Index.

944.   Hazell, Rebecca, author/illustrator. **Heroines: Great Women Through the Ages**. New York: Abbeville, 1996. 79p. $19.95. ISBN 0-7892-0289-1. 5-8

The text covers 12 women from ancient Greece to contemporary times. In addition to the information about each woman is background on the culture and the history of the times in which she lived. Among those included are Lady Murasaki Shikibu (973?-1025?), Sacagawea (1787-1812), Agnodice of ancient Greece, Anna Akhmatova (1888-1966), Madame Sun Yat-Sen (1893-1931), Frida Kahlo (1907-1954), Eleanor of Aquitaine (1122-1202), Joan of Arc (1412?-1431), Queen Elizabeth I (1533-1603), Harriet Tubman (1820?-1913), Marie Curie (1867-1934), and Amelia Earhart (1897-1937). Further Reading.

945.   Heater, Derek. **The Cold War**. New York: Bookwright Press, Franklin Watts, 1989. 63p. $12.90. ISBN 0-531-18275-4. (Witness History). 7 up

Short chapters present different aspects of the Cold War, which followed World War II between the western capitalist and eastern socialist countries. Brief biographies of leading figures and quotes further the information. Heater believes that the Cold War began with the Bolshevik Revolution in 1917. Maps and other illustrations enhance the text. Bibliography, Chronology, Glossary, and Index.

946.   Heiligman, Deborah. **Barbara McClintock: Alone in Her Field**. Janet Hamlin, illustrator. New York: W. H. Freeman, 1994. 64p. $14.95; $4.95pa. ISBN 0-7167-6536-5; 0-7167-6548-9pa. (Science Superstars). 3-7

Barbara McClintock (1902-1992) enrolled in Cornell University and loved her studies. She discovered genetics, but she could only enter the graduate school in botany because she was a woman. She researched cytogenetics, the study of cells in maize plants. She discovered that genes "jumped," but her colleagues throughout the world ignored her discovery for 30 years. When they replicated her experiments, they saw she was right. In 1983, she won the Nobel Prize for her work. Index/Glossary.

947.   Heiss, Arleen McGrath. **Barbara Bush**. New York: Chelsea House, 1991. 128p. $18.95. ISBN 0-7910-1627-7. (Library of Biography). 5 up

Barbara Bush (b. 1925), as wife of the 41st President of the United States, accompanied her husband George on all of his missions for the United States, and fulfilled her role of mother of six as well. She campaigned for her husband and served as hostess in the White House. She also has volunteered for many important organizations, especially those concerned with illiteracy. Photographs, Further Reading, Chronology, and Index.

948.   Helmer, Diana Star. **Belles of the Ballpark**. Brookfield, CT: Millbrook Press, 1993. 96p. $14.90. ISBN 1-56294-230-1. 5-9

During World War II, when Wrigley had the idea to form female teams, the All-American Girls Professional Baseball League came into existence. The text describes their recruitment, their training in baseball and etiquette, and the chaperoning necessary to take females on the road. The games continued for five years. Bibliography, Chronology, and Index. *New York Public Library Books for the Teen Age*.

949.   Henricksson, John. **Rachel Carson: The Environmental Movement**. Brookfield, CT: Millbrook Press, 1990. 96p. $15.90. ISBN 1-87884-116-5. 7 up

Highly educated and interested in the ocean, Rachel Carson (1907-1964) shocked Americans with her book *Silent Spring*, published in 1962, which outlined the destruction caused by chemical pesticides if their use was not diminished. In essence, the book marked the beginning of the environmental movement. The various events that led to this book and her others appear here. Important Events, Notes, Suggested Reading, and Index. *Bulletin Blue Ribbon Book* and *Child Study Association Children's Books of the Year*.

950. Henry, Sondra, and Emily Taitz. **Betty Friedan: Fighter for Women's Rights**. Springfield, NJ: Enslow, 1990. 128p. $17.95. ISBN 0-89490-292-X. (Contemporary Women). 5-7

Betty Friedan excelled at her schoolwork during the 1930s and 1940s but wanted to have a family. After her children went to school, she saw her own lack of fulfillment and wrote about it in *The Feminine Mystique*. When she found that many others agreed with her, she established the National Organization for Women (NOW) to fight for women's rights. Chronology and Index.

951. Henry, Sondra, and Emily Taitz. **Coretta Scott King: Keeper of the Dream**. Springfield, NJ: Enslow, 1992. 128p. $17.95. ISBN 0-89490-334-9. (Contemporary Women). 6 up

In this biography of Coretta Scott King (b. 1927), the authors introduce her with a series of quotes as the chapter titles. They are "As good as anyone else"; "Wherever Martin lives, I will live there too"; "Much bigger than Montgomery"; "Our faith has now been vindicated"; "Lord, I hope this isn't the way Martin has to go"; "Everything we can to help"; "Watch it, man, that's Mrs. King"; "I have to resist worry"; "You must be prepared to continue"; "I am acting in the name of Martin Luther King, Jr."; "The right time and the right thing to do"; and "I have done things . . . most women could never do." Chronology, Further Reading, Sources, and Index.

952. Henry, Sondra, and Emily Taitz. **Everyone Wears His Name: A Biography of Levi Strauss**. New York: Dillon Press, 1990. 128p. $13.95. ISBN 0-87518-375-1. (People in Focus). 5-9

An immigrant from Germany who arrived via steerage class in the United States, Strauss became a peddler of merchandise like other merchants whose names are now well known—Gimbel, Altman, and Marshall Field. He moved west and supplied gold rush participants with durable canvas pants. Another man discovered that rivets added to Strauss's canvas helped the pants last longer. He and Strauss patented the idea, and jeans took their place in American culture. Strauss never married but always took an interest in his family and society. He was fair and ethical to his employees. Selected Bibliography and Index.

953. Herald, Jacqueline. **The 1920s**. New York: Facts on File, 1991. 64p. $18.95. ISBN 0-8160-2465-0. (Fashions of a Decade). 7 up

After World War I, in the 1920s, fashion was a response to the devastation of the previous decade. The text looks at the fashion changes influenced by the media, economics, jazz, and dances like the Lindy with many illustrations. Among the personalities of the time were Charles Lindbergh and F. Scott Fitzgerald. Glossary, Time Line, Reading List, Bibliography, and Index.

954. Herald, Jacqueline. **The 1970s**. New York: Facts on File, 1992. 64p. $18.05. ISBN 0-8160-2470-7. (Fashions of a Decade). 7 up

In this look at the 1970s, the chapters, with photographs, cover the nostalgic clothes look, "Black is Beautiful," glamour, dressed to clash, the trash culture, disco kings and queens, and the rebirth of style. Figures, television shows, and movies such as *Happy Days* and *The Great Gatsby* were influential, while the women's movement and the drug culture also had their own styles. Glossary, Reading List, Time Chart, and Index.

955. Herb, Angela M. **Beyond the Mississippi: Early Westward Expansion of the United States**. New York: Lodestar, 1996. 138p. $16.99. ISBN 0-525-67503-5. (Young Readers' History of the West). 7-10

Herb includes stories about women as well as men in this look at the various trails that opened the West during the early nineteenth century. Among those events and movements that lack much coverage elsewhere are the Black Hawk War, the Whitman Mission in Oregon, the British outpost at Fort Vancouver, and the opening of the Mormon Trail. Herb also covers the Lewis and Clark expedition, the Oregon Trail, and the California gold rush. She uses primary sources to introduce the people who participated in this shift across the country. Further Reading, Glossary, and Index.

956. Herda, D. J. **The Dred Scott Case: Slavery and Citizenship**. Springfield, NJ: Enslow, 1994. 104p. $17.95. ISBN 0-89490-460-4. (Landmark Supreme Court Cases). 6-9

With background on the life of Dred Scott and his family, the reader can understand some of the aspects of the Dred Scott case that began in 1840 in Missouri. After a series of appeals, the Supreme Court under Justice Taney finally ruled in 1857 that Dred Scott, a slave, was not a citizen of the United States, and therefore had no rights in deciding where he would live. The case was one more decision that led to the Civil War. Drawings enhance the text. Notes, Further Reading, and Index.

957. Herda, D. J. **Earl Warren: Chief Justice for Social Change**. Springfield, NJ: Enslow, 1995. 104p. $17.95. ISBN 0-89490-556-2. (Justices of the Supreme Court). YA

Earl Warren (1891-1974) served as governor of California before he tried to become Vice President, an unsuccessful attempt when Harry Truman beat his running mate Thomas Dewey for President. Warren helped Eisenhower win the Republican nomination in 1952, and Eisenhower appointed him as chief justice of the Supreme Court in 1953. On the court he presided over *Brown v. Board of Education of Topeka, Kansas*; *Baker v. Carr*, the decision giving every person one vote; and *Miranda v. Arizona*, giving prisoners more rights. The text looks at these and other aspects of Warren's life. Chronology, Notes, Further Reading, and Index.

958.   Herda, D. J. **Furman v. Georgia: The Death Penalty Case**. Springfield, NJ: Enslow, 1994. 104p. $17.95. ISBN 0-89490-489-2. (Landmark Supreme Court Cases). 6-9

In 1972, the Supreme Court was asked to judge whether the death penalty could be considered cruel and unusual punishment. William Furman had been convicted of murder in Georgia and hoped to get out of that penalty. The Court did declare that it was unconstitutional and spared his life and those of others on "death row." The text looks at the ideas and arguments behind this case as well as the people who brought it to court. Notes, Glossary, Further Reading, and Index.

959.   Herda, D. J. **Outlaws of the American West**. Brookfield, CT: Millbrook Press, 1995. 64p. $17.40. ISBN 1-56294-449-5. 5-7

As the American West grew, people began to take the law into their own hands. Some broke the law, while others tried to apprehend those that did. The text recounts stories of Frank and Jesse James, Billy the Kid, and Butch Cassidy and the Wild Bunch. Photographs augment the text. Further Reading and Index.

960.   Herda, D. J. **Roe v. Wade: The Abortion Question**. Springfield, NJ: Enslow, 1994. 104p. $17.95. ISBN 0-89490-459-0. (Landmark Supreme Court Cases). 6-9

In 1969, a woman in Texas needed an abortion after being raped, and lawyers wanted her to sue the state. In 1970, Jane Roe did sue, and the case went to the Supreme Court. When it was settled in 1973, women gained the right to have abortions under certain circumstances. Since then, the issue has continued to be controversial. Further Reading and Index.

961.   Herda, D. J. **Thurgood Marshall: Civil Rights Champion**. Hillside, NJ: Enslow, 1995. 112p. $17.95. ISBN 0-89490-557-0. 7 up

Thurgood Marshall (1908-1993) grew up in a poor Baltimore home, but the members of his family respected each other. He recalled the injustices he suffered as a child, including management's refusal to give him a uniform with pants long enough when he worked on a train. He remembered this as a lawyer working for the rights of all and as the man who argued before the Supreme Court so that all children could receive an equal education. He then became the first African American on the Supreme Court. Chronology, Notes, Glossary, Further Reading, and Index.

962.   Herda, D. J. **United States v. Nixon: Watergate and the President**. Springfield, NJ: Enslow, 1996. 112p. $17.95. ISBN 0-89490-753-0. (Landmark Supreme Court Cases). 6-9

President Richard Nixon resigned from office in August 1974 after admitting that he had knowledge of the Watergate break-in. The text looks at presidential power and executive privilege as it explains how the Supreme Court decided unanimously that Nixon had to relinquish tapes made in his White House office to the special prosecutor assigned to his case. The book discusses various groups involved and activities relating to the scandal as well as biographical information about Nixon. Photographs, Appendix, Chronology, Further Reading, Glossary, Notes, and Index.

963.   Herman, Charlotte. **Millie Cooper, Take a Chance**. Helen Cogancherry, illustrator. New York: Dutton, 1988. 101p. $5. ISBN 0-525-44442-4. 3-7

In this sequel to *Millie Cooper, 3B*, Millie, a third grader in 1947, worries that she will not get any valentines at school. To keep from being disappointed, she tells people not to give her any. When getting only one hurts her, she realizes that she has to take risks in order to have pleasures. She recites her favorite poem for class, and her parents reward her by giving her a bicycle like one she had tried to win.

964.   Herman, Charlotte. **Millie Cooper, 3B**. Helen Cogancherry, illustrator. New York: Dutton, 1985. 74p. $5. ISBN 0-525-44157-3. 3-7

What Millie Cooper wants in 1946, at the beginning of third grade in Chicago, is a ball-point pen. She thinks it will help her make her spelling tests neater. She also wants to write an especially good composition on "Why I Am Special." Her father gives her a pen that does not work as she expects. But when her teacher compliments her as artistic and the first snow comes, she begins to feel special.

965.   Herman, Charlotte. **A Summer on Thirteenth Street**. New York: Dutton, 1991. 181p. $13.95. ISBN 0-525-44642-7. 3-7

Shirley Cohen, 11, plants her victory garden during the summer of 1944 and meets her friends on their Chicago street. When the local druggist's son enlists in the army, the war becomes real although the boy dies from a vaccination before leaving Chicago. Shirley suspects a man as a spy, but she finds out that he left Germany because his wife, killed in an accident, was Jewish. Shirley spends the summer learning that not everything turns out as expected.

966. Hesse, Karen. **A Time of Angels**. New York: Hyperion Press, 1995. 224p. $15.95. ISBN 0-7868-0087-9. 6-8

Hannah Gold lives with her two sisters, Tanta Rose, and the herbalist Vashti in Boston during the influenza epidemic of 1918. Her mother is in Russia, detained by the war in which her father fights. Hannah feels responsible for her sisters, but they get sick, and Tanta Rose dies. When Hannah becomes sick, Vashti sends her to relatives, but Hannah takes the wrong train and finds herself in Vermont. There, the Red Cross helps her, and an old German farmer, ostracized by the town for his heritage, nurses her to health. When she returns home, she discovers that her sisters have miraculously survived.

967. Hevly, Nancy. **Preachers and Teachers**. New York: Twenty-First Century Books, 1995. 96p. $16.98. ISBN 0-8050-2996-6. (Settling the West). 5-8

After settlers went west, those who wanted them to be religious and educated followed. People needed someone to organize their religious activities and to teach their children things for which they might be unprepared. The text, with photographs and drawings, looks at the influence of teachers and preachers in the settlement of the West. Source Notes, Further Reading, and Index.

968. Hibbert, Christopher. **Redcoats and Rebels: The American Revolution Through British Eyes**. 1990. New York: Avon, 1991. 375p. $12.50pa. ISBN 0-380-71544-9pa. YA

A different way to look at the American Revolution is from the British point of view. Hibbert discusses the blunders and decisions that the British could have changed to win the war. He also shows that the colonists were as hostile toward the Loyalist or Tory neighbors as the British had been toward the Scots. The biographical sketches here are not those of American military figures but of the British leaders such as Thomas Gage, Francis Smith, Huge Percy, William Howe, John Burgoyne, Nathaniel Green, and Charles Cornwallis. Bibliography and Index.

969. Higginsen, Vy, and Tonya Bolder. **Mama, I Want to Sing**. New York: Scholastic, 1992. 183p. $13.95. ISBN 0-590-44201-5. YA

In 1946, Doris joins the adult choir at church even though she is only 11. Her father dies soon after but tells her first that she must follow her dream. She wants to sing, but her mother thinks that all music outside the church is sinful. Doris secretly begins work at the Apollo Theater in Harlem, and she and her friends sing in a talent show there. She eventually convinces her mother that different types of music offer people comfort.

970. High, Linda Oatman. **The Summer of the Great Divide**. New York: Holiday House, 1996. 177p. $15.95. ISBN 0-8234-1228-8. 5-7

When she is 12 in 1969, Wheezie's parents consider separating, and they send her to her uncle's farm. She hates it and her cousin Slow Roscoe with his greasy hair. Among the traumas of the summer are the arrival of her period, Roscoe's speech impediment, the slaughter of farm animals, and news that their uncle, missing in action in Vietnam, is dead. Wheezie decides to run away to her parents so that she can get them back together. But she reconciles to her situation when she realizes that the "divide" will continue.

971. Highwater, Jamake. **The Ceremony of Innocence**. New York: HarperCollins, 1985. 192p. $12.89. ISBN 0-06-022302-2. (The Ghost Horse Cycle). 7 up

Three years after Amana's husband dies (*Legend Days*), the Blood people drive her out because she has been acting as a warrior-hunter. She begs, then finds brief happiness with a French Canadian, but he abandons her before her child Jemina is born. Her daughter, separate from the tribal rituals and without identity, marries Jamie Ghost Horse and bears two children. One of the children, Sitko, loves his grandmother's stories and imagines the sacred ceremonies.

972. Highwater, Jamake. **Eyes of Darkness**. New York: Lothrop, Lee & Shepard, 1985. 189p. $13. ISBN 0-688-41993-3. 6 up

In 1890, Alexander East surveys the hundreds of dead Sioux Indians massacred at Wounded Knee, and he recalls his own life as a young Native American. He had gone to live with whites at his father's request and lost touch with his identity. He remembers hearing his name Yesa, or "Winner," when he was eight after leading his lacrosse team to victory. He also recalls dancing the Bear Dance for his dying friend. When he left the reservation, he attended white men's schools and became a physician. After Wounded Knee, he returned to the home of his youth.

973. Highwater, Jamake. **I Wear the Morning Star**. New York: HarperCollins, 1986. 148p. $12.89. ISBN 0-06-022355-3. (The Ghost Horse Cycle). 7 up

Sitko (*The Ceremony of Innocence*), orphaned and living in a home where teachers beat him and students ignore him, suffers humiliation but remembers the tribal stories his grandmother Amana had told him. Delighted when his older brother Reno appears, he can only be disappointed when Reno clarifies his intent to become more like the white man. Sitko refuses to change his dreams. He becomes a painter who recreates his Indian heritage through pictures.

974. Highwater, Jamake. **Legend Days**. New York: HarperCollins, 1984. 147p. $12.89. ISBN 0-06-022304-9. (The Ghost Horse Cycle). 8 up

Amana's Northern Plains Indian parents die of smallpox when she is 10. A grandfather who rescues her gives her a warrior's tools and tells her not to use them until she must. She has great strength, and people embellish their stories of her with tales of it. After she marries her ill sister's old husband, she shares adventure with him until a buffalo hunt, when she kills buffalo, but the herd tramples him.

975. Hildick, E. W. **Hester Bidgood: Investigatrix of Evill Deedes**. New York: Macmillan, 1994. 141p. $14.95. ISBN 0-02-743966-6. 4-7

In 1692, people in Willow Bend, Massachusetts, discuss the witch hunt in Salem. When someone finds an unconscious cat, they think the devil has come to their town. Hester, 13, and her friend Rob, who has lived with the Indians, begin their investigation. What they find shows that the cat's owner Mistress Willson has nothing to do with the cat's problems.

976. Hill, Elizabeth Starr. **The Banjo Player**. New York: Viking, 1993. 197p. $14.99. ISBN 0-670-84967-7. 4-8

Jonathan, 12, takes the Orphan Train to New Orleans in 1888 after he almost dies in New York City's Great Blizzard. A family adopts him, and he enjoys playing the banjo that a hired man on the farm gives him. When he meets another orphan who works in a restaurant, they decide to trade places. Soon Jonathan becomes a banjo player on a riverboat, where he meets another orphan whom he had known in New York.

977. Hill, Prescott. **Our Century: 1920-1930**. Milwaukee, WI: Gareth Stevens, 1993. 64p. $23.93. ISBN 0-8368-1034-1. 3 up

Written as if a newspaper, this book's short articles give an overview of the decade. Included are statistics, daily life in America, immigration quotas, the end of the Russian Civil War, Lenin's death, Fascists and *Il Duce* in Italy, Hitler gaining power, the refusal of the United States to join the League of Nations, Sacco and Vanzetti, Calvin Coolidge, the Scopes "Monkey Trial," the court martial of Billy Mitchell, Herbert Hoover, the stock market crash, the Egyptian treasures discovery, Charles Lindbergh, John McGraw, Babe Ruth, Red Grange, the Demsey-Tunney rematch, Charles Lindbergh, Lady Astor, Mohandas Gandhi, and Leon Trotsky. Glossary, Books for Further Reading, Places to Write or Visit, and Index.

978. Hill, Prescott. **Our Century: 1940-1950**. Milwaukee, WI: Gareth Stevens, 1993. 64p. $23.93. ISBN 0-8368-1036-8. 3 up

Written as if a newspaper, this book's short articles give an overview of the decade. Included are statistics, daily life in America, Germany sweeping Europe and the Soviet Union, the Japanese bombing of Pearl Harbor, America in World War II, Edward R. Murrow, Ernie Pyle, the Warsaw ghetto, the siege of Leningrad, the atomic bomb, the Nuremberg trials, the United Nations, Israel, India and independence, Gandhi assassinated, the Communist victory in the Chinese war, the Berlin airlift, Roosevelt's death, Admiral Byrd in Antarctica, Ted Williams, Joe DiMaggio, William Faulkner, Tennessee Williams, Arthur Miller, Dwight Eisenhower, Eleanor Roosevelt, and Jackie Robinson. Glossary, Books for Further Reading, Places to Write or Visit, and Index.

979. Hill, Prescott. **Our Century: 1970-1980**. Milwaukee, WI: Gareth Stevens, 1993. 64p. $23.93. ISBN 0-8368-1039-2. 3 up

Written as if a newspaper, this book's short articles give an overview of the decade. Included are statistics, daily life in America, Vietnam, Arabs and Israelis at war, Chile's Allende overthrow, bombs in Beirut, the Guyana mass suicide, the Sandinistas taking control, the Islamic overthrow of the Shah of Iran, the Attica prison revolt, Jimmy Carter, the first test-tube baby, Arab terrorists, Hank Aaron, O. J. Simpson, Billie Jean King, Muhammad Ali, Golda Meir, George Wallace, and Barbara Jordan. Glossary, Books for Further Reading, Places to Write or Visit, and Index.

980. Hilton, Suzanne. **A Capital Capital City, 1790-1814**. New York: Atheneum, 1992. 156p. $14.95. ISBN 0-689-31641-0. 7-12

The capital of 10 square miles, Washington, D.C., was first swampland, thick forests, and cornfields. Pierre-Charles L'Enfant saw wide avenues, manicured parks, and huge state buildings. George Washington kept the two views in perspective as the wilderness became a city. Among the interesting pieces of information that appear in the text are that malaria spread during the summer months and congressmen shared rented rooms. Bibliography and Index.

981.   Hilton, Suzanne. **Miners, Merchants, and Maids**. New York: Twenty-First Century Books, 1995. 96p. $16.98. ISBN 0-8050-2998-2. (Settling the West). 5-8

Miners went west when they heard about gold, and merchants went to sell the items that people could not make for themselves. Maids came for a variety of reasons, including the desire for adventure. The text looks at their roles with photographs and drawings. Source Notes, Further Reading, and Index.

982.   Hilton, Suzanne. **The World of Young Andrew Jackson**. Patricia Lynn, illustrator. New York: Walker, 1988. 118p. $13.85. ISBN 0-8927-6814-8. 5-8

In this biography, Hilton looks at the youth of Andrew Jackson (1767-1845) and tries to recreate it. She uses diaries and news reports from the times and from places where Jackson would have been during his youth. Jackson's father died two weeks before he was born, and his Irish mother's superstitions kept her from revealing his chosen name before he was baptized. He disliked school, preferring to fight during the Revolutionary War. He wore a saber scar from those battles all his life, but he was shrewd and courageous. As a young man, he won an inheritance that he spent frivolously. Then he decided to "read law," the beginning of his adult achievements. Andrew Jackson: The Man, Bibliography, and Index.

983.   Hilton, Suzanne. **The World of Young George Washington**. William Sauts Bock, illustrator. New York: Walker, 1987. 112p. $12.95. ISBN 0-8027-6657-9. 5-9

The text looks at the boyhood of George Washington (1732-1799) and places his life in the context of the times in which he lived. It gives a different insight on the very private George Washington who loved the outdoors, rather than the legends that have grown up about his childhood. George Washington: The Man and Index.

984.   Hilton, Suzanne. **The World of Young Tom Jefferson**. William Sauts Bock, illustrator. New York: Walker, 1986. 92p. $12.95. ISBN 0-8027-6621-8. 5-9

As a youngster, Tom Jefferson (1743-1826) lived in Virginia, where his father mastered woodlore and his mother learned herbal cures from their Indian friends. He hated school but loved the violin. He watched after younger siblings and decided early to study law. People he knew traded tobacco instead of money; the parson was the schoolmaster; and few could afford a carriage. Other facts reveal Jefferson's boyhood. Thomas Jefferson: The Man and Index.

985.   Hilts, Len. **Quanah Parker: Warrior for Freedom, Ambassador for Peace**. San Diego, CA: Harcourt Brace, 1987. 148p. $12.95; $4.95pa. ISBN 0-15-200565-X; 0-15-264447-4pa. (Great Episodes). 3-7

Quanah Parker (1854-1911) was a Comanche leader who fought white intruders to protect the buffalo hunting grounds on the Plains. He especially angered General Sherman when he attacked Adobe Walls and the army. Eventually the army found Parker and his band, and they had to go to a reservation. Parker went peacefully, but he refused to give up all of the Comanche traditions. Historical Note, Glossary, and Index.

986.   Hintz, Martin. **Farewell, John Barleycorn: Prohibition in the United States**. Minneapolis, MN: Lerner, 1996. 88p. $14.21. ISBN 0-8225-1743-5. (People's History). 5 up

Before Prohibition began on January 17, 1920, people called liquor "John Barleycorn." Those who wanted a ban on alcohol hoped that Prohibition would improve society. Instead, people made their liquor in basements or in the woods, and gangsters bought and sold liquor, while speakeasies filled. The text looks at the various aspects of a period that lasted until its repeal by the Volstead Act on April 7, 1933. Bibliography and Index.

987.   Hirsch, Charles. **Taxation: Paying for Government**. Austin, TX: Blackbirch/Steck-Vaughn, 1993. 48p. $15.49. ISBN 0-8114-7356-2. (Good Citizenship). 5-9

After defining what taxes are, the text tells what the government uses taxes for and the kinds of taxes. A history shows that taxes were first mentioned in 3500 BC in Sumer (currently Iraq). Egyptians, Greeks, and Romans all paid taxes. Spanish taxes financed Columbus's trip to the New World. However, many have complained about unfair taxes, one of the major reasons that the American Revolution began. A final presentation on the Internal Revenue Service completes the information. Photographs and drawings supplement the text. Further Reading, Glossary, and Index.

988.   Hite, Sid. **It's Nothing to a Mountain**. New York: Henry Holt, 1994. 214p. $15.95. ISBN 0-8050-2769-6. 6-9

In 1969, Lisette, 14, and Riley, 12, live with their grandparents in the Virginia mountains after their parents die in a car accident. Lisette wears her mother's gold locket and sees it as good luck and symbolic of a guardian angel looking after her. Riley meets a boy who lives in the woods trying to survive after his mother went to prison. Riley tries to help him but has difficulty deciding what to do. Lisette searches for her guardian angel with the aid of an elderly neighbor, and Riley's friend becomes interested in Lisette from afar.

989. Hobbs, Valerie. **How Far Would You Be If I Hadn't Called You Back?** New York: Jackson, Orchard, 1995. 320p. $19.95. ISBN 0-531-09480-4. 9-12

Bron, 16, leaves New Jersey in the 1950s to go to California, where her parents open a restaurant. She feels out of place, but when she finds a friend, she begins to socialize with hot rodders and drag racers. She begins to race herself and does well enough so that a male opponent intentionally crashes rather than lose to her. She then falls in love with a boy who plans to attend West Point, but he dies first. Bron has several different aspects of her personality that her choice of friends does not reveal, but after the summer she begins to come to terms with herself.

990. Hogan, Linda. **Mean Spirit**. New York: Atheneum, 1990. 374p. $19.95. ISBN 0-689-12101-6. New York: Ivy, 1992. 374p. $4.99pa. ISBN 0-8041-0863-3pa. YA

Grace Blanket, a Hill Indian, chooses a piece of dry land in 1922 according to the provisions of the Dawes Act. She soon discovers oil on the land and jeopardizes the safety of her family, the Grayclouds. White government officials and businessmen try to take the land from her when they hear about its previously unknown value.

991. Hoig, Stan. **It's the Fourth of July**. New York: Cobblehill, Dutton, 1995. 81p. $15.99. ISBN 0-525-65175-6. 4-8

Using old prints and photographs to complement the text, Hoig shows how people have celebrated and commemorated the Fourth of July since its first anniversary in 1777. He includes a chapter on the Centennial celebration in 1876 and another about the arrival of the Statue of Liberty. Bibliography and Index.

992. Holland, Cecelia. **The Bear Flag**. Boston: Houghton Mifflin, 1990. 422p. $19.95. ISBN 0-395-48886-9. Windsor, NY: Pinnacle, 1992. 422p. $5.99pa. ISBN 1-55817-635-7pa. YA

Cat wants to keep the control of California out of the hands of people like Kit Carson and John Frémont in 1846, when the flag proclaiming California's independence begins to fly. Widowed on the trip from Boston to California, she meets a Russian who helps her oppose these men. She falls in love with him.

993. Holland, Cecelia. **Pacific Street**. Boston: Houghton Mifflin, 1992. 260p. $21.95. ISBN 0-395-56144-2. YA

Mitya comes to San Francisco in 1850 where he meets Daisy, Mammy, and Gil, who work in The Shining Light saloon after Mitya helps to build it. San Francisco's lawlessness becomes uncontrollable, and Mammy tries to kill Gil so that Daisy will stay with her at the saloon. Mitya saves him, and they all escape from Mammy.

994. Holland, Isabelle. **Behind the Lines**. New York: Scholastic, 1994. 194p. $13.95. ISBN 0-590-45113-8. 6-10

While the United States is torn apart in 1863, Katie O'Farrell, 14, must help keep her motherless Irish immigrant family together by working as a maid on New York City's Washington Square for the Lacey family. What disturbs her is that the wealthy can pay someone $300 to go to war for them. The rich buy the Irish, who do not see this war as theirs but need the money. The Irish, however, are fearful that the free Blacks will take their jobs while they are gone. What erupts are the New York Draft Riots of 1863, which last for four days. Katie helps one of the Blacks escape from certain hanging, and her kindness helps her gain something she has always wanted.

995. Holler, Anne. **Pocahontas: Powhatan Peacemaker**. New York: Chelsea House, 1993. 103p. $18.95; $7.95pa. ISBN 0-7910-1705-2; 0-7910-1952-7pa. (North American Indians of Achievement). 5-8

As the favorite child of Powhatan, Pocahontas had all that she wanted when she was growing up. When she was 12 in 1607, however, the colonists arrived and changed her life. She began to visit them and developed close ties while learning the language and the customs. She took food to them, and Captain John Smith said that her kindness was the "instrument [saving] the colony from death, famine and utter confusion." She had to choose either her family or her friends, and she ended up marrying the colonist John Rolfe and going to London with him, where she died. Engravings and drawings enhance the text. Chronology, Further Reading, and Index.

996. Holmas, Stig. **Apache Pass**. Anne Born, translator. John Hurford, illustrator. New York: Harbinger House, 1996. 140p. $15.95; $9.95pa. ISBN 1-57140-010-9; 1-57140-011-7pa. 6-8

In the area now New Mexico during 1861 at the Apache Pass in the Chiricahua Mountains, Indians steal a white boy of 12. White soldiers search for him but are unsuccessful in their attempts to rescue him without losing other lives. Interesting details of Apache life and customs fill the story. Bibliography.

997. Holmes, Burnham. **Cesar Chavez: Farm Worker Activist**. Austin, TX: Raintree/Steck-Vaughn, 1994. 128p. $16.98. ISBN 0-8114-2326-3. (American Troublemakers). 6 up

Although Cesar Chavez (1927-1993) only had an eighth grade education, he rose to defend the injustices imposed on migrant farmworkers. His own family lost its farm in 1937, and he had to work as a field hand doing backbreaking work for minimum compensation. He established the United Farm Workers in 1962 and organized the California grape pickers' strike. He won increases in pay and better working conditions for migrant workers. Maps, Photographs, Key Dates, Glossary, Places to Visit, Bibliography and Recommended Readings, and Index.

998. Holmes, Burnham. **Paul Robeson: A Voice of Struggle**. Austin, TX: Raintree/Steck-Vaughn, 1994. 128p. $16.98. ISBN 0-8114-2381-6. (American Troublemakers). 6 up

Paul Robeson (1898-1976) was multitalented. He excelled in athletics, went to law school, and became an internationally acclaimed singer and actor. When he increased his political involvement, his stage career declined. His association with Communists in the 1950s caused the United States to revoke his passport, but when he regained it, he went to England to pursue his career. After he returned and retired, he wrote a book called *Here I Stand*. Maps, Key Dates, Glossary, Places to Visit, Bibliography and Recommended Readings, and Index.

999. Holmes, Mary Z. **Cross of Gold**. Geri Strigenz, illustrator. Austin, TX: Raintree/Steck-Vaughn, 1992. 48p. $20.70. ISBN 0-8114-3507-5. (History's Children). 4-8

In 1615, Felipe, 14, lies ill in Santa Fe. He promises God that he will give him his newfound gold if he gets well. A friar sent by the Viceroy of Spain helps Felipe recover, and Felipe gives him the gold to make a cross for the town's church.

1000. Holmes, Mary Z. **For Bread—1893**. Geri Strigenz, illustrator. Austin, TX: Raintree/Steck-Vaughn, 1992. 48p. $20.70. ISBN 0-8114-3501-6. (History's Children). 4-8

Stefan, 13, lives with his family in Buffalo, New York, during 1893. His Polish father loses his job, but rather than work as his father wants him to do, Stefan uses his artistic talent to make and sell drawings so that the family can survive the hard times. He draws pictures of business buildings and sells them to the owners.

1001. Holmes, Mary Z. **Thunder Foot—1730**. Geri Strigenz, illustrator. Austin, TX: Raintree/Steck-Vaughn, 1992. 48p. $20.70. ISBN 0-8114-3500-8. (History's Children). 4-8

In 1730, Running Dog, 14, finds a horse, an animal his Cheyenne Indian tribe has never seen. He brings it back, and it guides him on his vision quest. When he learns how to ride the horse, he earns the name Wind Chaser.

1002. Holmes, Mary Z. **Year of the Sevens—1777**. Geri Strigenz, illustrator. Austin, TX: Raintree/Steck-Vaughn, 1992. 48p. $20.70. ISBN 0-8114-3505-9. (History's Children). 4-8

In 1777, Polly and her family move to the Kentucky frontier. The country is fighting the Revolutionary War on the East Coast, and the Indians are at war near Polly's home. They raid and burn the house and kill her mother. She has to adjust to her father's remarriage and the new wife, who has lost a husband and a daughter.

1003. Hoobler, Dorothy, and Thomas Hoobler. **The Chinese American Family Album**. New York: Oxford University Press, 1994. 128p. $22.95. ISBN 0-19-509123-X. (American Family Albums). 5 up

In the 1830s, Chinese sugarcane workers arrived in Hawaii, and Chinese sailors entered New York City's harbor. From then to the present, the Chinese culture has enriched the experiences of all Americans. Chinese Americans have endured serious prejudice, including a law in 1924 that prohibited Chinese American citizens from bringing their wives and children into the country. The act was not repealed until 1943, after the United States and China became allies during World War II. The text, complemented by photographs, traces the history of Chinese immigrants, indicating that most have continued to live in groups or Chinatowns as they worked in laundries, restaurants, and sweatshops. Without the Chinese workers in the nineteenth century, the transcontinental railroad might not have been completed so rapidly. The diary entries of immigrants, tracing families as they live, work, and rest in America, enliven the text. Chinese American Timeline, Further Reading, and Index.

1004. Hoobler, Dorothy, and Thomas Hoobler. **The Irish American Family Album**. New York: Oxford University Press, 1995. 128p. $19.95. ISBN 0-19-509461-1. (American Family Albums). 5 up

Using diary entries, letters, clippings, and interviews, the authors present the story of Irish Americans. More than 39 million Americans claim their ancestry to be Irish. Between 1841 and 1850, more than 800,000 Irish arrived, and another 900,000 followed in the next decade. During that 20-year period, one in five Irish natives left for the United States. First employed as laborers, miners, and servants, the Irish soon formed political organizations that became major forces throughout the country. The Irish count among their numbers the Kennedy family, John Wayne, Georgia O'Keeffe, F. Scott Fitzgerald, and Sandra Day O'Connor. Irish American Timeline, Further Reading, and Index.

1005. Hoobler, Dorothy, and Thomas Hoobler. **The Italian American Family Album**. New York: Oxford University Press, 1994. 127p. $22.95. ISBN 0-19-509124-8. (American Family Albums). 5 up

Italian influences in all areas of society have helped create America since Cristofor Colombo arrived in 1492. The text traces the lives of individuals through their diaries and photographs of those who immigrated to America, especially during the nineteenth and early twentieth centuries: their work, living environment, religious activities, and burden of prejudice. Italian American Timeline, Further Reading, and Index.

1006.   Hoobler, Dorothy, and Thomas Hoobler. **The Japanese American Family Album**. New York: Oxford University Press, 1996. 127p. $22.95. ISBN 0-19-508131-5. (American Family Albums). 4-10

Through their own words and scrapbook pictures, Japanese American immigrants tell their stories. The first wave of Japanese immigration occurred in the nineteenth century, with another in the twentieth century. The text looks at treatment of Japanese Americans, including the deplorable chapter of internment during World War II. Japanese American Timeline, Further Reading, and Index.

1007.   Hoobler, Dorothy, and Thomas Hoobler. **The Jewish American Family Album**. New York: Oxford University Press, 1995. 128p. $22.95. ISBN 0-19-508135-8. (American Family Albums). 6-9

Through their own words and scrapbook pictures, Jewish immigrants tell their stories. A brief history of Jewish life through the centuries precedes chapters that describe special taxes, the limit on Jewish marriages, and occupational restrictions that caused many Ashkenazi Jews to flee central Europe from 1840 to 1860. Other waves followed in the early twentieth century. Chapters include the earliest arrivals in the sixteenth century, new life in New York in the garment trade, going west, the neighborhoods and Yiddish theater, Jewish religious rituals, and becoming part of America. Jewish American Timeline, Further Reading, and Index.

1008.   Hooks, William H. **Circle of Fire**. New York: Atheneum, 1982. 147p. $15. ISBN 0-689-50241-9. 5-9

Harrison, 11 in 1936, sees two disparate happenings at Christmas in North Carolina. He watches the gypsies' lovely candlelight mummer's play as well as the Ku Klux Klan burn one of their crosses on the way to punish a man married to a South Carolina woman. Because his two best friends are Black, he cannot understand the Klan's hatred toward Blacks, Catholics, and Jews.

1009.   Hooks, William H. **A Flight of Dazzle Angels**. New York: Macmillan, 1988. 169p. $13.95. ISBN 0-02-744430-9. 7-10

Annie Earle, 15 in 1908, has a club foot, an invalid mother, and a feebleminded brother. Additionally, her aunt looks forward to her mother's death so she can take her wealth. Annie Earle's only friends in her small southern town are the elderly Black housekeeper and her granddaughter, Queen Esther. What Annie Earle wants is to dance, and her friends try to help her accomplish that goal. A chance encounter also helps her overcome her feelings of inadequacy.

1010.   Hooks, William H. **The Legend of the White Doe**. Dennis Nolan, illustrator. New York: Macmillan, 1988. 48p. $13.95. ISBN 0-02-744350-7. 5-7

The first English child born in the colonies was Virginia Dare in North Carolina during 1587. This historical fantasy suggests that she escaped the hostile Indians who raided the settlement, and the Croatan Indians raised her after her mother walked into the sea. She refused to marry the medicine man who claimed her in favor of a brave whom she loved. She ran away with him, was killed, and supposedly roams through the Great Dismal Swamp as a white deer.

1011.   Hoppe, Joanne. **Dream Spinner**. New York: Morrow, 1992. 228p. $14. ISBN 0-688-08559-8. 7 up

After her father remarries, Mary, 15, goes with him and his new wife to live in a house built in 1893. She reads an article about dreaming in a science magazine and begins dreaming about the people who lived in the house and their use of an old railroad station on the property. No one has been aware of the station until she dreams about it.

1012.   Horton, Madelyn. **Mother Jones**. San Diego, CA: Lucent, 1996. 95p. $16.95. ISBN 1-56006-057-3. (The Importance Of). 6-9

In addition to telling about the life of Mary Harris or "Mother" Jones (1830-1930), the text also gives an overview of the labor movement in the United States, in which Mother Jones played a prominent role. She was imprisoned for activities on behalf of West Virginia and Colorado coal miners, and she exposed some of the abuses in child labor. Among them were that children who had been wounded, such as losing a limb in the mines, were the only ones who went to school. Primary source documents give an immediacy to the information. Bibliography, Chronology, Further Reading, Notes, and Index.

1013.   Horvath, Polly. **The Happy Yellow Car**. New York: Farrar, Straus & Giroux, 1994. 150p. $15. ISBN 0-374-32845-5. 4-7

Living in Missouri during the 1930s Depression with her family, Betty Grunt cannot get the dollar she needs for flowers so she can be crowned Pork-Fry Queen of her sixth grade class. A story of family money hidden in the area leads Betty and her brothers on a big search. When her father comes home with a yellow car, everyone wonders where he will find money to pay for the gas. Then her sister Gretel says that she is going to marry Clarence but has told him her family is in Italy and cannot come to the wedding. They do not find the family money, but the family's positive attitudes contrast to most stories set in the Depression.

1014. Hotze, Sollace. **Acquainted with the Night**. New York: Clarion, 1992. 230p. $13.95. ISBN 0-395-61576-3. 7 up

Molly, 17, and her cousin Caleb, 21 and wounded in Vietnam, find more to the summer than they expect when Caleb comes to stay with her family on their Maine island while he recuperates in 1979. They find the ghost of Evaline Cobb Bloodsworth and read her diary, which talks of her boss seducing her while she worked in a mill, and of her baby that had to be placed for adoption. As an older woman, she had the double horror of being shunned by the townspeople, of falling in love with a much younger visitor to the town, and of finding from the man's family that he was her son. Molly and Caleb try to help her ghost rest, as well as their own shadows.

1015. Hotze, Sollace. **A Circle Unbroken**. New York: Clarion, 1988. 224p. $13.95. ISBN 0-89919-733-7. 6 up

When she is 17, Rachel's father steals her back from the Dakota Sioux tribe that had taken her when she was 10. He wants to hear nothing about her life as Kata Wi and refuses to acknowledge that her kidnapping ever occurred. She enjoys her siblings and her stepmother but remembers the kindness and love of her other family. She becomes ill and fears that she will die like her Aunt Sarah, who died after she returned from being captured for the same seven years. Rachel realizes that she must go back to her Indian family in order to save her life. *Carl Sandburg Literary Arts Award*.

1016. Hotze, Sollace. **Summer Endings**. New York: Clarion, 1991. 176p. $13.95. ISBN 0-395-56197-3. 4-7

Christine Kosinski, 12, has a mixed summer in 1945. World War II ends, and her sister gets married. Christine enjoys watching the Chicago Cubs play baseball from her apartment window that overlooks the field, and she gets her first job working in the drugstore. She and her sister worry about their father, who has been a political prisoner in Poland during the war, but as the summer ends, they hear that he has survived Dachau. Finally, Christine gets her first kiss at Rosie's wedding.

1017. Houston, Gloria. **Littlejim's Dreams**. Thomas B. Allen, illustrator. San Diego, CA: Harcourt Brace, 1997. 240p. $16. ISBN 0-15-201509-4. 4-7

Littlejim, 14, wants to attend the academy in 1920 so that he can become a teacher like his Aunt Zony. His mother gets sick, however, and Littlejim has to do chores on the farm. Then the timber company's plans are going to change the family's life, and Littlejim has to devise a way to make his dreams come true.

1018. Houston, Gloria. **Mountain Valor**. Thomas B. Allen, illustrator. New York: Philomel, 1994. 227p. $14.95. ISBN 0-399-22519-6. New York: Paper Star, 1996. 227p. $5.95pa. ISBN 0-698-11383-7pa. 5-8

While Valor's father fights with a North Carolina regiment and her uncle with a Tennessee cavalry, Valor has to stay home with her mother and her cousin Jed. Jed is one year younger but recognized as the master of the house because he is a boy. When a soldier threatens her family's safety, Valor decides to pretend she is a Southern boy and join the army. She brings home the family's stolen livestock but catches pneumonia. Everyone hears of her exploits and knows that she is properly named.

1019. Houston, Jeanne Wakatsuki, and James D. Houston. **Farewell to Manzanar**. 1973. New York: Bantam, 1983. 145p. $4.50pa. ISBN 0-553-27258-6pa. 7 up

When Jeanne Wakatsuki was seven years old in 1942, the U.S. government sent her and her family to the Manzanar internment camp with 10,000 other Japanese Americans. The camp inhabitants tried to recreate life outside the fence by having Boy Scouts, sock hops, cheerleaders, and baton twirling lessons within, but the life lost outside could never be retrieved. Jeanne's story gives insight into the personalities and pains of those who had to endure this sordid time in American history.

1020. Hovde, Jane. **Jane Addams**. New York: Facts on File, 1989. 131p. $17.95. ISBN 0-8160-1547-3. (Makers of America). 7 up

Jane Addams (1860-1935), who acknowledged that her father was a great influence on her life, helped achieve suffrage for women. The text tells of her career, her founding of Hull House, and her seconding of Theodore Roosevelt's nomination for President in 1912. Bibliography and Index.

1021. Howard, Elizabeth. **Out of Step with the Dancers**. New York: Morrow, 1978. 223p. $10.75. ISBN 0-688-32141-0. 7 up

When Damaris is 16 in 1853 and in love with Matthew, her father announces that the family is moving to New Lebanon, New York, to join the Shakers. Shocked by this shift in her life, she tries to adjust to the community and to the idea that she can never marry, but she cannot. She returns to her hometown to live with friends and follow a lifestyle that she can more easily accept.

1022. Howard, Ellen. **Edith Herself**. Ronald Himler, illustrator. New York: Atheneum, 1987. 132p. $12.95. ISBN 0-689-31314-4. 5-7

Edith's mother dies around 1890, and Edith has to move in with her sister and her strict Christian husband John as well as his sour-smelling mother. Edith has blackouts, later diagnosed as epilepsy, and her sister wants her to stay home from school in case she has a seizure in front of the other children. But Edith wants to go to school, and, ironically, John supports her desire. *School Library Journal Best Book.*

1023. Howard, Ellen. **The Log Cabin Quilt**. Ronald Himler, illustrator. New York: Holiday House, 1996. 32p. $15.95. ISBN 0-8234-1247-4. K-2

Although Elvirey's father does not want to bring anything on their journey to Michigan from Carolina that will remind him of his deceased wife, her grandmother decides to bring her bag of scraps for quilting. After their arrival and construction of a cabin, Elvirey's father goes to hunt. During his absence, the mud freezes and falls out of the chinks in the wall. Elvirey uses the scraps to fill the holes, and when her father returns and sees her ingenuity, he declares that her mother would be proud of her.

1024. Howard, Ellen. **Sister**. New York: Atheneum, 1990. 148p. $12.95. ISBN 0-689-31653-4. 5-7

In 1886 in the Midwest, Alena wants to stay in school, but the birth and death of her sister depresses her mother so much that Alena has to stay home to help her. Because Alena delivered the baby, she also grieves over the child's death. Her teacher knows her desires and helps her find a way to get a diploma and to help her mother. *American Library Association Notable Books for Children.*

1025. Howard, Ellen. **The Tower Room**. New York: Atheneum, 1993. 137p. $13.95. ISBN 0-689-31856-1. 5-7

After her mother dies during the 1950s, Mary Brooke has to go live with her aunt in Michigan. While she waits for her father to come for her, another classmate in the fifth grade taunts her about her mother dying from an illegal abortion. In the tower room of the house where her grandfather died, Mary Brooke hides, and her aunt comes to the room for the first time since her own father's death. Together they mourn their losses and learn about each other.

1026. Howarth, Sarah. **Colonial People**. Brookfield, CT: Millbrook Press, 1994. 47p. $15.40. ISBN 1-56294-512-2. (People and Places). 4-8

Quotations and case studies provide insight into the everyday lives of 13 people typical of those who settled in North America. Each chapter shows how this person would have fit (or not) into society. The people are governor, newcomer, Puritan, planter, servant, goodwife, Native American, apprentice, slave, fur trader, constable, smuggler, and patriot. Glossary, Further Reading, and Index.

1027. Howarth, Sarah. **Colonial Places**. Brookfield, CT: Millbrook Press, 1994. 47p. $15.40. ISBN 1-56294-513-0. (People and Places). 4-8

Each chapter shows a typical place in the early days of European settlement in North America and how it fit into the life of the community. Places covered are the colony, cornfield, meetinghouse, church, tobacco field, hunting ground, street post office, harbor, governor's house, college, and the Old World (because many people spoke of it as "home"). Glossary, Further Reading, and Index.

1028. Howe, Russell Warren. **The Hunt for Tokyo Rose**. Lanham, MD: Madison, 1990. 354p. $19.95. ISBN 0-8191-7456-4. YA

Iva Toguri d'Aquino, or Tokyo Rose (b. 1916), was a California-born Nisei woman stranded in Japan at the beginning of the Pacific war. She began broadcasting to the American troops for the Japanese military and was later convicted of treason. Howe questions whether she cooperated freely or under duress by the Japanese or if Tokyo Rose was more than one person. The case as Howe presents it seems to have been contrived and probably based on racial prejudice with the government and press exaggerating it. Index.

1029. Hudson, Karen E. **The Will and the Way: Paul R. Williams, Architect**. New York: Rizzoli, 1994. 64p. $14.95. ISBN 0-8478-1780-6. 7-10

Paul R. Williams (1894-1980), the first African American member and Fellow of the American Institute of Architects, designed more than 3,000 buildings. The biography takes the form of a journal with Williams writing about his life to his grandson. Williams tells what architects do and about his experiences as an African American growing up in Los Angeles during the early twentieth century. Glossary.

1030. Hull, Mary. **Rosa Parks: Civil Rights Leader**. New York: Chelsea House, 1994. 110p. $18.95; $7.95pa. ISBN 0-7910-1881-4; 0-7910-1910-1pa. (Black Americans of Achievement). 5 up

This biography of Rosa Parks (b. 1913) traces her life from the eventful day in 1955, when she refused to move from her seat on the bus because she "had had enough," through her life afterward. It is also a story of the Civil Rights movement from her perspective. Photographs and reproductions enhance the text. Chronology, Further Reading, and Index.

1031.　Hull, Robert, sell. **Breaking Free: An Anthology of Human Rights Poetry**. New York: Thomson Learning, 1994. 64p. $17.95. ISBN 1-56847-196-3. All ages

This anthology of international poems written over several centuries presents such themes as imprisonment, liberation, slavery, hunger, education, and family and human relations. Photographs and drawings illustrate the text. Poet Biographies, Glossary, Bibliography, and Index.

1032.　Humble, Richard. **Ships**. Peter Cornwall, illustrator. Austin, TX: Raintree/Steck-Vaughn, 1994. 32p. $21.40. ISBN 0-8114-6158-0. (Pointers). 3-7

Two-page spreads on each type of ship tell its structure and give historical information and an illustration. The types of ships presented are Egyptian warships, Greek triremes, Viking long ships, man-of-war ships, ships of the Line, early steamships, clipper ships, ironclads, turret rams, submarines, aircraft carriers, and ocean liners. Glossary and Index.

1033.　Humble, Richard. **A World War Two Submarine**. Mark Bergin, illustrator. New York: Peter Bedrick, 1991. 48p. $18.95. ISBN 0-87226-351-7. (Inside Story). 4-7

The very first submarine used in the United States was in 1776, when the *Turtle* was put to service to explode British ammunition. It failed, but it caused engineers to began searching for a submarine that would work. The text looks at submarine warfare during the World Wars and how they were designed and built. Diagrams and drawings show the midships, bow tubes, sleeping and eating arrangements, sonar, torpedoes and guns, and uniforms worn by the crew. A brief discussion of the Battle of the Atlantic from 1940 to 1943 describes subs in action. Chronology, Glossary, and Index.

1034.　Humphrey, Hubert H. **The Education of a Public Man: My Life and Politics**. 1976. Minneapolis, MN: University of Minnesota, 1991. 391p. $16.95pa. ISBN 0-8166-1897-6pa. YA

Starting with the day he lost the presidential election to Richard Nixon, then-Vice President Hubert Humphrey (1911-1978) recounts his life, much of it serving his state and his country in political roles. During the year in which he was running for President, the Tet Offensive in Vietnam, riots, backlash, assassinations, and George Wallace all grabbed media attention. He was a champion of the Civil Rights movement, public education, arms control, and health care. The text presents a man who might have made a difference in the presidency. Notes and Index.

1035.　Hunt, Conover. **JFK for a New Generation**. New York: Southern Methodist University, 1996. 159p. $34.95; $19.95pa. ISBN 0-87074-415-1; 0-87074-395-3pa. YA

John F. Kennedy (1917-1963) died in Dallas on a November day in 1963. The text looks at the man in light of his presidency and his times and shows how the press and others perpetrated the myth of Camelot and of a great presidency. It looks at the preparations for the visit, the weather, the news of the day, and the music of the time to set the stage for a tragedy that made the nation and the world mourn. Hunt also examines the theories about the assassination and documents the pros and cons of each. Photographs, Bibliography, Notes, and Index.

1036.　Hunt, Irene. **Across Five Aprils**. 1965. Parsippany, NJ: Silver Burdett, 1994. 190p. $12.95. ISBN 0-382-24358-7. New York: Berkley, 1990. 190p. $3.99pa. ISBN 0-425-10241-6pa. 6 up

Jethro turns nine in 1861, and his life changes. The story traces the activities of his Illinois family during the four years of the Civil War, where brothers fight on opposite sides of the conflict. Jethro assumes the male responsibilities of the household when his father has a heart attack, and he learns about Abraham Lincoln and Robert E. Lee, both greatly respected by some and greatly reviled by others. When one of his brothers deserts, Jethro writes to Lincoln requesting amnesty. At Lincoln's death, the family mourns along with the nation. *Newbery Honor Book* and *Society of Midland Authors Book Award*.

1037.　Hunt, Irene. **No Promises in the Wind**. 1970. New York: Berkley, 1987. 224p. $3.50pa. ISBN 0-425-09969-5pa. YA

Josh, 15 in 1932 during the Depression, leaves home with his brother to find work. After Josh obtains a job playing the piano for a carnival, the business burns, and he has to look again. Several difficulties occur during this journey where they see homeless and illegal activity, but they finally decide to return to Chicago and their father. Because they had left home after an argument with their father, he is relieved to see them and hopeful that Franklin Delano Roosevelt, the new President, will help solve the economic problems.

1038.　Hunter-Gault, Charlayne. **In My Place**. New York: Farrar, Straus & Giroux, 1992. 256p. $19. ISBN 0-374-17563-2. New York: Vintage, 1993. 256p. $11pa. ISBN 0-679-74818-0pa. YA

Charlayne Hunter-Gault grew up in Georgia and was one of the first Blacks to attend the University of Georgia, from which she graduated in 1963. She discusses her life in terms of the Civil Rights movement, which began as she left high school and entered college.

1039.   Hurmence, Belinda. **Dixie in the Big Pasture**. New York: Clarion, 1994. 169p. $13.95. ISBN 0-395-52002-9. 5-7

In 1907, Dixie, 12, and her family move to Oklahoma with its wide plains. After her dog disappears, her father buys her a horse from a Kiowa Indian, but the Indian's son believes the horse still belongs to him. After this experience, plus a prairie fire, Dixie is unconvinced that the move from Tennessee was the right thing to do. But her family gains respect for being good neighbors and for her mother's medicinal knowledge.

1040.   Hurmence, Belinda. **Tancy**. Boston: Houghton Mifflin, 1984. 224p. $12.95. ISBN 0-89919-228-9. 8-10

When 16 in 1865, Tancy gains her freedom at the end of the American Civil War. She wants to find her mother, sold when she was two, and she leaves her North Carolina plantation home in search of her. Because her mistress taught her to read and write, she takes a job registering other former slaves. She finds out that her former master is her father as she looks for her mother and the mother of a young child who remains in her care. *Golden Kite Award, School Library Journal Best Book, American Association of University Women,* and *North Carolina Literary and Historical Association Award.*

I

1041. Iida, Deborah. **Middle Son: A Novel.** New York: Algonquin, 1996. 228p. $18.95. ISBN 1-56512-119-8. YA

Of the three brothers in Hawaii of the 1950s, the youngest has as his surrogate father a childless uncle. The three are close but the two oldest never refer to the youngest as a brother. The oldest drowns accidentally, and the other two split. Not until the middle brother leaves Hawaii, serves in the Vietnam War, and returns as a newspaper photographer married to a Caucasian do they face and make amends about the tragedy of their youth.

1042. IlgenFritz, Elizabeth. **Anne Hutchinson.** New York: Chelsea House, 1990. 111p. $18.95. ISBN 1-55546-660-5. (American Women of Achievement). 5 up

Born in Alford, England, in 1591 during the reign of Queen Elizabeth I, Anne Marbury was the daughter of a dissident clergyman. He gave her an excellent education, and after her marriage to William Hutchinson, she spent 20 years as his wife and a village folk medicine expert. During the reign of James I, religious turmoil changed their lives, and they joined the earliest settlers in the Massachusetts Bay Colony. There, Anne criticized the ministers and spoke about religion in her home. Although some people supported her ideas, the issues she raised divided the settlement. Because women had no power, the governor in Boston, John Winthrop, called her to trial and condemned her. At her trial, she spoke with intelligence and integrity, never shrinking from her beliefs. She was one of the first settlers to request religious tolerance in this new land, and she and her followers moved to Rhode Island where Roger Williams had earlier been banished. She went to New York after her husband died. She and five of her children, caught in a Native American and Dutch war, were killed in 1643. Photographs and reproductions enhance the text. Chronology, Further Reading, and Index.

1043. Irwin, Hadley. **I Be Somebody.** New York: Macmillan, 1984. 170p. $13.95. ISBN 0-689-50308-3. Bergenfield, NJ: New American Library, 1988. 170p. $2.50pa. ISBN 0-4511-5303-0pa. 4-8

Rap, 10, lives with his Aunt Spicy in Oklahoma. In 1910, she decides that the two will move with others from their town to Athabasca, Canada. On the train north, she dies, but before she dies, she tells Rap his father's identity. With that information, he can be "somebody" who has both a past and a future.

1044. Irwin, Hadley. **Jim-Dandy.** New York: Margaret K. McElderry, 1994. 144p. $14.95. ISBN 0-689-50594-9. 5-8

In the late 1860s, Caleb, 12, hates life with his stepfather on the empty Kansas plains after his mother dies. A foal, Dandy, is born and gives Caleb a new interest. His stepfather has to sell Dandy to Custer's Seventh Cavalry at nearby Fort Hays, and Caleb follows. He sees their campaign against the Cheyenne when they massacre Black Kettle at Washita and realizes the horrible results of the Indian Wars.

1045. Irwin, Hadley. **Kim/Kimi.** New York: Margaret K. McElderry, Macmillan, 1987. 200p. $16. ISBN 0-689-50428-4. New York: Penguin, 1988. 200p. $4.99pa. ISBN 0-14-032593-Xpa. 7-10

Adopted by her Caucasian stepfather because her Nisei father died before she was born, Kim has always been known as Caucasian. When at 16 she goes from Iowa to Sacramento, California, with her younger stepbrother to find out about her father's family, she discovers the pain of Japanese Americans during World War II, who lost all that they had when the American government put them into internment camps.

1046. Israel, Fred L. **Franklin Delano Roosevelt.** New York: Chelsea House, 1985. 112p. $18.95. ISBN 0-87754-573-1. (World Leaders Past and Present). 5 up

Elected in 1932 to the presidency, Franklin D. Roosevelt (1882-1945) ignored those who disagreed with his New Deal programs to stop the economic devastation throughout the country. Not everything worked, but the United States entered World War II, and then true recovery could begin. Roosevelt was a great leader in both war and peace. Photographs enhance the text. Chronology, Further Reading, and Index.

1047. Isserman, Maurice. **The Korean War: America at War.** New York: Facts on File, 1992. 117p. $17.95. ISBN 0-8160-2688-2. (America at War). 7 up

The Korean War (1950-1953), called by some the "forgotten" war, was the first "undeclared" war fought under the United Nations flag. The text tells about the miscalculation of military personnel who believed that the invading North Koreans would not fight, followed by a chronological account of the war. Pertinent quotes from participants show what this war was like. Bibliography and Index.

1048. Isserman, Maurice. **World War II.** New York: Facts on File, 1991. 184p. $17.95. ISBN 0-8160-2374-3. (America at War). 7 up

This volume gives an overview of World War II, beginning with Leo Szilard's concern in 1939 that the best people working on nuclear fission were in Hitler's Germany. Szilard was a Hungarian scientist who had recently come to America. His advice led to the Manhattan Project and the development of the atomic bomb later used in

Japan. The text presents the major events of the war, the major objectives and strategies of the war's leaders, and significant innovations in weapons and tactics. Biographical references to many of the leaders also appear. Recommended Reading and Index.

1049.   Italia, Robert. **Courageous Crimefighters**. Minneapolis, MN: Oliver Press, 1995. 160p. $14.95. ISBN 1-881508-21-8. (Profiles). 6-9

People who lived the adventures that make mystery and detective books so appealing risk their lives to catch criminals. The text looks at eight of these people: Sir Robert Peel (1788-1850) of Scotland Yard in England; Allan Pinkerton (1819-1884), the original private eye in America; Samuel Steele (1851-1919), a Canadian mountie; Leander H. McNelly (1844-1877), captain of the Texas Rangers; Melvin Purvis (1903-1960) and Eliot Ness (1902-1957), top agents in the Federal Bureau of Investigation; Estes Kefauver (1903-1963), a crusader in Congress; and Simon Wiesenthal (b. 1908), hunter of Nazis. Bibliography and Index.

1050.   Ito, Tom. **John Steinbeck**. San Diego, CA: Lucent, 1994. 112p. $16.95. ISBN 1-56006-049-2. (The Importance Of). 7 up

John Steinbeck (1902-1968) has been considered one of the most important writers of the twentieth century. He won the Nobel Prize for his work, which featured impoverished and dispossessed people. He began his writing career during the Great Depression of the 1930s, and his account of migrant farmworkers trying to survive in *The Grapes of Wrath* leaves an indelible impression on serious readers. Notes for Further Reading, Additional Works Consulted, and Index.

$\boxed{\text{J}}$

1051.   Jacobs, Francine. **The Tainos: The People Who Welcomed Columbus**. Patrick Collins, illustrator. New York: Putnam, 1992. 103p. $15.95. ISBN 0-399-22116-6. 5-9

The Indians who met Christopher Columbus and his crews in 1492 were called Tainos. They had no written language, so all that survives about them are the writings made during the time of Columbus and pictographs discovered in caves on the islands. They were peaceful farming people whose ancestors had come from South America hundreds of years before. Although the Tainos welcomed Columbus and his men, the visitors called them Indians because they thought they were in India. Then they destroyed the Taino culture in their greed for gold. In 50 years, the Tainos became extinct. Notes, Museums, Bibliography, and Index.

1052.   Jacobs, Paul S. **James Printer: A Novel of King Philip's War**. New York: Scholastic, 1997. 224p. $15.95. ISBN 0-590-97541-2. 6-8

This fictionalized biography of James Printer tells about his experiences as a master apprentice in seventeenth-century Cambridge to the printer and bookmaker Samuel Green. Printer, a Nipmuc Indian raised and educated by the English, struggles to understand his role in the strife that erupts between the Indians and the colonists. When the colonists force him into exile, he joins King Philip, the Pokanoket leader, and helps his English prisoners. Throughout, the narrator, Bartholomew Green, the printer's devil in the shop, is more and more shocked by the horrible things he observes.

1053.   Jacobs, William. **War with Mexico**. Brookfield, CT: Millbrook Press, 1994. 64p. $15.90; $5.95pa. ISBN 1-56294-366-9; 1-56294-776-1pa. (Spotlight on American History). 5-8

War between Mexico and the United States started in 1846 over territories that both claimed. Battles occurred at Monterey and Buena Vista as the United States drove toward Mexico City. When the United States won the war, many thought the boundaries of the country would extend with the Treaty of Guadalupe Hidalgo. What ensued after 1848 was anything but peaceful because of the bills in Congress to keep slavery from being legal in the new territories. The text discusses these various aspects of this war. Chronology, Further Reading, Bibliography, and Index.

1054.   Jacobs, William Jay. **Great Lives: Human Rights**. New York: Scribner's, 1990. 278p. $22.95. ISBN 0-684-19036-2. 4-7

People concerned with the rights of all humans have been expressing their beliefs throughout history. The text chronologically organizes profiles of some of these people. In the early New World, human rights advocates included Anne Hutchinson and Roger Williams. In the nineteenth century, such people as Dorothea Dix and Frederick Douglass professed their beliefs. In the Industrial Age, Susan B. Anthony and Andrew Carnegie are examples. The twentieth century contained such figures as Emma Goldman, Jacob Riis, Cesar Chavez, and Martin Luther King, Jr. For Further Reading and Index.

1055.   Jacobs, William Jay. **Great Lives**: **World Religions**. New York: Atheneum, 1996. 280p. $23. ISBN 0-689-80486-5. 4-7

The text covers religions and religious leaders throughout world history. Beginning with the religions of ancient Egypt and Persia, it continues with Asian religions, Judaism, Christianity, and Islam. Among the figures presented are Amenhotep IV, Zarathustra, Confucius, Buddha, Muhammad, Mahavira, Gandhi, Jesus, Khomeini, Moses, Jeremiah, Meir, Erasmus, Thomas Aquinas, John Calvin, John Wesley, George Fox, Roger Williams, Anne Hutchinson, Martin Luther King, Jr., Mother Teresa, and Joseph Smith. If appropriate, a brief interpretation of a person's theology also appears. Further Reading and Index.

1056.   Jacobs, William Jay. **Search for Peace: The Story of the United Nations**. New York: Scribner's, 1994. 144p. $14.95. ISBN 0-684-19652-2. 7-12

World War II may have been the result of the failed League of Nations. But in 1945, countries realized that they needed to find some way to keep peace. Thus, the United Nations was founded. The text discusses the events that led to its beginning, the structure of the organization, some of its notable successes and disappointments at peacekeeping, and its specialized agencies. Conclusion, Universal Declaration of Human Rights, Important Events in the History of the United Nations, For Further Reading, and Index.

1057.   Jacobs, William Jay. **World Government**. New York: Scribner's, 1992. 288p. $22.95. ISBN 0-684-19285-3. (Great Lives). 7 up

The text includes short biographies of up to 14 pages on such leaders as Napoleon Bonaparte (1769-1821), Vladimir Lenin (1870-1924), Adolf Hitler (1889-1945), Winston Churchill (1874-1965), Mohandas Gandhi (1869-1948), Mao Tse-tung (1893-1976), Charles de Gaulle (1890-1970), Golda Meir (1898-1978), Ruholla Khomeini (1900-1989), and Mikhail Gorbachev (b. 1931). Each entry presents the early lives of these people and shows what events led them to become leaders. Among the resources Jacobs used are diary entries, excerpts from published writings, and quotations. Photographs and For Further Reading.

1058. Jaffe, Steven. **Who Were the Founding Fathers? Two Hundred Years of Reinventing American History**. New York: Henry Holt, 1996. 227p. $16.95. ISBN 0-8050-3102-2. 6 up
The text looks at the way generations have reinterpreted history based on their own needs and politics. It examines the decisions of the founders such as Jefferson and Adams and uses cartoons and reproductions to enhance the idea that values taken for granted may not be as old or as entrenched as one supposes. Bibliography, Notes, and Index.

1059. Jakes, John. **Homeland**. New York: Doubleday, 1993. 785p. $6.99pa. ISBN 0-553-56499-4pa. YA
Pauli Kroner, 14 in 1892, leaves Berlin via steerage for the United States with monetary help from his dying Aunt Lotte for the fare. He goes to Chicago to be with his uncle, a brewer. After he becomes involved in the family's bickering, he helps an older cousin run away and is, in turn, banished from the family. Although Paul (his name changed in Chicago) wants to be a painter, he has little skill. However, he has the good luck to use George Eastman's recently invented Kodak, and his life changes. Among the people living during the time who appear in the novel are corrupt politicians and social reformers such as Eugene Debs, Carl Schurz, Jane Addams, and Clara Barton. Labor battles and Theodore Roosevelt's Rough Riders charging up San Juan Hill also have roles in Paul's story.

1060. Jakoubek, Robert. **Adam Clayton Powell, Jr.** New York: Chelsea House, 1988. 112p. $18.95; $7.95pa. ISBN 1-55546-606-0; 0-7910-0213-6pa. (Black Americans of Achievement). 5 up
Adam Clayton Powell, Jr. (1908-1972) was a minister of the Abyssinian Baptist Church in Harlem. He gave impassioned sermons and organized protests against racial discrimination in business practices. He won election to the New York City Council in 1941 and to the U.S. House of Representatives in 1944. He wanted civil rights legislation and social welfare programs. When he became chair of the House Education and Labor Committee in the 1960s, he was in a position to guide civil rights bills through Congress. He remained committed to racial equality even while being maligned by others in the latter part of his career. Photographs enhance the text. Chronology, Further Reading, and Index.

1061. Jakoubek, Robert E. **The Colonial Mosaic: American Women 1600-1700**. New York: Oxford University Press, 1994. 144p. $15. ISBN 0-19-508015-7. (The Young Oxford History of Women in the United States). 9 up
The text looks at the birth of the United States and the roles of women who used their wills when they could not use their votes. Topics covered include race relations, women in the colonial economy, life on the plantation, and the introduction of slavery into the colonies. Chronology, Further Reading, and Index.

1062. Jakoubek, Robert E. **Harriet Beecher Stowe**. New York: Chelsea House, 1989. 110p. $18.95. ISBN 1-55546-683-4. (American Women of Achievement). 5 up
Harriet Beecher Stowe (1811-1896) grew under the guidance of a stern religious father. She moved with her family to Cincinnati, Ohio, where she met the theologian Calvin Stowe and married him. She began publishing articles after talking to both abolitionists and fugitive slaves who lived across the Ohio River in the slave state of Kentucky. When she, her husband, and five children left for Maine, she was convinced that slavery had to be abolished. Abraham Lincoln commented that her book, *Uncle Tom's Cabin*, was one of the factors leading to the Civil War. After the war, she spoke on various topics, including feminism. Photographs, engravings, and reproductions enhance the text. Chronology, Further Reading, and Index.

1063. Jakoubek, Robert. **Joe Louis: Heavyweight Champion**. New York: Chelsea House, 1990. 128p. $18.95. ISBN 0-7910-0244-6. (Black Americans of Achievement). 5 up
Joe Louis Barrow (1914-1981) grew up in Alabama and a Detroit ghetto, where he began boxing. He was soundly defeated in his first two bouts and spent the next six months shoving truck bodies onto a conveyor belt. Then he returned to the ring, winning 50 of his next 53 fights. He became the leading contender for the heavyweight title in 1935, but in 1936 his loss to Hitler's favorite, Max Schmeling, cost him approval. In 1937, however, he won the championship, and a year later fought Schmeling again, knocking him out in the first round. His victory was a blow to the myth of racial inferiority. Photographs enhance the text. Chronology, Further Reading, and Index.

1064. Jakoubek, Robert. **Martin Luther King, Jr.** New York: Chelsea House, 1989. 143p. $18.95; $7.95pa. ISBN 1-55546-597-8; 0-7910-0243-8pa. (Black Americans of Achievement). 5 up
Martin Luther King, Jr. (1929-1968) grew up in the South, where he attended Atlanta's Morehead College and then went to Crozer Seminary and Boston University for advanced theological degrees. He returned to the South in 1954 to begin his pastorate in Montgomery, Alabama, and his fight for civil rights. The text tells of his important affiliations and his philosophy of nonviolence. Photographs enhance the text. Chronology, Further Reading, and Index.

1065.   James, Cary. **Julia Morgan: Architect**. New York: Chelsea House, 1988. 110p. $18.95. ISBN 1-55546-669-9. (American Women of Achievement). 5 up

Julia Morgan (1872-1957) was the first well-known female architect. She received many commissions for women's organizations and private homes as she developed her style. In 1919, she started building William Randolph Hearst's private estate, San Simeon, and worked on it for 20 years. By the end of her career, she had designed more than 700 buildings. Photographs enhance the text. Chronology, Further Reading, and Index.

1066.   James, J. Alison. **Sing for a Gentle Rain**. New York: Atheneum, 1990. 211p. $14.95. ISBN 0-689-31561-9. 7-10

James, a contemporary teenager of 16, has dreams of heat and thirst and an Indian girl whom he does not recognize, while Spring Rain, an Anasazi girl of AD 1300, worries about the drought in the desert where her people live. When James discovers information about the Anasazi in his grandfather's library, he goes to a local museum and sees an Anasazi pot. Then he searches for the place where the pot was found and experiences a unification with the past and the Native American identity of his father, whom he has never known. He and Spring Rain have a romance in which tribal customs become clear, especially when elders require that he participate in a hunting competition to show his worth.

1067.   Jantzen, Steven L. **Hooray for Peace, Hurrah for War: The United States During World War I**. New York: Facts on File, 1991. 181p. $17.95. ISBN 0-8160-2453-7. (Library of American History). 8 up

Using many personal accounts, Jantzen tells of the attitudes of Americans as they prepared for World War I and went through it. The chapters give the background of events leading to its beginning at Sarajevo and the American entrance in 1917. America was proud to fight for its ideals when it made the decision to go to war, but the horror of trench warfare shocked men, and that peace was not everlasting was an even greater blow. Among the people presented are a Princeton student who toughened himself by bathing in ice-cold water before he joined the American Ambulance Service, a pilot shot down behind German lines, Emma Goldman's quiet speeches to soldiers that war was wrong, and a man who refused to put on his uniform after being drafted against his will. Bibliography and Index.

1068.   Jenkins, Tony. **Nicaragua and the United States: Years of Conflict**. New York: Franklin Watts, 1989. 187p. $21.29. ISBN 0-531-10795-7. 9 up

Eleven chapters give the history of the relationship between the United States and Nicaragua, from William Walker and the Manifest Destiny of 1848 up to the Bush and Ortega administrations in 1989. Among the thoughtful topics included are the Sandinistas, Contras, the non-Communists' fear of total suppression, the internal polarization in the church, and liberation theology. Bibliography, Chronology, and Index.

1069.   Jezer, Marty. **Rachel Carson: Biologist and Author**. New York: Chelsea House, 1988. 112p. $18.95. ISBN 1-55546-646-X. (American Women of Achievement). 5 up

An environmentalist who realized that people were destroying the Earth, Rachel Carson (1907-1964) wrote a book, *The Silent Spring*, in 1962. Its publication caused an uproar by companies who tried to convince the public that pesticides were not as dangerous as she claimed. However, the public believed her, and the ecology movement gained much momentum from her words. She died of cancer. Photographs enhance the text. Chronology, Further Reading, and Index.

1070.   Johnson, Cecil. **Cuts: Legendary Black Rodeo Cowboy Bill Pickett**. Fort Worth, TX: Summit, 1994. 224p. $19.95. ISBN 1-56530-162-5. YA

Bill Pickett (c. 1860-1932) became the first Black cowboy inducted into the National Rodeo Cowboy Hall of Fame after a career that spanned 40 years. He invented the rodeo sport of bulldogging, and he was able to grab a steer by the horns, twist its neck, and bite it on the lip before pulling it to the ground. He went around the world displaying his skills and became known as the "Dusky Demon." He was also a man of courage and dignity as this biography shows. Appendix and Bibliography.

1071.   Johnson, Dick, and Glenn Stout. **Ted Williams**. New York: Walker, 1991. 225p. $24.95. ISBN 0-8027-1140-5. 7 up

Ted Williams (b. 1918) wanted people to say that he was the best baseball hitter who ever lived. His .406 average in the 1941 season still remains a triumph. He was a Naval Air Cadet and spent time visiting sick children in hospitals. The text looks at his life and statistics, with many photographs to help tell his story. Bibliography and Index.

1072. Johnson, Jacqueline. **Stokely Carmichael: The Story of Black Power**. Eric Velasquez, illustrator. Englewood Cliffs, NJ: Silver Burdett, 1990. 130p. $12.95. ISBN 0-382-09920-6. (History of the Civil Rights Movement). 5-12

Stokely Carmichael (b. 1941) raised his fist when he was 20 years old and said the words "Black power." He grew up in Trinidad in a well-off family and felt sympathy for those who did not have what he had. When he was 12, the family came to the United States and Harlem, a different world where his color mattered more than anything. The text continues with Carmichael's life as the originator of the Black Panthers and as a leader in the Civil Rights movement. Timetable, Suggested Reading, Sources, and Index.

1073. Johnson, James E. **The Irish in America**. Minneapolis, MN: Lerner, 1981. 80p. $17.50; $5.95pa. ISBN 0-8225-1954-2; 0-8225-3475-4pa. 5-8

More people of Irish descent live in the United States than in Ireland. The potato blight, which began in 1845 and lasted for five years, was a turning point in the history of the country. People either had to stay and starve or leave their homes for another country. Many men who came fought in the Civil War, mainly for the North, in the Irish Brigade. After the war, some men working in the coalfields of Pennsylvania formed the Molly Maguires, a secret organization that terrorized cruel bosses who exploited them. Other difficulties the Irish faced stemmed from their Catholicism. Notable Americans of Irish descent are Eugene O'Neill, F. Scott Fitzgerald, John O'Hara, Mary McCarthy, John McCormack, the Barrymore family, Helen Hayes, John Wayne, Louis Henry Sullivan, John F. Kennedy, and Ronald Reagan. Index.

1074. Johnston, Julie. **Hero of Lesser Causes**. Boston: Joy Street, 1993. 192p. $14.95. ISBN 0-316-46988-2. 5-8

Keely Connor, 12, loves to imagine that she is a knight riding a steed instead of a breadwagon horse. When her brother becomes paralyzed from polio in 1946, she spends the next year trying to interest him in living. He nearly dies before he realizes the value of his life.

1075. Johnston, Norma. **Harriet: The Life and World of Harriet Beecher Stowe**. New York: Four Winds, 1994. 239p. $16.95. ISBN 0-02-747714-2. 6 up

In 1852, after the passage of the Fugitive Slave Law and in the years preceding the Civil War, Harriet Beecher Stowe (1811-1896) and her book *Uncle Tom's Cabin* were important lights in the culture. As a middle-class white Calvinist, Stowe believed that everyone had equal rights under God. She faced the knowledge that her parents had wanted a boy, the loss of her mother and her sons, depression and physical illnesses, a husband who loved and respected her but could never quite support their family, and the misuse of her book when people retold it in a pejorative manner. Books for Further Reading and Index.

1076. Jones, Adrienne. **Long Time Passing**. New York: HarperCollins, 1990. 245p. $14.98. ISBN 0-06-023056-8. 7 up

In 1969, Jonas's life changed because his mother died in a car accident and his father left for Vietnam. Jonas goes to live with a cousin in northern California, and there he meets a one-armed sailor and a beautiful girl, Auleen, who is commited to peace rather than war. Jonas hears that his father is missing in action, and he leaves Auleen to enlist and search for his father. Unfortunately, he does not fit the military psyche. *New York Public Library Books for the Teen Age.*

1077. Jones, Douglas C. **The Barefoot Brigade**. New York: Henry Holt, 1980. 311p. $15.50. ISBN 0-03-060041-3. YA

Noah's sentence in 1861 for stealing a pig is to serve in the Rebel army fighting against the North. Away for four years, he meets several people, including Martin Hasford. Martin wants to be a minister, but he has left his family to fight for a cause in which he believes. After the war, they begin the long walk to Arkansas, but soldiers in Virginia shoot Noah because they think he might be connected to Abraham Lincoln's assassination.

1078. Jones, Douglas C. **Come Winter**. 1989. Fayetteville, AR: University of Arkansas Press, 1992. 418p. $14.95pa. ISBN 1-55728-259-5pa. YA

In *Elkhorn Tavern*, Roman stays home during the Civil War, and in *Roman*, he makes money in Kansas. As the protagonist in this novel, Roman returns to Arkansas where he lives until his death in 1899. After his marriage is not what he expected, he fathers a child out of wedlock and continues his role as the town's leading banker and political power although some of his decisions seem to ignore the law.

1079. Jones, Douglas C. **Elkhorn Tavern**. New York: Henry Holt, 1980. 311p. $12.95. ISBN 0-03-050926-2. New York: HarperCollins, 1996. 311p. $4.99pa. ISBN 0-06-100923-7pa. YA

Roman, 15, sees jayhawkers, or Northern partisans, arriving from Missouri and passing through his Arkansas valley in 1861 after his father has left to join the Rebel forces. He, his mother, and his sister prepare for their destruction. The armies fight the Battle of Pea Ridge nearby and ruin the area, but their home remains reasonably untouched. After the battle, an Indian brings a Yankee with a severed arm to their home, and while they nurse the man back to health, Roman's sister falls in love with him.

1080. Jones, Douglas C. **Gone the Dreams and Dancing**. New York: Henry Holt, 1984. 323p. $15.95. ISBN 0-03-060043-X. New York: HarperCollins, 1995. 323p. $4.50pa. ISBN 0-06-100850-8pa. YA

Liverpool Morgan helps Kwahadi, the half-white Comanche leader, find the bones of his white mother in 1875. He wants the bones to be buried next to those of his Comanche mother so the cycle of that part of his life can end. Liver continues the story of the Comanches as the white government finally destroys their power.

1081. Jones, Douglas C. **Remember Santiago**. New York: Henry Holt, 1988. 354p. $19.95. ISBN 0-8050-0776-8. YA

When Eben Pay comes to Fort Smith, Arkansas, he meets a Cherokee woman, marries her, and fathers a child. His wife dies in childbirth, and in his distraught state, he leaves to join the army fighting in Cuba during 1898. Even though Clara Barton and Theodore Roosevelt also participate, the battle plan is disorganized and frustrating, so he returns home ready to accept his son.

1082. Jones, Douglas C. **Roman**. New York: Henry Holt, 1986. 389p. $15.95. ISBN 0-03-060044-8. New York: HarperCollins, 1996. 389p. $5.50pa. ISBN 0-06-100922-9pa. YA

The protagonist of *Elkhorn Tavern*, Roman, leaves his Arkansas home for Leavenworth, Kansas, at his father's return from the Civil War. He stops fighting the Cherokee, and people encourage him to become a politician. He chooses to buy his partner's shares of their businesses so that he can return to Arkansas to the woman he loves as a wealthy man.

1083. Jones, Douglas C. **The Search for Temperance Moon**. New York: Henry Holt, 1991. 324p. $22.50. ISBN 0-8050-1387-3. New York: HarperCollins, 1994. 324p. $4.50pa. ISBN 0-06-100755-2pa. YA

Someone murders Temperance Moon, an outlaw queen from the Indian nations, after the Civil War ends. Her daughter has become the madam of Fort Smith, Arkansas's best brothel, and she hires an ex-marshal to find her mother's murderer. People remember Temperance for both her wildness and her kindness, and they help with the investigation.

1084. Jones, Douglas C. **Weedy Rough**. New York: Henry Holt, 1981. 345p. $13.95. ISBN 0-03-050931-9. YA

Eben Pay's half-breed son, Barton, comes to Weedy Rough, Arkansas, and begins to invest money in it. Most of the town hates Cherokees, and as part Cherokee, he is no less suspect. When someone robs a bank in 1925, a witness accuses Barton Pay's son. The expert defense by Eben Pay proves the boy's innocence.

1085. Jones, Douglas C. **Winding Stair**. 1979. New York: Tor Books, 1991. 277p. $4.95pa. ISBN 0-8125-8461-9pa. YA

Four murders and a rape occur soon after Eben Pay, a young lawyer, arrives in Fort Smith, Arkansas. Jennie, 18, is the lone survivor of the crime. Pay worries about the effects of the crime on her even after the capture, conviction, and hanging of the four men involved.

1086. Jones, Hettie. **Big Star Fallin' Mama: Five Women in Black Music**. 1974. New York: Viking, 1995. 147p. $14.99. ISBN 0-670-85621-5. 8 up

The role of African American women is very strong in the musical heritage of the United States. After defining the blues, Jones presents profiles of Ma Rainey (1886-1939), Bessie Smith (c. 1894-1937), Mahalia Jackson (1911-1972), Billie Holiday (1916-1959), and Aretha Franklin (b. 1942). Afterword: Old Blues and News, Selected Bibliography, Selected Discography, Other Notable Women in Black Music, and Index.

1087. Jones, Jayne Clark. **The American Indians in America**. Minneapolis, MN: Lerner, 1991. 72p. $9.95; $3.95pa. ISBN 0-8225-0240-2; 0-8225-1037-5pa. (In America). 7 up

The first half of this history of Native American–white relationships begins with Tecumseh's attempts to stop white expansion in 1812 and continues through the remainder of the nineteenth century. The second half concentrates on the twentieth century while describing fishing rights, treaty issues, and the situations at Alcatraz and Wounded Knee. A final chapter highlights the contributions of Native Americans in sports, the arts, and government. Index.

1088. Jones, Mary, ed. **The American Frontier: Opposing Viewpoints**. San Diego, CA: Greenhaven, 1994. 307p. $19.95. ISBN 1-56510-085-9. (Opposing Viewpoints). 10 up

Many historians might see the frontier experience as a defining attribute of the American character because it has happened repeatedly. In short essays both pro and con written by public figures thinking about the many times a new frontier has been conquered, the text examines different viewpoints toward its importance in the American psyche. Disagreement over the role of the frontier includes the concern as to whether the Indian was civilized or not, the role of the military in defending against "savages," and whether the Indians should assert their ethnic identity or submerge it in the dominant culture. A look at the fur trader and the miner before and after the advent of technology gives concepts of trade. Women are either supportive or independent, and the racial question centers on the Chinese staying or leaving. The frontier's mythic heroes might also be considered psychopaths: white and Black cowboys, Calamity Jane, and Billy the Kid. When seeing how the contemporary media portrays the West, one must question the motives—mere entertainment, cultural accuracy, historical importance, or advertisement of a product. For Discussion, Chronology, Annotated Bibliography, and Index.

1089.   Jones, Rebecca C. **The President Has Been Shot: True Stories of the Attacks on Ten U.S. Presidents**. New York: Dutton, 1996. 134p. $14.99. ISBN 0-525-45333-4. 4-9

The text looks at four assassinations and another seven attacks that were unsuccessful. It presents a chronology of these attacks and the resulting changes in security for the presidents. It also notes that when doctors could not find the bullet in President McKinley, they did not think to use the latest medical advance, the x-ray machine. Further Reading and Index.

1090.   Jones, S. D. **Our Century: 1950-1960**. Milwaukee, WI: Gareth Stevens, 1993. 64p. $23.93. ISBN 0-8368-1037-6. 3 up

Written as if a newspaper, the book's short articles give an overview of the decade. Included are statistics, daily life in America, Red China entering the Korean conflict, the Hungarian revolt, Fidel Castro in Cuba, Joseph McCarthy, civil rights, Edmund Hillary, Albert Schweitzer, *Sputnik*, Jonas Salk, Evita Peron, and Marilyn Monroe. Glossary, Books for Further Reading, Places to Write or Visit, and Index.

1091.   Jones, Ted. **The Fifth Conspiracy: A Novel**. Novato, CA: Presidio Press, 1995. 464p. $21.95. ISBN 0-89141-515-7. YA

The story of the Healy and Thornton families begun in *Hard Road to Gettysburg* continues here as the Battle of Gettysburg begins in 1863. The twin brothers, Samuel and Simon, fight in the opposing armies and meet in battle. Military strategy and love situations propel the plot forward as the troops move from Gettysburg to Georgia and from Vicksburg to Richmond.

1092.   Jones, Ted. **Hard Road to Gettysburg: A Novel**. San Francisco: Presidio Press, 1993. 316p. $21.95. ISBN 0-89141-445-2. YA

Twins born in 1839 become separated, one living on one side of the Mason-Dixon line and one on the other. Neither knows that the other exists until the Civil War starts. Jones uses the device of the aunt's diary to show what happened to the two boys during their childhoods. Their situation in the war becomes the focus as the novel progresses.

1093.   Josephson, Judith Pinkerton. **Allan Pinkerton: The Original Private Eye**. Minneapolis, MN: Lerner, 1996. 128p. $17.21. ISBN 0-8225-4923-9. (Lerner Biographies). 5 up

Allan Pinkerton (1819-1884) came to the United States from Scotland and began the detective trade. He and his workers recorded their facts and codes in small black notebooks and worked undercover with disguises. He helped to find many criminals and rebuilt his business after the Great Chicago Fire destroyed it. Detective work today is based on his solid beginning. Sources, Bibliography, and Index.

K

1094.   Kadohata, Cynthia. **The Floating World**. New York: Viking, 1989. 196p. $17.95. ISBN 0-670-82680-4. New York: Ballantine, 1991. 196p. $5.99pa. ISBN 0-345-36756-1pa. YA

Olivia, a Japanese American, goes with her grandmother, her stepfather, her mother, and her brothers along the coast of California in the 1950s. Her stepfather works at transient jobs along the way, and her grandmother talks incessantly. Eventually the family settles in Arkansas, but Olivia moves to California, where she continues to hear in her mind the stories of her youth, although her grandmother has long since died. They give her guidance in her new life.

1095.   Kallen, Stuart A. **Martin Luther King: A Man and His Dream**. Minneapolis, MN: Abdo, 1993. 48p. $21.36. ISBN 1-56239-256-5. 7 up

The text examines the life of Martin Luther King, Jr. (1929-1968): his growing up with Jim Crow laws, his concerns about Gandhi and marriage, the bus boycott, the various conflicts in the streets of cities in the nation, and his work in Alabama before his death in Memphis. Photographs, Glossary, and Index.

1096.   Kallen, Stuart A. **Thurgood Marshall: A Dream of Justice for All**. Minneapolis, MN: Abdo, 1993. 40p. $14.96. ISBN 1-56239-258-1. (I Have a Dream). 5-9

This biography of Thurgood Marshall (1908-1993) begins with his boss ordering him to go to the White House to see Lyndon Johnson in 1967. He did, and when he arrived, Johnson told him, "I'm going to put you on the Supreme Court." Marshall's response was "Oh, yippee, what did you say?" The rest of the text presents Marshall's life as a civil rights lawyer who helped diminish racial injustice. Glossary and Index.

1097.   Kantor, MacKinlay. **Gettysburg**. 1952. New York: Random House, 1987. 151p. $4.99pa. ISBN 0-394-89181-3pa. (Landmark Books). 7 up

More than 7,000 soldiers were killed at Gettysburg and more than 30,000 were wounded. Beginning on July 1, 1863, the battle lasted three days. Louisa May Alcott, Dorothea Dix, Walt Whitman, and Clara Barton tried to nurse these men, but even they could not stop the dying. This text humanizes this dreadful event by seeing it in terms of individuals who lived or fought in Gettysburg. Ending the account is Abraham Lincoln's Gettysburg address, delivered to the people in November of that year when the cemetery for those who fought was dedicated. Index.

1098.   Karl, Jean. **America Alive: A History**. Ian Schoenherr, illustrator. New York: Philomel, 1994. 120p. $22.95. ISBN 0-399-22013-5. 5-8

This history of the United States, tagged as a personal history, touches on almost every subject, from the crossing of the Bering Strait to the election of Bill Clinton as President. Karl sees history as a continuum and writes about it as if it occurs sequentially. She tries to give an overall view, such as telling what the Blacks and Indians were doing while the whites fought in battles. Illustrations, including pictures of appropriate individuals, appear in the borders of the pages. Bibliography and Index.

1099.   Karr, Kathleen. **The Cave**. New York: Farrar, Straus & Giroux, 1994. 165p. $16. ISBN 0-374-31230-3. 5-7

Christine, 12, and her family cope with dust during the Depression in the Black Hills of South Dakota. She finds a cave with white fish swimming in a stream inside. She reluctantly tells her brother, and the two visit the cave repeatedly without telling their parents. When her father decides that they will have to leave if it does not rain, she tries to show him the cave, but a tornado has destroyed it. However, she and her brother saved the perfectly formed geodes that they found on prior visits to the cave and can sell them for the family's survival.

1100.   Karr, Kathleen. **Gideon and the Mummy Professor**. New York: Atheneum, 1993. 137p. $16. ISBN 0-374-32563-4. 5-8

In the mid-nineteenth century, Gideon, 12, and his father travel through the South in Mississippi with a mummy that intermittently sheds jewels from its wrappings. Gideon grew up in Egypt while his father was in diplomatic service, and when George, the mummy, and his father are at odds, Gideon joins George. George saves them by producing a scarab. They are pursued by jewel thieves and a criminal from New Orleans, but a voodoo queen rescues them during their adventures.

1101.   Karr, Kathleen. **Go West, Young Women!** New York: HarperCollins, 1996. 160p. $14.95; $4.50pa. ISBN 0-06-027151-5; 0-06-440495-1pa. (The Petticoat Party, Book 1). 4-7

Because falling buffalo have killed the ineffectual men in the wagon party going to Oregon, their women have to finish the journey without them. Phoebe, 12, tells about their humorous escapades and the romance that begins between two teenage girls and two Pawnee braves that they meet on the trail. The group finally arrives in Fort Laramie, but the journey is not complete.

1102.   Karr, Kathleen. **In the Kaiser's Clutch**. New York: Farrar, Straus & Giroux, 1995. 144p. $15. ISBN 0-374-33638-5. 5-8

The twins Fritz and Nelly, 15 in 1918, star in their mother's silent-movie serial, *In the Kaiser's Clutch*, after the mysterious death of their father in a munitions store explosion. Their real lives mirror their movie lives when they discover that someone is pursuing them and trying to keep them from finding out about their father's death. The story reveals the problems of making films on low budgets and the need to make money to pursue one's art.

1103.   Karr, Kathleen. **It Ain't Always Easy**. New York: Farrar, Straus & Giroux, 1990. 229p. $14.95. ISBN 0-374-33645-8. 5-8

Jack, 11, tells the story of how the New York Children's Aid Society planned to take him and Mandy, eight, on the orphan train west in 1882. They miss the train and live in a coal bin. They then have problems in Pennsylvania that cause Jack to return to New York for help from Miss Blackman of the Children's Aid Society. Mandy goes west, and a farmer mistreats her, but Miss Blackman and her suitor rescue her. The four then go to Nebraska to become a family.

1104.   Karr, Kathleen. **Oh, Those Harper Girls!** New York: Farrar, Straus, & Giroux, 1992. 182p. $16; $4.95pa. ISBN 0-374-35609-2; 0-374-45599-6pa. 7 up

When Lily's father has a payment due on the Texas ranch in 1869, he has difficulty getting the money. Lily, 13, convinces her five older sisters to try cattle rustling. Their scheme fails, and they try to rob a stage coach. After their arrest, they are proclaimed innocent, but their exploits attract media attention from reporters willing to pay for their story and a stage tour that earns them enough money to save the ranch.

1105.   Karr, Kathleen. **Phoebe's Folly**. New York: HarperCollins, 1996. 199p. $14.95; $4.50pa. ISBN 0-06-027153-1; 0-06-440496-Xpa. (The Petticoat Party, Book 2). 5 up

While in Fort Laramie, the women of the Petticoat Party arm themselves with rifles and show their ability to use them on the next leg of their Oregon Trail journey. Phoebe, 12, makes a comment that prompts the Snake Indians to challenge them to a shooting contest. They survive the challenge and eventually have the thrill of seeing Mount Hood rise in the distance.

1106.   Kassem, Lou. **Listen for Rachel**. New York: Margaret K. McElderry, Macmillan, 1986. 176p. $11.95. ISBN 0-689-50396-2. 6-9

At 14, Rachel has to leave Nashville to live with her grandparents in Appalachia after her parents die in a fire. She adjusts to the new home because she loves to ride her grandfather's horses and thinks that the mountains are beautiful. But discord arrives when the Civil War looms; her cousins and her fiancé go to fight, and the "poor white trash" threaten to rape her. An old woman, however, encourages her ability to heal with herbs, and this reassurance comforts her.

1107.   Kastner, Joseph. **John James Audubon**. New York: Harry N. Abrams, 1992. 92p. $19.95. ISBN 0-8109-1918-4. (First Impressions). YA

When John James Audubon (1785-1851) arrived from France at 18, he spoke little English. But his social graces helped him to find friends and entertainment. He loved the outdoors, and soon his passion for American birds became an obsession. He began tracking, observing, sketching, and painting every bird he could find. He developed the largest and most accurate collection of paintings, but he had to go to England to get them published. Index.

1108.   Katcher, Philip. **The Civil War Source Book**. New York: Facts on File, 1992. 318p. $35. ISBN 0-8160-2823-0. YA

Katcher discusses 40 topics that tell about the Civil War from both sides. Among the topics are equipment, Union and Confederate military tactics on land and sea, and biographies of the leaders. Photographs, charts, maps, and newspaper stories from the times clarify the text. Bibliography and Index.

1109.   Katz, Jane B., comp. **We Rode the Wind: Recollections of Native American Life**. 1975. Minneapolis, MN: Runestone, 1995. 128p. $19.95. ISBN 0-8225-3154-2. 7 up

In this collection of memories from nineteenth-century Native Americans of the Plains, Katz includes Charles A. Eastman of the Santee, John Stands in Timber of the Cheyenne, Two Leggings of the Crow, Chief Luther Standing Bear of the Oglala band of the Teton Lakota Sioux, William Whipple Warren of the Ojibway, Waheenee of the Hidatsa, Jim Whitewolf of the Kiowa-Apache, and Black Elk of the Oglala Sioux. Photographs and drawings highlight the text. Glossary, Sources, and Index.

1110. Katz, William L. **The Black West**. 2d ed. Seattle, WA: Open Hand, 1987. 348p. $14.95pa ISBN 0-940880-18-0pa. YA

Photographs complement this text about the Blacks who settled the West. Chapter topics include explorers, fur traders, early settlers, slavery in the West, California, cowboys, homesteaders, the Black infantry and cavalry, dreams crushed in Oklahoma, the Spanish-American War, and Black women on the last frontier. Among the specific names are Estevan (c. 1500-1539), Jean Baptiste Pointe du Sable (1745-1818), the Bonga family (c. 1800-1850), James P. Beckwourth (1798-1866), Lucy and Abijah Prince (c. 1750-1821), Greenbury Logan (c. 1831), John Jones (1816-1879), George Washington Bush (c. 1800-1863), Aunt Clara Brown (1803-c. 1880), Mifflin W. Gibbs (1828-1903), Nat Love or "Deadwood Dick" (1854-c. 1900), Cherokee Bill (c. 1865-1896), Mary Fields (c. 1830-1914), Ben Hodges (?-1929), Isom Dart (1849-1900), and Barney Ford and Henry O. Wagoner (c. 1850-1900). Appendix, Bibliography, and Index.

1111. Katz, William Loren. **Black Women of the Old West**. New York: Atheneum, 1995. 84p. $18. ISBN 0-689-31944-4. 5-8

The text looks at African American women who helped settle the West since colonial times. Because finding documentation on their achievements is difficult, Katz presents vignettes of them. Among those discussed are Sarah Lester, expelled from a San Francisco school for being too bright by her white neighbors; Mary Pleasant, both a civil rights activist and a bordello owner; Harriet Scott, wife of Dred; and Lucy Parsons, wife of Alfred. Photographs, Bibliography, and Index. *Notable Children's Trade Books in the Field of Social Studies.*

1112. Katz, William Loren. **Breaking the Chains: African-American Slave Resistance**. New York: Atheneum, 1990. 194p. $16. ISBN 0-689-31493. 5 up

Katz posits that slavery in the New World began the day that Christopher Columbus arrived. Columbus bought with him the knowledge that other slave owners, including African slave holders, had: Slaves had to be removed from their homes because their kinsmen would fight to regain their freedom. For this reason (among others), Africans were shipped to America. The chapters cover the difficulties and deprivations slaves endured, those who attempted to escape, the abolitionists who tried to help, and the freedom that the Civil War brought. Bibliography and Index.

1113. Katz, William Loren. **The Civil War to the Last Frontier: 1850-1880s**. Austin, TX: Raintree/Steck-Vaughn, 1993. 96p. $25.68; $6.96pa. ISBN 0-8114-6277-3; 0-8114-2914-8pa. (A History of Multicultural America). 7 up

This interpretation of American history recounts the contributions of all Americans: people of color, women, religious groups, and ethnic groups. In this volume, sidebars give information about such people and topics as Wladimir Kryzyzanowski, women in the Civil War, Robert Smalls and the *Planter*, Carl Schurz, Elias Hill, Black senators from Mississippi, the Cherokee, Seminole Negro Indian scouts, women's clubs, Chinese American theater, Oscar Ameringer of the Knights of Labor, Apaches, Black women in the West, the Goldwater brothers, and "Stagecoach Mary" Fields. Further Reading and Index.

1114. Katz, William Loren. **Exploration to the War of 1812: 1492-1814**. Austin, TX: Raintree/Steck-Vaughn, 1993. 96p. $25.68; $6.96pa. ISBN 0-8114-6275-7; 0-8114-2912-1pa. (A History of Multicultural America). 7 up

This interpretation of American history recounts the contributions of all Americans: people of color, women, religious groups, and ethnic groups. Sidebars give information about such people and topics as Borinquen, Pee Dee River bonding, alternate societies in the Americas, Jacob Leisler, Phyllis Wheatley, Benjamin Lay, Anthony Benezet, Benjamin Banneker, David Rittenhouse, John Peter Zenger, and Albert Gallatin. Further Reading and Index.

1115. Katz, William Loren. **The Great Migrations: 1880s-1912**. Austin, TX: Raintree/Steck-Vaughn, 1993. 96p. $25.68; $6.96pa. ISBN 0-8114-6278-1; 0-8114-2915-6pa. (A History of Multicultural America). 7 up

This interpretation of American history recounts the contributions of all Americans: people of color, women, religious groups, and ethnic groups. In this volume, sidebars give information about such people and topics as New York City's Lower East Side, Baltic peoples, Jews, baseball, Dr. Daniel Hale Williams, the Balkans and Greece, Armenians, Czechs, Slovaks, Poles, Italians, Japanese, Koreans, Arabs, journalists, Jonas Sliupas, Khalil Gibran, Madam C. J. Walker, Ida B. Wells, Paul Lawrence Dunbar, and Peter Finley Dunne. Further Reading and Index.

1116. Katz, William Loren. **The Great Society to the Reagan Era: 19641990**. Austin, TX: Raintree/Steck-Vaughn, 1993. 96p. $25.68; $6.96pa. ISBN 0-8114-6282-X; 0-8114-2937-7pa. (A History of Multicultural America). 7 up

This interpretation of American history recounts the contributions of all Americans: people of color, women, religious groups, and ethnic groups. In this volume, sidebars give information about such people and topics as the Black Panthers, the Vietnam War, *La Raza*, Native Americans, the "Benign Neglect" policy, Thurgood Marshall, Arabs, immigrants, Ralph Nader, Bella Abzug, and Ralph Bunche. Further Reading and Index.

1117. Katz, William Loren. **Minorities Today**. Austin, TX: Raintree/Steck-Vaughn, 1993. 96p. $25.68; $6.96pa. ISBN 0-8114-6281-1; 0-8114-2918-0pa. (A History of Multicultural America). 7 up

This interpretation of American history recounts the contributions of all Americans: people of color, women, religious groups, and ethnic groups. In this volume, sidebars give information about such people and topics as Guillermo Linares, Dennis Rivera, Ron Dellums, Mae Carol Jemison, sports, immigrants, and Reverend Cecil Murray. Further Reading and Index.

1118. Katz, William Loren. **The New Freedom to the New Deal: 1913-1939**. Austin, TX: Raintree/SteckVaughn, 1993. 96p. $25.68; $6.96pa. ISBN 0-8114-6279-X; 0-8114-2916-4pa. (A History of Multicultural America). 7 up

This interpretation of American history recounts the contributions of all Americans—people of color, women, religious groups, and ethnic groups. In this volume, sidebars give information about such people and topics as Ole Rolvaag, Louis B. Mayer, Rudolph Valentino, Walter White, W. E. B. Du Bois, Bessie Smith, Eugene Debs, A. Philip Randolph, Mother Jones, Helen Keller, Dr. Carlos Montezuma, Frank Murphy, Carlos Bulosan, Salaria Key, and Frances Perkins. Further Reading and Index.

1119. Katz, William Loren. **The Westward Movement and Abolitionism: 1815-1850**. Austin, TX: Raintree/Steck-Vaughn, 1993. 96p. $25.68; $6.96pa. ISBN 0-8114-6276-5; 0-8114-2913-Xpa. (A History of Multicultural America). 7 up

This interpretation of American history recounts the contributions of all Americans: people of color, women, religious groups, and ethnic groups. In this volume, sidebars give information about such people and topics as Irish in the city, German immigrants, mountain men, the war in Florida, southern cities and slavery, New Orleans, Texas, the Oregon Trail, women, Prudence Crandall, Dr. Elizabeth Blackwell, and Yung Wing. Further Reading and Index.

1120. Katz, William Loren. **World War II to the New Frontier: 1940-1963**. Austin, TX: Raintree/Steck-Vaughn, 1993. 96p. $25.68; $6.96pa. ISBN 0-8114-6280-3; 0-8114-2917-2pa. (A History of Multicultural America). 7 up

This interpretation of American history recounts the contributions of all Americans: people of color, women, religious groups, and ethnic groups. In this volume, sidebars give information about such people and topics as Japanese American soldiers, postwar women, Eleanor Roosevelt, the Red scare, Puerto Ricans, desegregating the schools, Kennedy and civil rights, Montgomery and Birmingham, Bernard Baruch, Jackie Robinson, and Fannie Lou Hamer. Further Reading and Index.

1121. Katz, William Loren, and Paula A. Franklin. **Proudly Red and Black: Stories of African and Native Americans**. New York: Atheneum, 1993. 88p. $13.95. ISBN 0-689-31801-4. 5-8

Because official birth and death records were not kept for people of color for many years, the ancestry of African and Native Americans is cloudy. The text looks at Black Indians who made contributions to society even though they faced many barriers. Those profiled include Paul Cuffe (1759-1817), a New England trader; Edward Rose (1780?-1830?), a frontiersman; John Horse (1812-1882), a Black Seminole leader; Edmonia Lewis (1845-1911?), sculptor; George Henry White (1852-1918), militant Congressman; and Bill Pickett (1870-1932), rodeo star. Bibliography and Index.

1122. Kaye, Judith. **The Life of Alexander Fleming**. New York: Twenty-First Century Books, 1993. 80p. $13.95. ISBN 0-8050-2300-3. (Pioneers in Health and Medicine). 5-7

Alexander Fleming (1881-1955) told people that he "played with microbes" for a living. He discovered penicillin, the first antibiotic, which increased lifespan by an average of 30 years for humans. Although he said that its discovery was a matter of chance and fortune, he was curious, creative, and dedicated to fighting infection and disease. For his work, he won the Nobel Prize. For Further Reading and Index.

1123. Kaye, Judith. **The Life of Benjamin Spock**. New York: Twenty-First Century Books, 1993. 80p. $13.95. ISBN 0-8050-2301-1. (Pioneers in Health and Medicine). 4-7

Benjamin Spock (b. 1903) told parents to trust themselves as they tried to raise their children. He first published his book, *Baby and Child Care*, in 1946, and it changed the way parents raised American children, for good or for bad. In his later life, he involved himself in larger issues, such as nuclear disarmament and world peace. He even went to jail for his beliefs. For Further Reading and Index.

1124. Kaye, Judith. **The Life of Daniel Hale Williams**. New York: Twenty-First Century Books, 1993. 80p. $13.95. ISBN 0-8050-2302-X. (Pioneers in Health and Medicine). 5 up

Daniel Hale Williams (1856-1931) was an African American doctor who performed the first surgery on the human heart in the nineteenth century and founded the first interracial hospital in the United States. Black-and-white photographs illustrate the text. For Further Reading and Index.

1125.   Kaye, Judith. **The Life of Florence Sabin**. New York: Twenty-First Century Books, 1993. 80p. $13.95. ISBN 0-8050-2299-6. (Pioneers in Health and Medicine). 4-7
    Florence Sabin (1871-1953) spent the first part of her life as a medical researcher and helped discover a cure for tuberculosis. Then she went back to her home state of Colorado, discovered the miserable state of public health, and began working to change the laws and the poor sanitary conditions. One of her last activities was to offer free x-rays on Denver streets so that doctors could identify tuberculosis early for easier treatment. For Further Reading and Index.

1126.   Kaye, Tony. **Lyndon B. Johnson**. New York: Chelsea House, 1988. 112p. $18.95. ISBN 0-87754-536-7. (World Leaders Past and Present). 5 up
    Lyndon B. Johnson (1908-1973) had a grand vision of the American society. He had seen the depressed farmers in Texas in his youth, and he wanted to help them by changing things in Washington. When he became an elected President (after finishing the term of John F. Kennedy), he started his "Great Society" program and brought reform to Medicare, civil rights, pollution laws, and federal aid for the poor. By 1966, the Vietnam War occupied him. He said that the United States was not at war while simultaneously ordering bombing raids and deploying ground troops. Although he achieved much on the national level, the Vietnam War scarred his legacy. Photographs enhance the text. Chronology, Further Reading, and Index.

1127.   Keegan, John. **History of Warfare**. New York: Knopf, 1993. 432p. $30; $15pa. ISBN 0-394-58801-0; 0-679-73082-6pa. YA
    This survey of warfare starts with the beginning of history and continues to the atomic bomb's explosions in Hiroshima and Nagasaki during 1945. Keegan believes not that war is an extension of politics, as Clausewitz does, but that war is an extension of a culture. He draws on various resources from history, anthropology, ethnology, and psychology to express his theories that the threats to peace today are countries who wage war as they did before government or politics were invented. Bibliography and Index.

1128.   Keehn, Sally. **I Am Regina**. New York: Philomel, 1991. 240p. $14.95. ISBN 0-399-21797-5. 4-8
    In 1755, Regina is 11. Allegheny Indians kidnap her and her sister after killing her father and brother. She spends eight years with them, forgets German, and speaks the Allegheny language. Within the tribe, she has both a helpful friend and a spiteful enemy. When they die of smallpox, she knows them well enough to grieve, but she and her sister still miss their mother, who sang a song they cannot forget.

1129.   Keehn, Sally M. **Moon of Two Dark Horses**. New York: Putnam, 1995. 218p. $16.95. ISBN 0-399-22783-0. 4-8
    The ghost of Coshmoo, a young Indian boy killed in the Revolutionary War, relates how he and his friend, son of a white settler, tried to end the hostilities between their people. When the Delaware need money to survive, the differences surge, and fighting begins that eventually kills Coshmoo.

1130.   Keith, Harold. **The Obstinate Land**. 1977. Norman, OK: Levite of Apache, 1993. $12.95pa. ISBN 0-927562-15-4pa. 7-10
    Fritz Romberg, 13, travels with his German-American family from Texas to Cherokee land in northwest Oklahoma during 1893. They suffer drought, hailstorms, robbery, and malicious destruction at the hands of jealous ranchers who want no new settlers. After his father dies in a snowstorm, Fritz becomes the family's sole supporter and earns a reputation for his hard work and honesty.

1131.   Keith, Harold. **Rifles for Watie**. New York: HarperCollins, 1957. 334p. $14.89; $3.95pa. ISBN 0-690-70181-0; 0-06-447030-Xpa. 7 up
    Jeff, 16, looks forward to leaving the Kansas farm in 1861 to fight for the Union cause against Stand Watie, the Cherokee Indian Rebel leader. In the infantry, he watches friends die, but then he becomes a spy. What he discovers is that his enemy is not necessarily on the Confederate side. *Newbery Medal, American Library Association Notable Books for Children,* and *Lewis Carroll Shelf Award.*

1132.   Keller, Emily. **Margaret Bourke-White: A Photographer's Life**. Minneapolis, MN: Lerner, 1996. 128p. $17.21. ISBN 0-8225-4916-6. (Lerner Biographies). 5 up
    The person who helped to develop the photo-essay style of *Life* magazine's news reporting was Margaret Bourke-White (1904-1971). Her photographs of industrial scenes and machinery, people coping during the Depression, World War II battlefields, and a variety of other subjects helped people see these things in a different way. Her work retains its timeless quality. Photographs, Sources, Bibliography, and Index.

1133.   Keller, Helen. **The Story of My Life**. 1954. Mineola, NY: Dover, 1996. 225p. $10.01pa. ISBN 0-486-29249-5pa. 7 up

When 19 months old, Helen Keller (1880-1968) contracted an illness that left her deaf and blind. Her frustration at not being able to communicate led her to be hostile and uncontrollable, behavior that her parents were able to correct through an incredible teacher who came into her life, Annie Sullivan. Keller recounts the things that influenced her in her journey to attend Radcliffe and become a writer.

1134.   Kelley, Robin D. G. **Into the Fire: African Americans Since 1970**. New York: Oxford University Press, 1996. 142p. $21. ISBN 0-19-508701-1. (Young Oxford History of African Americans). 8 up

Among the topics of discussion in this history of the politics, social and economic conditions, and culture of Blacks in America are the rebirth of Black nationalism, the neoconservative movement, Black feminism, interethnic tension, rap music, and the hip-hop culture. Photographs, posters, prints, letters, and additional artwork complement the text. Chronology, Further Reading, and Index.

1135.   Kelly, Kate. **Election Day: An American Holiday, An American History**. New York: Facts on File, 1991. 282p. $24.95. ISBN 0-8160-1871-5. YA

In 1845, a Congressional Act declared that Election Day would be a national holiday; therefore, the presidential election of 1848 was the first holiday. The text covers the history of this day, including the boisterous behavior, fraud, rioting, and general disarray of past election days, with anecdotes and information. It also presents the voting and reporting process as it evolved, the secret ballot, woman suffrage, and voting during the civil rights era. Kelly suggests that modern election-day rituals stem from the election in 1960, when television became an important part of the process. Notes and Index.

1136.   Kelly, Lawrence C. **Federal Indian Policy**. New York: Chelsea House, 1989. 111p. $19.95. ISBN 1-55546-706-7. (Indians of North America). 7 up

The text looks at four centuries of white-Indian relations in the United States beginning with colonial policies. It covers the presidencies of Jefferson through Jackson as they purchased land belonging to the Indians, removal policies before the Civil War, the Post War Reservation Policy, the 1887 Dawes Act, the New Deal, the War on Poverty, the American Indian Movement, and the Reagan presidency. Although not sensational, the text relates fully what the U.S. government has done to the Indians. Photographs, maps, and drawings enhance the text. Further Reading, Glossary, and Index.

1137.   Kelly, Mary Pat. **Proudly We Served: The Men of the USS Mason**. Annapolis, MD: Naval Institute Press, 1995. 198p. $31.95. ISBN 1-55750-453-9. YA

In World War II, the USS *Mason*, with its largely African American crew, escorted six convoys across the Atlantic. The crew performed all the duties of seamanship necessary to take the warship into combat, and they told Kelly their stories. Crews from other ships discriminated against them in ports of call. During a storm on the North Atlantic in 1944, they helped 20 vessels reach safety before repairing damage to the *Mason* despite 40-foot waves. A recommendation that each sailor have a Letter of Commendation placed in their files was ignored. When they went to Belfast, Ireland, they had the first taste of being considered "American," like white navy men. The Irish called them "Yanks," not "tan Yanks" as others did. These stories and others appear in the text. Appendices and Index.

1138.   Kelso, Richard. **Days of Courage: The Little Rock Story**. Mel Williges, illustrator. Austin, TX: Raintree/Steck-Vaughn, 1993. 88p. $24.96; $5.95pa. ISBN 0-8114-7230-2; 0-8114-8070-4pa. (Stories of America—Stand Up and Be Counted). 4-7

When Elizabeth Eckford was 15 in 1957, she was one of nine Black students chosen to integrate Little Rock High School in Alabama. She and the other eight faced danger from hostile white adults determined that their children would not attend school with Blacks. Governor Faubus of Alabama was no help because he supported the white parents, defying a Supreme Court order for immediate integration. Finally, President Eisenhower had to intervene so that these young people could go to school. Epilogue, Afterword, and Notes.

1139.   Kelso, Richard. **Walking for Freedom: The Montgomery Bus Boycott**. Michael Newton, illustrator. Austin, TX: Raintree/Steck-Vaughn, 1993. 52p. $22.83; $4.95pa. ISBN 0-8114-7218-3; 0-8114-8058-5pa. (Stories of America—Working Together). 3-7

In 1949, Mrs. Robinson, who usually drove her car, rode a Montgomery, Alabama, bus instead and inadvertently sat in the whites-only section. The driver's hostile and rude treatment toward her led her to suggest a bus boycott to the Woman's Political Council. They waited six years until the time was right to put the plan into effect. When Rosa Parks refused to rise from her seat in the Black section of the bus for a white man in 1955, the boycott began. It lasted until November 1956, when Montgomery officials changed their laws. Epilogue, Afterword, and Notes.

1140. Kenan, Randall. **James Baldwin**. New York: Chelsea House, 1994. 144p. $19.95; $9.95pa. ISBN 0-7910-2301-X; 0-7910-2876-3pa. (Lives of Notable Gay Men and Lesbians). 9 up

Born in Harlem, James Baldwin (1924-1987) thought he wanted to be a minister until he went to high school and enjoyed writing for the school newspaper. He met Richard Wright in 1945 and began publishing his work after he left for Paris in 1948. His novel *Giovanni's Room*, published in 1956, was a groundbreaking novel about homosexuality. He visited the American South in 1957 and wrote articles for such publications as *Harper's*, where he noted the division of the races. Further Reading, Chronology, and Index.

1141. Kendall, Martha E. **Susan B. Anthony: Voice for Women's Voting Rights**. Springfield, NJ: Enslow, 1997. 128p. $18.95. ISBN 0-89490-780-8. (Historical American Biographies). 6-9

Susan B. Anthony (1820-1906) was an intelligent and educated woman who refused to accept a double standard for women, and she fought for women's rights. The biography looks at her impact on American history as it examines her life. Fact boxes and maps augment the text. Notes, Glossary, Further Reading, and Index.

1142. Kennett, Lee. **Marching Through Georgia: The Story of Soldiers & Civilians During Sherman's Campaign**. New York: HarperCollins, 1995. 418p. $27.50. ISBN 0-06-016815-3. YA

The Union general Sherman began his march toward Georgia with an opening altercation at Buzzard Roost Gap; he entered Savannah 10 months later. His campaign changed the ways wars were waged because he caused havoc in the lives of many civilians who thought their status would protect them from the war. Sherman fought everyone with no exception. The three parts of the text cover the invasion of Joe Brown's Georgia, Atlanta, and the march. Notes, Bibliography, and Index.

1143. Kent, Deborah. **Dorothy Day: Friend to the Forgotten**. Grand Rapids, MI: William B. Eerdman, 1996. 137p. $15; $8pa. ISBN 0-8028-5117-7; 0-8028-5100-2pa. 5-9

Dorothy Day (1897-1980) became known throughout the world as the leader of the Catholic Worker movement. She was a journalist who thought that community service and social justice defined what it means to be human. In her work, she helped publish a newspaper, reached out to all in need, gave solace to the indigent, and guided those who wanted to pursue their inner life of contemplation. She went to jail many times in the 1950s for protesting against nuclear weapons. Photographs and Index.

1144. Kent, Zachary. **Andrew Johnson: Seventeenth President of the United States**. Chicago: Childrens Press, 1989. 100p. $19.80. ISBN 0-516-01363-7. (Encyclopedia of Presidents). 4-9

Andrew Johnson (1808-1875) lived a life filled with contradictions. He was born into extreme poverty, but apprenticed himself to a tailor and learned a trade to propel him into another life. He struggled to learn to read; he taught himself to give speeches; and he became President of the United States. People admired him for pardoning Confederates, but at the same time, they perceived him as a failure for being unable to engineer a speedy, peaceful reconstruction of the South. He was accused of misdeeds and suffered an impeachment trial, but emerged without guilt. Chronology of American History and Index.

1145. Kent, Zachary. **The Battle of Chancellorsville**. Chicago: Childrens Press, 1994. 31p. $17.30; $4.95pa. ISBN 0-516-06679-X; 0-516-46679-8pa. (Cornerstones of Freedom). 3-7

The Battle of Chancellorsville, Virginia, May 2-4, 1863, was Robert E. Lee's last major victory in the Civil War. He fought Joseph Hooker's Union army with the help of Stonewall Jackson, but Jackson's own troops mortally wounded Jackson in the fray. Black-and-white photographs and engravings enhance the text. Index.

1146. Kent, Zachary. **The Battle of Shiloh**. Chicago: Childrens Press, 1991. 32p. $4.95pa. ISBN 0-516-44754-8pa. (Cornerstones of Freedom). 3-7

The second great battle of the Civil War was the Battle of Shiloh fought in Tennessee on April 6-7, 1862. At the time, it was the bloodiest battle fought on American soil, with 10,000 men losing their lives before the Confederates retreated. Index.

1147. Kent, Zachary. **Calvin Coolidge**. Chicago: Childrens Press, 1988. 100p. $19.80. ISBN 0-516-01362-9. (Encyclopedia of Presidents). 4-9

Calvin Coolidge (1872-1933), a shy man from Vermont, moved to Massachusetts, where he held state offices, including governor. When refusing reelection for President, he said "I do not choose to run." Photographs, Chronology of American History, and Index.

1148. Kent, Zachary. **George Bush: Forty-First President of the United States**. Chicago: Childrens Press, 1993. 100p. $19.80. ISBN 0-516-01374-2. (Encyclopedia of Presidents). 4-9

Kent uses many of George Bush's direct quotes to give insight into his life. Bush (b. 1924) discusses his reactions to being shot down in World War II, his life as a father and as a Texas oilman, his service in the United States and China, his role as Vice President when he was a "heartbeat" away from the presidency, and his life as President. Photographs, Chronology of American History, and Index.

1149.   Kent, Zachary. **Geronimo**. Chicago: Childrens Press, 1989. 31p. $4.95pa. ISBN 0-516-44743-2. (Cornerstones of Freedom). 3-7

In the 1870s and 1880s, Geronimo (1829-1909), the Apache chief, led attacks on settlers and soldiers in Mexico and the southwestern United States. He tried to protect his tribe, but he eventually had to surrender in 1886. The government took the Apaches as prisoners of war to Florida, but Geronimo returned to Fort Sill, Oklahoma, where he became a farmer and marched in Theodore Roosevelt's inaugural parade. Index.

1150.   Kent, Zachary. **Grover Cleveland: Twenty-Second and Twenty-Fourth President of the United States**. Chicago: Childrens Press, 1988. 100p. $19.80. ISBN 0-516-01360-2. (Encyclopedia of Presidents). 4-9

Grover Cleveland (1837-1908) served as president during a depression that gripped the nation during 1893. He urged that the Sherman Act, which allowed gold to be drained from the national treasury, be repealed. At the same time, a cancerous growth discovered in his mouth had to be removed. He demanded secrecy, and the operation took place on a yacht near his Buzzards Bay, Massachusetts, home. Part of his jaw was removed, and during public appearances he wore a rubber jaw. Not until nine years after he died did the public find out about his ordeal. This was one case in which Cleveland did not tell the truth, but he did not otherwise lie. He believed that one must always be truthful, and he never changed. Chronology of American History and Index.

1151.   Kent, Zachary. **John F. Kennedy: Thirty-Fifth President of the United States**. Chicago: Childrens Press, 1987. 100p. $19.80. ISBN 0-516-01390-4. (Encyclopedia of Presidents). 4-9

John Fitzgerald Kennedy (1917-1963) was in a boat sunk by the Japanese in World War II, and the chapter covering this event in his life is "They sank my boat." The text looks at his youth, his experience in the war that made him a hero, his political races, his book *Profiles of Courage*, the call for "Let's Back Jack!" as the President, his time in the White House, space as the new frontier, and the eternal flame still burning on his grave. Photographs, Chronology of American History, and Index.

1152.   Kent, Zachary. **Ronald Reagan: Fortieth President of the United States**. Chicago: Childrens Press, 1989. 100p. $19.80. ISBN 0-516-01373-4. (Encyclopedia of Presidents). 4-9

Ronald Reagan (b. 1911) was shot as he left a Washington, D.C., hotel in 1981, and this biography begins with that story. It returns to his childhood and his life, from actor to politician in California to President of the United States. Chronology of American History and Index.

1153.   Kent, Zachary. **Rutherford B. Hayes: Nineteenth President of the United States**. Chicago: Childrens Press, 1989. 100p. $19.80. ISBN 0-516-01365-3. (Encyclopedia of Presidents). 5-8

Born prematurely in Ohio, Rutherford Hayes (1822-1893) had his uncle persuade his overprotective mother to let him have more freedom, and he left home for boarding school and college. Encouraged to do the best that he could, he attended Harvard Law School. When he returned to Ohio, he gave legal advice to those working for the Underground Railway. He fought in the Civil War for the Union and was much loved and respected by the soldiers in the 23rd Regiment. He became the nineteenth President in 1876 (winning by one electoral vote), a job in which he served as conscientiously as possible but hated so much that he never considered running for a second term. At his death he was looking forward to joining his beloved wife. Chronology of American History and Index.

1154.   Kent, Zachary. **The Story of the Battle of Bull Run**. Chicago: Childrens Press, 1986. 30p. $4.95pa. ISBN 0-516-44703-3pa. (Cornerstones of Freedom). 3-7

The first Battle of Bull Run occurred on July 21, 1861, near Manassas, Virginia. It was also the first battle of the Civil War, a war not expected to last very long. Because people only expected a minor skirmish at Bull Run, sightseers went there with picnic baskets. The text presents the events that led to that battle and its aftermath. Index.

1155.   Kent, Zachary. **The Story of the Surrender at Yorktown**. Chicago: Childrens Press, 1989. 32p. $14.60. ISBN 0-516-04723-X. (Cornerstones of Freedom). 3-7

On October 25, 1781, the announcement of Cornwallis's surrender on October 19 at Yorktown reached Philadelphia. With a brief overview of the American Revolution and its most significant dates, Kent leads to Washington's unification with the French soldiers as he neared the British stronghold at Yorktown. The text, with accompanying illustrations, gives a good summary of the situation before the surrender.

1156.   Kent, Zachary. **Theodore Roosevelt: Twenty-Sixth President of the United States**. Chicago: Childrens Press, 1988. 100p. $19.80. ISBN 0-516-01354-8. (Encyclopedia of Presidents). 4-9

Theodore Roosevelt (1858-1919) led a volunteer regiment of western cowboys and Indians along with Ivy League college graduates up San Juan Hill during the Cuban war of independence from Spain. He helped Cuba win. With his relentless charging ahead, he became America's new folk hero. Roosevelt said to America, "Get action, do things; be sane; don't fritter away your time; create, act, take a place wherever you are, and be somebody!" He took his own advice while serving in various roles, including President. Chronology of American History and Index.

1157.   Kent, Zachary. **Ulysses S. Grant: Eighteenth President of the United States**. Chicago: Childrens Press, 1989. 100p. $19.80. ISBN 0-516-01364-5. (Encyclopedia of Presidents). 4-9

Ulysses S. Grant (1822-1885) experienced years of glory followed by years of failure and repeated the cycle. He graduated from West Point and served ably in the Mexican War, but he left the army at a low point in his life. He returned and became a Civil War hero, which led to his election as President of the United States. Chronology of American History and Index.

1158.   Kent, Zachary. **William McKinley: Twenty-Fifth President of the United States**. Chicago: Childrens Press, 1988. 100p. $19.80. ISBN 0-516-01361-0. (Encyclopedia of Presidents). 3 up

William McKinley (1843-1901) served Ohio as a representative in Congress and as its governor before he became President of the United States. During his second term, an assassin's bullet killed him, and Theodore Roosevelt took his place. He had a reputation as a kind man, concerned about everyone. Chronology of American History and Index.

1159.   Kent, Zachary. **World War I: "The War to End Wars."** Springfield, NJ: Enslow, 1994. 128p. $17.95. ISBN 0-89490-523-6. (American War). 6 up

Starting with the sinking of the *Lusitania* in 1915, the text relates the progress of World War, I from its beginning in Sarajevo in August 1914 until its end in November 1918. It presents the major battles starting with the Hindenburg Line marked by the Germans, Belleau Wood, the Marne, Saint-Mihiel, and the Meuse-Argonne offensive. Among the leaders on both sides were Captain Baron Manfred von Richthofen, "The Red Baron"; Sergeant York; General Douglas MacArthur; and General John J. (Black Jack) Pershing. During the war, more than 116,000 American soldiers died, and 4 million more from other nations. Afterward, President Woodrow Wilson tried to start the League of Nations, but American isolationism defeated his plan. Photographs complement the text. Chronology, Notes, Further Reading, and Index.

1160.   Kent, Zachary. **Zachary Taylor: Twelfth President of the United States**. Chicago: Childrens Press, 1988. 100p. $19.80. ISBN 0-516-01352-1. (Encyclopedia of Presidents). 4-9

Zachary Taylor (1784-1850) attacked Buena Vista in the Mexican War, and against great odds, he won. His many years of experience and his fearless leadership earned him the name "Old Rough and Ready." His popularity spread, and his fame swept him into the White House in 1849. As President, he tried to help domestic policy, but he had no solution to the problem of slavery. Chronology of American History and Index.

1161.   Kerby, Mona. **Robert E. Lee: Southern Hero of the Civil War**. Springfield, NJ: Enslow, 1997. 128p. $18.95. ISBN 0-89490-782-4. (Historical American Biographies). 6-9

Robert E. Lee (1807-1870) had a reputation as a gentleman general, and he fought only for the South because he lived in Virginia. He owned no slaves. This biography looks at his impact on American history as it examines his life. Fact boxes and maps augment the text. Notes, Glossary, Further Reading, and Index.

1162.   Kerr, Daisy. **Keeping Clean**. New York: Franklin Watts, 1995. 48p. $14.42. ISBN 0-531-15353-8. 4-7

This text relates a history of bathing, plumbing, and waste removal. Each two-page spread deals with a different time or region as they cover such topics as the ancient world, the Middle Ages, Roman baths, spaceship hygiene, and lavatories on board ships. Illustrations augment the text. Glossary and Index.

1163.   Kessler, Lauren. **Stubborn Twig: Three Generations in the Life of a Japanese American Family**. 1993. New York: Plume, 1994. 347p. $12.95pa. ISBN 0-452-27301-3pa. YA

From 1908 to the present, Kessler traces the life of Masuo Yasui based on her interviews and information from the Oregon Historical Society. Yasui came to America to work on the railroads and became a successful businessman in Hood River, Oregon. During World War II, the government accused him of being a spy and moved him from one internment camp to another. His son used himself as a test case to prove that evacuating Japanese Americans from the West Coast was illegal, but other family members were still relocated. The family lost everything, and Masuo Yasui committed suicide after returning home. Annotated Bibliography and Index.

1164.   Ketchum, Liza. **The Gold Rush**. Boston: Little, Brown, 1996. 144p. $19.95; $10.95pa. ISBN 0-316-59133-5; 0-316-49047-4-0pa. 3-7

On January 24, 1848, someone discovered a tiny nugget of gold about the size of a dime. Thousands of people all over the world heard about this event and rushed to California hoping to find gold for themselves. Many lost money or even their lives, but others found adventure and new hope for the future. The text tells the story of some of the people whose lives changed, and what they did for themselves and others after the height of the gold rush ended. Black-and-White Photographs, Bibliography, and Index. *Notable Children's Trade Books in the Field of Social Studies* and *New York Public Library Books for the Teen Age.*

1165. Kherdian, David. **Bridger: The Story of a Mountain Man**. New York: Greenwillow, 1987. 147p. $11.75. ISBN 0-688-06510-4. 5-8

After fulfilling his duty as a bound-out servant, Jim Bridger journeys up the Missouri River when he is 18 and begins his life as a trapper. He becomes friends with the Crow Indians and "discovers" the Great Salt Lake (long known to the Indians). He delights in his experiences of freedom.

1166. Kilian, Pamela. **What Was Watergate**. New York: Thomas Dunne, St. Martin's Press, 1990. 133p. $16.95. ISBN 0-312-04446-1. 8 up

The Watergate affair came to a climax in 1973 with the resignation of Richard Nixon from the presidency of the United States. Kilian looks at the pressure that the administration felt from the Vietnam War and posits that this led to such decisions as the burglary of the Democratic National Committee's offices in the Watergate. The text starts with the break-in and continues with the chronological order of events leading to Nixon's resignation. Chronology, Bibliography, and Index.

1167. Kimmel, Eric. **Bar Mitzvah: A Jewish Boy's Coming of Age**. Erika Weihs, illustrator. New York: Viking, 1995. 143p. $15. ISBN 0-670-85540-5. 6-8

The text presents the importance of the bar mitzvah in the life of a 13-year-old Jewish boy by comparing it to rituals in other cultures and describing it in detail. Kimmel includes the origins and teachings of Judaism, the place of the synagogue in worship, the structure of the prayer service, the Torah ritual, the bar mitzvah ceremony, and the importance of ritual objects. Glossary and Index.

1168. King, Coretta Scott. **My Life with Martin Luther King, Jr.** New York: Henry Holt, 1993. 335p. $17.95. ISBN 0-8050-2445-X. New York: Puffin, 1994. 335p. $4.99pa. ISBN 0-14-036805-1pa. 7 up

In the text, Coretta Scott King describes her life with her husband, Martin Luther King, Jr. (1929-1968), and says that no one will ever replace him. His nonviolent approach to the Civil Rights movement has given African Americans a place in government and business that might not have occurred without his willingness to practice and push for what he believed. Chronology and Index.

1169. King, John. **The Gulf War**. New York: Dillon Press, Macmillan, 1991. 48p. $13.95. ISBN 0-87518-514-2. 5-10

Questions arise as to why the United States fought the Gulf War in 1991. The text looks at geography in the area, history, the role of oil, and Saddam Hussein's Iraq as it asks why Hussein initially invaded Kuwait. The crisis began in August 1990 and escalated to the attack in January 1991. Glossary, Key Events, Further Reading, and Index.

1170. King, Perry Scott. **Jefferson Davis**. New York: Chelsea House, 1990. 112p. $18.95 ISBN 1-55546-806-3. (World Leaders Past and Present). 5 up

In 1861, Jefferson Davis (1808-1889) left the U.S. Senate to join the revolt of the southern states. His West Point education prepared him to fight in the Mexican War, serve as Secretary of War for Franklin Pierce, and become the South's president while it fought the Civil War. He was the opposite of Lincoln as he tried to preserve the rights of slave owners in the South. The text, augmented by photographs and reproductions, looks at his life and influences. Chronology, Further Reading, and Index.

1171. Kinsey-Warnock, Natalie. **The Canada Geese Quilt**. Leslie W. Bowman, illustrator. New York: Dutton, 1989. 64p. $12.95. ISBN 0-525-65004-0. 4 up

When Ariel is 10 in 1946, she and her grandmother work on a quilt for the new baby. Her grandmother has a stroke and begins to act in ways that Ariel cannot understand, and Ariel refuses to talk to her for a while. Ariel does overcome her feelings and helps finish the Canada geese quilt before the baby arrives. But what makes her happiest is the quilt that her grandmother gives her that she secretly made. *American Library Association Notable Books for Children.*

1172. Kinsey-Warnock, Natalie. **The Night the Bells Rang**. Leslie W. Bowman, illustrator. New York: Cobblehill, 1991. 76p. $12.95. ISBN 0-525-65074-1. 4 up

In Vermont during 1918, Mason tries to avoid Aden, the big boy who knocks him down and fills his hat with snow. But Aden also helped Mason retrieve a drawing created for his father that flew out of his hand. Thus, Mason has mixed feelings when Aden enlists. His feelings change to sadness when he hears that Aden has died. As the bells ring to signal the end of the war, Mason knows that he has changed in his attitude toward Aden as well as others who have bothered him, including his younger brother.

1173.	Kirby, Philippa. **Glorious Days, Dreadful Days: The Battle of Bunker Hill**. John Edens, illustrator. Austin, TX: Raintree/Steck-Vaughn, 1993. 88p. $24.26; $4.95pa. ISBN 0-8114-7226-4; 0-8114-8066-6pa. (Stories of America—Stand Up and Be Counted). 4-8

The Battle of Bunker Hill (actually Breed's Hill), which occurred in 1775, began the Revolutionary War. In that war, a group of ordinary citizens overcame the most powerful army in the world. The text presents the causes of the battle, its story, and its results. Epilogue, Afterword, and Notes.

1174.	Kirchberger, Joe H. **The Civil War and Reconstruction**. New York: Facts On File, 1991. 389p. $45. ISBN 0-8160-2171-6. (Eyewitness History). YA

The Civil War affected everyone in the Union and in the Confederacy, unlike any war before or after. More people died in it than in the sum total of all other wars in which America has fought. One reason for all the destruction may have been the advancement in weapons, which the generals did not expect as they continued to fight at close range in the old style. Railroads, telegraphs, and rivers also played important roles in the war. The text looks at these aspects through primary sources from these four traumatic years in the nation's history. Appendix, Bibliography, and Index.

1175.	Kirchberger, Joe H. **The First World War**. New York: Facts on File, 1992. 402p. $45. ISBN 0-8160-2552-5. (Eyewitness History). YA

In 1914, Austria-Hungary and Serbia had a disagreement that, with the assassination of Archduke Francis Ferdinand of Austria, escalated into a major war involving Russia, Germany, France, Britain, Japan, and Turkey. By 1917, the United States had joined. This war, also known as the Great War, changed European history. The text includes many firsthand accounts of the war from memoirs, speeches, newspapers, and letters. Some of the commentaries come from T. E. Lawrence (Lawrence of Arabia), Woodrow Wilson, Otto von Bismarck, and Vladimir Lenin. Each chapter includes an essay about the area of the war it presents and a chronology of events. Appendices, Bibliography, and Index.

1176.	Kirkpatrick, Katherine. **Keeping the Good Light**. New York: Delacorte, 1995. 220p. $14.95. ISBN 0-385-32161-9. 5-9

Eliza Brown, 16 in 1903, thinks that her chores are endless at the Stepping Stones Lighthouse. She is isolated on the island with her quiet brother Sam, her father, and a mother who always criticizes her. She is happiest when she goes by rowboat to school on another island. After she goes out unchaperoned with a boyfriend at night and because she thinks independently—two unacceptable attributes in her closed society—she is expelled from school. As she tries to decide if she will accept a marriage without love, a job offer lets her escape the island's rigid expectations.

1177.	Kitano, Harry. **The Japanese Americans**. New York: Chelsea House, 1988. 92p. $19.95; $8.95pa. ISBN 0-7910-3766-5; 0-7910-3380-5pa. (The Immigrant Experience). 5 up

The Japanese began to arrive in America in the late nineteenth century, and since their arrival, they have faced hostility. The text, with photographs, looks at their religion and politics, the situation in the West, their wartime evacuation in World War II, their traditions and the difficult transition from them, their contributions to the country, and their lives. Selected References and Index.

1178.	Kittredge, Mary. **Barbara McClintock**. New York: Chelsea House, 1990. 103p. $18.95. ISBN 1-55546-666-4. (American Women of Achievement). 5 up

As a young woman working for a male scientist studying genes in maize (corn), Barbara McClintock (1902-1992) realized that he was looking in the wrong places for the differences among the 10 genes. She looked in the right place, made him furious, and lost her job. But she began to establish her name in the study of cytogenetics. She worked mainly at the labs of Carnegie Institution in Cold Spring Harbor, New York, researching maize. She cross-pollinated various kinds of corn to see what happened to the offspring. Her major discovery that genetic material moved from place to place on chromosomes occurred 30 years before scientists realized that she was right. They refused to acknowledge her research at a time when they were more interested in the discovery of DNA. She won the Nobel Prize in 1983 for her work, and other awards and prizes followed. But none of them changed her methods or her appreciation of life. She said that her work had given her much pleasure through the years. Photographs enhance the text. Chronology, Further Reading, and Index.

1179.	Kittredge, Mary. **Helen Hayes: Actress**. New York: Chelsea House, 1988. 112p. $18.95. ISBN 1-55546-656-7. (American Women of Achievement). 5 up

Helen Hayes (1900-1993) began her theatrical career at the age of five and made a Broadway debut at nine, achieving major stardom before she was 20. She won two Oscars for her movie work and much acclaim for her stage work. Her daughter died at 19 from polio, and Hayes constantly publicized the new polio vaccine and encouraged parents to inoculate their children. When she retired at 85, she started a campaign to aid the elderly. Photographs and reproductions enhance the text. Chronology, Further Reading, and Index.

1180.   Kittredge, Mary. **Jane Addams**. New York: Chelsea House, 1990. 111p. $18.95. ISBN 1-55546-636-2. (American Women of Achievement). 4-7

As a pioneering social worker, Jane Addams (1860-1935) revolutionized America's attitude toward the poor. She was born into a prosperous family and went to college, graduating in 1881. When she could not find other avenues to help people, she moved into the Chicago slums and opened Hull House. She always defended poor and unpopular minorities, and in 1920 she was called "the most dangerous woman in America." Black-and-white photographs supplement the text. Bibliography and Index.

1181.   Klausmeier, Robert. **Cowboy**. Richard Erickson, illustrator. Minneapolis, MN: Lerner, 1996. 48p. $14.96. ISBN 0-8225-2975-0. (American Pastfinder). 4-7

The cowboy has domesticated cattle and horses, built empires, and helped open the West to settlement. The text looks at the daily routine of a cowboy, his uniform, the roundup, branding, trail drives, chuckwagon stops, winter on a ranch, and living in a bunkhouse. It shows that a cowboy's real life rarely resembles the romantic image created in movies and books. Glossary and Index.

1182.   Klausner, Janet. **Sequoyah's Gift: A Portrait of the Cherokee Leader**. New York: HarperCollins, 1993. 111p. $14.89. ISBN 0-06-021235-7. 4-8

When Sequoyah (1773?-1843) saw that Cherokees were losing land to white settlers, he noted that the whites communicated through symbols as well as through speech. He did not want the Cherokees to lose their culture by succumbing to all of the white customs. He then began working on a system of written Cherokee and eventually accomplished his goal. The text looks at his life as a man who overcame the physical disability of one leg shorter than the other, his achievements, and the times. The information about him comes from people who knew or met him. Photographs, Bibliography, and Index. *Notable Children's Trade Books in the Field of Social Studies.*

1183.   Kliment, Bud. **Billie Holiday: Singer**. New York: Chelsea House, 1990. 112p. $18.95; $7.95pa. ISBN 1-55546-592-7; 0-7910-0241-1pa. (Black Americans of Achievement). 5 up

Born Eleanor Fagan in 1915, Billie Holiday moved to New York City with her mother in 1927; she made her professional debut at age 15 in a Harlem nightclub. She toured with big bands such as Count Basie and Artie Shaw during the 1930s, and in the early 1940s she was a star attraction. In 1941, however, she became addicted to heroin, and by 1947 she was imprisoned for possession of narcotics. Regardless of her meteoric rise and fall, she was extremely talented. Photographs enhance the text. Chronology, Further Reading, and Index.

1184.   Kliment, Bud. **Count Basie: Bandleader and Musician**. New York: Chelsea House, 1992. 128p. $18.95. ISBN 0-7910-1118-6. (Black Americans of Achievement). 5 up

Count Basie (1904-1984) was a drummer who switched to playing the piano. He toured in vaudeville acts to sharpen his timing and to learn a variety of styles. In 1935, he formed his own group, backing such vocalists as Billie Holiday. Photographs and reproductions enhance the text. Chronology, Further Reading, and Index.

1185.   Kliment, Bud. **Ella Fitzgerald: Singer**. New York: Chelsea House, 1988. 112p. $18.95; $7.95pa. ISBN 1-55546-586-2; 0-7910-0220-9pa. (Black Americans of Achievement). 5 up

For more than 50 years, Ella Fitzgerald (1918-1996) entertained the world with her unique jazz vocal stylings. She grew up in Yonkers, in New York City, where she started her career at 14 by winning a contest. She became the featured singer in the Chick Webb orchestra, one of the country's best-known swing bands. Her recordings made her famous across the nation by the time she was 20. Eventually she toured with her own band while promoting racial equality around the world. Photographs and reproductions enhance the text. Chronology, Further Reading, and Index.

1186.   Klots, Steve. **Ida Wells-Barnett: Civil Rights Leader**. New York: Chelsea House, 1994. 128p. $18.95. ISBN 0-7910-1885-7. (Black Americans of Achievement). 5 up

Ida Wells-Barnett (1862-1931), born in Mississippi, decided when she was very young that she would help her people. She became a teacher and the editor of a Black newspaper in Tennessee. Her editorials upset the white population so much that they exiled her from the South. She continued to write in the *New York Age*, one of the country's leading Black newspapers. She wanted to expose the gruesome practice of lynching, and she continually attacked racial injustice. Neither women nor African Americans were expected to speak out about problems during Wells-Barnett's lifetime. She refused to stay quiet and became a fearless leader for civil rights. Photographs enhance the text. Chronology, Further Reading, and Index.

1187.   Klots, Steve. **Richard Allen: Religious Leader and Social Activist**. New York: Chelsea House, 1990. 111p. $18.95. ISBN 1-55546-570-6. (Black Americans of Achievement). 5 up

When Methodist circuit rider preachers convinced Richard Allen's master that owning slaves was sinful, the master allowed his slaves to buy their freedom. Allen (1760-1831) went to Philadelphia and tried to use his strong Methodist beliefs to serve the Black community. The church grew until whites who still supported slavery infiltrated it, and the Black members suffered. Allen, after many years and many setbacks, established the American Methodist Episcopal Church with the first Black congregation of Bethel Church in Philadelphia. He was also the first Black ordained to the deaconate of the church and allowed to serve the sacraments. Those supporting him in his endeavors, especially after his service to the city during the yellow fever epidemic in 1793, included the vocal abolitionist William Lloyd Garrison. Chronology, Further Reading, and Index.

1188.   Knappman, Edward W., ed. **Great American Trials: From Salem Witchcraft to Rodney King**. Detroit: Visible Ink, 1994. 872p. $50; $17.95pa. ISBN 0-8103-8875-8; 0-8103-9134-1pa. 9-12

Two hundred trials, arranged chronologically and chosen for their notoriety, touch on subjects such as corruption, impeachment, rape, murder, and civil liberties. For each trial, the reader learns the facts, a narrative account of the crime, the pretrial activities, the trial itself, the aftermath of the trial, and any impact that the trial might have had on American life. The accounts are written in lay language so that they can be easily understood. Bibliography and Index.

1189.   Koller, Jackie French. **Nothing to Fear**. San Diego, CA: Harcourt Brace, 1991. 279p. $14.95. ISBN 0-15-200544-7. 5-7

Danny worries about his pregnant mother and his father, who has left home in Manhattan to seek work during the Depression in 1932. When his mother goes to the hospital in a coma, Danny finds a letter saying that his father had died on the rails four months earlier. Another victim of the Depression from Oklahoma, whom they have nursed back to health, helps them in turn, and Danny's mother decides she will marry him. *IRA Young Adults' Choices*.

1190.   Koller, Jackie French. **The Primrose Way**. San Diego, CA: Gulliver, Harcourt Brace, 1995. 352p. $15.95; $5pa. ISBN 0-15-256745-3; 0-15-200372-Xpa. 6 up

After Rebekah meets the Pawtucket people in 1633, she begins to make friends with them. Knowing that the colonists consider the Pawtuckets savages, Rebekah expects them to be very different. She sees that they have their own valid beliefs, especially when she falls in love with the Pawtucket medicine man, a defiant individualist. *American Library Association Best Books for Young Adults* and *New York Public Library Books for the Teen Age*.

1191.   Koral, April. **An Album of War Refugees**. New York: Franklin Watts, 1989. 96p. $13.90. ISBN 0-531-10765-5. (Picture Album). 6-9

The text presents refugees from different countries who have come to the United States since the Armenians arrived in 1915. The latest refugees have come from Central America. Personal stories bring immediacy to situations in which people have had to leave their homes, usually having lost all material items, in order to save their lives. In their land of exile, they have faced new political, social, and economic problems. Bibliography and Index.

1192.   Kort, Michael G. **The Cold War**. Brookfield, CT: Millbrook Press, 1994. 160p. $17.40. ISBN 1-56294-353-7. 7 up

From 1945 to 1990, the United States was involved in a rivalry of ideologies between the capitalist countries of the West and the Communist nations led by the Soviet Union. The text looks at the origins of the conflict and the buildup of nuclear weapons with which each side could destroy the other. The two sides encouraged spying and other secret activities. The topics covered are the rise of the Berlin Wall; Soviet Russia and Communism; the Korean War; the Cold War underground and in the United States; adjustments to new leaders; the Cuban Missile Crisis with Kennedy, Khrushchev, and Castro; Vietnam; détente; and the end of the Cold War in 1990 with the fall of the Berlin Wall. For Further Reading and Index.

1193.   Koslow, Philip. **The Seminole Indians**. New York: Chelsea House, 1994. 79p. $14.95; $6.95pa. ISBN 0-7910-1672-2; 0-7910-2486-5pa. (The Junior Library of American Indians). 3-7

People trying to escape subjugation eventually banded together and ended up in the Florida Everglades. They called themselves "Seminoles," and they are the one Native American tribe that the U.S. government never defeated. Two bloody wars, the Seminole wars, showed that the government could not fight in the swamps of Florida. Other aspects of history appear as well. Photographs and engravings enhance the text. Glossary, Chronology, and Index.

1194.   Kozodoy, Ruth. **Isadora Duncan: Dancer**. New York: Chelsea House, 1988. 112p. $18.95. ISBN 1-55546-650-8. (American Women of Achievement). 5 up

Isadora Duncan (1878-1927) was a self-described "revolutionist" with an unconventional lifestyle. After dancing barefoot to classical music and rejecting orthodox ballet techniques throughout Europe and Russia, she created a new form of dance that evolved into modern expressive dance. Photographs enhance the text. Chronology, Further Reading, and Index.

1195.   Kraft, Betsy Harvey. **Mother Jones: One Woman's Fight for Labor**. New York: Clarion, 1995. 116p. $16.95. ISBN 0-395-67163-9. 5-9

Although Mary Harris Jones, known as Mother Jones (1843?-1930), looked like a grandmother wearing a modest black dress and glasses, she was one of America's most effective union organizers. An Irish immigrant, she used her oratorical gifts to help abused workers. She wanted children out of the coal mines, and while she bullied the officials, she lived with the coal miner families. Titles of the chapters give insight into her thoughts and those of her enemies: "I have been in jail more than once," "My people were poor," "I sat alone through nights of grief," "A quick brain and an even quicker tongue," "Just an old woman," "Good fight against wrong," and "I didn't come out on a stretcher." Additional topics include the miners' angel, coal wars in West Virginia, a march for the children, and the woman with an excess of courage. Photographs, Engravings, Notes, More About Mother Jones, and Index.

1196.   Krass, Peter. **Sojourner Truth: Antislavery Activist**. New York: Chelsea House, 1988. 110p. $18.95; $7.95pa. ISBN 1-55546-611-7; 0-7910-0215-2pa. (Black Americans of Achievement). 5 up

As a child, Isabella (1797-1883) was sold to another slave owner and separated from her family. She won her freedom in 1827 and became a traveling preacher who took the name Sojourner Truth. Eventually renowned throughout the East Coast for her beliefs, she published the story of her life as a slave in 1850. Afterward, she began lecture tours to advocate the end of slavery and the beginning of women's rights. She worked as a counselor to former slaves and started campaigns to help Blacks obtain federal grants for farmland. Photographs and engravings highlight the text. Chronology, Further Reading, and Index.

1197.   Krause, Corinne Azenn. **Grandmothers, Mothers, and Daughters: Oral Histories of Three Generations of Ethnic American Women**. Boston: Twayne, 1991. 230p. $24.95. ISBN 0-8057-9105-1. (Twayne's Oral History). YA

The immigrant experience in the United States extended to many different groups. Three groups that settled in Pittsburgh, Pennsylvania, were Italian, Slavic, and Jewish families. The text uses the voices of three generations of women from these groups to tell about their Americanization. The areas of their lives that highlight the discussion are their ethnic assimilations, marriages, child rearing, roles, and sexual myths to which they were exposed. Bibliography and Index.

1198.   Kremer, Gary R., ed. **George Washington Carver: In His Own Words**. Columbia, MO: University of Missouri, 1987. $15.95pa. ISBN 0-8262-0785-5pa. YA

One way to get to know George Washington Carver (c. 1864-1943) better is to read what he actually said about things. The text quotes Carver's comments about himself and about various times in his life. Topics include the pre-Tuskegee years, his time at Tuskegee plantation, trying to motivate his students, the role of scientist as servant and as mystic, and the relationship of a Black man to white America. Notes and Index.

1199.   Krensky, Stephen. **The Printer's Apprentice**. Madeline Sorel, illustrator. New York: Delacorte, 1995. 103p. $13.95. ISBN 0-385-32095-7. 5-7

Gus Croft tells the story of the 1734 arrest and trial of New York printer Peter Zenger, indicted for slandering the colonial governor. Gus wonders why Zenger's words, which are true, should not be printed, and why his boss, a rival printer, does not report on the trial. Gus helps Zenger retain a lawyer from Philadelphia who thinks that slander will become the concern that leads to a discussion on the freedom of the press. Through Zenger's ordeal, the reader begins to understand the importance of free speech.

1200.   Krisher, Trudy. **Spite Fences**. New York: Delacorte, 1994. 283p. $14.95. ISBN 0-385-32088-4. 8 up

Maggie Pugh, 13, receives her first camera and sees a group of whites beat up her best friend Zeke for breaking a segregation law in the summer of 1960. In her first-person narrative, she relates how her next-door neighbor tries to molest her and treats her little sister cruelly. Zeke gets her a job with a well-educated Black man who comes to Kinship, Georgia, to help with nonviolent segregation. She eventually decides to testify for Zeke and earns money for her photographs of segregation attempts from *Life* magazine, but her relationship with her mother does not improve. *Jefferson Cup Runner-Up.*

1201. Kroeber, Theodora. **Ishi: Last of His Tribe**. Ruth Robbins, illustrator. 1964. New York: Bantam, 1990. 213p. $4.50. ISBN 0-553-24898-7pa. 7 up

Until the early 1900s, the Yahi, an American Indian tribe, lived peacefully in California. Then the white settlers arrived and destroyed them. Of the few who were able to escape, one was Ishi, who, when around 10 in 1871 or 1872, hid with the others in nearby canyons. When the others died, only Ishi remained. Workers discovered him in a small mining town around 1911, and he told his story to anthropologists so that they were able to recreate what life was like in the Yahi tribe.

1202. Krohn, Katherine E. **Elvis Presley: The King**. Minneapolis, MN: Lerner, 1994. 64p. $15.95. ISBN 0-8225-2877-0. 4-8

In January 1956, Elvis Presley (1935-1977) recorded his first hit single, "Heartbreak Hotel." The next January, Ed Sullivan wanted to improve the ratings on his television show so he paid Elvis the huge sum of $50,000 to appear. Sullivan's assessment of the man was that he was polite and pleasant. Presley entered the army, but as soon as he exited, his career resumed. This poor boy became a millionaire and the focus of people all over the world. His fans created a shrine to his memory at Graceland, his home in Memphis, Tennessee.

1203. Kroll, Steven. **By the Dawn's Early Light: The Story of the Star-Spangled Banner**. New York: Scholastic, 1994. 40p. $15.95. ISBN 0-590-45054-9. 4-7

Francis Scott Key wrote a poem to verbalize his feeling of relief when he looked across the water at Fort McHenry in Baltimore, Maryland, at dawn in September 1814 and saw the Stars and Stripes still flying after a British attack. The text tells the story of Key's days after the British burned Washington. He was trying to save Dr. Beanes, a friend, from British injustice and found himself at Fort McHenry during the battle. Author's Note, Manuscript, Music, Maps, Bibliography, and Index. *Notable Children's Trade Books in the Field of Social Studies*.

1204. Kroll, Steven. **Ellis Island: Doorway to Freedom**. New York: Holiday House, 1995. 32p. $15.95. ISBN 0-8234-1192-3. 4-7

Until 1954, Ellis Island was a symbol of both hope and fear for immigrants arriving in New York Harbor. The text tells the island's history from its beginning in colonial times until it became an immigrant station for the federal government. More than 16 million foreigners began their quest for American citizenship at its gates. Now a national monument, the buildings house an immigration museum. Glossary and Index.

1205. Kronenwetter, Michael. **Capital Punishment**. Santa Barbara, CA: ABC-CLIO, 1993. 242p. $39.50. ISBN 0-87436-718-2. (Contemporary World Issues). 9 up

After an overview of contemporary attitudes about capital punishment, the text gives events, biographies of pro- and anti-death penalty personalities and victims, and source materials that relate to the topic. The history begins with the Code of Hammurabi and continues to the present, looking at the death penalty in the United States and Great Britain and the methods by which victims have been executed. Annotated Bibliography, Glossary, and Index.

1206. Kronenwetter, Michael. **Covert Action**. New York: Franklin Watts, 1991. 144p. $12.90. ISBN 0-531-13018-5. (Impact). 7-12

Beginning with the presidency of George Washington, the United States has used covert intelligence operations to protect its interests. The text focuses on the roles of the Office of Strategic Services (OSS) from 1942 to 1947 and the Central Intelligence Agency (CIA), chartered in 1947, which evolved from the OSS as a method of furthering American foreign and military policy. Bibliography and Index.

1207. Kronenwetter, Michael. **United They Hate: White Supremacist Groups in America**. New York: Walker, 1992. 133p. $14.95. ISBN 0-8027-8162-4. 8 up

By focusing mainly on the Ku Klux Klan, the text gives a history of white supremacy hate groups in the United States. Other groups also presented are neo-Nazis, the Order, the Posse Comitatus, the Aryan Nations, and the Skinheads. A balanced report of some of the known activities, recruitment practices, and philosophies of these groups, as well as the ways police are trying to combat their crimes, completes the information. Bibliography and Index.

1208. Kronenwetter, Michael. **The War Against Terrorism**. Englewood Cliffs, NJ: Julian Messner, 1989. 130p. $13.98. ISBN 0-671-69050-7. 7 up

Since the mid-1960s, international terrorism has escalated. With instant communication, people throughout the globe know immediately when a terrorist act occurs. The text discusses the history of terrorism and includes overviews of terrorist and antiterrorist groups. Terrorism comes in varied forms, and the United States has had to create a policy and a response toward the acts that sometimes seem appropriate to everyone except those directly involved in the situation. Among the specific situations noted are the Munich Olympic Game murders and terrorism in Latin America, Northern Ireland, and the Middle East. Bibliography and Index.

1209.   Kronstadt, Janet. **Florence Sabin: Medical Researcher**. New York: Chelsea House, 1990. 110p. $18.95. ISBN 1-55546-676-1. (American Women of Achievement). 5 up

Florence Sabin (1871-1953) was the first woman to be elected to the National Academy of Sciences and was recognized as the most eminent of living women scientists in the early twentieth century. After graduating from Smith College and going to Johns Hopkins, she began studying the lymphatic system. Her work allowed her to join a team of scientists that found how to control tuberculosis, the chief cause of death in the United States at the time. She spent her later years trying to improve public health in Colorado. Photographs enhance the text. Chronology, Further Reading, and Index.

1210.   Krull, Kathleen. **Lives of the Artists: Masterpieces, Messes (and What the Neighbors Thought)**. Kathryn Hewitt, illustrator. San Diego, CA: Harcourt Brace, 1995. 96p. $19. ISBN 0-15-200103-4. 4-8

Vignettes on artists, arranged chronologically, give interesting insights into their lives and sometimes their relationships to each other. The artists are Leonardo da Vinci (Italy, 1452-1519), Michelangelo Buonarroti (Italy, 1475-1564), Peter Bruegel (Netherlands, 1525-1569), Sofonisba Anguissola who served King Philip II of Spain although Italian (1532-1625), Rembrandt van Rijn (Holland, 1606-1669), Katsushika Hokusai (Japan, 1760-1849), Mary Cassatt (American relocated in France, 1845-1926), Vincent van Gogh (Holland, 1853-1890), Käthe Kollwitz (Germany, 1867-1945), Henri Matisse (France, 1869-1954), Pablo Picasso (Spain 1881-1973), Marc Chagall (Russia, 1887-1985), Marcel Duchamp (France, 1887-1968), Georgia O'Keeffe (United States, 1887-1986), William H. Johnson (United States, 1901-1970), Salvador Dali (Spain, 1904-1989), Isamu Noguchi (United States, 1904-1988), Diego Rivera (Mexico, 1886-1957), Frida Kahlo (Mexico, 1907-1954), and Andy Warhol (United States, 1928-1987). Artistic Terms, Index of Artists, and For Further Reading and Looking. *IRA Teachers' Choices*, *American Bookseller Pick of the Lists*, and *New York Public Library Books for the Teen Age*.

1211.   Krull, Kathleen. **Lives of the Athletes: Thrills, Spills (and What the Neighbors Thought)**. Kathryn Hewitt, illustrator. San Diego, CA: Harcourt Brace, 1997. 96p. $19. ISBN 0-15-200806-3. 4-7

In capsule biographies, Krull tells a little about the lives of some international athletes away from their sports. She includes commentary on Jim Thorpe (1888-1953), Duke Kahanamoku (1890-1968), Babe Ruth (1895-1948), Red Grange (1903-1991), Johnny Weissmuller (1903-1984), Gertrude Ederle (b. 1906), Babe Didrikson Zaharias (1911-1956), Sonja Henie (1912-1969), Jesse Owens (1913-1980), Jackie Robinson (1919-1972), Sir Edmund Hillary (b. 1919), Maurice Richard (b. 1921), Maureen Connolly (1934-1969), Roberto Clemente (1934-1972), Wilma Rudolph (1940-1994), Arthur Ashe (1943-1993), Pete Maravich (1947-1988), Bruce Lee (1940-1973), Pelé (b. 1940), and Flo Hyman (1954-1986). Selected Bibliography.

1212.   Krull, Kathleen. **Lives of the Musicians: Good Times, Bad Times (and What the Neighbors Thought)**. Kathryn Hewitt, illustrator. San Diego, CA: Harcourt Brace, 1993. 96p. $18.95. ISBN 0-15-248010-2. 4-8

Vignettes on musicians, arranged chronologically, give interesting insights into their lives and sometimes their relationships to each other. The musicians included are Antonio Vivaldi (Italy, 1876-1741), Johann Sebastian Bach (Germany, 1685-1750), Wolfgang Amadeus Mozart (Austria, 1756-1791), Ludwig van Beethoven (Germany, 1770-1827), Frédéric Chopin (Poland, 1810-1849), Giuseppe Verdi (Italy, 1813-1901), Clara Schumann (Germany, 1819-1896), Stephen Foster (America, 1826-1864), Johannes Brahms (Germany, 1833-1897), Peter Ilich Tchaikovsky (Russia, 1840-1893), William Gilbert (England, 1836-1911) and Arthur Sullivan (England, 1842-1900), Erik Satie (France, 1866-1925), Scott Joplin (America, 1868-1917), Charles Ives (1874-1954), Igor Stravinsky (Russia, 1882-1971), Nadia Boulanger (France, 1887-1979), Sergei Prokofiev (Ukraine, 1891-1953), George Gershwin (America, 1898-1937), and Woody Guthrie (America, 1912-1967). Musical Terms, Index of Composers, and For Further Reading . . . and Listening. *Boston Globe-Horn Book Honor*, *American Library Association Notable Books for Children*, *Notable Children's Trade Books in the Field of Social Studies*, *PEN Center USA West Literary Award*, *IRA Teachers' Choices*, *New York Public Library Books for the Teen Age*, and *Golden Kite Honor*.

1213.   Krull, Kathleen. **Lives of the Writers: Comedies, Tragedies (and What the Neighbors Thought)**. Kathryn Hewitt, illustrator. San Diego, CA: Harcourt Brace, 1994. 96p. $19. ISBN 0-15-248009-9. 4 up

Vignettes on writers, arranged chronologically, give interesting insights into their lives and sometimes their relationships to each other. Writers covered are Murasaki Shikibu (Japan, 973?-1025?), Miguel de Cervantes (Spain, 1547-1616), William Shakespeare (England, 1564-1616), Jane Austen (England, 1775-1817), Hans Christian Anderson (Denmark, 1805-1875), Edgar Allan Poe (America, 1809-1849), Charles Dickens (England, 1812-1870), Charlotte Brontë (England, 1816-1855) and Emily Brontë (England, 1818-1848), Emily Dickinson (America, 1830-1886), Louisa May Alcott (America, 1832-1888), Mark Twain (America, 1835-1910), Frances Hodgson Burnett (England, 1849-1924), Robert Louis Stevenson (Scotland, 1850-1894), Jack London (America, 1876-1916), Carl Sandburg (America, 1878-1967), E. B. White (America, 1899-1985), Zora Neale Hurston (America, 1901?-1960), Langston Hughes (1902-1967), and Isaac Bashevis Singer (Poland and America, 1904-1991). Literary Terms, Index of Writers, and For Further Reading and Writing. *American Bookseller Pick of the Lists*, *NCTE Notable Children's Trade Books in the Language Arts*, and *IRA Teachers' Choices*.

1214.   Krull, Kathleen. **V Is for Victory: America Remembers World War II**. New York: Apple Soup, Knopf, 1995. 116p. $24. ISBN 0-679-86198-X. 5-8

In this text, photographs of memorabilia such as postcards, posters, ration books, and newspapers give a view of life during World War II. The book covers many aspects of the war, including Pearl Harbor, weapons, soldiers, civilian life, Japanese American internment camps, and the Holocaust. It presents people from both the Axis and Allied sides. Chronology, Bibliography, Map, and Index.

1215.   Kudlinski, Kathleen. **Pearl Harbor Is Burning! A Story of World War II**. Ronald Himler, illustrator. New York: Viking, 1991. 54p. $11.95. ISBN 0-670-83475-0. (Once Upon America). 4-7

Lonely and isolated from his friends while he lives in Hawaii during 1941, Frank, 10, meets Kenji, a Japanese American boy. As they play in Frank's tree house one morning, they see planes bomb the harbor below, and Kenji realizes that they are Japanese. During this time, the families have to learn how to deal with their conflicting emotions of loyalty to friends versus patriotism.

1216.   Kunhardt, Philip B., Jr., Philip B. Kunhardt, and Peter W. Kunhardt. **Lincoln: An Illustrated Biography**. New York: Knopf, 1993. 415p. $50. ISBN 0-679-40862-2. YA

Although this is not an easy text to read, the photographs of Abraham Lincoln (1809-1865) give a strong sense of the man who led the nation through the Civil War. Additional photographs of family, scenes, and artifacts broaden the perspective of his life to the people around him. Bibliography and Index.

1217.   Kuropas, Myron B. **Ukrainians in America**. 1972. Minneapolis, MN: Lerner, 1996. 80p. $13.13. ISBN 0-8225-1043-X. (In America). 6 up

This revised edition includes the history of the Ukraine up through the country's recent independence in 1991. It discusses the periods under foreign rule of the Poles, Lithuanians, Austro-Hungarians, Hungarians, and Russians. As Ukrainians have come to the United States, they have found ways to organize themselves into communities. The text covers the concern over preservation of identity in the Ukrainian population. Photographs, Glossary, and Notes.

L

1218.   La Farge, Ann. **Pearl Buck**. New York: Chelsea House, 1988. 111p. $18.95. ISBN 1-55546-645-1. (American Women of Achievement). 5 up

The first American woman to win the Nobel Prize for Literature, Pearl Buck (1892-1972) did more than write vivid stories about China (her best-known book is *The Good Earth*), where she grew up as the daughter of missionaries. When she returned to the United States, she opened a home for children of mixed American and Asian descent who were orphaned or abandoned, trying to help them have better lives. Photographs and reproductions enhance the text. Chronology, Further Reading, and Index.

1219.   La Pierre, Yvette. **Native American Rock Art: Messages from the Past**. Lois Sloan, illustrator. Charlottesville, VA: Thomasson-Grant, 1994. 48p. $16.95. ISBN 1-56566-063-3. 3-7

The English settlers in the Massachusetts colony were the first to note prehistoric rock drawings in North America and wonder what they meant, but the first scientific study of rock art was not made until the late 1880s. Now archaeologists study the two types of rock art: *petroglyphs*, or images pecked or carved on stone surfaces, and *pictographs*, paintings on rocks. The first Americans who came across the Bering Sea land bridge may have left rock art that still exists. Scientists study where the art can be found, the pictures it presents, the culture of the Native Americans who created it, and what age it might be. Photographs of rock art in North America enhance the text. Rock Art Sites to Visit and Glossary.

1220.   Lacey, Dan. **The Essential Immigrant**. New York: Hippocrene, 1990. 256p. $16.95. ISBN 0-87052-610-3. YA

In a somewhat unexpected stance, the text supports the United States admitting immigrants. Research shows that immigrants have helped the economy through the years that they have been accepted. The history of immigration law in the United States, however, is uneven at best. Index.

1221.   Lackmann, Ronald W. **Same Time . . . Same Station: An A-Z Guide to Radio from Jack Benny to Howard Stern**. New York: Facts on File, 1995. 370p. $45. ISBN 0-8160-2862-1. YA

The history of radio shows a medium that has presented both entertainment and news. The text looks at many early shows beginning in the 1920s and continues to the present by giving synopses of the programs' contents. Information on news broadcasts such as Roosevelt's Fireside Chats and Edward R. Murrow's "You Are There" series also appears. Photographs, Appendix, Bibliography, and Index.

1222.   LaFarelle, Lorenzo G. **Bernardo de Gálvez: Hero of the American Revolution**. Austin, TX: Eakin Press, 1992. 76p. $14.95. ISBN 0-89015-849-5. 5-8

The family of Bernardo de Gálvez (1746-1786) lived in Spain during the time of Queen Isabel and Columbus's journey to the New World. Bernardo de Gálvez attended a military academy in Avila, Spain, before coming to New Spain with his father. Later, he became the commander of Spanish forces that supported the American Revolution. He directed the offense against the British in Louisiana, Alabama, and Florida. He first served in northern Mexico and the Spanish territory before he fought the British. Then he became the Viceroy of New Spain before he died in Mexico City. Galveston, Texas, is named for him. Glossary and Bibliography.

1223.   Lampman, Evelyn Sibley. **White Captives**. New York: Atheneum, 1975. 181p. $1.79. ISBN 0-689-50023-8. YA

Olive's family travels from Illinois to New Mexico in 1851 when she is 12 . After Apaches ambush their lone wagon and retaliate for tribal deaths by killing family members, only Olive and her younger sister survive. The Apaches take the two girls and make them slaves, but Olive's frail sister dies before she can be traded to other whites for a horse.

1224.   Landau, Elaine. **Armed America: The Status of Gun Control**. Englewood Cliffs, NJ: Silver Burdett, 1991. 102p. $12.95; $5.95pa. ISBN 0-671-72386-3; 0-671-72387-1pa. 7 up

Although gun control laws have changed in recent years and will likely continue to do so, the text gives a history of gun ownership in America since colonial times. Some of the state experiments mentioned have proven to be ineffective, but the text still has interesting information, including opposing viewpoints about state legislation and federal laws, including the Brady Bill and the McCallum Amendment. Bibliography and Index.

1225.   Landau, Elaine. **Cowboys**. New York: Franklin Watts, 1990. 64p. $19.90. ISBN 0-531-10866-X. (First Books). 5-8

Photographs and illustrations tell the story of the cowboys of the American West during the nineteenth century. Topics cover the range, the roundup, the trail drive, and cowboy social life until the end of the era. Glossary, Further Reading, and Index.

1226. Landau, Elaine. **The White Power Movement: America's Racist Hate Groups**. Brookfield, CT: Mill-brook Press, 1993. 96p. $17.40. ISBN 1-56294-327-8. 7 up

The history of the Ku Klux Klan in America shows the activity of a racist hate group from its inception to the attempt to gain national political office by one of its leaders, David Duke. The text also gives the history of other groups such as the Skinheads, who started in England, and the neo-Nazis, who function in the United States as well as other countries. Photographs and drawings enhance the text. Further Reading and Index. *New York Public Library Books for the Teen Age.*

1227. Landrum, Gene N. **Profiles of Female Genius: Thirteen Creative Women Who Changed the World**. Amherst, NY: Prometheus, 1994. 437p. $24.95. ISBN 0-87975-892-9. YA

In looking at female genius, Landrum examines self-esteem, birth order, childhood transience, role models, education, intelligence, crisis, personality traits, and temperament. With strict criteria for selection, he presents the profiles of 13 women who helped make significant changes in their fields. The women are Mary Kay Ash in cosmetics (b. 1917), Maria Callas in opera (1923-1977), Liz Claiborne in women's clothes (b. 1929), Jane Fonda in video and movies (b. 1937), Estée Lauder in cosmetics (b. 1908), Madonna in entertainment (b. 1958), Golda Meir in politics (1898-1978), Ayn Rand in philosophical literature (1905-1982), Gloria Steinem in women's is-sues (b. 1934), Margaret Thatcher in politics (b. 1925), Lillian Vernon in catalog sales (b. 1928), Linda Wachner in lingerie (b. 1946), and Oprah Winfrey in television talk (b. 1954). References and Index.

1228. Landrum, Gene N. **Profiles of Genius: Thirteen Creative Men Who Changed the World**. Amherst, NY: Prometheus, 1993. 263p. $24.95. ISBN 0-87975-832-5. YA

By examining innovation, change, and personality, Landrum suggests 10 reasons why traditional managers are not innovative. Using strict criteria for selection, he chooses 13 innovators and discusses their characteristics. He presents Steven Jobs (b. 1955) and Apple Computers, Fred Smith (b. 1944) and Federal Express, Tom Mona-ghan (b. 1937) and Domino's Pizza, Nolan Bushnell (b. 1943) and Atari and Pizza Time Theater, William Gates III (b. 1955) and Microsoft, Marcel Bich (b. 1914) and Bic Pens, Solomon Price (b. 1916) and Price Club, Howard Head (1914-1991) and Head Ski and Prince Tennis, William Lear (1902-1978) and Learjet, Soichiro Honda (1906-1991) and Honda Motors, Akio Morita (b. 1921) and Sony, Arthur Jones (b. 1923) and Nautilus, and Ted Turner (b. 1938) and Turner Broadcasting. Bibliography and Index.

1229. Lane, Joyce. **Our Century: 1960-1970**. Milwaukee, WI: Gareth Stevens, 1993. 64p. $23.93. ISBN 0-8368-1038-4. 3 up

Written as if a newspaper, the book's short articles give an overview of the decade. Included are statistics, daily life in America, Vietnam on television, Soviets and the U-2 spy plane, the Berlin Wall, Israel, the Czechos-lovakian revolt, the Kennedy years, the riots of 1968, the first man on the moon, Roger Maris, Sandy Koufax, Robert Frost, Martin Luther King, Jr., and Malcolm X. Glossary, Books for Further Reading, Places to Write or Visit, and Index.

1230. Lang, Susan. **Extremist Groups in America**. New York: Franklin Watts, 1990. 174p. $12.90. ISBN 0-531-10901-1. 6 up

Extremist groups in the United States include religious, paramilitary, and racist factions. Among them are the White Aryan Resistance, Chicago Area Skinheads (CASH), Christian Patriots Defense League (CPDL), David Duke, Lyndon LaRouche, Louis Farrakhan, and others. The text looks at the history of these groups, how they recruit, and what effects they have on society as a whole. Bibliography and Index.

1231. Langley, Myrtle. **Religion**. New York: Knopf, 1996. 59p. $19. ISBN 0-679-88123-9. (Eyewitness Books). 4-7

The text looks at different religions or facets of religions and relates them in double-page spreads illustrated with photographs, drawings, and reproductions. Among the religions and beliefs introduced in this overview are the Egyptian, Greek, Primitive, Hindu, Buddhist, Confucian, Taoist, Jainist, Sikh, Zoroastrian, Judaic, Christian, and Islamic faiths. Index.

1232. Langone, John. **Spreading Poison: A Book About Racism and Prejudice**. Boston: Little, Brown, 1993. 192p. $15.95. ISBN 0-316-51410-1. 7-12

By looking at various incidents in history, the text shows how prejudice can spread. Specific events include the Holocaust, Ku Klux Klan lynchings of Blacks, the internment of Japanese Americans, and the mistreatment of Native Americans. Specific topics include racism, anti-Semitism, homophobia, ethnic intolerance for immigrants, discrimination against the disabled, and sexism. Notes and Index.

1233.   Lansche, Jerry. **Stan "The Man" Musial: Born to Be a Ballplayer**. Dallas, TX: Taylor, 1994. 212p. $19.95. ISBN 0-87833-846-2. 7 up

Stan Musial (b. 1920) had no wasted energy in his swing at the plate. He had the eyesight, coordination, instinct, timing, and speed to make all pitchers dislike facing him at bat. He retired in 1963, holding almost every possible Cardinal record. He had more than 3,000 hits and more than 400 home runs. He had many major awards; some of them he earned more than once. He never embarrassed teammates or opponents, as he was concerned mainly with being decent and playing the game well. Photographs, Playing Record, Bibliography, and Index.

1234.   Larsen, Anita. **Amelia Earhart: Missing, Declared Dead**. Marcy Ramsey, illustrator. New York: Crestwood House, 1992. 48p. $11.95. ISBN 0-89686-613-0. (History's Mysteries). 5 up

When Amelia Earhart and Fred Noonan disappeared in 1937 on their trip around the world at the equator, various theories arose as to what had happened to them. Some thought they were spying on the Japanese; others thought they might be lost at sea. The mystery continues because no one has found any remains of either the aviators or the plane. Chronology, Resources, and Index.

1235.   Larsen, Rebecca. **Franklin D. Roosevelt: Man of Destiny**. New York: Franklin Watts, 1991. 208p. $23.40. ISBN 0-531-11068-0. 8-12

While Franklin Delano Roosevelt (1882-1945) was in the White House for 12 years, the nation emerged from the Depression of the early 1930s to the prosperity brought by production for the war. Legacies of the era included Social Security, federal deposit insurance, the Securities and Exchange Commission, and collective bargaining in labor relations. Roosevelt's wife Eleanor supported him after he was stricken with polio in 1921 and helped him in his quest for the presidency and in his performance while in office. Notes, For Further Reading, and Index.

1236.   Larsen, Rebecca. **Paul Robeson: Hero Before His Time**. New York: Franklin Watts, 1989. 158p. $13.95. ISBN 0-531-10779-5. 6-9

Paul Robeson (1890-1976) was an all-American football player, a Phi Beta Kappa member, a debater, and the class valedictorian at Rutgers University. He then graduated from Columbia University Law School. But he became famous as an actor and singer when he played in *Show Boat*, *Othello*, and *The Emperor Jones*. He was always outraged at the way Blacks were treated, and he was an early activist in many of the civil rights and labor movement struggles. He thought the Soviet Union must be better after he saw how poorly the United States treated Blacks. In the 1950s, during the Joseph McCarthy era, his pro-Soviet sentiments became targeted, and his career was ruined. He spent much of his later life in the Soviet Union. Notes, Bibliography, and Index.

1237.   Larsen, Rebecca. **Richard Nixon: Rise and Fall of a President**. New York: Franklin Watts, 1991. 208p. $23.40. ISBN 0-531-10997-6. 6-9

Richard Milhous Nixon (1913-1994) was elected to the presidency in 1968 and reelected in 1972 only to resign in ignominy when found to have known about people breaking into the Democratic Committee's headquarters at the Watergate. The text looks at Nixon's life and the variety of influences that may have affected his choices during his political career. Notes, Sources, and Index.

1238.   Larsen, Rebecca. **Ronald Reagan**. New York: Franklin Watts, 1995. 191p. $21.20. ISBN 0-531-11191-1. (Impact Biography). 7 up

The 40th President of the United States, Ronald Reagan (b. 1911) first found his voice in front of an audience when he was a college freshman speaking out against the administration's treatment of students and faculty. Son of an alcoholic father, he had to find his own place in life, and after college in 1932, he wanted to go to Hollywood and become an actor. He did, and he became the governor of California before he became the President. Bibliography and Index.

1239.   Lasky, Kathryn. **Beyond the Burning Time**. New York: Blue Sky, Scholastic, 1994. 272p. $13.95. ISBN 0-590-47331-X. 5-9

In 1691, Mary Chase, 12, works hard with her mother on their Salem farm while her brother Caleb serves his shipbuilding apprenticeship. At the same time, the strange actions of the girls who have been visiting Tituba, Reverend Parris's slave, begin to frighten the town. Then a boy who works for the family accuses Mary's mother Virginia of being a witch. Mary and Caleb threaten Mary Warren, and she tells them where their mother is hidden after she is taken from prison to be hanged. They save her and escape. The ending reveals that the story, in omniscient point of view, is a flashback. *American Library Association Best Books for Young Adults*.

1240. Lasky, Katheryn. **Beyond the Divide**. New York: Macmillan, 1983. 264p. $17. ISBN 0-02-751670-9. New York: Aladdin, 1995. 264p. $3.95pa. ISBN 0-689-80163-7pa. 7 up

When the Amish community in Holly Springs, Pennsylvania, shuns Meribah's father in 1849, the family leaves for the West. In their group of wagons are several unsavory people who refuse to respect the rights of others on the journey. The men rape the friend that Meribah has made. Later, Meribah learns about herbs from a woman at one of the wagon stops. After she runs out of herbs, she has to leave the train with her father and try to save him from gangrene. She is unsuccessful, but Yani (Mill Creek) Indians find her and give her food so that she can learn about survival in the wild and gain confidence for her future. *American Library Association Best Book for Young Adults, American Library Association Notable Books for Children,* and *NCTE Recommended Book.*

1241. Lasky, Kathryn. **A Journey to the New World: The Diary of Remember Patience Whipple: Mayflower/Plimoth Colony, 1620**. New York: Scholastic, 1996. 173p. $9.95. ISBN 0-590-50214-X. (Dear America 3). 5-9

When Mem is 12, she and her family sail on the *Mayflower* to the New World. She writes in her journal beginning on October 1, 1620, and ends it on November 10, 1621, as she watches another ship come into the harbor and hopes that a girl her age will be arriving soon. She talks of the difficult times in the year as well as the Thanksgiving celebration, and dares to dream that someday their settlement will have a bakery. An epilogue gives further information about her after her diary ends.

1242. Lasky, Kathryn. **The Night Journey**. Trina S. Hynam, illustrator. New York: Viking, 1986. 152p. $12.95. ISBN 0-670-80935-7. New York: Penguin, 1986. 152p. $4.99pa. ISBN 0-14-032048-2pa. 5-9

Not until she is 13 does Rache hear the story of Jewish pogroms and her grandmother's escape from Russia with her family in 1900. Her grandmother hid under chicken crates, paraded as a Purim player, and crossed the border with her cookies. The cookies held the family's gold. *National Jewish Awards, American Library Association Notable Books for Children, Association of Jewish Libraries Award,* and *Sydney Taylor Book Award.*

1243. Lasky, Kathryn. **Pageant**. New York: Macmillan, 1986. 221p. $14.95. ISBN 0-02-751720-9. New York: Dell, 1988. 221p. $3.95pa. ISBN 0-440-20161-6pa. 8 up

Sarah, a Jewish teenager, recalls her four years of high school in Indianapolis as she prepares to participate in the Christmas pageant as a shepherd, a role she has played each year. As a senior, she walks out of the rehearsal, gets into her parents' car, and drives to see her sister in New York. Still shocked over John Kennedy's assassination in 1963, she cannot yet find a coherent reason underlying her life. Her aunt's friend helps her face some of the choices she must make.

1244. Lasky, Kathryn. **True North: A Novel of the Underground Railroad**. New York: Scholastic, 1996. 267p. $14.95. ISBN 0-590-20523-4. 7 up

When Lucy Bradford is 14 in 1858 and living in Boston, she finds out that her grandfather, who has taught her to sail, is a stationmaster on the Underground Railroad. When Lucy meets Afrika, a girl fleeing from the South, she knows that she has to help her. Lucy is gone from home so long that her family thinks that she is dead. When she returns on the day of her sister's wedding, everyone is overcome, but Lucy has helped Afrika to freedom.

1245. Latham, Jean Lee. **Carry On, Mr. Bowditch**. John O'Hara Cosgrave II, illustrator. Boston: Houghton Mifflin, 1955. 256p. $14.95; $6.95pa. ISBN 0-395-06881-9; 0-395-13713-6pa. 6 up

Several years after Nathaniel Bowditch was born in 1773, his sailing captain father ran aground and lost his ship. This reversed the family's fortunes, as recounted in this fictional biography, and when 12, Nat was indentured for nine years. He had desperately wanted to go to Harvard, but instead, he read widely and taught himself languages (including Latin word-by-word so that he could read Newton) with the help of mentors who were impressed with his enormous intelligence. His abilities helped him navigate by using the moon's position. He found mistakes in charts used by sailors and dedicated himself to checking every one of the entries and correcting the wrong ones that were published in *The New American Practical Navigator* (1802). He taught others how to navigate before his death in 1838. *Newbery Medal.*

1246. Lauber, Patricia. **Lost Star: The Story of Amelia Earhart**. New York: Scholastic, 1988. 106p. $3.50. ISBN 0-590-41615-4. 5-8

In 1937, Amelia Earhart (1897-1937) attempted to fly around the world at the equator. Her plane was lost, and no one has ever found a trace of it. Earhart's mother was the first woman to reach Pikes Peak and made bloomers for Amelia and her sister like those introduced by Amelia Jenks Bloomer. While alcoholism was destroying her father, Amelia became interested in airplanes and eventually flying. She married a publicist, George Putnam, who supported her interests. She was the first woman to cross the Atlantic and the first person to cross the Pacific. People speculate that Earhart might have crashed in the Pacific islands controlled by the Japanese, where no one was allowed to search. For Further Reading and Index.

1247.   Lavender, David. **Snowbound: The Tragic Story of the Donner Party**. New York: Holiday House, 1996. 87p. $16.95. ISBN 0-8234-1231-8. 4-8

In 1846, the Donner party became stranded in a blizzard in the Sierra Nevada Mountains as they tried to negotiate the Overland Trail. Lavender looks at their journey by focusing mainly on the group that stayed near the lake during the winter and tries to assess what caused the tragedy. He says that part of the blame belongs to the guidebook author Lanford Hastings, who misled the group. The other part belongs within the party because supplies were not equally distributed. Lavender downplays the accusations against those who survived for engaging in cannibalism by noting that it was the one means to keep themselves alive. Maps, Photographs, Bibliography, and Index.

1248.   Law, Kevin J. **Milliard Fillmore: 13th President of the United States**. Ada, OK: Garrett Educational, 1990. 122p. $19.80. ISBN 0-944483-61-5. (Presidents of the United States). 5-9

Millard Fillmore (1800-1874) lived in poverty as a young boy. His father apprenticed him to a mill owner, a job that he hated. While there, he realized that he needed more education and began studying. His father secured another position for him to read law in the summer, and the kindness of the judge who saw his potential changed the course of his life. He went to Washington as a congressman and became Zachary Taylor's Vice President. When Taylor died in 1849, Fillmore rose to the presidency. He served in office during a difficult time and did not want to run again. His party members begged him, but because of various strategies by his enemies, he lost the nomination, and the Whigs lost the election to Franklin Pierce. Fillmore was not displeased with the results because he was able to leave a job he never really wanted. Bibliography and Index.

1249.   Lawler, Mary. **Marcus Garvey: Black Nationalist Leader**. New York: Chelsea House, 1988. 112p. $18.95; $7.95pa. ISBN 1-55546-587-0; 0-7910-0203-9pa. (Black Americans of Achievement). 5 up

Marcus Garvey (1887-1940) believed in the Back to Africa movement for Blacks to return to Africa and establish a central homeland. He began his fight for Black rights in 1914 as he tried to heighten racial pride and improve economics and education. People called him "Black Moses" for his efforts, but a failed business venture led to his loss of power. Photographs enhance the text. Chronology, Further Reading, and Index.

1250.   Lawlor, Laurie. **Daniel Boone**. Bert Dodson, illustrator. Niles, IL: Albert Whitman, 1989. 160p. $13.95. ISBN 0-8075-1462-4. 4-8

Daniel Boone (1734-1820) would not want to be remembered as a man who fought the Native Americans. As a Quaker, he did not hold grudges, and he was not particularly tall or imposing. Shawnee Chief Blackfish adopted him as his son. What motivated Boone was a love of the wilderness and a desire to explore. He was a leader who moved beyond the Appalachian Mountains to open the area for others. Chronology, Bibliography, and Index.

1251.   Lawlor, Laurie. **Gold in the Hills**. New York: Walker, 1995. 146p. $15.95. ISBN 0-8027-8371-6. 4-7

Hattie, 10, and her brother Pheme, 12, go to live with a cousin after their mother dies, while their father goes to mine gold in the mountains around 1880. After a mine owner tries to get their cousin to commit them to slave labor, the two make friends with a neighbor, an old woodsman who teaches them the secrets of the Colorado forest. After Hattie nearly drowns and Pheme meets a nine-foot grizzly bear, they feel more comfortable with their changed life.

1252.   Lawlor, Laurie. **Shadow Catcher: The Life and Work of Edward S. Curtis**. New York: Walker, 1994. 132p. $20.85. ISBN 0-8027-8289-2. 8-10

Edward S. Curtis (1868-1952) began documenting North American Indian cultures at the beginning of the twentieth century, creating 20 volumes of text and oversized photogravure plates to record their lives. He finished his project around 1930. During his lifetime, the work was never appreciated, but as people became more concerned about the Native American tribal way of life and his plates were discovered in the basement of a Boston bookstore, their full worth is now known. He recorded the dignity and pain of the Indians. Photographs of many tribes, including the Zuni, Hopi, Quahatika, Kutenai, Tewa, Lummi, Achomawi, and Assiniboin, enhance the text. Among the warriors he photographed were Chief Red Cloud and Picket Pin of the Oglala Sioux, the aged daughter of Chief Seatlh (Seattle), Chief Joseph of the Nez Percé, Geronimo of the Apache, Black Eagle of the Assiniboin, Hollow Horn Bear of the Brulé Sioux, and Two Moons of the Cheyenne. Appendix, Selected Bibliography for Children, and Index. *American Library Association Best Books for Young Adults, Golden Kite Honor Book, Hungry Mind Review Children's Books of Distinction*, and *Notable Children's Trade Books in the Field of Social Studies.*

1253.   Lawlor, Laurie. **Where Will This Shoe Take You? A Walk Through the History of Footwear**. New York: Walker, 1996. 132p. $17.95. ISBN 0-8027-8434-8. 4-8

Among a number of facts, Lawlor shows that footwear reflects economic class, social status, authority level, and sometimes political beliefs of the wearer. She presents the invention and development of shoes in seven categories: sandals, boots, oxfords, pumps, clogs, mules, and moccasins as well as shoe-related customs. Photographs, Bibliography, and Index.

1254.   Lawlor, Veronica, selector/illustrator. **I Was Dreaming to Come to America: Memories from the Ellis Island Oral History Project**. New York: Viking, 1995. 40p. $14.99. ISBN 0-670-86164-2. 5 up
    This collection of images and memories from children and adults who passed through Ellis Island from 1900 to 1925 gives a vibrant view of the immigrant experience. *Notable Children's Trade Books in the Field of Social Studies*.

1255.   Lawrence, Jacob, author/illustrator. **The Great Migration**. New York: HarperCollins, 1993. Unpaged. $23.89; $6.95pa. ISBN 0-06-023038-X; 0-06-443428-1pa. 3-7
    Around the time of World War I, African Americans began leaving their homes in the rural South and moving to the North. This sequence of paintings shows this Great Migration. The accompanying text tells about the movement of a people who wanted to improve their lives with better opportunities. *Notable Children's Trade Books in the Field of Social Studies, American Library Association Notable Books for Children, Booklist Books for Young Editors' Choices, IRA Teachers' Choices, Carter G. Woodson Outstanding Merit Book*, and *New York Public Library Books for the Teen Age*.

1256.   Lawson, Don. **Famous Presidential Scandals**. Springfield, NJ: Enslow, 1990. 128p. $15.95. ISBN 0-89490-247-4. 8-12
    In a look at a few Presidents since the Civil War who have had scandal rip through their administrations, Lawson finds some similarities. Among them are corruption, unethical behavior, deceit, and popularity. Graft tarnished Grant; greed toppled Harding; Watergate was larger than Nixon; and the Iran-Contra scandal infiltrated Reagan. Although he makes few parallels among the men, he tries to set the situations in their historical contexts. Further Reading and Index.

1257.   Lawson, John. **If Pigs Could Fly**. Boston: Houghton Mifflin, 1989. 136p. $13.95. ISBN 0-395-50928-9. 6-9
    During the War of 1812, innocent and naive Morgan James becomes involved with some interesting characters. Perhaps a Scottish regiment was defeated when bees flew under their kilts, but documentation may not be available. Morgan is moral and true and loves with great idealism in this entertaining rendition of the war.

1258.   Lazar, Jerry. **Red Cloud: Sioux War Chief**. New York: Chelsea House, 1995. 111p. $18.95; $7.95pa. ISBN 0-7910-1718-4; 0-7910-2044-4pa. (North American Indians of Achievement). 6-9
    Red Cloud (1822-1909) was an able warrior by the time the first settlers arrived in Sioux territory, where he lived as a Teton Sioux. To keep the lands, he united more than 2,000 Sioux, Cheyenne, and Arapaho to drive the U.S. Army from the Black Hills of South Dakota. He won, stopped fighting, and moved to the Sioux reservation. He spent the last 40 years of his life trying to keep the government from taking the remainder of his people's homeland and culture. Photographs enhance the text. Chronology, Further Reading, and Index.

1259.   Lazo, Caroline. **Eleanor Roosevelt**. New York: Dillon Press, 1993. 64p. $13.95. ISBN 0-87518-594-0. (Peacemakers). 4-8
    Eleanor Roosevelt (1884-1962) had a sad childhood after her parents died, living with a strict grandmother. She went to study in England, however, and one of her teachers saw her potential and encouraged her. She became reacquainted with and married Franklin Roosevelt, her distant cousin, when she returned to the United States. Among the early disappointments of the marriage was finding love letters from another woman in his luggage and his bout with polio, which left him in a wheelchair. She spoke for issues in which she believed. Photographs, For Further Reading, and Index.

1260.   Lazo, Caroline. **Wilma Mankiller**. New York: Dillon Press, 1995. 64p. $13.95; $7.95pa. ISBN 0-87518-635-1; 0-382-24716-7pa. (Peacemakers). 4-8
    Wilma Mankiller (b. 1945) became the leader of the Cherokee Nation when the chief for whom she worked resigned in 1985. Two years later, she was elected in her own right. The name "Mankiller" in the eighteenth century referred to a top military rank of the Cherokee's warring ancestors. Because of the pride associated with the name, Wilma Mankiller continued to use it after she was married. But contrary to what the name implies, she has been working for peace with her nation of 130,000 members. The text looks at her life. For Further Reading and Index.

1261.   Learmon, Warren. **Unheard Melodies**. Marietta, GA: Longstreet, 1990. 214p. $16.95. ISBN 0-929264-26-6. YA
    The narrator's story starts in 1948, when he remembers hearing his mother and uncle discuss the changed attitude of their brother after his return from World War II. He continues to observe his family as he goes through school, plays on his Atlanta high school basketball team, and chooses a college. As he assesses what he has learned, he realizes that what he thought he knew about his family and friends was only an illusion. The reality is very different.

1262.   Leathers, Noel L. **The Japanese in America**. Minneapolis, MN: Lerner, 1991. 64p. $17.50; $5.95pa. ISBN 0-8225-0241-0; 0-8225-1044-8pa. (In America). 5 up

Photographs, maps, and text tell about the Japanese immigration to America, their way of life, the prejudice they faced during World War II, and their contributions to American life. Index.

1263.   Leavell, J. Perry, Jr. **Harry S. Truman**. New York: Chelsea House, 1988. 112p. $18.95. ISBN 0-87754-558-8. (World Leaders Past and Present). 5 up

Harry S. Truman (1884-1972) became President when Franklin Roosevelt died in office. He first worked in the Senate for Missouri, where he earned a reputation for honesty and efficiency. He began the atomic age when he authorized the bombing of Hiroshima. After the war, he committed the United States to a program of economic aid for war-torn countries, even the enemies. Blacks and labor helped him win a second term, but Congress defeated most of his proposals. His last years in office saw the Korean War and Senator Joseph McCarthy's crusade against Communism. Photographs enhance the text. Chronology, Further Reading, and Index.

1264.   Leavell, J. Perry, Jr. **James Madison**. New York: Chelsea House, 1988. 112p. $18.95. ISBN 55546-815-2. (World Leaders Past and Present). 5 up

James Madison (1751-1836) is the father of the Constitution. He and Thomas Jefferson outlined the ideas of freedom and democracy that appear in that document. During his presidency, he established the second national bank, and the "era of good feeling," a time of economic growth, ensued. He was intelligent, philosophical, and democratic. Engravings and reproductions enhance the text. Chronology, Further Reading, and Index.

1265.   Leavell, J. Perry, Jr. **Woodrow Wilson**. New York: Chelsea House, 1987. 116p. $18.95. ISBN 0-87754-557-X. (World Leaders Past and Present). 5 up

Woodrow Wilson (1856-1924) was a college professor and university president before he became New Jersey's governor. Later, as President of the United States, he started "trust-busting." He helped create the federal reserve system and the graduated income tax. He was reelected in 1916 for keeping America out of the Great War, but he had to declare war on Germany in 1917. After the war, he could not get support at home for the League of Nations, but the United States became a military power during his terms of office. Wilson was alternately pragmatic, idealistic, pacifistic, and militaristic, but he was always dedicated to world peace. Photographs enhance the text. Further Reading, Glossary, and Index.

1266.   Leckie, Robert. **None Died in Vain: The Saga of the American Civil War**. New York: HarperCollins, 1990. 682p. $29.95; $17pa. ISBN 0-06-016280-5; 0-06-092116-1pa. YA

The text includes introductory background on the economic, political, and social forces that shaped the secession of the states leading to the Civil War. Anecdotes about the political and military leaders help the reader understand some of the choices they made, or did not make. To highlight the text, Leckie has added photographs and detailed maps. Bibliography and Index.

1267.   Leckie, Robert. **Okinawa: The Last Battle of World War II**. New York: Viking, 1995. 220p. $24.95; $13.95pa. ISBN 0-670-84716-X; 0-14-017389-7pa. YA

The text presents all aspects of the Okinawa landing, from its planning to its execution, as well as the ground fighting and the fierce action of the Japanese at sea with their kamikaze planes and ships. Leckie believes that Japan would have surrendered without either bomb or invasion and that Truman dropped the bomb to show Stalin his power. However, Okinawa was decisive because a Japanese victory would have heightened the conviction of the Japanese military inner sanctum that Japan should never accept an Allied surrender offer, even with Hirohito's influence to the contrary. Bibliography and Index.

1268.   Ledbetter, Cynthia, and Richard C. Jones. **John Muir**. Vero Beach, FL: Rourke, 1993. 112p. $19.93. ISBN 0-86625-494-3. (Pioneers). 5-9

John Muir (1838-1914) was one of the first to speak out for the protection of the country's natural areas. He was an expert in botany and geology, largely self-taught. He observed nature closely and saw that glaciers had formed Yosemite's landscape. He saw that nature and humans were interconnected, and he wrote articles to ensure that humans would know their responsibilities to nature and to keep it healthy. As perhaps the first ecologist, he was able to influence Theodore Roosevelt to save as much land as he could. Time Line, Glossary, Bibliography, Media Resources, and Index.

1269.   Leder, Jane. **Amelia Earhart: Opposing Viewpoints**. San Diego, CA: Greenhaven, 1990. 111p. $19.95. ISBN 0-89908-070-7. (Great Mysteries—Opposing Viewpoints). 6-9

The text explores the mystery of the disappearance of Amelia Earhart, the first woman to cross the Atlantic, in 1937 when she was flying over the Pacific. Because no one knows what happened to her, the speculation continues as to whether she was lost at sea or survived and was unable to communicate her whereabouts. Quotes, black-and-white illustrations, and maps complement the text. Bibliography and Index.

1270. Lee, Gus. **China Boy**. New York: Dutton, 1991. 322p. $19.95. ISBN 0-525-24994-X. New York: Plume, 1994. 322p. $11.95pa. ISBN 0-452-27158-4pa. YA

When he is seven in the 1950s, Kai Ting begins boxing lessons at the neighborhood YMCA in a Black San Francisco community. Although he learns how to defend himself, he still has difficulty balancing the reality of his Chinese culture, the cultures around him, and his stepmother, a product of Philadelphia society.

1271. Lee, Helen Elaine. **The Serpent's Gift**. New York: Atheneum, 1994. 374p. $21; $12pa. ISBN 0-689-12193-8; 0-684-80168-4pa. YA

In 1910, after her husband beats her, Eula Smalls and her children look for refuge, but only another mid-western Black woman, Ruby, who has a daughter of her own, will take them in. The two families live together during the twentieth century with Eula and one daughter isolating themselves from pain while Ruby and her daughter and Eula's other daughter cope with their lives through storytelling and community involvement.

1272. Lefer, Diane. **Emma Lazarus**. New York: Chelsea House, 1988. 110p. $18.95. ISBN 1-55546-664-8. (American Women of Achievement). 5 up

The poet who made the Statue of Liberty a symbol of hope, Emma Lazarus (1849-1887) grew up in a wealthy New York Jewish family. She published her first poems at 18. Her strong beliefs surfaced 14 years later when she heard of the anti-Semitic violence abroad and realized that it was a part of her own heritage. She became a spokeswoman for Jewish unity, religious tolerance, and an "open-door" immigration policy in the United States. Not until 10 years after she died were her verses inscribed on the base of the Statue of Liberty: "Give me your tired, your poor, your huddled masses yearning to breathe free." Photographs and engravings enhance the text. Chronology, Further Reading, and Index.

1273. Lehrer, Brian. **The Korean Americans**. New York: Chelsea House, 1988. 108p. $19.95. ISBN 0-87754-888-9. (The Immigrant Experience). 5 up

Although Koreans had migrated to Hawaii during the twentieth century, they did not began settling around New York and Los Angeles until 1965, when the anti-Asian quota system was abolished. At that time, many educated Koreans arrived. Recorded Korean history begins in the first century AD with the words of a Chinese scholar, Ki-tze. At the end of the Sino-Japanese war in 1895, troops of Japanese soldiers controlled Korean civilians until 1945. After World War II, Korea was split with the Communists in the north above the 38th parallel. Further Reading and Index.

1274. Lehrman, Robert. **The Store That Mama Built**. New York: Macmillan, 1992. 126p. $13.95. ISBN 0-02-754632-2. 3-7

Almost ready to open his grocery store in Harrisburg, Pennsylvania, in 1917, Birdie's father, a Russian Jewish immigrant, dies of influenza. Birdie's mother decides that she will open the store as planned, and the entire family helps. His mother decides that she will offer credit to Black families, and the store begins to make money even though the family closes it on Friday nights and Saturdays so that they can keep their Sabbath.

1275. Leiner, Katherine. **First Children: Growing Up in the White House**. Katie Keller, illustrator. New York: Tambourine, 1996. 224p. $20. ISBN 0-688-13341-X. 6-9

Leiner limits the text to information about 17 first families as she presents Presidents' children and grandchildren as well as the offspring of staff and visitors who stay in the White House for a long time. She also shows an angle such as Luci Johnson's wedding, Quentin Roosevelt and his gang, Letitia Tyler's response to her father's new wife being the same age as she, Caroline Kennedy's White House school, or Andrew Johnson's son Frank waiting to hear if his father has been impeached. Appendix and Bibliography.

1276. Leinwand, Gerald. **Do We Need a New Constitution?** New York: Franklin Watts, 1994. 144p. $20.30. ISBN 0-531-11127-X. (Democracy in Action). 7-12

Beginning with the Constitutional Convention of 1787, Leinwand discusses the decisions of the representatives about what type of government would be formed within the new nation. It chose a federal system in which states would be gathered under one national government and power parceled to three branches. Leinwand questions the validity of this government in modern times by looking at the checks and balances system, the roles of political parties, and the power of the Supreme Court. But he notes that any decision for change lies in debate and careful consideration. Glossary, For Further Reading, Appendices, and Index.

1277. Lelchuk, Alan. **On Home Ground**. Merle Nacht, illustrator. San Diego, CA: Harcourt Brace, 1987. 72p. $9.95. ISBN 0-15-200560-9. 5-7

When Aaron is almost 10 in 1947, three males are important in his life. One, a veteran suffering from war wounds, takes him to baseball games. The second, Jackie Robinson, plays in those games. The third, his father, feels uncomfortable with his new life in the United States after leaving Russia. When Aaron sees his father in the country, galloping on a large horse, he understands that his father has a side to his personality that he had never seen.

1278.   Lenski, Lois. **Indian Captive: The Story of Mary Jemison**. 1941. New York: Trophy, 1995. 304p. $16; $4.95pa. ISBN 0-397-30072-7; 0-06-446162-9pa. 5 up

This book is based on a true story. Seneca Indians captured Mary Jemison, 12, in 1758, and massacred her family in retaliation for white settlers killing their own people. After two years, she felt like she belonged to this group, which was mostly kind and courageous, and refused to go with the English conquerors of Quebec. Although the book was first published in 1941, Lenski presents a balanced view of Native American and white settlers—none of them all bad or all good. The blond Mary, first known as "Corn Tassel," earned her name "Little-Woman-of-Great-Courage" by realizing that being with people who loved her was more important than being with people of the same race who only saw her as a pawn in a distant war. *Newbery Honor Book*.

1279.   Lenski, Lois. **Strawberry Girl**. 1945. New York: HarperTrophy, 1995. 194p. $4.50pa. ISBN 0-06-440585-0pa. 5 up

Two families in Florida during the early 1900s, the Slaters and the Boyers, have to adjust to each other's ways. The Boyers strive to succeed through work and education, but the Slater family's father seems to thrive on destroying their efforts. When the Slater mother and children become ill while the father is away, Mrs. Boyer comes to nurse them back to health. Her kindness and the influence of an itinerant preacher help Mr. Slater realize the value of being a good neighbor and an honest employee. *American Library Association Notable Books for Children* and *Newbery Medal*.

1280.   Leonard, Laura. **Saving Damaris**. New York: Jean Karl, Atheneum, 1989. 192p. $14.95. ISBN 0-689-31553-8. 5-7

Abby is 12 on July 4, 1904. That day she begins a diary in which she tells of her father leaving home, her sewing, and her sister Damaris, 16, taking a job in Mr. Buttenbacher's emporium. After their mother dies, Mr. Buttenbacher wants Damaris to marry him. Although Damaris does not love him, she knows she must accept the offer. Before Abby can figure out how to stop the engagement, Mr. Buttenbacher realizes he will have to care for the other two children as well as Damaris. He changes his mind.

1281.   Leuzzi, Linda. **Urban Life**. New York: Chelsea House, 1995. 104p. $18.95. ISBN 0-7910-2841-0. (Life in America One Hundred Years Ago). 5-9

Cities in the United States began to flourish only a century ago. In the second half of the nineteenth century, construction of huge buildings, electric lights, elevators, parks, suspension bridges, and mansions furthered their growth. At the same time, however, they became places of dingy tenements for poorly paid immigrants who worked long hours. Social workers and muckrakers had to expose their existence and the political system that allowed it. The text looks at all of these complexities underlying the growth of cities. Photographs, Further Reading, and Index.

1282.   LeVert, Suzanne. **Edgar Allan Poe: Mournful and Never Ending Remembrance**. New York: Chelsea House, 1992. 111p. $18.95. ISBN 0-7910-1640-4. (Library of Biography). 7-10

Edgar Allan Poe (1809-1849) was one of the most accomplished short story writers of the nineteenth century. His tempestuous and unstable nature fought with his literary abilities, and his fame was greater in France than in the United States. However, he approached writing very systematically, knowing exactly what kinds of effects he wanted to achieve. Bibliography and Index.

1283.   LeVert, Suzanne. **Huey Long: The Kingfish of Louisiana**. New York: Facts on File, 1995. 134p. $17.95. ISBN 0-8160-2880-X. (Makers of America). 7 up

As governor and later U.S. senator from Louisiana, Huey Long (1893-1935) tried to improve the lives of poor Americans. He campaigned for workers' compensation, higher taxation of the wealthy, and better education for Louisiana citizens. However, he ran the Louisiana legislature tightly and implemented his policies in questionable, probably illegal ways. As a young man, he was a traveling salesman, and the qualities he learned there aided him in his political career. He brought roads, electricity, and jobs to his state. Bibliography and Index.

1284.   Levi, Steven C. **Cowboys of the Sky: The Story of Alaska's Bush Pilots**. New York: Walker, 1996. 114p. $17.95. ISBN 0-8027-8331-7. 5-9

The size of the state of Alaska and the portions isolated by ice and snow in the winter have made the role of bush pilots important. The text looks at the history of pilots since the 1920s who have brought mail, supplies, and contact to citizens in the outer areas. Anecdotes about the adventures of men with such nicknames as "the craziest pilot in the world" or "Thrill 'Em, Chill 'Em, Spill 'Em, But No Kill 'Em" include encounters with weather, animals such as polar bears, planes barely holding together, and dangerous landing places. The people who fly these planes have their own unusual histories. Photographs, Bibliography, Glossary, and Index.

1285.   Levin, Betty. **Fire in the Wind**. New York: Greenwillow, 1995. 176p. $15. ISBN 0-688-14299-0. 5-7

Meg and her brother wait for the fire ravaging through the Maine woods to reach their two-room school-house in 1947. Her slightly retarded cousin Orin knows the way to the school so well that he is able to beat the fire and rescue the two by thrusting them into a culvert. His quick response leads his parents to recognize his worth and stop revering their other son, a dead hero of World War II.

1286.   Levin, Betty. **Mercy's Mill**. New York: Greenwillow, 1992. 241p. $14. ISBN 0-688-11122-X. 7 up

In this historical fantasy, Sarah, 13, feels neglected while her mother and stepfather renovate an old mill to which they have moved. She meets a boy who does not understand some of the simple things that she mentions although he otherwise seems normal. She finds that he, a runaway slave, looks for a girl he thinks is in danger who lived both in colonial times and in the pre–Civil War period with him. While her own family life is difficult, Sarah helps him and the girl in unexpected ways.

1287.   Levine, Ellen. **A Fence Away from Freedom: Japanese Americans and World War II**. New York: Putnam, 1995. 288p. $17.95. ISBN 0-399-22638-9. 5 up

Using the memories of 35 people who lived in several different camps during the World War II internment of Japanese Americans, Levine tells a story about the people and the camps. The government even brought some Japanese from Peru and placed them in the camps, probably as a bait for exchange of prisoners of war. The text is arranged both chronologically and topically, with the stories of the 35 people appearing as parts in more than one chapter. Appendix and Index. *Notable Children's Trade Books in the Field of Social Studies.*

1288.   Levine, Ellen. **Freedom's Children: Young Civil Rights Activists Tell Their Own Stories**. New York: Putnam, 1993. 152p. $16.95. ISBN 0-399-21893-9. 7-12

During the 1950s and 1960s, many people were jailed for their participation in civil rights activities. Among them were children. Claudette Colvin was arrested for not giving up her seat on a bus before Rosa Parks was ar-rested. Audrey Faye Hendricks, nine, went to jail along with Dr. Martin Luther King, Jr. in Birmingham for par-ticipating in the demonstration. Euvester Simpson was in the same jail with Fannie Lou Hamer in Mississippi. Sheyann Webb was eight when she went to the Selma march that turned into "Bloody Sunday." These and others are the 30 subjects of this book who tell about their experiences during this important political and social move-ment. Chronology, Bibliography, and Index.

1289.   Levinson, Nancy Smiler. **I Lift My Lamp: Emma Lazarus and the Statue of Liberty**. New York: Lodestar, Dutton, 1992. 102p. $13.95. ISBN 0-525-67180-3. (Jewish Biography). 5-9

Emma Lazarus (1849-1887) grew up in a privileged family, but seeing Jewish refugees fleeing from perse-cution affected her so much that she began to write about their problems. She wrote her now-famous poem about the Statue of Liberty before the statue was unveiled. She had composed it as part of a portfolio of works created to entice people to contribute to a fund to pay for the statue's base. Not until 1903, when a woman discovered the port-folio in a book store, did the poem become famous. "The New Colossus," with its words, "Give me your tired, your poor," became symbolic of what the United States could offer to its immigrants. The text looks at Emma's life and the background of the statue's sculptor, Frédéric-Auguste Bartholdi. Books for Further Reading and Index.

1290.   Levinson, Nancy Smiler. **Turn of the Century: Our Nation One Hundred Years Ago**. New York: Lodestar, Dutton, 1994. 134p. $16.99. ISBN 0-525-67433-0. 7 up

Integrating anecdotes and facts, Levinson recreates what was happening at the turn of the nineteenth century to the twentieth century in the United States. She talks about the influence of the railroads, the robber barons, the need for workers to unite, the entry and isolation of immigrants, the increase in population of the cities, the needs of Black citizens, families and their expectations, and the changes in the West. She ends with the note that this time was the beginning of the nation's power throughout the world. Suggested Reading and Index.

1291.   Levinson, Nancy Smiler. **Your Friend, Natalie Popper**. New York: Lodestar, 1991. 113p. $13.95. ISBN 0-525-67307-5. 5-7

After Natalie, 12, and her friend Corinne finish sixth grade, they go to camp. At first, Natalie clings to Cor-rine, who had attended camp the previous summer. But living in a different cabin, Natalie meets a variety of people, including a motherless girl, a girl who stutters, and a girl who makes anti-Semitic remarks. The latter girl contracts polio at camp, and the camp closes. What happened was very different from what Natalie had anticipated.

1292.   Levitin, Sonia. **Annie's Promise**. New York: Atheneum, 1993. 192p. $14.95; $3.99pa. ISBN 0-689-31752-2; 0-689-80440-7pa. 5 up

In this sequel to *Journey to America* and *Silver Days*, Annie, 12 in 1945, wants to become independent from her parents and follow her older sisters. Still suffering from migraine headaches of the year before, she thinks that her parents are overly protective. In the summer, she has the opportunity to go to a Quaker camp in the moun-tains. Although not the expected solace, the camp offers her a chance to meet others and to personally combat the anti-Semitic sentiment lingering from World War II. *Publishers Weekly Starred Review.*

1293.   Levitin, Sonia. **Silver Days**. New York: Atheneum, 1989. 186p. $13.95. ISBN 0-689-31563-5. 6-8

Lisa, 13, tells of her family's move from New York to California, where her father thinks that he can make money. They have had to leave all of their assets in Nazi Germany and are still concerned about Lisa's grandmother, whom they hear has had to go to Auschwitz. In this sequel to *Journey to America*, Lisa's father reenters the garment-making business, and she succeeds when she returns to her dancing.

1294.   Levoy, Myron. **Alan and Naomi**. New York: Harper, 1977. 176p. $12.89; $4.50pa. ISBN 0-06-023800-3; 0-06-440209-6pa. 10 up

When Alan's mother asks him to befriend 12-year-old Naomi, a French refugee from World War II in 1943, he is displeased. He knows that he must because Naomi will not communicate with anyone; she is still in shock after seeing Nazis beat her father to death. When she finally talks to him and even goes to school, a neighborhood bully calls them "Jews." Naomi returns to her shell and must be placed in an asylum. *American Library Association Best of the Best Books for Young Adults 1969-1992, Boston Globe-Horn Book Award Honor Book, Horn Book Fanfare Honor List*, and *Jane Addams Children's Book Award Honor Book*.

1295.   Lewis, David Levering. **W. E. B. Du Bois: Biography of a Race, 1868-1919**. New York: Henry Holt, 1993. 735p. $35; $17.95pa. ISBN 0-8050-2621-5; 0-8050-3568-0pa. YA

The first of a projected two volumes follows W. E. B. Du Bois from his birth in 1868 to 1919, when he organized a Pan-African Congress in Paris. Besides looking at Du Bois through his personal papers and his writings in history, sociology, literature, and journalism, Lewis also looks at the Civil Rights movement in the late nineteenth and early twentieth centuries. Bibliography. Index.

1296.   Lewis-Ferguson, Julinda. **Alvin Ailey, Jr.: A Life in Dance**. New York: Walker, 1994. 96p. $12.95. ISBN 0-8027-8239-6. 5-7

The text looks at Alvin Ailey's professional career in detail, from work with Lester Horton to the formation of his own ballet company. Quotes from Ailey and people with whom he was associated help reveal his personality and talent. Also included are interpretations of the dances that he choreographed. Bibliography and Reviews.

1297.   Lhamon, W. T., Jr. **Deliberate Speed: The Origins of a Cultural Style in the American 1950s**. Washington, DC: Smithsonian Institution Press, 1990. 274p. $15.95. ISBN 1-56098-316-7. YA

Although some think that the 1950s were a decade that bridged the time between World War II and the demonstrations of the 1960s, Lhamon shows that they shaped much of contemporary culture. The essays cover such topics as electronics; civil rights and Martin Luther King, Jr.; art forms such as abstract expressionists and Jackson Pollock; the Beat poets including Allen Ginsberg; Ralph Ellison's *Invisible Man*; Little Richard, Elvis Presley, and rock and roll; movie stars such as Marilyn Monroe, James Dean, and Marlon Brando; and other writers, including Joseph Heller, Norman Mailer, and Flannery O'Connor. The Supreme Court's Brown vs. Topeka Board of Education decision, which said that desegregation be carried out with "deliberate speed," was, according to Lhamon, the metaphor of the decade. Bibliography and Index.

1298.   Libreatore, Karen. **Our Century: 1910-1920**. Milwaukee, WI: Gareth Stevens, 1993. 64p. $23.93. ISBN 0-8368-1033-3. 3 up

Written as if a newspaper, this book's short articles give an overview of the decade. Included are statistics, daily life in America, the *Titanic* sinking, Archduke Ferdinand's murder, World War I, Nicholas I of Russia's overthrow, Bolsheviks, the flu epidemic, suffragettes, Prohibition, Pancho Villa's border town raids, the first assembly line, Panama Canal progress, the Black Sox baseball scandal, Woodrow Wilson, Vladimir Lenin, Louis B. Brandeis, Eugene Debs, Margaret Sanger, D. W. Griffith, Mary Pickford, and Charlie Chaplin. Glossary, Books for Further Reading, Places to Write or Visit, and Index.

1299.   Liles, Maurine Walpole. **Sam and the Speaker's Chair**. Austin, TX: Eakin Press, 1994. 143p. $14.95. ISBN 0-89015-946-7. 7 up

Sam Rayburn (1882-1961) became a legend in his own lifetime. Born in Tennessee, he and his family went to Texas when he was only five. When he started serving in Congress, he rose in prominence and served eight Presidents as the Speaker in the House of Representatives. In his work, he accomplished much for the average citizen. He brought electricity to farms, the farm-to-market road program, the regulation of Wall Street, insurance and veterans' disability payments, soil conservation and flood control, and other changes in the law. During his career of almost 49 years, he had only 38 employees; they loved him for his common sense, ability, and kindness. Notes, Bibliography, and Index.

1300.   Lillegard, Dee. **James A. Garfield: Twentieth President of the United States**. Chicago: Childrens Press, 1987. 100p. $19.80. ISBN 0-516-01394-7. (Encyclopedia of Presidents). 4-9

Although James Garfield (1831-1881) liked Abraham Lincoln personally, he opposed some of his decisions. And when Lincoln died, Garfield mourned. Garfield attended Williams College before serving Ohio in the U.S. Senate. Then he went to the House of Representatives from which he was elected President of the United States in 1880. A disappointed office seeker, however, kept him from serving long because he assassinated him. Chronology of American History and Index.

1301.   Lillegard, Dee. **James K. Polk: Eleventh President of the United States**. Chicago: Childrens Press, 1988. 100p. $19.80. ISBN 0-516-01351-3. (Encyclopedia of Presidents). 4-9

James K. Polk (1795-1849) of Tennessee wanted to be the Vice President for Martin Van Buren, but he had been defeated for governor and various other positions. Andrew Jackson decided to support him, so Polk persuaded Democrats to write letters saying that if Henry Clay were elected, he would give the federal government too much control over the states. Instead of the nomination for Vice President, Polk actually won the nomination for President because he favored immediate annexation of Texas even though it was a slave state. Jackson decided not to support Van Buren because he would not annex Texas. Polk was nominated on the ninth ballot as the first "dark horse" President. Although his accomplishment was not recognized for years, he was one of the great Presidents. Chronology of American History and Index.

1302.   Lillegard, Dee. **John Tyler: Tenth President of the United States**. Chicago: Childrens Press, 1987. 100p. $19.80. ISBN 0-516-01393-9. (Encyclopedia of Presidents). 4-9

John Tyler (1790-1862) became President after being a senator from Virginia and William Henry Harrison's vice presidential running mate. He did not plan to be President, but when he took office, he began to battle with the Whigs in Congress who expected him to pass their laws. But his friends had already nicknamed him "Honest John." After he left office, he did not leave politics. Seeing the Union moving toward civil war distressed him; he was trying to save the Union at his death. Chronology of American History and Index.

1303.   Lillegard, Dee. **Richard Nixon: Thirty-Seventh President of the United States**. Chicago: Childrens Press, 1988. 100p. $19.80. ISBN 0-516-01356-4. (Encyclopedia of Presidents). 4-9

This biography of Richard Milhaus Nixon (1913-1994) presents Nixon's famous "Checkers" speech with his dog, his background, his marriage and family, and his service for California and as Vice President. It also comments on his victories and defeats before he had to resign during the Watergate controversy. Chronology of American History and Index.

1304.   Lincoln, Abraham. **The Gettysburg Address**. Michael McCurdy, illustrator. Boston: Houghton Mifflin, 1995. Unpaged. $14.95. ISBN 0-395-69824-3. K up

McCurdy has carefully illustrated the words of the Gettysburg Address so that they are accessible to all readers. By having only a few words per page, he shows the shortness of the speech as well as its power. *Notable Children's Trade Books in the Field of Social Studies.*

1305.   Lindop, Edmund. **Dwight D. Eisenhower, John F. Kennedy, Lyndon B. Johnson**. New York: Twenty-First Century Books, 1996. 64p. $15.98. ISBN 0-8050-3404-8. (Presidents Who Dared). 5-8

The text covers the childhood, educations, and prepresidential careers of Dwight Eisenhower, John Kennedy, and Lyndon Johnson. It then describes their administrations by noting their goals and their achievements in office. The inclusion of each man's strengths and weaknesses lends objectivity to the presentation. Bibliography, Further Reading, Notes, and Index.

1306.   Lindop, Edmund. **George Washington, Thomas Jefferson, Andrew Jackson**. New York: Twenty-First Century Books, 1996. 64p. $15.98. ISBN 0-8050-3401-3. (Presidents Who Dared). 5-8

The text covers the childhood, educations, and prepresidential careers of George Washington, Thomas Jefferson, and Andrew Jackson. It then describes their administrations by noting their goals and their achievements in office. The inclusion of each man's strengths and weaknesses lends objectivity to the presentation. Washington set the major precedents for the government, while Jefferson established the Democratic-Republican Party and abolished slave trade. Jackson decided that the South had no right to nullify federal laws. Bibliography, Further Reading, Notes, and Index.

1307.   Lindop, Edmund. **James K. Polk, Abraham Lincoln, Theodore Roosevelt**. New York: Twenty-First Century Books, 1996. 64p. $15.98. ISBN 0-8050-3402-1. (Presidents Who Dared). 5-8

The text covers the childhood, educations, and prepresidential careers of James Polk, Abraham Lincoln, and Theodore Roosevelt. It then describes their administrations by noting their goals and their achievements in office. The inclusion of each man's strengths and weaknesses lends an objectivity to the presentation. Polk pushed the idea of Manifest Destiny while Lincoln tried to guide the country through the Civil War. Roosevelt realized the importance of conservation and broke the trusts and monopolies of large businesses. Bibliography, Further Reading, Notes, and Index.

1308. Lindop, Edmund. **Presidents by Accident**. New York: Franklin Watts, 1991. 224p. $15.40. ISBN 0-531-11059-1. 7-12

Nine Vice Presidents of the United States have become Presidents when the elected President died or resigned. The text discusses these men, what happened to their predecessors, and what they had to face when they took office. Bibliography and Index.

1309. Lindop, Edmund. **Presidents Versus Congress: Conflict and Compromise**. New York: Franklin Watts, 1994. 176p. $20.30. ISBN 0-531-11165-2. (Democracy in Action). 8-12

In the text, Lindop looks at the relationship between several Presidents and their Congresses to see what causes gridlock over crucial national issues such as civil rights, conduct of war, foreign policy, appointment of cabinet officials, and the makeup of the Supreme Court. The Presidents and their conflicts are George Washington, Andrew Jackson, Abraham Lincoln, Andrew Johnson, Woodrow Wilson, Franklin D. Roosevelt, Harry Truman, Dwight D. Eisenhower, John F. Kennedy, Lyndon B. Johnson, Richard Nixon, Jimmy Carter, Ronald Reagan, and George Bush. Epilogue, Notes, For Further Reading, and Index.

1310. Lindop, Edmund. **Richard M. Nixon, Jimmy Carter, Ronald Reagan**. New York: Twenty-First Century Books, 1996. 64p. $15.98. ISBN 0-8050-3405-6. (Presidents Who Dared). 5-8

The text covers the childhood, educations, and prepresidential careers of Richard Nixon, Jimmy Carter, and Ronald Reagan. It then describes their administrations by noting their goals and their achievements in office. Nixon had to resign or be impeached while Carter had to face the Iranian hostage crisis. Reagan kept office for eight years but left a huge budget deficit after his term ended. The inclusion of each man's strengths and weaknesses lends objectivity to the presentation. Bibliography, Further Reading, Notes, and Index.

1311. Lindop, Edmund. **Woodrow Wilson, Franklin D. Roosevelt, Harry S. Truman**. New York: Twenty-First Century Books, 1996. 64p. $15.98. ISBN 0-8050-3403-X. (Presidents Who Dared). 5-8

The text covers the childhood, educations, and prepresidential careers of Woodrow Wilson, Franklin D. Roosevelt, and Harry Truman. It then describes their administrations by noting their goals and their achievements in office. The inclusion of each man's strengths and weaknesses lends objectivity to the presentation. Wilson helped create the Federal Trade Commission and the Federal Reserve System. Roosevelt used the powers of the government to help lessen the horror of the Depression. Truman used the first atomic weapon while also supporting the Marshall Plan and the United States' involvement in Korea under the aegis of the United Nations. Bibliography, Further Reading, Notes, and Index.

1312. Lipsyte, Robert. **Jim Thorpe: Twentieth-Century Jock**. New York: HarperCollins, 1993. 103p. $13.89. ISBN 0-06-022988-8. 3-7

An American Indian, Jim Thorpe (1887-1953) surprised everyone with his athletic ability. He won two gold medals at the 1912 Olympics, but the next year someone reported that he had played professional baseball during the previous summer, so the medals were stripped from him. He won fairly, and many think that he was made a scapegoat for something that others also did. The National Football League Most Valuable Player award bears his name. Further Reading and Index.

1313. Lipsyte, Robert. **Joe Louis: A Champ for All America**. New York: HarperCollins, 1994. 64p. $13.89. ISBN 0-06-023410-5. (Superstar Lineup). 4-9

In this fictional biography, when Joe Louis (1914-1981) beat the German Max Schmeling on the eve of World War II after losing to him in 1936, he became a symbol of American power, although whites continued to discriminate against him in his home country. Louis's own hero was Jack Johnson, a Black boxer who won the heavyweight championship in 1908. When Louis served in the Armed Forces, he met and helped Jackie Robinson. In his own life, his mother, stepfather, and boxing trainer served as strong reminders that he must do the best that he could in order to represent his race well. For Further Reading and Index.

1314. Lisle, Janet Taylor. **Sirens and Spies**. New York: Bradbury, 1985. 169p. $14.95. ISBN 0-02-759150-6. 7 up

When Elsie is 14, she begins researching World War II in her library to see what she can find out about her violin teacher, a woman who came from France. She finds a photograph of the woman with a child. Elsie starts spying on her, but after an intruder wounds the teacher, Elsie's sister suggests that she confront the teacher rather than cause any more harm. When the teacher reveals her experiences as a teenager suffering through the war, Elsie's attitude changes.

1315. Loewen, Nancy. **Elvis**. Vero Beach, FL: Rourke, 1989. 111p. $18.60. ISBN 0-86592-606-9. 5 up

One of the best-known entertainers in the twentieth century was Elvis Presley (1935-1977). The text looks at his life and career from his early years in Mississippi to his unexpected death. Index.

1316.   Loewen, Nancy. **Poe: A Biography**. Mucci, photographer. Mankato, MN: Creative Education, 1993. Unpaged. $16.95. ISBN 0-15-200920-5. 7-10
This look at Edgar Allan Poe (1809-1849) emphasizes how his life affected his works. Each chapter begins with a passage from his writing or an incident from his life. The illustrations enhance the text with their dreamlike quality by showing Poe's unhappiness and the personal difficulties that he could not seem to overcome. Lacking documentation, the text is more an aesthetic approach to Poe's life than a scholarly one. *Publishers Weekly Starred Review* and *Recommended Books for Reluctant Young Adult Readers for YALSA and American Library Association.*

1317.   Loewen, Nancy, ed. **Walt Whitman**. Rob Day, illustrator. Mankato, MN: Creative Education, 1994. 45p. $18.95. ISBN 0-15-200919-1. YA
Walt Whitman (1819-1892) was the first American poet who used the language of the new country. The text looks at his poetry and his life by dividing it into such periods as "Childhood," "Education," and "Civil War." Among the poems are sections of "Song of Myself," "When Lilacs Last in the Dooryard Bloom'd," and "Out of the Cradle Endlessly Rocking." Historical photographs and reproductions represent the man and his work, *Leaves of Grass*. Bibliography and Index. *School Library Journal Starred Review, New York Public Library Books for the Teen Age,* and *Parents' Choice Award.*

1318.   Lomask, Milton. **Great Lives: Exploration**. New York: Scribner's, 1988. 258p. $23. ISBN 0-684-18511-3. YA
The text looks at famous explorers who have changed the world. Included are Pytheas (4th c. BC) and his discovery that the pull of the moon controls the tides in the ocean; Hoei-shin (5th c. BC), one of the first Asians to find and explore portions of North and Central America; Leif Erikson (10th c. AD) and his exploration of the North American coast; Prince Henry the Navigator (1394-1460) of Portugal; Christopher Columbus (1451-1506); John Cabot (1450-1499) and his claim of North America for England; Vasco da Gama (1460?-1524) and his sea-lane to the Orient going to the east from Portugal; Marco Polo (1254-1324) to Asia; Amerigo Vespucci's (1454-1512) discovery of Brazil; Fernão de Magalhães, known as Magellan (c. 1480-1521) and his circumnavigation of the globe; Jacques Cartier (1491-1557) and the St. Lawrence River claimed for France; Balboa (1475-1519) and the discovery of the Pacific Ocean; La Salle (1643-1687) and his expedition up the Mississippi River to its mouth; Orellana (c. 1490-1546) and his navigation of the Amazon River; Meriwether Lewis (1774-1809) opening the American West; Roald Amundsen (1872-1928) and the North and South Poles; Nordenskiöld (1832-1901) and the Northeast Passage; James Cook (1728-1779) with Australia and the Antarctic Circle; Alexander MacKenzie (1764-1820) and the first expedition to cross North America; Robert O'Hara Burke (1820-1861) and the first expedition to cross the continent of Australia; Sir Richard Francis Burton (1821-1890) as one of the few non-Muslims to enter Mecca in Arabia, and the first to enter Harar in Africa, another Muslim shrine; David Livingstone (1813-1873), discoverer of Africa's Victoria Falls, several central African lakes, and the source of the Congo River; Mary Henrietta Kinglsey (1862-1900) and her trips to Africa; Robert Edwin Peary (1856-1920) and the North Pole; and Richard Evelyn Byrd (1888-1957) and trips to both the North and South Poles. Photographs, Important Dates in the History of Geographical Exploration, Further Reading, and Index.

1319.   Looby, Chris. **Benjamin Franklin**. New York: Chelsea House, 1990. 112p. $18.95. ISBN 1-55546-808-X. (World Leaders Past and Present). 5 up
Benjamin Franklin (1706-1790) is reported to have said to the signers of the Declaration of Independence in July 1776 that "Gentlemen, we must now all hang together, or we shall most assuredly hang separately." His wit and wisdom as a self-made man permeated all aspects of his life as statesman, revolutionary, publisher, philanthropist, and inventor. His many professions prepared him to represent the new government abroad. Photographs and reproductions enhance the text. Chronology, Further Reading, and Index.

1320.   Lord, Athena. **The Luck of Z.A.P. and Zoe**. Jean Jenkins, illustrator. New York: Macmillan, 1987. 154p. $13.95. ISBN 0-02-759560-9. 4-7
In 1940, Zach, 12, and his family move to Albany, New York, where many Greek Americans live. He has adventures with his little sister Zoe and becomes friends with a Jewish boy who lived in Austria and Cuba before coming to America. When his mother hears that Axis forces have bombed her Greek hometown, she worries about the people she knows. But the family has Greek friends who support them.

1321.   Lord, Athena. **Today's Special: Z.A.P. and Zoe**. Jean Jenkins, illustrator. New York: Macmillan, 1984. 150p. $13.95. ISBN 0-02-761440-9. 4-7
Zach, 11, has to babysit for his sister in 1939 while his parents work in their Greek family restaurant. Because he teaches Zoe her letters and numbers, she is prepared to enter kindergarten at an earlier age. She also learns to take more responsibility for herself.

1322. Lord, Athena. **Z.A.P., Zoe, & the Musketeers**. New York: Macmillan, 1992. 157p. $13.95. ISBN 0-02-759561-7. 4-7

In 1941, Zach, 13, and his sister Zoe, Greek Americans, enjoy their friends in Albany, New York. But as Zach's body begins to change, he begins to worry about himself. He realizes that the changes have nothing to do with his tonsillectomy.

1323. Lord, Bette Bao. **In the Year of the Boar and Jackie Robinson**. New York: Trophy, 1986. 176p. $4.50pa. ISBN 0-06-440175-8pa. 3-7

In 1947, Bandit Wong immigrates to America from China. She tries to assimilate into the idea of the Chinese American Shirley Temple Wong but faces hostility from her classmates. When she makes friends with the toughest girl in class, she begins playing in stickball games and becomes a loyal fan of the Brooklyn Dodgers. *American Library Association Notable Books for Children, School Library Journal Best Book, Notable Children's Trade Books in the Field of Social Studies, New York Public Library Children's Books*, and *Jefferson Cup Award*.

1324. Lord, Bette Bao. **Legacies: A Chinese Mosaic**. New York: Knopf, 1990. 242p. $19.95. ISBN 0-394-58325-6. YA

While Lord lived in China from 1985 to 1989, she interviewed many Chinese persecuted by Mao's Cultural Revolution. This book relates those interviews while also describing her experiences and her family's history. Among the accounts included are those of a veteran of Mao's Long March in 1934, an artist, an actress, a teacher, an entrepreneur, a journalist, and a peasant. Chronology.

1325. Lowell, Susan. **I Am Lavinia Cumming**. Paul Mirocha, illustrator. Minneapolis, MN: Milkweed Press, 1993. 198p. $14.95. ISBN 0-915943-39-5. 5-7

Lavinia, 10, loves the Bosque Ranch in Arizona Territory where she lives with her parents, five brothers, and pony. Her mother dies, and she has to go to California in 1905 to live with her aunt. Her aunt has a telephone and oak floors and an annoying eight-year-old child, Aggie. Lavinia has to deal with a new school, homesickness, Aggie, and the earthquake that nearly demolishes the city. But her aunt helps her see that life outside the ranch also has its value, and Lavinia decides to pursue her schooling.

1326. Lubetkin, Wendy. **George Marshall**. New York: Chelsea House, 1989. 112p. $18.95. ISBN 1-55546-843-8. (World Leaders Past and Present). 5 up

General George C. Marshall (1880-1959) distinguished himself under General Pershing in Europe during World War I. On the day that Nazi Germany invaded Poland, he became the U.S. Army chief of staff. After the Allies won, he became the Secretary of State. He introduced a plan for the reconstruction of Europe after the war that offered relief to the war-torn nations. For the Marshall Plan he received the Nobel Peace Prize in 1953, the first military man to do so. Photographs enhance the text. Chronology, Further Reading, and Index.

1327. Lucas, Eileen. **The Cherokees: People of the Southeast**. Brookfield, CT: Millbrook Press, 1993. 64p. $15.90. ISBN 1-56294-312-X. (Native Americans). 5-8

Four chapters of the text cover the origins of the Cherokee, their culture, their interaction with white settlers, and the current status of the Cherokee Nation. Photographs and maps enhance the text. Bibliography, Chronology, Glossary, and Index.

1328. Lucas, Eileen. **Civil Rights: The Long Struggle**. Springfield, NJ: Enslow, 1996. 112p. $18.95. ISBN 0-89490-729-8. 5-8

The text covers the long history of civil rights beginning with the first 10 amendments to the Constitution, the abolition of slavery, the desegregation of the South, and the most recent developments such as the Million Man March. It also looks at the activities of militias through this time. Photographs, Further Reading, Glossary, and Index.

1329. Luhrmann, Winifred Bruce. **Only Brave Tomorrows**. Boston: Houghton Mifflin, 1989. 190p. $13.95. ISBN 0-395-47983-5. 7-9

After Faith, 15, arrives in the Massachusetts Colony in 1675 with a father she has hardly known, Indians raid the settlers' compound and kill her father and others during King Philip's War. As she has no one else, she marries the man who had been her family's guide. As she learns to cope with household chores, her husband finally realizes that he loves her and not another man who was on the voyage with her and her father.

1330. Lukes, Bonnie L. **The American Revolution**. San Diego, CA: Lucent, 1996. 128p. $16.95. ISBN 1-56006-287-8. (World History). 7 up

Primary and secondary sources give basic historical facts from the points of view of those who lived during the time of the American Revolution. Bibliography, Chronology, Further Reading, Notes, and Index.

1331.   Lynch, Daniel. **Yellow: A Novel**. New York: Walker, 1992. 211p. $19.95. ISBN 0-8027-1226-6. YA

During the Spanish-American War of 1898, journalist Richard Davis and artist Frederic Remington travel to meet Cuban resistance fighters while trying to get a story for William Randolph Hearst's "scandal" newspaper. The dying writer Ambrose Bierce tells the story of the adventure as a prostitute told it to him.

1332.   Lynn, Elizabeth A. **Babe Didrikson Zaharias**. New York: Chelsea House, 1988. 108p. $18.95. ISBN 1-55546-684-2. (American Women of Achievement). 5 up

Babe Didrikson Zaharias (1911-1956) had an amazing athletic career, starring in basketball, baseball, swimming, tennis, and volleyball in high school. At the 1932 Olympics, she won three track and field medals. Then she added boxing, football, and hockey to her games as a professional before becoming a professional golfer. Dissatisfied with treatment given to women golfers, she helped establish the Ladies Professional Golf Association before succumbing to cancer. Some of her records remain unequaled. Photographs enhance the text. Chronology, Further Reading, and Index.

1333.   Lyon, George Ella. **Borrowed Children**. New York: Orchard, 1988. 154p. $12.95. ISBN 0-532-08351-9. 5-7

Amanda, 12, the oldest in a Kentucky family suffering during the Depression, quits school to help her mother recover from a difficult childbirth. For all her work, she gets a vacation with her grandparents in Memphis. Although the Memphis family members have few worries, Mandy observes the unhappy marriage of her alcoholic aunt and appreciates her own home, sparse as it is, much more. *Golden Kite Award* and *School Library Journal Best Book*.

1334.   Lyon, George Ella. **Here and Then**. New York: Orchard, 1994. 114p. $14.95. ISBN 0-531-06866-8. 5-7

After Abby, 12, returns from a Civil War reenactment with her parents, she finds that in the journal in which she writes about her character Eliza, she "becomes" Eliza. Abby searches for supplies to help the wounded that Eliza Hoskins, 40, needed as the "Angel of Camp Robinson." In an interesting twist, Abby, with the help of her practical friend Harper, delivers them to 1861.

1335.   Lyon, George Ella. **Red Rover, Red Rover**. New York: Jackson, Franklin Watts, 1989. 131p. $12.95. ISBN 0-531-05832-8. 6-9

In the early 1960s, Sumi, 12, reviews the year past when she has had to cope with two losses—the death of her grandfather and the departure of her favorite older brother for music school. She also starts her menstrual period; enjoys the music of Peter, Paul, and Mary; and gets a crush on her teacher. She admits that she has a hard time getting used to new things.

1336.   Lyons, Joseph. **Clare Boothe Luce**. New York: Chelsea House, 1988. 110p. $18.95. ISBN 1-55546-665-6. (American Women of Achievement). 7 up

Clare Boothe Luce (1903-1987) grew up in New York City with the unorthodox childhood of a stage family. She was a feminist before she married a wealthy man, but the marriage ended, and she began writing and magazine publishing. Her professional positions included political commentator, war correspondent, and Connecticut's first congresswoman in 1942. She went to Italy in 1952 as the first female U.S. ambassador. Until her death, she continued to advise politicians. She was politically conservative but pressed for liberal social reforms. Photographs enhance the text. Chronology, Further Reading, and Index.

1337.   Lyons, Mary E. **Keeping Secrets: The Girlhood Diaries of Seven Women Writers**. New York: Henry Holt, 1995. 180p. $15.95. ISBN 0-8050-3065-4. 7 up

To understand other people requires knowing exactly what they think. The text presents excerpts from the diaries of seven women who confessed their concerns, their doubts, and their dreams to themselves. The women are Louisa May Alcott, Charlotte Forten, Sarah Jane Foster, Kate Chopin, Alice Dunbar-Nelson, Ida B. Wells, and Charlotte Perkins Gilman. Looking at these words and knowing what the women accomplished reveals them in new ways. Notes, Bibliography, and Index.

1338.   Lyons, Mary E. **Letters from a Slave Girl: The Story of Harriet Jacobs**. New York: Scribner's, 1992. 146p. $13.95. ISBN 0-684-19446-5. New York: Aladdin, 1996. 160p. $3.95pa. ISBN 0-689-80015-0pa. 7 up

Harriet Lyons, daughter and granddaughter of North Carolina slaves, hopes that her deceased mistress has given her freedom in her will. But in 1825, Harriet finds that she has only changed owners to her mistress's sister and evil husband. Rather than face the indignities that the husband inflicts on her, Harriet escapes to the North and is separated from her family. This story is based on Harriet Jacobs's biography, written in 1861. *American Library Association Notable Books for Children*, *American Library Association Best Books for Young Adults*, *School Library Journal Starred Review*, and *Horn Book Fanfare Honor List*.

1339.	Lyons, Mary E. **Painting Dreams: Minnie Evans, Visionary Artist**. Boston: Houghton Mifflin, 1996. 47p. $14.95. ISBN 0-395-72032-X. 4-8

Minnie Evans (b. 1892) had tormenting visions. In her middle age, she began to paint with scrap materials using her imagination as a subject source for her pictures. Her family thought she was mentally unstable, and although the individual members accepted her need to paint, no one thought much of the results. In the 1960s, a photographer saw her work and helped her exhibit it. Interviews with people who knew the artist and reproductions of her work highlight the text. Index.

1340.	Lyons, Mary E. **Sorrow's Kitchen: The Life and Folklore of Zora Neale Hurston**. New York: Scribner's, 1990. 160p. $15. ISBN 0-684-19198-9. New York: Collier, 1993. 160p. $6.95pa. ISBN 0-02-044445-1pa. (Great Achievers). 7 up

When Zora Neale Hurston (1891-1960) was nine and living in Florida, her mother died, and her father's new wife did not want her. Her writing gave her an outlet as she moved around. In Harlem, she won four prizes in a literary contest in which Langston Hughes also competed. Hurston spent time at Howard University and decided to collect folklore as an anthropologist. The Mrs. Mason who supported Langston Hughes also supported Hurston, and their relationship caused Hughes to break with Mrs. Mason. Hurston's unusual interests, including voodoo rituals in Haiti, led to *Their Eyes Were Watching God*. The African American community shunned her when she opposed the 1954 school segregation ruling; she thought it insulted Black teachers. At the end of her life, she lived poor and alone although seemingly content with her choices.

1341.	Lyons, Mary E. **Starting Home: The Story of Horace Pippin, Painter**. New York: Scribner's, 1993. 42p. $14.95. ISBN 0-684-19534-8. (African-American Artists and Artisans). 4-7

Horace Pippin (1885-1946) once penciled pictures on a piece of cloth that he sold to a woman. She returned to tell him that they disappeared when she washed it. He had other memories of trying to work because each piece of art revealed a piece of his life. A disabling wound in World War I did not keep him from painting, especially the horrors he saw on the battlefield, and he continued to paint those memories as well as others. Index.

1342.	Lyttle, Richard B. **Mark Twain: The Man and His Adventures**. New York: Atheneum, 1994. 230p. $15.95. ISBN 0-689-31712-3. 7 up

Mark Twain, or Samuel Clemens (1835-1910), was a printer, riverboat pilot, miner, newspaper reporter, and lecturer. He was also an inventor, an experienced traveler, a conversationalist, and a humorist. He was both hysterically funny and deadly serious. He published more than 20 books during his life, lost money, and earned it again. He was a dedicated family man who became distraught at the deaths of his daughter and wife. Notes, Books by Mark Twain, Select Bibliography, and Index.

M

1343.   MacBride, Roger Lea. **Little House on Rocky Ridge**. David Gilleece, illustrator. New York: HarperCollins, 1993. 353p. $15.95; $3.95pa. ISBN 0-06-020842-2; 0-06-440478-1pa. (Rocky Ridge Years). 3-7
    Rose, Laura Ingalls Wilder's daughter, begins her story in 1894, when she is seven. She and her parents take their possessions on a covered wagon to southern Missouri. The farm needs a barn, and when the neighbors gather from around the area to raise the barn, the family begins to feel like a part of the community.

1344.   Macht, Norman L. **Lou Gehrig**. New York: Chelsea House, 1993. 64p. $14.95; $7.95pa. ISBN 0-7910-1176-3; 0-7910-1210-7pa. (Baseball Legends). 6-9
    Lou Gehrig (1903-1941) played in 2,140 consecutive games, which earned him the nickname of "The Iron Man." He also hit 493 home runs. Black-and-white photographs complement the text. Chronology, Further Reading, and Index.

1345.   Mack-Williams, Kibibi. **Malcolm X**. Vero Beach, FL: Rourke, 1993. 112p. $22.60. ISBN 0-86625-493-5. YA
    Malcolm Little (1925-1965) changed his name to Malcolm X, and on his coffin was the name El-Hajj Malik El-Shabazz, the Islamic name he took after his trip to Mecca, the Holy City of Islam, in 1964. He had a difficult life, losing both parents when he was young during the Depression years and then going to prison. As an adult, he supported and then separated from Elijah Muhammad, head of the Nation of Islam. He was a loving family man with four daughters, but he refused to temper his public remarks about racial discrimination. Speeches and Writings, Time Line, Glossary, Bibliography, Media Resources, and Index.

1346.   Macy, Sue. **A Whole New Ballgame: The Story of the All-American Girls Professional Baseball League**. New York: Henry Holt, 1993. 140p. $14.95. ISBN 0-8050-1942-1. 5-9
    The All-American Girls Professional Baseball League played during World War II, but interest declined when the men and normality returned in the early 1950s. The text looks at some tense games and reconstructs them play-by-play while showing statistics for the best players. It notes that women players faced both encouragement and prejudice in their roles and tells what they did after the league play ended. Photographs, Notes, Further Reading, and Index.

1347.   Macy, Sue. **Winning Ways: A Photohistory of American Women in Sports**. New York: Henry Holt, 1996. 217p. $15.95. ISBN 0-8050-4147-8. 7-10
    Women have attempted to participate in sports since the early 1800s, and the text looks at their struggles. In 1827, according to Macy, a warning appeared in a magazine that women who exercised too much could develop small tumors in their ankles. Changes in female education and clothing, greater acceptance of women in the mass media, and World War II helped women find a place as athletes. The text looks at the difficulties and achievements from the 1800s until the present. Chronology and Index.

1348.   Madden, O. T., and Ann L. Miller. **We Were Always Free: The Maddens of Culpeper County Va.** New York: Norton, 1992. 218p. $19.95. ISBN 0-393-03347-3. New York: Vintage, 1993. 218p. $12pa. ISBN 0-679-74518-5pa. YA
    Madden's family line extends through the past two centuries from a white Irish woman who had an affair with a Black man; therefore, after her period of indentured servitude ended, the family was free. He describes their lives as free Blacks, distrusted by other Blacks because they owned land and were educated, and sometimes irritating to whites who disliked free Blacks. Madden describes the family in endearing terms and for the family's sake rather than for any hidden agenda. Bibliography and Index.

1349.   Magocsi, Paul R. **The Russian Americans**. New York: Chelsea House, 1995. 110p. $19.95. ISBN 0-7910-3367-8. (The Immigrant Experience). 6-9
    Russians came to North America before the fur trade drew them to Alaska in the 1740s. In the early twentieth century, before World War I, more than 2 million Russians settled along the East Coast. After the Russian Revolution in 1917, a large wave of Russians came, and after World War II, another group arrived. Since the 1970s, a third group has come to America to escape the harsh life in the Soviet Union. Photographs and text tell their history and their contributions to American life. Further Reading and Index.

1350.   Mahone-Lonesome, Robyn. **Charles R. Drew**. New York: Chelsea House, 1990. 109p. $18.95. ISBN 1-55546-581-1. (Black Americans of Achievement). 5 up
    Charles Drew (1904-1950) became a surgeon and researcher. He helped establish blood banks and found out how to preserve blood plasma after studying its properties. Bibliography and Index.

1351.   Mahoney, M. H. **Women in Espionage: A Biographical Dictionary**. Santa Barbara, CA: ABC-CLIO, 1993. 253p. $65. ISBN 0-87436-743-3. 9 up

As a former CIA operative, Mahoney presents alphabetical entries on 150 women who have been involved in espionage. She includes Delilah in the Bible as well as those from the American Revolution and the Civil War. Most of the women are American or European, but some come from other countries. In the introduction, Mahoney lists some of the roles that women have played as spies. Bibliography and Index.

1352.   Malone, Mary. **Maya Lin: Architect and Artist**. Springfield, NJ: Enslow, 1995. 112p. $17.95. ISBN 0-89490-499-X. 7 up

Maya Lin (b. 1959) won the design contest for the Vietnam Memorial planned for Washington, D.C., to honor those who died in that war, and her life filled with controversy. Some did not like the design and tried to stop the construction of the monument. Her concept, however, proved them wrong, because it remains one of the most sacred of national monuments. One of her recent designs is "Eclipsed Time," a clock in the Penn Station concourse in New York City. The text looks at her life. Chronology, Notes, Further Reading, and Index.

1353.   Malone, Mary. **Will Rogers: Cowboy Philosopher**. Springfield, NJ: Enslow, 1996. 128p. $17.95. ISBN 0-89490-695-X. (People to Know). 6-10

Will Rogers (1875-1935), part Cherokee, wanted to be a cowboy, but he became a performer in vaudeville, in Ziegfeld's Follies, and on his own. He twirled a lariat as he told jokes. He also traveled widely and wrote a newspaper column. When he died in an airplane crash, the nation mourned. Chronology, Further Reading, Notes, and Index.

1354.   Manchester, William. **One Brief Shining Moment: Remembering Kennedy**. Boston: Little, Brown, 1983. 280p. $25. ISBN 0-316-54491-4. YA

Although the author knew Kennedy, and the book is adulatory, the text and the photographs give a strong sense of the time in which Kennedy lived. The times were "shining" moments, and seeing Kennedy and Mrs. Kennedy with world leaders and in foreign countries recreates the few years in the early 1960s before the rash of assassinations began in the United States.

1355.   Manchester, William Raymond. **The Death of a President, November 20-November 25, 1963**. 1967. New York: HarperCollins, 1988. 710p. $18pa. ISBN 0-06-055136-4pa. YA

John Fitzgerald Kennedy (1917-1963) was assassinated by Lee Harvey Oswald in Dallas, Texas, on November 22, 1963. The text examines the six days surrounding this incident, giving a thorough analysis of all the persons involved and starting with the decision to go to Dallas where Kennedy would show support for the Democrats in the state. Manchester captures personalities and problems in this intriguing tale, which he enlarges by comparing Kennedy's death to that of kings in societies that sacrificed their kings in the autumn so that the next year's crops would be plentiful. Sources and Index.

1356.   Mancini, Richard. **American Legends of the Wild West**. Philadelphia: Courage, Running Press, 1992. 128p. $19.98. ISBN 1-56138-119-5. 9 up

The text, divided into three parts called "Blazing the Trails," "Westward, Ho!" and "The Winning of the West," gives information about those who settled the area: explorers, western women, Native Americans, and soldiers. Biographical information, photographs, maps, and a timeline enhance the text. Bibliography and Index.

1357.   Mangione, Jerry and Ben Morreale. **La Storia: Five Centuries of the Italian-American Experience**. New York: HarperCollins, 1992. 508p. $17. ISBN 0-06-016778-5. YA

The text covers Italian American history from the colonial period through the major immigration from 1880 to 1920 and into the present. Various facets covered are the reasons for the mass migration, prejudice in the new land, integration into the community, and the subsequent loss of tradition and religion. The book relates the stories of individuals who have come and thrived, such as Frank Capra, Lee Iacocca, Fiorella LaGuardia, and Mario Cuomo, as well as others who are not famous. Bibliography and Index.

1358.   Manley, Joan B. **She Flew No Flags**. Boston: Houghton Mifflin, 1995. 269p. $15.95. ISBN 0-395-71130-4. 4-8

In 1944, Janet, 10, returns to the United States with her family after living in India for seven years. The ship travels through enemy waters with no lights or radio contact, zigzagging to avoid torpedoes. It has no name and flies no flag so that the enemy will not attack it. She and her brothers explore the ship, and she wonders about other people aboard. When she arrives in America, it is not what she expects, and she has to adjust not only to wartime but also to her new country.

1359.   Marable, Manning. **W. E. B. Du Bois: Black Radical Democrat**. Boston: Twaine, G. K. Hall, 1986. 286p. $13.95pa. ISBN 0-8057-7771-7pa. (Twentieth-Century American Biography). YA

As a social scientist, W. E. B. (William Edward Burghardt) Du Bois (1868-1963) reluctantly became a politician, but the relationship of race, class, and democracy began to preoccupy him. As a Calvinist, he believed in the democratic ideal. He was a cultural pluralist and Pan-Africanist who showed the tensions in American culture. The text looks at his education, his involvement in the Tuskegee and Niagara movements, his role in the NAACP, his Pan-Africanism, his life during the Great Depression and the World Wars, his politics of peace, and his later life. Chronology, Notes, Bibliographic Essay, Bibliography, and Index.

1360.   Marino, Jan. **The Day That Elvis Came to Town**. Boston: Little, Brown, 1991. 204p. $15.95. ISBN 0-316-54618-6. 5 up

In 1964, a new boarder, Mercedes Washington, moves into Wanda's family's boardinghouse. A jazz singer, Mercedes knows everyone, and Wanda, 13, is delighted that she even knows her hero, Elvis Presley. When Wanda hears that Elvis is coming to nearby Savannah, Georgia, for a concert, she expects Mercedes to take her backstage. Instead, Wanda finds out that Mercedes is not what she pretends to be. Most shocking of all, she is part Black, something that Wanda has difficulty accepting in her Southern home. *Bulletin Blue Ribbon Book* and *School Library Journal Best Book*.

1361.   Marino, Jan. **For the Love of Pete**. Boston: Little, Brown, 1993. 197p. $14.95. ISBN 0-316-54627-5. 5 up

Phoebe, nine in 1977, lives with her grandmother in Lubelle, Georgia, until the grandmother begins to grow senile and must go to a nursing home. Bertie, the cook; her brother Billy; and Bishopp, the English butler, take Phoebe north to meet her father whom she has never known except for the letter that she found in the attic. What she discovers is that her grandmother had never told him about her because her grandmother, once a famous opera singer, was afraid she would lose her granddaughter. The four have encounters on the journey including a racial incident and a restaurant owner's kindness.

1362.   Marius, Richard, ed. **The Columbia Book of Civil War Poetry: From Whitman to Wolcott**. New York: Columbia University Press, 1994. 560p. $24.95. ISBN 0-231-10002-7. YA

This presentation of the Civil War gives a different perspective. Marius introduces the Civil War with background information on the war years and those years immediately after it. He then prefaces each poetry selection with information that gives its historical perspective. The thematic organization highlights poetry by men, women, African Americans, modern poets, and those writing during the war. Individuals include Melville, Whittier, Dunbar, and Whitman. Index.

1363.   Markham, Lois. **Helen Keller**. New York: Franklin Watts, 1993. 64p. $12.90. ISBN 0-531-20101-X. (First Books). 5-8

Helen Keller (1880-1968) lived a remarkable life after Annie Sullivan taught her to talk, read, and write. Blind and deaf from disease at 18 months, the struggle Keller and her family endured was difficult. Sullivan helped her, and after Keller attended Radcliffe College, she continued to amaze people with what she was able to achieve. For Further Reading and Index.

1364.   Markham, Lois. **Inventions That Changed Modern Life**. Austin, TX: Raintree/Steck-Vaughn, 1994. 48p. $15.96. ISBN 0-8114-4930-0. (20 Events Series). 6 up

In the late eighteenth century, James Watt's steam engine was produced for sale, Nicolas Appert began working with food preservation, and Eli Whitney designed interchangeable parts for guns. In the nineteenth century, Richard Trevithick and George Stephenson worked with locomotives. Photography began with experiments in France and England by Josiah Wedgwood, Joseph-Nicéphore Niepce, Louis Daguerre, and W. H. Fox Talbot. Cyrus McCormick began work on the combine harvester, and Isaac Singer patented the sewing machine begun by Elias Howe. Work on refrigeration, plastics, the telephone, electric light, and the automobile ended the century. In 1901, Marconi's radio worked. Also in the twentieth century, the airplane, assembly line, rocket, nuclear fission, television, computers, and lasers have changed the way people live. Each topic covers two pages. Glossary, Suggested Readings, and Index.

1365.   Markham, Lois. **Theodore Roosevelt**. New York: Chelsea House, 1984. 112p. $18.95. ISBN 0-87754-553-7. (World Leaders Past and Present). 5 up

Theodore Roosevelt (1858-1919) was a sickly child, but he decided when he was 12 that he would become strong and active. He became a cowboy, a war hero, a cavalry officer, an author, a husband, a father, an explorer, a conservationist, a police commissioner, a governor, and a President. In all of his professions, he wanted Americans to have a "square deal." Photographs enhance the text. Chronology, Further Reading, and Index.

1366.   Marling, Karal Ann. **George Washington Slept Here: Colonial Revivals and American Culture, 1876-1986**. Cambridge, MA: Harvard University Press, 1988. 453p. $47.50. ISBN 0-674-34951-2. YA

The text, filled with information and trivia about George Washington, shows that contemporary society uses its connection to colonial society to validate itself in some cases. Popular culture can reveal problems in social history, and Marling comments on this and many other aspects about where "George Washington slept." Illustrations and Index.

1367.   Marling, Karal Ann, and John Wetenhall. **Iwo Jima: Monuments, Memories, and the American Hero**. Cambridge, MA: Harvard University Press, 1991. 300p. $24.95. ISBN 0-674-46980-1. YA

Marling and Wetenhall examine the motivation and the politics behind the creation of the Iwo Jima monument designed by de Weldon, based on a Rosenthal photograph taken as marines raised the American flag over Iwo Jima in World War II. They discuss how such a commemoration is a way to create wartime heroes in the popular culture. They also discuss its use as a symbol in political cartoons and even in the movies, where it helped John Wayne gain the reputation of being a tough marine. Index.

1368.   Marrin, Albert. **The Airman's War: World War II in the Sky**. New York: Atheneum, 1982. 213p. $11.95. ISBN 0-689-30907-4. 5 up

In 1939, German Reichsmarshal Hermann Goering boasted that no one would ever bomb Germany. He thought that Germany controlled the skies. He was wrong. The text looks at the importance of air power in World War II after many leaders of the American armed services had ignored the value of an air force in the early 1930s. Three men, "Hap" Arnold, "Tooey" Spaatz, and Ira Eaker, fulfilled "Billy" Mitchell's goal for a strong air fleet. The text tells their stories; the stories of pilots in the war flying bombers and fighter planes; the stories of the planes they flew, such as the B-17s, the Liberators, the Spitfires, and the Messerschmitts; and the battles they fought, some of them bombing raids that lasted around the clock. Photographs, Maps, Some More Books, and Index.

1369.   Marrin, Albert. **America and Vietnam: The Elephant and the Tiger**. New York: Viking, 1992. 256p. $16. ISBN 0-670-84063-7. 9 up

The text presents a background history of Vietnam followed by a capsule biography of Ho Chi Minh before telling how the war affected both Vietnam and the United States. Marrin attempts to show both the atrocities and the admirable acts on both sides of the battlefield as he explains the motivations and mistakes behind the war. Glossary, Bibliography, and Index.

1370.   Marrin, Albert. **Cowboys, Indians and Gunfighters: The Story of the Cattle Kingdom**. New York: Atheneum, 1993. 196p. $22.95. ISBN 0-689-31774-3. 6 up

The cattle industry began when horses arrived from Spain. Men used them to drive longhorn cattle across the plains where cowboys, Indians, and gunfighters merged in their dealings. The text looks at the drives; the different areas of the country; leisure time in town; and other facts about these people, who thrived through the reign of the cattle barons in the late nineteenth century. Photographs and reproductions enhance the text. Further Reading, Some More Books, and Index. *Bulletin Blue Ribbon Book*.

1371.   Marrin, Albert. **1812: The War Nobody Won**. New York: Atheneum, 1985. 176p. $12.95. ISBN 0-689-31075-7. 5 up

While Dolley Madison was waiting for her husband to return from inspecting the U.S. troops defending Washington, she got word that the British were advancing. She had to flee the White House. She took George Washington's portrait and an original copy of the Declaration of Independence, but not her husband's bags. The British arrived and destroyed most of the buildings. The text looks at the events that led up to the "Second War of Independence" and the results. Neither country gained territory, but the United States proved to the British that it could retain what it had won in the Revolution. Some More Books and Index.

1372.   Marrin, Albert. **Empires Lost and Won: The Spanish Heritage in the Southwest**. New York: Simon & Schuster, Atheneum, 1997. 224p. $19. ISBN 0-689-80414-8. 5 up

In 1540, Francisco Vásquez de Coronado left Mexico City to go north and claim the wealth of the fabled cities. Although only Pueblo villages awaited him, Santa Fe became their capital and the capital of New Mexico by 1610. The Texans voted for independence from Mexico in the nineteenth century, and the ensuing battle caused Mexico to lose all of its northern conquests. The text looks at the history of this process with accompanying photographs. Index.

1373.   Marrin, Albert. **OVERLORD: D-Day and the Invasion of Europe**. New York: Atheneum, 1982. 176p. $12.95. ISBN 0-689-30931-7. 7 up

In 1942, Winston Churchill flew to the United States to meet with Franklin Roosevelt about ways to stop Adolf Hitler from taking over Europe. What evolved was a plan called Operation OVERLORD, the Allied plan for freeing Europe and winning the war. The project took extraordinary planning, with supplies collected in

England along with ships, tanks, planes, and gliders. Dummy airfields with fake tanks and planes had to be prepared as lures for Hitler's air force. Germany knew the invasion would occur and fortified the coast of France along the English Channel closest to England. The landing at Omaha Beach along with Juno and Utah on June 6, 1944, was difficult. Photographs, Maps, Some More Books, and Index.

1374.   Marrin, Albert. **Plains Warrior: Chief Quanah Parker and the Comanches**. New York: Atheneum, 1996. 208p. $18. ISBN 0-689-80081-9. 6-9

Beginning with the Comanche kidnapping of Cynthia Ann Parker, Quanah Parker's mother, when she was nine, Marrin tells the story of the Comanches and their fight to preserve their land on the Great Plains during the nineteenth century. Without making the government all bad or the Comanches all good, Marrin uses eyewitness sources that describe many of the events during this time. Photographs, Notes, Further Reading, and Index.

1375.   Marrin, Albert. **The Sea Rovers: Pirates, Privateers, and Buccaneers**. New York: Atheneum, 1984. 173p. $15.95. ISBN 0-689-31029-3. 5 up

In the early history of Europeans coming to American shores, pirates rode the seas in search of other peoples' wealth. English sea dogs such as Jack Hawkins and Francis Drake helped Queen Elizabeth declare war on Spain. Henry Morgan, Blackbeard, and Captain Kidd looked for booty on all the ships sailing the Atlantic. On the Mediterranean, the Barbary pirates patrolled the northern coast of Africa, but the U.S. Navy proved itself by thwarting their progress. The text looks at these pirates as well as women who also sailed under the pirate flag, the Jolly Roger. Some More Books and Index.

1376.   Marrin, Albert. **The Secret Armies: Spies, Counterspies, and Saboteurs in World War II**. New York: Atheneum, 1985. 239p. $13.95. ISBN 0-689-31165-6. 5 up

Spies and counterspies worked in Europe during World War II under code names, such as Hedgehog, Zigzag, and Tricycle, to gather information behind German lines and pass misinformation to Nazi intelligence. People participated in the Resistance movement, in the Maquis in France, in the Netherlands, and in other conquered countries where people risked their lives. These undercover agents cracked the German secret code with the Enigma machine and helped ensure an Allied victory. The text looks at all aspects of these important participants in the war. Photographs, More Books, and Index.

1377.   Marrin, Albert. **The Spanish-American War**. New York: Atheneum, 1991. 182p. $15.95. ISBN 0-689-31663-1. 7 up

In 1898, the United States fought "a splendid little war" according to diplomat John Hay. Using inconclusive data to blame the Spanish for an attack on the USS *Maine*, a battleship, the United States joined the war to free Cuba from Spain. Marrin uses the facts along with biographical sketches of figures important in the decision to fight the war, such as William Randolph Hearst, whose newspaper blamed the Spanish for the deaths of the 260 men on the *Maine;* George Dewey, the man who destroyed the Spanish fleet in Manila Bay, the Philippines; and Theodore Roosevelt, the hero of San Juan Hill in Puerto Rico. Although the United States won in Puerto Rico and the Philippines, Marrin shows through text and photographs that jingoists, expansionists, and yellow journalists encouraged the country to intervene in the war for the wrong reasons. Bibliography and Index.

1378.   Marrin, Albert. **Struggle for a Continent: The French and Indian Wars: 1690-1760**. New York: Atheneum, 1987. 218p. $15.95. ISBN 0-689-31313-6. 5 up

On February 8, 1690, raiders entered the settlement of Schenectady on the Mohawk River in New York and murdered almost all of the members of 50 families. The Indians took the rest as prisoners. This massacre began the series of wars called King William's War, Queen Anne's War, King George's War, and the French and Indian War. However, they were all part of the same war, and Marrin presents them as he narrates this episode in American history. Some More Books and Index.

1379.   Marrin Albert. **Unconditional Surrender**. New York: Atheneum, 1994. 200p. $21. ISBN 0-689-31837-5. 7 up

When Ulysses S. Grant (1822-1885) took command of the Union army during the Civil War, he had attended West Point and served in the Mexican-American War, but had become an unsuccessful shopkeeper after ending his military career. He had appeared to be a man who could do nothing right, but his wife had faith in him, which he fulfilled by keeping his troops focused, organized, and effective in the Civil War. He attended West Point only because a senator owed his father a favor. Once there, Marrin notes that "Napoleon, for all he [Grant] cared, could have been the inventor of a cream-filled pastry." His friend at West Point happened to be William T. Sherman, a man who would serve under him in the Civil War. Although a biography of Grant, this book relates much more information on such topics as Lincoln's discriminatory attitude toward Blacks and his understanding that the war could be won only if they were freed, the composition of an army, and military strategy. Grant asked for "unconditional surrender," but once he got it, he did not unnecessarily punish his defeated enemy. His fame got him elected President, a job for which he was unfit. His family was always the most important aspect of his life. Notes, Some More Books, and Index. *American Library Association Best Books for Young Adults* and *Bulletin Blue Ribbon Book*.

1380.   Marrin, Albert. **Victory in the Pacific**. New York: Atheneum, 1983. 217p. $12.95. ISBN 0-689-30948-1. 7 up

When the Japanese attacked Pearl Harbor on December 7, 1941, 96 U.S. warships were in the harbor for the weekend with only a few people looking after them. The text looks at the events leading to that defeat and the battles afterward in the Pacific. Those included are Midway, Guadalcanal, Betio, and the movement toward Japan to the Caroline and Mariana Islands and the Philippines. Taking Iwo Jima and Okinawa allowed the Allied bombing of mainland Japan. Among the other topics are the basic structures of the ships, the torpedo charges, and how the big guns fired aboard ship. Photographs, Some More Books, and Index.

1381.   Marrin, Albert. **Virginia's General: Robert E. Lee and the Civil War**. New York: Atheneum, 1994. 218p. $19.95. ISBN 0-689-31838-3. 6 up

Robert E. Lee (1807-1870) attended West Point because it was free. His father, "Light-Horse Harry," Revolutionary War hero, had abandoned the family and left them with no money. Robert E. Lee, admired for his kindness, generosity, and courtesy, was also loyal to his family and to his own state of Virginia, even though he disliked slavery and opposed secession. His victory at Chancellorsville still intrigues military strategists with its masterful planning. Even as the loser at the end of the Civil War, however, he kept his dignity. Notes, Some More Books, and Index. *American Library Association Best Books for Young Adults*.

1382.   Marrin, Albert. **War Clouds in the West: Indians and Cavalrymen 1860-1890**. New York: Atheneum, 1984. 219p. $14.95. ISBN 0-689-31066-8. 7 up

Although the Indians first helped settlers who came west, they soon realized that these people were taking their lands and killing their animals. The settlers expected the Indians to live like whites, and the Indians refused. The text looks at the buffalo hunters; the Southern Plains Indians; Sitting Bull, the Sioux, and Custer; the long march of the Nez Percé; the Apaches; and the aftermath of Wounded Knee. Some More Books and Index.

1383.   Marrin, Albert. **The War for Independence: The Story of the American Revolution**. New York: Atheneum, 1988. 276p. $19. ISBN 0-689-31390-X. 7 up

In this history of the Revolutionary War, Marrin begins with a scene at Mount Vernon as George Washington, who always wears a miniature portrait of his wife Martha, says good-bye to her as he, troubled, departs for the Second Continental Congress. Marrin links other events in the war with the people involved so that the war becomes personal from its beginning through the surrender at Yorktown. Some More Books and Index.

1384.   Marrin, Albert. **The Yanks Are Coming: The United States in the First World War**. New York: Atheneum, 1986. 248p. $14.95. ISBN 0-689-31209-1. 7 up

Furious that German U-boats had sunk an American passenger ship, the *Lusitania,* in 1915, Americans began to think that they should enter World War I. President Wilson believed in peace, but finally, on April 2, 1917, he declared war. The United States had to mobilize rapidly by coordinating industry, training doughboy soldiers, and promoting the war to those who did not want to fight. The text recounts these achievements; the battles on the front line such as Chateau Thierry and Belleau Woods, where more U.S. Marines died in one day than in their entire history; and Meuse-Argonne, where the Lost Battalion became trapped behind German lines. Leaders such as Foch, Pershing, Mitchell, and Marshall appear within the pages as they tried to give morale and direction to their men. Some More Books and Index.

1385.   Marshall, Michael W. **Ocean Traders: From the Portuguese Discoveries to the Present Day**. New York: Facts on File, 1990. 192p. $24.95. ISBN 0-8160-2420-0. 7-12

From 2600 BC, when Pharaoh Sneferu supposedly sent 40 ships to Phoenicia, until the present, ships for ocean trading have kept countries wealthy. Not until the Portuguese in the 1400s, however, was a ship designed that was fast enough to actually trade. Previously, ships carried cargo rather than salable goods. Chapters emphasize the long dawn of trading ships, the ocean trader coming of age from 1400 to 1600, the ocean highways developing from 1500 to 1700, the wars at sea from 1700 to 1800, the rise and fall of the sailing trader from 1800 to 1910, and the compound engine and container ships that evolved from 1890 through the twentieth century. Diagrams complement photographs and text on life aboard as well as the design of all these ships. Selected Bibliography and Index.

1386.   Marston, Hope Irvin. **Isaac Johnson: From Slave to Stonecutter**. Maria Magdalena Brown, illustrator. New York: Cobblehill, Dutton, 1995. 80p. $14.99. ISBN 0-525-65165-9. 4-7

When Isaac Johnson was seven, a sheriff came to the family farm while his father was away and took him, his mother, and brothers away and sold them into slavery. After the Civil War began, Johnson joined the Union army, and when the war ended, he went to Canada. There he became an accomplished stonecutter, with churches, bridges, and other structures to his credit. He wrote the story of his slave days, *Slavery Days in Old Kentucky*, to earn money for his children to attend college. The text, based on this book, also includes conversations with his descendants. Important Dates, For Further Reading, and Index.

1387.   Martin, Katherine. **Night Riding**. New York: Knopf, 1989. 197p. $12.95. ISBN 0-679-90064-0. 5-8

Prin's father has to go to the hospital for tuberculosis treatment in 1958 when she is 11. At the same time, new neighbors move in next door to their Tennessee home. Prin does not understand why her mother will not let her visit the neighbors, and her sister tells her that the girl is pregnant without being married. The girl's father makes overtures to Prin one night when she is out riding her horse, and she realizes that the father has abused his own daughter and would do the same to her.

1388.   Martinello, Marian L., and Samuel P. Nesmith. **With Domingo Leal in San Antonio 1734**. San Antonio, TX: University of Texas Institute of Texas Culture, 1980. 78p. $6.95. ISBN 0-933164-40-8pa. 5-8

When he becomes bored with watching the cattle in 1734, Domingo, 10, happily takes an adze to the mission for repair. He loiters at the blacksmiths and finally rides his horse toward home in the company of a soldier. On the way, he sees enemy Indians stopping by the river for their horses to drink. He realizes that everyone must do boring chores in order to look after themselves and their animals.

1389.   Marvin, Isabel R. **A Bride for Anna's Papa**. Minneapolis, MN: Milkweed Press, 1994. 136p. $6.95pa. ISBN 0-915943-93-Xpa. 5-7

At 13 in 1907, Anna Kallio has to manage the house and look after her nine-year-old brother and her father, who works in the dangerous Minnesota iron mines. Now that her mother is dead, she realizes that her father is very lonely, so she and her brother try to arrange a marriage for him, even with a mail-order bride from Finland. Although she wants her father to be happy, she still has to deal with her feelings about having someone else, someone unexpected, running the household.

1390.   Mason, Antony. **Peary and Amundsen: Race to the Poles**. Austin, TX: Raintree/Steck-Vaughn. 1995. 46p. $15.96. ISBN 0-8114-3977-1. (Beyond the Horizons). 5-8

Robert Peary (1856-1920) tried to reach the North Pole first, and Roald Amundsen (1872-1928) raced for the South Pole. Peary tried for the North Pole in 1898 and 1899, when he lost several toes. He made further expeditions in 1902 and 1906 before reaching it in 1909. Another American, however, claimed to have gotten to it in 1908, having taken a year to return by dogsled. Amundsen reached the South Pole two weeks before Robert Scott, who arrived crestfallen to find that someone had already been there. Neither he nor his companions survived, only his diary and photographs. The text also includes historical background, information about the people who live in the Arctic region, and what happened as a result of these expeditions. Photographs, paintings, drawings, and maps augment the text. Glossary, Further Reading, and Index.

1391.   Mason, Bobbie Ann. **Feather Crowns: A Novel**. New York: HarperCollins, 1993. 454p. $23; $13pa. ISBN 0-06-016780-7; 0-06-092549-3pa. YA

One night in the early 1900s, after Christianna Wheeler goes to a camp meeting in her Hopewell, Kentucky, home, she has erotic dreams about the preacher. In the spring of that year, she gives birth to the first quintuplets to be recorded in North America. Everyone comes to see the babies, and Christianna and her husband and three other children have to accept being the center of attention. Months later, the babies begin dying one by one. They preserve the children in a glass case and travel around the South lecturing. The details of daily life and raising babies make their lives seem real as they endure the attention and then the pain of their loss.

1392.   Matthews, Rupert. **Power Brokers: Kingmakers & Usurpers Throughout History**. New York: Facts on File, 1990. 326p. $27.95. ISBN 0-8160-2156-2. 8 up

Beginning in c. 2875 BC with Khufu, or Cheops, who usurped the throne of the Pharaoh Sneferu, the author presents nearly 300 people throughout the world who used power or position to gain more power or position. The most recent listed is Idi Amin, who took power in Uganda in 1971. Many familiar names, both male and female, eastern and western, fill the interesting text. The book is relevant for all historical time periods. Bibliography and Index.

1393.   Matthiessen, Peter. **Killing Mister Watson**. New York: Random House, 1990. 372p. $21.95. ISBN 0-394-55400-0. YA

Some people in the Florida Everglades during the 1890s think that E. J. Watson is a murderer; others think that he is a loving father. Those that think ill of him are ready to blame the Great Hurricane of 1910 on him and attempt to accuse, try, and punish him without justice.

1394.   Maurer, Richard. **Airborne: The Search for the Secret of Flight**. New York: Aladdin, 1990. 48p. $5.95pa. ISBN 0-671-69423-5pa. (NOVA). 5-8

A history of flight, the text begins with experiments and designs for various types of aircraft, gliders, and hot-air balloons from the 1600s. It continues through the history of experimentation until the Wright brothers flew their heavier-than-air craft in 1903. Drawings, photographs, and diagrams illustrate the principles of flight that had to be understood before flying became possible. When such terms as *aileron, elevator, rudder*, and *throttle* became attached to the principles, human flight began. Index.

1395. May, Elaine Tyler. **Pushing the Limits: American Women 1940-1961**. New York: Oxford University Press, 1994. 144p. $22. ISBN 0-19-508084-X. (The Young Oxford History of Women in the United States). 7 up

The diverse experiences of women become apparent when compared in the text. Luisa Moreno, a migrant worker of Hispanic origin, organizes Mexican workers in California. Margaret Starks moves from the South to the West in search of work and becomes active in the NAACP (National Association for the Advancement of Colored People). Betty Goldstein, a college-educated Jew who relinquishes her Ph.D. fellowship to marry and move to the suburbs as Mrs. Friedan, writes *The Feminine Mystique*. The text discusses World War II's chance for change and the disappointment after it ended, the nuclear family, the homemaker's workplace in suburbia, the double standard in sex, the hot topics of birth control and abortion, the baby boom, and women's inequality in public life. In 1946, Congress narrowly defeated the Equal Rights Amendment. Levittown opened in 1949, and television entered American homes in 1950. *Brown v. Board of Education* desegregated schools in 1954, and in 1955, Rosa Parks sparked the Montgomery Bus Boycott. In 1960, the Food and Drug Administration approved oral contraceptives, and in 1961, women organized a strike for peace and an end to the bomb shelter mentality. Chronology, Further Reading, and Index.

1396. Mayberry, Jodine. **Business Leaders Who Built Financial Empires**. Austin, TX: Raintree/Steck-Vaughn, 1995. 48p. $24.26. ISBN 0-8114-4934-3. (20 Events). 5-8

Two-page spreads with accompanying photographs and drawings give capsule biographies of Levi Strauss (1829?-1902), Andrew Carnegie (1835-1919), John D. Rockefeller (1839-1937), W. K. Kellogg (1860-1951), Richard Sears (1863-1914), William Randolph Hearst (1863-1951), Madame C. J. Walker (1867-1919), A. P. Giannini (1870-1949), Alfred Fuller (1885-1973), David Sarnoff (1891-1971), Roy Herbert Thomson (1894-1976), Walt Disney (1901-1966), Ray Kroc (1902-1984), Walter Annenberg (b. 1908), Sam Walton (1918-1992), Phil Knight (b. 1938), Ted Turner (b. 1938), Anita Roddick (b. 1942), Ben Cohen (b. 1951), Jerry Greenfield (b. 1951), and Steven Jobs (b. 1955). Glossary, Suggested Readings, and Index.

1397. Mayberry, Jodine. **Leaders Who Changed the 20th Century**. Austin, TX: Raintree/Steck-Vaughn, 1993. 48p. $15.96. ISBN 0-81144-926-2. (20 Events). 7-12

To understand what happened during the twentieth century, one must know something about those who became leaders and who changed things close to them. Among the leaders presented here in two-page spreads are Woodrow Wilson, Jane Addams, Ho Chi Minh, Lech Walesa, Vladimir Lenin, Mohandas Gandhi, Adolf Hitler, Winston Churchill, Franklin Roosevelt, Joseph Stalin, Mao Zedong, Fidel Castro, Martin Luther King, Jr., Anwar Sadat, Menachem Begin, the Ayatollah Khomeini, Margaret Thatcher, Mikhail Gorbachev, and Nelson Mandela. Photographs and drawings enhance the text. Further Reading, Glossary, and Index.

1398. Mayo, Edith, ed. **Smithsonian Book of the First Ladies**. New York: Henry Holt, 1996. 302p. $24.95. ISBN 0-8050-1751-8. 6 up

The text gives a brief account of women who have married Presidents, from Martha Washington to Hillary Rodham Clinton, as well as those who have served as hostesses in the White House for unmarried Presidents. Also included is how the role has changed, the question of suffrage, temperance, and other historical movements that have affected these women. Bibliography, Further Reading, and Index.

1399. Mazer, Harry. **Cave Under the City**. New York: Crowell, 1986. 152p. $13.89. ISBN 0-690-04559-X. New York: HarperCollins, 1986. 152p. $3.95pa. ISBN 0-06-440303-3pa. 5-8

During the early years of the Depression, Tolley, 12, and his younger brother decide to stay in the streets rather than go to the children's shelter when their father leaves New York to look for work and their mother is hospitalized for tuberculosis. They survive day by day doing little jobs, begging, and stealing until Tolley himself becomes sick. When they return home, they find their father waiting for them.

1400. Mazzio, Joann. **Leaving Eldorado**. Boston: Houghton Mifflin, 1993. 170p. $13.95. ISBN 0-395-64381-3. 5-9

In 1896, Maude, 14, decides that she will stay in Eldorado, New Mexico, after her father goes to search for gold in the Yukon. She begins work at the boardinghouse, where she meets an unusual group of people, including a woman who calls herself Venus Adonna and a schoolteacher. In diary entries addressed to her deceased mother, she tells about her experiences. Maude is surprised that she likes a "fallen" woman and that she would rather take art lessons than marry. After she receives unexpected money for saving someone from a fire, she decides that she does not have to marry someone she does not love.

1401. McCall, Edith. **Better than a Brother**. Minneapolis, MN: Walker, 1988. 133p. $13.95. ISBN 0-8027-6783-4. 5-7

Hughie, 13 and the oldest of six children in 1900, lives with her family in their house free because they board a team of ice cutters. Hughie loses a gold locket given her by her grandmother in the snow. When an ice cutter tells her he has found it, he says that he will give it to her for sexual favors. Hughie's friend, a boy whom she likes, hears about the proposition and finally gets her to tell her father.

1402.   McCall, Edith S. **Message from the Mountains**. New York: Walker, 1985. 122p. $11.95. ISBN 0-8027-6582-3. 6-9

In 1826, Jim, 15, tries to get information about his father when a caravan returns to Franklin, Missouri, from Santa Fe. Concerned, he decides to join Kit Carson on his caravan leaving soon, but Jim's boss breaks his leg before he can leave. Jim then finds a note from his father telling him to wait for his return. He does.

1403.   McClard, Megan. **Harriet Tubman: Slavery and the Underground Railroad**. Den Schofield, illustrator. Englewood Cliffs, NJ: Silver Burdett, 1991. 133p. $12.95; $7.95pa. ISBN 0-382-09938-9; 0-382-224047-2pa. (History of the Civil War). 6-9

As an illiterate slave, Harriet Tubman (1820-1913) fought one of the great battles against the power structure by conducting on the Underground Railroad and freeing more than 300 slaves. She also served as a nurse and scout in the South during the Civil War and later started speaking out for women's rights. John Brown, the abolitionist, called her "General Tubman," and her people called her "Moses." Time Table, Selected Sources, Suggested Reading, and Index.

1404.   McClard, Megan, and George Ypsilantis. **Hiawatha and the Iroquois League**. Frank Riccio, illustrator. Englewood Cliffs, NJ: Silver Burdett, 1989. 123p. $12.95; $7.95pa. ISBN 0-382-09568-5; 0-382-09757-2pa. (Biography of American Indians). 5-8

Hiawatha grew up as an Iroquois in the area of the current New York State during the fifteenth century. His concern over the blood feuds of tribes and the determination to avenge the death of anyone in the tribe led him to want peace. At great personal sacrifice, he eventually led, with the Huron Degandawida, the formation of the Iroquois League, consisting of five tribes, which became the example for the U.S. government. Suggested Reading.

1405.   McClung, Robert. **Hugh Glass, Mountain Man**. New York: Morrow, 1990. 142p. $12.95. ISBN 0-688-08092-8. 6 up

Hugh Glass has an amazing history of capture and escape from pirates and from death at the hands of Indians before he joins the Rocky Mountain Fur Company. In August 1823, on a hunting expedition for his new employer, a grizzly bear attacks him. Two trappers, Jim Bridger and John Fitzgerald, fearful of Indian attack, leave him for dead, without supplies, food, or weapons. He survives and begins to crawl toward the area of present-day South Dakota, 200 miles away, to the nearest settlement. He determines to reunite with the two who left him and get his retribution. He succeeds.

1406.   McClung, Robert M. **The True Adventures of Grizzly Adams**. New York: Morrow, 1985. 208p. $11.95. ISBN 0-688-05794-2. 5 up

Grizzly Adams (1812-1860) was one of the best-known frontiersmen in the Old West. He went to the goldfields in California where the greed of the miners disillusioned him. He disappeared into the western wilderness of the Sierra Nevadas, where he confronted jaguars and bears. He captured the largest grizzly of his day, a 1,200-pound animal he named Samson. When his menagerie starred as one of P. T. Barnum's leading attractions, he became a legend. Bibliography and Index.

1407.   McCullough, David. **Brave Companions: Portraits in History**. 1991. New York: Touchstone, Simon & Shuster, 1992. 240p. $12pa. ISBN 0-671-79276-8pa. YA

The 17 essays and speeches in this book contain portraits throughout the history of the United States of such people as Alexander von Humboldt and his South American explorations, Louis Agassiz and his impact on American families and their education, Teddy Roosevelt and his conservationism, Miriam Rothschild and her work in zoology, and Harriet Beecher Stowe's writing. Others come from the professions of social work, architecture, literature, etymology, and history. They include the Marquis de Morès, Frederick Remington, W. A. Roebling, Beryl Markham, Conrad Richter, Harry Caudill, David Plowden, and Simon Willard. Index.

1408.   McCullough, David G. **Truman**. New York: Simon & Schuster, 1992. 1117p. $30; $16pa. ISBN 0-671-45654-7; 0-671-86920-5pa. YA

By devoting a large section of text (around 100 pages) to the 1948 election, McCullough uses the other 1,000 to tell about Harry Truman (1884-1972) the man. He tries to show Truman's qualities as well as his times so that the decisions he made have a basis in history. Truman had to decide whether to drop a bomb on Hiroshima, whether to begin the Cold War, and whether the United States should aid South Korea after North Korea's invasion. McCullough gives the reader as many facts as Truman might have had for each of these situations and implies that the reader can make a similar informed decision. Truman had both wonderful and terrible traits such as honesty and determination along with obstinacy and insecurity. Bibliography and Index.

1409. McDonough, Yona Zeldis. **Frank Lloyd Wright**. New York: Chelsea House, 1991. 111p. $18.95; $7.95pa. ISBN 0-7910-1626-9; 0-7910-1633-1pa. (Library of Biography). 7 up

His architectural career spanning more than 72 years, Frank Lloyd Wright (1867-1959) wanted to harmonize the interiors and exteriors of his buildings with the environment in which they existed. He called his approach "organic architecture." Many of his buildings attracted the public because of their unconventionality and their attempt to use space. Among his best-known buildings are the Imperial Hotel in Tokyo, the Guggenheim Museum in New York, Fallingwater in Pennsylvania, and the Robie House in Chicago. Photographs highlight the text. Chronology, Further Reading, and Index.

1410. McGowen, Tom. **The Great Monkey Trial: Science vs. Fundamentalism in America**. New York: Franklin Watts, 1990. 110p. $20.50. ISBN 0-531-10965-8. YA

The Scopes trial or the Great Monkey trial lasted 10 days in July 1925, when a young biology teacher, John Scopes, was accused of teaching evolution in a public high school. Fundamentalist Christians believed in a literal interpretation of the Bible and saw no place for Charles Darwin's theory in the classroom. The two lawyers who verbally sparred with each other, William Jennings Bryan and Clarence Darrow, were two of the best. The text gives a history of the dispute through the decision in 1987 in the Supreme Court that struck down laws in Arkansas and Louisiana requiring the public schools to teach creationism (a literal interpretation of the Book of Genesis). Bibliography and Index.

1411. McGrath, Patrick. **The Lewis and Clark Expedition**. Englewood Cliffs, NJ: Silver Burdett, 1985. 64p. $14.95. ISBN 0-382-06828-9. 4-9

In 1803, Thomas Jefferson commissioned the expedition that sent Meriwether Lewis and William Clark to explore the Louisiana Purchase territory. During this journey across land, they and members of the group cataloged plant and animal life and established relations with Indian inhabitants while collecting information about their cultures. The leaders of the expedition were two Virginians who shared a similar military background but who had dissimilar personalities and temperaments. The text looks at them and their achievements. Index and Suggested Reading.

1412. McGraw, Eloise Jarvis. **Moccasin Trail**. 1952. New York: Penguin, 1986. 256p. $4.99pa. ISBN 0-14-032170-5pa. 6-10

A bear mauls Jim when he is 12, and the Crow tribe adopts him. He spends six years living with them and counting coup (the number of whites scalped), wearing his eagle feathers as a young brave. When he meets his younger siblings in a nearby settlement, they tell him that they need his signature as the oldest son. They need it to get the land that their father had identified in Willamette Valley, Oregon, before dying on the trail with their mother. Jim agrees, and he goes with them although they distrust each other. They eventually learn that each has talents that will help them all be successful. *Newbery Honor Book, Junior Literary Guild Selection*, and *Lewis Carroll Shelf Award*.

1413. McHale, John E., Jr. **Dr. Samuel A. Mudd and the Lincoln Assassination**. New York: Dillon Press, Silver Burdett, 1995. 144p. $7.95. ISBN 0-87518-629-7. (People in Focus). 6-9

On April 15, 1865, two men, one with a broken leg, rode to the southern Maryland farmhouse of Dr. Samuel A. Mudd. As a doctor obligated to heal the sick, Dr. Mudd set the man's leg and gave the two a place to sleep for the night. Because the injured man was John Wilkes Booth, the man who had just assassinated Abraham Lincoln, Dr. Mudd was convicted and sent to prison for helping the criminals. The text looks at his story and asks questions such as whether he knew who the patient was, if he waited to tell authorities about the strangers, if he showed the men through the Zekiah Swamp as an escape route, if he hid the assassin's boots from War Department detectives, and if he lied when he said he did not recognize a picture of Booth after the incident. Bibliography and Index.

1414. McHugh, Christopher. **Western Art 1600-1800**. New York: Thomson Learning, 1994. 48p. $16.95. ISBN 1-56847-219-6. (Art and Artists). 7-10

In the text, McHugh covers major art movements in the western world by focusing on the Dutch, the Italian Renaissance, Spain, France, and England. Boxes include capsule biographies and commentaries of and on women artists, El Greco (1541-1614), Jan Vermeer (1632-1675), *Commedia dell'arte* (sixteenth-century drama), William Hogarth (1697-1764), Francisco de Goya (1746-1828), the arts of Native Americans, and Greco-Roman painting. Glossary, Further Reading, Where to See Seventeenth and Eighteenth Century Art (United States), and Index.

1415. McKee, Lynn Armistead. **Woman of the Mists**. New York: Diamond, Berkley, 1991. 343p. $4.95pa. ISBN 1-55773-520-4pa. YA

Around 500 BC in the area now known as southern Florida, Kaho kidnaps Teeka from a hostile tribe. She has pledged love to Auro, son of her tribe's shaman, but she stays with Kaho because she wants to protect her people. When Auro becomes morose after she refuses to return, she tries to convince him and Kaho that living in peace is preferable. Finds of a burial site, a habitation mound, and a ceremonial complex from an archaeological dig form the basis of the story.

1416.   McKenzie, Ellen Kindt. **Under the Bridge**. New York: Henry Holt, 1994. 140p. $14.95. ISBN 0-8050-3398-X. 4-7

Ritchie, 10, and his little sister Rosie in Illinois during 1939 try to cope while their mother is away. She disappears one day, but their father does not tell them where she is. Someone finally says that she has had a nervous breakdown. Rosie gets sick, and she starts getting letters from a troll that she thinks might be living under a nearby bridge after hearing "Billy Goats Gruff." The letters help her get better, and they eventually stop when their mother returns and a musician who lives next to the bridge goes to fight in World War II. Although they never know who sent the letters, Ritchie realizes after the war in 1945, when they receive a letter from England saying "we won" and signed by the troll, that the musician is safe.

1417.   McKissack, Patricia C., and Fredrick McKissack, Jr. **Black Diamond: The Story of the Negro Baseball Leagues**. New York: Scholastic, 1994. 184p. $14.95; $3.99pa. ISBN 0-590-45809-4; 0-590-45810-8pa. 4-9

Because African Americans were not allowed to play in white baseball leagues for nearly a century, they formed leagues of their own. Many participants were superb players like Cool Papa Bell, Josh Gibson, and Satchel Paige. The text covers their history from the beginning of baseball through some of the first African Americans to play in the major leagues: Jackie Robinson, Willie Mays, and Hank Aaron. Player Profiles, Hall of Fame, Time Line, Bibliography, and Index. *Coretta Scott King Honor* and *Notable Children's Trade Books in the Field of Social Studies.*

1418.   McKissack, Patricia, and Fredrick McKissack. **A Long Hard Journey: The Story of the Pullman Porter**. New York: Walker, 1989. 144p. $17.95; $9.95pa. ISBN 0-8027-6884-9; 0-8027-7437-7pa. (American History). 7 up

Train travel needed people who served passengers during its early years. The Pullman porters were Black men who smiled at the passengers but suffered from unfair labor practices. A. Philip Randolph organized them so that they could fight management with a strike. The text, in three parts covering 1829-1900, 1900-1934, and 1935-1979, details their trials, concessions, and successes. Photographs give a sense of the time and place. Bibliography and Index. *Coretta Scott King Award, Carter G. Woodson Book Award, American Library Association Notable Books for Children, New York Public Library Books for the Teen Age,* and *Jane Addams Children's Book Award.*

1419.   McKissack, Patricia C., and Frederick L. McKissack. **Rebels Against Slavery: American Slave Revolts**. New York: Scholastic, 1996. 176p. $14.95. ISBN 0-590-45735-7. 5-8

The text looks at several slave revolts and posits that each one was more intense than the previous one with all leading to the organized attempts that eventually overcame slavery. Toussaint L'Ouverture, Cato, Denmark Vesey, Gabriel Prosser, Harriet Tubman, and John Brown led the way, with others operating on the fringes. Tubman was willing to shoot any runaway who could not complete the journey to freedom. But the McKissacks think that even the nonviolent resistance had its place because it helped the final goal. Photographs, Chronology, and Index.

1420.   McKissack, Patricia, and Frederick McKissack. **Red-Tail Angels: The Story of the Tuskegee Airmen of World War II**. New York: Walker, 1995. 136p. $19.95. ISBN 0-8027-8292-2. 5-9

Because of prejudice, the United States denied African Americans the right to make contributions to various war efforts or shunned them when they returned home from fighting. The text looks at the history of African American participation in the U.S. military, including decisions, assignments, and experiences of those involved. For World War II, the text gives a chronological account of African American participation. The flying squadron of the Tuskegee Airmen showed that prior decisions to exclude African Americans were a mistake, and they helped others have a better chance for promotion in the military. Photographs, Bibliography, and Index. *American Library Association Best Books for Young Adults, IRA Teachers' Choices, Carter G. Woodson Book Award,* and *Notable Children's Trade Books in the Field of Social Studies.*

1421.   McKissack, Patricia, and Frederick McKissack. **Sojourner Truth: Ain't I a Woman?** New York: Scholastic, 1992. 186p. $13.95; $3.50pa. ISBN 0-590-44690-8; 0-590-44691-6pa. 5-8

Isabella (1797-1883) was born a slave in New York and freed in 1827. Mother of five children, she sued because her son had been illegally sold to someone in the South and became one of the first Black women to win a lawsuit against a white. Not until later in her life did she choose the name Sojourner Truth. She wandered from place to place speaking against slavery to anyone who would listen. Six feet tall with a resonant voice, she was a visible and vocal fighter against injustice. Although she could not read, she was a preacher who could quote the Bible word-for-word, an abolitionist, and an activist for the rights of women. Bibliography and Index. *Coretta Scott King Honor Book, American Library Association Best Books for Young Adults, American Library Association Notable Books for Children,* and *Boston Globe-Horn Book Award.*

1422. McKissack, Patricia, and Fredrick McKissack. **W. E. B. Du bois**. New York: Franklin Watts, 1990. 143p. $21.20. ISBN 0-531-10939-9. (Impact Biography). 9 up

W. E. B. DuBois (1868-1963) had a career that saw Booker T. Washington, Martin Luther King, Jr, the Jim Crow laws, and the *Brown vs. Board of Education* decision ending school segregation. As the son of free blacks, he achieved distinction which he credited to his college habit of going to bed at ten o'clock every night. He was a founder of the National Association for the Advancement of Colored People, and he edited *Crisis* magazine. The last years of his life he spent in Ghana. Photographs, Source Notes, Bibliography, and Index.

1423. McLanathan, Richard B. K. **Gilbert Stuart**. New York: Harry N. Abrams, 1986. 159p. $39.95. ISBN 0-8109-1501-4. YA

As the first settlers in the Protestant colonies had little use for fine arts, the first important artworks were portraits to preserve the family's likeness. Gilbert Stuart (1755-1828) was, in his day, the most famous and best-employed portraitist. Although born in the colonies, Stuart spent some years in London, where he knew other American painters. Because he lived extravagantly, he overspent his income and had to return to America. He created portraits of Thomas Jefferson, John Jay, James and Dolley Madison, John Adams, Paul Revere, and others; he caught their appearances as well as their characters. Through him, the world sees the people who began and completed the shift of British power to American democracy. The oversized book includes color reproductions of 50 plates. Chronology, Bibliography, and Index.

1424. McLaurin, Melton A. **Celia, A Slave**. Athens, GA: University of Georgia, 1991. 148p. $19.95. ISBN 0-8203-1352-1. New York: Avon, 1993. 148p. $10pa. ISBN 0-380-71935-5pa. YA

In 1855, Celia, a slave in Missouri, killed her sexually abusive master, Robert Newsom. After an inquest and a jury trial, she was hung for the murder. McLaurin reconstructs the story from court records, local histories, census data, and contemporary newspapers. Because of the paucity of information, he has to be creative in his interpretations for some points. More important is the ethical and moral issue that nineteenth-century America tacitly condoned the rape and sexual abuse of Black slaves by their masters. Bibliography and Index.

1425. McLynn, F. J. **Famous Trials: Cases That Made History**. New York: Reader's Digest, 1996. 182p. $27.95. ISBN 0-89577-655-3. YA

Although McLynn includes no criteria for selection, the cases here have influenced history. Arranged into groups according to the types of court that heard the case—special, military, church, or jury—those discussed include the trials of Socrates, Jesus, Thomas More, Danton of the French Revolution, Dreyfus in France, the Chinese Gang of Four, Galileo, John Brown, Tojo, Scopes, and Nelson Mandela. Commentary adds information about the importance of each case to history. Bibliography, Chronology, and Index.

1426. McMurtry, Larry. **Lonesome Dove: A Novel**. New York: Simon & Schuster, 1985. 843p. $24.95; $6.99pa. ISBN 0-671-50420-7; 0-671-68390-Xpa. YA

In the 1870s, partners of a business in Lonesome Dove, Texas, decide to lead the cattle they have stolen from Mexico into Montana where they can stake their own settlements. Gus and Call take an assortment of people with them on the drive, and their journey includes stampedes, lynchings, outlaws, drought, gunfights, Indian raids, and other events. *Pulitzer Prize*.

1427. McNeese, Tim. **America's Early Canals**. New York: Crestwood House, 1993. 48p. $11.95. ISBN 0-89686-730-7. (Americans on the Move). 4-8

By the 1790s, 30 canal companies were working on canals. One such place was Middlesex in Massachusetts, which connected the Merrimack River to Boston Harbor. The companies built hundreds of canals before the Civil War including the Potomac Canal, to connect the Potomac with the Ohio, and the Erie Canal, to connect the Hudson River with Lake Erie at Buffalo. After the war, canal travel began to decline. Drawings augment the text. Further Reading, Glossary, and Index.

1428. McNeese, Tim. **America's First Railroads**. Chris Duke, illustrator. New York: Crestwood House, 1993. 48p. $11.95. ISBN 0-89686-729-3. (Americans on the Move). 4-8

In 1828, work began on the Baltimore and Ohio Railroad, and its first miles were completed in 1830. It stretched to Cumberland, Maryland, by 1842. During that time and after, locomotives changed. Matthias Baldwin designed and made a full-size locomotive nicknamed "Old Ironsides" in the 1830s. Then railroads began to stretch to the West after the transcontinental line was finished. Drawings highlight the text. Further Reading, Glossary, and Index.

1429. McNeese, Tim. **Clippers and Whaling Ships**. Chris Duke, illustrator. New York: Crestwood House, 1993. 48p. $11.95. ISBN 0-89686-735-8. (Americans on the Move). 4-8

In the mid-1840s and for 30 years, privateers changed to clipper ships. Some of those built were the *Ann McKim*, *Rainbow*, and *Sea Witch*. American whalers traveled the world. The text covers life on ship, killing and carving the whales, and the sources for oil. Drawings and diagrams highlight the text. Further Reading, Glossary, and Index.

1430.   McNeese, Tim. **Conestogas and Stagecoaches**. Chris Duke, illustrator. New York: Crestwood House, 1993. 48p. $11.95. ISBN 0-89686-732-3. (Americans on the Move). 4-8

Among those vehicles carrying passengers and mail during the eighteenth and nineteenth centuries were Conestoga wagons and stagecoaches. The text discusses the differing functions of wagons and stagecoaches along with the facilities for passengers along the travel routes, like sleeping and eating at taverns. Among the trails were the National Road from Cumberland, Maryland, to Wheeling, Virginia (West Virginia today). Some of the companies were the Butterfield Overland mail, which traveled 2,000 miles across Texas, New Mexico, and Arizona; the Western Stage Trail; and the Colorado stages. By 1920, mass-produced vehicles took over the roads. Drawings enhance the text. Further Reading, Glossary, and Index.

1431.   McNeese, Tim. **Early River Travel**. New York: Crestwood House, 1993. 48p. $11.95. ISBN 0-89686-733-1. (Americans on the Move). 4-8

The earliest ships were canoes, but when Americans moved west, people needed new crafts. Flatboats and keelboats floated the Mississippi, and steamboats became the mode of travel for passengers. Men who helped develop the steamboat were John Fitch in 1790 and Robert Fulton, who, after an initial failure, built the Clermont in New York in 1807. Helping Fulton was Robert Livingston. Drawings enhance the text. Further Reading, Glossary, and Index.

1432.   McNeese, Tim. **From Trails to Turnpikes**. New York: Crestwood House, 1993. 48p. $11.95. ISBN 0-89686-731-5. (Americans on the Move). 4-8

Buffalo and the Native Americans created paths that became colonial roads. In 1775, Daniel Boone built the Wilderness Road into Kentucky. Other turnpikes were Lancaster Pike, first opened in Philadelphia in 1797. The National Road from Maryland to Ohio was built between 1827 and 1850 with Conestogas, pack trains, and stagecoaches taking advantage of its convenience. In the early 1800s, western trails included the Santa Fe, the Oregon, and the California. Drawings enhance the text. Further Reading, Glossary, and Index.

1433.   McNeese, Tim. **West by Steamboat**. Chris Duke, illustrator. New York: Crestwood House, 1993. 48p. $11.95. ISBN 0-89686-728-5. (Americans on the Move). 4-8

Once the first steamboat became a vessel, rivers became two-way streets because boats could travel against the current. Nicholas J. Roosevelt constructed the first western steamer and launched it in 1811. Others followed, and the text chronicles the golden age of the steamboat, which took passengers on the Mississippi. With the advent of the locomotive, the boats lost their attraction. Illustrations enhance the text. Glossary, Further Reading, and Index.

1434.   McPherson, James M. **Abraham Lincoln and the Second American Revolution**. New York: Oxford University Press, 1991. 173p. $20; $9.95pa. ISBN 0-19-505542-X; 0-19-507606-0pa. YA

Seven essays in this text look at Abraham Lincoln and the meaning of the Civil War. The first and last discuss the different notions of liberty that the two sides had and what the war achieved, if anything. The five central essays look at Lincoln's political philosophies and how he had to create a situation after emancipation in which government could control freedom without intruding on the rights of its citizens. McPherson believes that Lincoln's visions were what made emancipation successful. Bibliography and Index.

1435.   McPherson, James M. **Battle Cry of Freedom: The Civil War Era**. New York: Oxford University Press, 1988. 904p. $39.95; $16.95pa. ISBN 0-19-503863-0; 0-345-35942-9pa. (Oxford History of the United States, 6). YA

James McPherson writes that casualties at the Battle of Antietam (or the Battle of Sharpsburg, according to the Southern troops) on September 17, 1862, totaled four times the number lost at Normandy on June 6, 1944. Then he adds that twice as many died that day than fell during the combined War of 1812, Mexican War, and Spanish-American War. The lives lost during the Civil War were more than in all other wars together that the United States has ever fought. In this history of the Civil War, the text covers in detail the battles on land and sea in the North and South. Bibliography and Index. *Pulitzer Prize*.

1436.   McPherson, James M. **Images of the Civil War**. Mort Kunstler, illustrator. Richmond VA: Gramercy, 1992. 189p. $19.99. ISBN 0-517-07356-0. YA

The text is a combination of McPherson's descriptions of happenings in the Civil War with 72 paintings of sites including portraits of generals on both sides. Also included are maps so that one may gain a sense of the war emotionally and intellectually. Index.

1437.   McPherson, James M. **Marching Toward Freedom: Blacks in the Civil War 1861-1865**. 1967. New York: Facts on File, 1991. 142p. $17.95; $8.95pa. ISBN 0-8160-2337-9; 0-8160-3092-8pa. YA

Although many people think that the Civil War was fought to end slavery, it did not begin with that as the main purpose. Not until two years after the start was the Emancipation Proclamation signed saying that the Union was also fighting for slavery to be abolished. Because they were not allowed to fight in the beginning of the war, patriotic Blacks served as spies, cooks, teachers, nurses, and laborers. They inspired civilians, both Black and white, to struggle for equal rights; they earned respect from the Union command; and they contributed to the downfall of the Confederacy. Eyewitness accounts, newspaper articles, diaries of abolitionists, slave tales, and marching songs contribute to this presentation. Bibliography and Index.

1438.   McPherson, James M. **What They Fought For, 1861-1865**. Baton Rouge, LA: Louisiana State University Press, 1994. 88p. $16.95. ISBN 0-8071-1904-0. New York: Anchor, 1995. 88p. $10pa. ISBN 0-385-47634-5pa. YA

After reviewing thousands of letters and diaries of frontline soldiers in the Civil War, McPherson argues that the men who fought in the Civil War felt strongly about what they were fighting for, and many were prepared to die for their political views. Their patriotism led to the deaths of more than 620,000 of them. He contrasts them to soldiers in World War II, whom many military historians have thought were fighting to save their compatriots rather than for a particular cause. In the Civil War, however, the soldiers were on their home soil, and they had strong beliefs. The text includes excerpts from the letters and diaries to prove McPherson's conclusion. Bibliography and Index.

1439.   McPherson, James M., and G. S. Borritt, eds. **Why the Confederacy Lost**. New York: Oxford University Press, 1992. 209p. $25. ISBN 0-19-507405-X. YA

These essays by five major military historians posit that the Union won the Civil War because of Grant and Sherman's innovative battlefield decisions. The Union used its troops more effectively, which kept the Union soldiers' morale higher. When the Confederates felt that they were losing, they lost confidence, and that was a consequence rather than a cause of the defeat. Additional discussions include the concept that North and South both developed strategies appropriate to their political needs. The use of Black troops appears as well as commentary as to why generals failed to pursue defeated enemies when they retreated. McPherson notes that the war's outcome was not inevitable; the ending could have been reversed. Bibliography and Index.

1440.   McPherson, Stephanie Sammartino. **Peace and Bread: The Story of Jane Addams**. Minneapolis, MN: Carolrhoda, 1993. 96p. $19.95. ISBN 0-87614-792-9. (Trailblazers). 4-7

As a child, Jane Addams (1860-1935) helped her neighbors. As an adult, she saw a problem and tried to solve it. She rented a house in one of the poorest areas of Chicago, on Halsted Street, and in it she created the first settlement house for the poor. She spent more than 40 years at Hull House, and her years with the Women's International League for Peace and Freedom led her to become one of the leading figures battling for the less fortunate. Photographs, Bibliography, and Index.

1441.   McPherson, Stephanie Sammartino. **TV's Forgotten Hero: The Story of Philo Farnsworth**. Minneapolis, MN: Carolrhoda, 1996. 96p. $19.95. ISBN 1-57505-017-X. 4-7

In the 1920s, Philo Farnsworth (1906-1971) developed the basic components for electronic television. When he was 12, he saw electric lines for the first time, and he began experimenting. What he created changed the twentieth century. He needed to control electrons so that they would change speed or direction, change light into electricity, and change electricity into pictures. After much effort, he succeeded. In honor of his achievement, children from Utah voted to have him be the subject of the second statue from their state to be displayed in the capitol building. Notes, Bibliography, and Index.

1442.   Medearis, Angela Shelf. **Come This Far to Freedom: A History of African Americans**. New York: Atheneum, 1993. 148p. $14.95. ISBN 0-689-31522-8. 5 up

Medearis divides the history of African Americans into five parts: coming from Africa to the hardships of slavery, the fight for freedom, the fresh start during Reconstruction after the Civil War, the movement for equality, and the people who have continued to break down the barriers in politics, the military, the sciences, and other fields. Important Dates, Bibliography, and Index.

1443.   Meigs, Cornelia. **Invincible Louisa**. 1933. Boston: Little, Brown, 1968. 195p. $17.95; $5.95pa. ISBN 0-316-56590-3; 0-316-56594-6pa. YA

Louisa May Alcott (1832-1888), born in Germantown, Pennsylvania, was raised in Boston with tutors such as the American writers Ralph Waldo Emerson and Henry David Thoreau. In addition to writing *Little Women* and *Jo's Boys,* she also wrote other works anonymously to help support her family. While serving as a nurse during the American Civil War, she wrote letters to her family that were also eventually published. Chronology and Index. *Newbery Medal.*

1444.   Melder, Keith. **Hail to the Candidate: Presidential Campaigns from Banners to Broadcasts**. Washington, DC: Smithsonian Institution Press, 1992. 224p. $24.95pa. ISBN 1-56098-178-4pa. YA

This story of U.S. campaigns highlights the memorabilia, including banners, posters, and buttons. It discusses how such objects have related to the political process since 1840. These items have allowed people to feel as if they were participating in the process, although recently people have tended to observe from afar. The text includes 200 illustrations of these artifacts, half of them in color. They make learning about politics a more interesting and more concrete endeavor. Bibliography and Index.

1445.   Meltzer, Milton. **The American Promise: Voices of a Changing Nation 1945-Present**. New York: Bantam, 1990. 184p. $15.90. ISBN 0-553-07020-7. 10 up

Topics that have shaped and influenced American society since the end of World War II are the Cold War, the Korean and Vietnamese fighting, the Civil Rights movement, the women's rights movement, poverty, and environmental issues. Persons presented in the discussions associated with these topics are Betty Friedan, the Berrigans, Howell Raines, Rachel Carson, and others. Bibliography and Index.

1446.   Meltzer, Milton, ed. **The American Revolutionaries: A History in their Own Words, 1750-1800**. New York: Crowell, 1987. 256p. $12.95. ISBN 0-690-04643-X. New York: Trophy, 1993. 256p. $6.95pa. ISBN 0-06-446145-9pa. 7 up

Eyewitness accounts of the Revolution through letters, diaries, speeches, and other documents help give a chronological account of the times from those who lived through the war. Meltzer incorporates various points of view to show that colonists disagreed about fighting a war. The additional turmoil between Indians and white settlers also appears as well as the women and Blacks who either went with the troops or fought with them. Sources and Index. *American Library Association Best Books for Young Adults, American Library Association USA Through Children's Books, School Library Journal Best Book, Notable Children's Trade Books in the Field of Social Studies, New York Public Library Children's Books,* and *New York Public Library Books for the Teen Age.*

1447.   Meltzer, Milton. **Andrew Jackson and His America**. New York: Franklin Watts, 1993. 207p. $24.90. ISBN 0-531-11157-1. 7-10

Born to poor Irish immigrants in 1767, Andrew Jackson (d. 1845) always aspired to greatness. He became a frontiersman and Indian fighter, defeated the British in 1815, and served his state of Tennessee as congressman, senator, and judge. He earned money after studying law and making smart real estate investments. As President, he preserved the country against factionalism and from the power of the Bank of the United States. At the same time, he ordered the forced relocation of thousands of Native Americans from their homes. He refused to change his mind, once made, and after he left the presidency, he served the country as one of its beloved elder statesmen. Sources and Index.

1448.   Meltzer, Milton. **Benjamin Franklin: The New American**. New York: Franklin Watts, 1988. 287p. $23.40. ISBN 0-531-10582-2. YA

Meltzer attributes Benjamin Franklin's (1706-1790) "energy, humor, patience, tact, [and] understanding of people and politics" as having helped the new country of America gain a positive response in France. Using comments from Franklin's writing, including letters, Meltzer shows Franklin's love of ordinary pleasures and his various professions such as printer, inventor, author, publisher, scientist, businessman, diplomat, and politician. He helped with the Declaration of Independence and the writing of the Constitution. Yet he also had his weaknesses, which Meltzer also presents in this balanced account of Franklin's life. A Note on Sources and Index.

1449.   Meltzer, Milton. **Betty Friedan: A Voice for Women's Rights**. Stephen Maarchesi, illustrator. New York: Viking, 1985. 58p. $9.95. ISBN 0-670-80786-9. (Women of Our Lifetime). 5 up

Betty Friedan (b. 1921) grew up in Peoria, Illinois, and left her unhappy family to attend Smith College. After college, she began graduate school at Berkeley, and then went to New York to work as a writer. She met a man whom she married. After she gave up her work to raise his children in the suburbs, she felt she had given up her self. As she became more and more unhappy and talked to others like her, she found out that many women wanted to work. She wrote a book called *The Feminine Mystique* in 1963, which furthered the feminist movement. She saw that women had more to offer than roles as housecleaners and babysitters, and this book led them to recognize and use their abilities.

1450.   Meltzer, Milton. **The Bill of Rights: How We Got It and What It Means**. New York: HarperCollins, 1990. 179p. $14.89. ISBN 0-690-04805-X. 9 up

People ask questions about their rights every day, and the Bill of Rights can offer many of the answers. Adopted as an amendment to the U.S. Constitution in 1791, this document has its roots in England in 1215, when angry barons forced King John to grant them the Magna Carta. Additionally, the text explains the reasons behind the American colonies' struggles to expand their liberties and gain independence. Then it looks at the internal difficulties that the colonists encountered on their way to the Revolution and democracy. Bibliography and Index.

1451.   Meltzer, Milton. **The Black Americans: A History in Their Own Words**. 1964. New York: Trophy, 1987. 306p. $9.95pa. ISBN 0-06-446055-Xpa. 5 up

Meltzer has collected documents showing 350 years of Black life in America. His subjects range from the sharecropper's struggle to the scholar Maya Angelou. Using the words of those who endured, he relates a history that stretches from 1619 to 1983. Sources and Index. *American Library Association Notable Books for Children* and *Notable Children's Trade Books in the Field of Social Studies.*

1452.   Meltzer, Milton. **Brother Can You Spare A Dime? The Great Depression, 1929-1933**. New York: Facts on File, 1991. 130p. $17.95. ISBN 0-8160-2372-7. (Library of American History). 7-12

In October 1929, when the stock market crashed, a decade of unemployment and poverty began that became known as the Great Depression. The first four years were the most severe, and the text looks at these difficult times by incorporating firsthand accounts of workers, farmers, professionals, sharecroppers, men and women, and young and old. Meltzer also includes songs, poems, and short writings to recreate the traumatic feelings of the times. Bibliography and Index.

1453.   Meltzer, Milton. **Cheap Raw Material: How Our Youngest Workers Are Exploited and Abused**. New York: Viking, 1994. 167p. $14.95. ISBN 0-670-83128-X. 7-9

Meltzer looks at the history of child labor since the beginning of civilization to show that children have always worked. He investigates the mills, mines, and sweatshops in which they have labored. He also notes how they have been maligned and abused with no rights as long as no one outside the workplace knew what was happening inside. Accidents have been common, disabling children for the rest of their lives. Bibliography, Source Notes, and Index.

1454.   Meltzer, Milton, ed. **Frederick Douglass: In His Own Words**. Stephen Alcorn, illustrator. San Diego, CA: Harcourt Brace, 1995. 220p. $22. ISBN 0-15-229492-9. 7 up

Frederick Douglass (1818-1895) was one of the most influential Black leaders of the nineteenth century. He was also an orator and an editor whose words helped to win freedom for slaves. The text collects his words with interesting information about his achievements as a fighter against slavery, injustice, inequality, and racism. Following the text are brief biographical profiles of Susan Bronell Anthony, Anthony Burns, Anna Murray Douglass, Abby Kelley Foster, William Lloyd Garrison, Wendell Phillips, Charles Sumner, Toussaint L'Ouverture, Harriet Tubman, and Ida B. Wells-Barnett. A Note on Sources and Further Reading and Index. *New York Public Library Books for the Teen Age, Parents' Choice Awards,* and *Notable Children's Trade Books in the Field of Social Studies.*

1455.   Meltzer, Milton. **George Washington and the Birth of Our Nation**. New York: Franklin Watts, 1986. 188p. $21.90. ISBN 0-531-10253-X. YA

George Washington (1732-1799) was ambitious, energetic, impulsive, and vulnerable. Meltzer tries to find the real man behind the legends that have evolved. He sees him as a surveyor and a soldier on the wilderness frontier who also had the difficulties of managing his plantations. But he had to fulfill the roles of general and President as well. Further Reading and Index.

1456.   Meltzer, Milton. **Gold: The True Story of Why People Search for It, Mine It, Trade It, Steal It, Mint It, Hoard It**. New York: HarperCollins, 1993. 167p. $15. ISBN 0-06-022983-7. 4-8

Photographs complement the text, which tells of humankind's 5,000-year quest for gold. Included are such topics as shekels, bezants, florins, ducats, and guineas. Other chapters look at where to get gold in the mines and the slaves who mined it, African empires built on gold, the gold rush in California, the search from Australia to South Africa, and what people endured when others came to their lands looking for gold. Bibliography and Index.

1457.   Meltzer, Milton, ed. **Lincoln in His Own Words**. Stephen Alcorn, illustrator. San Diego, CA: Harcourt Brace, 1993. 226p. $22.95. ISBN 0-15-245437. 7 up

Meltzer has taken Abraham Lincoln's speeches and letters and organized them so that he presents Lincoln's beliefs with Lincoln's words appearing as bold text. Meltzer adds brief profiles of Lincoln's contemporaries including Lydia Maria Child, Henry David Thoreau, Harriet Beecher Stowe, and Walt Whitman. Chronology, Sources, Illustrator's Note, and Index. *Notable Children's Trade Books in the Field of Social Studies, IRA Teachers' Choices*, and *New York Public Library Books for the Teen Age.*

1458.   Meltzer, Milton. **Starting from Home: A Writer's Beginnings**. 1988. New York: Puffin, 1991. 145p. $3.95pa. ISBN 0-14-032299-Xpa. YA

The author of many biographies and history trade books for juveniles, Milton Meltzer (b. 1915) recounts the discoveries, hardships, and triumphs of his early life as he identifies the influences that shaped him as a person and writer.

1459. Meltzer, Milton. **Theodore Roosevelt and His America**. New York: Franklin Watts, 1994. 191p. $24.90. ISBN 0-531-11192-X. 9-12

Teddy Roosevelt (1858-1919) reflects the words carved into the stone wall of the American Museum of Natural History in New York: "Statesman, Conservationist, Naturalist, Patriot, Historian." During his lifetime, America was making the transition into an industrialized nation where huge financial empires were growing. He worked hard for the poor, fought the political powers of the time, and passed appropriate laws in government. Roosevelt also had his faults; among them was his suspicion of foreigners. Yet he tried to keep America going on an honest path. Sources and Index.

1460. Meltzer, Milton. **Thomas Jefferson: The Revolutionary Aristocrat**. New York: Franklin Watts, 1991. 255p. $15.95. ISBN 0-531-15227-8. 7-9

Thomas Jefferson (1743-1826) was a complicated man whose beliefs were sometimes at odds with his actions. His political career lasted approximately 50 years but gave him little pleasure. He believed in rights but wanted to take them away from his critics. He condemned the evils of slavery but owned slaves. He was a diplomat, scientist, architect, philosopher, educator, and agriculturalist. Sources and Index.

1461. Meltzer, Milton. **Tom Paine: Voice of Revolution**. New York: Franklin Watts, 1996. 175p. $25.80. ISBN 0-531-11291-8. 9 up

Tom Paine (1737-1809) was a complex man who questioned, suffered for his assertions, and died penniless. Meltzer presents his life and explains why Paine turned against Washington, how he ended up in a French prison during the French Revolution, and other aspects that place Paine in his historical period. Index.

1462. Meltzer, Milton, ed. **Voices from the Civil War**. New York: Crowell, 1989. 203p. $13.95. ISBN 0-690-04802-5. New York: Trophy, 1992. 224p. $6.95pa. ISBN 0-06-446124-6pa. 7 up

Using excerpts from letters, speeches, songs, and diaries, Meltzer tells the story of the Civil War through the words of those who participated. The selections, arranged chronologically from the beginning to the end of the war, include battle accounts, Lincoln's words, Mark Twain, and others with diverse perspectives. Photographs, Illustrations, Bibliography, and Index. *American Library Association Best Books for Young Adults, School Library Journal Best Book, Notable Children's Trade Books in the Field of Social Studies, New York Public Library Children's Books,* and *New York Public Library Books for the Teen Age.*

1463. Meltzer, Milton. **Weapons & Warfare: From the Stone Age to the Space Age**. Sergio Martinez, illustrator. New York: HarperCollins, 1996. 85p. $16.95. ISBN 0-06-024875-0. 7 up

Meltzer looks at the creation and use of weapons throughout history in chronological order. Within the chapters are short essays asking such questions as "Do women war?" and commenting on such topics as "The profits of death-dealing." The philsophical tone wonders why humans would do such a thing to themselves. Bibliography and Index.

1464. Mendelsohn, Jane. **I Was Amelia Earhart**. New York: Knopf, 1996. 145p. $18; $10pa. ISBN 0-679-45805-0; 0-679-77636-2pa. YA

Using a fictitious log that Earhart might have written in the days after her disappearance with her navigator Fred Noonan, Mendelsohn creates a story of two people who were trying to find a good life away from Earhart's manipulative husband. She names Earhart's island "Heaven" in this unusual speculation.

1465. Mendez, Adriana. **Cubans in America**. Minneapolis, MN: Lerner, 1994. 80p. $17.50; $5.95pa. ISBN 0-8225-1953-4; 0-8225-1039-1pa. (In America). 5-9

Cuba's position at 90 miles from Florida puts it at a location strategic to the United States. When Columbus arrived, he wrote about its beauty, and other explorers landed there. Cuba's history has been one of people who have had to survive. The Taino Indians, natives when Columbus came, were conquered and became slaves to the Spanish. In the nineteenth century, José Martí finally helped free the country from Spain. In 1959, Batista lost Cuba to Fidel Castro. Castro set up a socialist government from which people now want to escape. The text compares the different Cubas that have existed on this beautiful island. Glossary, Selected Bibliography, and Index.

1466. Meriwether, Louise. **Fragments of the Ark**. New York: Pocket Books, 1994. 342p. $21. ISBN 0-671-79947-9. YA

In 1861, Peter Mango, a slave trained as a navigator, pilots a gunboat out of Charleston Harbor into the Union army. He adds his voice to those trying to allow Blacks to fight against the Confederacy. After the war, he becomes a riverboat captain, buys his former master's home, and becomes a delegate to the Freedman's Convention. Based on the life of Robert Small, this fictional work gives insight into the times from the view of a person determined to become free.

1467.	Meryman, Richard. **Andrew Wyeth**. New York: Harry N. Abrams, 1991. 92p. $19.95. ISBN 0-8109-3956-8. (First Impressions). 6-9

Andrew Wyeth (b. 1917) was born into a family of artists. Not until his father died was he able to develop his own painting and become an artist in his own right, with pictures such as *Christina's World*. Reproductions and Index.

1468.	Mettger, Zak. **Reconstruction: America After the Civil War**. New York: Lodestar, 1994. 122p. $16.99. ISBN 0-525-67490-X. (Young Readers' History of the Civil War). 5-9

After the Civil War, not only were cities and farms ruined but also the South's entire way of life. The years 1865-1877 are known as Reconstruction. Northern politicians discussed whether to punish Southern traitors before allowing them to rejoin the United States. Freed slaves had to fight for their rights in the South to vote, own land, and earn wages. Mettger discusses these problems and how the people confronted them as they tried to rebuild their lives. Glossary, Further Reading, and Index.

1469.	Mettger, Zak. **Till Victory Is Won: Black Soldiers in the Civil War**. New York: Lodestar, 1994. 118p. $16.99. ISBN 0-525-67412-8. (Young Readers' History of the Civil War). 5-9

Photographs, prints, and reproductions of newspaper notices complement the text, which presents the attempts of Black men to fight in the Civil War. At first their services were refused in the "white man's war," but they finally gained the right to fight. Their enormous contribution helped the Union win. In addition, they fought for equal pay and equal rights. Mettger discusses their recruitment, their battles behind the lines, the treatment of women and children, and how Black occupation forces helped to both liberate and protect the slaves in the South. Glossary, Selected Bibliography, and Index.

1470.	Meyer, Carolyn. **Gideon's People**. San Diego, CA: Gulliver, Harcourt Brace, 1996. 320p. $12; $6pa. ISBN 0-15-200303-7; 0-15-200304-5pa. 7-10

When Isaac Litsky goes with his father Peddlar Jakob on his route for the first time in 1911, the wagon overturns in front of the Amish Stolzfus family's home, and Isaac is injured. Isaac has to remain with the family while his father returns to his pregnant wife. Isaac sees the animosity between Mr. Stolzfus and his son Gideon, 16. When the sister Annie solicits Isaac's help to keep Gideon from going to his less-strict uncle, Isaac has to disagree with her. After Gideon leaves, he writes Annie to show he has not broken with the family as much as with the intolerant religious sect they espouse. *American Bookseller Pick of the Lists*.

1471.	Meyer, Carolyn. **White Lilacs**. San Diego, CA: Gulliver, Harcourt Brace, 1993. 256p. $10.95. ISBN 0-15-200641-9. 7-10

Rose Lee Jefferson, 12 in Texas during the 1920s, hears while serving food at a social luncheon that the whites plan to tear down Freedomtown, where the Blacks live, and make a park from it. The family for whom she and her grandfather work want the park, and they use more and more force, including a Ku Klux Klan attack, to displace the people who live there. Rose Lee is an artist, and a girl from the North, recently arrived, suggests that Rose Lee draw the houses and churches so that she will have a picture of them after they are destroyed. The friendship between the Black Rose Lee and the Bells's daughter is also a place where racial tensions occur. *American Library Association Best Books for Young Adults, IRA Young Adult Choices,* and *New York Public Library Books for the Teen Age*.

1472.	Meyer, Susan E. **Mary Cassatt**. New York: Harry N. Abrams, 1990. 92p. $19.95. ISBN 0-8109-3154-0. (First Impressions). 4-8

Born into a wealthy family during the Victorian age, Mary Cassatt (1844-1926) became a painter when "nice girls didn't do that sort of thing." She went to Paris to work and study, met the Impressionists, and began to work in a similar style. Photographs and reproductions enhance the text. Index.

1473.	Meyers, Jeffrey. **Robert Frost: A Biography**. Boston: Houghton Mifflin, 1996. 424p. $30. ISBN 0-395-72809-6. YA

In this biography, Meyers examines Robert Frost's (1874-1963) development as a poet by relating it to Frosts' experiences, relationships with others, and his personal statements. He also integrates interpretations of Frost's poems with stories about Frost's life so that they become one. Bibliography and Index.

1474.	Meyers, Maan. **The Dutchman: An Historical Mystery**. New York: Doubleday, 1992. 307p. $18.50. ISBN 0-385-42603-8. YA

In 1664 in New Amsterdam, Tonneman, the Dutch schout (sheriff), mourns his wife's death with extra stout and worries about the Dutch citizens who are uninterested in fighting the British arriving on warships and demanding surrender. But Tonneman must also investigate recent crimes and find out if Racquel Mendoza is interested in him for himself or because he can serve as a political informer. He solves the puzzle, but not without difficulty and danger.

1475. Meyers, Maan. **The Dutchman's Dilemma: An Historical Mystery**. New York: Bantam, 1995. 255p. $21.95. ISBN 0-553-09705-9. YA

New York, under British rule, has a population of 3,000 in 1675. Pieter Tonneman has been married to Racquel Mendoza (from *The Dutchman*), a Jew, for 11 years and has become a businessman, husband, and father. But strange animal deaths make people speak of devil worship and witchcraft, and because some are blaming Racquel, Tonneman becomes involved. After he identifies the criminals and their crimes, he thinks about converting to Judaism.

1476. Meyers, Maan. **The High Constable: An Historical Mystery**. New York: Doubleday, 1994. 307p. $19.95. ISBN 0-385-46984-5. New York: Fanfare, 1995. $5.50pa. ISBN 0-553-56889-2pa. YA

The third installment about the Tonneman family in New York City takes them into the nineteenth century. A man is found suffocated from being buried alive, and the skull of a young woman appears nearby. Baffled, the high constable asks John Tonneman to help him. Tonneman is a physician who has troubles with his wife and son and wants a diversion.

1477. Meyers, Maan. **The Knightsbridge Plot: An Historical Mystery**. New York: Doubleday, 1993. 321p. $18.50. ISBN 0-385-46951-9. YA

In 1775, the discovery of a decapitated body in New York captures everyone's attention. Recently returned from studying to be a physician in England is John Tonneman, descendant of Pieter Tonneman (*The Dutchman* and *The Dutchman's Dilemma*). John Tonneman becomes involved in the murder although he has wanted to stay away from politics. What he finds is a plot to murder George Washington. As soon as the criminals have been caught and punished, John is free to marry the woman he loves.

1478. Michener, James Albert. **Centennial**. 1974. New York: Fawcett, 1994. $6.99pa. ISBN 0-449-21419-2pa. YA

Centennial, Colorado, begins its life in 1760 and grows through the Civil War before its demise in the 1890s. An assortment of people live inside its boundaries, among them an Arapaho brave, a French trapper with two wives, a disillusioned Mennonite and his child bride, and an unscrupulous actor who invests a dead banker's money for himself. With the passing of the cattle empires, Centennial loses its economic base, and the people gradually move away.

1479. Mickle, Shelly Fraser. **The Queen of October**. Chapel Hill, NC: Algonquin, 1989. 301p. $15.95; $8.95pa. ISBN 0-945575-21-1;1-56512-003-5pa. YA

In 1959, Sally's parents divorce, and she goes to live with her grandparents in Coldwater, Arkansas. During her eighth grade year, while she tries to cope with her emotional upheavals, she meets old friends and makes new ones. Among her experiences are thinking that one man will wait until she grows up and marry her, having a parrot that curses, and becoming Coldwater's October queen.

1480. Migneco, Ronald, and Timothy Levi Biel. **The Crash of 1929**. Maurie Manning, et al., illustrators. San Diego, CA: Lucent, 1990. 64p. $12.95. ISBN 1-56006-003-4. (World Disasters). 5-7

After the "Roaring Twenties," with stocks on Wall Street rising in a bull market, the market crashed on October 29, 1929. With its fall began the Depression, which finally ended after Franklin Delano Roosevelt instituted the New Deal and America entered World War II. The text discusses aspects of the stock market and why it fell so radically. Additionally, it considers the market today and whether it could do the same thing. Photographs augment the text. Further Reading, Glossary, Other Works Consulted, and Index.

1481. Miller, Brandon Marie. **Buffalo Gals: Women of the Old West**. Minneapolis, MN: Lerner, 1995. 88p. $18.95. ISBN 0-8225-1730-2. 4-8

Reproductions and text give a good view of women who went west during the nineteenth century. Topics covered include why they left home, the homes they tried to create, their use of leisure time, their hopes for the future, falling in love, and the clash between Native American and white women. Bibliography and Index. *Notable Children's Trade Books in the Field of Social Studies*, *IRA Teachers' Choices*, *Scientific American Young Readers Book Award*, and *Society of School Librarians Outstanding Book*.

1482. Miller, Douglas T. **Henry David Thoreau: A Man for All Seasons**. New York: Facts on File, 1991. 110p. $17.95. ISBN 0-8160-2478-2. (Makers of America). 7 up

Henry David Thoreau (1817-1862) based his life on the principles of liberty, self-sufficiency, and simplicity. To test himself, he lived for two years alone on the shores of Walden Pond in Concord, Massachusetts. He wrote an essay called "Civil Disobedience," which inspired Mahatma Gandhi's Indian independence and Martin Luther King, Jr. He suggested in this and other works that people reject materialism and seek fulfillment in the world of the mind and spirit. Selected Bibliography and Index.

1483.   Miller, Robert H. **The Buffalo Soldiers**. Richard Leonard, illustrator. Englewood Cliffs, NJ: Silver Burdett, 1991. 89p. $12.95; $4.95pa. ISBN 0-382-24080-4; 0-382-24085-5pa. (Reflections of a Black Cowboy). 7-10

During the time of the Civil War, the Indian wars, and the Spanish-American War in the nineteenth century, African American soldiers made major contributions. Among those who should be recognized are the men of the Ninth and Tenth cavalries, the Buffalo Soldiers, and Lieutenant Henry O. Flipper. Pen-and-ink drawings highlight the text. Bibliography.

1484.   Miller, Robert H. **Cowboys**. Richard Leonard, illustrator. Englewood Cliffs, NJ: Silver Burdett, 1991. 80p. $4.95pa. ISBN 0-382-24084-7pa. (Reflections of a Black Cowboy). 7-10

More than 8,000 men, or one in four, who worked as cowboys driving cattle in the early West were African Americans. Among them were Nat Love and "Cherokee Bill." Others who were in the West with the cowboys were Mary Fields, Bill Pickett, and Willie Kennard, who transformed the lawless mining town of Yankee Hill, Colorado, into a safe place. Pen-and-ink drawings highlight the text. Bibliography.

1485.   Miller, Robert H. **Pioneers**. Richard Leonard, illustrator. Englewood Cliffs, NJ: Silver Burdett, 1991. 80p. $12.95. ISBN 0-382-24081-2. (Reflections of a Black Cowboy). 7-10

Among the African Americans who went West in the nineteenth century were York, a former slave who traveled with Lewis and Clark; Ed "Cut Nose" Rose, a fur hunter and trapper; Alvin Coffee, a miner; Biddy Mason, a woman sheepherder who sued for her and her daughters' freedom in California; and George Monroe, a Pony Express rider. Pen-and-ink drawings highlight the text. Bibliography.

1486.   Miller, Russell. **Nothing Less than Victory: The Oral History of D-Day**. New York: Morrow, 1994. 556p. $27.50; $15pa. ISBN 0-688-10209-3; 0-688-14344-Xpa. YA

Miller compiled information from sources such as letters, diaries, memoranda, and official reports as well as interviews with veterans who fought on D-Day, June 6, 1944, to write a history of that day. What he discovered was that the statistics meant nothing to the individuals who participated in the greatest amphibious operation ever staged. They were only interested in survival and coping with the changes around them. Notes, Select Bibliography, and Index.

1487.   Mills, Claudia. **What About Annie?** New York: Walker, 1985. 68p. $9.95. ISBN 0-8027-6573-4. 5 up

When Annie is 13 in 1931, her father loses his job, and her family has to find support during the Depression. Her friends and their families have similar problems during this difficult period. As she passes through her teenage years toward 18, she becomes intrigued with flying. The Lindbergh baby's kidnapping and murder sadden her, but Amelia Earhart's achievements in the air are delightful. Becoming interested in this whole new aspect of life helps her cope with daily difficulties.

1488.   Mills, Judie. **John F. Kennedy**. New York: Franklin Watts, 1988. 370p. $14.90. ISBN 0-531-10520-2. 7 up

John Fitzgerald Kennedy (1917-1963), the second son in his family, had poor grades and poor health as a youngster. He lived in the shadow of his brother whom his father had decided would be President of the United States. But Kennedy's brother was killed in World War II, so his father chose John to fulfill the dream. Kennedy began serving in the House of Representatives and then in Congress as a senator. He became President and served for nearly 1,000 days before being assassinated. His legacy is uncertain, but his era is memorable. Notes, Bibliography, and Index.

1489.   Mills, Kay. **This Little Light of Mine: The Life of Fannie Lou Hamer**. New York: Dutton, 1993. 390p. $13.95pa. ISBN 0-452-27052-9pa. YA

Fannie Lou Hamer (1917-1977) risked her life by staying in Mississippi, her home state, and trying to increase voter registration and to improve educational and economic opportunities for Blacks during the 1960s, when the Civil Rights movement became a public effort. She first heard about the attempts to increase voter registration among Blacks in 1962. The text includes interviews with Blacks such as Andrew Young and Marian Wright Edleman, who spent hot summers in Mississippi along with Hamer to try to change the white control of the state. What Mills tries to show is why Hamer and others like her would take such risks during that time. Bibliography and Index.

1490.   Milner, Clyde A. II, Carol A. O'Connor, and Martha A. Sandweiss. **The Oxford History of the American West**. New York: Oxford University Press, 1994. 872p. $49.95; $25pa. ISBN 0-19-505968-9; 0-19-511212-1pa. YA

The text defines the American West as lying west of the 98th meridian, but most of the authors find defining the term "frontier" to be problematic. Twenty-eight essays cover the political, social, and economic history of the West by looking at the Native American culture, families, labor, agriculture, and the evolution of the cities. A final section presents the views of the West present in literature, art, and popular entertainment. These views give an idea of how the West developed. Chapter Annotated Bibliographies and Index.

1491.   Mintz, Penny. **Thomas Edison: Inventing the Future**. New York: Fawcett, 1990. 118p. $3.95pa. ISBN 0-449-90378-8pa. (Great Lives). 5-8

Although this look at Thomas Edison (1847-1931) covers his entire life, it emphasizes the years during which he was trying to develop the incandescent light bulb. He was a man focused on his work to such an extent that he could be unpleasant in his relationships with others. Bibliography.

1492.   Mitchell, Margaret. **Gone with the Wind**. New York: Scribner's, 1996. 1024p. $40. ISBN 0-684-82625-9. YA

Scarlett O'Hara is 16 when the Civil War begins in 1861. She is in love with Ashley, the heir to a local plantation, but he decides to marry Melanie. In retaliation, Scarlett marries Melanie's brother but within a year becomes a war widow with a child she does not want. She leaves the plantation for Atlanta while Sherman ruins the city, and when she returns to her home Tara, similar destruction abounds. She marries a businessman to keep the plantation solvent, and when he dies, she marries Rhett Butler, a Southerner who made money by blockade running. Only when Rhett decides to leave her does she realize that she loves him and not the weak Ashley, for whom she has been pining since he first married Melanie.

1493.   Mitchell, Sara. **Trial of the Innocent**. Minneapolis, MN: Bethany House, 1995. 336p. $9.95pa. ISBN 1-55661-497-7pa. YA

In Richmond, Virginia, during 1891, Eve Sheridan develops a mistrust for her new brother-in-law although she at first cannot identify the problem. As she sees him more, she notes his greed and the violent attitudes of his friends. She and her friend, a Pinkerton detective, have to decide how to stop the evil. Part of her help is her religious faith.

1494.   Mizell, Linda. **Think About Racism**. New York: Walker, 1992. 230p. $15.85. ISBN 0-8027-8113-6. (Think). 6-10

Mizell's theory is that the history of racism in the United States is actually the history of people of color. Among the topics she presents are an assessment of Christopher Columbus, an overview of the slave trade and slavery laws, the Jim Crow laws, lynching, white supremacist groups, and relationships with Mexican and Japanese Americans, including the Japanese internment during World War II. She focuses on African Americans, Native Americans, Latinos, and Asian Americans through the Civil Rights movements of the 1960s. Glossary, Bibliography, and Index.

1495.   Moates, Marianne M. **A Bridge of Childhood: Truman Capote's Southern Years**. New York: Henry Holt, 1989. 240p. $19.95. ISBN 0-8050-0971-X. YA

Truman Capote's dysfunctional family thought he was strange and refused to accept him for who he was rather than what they wanted him to be. This account was written by someone who moved to his hometown during the time that Harper Lee's *To Kill a Mockingbird* hit the best-seller lists and before Capote's *In Cold Blood* gained him fame. Index.

1496.   Moeri, Louise. **Save Queen of Sheba**. 1981. New York: Puffin, 1994. 116p. $3.99pa. ISBN 0-14-037148-6pa. 5-8

After a Sioux raid on their portion of the wagon train, King David, 12, and Queen of Sheba, six, cannot find their father or his wagon. Although almost scalped himself, King David looks after Queen of Sheba as they walk along the trail. He eventually recovers and becomes reunited with his father.

1497.   Monceaux, Morgan. **Jazz: My Music, My People**. New York: Knopf, 1994. 64p. $18. ISBN 0-679-85618-8. 6 up

The text looks at the history of jazz through profiles of its greatest performers. The first segment covers the early years when jazz was taking shape under such talents as W. C. Handy, Leadbelly, Jelly Roll Morton, Ma Rainey, and Louis Armstrong. The second part continues with the swing years and dance music from Duke Ellington, Billie Holiday, Ella Fitzgerald, and Dorothy Dandridge. The third section on bebop and modern jazz poses questions about what will come next in the jazz world. Some of the performers mentioned here are Charlie Parker, Nat King Cole, Sarah Vaughan, and Pearl Bailey. Glossary and Index.

1498.   Monjo, F. N. **A Namesake for Nathan**. Eros Keith, illustrator. New York: Coward, McCann & Geoghegan, 1977. 48p. $6.95. ISBN 0-698-20411-5. 4-7

Joanna Hale, 12, and her family prepare for her brother Nathan's leave from the army during 1776. The women support the six family men serving in the Continental army by spinning, weaving, and knitting. As the story progresses, Joanna and her family learn that the British have executed Nathan, 21, for spying.

1499.   Monroe, Jean Guard, and Ray A. Williamson. **First Houses: Native American Homes and Sacred Structures**. Susan Johnston Carlson, illustrator. Boston: Houghton Mifflin, 1993. 160p. $14.95. ISBN 0-395-51081-3. 5-9

The text, with pen-and-ink drawings, presents the homes of various Native American tribes while noting that their different creation myths served as patterns for how the homes and ritual structures would be built. The dwellings also relate closely to the climate and the local building materials. Buildings discussed include the Iroquois longhouse, the Pueblo kiva, the Navajo hogan, Mohave houses, Pawnee earth lodges, the Plains tipi, Northwest Coast dwellings, and the sweatlodge, an important structure in many tribes. Bibliography and Index.

1500.   Moore, Ruth Nulton. **Distant Thunder**. Allan Eitzen, illustrator. Scottdale, PA: Herald, 1991. 160p. $5.95pa. ISBN 0-8361-3557-1pa. 4-8

When the War of Independence begins, prisoners of war come to Bethlehem, Pennsylvania, in 1777, where Kate, 15, lives with her aunt's family while her parents serve in the mission field. The Moravians do not believe in war, but they know they must help with peaceful ways. They welcome wounded soldiers to their buildings and try to feed as many as possible. Kate, her cousin, and their Indian friend help a Hessian drummer boy escape capture by the American guards and meet the young Marquis de Lafayette, a French nobleman come to help the fight. It is a difficult year, but Kate's mother reunites with her brother, adopted years before by the Seneca Indians.

1501.   Moore, Yvette. **Freedom Songs**. New York: Orchard, 1991. 168p. $14.99. ISBN 0-531-05812-3. 7-10

Sheryl, 14 and living in Brooklyn, New York, visits Wingate, North Carolina, on Easter 1963. For the first time she experiences being called "nigra" and told not to drink out of a water fountain; she also watches white customers in a store being served before the Blacks who arrived first. When she returns home, she reads about groups trying to support Blacks in their quest for equal rights, and she urges her school to give a benefit concert for the Freedom Riders. Just before the concert, her young uncle is murdered at the school where he teaches Black southerners registering to vote.

1502.   Morey, Eileen. **Amelia Earhart**. San Diego, CA: Lucent, 1995. 112p. $16.95. ISBN 1-56006-065-4. (The Importance Of). 7-9

Amelia Earhart (1897-1937) became an American hero when she became the first woman to cross the Atlantic in an airplane. She flew from Newfoundland to Wales as a passenger in a Fokker. After she became a pilot, she preferred to fly alone, but she promoted the development of passenger service with a group that later became Trans World Airlines. She also invested money in arranging flights between New York City and Washington, D.C. She also became a member of the Ninety-Nines, a group of women pilots, to show that she supported other women as pilots while she led the way. She thought that women should be independent and self-reliant, in control of their own lives. Photographs, For Further Reading, Works Consulted, and Index.

1503.   Morin, Isobel V. **Impeaching the President**. Brookfield, CT: Millbrook Press, 1996. 159p. $16.40. ISBN 1-56294-668-4. 8 up

The text defines impeachment, how it takes place, and its role in American history. Most of it deals with the investigations that led to the impeachment trial of Andrew Johnson in 1868 and to the possibility of impeaching Richard Nixon before he resigned from the presidency in 1974. Bibliography, Glossary, Notes, and Index.

1504.   Morin, Isobel V. **Women Chosen for Public Office**. Minneapolis, MN: Oliver Press, 1995. 160p. $14.95. ISBN 1-881508-20-X. (Profiles). 7 up

The text presents profiles of nine women who have held appointed offices in the federal government, some of them unpaid. The women are: Dorothea Dix (1802-1887), superintendent of army nurses; Julia Lathrop (1858-1932), director of the U.S. Children's Bureau; Mary Anderson (1872-1964), director of the U.S. Women's Bureau; Frances Perkins (1880-1965), secretary of labor; Ruth Bryan Owen Rohde (1885-1954), congresswoman-turned-diplomat; Florence Ellinwood Allen (1884-1965), Court of Appeals judge; Constance Baker Motley (b. 1922), civil rights lawyer and judge; Patricia Roberts Harris (1924-1985), diplomat and cabinet member; and Ruth Bader Ginsburg (b. 1933), Supreme Court justice. Bibliography and Index.

1505.   Morin, Isobel V. **Women of the U.S. Congress**. Minneapolis, MN: Oliver Press, 1994. 160p. $14.95. ISBN 1-881508-12-9. (Profiles). 5-7

This book looks at 11 of the women voted into Congress during the twentieth century: Jeannette Rankin (1880-1973); Margaret Chase Smith (1897-1994); Helen Gahagan Douglas (1900-1980); Shirley Chisholm (b. 1924); Barbara Jordan (1936-1996); Nancy Landon Kassebaum (b. 1932); Barbara Mikulski (b. 1936); and the women elected in 1992, who were Dianne Feinstein, Barbara Boxer, Patty Murray, and Carol Moseley Braun. Women Who Served in the U.S. Congress, Bibliography, and Index.

1506.   Morin, Isobel V. **Women Who Reformed Politics**. Minneapolis, MN: Oliver Press, 1994. 160p. $14.95. ISBN 1-881508-16-1. (Profiles). 6 up

Women who saw connections between social problems, the second-class status of women, and racial justice worked for reforms in politics. The women included in this text are Abby Kelley Foster, crusader against slavery (1811-1887); Frances Willard, temperance fighter (1839-1898); Ida Wells-Barnett, intolerant of mob violence (1862-1931); Carrie Chapman Catt, right to vote (1859-1947); Molly Dewson, political boss (1874-1962); Pauli Murray, for integration (1910-1985); Fannie Lou Hamer, civil rights (1917-1977); and Gloria Steinem, women's rights (b. 1934). Major Reforms in U.S. History, Bibliography, and Index.

1507.   Morley, Jacqueline. **Clothes: For Work, Play and Display**. Vanda Baginskia, Mark Bergin, John James, Carolyn Scrace, and Gerald Wood, illustrators. New York: Franklin Watts, 1992. 48p. $7.95pa. ISBN 0-531-15740-7pa. (Timelines). 5-8

Two-page spreads divide the text into minichapters with many illustrations to show clothes throughout history. The time periods covered are the first clothes people wore; classical clothes of the Minoans, Greeks, and Romans; the Dark Ages; armor and tournament gear; medieval and Renaissance Italy; farthingales with Spanish influence in the sixteenth century; seventeenth-century Cavaliers and Puritans in England; court clothes and politics of France; crinoline petticoats introduced in 1857; folk costumes; dress reforms like bloomers; sportswear; between the World Wars; work clothes; clothes today; and clothes of the future. Timeline, Glossary, and Index.

1508.   Morpurgo, Michael. **Twist of Gold**. New York: Viking, 1993. 246p. $14.99. ISBN 0-670-84851-4. 5-9

When Sean O'Brien's mother is too sick from hunger to travel during the 1850s, he and his sister leave Ireland to join their father in America. They carry with them the symbol of their clan: the golden torc (necklace) of their ancestors. Thieves who know of their possession try to steal it, and twice they lose it. But twice they find it again as they travel from Boston to California to meet their father, and surprisingly, their mother, who has been able to make a quicker, safer journey.

1509.   Morris, Jeffrey. **The FDR Way**. Minneapolis, MN: Lerner, 1996. 128p. $22.95. ISBN 0-8225-2929-7. (Great Presidential Decisions). 5 up

Franklin Delano Roosevelt was elected President for four terms. During those years, he had to make many decisions, beginning with what to do about the Depression, which had destroyed many lives before he took office in 1933. The text looks at his style, the first 100 days of his presidency, his fight for social security, his choices for the Supreme Court, how he traded destroyers to Great Britain in World War II for 99-year leases in the Western Hemisphere, his decision to seek a third term, his creation of the United Nations, and his death. Index.

1510.   Morris, Jeffrey. **The Jefferson Way**. Minneapolis, MN: Lerner, 1994. 128p. $23.95. ISBN 0-8225-2926-2. (Great Presidential Decisions). 6-9

The text presents some of the major decisions, good and bad, that Thomas Jefferson (1743-1826) made as President. These decisions and their effects on the country's life are part of the examination of his presidency. Photographs and reproductions enhance the text. Glossary, Further Reading, and Index.

1511.   Morris, Jeffrey. **The Lincoln Way**. Minneapolis, MN: Lerner, 1996. 136p. $22.95. ISBN 0-8225-2930-0. (Great Presidential Decisions). 5 up

The text looks at Lincoln while he was President and the decisions that he had to make. The chapter topics include the election of 1860, Lincoln's qualifications for the presidency, how Lincoln made decisions, what kind of man he was, the decision he made to preserve the Union and to back down in the *Trent* affair, the decision not to change the cabinet but to free the slaves, his attempt to find a general, his final days, and his questions about how to reconstruct the South. Index.

1512.   Morris, Jeffrey. **The Truman Way**. Minneapolis, MN: Lerner, 1995. 128p. $22.95. ISBN 0-8225-2927-0. (Great Presidential Decisions). 7-9

The first decision that Harry Truman made as President when Franklin Delano Roosevelt died on April 12, 1945, was that the conference for creating the United Nations would proceed as planned. Morris looks at other decisions that Truman had to make while President such as dropping the atomic bomb on Japan, aiding Europe after the end of World War II, and standing against Communist aggression with the Truman Doctrine. Morris asks what led to the decisions, what other options the President might have had, and what the long-term effects have been. Photographs complement the text. Index. *Society of School Librarians International Outstanding Book.*

1513.   Morris, Jeffrey. **The Washington Way**. Minneapolis, MN: Lerner, 1994. 128p. $22.95. ISBN 0-8225-2928-9. 6-9

As the first President, George Washington set many precedents. He established traditions that have influenced the role of the Presidents throughout the years. Most of his decisions worked well, and the text looks at his time in office and examines the situations and the solutions that he offered. Photographs and reproductions enhance the text. Glossary, Further Reading, and Index.

1514. Morris, Jeffrey Brandon. **The Reagan Way**. Minneapolis, MN: Lerner, 1995. 124p. $22.95. ISBN 0-8225-2931-9. (Great Presidential Decisions). 6-9

Beginning with a biographical overview of Ronald Reagan's life, the text looks at the major decisions that he made during his presidency from 1980 to 1988. He cut taxes and increased defense spending, sent American troops to Lebanon, supported tax reform, traded arms for hostages in the Iran-Contra situation, and talked to the Soviets about arms reduction. In his attempt to be fair, Morris decides not to assess Reagan's decisions because time has not yet proven them either good or bad. Index.

1515. Morris, Juddi. **The Harvey Girls: The Women Who Civilized the West**. New York: Walker, 1994. 101p. $15.95. ISBN 0-8027-8302-3. 6-9

Fred Harvey started railroad restaurants and hotels in the American West at such places as Dodge City, Topeka, Santa Fe, and Albuquerque. To staff these establishments, he imported young, single white women who had character references as spotless as their uniforms. The text discusses what being a "Harvey girl" meant and why the women went west initially. Economic circumstances were usually the prime reason that the women took jobs with Harvey. After World War II, the chain began to decline, and Morris discusses reasons why this might have happened. Photographs, Notes, Bibliography, and Index.

1516. Morrison, Dorothy Nafus. **Chief Sarah: Sarah Winnemucca's Fight for Indian Rights**. New York: Atheneum, 1980. 170p. $9.95. ISBN 0-689-30752-7. 6-8

An Indian woman with only three weeks of formal education, Sarah Winnemucca (1844-1891) became a successful lecturer, wrote the first book published in English by any Native American, and started the first school taught and administered by Indians. Her people, the Paiutes, suffered when miners and settlers moved into Nevada, taking their land and resources. Sarah often argued with the corrupt Bureau of Indian Affairs about the rights of Indians. The text relies on her autobiography, newspaper accounts, and her letters. She is sometimes called the Indian Joan of Arc because of her willingness to support the cause of her people. Photographs and prints enhance the text. Bibliography and Index.

1517. Morrow, Honoré. **On to Oregon!** 1927. New York: Beech Tree, Morrow, 1991. 239p. $4.95pa. ISBN 0-688-10494-0pa. 5-9

John, 13, leaves Missouri with his family in 1844 for a journey to Oregon. Both of his parents die on the way, and he takes the other six children the remaining 1,000 miles through snow and mountains.

1518. Mosher, Howard Frank. **Northern Borders**. New York: Doubleday, 1994. 291p. $11.95pa. ISBN 0-385-31487-6pa. YA

When he is six in 1947, Austen Kittredge goes to Lost Nation Hollow, Vermont, to live with his widowed father's parents. The area is so remote that it has no electricity until the mid-1950s. Austen observes the constant battles between his grandparents, and as he grows up, he begins to understand what they mean. At 18, he goes with his grandfather to Labrador to explore and to map the beautiful but mysterious area; this experience contributes to Austen's maturity.

1519. Mosley, Walter. **A Little Yellow Dog**. New York: Norton, 1996. 300p. $23. ISBN 0-393-03924-2. YA

In the 1960s, Easy Rawlins works as a supervisory janitor in the Sojourner Truth Junior High School of Los Angeles while supporting two children that he found abandoned on the streets. When one of the teachers, her husband, and her husband's twin brother are found murdered, Rawlins uses his underground contacts and the slain woman's little yellow dog as a way to solve the murders.

1520. Muggamin, Howard. **The Jewish Americans**. New York: Chelsea House, 1995. 128p. $19.95; $8.95pa. ISBN 0-7910-3365-1; 0-7910-3387-2pa. (The Immigrant Experience). 6-9

The first Jewish immigrants to settle in America came in 1654 because they wanted to worship in their own congregations. In the eighteenth century, more than 150,000 Jews arrived from Germany. In the decades following, more than 4 million came, fleeing the anti-Semitism of their homelands. The text, with accompanying photographs, tells of their history and their contribution to American culture. Further Reading and Index.

1521. Muhlberger, Richard. **What Makes a Cassatt a Cassatt?** New York: Viking, 1994. 48p. $11.99. ISBN 0-670-85742-4. 5-9

Although born an American, Mary Cassatt (1844-1926) lived most of her life in Paris, painting in the style of the French Impressionists. She traveled to Spain, and her study of the work of Velásquez and Goya led her to focus on people and eliminate almost all background detail. Japanese work inspired her to use contrasting colors and tilted perspective. She used solid lines and clear colors to present relationships between people. Included are reproductions and discussions of *Offering the Panale to the Bullfighter*, *Little Girl in a Blue Armchair*, *At the Opéra*, *Lydia Crocheting in the Garden at Marly*, *Five O'Clock Tea*, *Reading Le Figaro*, *Children Playing on the Beach*, *The Letter*, *Baby Reaching for an Apple*, *The Boating Party*, *Breakfast in Bed*, and *Mother and Child*.

1522. Mulcahy, Robert. **Diseases: Finding the Cure**. Minneapolis, MN: Oliver Press, 1996. 144p. $14.95. ISBN 1-881508-28-5. 7 up

Why people get sick has been a mystery for centuries. In the eighteenth century, James Lind (1716-1794) conducted the first clinical trials to discover a cure for scurvy. Edward Jenner (1749-1823) worked to find an inoculation against smallpox. Louis Pasteur (1822-1895) suggested finding the germ and turning it into a vaccine to kill itself. Since then, Paul Ehrlich founded chemotherapy, Frederick Banting refined insulin, Alexander Fleming discovered penicillin, and Jonas Salk developed the polio vaccine. Currently, researchers work frantically to find a cure for AIDS. Nobel Prize Winners, Glossary, Bibliography, and Index.

1523. Murdoch, David H. **Cowboy**. New York: Dorling Kindersley, 1993. 64p. $19. ISBN 0-679-84014-1. (Eyewitness). 3 up

This overview of cowboys includes brief topics on dress such as hats, boots, chaps, and spurs. It also looks at the *charros* and *vaqueros*, the best horses, saddles, life on the ranch, cattle and branding, ranges, trail drives, law and order, guns and gunslingers, the South American gaucho, Camargue *Gardians* of France, cowgirls, cowboys in Australia, the rodeo, and the culture of the cowboy. Index.

1524. Murdoch, David H. **North American Indian**. New York: Dorling Kindersley, 1995. 62p. $19. ISBN 0-679-096169-0. 4 up

In conjunction with the artifacts of the American Museum of Natural History, the text gives an overview of the North American Indian. Two-page spreads cover such topics as the peopling of the Americas, medicine and the spirit world, the League of the Iroquois, the Mid-Atlantic Seaboard, the Ohio River Valley, the western Great Lakes, the Southeast, the Great Plains, the Dakota Sioux, Mandan and Hidatsa, war and peace, the Sun Dance, the Plateau, the Great Basin, California, the Southwest, the Pueblo peoples, Apache and Navajo, Papago and Pima, totem pole land, art, the potlatch, northern hunters, the Arctic, and modern times. Index.

1525. Murphy, Claire Rudolf. **Gold Star Sister**. New York: Lodestar, 1994. 166p. $14.99. ISBN 0-525-67492-6. 6-9

In a first-person narrative, Carrie, 13, describes her pleasure at her Gram coming to live with the family and her consternation at Gram's rapid surrender to the cancer invading her body. She and Gram spend time looking at Gram's memorabilia. She discovers letters from Billy Sweeney, a brother killed by friendly fire in a World War II Aleutian Islands battle. She also finds a letter that Billy was supposed to give to a dying soldier's baby son, but his own death prevented the delivery. Carrie determines that she must find the son and give him the letter before Gram dies.

1526. Murphy, Jim. **Across America on an Emigrant Train**. New York: Clarion, 1993. 150p. $16.95. ISBN 0-395-63390-7. 5-8

The text looks at a journey that the young writer Robert Louis Stevenson made in 1879 when he traveled from Scotland to see the woman he loved in California. He took the cheapest transportation and wrote about it. Murphy uses Stevenson's words to tell about the construction of the transcontinental railroad and steam travel. Photographs, Drawings, Bibliography, and Index. *Orbis Pictus Award*.

1527. Murphy, Jim. **The Boys' War: Confederate and Union Soldiers Talk About the Civil War**. New York: Clarion, 1990. 110p. $15.95. ISBN 0-89919-893-7. 6 up

Using quotes from boys who actually fought in the Civil War, Murphy shows that they left home at 16 or even younger for what they thought would be an exciting adventure. What they found was different, a savage slaughter of humans and animals from which many, if they survived, never psychologically recovered. The text looks at the thrill of enlistment, the rigors of camp life, and the terror of the battlefield. Bibliography and Index.

1528. Murphy, Jim. **The Great Fire**. New York: Scholastic, 1995. 144p. $16.95. ISBN 0-590-47267-4. 5 up

One of the major disasters in American history was the Great Fire of 1871, when Chicago became a wasteland. The damage was so widespread that few believed the city could ever recover. It began when a small fire broke out in O'Leary's barn on a Sunday evening. The fire department could not locate the fire, and no one was particularly concerned. But the city's wooden sidewalks and roads burned when a steady wind fueled the flames. The text includes personal accounts of survivors and facts about this devastation as the people began to rebuild the city. Bibliography and Sources and Index. *Bulletin Blue Ribbon Book, American Library Association Notable Books for Children, American Library Association Best Books for Young Adults, Newbery Honor Book, Orbis Pictus Award, American Library Association Booklist Editors' Choices, Horn Book Fanfare Honor List, American Library Association Quick Picks for Reluctant Young Adult Readers, Notable Children's Trade Books in the Field of Social Studies, School Library Journal Best Book,* and *Boston Globe-Horn Book Honor*.

1529. Murphy, Jim. **The Long Road to Gettysburg**. New York: Clarion, 1992. 116p. $15.95. ISBN 0-395-55965-0. 6 up

This story of the Battle of Gettysburg, fought in 1863, includes firsthand accounts by young soldiers and others. It reveals the hardships, the anxieties accompanying the preparation and wait for the battle, the long days of the actual battle, and the anguish of treating the wounded and burying the dead. The address that President Lincoln delivered helped the families of the dead to think of their losses as being a sacrifice for liberty and equality. Photographs, Bibliography, and Index.

1530. Murphy, Jim. **Young Patriot: The American Revolution as Experienced by One Boy**. New York: Clarion, 1996. 101p. $15.95. ISBN 0-395-60523-7. 6 up

Joseph Plumb Martin, a 15-year-old from Connecticut, enlisted in the Continental army in 1776. Murphy uses Martin's self-published memoir to tell about his fears, boredom, and hardships in winter camp as well as other aspects of the American Revolution. Figures known to history, including Burgoyne, Cornwallis, and Washington, become indivduals in this intriguing view of the Revolution. Bibliography, Chronology, and Index. *School Library Journal Best Book.*

1531. Murphy, Virginia Reed. **Across the Plains in the Donner Party**. Karen Zeinert, ed. New York: Linnet, 1996. 112p. $19.50. ISBN 0-208-02404-2. 5-10

Virginia Reed, 12, went with her stepfather and her family to California with the Donners in 1846. Zeinert uses Reed's account of the ordeal published in a magazine after her marriage, along with information from Patrick Breen and notes from Virginia's stepfather James. The memoirs show that people in the group enjoyed their hunting parties, each other's company, and the scenery until they decided to take the Hastings Cutoff, advertised by Lanford Hastings as the quickest way through the Sierra Nevadas. As she keeps record of the increasing snow, Virginia Reed promises God that she will become a Catholic if she survives. Index.

1532. Murphy, Wendy Buehr. **Frank Lloyd Wright**. Englewood Cliffs, NJ: Silver Burdett, 1990. 128p. $14.95. ISBN 0-382-24033-2. (Genius! The Artist and the Process). 7-9

Frank Lloyd Wright (1867-1959) lived in a household where his mother concentrated all of her attention on him and abused her other children, both her own and her stepchildren. He seems to have seen her as the source of everything important in his life. However, his father had a love of music and that also influenced Wright, because he could play the viola and piano. Throughout his long career, he compared the goals of an architect to those of a musician concerned with balance, rhythm, theme, and variation. Chronology, Glossary, Bibliography, and Index.

1533. Murrow, Liza K. **West Against the Wind**. New York: Holiday, 1987. 232p. $15.95. ISBN 0-8234-0668-7. New York: Troll, 1988. 232p. $2.50pa. ISBN 0-8167-1324-3pa. 7 up

In 1850, Abigail Parker, 14, has a touch of gold fever like the men in the wagon train in which she is traveling from Independence, Missouri, to Yuba City, California. She thinks of land that she wants to buy for herself and her father, who went west the year before. As the family faces the endless flatness of the prairie and the deep snow of the Sierras, Abigail also wonders about the man who joined the family for the journey but keeps disappearing unexpectedly. After they arrive, she realizes that "gold" is something she has had with her all the way.

1534. Myers, Anna. **Fire in the Hills**. New York: Walker, 1996. 176p. $15.95. ISBN 0-8027-8421-6. 7-10

Hallie, 16, has to take charge of the house and her four siblings when her mother dies in childbirth. Meanwhile, her father and brother tend their Oklahoma farm. After her brother leaves to fight in World War I, her burdens increase, but a neighboring woman gives her unexpected support. A draft dodger hiding in the woods saves her from the lechery of the woman's son, and Hallie struggles with this and her home problems, the area's anti-German sentiment, and the almost fanatical patriotism for those serving in the military.

1535. Myers, Anna. **Red-Dirt Jessie**. New York: Walker, 1992. 107p. $13.95. ISBN 0-8027-8172-1. 6-9

After Jessie's baby sister dies in 1930, Jessie's father stops talking. Her aunt and uncle leave for California, and when Jessie tries to get their dog to come home with her, the dog will not move. Only when the dog becomes wounded and cannot walk can she get it away from its house. But when the dog arrives and becomes part of the family, it saves Jessie from a wild dog and helps her father escape from his depression. *Oklahoma Book Award, Parents' Choice Award, Sequoyah Children's Book Award Masterlist, Volunteer State Book Ward Masterlist*, and *Land of Enchantment Book Award Masterlist.*

1536. Myers, Anna. **Rosie's Tiger**. New York: Walker, 1994. 121p. $14.95. ISBN 0-8027-8305-8. 5-7

Rosie adores her brother Ronny, especially after her mother dies, and she misses him while he is fighting in Korea during the 1950s. When she and her father hear that he is coming home, not alone but with a Korean wife who has a child, Rosie is distressed. Her new friend Cassandra tells her that she makes magic, and Rosie depends on Cassandra to help her get rid of the two extra people after they arrive. Rosie's wish almost comes true when the child Yong So falls into a cemetery cistern. But Rosie is surprised at what she learns about herself and her friend during the rescue and its aftermath.

1537. Myers, Anna. **Spotting the Leopard**. New York: Walker, 1996. 176p. $15.95. ISBN 0-8027-8459-3. 4-8

Jessie, from *Red-Dirt Jessie*, wants to go to college, but her father cannot afford to send her even though he has recovered from his Depression losses. Her brother H. J. knows that Jessie feels caged and wants to be free, just like the leopard named Lucky he has seen in the Oklahoma City zoo. When Lucky escapes, zoo officials search for him in fields near H. J. and Jessie's home. H. J. wants to find Lucky before the hunters kill him. He seems to think that saving Lucky will somehow help him save Jessie.

1538. Myers, Walter Dean. **Fallen Angels**. New York: Scholastic, 1988. 369p. $14.95; $3.50pa. ISBN 0-590-40942-5; 0-590-40943-3pa. 8 up

Richie, a 17-year-old African American, enlists in the army and leaves for Vietnam in 1967. He plans to use the money he earns to pay for his brother's school clothes. When he arrives on the front, he realizes that war is quite different from what he expected. After hours of doing nothing, he and his squad have to battle the sly Viet Cong, who often kill before the squad knows they are present. Richie has the "good" fortune of being wounded so that he can return home, but what he has seen continues to disturb his thoughts. *Coretta Scott King Award, American Library Association Best Books for Young Adults, American Library Association Quick Picks for Reluctant Young Adult Readers, American Library Association Booklist Editors' Choice, Horn Book Fanfare Honor List,* and *School Library Journal Best Book.*

1539. Myers, Walter Dean. **The Glory Field**. New York: Scholastic, 1994. 333p. $14.95; $4.99pa. ISBN 0-590-45897-3; 0-590-45898-1pa. 7 up

Although Curry Island, South Carolina, had many fields, only one of them meant something to the Lewis family. Beginning in the 1750s, an African boy captured into slavery worked the land. In 1864, Lizzy, 13, worked the land until she left to find the Union army and freedom. Thirty years later, Elijah bargained for it, but had to flee north to save his life. In 1930, Luvenia does not want to leave Chicago during the Depression to return to it. Other family connections occur in 1964. *American Library Association Best Books for Young Adults.*

1540. Myers, Walter Dean. **Malcolm X: By Any Means Necessary**. New York: Scholastic, 1993. 210p. $13.95. ISBN 0-590-46484-1. 5 up

Malcolm Little's father died during the Depression, and his mother slowly went insane trying to feed her children and keep shelter over their heads. After she was committed to an asylum, he resented having to live in a foster home. He left for Boston and New York, where he was eventually arrested for theft and imprisoned for 10 years. After he was released, he began working with the Nation of Islam and Elijah Muhammad. Malcolm (1925-1965) took the last name "X" and spoke out against racial discrimination. When the two men split because Malcolm refused to curb his comments, Malcolm went on a *hajj* to Mecca. When he returned, he established his own group, but he was soon assassinated as he prepared to give a public speech. Chronology, Bibliography, and Index. *Coretta Scott King Honor Book, American Library Association Best Books for Young Adults, American Library Association Notable Books for Children,* and *Horn Book Fanfare Honor List.*

1541. Myers, Walter Dean. **Now Is Your Time: The African-American Struggle for Freedom**. New York: HarperCollins, 1991. 292p. $17.95; $10.95pa. ISBN 0-06-024370-8; 0-06-446120-3pa. 6 up

The text looks at three centuries of African American life with many individual stories. It includes anecdotes about Ibrahima, an educated Islamic scholar and Fula prince who was abducted into slavery; Meta Vaux Warrick, an artist; Dolly Dennis, Myers's great-grandmother; and many others. Myers shows how a group of people has been kept from its rightful heritage for several centuries. Photographs, Bibliography, and Index. *Coretta Scott King Author Award, American Library Association Notable Books for Children, American Library Association Best Books for Young Adults, Horn Book Fanfare Honor List, Orbis Pictus Honor Book, Golden Kite Honor Book for Nonfiction, Carter G. Woodson Book Award Outstanding Merit Book, Jane Addams Children's Book Award Honor Book,* and *New York Public Library Books for the Teen Age.*

1542. Myers, Walter Dean. **A Place Called Heartbreak: A Story of Vietnam**. Frederick Porter, illustrator. Austin TX: Raintree/Steck-Vaughn, 1993. 71p. $24.26; $6.64pa. ISBN 0-8114-7237-X; 0-8114-8077-1pa. (Stories of America—Personal Challenge). 5-9

In 1965, Major Fred Cherry was shot down on a routine mission near Hanoi in North Vietnam. He was the 43rd American and the first Black American to be captured. The Viet Cong beat him for 92 days straight even though his arm and ankle were broken. They finally hospitalized him, and afterward, he lived in solitary for almost a year before being imprisoned with other Americans. To communicate, the prisoners used a code of tapping on the walls that the guards could not hear. After being a prisoner for seven-and-a-half years, the war ended, and Fred Cherry became free. Epilogue, Afterword, and Notes.

1543. Myers, Walter Dean. **The Righteous Revenge of Artemis Bonner**. New York: HarperCollins, 1992. 140p. $14. ISBN 0-06-020846-5. 5-9

At 15 in 1880, Artemis leaves New York City to avenge the murder of his uncle, Ugly Ned Bonner, and find a gold mine. He has a map his uncle made on his deathbed. Artemis travels from Mexico to the Alaskan Territory tracking Catfish Grimes and his female companion, Lucy Featherdip. In New Mexico he meets half-Cherokee Frolic, 12, who aids him in his search. *American Library Association Best Books for Young Adults* and *New York Public Library Books for the Teen Age.*

N

1544. Naden, Corinne J., and Rose Blue. **The U.S. Coast Guard**. Brookfield, CT: Millbrook Press, 1993. 64p. $14.90. ISBN 1-56294-321-9. (Defending Our Country). 5-8

The text gives the origins of the U.S. Coast Guard and traces its combat history in America's wars. Chapters on weapons, equipment, personnel, organization, and work give an overview of this branch of the U.S. military. Photographs and drawings enhance the text. Further Reading, Glossary, and Index.

1545. Nardo, Don. **Braving the New World: 1619-1784**. New York: Chelsea House, 1994. 117p. $19.95; $7.95pa. ISBN 0-7910-2259-5; 0-7910-2685-Xpa. (Milestones of Black American History). 7-9

In covering the roles of Black Americans from 1619 to 1784, the text and illustrations present the sugar revolution when the slave trade developed, early colonial slavery, the increase in the number of slaves imported as plantation needs grew, the trip from Africa to America, the relationship between master and slave, and the growth of African American culture. Further Reading and Index.

1546. Nardo, Don. **Franklin D. Roosevelt: U.S. President**. New York: Chelsea House, 1995. 111p. $18.95; $7.95pa. ISBN 0-7910-2406-7; 0-7910-2407-5pa. (Great Achievers: Lives of the Physically Challenged). 7-10

Franklin D. Roosevelt (1882-1945) became President of the United States even though he had been stricken with polio at an earlier age. The text looks at the hardships that this physical disability caused him and how he overcame it and achieved great success. Nardo uses primary sources along with quotes from Roosevelt and those who knew him. Chronology, Further Reading, and Index.

1547. Nardo, Don. **Jim Thorpe**. San Diego, CA: Lucent, 1994. 95p. $16.95. ISBN 1-56006-045-X. (The Importance Of). 7 up

During the first half of the twentieth century, Jim Thorpe (1887-1953) was perhaps the world's greatest athlete. He could kick a field goal from the 50-yard line and high jump more than six feet. At the 1912 Olympic Games in Sweden, he competed in both the decathlon and pentathlon, 15 grueling events, and won both. Because he had played semiprofessional baseball in the summer, his medals were taken from him, but they were posthumously restored in 1983. A Sac and Fox Indian, he and others on his Native American football team at the Indian School in Carlisle, Pennsylvania, showed their abilities only 14 years after the massacre at Wounded Knee. Whites had difficulty accepting the notion of an American Indian hero. Photographs, Notes, For Further Reading, Works Consulted, and Index.

1548. Nardo, Don. **The Mexican-American War**. San Diego, CA: Lucent, 1991. 96p. $16.95. ISBN 1-56006-402-1. (America's Wars). 9-12

The Mexican-American War lasted from 1845 to 1848, with the immediate cause of the war being the U.S. annexation of Texas in December 1845. Other factors were the existence of long-standing claims by U.S. citizens against Mexico and the American ambition to acquire California. When the attempt to buy California and Mexico in 1845 failed, President James Polk prepared for war, and in March 1846, General Zachary Taylor began the aggression. The text also presents other historical and cultural backgrounds in the conflict. Diagrams, boxed comments, maps, and black-and-white photographs augment the text. Bibliography, Glossary, Appendix, and Index.

1549. Nardo, Don. **Thomas Jefferson**. San Diego, CA: Lucent, 1993. 112p. $16.95. ISBN 1-56006-037-9. (The Importance Of). 5-8

Chapter headings in this biography of Thomas Jefferson (1743-1826) include topics that show his thirst for knowledge, his role in the colonies' rebellion, his writing of the Constitution, his reluctance to become a diplomat, his realization that he had to serve as President, his return to Monticello, and his legacy. Notes, For Further Reading, Works Consulted, and Index.

1550. Nardo, Don. **The War of 1812**. San Diego, CA: Lucent, 1991. 112p. $16.95. ISBN 1-56006-401-3. (America's Wars). 9-12

The War of 1812, the second war between the Americans and the British, has been called an unnecessary and impractical war. The text discusses how these terms define this conflict by giving an account of the strategies, personalities, and results of the encounter. Diagrams, boxed comments, maps, and black-and-white photographs augment the text. Bibliography, Glossary, Appendix, and Index.

1551. Nardo, Don. **World War II: The War in the Pacific**. San Diego, CA: Lucent, 1991. 96p. $16.95. ISBN 1-56006-408-0. (America's Wars). 9-12

In addition to facts about the progress of World War II in the Pacific, the text also gives information about the Japanese culture before the war began. Because the Japanese government focused on militarism, its choice to bomb Pearl Harbor was understandable although unexpected at the time it occurred. Diagrams, boxed comments, maps, and black-and-white photographs augment the text. Bibliography, Glossary, Appendix, and Index.

1552. Nash, Bruce, and Allan Zullo. **The Baseball Hall of Shame: Young Fans Edition**. New York: Archway, Pocket Books, 1990. 133p. $2.99pa. ISBN 0-671-69354-9pa. 5-8

The authors think that one of the reasons baseball is such an interesting sport is "the losers, the flakes, the buffoons, the boneheads, and the outrageous." Twenty-three chapters include topics such as coaching mistakes, misplayed games, and inept fielding. The text also recalls other entertaining mistakes, mainly in the twentieth century, that have made baseball fun to watch.

1553. Nash, Sunny. **Bigmama Didn't Shop at Woolworth's**. Lubbock, TX: Texas A&M University, 1996. 186p. $19.95. ISBN 0-890-96716-4. YA

The author narrates her experiences of growing up in a segregated community in Bryan, Texas, during the 1950s. Her grandmother, born in 1896, remembered events from the history of civil rights and shared them. Nash endured poverty and prejudice during her childhood, but the neighborhood people cared for each other, which lessened the pain. Photographs.

1554. Neimark, Anne E. **A Deaf Child Listened: Thomas Gallaudet, Pioneer in American Education**. New York: Morrow, 1983. 116p. $11.95. ISBN 0-688-01719-3. 7 up

After Thomas Gallaudet (1787-1851) graduated from Yale, his poor health caused him to move from one occupation to another. In 1814, he met a nine-year-old deaf girl to whom he was able to teach the names of things through finger and hand signs. He studied sign language in Paris and returned to Hartford, Connecticut, to become headmaster of the first school for the deaf in the United States. He stayed there for 13 years while he taught and developed American Sign Language. Even though his health never improved, he continued to work for better conditions in the lives of the deaf. Bibliography and Index.

1555. Nelson, Theresa. **And One for All**. New York: Orchard, 1989. 182p. $12.95. ISBN 0-531-08404-3. 7 up

Geraldine, 12, tells about the years 1966 to 1968 when Wing, her brother, serves in the Marines in Vietnam. She discloses his school problems, his friendship with a boy in high school who becomes an antiwar demonstrator, and family conflicts that led to his enlistment midway through his senior year in high school. After he returns in a coffin, his friend eulogizes him, and Geraldine has problems with his friend's rejection of the war in which her brother died. *American Library Association Notable Books for Children* and *School Library Journal Best Book.*

1556. Nelson, Theresa. **Devil Storm**. New York: Orchard, 1987. 214p. $12.95. ISBN 0-531-08311-X. 5-8

Walter, 13, and his sister befriend old Tom in 1900, even though their father has told them not to talk to the man, who says he is the son of pirate Jean LaFitte. They like his stories, and in return they give him food. When a hurricane begins blowing through their Texas town, old Tom rushes to help the family escape while Walter's father is away on business.

1557. Nelson, Vaunda M. **Mayfield Crossing**. Leonard Jenkins, illustrator. New York: Putnam, 1993. 96p. $14.95. ISBN 0-399-22331-2. 3-7

In 1960, Meg looks forward to going to a new school that has a larger baseball field. When she and her friends arrive, they find that they are outsiders, and no one wants them at the school because they are Black. When Meg and her friends challenge the others to a baseball game, one of the Parkview students refuses to continue the hostility and joins their team so they will have enough players.

1558. Neufeld, John. **Gaps in Stone Walls**. New York: Atheneum, 1996. 192p. $16. ISBN 0-689-80102-5. 5-8

In this nineteenth-century story Merry Skiffe, 12, finds herself a suspect for the murder of Ned Nickerson, the most despised man in her town. She cannot verify where she was when he died, and her deafness makes it difficult to communicate with the investigator. Her town of Chilmark on Martha's Vineyard has an unusually high population of deaf people. She has to devise a way to prove her innocence.

1559. Neumann, Peter J. **Playing a Virginia Moon**. Boston: Houghton Mifflin, 1994. 240p. $14.95. ISBN 0-395-66562-0. 8-10

In the 1970s, Chet wants to break the cross-country record of the high school legend Johnny Fiske, but Fiske's younger brother Jimmy returns from military school and seems to have his brother's running ability. The novel looks at Chet and his attempts to beat Jimmy as they go back and forth in winning first place at the races. Chet sees the challenge as a battle that he tried to plan like his hero Robert E. Lee might have done. The novel gives specifics about running, including scorecards and advice from Chet's coach.

1560. Newton, David E. **Gun Control: An Issue for the Nineties**. Springfield, NJ: Enslow, 1992. 128p. $17.95. ISBN 0-89490-296-2. (Issues in Focus). 7 up

After giving the history of gun ownership in the United States and the concern about the freedom to bear arms, the text uses incidents to show how statistics can skew debates so that one can argue for either side. The balanced view offers much to consider. Illustrations highlight the text. Bibliography and Index.

1561. Newton, David E. **Linus Pauling: Scientist and Advocate**. New York: Facts on File, 1994. 136p. $17.95. ISBN 0-8160-2959-8. (Makers of Modern Science). YA

Linus Pauling (1901-1995) received two unshared Nobel Prizes, one for chemistry and one for peace. He discovered the alpha helix and wrote about it in the early 1950s. Scientists had difficulty understanding his assessment of the number of amino acids in the complete twist, and he planned to go to England to explain it at a 1952 conference. But because he had spoken against Joseph McCarthy's tactics against Communists, he was denied a passport. Speculation still continues that if he had gone to the meeting and seen x-rays that revealed a missing link to DNA, he might have been the one to win the Nobel Prize for DNA research. He was an expert problem solver and superior scientist who started people thinking about the chemical bond, but he was also concerned about the role of radioactive fallout on hereditary diseases, which made him become a fierce opponent of nuclear testing. Glossary, Further Reading, and Index.

1562. Nichols, Joan Kane. **A Matter of Conscience: The Trial of Anne Hutchinson**. Dan Krovatin, illustrator. Austin, TX: Raintree/Steck-Vaughn, 1993. 101p. $24.26; $6.64pa. ISBN 0-8114-7233-7; 0-8114-8073-9pa. (Stories of America—Personal Challenge). 5-9

Because she wanted to follow John Cotton and his teachings, Anne Hutchinson (1591-1643) left England in 1634 for the New World. On board ship, she disagreed with the preaching of Reverend Symmes. He refused to think that anyone not a minister, much less a woman, could know what God wanted. After they landed, he accused her of being a witch. Eventually even John Cotton turned against her, and in 1838 she and her husband moved outside the colony to Rhode Island because the Boston Puritan community would not tolerate different beliefs. Epilogue, Afterword, and Notes.

1563. Nicholson, Dorinda Makanaonalani Stagner. **Pearl Harbor Child: A Child's View of Pearl Harbor—From Attack to Peace**. Honolulu, HI: Woodson House, Arizona Memorial Museum Association, 1993. 64p. $9pa. ISBN 0-9631388-6-3pa. 4-8

In 1941, Nicholson was in first grade in Pearl Harbor when the Japanese bombs fell. She remembers that the noise of the planes kept her from hearing the incendiary bullets, but they found their targets because her family's kitchen and parts of the roof burned. She tells of the evacuation afterward, the increase in military personnel, blackouts, and rationing. Her mother would rub pieces of newspaper together so they would soften enough to become effective toilet paper. Photographs.

1564. Nicholson, Lois. **Babe Ruth: Sultan of Swat**. Woodbury, CT: Goodwood, 1995. 119p. $17.95. ISBN 0-9625427-1-7. 5-9

George Herman Ruth (1895-1948) was one of the greatest ballplayers who ever lived. He said of his childhood that he was a bum, and he continued to resist authority throughout his adulthood, an attitude that cost him the chance to manage the Yankees after he retired from playing. But he loved children, and his honest appreciation of them showed in his personality. The text looks at this man and what he accomplished. Chronology, Statistical Record, Further Readings, and Index.

1565. Nicholson. Lois. **Georgia O'Keeffe**. San Diego, CA: Lucent, 1995. 112p. $16.95. ISBN 1-56006-005-7. (The Importance Of). 7 up

Georgia O'Keeffe's (1887-1986) influence as an artist began to rise around 1920, when women earned the right to vote. She studied art in Chicago and New York in between teaching jobs because her family's fortunes continued to decrease. When she returned to New York after the Armory Show in 1913 and saw what the Modernists were doing, she began to feel more freedom to paint what pleased her rather than what her teachers requested. She met Alfred Steiglitz on her first trip in New York, but not until she completely changed her style at the age of 27 did he become a major part of her life. They wrote letters, and she sent him pictures. Eventually he divorced his wife and hounded O'Keeffe to marry him. After their marriage, O'Keeffe spent much of her time in the West because she loved the emotion of the spaces and natural objects that she wanted to paint. Notes for Further Reading, Additional Works Consulted, and Index.

1566. Nicholson, Lois. **Helen Keller: Humanitarian**. New York: Chelsea House, 1996. 111p. $18.95. ISBN 1-55546-662-1. (American Women of Achievement). 5 up

Helen Keller (1880-1968) said that "Life is either a daring adventure or nothing." She was blind and deaf from a childhood illness at 18 months, but her teacher Anne Sullivan gave her the world by teaching her to read and write. She became one of the best-educated and most influential women in the world. She graduated from

Radcliffe College in 1904 and became an author, lecturer, and political activist. Mark Twain said that the two most interesting people in the nineteenth century were Napoleon and Helen Keller. Photographs enhance the text. Chronology, Further Reading, and Index.

1567. Nirgiotis, Nicholas. **Erie Canal: Gateway to the West**. New York: Franklin Watts, 1993. 64p. $19.90. ISBN 0-531-20146-5. (First Books). 4-7

The text describes the construction of the Erie Canal, begun in 1817, to connect the Hudson River in Albany to Lake Erie in Buffalo. This transportation route had political, historical, economic, and sociological impact on the area and on the country. Photographs, maps, and drawings enhance the text. Further Reading, Glossary, and Index.

1568. Nixon, Joan Lowery. **Caught in the Act: The Orphan Quartet Two**. New York: Bantam, 1988. 151p. $13.95. ISBN 0-553-05443-0. 5-7

When Mike, 11, leaves his brothers and sisters after they take the orphan train to the West, he goes to live with the Friedrichs in Missouri. The father is harsh and hostile, always willing to believe his natural son Gunter instead of Mike, whom he knows once stole money in New York. When Gunter makes problems on the farm, he blames Mike, but Mike has a chance to prove he is innocent before he goes to live with another family.

1569. Nixon, Joan Lowery. **Circle of Love**. New York: Bantam, 1997. 160p. $15.95. ISBN 0-385-32280-1. (Orphan Train Adventures). 4-8

After the Civil War, Frances Mary Kelly's love returns home. He, however, is reluctant to marry her, and to escape from her distress, she decides to go to New York City to accompany a group of orphans out west. During the journey, she has to cope with her memories and with the threats of a stranger.

1570. Nixon, Joan Lowery. **A Dangerous Promise**. New York: Delacorte, 1994. 148p. $15.95; $3.99pa. ISBN 0-385-32073-6; 0-440-21965-5pa. (Orphan Train Adventures). 4-8

In 1861, Mike Kelly and his friend Todd practice to become army drummers. They run away to join the Kansas Infantry and fight for the Union. In a Missouri battle, Mike is left for dead and Todd is killed. After Mike watches a thief steal Todd's watch, someone he met on the orphan train to the Midwest from New York finds and rescues him. Because Mike had promised to return Todd's watch to his sister, he spends much time behind Confederate lines looking for the thief. He eventually locates the watch, and after being accused of stealing, returns it and fulfills a second promise as well.

1571. Nixon, Joan Lowery. **A Deadly Promise**. New York: Bantam, 1992. 169p. $16. ISBN 0-553-08054-7. 7-9

In the sequel to *High Trail to Danger*, Sarah, 17, tries to clear her father's name in Leadville, Colorado, in 1880. She needs to solve the mystery as to why someone has accused him of murder and where to find what he mentioned as he died. Her sister Susannah, 15, joins her from Chicago and tries to win one of her suitors while Sarah investigates her father's situation. What Sarah finds is that before her father's death, he found out about the schemes of wealthy men in town to defraud illiterate silver miners. They had him killed before he could reveal their dishonesty.

1572. Nixon, Joan L. **A Family Apart**. New York: Bantam, 1987. 163p. $13.95. ISBN 0-553-05432-5. 5-7

When Frances is 13 in 1860, her mother relinquishes her and her five siblings to the Children's Aid Society so they can be adopted by people in the West who have enough money to care for them. Frances cuts her hair and pretends to be a boy so she can be placed with her little brother. The family with whom they live soon discovers that she is not "Frankie," but they are pleased. She works hard and courageously when she helps her new family transport slaves along the Underground Railway. *Western Writers of America Spur Award*.

1573. Nixon, Joan Lowery. **High Trail to Danger**. New York: Bantam, 1991. 168p. $15. ISBN 0-553-07314-1. 7-9

Sarah, 17 in 1879, goes from Chicago to Leadville, Colorado, to see her father after her mother dies. He has been gone for 10 years trying to find his fortune. As the journey progresses from train to stagecoach, two men fall in love with Sarah, and tidbits of information reveal that her father has actually been in hiding because he shot a man in self-defense. Once in Leadville, Sarah finds that things are not going as they should, and she will probably stay to help clear her father's name.

1574. Nixon, Joan. **In the Face of Danger: The Orphan Train Quartet Three**. New York: Bantam, 1988. 152p. $16; $3.99pa. ISBN 0-553-05490-2; 0-553-28196-8pa. 7 up

Unhappy to be separated from her family and blaming herself for all of their problems, Meg, 12, goes to Ben and Emma's house in Kansas Territory. She tries to adjust to the change, and she shows that she has learned to cope when she bravely saves the neighbors and Emma from a known killer. She suggests he show his marksmanship by shooting at targets she selects, and he uses all his ammunition. The birth of Emma's baby soon after makes the effort worthwhile. *Western Writers of America Spur Award*.

1575. Nixon, Joan Lowery. **Keeping Secrets**. New York: Delacorte, 1995. 163p. $15.95; $3.99pa. ISBN 0-385-32139-2; 0-440-21992-2pa. (Orphan Train Adventures). 5-8

When she is 11 in 1863, Peg Kelly thinks her mother should treat her like the young woman she almost is. Peg meets and helps a woman escaping from the Confederates, Violet Hennessey. Violet needs Peg to pretend to be her daughter so she can safely deliver secrets to the Union army. Peg agrees, and their efforts help the army win, but not quickly enough to save Peg's brother from the Confederates.

1576. Nixon, Joan Lowery. **Land of Dreams**. New York: Delacorte, 1994. 160p. $14.95; $3.99pa. ISBN 0-385-31170-2; 0-440-21935-5pa. (Ellis Island). 7 up

In the third book of the Ellis Island series, Kristin Swenson, 17, reaches the colony of Great Rock Lake, Minnesota, in 1902 with her parents. There she refuses to follow the traditions of her Swedish heritage by rejecting an arranged marriage. After the family's home burns and she sees how the community works together, she realizes that compromising does not mean that she has to lose her individuality. With an empathetic husband, she can also continue her support of a woman's right to vote and other causes important to her.

1577. Nixon, Joan Lowery. **Land of Hope**. 1992. New York: Laurel, 1995. 172p. $3.99pa. ISBN 0-440-21597-8pa. (Ellis Island). 7 up

Rebekah arrives in New York in 1902 after her family left Russia to flee the Jewish pogroms. She wants to get an education, but her family needs money, so she has to work seven days a week in a sweatshop. She hears from Rose in Chicago and Kristin in Minnesota, two girls she met on the crossing, and they tell her about their new lives. But when her brother refuses his opportunity to study, Rebekah's father finally agrees to escort her to class.

1578. Nixon, Joan Lowery. **Land of Promise**. New York: Bantam, 1993. 170p. $16; $3.99pa. ISBN 0-553-08111-X; 0-440-21904-3pa. (Ellis Island). 7 up

Rose, 15, arrives in Chicago from Ireland in 1902, and her brother's political connections there help her get a job as a shop girl. She plans to use her salary to pay for her mother and sister to come to America, because she thinks her mother will curb her father's drinking and her brother's radical activities. But her mother does not arrive in time to solve all of these problems. Rose joins Jane Addams's campaign to clean up Chicago and fight for world peace.

1579. Nixon, Joan Lowery. **A Place to Belong**: The Orphan Train Quartet Four. 1989. New York: Bantam, 1996. 149p. $3.50pa. ISBN 0-553-28485-1pa. 7 up

Danny and Peg's foster mother dies around 1860, and Danny suggests that his foster father Alfrid invite his real mother to the West. He hopes that the two will marry. They are very different, but both find unexpected happiness in knowing each other.

1580. Noble, William. **Bookbanning in America: Who Bans Books? And Why**. Middlebury, VT: Paul S. Eriksson, 1990. 349p. $14.95pa. ISBN 0-8397-1080-1pa. YA

Those who believe that written texts threaten their perception of life sometimes try to keep others from reading these texts. People have been attempting to ban various books in America since the seditious libel case of John Peter Zinger in 1734. Noble thinks that censorship threatens all aspects of life, including "politics, religion, social status, education and publishing." He discusses various cases of censorship and book banning while noting that the people who try to censor are rarely zealots, just those who think their way is the only right one. Bibliography and Index.

1581. Norman, Winifred Latimer, and Lily Patterson. **Lewis Latimer: Scientist**. New York: Chelsea House, 1993. 100p. $18.95. ISBN 0-7910-1977-2. (Black Americans of Achievement). 5 up

Lewis Latimer (1848-1928), the son of fugitive slaves living in Boston, worked closely with Alexander Graham Bell and Thomas Edison. He became a master draftsman, engineer, and inventor. Because Blacks went unrecognized, his name was not associated with his achievements, which included the creation and design of electric street lighting. Photographs and reproductions enhance the text. Chronology, Further Reading, and Index.

1582. Norrell, Robert J. **We Want Jobs! A Story of the Great Depression**. Jan Naimo Jones, illustrator. Austin, TX: Raintree/Steck-Vaughn, 1993. 40p. $24.26; $5.95pa. ISBN 0-8114-7229-9; 0-8114-8069-0pa. (Stories of America—Stand Up and Be Counted). 4-8

In 1929, John Waskowitz, a Pennsylvania steelworker, loses his job like millions of others during the Great Depression. His family and the others suffer while everyone looks for nonexistent jobs. Some despair, but all call for government intervention. Not until 1933 does work start to become more available. Epilogue, Afterword, and Notes.

1583.   Norton, Mary Beth. **Founding Mothers & Fathers: Gendered Power and the Forming of American Society**. New York: Knopf, 1996. 496p. $35. ISBN 0-679-42965-4. YA

Thomasine Hall, born in England during the early seventeenth century, decided to dress like a man and immigrate to the American colonies. She then became a soldier. When she returned from duty, she changed to a woman and started making a living by doing needlework. Her story survives because people could not decide if she was a man or a woman, and her society allowed privilege based on sex. By refusing to say that Hall was a woman, the women of her time showed power over the men in the court, according to Norton. The men had to accept the verdict of women who refused to positively identify Hall. Discussions of other aspects of colonial society give further insight into the roles of women within the family and neighborhoods. Bibliography and Index.

O

1584. O'Brien, Steven. **Alexander Hamilton**. New York: Chelsea House, 1988. 112p. $18.95. ISBN 1-55546-810-1. (World Leaders Past and Present). 5 up

Alexander Hamilton (1757-1804), a political thinker, essayist, and statesman, devoted his life to building the nation. But his volatile personality led him to bitter feuds with Thomas Jefferson and John Adams. He arrived in New York at 17 to study at Columbia after an impoverished life as an illegitimate child on the island of St. Croix. He later joined the Continental army and became Washington's trusted personal aide. He favored a strong national government and, as a lawyer able to articulate many of the Constitution's central principles, led the fight with John Madison to ratify the Constitution. He was the first secretary of the Treasury, but his policies advocating expansion of the nation's economy drew opposition. He died in a duel with Aaron Burr, the Vice President. Reproductions enhance the text. Chronology, Further Reading, and Index.

1585. O'Brien, Steven. **Ulysses S. Grant**. New York: Chelsea House, 1991. 112p. $18.95. ISBN 1-55546-809-8. (World Leaders Past and Present). 5 up

Ulysses S. Grant (1822-1885), a graduate of West Point, fought in the Mexican War, but he was discharged from the army in 1854 suffering from alcoholism and depression. He reenlisted during the Civil War, and he rose to become the Union's boldest commander, taking charge of the Union forces in 1864. He refused to accept any type of surrender in the Civil War except an unconditional one. That decree led to a longer war, but he received the surrender in 1865. From 1869 to 1877, he served as President of the United States, but he remains best known as the man who defeated Robert E. Lee. Photographs and reproductions enhance the text. Chronology, Further Reading, and Index.

1586. O'Brien, Steven, et al. **American Political Leaders: From Colonial Times to the Present**. Santa Barbara, CA: ABC-CLIO, 1991. 473p. $65. ISBN 0-87436-570-8. YA

The alphabetical entries in this collection cover 409 people either elected or appointed to a national political office. Included are major and third-party presidential candidates, Vice Presidents, Speakers of the House, Supreme Court chief justices, secretaries of state, revolutionary and colonial figures, senators, representatives, and presidential advisors. The entries, which interpret the lives of each figure, have cross-references and brief bibliographies. Timeline.

1587. O'Connor, Barbara. **The Soldier's Voice: The Story of Ernie Pyle**. Minneapolis, MN: Carolrhoda, 1996. 80p. $14.96. ISBN 0-87614-942-5. (Trailblazers). 4-7

Ernie Pyle (1900-1945) grew up on a farm in Indiana, but he wanted to travel. When he discovered his talent for newspaper writing, he was able to see the world. He wrote the first daily aviation column and then used his words to take people across America to visit a variety of places. In World War II, he began to speak for the soldiers by sharing their thoughts and experiences with the people who waited for them at home. President Truman complemented him for being the voice of "American fighting [men] as [they] wanted [their story] told." The text looks at Pyle's life and accomplishments. Notes, Bibliography, and Index.

1588. O'Connor, Jim. **The Story of Roberto Clemente: All-Star Hero**. Stephen Marchesi, illustrator. 1991. Minneapolis, MN: Gareth Stevens, 1995. 112p. $13.95. ISBN 0-8368-1384-7. (Famous Lives). 3-7

Roberto Clemente (1934-1972) went against his mother's wishes when he became a baseball player. A Puerto Rican when few minorities were playing in the major leagues, he joined the Pittsburgh Pirates and helped them become victorious in the 1960 and 1961 World Series. He died when his plane crashed while on the way to Nicaragua with supplies after a huge earthquake there. Baseball writers honored him by voting him into the Hall of Fame a few weeks after his death rather than waiting the customary five years. Highlights in the Life, For Further Study, and Index.

1589. O'Dell, Scott. **Island of the Blue Dolphins**. Ted Lewin, illustrator. 1960. Boston: Houghton Mifflin, 1990. 192p. $18.95. ISBN 0-395-53680-4. New York: Scholastic, 1994. 192p. $3.95pa. ISBN 0-590-22165-5pa. 5 up

Karana is the only remaining human on her island after Aleuts kill most of the men and the others sail to the mainland. Her brother survives for a while, but a wild dog kills him. Karana learns how to live by overcoming tribal taboos such as women not making weapons. Her experiences as she lives each day show that people can adapt to and work with nature. *Newbery Medal, Southern California Council on Literature for Children and Young People Awards, International Board of Books for Young People, Friends of Children and Literature Award, American Library Association Notable Books for Children,* and *School Library Journal Best Book.*

1590. O'Dell, Scott. **The King's Fifth**. Samuel Bryant, illustrator. Boston: Houghton Mifflin, 1966. $15.95. ISBN 0-395-06963-7. 7-10

In 1541, Esteban, 17, waits to be tried in a California prison for hoarding a fifth of the king's gold. The story, told through flashbacks, shows that Esteban was the cartographer for Captain Mendoza's expedition in the West. Esteban threw gold into a desert sinkhole because he saw how much the desire for gold was destroying the men in the group. *Newbery Honor Book.*

1591. O'Dell, Scott. **Sarah Bishop**. Boston: Houghton Mifflin, 1980. 240p. $14.95. ISBN 0-395-29185-2. New York: Point, Scholastic, 1991. 240p. $3.50pa. ISBN 0-590-44651-7pa. 7 up

In 1776, Sarah Bishop has to escape from the British after rebels kill her father. She disguises herself as a male and travels north until she thinks she has reached safety. She establishes her home in a cave and learns to survive in the wild. When a local Quaker sells her supplies, he tells her that the British still search for her. A disease sweeps the area, and the people begin to blame her until a mail carrier tells them that Boston's drought has caused this disease.

1592. O'Dell, Scott. **The Serpent Never Sleeps: A Novel of Jamestown and Pocahontas**. Ted Lewin, illustrator. Boston: Houghton Mifflin, 1987. 240p. $15.95. ISBN 0-395-4424-7. 6-9

Serena Lynn, supposed to come to the court of King James in London, decides instead to join the company sailing from Plymouth to Jamestown in 1609. The king has given her a ring engraved with a serpent that supposedly will protect her. As she follows the man she loves, she can only hope that the ring will perform if necessary. Serena arrives in Jamestown, gets to know Pocahontas, and experiences the tragedy of the colony.

1593. O'Dell, Scott. **Sing Down the Moon**. Boston: Houghton Mifflin, 1970. 137p. $14.95. ISBN 0-395-10919-1. New York: Dell, 1992. 137p. $3.99pa. ISBN 0-400-40673-0pa. 5 up

Spanish slavers enter the Canyon de Chelly in 1864 and take the Navajo girl Bright Morning and her friend south with them to sell. Soon after, the white soldiers burn the crops and force the remaining Navajos to march toward Fort Sumner. The boy she intends to marry, Tall Boy, helps her escape from the slavers, but the soldiers retake them all. Bright Morning and Tall Boy have to endure the ignominy of the camp before they escape and return to live in the crevices of their canyon with their son. *Newbery Honor Book.*

1594. O'Dell, Scott. **Streams to the River, River to the Sea**. Boston: Houghton Mifflin, 1986. 164p. $15.95. ISBN 0-395-40430-4. New York: Fawcett, 1988. 164p. $4.50pa. ISBN 0-449-70244-8pa. YA

Indian braves from an enemy tribe capture Sacagawea when she is 13 and take her away. Those who buy her then marry her to a French trader. She, the trader, and their son accompany Lewis and Clark on their expedition to the West. On the trip, she falls in love with Clark, but she knows that they cannot be happy together because she is Shoshone, so she leaves her husband and returns to her tribe. *Scott O'Dell Award for Historical Fiction.*

1595. O'Dell, Scott. **Zia**. Ted Lewin, illustrator. Boston: Houghton Mifflin, 1976. 224p. $14.95. ISBN 0-395-24393-9. New York: Laurel, 1996. 144p. $4.50pa. ISBN 0-440-21956-6pa. 4-8

Karana's niece Zia tries to rescue her in this sequel to *Island of the Blue Dolphins*. Zia and her brother get a boat to sail to the island, but a ship sees and captures them, and the captain enslaves them on board. They steal another boat and return to the Santa Barbara mission. When Zia tells her story to another captain, he promises to bring Karana back to the mainland on his next trip. He does as he promised, but Karana cannot adjust to mission life and its rules after living alone for so many years and learning to survive without anyone else around.

1596. O'Dell, Scott, and Elizabeth Hall. **Thunder Rolling in the Mountains**. Boston: Houghton Mifflin, 1992. 128p. $14.95. ISBN 0-395-59966-0. 6-9

Sound of Running Feet, daughter of Chief Joseph of the Nez Percé Indians, tells about the Blue Coats (American soldiers) pursuing her people in 1877. The army forces them to leave their Oregon valley and then attacks them so that they have to fight. She walks toward Canada with her intended husband, but another tribe, the Assiniboin, betray them. She escapes again and goes to join Sitting Bull. *Notable Children's Trade Books in the Field of Social Studies.*

1597. O'Grady, Scott, and Michael French. **Basher Five-Two**. New York: Doubleday, 1997. 144p. $16.95. ISBN 0-385-32300-X. 5-9

Captain Scott O'Grady was flying an F-16 during a NATO peacekeeping mission when he was shot down over Bosnia in 1995. He survived in hostile territory for six days with no food or water and without survival equipment. O'Grady tells of his experience and credits the U.S. Marines with saving his life. He sees himself not as a hero but as one who was lucky enough to escape in this recounting of his experience.

1598. Oke, Janette. **The Bluebird and the Sparrow**. Minneapolis, MN: Bethany House, 1995. 251p. $12.99; $8.99pa. ISBN 1-55661-613-9; 1-55661-612-0pa. 7 up

In the early 1900s, Berthe feels inadequate when compared to her lovely, vivacious sister Glenna. She decides she will be the opposite of her sister and not be hurt by all of the compliments that Glenna receives. When the pretense becomes too burdensome, Berthe goes to her minister, and he suggests that the two discuss their perceptions of each other. This approach frees Berthe to be herself, not the "sparrow" that she has decided must contrast a "bluebird."

1599. Okihiro, Gary Y. **Whispered Silences: Japanese Americans and World War II**. Joan Myers, photographer. Seattle, WA: University of Washington, 1996. 249p. $60; $29.95pa. ISBN 0-295-97497-4; 0-295-97498-2pa. YA

This text covers the history of Japanese life in Hawaii and the mainland of the United States since the first migration in the late 1860s. As Okihiro, a *sansei* (third generation Japanese American) researched the book, he found out about the treatment of Japanese Americans during World War II about which many Japanese, including his parents, had remained silent. The text is an essay in four parts using primary sources such as interviews. Powerful photographs of the abandoned camps enhance the text. Bibliography.

1600. Olds, Bruce. **Raising Holy Hell: A Novel**. New York: Henry Holt, 1996. 333p. $22.50. ISBN 0-8050-3856-6. YA

John Brown, a religious fanatic, was also a self-flagellator and an inept businessman whose family suffered while he tried to rid America of slavery. Interviews, documents, and journal articles make his story seem less horrifying than it might have been for those who had to live or work with him. Part of the text discusses the terrors of slavery that Brown did help to overcome even though he failed at Harpers Ferry.

1601. Oleksy, Walter. **Military Leaders of World War II**. New York: Facts on File, 1994. 154p. $17.95. ISBN 0-8160-3008-1. (American Profiles). 8 up

Because World War II involved every major power in the world, the decisions of those who led the U.S. military units became very important. In the Pacific, leaders were Colonel Claire Lee Chennault of the "Flying Tigers"; Lieutenant Colonel Evans Carlson of "Carlson's Raiders"; General Douglas MacArthur of the United States Far East Command; Admiral Chester W. Nimitz, Commander of the United States Pacific Fleet; and Admiral William F. "Bull" Halsey, Commander of the Third Fleet. In Europe were General Dwight D. Eisenhower, Supreme United States Commander in Europe; Jacqueline Cochran, Director of the Women's Air Force Service pilots; General Omar Bradley, Commander of the Second Army and Twelfth Army Corps; Captain Curtis E. LeMay, Army Air Corps Commander in Europe and the Pacific; and General George S. Patton, Jr., Commander, 2nd Armored Division and Third Army. Index.

1602. Olsen, Victoria. **Emily Dickinson: Poet**. New York: Chelsea House, 1990. 110p. $18.95. ISBN 1-55546-649-4. (American Women of Achievement). 5 up

Emily Dickinson (1830-1886) lived her entire life in Amherst, Massachusetts. She left only to visit Washington, D.C., and Boston. She had strong convictions about Christianity and nature that seemed contrary to many who knew her. After she was 30 years old, she avoided society, choosing to stay inside her home. Because only seven of her poems were published during her lifetime, she gained most of her fame in the twentieth century, when the originality and thoughtfulness of her poems were better understood. Photographs and reproductions enhance the text. Chronology, Further Reading, and Index.

1603. Olsen, Violet. **The View from the Pighouse Roof**. New York: Atheneum, 1987. 176p. $13.95. ISBN 0-689-31324-1. 5-7

Marie, 12, misses her older sister Rosie, who has left the home of her Danish-American farm family with her husband and child to go around the country looking for a job during the Great Depression. But Rosie dies in a motorcycle accident. Marie plans not to attend high school so she can look after Rosie's two-year-old child, but Marie's mother says that she must. Marie realizes that her view of life has changed and equates it with looking from the pighouse roof. *Society of Midland Authors' Award.*

1604. O'Neal, Michael. **The Assassination of Abraham Lincoln**. San Diego, CA: Greenhaven, 1991. 96p. $13.95. ISBN 0-89908-092-8. (Great Mysteries). 5-9

A prologue gives the facts behind the assassination of Abraham Lincoln on April 14, 1865. In two-page spreads, the text presents the theories behind the murder at Ford's Theater in Washington. Captions and quotes from sources, as well as black-and-white photographs and drawings, enhance the text. Bibliography and Index.

1605. O'Neal, Michael. **President Truman and the Atomic Bomb: Opposing Viewpoints**. San Diego, CA: Greenhaven, 1990. 112p. $13.95. ISBN 0-89908-079-0. (Great Mysteries—Opposing Viewpoints). 6-9

When President Truman gave the command to drop the atomic bomb on Hiroshima in 1945, he relied on information from various sources to assist him in reaching the decision. The text examines the events and the facts that Truman might have used as his basis for initiating this situation. Bibliography and Index.

1606. Oneal, Zibby. **Grandma Moses: Painter of Rural America**. Donna Ruff, illustrator. New York: Puffin, 1986. 58p. $4.99pa. ISBN 0-14-032220-5pa. (Women of Our Time). 5 up

Called a primitive painter because she never had formal lessons, Anna Mary Moses (1860-1961) began painting after she was 70 years old. She gave her landscapes away as gifts, and her first "show" was in the local drugstore window. A man saw her paintings in the drugstore, bought them, and eventually got them displayed in the Museum of Modern Art in New York City. The year she was 80, she had a real gallery show.

1607. O'Neil, Buck, Steve Wulf, and David Conrads. **I Was Right on Time**. New York: Simon & Schuster, 1996. 254p. $23; $12pa. ISBN 0-684-80305-4; 0-684-83247-Xpa. YA

Buck O'Neil tells about his experiences in the Negro Baseball Leagues during the 1940s and 1950s. He grew up in Florida and spent time in Kansas City during his playing years. He enjoyed his experience and encourages young people to enjoy what they choose to do.

1608. O'Neill, Laurie. **Little Rock: The Desegregation of Central High**. Brookfield, CT: Millbrook Press, 1994. 64p. $15.40. ISBN 1-56294-354-5. (Spotlight on American History). 4-8

On September 25, 1957, nine Black teenagers entered high school in Little Rock, Arkansas. Little Rock's white citizens refused to accept that Blacks and whites were equal, and a mob shouted for them to go home and leave the white school alone. In fact, they closed the high school during 1958-1959 to avoid integration. The text tells about these nine students and what they had to endure as they tried to take their rightful places in the classroom. Photographs illustrate the text. Chronology, Sources, Further Reading, and Index.

1609. O'Neill, Laurie. **Wounded Knee: The Death of a Dream**. Brookfield, CT: Millbrook Press, 1993. 64p. $14.40. ISBN 1-56294-253-0. (Spotlight on American History). 3-7

In 1890, U.S. Cavalry troops massacred men, women, and children at Wounded Knee, South Dakota. The text places the incident in a historical context by looking at the relationships between whites and the Lakota Sioux, the early Sioux Plains settlements in the 1700s and their interaction with nature, the reservation plan, the ghost dance ceremony, and other topics. Archival photographs and drawings enhance the text. Further Reading, Glossary, and Index. *Child Study Association Children's Books of the Year.*

1610. O'Rear, Sybil J. **Charles Goodnight: Pioneer Cowman**. New York: Eakin, 1990. 69p. $10.95. ISBN 0-89015-741-3. 5-8

Charles Goodnight (1836-1929) lived in the Texas panhandle all his life and served his state by remaining there to fight during the Civil War. He developed the idea of the chuckwagon, and he improved the sidesaddle for women. He experimented with plants and fought against cattle diseases, trying to have laws passed protecting cattle. He loved children, and he helped the people of his state in any way he could. Glossary and Bibliography.

1611. Ortiz Cofer, Judith. **Silent Dancing: A Partial Remembrance of a Puerto Rican Childhood**. Houston, TX: Arte Publico Press, 1990. 167p. $9.50pa. ISBN 1-55885-015-5pa. YA

As a young girl, Judith Ortiz Cofer spent her childhood moving back and forth between Puerto Rico and New Jersey. In this book, she recalls her bilingual-bicultural childhood and shows what life was like for her. Poems that encompass the themes appear throughout the text. *New York Public Library Best Books for the Teen Age.*

1612. Osborn, Karen. **Between Earth and Sky**. New York: Morrow, 1996. 305p. $23. ISBN 0-688-14123-4. YA

Abigail Conklin and her husband leave the South after the Civil War in 1867 for land and economic opportunity in the West. She writes letters to her sister telling her about the wagon train, the boredom of traveling all day, and keeping her dusty, hot children happy. After they arrive, and as time passes, she begins to appreciate the beauty of her new home, and she continues to write into the 1930s, after the frontier has disappeared. The letters give a glimpse into her life and the lives of pioneer women like her.

1613. Osborne, Angela. **Abigail Adams: Women's Rights Advocate**. New York: Chelsea House, 1989. 112p. $18.95; $7.95pa. ISBN 1-55546-635-4; 0-7910-0405-8pa. (American Women of Achievement). 5 up

As America's First Lady from 1796 to 1800, Abigail Adams (1744-1818) was a political advisor, dedicated wife and mother, and defender of women. She insisted that women deserved the same rights as men, and in many letters she makes these assertions. She lived in five world capitals, raised four children, and enjoyed more than 50 years of marriage. Photographs and reproductions enhance the text. Further Reading, Chronology, and Index.

1614. Osborne, Mary Pope. **George Washington: Leader of a New Nation**. New York: Dial Press, 1991. 117p. $14. ISBN 0-8037-0947-1. 4-7

Osborne believes that the greatness of George Washington (1732-1799) lay in his courage and humility. When offered the chance to be the leader of a new country, he refused to become either a dictator or a king. He did not capitalize on his popularity to become an absolute ruler. When he was elected President, he felt that he had to serve even though he preferred life on his Virginia farm. He gained power by giving it up and, in turn, laid the foundation for America to become a free and self-governing nation. The text looks at his life and his choices. Timeline, Bibliography, and Index.

1615. Osborne, Mary Pope. **The Many Lives of Benjamin Franklin**. New York: Dial Press, 1990. 129p. $13.95. ISBN 0-8037-0679-0. 4-7

When Benjamin Franklin was a small boy, his family gave him some money. He spent it on a whistle that he bought from another boy. His family laughed and said that he had spent too much. He never forgot the lesson because he was frugal for the rest of his life. He was an apprentice, a journeyman, and a printer; a scientist and inventor; an agent to England; the oldest revolutionary; and one of the founding fathers of the nation. The text looks at his contributions, including his tenure as the president of the first abolitionist society. Timeline, Bibliography, and Index.

1616. Osinski, Alice. **Andrew Jackson: Seventh President of the United States**. Chicago: Childrens Press, 1987. 100p. $19.80. ISBN 0-516-01387-4. (Encyclopedia of Presidents). 4-9

The 6'1" Andrew Jackson (1767-1845) became President of the United States in 1829. Face scarred by smallpox and battle wounds, he told his audience, "I will not fail you." People were invited to the White House for a reception, but they destroyed the furniture. Others said that Jackson was beginning "the reign of King Mob." He was the first President since George Washington not to have a college education, and he was determined to govern for all people. Chronology of American History and Index.

1617. Osofsky, Audrey. **Free to Dream: The Making of a Poet, Langston Hughes**. New York: Lothrop, Lee & Shepard, 1996. 112p. $16. ISBN 0-688-10605-6. 5-9

This biography of Langston Hughes (1902-1967) concentrates on the childhood influences that shaped his life when he was interested in writing, and his absent father who was against his choice. He accomplished extraordinary things as a Black author who wrote in a variety of genres while establishing the unique language of African Americans. Bibliography, Notes, and Index.

1618. Otfinoski, Steven. **Great Black Writers**. New York: Facts on File, 1994. 118p. $17.95. ISBN 0-8160-2906-7. (American Profiles). 8 up

With each of the 10 writers profiled here is a chronology of the author's life and a list of books for further reading both by and about the author. The writers are Phillis Wheatley, mother of African American literature (c. 1753-1784); Charles Waddell Chestnutt, father of Black American fiction (1858-1932); James Weldon Johnson, Black writer as public figure (1871-1938); Langston Hughes, the dean of Black writers (1902-1967); Zora Neale Hurston, folklorist and feminist (1891-1960); Countee Cullen (1903-1946); Richard Wright (1908-1960); James Baldwin (1924-1987); Lorraine Hansberry (1930-1965); and Alex Haley (1921-1992). Index.

1619. Otfinoski, Steven. **Lewis and Clark: Leading America West**. New York: Fawcett, 1992. 114p. $4pa. ISBN 0-449-90398-2pa. (Great Lives). 7 up

This look at the men who went west to map the Louisiana Purchase tells about their relationship, their decisions, and their adventures on the journey, which began in 1803 from St. Louis, Missouri, and lasted until 1806, when they returned to the same spot. Afterward, Lewis was either murdered or, most likely, committed suicide. Appendix.

1620. Otfinoski, Steven. **Nineteenth-Century Writers**. New York: Facts on File, 1991. 122p. $17.95. ISBN 0-8160-2486-3. (American Profiles). 8-12

Short biographies of 10 nineteenth-century writers begin with anecdotes that place them within their times. The authors include Washington Irving, Edgar Allan Poe, Herman Melville, Mark Twain, Stephen Crane, and Emily Dickinson. Otfinoski includes information about the political, historical, economic, and social situation of the times as well. Photographs, Bibliography, and Index.

1621. Oughton, Jerrie. **Music from a Place Called Half Moon**. Boston: Houghton Mifflin, 1995. 160p. $13.95. ISBN 0-395-70737-4. 6-9

Edie Jo, 13, realizes that the prejudice between the Indians and the whites in Half Moon, North Carolina, during 1956 affects all of them when her father suggests that the church allow Indians to attend. She becomes even more involved when she falls in love with Cherokee Fish, a local Indian boy. That year, however, a fire in the town causes enormous hostility. Cherokee dies when his brother, who started the fire but wants Cherokee to protect him, hits him in a fight. After a few months, Edie Jo's family seems to forget the incident, but she retains her changed attitude. *Bank Street College's Children's Book Award.*

1622. Oughton, Jerrie. **The War in Georgia**. Boston: Houghton Mifflin, 1997. 192p. $14.95. ISBN 0-395-81568-1. 5-8

Shanta, 13, lives with her grandmother and her bedridden uncle during World War II. They have difficult times during the summer of 1945, and she learns about helping others during a time of local war in Georgia that creeps through her town.

1623. Owen, Marna. **Our Century: 1930-1940**. Milwaukee, WI: Gareth Stevens, 1993. 64p. $23.93. ISBN 0-8368-1035-X. 3-10

Written as if a newspaper, the book's short articles give an overview of the decade. Included are statistics, daily life in America, the Spanish king's abdication and civil war in Spain, General Franco, Edward of England abdicating, the Nazis' rise, Stalin and Hitler, Hoover, Roosevelt, the end of Prohibition, the Scottsboro case, the rise of the Empire State Building, Boulder Dam, New York's World Fair, Babe Didrikson, Lou Gehrig, Joe Louis, Eugene O'Neill, Jane Addams, Huey Long, and Amelia Earhart. Glossary, Books for Further Reading, Places to Write or Visit, and Index.

1624. Owens, Jesse, with Paul Neimark. **Jesse: The Man Who Outran Hitler**. New York: Fawcett, 1985. 224p. $4.95pa. ISBN 0-449-13056-8pa. YA

Jesse Owens (1913-1980) tells about the influences in his life as he grew up in a segregated America. One of his first memories is almost bleeding to death at five and praying with his father for it to stop so his mother would not die herself from mourning. The family moved from Alabama to Cleveland, and there he met the man who interested him in running. After taking him to watch the horses' faces during a race, the coach continued to influence his approach to the rest of his life and fueled his desire to be the best. When he won gold medals in Hitler's Olympics in 1936, he surprised the world and undermined Hitler's concept of the Aryan race.

P

1625. Paiewonsky, Michael. **Conquest of Eden, 1493-1515**. 1991. Chicago: Academy, 1993. 176p. ISBN 0-926330-04-7. YA

Paiewonsky uses reports and letters of Spanish explorers to reveal their lust for gold and their willingness to destroy the native life in the New World to get it after Columbus's initial voyage in 1492. The text looks at the significance of Columbus's "discovery," and the resulting destruction of native peoples in St. Croix during 1515. It includes Columbus's letter to Queen Isabella describing the beauty and the wealth of the area as well as the journals and logs of Columbus's sons and brothers telling of the Indians' reactions to intruders, the disappearance of exploring parties, meetings with cannibals, and the cruel treatment of Indians who interfered with the collection of wealth for the Spanish crown. Woodcuts, engravings, and photographs complement the text. Bibliography and Index.

1626. Palmer, Bruce. **The Karma Charmer**. New York: Harmony, 1994. 245p. $20. ISBN 0-517-59919-8. YA

Howser, a 46-year-old hippie in Woodstock, New York, during the 1960s falls in love with a college senior who has been living with him since her dormitory burned down. She, however, is only interested in making a lot of money in a Wall Street job. When Howser's 10-year-old son, whom he has only seen once, arrives, the two become acquainted, and together they plot to make the girl fall in love with Howser.

1627. Palmer, Colin A. **The First Passage: Blacks in the Americas, 1502-1617**. New York: Oxford University Press, 1995. 126p. $21. ISBN 0-19-508699-6. (Young Oxford History of African Americans). 7 up

In an attempt to discuss all slaves in the first of an 11-volume series, the text talks about the differences among African cultures and how those who were enslaved had to change their traditions and religions. It centers on slaves in Peru, Brazil, and Mexico who might also have been miners or pearl fishers instead of domestic field hands. Black-and-white reproductions enhance the text. Bibliography and Index.

1628. Palmer, Leslie. **Lena Horne: Entertainer**. New York: Chelsea House, 1989. 127p. $18.95. ISBN 1-55546-594-3. (Black Americans of Achievement). 5 up

Lena Horne, born into a privileged family in 1917, grew up in Brooklyn and several towns in the racially segregated South. She made her professional debut as a singer at 16 at the Cotton Club in Harlem, a place that featured Black performers. Her career as a solo nightclub performer began in 1941, and she became the first Black singer to be promoted by the movie industry. She has crossed color barriers while pushing civil rights issues. Photographs, Chronology, Further Reading, and Index.

1629. Parker, Steve. **Benjamin Franklin and Electricity**. New York: Chelsea House, 1995. 32p. $14.95. ISBN 0-7910-3006-7. (Science Discoveries). 3 up

The text gives a brief overview of Benjamin Franklin's life (1706-1790) while emphasizing the contributions he made to science through inventions that have influenced contemporary life. He was the first person to use the terms "positive" and "negative" when referring to electricity. In addition to inventing bifocals, the Franklin stove, and a musical instrument, he also studied oceans and their water currents. His most famous experiments occurred in the field of static electricity. The World in Franklin's Time, Glossary, and Index.

1630. Parker, Steve. **Thomas Edison and Electricity**. New York: Chelsea House, 1995. 32p. $14.95. ISBN 0-7910-3012-1. (Science Discoveries). 4-8

Through his understanding of science, Thomas A. (Alva) Edison (1847-1931) made major contributions to humanity. Some see him as the greatest inventor in history because of electricity. The text examines his wizardry and perseverance. Glossary, Timeline, and Index.

1631. Parker, Steve. **The Wright Brothers and Aviation**. Tony Smith, illustrator. New York: Chelsea House, 1995. 32p. $14.95. ISBN 0-7910-3013-X. (Science Discoveries). 3-7

The text presents the early years of the Wright brothers, Wilbur and Orville, and their gliding skills learned from their early experiments with bicycles. They taught themselves much about machines and mechanics and even made a small combustion engine. Although they were not the first to attempt powered flight, they were the first to be successful when they overcame the three basic problems in flying: designing wings that would lift the craft, figuring out how to control it in the air, and building a power plant that would propel it. The final chapter looks at aviation after the Wrights made their flight on December 17, 1903. The World in the Wrights' Time, Glossary, and Index.

1632. Parks, Rosa, with Gregory J. Reed. **Quiet Strength**. Grand Rapids, MI: Zondervan Publishing, 1994. 94p. $12.99. ISBN 0-310-50150-4. 8 up

Rosa Parks (b. 1913) started a bus boycott, but she wants to be remembered as a person who made life better for the young people of the world. She says that whenever she has problems she thinks about the strength of her mother and grandmother, who taught her to have faith in God and to read the Bible. Other notes in the text tell about her personal strength in facing life in the twentieth century. Chronology.

1633. Partnow, Elaine, comp. and ed. **The New Quotable Woman**. Rev. ed. New York: Facts on File, 1992. 714p. $40. ISBN 0-8160-2134-1. YA

Some 15,000 quotations represent 2,500 women. The entries are arranged in chronological order according to the birth year of the woman quoted. Within years, entries are alphabetical. Perhaps as helpful and interesting as the quotes are the indices, which include a biographical index, a subject index, an occupation index, and an index of nationality and ethnicity.

1634. Partridge, Elizabeth, ed. **Dorothea Lange: A Visual Life**. Washington, DC: Smithsonian Institution Press, 1994. 168p. $29.95pa. ISBN 1-56098-455-4pa. YA

Dorothea Lange (1895-1965) was a feminist, a wife, a mother, and a photographer. As a child, she had polio, and for the rest of her life she had a limp. One of the essays on Lange indicates that this disability influenced the subjects that she chose to photograph. Her photographs of the Depression are well known, and she also made studies of the Japanese internment camps created by the War Relocation Authority. A son says that Lange saw herself as a "witness" and an "observer" rather than a photographer or artist. The story of her life and work is a history of the 1930s, 1940s, and 1950s in America. Index.

1635. Pasachoff, Naomi. **Alexander Graham Bell: Making Connections**. New York: Oxford University Press, 1996. 140p. $20. ISBN 0-19-509908-7. 6-9

The text looks at Alexander Graham Bell (1847-1922) and his contributions as an educator and inventor more than at his personal life. Clear explanations of his experiments and the scientific principles behind them enliven the text and clarify his work, especially as a teacher of the deaf. Photographs and reproductions highlight the text. Further Reading and Index.

1636. Pascoe, Elaine. **First Facts About the Presidents**. New York: Blackbirch, 1996. 112p. $22.95. ISBN 1-56711-167-X. (First Facts). 4-8

Four main sections in the text introduce the first Presidents, the Presidents as America grew, the Civil War and after, and the twentieth century. Within each area, full-page portraits of each President appear with personal statistics and paragraphs about the term of office. Also included are sidebars listing contemporary events and information about family and cabinet members. Chronology, Further Reading, and Index.

1637. Pascoe, Elaine. **Freedom of Expression: The Right to Speak Out in America**. Brookfield, CT: Millbrook Press, 1988. 128p. $16.40. ISBN 1-56294-255-7. (Issue and Debate). 7 up

The text traces the First Amendment's history by examining how the right to speak one's mind has been tested and interpreted from colonial times to the present in various types of media as well as individually. Black-and-white photographs enhance the text. Bibliography and Index. *Child Study Association Children's Books of the Year* and *New York Public Library Books for the Teen Age.*

1638. Pascoe, Elaine. **Mexico and the United States: Cooperation and Conflict**. New York: Twenty-First Century, 1996. 126p. $17.98. ISBN 0-8050-4180-X. 7 up

The text discusses the relationship between the United States and Mexico from the Spanish colonial period to the present with details and humorous anecdotes. It also looks at the anti-Mexican attitudes that prevail in some areas of the country and tries to assess them. Photographs, Further Reading, Notes, and Index.

1639. Paterson, Katherine. **Jacob Have I Loved**. New York: HarperCollins, 1980. 256p. $14.95; $4.50pa. ISBN 0-690-04078-4; 0-06-447059-8pa. 5 up

Louise (Wheeze) grows up in the early 1940s on her Chesapeake Bay island thinking that everyone loves her younger twin Caroline more than they do her. Wheeze learns about crabbing and being a waterman from her father, while Caroline sings and wins money to go to school on the mainland. Not until Wheeze leaves the island herself does she understand that everyone has always thought she was strong but that Caroline needed help. *Newbery Medal, American Book Award for Children's Literature Nominee, American Library Association Notable Children's Books of 1976-1980, American Library Association Best Books for Young Adults, Horn Book Fanfare Honor List, School Library Journal Best Book, Booklist Children's Editors' Choices, New York Times Outstanding Books of 1980*, and *New York Public Library Children's Books.*

1640.   Paterson, Katherine. **Jip: His Story**. New York: Lodestar, 1996. 181p. $15.99. ISBN 0-525-67543-4. 5-9

Jip works for lazy Vermont farm owners in the late 1850s. They told him that he fell out of a wagon near the house when a toddler, and they have supported him since. A stranger arrives and tells Jip that his father might be looking for him, and Jip wants to leave the farm. The stranger turns out to be a slave catcher, and to give the story an acceptable ending, Lyddie, from Paterson's book of the same title, now Jip's teacher, and her Quaker sweetheart Luke help Jip escape to Canada. The complex story presents the dark times before the Civil War. *School Library Journal Best Book.*

1641.   Paterson, Katherine. **Lyddie**. New York: Lodestar, 1991. 192p. $15. ISBN 0-525-67338-5. New York: Puffin, 1994. 192p. $3.99pa. ISBN 0-14-037389-6pa. 6-9

Lyddie, 13, has to take charge of the family after her father dies because her mother seems to have lost her mind. Without economic support, the family must separate, and Lyddie goes to the mills in Lowell, Massachusetts, to work in 1843. There she has to overcome the Quaker prejudice instilled by her mother and begin to assert her rights as a worker and a woman. Because she refuses to comply with the overseer's advances, she loses her job, but by that time she has enough money to save the farm. She also knows that the Quaker in love with her will wait until she finishes college for them to marry. *Bulletin Blue Ribbon Book.*

1642.   Patrick, Diane. **Coretta Scott King**. New York: Franklin Watts, 1991. 128p. $22.10. ISBN 0-531-13005-3. (Impact Biography). 6-9

As the wife of Martin Luther King, Jr., Coretta Scott King (b. 1927) has spent her life supporting a man who was always at the forefront of controversy. When she met King, she was studying in New England to be a concert singer. She works today for civil rights and for world peace. The text examines her early life, her education, her courtship and marriage, her early years of marriage, her work for civil rights with her husband, and her continued endeavors. Notes, Bibliography, and Index.

1643.   Patrick, John J. **The Young Oxford Companion to the Supreme Court of the United States**. New York: Oxford University Press, 1994. 368p. $40. ISBN 0-19-507877-2. 6 up

Alphabetically arranged articles include biographies of all chief justices and associate justices of the Supreme Court, from John Jay in 1789 through Ruth Ginsberg. There are discussions of 100 of the most historically significant cases and decisions with their official citations. Other essays present the core concepts of constitutionalism, ideas and issues, and the procedures and practices of the Court. Each article has cross-references and a recommendation for further reading. Photographs and drawings complement the text. The appendices list the justices in chronological order since the beginning of the Court, with their terms, and information about visiting the Supreme Court. Further Reading and Index.

1644.   Patterson, Charles. **Marian Anderson**. New York: Franklin Watts, 1988. 157p. $22.10. ISBN 0-531-10568-7. (Impact Biography). 7 up

Marian Anderson (1897-1993) was one of the great singers of the twentieth century. As an African American, she was denied entry into various places. Eleanor Roosevelt supported her artistry by arranging for her to sing at the Lincoln Memorial. In 1955, she became the first Black soloist to perform with the Metropolitan Opera Company. The text looks at her career at home and in Europe, where she was a star. Bibliography and Index.

1645.   Patterson, Charles. **The Oxford 50th Anniversary Book of the United Nations**. New York: Oxford University Press, 1995. 237p. $40. ISBN 0-19-508280-X. 7 up

The text gives the history of the United Nations by discussing the various attempts in history to establish such a body before the current United Nations was chartered in 1945. Chapters include peacekeeping missions, disarmament and arms control, helping to establish human rights, the appearance of new nations, international law, and the specialized agencies within the body. Photographs highlight the text. Further Reading and Index.

1646.   Patterson, Charles. **Thomas Jefferson**. New York: Franklin Watts, 1987. 95p. $10.40. ISBN 0-531-10306-4. (First Book). 5-9

Before becoming the third President of the United States, Thomas Jefferson (1743-1826) had participated fully in the life of the new government. The text includes a discussion of his beliefs and their influence on the Declaration of Independence. Index.

1647.   Patterson, Lillie. **A. Philip Randolph: Messenger for the Masses**. New York: Facts on File, 1995. 115p. $17.95. ISBN 0-8160-2827-3. (Makers of America). 7-10

After being born in a poor Florida household, A. Philip Randolph (1889-1979) moved to New York, where he later became a strong advocate for labor and civil rights. The text looks at his life and his contributions, such as leading the Pullman Porter Strike after organizing the union in 1925 and his planning of the March on Washington in 1963. Bibliography, Further Reading, and Index.

1648.   Patterson, Lillie. **Martin Luther King and the Montgomery Bus Boycott**. New York: Facts on File, 1989. 178p. $17.95; $8.95pa. ISBN 0-8160-1605-4; 0-8160-2997-0pa. (Makers of America). 6-9

Martin Luther King, Jr. (1929-1968) reflected the times in which he lived. Primary sources such as his letters, speeches, documents, and diaries help to define him in this text. He believed that America's moral progress was much behind its scientific progress because Americans so often failed to see others as human beings. He led the Civil Rights movement, but from that came other movements—for women, for peace, and for the survival of the planet. Chapters cover the Montgomery bus boycott, King's childhood, his trip to India, the sit-ins, the Freedom Ride, Albany and Birmingham, Washington, the Selma Protest, and his Nobel Peace Prize. Significant Events, For Further Reading, and Index.

1649.   Paulsen. Gary. **Call Me Francis Tucket**. New York: Delacorte, 1995. 97p. $14.95. ISBN 0-385-32116-3. 4-8

While Francis Tucket, 14, is taking a wagon train from Missouri to Oregon in 1848, Pawnee Indians kidnap him. A mountain man helps him escape and teaches him to survive. When he is on his own, he thinks he can handle anything. But he has not considered the difficulties of caring for two abandoned children, Lottie and Billy. When he tries to leave them, he realizes he has made a mistake and returns to find that their benefactor beat them for not working hard enough.

1650.   Paulsen, Gary. **The Cookcamp**. New York: Orchard, 1991. 116p. $13.95. ISBN 0-531-05927-8. 5-8

In this 1944 story, when the five-year-old unnamed protagonist's mother comes home with a man whom she identifies as his uncle and makes sounds with the man on the couch that bother him, his mother sends him to stay with his grandmother in Minnesota, who cooks for a group of men building a road into Canada. The huge men frighten the boy at first, but then they invite him to sit in their trucks and tractors with them, and he begins to feel comfortable in their company. He regrets having to leave. *School Library Journal Best Book.*

1651.   Paulsen, Gary. **Eastern Sun, Winter Moon**. San Diego, CA: Harcourt Brace, 1993. 244p. $11. ISBN 0-15-600203-5pa. YA

Gary Paulsen writes this strong story of his childhood at nine, during World War II, when he went with his mother to live with his military father in the Philippines. The sense of life from a child's microcosmic view of the war raging around him is unsentimental in the telling. Author of books that include *Dogsong, Call Me Francis Tucker*, and *The Rifle*, he survived his childhood by realizing that everything stays the same while everything changes. Nothing ever ends.

1652.   Paulsen, Gary. **Harris and Me: A Summer Remembered**. San Diego, CA: Harcourt Brace, 1993. 157p. $13.95. ISBN 0-15-292877-4. 6-8

The nameless protagonist, victim of alcoholic parents who have abused him, travels in a 1949 pickup to live on his uncle's farm. The dirty farm disgusts him, but he meets Harris, a boy who leads him into surprising adventures. They pretend to be Tarzan in the hayloft, GI Joes in the pigpen with its mire, and Gene Autry riding his horse. The protagonist learns that a real farm and those associated with it can give him a sense of belonging.

1653.   Paulsen, Gary. **Mr. Tucket**. New York: Delacorte, 1994. 176p. $14.95. ISBN 0-385-31169-9. 6-9

Jason Grimes, a mountain man, finds and frees Francis Alphonse Tucket, 14, after Pawnee Indians kidnap him. Grimes calls Francis "Mr. Tucket" and teaches him how to survive on the frontier. Francis meets Jim Bridger and fights the Pawnee while serving his apprenticeship in which he learns to shoot, ride, trap, and trade with the Indians.

1654.   Paulsen, Gary. **Nightjohn**. New York: Delacorte, 1993. 92p. $14. ISBN 0-385-30838-8. 7 up

In the 1850s, the young slave Sarny, 12, knows her owner is raising her to become a breeder like her mother. When the master sees Sarny write in the dirt, he knows someone has been teaching her to read. When no one will tell who is teaching her, he strips the woman who looks after Sarny, harnesses her to a cart, and beats her for not pulling him fast enough. Then he cuts the toes off John, the new slave, who says that he taught her. John escapes but returns at night to continue teaching her so that she can help others become free.

1655.   Paulsen, Gary. **The Rifle**. San Diego, CA: Harcourt Brace, 1995. 105p. $16. ISBN 0-15-292880-4. 7-10

In 1768, Cornish McManus built a rifle that John Byam took into battle during the Revolutionary War. The gun continued to change ownership until one night when Harv exchanged his services for a black velvet portrait of his favorite, Elvis, and the old rifle. He hung the gun over his mantle, never checking to see if it was loaded. It was, and when a spark from the fireplace ignited the black powder, it took the life of an innocent boy in the next house. *New York Public Library Books for the Teen Age* and *Notable Children's Trade Books in the Field of Social Studies.*

1656. Paulsen, Gary. **Tucket's Ride**. New York: Bantam, 1997. 112p. $15.95. ISBN 0-385-32199-6. 5-8
Francis Tucket and his adopted family of Lottie and Billy head west to look for Francis's parents on the Oregon Trail. When they turn south to avoid the early winter, they enter enemy territory during the war between the United States and Mexico. Outlaws capture them, and their loyalty to each other, ability to endure, and intelligence give them hope of escape.

1657. Paulsen, Gary, with Ruth Wright Paulsen. **Woodsong**. New York: Bradbury, 1990. 132p. $15. ISBN 0-02-770221-9. New York: Puffin, 1991. 132p. $4.99pa. ISBN 0-14-034905-7pa. 6 up
Gary Paulsen tells his story of participating in the Iditarod Race for 1,180 miles through Alaska. He describes the physical endurance needed to complete the race across ice and snow and the importance of the sled dogs as a team and individually.

1658. Paulson, Timothy J. **Days of Sorrow; Years of Glory: 1831-1850: From the Nat Turner Revolt to the Fugitive Slave Law**. New York: Chelsea House, 1994. 111p. $18.95; $7.95pa. ISBN 0-7910-2263-3; 0-7910-2552-7pa. (Milestones in Black American History). 6-9
In 1831, Nat Turner led a slave revolt in Virginia. In 1850, the Fugitive Slave Law passed, allowing masters to hunt for fugitive slaves in other states. Among the topics presented about the years in between are the Underground Railway, the abolitionist movement, and the Seminoles in Florida, who harbored escaped slaves in the Everglades. The text shows the desperate desire of people wanting to be free at any cost. Black-and-white reproductions enhance the text. Further Reading and Index.

1659. Peck, Richard. **Voices After Midnight**. New York: Delacorte, 1989. 182p. $14.95. ISBN 0-385-29779-3. New York: Yearling, Dell, 1990. 182p. $3.99pa. ISBN 0-440-40378-2pa. 5-8
Three contemporary children, Chad, Luke, and Heidi, spend two weeks in New York City at a house built in 1888. The three children find themselves in 1888 with the people who lived in the house then. Luke, eight, is fascinated, and his intense love of history shows through the experience. He understands how the people felt then, and he wants to know more about them.

1660. Peduzzi, Kelli. **Ralph Nader**. Milwaukee, WI: Gareth Stevens, 1990. 68p. $16.95. ISBN 0-8368-0098-2. (People Who Have Helped the World). 7-9
Born in 1934 to Lebanese parents, Ralph Nader was always interested in how government worked, but both Princeton and Harvard disappointed him because of their interests in big business rather than the average consumer. In 1965, Nader published a book saying that unsafe cars caused unnecessary accidents and deaths, but automobile manufacturers were uninterested in safety measures. The worst car, he said, was General Motors' Corvair. When Corvair sales fell 93 percent, GM had private detectives investigate Nader's life, trying to find something bad about him. They could not. But Nader found out about the spying, sued, and won a settlement that allowed him to start his public-interest law firm. Among the changes to which his lawyers have contributed are seat belt laws, shock-absorbing car bumpers, and padded dashboards. He is associated with honesty, fairness, and attention to careful research, which has given him the facts that back his claims of unfair business practices. Organizations, Books, Glossary, Chronology, and Index.

1661. Peifer, Charles, Jr. **Soldier of Destiny: A Biography of George Patton**. New York: Dillon Press, 1989. 126p. $13.95. ISBN 0-87518-395-6. (People in Focus). 5 up
George Patton (1885-1945) knew he wanted to be a soldier very early in life because he loved the stories his father read to him about military men in history and literature. Although he had a reading disability, he was able to go to West Point, where his athleticism propelled him into the 1912 Olympics and a fifth-place finish in the pentathlon. His 3rd Army in World War II became an important key to winning the war, spurred onward by his inspiring (and scatological) speeches earning him the nickname "Old Blood and Guts." The text looks at his life and his burial in Luxembourg as he requested. Appendix, Major Events, Bibliography, and Index.

1662. Pellowski, Anne. **First Farm in the Valley: Anna's Story**. Wendy Watson, illustrator. New York: Philomel, 1982. 192p. $9.95. ISBN 0-399-20887-9. 4-7
In 1876, Anna and her family live on their Wisconsin farm. She is happy to have a friend of her age who is also Polish. She helps her mother do chores and enjoys the Fourth of July fireworks, but does not understand what the adults mean when they talk about a Polish government ruled by people who speak German. She wonders how the Kaiser and Bismarck can have more power than kings and queens, but she knows that the reason influences why some of the Polish immigrants have come to Wisconsin.

1663. Pemberton, William E. **George Bush**. Vero Beach, FL: Rourke, 1993. 112p. $22.60. ISBN 0-86625-478-1. 4 up
The text starts with the 1990s crisis that led to the Persian Gulf War and returns to George Bush's childhood, when he was a child of privilege in New England born in 1924. It looks at his achievements in business and public service before he became Vice President and then President. Photographs, Time Line, Glossary, Bibliography, Media Resources, and Index.

1664.   Pendergraft, Patricia. **As Far as Mill Springs**. New York: Philomel, 1991. 153p. $15.95. ISBN 0-399-22102-6. 5 up

After living most of his life in foster homes and enduring much abuse, Robert hears adults talking through a closed door in 1932. They say that his biological mother lives in a nearby town. He and one of the girls from the home leave for the town by riding in boxcars with hobos. They become separated but find each other on Christmas, the day after Robert turns 13. Robert does not find his mother, but he finds an old woman who needs him as much as he needs her.

1665.   Pendergraft, Patricia. **Brushy Mountain**. New York: Philomel, 1989. 207p. $14.95. ISBN 0-399-21610-3. 5-7

Arney, 13, lives with his mother and sister in a tiny mountain town after his father died in World War II. He hates one of the town's old men and wants to kill him, but instead, he ends up saving him three times: from drowning, from a fire, and from an explosion. He also helps his sister deliver Old Man Hooker's twin grandsons, one of them dead. The mother names the remaining one Arney.

1666.   Pendergraft, Patricia. **Hear the Wind Blow**. New York: Philomel, 1988. 208p. $14.95. ISBN 0-399-21528-X. New York: Point, Scholastic, 1989. 208p. $2.75pa. ISBN 0-590-42273-1pa. 5 up

Isadora, 12, attends school in a small town near the beginning of the twentieth century. Various things happen in the town, and people talk about the male schoolteacher, who marries a woman already pregnant, and Isadora's best friend, who dies when her parents choose herbal over medicinal treatment. One of the good things that happens is that Isadora gets her wish, which is to take dancing lessons.

1667.   Pennebaker, Ruth. **Don't Think Twice**. New York: Henry Holt, 1996. 196p. $15.95. ISBN 0-8050-4407-8. 7-12

In 1967, Anne, 17, finds herself in a home for unwed mothers rather than in her senior year of high school. She remembers her mistake of thinking she was in love, which got her into her situation. Then she relates the reasons that others are there. A father raped one, a pastor seduced another, and contraception failed a third. Because she has alienated her family, her focus falls on the others from other faiths, social classes, and regions of the country who are waiting with her.

1668.   Perez, N. A. **Breaker**. Boston: Houghton Mifflin, 1988. 206p. $13.95. ISBN 0-395-34437-5. 7-9

Pat and his brother are "breaker boys" in a Pennsylvania coal mine where their father died. The boys are also members of the Irish Catholic community, which does not welcome the more recent Polish immigrants. When Pat gets to know some of his Polish neighbors while working in the union war leading to the coal miners' strike of 1902, he realizes that they are likable people.

1669.   Perez, N. A. **The Slopes of War**. Boston: Houghton Mifflin, 1984. 202p. $14.95. ISBN 0-395-35642-3. 7 up

Buck, 18, fights for the Union army in Gettysburg while Bekah, 15, stays at home. When that battle ends on July 4, 1863, they find that their lives have changed dramatically.

1670.   Perl, Lila. **From Top Hats to Baseball Caps, from Bustles to Blue Jeans: Why We Dress the Way We Do**. New York: Clarion, 1990. 118p. $14.95. ISBN 0-899-19872-4. 5-9

Perl thinks that through the years in Western Europe and the United States such things as social class, women's liberation, war, and technology have influenced styles of clothing. She includes chapters on pants, skirts, shoes, and hats. The text is complemented with photographs and drawings. Bibliography and Index.

1671.   Perry, James M. **Arrogant Armies: Great Military Disasters and the Generals Behind Them**. New York: Wiley, 1996. 301p. $27.95. ISBN 0-471-11976-8. YA

During two-and-one-half centuries of colonialism, many military expeditions failed. Among them recounted here are General Edward Bradock's failure in the Ohio Valley, General Gordon's loss of Khartoum in the Sudan, General Baratieri's defeat in Ethiopia, and General Townshend's loss in the Mesopotamian campaign of World War I. The last segment concerns General Silvestre's Spanish troops battling the Rifs in Morocco from 1921 to 1926. Loss of life and degradation of situation was immeasurable in these displays of egotism. Bibliography and Index.

1672.   Peters, Arthur King. **Seven Trails West**. New York: Abbeville, 1996. 252p. $39.95. ISBN 1-55859-782-4. YA

The text documents the creation and the utilization of the seven major trails across the American continent from 1804 to 1869. They are the Lewis and Clark expedition, the Santa Fe Trail, the Oregon-California Trail, the Mormon Trail, the Pony Express, the Transcontinental Telegraph, and the Transcontinental Railroad. Illustrations and reproductions enhance the text along with capsule biographies of people who traveled the trails. Chronology, Bibliography, Notes, and Index.

1673. Petersen, David. **Meriwether Lewis and William Clark: Soldiers, Explorers, and Partners in History**. Chicago: Childrens Press, 1988. 152p. $19.30. ISBN 0-516-03264-X. 6 up

Meriwether Lewis (1774-1809) and William Clark (1770-1838) explored Thomas Jefferson's new addition to the United States, the Louisiana Purchase. They traveled from St. Louis to the mouth of the Columbia River in the Pacific Northwest. This biography of their lives emphasizes the value of the many scientific contributions of their expedition. Timeline and Index.

1674. Peterson, Robert W. **Cages to Jump Shots: Pro Basketball's Early Years**. New York: Oxford University Press, 1990. 224p. $19.95; $9.95pa. ISBN 0-19-505310-9; 0-19-507261-8pa. YA

In 1891, James Naismith created the rules for professional basketball. Teams played in gas-lit social halls long before they went to Madison Square Garden. In looking at the first 50 years of the game, Peterson believes that changes in society have greatly affected the game and the teams. He chronicles events during that time and includes interviews with some of the players. Chronology, Bibliography, and Index.

1675. Petrillo, Daniel J. **Robert F. Kennedy**. New York: Chelsea House, 1989. 112p. $18.95; $7.95pa. ISBN 1-55546-840-3; 0-7910-0581-Xpa. (World Leaders Past and Present). 7 up

Robert Kennedy (1925-1968) was assassinated while attempting to get the Democratic Party's nomination for President of the United States. He had served as attorney general for his brother, John F. Kennedy, and then became a senator from New York. The text looks at his life and the political climate in which this tragedy occurred. Photographs enhance the text. Chronology, Further Reading, and Index.

1676. Petry, Ann. **Tituba of Salem Village**. New York: Crowell, 1988. 254p. $14.89; $3.95pa. ISBN 0-690-04766-5; 0-06-440403-Xpa. 7 up

The minister's slave Tituba tells fortunes with tarot cards and can spin fine threads. In 1692, these abilities make her a focus of witchcraft accusations in Salem, Massachusetts, when five girls tell the town of her skills. The town convicts her of being a witch, and she suffers accordingly.

1677. Pfeffer, Susan B. **Justice for Emily**. New York: Delacorte, 1997. 160p. $14.95. ISBN 0-385-32259-3. 5-7

In the sequel to *Nobody's Daughter*, Emily has to face a town that dislikes her because she has told the truth about the death of a child in the orphan home where she once stayed. Her best friend is also an outcast because her father is a mill labor organizer and her mother a suffragette in this early-twentieth-century New England town. The school board has to decide whether it will expel Emily for misdeeds that she did not commit.

1678. Pfeffer, Susan Beth. **Nobody's Daughter**. New York: Delacorte, 1995. 154p. $14.95. ISBN 0-385-32106-6. 4-7

Emily, 11, has to go to the Austen Home for Orphaned Girls when her great-aunt Mabel dies. She expects to join her sister, adopted at birth, but the sister's family refuses her. After enduring the taunts of the town's wealthy young girls, having her braids cut, knowing how one of the orphans died, and not being able to play her beloved piano, she finds a home with the librarian, who has one of the new automobiles, and her mother in the early twentieth century.

1679. Pfeifer, Kathryn Browne. **Henry O. Flipper**. New York: Twenty-First Century Books, 1993. 80p. $14.95. ISBN 0-8050-2351-8. (African-American Soldiers). 4-7

Henry Ossian Flipper (1856-1940) was the first African American graduate of West Point, but he was dishonorably discharged from the army in 1881. Nearly 100 years later, attempts were made to have this decision reversed. Photographs supplement the text. Bibliography, Chronology, and Index.

1680. Pflueger, Lynda. **Stonewall Jackson: Confederate General**. Springfield, NJ: Enslow, 1997. 128p. $18.95. ISBN 0-89490-783-2. (Historical American Biographies). 6-9

Stonewall Jackson (1824-1863) led Confederate troops who followed him faithfully because he planned carefully and was fearless in battle. This biography looks at his impact on American history as it examines his life. Fact boxes and maps augment the text. Notes, Glossary, Further Reading, and Index.

1681. Phelan, Mary Kay. **The Story of the Boston Massacre**. Allan Eitzen, illustrator. New York: Crowell/HarperCollins, 1990. 160p. $13.89. ISBN 0-690-04883-1. 4-7

On the evening of March 5, 1770, angry Boston citizens stormed the Custom House. Soldiers began to fire on the crowd, and five men are killed, along with six others wounded. People, however, think the men must have a fair trial, and John Adams decides to defend them. The text looks at the actions prior to the killings and the trial and verdict after. Bibliography and Index.

1682.   Phelps, J. Alfred. **Chappie: Daniel James, Jr., America's First Black Four Star General**. Novato, CA: Presidio, 1991. 358p. $9.95pa. ISBN 0-89141-464-9pa. YA

Daniel James (1920-1978) was an air force officer who happened to be Black rather than a "Black" air force officer. He worked within the established system, showed his worth, and took increasingly responsible positions until he became the spokesman for America's Vietnam policies. He excelled in the service, and he had strong relationships outside the military with family and friends. Bibliography and Index.

1683.   Phelps, J. Alfred. **They Had a Dream: The Story of African-American Astronauts**. Novato, CA: Presidio, 1994. 291p. $24.95. ISBN 0-89141-497-5. YA

The text recounts the history of African Americans' involvement in the U.S. space program. The first African American accepted into the program, Edward J. Dwight, Jr., was released after John F. Kennedy's death in 1963. Others continued where he did not. The astronauts profiled here are Robert H. Lawrence, Jr.; Guion S. Bluford, Jr.; Ronald E. McNair; Frederick D. Gregory; Charles F. Bolden, Jr.; Mae C. Jemison; and Bernard Harris, Jr. Other chapters discuss the difficulties of the *Challenger* explosion and what followed it in the space program. Epilogue, Notes, Selected Bibliography, and Index.

1684.   Philip, Neil, ed. **Singing America: Poems That Define a Nation**. Michael McCurdy, illustrator. New York: Viking, 1995. 160p. $19.99. ISBN 0-670-86150-2. 6 up

This collection of American poems that give different views of the country begins with Walt Whitman's "I Hear America Singing" and ends with Woody Guthrie's "This Land Is Your Land." In between are poems about cities, tribes, animals, people, and places. The overview of American life collected in such a way is varied and interesting. Index of Poets, Index of First Lines and Titles, Subject Index, and Further Reading.

1685.   Phillips, Ann. **A Haunted Year**. Teresa Flavin, illustrator. New York: Macmillan, 1994. 175p. $14.95. ISBN 0-02-774605-4. 5-8

Florence, bored with Sunday life in 1910, finds 12-year-old George's photograph in a family album. Her aunts do not want to talk about him. With the photograph and a magic-circle ritual, she calls up the ghost of George, and he becomes her playmate. But George soon realizes that he can come to her whenever he wants, and he takes control of the situation by coming at night and keeping her up. With the help of cousins who become friends, she finally rids herself of the unexpected burden.

1686.   Pickford, Nigel. **The Atlas of Shipwrecks & Treasure**. New York: Dorling Kindersley, 1994. 200p. $29.95. ISBN 1-56458-599-9. YA

Maps identify the locations of ships that were wrecked during a particular period of history. Following these are a description of the find and facts about the history of shipbuilding and cargo gleaned from the recovery of the ruin. Photographs complement the text. Periods covered are the Bronze Age to Byzantium (up to AD 1000), the Vikings (beginning in the ninth century AD), Chinese junks (early fifteenth century), the Levantine trade (1000-1500), Portuguese carracks (sixteenth century to mid-seventeenth), the Armada (sixteenth century), Spanish plate fleets (sixteenth and seventeenth centuries), pirates and privateers (late sixteenth to eighteenth centuries), East Indiamen (seventeenth and eighteenth centuries), the Age of Revolution (eighteenth and early nineteenth centuries), great collections (eighteenth and nineteenth centuries), the rush for gold (nineteenth century), mail ships and liners (nineteenth and twentieth centuries), and World War II (1940-1945). Gazetteer Maps, Shipwreck Listings, Glossary, Bibliography, and Index.

1687.   Pietrusza, David. **The End of the Cold War**. San Diego, CA: Lucent, 1995. 112p. $16.95. ISBN 1-56006-280-0. (World History). 7-9

To persons familiar with the oppression of the Soviet regime and its tentacles, the fall of the Berlin Wall on November 9, 1989, almost 30 years after its erection in 1961, was an astonishing sight broadcast on international television. The text traces the beginnings of Eastern European Communism in the twentieth century and the living conditions of those caught in its clutches. It establishes that the first breach with Communist leaders occurred in 1948 in Yugoslavia, but Stalin quickly quelled the revolt. The text presents Poland's Solidarity stand and subsequent defeat before Gorbachev's rise to leadership and Solidarity's triumph after Gorbachev took office as well as other uprisings and failures throughout the regime. The chipping of the Soviet Bloc led to its collapse and the period afterward—still uncertain, but at least unfettered. Notes, Glossary, For Further Exploration, Works Consulted, and Index.

1688.   Pietrusza, David. **The Invasion of Normandy**. San Diego, CA: Lucent, 1995. 110p. $19.95. ISBN 1-56006-413-7. (Battles of World War II). 7 up

Photographs, maps, and sidebars help tell the story of the Allied forces' invasion of Normandy on June 6, 1944. The text discusses the prior catastrophes at Slapton Sands and Dieppe, which gave the Allies reason to think that the invasion might not work. The text gives background on the planning involved and the people who helped it occur. It also discusses the problems that occurred on beaches other than the ones on which the Americans landed, Omaha and Utah. Bibliography, Chronology, Further Reading, Glossary, and Index.

1689. Pietrusza, David. **John F. Kennedy**. San Diego, CA: Lucent, 1997. 128p. $16.95. ISBN 1-56006-263-0. (Mysterious Deaths). 7 up

The text begins with John F. Kennedy's trip to Dallas, Texas, and details the shooting, Lee Harvey Oswald's life, and the weakness of the Warren Commission Report. It also looks at the various conspiracy theories that have surfaced in the years since the assassination and gives objective critiques of their strengths and weaknesses. Sidebars display other information such as capsule biographies of other people, photographs, or events. Bibliography, Further Reading, and index.

1690. Piggins, Carol Ann. **A Multicultural Portrait of the Civil War**. Freeport, NY: Marshall Cavendish, 1994. 80p. $18.95. ISBN 1-85435-660-7. (Perspectives). 7 up

The slave trade, necessary for supporting the Southern economy, and Andrew Jackson's removal of Native Americans from their land (contrary to a Supreme Court directive) were just some of the seeds of the Civil War. Not everyone supported slavery, and many risked their own lives to help escaped slaves. During and after the war, other minority groups also suffered consequences. The text looks at their problems as well. Chronology, Glossary, Further Reading, and Index.

1691. Pile, Robert B. **Top Entrepreneurs and Their Businesses**. Minneapolis, MN: Oliver Press, 1993. 159p. $14.95. ISBN 1-881508-04-8. 4-7

In this collective biography are several profiles of twentieth-century Americans who have created their own businesses. They are Lewis Brittin, a Connecticut Colonel, and his flying; L. L. Bean, who hated wet feet; Walt Disney and his animation; Bruce Barton, an advertising wizard; Nathan Cummings and his Sara Lee brand; Bud Hillerich, who made baseball bats; Sam Walton and Walmart Drugs; Rose Totino and her pizza; and John Johnson, an African American who founded a publishing company and who said "don't get mad, get smart."

1692. Pile, Robert B. **Women Business Leaders**. Minneapolis, MN: Oliver Press, 1995. 160p. $14.95. ISBN 1-881508-24-2. (Profiles). 5 up

The women included here actively pursued their goals to create businesses of significance in the economy. Some of them had to overcome physical impairments as well as gender bias. They are Mary Kay Ash (cosmetics), Helen Boehm (porcelain figures), Leeann Chin (Chinese food products), Ellen Terry (real estate), Ella Musolina-Alber (sports and entertainment promoter), Louise Woerner (health care), Masako Boissonnault (commercial design), and Marilyn Hamilton (wheelchair design). More Notable Twentieth-Century Businesswomen, Bibliography, and Index.

1693. Pimlott, John, ed. **The Elite: The Special Forces of the World, Vol. 1**. New York: Marshall Cavendish, 1987. 160p. $189.95 set. ISBN 0-86307-792-7. YA

Articles laid out as collages of text, photographs of soldiers and battles, maps, and illustrations of equipment tell about the elite forces in the world that have developed and controlled warfare in the twentieth century. Included in this volume are stories about the Nachtjagdgeschwader 1 in Nuremberg, 1944; German 7th Armored Division in France, 1940; the 7th Duke of Edinburgh's Own Gurkha Rifles in the Falklands, 1982; South African Recce Commandos in Namibia, 1980s; training in the Royal Marines; weapons and equipment of British paratroops of World War II; D-Day landing of the 9th Battalion, the Parachute Regiment, in Normandy, 1944; and the 1st Airborne Division at Arnhem, 1944. Index.

1694. Pimlott, John, ed. **The Elite: The Special Forces of the World, Vol. 2**. New York: Marshall Cavendish, 1987. 160p. $189.95 set. ISBN 0-86307-794-3. YA

Articles laid out as collages of text, photographs of soldiers and battles, maps, and illustrations of equipment tell about the elite forces in the world that have developed and controlled warfare in the twentieth century. Included in this volume are stories about the Israeli Golani Brigade and the Golan Heights in 1967 and Lebanon in 1982; the No. 11 Squadron of the Pakistan Air Force at Punjab in 1965; Operation Kipling and the SAS in France 1944 and Germany 1945; Scorpions and Scimitars in the Falklands, 1982; French 3rd Colonial Parachute, chasseurs alpins, and 9th Zouave Regiment, Algeria, 1956-1960; Suffolk Regiment in Malaya, 1949-1953; Soviet 105th Guards Airborne Division in Afghanistan, 1979; American Flying Tigers in China, 1941-1942; Grossdeutschland Regiment in France 1940 and Soviet Union 1943; Japanese suicide units, 1944-1945; South Vietnamese marines, 1971; Explosive Ordnance Disposal Units in Northern Ireland, 1972; Popski's Private Army in the Western Desert and Italy, 12th Submarine Flotilla of the Royal Navy in Norway, 1943; and the 22nd Special Air Service Regiment in Oman, 1958-1959. Index.

1695. Pimlott, John, ed. **The Elite: The Special Forces of the World, Vol. 3**. New York: Marshall Cavendish, 1987. 160p. $189.95 set. ISBN 0-86307-793-5. YA

Articles laid out as collages of text, photographs of soldiers and battles, maps, and illustrations of equipment tell about the elite forces in the world that have developed and controlled warfare in the twentieth century. Included in this volume are stories about the German Brandenburgers in Europe, 1939-1940;

training and deployment of the Spetsnaz, Soviet Special Forces; RAF Glider Pilot Regiment at D-day, 1944; Israeli 202nd Parachute Brigade in the Sinai, 1967; Chindits in Burma, 1943; Green Berets, formation and training; the U.S. Special Forces in Vietnam; the Special Air Service (SAS) formation in 1941; Egyptian Commandos in the Yom Kippur War, 1973; and the U.S. 82nd Airborne Division invasion of Grenada, 1983. Index.

1696. Pimlott, John, ed. **The Elite: The Special Forces of the World, Vol. 4**. New York: Marshall Cavendish, 1987. 160p. $189.95 set. ISBN 0-86307-796-X. YA

Articles laid out as collages of text, photographs of soldiers and battles, maps, and illustrations of equipment tell about the elite forces in the world that have developed and controlled warfare in the twentieth century. Included in this volume are stories about the Royal Netherlands Marine Corps and the South Moluccan hijack in 1977; U.S. 4th Fighter-Interceptor Wing in Korea, 1950-1953; USAF 3rd Aerospace Rescue and Recovery Group in Vietnam; SAS in Yemen, 1963, World War II; World War I; and training for the West German Fallschirmjäger Paratroops. Index.

1697. Pimlott, John, ed. **The Elite: The Special Forces of the World, Vol. 5**. New York: Marshall Cavendish, 1987. 160p. $189.95 set. ISBN 0-86307-795-1. YA

Articles made up of collages of text, photographs of soldiers and battles, maps, and illustrations of equipment tell about the elite forces in the world that have developed and controlled warfare in the twentieth century. Included in this volume are stories about the Rhodesian SAS in Zambia, 1979; the U.S. 322nd Bombardment Group in Europe during 1943; Kampfgruppe Peiper in Ardennes, 1944; 73rd Hanoverian Fusilieres in World War I, France, 1918; Israeli Defence Force, Entebbe, 1976; USAF 44th Tactical Fighter Squadron in Vietnam, 1964-1971; U.S. 2nd Marine Raider Battalion, Guadalcanal in 1942; No. 249 RAF Squadron in Malta, 1941-1943; U.S. Army Tunnel Rats in Vietnam; 28th Marine Regiment in Iwo Jima, 1945; and the Soviet Air Force 16th Guards Fighter Regiment, 1943. Index.

1698. Pimlott, John. **Middle East: A Background to the Conflicts**. New York: Gloucester, Franklin Watts, 1991. 36p. $11.90. ISBN 0-531-17329-1. (Hotspots). 3-7

The text, starting with a brief summary of the Gulf War in 1991, gives an examination of the nineteenth-century conflicts leading to this war. Additional information about the Arab-Israeli difficulties shows that peace in this area has a history of violence and discord to overcome. Photographs supplement the text. Chronology, Glossary, and Index.

1699. Pinchot, Jane. **The Mexicans in America**. Minneapolis, MN: Lerner, 1989. 94p. $17.50; $5.95pa. ISBN 0-8225-0222-4; 0-8225-1016-2pa. (In America). 5 up

This brief history of the Mexicans in the United States tells about their life in the American Southwest before statehood, the United States's acquisition of their land, and their individual contributions to American life. Index.

1700. Plain, Nancy. **Mary Cassatt: An Artist's Life**. New York: Dillon Press, 1994. 168p. $13.95; $7.95pa. ISBN 0-87518-597-5; 0-382-24720-5pa. (People in Focus). 6 up

Mary Cassatt (1844-1926) knew by the time she was 16 that she wanted to become a professional artist. She was willing to take what she viewed as the narrow and hard path to achieve her goal. In Paris, she initially found a stuffy, aristocratic view of painting. In rebellion, she joined Degas and other Impressionists in creating a different style of painting. Photographs and reproductions of her work highlight the text. Bibliography and Index.

1701. Platt, Randall B. **Honor Bright**. New York: Delacorte, 1997. 224p. $14.95. ISBN 0-385-32216-X. 7-10

Teddy, 14, feels as if she is fighting a private war against the backdrop of World War II in 1944. Her mother is too perfect, and her twin brother is disagreeable. She has to spend the summer at the beach with her grandmother, a woman she has never met. But her stay with her grandmother opens up the past and the wounds that separated her mother and her grandmother years previously. What she learns ultimately keeps her from making a similar decision.

1702. Platt, Richard. **Pirate**. Tina Chambers, illustrator. New York: Knopf, 1995. 64p. $19. ISBN 0-679-87255-8. (Eyewitness). 5-8

Photographs of artifacts and drawings complement the text, presented in two-page spreads that cover different topics. They include the pirates of ancient Greece and Rome, the raiders of the north, the Barbary Coast in the eleventh century, the corsairs of Malta during the sixteenth and seventeenth centuries, and the privateers, buccaneers, and pirates of the Caribbean. Other topics are women pirates like Mary Read, the Jolly Roger flag, pirate life, pirates in the Indian Ocean, American privateers, the French corsairs, and pirates of the China Sea. Index.

1703. Platt, Richard. **The Smithsonian Visual Timeline of Inventions**. New York: Dorling Kindersley, 1994. 64p. $16.95. ISBN 1-56458-675-8. 5-9

Each segment contains an overview of the period followed by a timeline presenting inventions helpful to counting and communication, daily life and health, agriculture and industry, and travel and conquest. A brief list of world events correlates to the inventions. For example, the closed-eye needle appeared in 1450. Time segments are 600,000 BC (Fire, etc.) to AD 1299 for the first inventions; 1300-1779 for inventions motivated by printing and the spread of ideas; 1780-1869 and the rise of steam power and the Industrial Revolution; 1870-1939 and the use of electric power in the modern world; and 1940-2000, when transistors and information seem most important. Index of Inventions and Index of Inventors.

1704. Pleasant Company. **Addy's Cook Book 1864**. Middleton, WI: Pleasant, 1994. 44p. $5.95pa. ISBN 1-56247-123-6pa. (American Girls Pastimes). 3-7

Addie cooks the foods available during the Civil War using recipes and cooking utensils then in use. The recipes for breakfast and dinner are updated for contemporary kitchens and include such foods as pork sausage and gravy, sweet potato pone, and hoppin' John (a mixture of black-eyed peas, bacon, and other ingredients).

1705. Pleasant Company. **Kirsten's Cookbook**. Middleton, WI: Pleasant, 1994. 44p. $5.95pa. ISBN 1-56247-111-2pa. (American Girls Pastimes). 3-7

In 1854, Kirsten lives in a one-room log cabin on the Minnesota frontier. Her family came from Sweden and joined other immigrants who had come to the new land. Their recipes and menus reflect their Swedish heritage. After the breakfast and dinner recipes, the favorite foods presented are potato soup, Swedish meatballs, fresh applesauce, Swedish pancakes, St. Lucia buns, and *pepparkakor* cookies.

1706. Pleasant Company. **Samantha's Cookbook**. Middleton, WI: Pleasant, 1994. 44p. $5.95pa. ISBN 1-56247-114-7pa. (American Girls Pastimes). 3-7

In 1904, when Samantha, an orphan, lives with her grandmother, she follows strict rules of etiquette in setting the table and serving the food. Menus and recipes for breakfast, dinner, and tea show that the favorite foods are apple brown betty, jelly biscuits, cream cheese and walnut sandwiches, chicken salad sandwiches, gingerbread, and lemon ice.

1707. Plowden, Martha Ward. **Famous Firsts of Black Women**. Ronald Jones, illustrator. Gretna, LA: Pelican, 1993. 155p. $15.95. ISBN 0-88289-973-2. 6-9

The text focuses on notable African American women who have helped shape American life, including contributors in the fields of politics, sports, and the arts. The women selected are Marian Anderson (1902-1993), Mary McLeod Bethune (1875-1955), Gwendolyn Brooks (b. 1917), Diahann Carroll (b. 1935), Shirley Chisholm (b. 1924), Althea Gibson (b. 1927), Patricia Roberts Harris (1924-1985), Barbara Jordan (1936-1996), Elizabeth Duncan Koontz (b. 1919), Edmonia Lewis (1845-1890), Hattie McDaniel (1898-1952), Constance Baker Motley (b. 1920), Rosa Parks (b. 1913), Leontyne Price (b. 1927), Wilma Rudolph (b. 1940), Sojourner Truth (1797?-1883), Harriet Tubman (1820-1913), Maggie Lena Walker (1867-1934), Ida B. Wells-Barnett (?-1931), and Phillis Wheatley (1753-1784). Illustrations complement the text. Further Reading.

1708. Polacco, Patricia, author/illustrator. **Pink and Say**. New York: Philomel, 1994. Unpaged. $15.95. ISBN 0-399-22671-0. 4 up

Pinkus (Pink) Aylee saves Sheldon (Say), 15, after he has been shot in the leg for deserting his unit of the Union army during the Civil War. Pink takes him home to his mother, a slave still living on the plantation after everyone else has left. While they are healing, marauders come and murder Pink's mother, the woman who has made Say feel like he belonged to her. The two boys, almost immediately captured, end up at Andersonville, where Say survives; Pink is most likely hung hours after they arrive. *Jefferson Cup Award*.

1709. Polikoff, Barbara G. **Herbert C. Hoover: 31st President of the United States**. Ada, OK: Garrett Educational, 1990. 120p. $17.26. ISBN 0-944483-58-5. (Presidents of the United States). 5-9

Herbert C. Hoover (1874-1964) attended Stanford University and became a mining engineer. He served presidents Wilson, Harding, and Coolidge before being elected to the presidency himself. As the Depression developed, people accused Hoover of refusing to pay hungry veterans and then routing them with army troops. What Hoover did not know was that MacArthur, charged with looking after the veterans, was disobeying Hoover's directions and choosing to act as he wanted. Hoover, in turn, dismayed by the harsh charges, accused many rebellious veterans of being Communists. These and other problems led to Roosevelt defeating him in his bid for a second term. Bibliography and Index.

1710. Polikoff, Barbara G. **James Madison: 4th President of the United States**. Ada, OK: Garrett Educational, 1989. 118p. $17.26. ISBN 0-944483-22-4. (Presidents of the United States). 5-9

James Madison (1751-1836), born in Virginia, attended Princeton University (then the College of New Jersey), and returned home to serve on the Virginia Council of State under Governors Thomas Jefferson and Patrick Henry. He was a delegate to the Second Continental Congress, where he advocated separation of church and state and a strong central government. He wrote the *Federalist* essays, married Dolley Payne Todd, and served as President for two terms. Bibliography and Index.

1711. Pollack, Jill S. **Shirley Chisholm**. New York: Franklin Watts, 1994. 64p. $19.90. ISBN 0-531-20168-6. (First Book). 6 up

In her grandparents' Barbados home, Shirley St. Hill (Chisholm) learned to read by age four. She stayed with them until 1934, when she went to be with her parents in Brooklyn during the Depression. There, she heard her father discussing politics with friends, and became interested in it herself. Although she became a teacher after college, she still loved politics. Soon she ran for office and went to the state capital of New York as an assemblywoman. She followed this job by becoming a representative to Congress. She retired in 1982, and in 1985 became the first president of the national Political Congress of Black Women.

1712. Pollack, Jill S. **Women on the Hill: A History of Women in Congress**. New York: Franklin Watts, 1996. 207p. $22.70. ISBN 0-531-11306-X. (Women Then—Women Now). 9 up

This history of the women who have served in the House of Representatives and in the Senate begins with the election of Jeanette Rankin to the House of Representatives in 1917. Special emphasis is given to Rankin, Margaret Chase Smith, and Geraldine Ferraro. Also included are capsule biographies of some of the men around them describing their campaign styles and their interests. A flowchart shows the process of an idea becoming a law. Photographs, Further Reading, Notes, and Index.

1713. Pollard, Michael. **The Nineteenth Century**. New York: Facts on File, 1993. 78p. $17.95. ISBN 0-8160-2791-9. (Illustrated History of the World). 4-7

In the nineteenth century, towns and the cities showed changes from the old way of life. The British went into India and Americans went West in attempts to build empires. The slave trade led to the Civil War in the United States. Other changes affected Europe, Africa, Australia, and New Zealand as steamships reshaped travel, the oil age began, and the communication revolution started. Illustrations highlight the text. Glossary, Further Reading, and Index.

1714. Pollard, Michael. **The Red Cross and the Red Crescent**. New York: New Discovery, 1994. 64p. $7.95. ISBN 0-02-774720-4. (Organizations That Help the World). 4-8

The Red Cross and the Red Crescent are two organizations created in the nineteenth century to help soldiers on the battlefield receive help more quickly. Neutral emergency units became available that could offer medical aid without threatening the enemy. In Europe, Jean-Herni Dunant watched the Battle of Solferino in 1859. In 1862, he wrote a book about it in which he suggested ways to alleviate some of the deaths. At the same time, Clara Barton in America had become interested in helping prisoners and the wounded. In 1863, an international conference to launch the Red Cross movement opened in Geneva with representatives from 16 countries. On August 22, 1964, the first Geneva Convention had signatures from 12 countries. During the Franco-Prussian war of 1870-1871, the Red Cross helped trace and report on prisoners of war, and Clara Barton provided relief on the battlefields. In 1873, Barton returned to the United States to begin setting up the Red Cross in America. Various other treaties and disagreements continued to refine the process. Since then, the Red Cross (Red Crescent in Islamic countries) has been a major relief organization. Glossary, Important Dates, How You Can Help, and Index.

1715. Pope, Elizabeth. **The Sherwood Ring**. 1958. Magnolia, MA: Peter Smith, 1989. $19.30. ISBN 0-8446-6416-2. New York: Puffin, Penguin, 1992. $3.99pa. ISBN 0-14-034911-1pa. 7 up

After her father's death in Scotland, Peggy goes to live in the family's home in New York State in this historical fantasy. When Peggy tries to find out who the girl was who met her at the train on horseback, she discovers that the girl, Barbara Grahame, lived in 1773. Peggy is transported into the time and learns much about the American Revolution and family intrigues. *Newbery Honor Book* and *American Library Association Notable Books for Children*.

1716. Posner, Gerald L. **Case Closed: Lee Harvey Oswald and the Assassination of JFK**. New York: Random House, 1993. 607p. $14.95pa. ISBN 0-385-47446-6pa. YA

Posner believes that Lee Harvey Oswald was the only person who shot at President John F. Kennedy on November 22, 1963. He uses computerized enhancements of bullet trajectories as conclusive evidence for the case. He examines all of the conspiracy theories and discards them one by one. What the conspiracy theories do not have is a motivation, while Oswald's unhappy childhood and disillusionment with the American and Soviet political systems might be the motivation necessary. Bibliography and Index.

1717.   Potter, Joan, and Constance Claytor. **African-American Firsts**. Alison Munoz, illustrator. Elizabethtown, NY: Pinto Press, 1994, 336p. $14.95pa. ISBN 0-9632476-1-1pa. YA

Presented as questions with answers, the text covers many facts about African Americans throughout history. The information is arranged according to general categories and includes business, education, entertainment, film, history, journalism, law and government, literature, the military, music, religion, science and medicine, sports, theater and dance, and visual arts. Select Bibliography and Index.

1718.   Potter, Robert R. **Benjamin Franklin**. Englewood Cliffs, NJ: Silver Burdett, 1991. 138p. $10.95; $6.95pa. ISBN 0-382-24173-8; 0-382-24178-9pa. (Pioneers in Change). 5-9

This text on Benjamin Franklin (1706-1790) starts with his firsts: flying the kite to test electricity; suggesting that the union begin with the 13 original colonies; and inventing the lightning rod, bifocal glasses, and the Franklin stove. He also wrote documents for publication and for the public good in the Declaration of Independence and the Constitution. As a youth, he and his family faced one of the main enemies of the time: disease, and the losses there helped prepare him for his future disappointments. His humor and intelligence as a self-made man propelled him into a prominent role during the creation of the new country. Engravings, Important Dates, Bibliography, and Index.

1719.   Potter, Robert R. **Buckminster Fuller**. Englewood Cliffs, NJ: Silver Burdett, 1990. 152p. $13.98. ISBN 0-382-09967-2. (Pioneers in Change). 5-9

Buckminster Fuller (1895-1983) attributed his interest in shapes to the poor eyesight he had as a child, when he saw everything in large squares, triangles, or circles. He was, therefore, always interested in "the big picture." Among his accomplishments were 25 inventions, one of them the famous geodesic dome; 52 trips around the world; 17 books; 47 honorary degrees; and many other things. He was a scientist, an inventor, an architect, a mathematician, a historian, a philosopher, an economist, and a prophet. The text looks at this many-faceted man and his interests. Bibliography and Index.

1720.   Potter, Robert R. **Jefferson Davis: Confederate President**. Austin, TX: Raintree/Steck-Vaughn, 1994. 128p. $16.98. ISBN 0-8114-2330-1. (American Troublemakers). 6 up

Jefferson Davis (1808-1889) was born eight months before and only 100 miles from Abraham Lincoln. He went to West Point but resigned to become a plantation owner where he became thoroughly committed to the aristocratic Southern way of life and the value of states' rights. He was selected to be President of the Confederacy after the South seceded from the Union, was imprisoned without trial after the South's defeat, and refused to swear allegiance to the United States. Maps, Photographs, Key Dates, Glossary, Places to Visit, Bibliography and Recommended Readings, and Index.

1721.   Potter, Robert R. **John Brown: Militant Abolitionist**. Austin, TX: Raintree/Steck-Vaughn, 1994. 128p. $16.98. ISBN 0-8114-2378-6. (American Troublemakers). 6 up

As a member of a religious family, John Brown (1800-1859) first became a minister. When that line of work failed him, he ran a tannery. In 1836 at an Ohio church meeting, he vowed to dedicate his life to end slavery in America, a practice he had always abhorred. In 1855, he went to Kansas Territory to help antislavery forces, and the next year led a massacre in a proslavery settlement. In 1859, he led the Harper's Ferry raid and was tried for treason, convicted, and hanged. Maps, Photographs, Key Dates, Glossary, Places to Visit, Bibliography and Recommended Readings, and Index.

1722.   Powers, Richard G. **Secrecy and Power: The Life of J. Edgar Hoover**. New York: Free Press, Macmillan, 1987. 624p. $27.95. ISBN 0-02-925060-9. YA

This biography covers a man who wanted to keep America as it had been rather than accept it as it had come to be. J. Edgar Hoover (1895-1972) took over the Federal Bureau of Investigation in 1924 and changed it into an organization that fought against all crime. He hated those who questioned the American society or who did not fit the preconception that he had of a good citizen. He kept files on many Americans and used his power to help or hinder. Hoover's personal life was questionable as well. The text draws on personal documents, thousands of FBI files, interviews with former agents, and presidential papers from nine administrations. Notes, Bibliography, and Index.

1723.   Powledge, Fred. **We Shall Overcome: Heroes of the Civil Rights Movement**. New York: Atheneum, 1993. 214p. $17. ISBN 0-684-19362-0. 7-10

In this presentation of the Civil Rights movement in America, Powledge explains the reasons for the movement's beginning and illustrates that tacit approval of segregation existed in the government through its laws. He lists the milestones of the movement, which include the Montgomery bus boycott in 1955, Emmett Till's lynching, the Southern Christian Leadership Conference, and the Student Nonviolent Coordinating Committee. He also presents biographies of 10 individuals, both white and Black, who were strongly affected by the Civil Rights movement and who wanted to change what they saw as a terrible wrong. Time Line of African American History and Index.

1724. Poynter, Margaret. **A Time Too Swift**. New York: Atheneum, 1990. $12.95. 216p. ISBN 0-689-31146-X. 6-9

In 1941, Marjorie, 15, undergoes several experiences. She meets a boy whom she likes, but he has to go to Pearl Harbor after the bombing. Her brother enlists in the Marines, and her friend's father is killed. She has Japanese-American friends who have to go to an internment camp, and she has to listen to her father's prejudiced remarks. Eventually the strands resolve as her brother returns injured but alive, and Marjorie falls in love with her brother's best friend, who is not physically fit to fight in the war.

1725. Pratt, Paula. **Martha Graham**. San Diego, CA: Lucent, 1995. 112p. $16.95. ISBN 1-56006-056-5. (The Importance Of). 6 up

Martha Graham (1894-1991), a pioneer in dance and choreography, exposed the hard work of the dancer to the audience rather than hiding it, as in traditional ballet, and became the creator of modern dance. Most of her major work was begun in the 1930s and 1940s. Modern dancers work into the ground rather than leap into the air. To her, every dancer was trying to show the trials of the human spirit and the triumphs over those trials. She showed courage by being different, and today her methods are taught worldwide. Notes, For Further Reading, Additional Works Consulted, and Index.

1726. Presnall, Judith Janda. **Rachel Carson**. San Diego, CA: Lucent, 1995. 96p. $16.95. ISBN 1-56006-052-2. (The Importance Of). 6 up

Although a biologist by training, Rachel Carson (1907-1964) loved writing; her first published story appearing in *St. Nicholas* magazine when she was only 12. Her talent led to *The Sea Around Us* (1951), a best-seller that introduced readers to the life under the ocean surface. Her intense concern with the proliferation of pesticides between 1947 and 1960, when the number of them increased fivefold, led her to write *Silent Spring* (1962). The public had been unaware of the dangers of chemicals being sprayed almost everywhere and on almost everything. Her book caused a furor in the chemical industry, but it led to the passage of more than 40 bills controlling the use of chemicals in daily life. She is the founder of today's ecology movement. Notes, For Further Reading, Additional Works Consulted, and Index.

1727. Press, David. **A Multicultural Portrait of Professional Sports**. Freeport, NY: Marshall Cavendish, 1994. 80p. $18.95. ISBN 1-85435-661-5. (Perspectives). 7 up

The text presents the history of various minorities in professional sports in the United States. It covers major league baseball; pro basketball; pro football; women's pro baseball, basketball, and football; and the Jackie Robinson "revolution" that opened sports to everyone. Chronology, Glossary, Further Reading, and Index.

1728. Press, Skip. **Mark Twain**. San Diego, CA: Lucent, 1994. 112p. $16.95. ISBN 1-56006-043-3. (The Importance Of). 6-9

Born in 1835 when Halley's comet blazed through the sky, Mark Twain (Samuel Langhorne Clemens) was arguably the most recognized man in America by the time of his death, when Halley's comet reappeared in 1910. His bushy white hair and mustache, white suits, and cigar on the lecture circuit had made him famous. His friends included Nikola Tesla (discoverer of alternating current), Andrew Carnegie, and Thomas Edison. Twain's life, filled with writing and traveling, had moments of intense happiness and intense sadness. He seemed to recover from the bad and regain his composure, but his writing became more cynical in his later years. Still, he is the dean of American letters because he wrote the first truly American novel, *Huckleberry Finn*. Notes, For Further Reading, Additional Works Consulted, and Index.

1729. Prior, Katherine. **Initiation Customs**. New York: Thomson Learning, 1993. 32p. $13.95. ISBN 1-56847-035-5. (Comparing Religions). 4-8

Six major religions—Buddhism, Christianity, Hinduism, Judaism, Islam, and Sikhism—have specific ideas about the introduction to adulthood. The text examines the age for initiation ceremonies, how much study and preparation each requires, the special clothing worn, and the symbols that represent the religion. Topics such as baptism and confirmation for Christians, bar mitzvah for Jews, *uanayana* for Hindus, *anint* for Sikhs, and *pravrajya* for Buddhists show these rituals.

1730. Prior, Katherine. **Pilgrimages and Journeys**. New York: Thomson Learning, 1993. 32p. $13.95. ISBN 1-56847-032-0. (Comparing Religions). 4-8

Six major religions—Buddhism, Christianity, Hinduism, Judaism, Islam, and Sikhism—have used pilgrimages and journeys as part of their faith. The text looks at why people go on pilgrimages, where they go, how they behave and dress, and what journeys they took in the past. Photographs of holy sites such as Jerusalem augment the text. Glossary, Books to Read, and Index.

1731. Probosz, Kathilyn Solomon. **Martha Graham**. Englewood Cliffs, NJ: Dillon Press, 1995. 184p. $13.95. ISBN 0-87518-568-1. 5 up

As a child, Martha Graham (1894-1991) preferred to jump rope in a tree rather than on the ground. At 16, she saw Ruth St. Denis perform and knew that she wanted to dance. People thought she was too old to begin lessons, but she proved them wrong as she became accomplished. She revolutionized the dance world by choreographing nearly 200 dances and creating a dance company. Although her beliefs cost her personal relationships, she thought that a person should listen to their inner voice in deciding what to do with life. Chapter Notes, For Further Reading, and Index.

1732. Prochnau, William. **Once upon a Distant War: David Halberstam, Neil Sheehan, Peter Arnett—Young War Correspondents and Their Early Vietnam Battles**. New York: Times Books, 1995. 546p. $27.50. ISBN 0-8129-2633-1. YA

Prochnau says that the print correspondents lost control of the news with the advent of satellite communication. He tells the story of the last group who had such power to control America's understanding of other countries during the Vietnam War. The persons discussed brought back news that contradicted what the government said, and they established the "credibility gap" between the people and the government. Bibliography, Notes, and Index.

Q

1733. Qualey, Marsha. **Come In from the Cold**. Boston: Houghton Mifflin, 1994. 219p. $14.95. ISBN 0-395-68986-4. 7 up

Jeff, the only person in his Minnesota town to oppose the Vietnam War, becomes even more distressed when his brother dies fighting in it. In Minneapolis, Maud is rethinking her beliefs about country and family when her sister blows herself up with a bomb rather than report her antiwar activities to the police. In 1969, Jeff and Maud meet, and they eventually settle together in a Minnesota commune named Woodlands in this prequel to *Everybody's Daughter* (where they become the parents). The story gives a clear picture of the conflicts that people experienced when they felt morally opposed to the war in Vietnam.

1734. Qualey, Marsha. **Everybody's Daughter**. Boston: Houghton Mifflin, 1991. 208p. $13.95. ISBN 0-395-55870-0. 7-12

Beamer, 16, hates the comments made by the people who hover in her parents' bait and tackle store. Most of them are former commune dwellers with whom she has grown up since her birth in the commune as Merry Moonbeam. As a teenager, she falls in love with two boys, one a local and the other a visiting college intern, while she has a realistic exchange with these adults who acknowledge the normal progress of her rebellion.

R

1735. Rabinowitz, Ann. **Bethie**. New York: Macmillan, 1989. 208p. $13.95. ISBN 0-02-775661-0. 7-10

Beth, 15 in 1943, lives in New York City. She loves her father, but he is preoccupied with helping to rescue European Jews. Her stepmother has little warmth, and her mother is depressed. Her friend Grace becomes more withdrawn after the divorce of her own parents, and when Grace commits suicide, Beth has to deal with that change in her life.

1736. Randall, Marta. **John F. Kennedy**. New York: Chelsea House, 1988. 112p. $18.95; $7.95pa. ISBN 0-87754-586-3; 0-7910-0580-1pa. (World Leaders Past and Present). 5 up

John F. Kennedy (1917-1963) was full of determination and competitiveness. As President, he created the Peace Corps and the Alliance for Progress, revamped the space program, and instituted welfare reforms. His first foreign policy foray, the invasion at the Bay of Pigs in 1961, was a disaster. Photographs enhance the text. Chronology, Further Reading, and Index.

1737. Randolph, Blythe. **Amelia Earhart**. New York: Franklin Watts, 1987. 121p. $11.90. ISBN 0-531-10331-5. (Impact Biography). 5-8

Amelia Earhart refused to accept traditional feminine roles in order to pursue her interest in flying. When she married George Putnam, he promoted her relentlessly. The text looks at her life and the records that she broke before she attempted to fly around the world. She disappeared in the Pacific. Bibliography and Index.

1738. Randolph, Blythe. **Charles Lindbergh**. New York: Franklin Watts, 1990. 160p. $11.90. ISBN 0-531-10918-6. 6-12

Charles Lindbergh (1902-1974) gained fame when he became the first person to fly across the Atlantic Ocean. Five years later, he and his wife suffered the kidnapping and death of their firstborn son. With emotions from the highest jubilation to the lowest despair, his demeanor became well known to the American public. When he went to Germany in 1936 and professed admiration for Hitler and his country, many accused him of being a traitor. The text looks at the controversies in Lindbergh's life. Bibliography and Index.

1739. Randolph, Sallie G. **Woodrow Wilson: President**. New York: Walker, 1992. 124p. $15.85. ISBN 0-8027-8143-8. 6-9

Woodrow Wilson (1856-1924) made massive labor reforms, overhauled the banking system, and solved problems in international trade and tariffs while facing the threat of world war. He changed from an allegiance to his privileged social class to a fighter for the common people, a decision that shocked his political associates. Although a dreamer and an idealist, he declared war on Germany when he had to save Great Britain. He worked for a lasting peace and was disappointed when the United States would not ratify the League of Nations charter. Index.

1740. Rappaport, Doreen. **The Alger Hiss Trial**. New York: HarperCollins, 1993. 184p. $14.89. ISBN 0-06-025120-4. (Be the Judge/Be the Jury). 6 up

In 1948, Whittaker Chambers, a former Communist, accused Alger Hiss of giving him secret documents. In 1949, a second trial began after the first jury could not reach a verdict. In 1950, Alger Hiss was declared guilty, and he had to go to prison. However, he never stopped trying to clear his name. The text looks at all the facts available from the trial and asks the reader to make a decision before reading the verdict. Photographs and drawings enhance the text. Bibliography and Stenographer's Notes.

1741. Rappaport, Doreen, ed. **American Women: Their Lives in Their Words**. New York: Crowell, 1990. 318p. $17.89. ISBN 0-690-04819-X. New York: HarperCollins, 1992. 318p. $7.95pa. ISBN 0-06-446127-0pa. 7-12

Presenting a history of America, the text quotes letters, diaries, interviews, and speeches of approximately 60 women in thematically arranged chapters such as "Settling the West" and "Work and Politics." Those quoted include Anne Bradstreet, Abigail Adams, Sojourner Truth, Margaret Sanger, Eleanor Roosevelt, Fannie Lou Hamer, Jane Addams, Jacqueline Cochran, and Ida B. Wells. By using these sources, Rappaport reveals women who are rich and poor, old and young, in love and in pain, and from different ethnic backgrounds, including Spanish American. Bibliography and Index. *American Library Association Best Books for Young Adults, Horn Book Fanfare Honor List, Notable Children's Trade Books in the Field of Social Studies*, and *New York Public Library Books for the Teen Age*.

1742. Rappaport, Doreen. **The Flight of the Red Bird**. New York: Dial Press, 1997. 208p. $15.99. ISBN 0-8037-1438-6. 5 up

Gertrude Bonnin was a writer, lecturer, and activist known as Zitkala-Sa, one of the most important Native American reformers of the early twentieth century. After authorities took her from her South Dakota home, she went to a Quaker school in Indiana where she was forced to abandon her Yankton Sioux language and other aspects of her heritage. She spent her adulthood trying to inform white audiences of her distressful childhood and to encourage them to better the lives of Native Americans in ways not previously practiced. Photographs and Index.

1743. Rappaport, Doreen. **The Lizzie Borden Trial**. New York: HarperCollins, 1992. 175p. $15. ISBN 0-06-025114-X. (Be the Judge/Be the Jury). 6 up

Eight days after Andrew and Abby Borden were bludgeoned to death with an ax, Lizzie Borden (1860-1927) was accused of the murder. Because she was wealthy and a regular church attendee, the jury acquitted her. Although she was declared not guilty, the town thought that she was, and she was ostracized. The text looks at all the facts available from the trial and asks the reader to make a decision before reading the verdict. Photographs and drawings enhance the text. Bibliography and Stenographer's Notes.

1744. Rappaport, Doreen. **The Sacco-Vanzetti Trial**. John Palencar, illustrator. New York: HarperCollins, 1992. 175p. $15. ISBN 0-06-0251116-6. (Be the Judge/Be the Jury). 5 up

When a paymaster and a guard were shot and killed on April 15, 1920, the two men accused of the crime were Italian immigrants Sacco and Vanzetti. Most likely, the trial that convicted them of the murders was not fair because of their background. They were electrocuted on August 22, 1927, after appeals failed. The text looks at all the facts available from the trial and asks the reader to make a decision before reading the verdict. Photographs and drawings enhance the text. Bibliography and Stenographer's Notes.

1745. Rappaport, Doreen. **Tinker vs. Des Moines: Student Rights on Trial**. New York: HarperCollins, 1993. 153p. $15. ISBN 0-06-025118-2. (Be the Judge/Be the Jury). 5 up

In 1965, John Frederick Tinker and two other students protested the Vietnam War by wearing black armbands in memory of those who had died. They were expelled from school. Appeals to this decision reached the Supreme Court, which decided in favor of the students in 1969 because they were exercising their freedom of speech according to the First Amendment. The text looks at all the facts available from the trial and asks the reader to make a decision before reading the verdict. Photographs and drawings enhance the text. Bibliography and Law Clerk's Notes.

1746. Rappaport, Doreen. **Trouble at the Mines**. Joan Sandin, illustrator. New York: HarperCollins, 1987. 96p. $14.89. ISBN 0-690-04446-1. 3-7

When they get neither improvement in working conditions nor pay raises in the Arnot, Pennsylvania, mines by 1898, Mother Jones comes to the area and helps the miners strike. The wives and daughters keep the men from succumbing to the mine owners' demands and stand by their needs. They also have to keep them from hurting their friends who choose to support the mine owners.

1747. Ravage, Barbara. **George Westinghouse: A Genius for Invention**. Austin, TX: Raintree/Steck-Vaughn, 1997. 112p. $18.98. ISBN 0-8172-4402-6. (Innovative Minds). 7-8

George Westinghouse (1846-1914) was a difficult child, but by the time he was 14, he had begun working on an invention that would earn him the first of the 361 patents that he held when he died. Among the results of his inventions were safe, high-speed train travel, electricity and natural gas flowing into homes, and a way to use the power of Niagara Falls. After he had won a patent for his rotary steam engine invention when he was only 19, he realized after several tries that college was not for him, and he continued working on his inventions alone. Glossary, Further Reading, Sources, and Index.

1748. Ravage, Barbara. **Rachel Carson, Gentle Crusader**. Austin, TX: Raintree/Steck-Vaughn, 1997. 112p. $18.98. ISBN 0-8172-4406-9. (Innovative Minds). 7-8

When Rachel Louise Carson (1907-1964) published her book, *The Sea Around Us*, she created a controversy among scientists who did not believe her dire warnings about the environment's destruction. Her careful study proved correct, and her ideas reached nonscientists because she could write well. Because she advocated the reduction of pesticide use, she helped to save many natural habitats that would have been otherwise systematically destroyed. She was a scholar, scientist, and pioneer environmentalist. Glossary, Further Reading, Sources, and Index.

1749. Rawls, Jim. **Dame Shirley and the Gold Rush**. John Holder, illustrator. Austin, TX: Raintree/Steck-Vaughn, 1993. 55p. $22.83; $6.64pa. ISBN 0-8114-7222-1; 0-8114-8062-3pa. (Stories of America—Against All Odds). 3-7

Louise Amelia Knapp Smith Clappe (1819-1906) called herself Dame Shirley when she wrote letters in which she described the truth about the California Gold Rush of the early 1850s. Rumors said gold was everywhere for anyone who wanted it, but that was not the reality. Epilogue, Afterword, and Notes.

1750. Rawls, Jim. **Never Turn Back: Father Serra's Mission**. George Guzzi, illustrator. Austin, TX: Raintree/Steck-Vaughn, 1993. 54p. $22.83; $6.64pa. ISBN 0-8114-7221-3; 0-8114-8061-5pa. (Stories of America—Against All Odds). 5-9

In 1749, Father Serra and a friend left Spain to become missionaries to New Spain. They established a mission in San Xavier, Baja California. But in April 1769, Father Serra left there to help the Tipais Indians in Alta California. He established San Diego de Alacalá, where he lived until his death five years later. Epilogue, Afterword, and Notes.

1751. Ray, Delia. **Behind the Blue and the Gray: The Soldier's Life in the Civil War**. New York: Lodestar, 1991. 112p. $16.99. ISBN 0-525-67333-4. (Young Reader's History of the Civil War). 7 up

The text looks at the lives of the soldiers in the Civil War as they went to war, made their camps, and sat by the fires at night; how quickly they became used to and bored by the routine; the results of battles in which soldiers often became patients or prisoners; the attempt to keep the armies together by patching separate groups; and the road home after the battle's end. Photographs, Glossary, Bibliography, and Index.

1752. Ray, Delia. **Gold! The Klondike Adventure**. New York: Lodestar, 1989. 90p. $14.95. ISBN 0-525-67288-5. 5 up

In 1897, three men spread the word that they had found gold in a remote corner of Canada. Thousands headed north, some not even knowing where Klondike was located. They all hoped to escape the depressed American economy. Their route started with a steamship journey to Alaska. Then they had to go through mountain passes and build boats for a trip of 500 miles up the Dawson River. Highlighting the text are more than 50 photographs of the people who went on this last major North American adventure. Glossary and Index.

1753. Ray, Delia. **A Nation Torn: The Story of How the Civil War Began**. New York: Lodestar, 1990. 102p. $15.95. ISBN 0-525-67308-3. 5-8

In the mid-1800s, the North and South were very different. They had contrasting economies and differing ideas about slavery. The text looks at the various events that led to the beginning of the war over slavery on April 12, 1861, when the rebels attacked Union troops at Fort Sumter, South Carolina. It also presents influential figures of the time, such as Henry Clay, Harriet Tubman, and John Brown. Photographs, letters, diaries, and eyewitness accounts help tell this story. Glossary, Bibliography, and Index.

1754. Raymer, Edward C. **Descent into Darkness: Pearl Harbor, 1941: A Navy Diver's Memoir**. San Francisco: Presidio Press, 1996. 240p. $21.95. ISBN 0-89141-589-0. YA

After the Japanese bombed Pearl Harbor in 1941, three battleships, *Arizona*, *Oklahoma*, and *Utah*, were burning off the island of Oahu. The Navy flew their salvage divers to the island, trying to rescue as many trapped sailors and Marines as possible. Raymer, one of the divers, tells of his experiences while trying to recover drowned humans and raise the battleships. He and the crew used previously untested methods in total blackness. They could not even see faceplates on their helmets. They memorized the blueprints of the ships so they could grope inside for war materials. Among the dangers were falling objects, human bodies, sharks, and the threat of another air strike from the Japanese. Photographs and Index.

1755. Reader's Digest. **America's Fascinating Indian Heritage: The First Americans: Their Customs, Art, History and How They Lived**. 1978. New York: Reader's Digest, 1990. 415p. $30. ISBN 0-89577-372-4. YA

After discussing the point that Indians probably came over the land bridge from Siberia 20,000 to 40,000 years ago, the text looks at their history and customs. The topics include the first Indians, the lost Indian civilizations, the Five Civilized tribes of the Iroquois Confederacy, the Woodland warriors of the Northeast and Great Lakes, the nomadic horsemen of the Great Plains, the planters and herdsmen of the Southwest, the foragers and gatherers of the Great Basin and California, the traders and fisherman of the Northwest coast, the people of the caribou in the Subarctic, the dwellers on ice in the Arctic, and contemporary Indians. Index.

1756. Reaves, Wendy Wick. **Oliphant's Presidents: Twenty-Five Years of Caricature by Pat Oliphant**. Kansas City, MO: Andrews and McMeel, 1990. 96p. $12.95. ISBN 0-83621-813-2. YA

Although not documented history in the manner of other pieces of writing, the political cartoons of a time reveals much about that time's problems and concerns. These caricatures and cartoons present the state of the nation over the past 25 years with wit and insight.

1757. Reck, W. Emerson. **A. Lincoln: His Last 24 Hours**. Jefferson, NC: McFarland, 1987. 232p. $23.95. ISBN 0-89950-216-4. YA

This scholarly look at Abraham Lincoln (1809-1865) on the day that he was assassinated has quotes in the chapter titles that reveal Lincoln's mood as the day passed. One person said, "He was full of hope and happiness"; other visitors noted his "exuberant mood." He had urgent business but time for good deeds. Another said, "I never saw him so supremely cheerful." He went reluctantly to the theater, and while he was there, his guard left his post. During that interlude, Booth shot Lincoln while the President held his wife Mary's hand. After the shooting, someone else said "It is impossible for him to recover." And after his death, a friend pronounced, "Now he belongs to the ages." Appendix: Some Unsolved Mysteries, Notes, Bibliography, and Index.

1758. Reeder, Carolyn. **Across the Lines**. Robin Moore, illustrator. New York: Simon & Schuster, Atheneum, 1997. 224p. $16. ISBN 0-689-81133-0. 3-7

Edward, 12, is surprised when his young slave, Simon, runs away at the Union army's arrival. Edward's family flees to Petersburg, and the constant shell bombardment frays Edward's nerves. Simon finds that being free and serving in the army can also be lonely. The two points of view in the novel give differing perspectives on the same conflict.

1759. Reeder, Carolyn. **Moonshiner's Son**. New York: Macmillan, 1993. 208p. $14.95. ISBN 0-02-775805-2. 3-7

Because Tom, 12, only wants to please his father, he tries to make whiskey as best as he can even though it is illegal during Prohibition in 1919. A new preacher arrives and speaks against the liquor, and police arrest Tom's father. Tom observes wife beating and fighting, both caused by drunkenness. He slowly realizes that his wood carvings, which he can sell to the townsfolk, will fulfill his creative urges. His father, remorseful at having beaten his son, stops running the still.

1760. Reeder, Carolyn. **Shades of Gray**. New York: Macmillan, 1989. 152p. $12.95. ISBN 0-02-775810-9. New York: Camelot, 1992. 152p. $3.99pa. ISBN 0-380-71232-6pa. 5-7

During the Civil War, Jed's sisters die of typhoid, Yankees kill his father and brother, and his mother dies of grief. At 12, he must go to his mother's sister's home. There he has to adjust to the rural life of Virginia and to an uncle who refuses to fight for the South or the North. Jed has to overcome his own prejudices and ignore the neighbors' jeers as he begins to understand the strength that his uncle shows in standing firm to his own convictions. *Scott O'Dell Award for Historical Fiction*, *Child Study Children's Book Award*, *Jefferson Cup Award*, and *American Library Association Notable Books for Children*.

1761. Reef, Catherine. **Buffalo Soldiers**. New York: Twenty-First Century Books, 1993. 80p. $14.98. ISBN 0-8050-2372-0. (African-American Soldiers). 7 up

After the Civil War, which proved the bravery of African American soldiers, the government decided to let Black regiments form. The first four regiments were the Buffalo Soldiers. Their lives on the frontier were difficult because they had to fight outlaws and Indian criminals as well as face prejudice in the army and from settlers. But they all contributed to a tradition of excellence in their service. Chronology, Bibliography, and Index.

1762. Reef, Catherine. **Civil War Soldiers**. New York: Twenty-First Century Books, 1993. 80p. $14.98. ISBN 0-8050-2371-2. (African-American Soldiers). 7 up

On June 7, 1863, Union and Confederate soldiers faced each other at Millikin's Bend, Louisiana, in a bloody battle. African American soldiers helped the Union win that battle, and they fought in more than 400 others during the Civil War. The army's first Black major, Dr. Martin Delany, told the group of former slaves that their participation won the war for the Union. At the same time they fought the Confederacy, Black soldiers fought within the Union army to gain the same treatment as white soldiers and for the respect of other American citizens. The text tells the story of their contribution in the Civil War. Chronology, Bibliography, and Index.

1763. Reef, Catherine. **Henry David Thoreau: A Neighbor to Nature**. Larry Raymond, illustrator. New York: Twenty-First Century Books, 1992. 72p. $14.98. ISBN 0-941477-39-8. (Earth Keepers). 4-8

Henry David Thoreau (1817-1862) believed that many answers to life could be found by observing nature. His most famous account of nature appears in *Walden Pond*, a book he wrote about his two-year stay on its shores. Glossary and Index.

1764. Reef, Catherine. **John Steinbeck**. New York: Clarion, 1996. 163p. $17.95. ISBN 0-395-71278-5. 7-10

John Steinbeck (1902-1968) grew up in California, where he saw much social injustice toward the migrant workers who came from Mexico. During the Depression, he saw the "Oakies" coming from the Dust Bowl in search of work so they could feed their families. The text looks at Steinbeck's books such as *Grapes of Wrath* and *Of Mice and Men* as it talks about his politics, his private life, and his philosophy for living. Photographs, Bibliography, and Index.

1765. Reef, Catherine. **Rachel Carson: The Wonder of Nature**. Larry Raymond, illustrator. New York: Twenty-First Century Books, 1992. 68p. $14.95. ISBN 0-941477-38-X. (Earth Keepers). 4-8

The text presents the life of Rachel Carson (1907-1964) by looking at the events in her childhood that influenced her adult choices. Quotes from her writing show her personal philosophy about life and nature. Her book *The Silent Spring* (1962) probably marks the date when people began to realize that progress was not necessarily good for the environment. Glossary and Index.

1766. Reef, Catherine. **Ralph David Abernathy**. New York: Dillon Press, 1995. 168p. $13.95; $7.95pa. ISBN 0-87518-653-X; 0-382-24965-8pa. (People in Focus). 7 up

Ralph David Abernathy (1926-1990) earns credit as the launcher of the Civil Rights movement in Montgomery, Alabama, in December 1955. He led the boycott of public buses in the city that kept thousands of African Americans off them for more than a year, leading to the landmark federal court decision outlawing segregation on public transportation. The text starts with this story, highlighted with photographs, and returns to Abernathy's beginnings as it traces his life. Bibliography and Index.

1767. Reef, Catherine. **Walt Whitman**. New York: Clarion, 1995. 148p. $16.95. ISBN 0-395-68705-5. 7-10

Walt Whitman (1819-1892) described himself as a "born loafer." But he worked at a variety of jobs while writing his poetry. The first edition of *Leaves of Grass*, published in 1855, showed his free poetic style in its exploration of nineteenth-century life. The last edition of *Leaves of Grass* contained more than 400 poems that Whitman had published during his lifetime. During the Civil War he helped wounded soldiers in Washington and admired Abraham Lincoln. Because he refused to omit any subject from his poetry, some critics hated his work and censored it. However, he always included the weak, the poor, and the scorned. Bibliography and Index. *American Library Association Notable Books for Children* and *American Library Association Best Books for Young Adults*.

1768. Reinberg, Linda. **In the Field: The Language of the Vietnam War**. New York: Facts on File, 1991. 288p. $22.95. ISBN 0-8160-2214-3. YA

The Vietnam War lasted from 1961 to 1975. Direct American involvement covered a shorter period, but Reinberg has found more than 5,000 terms that relate to the time. Among the terms are "body count," "domino theory," and "Agent Orange." She defines them in the text. Bibliography and Index.

1769. Rennert, Richard, ed. **Book of Firsts: Leaders of America**. New York: Chelsea House, 1994. 63p. $14.95; $5.95pa. ISBN 0-7910-2065-7; 0-7910-2066-5pa. (Profiles of Great Black Americans). 6-9

This collection of succinct biographies gives an overview of African American leaders. Those profiled are Blanche K. Bruce (1841-1898), Ralph Bunche (1904-1971), Shirley Chisholm (b. 1924), Benjamin O. Davis (1877-1970), William H. Hastie (1904-1976), Thurgood Marshall (1908-1993), Colin Powell (b. 1937), and L. Douglas Wilder (b. 1931). Black-and-white illustrations highlight the text. Bibliography and Index.

1770. Rennert, Richard, ed. **Civil Rights Leaders**. New York: Chelsea House, 1993. 63p. $14.95; $5.95pa. ISBN 0-7910-2051-7; 0-7910-2052-5pa. (Profiles of Great Black Americans). 6-9

This collection of biographical profiles gives an overview of African Americans who led the Civil Rights movement. Those presented are James Weldon Johnson (1871-1938), Martin Luther King, Jr. (1929-1968), Thurgood Marshall (1908-1993), Malcolm X (1925-1965), Adam Clayton Powell, Jr. (1908-1972), Asa Philip Randolph (1889-1979), Walter White (1893-1955), and Jesse Jackson (b. 1941). Black-and-white illustrations highlight the text. Bibliography and Index.

1771. Rennert, Richard, ed. **Female Writers**. New York: Chelsea House, 1994. 63p. $14.95; $5.95pa. ISBN 0-7910-2063-0; 0-7910-2064-9pa. (Profiles of Great Black Americans). 6-9

This collection of biographical profiles gives an overview of African American female writers. Those included are Maya Angelou (b. 1928), Gwendolyn Brooks (b. 1917), Nikki Giovanni (b. 1943), Lorraine Hansberry (1930-1965), Zora Neale Hurston (1901?-1960), Toni Morrison (b. 1931), Alice Walker (b. 1944), and Phillis Wheatley (1753?-1784). Black-and-white illustrations highlight the text. Bibliography and Index.

1772. Rennert, Richard, ed. **Jazz Stars**. New York: Chelsea House, 1993. 63p. $14.95; $5.95pa. ISBN 0-7910-2059-2; 0-7910-2060-6pa. (Profiles of Great Black Americans). 5-8

The text looks at people who starred in the jazz music world of the twentieth century. Given are an account of each performer's life, his or her early interest in music, and career development. The book includes capsule biographies of Louis Armstrong (1900-1971), Count Basie (1904-1984), John Coltrane (1926-1967), Duke Ellington (1899-1974), Ella Fitzgerald (1918-1996), Dizzy Gillespie (1917-1993), Billie Holiday (1915-1959), and Charlie Parker (1920-1955). Bibliography and Index.

1773. Rennert, Richard, ed. **Pioneers of Discovery**. New York: Chelsea House, 1994. 63p. $14.95; $5.95pa. ISBN 0-7910-2067-3; 0-7910-2068-1pa. (Profiles of Great Black Americans). 6-9

This collection of biographies gives an overview of African American scientists. Those profiled are Benjamin Banneker (1731-1806), George Washington Carver (1864?-1943), James Beckwourth (1798-1867?), Guion Bluford (b. 1942), Charles Drew (1904-1950), Matthew Henson (1866-1955), Ernest Everett Just (1883-1941), and Lewis Latimer (1848-1928). Black-and-white illustrations highlight the text. Bibliography and Index.

1774. Rice, Earle. **The Battle of Midway**. San Diego, CA: Lucent, 1995. 110p. $19.95. ISBN 1-56006-415-3. (Battles of World War II). 7 up

The Battle of Midway was one of World War II's most important battles. In June 1942, Raymond Spruance led the outnumbered Americans against the Japanese naval forces commanded by Isoruko Yamamoto. In relating the American victory, the text uses contemporary observations to enhance knowledge gleaned through historical scholarship. Appendix, Bibliography, Chronology, Further Reading, and Index.

1775. Richardson, Joy. **Inside the Metropolitan Museum**. New York: Metropolitan Museum of Art, Harry N. Abrams, 1993. 72p. $12.95pa. ISBN 0-8109-2561-3pa. 4-8

Photographs and reproductions show what one might see on a visit to the Metropolitan Museum in New York. An aerial photograph locates the museum's position in New York City. Inside the book, one may look behind the scenes and then visit some of the exhibits, including Egyptian art, ancient Near Eastern art, Asian art, Islamic art, Greek and Roman art, medieval art, arms and armor, European sculpture and decorative arts, arts of Africa, Oceania, and the Americas, musical instruments, American art, European paintings, costumes, and twentieth-century art. Quiz.

1776. Richman, Daniel A. **James E. Carter: 39th President of the United States**. Ada, OK: Garrett Educational, 1989. 122p. $17.26. ISBN 0-944483-24-0. (Presidents of the United States). 5-9

As a farm boy from Georgia, Jimmy Carter (b. 1924) grew up to become state senator, governor, and President of the United States. The text tells his story and gives information about his family. Bibliography and Index.

1777. Richmond, Merle. **Phillis Wheatley**. New York: Chelsea House, 1987. 111p. $18.95; $7.95pa. ISBN 1-55546-683-4; 0-7910-0218-7pa. (American Women of Achievement). 5 up

Before Phillis Wheatley (1753-1784) became America's first Black poet, slavers captured her when she was seven and brought her from Africa. The prosperous Wheatley family in Boston bought her in 1761 and taught her Latin and English. The neighbors knew her talents when she was a teenager, and she recited poems for the elite even though she could not sit at their tables. After the American Revolution, people seemed no longer interested in poetry, and she had to struggle to be recognized. She died penniless at 31, but today people realize that she was an important colonial poet. Engravings enhance the text. Chronology, Further Reading, and Index.

1778. Richter, Conrad. **The Light in the Forest**. 1953. Cutchogue, NY: Buccaneer, 1996. 180p. $21.95. ISBN 1-568-49064-X. New York: Juniper, Fawcett, 1995. 180p. $4.50pa. ISBN 0-449-70437-8pa. 5 up

True Son, 15 in 1765, has lived with the Cuyloga (Delaware Indians) for 11 years and thinks of himself as a Cuyloga. When the whites demand that the Cuyloga release the white captives living with them, True Son has to leave. He cannot adjust to the whites, whom he has learned to hate, including his biological parents.

1779. Rickaby, Laura Ann. **Ulysses S. Grant and the Strategy of Victory**. Den Schofield, illustrator. Englewood Cliffs, NJ: Silver Burdett, 1991. 125p. $16.98; $7.95pa. ISBN 0-382-09944-3; 0-382-24053-7pa. (History of the Civil War). 7-9

Ulysses S. Grant (1822-1885) grew up in Ohio before he went to West Point. After fighting in the Mexican War and resigning from the army, he joined again during the Civil War and distinguished himself at Fort Henry, Vicksburg, and Shiloh before taking command of the Union forces. After the war, he entered politics and served two troubled terms as President. Timetable of Events, Selected Sources, Suggested Reading, and Index.

1780. Ride, Sally. **To Space and Back**. New York: Lothrop, Lee & Shepard, 1986. 96p. $19. ISBN 0-688-06159-1. 5-9

The text and photographs help describe what it is like to be an astronaut on the space shuttle through Sally Ride's experiences. Glossary.

1781. Riefe, Barbara. **For Love of Two Eagles**. New York: Tom Doherty, Forge, 1995. 378p. $22.95. ISBN 0-312-85703-9. YA

This sequel to *The Woman Who Fell from the Sky* occurs in 1700. Margaret Addison, an Englishwoman, has married the Oneida warrior Two Eagles and is adapting to his tribal life in northern New York State. After Two Eagles leaves to fight against the white man in a matter of honor, his companions return to tell her he is dead. She and her young son must return to England. Getting to Boston in the company of a lecherous missionary while trying to avoid the Mohawks, enemies of Oneida allies, becomes a dangerous journey. Once in Boston, and even on the boat, Margaret senses that rumors about Two Eagles are untrue.

1782. Riley, Gail Blasser. **Miranda v. Arizona: Rights of the Accused**. Springfield, NJ: Enslow, 1994. 128p. $17.95. ISBN 0-89490-504-X. (Landmark Supreme Court Cases). 6 up

Ernesto Miranda was arrested and questioned about a rape and kidnapping. He was charged without being advised that he had the right to an attorney. The case came before the Supreme Court in 1966, and on June 13 of that year, the court said that police must tell all people being questioned that they have a right to remain silent. The text looks at the background of this case and what brought it to the Supreme Court. Notes, Further Reading, Glossary, and Index.

1783. Riley, James, A. ed. **The Biographical Encyclopedia of Negro Baseball Leagues**. New York: Carroll & Graf, 1994. 926p. $39.95. ISBN 0-7867-0065-3. YA

The text, beginning with a brief history of the Negro Leagues, documents the careers of 4,000 baseball players from the Negro League into the major league teams from 1872 to 1950. The book contains a brief biographical sketch of each player and statistics for that person's career. Appendix, Bibliography, and Index.

1784. Rinaldi, Ann. **The Blue Door**. New York: Scholastic, 1996. 273p. $15.95. ISBN 0-590-46051-X. (Quilt Trilogy, 3). 7-10

In 1841, Amanda, 14, annoys her stepmother, an opium addict, and her father and grandmother decide that she should go north to Lowell, Massachusetts, to meet her grandmother's family. Her grandmother gives her a section of the quilt that she made to join with those of her sisters so that the quilt can be completed. Amanda sees a crime, survives a shipwreck, has to work in her great-grandfather's mill, and petitions for better conditions before she receives an honorable welcome in her great-grandfather's home. Like the slaves' quarters at her home in the South, the door on the Lowell family home is blue.

1785. Rinaldi, Ann. **A Break with Charity**. San Diego, CA: Harcourt Brace, 1992. 257p. $16.95. ISBN 0-15-200353-3. YA

When Susanna English gets her wish in 1692 to join the girls when Tituba tells their fortunes in Salem, Massachusetts, she watches the beginning of the witch-hunt panic. Ann Putnam leads the girls in their identification of the witches, but Susanna keeps the knowledge of their lies to herself, fearful to "break charity" because they might identify her own family. In 1706, she recalls her participation as she remembers the situation. *American Library Association Best Books for Young Adults* and *New York Public Library Books for the Teen Age*.

1786. Rinaldi, Ann. **The Fifth of March: A Story of the Boston Massacre**. San Diego, CA: Gulliver, Harcourt Brace, 1993. 333p. $10.95. ISBN 0-15-227517-7. 7-10

Rachel Marsh is an indentured servant in John Adams's family in Boston during the early days of the American revolts around 1770. She is free to obtain books from Henry Knox's store for her education, have a British soldier as a boyfriend, and find out about riots from her friend Jane, an activist. She also hears conversations in the Adams home when visitors come to discuss the politics of the time with her master. Jane alerts her about the riot that becomes the Boston Massacre on March 5th. *New York Public Library Books for the Teen Age*.

1787. Rinaldi, Anne. **Finishing Becca: A Story About Peggy Shippen and Benedict Arnold**. San Diego, CA: Gulliver, Harcourt Brace, 1994. 362p. $12; $6pa. ISBN 0152008802; 0-15-200879-9pa. (Great Episodes). 7 up

In 1778, when she is 14, Becca Syng goes to Philadelphia for "finishing" by becoming Peggy Shippen's maid. In first person, she gives her account of the war, the romance and marriage of Benedict Arnold to Peggy, and her stepfather serving as a double agent. When she returns to the farm and reflects on her past four years, she understands that no one ever "finishes" and that happiness and understanding can appear near one's own house.

1788. Rinaldi, Anne. **Hang a Thousand Trees with Ribbons: The Story of Phillis Wheatley**. San Diego, CA: Gulliver, Harcourt Brace, 1996. 352p. $12; $6pa. ISBN 0152008764; 0-15-200877-2pa. (Great Episodes). 7 up

After kidnappers bring a young girl from Senegal to Boston, they sell her as a slave to the wealthy Wheatley family. She becomes known as Phillis Wheatley, and she has the ability to write poetry. Mrs. Wheatley has her perform for influential guests, but when American publishers will not print her work, the Wheatleys send her to England in 1773. There she gains fame, but she also has to face the difficulties that accompany it.

1789. Rinaldi, Anne. **In My Father's House**. New York: Scholastic, 1993. 323p. $13.95. ISBN 0-590-44730-0. 7 up

Oscie does not want the South to change as she grows up during the Civil War, and she refuses to accept anything her stepfather believes. But he, her Yankee tutor, the slave to whom she has been unkind, and a brave freedwoman finally show her that the Confederate way is not the best. When generals Lee and Grant meet in the family living room at Appomattox where Lee surrenders in 1865, Oscie is ready for the change that must occur. *American Library Association Best Books for Young Adults*.

1790. Rinaldi, Ann. **Keep Smiling Through**. San Diego, CA: Harcourt Brace, 1996. 208p. $11; $5pa. ISBN 0-15-200768-7; 0-15-201072-6pa. 4-7

Kay, a fifth grader in 1943, thinks that World War II gives her penurious father another reason not to spend money, and because her stepmother uses any excuse, the rationing does not cause her much stress. Her problems come from the death of her stepmother's baby and deciding who is on what side during the war. A German neighbor is kind and helpful, while her own grandfather's comments let her know that he sympathizes with the Germans. Ann has to learn that nationality does not automatically reveal one's political or moral direction and that she is not guilty for the baby's death.

1791. Rinaldi, Ann. **The Last Silk Dress**. New York: Holiday House, 1988. 350p. $15.95. ISBN 0-8234-0690-3. New York: Bantam, 1996. 350p. $4.99pa. ISBN 0-553-28315-4pa. 5 up

At 14, Susan wants to do something meaningful in support of the Confederacy during the Civil War. Her mother, however, worries that Susan's older brother's scandalous reputation will hurt Susan, so she makes her stay home. When the Yankees approach Richmond, Susan and her friend convince their mothers to let them collect silk dresses to make a balloon that will help spy on the Yankees. In the meantime, Susan has met her brother, banished from the house, and he has told her family secrets. When she almost faces treason for her actions and falls in love with a Yankee, she knows she must hurt someone she loves.

1792. Rinaldi, Anne. **A Ride into Morning: The Story of Tempe Wick**. San Diego, CA: Harcourt Brace, 1991. 289p. $15.95. ISBN 0-15-200573-0. (Great Episodes). 7-9

Mary Cooper, 14-year-old cousin of Tempe Wick, tells the story of her stay with Tempe in 1772. She expects to be welcomed because she and Tempe are both ardent Patriots, but Tempe is hostile, especially when Mary befriends Henry, Tempe's brother, who is thought to have mental problems. Henry pretends to be ill so no one stops him from going around the countryside because they think he is harmless. When a Pennsylvania regiment camps on the farm, he hides in the billet, and Tempe must decide whether to tell her mother that Henry has reappeared or to let her think he is dead, as she has been told.

1793. Rinaldi, Anne. **The Second Bend in the River**. New York: Scholastic, 1997. 288p. $15.95. ISBN 0-590-74258-2. 5-8

Rebecca Galloway likes the kindly Tecumseh who has visited her father's farm since she was seven. In fact, she falls in love with him when she is in her early twenties although he has been married twice before. She admires his diplomatic abilities with the Revolutionary War veterans who have come to the area. When he wants her to live with him on Indian lands, she realizes that she cannot leave the white settlers in her Ohio frontier home.

1794. Rinaldi, Anne. **The Secret of Sarah Revere**. San Diego, CA: Gulliver, Harcourt Brace, 1995. 320p. $11; $5pa. ISBN 0-15-200393-2; 0-15-200392-4pa. (Great Episodes). 7 up

Sarah at 13 is her father Paul's favorite daughter. But she has feelings for Dr. Warren, a frequent visitor to the house and her father and stepmother's friend. She thinks her stepmother is also overly fond of Dr. Warren. But her father and Dr. Warren are involved in the beginning of the war against the British, and Dr. Warren is in charge of propaganda. Only from Warren does she hear that Revere believed that the revolutionaries fired the first shot at Lexington rather than the British, and Warren wants no one else to know. Sarah quarrels with Warren and tries to retract her words when he goes off to battle at Breed's Hill (called Bunker Hill), but does not confront him when they have time to talk. His death leaves this part of her life less than satisfactory. Bibliography. *American Bookseller Pick of the Lists*.

1795. Rinaldi, Anne. **A Stitch in Time**. New York: Scholastic, 1994. 305p. $13.95. ISBN 0-590-46055-2. (Quilt Trilogy). YA

In the first book of the quilt trilogy about the Chelmsford family, introduced in *A Break with Charity*, Hannah tries to keep her family together. All of them have goals, but their father tries to control them in whatever way he can. In the end, he even tries to control Hannah and the man she loves by buying shares in the man's cargo through other people. Throughout, Hannah works on a quilt to try to unite the family with those people who have been part of their lives in Salem before 1788.

1796. Rinaldi, Anne. **Time Enough for Drums**. New York: Holiday House, 1986. 249p. $15.95. ISBN 0-8234-0603-2. 7 up

Jem, 15, looks forward to her birthday while passing time doing her lessons with a handsome Tory tutor. She finds out, however, that he is a spy for the Americans during the Revolutionary War in Trenton, New Jersey, and that he loves her. He helps her cope with the difficulties in her family, including deaths and a sister who runs away to marry a British officer.

1797. Rinaldi, Anne. **Wolf by the Ears**. New York: Scholastic, 1991. 252p. $13.95. ISBN 0-590-43413-6. 7 up

Harriet Hemings, called a servant, is actually a slave, but she might also be the daughter of her master, Thomas Jefferson, as rumored around Monticello. What Harriet cannot understand is why her mother Sally is determined that her children will be free and has extracted a promise from Jefferson that they will be freed when they reach 21. Harriet keeps a diary of her emotions from the time she is 18 in 1819 until she leaves the security of Monticello, against her wishes, to pass as a white woman so that she can help her own people. No one verifies her position as Jefferson's daughter, but she looks like him, and he pays for her education. *American Library Association Best Books for Young Adults* and *American Library Association Best of the Books, 1966-1992*.

1798. Ripple, Ezra Hoyt, and Mark A. Snell, ed. **Dancing Along the Deadline: The Andersonville Memoir of a Prisoner of the Confederacy**. New York: Presidio, 1996. 192p. $19.95. ISBN 0-89141-577-7. YA

In July 1864, rebel troops captured Ezra Hoyt Ripple, a private in the 52nd Pennsylvania Volunteer Infantry Regiment. He spent the rest of the war as a prisoner in Andersonville Prison. He tells about the horror of a place designed to hold 10,000 men but holding more than 31,000 instead. They had no chance to escape because the rebels had created a series of posts in a line that they called the "deadline." Anyone who crossed the line would be shot. To cope with the place, Ripple played his fiddle at night while his fellow prisoners danced. Other prisoners joined him in an orchestra that played at Confederate social functions outside the prison. After the war, Ripple had many speaking engagements during which he discussed his experiences. Photographs and Index.

1799. Riskind, Mary. **Apple Is My Sign**. Boston: Houghton Mifflin, 1981. 146p. $14.95; $4.95pa. ISBN 0-395-30852-6; 0-395-65747-4pa. 5-9

Harry, 10, bravely travels to Philadelphia in 1899 by train to enter the school for the deaf. Worried about being accepted, he soon finds a place for himself when he begins to play football and make clever drawings for the people around him. He thrives in an environment that accepts him as he is, and he carries his newly found confidence home with him. *American Library Association Notable Books for Children*.

1800. Ritchie, David. **Frontier Life**. New York: Chelsea House, 1996. 104p. $18.95. ISBN 0-7910-2842-9. (Life in America 100 Years Ago). 5-7

The frontier more than 100 years ago was not the romantic wild place that people imagine. To live there and survive, one had to be a farmer or rancher, a gunslinger or a lawman. These people and the army waged a war against Native Americans, taking their lands. Then they fought the railroad monopolies to lower the rates for freight. The Industrial Revolution at the end of the nineteenth century led to new factories and businesses. The shift to more people in industry than agriculture changed the frontier. Photographs and drawings enhance the text. Further Reading and Index.

1801. Ritchie, Michael. **Please Stand By: A Prehistory of Television**. Woodstock, NY: Overlook Press, 1994. 247p. $15.94pa. ISBN 0-87951-615-1pa. YA

The history of television began in the 1920s. The text looks at the early years of television up to 1948. In 1927, the first broadcast occurred, and after that all dates, according to Ritchie, may be debatable. In 1948, his "Year One" of the modern age, networks could not transmit live pictures from coast to coast, thus restricting news coverage. As pervasive as it is today, television took longer than expected to have such an influence. Included are anecdotes about famous people and many rare photographs. Bibliography and Index.

1802. Robbins, Neal E. **Ronald W. Reagan: 40th President of the United States**. Ada, OK: Garrett Educational, 1990. 124p. $17.26. ISBN 0-944483-66-6. (Presidents of the United States). 5-9

Ronald Reagan (b. 1911) grew up in Illinois before he began to work in radio and the movies in Hollywood. He married Nancy Davis, became the governor of California, and then the President of the United States. His ability to communicate with people helped his negotiations with Gorbachev in Moscow. Bibliography and Index.

1803. Roberts, David. **In Search of the Old Ones: Exploring the Anasazi World of the Southwest**. New York: Simon & Schuster, 1996. 272p. $24. ISBN 0-684-81078-6. YA

Basket making, pottery, and homes in the southwestern cliffs are all that remain of the mysterious Anasazi civilization, which flourished more than 1,000 years ago. The text looks at what archaeologists have discovered about the Anasazi past since finding the Cliff Palace in 1888 and what is happening to their ruins today. Appendix, Bibliography, Glossary, and Index.

1804. Roberts, Wills Davis. **Jo and the Bandit**. New York: Atheneum, 1992. 185p. $15. ISBN 0-689-31745-X. 4-7

While Jo and her brother are taking the stagecoach to Texas in the late 1860s, a gang robs it. She remembers details about the men because she is an artist who looks at things very carefully. Her drawings cover the wanted posters, and her ideas for capturing the men succeed. Her intelligence impresses her uncle, a judge, as he realizes she has unusual talents.

1805.   Robertson, James I., Jr. **Civil War! America Becomes One Nation: An Illustrated History for Young Readers**. New York: Knopf, 1992. 184p. $15pa. ISBN 0-679-88111-5pa. YA

Robertson explains the importance of cotton to the economy of the eighteenth century after Eli Whitney invented the cotton gin. The South became the wealthiest section of the nation when it had enough slaves to harvest the crops. The North had to industrialize itself, and in doing so, developed an economy that did not depend on the number of people available to work in the fields. The inhumane treatment of humans in the South caused abolitionists to object and begin a major split in perception between parts of the country. Thus the grounds for a civil war were set. The text looks at the war and its effects. Photographs, Chronology, Glossary, For Further Reading, and Index.

1806.   Robinet, Harriette Gillem. **If You Please, President Lincoln**. New York: Atheneum, 1995. 149p. $15. ISBN 0-689-31969-X. 7 up

When promoters transport 400 recently emancipated slaves to an island with little fresh water and poor soil, Moses, former slave of Father Fitzpatrick, organizes them. Moses had left his Jesuit master where he was a well-educated house slave so that he would not be sold to someone in the South. He becomes the leader of these people who had been promised land, transportation, tools, and seed in a scheme to get them out of the country so that they would not take jobs from white laborers. Moses learns how to control his irritation at people less educated and intelligent than himself and gets them to work together to create a colony in Haiti.

1807.   Robinet, Harriette Gillem. **Mississippi Chariot**. New York: Jean Karl, Atheneum, 1994. 116p. $14.95. ISBN 0-689-31960-6. 5-7

Shortning Bread Jackson's father, innocent of the crime for which he was convicted, serves on a Mississippi chain gang in 1936. Shortning, 12, wants to help his family, but first he saves Hawk Baker, a white boy, from drowning. Then he starts a rumor that he hopes will save his father. He and Hawk become friends, and Hawk's father saves Shortning's father when he tells how officials have hidden the truth. *New York Public Library Books for the Teen Age* and *Notable Children's Trade Books in the Field of Social Studies*.

1808.   Robinson, Jackie, and Alfred Duckett. **I Never Had It Made: An Autobiography**. Hopewell, NJ: Ecco, 1995. 275p. $24. ISBN 0-88001-419-9. YA

Jackie Robinson (1919-1972), grandson of a slave, became the first Black man to play major league baseball and to be inducted into the Baseball Hall of Fame. His mother, a minister, and a friend saved him from becoming a juvenile delinquent so that he was able to became the first four-letter sportsman at the University of California at Los Angeles. He remembers refusing to move to the back of a bus in the army and being court-martialed, but he continued to support equal rights throughout his life. His story places him in the twentieth century, a time in which people both revered and reviled him as a Black man. Epilogue.

1809.   Robinson, Ray. **Iron Horse: Lou Gehrig in His Time**. New York: HarperCollins, 1990. 300p. $22.50pa. ISBN 0-06-097408-7pa. YA

Lou Gehrig (1903-1941) played baseball in the shadow of Babe Ruth and Joe DiMaggio. He was kind and honest but not without fault. Robinson gives many details about Gehrig's life during his years as a baseball player until his death of the disease later named after him. Index.

1810.   Robison, Nancy. **Buffalo Bill**. New York: Franklin Watts, 1991. 64p. $19.90. ISBN 0-531-20007-8. (First Books). 5-8

When Buffalo Bill (1846-1917) was a young man, he was a scout and guide for the U.S. military and a Pony Express rider. Then he became well known as a hunter, an author, and a showman. His traveling Wild West show gave audiences a view of the early life in the American West. Photographs and reproductions enhance the text. Further Reading and Index.

1811.   Rochelle, Belinda. **Witnesses to Freedom: Young People Who Fought for Civil Rights**. New York: Lodestar, Dutton, 1993. 97p. $15.99. ISBN 0-525-67377-6. 5-8

Adults are not the only people who have fought for civil rights. The text tells the stories of several children who defied Jim Crow laws in the 1950s and 1960s. Claudette Colvin, 15, refused to give her bus seat to a white passenger. Elizabeth Eckford faced a crowd spitting on her and calling her names as she tried to enter Little Rock High School in Arkansas. Sheyann Webb, nine, marched in Selma, Alabama, to protest racism. Others profiled are Barbara Johns, Spottswood Thomas Bolling, Jr., Rosa Parks, Harvey Gantt, Dianne Nash, and Raymond Greene. Sources, Further Reading for Children, and Index.

1812.   Rochman, Hazel, and Darlene Z. McCampbell, selectors. **Bearing Witness: Stories of the Holocaust**. New York: Orchard, 1995. 136p. $15.95. ISBN 0-531-09488-X. 7 up

This collection of writings about the Holocaust presents selections from fiction and nonfiction written by people who lived during the Holocaust of World War II. Authors included are Elie Wiesel, Ida Vos, Erika Mumford, Art Spiegelman, Primo Levi, Cynthia Ozick, Claude Lanzmann, Carl Friedman, Ida Fink, Frank O'Conor, Dorothy Rabinowitz, Anna Deavere Smith, and Delbert D. Cooper. Bibliography. *Bulletin Blue Ribbon Book, Chicago Tribune's Year's Best Books,* and *American Library Association Best Books for Young Adults*.

1813. Rockwood, Joyce. **Groundhog's Horse**. Victor Kalin, illustrator. New York: Henry Holt, 1978. 115p. $12.95. ISBN 0-8050-1173-0. 4-7

In 1750, Groundhog goes to rescue his horse Midnight from the Creeks who stole it. His brother and their friends had refused to help him because they did not think the horse was worth the effort. But in addition to his horse, Groundhog is able to rescue a Cherokee boy, Duck, kidnapped two years before. He gets lost on his return, but Midnight brings him and Duck safely home.

1814. Rodgers, Eugene. **Beyond the Barrier: The Story of Byrd's First Expedition to Antarctica**. Annapolis, MD: Naval Institute Press, 1990. 354p. $29.95. ISBN 0-87021-022-X. YA

Rodgers tells the story of the 1928-1929 expedition that Richard E. Byrd took to the Antarctic where he and his team explored some of the lands beyond the great ice barrier called the Ross Ice Shelf. Rodgers sees Byrd as human rather than as the godlike explorer that people imagined. Byrd lied and pretended to be other than he was because he knew people would have to think him heroic before they would give him money to continue his exploration. However, he did achieve much for science and technology because of his use of airplanes and radios. Bibliography and Index.

1815. Rodowsky, Colby F. **Fitchett's Folly**. New York: Farrar, Straus & Giroux, 1987. 165p. $15. ISBN 0-374-32342-9. 4 up

When Sarey's father drowns around 1890 off the eastern coast of the United States, he is trying to save a child from a shipwreck in which all others died. Sarey resents the girl, Faith, even though the girl has lost both parents, and dislikes her staying in the house with Sarey's family. Faith runs away, and Sarey realizes that in their grief, they both need each other.

1816. Rodriguez, Consuelo. **Cesar Chavez**. New York: Chelsea House, 1991. 112p. $18.95. ISBN 0-7910-1232-8. (Hispanics of Achievement). 5 up

Cesar Chavez (1927-1993) helped win a contract for migrant farmworkers and thereby upheld some of the dignity of Mexican Americans. After the Depression, he and his own family had become migrant workers, so he knew their plight. He became a community organizer, and in 1965 the United Farm Workers, the union he began, went on strike against the grape growers. He organized a national boycott of grapes rather than resort to violence and fasted for 25 days. In 1970, the grape growers relented. Photographs enhance the text. Chronology, Further Reading, and Index.

1817. Roesch, Ethel, and Paul Roesch. **Ashana**. New York: Random House, 1990. 404p. $15.95. ISBN 0-394-56963-6. New York: Ballantine, 1991. 404p. $5.99pa. ISBN 0-345-37298-0pa. YA

Russian fur traders come to Alaska in the 1790s. One of them takes Ashana, 15, as his mistress even though she already has a husband. She bears the man two children but continues to see her husband secretly until someone kills him. She teaches her children her heritage, refusing to compromise her past regardless of what she must endure in the present.

1818. Rogers, James. **The Antislavery Movement**. New York: Facts on File, 1994. 118p. $17.95. ISBN 0-8160-2907-5. (Social Reform Movements). 7 up

The antislavery movement began before the Civil War, but in some ways slavery did not end in 1865. Blacks faced discrimination in housing, education, and jobs; even the government kept military units segregated in the two world wars. Not until after World War II did civil rights laws begin to bring about real improvements in the lives of Black men and women. The text traces the beginnings of this movement with abolitionists and continues with its history through the civil rights agreements. Chronology, Further Reading, and Index.

1819. Rogers, James T. **The Secret War: Espionage in World War II**. New York: Facts on File, 1991. 91p. $16.95. ISBN 0-8160-2395-6. (World Espionage). 7 up

In World War II, espionage was an important activity for the Japanese, the Germans, the Americans, and the British. Not until the British were able to break the German codes with "Ultra" and the Americans break the Japanese codes with "Magic" was the war winnable. The text looks at espionage in these countries. Suggested Reading and Index.

1820. Rogers, Teresa. **George Washington Carver: Nature's Trailblazer**. Antonio Castro, illustrator. New York: Twenty-First Century Books, 1992. 72p. $14.98. ISBN 0-8050-2115-9. (Earth Keepers). 4-7

George Washington Carver (c. 1864-1943), an American botanist, was the son of slave parents. He worked to gain an education. Among other achievements, he learned the value of crop diversification, which he promoted to Southern farmers. He also taught at Tuskegee Institute for many years. Glossary and Index.

1821. Roman, Joseph. **King Philip: Wampanoag Rebel**. New York: Chelsea House, 1991. 110p. $18.95. ISBN 0-7910-1704-4. (North American Indians of Achievement). 5 up

As the son of Massasoit, the leader of the Wampanoag Indians, Metacom became the chief when his father died. The English had named him "Philip," and when he took leadership of the tribe, they called him "king." He tried to relieve the growing tension between his tribe and the English, but to do so, he had to give away acres of land. In 1675, he tried to stop the continued encroachment, and King Philip's War began. He asked for help from other tribes, but they could not defeat the English. The colonists killed many people, including Philip, and the balance of power shifted to the colonists. Photographs and reproductions enhance the text. Chronology, Further Reading, and Index.

1822. Roop, Peter, and Connie Roop, eds. **Capturing Nature: The Writings and Art of John James Audubon**. Rick Farley, illustrator. New York: Walker, 1993. 39p. $16.95. ISBN 0-8027-8204-3. 4-8

Beautiful illustrations of birds accompany the story of John James Audubon (1785-1851) through his journal. He traveled around America painting birds, but he had to go to England to be published.

1823. Rosen, Dorothy Schack. **A Fire in Her Bones: The Story of Mary Lyon**. Minneapolis, MN: Carolrhoda, 1995. 88p. $19.95. ISBN 0-87614-840-2. 4-8

When Mary Lyon (1797-1849) had to give up schooling to work on the family farm, she found ways to save money so that she could return to school, an unusual desire for a female in her time. She wanted to make going to school easier for other females than it had been for her, and she wanted to start a school for young women. This desire was like "a fire, shut up in my bones." In 1837, she opened Mount Holyoke Female Seminary in South Hadley, Massachusetts. One of the students at this very demanding school was Emily Dickinson. Bibliography and Index. *Notable Children's Trade Books in the Field of Social Studies.*

1824. Rosen, Michael J. **A School for Pompey Walker**. Aminah Brenda Lynn Robinson, illustrator. San Diego, CA: Harcourt Brace, 1995. 48p. $16. ISBN 0-15-200114-X. 3-7

When Pompey Bibb is barely a teen in the 1840s, a white man, Jeremiah Walker, buys him and sets him free. But Black men could still be caught and accused of running away even if they were free. Jeremiah and Pompey decide that Jeremiah will sell him and help him escape enough times so that Pompey can earn the money to build a school for Black children in Ohio. He tells his story at the dedication of the school and explains that he changed his last name to "Walker" because Jeremiah Walker, although dead more than 30 years, was his best friend. *American Library Association Notable Books for Children.*

1825. Rosenburg, John M. **William Parker: Rebel Without Rights**. Brookfield, CT: Millbrook Press, 1996. 141p. $15.90. ISBN 1-56294-139-9. 4-8

On September 11, 1851, Maryland slave owner Edward Gorsuch tried to reclaim his human property of former slaves. William Parker and the others fought back, and Gorsuch died. Parker escaped to Canada via the Underground Railroad, but several of the men were arrested and tried for treason against the Fugitive Slave Act. The response to this act depended upon which side the person supported.

1826. Rosofsky, Iris. **Miriam**. New York: HarperCollins, 1988. 188p. $11.95. ISBN 0-06-024854-8. 7-10

Miriam narrates a story during the early 1960s that begins with the memory of her brother Moshe's *bris* and ends after his bar mitzvah and subsequent death from pneumonia. Her parents refuse to allow the children to assimilate into mainstream culture, preferring to remain separate as orthodox Jews. Miriam feels alienated from others her age and from the adults as she tries to cope with mourning and with her ideas, which become more contrary to those of her parents. Working in a bookstore helps her begin to coordinate her own orthodoxy with the world outside it.

1827. Ross, Ramon Royal. **The Dancing Tree**. New York: Atheneum, 1995. 59p. $14. ISBN 0-689-80072-X. 6-9

In 1934, Zeenie senses that her mother will leave, which she does when Zeenie is 12, after World War II starts. Although Zeenie does not tell her grandmother about the departure, her grandmother seems to know. She tells Zeenie of a day when she had been near Zeenie's age. She danced with the gypsies who once camped by a tree in the backyard and felt a love that she had not experienced since she was five before her mother died. Zeenie realizes that she will survive the desertion.

1828. Ross, Ramon Royal. **Harper & Moon**. New York: Atheneum, 1993. 181p. $14.95. ISBN 0-689-31803-0. 4 up

Harper, 12, has enjoyed his friends Moon, 17, and Olinger, an old storekeeper who lived alone up in the Blue Mountains of Washington. But during World War II, Moon enlists in the army, and that winter Olinger dies. Moon, whose parents abused him, cannot speak clearly, but he is very artistic. After he returns from the war, a hero and wounded, Moon tells Harper that Olinger lived alone in remorse over the young boy he killed during World War I and the medal he did not want.

1829. Ross, Rhea Beth. **The Bet's On, Lizzie Bingman!** Boston: Houghton Mifflin, 1988. 186p. $13.95; $4.95pa. ISBN 0-395-44472-1; 0-395-64375-9pa. 5-9

Elizabeth, 14, makes a bet with her brother in 1914 that she will remain self-sufficient for the entire summer. If she does, he will have to change his speech for a statewide oratory contest so that it promotes women's rights rather than denies them. Among the things that happen to her is that she witnesses a murder and has to testify in court, but she wins the bet. He changes the speech.

1830. Ross, Rhea Beth. **Hillbilly Choir**. Boston: Houghton Mifflin, 1991. 166p. $13.95. ISBN 0-395-53356-2. 5-7

Laurie, 15, returns to rural Arkansas in 1932 when her mother decides to relinquish her hope for an acting career in New York City. Laurie starts her career as a hillbilly musician, which helps her adjust to the different way of life. Various characters respond to her choices and admire her progress in her singing.

1831. Ross, Stewart. **The United Nations**. New York: Franklin Watts, 1990. 64p. $11.90. ISBN 0-531-18295-9. (Witness History). 7 up

The text examines the history of the United Nations from the days before the discussions about the League of Nations to the present. The responsibilities of the United Nations are peacekeeping, human rights, and human welfare for people around the world. Black-and-white photographs supplement the text. Bibliography, Chronology, Glossary, Notes, and Index.

1832. Rosset, Lisa. **James Baldwin: Author**. New York: Chelsea House, 1989. 110p. $18.95; $7.95pa. ISBN 1-55546-572-2; 0-7910-0230-6pa. (Black Americans of Achievement). 7-12

Born in New York City in Harlem, James Baldwin (1924-1987) became a storefront preacher at 14 but found while working on his school newspaper that he wanted to be a writer. In 1948, after writing several strong articles about racism, Baldwin left America and went to live in Europe. His novel *Go Tell It on the Mountain* looks at ghetto life and established him as a major author at its 1953 publication. He continued to write about the Civil Rights movement and the relationships between Blacks and whites. Photographs highlight the text. Chronology, Further Reading, and Index.

1833. Rossiter, Phyllis. **Moxie**. New York: Four Winds, 1990. 192p. $14.95. ISBN 0-02-777831-2. 5 up

Drew, 13, raises sheep in the Kansas dust bowl area during 1934. But the lack of rain to grow crops causes his family to have almost no money, and they worry about paying for their land. By using his mule Moxie, Drew helps save the family farm.

1834. Rostkowski, Margaret. **After the Dancing Days**. New York: HarperCollins, 1986. 217p. $14.89; $4.50pa. ISBN 0-06-025078-X; 0-06-440248-7pa. 6-9

Annie, 13, is delighted that her physician father is returning from World War I after her favorite uncle has been killed. She is surprised when he announces that he is going to work with returning wounded veterans in a nearby hospital. Annie's mother, a concert pianist, wants Annie to have nothing to do with the hospital, but Annie visits anyway and meets Andrew, a young man who lost part of his face when gassed without wearing his mask. She helps him regain confidence and finally her mother's acceptance. *American Library Association Notable Books for Children, American Library Association Best Books for Young Adults, USA Through Children's Books, Booklist Children's Editors' Choices, IRA Children's Book Award, IRA Young Adult Choices, Notable Children's Trade Books in the Field of Social Studies, NCTE Teachers' Choices, Golden Kite Award for Fiction, Judy Lopez Memorial Certificate of Merit*, and *Jefferson Cup Award Winner*.

1835. Rostkowski, Margaret I. **The Best of Friends**. New York: Harper, 1989. 183p. $12.95. ISBN 0-06-025105-0. 7-10

In 1969, Sarah, Dan, and Will assess their plans for the future and with each other as seniors in a Utah high school. Dan and Sarah's father fought in Korea, and he resents the flirtation that his daughter Sarah has with anti–Vietnam War activities. As the year ends, each of them has to become independent, and the choices each makes disappoint someone else.

1836. Rostkowski, Margaret I. **Moon Dancer**. San Diego, CA: Browndeer, Harcourt Brace, 1995. 224p. $11; $5pa. ISBN 0152766383; 0-15-200194-8pa. YA

Although set in the present, the book's focus is on discovery of ancient drawings of the Anasazi (Navajo for "ancient enemy"), or Hisatsinom (Hopi for "those who came before"). Sixteen-year-old Miranda Galbraith, her sister, a college friend, and Max go on a four-day hike into a Utah canyon where the drawings were discovered by someone named Katie Weston more than 100 years before. They see the pictures, including one of Kokopelli, the fertility god, and piece together a story of what life might have been like for these people during the tenth or eleventh century.

1837.   Roth-Hano, Renee. **Safe Harbors**. New York: Four Winds, 1993. 256p. $16.95. ISBN 0-02-777795-2. 9-12

Renee Roth arrives in America in 1951 to work as a governess in New York. She still remembers the horrors of World War II, when she had to convert to Catholicism so that no one would identify her family as Jewish, a situation presented in *Touch Wood*. She has to learn to say good-bye to the past and to her childhood and live independently. But she has to return to France and make peace with her mother before she can fully assert herself.

1838.   Rowland, Della. **Martin Luther King, Jr.: The Dream of Peaceful Revolution**. Englewood Cliffs, NJ: Silver Burdett, 1990. 138p. $12.95. ISBN 0-382-09924-9. (History of the Civil Rights Movement). 6-9

Martin Luther King, Jr. (1929-1968), along with others, helped shape the Civil Rights movement with some of the highlights being his "I Have a Dream" speech at the Lincoln Memorial in 1963, the beginning of the Poor People's Campaign in 1967, and his "I've Been to the Mountaintop" speech in 1968. Photographs, Timetable, Suggested Reading, Sources, and Index.

1839.   Rubel, David. **Elvis Presley: The Rise of Rock and Roll**. Brookfield, CT: Millbrook Press, 1991. 96p. $15.90. ISBN 1-878841-18-1. (New Directions). 7 up

Elvis Presley (1935-1977) was born as a twin, but his brother died at birth. He did not invent rock and roll but made it commercial by reflecting the conflict and tension of the times. Parents disliked his loud clothes, sideburns, swiveling hips, and sneer, as they symbolized teenagers' desires to be different, but his teen fans adored him. After a life of adulation, Presley died of a drug overdose. Stories of his death ran in newspapers all over the world. Notes, Suggested Reading, Index.

1840.   Rubel, David. **Fannie Lou Hamer: From Sharecropping to Politics**. Englewood Cliffs, NJ: Silver Burdett, 1990. 130p. $12.95. ISBN 0-8335-9870-8. (History of the Civil Rights Movement). 6-9

When Civil Rights workers came to her Mississippi town in 1962, Fannie Lou Hamer (1917-1977) was 45. She knew that any African American who registered to vote would suffer consequences, but she was one of the first to volunteer and spent the last 15 years of her life as a civil rights activist. She said "I'm sick and tired of being sick and tired!" She testified before the Democratic National Convention in 1968 and founded Freedom Farm Cooperative in 1969. She then ran unsuccessfully for the Mississippi state senate. Suggested Reading, Sources, and Index.

1841.   Rubel, David. **The Scholastic Encyclopedia of the Presidents and Their Times**. New York: Scholastic, 1994. 224p. $16.95. ISBN 0-590-49366-3. 4 up

Each page of the text corresponds to one year, beginning with 1789 and ending in 1994. In the first year of a President's term appears a list of statistics about him, including his nickname. Campaign information corresponds to the year in which the campaign occurred. Information on important events and people appears in boxed text during the appropriate year. At the end of the text, a chart gives results of every presidential election. Index.

1842.   Rubin, Susan Goldman. **Frank Lloyd Wright**. New York: Harry N. Abrams, 1994. 92p. $19.95. ISBN 0-8109-3974-6. (First Impressions). 7-9

Frank Lloyd Wright (1867-1959) built new forms of houses, offices, museums, churches, and hotels. He grew up in the Midwest before becoming an apprentice to the architect Louis Sullivan in Chicago. After he finished his schooling, he began teaching his style of architecture in schools he established in Wisconsin and Arizona. He continued to work well into his eighties; when he died, he was trying to design a mile-high skyscraper. Photographs and Index.

1843.   Ruby, Lois. **Steal Away Home**. New York: Simon & Schuster, 1994. 192p. $15.95. ISBN 0-02-777883-5. 5-8

Dana, 12, in contemporary Kansas, reluctantly strips away wallpaper, and she finds a secret room with a skeleton and a black book inside. As she studies the black book, she pieces together the mystery of the skeleton and the life inside the house before the Civil War. The Quaker inhabitants protected a young Underground Railroad conductor who died in the house while guards were outside searching for runaway slaves.

1844.   Rumbaut, Hendle. **Dove Dream**. Boston: Houghton Mifflin, 1994. 119p. $13.95. ISBN 0-395-68393-9. 7-10

In 1963, Dove, 13, goes to live with her aunt in Kansas while her parents reassess their relationship. Dove likes her aunt's life as waitress at a truck stop, and she expects to learn something about adult attitudes. During that summer, she prays for her parents, Marilyn Monroe, the Russians, and the astronauts. She gets more than her desires when she reads her grandmother's letters and begins to think about, and practice, her Chickasaw heritage.

1845.   Rummel, Jack. **Langston Hughes**. New York: Chelsea House, 1988. 112p. $18.95; $7.95pa. ISBN 1-55546-595-1; 0-7910-0201-2pa. (Black Americans of Achievement). 7 up

At 19, Langston Hughes (1902-1967) published his first piece of poetry in a major magazine. Soon he became a force in the Harlem Renaissance, a movement in New York City. His poetry introduced a new form incorporating elements of jazz and blues music with Black speech patterns. He traveled all over the world as he expanded his literary achievements to drama, essay, and prose. He had his own difficulties, however, during the 1950s. He faced the American government as an African American who had had ties to Communism. Photographs highlight the text. Chronology, Further Reading, and Index.

1846.   Rummel, Jack. **Robert Oppenheimer: Dark Prince**. New York: Facts on File, 1992. 140p. $17.95. ISBN 0-8160-2598-3. (Makers of Modern Science). 7 up

Robert Oppenheimer (1904-1967) grew up in a wealthy Jewish family, attended Harvard, and studied physics at Cambridge in England. He returned to California and Berkeley to teach nuclear physics. In the late 1930s, physicists discovered that uranium atoms split, and they realized that one could make an enormous bomb from this phenomenon. The government recruited Oppenheimer, a difficult and arrogant man, to organize a laboratory to oversee creation of a bomb for the United States, and he began the Manhattan Project. But after nuclear arms became available to many countries, Oppenheimer encouraged treaties and negotiations because he knew the bomb could destroy Earth. Glossary, Further Reading, and Index.

1847.   Rushton, Lucy. **Birth Customs**. New York: Thomson Learning, 1993. 32p. $13.95; $5.95pa. ISBN 1-56847-034-7; 1-56847-502-0pa. (Comparing Religions). 4-8

Six major religions—Buddhism, Christianity, Hinduism, Judaism, Islam, and Sikhism—have customs surrounding the birth of a child. The text looks at the choosing of a name, the prayers said over the child, the ceremonies, and gifts to the child and family. Photographs enhance the information. Glossary, Books to Read, and Index.

1848.   Rushton, Lucy. **Death Customs**. New York: Thomson Learning, 1993. 32p. $13.95; $5.95pa. ISBN 1-56847-031-2; 1-56847-503-9pa. (Comparing Religions). 4-8

Six major religions—Buddhism, Christianity, Hinduism, Judaism, Islam, and Sikhism—have specific rituals for approaching death. The text looks at the practices, the attitudes toward death, mourning customs, and ways to remember the dead. Glossary, Books to Read, and Index.

1849.   Russell, Sharman. **Frederick Douglass: Abolitionist Editor**. New York: Chelsea House, 1988. 110p. $18.95; $7.95pa. ISBN 1-55546-580-3; 1-7910-0204-7pa. (Black Americans of Achievement). 5 up

Frederick Douglass (1817?-1895) escaped slavery and became an orator, writer, and leader in the antislavery movement during the early nineteenth century. His newspaper, *The North Star*, helped others learn what was happening in the abolitionist movement. Black-and-white illustrations enhance the text. Bibliography, Chronology, and Index.

1850.   Rutberg, Becky. **Mary Lincoln's Dressmaker**. New York: Walker, 1994. 176p. $15.95. ISBN 0-8027-8224-5. 5 up

Elizabeth Keckley (c. 1818-1907) was a servant in the Lincoln White House, and she kept a diary. But she was much more than a servant; she was also Mary Lincoln's confidante. The text uses information from her writing and facts about the times to recreate a story of Mary Lincoln, Abraham Lincoln's wife. It also reveals the life of a slave before and after freedom and the perils of a Black businesswoman. Bibliography, Further Reading, and Index. *Notable Children's Trade Books in the Field of Social Studies.*

1851.   Ryan, Cary, ed. **Louisa May Alcott: Her Girlhood Diary**. Mark Graham, illustrator. Mahwah, NJ: Troll, BridgeWater, 1993. 42p. $14.95; $4.95pa. ISBN 0-8167-3139-X; 0-8167-3140-3pa. 5 up

Through her diaries, Louisa May Alcott (1832-1888) reveals the influences of her father, her mother, and her sisters in her life. She confides about her moods as a young girl and shows her feelings of doubt as she grew up.

1852.   Rylant, Cynthia. **I Had Seen Castles**. San Diego, CA: Harcourt Brace, 1993. 97p. $10.95. ISBN 0-15-238003-5. 7 up

John, 17 in 1941, wants to enlist immediately when the Japanese bomb Pearl Harbor. He meets Ginny, who is against all war, and when he enlists, he sacrifices their relationship. As he reflects 50 years later while he lives alone in Canada, he thinks of his losses, including Ginny and his country. Although he had wanted to see castles since he was nine, and he did see them during the war, he wonders if the sacrifices were worth it. No one in the United States had understood his suffering, and he had had to move to Canada. *New York Public Library Books for the Teen Age.*

1853.   Rylant, Cynthia. **Something Permanent**. Walker Evans, photographer. San Diego, CA: Harcourt Brace, 1994. 61p. $17. ISBN 0-15-277090-9. 8 up

These short poems, some suggestive, react to photographs taken by Walker Evans during the Great Depression. Both poetry and picture reveal an emotional view of life at that time. *American Library Association Best Books for Young Adults, American Library Association Recommended Books for the Reluctant Young Reader,* and *Booklist Editors' Choice.*

S

1854. Safer, Morley. **Flashbacks: On Returning to Vietnam**. 1990. New York: St. Martin's Press, 1991. 206p. $5.99pa. ISBN 0-312-92482-8pa. YA

In 1965, 4 years after the Vietnam War's beginning and 10 years before its end, Morley Safer, a CBS news correspondent, traveled to Vietnam and went on a search-and-destroy mission with the U.S. Marines to the hamlet of Cam Ne. His television footage of troops burning peasant huts brought the horrors of the war into family rooms throughout America. He returned to Vietnam in 1990 and interviewed both South and North Vietnamese. His contrast of the past to the present emphasizes the changes in politics, the folly of war, and the consequences of defeat.

1855. Sagan, Miriam. **Women's Suffrage**. San Diego, CA: Lucent, 1995. 96p. $16.95. ISBN 1-56006-290-8. (World History). 7 up

Women's rights concerns began many years ago, and the text traces them from Mary Wollstonecraft's *A Vindication of the Rights of Women*, published in England in 1792. In nineteenth-century America, Susan B. Anthony refused to accept the fact that she was ineligible to vote, and in 1872, she and friends registered to vote by intimidating the registrar. They voted in the election but were immediately arrested. Anthony, however, defended herself in court by saying that the Constitution gave her the right, and although the judge disagreed and fined her, she refused to pay. Beliefs like hers led to the eventual constitutional amendment that gave women the right to vote in 1920. The text looks at the history of these attempts for justice with chapters on women and the abolitionist movement; the Convention for Women's Rights in 1848 at Seneca Falls, New York; Susan B. Anthony in the 1850s; the Civil War and passage of the Civil Rights amendments; the changing roles of women; the final push for suffrage; and the development of feminism. Notes, For Further Reading, Additional Works Consulted, and Index.

1856. Salisbury, Graham. **Blue Skin of the Sea**. New York: Delacorte, 1992. 215p. $15.95. ISBN 0-385-30596-6. New York: Laurel, 1994. 215p. $3.99pa. ISBN 0-440-21905-1pa. 4-7

In 1953, Sonny at six fears the sea, and he lives in Hawaii. He does not know why he hates it until after his father disappears in his sampan. Then Sonny remembers falling into the water at the age of one. A yachter finds his father and brings him home. Sonny realizes that he must get to know his father, although they are very different, and learn something about his mother, who died when Sonny was only a few months old.

1857. Salisbury, Graham. **Under the Blood-Red Sun**. New York: Delacorte, 1994. 246p. $15.95. ISBN 0-385-32099-X. 5-8

When Tomi Nakaji is in eighth grade in Hawaii, the Japanese bomb Pearl Harbor. As the son and grandson of Japanese immigrant workers who have been proud of their heritage but who are interred as a result of the bombing, Tomi becomes an enemy himself. He, his sister, and mother live through the trauma of the times with the help of others who know that they are not guilty for decisions made by others who happen to be of the same heritage. *Scott O'Dell Award for Historical Fiction.*

1858. Salmon, Marylynn. **The Limits of Independence: American Women 1760-1800**. New York: Oxford University Press, 1994. 141p. $22. ISBN 0-19-508125-0. (The Young Oxford History of Women in the United States). 7 up

The text discusses life for American women from 1760 to 1800. Childbirth practices changed for some women during this period as new methods evolved. Iroquois women, however, still preferred their secluded forest bed, while some wealthy white women began to use birthing chairs. Yet the sexual division of work continued. After the War of Independence, women wanted a public role for mothers, although in the new republic, women of color had to cope with the additional problem of their race. Women both gained and lost the right to vote in New Jersey, raised funds for the American Army, had a private ladies' academy founded in Philadelphia, began charitable and reform societies after the Second Great Awakening, and saw the slave trade end. Chronology, Further Reading, and Index.

1859. Salmoral, Manuel Lucena. **America 1492: Portrait of a Continent 500 Years Ago**. New York: Facts on File, 1990. 239p. $50. ISBN 0-8160-2483-9. YA

The text gives details about the Incan, Aztec, and Mayan societies of Latin America as well as the cultures in the southwestern area of the current United States. Among the topics presented are the customs of these people, including birth, death, eating, music, sports, medicine, and stimulants. Also included are the achievements of the people in architecture, art, and science. The rigidity of the societies may have led to their destruction. Photographs and drawings enhance the text. Bibliography, Glossary, and Index.

1860. San Souci, Robert. **N. C. Wyeth's Pilgrims**. San Francisco: Chronicle, 1991. Unpaged. $13.95. ISBN 0-87701-806-5. 3 up

The text uses the beautiful illustrations by N. C. Wyeth (1882-1945), completed in the 1940s, of the Pilgrims coming to America. The pictures are a way of retelling the story of their arrival at New Plymouth, Massachusetts, in 1620. The facts are less important than the pictures in this text.

1861. Sandak, Cass R. **The Eisenhowers**. New York: Crestwood House, 1993. 48p. $12.95. ISBN 0-89686-653-X. (First Families). 5 up

The text examines the life of the World War II general Dwight D. Eisenhower (1890-1969), who became the 34th President of the United States. It describes his relationship with his wife, Mamie. Illustrations highlight the text. Bibliography and Index.

1862. Sandak, Cass R. **The Franklin Roosevelts**. New York: Crestwood House, 1992. 48p. $12.95. ISBN 0-89686-639-4. (First Families). 5 up

Franklin Delano Roosevelt (1882-1945) became the 32nd President of the United States during the Depression. He and his wife Eleanor (1884-1962) had an unusual partnership during his unprecedented four terms in the White House. Illustrations highlight the text. Bibliography and Index.

1863. Sandak, Cass R. **The Jacksons**. New York: Crestwood House, 1992. 48p. $12.95. ISBN 0-89686-636-X. (First Families). 5 up

Andrew Jackson (1767-1845), the 7th President of the United States from 1829 until 1837, was married to Rachel Jackson (1767-1828), who died as he took office. The text emphasizes his years in office. Illustrations highlight the text. Bibliography and Index.

1864. Sandak, Cass R. **The Jeffersons**. New York: Crestwood House, 1992. 48p. $12.95. ISBN 0-89686-637-8. (First Families). 5 up

Thomas Jefferson (1743-1826) was the 3rd President of the United States. Jefferson was a widower when he reached office. The text gives an overview of the private and political situations in which he was involved, including the Louisiana Purchase. Illustrations highlight the text. Bibliography and Index.

1865. Sandak, Cass R. **The John Adamses**. New York: Crestwood House, 1992. 48p. $12.95. ISBN 0-89686-640-8. (First Families). 5 up

John Adams (1735-1826), the second American President, and Abigail Adams (1744-1818) were happily married for many years. Their letters revealed much about their relationship. The text also discusses other periods of Adams's life. Illustrations highlight the text. Bibliography and Index.

1866. Sandak, Cass R. **The Lincolns**. New York: Crestwood House, 1992. 48p. $12.95. ISBN 0-89686-641-6. (First Families). 5 up

Abraham Lincoln (1809-1865) had a stormy marriage to Mary Todd Lincoln (1818-1882), but reports indicate that Lincoln was devoted to his family. The text examines his family life and political career. Illustrations highlight the text. Bibliography and Index.

1867. Sandak, Cass R. **The Lyndon Johnsons**. New York: Crestwood House, 1993. 48p. $12.95. ISBN 0-89686-644-0. (First Families). 5 up

Lyndon Baines Johnson (1908-1973) was the 36th President of the United States, taking his post after John Kennedy was assassinated in 1963. He, his wife, and his two daughters lived in the White House. Although Johnson had a long career in Congress, the text discusses his family's life in the White House. Bibliography and Index.

1868. Sandak, Cass R. **The Madisons**. New York: Crestwood House, 1992. 48p. $12.95. ISBN 0-89686-642-4. (First Families). 5 up

James Madison (1751-1836), known as the "Father of the Constitution," was the 4th President of the United States. Dolley Madison (1768-1849), his wife, was beloved by those who knew her and served as the hostess for Thomas Jefferson when he occupied the White House. The text emphasizes the White House years of the Madison family. Illustrations highlight the text. Bibliography and Index.

1869. Sandak, Cass R. **The Nixons**. New York: Crestwood House, 1992. 48p. $12.95. ISBN 0-89686-638-6. (First Families). 5 up

Richard Nixon (1913-1994) became the 37th President of the United States. When he was in the White House, his wife Pat was with him, and he had a close relationship with his two daughters. The text emphasizes their time in the White House until Nixon resigned from his office in 1974. Illustrations highlight the text. Bibliography and Index.

1870. Sandak, Cass R. **The Reagans**. New York: Crestwood House, 1993. 48p. $12.95. ISBN 0-89686-646-7. (First Families). 5 up

Ronald Reagan (b. 1911) was President from 1982 until 1990. He and his wife, Nancy Davis Reagan, lived in the White House while his older children were elsewhere. The text discusses his life and his relationship with his wife. Illustrations highlight the text. Bibliography and Index.

1871. Sandak, Cass R. **The Tafts**. New York: Crestwood House, 1993. 48p. $12.95. ISBN 0-89686-647-5. (First Families). 5 up

William Howard Taft (1857-1930) occupied the White House as the 27th President from 1909 to 1913. He was the only President to also serve as Supreme Court justice. The text discusses his life, especially his time in the White House, and his relationship with his wife Nellie Herron Taft (1861-1943).

1872. Sandak, Cass R. **The Theodore Roosevelts**. New York: Crestwood House, 1991. 48p. $12.95. ISBN 0-89686-634-3. (First Families). 5 up

Theodore Roosevelt (1858-1919) became President of the United States in 1901 when William McKinley was assassinated. He initiated lawsuits against big companies in order to "trust bust." He met John Muir and created important conservation legislation. He wanted to help people who had little power, and this commitment reelected him in 1904. He also mediated the end of the Russo-Japanese War, and for these efforts, he won the Nobel Peace Prize. While he was working internationally, he also had a family with him, and the text presents these important people in his life. Illustrations highlight the text. Bibliography and Index.

1873. Sandak, Cass R. **The Trumans**. New York: Crestwood House, 1992. 48p. $12.95. ISBN 0-89686-643-2. (First Families). 5 up

The text focuses on Harry Truman (1884-1972), his wife, and his daughter Margaret as well as his years in the presidency, from 1945 to 1952 after the beginning of the Cold War. Illustrations highlight the text. Bibliography and Index.

1874. Sandak, Cass R. **The Washingtons**. New York: Crestwood House, 1991. 48p. $12.95. ISBN 0-89686-635-1. (First Families). 5 up

George Washington (1732-1799), the first President of the United States, inherited Mount Vernon in Virginia when his half-brother died. He married Martha Custis, and they lived on the estate. The text emphasizes Washington's years as President and his relationship with his family. Illustrations enhance the text. Bibliography and Index.

1875. Sandak, Cass R. **The Wilsons**. New York: Crestwood House, 1993. 48p. $12.95. ISBN 0-89686-651-3. (First Families). 5 up

Woodrow Wilson (1856-1924) was the 28th President of the United States. The text describes his time in office as well as his relationship with his family. Illustrations highlight the text. Bibliography and Index.

1876. Sandberg, Peter Lars. **Dwight D. Eisenhower**. New York: Chelsea House, 1986. 116p. $18.95. ISBN 0-87754-521-9. (World Leaders Past and Present). 5 up

In 1911, Dwight David Eisenhower (1890-1969) entered West Point and began his illustrious career in the military. Franklin D. Roosevelt appointed him to lead the Allied Forces in Europe, where he controlled the Normandy landing on June 6, 1944, known as D-Day. He was elected to the U.S. presidency in 1952 and reelected in 1956, but while becoming a shrewd Cold War negotiator, he did little to curb the anti-Communist hysteria throughout the country. Photographs highlight the text. Chronology, Further Reading, and Index.

1877. Sandburg, Carl. **Abe Lincoln Grows Up**. James Daugherty, illustrator. 1928. San Diego, CA: Harcourt Brace, 1985. 222p. $20.00 ISBN 0-15-201037-8. 4-8

The first 27 chapters of Carl Sandburg's biography of Abraham Lincoln (1809-1865) concern his years of maturity. As a boy, Lincoln walked four miles to school, did chores on the family farm, helped his father cut down trees, and shot wild turkeys. At 17, he split rails and became a champion "rassler" as well as an expert at skinning animals and curing hides. He saw a slave auction in New Orleans, and at 19 he set off to make his fortune. Throughout all, he always read as much as he could.

1878. Sanders, Scott R. **Badman Ballad**. New York: Bradbury, 1986. 241p. $14.95. ISBN 0-02-778230-1. 7-9

In 1813, Eli searches for his brother on the Ohio Valley frontier with a lawyer who knows nothing about the woods. They begin to search for a giant who killed a dwarf with the girl whom the giant saved from the dwarf. Because the giant cannot speak, people in the nearby town are ready to prosecute him unfairly. Eli, the girl, and the lawyer eventually find the gentle giant and protect him from those who would take revenge on the wrong person.

1879.   Sandler, Martin. **Immigrants**. New York: HarperCollins, 1995. 92p. $19.95. ISBN 0-06-024507-7. (Library of Congress Books). 4-8

Using photographs and paintings from the Library of Congress collection, Sandler tells a story of America's immigrants since the late 1800s as they entered Ellis Island, settled in New York and other cities, and worked hard. Some became pioneers and went west. Immigration continues, but immigrants go to a variety of places throughout the country. The Library of Congress and Index. *Notable Children's Trade Books in the Field of Social Studies*.

1880.   Sandler, Martin. **Presidents**. New York: HarperCollins, 1995. 94p. $19.95. ISBN 0-06-024534-3. (Library of Congress Books). 4-8

In a text complemented by photographs and paintings available in the Library of Congress collection, the reader meets many of the Presidents and their wives and children, sees them relaxing, and hears about their pets. The Library of Congress and Index.

1881.   Sandomir, Larry. **Isadora Duncan: Revolutionary Dancer**. Austin, TX: Raintree/Steck-Vaughn, 1994. 128p. $16.98. ISBN 0-8114-2380-8. (American Troublemakers). 6 up

Isadora Duncan (1877-1927) grew up in a fatherless household, and to earn money she and her sister taught children to dance. She revolutionized the art of ballet by moving away from the rigidity of the classical to find other forms of expressing music. She loved Greek art and unsullied nature, but her choice of immodest costumes to represent these ideas upset her audiences. Thus her innovation in dance and her private life caused both acclaim and criticism. Maps, Photographs, Key Dates, Glossary, Places to Visit, Bibliography and Recommended Readings, and Index.

1882.   Sandoz, Mari. **The Horsecatcher**. 1957. Lincoln, NE: University of Nebraska Press, 1986. 192p. $7.95pa. ISBN 0-8032-4166-6pa. 6 up

Young Elk's Cheyenne tribe expects him to be a warrior in the 1830s, but he prefers to catch and tame mustangs. The idea of killing makes him ill. As he proves his ability to find horses, he captures the Ghost Horse, a beautiful white horse that he wants more than anything. But he sees Kiowa warriors on the way to invade his village, so he must free the horses he has caught, including the white one, to rush home and warn his people. The Kiowa tell that he had caught and freed the Ghost Horse, and his village gives him his new name, "Horsecatcher."

1883.   Sanford, William R. **Chief Joseph: Nez Percé Warrior**. Springfield, NJ: Enslow, 1994. 48p. $14.95. ISBN 0-89490-509-0. (Native American Leaders of the Wild West). 5-7

A Nez Percé warrior was urged by his friends to take retribution because a white man killed his father. He killed four whites who had harmed the Indians but were not the ones responsible for his father's death, and triggered government retaliation. Although this warrior was not a member of Chief Joseph's band, Chief Joseph (1840-1904) knew that the army would not care who had killed the whites because soldiers would kill any group of Indians that they saw. He was right. He led his people during this warring period, the Nez Percé-American War, all the while trying to get peace. He led his tribe toward safety in Canada but was detained 30 miles from the border. He spent the rest of his life in Washington State working to get his people back to their Oregon land, but whites who had settled on it would not leave. Glossary, More Good Reading, and Index.

1884.   Sanford, William R. **Crazy Horse: Sioux Warrior**. Springfield, NJ: Enslow, 1994. 48p. $14.95. ISBN 0-89490-511-2. (Native American Leaders of the Wild West). 5-7

As one of the greatest chiefs of the Oglala Sioux, Crazy Horse (1842-1877) led his warriors against the U.S. Army and won many battles. His famous victory at the Battle of the Little Bighorn caused the defeat of the 7th Cavalry and Lt. Colonel George A. Custer, but Sanford believes he should be remembered for his wise leadership of his people. He was eventually forced to surrender, and he died mysteriously in Fort Robinson, Nebraska. Photographs and reproductions highlight the text. Notes, More Good Reading, Glossary, and Index.

1885.   Sanford, William R. **Geronimo: Apache Warrior**. Springfield, NJ: Enslow, 1994. 48p. $14.95. ISBN 0-89490-510-4. (Native American Leaders of the Wild West). 5-7

Geronimo (1829-1909) spent much of his life trying to avenge the deaths of his wife, mother, and children by Mexicans after they had promised peace in 1848. He became a leader of the Apaches as they fought against the U.S. Army in the later half of the nineteenth century and escaped from several reservations where the army had imprisoned him with other Apaches. Geronimo told his life story in 1906, and he lived in depression until his death in 1909. Glossary, More Good Reading About Geronimo, and Index.

1886. Sanford, William R. **Osceola: Seminole Warrior**. Springfield, NJ: Enslow, 1994. 48p. $14.95. ISBN 0-89490-535-X. (Native American Leaders of the Wild West). 4-10

Osceola (1804-1838), once known as Billy Powell, tried to keep the U.S. government from removing Seminoles from their land in Florida. He led the Second Seminole War, which began in 1835, but the white Jesup betrayed Osceola when he tried to negotiate. Glossary, Notes, More Good Reading, and Index.

1887. Sanford, William R. **Quanah Parker: Comanche Warrior**. Springfield, NJ: Enslow, 1994. 48p. $14.95. ISBN 0-89490-512-0. (Native American Leaders of the Wild West). 5-7

Quanah Parker (1854-1911) was the last great Comanche chief. He led his people in their resistance to resettlement in Texas when white ranchers wanted the land on which they lived. They survived the onslaught of the U.S. Army trying to take their lands, but the cavalry destroyed Parker's herd of more than 1,400 horses before he stopped the Comanche protest. After he took his people on a reservation, he taught them to acquiesce as necessary but to keep their traditional ways as well. Photographs, Notes, More Good Reading, Glossary, and Index.

1888. Sanford, William R. **Red Cloud: Sioux Warrior**. Springfield, NJ: Enslow, 1994. 48p. $14.95. ISBN 0-89490-513-9. (Native American Leaders of the Wild West). 5-7

Red Cloud (1822-1909) led the Oglala Sioux against the U.S. government in Bozeman, Montana, when they began to build forts for white settlers after gold was discovered around 1863. Red Cloud fought many battles, but the one remembered is the Fetterman Fight, which forced the United States to abandon its forts. Notes, Glossary, More Good Reading, and Index.

1889. Sanford, William R. **Sitting Bull: Sioux Warrior**. Springfield, NJ: Enslow, 1994. 48p. $14.95. ISBN 0-89490-514-7. (Native American Leaders of the Wild West). 4-10

Sitting Bull, the Hunkpapa Sioux chief (1834?-1890), led the Plains Sioux for many years and helped to defeat Custer at Little Bighorn. Before his death (while white soldiers were taking him away from his home), he toured with Buffalo Bill Cody. Glossary, Notes, More Good Reading, and Index.

1890. Sante, Luc. **Low Life: Lures and Snares of Old New York**. New York: Farrar, Straus & Giroux, 1991. 414p. $27.50. ISBN 0-374-19414-9. New York: Vintage, 1992. 414p. $16pa. ISBN 0-679-73876-2pa. YA

The book covers Manhattan in New York City during 1840 to 1919 in four sections. Sante examines the streets and buildings (Landscape); the theaters, saloons, gambling, drugs, and prostitution (Sporting Life); street gangs, police, and politics (Arm); and orphans, drifters, and "Bohemians" (Invisible City). What he finds is that the underclass in Manhattan was largely responsible for popular culture and that areas such as the Bowery began to have low-life reputations during colonial times. Anecdotes and character sketches about vice lords and corrupt policemen add to this sociological study of the city during its rise. Bibliography and Index.

1891. Santmyer, Helen H. **And Ladies of the Club**. 1982. New York: Putnam, 1984. 1440p. $19.95. ISBN 0-399-12965-0. New York: Berkley, 1988. 1440p. $5.98pa. ISBN 0-425-10243-2pa. YA

In 1868, Sally and Anne start a group with some of the women in Waynesboro, Ohio. Other members are a judge's wife who believes in temperance and women's suffrage; her daughter, who has had the audacity to marry because she loved the man; a lonely female intellectual; a general's wife whose family later has to endure a scandal; and a teacher who gives her life for her students. Anne marries a physician, and Sally marries a German who makes her the town's wealthiest woman. The events in the lives of these women give the history of the town until Anne, the last charter member, dies of old age.

1892. Sattler, Helen Roney. **The Earliest Americans**. Jean Day Zallinger, illustrator. New York: Clarion, 1993. 125p. $16.95. ISBN 0-395-54996-5. 5-9

The text looks at the earliest people known to have been on the American continent. Chapters include discussions of the Paleo-Indians in Beringia before they came across the Bering Strait, the Paleo-Indians in North America approximately 12,500-22,000 years ago, the big game hunters approximately 7,000-12,000 years ago, the beginnings of civilization from 2,000 to 8,000 years ago, and the rise of empires and nations from 500 to 2,000 years ago. Time Chart, Bibliography, and Index.

1893. Sattler, Helen Roney. **Hominids: A Look Back at Our Ancestors**. Christopher Santoro, illustrator. New York: Lothrop, Lee & Shepard, 1988. 125p. $15.95. ISBN 0-688-06061-7. 4-8

Drawings of early fossil remains decorate this story of our early ancestors: the Australopithecines, Genus Homo, Homo Habilis, Homo Erectus, Homo Sapiens Neanderthalensis, and modern humans (Homo Sapiens). Time Chart, Species Chart, Bibliography, and Index.

1894. Sauerwein, Leigh. **The Way Home**. Miles Hyman, illustrator. New York: Farrar, Straus & Giroux, 1994. 118p. $15. ISBN 0-374-38247-6. 7 up

In a series of short stories set at different times in American history, Sauerwein highlights those who find themselves in minorities. The characters include a boy in 1989 whose Lakota friend is also his father; a lonely pioneer woman in 1860 rescued by a cowhand; an 1853 escape of two slaves pretending to be a prostitute and her bodyguard; a girl learning in 1876 that soldiers had killed her aunt, Cheyenne husband, and her children; a severely disabled boy meeting Geronimo in 1902; and a 1992 series of responses to pictures picked from an album at random that unites the other characters in the book.

1895. Saunders, Alan. **George C. Marshall: A General for Peace**. New York: Facts on File, 1996. 134p. $17.95. ISBN 0-8160-2666-1. 7 up

As a young boy, George C. Marshall (1880-1959) was uninterested in studying, and he suffered the consequences from a father who believed that a warm backside would create intellectual excellence. In essence, his father proved right, as Marshall matured into the man whom President Harry Truman called "the greatest living American." He was the chief coordinator of training and strategy for the military throughout World War II. Chronology, Bibliography, and Index.

1896. Savage, Deborah. **To Race a Dream**. Boston: Houghton Mifflin, 1994. 245p. $14.95. ISBN 0-395-69252-0. 7-10

At 16 in 1906, Theo (Theodora) wants to find her own life after the family moves to Minnesota where her sister is a concert violinist for the Minneapolis Symphony. Theo loves horses and wants to drive them, and the International Stock Feed Farm that keeps harness-racing horses is nearby. Her friend Carl helps her dress like a boy so she can get a job on the farm. She struggles to achieve her dream, and unpretentious Carl helps her while they become enamored of each other.

1897. Savage, Jeff. **Cowboys and Cow Towns of the Wild West**. Springfield, NJ: Enslow, 1995. 48p. $14.95. ISBN 0-89490-603-8. (Trailblazers of the Wild West). 4-7

The text looks at the personal experiences of the cowboys, ranchers, and businesspeople who started the cattle trails and the towns that sprang up to serve them. Among the trails that cowboys followed were the Goodnight-Loving Trail, the Western Trail, the Chisholm Trail, and the Shawnee Trail. A gunshot could start a stampede, and these men (and some women) had to be prepared for such situations. Among the topics discussed are dangers, equipment, cattle drives, the boredom between drives, and roundups. Notes, Glossary, Further Reading, and Index.

1898. Savage, Jeff. **Gold Miners of the Wild West**. Springfield, NJ: Enslow, 1995. 48p. $14.95. ISBN 0-89490-601-1. (Trailblazers of the Wild West). 4-7

The California gold rush period began in 1849 and ended with the Yukon gold rush in 1897. People from all over the world came to the western United States hoping to find money. The text tells of those who found hoards and those who found nothing, of claim-jumpers and of people who helped or hindered the miners. Notes, Glossary, Further Reading, and Index.

1899. Savage, Jeff. **Gunfighters of the Wild West**. Springfield, NJ: Enslow, 1995. 48p. $14.95. ISBN 0-89490-600-3. (Trailblazers of the Wild West). 4-7

In the second half of the nineteenth century, gunfighters were notorious in the Wild West. The text looks at some of these men, from the Shootout at O.K. Corral until their end. The topics include background on the gunfighters, the outlaws, the gangs, and the lawmen who eventually put them out of business. Notes, Glossary, Further Reading, and Index.

1900. Savage, Jeff. **Pioneering Women of the Wild**. Springfield, NJ: Enslow, 1995. 48p. $14.95. ISBN 0-89490-604-6. (Trailblazers of the Wild West). 4-7

Many women lived on the frontier in America. To survive, they had to exhibit great courage. They were teachers, homesteaders, ranchers, outlaws, miners, and reformers. They included such women as Sacajawea, Carrie Nation, Calamity Jane, Belle Starr, Carrie Chapman Catt, and Anna Howard Shaw. Notes, Glossary, Further Reading, and Index.

1901. Savage, Jeff. **Pony Express Riders of the Wild West**. Springfield, NJ: Enslow, 1995. 48p. $14.95. ISBN 0-89490-602-X. (Trailblazers of the Wild West). 4-7

On April 3, 1860, the Pony Express began carrying mail the 2,000 miles between St. Joseph, Missouri, and Sacramento, California. In only 18 months, the telegraph put it out of business, but during that time, men showed that they could ride fast enough to get the mail delivered within 10 days. The text looks at these riders, who dodged angry Native Americans and thieves. Notes, Glossary, Further Reading, and Index.

1902.   Savage, Jeff. **Scouts of the Wild West**. Springfield, NJ: Enslow, 1995. 48p. $14.95. ISBN 0-89490-605-4. 4-7

Pioneers and settlers in the Wild West of the 1800s needed people to find out what was in the territory before they came. Scouts such as Kit Carson and Jim Bridger helped them find their way by leading trapping parties and mapping expeditions and guiding wagon trains. They also protected them from wild animals and bandits. Notes, Glossary, Further Reading, and Index.

1903.   Savin, Marcia. **The Moon Bridge**. New York: Scholastic, 1992. 232p. $13.95. ISBN 0-590-45873-6. 4-7

The war does not affect Ruthie in 1942 until her best friend tells her not to make friends with the new girl in school, Mitzi Fujimoto. Because Ruthie dislikes being told what to do, she defies her friend and begins to talk with Mitzi. What she discovers is a "better" best friend until Mitzi and her family disappear, having been taken to the internment camps. While she is gone, Ruthie writes her about her life, but does not mail the letters. As the end of the war arrives, Mitzi writes and asks to meet Ruthie. When they meet, Mitzi tells her that she had stopped talking during the war. After her family convinced her that to hate would make her the same as those who had imprisoned her, she changed. However, she can never recover the years lost behind the chain fences.

1904.   Sawyer, Kem Knapp. **Marjory Stoneman Douglas: Guardian of the Everglades**. Lowell, MA: Discovery, 1992. 72p. $14.95; $7.95pa. ISBN 1-878668-20-X; 1-878668-28-5pa. 6-8

Marjory Stoneman Douglas (b. 1890) was born into a privileged household in New England, and she attended Wellesley College. Among her jobs was working with the Red Cross. When she moved to Florida, she realized the Everglades were unique, and she has spent much of her life trying to protect the area from poachers and developers. The text looks at her life and the events that made her become the advocate of the Everglades. Index.

1905.   Sawyer, Kem Knapp. **Refugees: Seeking a Safe Haven**. Springfield, NJ: Enslow, 1995. 128p. $17.95. ISBN 0-89490-663-1. (Multicultural Issues). 7-10

Although the text only spends one chapter on the historical aspect of refugees, it includes information about the history of current refugee groups. The United Nations estimates that 1 out of every 125 people is a refugee, forced from home because of human rights violations and loss of freedom. The main groups presented here are refugees from Latin America and the Caribbean, Africa, the Middle East, Asia, and Bosnia. Chapter Notes, Bibliography, and Index.

1906.   Saxby, Maurice. **The Great Deeds of Heroic Women**. Robert Ingpen, illustrator. New York: Peter Bedrick, 1992. 151p. $24.95. ISBN 0-87226-348-7. 6-12

The women, both real and legendary, featured in the text have displayed their courage, intelligence, boldness, forcefulness, and strength in whatever task they had to accomplish. Those discussed are Athena, Aphrodite, Demeter, Circe, Medea, Esther, Judith, Scheherazade, the Queen of Sheba (1000 BC), Boadicea (50 BC), Joan of Arc (1412?-1431), the Hunter Maiden, Vasilissa, Pocahontas (1595?-1617), and Mary Bryant. Bibliography and Index.

1907.   Saxon-Ford, Stephanie. **The Czech Americans**. New York: Chelsea House, 1989. 110p. $14.95. ISBN 0-87754-870-6. (Peoples of North America). 5 up

In the 1880s and 1890s, nearly 100,000 Czechs came to America from central Europe and regions of Bohemia and Moravia. They were skilled, literate, and able to function in many areas of society. The text looks at their arrival, their history, what they did after they came, their religion and community, and their future. Photographs augment the text. Further Reading and Index.

1908.   Scheader, Catherine. **Shirley Chisholm: Teacher and Congresswoman**. Springfield, NJ: Enslow, 1990. 138p. $17.95. ISBN 0-89490-285-7. (Contemporary Women). 6 up

Shirley Chisholm (b. 1924) was the first Black woman elected to Congress and the first to make a serious bid for the presidency when George McGovern won the nomination. She has always wanted to be known as a woman who fought for women and for Blacks. Chronology and Index.

1909.   Schimmel, Annemarie, and Franz Carl Endres. **Mystery of Numbers**. New York: Oxford University Press, 1993. 314p. $25; $12.95pa. ISBN 0-19-506303-1; 0-19-508919-7pa. YA

After reading the various interpretations of numbers from 1 to 40 and various numbers from 42 to 10,000 based on "symbolism, religious connotation, and linguistic correlation," one may decide that numbers have more meaning than one would like. Many of the ideas concern numbers in the Judaic, Christian, and Islamic heritages, as Schimmel looks at the origin of Arabic numbers, the evolution of modern superstitions, number games, the Gnostic relationship, and mysticism. Some numbers may be merely lucky, "feminine," or "perfect." Reproductions and drawings complement the text. Bibliography and Index.

1910.   Schleichert, Elizabeth. **The Life of Dorothea Dix**. Antonio Castro, illustrator. New York: Twenty-First Century Books, 1992. 80p. $13.98. ISBN 0-941477-68-1. (Pioneers in Health and Medicine). 4-7

When Dorothea Dix (1802-1887) visited a prison in 1841, she found women in cells with no furniture, no heat, and no sanitary facilities. When she asked why they were there, the jailer told her that they were insane. For women who had no money and no one to care for them, they had no place to go but to the jails. Dix began to try to establish mental hospitals to look after those who could not help themselves. When the Civil War started, she came to Washington, where she was appointed the Superintendent of U.S. Army Nurses, the highest post in the nation held by a woman. After her death, the study of the mentally ill became a significant branch of medicine. For Further Reading and Index.

1911.   Schleichert, Elizabeth. **The Life of Elizabeth Blackwell**. New York: Twenty-First Century Books, 1992. 80p. $14.95. ISBN 0-941477-66-5. (Pioneers in Health and Medicine). 4-7

Elizabeth Blackwell (1821-1910) became the first female physician in the United States in 1849 and opened the medical field to women. In 1857, she founded the Hospital for Women and Children in New York and announced her desire to have women medical students living there. For Further Reading and Index.

1912.   Schlissel, Lillian. **Black Frontiers: A History of African American Heroes in the Old West**. New York: Simon & Schuster, 1995. 80p. $18. ISBN 0-689-80285-4. 3-7

The text includes short chapters on both individuals and groups in this look at the contributions of Black Americans toward settling the West. Topics such as early Black businesspeople and dime-novel images of Blacks add a broad view of the West to the more widely known stories of Black cowboys. Photographs, Notes, Bibliography, and Index. *Notable Children's Trade Books in the Field of Social Studies.*

1913.   Schlissel, Lillian. **Women's Diaries of the Westward Journey**. 2d ed. New York: Schocken, 1992. 278p. $14pa. ISBN 0-8052-1004-0pa. YA

The text presents excerpts from the diaries of more than 100 women who went on the Overland Trail during the nineteenth century. Schlissel looked for passages that would show a different experience from the writings about men who made the journey. These women wrote while riding in the wagons, when they stopped, or long after the journey's end. Many were pregnant, but the mores of the time kept them from saying anything in their diaries except that they had borne a child. Their greatest trials were not the Indians but disease and accidents; one of the major cholera epidemics occurred on the trail. Women whose husbands either died or left for other reasons raised their families independently, a fact that has generally been ignored. The entries cover three periods: the first migration of families from 1841 to 1850, a second migration of families from 1851 to 1855, and the later journeys, some of wealthy travelers in stagecoaches, from 1856 to 1867. A table of the women included with vital information follows the text. Sources and Index.

1914.   Schlissel, Lillian, Byrd Gibbens, and Elizabeth Hampsten. **Far from Home: Families of the Westward Journey**. New York: Schocken, 1989. 264p. $14pa. ISBN 0-8052-0977-8pa. YA

The text uses the correspondence and autobiographical writings of mothers and daughters who were pioneers as a basis for the stories of three pioneering families. The words show women's roles in the westward movement and the strain that the harshness of frontier life put on the entire family unit. Bibliography and Index.

1915.   Schneider, Dorothy. **American Women in the Progressive Era: 1900-1920**. New York: Facts on File, 1993. 276p. $27.95. ISBN 0-8160-2513-4. YA

The text presents the role of women in American history during 1900-1920. It includes a chapter on Black women but does not mention women from other minorities. It shows how women helped reform society by changing the definitions of housekeeping, raising families, and farm employment. Women learned organizational skills from joining clubs, and they used these to make changes in labor, peace activism, sexual mores, health, labor, and civil liberties. Photographs, Bibliography, and Index.

1916.   Schneider, Dorothy, and Carl J. Schneider. **Into the Breach: American Women Overseas in World War I**. New York: Viking, 1991. 368p. $29.95. ISBN 0-670-83936-1. YA

Twenty-five thousand middle-class, educated American women served in Europe during World War I. They were peace activists, journalists, nurses and Red Cross workers, physicians, Salvation Army and YMCA workers, and canteen workers. This account uses primary sources such as written memoirs, diaries, letters, and interviews, with secondary sources such as novels, to tell the story of these women serving in Europe, Asia, and the Middle East, where more than 348 died. An appendix lists the occupations and organizations in which the women served and the number for each. Because their experiences were soon forgotten, women serving in World War II had similar problems in establishing themselves abroad. Bibliography and Index.

1917.   Schouweiler, Tom. **The Lost Colony of Roanoke: Opposing Viewpoints**. San Diego, CA: Greenhaven, 1991. 80p. $16.95. ISBN 0-89908-093-6. (Great Mysteries—Opposing Viewpoints). 5-9

The Colony of Roanoke on the coast of North Carolina disappeared without much of a trace between 1587 and 1590. The text tries to piece together the mystery by examining the colony's founding by Sir Walter Raleigh and what might have happened based on the members' relationships to each other and to the Native Americans who lived in the area. Reproductions highlight the information. For Further Exploration, Works Consulted, and Index.

1918.   Schraff, Anne E. **American Heroes of Exploration and Flight**. Springfield, NJ: Enslow, 1996. 112p. $17.95. ISBN 0-89490-619-4. (Collective Biographies). 5-9

The text profiles 10 people who have contributed to exploration and flight in America. Included in the profiles are information about their lives, beginning with an exciting event and a brief overview of history to show why their particular contribution was important. Those profiled include Matthew Henson (1866-1955) and Robert Peary (1856-1920), who discovered the North Pole together; Amelia Earhart (1897-1937); Jacqueline Cochran (1910-1980); Sally Ride (b. 1951); and Christa McAuliffe (d. 1986). Notes and Index.

1919.   Schraff, Anne E. **The Great Depression and the New Deal: America's Economic Collapse and Recovery**. New York: Franklin Watts, 1990. 111p. $12.90. ISBN 0-531-10964-X. (Twentieth Century American History). 7 up

When the stock market crashed the American economy in 1929, the aftermath was a depression that changed the United States. The text looks at the crash and President Franklin D. Roosevelt's programs to restore the nation's financial health, which revitalized completely during and after World War II. Photographs supplement the text. Bibliography, Chronology, and Index.

1920.   Schraff, Anne. **Women of Peace: Nobel Peace Prize Winners**. Springfield, NJ: Enslow, 1994. 112p. $17.95. ISBN 0-89490-493-0. (Collective Biographies). 5-9

The first Nobel Peace Prize was awarded in 1901, and since then, nine women have been named winners for their attempts to establish peace in the world. They are Baroness von Suttner (1905), Jane Addams (1931), Emily Green Balch (1946), Mairead Corrigan and Betty Williams (1976), Mother Teresa (1979), Alva Myrdal (1982), Daw Aung San Suu Kyi (1991), and Rigoberta Menchu (1992). Index.

1921.   Schreiner, Samuel A., Jr. **Mayday! Mayday! The Most Exciting Missions of Rescue, Interdiction and Combat in the 200-year Annals of the U.S. Coast Guard**. New York: Donald I. Fine, 1990. 264p. $19.95. ISBN 1-55611-195-9. YA

Since 1790, the Coast Guard, first known as the Revenue and Cutter Service, has protected U.S. coastal areas from foreign enemies, illegal aliens, and smugglers. It has served as a search and rescue (SAR) unit and recently has worked to cut pollution. The text includes 14 narratives that describe these activities and show how important a calm and intelligent response can be in frightening situations. Real-life radio communications and interviews add to the immediacy. Bibliography and Index.

1922.   Schroeder, Alan. **Booker T. Washington: Educator and Racial Spokesman**. New York: Chelsea House, 1992. 142p. $18.95; $7.95pa. ISBN 1-55546-616-8; 0-7910-0252-7pa. (Black Americans of Achievement). 5 up

Booker T. Washington (1856-1915) was born a slave on a Virginia farm and got his freedom when the Civil War ended. He then went to work in the salt furnaces and coal mines of West Virginia. At 16, he walked 200 miles to enroll at Virginia's Hampton Institute. He became a teacher, and in 1881 he went to Tuskegee, Alabama, where he founded a school that became one of the largest and best-endowed of the Black institutions. He worked for a better life for Blacks and wanted them to accept white society in their attempts to raise themselves economically. Photographs enhance the text. Chronology, Further Reading, and Index.

1923.   Schroeder, Alan. **Jack London**. New York: Chelsea House, 1991. 127p. $18.95. ISBN 0-7910-1623-4. (Library of Biography). 5-8

Jack London (1876-1916) was one of the highest paid and most widely read American authors in the early twentieth century, with such novels as *Call of the Wild* and stories like "To Build a Fire." After growing up in the San Francisco area, he started working in a pickle cannery at 13. He became an oyster pirate two years later, then a sailor, next a hobo. By 21, he was a gold miner. When he returned from the Klondike gold rush in 1898, he had much material for future stories but no gold. He was known for many things, including being a socialist and a correspondent during the Russo-Japanese War. Photographs enhance the text. Chronology, Further Reading, and Index.

1924.   Schroeder, Alan. **Josephine Baker**. New York: Chelsea House, 1991. 127p. $18.95. ISBN 0-7910-1116-X. (Black Americans of Achievement). 5 up

Josephine Baker (1906-1975) tried to escape her poverty in St. Louis, Missouri, by entertaining her friends and visiting the city's Black vaudeville houses. At 13, when she made her debut, she realized that she should make an ill-fitting costume be the focus of her act and thus began her comedy. In 1925, she sailed to France, and the French loved both her beauty and her dancing. During World War II, the French Resistance recruited her to be a secret agent. After the war, she turned her estate in southern France into a tourist resort. She was one of the first civil rights crusaders, and she adopted 12 children from different nations to show that people of different backgrounds could live in peace. Photographs complement the text. Chronology, Further Reading, and Index.

1925.   Schultz, Duane P. **Glory Enough for All: The Battle of the Crater: A Novel of the Civil War**. New York: St. Martin's Press, 1993. 360p. $22.95; $5.99pa. ISBN 0-312-09817-0; 0-312-95579-0pa. YA

In 1864, Colonel Pleasants leads a group of Pennsylvania miners to dig a mine shaft under the Confederate fort on Cemetery Hill in preparation for breaking the siege of Petersburg. But the white commanders who lead the ensuing battle bungle it so badly that they sacrifice an entire division of African American troops. The story of Pleasants, his fiancée, and those with him gives a good view of 1864 in Petersburg.

1926.   Schultz, Duane P. **Hero of Bataan: The Story of General Jonathan M. Wainwright**. New York: St. Martin's Press, 1981. 479p. $19.95pa. ISBN 0-312-37011-3pa. YA

A 1906 graduate of West Point, General Jonathan M. Wainwright (1883-1953), or "Skinny," served his country during World War II with such courage that he became a national hero. At Bataan and Corregidor, he led U.S. Army troops when they had few supplies, little food, no backup from the air force or navy, and outdated weapons against Japan's modern and well-equipped army. He held the Japanese for five months. Then he became the highest-ranking American captive during World War II. After he was freed, he received a fourth star and the Medal of Honor. The text looks at Wainwright, a complex man who walked around outside his guard post while the Japanese bombed the Philippines on December 8, 1941, and rallied his men by refusing to be defeated. Bibliography and Index.

1927.   Schultz, Duane P. **The Maverick War: Chennault and the Flying Tigers**. New York: St. Martin's Press, 1987. 335p. $4.95pa. ISBN 0-312-92054-7pa. YA

On July 23, 1941, President Roosevelt signed a secret executive order that authorized the bombing of Tokyo and other Japanese cities. Although this mission was never completed, it shows that America had ventured into the world of covert operations. The person who instituted the plan was Claire Lee Chennault, a controversial ex-army captain. As a consolation, Roosevelt gave him a force of 100 fighter planes and the men to fly them. Chennault had observed the Japanese from China, where he had been working to build airstrips. He knew about their tactics and planes, but the people to whom he gave this information discarded it before the Japanese bombed Pearl Harbor. Chennault's pilots became the Flying Tigers, a group of undisciplined men who became the most successful and unorthodox squadron in World War II. The text uses Chennault's papers, diaries, personal interviews, and military archives in this intriguing story of the First American Volunteer Group or AGV.

1928.   Schultz, Duane P. **Month of the Freezing Moon: The Sand Creek Massacre, November 1864**. New York: St. Martin's Press, 1990. $12.95pa. ISBN 0-312-06417-9pa. YA

In November 1864, J. M. Chivington led the U.S. cavalry into Sand Creek, Colorado, and massacred the Cheyenne families in an encampment there. The text recounts the events that led to the killing and places them in the context of the American West before the 1860s and after. It shows how the insatiable desire for gold and power among the U.S. militia destroyed so many, including Custer at Little Bighorn in 1876. Bibliography and Index.

1929.   Schuman, Michael A. **Eleanor Roosevelt: First Lady and Humanitarian**. Springfield, NJ: Enslow, 1995. 128p. $17.95. ISBN 0-89490-547-3. (People to Know). 5-9

Among the titles used to describe Eleanor Roosevelt (1884-1962) are First Lady, journalist, activist, and delegate to the United Nations. Her concern for others showed in her attempts to help people of all races and economic levels although she had a wealthy and privileged background. She was an early advocate of women's rights, child labor laws, the eight-hour workday, and equality for African Americans. Chronology, Notes, and Index.

1930.   Schuman, Michael A. **Elie Wiesel: Voice from the Holocaust**. Springfield, NJ: Enslow, 1994. 128p. $17.95. ISBN 0-89490-428-0. (People to Know). 5-8

In 1986, Elie Wiesel (b. 1928) won the Nobel Peace Prize. After growing up in Rumania, he almost died because he and his family were taken to Auschwitz, Poland, in 1944, to Hitler's death camp because they were Jewish. He was later transferred to Buchenwald, where he was rescued when the U.S. Army liberated the prisoners. The rest of his family died. He has written books and lectured on his experience while trying to get people to reject bigotry, hatred, and violence. Chronology, Further Reading, and Index.

1931.   Schuman, Michael A. **Martin Luther King, Jr.: Leader for Civil Rights**. Springfield, NJ: Enslow, 1996. 128p. $18.95. ISBN 0-89490-687-9. 5-8

The text begins with Martin Luther King, Jr.'s (1929-1968) "I Have a Dream" speech delivered in 1963. It has enough detail and information about collections at museums and historical sites that the text is worthwhile. Other information is standard and available in other places.

1932.   Schwartz, Barry. **George Washington: The Making of a Symbol**. New York: Free Press, 1987. 250p. $35. ISBN 0-02-928141-5. Ithaca, NY: Cornell University Press, 1990. 250p. $14.95pa. ISBN 0-8014-9747-7pa. 7 up

George Washington (1732-1799) was neither brilliant nor self-confident, and he had no experience with large armies when he began to lead the American forces in the revolution. Washington seems to have been politically ambivalent, with a disrespect for political leaders and a suspicion of the powers that these people seemed to have. He won approval from others because he was careful to avoid power, and when he got it, he relinquished it as soon as possible. The text continues with these ideas and an examination of the country that has idealized Washington over the past two centuries. Notes and Index.

1933.   Schwartzberg, Renée. **Ronald Reagan**. New York: Chelsea House, 1991. 134p. $18.95. ISBN 1-55546-849-7. (World Leaders Past and Present). 5 up

Ronald Reagan (b. 1911) became President after many things had disturbed the United States during the 1970s. As an actor, he had learned to communicate with people, and he made them believe in his conservative vision for a better United States. When he ran for President, he had already demonstrated his abilities as the governor in California. Concerns about his presidency included the reduction in help for the poor and education and the increase in the military budget. He said he would not deal with terrorists, but his subordinates secretly sold arms to Iran and the Nicaraguan rebels. Photographs enhance the text. Chronology, Further Reading, and Index.

1934.   Schwarz, Melissa. **Cochise, Apache Chief**. New York: Chelsea House, 1992. 119p. $18.95; $7.95pa. ISBN 0-7910-1706-0; 0-7910-1694-3pa. (North American Indians of Achievement). 5 up

Cochise (c. 1805-1874) was one of the greatest chiefs in Apache history. He earned respect from his people and fear from his enemies. He was an honest man whom soldiers called a liar when he denied their accusation that he had kidnapped a white boy. When the soldiers murdered his brother and two nephews, he vowed war and made revenge attacks against white settlers for a decade. During the Cochise wars, he became "public enemy number one" to Tucson officials. He continued attacking until 1872, when he concluded a peace treaty with the military. He became the only Apache ever to be granted a reservation for his people. Photographs and reproductions enhance the text. Chronology, Further Reading, and Index.

1935.   Schwarz, Melissa. **Geronimo: Apache Warrior**. New York: Chelsea House, 1991. 128p. $18.95; $7.95pa. ISBN 0-7910-1701-X; 0-7910-1691-9pa. (North American Indians of Achievement). 5 up

The Apaches thought that Geronimo (1823-1909) was a war shaman with mystical power, but the Mexicans and Americans, his enemies, thought he was a fearless and terrifying warrior. He led killing raids against his foes, and during the raids, he lost many family members, including his wife, mother, and children. Four times the U.S. Army forced Geronimo to surrender, and three times he escaped. The fourth time, he was imprisoned and not allowed to return to his homeland. He was relocated to an Oklahoma reservation where he died. Photographs and reproductions enhance the text. Chronology, Further Reading, and Index.

1936.   Schwarz, Melissa. **Wilma Mankiller: Principal Chief of the Cherokees**. New York: Chelsea House, 1994. 110p. $18.95. ISBN 0-7910-1715-X. (North American Indians of Achievement). 5 up

Wilma Mankiller (b. 1945) moved to San Francisco at 12 when a drought struck her family's Oklahoma region. In 1969, when Native Americans seized Alcatraz Island to protest U.S. government policy on Indians, Mankiller became a supporter. In 1976, she returned to Oklahoma and continued community development work. Then in 1985, she became the first woman to head the Cherokee Nation. She continues to encourage her people to work together. Photographs enhance the text. Chronology, Further Reading, and Index.

1937.   Scordato, Ellen. **Sarah Winnemucca: Northern Paiute Writer and Diplomat**. New York: Chelsea House, 1992. 126p. $18.95; $7.95pa. ISBN 0-7910-1710-9; 0-7910-1696-Xpa. (North American Indians of Achievement). 5 up

Sarah Winnemucca (1844-1891), a Northern Paiute, grew up in what is now the state of Nevada, where she learned English. She became an ambassador between the tribal and the non-Indian world by arguing against the displacement of her people, the taking of their lands, and the theft of their property. She served as a guide during the Bannock War of 1878 and tried to get Indians and whites to live together peacefully. To tell their story, she wrote *Life Among the Paiutes*, published in 1883, as the first book about Indians by an Indian woman. She traveled across the country trying to raise money for education and was able to start one of the first Indian-run schools. Photographs and engravings enhance the text. Chronology, Further Reading, and Index.

1938.   Scott, Elaine. **Funny Papers: Behind the Scenes of the Comics**. Margaret Miller, photographer. New York: Morrow, 1993. 90p. $15. ISBN 0-688-11575-6. 4-8

The first cartoon appeared in 1895 in a New York newspaper. Since that time, the comics have been newspaper features. The text looks at Hank Ketcham and *Dennis the Menace*, Charles Schulz and *Peanuts*, and Dean Young and *Blondie* to give insight about this aspect of our culture. Photographs supplement the text. Index.

1939.   Scott, John Anthony. **Settlers on the Eastern Shore: The British Colonies in North America 1607-1750**. New York: Facts on File, 1991. 133p. $17.95. ISBN 0-8160-2327-1. (Library of American History). 8 up

The people who first came to the eastern shores of America to colonize it faced more problems than they had expected. The people who came were geographers, explorers, fisherman, sea captains, and settlers. They found a beautiful country with wildfowl, fish, wild fruits, and, not so happily, rattlesnakes. Chapters include information on New England, Mary Rowlandson, the woods of William Penn, Virginia and its planters, the Africans who came, Manhattan, Jonathan Edwards, and the Great Awakening. Bibliography and Index.

1940.   Scott, John Anthony, and Robert Alan Scott. **John Brown of Harper's Ferry**. New York: Facts on File, 1988. 184p. $16.95. ISBN 0-8160-1347-0. (Makers of America). 5 up

John Brown (1800-1859) is best known for his raid on the arms factories in Harpers Ferry, West Virginia, in 1859. He was trying to spark a slave rebellion, but it ended unsuccessfully when most of his men were killed, and he had to surrender to the federal troops. He and seven of his men who survived were hanged because of their insurrection. The text shows that Brown's love of humans and his belief that all people were equal propelled him toward violence when he saw no other way. Maps, Bibliography, and Index.

1941.   Scott, Lynn H. **The Covered Wagon and Other Adventures**. Lincoln, NE: University of Nebraska Press, 1987. 134p. $15. ISBN 0-8032-4179-8. 4-7

Before 1910, Lynn Scott lived in the West when it was underdeveloped. He illustrated his stories about family experiences on their covered wagon in 1906, and other stories about encounters with Indians, sheepmen, and freighters; crises with rattlesnakes, black ants, and rock avalanches; and Rocky Mountain spotted fever. His story gives a view of life in western America at that time.

1942.   Scott, Richard. **Jackie Robinson**. New York: Chelsea House, 1987. 110p. $18.95; $7.95pa. ISBN 1-55546-609-5; 0-7910-0200-4pa. (Black Americans of Achievement). 5 up

Jackie Robinson (1919-1972), former All-American football player and army officer, was playing for the Kansas City Monarchs when asked to join the Brooklyn Dodgers as the first African American baseball player in the modern major leagues. After he stopped playing, he became vice president of Chock Full O'Nuts and a spokesman for the NAACP. He wanted equal opportunity at work, condemned drug use, and urged people to return to family values. Photographs and reproductions enhance the text. Chronology, Further Reading, and Index.

1943.   Scott, Robert A. **Chief Joseph and the Nez Percés**. New York: Facts on File, 1993. 134p. $17.95. ISBN 0-8160-2475-8. (Makers of America). 5 up

The American government attacked Chief Joseph's (1840-1904) Nez Percé tribe in June 1877, trying to kill the people before they could start another Sioux uprising as they marched from Oregon to a new home chosen by the government in Idaho. Women and children were slaughtered in their tipis, with soldiers saying later that they had to kill them because they were going to fight back. Chief Joseph tried to protect his people, but by October of that year, he knew they could not win. Even after this defeat, he continued to try to regain the ancestral home of his people, but he could not. A description of Chief Joseph at that time by a man who later regretted the horrible treatment of the Native Americans said that he was "a splendid looking man . . . fully six feet high . . . . His forehead is high, his eyes bright yet kind, his nose finely cut . . . ." Bibliography and Index.

1944.   **Scrawl! Writing in Ancient Times**. Minneapolis, MN: Runestone Press, 1994. 72p. $22.95. ISBN 0-8225-3209-3. (Buried Worlds). 6 up

Ancient writing, or paleography, the study of writing, gives an insight into what ancient civilizations had achieved in communication and what they thought was important. The text looks at various ancient scripts and what they reveal. Glossary and Index.

1945.   Sears, Stephen W., and G. S. Boritt, eds. **Lincoln's Generals**. New York: Oxford University Press, 1994. 248p. $22. ISBN 0-19-508505-1. YA

Civil War historians discuss five generals who served under Lincoln: Sherman, McClellan, Hooker, Meade, and Grant. Of the generals, the lack of aggression in McClellan, Hooker, and Meade finally led Lincoln to release them from command. McClellan, complex as well as talented, did not perform as he should have. Sherman's personality contrasted with Lincoln's, and he had differing views about slavery, Blacks in the military, and the reconstruction of the Confederate states. Hooker tended to be an excellent strategist, and while Grant understood the politics of war, they repelled him. Bibliography.

1946.   Seaver, James E. **A Narrative of the Life of Mrs. Mary Jemison**. Norman, OK: University of Oklahoma Press, 1992. 205p. $25.95. ISBN 0-8016-2381-8. YA

Around 1758, Shawnee Indians captured Mrs. Mary Jemison when she was a teenager after mutilating and killing her family. Two Seneca sisters bought her, and she willingly stayed with them. She eventually married twice and had several children. Her story shows amazing courage and a will to survive. Bibliography, Notes, and Index.

1947.   Sebestyen, Ouida. **Far from Home**. Boston: Little, Brown, 1980. 191p. $15.95. ISBN 0-316-77932-6. New York: Laurel, 1983. 191p. $2.95pa. ISBN 0-440-92640-8pa. 7 up

When his mute mother dies during the Depression, Salty, 13, asks for work at a boardinghouse where his mother had worked and where she wanted him to go before she died. While there, he meets the father who never acknowledged him while his mother lived. They and the others in the boardinghouse have to learn to adjust to each other and the difficulties of the Depression. *School Library Journal Best Book.*

1948.   Sebestyen, Ouida. **Words by Heart**. Boston: Little, Brown, 1979. 144p. $15.95. ISBN 0-316-77931-8. New York: Bantam, 1991. 144p. $3.99pa. ISBN 0-553-27179-2pa. 4-8

Lena Sills, 12 in 1910, wins a spelling contest instead of a white boy and refuses the first prize of a bow tie. Someone upset that a Black family lives in the small town leaves a big butcher knife stabbed through bread on their table. Because Lena has only been concerned with making her father proud, she has been unaware of the prejudice surrounding her. A tragedy causes the white sharecropper family to understand that they must all work together to be successful. *International Children's Books Awards* and *American Book Award.*

1949.   Selfridge, John W. **John F. Kennedy: Courage in Crisis**. New York: Fawcett Columbine, 1989. 120p. $3.95pa. ISBN 0-449-90399-0pa. 5-9

The text looks at the life of John Fitzgerald Kennedy (1917-1963), the youngest man to be elected President of the United States. Included are chapters on the Cuban crisis, what being a "Kennedy" meant, his heroic action in World War II, the beginning of his political career, his role as President and the "New Frontierism," his fight against the Cold War, his arguments for civil rights, and his death in Dallas. Glossary.

1950.   Senna, Carl. **The Black Press and the Struggle of Civil Rights**. New York: Franklin Watts, 1993. 160p. $21.40; $6.95pa. ISBN 0-531-11036-2; 0-531-15693-1pa. 8 up

The text looks at the history of Black newspapers and journalists and their roles in the civil rights struggles since slavery. Among those discussed are T. Thomas Fortune, Frederick Douglass, Ida B. Wells, W. E. B. Du Bois, Marcus Garvey, and Carl Rowan. Chapter topics include slavery, the Civil War, and Reconstruction. Photographs, Bibliography, and Index.

1951.   Seymour-Jones, Carole. **Refugees**. New York: New Discovery, 1992. 48p. $12.95. ISBN 0-02-735402-4. (Past and Present). 5-7

People have had to flee their homes because of war, poverty, starvation, or government persecution. Among the historical flights of people included in the text are the dispersions under Genghis Khan and the Mongols around 1214, the Trail of Tears in 1838 when the Cherokees had to leave their homes, the boat people fleeing to Thailand following the fall of Saigon in 1975, and the escape of the Israelites from Egypt around 1280 BC. The text looks at the way these people coped and how other societies have tried to help. Key Dates, Glossary, and Index.

1952.   Shaara, Michael. **The Killer Angels**. 1976. New York: Random House, 1993. 355p. $20; $5.99pa. ISBN 0-679-42541-1; 0-345-34810-9pa. YA

When Robert E. Lee led his Army of Northern Virginia into Gettysburg, Pennsylvania, to meet the Army of the Potomac, no one realized that those four days in July 1863 would be so momentous. Lee, a man who neither believed in slavery nor owned slaves, fought against the Union. The military leaders on both sides of the conflict made decisions that eventually led to Lee's defeat. The omniscient point of view allows the reader to muse along with these commanders and other people at the scene about the events in which they were involved. *Pulitzer Prize.*

1953.   Shapiro, Miles. **Charles Drew: Founder of the Blood Bank.** Austin, TX: Raintree/Steck-Vaughn, 1997. 112p. $18.98. ISBN 0-8172-4403-4. (Innovative Minds). 7-8

Charles Richard Drew (1904-1950) was the first African American to earn the degree of Doctor of Science in Medicine, and for his doctoral thesis, he had written about his discoveries in blood and plasma transfusion. Because of the need for blood during World War II, Charles Drew's expertise was called upon. He helped collect and preserve blood. His achievements were important milestones for blood banks and for African Americans. Glossary, Further Reading, Sources, and Index.

1954.   Sheafer, Silvia Anne. **Women in America's Wars**. Springfield, NJ: Enslow, 1996. 112p. $17.95. ISBN 0-89490-553-8. (Collective Biographies). 6-9

The text profiles 10 women who have helped America during times of war. Included in the profiles are information about their lives, beginning with an exciting event and a brief overview of history to show why their contribution was important. They include Mary Hays, known as Molly Pitcher (1754-1832), and Pamela Davis Dorman, the first female U.S. chaplain to serve in the Marines. Notes and Index.

1955.   Shenkman, Richard. **"I Love Paul Revere, Whether He Rode or Not," Warren Harding**. New York: HarperCollins, 1991. 226p. $12pa. ISBN 0-06-092330-Xpa. YA

Many "truths" about American history are stories that have grown into legends with idealized characters and situations. Among the stories that Shenkman has researched that are different from contemporary interpretation include Thoreau, the Pilgrims, the early republic, women's roles, and Betsy Ross. Bibliography and Index.

1956.   Sherman, Eileen B. **Independence Avenue**. Philadelphia, PA: Jewish Publication Society, 1990. 145p. $13.95. ISBN 0-8276-0367-3. 5-8

In 1907, Elias, 14, arrives in Kansas City from Russia, alone and with no job. He talks his way into a job in a department store, hoping to become a tailor, his family's trade. He meets the boss's daughter, but her aunt sees him as an immigrant, beneath Rebecca's attentions. He must learn how to cope in this new environment. He does, but he first hears of his parents' deaths in a pogrom, and his six-year-old brother arrives to live with him.

1957.   Sherr, Lynn. **Failure Is Impossible: Susan B. Anthony in Her Own Words**. New York: Times Books, 1995. 384p. $23; $15pa. ISBN 0-8129-2430-4; 0-8129-2718-4pa. YA

Susan B. Anthony (1820-1906) was a Quaker who believed that she could achieve anything she wanted. She left speeches, letters, and journals that reveal her unfailing belief in the equality of all people. The passages show Anthony's distress over the plight of women in all social classes and her willingness to support and fight for their rights under the law. Bibliography, Notes, and Index.

1958.   Sherr, Lynn, and Jurate Kazickas. **Susan B. Anthony Slept Here: A Guide to American Women's Landmarks**. 1977. New York: Times Books, 1994. 579p. $20pa. ISBN 0-8129-2223-9pa. YA

The 2,000 sites listed in the text connect to many women, including Alice Paul (Equal Rights Amendment), Golda Meir, Mother Clara M. Hale, and Madame C. J. Walker. The text shows that women's history begins at different times depending on the area of the United States in which the woman lived. In the East, it extends from the revolutionary period. In the West, it began during the pioneer period, and in the South, the Civil War period. Illustrations, Bibliography, and Index.

1959.   Sherrow, Victoria. **Gideon v. Wainwright: Free Legal Counsel**. Springfield, NJ: Enslow, 1995. 104p. $17.95. ISBN 0-89490-507-4. (Landmark Supreme Court Cases). 7 up

In 1961, Clarence Gideon, a Florida laborer, was convicted of burglary. Although poorly educated, he studied law in prison and saw that he could petition the higher courts for a reversal of the decision because he had been denied the constitutional right of "assistance of counsel." His case led the Supreme Court to require that courts appoint a lawyer if a criminal defendant who could not afford a lawyer might be sent to jail. The text shows each side of the argument as well as some of the results of the Court's decision. Bibliography, Glossary, and Index.

1960.   Sherrow, Victoria. **Linus Pauling: Investigating the Magic Within**. Austin, TX: Raintree/Steck-Vaughn, 1997. 112p. $18.98. ISBN 0-8172-4400-X. (Innovative Minds). 7-8

While still a chemistry student, Linus Pauling (1901-1994) became intrigued about chemical phenomena that caused substances to disappear and new ones to take their place. What he found during his research changed physics and biology. He discovered the helical structure of protein molecules and created controversy with his belief that vitamin C could prevent disease. Outside his laboratory, his social activism supported a ban on nuclear weapons and nuclear testing as he strongly encouraged world peace. Glossary, Further Reading, Sources, and Index.

1961.   Sherrow, Victoria. **Political Leaders and Peacemakers**. New York: Facts on File, 1994. 146p. $17.95. ISBN 0-8160-2943-1. (American Indian Lives). 7 up

Early founders of the Iroquois League to the present-day leaders of the Cherokee Nation show the varied roles of Indians as they have tried to retain their heritage in the United States. The leaders profiled here are Deganawida and Hayenwatha [Hiawatha] (Wendot and Mohawk peacemakers), Seathl (diplomat of the Pacific Northwest as a Coastal Salish), John Ross (father of the displaced Cherokee), Washakie (Shoshone leader), Black Kettle (Cheyenne betrayed by the government), Ouray (leader of the Southern Ute), Crowfoot (leader of the Blackfoot Confederacy), Spotted Tail (Sioux warrior), Winema, Tobey Riddle (mediator in the Modoc war), Annie Dodge Wauneka (Navajo health advocate), Ada Deer (Menominee leader in Washington), and Wilma Mankiller (first woman chief of the Cherokee). Selected Annotated Bibliography and Index.

1962. Sherrow, Victoria. **Separation of Church and State**. New York: Franklin Watts, 1992. 128p. $12.90. ISBN 0-531-13000-2. (Impact). 7-10

The First Amendment to the Constitution of the United States guarantees the separation of church and state. The text looks at the history of this decision by the colonial and then national leaders, including Thomas Jefferson and James Madison. It also discusses various court decisions, including those made by the Supreme Court, that resulted because of this amendment. Photographs, Bibliography, and Index.

1963. Sherrow, Victoria. **The Triangle Factory Fire**. Brookfield, CT: Millbrook Press, 1995. 64p. $15.90. ISBN 1-56294-572-6. (Spotlight on American History). 5-8

The text begins with an account of the 1911 fire in the Triangle factory, which killed young female workers trapped inside by doors locked from the outside. It then gives the background to the calamity in a chronological order of events, including dismal working conditions and the beginnings of the labor movement. Bibliography, Chronology, Further Reading, and Index.

1964. Shirley, David. **Satchel Paige**. New York: Chelsea House, 1993. 100p. $18.95; $7.95pa. ISBN 0-7910-1880-6; 0-7910-1983-7pa. (Black Americans of Achievement). 5 up

LeRoy "Satchel" Paige (1906-1982) was a great pitcher in the Negro Leagues. He got his nickname from carrying satchels at the local train station when he was seven. He learned to pitch while attending reform school and began playing baseball at 17. When he became the American League's first Black pitcher in 1948, he was also the oldest rookie ever. He had 2,000 lifetime victories before he quit playing in 1968. He was the first Negro League star to enter the Baseball Hall of Fame, and some consider him "the World's Greatest Pitcher." Photographs enhance the text. Chronology, Further Reading, and Index.

1965. Shore, Laura Jan. **The Sacred Moon Tree**: The Trials and Adventures of Phoebe Sands in the Great War Between the States, 1861-1865. New York: Bradbury, 1986. 209p. $13.95. ISBN 0-02-782790-9. 7 up

Phoebe pretends to be male as she travels from Pennsylvania to Richmond during the Civil War. She sees the battles, and after the war she reunites with her parents. Her father has had one leg shot off, and eventually he begins to care enough about life to invent a prosthesis that is neither heavy nor noisy. The family cherishes being together after a difficult time.

1966. Shore, Nancy. **Amelia Earhart: Aviator**. New York: Chelsea House, 1987. 110p. $18.95; $7.95pa. ISBN 1-55546-651-6; 0-7910-0415-5pa. (American Women of Achievement). 5 up

Amelia Earhart (1897-1937) received her pilot's license in 1922 and began to break many records as a female flyer. In 1932, she became the first woman to pilot a small plane across the Atlantic Ocean. In 1937, she planned to fly around the world at the equator. She left on June 1. On July 3, while she was flying over the Pacific, communication with her plane ceased. No trace of pilot or plane has been found. She believed in being an individualist throughout her life. Photographs, Chronology, Further Reading, and Index.

1967. Shorto, Russell. **Abraham Lincoln: To Preserve the Union**. Richard Loehle, illustrator. Englewood Cliffs, NJ: Silver Burdett, 1991. 135p. $12.95. ISBN 0-382-09937-0. (History of the Civil War). 7-9

Called a "peculiarsome" farm boy, Abraham Lincoln (1809-1865) did odd jobs before he left home to read for the law. He went to Washington, participated in the debates with Stephen Douglas, lost one election, and won another. As President of the United States, he had to find a general for the Union with the South rising against him. He mourned at Gettysburg and celebrated a victory before his assassination. Timetable, Suggested Reading, Sources, and Index.

1968. Shorto, Russell. **David Farragut and the Great Naval Blockade**. Englewood Cliffs, NJ: Silver Burdett, 1991. 128p. $12.95. ISBN 0-382-09941-9. (History of the Civil War). 5 up

David Farragut (1801-1870) became a midshipman for the U.S. Navy at the age of nine, helping to capture pirates in the Caribbean and journeying around the world in the War of 1812. At the beginning of the Civil War, he rose to the rank of captain and led two of the major sea battles of the war, the Battle of New Orleans and the Battle of Mobile Bay. History remembers his response to the cry "Torpedoes ahead!" as "Damn the torpedoes! Full speed ahead!" His achievements earned him the rank as the first admiral in the U.S. Navy's history. Timetables, Suggested Reading, Selected Sources, and Index.

1969. Shorto, Russell. **Geronimo and the Struggle for Apache Freedom**. Englewood Cliffs, NJ: Silver Burdett, 1989. 131p. $12.95; $7.95pa. ISBN 0-382-09571-5; 0-382-09760-2pa. (Biography of the American Indians). 5-8

Named Goyathlay at his birth (1823-1909), he became Geronimo after he proved his manhood to his Apache tribe. Geronimo's life changed when he saw the bodies of his wife, mother, and children mutilated in the dirt where U.S. Army soldiers had left them. He began planning revenge with Cochise and others. He continued to fight for Apache freedom until the army finally captured and imprisoned him. They would not allow him to return to his homeland. Suggested Reading.

1970.   Shorto, Russell. **Tecumseh and the Dream of an American Indian Nation**. Tim Sisco, illustrator. Englewood Cliffs, NJ: Silver Burdett, 1989. 123p. $12.95; $7.95pa. ISBN 0-382-09569-3; 0-382-09758-0pa. (Biography of American Indians). 5-8

Tecumseh (1768-1813) was a bold and talented Shawnee warrior as well as a statesman and powerful speaker who cared about others. He wanted a united Indian nation in the present Midwest, and tried to use European ways to his advantage. If he had not been killed during the War of 1812, he might have been successful. Suggested Reading.

1971.   Shuker, Nancy. **Elizabeth Arden**. Englewood Cliffs, NJ: Silver Burdett, 1989. 112p. $11.98. ISBN 0-382-09587-1. (American Dream). 7-10

Elizabeth Arden, or Florence Nightingale Graham (1884-1966), was highly successful in her business efforts but a difficult person to be friends with. Her behavior, contrasted to that of the first woman millionaire in America, Madame Walker, shows a woman whose cosmetics empire gave her great personal wealth that she did not use, as Madame Walker did, to benefit others. Arden used her genius and unstoppable ambition to build and market her business. Bibliography and Index.

1972.   Shuler, Linda Lay. **She Who Remembers**. 1988. New York: Signet, 1989. 478p. $6.99pa. ISBN 0-451-16053-3pa. YA

Because the Anasazi girl Kwani has blue eyes, her tribe banishes her. A Toltec magician finds her and takes her to the Place of the Eagle Clan. There she finds that she is the one chosen to carry knowledge of ancient secrets that she learns from an old woman, She Who Remembers. When Kwani has a child, she understands that she must return to her tribe to pass on the secrets rather than go with the Toltec to his people.

1973.   Shuler, Linda Lay. **Voice of the Eagle**. 1992. New York: Signet, 1993. 654p. $6.99pa. ISBN 0-451-17681-2pa. YA

The sequel to *She Who Remembers* shows Kwani, her baby, and Toloqua returning to Cicuye in 1272. After her long life, Kwani has a vision telling her to return to Mesa Verde, the House of the Sun, where she became "She Who Remembers." She leaves her pregnant daughter, who goes in the opposite direction. At the House of the Sun, Kwani dies, but simultaneously her granddaughter, blue-eyed like Kwani, enters another city with her parents; she is on her way to take Kwani's place.

1974.   Shumate, Jane. **Chief Gall: Sioux War Chief**. New York: Chelsea House, 1995. 118p. $18.95. ISBN 0-7910-1713-3. (North American Indians of Achievement). 5 up

Chief Gall (1840-1894), born in Dakota Territory, rose to a position of power in his tribe when U.S. officials began to pressure his people, the Hunkpapa Sioux, to let white settlers live on their lands. In 1863, he fought the U.S. Army. For the next 20 years, he continued to defend his home and culture until he had to surrender his weapons to the army during the winter of 1881. The army called him "the fighting cock of the Sioux." Photographs and reproductions enhance the text. Chronology, Further Reading, and Index.

1975.   Shumate, Jane. **Sequoyah: Inventor of the Cherokee Alphabet**. New York: Chelsea House, 1994. 112p. $18.95. ISBN 0-7910-1720-6. (North American Indians of Achievement). 5 up

Sequoyah (1773?-1843) was an artist, an inventor, and a Cherokee patriot. He developed a system of writing for the Cherokee language based on syllables. He worked many years on his efforts, and eventually his people recognized his great contribution and gave him the respect he deserved. Engravings and reproductions enhance the text. Chronology, Further Reading, and Index.

1976.   Shura, Mary Francis. **Gentle Annie: The True Story of a Civil War Nurse**. New York: Scholastic, 1991. 184p. $12.95; $3.50pa. ISBN 0-590-44367-4; 0-590-43500-0pa. 4-7

Annie, 16, enlists as one of 18 female volunteers from Michigan to defend the Union in the Civil War. She prepares to cook and sew but hopes to be a nurse. She is the only one who stays when the Army of the Potomac goes to battle. She becomes known for her letters and for her bravery as a nurse in almost every battle fought by this army.

1977.   Shura, Mary Francis. **Kate's Book**. New York: Scholastic, 1989. 204p. $2.75pa. ISBN 0-590-42381-9pa. 3-7

When her family decides to move from Ohio to Oregon in 1843, Kate, 11, has to go although her older brother stays to study medicine. Not many of the women seemed to want to be on the trip, but they have to go with their husbands and fathers. On the long journey, Kate finds a friend, Tildy, who helps her endure the trials of the journey. Kate is lonely when Tildy and her family go in a different direction.

1978. Shura, Mary Francis. **Kate's House**. New York: Scholastic, 1990. 183p. $3.25pa. ISBN 0-590-42380-0pa. 4-7

In 1843, Kate's family arrives in Oregon. To escape the animals roaming in the night, they have to build a house as quickly as they can. They have other problems, such as Kate's friend's brother's disappearance and another dying after falling off a horse. When they find out that Kate's mother will have a baby, they start to see Oregon as a place for new life.

1979. Shuter, Jane, ed. **Charles Ball and American Slavery**. Austin, TX: Raintree/Steck-Vaughn, 1995. 48p. $15.96. ISBN 0-8114-8281-2. (History Eyewitness). 6 up

Slavery started in the Americas about 1502, when the Spanish used slaves instead of hired labor in the silver mines of Mexico and on the sugar plantations of the West Indies. While slavery declined in South America during the early seventeenth century, it began growing in North America. Charles Ball grew up in the 1790s, when most slaves lived in Maryland and Virginia, working on tobacco plantations. His owner sold him away from his family to a Georgia landowner. Ball escaped, walking back to Maryland, and reunited with his family. Eventually he was recaptured and returned to Georgia, only to escape again, going to Philadelphia via ship. Once there, he found that his family had been sold to someone in the South; he never saw any of them again. He narrated his story to an abolitionist, who published it, with its detailed description of plantation life, during the early nineteenth century. Glossary and Index.

1980. Shuter, Jane, ed. **Parkman and the Plains Indians**. Austin, TX: Raintree/Steck-Vaughn, 1995. 48p. $15.96. ISBN 0-8114-8280-4. (History Eyewitness). 5 up

Although Francis Parkman (1823-1893) went to Harvard and enjoyed chemistry and acting, he always seemed to have "Indians on the brain." In 1846, he set off on the Oregon Trail. This text is a description of the summer of 1847, when he stayed with a group of Sioux Indians. He relates many of the customs and beliefs of these Plains Indians, including their dependence on the buffalo. Although Parkman had a weakness of the nervous system and was in bed for months at a time, he kept working on his American history books throughout his life. Glossary and Index.

1981. Shuter, Jane, ed. **Sarah Royce and the American West**. Austin, TX: Raintree/Steck-Vaughn, 1996. 48p. $15.96. ISBN 0-8114-8286-3. (History Eyewitness). 5-8

In 1849, Sarah Royce traveled with her husband and daughter across the western territories. She described illnesses, high rivers, drought, and difficult mountain passes that others experienced as well as more personalized events such as a cattle stampede and an encounter with tarantulas. In California her family moved from camp to camp, living in a portable tent, as she had several more children. Photographs, Reproductions, Glossary, and Index.

1982. Siegel, Beatrice. **Murder on the Highway: The Viola Luizzo Story**. New York: Four Winds, 1994. 125p. $14.95. ISBN 0-02-782632-5. 7 up

After driving to Selma, Alabama, in 1965 from Detroit, Michigan, because she was outraged by the treatment of Blacks when she viewed it on television, Viola Luizzo, student, housewife, and mother of five, stayed to help with the Freedom March as long as she was needed. One night as she drove along a dark stretch of Alabama highway, members of the Ku Klux Klan murdered her. Epilogue, Bibliography, Suggested Titles for Young Readers, and Index.

1983. Siegel, Beatrice. **The Year They Walked: Rosa Parks and the Montgomery Bus Boycott**. New York: Four Winds, 1992. 103p. $13.95. ISBN 0-02-782631-7. 4-7

With photographs and maps to highlight the text, Siegel recounts the year 1956, during which the Blacks of Montgomery, Alabama, refused to ride the public buses in protest of their treatment on board. They won a public victory, but privately many of them suffered personal consequences that Siegel documents. Bibliography, Suggested Titles for Young Readers, and Index.

1984. Sifakis, Carl. **Encyclopedia of Assassinations**. New York: Facts on File, 1991. 228p. $35. ISBN 0-8160-1935-5. YA

Among the 350 assassination victims from ancient to modern times presented in the text are Abraham Lincoln (d. 1865); Archduke Francis Ferdinand of Austria (d. 1914); Arsinoe III, Queen of Egypt (d. AD 204); Spencer Perceval (d. 1812); and Mohammed Sokolli (d. 1579). Some who had assassination attempts directed at them were Napoleon, Fidel Castro, Queen Victoria, and Adolf Hitler. Dates, places, times, names of victims, their assassins, conspirators if any, and other important information appears in the biographical entries. Index.

1985. Sifakis, Carl. **Hoaxes and Scams: A Compendium of Deceptions, Ruses, and Swindles**. New York: Facts on File, 1993. 308p. $45; $19.95pa. ISBN 0-8160-2569-X; 0-8160-3026-Xpa. 7 up

The text presents 700 entries on topics such as medical quackery, art forgeries, Bigfoot, Piltdown Man, the Tasaday tribe, "Kangaroo Monster Who Terrorized Tennessee," "King Tut's typewriter," and the local automobile repair garage. Biographical entries on infamous con artists describe their "mooches." Swindles and scams that can occur everyday happen in such places as the garage, the computer, or the real estate office. If a scam has been advertised, this text may have it. Personality Index and Subject Index.

1986. Sigerman, Harriet. **Laborers for Liberty: American Women 1865-1890**. New York: Oxford University Press, 1994. 144p. $22. ISBN 0-19-508046-7. (The Young Oxford History of Women in the United States). 7 up

In the aftermath of the Civil War, women had to attempt to reestablish their broken families. At the same time, they had to fight for their own rights and find new employment opportunities. Toward the end of the period, women began to work together for social change. In the next 20 years, Vassar College (1865), Smith and Wellesley (1875), and Bryn Mawr and Barnard (1884) were all founded. In 1868, Susan B. Anthony organized the Working Woman's Association, and with Elizabeth Cady Stanton in 1869, she formed the National Woman Suffrage Association. When that group refused to support the fifteenth Amendment calling for African American male voting rights, Lucy Stone and Henry Blackwell organized the American Woman Suffrage Association in 1869. The same year, a national labor union for women began. By 1873, literature considered obscene, such as birth control information, was not allowed to go through the mail, and in 1874, the Women's Christian Temperance Union started. In 1880, the Colored Woman's Progressive Franchise Association began to aid African American women. In 1890, the U.S. Army massacred the Sioux Indian tribe at Wounded Knee, South Dakota. Chronology, Further Reading, and Index.

1987. Sigerman, Harriet. **An Unfinished Battle: American Women 1848-1865**. New York: Oxford University Press, 1994. 144p. $22. ISBN 0-19-508110-2. (The Young Oxford History of Women in the United States). 7 up

Not until 1848 did a woman gain the right to own her own property after marriage. In the same year, the first women's rights convention drew attendees to Seneca Falls, New York, with a second gathering in Rochester, New York. In 1849, Amelia Bloomer established *Lily*, first a journal for temperance and then an advocate of women's rights. In 1850, the Female Medical College of Pennsylvania gave women a place to attend medical school. But despite these small advances for white women, African American women found themselves noncitizens and sole property of their owners after the Dred Scott Supreme Court decision in 1857. While women tried to help themselves, they simultaneously had to endure hard work in factories as weavers, stitchers, and domestics. When the Civil War began, their lives became even harder, but at least the African American women gained emancipation in 1863, with slavery outlawed in 1865. Chronology, Further Reading, and Index.

1988. Sills, Leslie. **Inspirations: Stories About Women Artists**. Ann Fay, illustrator. Morton Grove, IL: Albert Whitman, 1989. Unpaged. $16.95. ISBN 0-8075-4649-0. 5-8

Georgia O'Keeffe (1887-1986), Frida Kahlo (1907-1954), Alice Neel (1900-1984), and Faith Ringgold (b. 1930) have found different inspirations for their work. O'Keeffe loved nature and repeatedly painted the same subjects. Kahlo looked inward for her inspiration and painted what she thought about. Neel called herself a "collector of souls" and tried to capture the inner life of her subjects as well as the vulnerability of human nature. Ringgold tries to express the sense of community in Harlem, her relationships to other women, and life within her family.

1989. Sills, Leslie. **Visions: Stories About Women Artists**. Morton Grove, IL: Albert Whitman, 1993. 58p. $18.95. ISBN 0-8075-8491-6. 5-8

The text presents the works of and biographical information about Mary Cassatt, an American Impressionist living in Paris; Betye Saar, an African American assemblage artist; Leonora Carrington, a British surrealist painter; and Mary Frank, an American sculptor. Chapter Bibliographies.

1990. Silverman, Jerry. **Songs and Stories from the American Revolution**. Brookfield, CT: Millbrook Press, 1994. 71p. $18.90. ISBN 1-56294-429-0. 7 up

In the days of the American Revolution, balladeers sang songs and spread the music around the country. They sold broadsides with the printed words for the songs, and everyone sang those they liked best. Songs featured in the text, including the music and the stories behind them, are "The Drum," "The Wars of America," "The Sergeant," "Yankee Doodle," "Ballad of Bunker Hill," "The Riflemen of Bennington," "The Battle of Saratoga," "The Swamp Fox," "The Surrender of Cornwallis," and "In the Days of Seventy-Six." Further Reading and Index.

1991. Silverman, Kenneth. **Edgar A. Poe: Mournful and Never Ending Remembrance**. New York: HarperCollins, 1991. 564p. $15pa. ISBN 0-06-092331-8pa. YA

Silverman thinks that Poe's (1809-1849) exploration of life and death in his stories was the result of his mother's death when he was very young. Silverman uses public records, letters, and diaries to tell about Poe's battle with alcoholism and his hallucinations while an editor and a writer of stories such as "The Cask of Amontillado" and poems such as "Ligeia" and "The Raven." Bibliography and Index.

1992. Simon, Charnan. **Franklin Pierce**. Chicago: Childrens Press, 1988. 100p. $17.27. ISBN 0-516-01357-2. (Encyclopedia of Presidents). 4-9

As the 14th President, Franklin Pierce (1804-1869) wanted states to have more rights, with federal authority lessened. Stephen Douglas from Illinois put the idea into practice by negotiating with Kansas and Nebraska so that he could have the transcontinental railroad come through his state rather than through the South. Pierce served in the House and the Senate but loved the idea of going to war so much that he enlisted in 1846 to fight the Mexicans. He rose to the rank of general in little more than a year. On a personal level, Pierce's son died two months before Pierce took office, and the White House never had much happiness while he lived in it. Chronology of American History and Index.

1993. Simpson, Bland. **The Great Dismal: A Carolinian's Swamp Memoir**. Chapel Hill, NC: University of North Carolina Press, 1990. 185p. $18.95. ISBN 0-8078-1873-9. YA

In 1973, the Great Dismal Swamp, on the border between Virginia and North Carolina between the Jamestown restoration and Roanoke Island, became a national wildlife refuge. In 1728, surveyors established its boundaries, and humans enjoying its protective cover have included swamp rats, bird watchers, fugitive slaves, Indians, and hermits. During its life, it has also supported the professions of shingle cutting, cypress lumbering, hunting, and trapping. Simpson grew up on the border of this swamp; knows its tales, which he includes in the text; and shows how important conservation of such areas remains in the United States. Annotated Chapter Bibliographies and Index.

1994. Singer, Donna. **Structures That Changed the Way the World Looked**. Austin, TX: Raintree/Steck-Vaughn, 1995. 48p. $15.96. ISBN 0-8114-4937-8. (20 Events Series). 6 up

Humans in recorded history have built structures that have survived to tell something about the people who built them. The structures identified here and discussed in two-page spreads are the Great Pyramid (Cairo, Egypt), the Parthenon (Athens, Greece), the Great Wall of China, the Coliseum (Rome, Italy), Palenque (Chiapas, Mexico), Angkor (near Siem Reap, Cambodia), Great Zimbabwe (near Harare, Zimbabwe), the Tower of London (England), the Anasazi cliff dwellings (Mesa Verda, Colorado), Chartres Cathedral (France), dikes of the Netherlands, Alhambra (Granada, Spain), the Taj Mahal (Agra, India), Suez Canal (between Egypt and Israel), Statue of Liberty (New York), Eiffel Tower (Paris, France), Hoover Dam (near Las Vegas, Nevada), Golden Gate Bridge (San Francisco), Sears Tower (Chicago), and the English Channel Tunnel (between France and England). Glossary, Suggested Readings, and Index.

1995. Sinnott, Susan. **Chinese Railroad Workers**. New York: Franklin Watts, 1995. 63p. $19.30. ISBN 0-531-20169-4. (First Books). 5-8

By the 1850s, people realized that finding a way to get from coast to coast other than wagon train, stagecoach, or the Isthmus of Panama was going to be important. They began planning and constructing a transcontinental railroad. Theodore Dehone Judah was the visionary who began it, but Californians who forced it through were Collis P. Huntington, Mark Hopkins, Leland Stanford, and Charles Crocker. Those who made it exist were Chinese workers who worked through some of the worst snow ever, 44 blizzards, in the Sierra Nevada winter of 1866-1867. The railroad was finished and dedicated in 1869, carrying 30,000 passengers that year. For Further Reading and Index.

1996. Sinnott, Susan. **Extraordinary Asian Pacific Americans**. Chicago: Childrens Press, 1993. 270p. $33.80; $15.95pa. ISBN 0-516-03052-X; 0-516-43152-8pa. (Extraordinary People). 5 up

The text looks at topics and people of Asian Pacific descent who are now Americans. The 83 topics include people as well as groups of people. Brief biographies of individuals complement the lives of Gold Mountain travelers, Chinese benevolent associations, inmates in detention camps, and Korean-American grocery and convenience store businesspeople. Notes, Further Reading, and Index.

1997. Sinnott, Susan. **Zebulon Pike**. Chicago: Childrens Press, 1990. 128p. $28.20. ISBN 0-516-03058-2. (World's Great Explorers). 5-8

Zebulon Pike (1779-1813) was an army officer who explored the upper Mississippi, the Great Plains, and the Colorado area before the War of 1812. Jefferson sent him to look for the source of the Arkansas River. When he saw Cheyenne Mountain in Colorado, he climbed it to see the beauty of the Grand Peak, which was too far to reach in the cold Rocky Mountain winter. Although he did not know, the larger peak would become known as Pikes Peak. He returned to the army and died at the Battle of York. Timeline, Glossary, Bibliography, and Index.

1998. Sipiera, Paul P. **Gerald Ford: Thirty-Eighth President of the United States**. Chicago: Childrens Press, 1989. 100p. $19.80. ISBN 0-516-01371-8. (Encyclopedia of Presidents). 4-9

Gerald Ford (b. 1913) became President of the United States after Richard Nixon resigned on August 8, 1974, as a result of wrongdoing in the Watergate break-in before the 1972 election. Ford was not reelected to a second term. During his youth he was an Eagle Scout, a football player, and a member of the National Honor Society.

He received a football scholarship to the University of Michigan, but instead of playing professional football, he decided to study law at Yale. In 1948, he was elected to Congress, and he served 25 years in that role before becoming Vice President and then President of the United States. Photographs, Chronology of American History, and Index.

1999. Sklansky, Jeff. **James Farmer: Civil Rights Leader**. New York: Chelsea House, 1991. 112p. $18.95. ISBN 0-7910-1126-7. (Black Americans of Achievement). 5 up

James Farmer (1920-) was one of the most influential leaders in the fight against racial discrimination. He organized the first nonviolent protests after becoming a Methodist minister educated at Howard University in Washington, D.C. He formed the Congress of Racial Equality (CORE) in 1942 to end segregation in housing, restaurants, and other public facilities. He held boycotts, marches, sit-ins, jail-ins, Freedom Rides, and other demonstrations that filled the news. He has served the government and education since his departure from CORE in 1966. Photographs and reproductions enhance the text. Chronology, Further Reading, and Index.

2000. Skurzynski, Gloria. **Good-Bye, Billy Radish**. New York: Bradbury, 1992. 137p. $15. ISBN 0-02-782921-9. New York: Aladdin, 1996. 137p. $3.99pa. ISBN 0-689-80443-1pa. 5 up

Although Billy Radish (Bazyli Radichevych) is two years older than Hank, they are best friends living in Canaan, Pennsylvania, where their fathers work in the steel mills. Because Billy is Ukrainian, the two share their cultures and a love of beauty. They go to Pittsburgh to see the Greek sculptures, and they share each others' triumphs, such as Hank's successful delivery of his sister-in-law's baby and Billy's naturalization as a U.S. citizen. What they do not expect is for Billy to get influenza in 1917 and die. *School Library Journal Best Book*, *New York Public Library Books for the Teen Age*, and *Jefferson Cup Honor Book*.

2001. Skurzynski, Gloria. **The Tempering**. New York: Clarion, 1983. $11.95. ISBN 0-899-19152-5. 8 up

Pleased with his new job in the Pennsylvania steel mills in 1912, Karl, 15, is fired when his friend plays a trick on another worker. Karl returns to school, where he falls in love with the new teacher. He follows her, and when he sees her with a man, thinks that she is having an affair. He finds out that she is secretly married because married women may not teach. She notices Karl's musical ability, but he decides to return to the mills when he is 16 because he wants to start organizing unions so that the men can have better working conditions. *Golden Kite Award, School Library Journal Best Book*, and *Choice List of Internationale Jugenbibliothek of UNESCO*.

2002. Slavin, Ed. **Jimmy Carter**. New York: Chelsea House, 1989. 112p. $18.95. ISBN 1-55546-828-4. (World Leaders Past and Present). 5 up

Jimmy Carter (b. 1924), when President of the United States, allowed the exiled Shah of Iran into the United States for medical treatment, and Iranians took Americans as hostages. This crisis contributed to the problems that kept Carter from serving for more than one term. Before the presidency, Carter was a Georgia state senator and Georgia's governor. Some think he is an idealist who forgot the realities of the world while in office. Photographs and reproductions enhance the text. Chronology, Further Reading, and Index.

2003. Slepian, Jan. **Risk n' Roses**. New York: Philomel, 1990. 175p. $14.95. ISBN 0-399-22219-7. 6 up

In 1948, 11-year-old Skip wants to be accepted into the family's new neighborhood. She meets Jean, who has a group of followers, and Jean accepts her into the group. Jean manipulates all of them until even Angela, Skip's retarded sister, does what she asks. Angela tells her a secret that hurts the kind man in the neighborhood who keeps searching for any family who might have survived the Nazi concentration camps in World War II. Skip must choose, and she realizes that Jean has misled them all. *Bulletin Blue Ribbon Book*.

2004. Sloate, Susan. **Amelia Earhart: Challenging the Skies**. New York: Fawcett, 1990. 118p. $3.95pa. ISBN 0-449-90396-6pa. (Great Lives). 5-8

Amelia Earhart (1897?-1937) disappeared during her attempt to fly around the world. Sloate considers the idea that the Japanese took her prisoner and that she might have lived a quiet life with another identity somewhere else. Although this idea is interesting, it is insupportable. The rest of the text sees Earhart as a woman exuding feminism and compassion while she broke records in a field considered to be reserved for men. Bibliography.

2005. Smith, Adam, and Katherine Snow Smith. **A Historical Album of Kentucky**. Brookfield, CT: Millbrook Press, 1994. 64p. $16.40; $6.95pa. ISBN 1-56294-507-6; 1-56294-850-4pa. (Historical Album). 4-8

The text presents the land of Kentucky before it became a state, beginning with Native American civilizations and continuing through exploration and settlement. Early statehood developments and issues, and the role of large cities in the state's livelihood, lead to the present day. Prints, maps, and photographs illustrate the text. Gazetteer: Quick Facts, Key Events, Personalities, and Index.

2006. Smith, Carter, ed. **The Arts and Sciences: A Sourcebook on Colonial America**. Brookfield, CT: Millbrook Press, 1991. 96p. $18.90; $8.95pa. ISBN 1-56294-037-6;1-878841-67-Xpa. 7 up

One part of the two-part text covers colonial art and architecture with music, artists, and buildings. The second looks at advancements in sciences, including medicine and the discoveries of Benjamin Franklin. Resource Guide and Index. *Child Study Association Children's Books of the Year* and *Notable Children's Trade Books in the Field of Social Studies.*

2007. Smith, Carter, ed. **The Legendary Wild West: A Sourcebook on the American West**. Brookfield, CT: Millbrook Press, 1992. 96p. $18.90; $8.95pa. ISBN 1-56294133-X; 0-7613-0153-4pa. (American Albums from the Collections of the Library of Congress). 7 up

The American West from 1763 until 1912 was a time of great change as people streamed into the area from the East and from abroad. The text looks at the frontier and the stories that sprang from the many unusual things that occurred. The two-page discussions include paintings, prints, and photographs. Chronology and Index.

2008. Smith, Carter, ed. **Native Americans of the West: A Sourcebook on the American West**. Brookfield, CT: Millbrook Press, 1992. 96p. $18.90; $8.95pa. ISBN 1-56294131-3; 0-7613-0154-2pa. (American Albums from the Collections of the Library of Congress). 7 up

The first section in the text covers the first Americans from 1789 to 1861. It includes the struggle for the old Northwest, Indians and the War of 1812, the Council of the Prairie du Chien, the Trail of Tears, Black Hawk's War, the use and abuse of buffalo, Carl Bodmer, George Catlin, Stanley, and the fight for the West. The second part on the years between 1862 and 1890 looks at the Santee uprising, Red Cloud's War, the Modoc war, the war for the Black Hills, the Battle of Little Bighorn, the Nez Percé wars, the Apache wars, and the massacre at Wounded Knee. Supplemental material covers the civilizations before the arrival of the Europeans. Two-page spreads on topics include paintings, prints, and photographs. Chronology and Index.

2009. Smith, Carter, ed. **Battles in a New Land: A Sourcebook on Colonial America**. Brookfield, CT: Millbrook Press, 1991. 96p. $18.90; $8.95pa. ISBN 1-56294-034-1; 1-878841-65-3pa. (American Albums from the Collections of the Library of Congress). 7 up

Divided into three parts, the text examines explorations and rivalries in the New World from 1500 to 1676, the contests for North America from 1677 to 1753, and the French and Indian War from 1754 to 1763. Resource Guide and Index. *Notable Children's Trade Books in the Field of Social Studies.*

2010. Smith, Carter, ed. **Behind the Lines: A Sourcebook on the Civil War**. Brookfield, CT: Millbrook Press, 1993. 96p. $18.90; $8.95. ISBN 1-56294-265-4; 1-56294-882-2pa. (American Albums from the Collections of the Library of Congress). 7up

People who were not on the front line of battle tell about the Civil War in this text. Politicians, civilians, soldiers in their camps, and citizens show the effect of the war on the cities and towns away from the fighting in both the North and the South. Photographs and materials from the Library of Congress complement the text. Chronology, Notes, and Index.

2011. Smith, Carter, ed. **Bridging the Continent: A Sourcebook on the American West**. Brookfield, CT: Millbrook Press, 1992. 96p. $18.90; $8.95pa. ISBN 1-5629-413-0; 0-7613-0150-Xpa. (American Albums from the Collections of the Library of Congress). 7 up

With general and specific timelines, the text discusses the opening up and settling of the Old West. People traveled on trails, inland and ocean waterways, and early railroads in their quest for a better life. Two-page topics include paintings, prints, and photographs. Chronology and Index. *Child Study Association Children's Books of the Year.*

2012. Smith, Carter, ed. **The Conquest of the West: A Sourcebook on the American West**. Brookfield, CT: Millbrook Press, 1992. 96p. $18.90; $8.95pa. ISBN 1-56294-129-1; 0-7613-0151-8pa. (American Albums from the Collections of the Library of Congress). 7 up

The western expansion of the United States occurred after the 13 colonies became a nation. The text covers the period from 1783 to 1912, when the West was no longer a land of unlimited opportunity. Two-page spreads on topics include paintings, prints, and photographs. Chronology and Index. *Child Study Association Children's Books of the Year.*

2013. Smith, Carter, ed. **Daily Life: A Sourcebook on Colonial America**. Brookfield, CT: Millbrook Press, 1991. 96p. $18.90; $8.95pa. ISBN 1-56294-038-4;1-56294-168-8pa. (American Albums from the Collections of the Library of Congress). 7 up

The text looks at life and work on the colonial frontier as well as daily life in the towns. Among the topics are the people in the colonies and their varied backgrounds, farm life, slavery and tobacco, cloth, Pennsylvania, the South, fishing, New Amsterdam/New York, Philadelphia, leisure and recreation, traveling, crafts and trades, the upper classes, European fashion, publishing and printing, banking, fire fighting, and the western frontier. Resource Guide and Index. *Notable Children's Trade Books in the Field of Social Studies.*

2014. Smith, Carter, ed. **1863: The Crucial Year: A Sourcebook on the Civil War**. Brookfield, CT: Millbrook Press, 1993. 96p. $18.60; $8.95pa. ISBN 1-56294-263-8; 1-56294-880-6pa. (Sourcebook on Civil War from the Collections of the Library of Congress). 7-10

Photographs and materials from the Library of Congress complement the text, which describes and illustrates the situation in the United States during 1863, when battle raged at Gettysburg and Vicksburg (Mississippi) fell to Grant. It was also the year of the Emancipation Proclamation. Chronology, Notes, and Index. *Notable Children's Trade Books in the Field of Social Studies.*

2015. Smith, Carter, ed. **Exploring the Frontier: A Sourcebook on the American West**. Brookfield, CT: Millbrook Press, 1992. 96p. $18.90; $8.95pa. ISBN 1-56294-128-3; 0-7613-0152-6pa. (American Albums from the Collections of the Library of Congress). 7 up

The text discusses the early European explorers, the mountain men, the frontiersmen, and explorations sponsored by the government such as that of Lewis and Clark, the Corps of Topographical Engineers, and the surveying projects of the 1870s. Two-page discussions include paintings, prints, and photographs. Chronology and Index.

2016. Smith, Carter, ed. **The First Battles: A Sourcebook on the Civil War**. Brookfield, CT: Millbrook Press, 1993. 96p. $18.90; $8.95pa. ISBN 1-5629-426-2;1-56294-879-2pa. (American Albums from the Collections of the Library of Congress). 7 up

Photographs and materials from the Library of Congress complement the text, which describes and illustrates the early battles in the Civil War. These conflicts include the firing on Fort Sumter in April 1861 to the conflict at Fredericksburg at the end of 1862. Chronology, Notes, and Index. *Notable Children's Trade Books in the Field of Social Studies.*

2017. Smith, Carter, ed. **The Founding Presidents: A Sourcebook on the U.S. Presidency**. Brookfield, CT: Millbrook Press, 1993. 95p. $18.90. ISBN 1-56294-357-X. (American Albums from the Collections of the Library of Congress). 7 up

Photographs and materials from the Library of Congress complement the text, which describes and illustrates the political and personal lives of the Presidents of the United States from George Washington to James Monroe (1758-1831). Others were John Adams, Thomas Jefferson, and James Madison. Chronology, Notes, and Index. *Notable Children's Trade Books in the Field of Social Studies.*

2018. Smith, Carter, ed. **Governing and Teaching: A Sourcebook on Colonial America**. Brookfield, CT: Millbrook Press, 1991. 96p. $18.90; $8.95pa. ISBN 1-56294-036-8; 1-878841-66-1pa. 7 up

This examination of the government and education divides into three time periods: 1490 to 1649 with the first settlers; 1650 to 1754 and the changes and conflicts that occur; and 1755 to 1775, when the reach toward independence began and blossomed. Topics included are the Great Awakening and the Salem Witchcraft trials. Resource Guide and Index. *Child Study Association Children's Books of the Year, Society of School Librarians International Best,* and *Notable Children's Trade Books in the Field of Social Studies.*

2019. Smith, Carter, ed. **One Nation Again: A Sourcebook on the Civil War**. Brookfield, CT: Millbrook Press, 1993. 96p. $18.90; $8.95pa. ISBN 1-56294-266-2;1-56294-883-0pa. (American Albums from the Collections of the Library of Congress). 7 up

In looking at the nation as the Civil War ended, the first section of the text covers Washington, D.C., in 1865; Lincoln's assassination; the fate of Jefferson Davis; soldiers returning home maimed; plans for the South; Andrew Johnson and his allies; the end of slavery; and the Freedman's Bureau. The second section covers Reconstruction with the Civil Rights Act, the Fourteenth and Fifteenth Amendments, and Grant and his scandal. Chronology and Index. *Notable Children's Trade Books in the Field of Social Studies.*

2020. Smith, Carter, ed. **Prelude to War: A Sourcebook on the Civil War**. Brookfield, CT: Millbrook Press, 1993. 96p. $18.90; $8.95pa. ISBN 1-56294-261-1; 1-56294-878-4pa. (American Albums from the Collections of the Library of Congress). 7 up

Photographs and materials from the Library of Congress complement the text, which describes and illustrates the situation in the United States prior to the Civil War from 1820 to 1861, when the first shots were fired at Fort Sumter. Chronology, Notes, and Index. *Notable Children's Trade Books in the Field of Social Studies.*

2021. Smith, Carter, ed. **Presidents in a Time of Change: A Sourcebook on the U.S. Presidency**. Brookfield, CT: Millbrook Press, 1993. 96p. $18.90. ISBN 1-56294-362-6. (American Albums from the Collections of the Library of Congress). 6-9

Photographs and materials from the Library of Congress complement the text, which describes and illustrates the personal and political lives of the U.S. Presidents from Harry Truman to Bill Clinton. Other Presidents are Dwight Eisenhower, John F. Kennedy, Lyndon Johnson, Richard Nixon, Gerald Ford, Jimmy Carter, Ronald Reagan, and George Bush. Chronology, Notes, and Index.

2022. Smith, Carter, ed. **Presidents of a Divided Nation: A Sourcebook on the U.S. Presidency**. Brookfield, CT: Millbrook Press, 1993. 96p. $18.90. ISBN 1-56294-360-X. (American Albums from the Collections of the Library of Congress). 6-9

Photographs and materials from the Library of Congress complement the text, which describes and illustrates the personal and political lives of the U.S. Presidents during the time the nation was divided: Abraham Lincoln, Andrew Johnson, and Ulysses S. Grant. Chronology, Notes, and Index. *Notable Children's Trade Books in the Field of Social Studies.*

2023. Smith, Carter, ed. **Presidents of a World Power: A Sourcebook on the U.S. Presidency**. Brookfield, CT: Millbrook Press, 1993. 96p. $18.90. ISBN 1-56294-361-8. (American Albums from the Collections of the Library of Congress). 6-9

Photographs and materials from the Library of Congress complement the text, which describes and illustrates the personal and political lives of the U.S. Presidents from Theodore Roosevelt to Franklin Delano Roosevelt. Those in between were William Howard Taft, Woodrow Wilson, Warren Harding, Calvin Coolidge, and Herbert Hoover. Chronology, Notes, and Index.

2024. Smith, Carter, ed. **Presidents of a Young Republic: A Sourcebook on the U.S. Presidency**. Brookfield, CT: Millbrook Press, 1993. 96p. $18.90. ISBN 1-56294-359-6. (American Albums from the Collections of the Library of Congress). 6-9

Photographs and materials from the Library of Congress complement the text, which describes and illustrates the personal and political lives of the U.S. Presidents from John Quincy Adams to James Buchanan. Those in between were Andrew Jackson, Martin Van Buren, William Henry Harrison, John Tyler, James Polk, Zachary Taylor, Millard Fillmore, and Franklin Pierce. Chronology, Notes, and Index. *Notable Children's Trade Books in the Field of Social Studies.*

2025. Smith, Carter, ed. **The Revolutionary War: A Sourcebook on Colonial America**. Brookfield, CT: Millbrook Press, 1991. 96p. $18.90; $8.95pa. ISBN 1-56294-039-2;1-56294-169-6pa. (American Albums from the Collections of the Library of Congress). 7 up

The text divides into three major chronological sections telling about the Revolutionary War. The fighting for a new nation continues from April 1775 to June 1776. The colonies declare liberty and struggle to survive from July 1776 to January 1778. From February 1778 to February 1783, the colonies have to plan their nation. Other aspects discussed are the historical, political, military, social, and cultural aspects of the war period. Resource Guide and Index. *Child Study Association Children's Books of the Year* and *Notable Children's Trade Books in the Field of Social Studies.*

2026. Smith, Carter, ed. **The Riches of the West**: Sourcebook on the American West. Brookfield, CT: Millbrook Press, 1992. 96p. $18.90; $8.95pa. ISBN 1-56294-132-1; 0-7613-0155-0pa. (American Albums from the Collections of the Library of Congress). 7 up

The two-part text divides into the subjects of seizing the resources of the West and living on land taken from others. The timeline begins in 1763, when King George III forbade the colonists to move west of the Appalachians in order to keep peace with the Indians, and ends in 1910. Among the topics covered are the wilderness, the frontier life, buffalo, Native Americans, gold, silver, lead, and forests. Living on the land the involves the ranchers, those on the trail, cowherders, and sheep farmers as they become aware of the new technology that became available in the late nineteenth century. Maps and drawings augment the text. Resource Guide and Index. *Child Study Association Children's Books of the Year.*

2027. Smith, Carter, ed. **The Road to Appomattox**: A Sourcebook on the Civil War. Brookfield, CT: Millbrook Press, 1993. 96p. $18.90; $8.95pa. ISBN 1-56294-264-6;1-56294-881-4pa. (American Albums from the Collections of the Library of Congress). 7 up

Photographs and materials from the Library of Congress complement the text, which describes and illustrates the last years of the war, when Grant was appointed commander of the Union forces in January 1864 through the Confederate surrender in April 1865 at Appomattox. Chronology, Notes, and Index.

2028. Smith, Claude Clayton. **The Stratford Devil**. New York: Walker, 1984. 191p. $13.95. ISBN 0-8027-6544-0. YA

Ruth, 12, hates the Sunday meetings in her Puritan town and has felt very lonely since the death of her father. The townspeople question her behavior in 1650, and after she discovers who is her real father, she has to marry to protect herself from people who would punish her. On the day she marries, she also becomes a widow, and the townspeople quickly accuse her of witchcraft.

2029.   Smith, Elizabeth Simpson. **Coming Out Right: The Story of Jacqueline Cochran, the First Woman Aviator to Break the Sound Barrier**. New York: Walker, 1991. 114p. $14.95. ISBN 0-8027-6988-8. 5-8

Jacqueline Cochran (d. 1980) overcame a childhood of poverty in a foster home to become the first woman pilot to break the sound barrier after learning to pilot a plane in less than three weeks. At her death, she held more speed, altitude, and distance records than any pilot in history. In World War II, she headed WASP (the Women's Airforce Service Pilots), and she earned the Distinguished Service Medal and the Distinguished Flying Cross. In her later years, she owned a cosmetic company and was named American Business Woman of the Year. Appendices and Index.

2030.   Smith, Jeff. **The Frugal Gourmet on Our Immigrant Ancestors**. New York: Morrow, 1990. 539p. $22. ISBN 0-688-07590-8. YA

Although this is a cookbook, the text extends beyond this limiting definition to include essays about each immigrant group mentioned. Additional notes before each recipe give as much about the foods' origin as possible. For example, a Cuban recipe for yellow rice requires saffron. Saffron, however, is very expensive, and people often made the rice without it by using items with the yellow color of saffron. Other pieces of information appear about 35 different groups who have come to the United States as immigrants. Bibliography, Sources, and Index.

2031.   Smith, Karen Manners. **New Paths to Power: American Women 1890-1920**. New York: Oxford University Press, 1994. 142p. $22. ISBN 0-19-508111-0. (The Young Oxford History of Women in the United States). 7 up

At the World's Columbian Exposition in October 1893, women convened without male escort from every part of the country, ran offices, signed contracts, and finished all aspects of business, including the erection of three buildings, without going into debt. They did not change history or make progress, but they showed that women's public activity could be much more than mere volunteer work. In the next three decades, they still endured racism, class prejudice, and exclusion. In six chapters, the text discusses women during this period at home, at work, in public life, in rebellion to the status quo, and in war and peace. Some advances did occur when women in Wyoming became eligible to vote in 1890, and the Women's Trade Union League formed in 1903 to help women overcome discrepancies in gender, political powerlessness, limited job and career opportunities, and family claims on time. Finally in 1920, the Nineteenth Amendment was ratified, and women could vote. Chronology, Further Reading, and Index.

2032.   Smith, Lucinda Irwin. **Women Who Write: From the Past and the Present to the Future. Volume II**. New York: Julian Messner, 1994. 221p. $15. ISBN 0-671-87253-2. 7 up

The text discusses the nature and significance of authorship and uses interviews and biographical profiles to analyze the contributions of notable women writers. Writers from the past are Jane Austen, George Eliot, Emily Dickinson, Virginia Woolf, Anne Frank, Agatha Christie, and Lorraine Hansberry. Contemporary women are Dawn Garcia, Nikki Giovanni, Jan Goodwin, Beth Henley, Tama Janowitz, Maxine Hong Kingston, Norma Klein, Denise Levertov, Nancy Meyers, Joyce Carol Oates, Carolyn See, and Anne Tyler. Available photographs of writers are included. Suggested Reading and Index.

2033.   Smith, Norman F. **Millions and Billions of Years Ago: Dating Our Earth and Its Life**. New York: Venture, Franklin Watts, 1993. 127p. $13.40. ISBN 0-531-12533-5. 7 up

Divided into sections according to methodology, the text discusses the processes by which scientists determine the age of their specimens, such as counting the number of tree rings, reading the strata, using chemical analyses, and carbon-14 dating. It also looks at recent findings that estimate the age of the universe. Photographs and drawings enhance the text. Further Reading, Glossary, and Index.

2034.   Smith, Ronald D., and William L. Richter. **Fascinating People and Astounding Events from American History**. Santa Barbara, CA: ABC-CLIO, 1993. 274p. $29.95. ISBN 0-87436-693-3. YA

In the text, the author presents a series of short essays and articles about periods in history starting with the settlers and proceeding through the twentieth century. Facts and details fill these articles, which give a sense of the historical times discussed. Chronology and Index.

2035.   Smith-Baranzini, Marlene, and Howard Egger-Bovet. **USKids History: Book of the New American Nation**. T. Taylor Bruce, illustrator. Covelo, CA: Yolla Bolly Press; Little, Brown, 1995. 94p. $21.95; $12.95pa. ISBN 0-316-96923-0; 0-316-2206-2pa. (Brown Paper School). 5-7

The text covers the beginning of the American nation. Among the topics are building a flatboat, playing a cabinet game, a dance, the first inauguration, America's "first granddaughter," Benjamin Banneker, the Louisiana Purchase, the burning of the Capitol, the Erie Canal, frontier towns, prairie schools, the cotton gin, mill girls, and Texas. If You Want to Know More and Index.

2036.   Smothers, Ethel Footman. **Down in the Piney Woods**. New York: Knopf, 1992. 151p. $14.99; $3.99pa. ISBN 0-679-90360-7; 0-679-84714-6pa. 5-9

Annie Rye, 10, loves her Georgia summers with her grandfather. In the 1950s, she is surprised by having to share her experiences of the rolling store and going possum hunting with half-sisters. She also has to adjust to a little white girl who visits and to finding rattlesnakes in the house that have to be smoked out.

2037.   Smucker, Barbara. **Runaway to Freedom**. 1977. Magnolia, MA: Peter Smith, 1992. 154p. $17.55. ISBN 0-8446-6585-1. New York: Trophy, 1979. $4.50pa. ISBN 0-06-440106-5pa. 4-8

Julilly, 12, travels from Virginia to Mississippi after being sold and separated from her mother. The overseer on the journey whips the slaves without provocation. After they arrive at the new plantation, Julilly meets a white man who has come from Canada, and he leads her and three other slaves north to Canada. *IRA Children's Choices* and *Notable Children's Trade Books in the Field of Social Studies*.

2038.   Snyder, Zilpha Keatley. **And Condors Danced**. New York: Delacorte, 1987. 216p. $14.95; $3.50pa. ISBN 0-385-29575-8; 0-440-40153-4pa. 4-7

Carly keeps a journal when she is 11 in California in 1907. In it she tells of the feud between her family and the wealthy Mr. Quigley. She worries about her invalid mother and the two people who look after her, her great-aunt Mehitabel and her servant Woo Ying. She also has to cope with a young Quigley who attends school with her. When her mother dies and she loses her favorite dog, her aunt and Woo Ying give her emotional support.

2039.   Snyder, Zilpha Keatley. **Cat Running**. New York: Delacorte, 1994. 168p. $14.95. ISBN 0-385-31056-0. 5-8

Sixth-grader Cat, the fastest runner in her school, refuses to participate in the school's Play Day races during the Depression years because her father will not let her wear slacks like the other girls. She finds refuge in her secret spot by the river in California's Central Valley, where she hides her favorite things. When she goes there, she finds Sammy has invaded. Sammy, a young Okie girl with nothing of her own, has fallen in love with Cat's doll. Sammy's brother Zane wins a race in Cat's absence, and Cat struggles with disliking him and wanting to help Sammy. When Sammy catches pneumonia and nearly dies, Cat behaves honorably with Sammy's deprived family.

2040.   Sonder, Ben. **The Tenement Writer: An Immigrant's Story**. Meryl Rossne, illustrator. Austin, TX: Raintree/Steck-Vaughn, 1993. 72p. $15.49. ISBN 0-8114-7235-3. (Stories of America—Personal Challenge). 5-9

Around 1890, Anzia Yezierska (1880?-1970) and her family arrived in New York from Poland to join her brother, renamed "Mayer." Taking the name Hattie Mayer, Anzia had to adjust to a new life in a tenement, safer than Poland but drearier. After she had worked for a long time and attended school, she began to write about the life of an immigrant who hated being poor. By the 1920s, she had become a well-known American immigrant writer. Epilogue, Afterword, and Notes.

2041.   Sonneborn, Liz. **Will Rogers: Cherokee Entertainer**. New York: Chelsea House, 1993. 110p. $18.95; $7.95pa. ISBN 0-7910-1719-2; 0-7910-1988-8pa. (North American Indians of Achievement). 5 up

Will Rogers (1879-1935), born in Indian Territory (now the state of Oklahoma), was part Cherokee. He liked riding and roping as a youth and became a great lariat artist. He was also one of the most popular entertainers in the early twentieth century with his lariat and his humor. He said "I never met a man I didn't like." He lampooned the follies of the wealthy and powerful while showing concern for the rights of ordinary humans. Photographs enhance the text. Chronology, Further Reading, and Index.

2042.   Spangenburg, Ray, and Diane Moser. **The History of Science from 1895 to 1945**. New York: Facts on File, 1994. 164p. $18.95. ISBN 0-8160-2742-0. (On the Shoulders of Giants). 9-12

In the first half of the twentieth century, research in the physical sciences produced new information about the structure of an atom, the nature of light waves, outer space, and relativity. In the life sciences, the disciplines of microbiology, biochemistry, genetics, and archaeology became active, with many male and female scientists making new discoveries. Included in the text are anecdotes about the discoveries as well as biographical profiles. Photographs, Appendices, Glossary, Bibliography, and Index.

2043.   Spangenburg, Ray, and Diane K. Moser. **The History of Science from 1946 to the 1990s**. New York: Facts on File, 1994. 176p. $18.95. ISBN 0-8160-2743-9. (On the Shoulders of Giants). 9 up

This text, the final in the series, discusses the significant scientific discoveries since World War II, including increased specialization and the reliance on computers in research. In the physical sciences during the period, the areas of change include the subatomic world, quarks, the beginning of the universe, stars and the solar system, and space exploration. In the life sciences, DNA, RNA, protein, and a concern as to where humans came from are some of the main topics. Scientists associated with these ideas include Stephen Hawking, Stephen Jay Gould, Richard Feynman, Barbara McClintock, and Linus Pauling. Photographs and illustrations enhance the text. Chronology, Glossary, Further Reading, and Index.

2044. Spangenburg, Ray, and Diane K. Moser. **The History of Science in the Nineteenth Century**. New York: Facts on File, 1994. 142p. $18.95. ISBN 0-8160-2741-2. (On the Shoulders of Giants). 9 up

During the Industrial Revolution, science became a popular discipline with discoveries in the areas of atoms, the elements, chemistry, evolution, and energy. Other work in the physical sciences included magnetism, electricity, and light. In the life sciences, Darwin went on the *Beagle* to do his research, and the microscope found germs and cells. John Dalton, William Thomson (Lord Kelvin), Michael Faraday, Thomas Edison, Maria Mitchell, and Louis Pasteur were among the working researchers. Photographs and illustrations enhance the text. Chronology, Glossary, Further Reading, and Index.

2045. Spangenburg, Ray, and Diane Moser. **Opening the Space Frontier: Space Exploration**. New York: Facts on File, 1989. 111p. $18.95. ISBN 0-8160-1848-0. (On the Shoulders of Giants). 9-12

The text looks at the history of space flight, beginning with imaginary voyages, then moving to China's invention of the rocket, the V-2 rocket program in Germany during World War II, the X-15, the first unmanned satellites and the space race at the launch of Sputnik, the man-in-space program, and men on the moon. It presents test flight details and spacecraft information. Photographs, Glossary, Chronology, Bibliography, and Index.

2046. Speaker-Yuan, Margaret. **Agnes de Mille: Choreographer**. New York: Chelsea House, 1988. 112p. $18.95. ISBN 1-55546- 648-6. (American Women of Achievement). 5 up

Agnes de Mille (b. 1905) helped change American dance with her uniquely American dance patterns and rhythms. Her first success was *Rodeo*, presented in 1942. The next year, her choreography for *Oklahoma* delighted viewers. In the 1950s, she organized a dance troupe to introduce ballet to Americans around the country. She wanted to have a family and a career, and she did both. Photographs enhance the text. Chronology, Further Reading, and Index.

2047. Speare, Elizabeth George. **Calico Captive**. Witold T. Mars, illustrator. Boston: Houghton Mifflin, 1957. 288p. $15.95. ISBN 0-395-07112-7. New York: Dell, 1993. 288p. $4.50pa. ISBN 0-440-41156-4pa. 7-9

In 1754, Indians capture Miriam and her pregnant sister, as well as other members of her sister's family, and sell them to the French in Montreal at the beginning of the French and Indian War. Miriam must support the family, and she does so with her dress designing. She also undergoes an arduous prisoner exchange in which she sails from Montreal to England and back to Boston. She finds that helping others gives her unexpected rewards.

2048. Speare, Elizabeth George. **The Sign of the Beaver**. Boston: Houghton Mifflin, 1983. 144p. $14.95. ISBN 0-395-33890-5. New York: Bantam, 1995. 144p. $1.99pa. ISBN 0-440-21623-0pa. 4-7

Matt and his father go to Maine to build a new house in 1768. Matt's father has to leave him alone while he returns to Massachusetts for the rest of the family after the home is ready. Someone visits and steals Matt's gun, but his worst moment comes when bees sting him so badly that he loses consciousness. An Indian boy nearby hears him screaming and comes to nurse him back to health. Matt begins teaching the boy to read, and the boy teaches Matt how to trap, fish, and find trails. *Newbery Honor Book, Child Study Children's Book Committee and Bank Street College Award, Christopher Award, American Library Association Notable Books for Children, School Library Journal Best Book*, and *Scott O'Dell Award for Historical Fiction*.

2049. Speare, Elizabeth George. **The Witch of Blackbird Pond**. Boston: Houghton Mifflin, 1958. 256p. ISBN 0-395-07114-3. New York: Laurel, 1993. 256p. $4.99pa. ISBN 0-440-99577-9pa. 5 up

When Kit's grandfather dies in 1687, she has to leave Barbados and go to New England to live with her only relative, her deceased mother's sister. The bleak life with no entertainment or color depresses her, and she cannot adjust. A Quaker woman nearby, whom others in the community call a witch, helps her endure the agony. The people also decide that Kit is a witch when she tries to teach a child to read, and they try her in court. When the child reads for the court, the people can no longer condemn Kit. *Newbery Medal* and *International Board of Books for Young People*.

2050. Spinka, Penina Keen. **White Hare's Horses**. New York: Atheneum, 1991. 154p. $12.95. ISBN 0-689-31654-2. 6-8

In 1522, the Aztecs threaten the calm of the Chumash village in the area now known as southern California. White Hare, 13, knows that the Aztecs are preparing for war and that they will offer human sacrifices. To stop their plan, White Hare frees their horses by imitating a frightened colt. Without horses, the Aztecs no longer have an advantage, and the Chumash drive them from the village.

2051. Sproule, Anna. **Abraham Lincoln**. Milwaukee, WI: Gareth Stevens, 1991. 68p. $16.95. ISBN 0-8368-0216-0. (People Who Have Helped the World). 7-9

Along with general information about Abraham Lincoln (1809-1865), the author emphasizes that Lincoln's stepmother encouraged his reading and writing, unlike his father, who had little use for learning. Perhaps the most important thing that Lincoln signed was the Emancipation Proclamation on January 1, 1863, which freed 4 million slaves. Lincoln faced happiness and heartbreak; by the time he went to the White House, he had lost one son, and in the White House, another died. Organizations, Books, List of New Words, Important Dates, and Index.

2052.   St. George, Judith. **Crazy Horse**. New York: Putnam, 1994. 180p. $17.95. ISBN 0-399-22667-2. YA

As a young boy, Curly dressed himself for battle with a lightning streak painted on his face and hail spots on his body. He gained the name Crazy Horse (1842-1877) by the time he was 17. He led war parties to battle for the Oglala Sioux and beat Custer at Little Bighorn. He seems to personify what the Plains people were fighting for, which was their way of life, their land, and their freedom. Sources show that Crazy Horse was quiet and modest, and more than anything, he wanted to protect his people. Bibliography and Index.

2053.   St. George, Judith. **Dear Dr. Bell . . . Your Friend, Helen Keller**. New York: Putnam, 1992. 95p. $15.95. ISBN 0-399-22337-1. 5-9

When Helen Keller (1880-1968) and her father met Alexander Graham Bell, the inventor of the telephone and a teacher of the deaf, her life changed. Bell recommended a teacher for her, Anne Sullivan, and Keller, after being deaf and blind from disease since she was 19 months old, learned to read and write because of her. Keller wrote one of her first letters to Bell, and they corresponded until he died. He advised her and encouraged her to speak about issues of importance to give a sense of accomplishment and bravery to others with disabilities. The text recounts their friendship. Photographs, Bibliography, and Index.

2054.   St. George, Judith. **Mason and Dixon's Line of Fire**. New York: Putnam, 1991. 128p. $16.95. ISBN 0-399-22240-5. 4-8

Two English scientists came to America in 1763 to survey the line between Maryland and Pennsylvania. Trouble had already flared on that border before they arrived, and it continued after they left. Among those who fought along the line were William Penn, Lord Baltimore, George Washington, Chief Pontiac, Lafayette, Harriet Tubman, John Brown, Robert E. Lee, and Abraham Lincoln. Others included settlers, riverboat men, slaves, foot soldiers, and frontiersmen. The Line serves now as a landmark that signifies the growing pains of the nation with its bitter divisions. The text gives a history of the altercations along this boundary. Photographs, Bibliography, and Index.

2055.   St. George, Judith. **Panama Canal: Gateway to the World**. New York: Putnam, 1989. 159p. $16.95. ISBN 0-399-21637-5. 5 up

The construction of the Panama Canal began in 1904. Unfortunately, it was not a simple cutting through of the isthmus from one side to the other. It took 10 years of transforming a swamp, a jungle, and mountain ranges to create the 50-mile-long waterway. It was the biggest human-made lake in the world and the longest earthen dam ever built. Part of the problem in the construction was the personalities of the men behind it, such as Teddy Roosevelt, William Howard Taft, William Gorgas, and three chief engineers—indecisive John Wallace, frontiersman John Stevens, and professional George Goethals. The text, with photographs, tells the story of this difficult task. Bibliography and Index.

2056.   St. George, Judith. **To See with the Heart: The Life of Sitting Bull**. New York: Putnam, 1990. 182p. $17.95. ISBN 0-399-22930-2. 5-9

Sitting Bull (1834?-1890), the leader of the Hunkpapa Sioux, tried to preserve his tribe's hunting grounds, but he was unsuccessful. His attempts to protect his people from the army representing the federal government led to a victory against Custer at the Little Bighorn as well as his own death under unexplained circumstances. The text looks at his life, the stresses among the tribal members, and the government's policies during his leadership.

2057.   St. George, Judith. **The White House: Cornerstone of a Nation**. New York: Putnam, 1990. 160p. $15.95. ISBN 0-399-22186-7. 6 up

The text gives an anecdotal history of the White House, emphasizing times when history influenced the building. Statements from Presidents, Presidents' wives, servants, and architects tell about the construction, reconstruction, and remodeling of the White House. Additional anecdotes include information about guests' requests and varied influences on the Presidents who have resided there, such as the media or specific crises. Photographs, Bibliography, and Index.

2058.   Stacey, Tom. **The Titanic**. Maurie Manning and Michael Spackman, illustrators. San Diego, CA: Lucent, 1990. 64p. $22.95. ISBN 1-56006-006-9. (World Disasters). 5-7

The *Titanic* was advertised as the ship that could not sink, but a few days into its maiden voyage, on April 14, 1914, icebergs sank it. The text recounts the story as it has been pieced together by rescue teams and survivors. In 1985, Robert Ballard and his submarine *Jason* discovered the wreckage of the *Titanic*, thereby allowing new information to become available. Diagrams and drawings augment the text. Further Reading, Glossary, Other Works, and Index.

2059.   Stafford, Mark. **W. E. B. Du Bois: Scholar and Activist**. New York: Chelsea House, 1989. 127p. $18.95; $7.95pa. ISBN 1-55546-587-0; 0-7910-0238-1pa. (Black Americans of Achievement). 5 up

   W. E. B. Du Bois (1868-1963) had degrees from Fisk and Harvard and studied at the University of Berlin in Germany. At 26, as a college professor, he began publishing a series of sociological studies on Black life. In *The Souls of Black Folk*, he attacked Booker T. Washington's position that Blacks should wait until their economic status rose before they began to seek equality. He cofounded the National Association for the Advancement of Colored People (NAACP). In 1961, he went to live in Africa because of his dissatisfaction with American society. Photographs enhance the text. Chronology, Further Reading, and Index.

2060.   Stalcup, Brenda, ed. **Reconstruction**. San Diego, CA: Greenhaven, 1995. 310p. $19.95. ISBN 1-56510-227-4. (Opposing Viewpoints). 9 up

   Only one Southerner, General Henry Wirz, commander of Andersonville Prison, was convicted and executed as a result of the Civil War. Prior to the war, people were citizens of their states first and then of the nation. The concept of nationalism as it exists in the twentieth century did not exist before 1865. In short essays both pro and con written by public figures living during the time of Reconstruction, the text examines different viewpoints toward its progress. The question of Reconstruction was who should do it if it should be done. Another group supported moderate Reconstruction. A third saw radical Reconstruction as the only solution. In a new social order, decisions had to be made about allowing Blacks to have the right to vote, to hold public office, to be given land, or to be segregated. After Reconstruction, people wondered if the Compromise of 1877 would help or hinder, whether the Blacks should stay or flee the South, and whether the Civil Rights Act of 1875 was constitutional. In hindsight, Reconstruction failed either because the Republican reforms were too radical or they were not committed to racial equality. For Discussion, Chronology, Annotated Bibliography, Appendix, and Index.

2061.   Stallones, Jared. **Zebulon Pike and the Explorers of the American Southwest**. New York: Chelsea House, 1991. $19.95. ISBN 0-7910-1317-0. (World Explorers). 5 up

   Zebulon Pike (1779-1813) was sent to conduct a geographic survey of the Arkansas and Red Rivers. However, his boss, an army general and a double agent for Spain, may have directed his men into the Rocky Mountains during the winter so that he would not succeed. Pike's group finally reached the Rio Grande River, which Spain claimed, and Pike supposedly said, "What? Is this not the Red River?" Pike most likely conducted a secret surveillance of the Spanish, which may have been the real intent of his journey. Photographs and illustrations enhance the text. Chronology, Further Reading, and Index.

2062.   Stamper, Judith Bauer. **Save the Everglades**. Allen Davis, illustrator. Austin, TX: Raintree/Steck-Vaughn, 1993. 58p. $14.95. ISBN 0-8114-7219-1. (Stories of America—Working Together). 5-9

   By 1969, the U.S. government had decided to build a huge jetport near Miami, Florida, which would destroy much of the wetlands of the Big Cypress Swamp near the Everglades. Joe Browder and Marjory Douglas fought together to keep the wetlands. Disagreement in Washington led President Nixon to send an emissary to the area. Julie Nixon realized that the loss of this area would be a loss for the nation and supported the Browder and Douglas dissent. Epilogue, Afterword, and Notes.

2063.   Stanley, Jerry. **Big Annie of Calumet: A True Story of the Industrial Revolution**. New York: Crown, 1996. 102p. $18. ISBN 0-517-70097-2. 5-8

   In 1913, the copper miners working for Michigan's Calumet and Hecla Mining Company decided to strike for a shorter workday and safer working conditions. The woman who led their marches every morning for a year was a Croatian miner's wife, Annie Clemenc, who at 6´2″ became a media attraction. She realized that families should help their husbands and fathers, and their participation might get the concessions that the strike wanted. The text looks at her contribution to the strike and presents the events that comprised the strike, including a stampede, probably started by company supporters, that caused the deaths of many children. Photographs and Index.

2064.   Stanley, Jerry. **Children of the Dust Bowl: The True Story of the School at Weedpatch Camp**. New York: Crown, 1992. 85p. $15. ISBN 0-517-57821-5. 6 up

   Migrant workers who traveled from the Dust Bowl to California during the Depression were forced to live in federal labor camps. A school established in a camp helped the children. Photographs and maps augment the text, which talks about the situation in the camp. Index.

2065.   Stanley, Jerry. **I Am an American: A True Story of Japanese Internment**. New York: Crown, 1994. 102p. $17.00. ISBN 0-517-59786-1. 5-10

   When the Japanese bombed Pearl Harbor on December 7, 1941, the Japanese Americans who lived in the United States immediately attracted suspicion as possible Japanese spies. These Californians were taken from their homes and businesses and placed into internment camps where they lived through the war. The text looks at these 10 camps and what happened to the people who had neither home nor work after they were released. Photographs, Bibliographic Note, and Index.

2066. Stanley, Sandra Carson. **Women in the Military**. New York: Julian Messner, 1993. 138p. $14.95. ISBN 0-671-75549-8. 8 up

Among the women involved in military activity early in America's history were Molly Pitcher, in the American Revolution, and Deborah Sampson, pretending to be Robert Shurliff, in the Civil War. Dr. Mary Walker was the first woman doctor in the army, also serving in the Civil War. Since then, women have become more involved by working as nurses in World Wars I and II. In the 1970s, the opportunity for different types of jobs opened, and women today are an integral part of the military. Photographs and drawings highlight the text. Time Line, Further Reading, Glossary, and Notes.

2067. Steedman, Scott. **A Frontier Fort on the Oregon Trail**. Mark Bergin, illustrator. New York: Peter Bedrick, 1993. 48p. $18.95; $9.95pa. ISBN 0-87226-371-1; 0-87226-264-2pa. 5 up

Settlers, prospectors, and soldiers met in the western frontier forts because they were places in which to fend off tribal attacks. The text, with many illustrations, looks at life in these forts. Two-page spreads present such topics as the first forts, the Oregon Trail, the site for a fort, building the fort, inside the fort, feeding the troops, a soldier's day, fur and gold traders, Plains Indians, trappers and traders, a pioneer cabin, a woman's day, the railway, Indian wars, and famous folk on the frontier. Glossary and Index.

2068. Steele, James. **Freedom's River: The African-American Contribution to Democracy**. New York: Franklin Watts, 1995. 175p. $21.40. ISBN 0-531-11184-9. (African American Experience). 9 up

Using the image of the River of Freedom, Steele traces the contribution of African Americans to American history. After 1776, Northern states outlawed slavery, but the South refused. If the Constitution included a clause to outlaw slavery, the Southern states would not sign it, so the South held power in the nation for almost 80 years. African Americans could not stop working for freedom with the end of the Civil War; they had to continue through Reconstruction into the twentieth century and the Civil Rights movement before they could see much progress. Source Notes, For Further Reading, and Index.

2069. Steele, Philip. **Censorship**. New York: New Discovery, 1992. 48p. $12.95. ISBN 0-02-735404-0. (Past and Present). 5-7

The text looks at the history of censorship, including the Chinese emperor who burned books in 213 BC, Roman censors, religion and the printing press, revolution, and private censorship. It examines the reasons stated for censorship and assesses freedom or control as a motive. Key Dates, Glossary, and Index.

2070. Steele, Philip. **Little Bighorn**. Richard Hook, illustrator. New York: New Discovery, 1992. 32p. $13.95. ISBN 0-02-786885-0. (Great Battle and Sieges). 5 up

Plains wars in America began in 1854 and did not end until 1890. On June 25, 1876, Lieutenant Colonel George Armstrong Custer challenged the Cheyenne and Sioux Nations. Under Sitting Bull, they crushed him. The text covers events that led to the battle, including white settlers taking Native American lands. It looks at the weapons, the enemies, and the land on which the battle took place. It also tells about Ghost Dancers, who believed that their dances would cause warriors to rise from the dead, the Bluecoats (army) to disappear, and the buffalo to return. At Wounded Knee in 1890, they found that this was not true. Glossary, Further Reading, and Index.

2071. Steele, Philip. **Riots**. New York: New Discovery, 1993. 48p. $12.95. ISBN 0-02-786883-4. YA

Steele defines the term *riot* and then traces these "quarrels" through the centuries. Rioting occurred in ancient Greece during 464 BC, when an earthquake shook Sparta. In AD 532, rioting broke out in Constantinople between political groups, the "Greens" and the "Blues." Riots over money, religion, and politics have continued through the centuries. Steele also looks at the lawfulness of such displays and the ways in which they can be controlled. Key Dates, Glossary, and Index.

2072. Steele, William O. **The Buffalo Knife**. Magnolia, MA: Peter Smith, 1992. 123p. $16.50. ISBN 0-8446-6505-3. San Diego, CA: Harcourt Brace, 1990. 123p. $3.95pa. ISBN 0-15-213212-0pa. 3-7

In 1782, nine-year-old Andy's uncle gives him a knife to mark the beginning of the family's flatboat journey down the Tennessee River. After whitewater rapids and Chickamauga Indian attacks, they reach the end of the journey. Andy cannot find the knife when they arrive. He feels bad for his carelessness, but his uncle arrives and tells him what happened to it.

2073. Steele, William O. **Flaming Arrows**. Paul Galdone, illustrator. 1958. Magnolia, MA: Peter Smith, 1992. 146p. $17. ISBN 0-8446-6506-1. San Diego, CA: Harcourt Brace, 1990. 146p. $3.95pa. ISBN 0-15-228427-3pa. 3-7

When the Chickamaugas raid Cumberland in 1784, Chad, 11, and other settlers go to the nearby fort for protection. People inside accuse one boy's father of betraying them to the Indians, but that boy risks his life for those inside the fort during the ensuing battle.

2074.   Steele, William O. **The Lone Hunt**. Paul Galdone, illustrator. San Diego, CA: Harcourt Brace, 1957. 175p. ISBN 0-15-652983-1. $1.75pa. 3-7

In 1810, Yance, 11, finds buffalo tracks in the Cumberland Mountains. He knows that others will reach the buffalo before he has a chance, but he goes on the hunt anyway. He uses almost all his bullets before he sees a buffalo, and after he shoots it, a Cherokee helps him save his kill while he returns home for help.

2075.   Steele, William O. **The Magic Amulet**. San Diego, CA: Harcourt Brace, 1976. 114p. $6.95. ISBN 0-15-250427-3. 3-7

In prehistoric times, Tragg's family abandons him because his wounded leg keeps him from walking fast enough while they are hunting mastodons and mammoths. As he watches an armadillo defend itself from a wolf, he realizes that he can defend himself as well. He joins another tribe, and they fully accept him when he leads them to food that he has previously found. They think Tragg's amulet has protected him.

2076.   Steele, William O. **The Man with the Silver Eyes**. San Diego, CA: Harcourt Brace, 1976. 147p. $5.95. ISBN 0-15-251720-0. 4-7

Talatu, 11, hates to leave his home to go with the pale-eyed Quaker Shinn in 1780. Talatu thinks that the man must need him as a guide. When Cherokees capture Shinn, Talatu asks them, in Cherokee, to kill Shinn, but they respect Talatu's uncle and think that he must have a good reason for sending the two into enemy territory. During the winter with Shinn, Talatu gets smallpox, and Shinn saves him. Another man tries to kill the Quaker. As he dies, Shinn tells Talatu that he is his father. Talatu realizes that Shinn understood his request that the Cherokees kill him, and he begins to miss being with Shinn more than he could have imagined.

2077.   Steele, William O. **The Perilous Road**. 1958. Magnolia, MA: Peter Smith, 1991. 156p. $16.50. ISBN 0-8446-6507-X. San Diego, CA: Harcourt Brace, 1990. 156p. $4.95pa. ISBN 0-15-260647-5pa. 3-7

The Union troops take all of Chris's family's food, which it has carefully stored in the winter during the Civil War. At 11, Chris decides that he will support the Rebels. But his brother joins the Union army in 1863 without telling Chris. Before Chris knows, he almost gets his brother killed by telling the Rebels that a federal wagon train has moved into the region. *Newbery Honor Book* and *Jane Addams Children's Book Award*.

2078.   Steele, William O. **Tomahawk Border**. Charles Beck, illustrator. San Diego, CA: Harcourt Brace, 1965. 120p. $3.95. ISBN 0-03-058050-1. 3-7

In 1716, Dalk tries to be a ranger on the Virginia border. He stops a Seneca Indian from crossing the border, and he takes an Indian captive to Williamsburg. What he and a friend discover is that one of the rangers is betraying the friendly Indians and causing much unnecessary conflict.

2079.   Steele, William O. **Trail Through Danger**. Charles Beck, illustrator. San Diego, CA: Harcourt Brace, 1964. 186p. $4.95. ISBN 0-15-289661-9. 3-7

In 1775, Lafe Birdwell, 11, hires himself to Mr. Gibbs to hunt buffalo on the other side of the Carolina mountains. Of the men in the group, Lafe likes only Rice, and when he sees the other men trying to kill Rice, he becomes furious. The group collects many buffalo skins, but the Cherokees come and take everything because they have been hunting illegally on Cherokee lands. Rice advises Lafe to return to his father and forget that Lafe's father shamed Lafe by selling guns to the Shawnee.

2080.   Steele, William O. **Wayah of the Real People**. Isa Barnett, illustrator. New York: Henry Holt, 1964. 128p. $3.95. ISBN 0-03-045220-1. 5-9

Wayah, 11, leaves his Cherokee home for Williamsburg to attend school in 1752. The customs and the buildings of the white people surprise him in many ways. He has never seen steps, and the bell frightens him. He thinks the piano has teeth. When he returns home, he has to use his knowledge and become a translator between the whites and the Cherokee in an attempt to keep peace.

2081.   Steele, William O. **Wilderness Journey**. Paul Galdone, illustrator. San Diego, CA: Harcourt Brace, 1953. 209p. $6.75. ISBN 0-15-297318-4. 3-7

Flan's family leaves for Kentucky in 1782, but Flan, 10, remains behind to recover from an illness. After he recuperates, he goes with Chap to Kentucky, but without a gun to shoot, he feels useless. Chap teaches him how to shoot and how to survive when they escape from attacking Indians and save a trader. Flan also has to nurse Chap back to health after a fever, and they ride a raft on a swirling river. When he reaches his family, he has developed new confidence.

2082. Steele, William O. **Winter Danger**. Paul Galdone, illustrator. 1954. Magnolia, MA: Peter Smith, 1992. 131p. $16.50. ISBN 0-8446-6508-8. San Diego, CA: Harcourt Brace, 1990. 131p. $3.95pa. ISBN 0-685-51103-0pa. 3-7

After Caje's mother dies in the 1780s, his father takes him to his mother's sister's home for the winter. Caje, 11, worries about the family's meager food supply and decides to leave so he will not burden them further. He happens to see a bear hibernating, and he kills it and brings the carcass back to the house so they can have food for the rest of the winter.

2083. Stefoff, Rebecca. **Abraham Lincoln: 16th President of the United States**. Ada, OK: Garrett Educational, 1989. 122p. $17.26. ISBN 0-944483-14-3. (Presidents of the United States). 5-9

This biography of Abraham Lincoln (1809-1865) begins with the Battle of Gettysburg, after which Lincoln made his memorable speech. The text then returns to his frontier boyhood, his becoming a self-made man, his introduction to politics, his career as a lawyer, and his love. He became Congressman Lincoln and then President Lincoln. During his presidency, he had to face the question of slavery, try to reunite a divided nation, and decide that the slaves should be emancipated. Bibliography and Index.

2084. Stefoff, Rebecca. **The American Environmental Movement**. New York: Facts on File, 1995. 146p. $17.95. ISBN 0-8160-3046-4. (Social Reform Movements). 7 up

The first Earth Day, April 22, 1970, marked the beginning of overt recognition by American citizens of the concern about protecting the environment. Others, however, had already recognized the wanton destruction of natural resources, and eventually people heard their cries. John Wesley Powell proclaimed in the 1870s that scientific planning should precede western settlement; he was ignored. In 1864, George Perkins Marsh wrote a scientific study of American environmental ills. Others in the twentieth century include Rachel Carson, Aldo Leopold, and John Muir. The text also looks at current environmental practices. Further Reading and Index.

2085. Stefoff, Rebecca. **Andrew Jackson: 7th President of the United States**. Ada, OK: Garrett Educational, 1988. 119p. $17.26. ISBN 0-944483-08-9. (Presidents of the United States). 5-9

Andrew Jackson (1767-1845) served informally during the Revolutionary War before he became certified to practice law in North Carolina. He went to Tennessee and became both a congressman and a senator. He also became a judge. In 1812, he led a company from Tennessee in the war and defeated the British at New Orleans in 1815. Then he attacked the Seminoles in Florida. After losing his first presidential campaign to John Quincy Adams, he began serving as President in 1829. Bibliography and Index.

2086. Stefoff, Rebecca. **Children of the Westward Trail**. Brookfield, CT: Millbrook Press, 1996. 96p. $16.90. ISBN 1-56294-582-3. 6-9

More than 500,000 people went west during the nineteenth century looking for gold, land, or adventure. The text focuses on one man: Martin Gay, a farmer from Springfield, Missouri, who took his family on a five-month journey to the Willamette Valley of Oregon. What they faced were problems experienced by all those who risked the trip. Bibliography and Index.

2087. Stefoff, Rebecca. **George H. W. Bush: 41st President of the United States**. Ada, OK: Garrett Educational, 1992. 140p. $17.26. ISBN 1-56074-033-7. (Presidents of the United States). 5-9

The text examines George Bush's life (b. 1924) before he became the 41st President as well as after. Chapters cover his New England boyhood, his navy career, living in Texas, influence in the Republican Party, his service in China and as the Vice President, his campaign and election for President, his years in office, and his role in the Persian Gulf War. Bibliography and Index.

2088. Stefoff, Rebecca. **Herman Melville**. New York: Julian Messner, 1994. 156p. $15. ISBN 0-671-86771-7. (Classic American Writers). 7 up

Herman Melville (1819-1891) told the story of nineteenth-century whaling in his books. Stefoff tells his story and his adventures, beginning with the first chapter when he and his friend have just had to abandon their own whaling ship near an island on which cannibals were thought to live. He survived, just as he did as a child of 12, when he had to stop school after his father's death. He always had to worry about money even as he wrote books, including *Moby Dick* and *Billy Budd,* which Stefoff briefly discusses. Among the chapter titles are "Grim Beginnings," "First Voyage," The Restless Searcher," "Among the Cannibals," "Home Again," "The South Sea Novels," "White-jacket and a New Friend," "The Whale," and "I Have Written a Wicked Book." Bibliography and Index.

2089. Stefoff, Rebecca. **James Monroe: 5th President of the United States**. Ada, OK: Garrett Educational, 1988. 120p. $17.26. ISBN 0-944483-11-9. (Presidents of the United States). 5-9

James Monroe (1758-1831) served General Washington in the American Revolution when his troops crossed the Delaware River. He also participated in the Battle of Trenton, when the Americans defeated the Hessians. He was wounded, and the farmer-doctor who gave the troops food soon after they crossed the river saved his life. Forty years after being wounded, he was elected President of the United States. Among his other achievements was buying the Louisiana Purchase for Thomas Jefferson and serving as a foreign ambassador. Bibliography and Index.

2090. Stefoff, Rebecca. **John Adams: 2nd President of the United States**. Ada, OK: Garrett Educational, 1988. 118p. $17.26. ISBN 0-944483-10-0. (Presidents of the United States). 7 up

John Adams (1735-1826) had many roles as he grew up and served the nation. Two of these were husband to Abigail Adams and father to John Quincy Adams. The chapters identify him in the roles of Puritan, student, lawyer, patriot, ambassador, Vice President, President, and the "Old Man," the name he called himself. Bibliography and Index.

2091. Stefoff, Rebecca. **Richard M. Nixon: 37th President of the United States**. Ada, OK: Garrett Educational, 1995. 129p. $17.26. ISBN 1-56074-063-9. (Presidents of the United States). 5-9

Richard Milhaus Nixon (1913-1994) served as President after being a congressman from California and Vice President of the United States. He had to resign from office or face impeachment for his implication in the Watergate burglary during the campaign for his second term in office. Bibliography and Index.

2092. Stefoff, Rebecca. **Theodore Roosevelt: 26th President of the United States**. Ada, OK: Garrett Educational, 1988. 120p. $17.26. ISBN 0-944483-09-7. (Presidents of the United States). 5-9

Theodore Roosevelt (1858-1919) went to Harvard and served as New York legislative leader. After his wife died in 1884, he remarried and became the Assistant Secretary of the Navy in 1897-1898. He resigned to become a colonel in the Rough Riders, a volunteer cavalry in the Spanish-American War in Cuba, where he led the San Juan Hill battle. He returned, won the governorship of New York, and soon after, in 1900, became McKinley's Vice President. When President, he made the Panama Canal Treaty and started antitrust legislation. In his second term, he won the Nobel Peace Prize. In the last years of his life, he explored Brazil. Bibliography and Index.

2093. Stefoff, Rebecca. **Thomas Jefferson: 3rd President of the United States**. Ada, OK: Garrett Educational, 1988. 122p. $17.26. ISBN 9-44483-07-0. (Presidents of the United States). 5-9

This text about Thomas Jefferson (1743-1826) includes chapters on the Declaration of Independence, the rebellion of the colonies, his role during the American Revolution, his accomplishments as a statesman at home and abroad, the politics in his party, his tendency to philosophize, and his late years at Monticello. Bibliography and Index.

2094. Stefoff, Rebecca. **William Henry Harrison: 9th President of the United States**. Ada, OK: Garrett Educational, 1990. 120p. $17.26. ISBN 0-944483-54-2. (Presidents of the United States). 5-8

William Henry Harrison (1773-1841) fought in the Northwest Territory under General "Mad" Anthony Wayne before he became a delegate to the U.S. House of Representatives and defeated the Shawnee at the Battle of Tippecanoe in 1811. As a general in the War of 1812, he won a battle that secured American control of the western territory. He represented Ohio in the House from 1816 to 1829, lost his first bid for the presidency to Martin Van Buren, and beat Van Buren in 1840. One month after taking office in 1841, he died. Bibliography and Index.

2095. Stefoff, Rebecca. **Women Pioneers**. New York: Facts on File, 1995. 126p. $17.95. ISBN 0-8160-3134-7. (American Profiles). 6 up

The text looks at several women who played important roles in the settling of the West during the nineteenth century. They include Rebecca Burlend, Clara Brown, Virginia Reed, Tabitha Brown, Polly Bemis, Elinore Pruitt Stewart, and Martha Gay Masterson. Rebecca Burlend was raised in England; Polly Bemis grew up in China; Clara Brown was a slave in Virginia. Chronology, Further Reading, and Index.

2096. Stein, R. Conrad. **The Iran Hostage Crisis**. Chicago: Childrens Press, 1994. 32p. $15.27. ISBN 0-516-06681-1. (Cornerstones of Freedom). 5 up

On November 4, 1979, Iranian students seized 60 employees in the U.S. embassy in Tehran. They kept most of the hostages for 444 days in various places separated from each other. After Jimmy Carter lost the presidential election, Ronald Reagan took office on the same day the hostages were released, January 20, 1981. People displayed yellow ribbons everywhere so that others would not forget the hostages before the Iranians freed them. Index.

2097. Stein, R. Conrad. **The Korean War: "The Forgotten War."** Springfield, NJ: Enslow, 1994. 128p. $17.95. ISBN 0-89490-526-0. (American War). 6-9

Although 54,000 Americans died in the Korean War, fought from 1950 to 1953, many Americans at home lost interest because they did not understand the threat of Communist control spreading when the North Koreans invaded South Korea. This war did not have the media coverage common today, and no major event such as Pearl Harbor caused it to start. The text and photographs look at the war and its effects on those who fought and on their families. Chronology, Further Reading, and Index.

2098.   Stein, R. Conrad. **Valley Forge**. Chicago: Childrens Press, 1994. 28p. $16.40. ISBN 0-516-06683-8. (Cornerstones of Freedom). 3-8

After the British beat him at the Battle of Brandywine on September 11, 1777, George Washington and his soldiers retreated to Valley Forge, Pennsylvania. Soldiers who describe their loyalties and their frustration with struggling through the cold winter with few supplies give this account a personal touch. Black-and-white photographs and reproductions enhance the text. Index.

2099.   Stein, R. Conrad. **World War II in the Pacific: "Remember Pearl Harbor."** Springfield, NJ: Enslow, 1994. 128p. $17.95. ISBN 0-89490-524-4. (American War). 7 up

In chronological order, the text covers World War II in the Pacific from the bombing of Pearl Harbor on December 7, 1941, through the signing of the surrender on the USS *Missouri* on September 2, 1945. Black-and-white photographs and maps enhance the text. Further Reading, Chronology, and Index.

2100.   Stein, Wendy. **Witches: Opposing Viewpoints**. San Diego, CA: Greenhaven, 1995. 112p. $19.95. ISBN 1-56510-240-1. (Great Mysteries—Opposing Viewpoints). 6-9

In an attempt to define "witch," the author asserts that witches either destroy or heal, depending upon intent. Some researchers trace the etymology of "witch" to *witan* (to know) in Old English, and others select *wiccian* (to cast a spell). The text presents a history of witches from the Western world, mentioning the Inquisition; a trial in Arras, France, from 1459 to 1460; witchcraft in England, especially Chelmsford in Essex; witch covens in sixteenth-century Scotland (1591); and the Salem witch hunt in the American colonies from 1620 to 1725. Some believe that misogyny (hatred of women) is a leading cause of witch hunts because more than 80 percent of the people persecuted as witches have been female. Contemporary witches worship a goddess that is said to have been worshipped more than 35,000 years ago. In history, the most overt worship of the goddess occurred in Greece from approximately 1500 BC to 900 BC with Diana, Selene, and Hecate. But sources also indicate other pockets of goddess worship. For Further Exploration, Additional Works Consulted, and Index.

2101.   Steiner, Barbara. **Tessa**. New York: Morrow, 1988. 218p. $11.95. ISBN 0-688-07232-1. 7-9

Tessa, 14 in 1946, prefers her father's interest in archaeology to her mother's interest in money and society. After her mother leaves her father, Tessa spends the summer working with him in the Arkansas river bottom. An attractive university assistant makes the summer even more interesting, but Tessa decides at the end of the summer that she needs to return to town and finish high school. Then she will be prepared to major in archaeology in college.

2102.   Steins, Richard. **The Allies Against the Axis: World War II (1940-1950)**. New York: Twenty-First Century Books, 1994. 64p. $15.95. ISBN 0-8050-2586-3. (First Person America). 5-8

America entered World War II after the Japanese bombed Pearl Harbor in 1941, thus ending its isolationist policy. Steins looks at the war on both oceans and notes such situations as the challenges of army segregation, the fear and paranoia of the county according to a nisei (second-generation Japanese American), the women working in factories, soldiers returning to peacetime, and the descent of the Iron Curtain. Photographs enhance the text. Timeline, For Further Reading, and Index.

2103.   Steins, Richard. **The Nation Divides: The Civil War, 1820-1880**. New York: Twenty-First Century Books, 1993. 64p. $15.95. ISBN 0-8050-2583-9. (First Person America). 5-8

The text uses letters, poems, broadsides, speeches, lyrics, and newspaper articles to present the different aspects of the Civil War, including the debate over slavery, the secession of the Confederate states, the war itself, and life for the slaves after emancipation. Bibliography and Index.

2104.   Steins, Richard. **A Nation Is Born: Rebellion and Independence in America, 1700-1820**. New York: Twenty-First Century Books, 1993. 64p. $15.95. ISBN 0-8050-2582-0. (First Person America). 5-8

The text uses letters, poems, broadsides, speeches, lyrics, and newspaper articles to present the life of the settlers in the 13 colonies as they began to have problems with England and decided to fight for freedom. The pains of creating a new government of the United States are related. Bibliography and Index.

2105.   Steins, Richard. **The Postwar Years: The Cold War and the Atomic Age (1950-1959)**. New York: Twenty-First Century Books, 1994. 64p. $15.95. ISBN 0-8050-2587-1. (First Person America). 5-8

During the 1950s, television took hold at the same time Joseph McCarthy was creating a climate of terror by blacklisting anyone who had ever made pro-Communist remarks. War had not ended because many were fighting in Korea. The country was "white" because ethnic groups were "invisible" until the Montgomery bus boycott in Alabama. People noted here include Lillian Hellman, the Rosenbergs, Elvis Presley, Dr. Spock, and Martin Luther King, Jr. Photographs enhance the text. Timeline, For Further Reading, and Index.

2106. Steltenkamp, Michael F. **Black Elk: Holy Man of the Oglala**. Norman, OK: University of Oklahoma Press, 1993. 212p. $19.95. ISBN 0-8061-2541-1. 7 up

Much of the story of Black Elk (1866-1950) is based on information provided by his last surviving child and those who knew him personally. He led his Lakota people through the Wounded Knee massacre in 1890, but he survived. In 1904, he converted to Catholicism and served as a missionary to his fellow American Indians. New forms of religious involvement filled his life as he came to understand how traditional Indian religion merged with traditional Christian themes. Notes, Bibliography, and Index.

2107. Stephens, C. A. **Stories from the Old Squire's Farm**. Nashville, TN: Rutledge, 1996. 408p. $18.95. ISBN 1-55853-334-6. YA

These stories, written more than 100 years ago, describe life on Old Squire's farm in Maine. Six cousins, orphaned by the Civil War, live with their grandparents. The selections recount county fairs, the Fourth of July, elderberry wine, and swimming hole escapades as they also present the strong values of work and responsibility that formed the foundation of their lives.

2108. Stepto, Michele, ed. **Our Song, Our Toil: The Story of American Slavery as Told by Slaves**. Brookfield, CT: Millbrook Press, 1985. 95p. $18.40. ISBN 1-56294-401-0. 5-9

Some masters taught their slaves how to read and write. Excerpts from autobiographies and other documents tell the story of slavery in this text. Chapters include "born a slave," enslaved families, work of slavery, resistance, literacy, escaping slavery, and freedom. Photographs and reproductions enhance the text. Sources, Further Reading, and Index. *Notable Children's Trade Books in the Field of Social Studies*.

2109. Sterling, Dorothy. **Ahead of Her Time: Abby Kelley and the Politics of Antislavery**. New York: Norton, 1991. 436p. $14.95. ISBN 0-393-03026-1. YA

Abby Kelley, an abolitionist and feminist, was the wife of Stephen Foster, the composer. She had difficulties with the factions in the antislavery community and also had conflicts with her husband and daughter. According to Sterling, she was as important in the abolitionist movement as Frederick Douglass or William Lloyd Garrison, but did not receive like notice because she functioned as the workhorse of the movement. Unlike the others, she went to Ohio, Indiana, Michigan, and New York to see what needed to be done and to recruit rather than to stay at home. Photographs, Notes, Bibliography, and Index.

2110. Stern, Jane, and Michael Stern. **Sixties People**. New York: Knopf, 1990. 242p. $24.95. ISBN 0-394-57050-2. YA

The authors include every significant group that had a name in the 1960s and define them in this book about life during that decade. Among the groups are surfers, greasers, and women's libbers as well as hippie-freaks. The beginning of the decade, much happier and lighthearted, changed as it progressed to one in which many people became militant and fanatical by the end. The social customs, fashion, and culture of the 1960s appear in this text.

2111. Stevens, Bernardine S. **Colonial American Craftspeople**. New York: Franklin Watts, 1993. 128p. $19.60. ISBN 0-531-12536-X. (Colonial America). 5 up

The text looks at the craftwork performed in the early years of the United States. Among the craftspeople highlighted are coopers, joiners, woodworkers, masons, sawyers, bricklayers, metalworkers, leather workers, papermakers, printers, and bookbinders. The sources of these crafts and the lives of those who practiced them give an insight into the daily life of the times. Reproductions and drawings enhance the text. Glossary, Further Reading, and Index.

2112. Stevens, Bryna. **Frank Thompson: Her Civil War Story**. New York: Macmillan, 1992. 144p. $13.95. ISBN 0-02-788185-7. 4-9

A Canadian-born woman, Emma Edmonds, 15, disguised herself as "Frank Thompson" to serve in the Union army during the Civil War. She was too short to be a foot soldier so she became a nurse, a mail carrier, and later a spy. She had to leave the army after becoming sick and injured because a hospital stay would have revealed her secret. She published an account of her life in 1865, entitled *Nurse and Spy*. Sources and Index.

2113. Stevens, Leonard A. **The Case of Roe v. Wade**. New York: Putnam, 1996. 188p. $16.95. ISBN 0-399-22812-8. 8 up

The text covers the trial and litigation in the case of Jane Roe, who sued for the right to have an abortion. It looks at the history of contraception in the United States beginning with Margaret Sanger's efforts and continues through the current bombings and blockades of abortion clinics. It attempts to be objective in its presentation of emotionally-based material. Bibliography, Glossary, and Index.

2114. Stevens, Rita. **Andrew Johnson: 17th President of the United States**. Ada, OK: Garrett Educational, 1989. 122p. $17.26. ISBN 0-944483-16-X. (Presidents of the United States). 5-9

On April 14, 1865, five days after Robert E. Lee had surrendered to Ulysses S. Grant at Appomattox, Virginia, John Wilkes Booth shot Abraham Lincoln. As the sitting Vice President, Johnson (1808-1875) was also a target of the conspiracy, but his would-be assassin was too drunk and too scared to carry out his assignment. Three hours after Lincoln died, Johnson became President. The text looks at the rest of his life, including charges of impeachment against him. Bibliography and Index.

2115. Stevens, Rita. **Benjamin Harrison: 23rd President of the United States**. Ada, OK: Garrett Educational, 1989. 120p. $17.26. ISBN 0-944483-15-1. (Presidents of the United States). 5-8

The grandson of William Henry Harrison, Benjamin Harrison (1833-1901) was a member of the Ohio bar before he joined the Republican Party in 1856. During the Civil War, he served with the Indiana Infantry and reached the rank of brigadier general. At first a U.S. senator from Indiana, he was elected President in 1888. Because people disagreed with his policies, Grover Cleveland defeated him in 1892. Bibliography and Index.

2116. Stevens, Rita. **Calvin Coolidge: 30th President of the United States**. Ada, OK: Garrett Educational, 1990. 124p. $17.26. ISBN 0-944483-57-7. (Presidents of the United States). 5-9

Calvin Coolidge (1872-1933) grew up in New England and served in the Massachusetts legislature and as the state's governor. He became Vice President under Warren G. Harding in 1921, and when Harding died in 1923, he became President. Many people blamed him for the Great Depression. Others thought that he was merely lazy. A mediocre President, he did not make any serious mistakes. War did not occur while he was in office, and business, science, and industry were free to grow. He was thrifty, honest, and moral. Bibliography and Index.

2117. Stevens, Rita. **Chester A. Arthur: 21st President of the United States**. Ada, OK: Garrett Educational, 1989. 120p. $17.26. ISBN 0-944483-05-4. (Presidents of the United States). 5-9

At the death of James Garfield, Chester A. Arthur (1829-1886) became President. He had never been elected to an office, and no one knew what to expect, including himself. He chose good assistants and lived honorably while in office. He had never wanted to be President, but he did not succumb to any unsavory practices while serving his country. The text looks at his life and his presidency. Bibliography and Index.

2118. Stevenson, Augusta. **Sitting Bull: Dakota Boy**. Robert Jenney, illustrator. New York: Aladdin, 1996. 192p. $4.99pa. ISBN 0-689-80628-0pa. (Childhood of Famous Americans). 4-7

While Sitting Bull (1834?-1890) was still called Jumping Badger as a boy of 10, boys pretending to be his friends started calling him "Slow" so that he would begin to think that he could not win races or games. His father talked with the tribe's witch, and she told Jumping Badger to start believing in himself. She gave him a tooth to wear as a lucky charm. He began winning, and people began asking him to tell them about their fates based on the tooth. By the time he was 12, he needed to earn his adult Sioux name. In a dream, he saw many buffalo sitting down as if they were wounded. His father gave him the name "Sitting Bull" because he expected him to become a great hunter. He did.

2119. Stevenson, Brenda E. **Life in Black and White: Family and Community in the Slave South**. New York: Oxford University Press, 1996. 458p. $35. ISBN 0-19-509536-7. YA

Diaries, letters, journals, and firsthand accounts are the sources for this description of life in Loudon County, Virginia, during the nineteenth century before the Civil War. It focuses on slave holders, slaves, free Blacks, and poor whites, and their lifestyles. One half of the book looks at the whites; the other examines the marriage and family structure of both slaves and free Blacks. The text does not spare the details of the horrors of slave life from severe beatings and repeated rapes. Bibliography, Notes, and Index.

2120. Stewart, Gail B. **Benjamin Franklin**. San Diego, CA: Lucent, 1992. 127p. $16.95. ISBN 1-560-06026-3. (The Importance Of). 6-9

Quotes from a variety of sources give insight into the importance of Benjamin Franklin (1706-1790) to American history and to intellectual advancement. As a scientist, statesman, printer, and leader, he was one of the fathers of the concept of American ingenuity. Photographs, reproductions, and drawings enhance the text. Further Reading and Index.

2121. Stewart, Gail B. **Cowboys in the Old West**. San Diego, CA: Lucent, 1995. 112p. $22.59. ISBN 1-56006-077-8. (The Way People Live). 6-8

The myth of the cowboy in American legend remains although the era of the cowboy only lasted from approximately 1865 until 1890. During that time, cowboys drove almost 8 million head of cattle north from Texas into Kansas and beyond. Their time ended with the increased use of trains across the country. Some of the details that Stewart presents are that cowboys were often Black and Mexican, but only white cowboys seemed to get raises and promotions. Their vocabulary included swearing and simple words, and they were likely to "shoot" at words they considered pretentious. Their guns made them all equal, and most cowboys had a sense of when to stay quiet. Their life on the trail was hard work, but they always tried to stay friendly with the cook, head of the chuckwagon (invented by Charles Goodnight). Notes, For Further Reading, Works Consulted, and Index.

2122. Stewart, Gail B. **The Revolutionary War**. San Diego, CA: Lucent, 1991. 112p. $16.95. ISBN 1-56006-400-5. (America's Wars). 7 up

The text examines the causes, effects, events, results, and long-term influences of the Revolutionary War, "America's first civil war." Details about persons, battles, and atrocities help the war become real. Maps, timelines, photographs, drawings, and paintings augment the text. Bibliography, Chronology, and Index.

2123. Stewart, Gail. **Where Lies Butch Cassidy?** Yoshi Miyaki, illustrator. New York: Crestwood House, 1992. 48p. $11.95. ISBN 0-89686-618-1. (History's Mysteries). 5-8

Using pseudonyms such as Butch Cassidy, Billy Maxwell, and Jim Ryan, Robert Leroy Parker tried to spare his family shame while he continued his exploits. He robbed banks and trains but was only arrested once for cattle rustling, and he never killed anyone. Supposedly he and his partner, the Sundance Kid, died in Bolivia. Conflicting evidence arose during the 1930s, which indicated that he may have returned to the United States instead. The text examines what is known and what is guessed about Butch Cassidy. Chronology, For Further Reading, and Index.

2124. Stewart, Gail B. **World War I**. San Diego, CA: Lucent, 1991. 112p. $16.95. ISBN 1-56006-406-4. (America's Wars). 7-10

With photographs taken before, during, and after World War I, the text relates the process of war from before Archduke Ferdinand was murdered in Sarajevo through the Treaty of Versailles. It examines the effects of the war on other countries as well as the United States and looks at the armies, weapons, battles, and people who were intimately associated with this war. Works Consulted, Further Reading, and Index.

2125. Stiles, T. L. **Jesse James**. New York: Chelsea House, 1993. 111p. $18.95; $7.95pa. ISBN 0-7910-1737-0; 0-7910-1738-9pa. (Library of Biography). 6-12

Jesse James (b. 1847) grew up in western Missouri, site of guerrilla fighting during the Civil War, where he fought for the Bushwhackers on the losing Confederate side. By 16, he was an experienced killer who was almost killed himself. He recovered and married the woman who nursed him, but he decided to get revenge by robbing banks and railroads. He and his brother Frank's band of robbers worked for more than 10 years, giving Missouri the name "the bandit state." A member of his gang, Bob Ford, finally killed him in 1882 to get the reward money. Photographs, Chronology, Further Reading, and Index.

2126. Stine, Megan. **The Story of Malcolm X: Civil Rights Leader**. Minneapolis, MN: Gareth Stevens, 1995. 112p. $13.95. ISBN 0-8368-1383-9. (Famous Lives). New York: Dell, 1994. 102p. $3.50pa. ISBN 0-440-40900-4pa. 4-7

The author notes that even in his autobiography, Malcolm X (1925-1965) wrote incorrect information, a situation that mirrors other different versions about him. Knowing what might be true is often difficult. His father might have been a criminal. His mother went insane when Malcolm was 13, and he went into a juvenile detention home. He committed crimes and went to prison, where he learned about the Nation of Islam and wrote to Elijah Muhammad, the leader. He began to read. In 1952, after being paroled, he met Elijah, and in a few months converted and changed his name to Malcolm X. He continued his work until he was assassinated in 1965. Photographs included. Highlights in the Life, For Further Study, and Index.

2127. Stolz, Mary. **Cezanne Pinto: A Memoir**. New York: Knopf, 1994. 252p. $15. ISBN 0-679-84917-3. 5-9

Cezanne Pinto, an old man around 90, recalls his life as a young man around 12, when he was a slave on a Virginia plantation. He escaped to the North in 1860. His mother had been sold before he left, and he went to search for her. He saw the beginnings of the Civil War, tended horses on a Canadian farm, and became a teenage cowboy who decided to move to Chicago when a longhorn steer looked him in the eye. He decides at his advanced age that he, like Zora Neale Hurston, does not mind being colored. *Jane Addams Children's Book Award Honor Book.*

2128. Stolz, Mary Slattery. **Ivy Larkin**. 1986. New York: Yearling, 1989. 226p. $3.25pa. ISBN 0-440-40175-5pa. 5-7

Ivy, 14, resents the feelings of inadequacy that the other students in her private school make her suffer as a scholarship student in the early 1930s during the Depression. She cannot understand why her mother demands that she continue going to the school when its extra expenses strain the family's resources, especially when her father does not have a job. The close family and the changes in her sister when she looks after a puppy help the year seem more positive.

2129. Stone, Bruce. **Autumn of the Royal Tar**. New York: Laura Geringer, HarperCollins, 1995. 160p. $13.95. ISBN 0-06-021492-9. 5 up

In this first-person narrative, 12-year-old Nora tries to help the survivors of a ship, the *Royal Tar*, that sinks off the coast of her Maine home in 1835. Among them is a burned boy whose mother has died in the accident. Nora and Giles, a man working for her father, try to care for an elephant that survived, but it soon dies. Giles and the others mourn its death. More important, caring for the boy helps Nora empathize with the pain her mother has suffered since Nora's brother died three years before.

2130. **Stones and Bones: How Archaeologists Trace Human Origins**. Minneapolis, MN: Runestone Press, 1994. 64p. $11.95. ISBN 08225-3207-7. 4-9

Archaeology as a science is only a century old. During that time, scientists have learned a lot about prehistoric humans and ancient civilizations. The text explains the methodology of archaeology and gives theories that have sprung from this research. Glossary and Index.

2131. Strauch, Eileen Walsh. **Hey You, Sister Rose**. New York: Tambourine, 1993. 159p. $13. ISBN 0-688-11829-1. 3-7

In Baltimore, Maryland, Arlene enters sixth grade in 1951 during the Korean War, fearful of her teacher, the terror Sister Rose. But as the year progresses, Arlene learns about herself and her talent that Sister Rose encourages: writing. Arlene realizes that people who demand hard work can also be some of the kindest.

2132. Streissguth, Thomas. **Hatemongers and Demagogues**. Minneapolis, MN: Oliver Press, 1995. 160p. $14.95. ISBN 1-881508-23-4. (Profiles). 7 up

Some people have tried to create a definition of America through hatred. They have tried to change laws and stop people from having what is rightfully theirs. The text discusses Samuel Parris (Salen witch hunter), Lyman Beecher (anti-Catholic), Thomas Watson (white supremacist), William Simmons (Imperial Wizard of the Ku Klux Klan), Father Charles Coughlin (radio priest), Joseph McCarthy (anti-Communist), George Lincoln Rockwell (American Nazi), and Louis Farrakhan (black separatist). Bibliography and Index.

2133. Streissguth, Thomas. **Hoaxers & Hustlers**. Minneapolis, MN: Oliver Press, 1994. 160p. $14.95. ISBN 1-881508-13-7. (Profiles). 7 up

Throughout history, con artists have fooled some people. More recent con artists presented here are Lord Gordon-Gordon, thief (1811-1872); Charles Ponzi, fraudulent investor (1877-1949); Joseph "Yellow Kid" Weil, dishonesty (1877-1976); Oscar Hartzell, Sir Francis Drake heritage (1920's); Orson Welles, accidental hoax (1915-1985); Clifford Irving, writer (b. 1930); and Jim and Tammy Bakker, religious schemers (1980s). A Chronology of Con, Bibliography, and Index.

2134. Streissguth, Tom. **Rocket Man: The Story of Robert Goddard**. Minneapolis, MN: Carolrhoda, 1995. 88p. $19.95. ISBN 0-87614-863-1. (Trailblazers). 4-7

One of the experiments that 16-year-old Robert Goddard (1882-1945) tried was to make diamonds. He did not succeed, but his interests led him to rockets and to becoming the man who thought about traveling in space and tried to find a way to do it. He always suffered from tuberculosis, but he did not let his health keep him from making major advancements in science while he worked as a professor. The text looks at his many achievements. Notes, Glossary, Bibliography, and Index.

2135. Strickland, Brad. **The Hand of the Necromancer**. New York: Dial Press, 1996. 176p. $14.89. ISBN 0-8037-1830-6. 5-8

In the 1950s, John Dixon gets a job in the Gudge Museum with the help of his friend Professor Childermass and the professor's donation of artifacts created by the evil wizard Esdrias Blackleash during the Salem witch trials. Mattheus Mergal comes to town to steal the wooden hand from the collection, and with him come the supernatural beings that fill the rest of the story.

2136. Stwertka, Eve. **Duke Ellington: A Life of Music**. New York: Franklin Watts, 1994. 143p. $21.10. ISBN 0-531-13035-5. (Impact Biography). 7 up

Edward Ellington Kennedy (1899-1974) helped define the uniquely American musical form known as jazz. Growing up, he enjoyed a loving family that supported him. Because his charm and style were legendary, he earned the name "Duke." He added "Duke" to "Ellington" for his stage name and spent much of his adult life touring with his orchestra. Notes, Glossary, Bibliography, and Index.

2137. Sufrin, Mark. **George Catlin: Painter of the Indian West**. New York: Atheneum, 1991. 153p. $14.95. ISBN 0-689-31608-9. 5 up

To record the life of the Plains Indians through paintings became George Catlin's desire. During his life (1796-1872), he abandoned the study of law and started painting. Between 1831 and 1836, he traveled west by riverboat, canoe, and horseback. He saw and painted people in the Cheyenne, Sioux, Blackfeet, Crow, and Mandan tribes. He learned that these people were humans who had a variety of cultural backgrounds, and his work gave them an individuality that the public had never before seen. Bibliography and Index.

2138. Sufrin, Mark. **Stephen Crane**. New York: Atheneum, 1992. 160p. $13.95. ISBN 0-689-31669-0. 7-12

With his novel *Red Badge of Courage*, Stephen Crane (1871-1900) destroyed the romantic image of the Civil War. His writing was different from past authors because he used an impressionistic style and strong irony. He was the 14th child of a Methodist minister and graduated from a military academy, where he starred in athletics. He became a sometime college student before going to New York to live a bohemian life. He then went west, to Mexico, to Florida, and to battlefields in Greece and Cuba before his early death. Bibliography and Index.

2139. Sullivan, Charles, ed. **Children of Promise: African-American Literature and Art for Young People**. New York: Harry N. Abrams, 1991. 126p. $24.95. ISBN 0-8190-3170-2. 4 up

This book is a collection of poems, essays, speeches, and other writings by African Americans. Some of it is autobiographical, and some of it is fiction. All of it gives a picture of the lives of African Americans since Phillis Wheatley in the late eighteenth century. Photographs and drawings complement the text. Biographical Notes and Index.

2140. Sullivan, George. **Black Artists in Photography, 1840-1940**. New York: Cobblehill, 1996. 104p. $16.99. ISBN 0-525-65208-6. 6-9

Among the Black photographers who have made successful professions are Jules Lion, Augustus Washington, James P. Ball, the Goodridge brothers, Cornelius M. Battey, and Addison Scurlock. Although not detailing the problems with photographic processing, the text gives interesting insights into the lives of these men along with high-quality representations of their work. Further Reading and Index.

2141. Sullivan, George. **The Day We Walked on the Moon: A Photo History of Space Exploration**. New York: Scholastic, 1990. 72p. $5.95pa. ISBN 0-590-45587-7pa. 7 up

The text and photographs cover topics such as the dawn of the Space Age, the manned space flights, landing on the moon, astronaut training, the first spacewoman, shuttle missions, the tragedy of the *Challenger* in 1988, the voyage to Neptune, and future plans. For Further Reading and Index.

2142. Sullivan, George. **George Bush**. New York: Julian Messner, 1989. 170p. $12.98; $5.98pa. ISBN 0-671-64599-4; 0-671-67814-0pa. 6-10

George Bush (b. 1924) became the 41st president after serving as Vice President under Ronald Reagan. Chapters look at his life in Texas, as a loyal member of the Republican Party, as a candidate, as Vice President, and as President. Highlights of his public life include naval service, having the Japanese shoot down his plane in World War II, serving as a member of the House, becoming the U.S. ambassador to the United Nations, working as chief of the U.S. Liaison Office in the People's Republic of China in Beijing, and being the director of the Central Intelligence Agency. Photographs, Time Line, For Further Reading, and Index.

2143. Sullivan, George. **Matthew Brady: His Life and Photographs**. New York: Cobblehill, Dutton, 1994. 136p. $15.99. ISBN 0-525-65186-1. 6-10

On Matthew Brady's tombstone are the words "Renowned Photographer of the Civil War." He realized early that photographs could give visual records of people and events, so he and his assistants photographed most of the people serving in public life during his times. In 1862, when he exhibited a show called "The Dead at Antietam," viewers were shocked at the reality of war. The text, with photographs, gives the life of Brady (c. 1823-1896), who left an important view of the nineteenth century in America. Sources and Index.

2144. Sullivan, George. **Presidents at Play**. New York: Walker, 1995. 167p. $15.95. ISBN 0-8027-8334-1. 7-10

Presidents of the United States have played various sports as a method of relaxing. In short vignettes complemented with photographs, Sullivan recounts the Presidents and their leisure-time interests. These sports include golf, jogging, bowling, tennis, horseshoes, fishing, hunting, speedboating, softball, riding, swimming, calisthenics, bicycling, and skiing. The appendix lists each President, his physical characteristics, and his chosen sports.

2145. Sullivan, George. **Ronald Reagan**. New York: Julian Messner, 1991. 144p. $10.98. ISBN 0-671-74537-9. 5 up

Ronald Reagan (b. 1911) became the 40th President of the United States. The text covers his earlier years, life in Hollywood, the military, his family, his tenure as governor of California, the two terms as President, and his legacy. Important Dates, Further Reading, and Index.

2146. Sullivan, George. **Slave Ship: The Story of the Henrietta Marie**. New York: Cobblehill, Dutton, 1994. 80p. $15.99. ISBN 0-525-65174-8. 5-8

In 1972, divers found the remains of a sunken ship in the Gulf of Mexico. One of the first items found was a pair of shackles, which indicated that the ship had been a slave ship. On the ship's bell was engraved the name *Henrietta Marie* and the date 1699. Records show that the ship had unloaded its human cargo in Jamaica and had sunk in a storm while returning to London. Background information about slavers and photographs of the items discovered in the ship give an insight into what the people on board might have endured. This ship is the only slaver to have been scientifically studied. Bibliography and Index.

2147. Summers, Harry G., Jr. **Korean War Almanac**. New York: Facts on File, 1990. 330p. $29.95; $14.95pa. ISBN 0-8160-1737-9; 0-8160-2463-4pa. YA

This narrative overview of the Korean War, which lasted from 1950 to 1953, presents alphabetical entries on the war's actions; its weapons; military formations; personalities such as General Douglas MacArthur and his replacement, Lt. Gen. Matthew Ridgway; and the tactics for battles such as Old Baldy, Capital, Pork Chop, T-Bone, and Heartbreak Ridge. Photographs, Bibliography, and Index.

2148. Super, Neil. **Daniel "Chappie" James**. New York: Twenty-First Century Books, 1992. 80p. $14.95. ISBN 0-8050-2138-8. (African-American Soldiers). 5-9

Last in a family of 17 children, Daniel James (b. 1920) grew up in Florida in a racially segregated society. His parents taught him to dream, and he turned his dreams into a reality by becoming a fighter pilot, a four-star general in the U.S. Air Force, and a commander of the nuclear air defenses. Chronology, Bibliography, and Index.

2149. Super, Neil. **Vietnam War Soldiers**. New York: Twenty-First Century Books, 1993. 80p. $14.95. ISBN 0-8050-2307-0. (African-American Soldiers). 4-7

In looking at the contribution of African Americans in the Vietnam War (1961-1975), the author sees that they served in all branches of the service. However, they were less likely to be promoted or awarded medals than their white counterparts. Additionally, they were more likely to receive disciplinary action. These conclusions give insight into the treatment of African Americans while they were serving their country. Photographs supplement the text. Bibliography, Chronology, and Index.

2150. Suter, Joanne. **Our Century: 1980-1990**. Milwaukee, WI: Gareth Stevens, 1993. 64p. $23.93. ISBN 0-8368-1040-6. 3-10

Written as if a newspaper, this book's short articles give an overview of the decade. Included are statistics, daily life in America, technology, American hostages in Iran, civil war in Lebanon, Contra forces in Nicaragua, assassins killing Indira Gandhi, the battle against apartheid, Philippine unrest, U.S. forces in Panama, Eastern Europe falling, AIDS, Ronald Reagan, John Lennon, the *Challenger* explosion, George Bush, Mount St. Helens, Magic Johnson, Larry Bird, Steven Spielberg, George Lucas, Mikhail Gorbachev, Jesse Jackson, and Margaret Thatcher. Glossary, Books for Further Reading, Places to Write or Visit, and Index.

2151. Swanson, Diane. **Buffalo Sunrise: The Story of a North American Giant**. San Francisco: Sierra Club, 1996. 58p. $16.95. ISBN 0-87156-861-6. 4-7

The text looks at the importance of bison in American history by discussing their role in the survival and culture of Native Americans and the way that European settlers indiscriminately destroyed them. Anecdotes set in boxes give a liveliness to the text, along with accompanying photographs and reproductions. Index.

T

2152. Takaki, Ronald. **Democracy and Race: Asian Americans and World War II**. New York: Chelsea House, 1994. 126p. $18.95. ISBN 0-7910-2184-X. (Asian American Experience). 6 up

During World War II, the United States wanted other countries to think that it had no race problems, but for the Japanese community, the war intensified discrimination and resulted in loss of property and internment in concentration camps. However, young Japanese courageously fought on all fronts for the United States during the war. Chronology, Further Reading, and Index.

2153. Takaki, Ronald. **A Different Mirror: The Making of Multicultural America**. Boston: Little, Brown, 1993. 508p. $23.95; $13.95pa. ISBN 0-316-83112-3; 0-316-83111-5pa. YA

After taking the position that America's development has relied on people who fled from another country or wanted a new opportunity in another land, Takaki looks at immigrants who have settled in America. He focuses on the Japanese, African, Irish, Asian, and Jews. These people supported themselves and made others wealthy by working in sweatshops, on plantations, and with construction projects. According to Takaki, they created the multiculturalism that is America. Index.

2154. Takaki, Ronald. **Ethnic Islands: The Emergence of Urban Chinese America**. New York: Chelsea House, 1994. 125p. $18.95. ISBN 0-7910-2180-7. (Asian American Experience). 6-10

When the Chinese first came to the United States in the second half of the nineteenth century, discrimination, language barriers, and their own needs kept them from mixing with the general population. They established Chinatowns, which were not exotic places, like white Americans thought, but often full of poverty, overcrowding, and the fear of whites. Takaki describes their development and how the people organized to protect themselves from prejudice and as a way to fight for their rightful places as American citizens.

2155. Takaki, Ronald. **From the Land of Morning Calm: The Koreans in America**. New York: Chelsea House, 1994. 125p. $18.95. ISBN 0-7910-2181-5. (Asian American Experience). 6-10

The Japanese began invading Korea in the 1890s. Through 1945, thousands had to leave the country they called "Land of the Morning Calm" to avoid political repression and poor economic conditions. They came first to Hawaii and then to the California coast. They formed Korean patriotic associations wherever they were, hoping someday to return home to an independent Korea. But as they raised their children, they began to think of themselves as Americans. In 1965, the Immigration Act allowed a second wave of Koreans to come. Photographs enhance the text. Chronology, Further Reading, and Index.

2156. Takaki, Ronald. **Hiroshima: Why America Dropped the Atomic Bomb**. Boston: Little, Brown, 1995. 194p. $19.95. ISBN 0-316-83122-0. YA

A question that still remains about the dropping of the bomb on Hiroshima, August 6, 1945, is whether its purpose was to stop the war with Japan or to start the Cold War. The text looks at these possibilities as well as others. General Douglas MacArthur, the Pacific commander, did not know until 48 hours prior to the bombing that it would happen, and he thought it was unnecessary because Japan was losing the war already. Others think that Japanese stereotypes influenced public opinion against Japan and might have led to the decision. President Harry Truman always said that he made the decision and no one else, but the question remains as to what psychological influences might have led him to make it. People have wondered if his own inadequacies were reflected in the decision, or if he was trying to show Stalin what the United States had that could be used against him. Truman, however, regretted that civilians, especially children, had to die. Takaki takes the information available on the subject and tries to answer the questions. Notes and Index.

2157. Takaki, Ronald. **India in the West: South Asians in America**. New York: Chelsea House, 1994. 117p. $18.95. ISBN 0-7910-2186-6. (Asian American Experience). 5-10

In the early 1900s, Asian Indians came to Canada and the United States. Mainly Sikh men, they endured much prejudice. When the immigration laws became more liberal in 1965, more arrived. The text tells of the difficulties they encountered and how they have had to adjust their cultural expectations to their new country. Black-and-white photographs complement the text. Chronology, Further Reading, and Index. *New York Public Library Books for the Teen Age.*

2158. Takaki, Ronald. **Issei and Nisei: The Settling of Japanese America**. New York: Chelsea House, 1994. 126p. $18.95. ISBN 0-7910-2179-3. (Asian American Experience). 6-10

The Issei are first-generation Japanese Americans, and the Nisei were their American-born children. In 1868, the Meiji Emperor of Japan returned to power and bankrupted thousands of farmers by imposing new taxes. To deal with the problem, the government encouraged emigration. From the 1880s to the 1920s, many

Japanese immigrants came first to Hawaii and then to the mainland. They transformed California's marshes and deserts to orchards and gardens, but the discrimination they faced with laws made in 1913 kept them from buying their own farmland. In 1922, the Supreme Court said that they could not become naturalized citizens. In 1924, no new immigration from Asia was permitted. Photographs enhance the text. Chronology, Further Reading, and Index.

2159. Takaki, Ronald. **Journey to Gold Mountain: The Chinese in Nineteenth Century America**. New York: Chelsea House, 1994. 126p. $18.95. ISBN 0-7910-2177-7. (Asian American Experience). 5-10

When the Chinese came to America during the nineteenth century, they were searching for Gold Mountain, a way to gain success and money and return home to support their families. What they did was become the builders of the transcontinental railroad, farmers in California, or laundrymen. They also went to Mississippi and Massachusetts to work in the factories. They had to struggle against prejudice and for their few rights. They eventually settled, but Chinese men outnumbered women fourteen-to-one. Although the women had a variety of jobs, many were prostitutes in the early years while many of the men remained bachelors. Photographs supplement the text. Glossary, Further Reading, and Index.

2160. Takaki, Ronald. **Raising Cane: The World of Plantation Hawaii**. New York: Chelsea House, 1994. 125p. $18.95. ISBN 0-7910-2178-5. (Asian American Experience). 6-10

Many Asian immigrants coming to the United States stopped on the way in Hawaii, and many stayed. In the nineteenth century, sugarcane growers had a shortage of labor so they recruited Japanese, Chinese, Korean, and Filipino workers. The conditions were harsh with low wages, but workers from the different ethnic groups learned to work together. On Hawaii, unlike the United States, men could bring their spouses and children. These people helped to make Hawaii a multiracial society. Photographs enhance the text. Chronology, Further Reading, and Index.

2161. Takaki, Ronald. **Spacious Dreams: The First Wave of Asian Immigration**. New York: Chelsea House, 1994. 127p. $18.95. ISBN 0-7910-2176-9. (Asian American Experience). 5-10

In the early 1800s, the first Asian immigrants arrived in Hawaii and worked on the plantations. Others continued to the mainland United States, where they helped to build the transcontinental railroad. Asians from India arrived in the United States in the early twentieth century. Their difficulties as well as successes appear in the book. Photographs and reproductions enhance the text. Glossary, Further Reading, and Index.

2162. Takaki, Ronald. **Strangers at the Gates Again: Asian American Immigration After 1965**. New York: Chelsea House, 1995. 124p. $18.95. ISBN 0-7910-2190-4. (Asian American Experience). 6-10

In the United States, Asian citizens after World War II eventually won more rights through the Civil Rights movement. In 1965, Congress passed a new immigration act that permitted an increase in immigration from Asian countries. Many came from Japan, China, the Philippines, India, and Pakistan. After 1975, refugees came from Vietnam, Cambodia, and Laos. The old problems of racism, unequal employment, and cultural conflict continued, but America was more diverse and more democratic. Chronology, Further Reading, and Index.

2163. Talbert, Marc. **The Purple Heart**. New York: HarperCollins, 1992. 135p. $14. ISBN 0-06-020428-1. 4-8

Delighted that his father is returning early from Vietnam in 1967, Luke is surprised by his father's disinterest in everything around him. The Purple Heart his father won for being wounded fascinates Luke, and he thinks that in it lies the key to his father's attitude. Luke's father, however, dismisses the award as something one gets for being wounded—nothing special. Although his father needs much time to recover from the horrors of the war, he eventually learns to love his family again.

2164. Talmadge, Katherine. **The Life of Charles Drew**. Antonio Castro, illustrator. New York: Twenty-First Century Books, 1992. 84p. $13.98. ISBN 0-941477-65-7. (Pioneers in Health and Medicine). 5-8

Charles Drew (1904-1950), known as the "father of modern blood banking," was a surgeon and teacher who also fought for racial equality. He helped future generations of African Americans gain access to medical training. He devoted his life to helping others. For Further Reading and Index.

2165. Tames, Richard. **The 1930s**. New York: Franklin Watts, 1991. 48p. $19.14. ISBN 0-531-14059-8. (Picture History of the 20th Century). 7-9

In 20 chapters, photographs and reproductions along with brief text tell the story of Stalin's Russia, Hitler's Germany, Spain and Italy's fascists, and Asian problems in the 1930s. Other topics of interest such as transportation, science and technology, radio, movie stars, music, literature, fashion, art, sports, home life, and growing up also appear. Chronology and Index.

2166. Tames, Richard. **The 1950s**. New York: Franklin Watts, 1990. 48p. $19.14. ISBN 0-531-14403-4. (Picture History of the 20th Century). 7-9

Twenty chapters cover the 1950s on topics such as science, medicine, fashion, and sports. Rock and roll, the Suez Canal, and leaders important in this decade appear. Photographs and reproductions enhance the text. Chronology and Index.

2167.   Tames, Richard. **The 1980s**. New York: Franklin Watts, 1990. 48p. $19.14. ISBN 0-531-14079-2. (Picture History of the 20th Century). 7-9

In 20 chapters about the 1980s, such topics as the Reagan years, the "second" Russian revolution, the fight for freedom in Africa, science and medicine, music, lifestyles, record-breakers, Latin American situations, Middle East conflicts, Asian events, sports, and film are depicted in text and photographs. Chronology and Index.

2168.   Tanaka, Shelley. **The Disaster of the Hindenburg: The Last Flight of the Greatest Airship Ever Built**. New York: Scholastic, 1993. 64p. $6.95pa. ISBN 0-590-45751-9pa. (Time Quest). 5 up

The Hindenburg was 804-feet long and the most fashionable and elite way to cross the Atlantic. The journey took only four-and-a-half days, half the time sailing on a ship. On May 3, 1937, it was in its second season when it burst into flames because it contained flammable hydrogen instead of nonflammable helium. Photographs and drawings of cross-sections show the inside and outside of the ship. Glossary, Chronology, and Further Reading.

2169.   Tanenhaus, Sam. **Louis Armstrong: Musician**. New York: Chelsea House, 1989. 112p. $18.95; $7.95pa. ISBN 1-55546-571-4; 0-7910-0221-7pa. (Black Americans of Achievement). 5 up

Louis Armstrong (1900-1971) revolutionized jazz and helped establish it as one of the nation's most popular African American art forms. His father deserted the family, and his mother raised him until he was sent to reform school at 13. There he learned to play the coronet. He continued playing and perfecting his art as he watched others play in New Orleans' entertainment areas. He went to Chicago and then New York before he became America's official goodwill ambassador in 1960. Photographs complement the text. Chronology, Further Reading, and Index.

2170.   Tate, Eleanora E. **The Secret of Gumbo Grove**. 1987. New York: Yearling, 1996. 256p. $3.99pa. ISBN 0-440-41273-0pa. 7 up

Miss Effie talks Raisin, 11, into cleaning up the old church cemetery. Raisin loves history and finds information in the cemetery that leads her to research about slavery in the nineteenth century. What she finds helps her to realize the suffering that some have endured and to appreciate the present.

2171.   Taylor, Kimberly Hayes. **Black Abolitionists and Freedom Fighters**. Minneapolis, MN: Oliver Press, 1996. 160p. $14.95. ISBN 1-881508-30-7. (Profiles). 5 up

The text looks at eight African American leaders of the abolitionist and freedom fighter movements in the United States. They are Richard Allen (1760-1831), Sojourner Truth (1797?-1883), Nat Turner (1800-1831), Henry Highland Garnet (1815-1882), Frederick Douglass (1818-1895), Harriet Ross Tubman (1820-1913), Booker T. Washington (1856-1915), and Mary Church Terrell (1863-1954). An additional chapter presents capsules of information on more leaders in this area. Bibliography and Index.

2172.   Taylor, Kimberly Hayes. **Black Civil Rights Champions**. Minneapolis, MN: Oliver Press, 1995. 160p. $14.95. ISBN 1-881508-22-6. (Profiles). 7 up

People had to create organizations and strategies to fight racism by defeating Jim Crow laws. Some of these people who took leadership roles are presented in the text. They include W. E. B. Du Bois (founder of the National Association for the Advancement of Colored People), Thurgood Marshall (Supreme Court justice), James Farmer (Freedom Ride leader), Ella Baker ("Othermother" of civil rights), Andrew Young (ambassador), Martin Luther King, Jr. (minister and dreamer), and Malcolm X (Black Pride leader). Important Events in African-American History, Bibliography, and Index.

2173.   Taylor, M. W. **Harriet Tubman: Antislavery Activist**. New York: Chelsea House, 1990. 110p. $18.95; $7.95pa. ISBN 1-55546-612-5; 0-7910-0249-pa. (Black Americans of Achievement). 5 up

Harriet Tubman (1820-1913) led more slaves to freedom than anyone else. She first tried to escape from slavery when she was seven, but was caught, beaten, and put in the fields to work. Twenty years later, she did reach the North, and she began her career on the Underground Railroad. She was able to guide more than 300 people, including her parents, to freedom. In the Civil War, she went to South Carolina as a nurse and led raids on Confederate positions. She continued to work after the war by helping people who needed homes. People call her "Moses." Photographs and engravings enhance the text. Chronology, Further Reading, and Index.

2174.   Taylor, Marian W. **Chief Joseph: Nez Percé Leader**. New York: Chelsea House, 1993. 110p. $18.95. ISBN 0-7910-1708-7. (North American Indians of Achievement). 5 up

Chief Joseph (1840-1904) led the flight of the Nez Percé Indians from the government in 1877. His ancestors had lived in Oregon for centuries, but in 1874, the U.S. government decided that the tribe should move to Idaho. In 1877, he started leading his group of 800 toward resettlement, but an incident incited the army, and the U.S. cavalry pursued them, ambushing the group 42 miles from Canada. Joseph saved 418 of them. On October 5, 1877, he said "I will fight no more forever." He spent the next 27 years trying to get the Nez Percé back to their home, but he never succeeded. Photographs enhance the text. Chronology, Further Reading, and Index.

2175. Taylor, Mildred. **Let the Circle Be Unbroken**. New York: Dial Press, 1982. 432p. $16.99. ISBN 0-8037-4748-9. New York: Puffin, 1991. 432p. $4.50pa. ISBN 0-14-034892-1pa. 7 up

Cassie is 10 in 1934, and she sees several racial incidents that she objectively reports. During this year, she finds that she cannot drink at a "white only" water fountain in the courthouse. She hears about a woman who loses her sharecropper home when she tries to register to vote. A jury convicts a Black boy of killing a man when two white boys did it, and whites belittle Cassie's uncle for sleeping with a white woman who happens to be his wife. The strong character of the Logan family continues in this sequel to *A Song of the Trees* and *Roll of Thunder, Hear My Cry*. *Coretta Scott King Award, George C. Stone Center for Children's Books Recognition of Merit Award,* and *American Library Association Notable Books for Children*.

2176. Taylor, Mildred. **Mississippi Bridge**. New York: Dial Press, 1990. 64p. $15.99. ISBN 0-8037-0426-7. New York: Bantam, 1992. 64p. $3.50pa. ISBN 0-553-15992-5pa. 4-7

Jeremy Simms, 10, a white boy who wants to be friends with the Logan children of *Roll of Thunder, Hear My Cry* and *Let the Circle Be Unbroken,* watches a bus driver make Black people get off the bus in a heavy rainstorm for some late-arriving white passengers, even though the Black travelers urgently need to take the bus. What happens next shocks Jeremy: A bridge collapses under the bus, and people he knows on board drown. *Christopher Award*.

2177. Taylor, Mildred. **The Road to Memphis**. New York: Dial Press, 1990. 288p. $15. ISBN 0-8037-0340-6. New York: Puffin, 1992. 288p. $3.99pa. ISBN 0-14-036077-8pa. 9 up

Finishing high school in Jackson, Mississippi, Cassie Logan dreams of college and law school. She tries to save a friend from trouble in 1941 by taking him out of Mississippi. One of the passengers becomes ill, and they have to find shelter for him. Their car has trouble in Memphis, but Cassie's uncle wires money from Chicago to a Harvard lawyer friend who helps them in their severe difficulties. When they return home, their white friend Jeremy wants to know if the escapee reached safety. Reassured, he leaves, not to return. *Coretta Scott King Award* and *George C. Stone Center for Children's Books Recognition of Merit Award*.

2178. Taylor, Mildred. **Roll of Thunder, Hear My Cry**. Jerry Pinkney, illustrator. New York: Dial Press, 1976. 210p. $15.99. ISBN 0-8037-7473-7. New York: Puffin, 1991. 210p. $4.99pa. ISBN 0-14-034893-Xpa. 5 up

In 1933, Cassie Logan, nine, lives in Mississippi with her family and goes to the school for Black children, which only has old books. A white boy, Jeremy, wants to play with the Logan children, but his family hates Blacks and degrades the Logans. Because the family owns land, Mr. Logan has to leave home during the Depression to find work in order to keep their land. Another Black boy tries to make friends with Jeremy's brothers, but they kill a man and blame him for the murder. The love that the family members have for each other and the loyalty they have for their community directs the choices they must make. *Newbery Medal* and *George C. Stone Center for Children's Books Recognition of Merit Award*.

2179. Taylor, Mildred D. **The Well: David's Story**. New York: Dial Press, 1995. 92p. $14.99. ISBN 0-8037-1803-9. 4-7

When the father of the Logan family (in *Roll of Thunder, Hear My Cry* and other books) was young, he and his brother Hammer had to cope with the Simms brothers, Charlie and Ed-Rose. As Black children in the early twentieth-century white world of Mississippi, their word was never as good as that of a white man, even if the white man was lying. The Logan well was the only one not to dry up during a long spell, and they allowed neighbors to use their water until the Simms boys poisoned it with parts of a coon, skunk, and possum. A half-wit sees them hunting and reports to people gathered at the well so that their mischief becomes clear. *American Library Association Notable Books for Children*.

2180. Taylor, Theodore. **Air Raid-Pearl Harbor: The Story of December 7, 1941**. Rev. ed. San Diego, CA: Odyssey, Harcourt Brace, 1991. 179p. $4.95pa. ISBN 0-15-201655-4pa. 5-8

This look at the Japanese raid on Pearl Harbor examines what was happening throughout the world at the time and the sequence of events that led to the bombing. Taylor lists key figures and discusses the situation. Bibliography.

2181. Taylor, Theodore. **The Bomb**. San Diego, CA: Harcourt Brace, 1995. 197p. $15. ISBN 0-15-200867-5. 7 up

Introducing each chapter in this novel about 16-year-old Sorry Rinamu's concern about U.S. atomic bomb tests on his Pacific island, Bikini Atoll, are pages containing a single statement about various aspects of the bomb. Sorry does not believe the government when it tells the islanders before displacing them that they will be able to return to the island in two years. Sorry, Grandfather Jonjen, and Tara are the last to leave, thinking that they can be six miles away before the actual drop of Operation Crossroads occurs. They are wrong. The government was also wrong. Almost 50 years after the test, Bikini Atoll will poison anyone who tries to survive on its land. *American Library Association Best Books for Young Adults, New York Public Library Books for the Teen Age, Notable Children's Trade Books in the Field of Social Studies,* and *Scott O'Dell Award for Historical Fiction*.

2182.   Taylor, Theodore. **The Cay**. 1969. New York: Doubleday, 1989. 138p. $15.95. ISBN 0-385-07906-0. New York: Flare, 1995. 138p. $4.50pa. ISBN 0-380-01003-8pa. 6-9

In 1942, Phillip, 11, sails with his mother from Curaçao to Norfolk after German submarines begin torpedoing ships in the harbor. After Germans sink their ship, an old Black man, Timothy, saves Phillip and a cat. On the raft, Phillip finds that he is blind from a head injury sustained during the ship's explosion. On the island where they wash up, Timothy teaches Phillip how to be independent in spite of his disability so that Phillip can survive if Timothy dies. *Jane Addams Children's Book Award*.

2183.   Taylor, Theodore. **Walking Up a Rainbow**. 1986. San Diego, CA: Harcourt Brace, 1994. 275p. $4.50. ISBN 0-15-294512-1. New York: Flare, 1996. 275p. $4.50pa. ISBN 0-380-72592-4pa. 5 up

Susan's parents die in a buggy accident when she is 14 in 1852. To get the money to pay the debt her father left and keep the family home, she has to go across the United States, down through Panama, and back up to New Orleans and Iowa to achieve her goal. Along the way with her chaperone, she meets a variety of people.

2184.   Taylor-Boyd, Susan. **Betty Friedan: Voice for Women's Rights and Advocate of Human Rights**. Milwaukee, WI: Gareth Stevens, 1990. 68p. $16.95. ISBN 0-8368-0104-0. (People Who Have Helped the World). 7-9

After graduation from Smith College and attending one year of graduate school, Betty Friedan (b. 1921) went to New York, got a job, and got married. During her second pregnancy, she was fired. She had a lovely home, a husband, and children, but was discontent. What she found out from a survey of her college classmates was that many felt the same way she did, and felt guilty for not appreciating all that they had. She wrote about their situations in a book published in 1963, *The Feminine Mystique*. Her publisher expected little, but the book was successful because other women saw that they were not alone in their boredom. Friedan was not the first to write about the situation. Simone de Beauvoir wrote *The Second Sex* in 1949, Gloria Steinem wrote about the abuse of Playboy Bunnies in 1963, and Gwendolyn Brooks won a Pulitzer Prize in 1950 for her poetry, which explored the situation of African Americans and women in society. Friedan and others formed the National Organization for Women (NOW), which lobbied for women's rights. One of the first achievements of the group was to stop newspaper want ads from being divided into male and female segments. Additionally, Friedan was a battered wife who eventually had to divorce her husband to save herself. Organizations, Books, Glossary, Chronology, and Index.

2185.   Tchudi, Stephen. **Lock and Key: The Secrets of Locking Things Up, In, and Out**. New York: Scribner's, 1993. 113p. $14.95. ISBN 0-684-19363-9. 7-10

This history of locks and keys gives unusual information about their origins and uses. The text discusses security systems from those on Khufu's Tomb in Egypt to Fort Knox and atomic safes. It describes the development of different kinds of locks as well as relating stories about locks in history. Bibliography and Index.

2186.   Tedards, Anne. **Marian Anderson: Singer**. New York: Chelsea House, 1988. 111p. $18.95; $7.95pa. ISBN 1-55546-638-9; 0-7910-0216-0pa. (American Women of Achievement). 5 up

Marian Anderson (1897-1993) has been called the "voice of the American soul." Denied entrance to music school because she was African American, she began to perform for segregated audiences. By 1935, she was recognized as one of the century's greatest singers. When the Washington, D.C., Daughters of the American Revolution refused to let her sing in their hall, she sang for 75,000 Americans at the Lincoln Memorial, an event arranged by Eleanor Roosevelt. President Eisenhower appointed her to the U.S. Mission to the United Nations in 1958. Photographs, Further Reading, Chronology, and Index.

2187.   Terkel, Studs. **Giants of Jazz**. 1957. New York: Harpercrest, 1992. 215p. $16.89. ISBN 0-690-04917-X. YA

The text gives brief biographies of 13 jazz musicians who have made a major contribution to this style of music in the twentieth century. Among those profiled are Joe Oliver; Louis Armstrong; Bessie Smith; Bix, young man with a horn; Fats Waller; Count Basie; Billie Holiday; Woody Herman; Stan Kenton; and Dizzy Gillespie.

2188.   Terkel, Studs. **The Good War**. New York: New Press, 1996. 589p. $13. ISBN 1-56584-343-6. YA

Accounts of people who lived during World War II or are responding to what they think resulted from the war fill this book. They tell of going to the Far Pacific or confronting the Germans. One of the Andrews sisters visits a military hospital, and a soldier recounts the fear that General Patton put into his men. Others tell of racial inequalities and of the horror when liberating the first concentration camp. Admirals, politicians, intellectuals, and the average person all contribute their views of the war.

2189.   Terkel, Studs. **The Great Divide: Second Thoughts on the American Dream**. 1988. Avenel, NJ: Outlet, 1991. 439p. $5.99. ISBN 0-517-05081-1. YA

Terkel interviewed 96 Americans to find what people thought about the 1980s. Some of them wanted to return to other times, and some thought that people should live in the present. Americans tend to think of themselves as individuals rather than as alike, but they become distressed when they differ with their families or with public policy. The views of these people cover such topics as education, religion, work, race relations, and greed, with no conclusions as to what to do about the present in order to have a better future.

2190.   Terris, Susan. **Nell's Quilt**. New York: Farrar, Straus & Giroux, 1987. 162p. $12.95. ISBN 0-374-35504-5. 7-9

Nell, 18, says that she will marry the widower 10 years older than her whom her parents have chosen although she wants to attend Smith College. She starts making a quilt that she says she must finish before she marries, and she becomes thin and ill. Nell expects to die when she finishes the quilt, but she discovers that other people need her too much. Eventually her sister shows an interest in the widower, and the youth that Nell once loved may reappear.

2191.   Tessendorf, K C. **Wings Around the World: The American World Flight of 1924**. New York: Atheneum, 1991. 104p. $14.95. ISBN 0-689-31550-3. 4-8

The first world flight occurred in 1924 from April 6 to September 28. The airmen of the U.S. Army's Air Service decided to be the first to accomplish this feat, but they had to have the support of other branches of the services to be successful. The flight began in Seattle, Washington, and continued over two oceans and three continents. They crossed 22 foreign nations with all types of climate. In every country, they had to accept invitations and attend celebrations. The text, with photographs, gives the details of the preparations and the execution of this journey. On Further Reading and Index.

2192.   Tessitore, John. **The Hunt and the Feast: A Life of Ernest Hemingway**. New York: Franklin Watts, 1996. 224p. $22.70. ISBN 0-531-11289-6. (Impact Biography). 7 up

This look at Ernest Hemingway (1899-1961) gives a balanced picture of a man who lied and exaggerated but who was also courageous. It begins with Hemingway's service in World War I and then covers his life chronologically from its beginning to his suicide. Hemingway was self-destructive as well as being one of the twentieth-century writers able to capture a situation through dialogue. Bibliography, Notes, and Index.

2193.   Thesman, Jean. **Molly Donnelly**. Boston: Houghton Mifflin, 1993. 186p. $13.95. ISBN 0-395-64348-1. 5-9

Although her day in Seattle, Washington, begins normally, Molly Donnelly sees changes begin on December 7, 1941, after the Japanese bomb Pearl Harbor. That night, the blackouts begin. Her best friend Emily Tanaka and her family are taken away and placed in an internment camp. Her brother and father start to work longer shifts for Boeing Aircraft, and her mother begins working. During the war, two of her cousins die, she has her first date, and she becomes interested in a young soldier. What she realizes as she looks around is that getting a college education is the only way she can escape the limited choices for women.

2194.   Thesman, Jean. **The Ornament Tree**. Boston: Houghton Mifflin, 1996. 240p. $15.95. ISBN 0-395-74278-1. 5-8

Bonnie, 14, becomes an orphan and has to move to Seattle where her mother's relatives live. The women are well-educated liberals who distribute information on suffrage, birth control, and the horrors of child labor. They have no management skills, however, so they have to take in boarders to recover from World War I and survive the general strike of 1919. When Bonnie arrives, the Deveraux women have found out that they need kitchen skills, so she comes to their aid, and they, in turn, help her.

2195.   Thesman, Jean. **Rachel Chance**. Boston: Houghton Mifflin, 1990. 175p. $13.95. ISBN 0-395-50934-3. 6-9

In Seattle in the early 1940s, Rachel, 15, feels despair when someone kidnaps her four-year-old illegitimate brother Rider. Her grandfather, cousin, and widowed mother desperately search for him with the help of her grandfather's eccentric friend Druid Annie and a hired boy whom Rachel at first dislikes. Rachel suspects revivalists who have just left town. She finds them and Rider, as well as Rider's father, who did not know about his son.

2196.   Thomas, Herbert. **Human Origin: The Search for Our Beginnings**. Paul G. Bahn, translator. New York: Abrams, 1996. 159p. $12.95. ISBN 0-8109-2866-3. YA

The text covers the various theories of early human life and the people who were their proponents. As an introduction, it tells how the theories changed with new discoveries and increased scientific understanding. Photographs, maps, diagrams, and drawings augment the text. Bibliography, Chronology, Glossary, and Index.

2197. Thompson, Cliff. **Charles Chesnutt: Author**. New York: Chelsea House, 1992. 112p. $18.95. ISBN 1-55546-578-1. (Black Americans of Achievement). 7 up

As one of his era's most articulate spokespeople, Charles Waddell Chesnutt (1858-1932) became the first published Black novelist in America. Born in the South but frustrated by the lack of options for Black men, he moved to Cleveland, where he studied law, became a court reporter, raised a family, and wrote fiction. His main novels appeared at the turn of the century. He knew Booker T. Washington and W. E. B. Du Bois and received the Spingarn Medal in 1928, the highest award possible from the National Association for the Advancement of Colored People. Photographs enhance the text. Chronology, Further Reading, and Index.

2198. Thoreau, Henry. **Walden: An Annotated Edition**. Boston: Houghton Mifflin, 1995. 338p. $30. ISBN 0-395-72042-7. YA

In 1845, Henry David Thoreau (1817-1862) moved into a cabin on Walden Pond in Concord, Massachusetts. Ralph Waldo Emerson allowed Thoreau to use his land for the experiment of building a cabin and living in the woods by himself. Thoreau had not planned to write about his experience, but he kept a journal, and when he started incorporating his notes into lectures in 1847, he realized that he needed to make a formal, written collection. In the book, Thoreau tells about these two years of his life. Appendix and Works Cited.

2199. Thorleifson, Alex. **Ethel Barrymore**. New York: Chelsea House, 1991. 110p. $18.95. ISBN 1-55546-640-0. (American Women of Achievement). 7 up

Ethel Barrymore (1879-1959) maintained the tradition of acting in her family, and she became a star and remained one for more than 60 years. She raised three children while carrying on her career in both New York and London. After the Depression, she returned to the stage. In 1944, she won an Academy Award. Photographs and reproductions enhance the text. Chronology, Further Reading, and Index.

2200. Tilghman, Christopher. **Mason's Retreat**. New York: Random House, 1996. 290p. $22. ISBN 0-679-42712-0. YA

In 1936, Edward and Edith Mason return to the family Chesapeake Bay home from England. Their son Simon reflects 40 years later on how he and his brother adjusted to their new home. His brother Sebastian, although melancholic, enjoyed working on the farm with the laborer Robert who had suffered for many years from the family abuses. Edward returns to England to run a munitions factory. When he hears about his wife's infidelity, he forgets his own affairs and decides to sell the farm and take the family back to England. Simon relates the story as it evolved during those difficult years.

2201. Tilton. Rafael. **Clara Barton**. San Diego, CA: Lucent, 1995. 112p. $16.95. ISBN 1-56006-058-1. (The Importance Of). 7 up

From her early childhood, Clara Barton (1821-1912) was always fearful, but she learned to hide her fears so that no one knew. Her first nursing experience was looking after her brother, who was seriously injured from falling off a roof, for two years. She then became a teacher, wanting to share the excellent instruction her own teachers had given her. She never married, although she was pursued, because no one fulfilled her expectations for a husband. She came to Washington, D.C., before the Civil War and got a job as the first female clerk in the Patent Office. Her job was eliminated, but soon she was rehired because her copying skills were needed. What she saw in the city during the Civil War was men who needed supplies, and she advertised in newspapers for people to send food and clothing for the troops. She devised ways to improve supply distribution and eventually was allowed to work on the front. The capture of her brother, his imprisonment, and subsequent death led her to try to find soldiers reported missing in action with a letter-writing campaign. During her endeavors, she became friends with Susan B. Anthony, Julia Ward Howe, Lucy Stone, and Frances Willard. She went to Switzerland to recover from exhaustion, where she met Henry Dunant and found out about his book and work in trying to help soldiers find supplies. At the time, she did not know that the United States had refused to sign the Treaty of Geneva. After helping in Europe from 1876 to 1882, she returned to the United States and spent time lobbying for a reversal of that decision and for establishing the American chapter of the Red Cross. She also went to Armenia. Without her tireless and selfless efforts, organizations for providing aid might not have succeeded. Notes for Further Reading, Additional Works Consulted, and Index.

2202. Tilton, Rafael. **Margaret Mead**. San Diego, CA: Lucent, 1993. 112p. $16.95. ISBN 1-56006-039-5. (The Importance Of). 7 up

Margaret Mead (1901-1978) was a pioneering anthropologist who helped change the roles of men and women in society. She wrote about the limitations of these roles and that people should not be restricted by society's bounds. Her goals were world peace, multicultural understanding, and help for all children. She knew that she must spread this information to as many people as possible so that others would support her ideas. She wrote hundreds of articles and more than 40 books discussing marriage, prejudice, child rearing, education, and world heath and cooperation. She married and had children while continuing her career. Notes, For Further Reading, Works Consulted, and Index.

2203. Time-Life. **African Americans: Voices of Triumph: Leadership**. Alexandria, VA: Time-Life, 1994. 256p. $18.95. ISBN 0-7835-2254-1. 6 up

The text and the accompanying photographs give a view of African leadership throughout history. Brief commentaries on the seventeenth-century Queen Nzingha and her contemporary Okomfo Anokye of the Ashanti nation, Makeda of Ethiopia (who may have been the Queen of Sheba), the Islamic Ahmed Baba in the sixteenth century, and Imhotep around 2600 BC introduce the heritage of African American leaders. Included are African American leaders in science and invention, business and industry, religion, education, and politics. Bibliography and Index.

2204. Time-Life. **The Buffalo Hunters**. Alexandria, VA: Time-Life, 1993. 192p. $18.95. ISBN 0-8094-9426-4. (The American Indians). 6 up

On the land between the Mississippi River and the Rocky Mountains, more than 32 nomadic tribes lived for centuries depending on the buffalo for their food, clothing, and shelter. The text looks at these people, their family and clan traditions, their relationship to the buffalo, and the ceremonies and rituals in which they believed. Photographic essays discuss their sacred hills, their Sun Dance, the homes that they carried with them, their dreams, and the Crow fair. Photographs, Illustrations, Bibliography, and Index.

2205. Time-Life. **Cycles of Life**. Alexandria, VA: Time-Life, 1994. 176p. $18.95. ISBN 0-8094-9583-X. (The American Indians). 8 up

In this volume with accompanying photographs, the text looks at cycles in Native American lives. The topics are the promise of youth, the rites of passage, and closing the circle in making connections. Photo essays cover mothers and their children, dream seekers, a Hopi wedding, and the passion for games. Bibliography and Index.

2206. Time-Life. **The European Challenge**. Alexandria, VA: Time-Life, 1992. 192p. $18.95. ISBN 0-8094-9409-4. (The American Indians). 8 up

When Christopher Columbus came to America and brought others with him in 1492, he began the European migration that challenged the rights of Native Americans already living on the two continents. The text looks at these first encounters, the Northern woods, the pueblo problems, and the California coasts. Photo essays discuss a Powhatan village, the Greenland tragedy, the California missions, trade, and Pecos, New Mexico, then a city. Photographs, Illustrations, Bibliography, and Index.

2207. Time-Life. **The First Americans**. Alexandria, VA: Time-Life, 1992. 192p. $18.95. ISBN 0-8094-9401-9. (The American Indians). 8 up

The first Americans probably came over the Bering Strait during one of the Ice Ages, perhaps as long ago as 40,000 years, but probably around 20,000-30,000 years ago. Some 15,000 years ago, a land bridge existed that was so broad that it had its own name, Beringia. When the peoples migrated south, some of them left weapons now called Clovis points because they were first discovered in Clovis, New Mexico, and dated to around 9500 BC. The text continues with information gleaned from archaeological finds about these first inhabitants of North and South America. Essays cover the desert people, the mound builders, the whale hunters, corn, home on the mesas, everyday objects, stone legacies, and sea rituals. Photographs, Illustrations, Bibliography, and Index.

2208. Time-Life. **Hunters of the Northern Forest**. Alexandria, VA: Time-Life, 1995. $18.95. ISBN 0-8094-9570-8. (The American Indians). 6 up

To live in the northern forests of North America, Native Americans had to be in tune with the seasons. The text looks at their lives, the infiltration of fur traders in the mid-1500s who changed their traditions, and the political reshaping of their world when other groups such as the U.S. government took power. Photo essays cover the land, beaver hunting, the help of the spirits for good hunting, the alliance of the French and the Indians in the seventeenth century, and the Mask Dance of the Ingalik. Photographs, Illustrations, Bibliography, and Index.

2209. Time-Life. **The Indians of California**. Alexandria, VA: Time-Life, 1994. 192p. $18.95. ISBN 0-8094-9587-2. (The American Indians). 9 up

The text presents the peoples indigenous to the area now known as California and shows their interactions with the Europeans who came to explore and the settlers who came for gold. Photo essays include topics such as the Cupeno struggle to keep their homeland, the White Deerskin Dance of the Hupa people, Ishi as the last member of his tribe, domestic architecture, attempts to blend Christianity with native spiritual beliefs, and the arts. Archival Photographs, Bibliography, and Index.

2210. Time-Life. **Mound Builders & Cliff Dwellers**. Alexandria, VA: Time-Life, 1992. 168p. $18.95. ISBN 0-8094-9859-6. (Lost Civilizations). 8 up

In 1991, an archaeologist flying over Arizona's Coconino National Forest noticed three clay pots in the mouth of a cave that he had not seen from the ground below or the butte above the cave. When he investigated, he found intact prehistoric vessels that had been created sometime between 1250 and 1350. They had belonged to the Sinagua Indians, who had left their home in the cliffs and mingled with other communities. This find and others appear in the text as it discusses the mounds in the Midwest and Southwest, the Adena (500 BC-AD 1) and Hopewell (100 BC-AD 400), cultures, temple mound builders or Mississippians (AD 800-1500), the Anasazi's canyons and cliffs (AD 200-1450), the Hohokam culture (AD 200-1450) and the Mogollon culture (AD 200-1450). Photo essays look also at Chaco Canyon. Photographs, Bibliography, and Index.

2211. Time-Life. **People of the Ice and Snow**. Alexandria, VA: Time-Life, 1994. 192p. $18.95. ISBN 0-8094-9562-7. (The American Indians). 7 up

The Indians who live in the northern climates of Canada, Alaska, and the Arctic support themselves through hunting and crafts. The text looks at these people and their trades, their humor, and their struggle to preserve tradition. Photo essays cover the life of the Eskimo, pursuing the Great Nanook or polar bear, the shaman as the emissary to the gods, images from the netherworld, and the art of ivory carving. Photographs, Bibliography, and Index.

2212. Time-Life. **People of the Western Range**. Alexandria, VA: Time-Life, 1995. 192p. $18.95. ISBN 0-8094-9725-5. (The American Indians). 6 up

Photographs, maps, and reproductions help tell the story of the people who lived on the western range before they lost their land to the white settlers. These tribes included the Causes, Umatillas, Nez Percés, Flatheads, Shoshones, Bannocks, and Utes. The text discusses the land and its resources, the loss of land, and the desire to defend the homeland before all of it had been taken. A picture essay makes a comparison between tribal members in the nineteenth century with those in the twentieth century. Other picture essay topics are spotted horses on the plateau, a cleric's journal, and a horse race for honor. Photographs, Illustrations, Bibliography, and Index.

2213. Time-Life. **Realm of the Iroquois**. Alexandria, VA: Time-Life, 1993. 176p. $18.95. ISBN 0-8094-9438-8. (The American Indians). 6 up

The Iroquois formed a confederacy in the sixteenth century that gave each of five previously feuding tribes a portion of the land. They compared their political structure to a longhouse where the Mohawk guarded the eastern door, the Seneca looked to the west, and in between burned the fires of the Oneida, the Onondaga, and the Cayuga. The trail that linked the tribes was so efficient that it is almost the exact path of the current New York State Thruway. The text looks at their alliance, the intrusion of the Europeans, and the subsequent shattering of the confederacy. Photo essays cover their land, the communal shelters, the importance of wampum, lacrosse, and the Mohawks who built the New York skyscrapers. Photographs, Illustrations, Bibliography, and Index.

2214. Time-Life. **The Reservations**. Alexandria, VA: Time-Life, 1995. 192p. $18.95. ISBN 0-8094-9737-9. (The American Indians). YA

The U.S. government has a poor history of treatment of Native Americans and their homes. The text recounts the history of the reservations, the land tenure, the relationships between the government and the tribes, and the mistreatment of the Native American cultures. Bibliography, Chronology, and Index. *Notable Children's Trade Books in the Field of Social Studies.*

2215. Time-Life. **The Revolutionaries**. Alexandria, VA: Time-Life, 1996. 192p. $19.95. ISBN 0-7835-6250-0. 7 up

The text begins with Paul Revere's ride in 1775 and ends with the Yorktown surrender by Cornwallis. In between are thorough battle descriptions and biographical insights about the figures who were involved in this period. The four essays reveal facts about a Quaker woman through her diary, the Iroquois, the pamphleteers, and an average soldier. Illustrations, photographs, and maps enhance the text. Bibliography and Index.

2216. Time-Life. **The Spirit World**. Alexandria, VA: Time-Life, 1992. 176p. $18.95. ISBN 0-8094-9405-1. (The American Indians). 7 up

According to the text, Sitting Bull climbed to the top of a butte in 1876 to ask the Great Mystery, Wakan Tanka, to give him guidance in the next confrontation between the Sioux and the U.S. government. He offered a "scarlet blanket," 50 pellets of his flesh, cut from each arm with an awl and a sharp knife, and then he performed the most holy Sioux ritual, the Sun Dance. He danced for more than 36 hours until he fainted. His vision during the dance was of white soldiers falling "like grasshoppers" in the Indian camp. Soon after, Sitting Bull and his men defeated Custer at the Battle of Little Bighorn. Whether his summoning the spirit caused the victory is unknown, but the spirituality of the individual tribes cannot be underestimated. The text covers the Great Mystery, the wisdom of the creatures, the power in the green stalk, and crying for a vision. There are photo essays on the masks or faces of the supernatural, the winged messengers to the gods, Navajo ways of healing, and sacred shelters. Photographs, Bibliography, and Index.

2217. Time-Life. **This Fabulous Century: 1870-1900, Prelude**. Alexandria, VA: Time-Life, 1969. 290p. $24.95. ISBN 0-8094-5754-7. 7 up

Period photographs and illustrations accompany text that describes American life from 1870 to 1900. Among the topics presented are law and order, holidays, the frontier, cycling, occupations, education, newspapers and yellow journalism, cures or nostrums, life in the city, and entertainment. Bibliography and Index.

2218. Time-Life. **This Fabulous Century: 1900-1910**. Alexandria, VA: Time-Life, 1969. 288p. $24.95. ISBN 0-8094-5758-X. 7 up

Period photographs and illustrations accompany text describing American life from 1900 to 1910. Among the topics presented are the patriarchal society, immigrants, flying machines, children, hometowns, women, sport, the very rich, motorcars, road shows, and summer rituals. Bibliography and Index.

2219. Time-Life. **This Fabulous Century: 1910-1920**. Alexandria, VA: Time-Life, 1969. 287p. $24.95. ISBN 0-8094-5762-8. 7 up

Period photographs and illustrations accompany text describing American life from 1910 to 1920. Among the topics presented are the end of innocence, the new woman, the "flickers" or movies, the Tin Lizzie (automobile), culture, fun and games, the outdoors, winter fun, World War I, and Broadway. Bibliography and Index.

2220. Time-Life. **This Fabulous Century: 1920-1930**. Alexandria, VA: Time-Life, 1969. 288p. $24.95. ISBN 0-8094-5766-0. 7 up

Period photographs and illustrations accompany text describing American life from 1920 to 1930. Among the topics presented are the quest for normalcy, youth and their music, flight, jazz, business and credit, sports stars, Prohibition, the press and newspapers, famous people, fads, and traveling. Bibliography and Index.

2221. Time-Life. **This Fabulous Century: 1930-1940**. Alexandria, VA: Time-Life, 1969. 288p. $24.95. ISBN 0-8094-57. 7 up

Period photographs and illustrations accompany text describing American life from 1930 to 1940. Among the topics presented are radio, hard times and the Depression, comic book characters, criminals, Franklin Delano Roosevelt, cafe society, labor and the working man, movies, anti-Communists, swing music, and the 1939 World's Fair in New York. Bibliography and Index.

2222. Time-Life. **This Fabulous Century: 1940-1950**. Alexandria, VA: Time-Life, 1969. 288p. $24.95. ISBN 0-8094-5775-X. 7 up

Period photographs and illustrations accompany text describing American life from 1940 to 1950. Among the topics presented are teenagers, clubwomen, World War II, the home front, after the war, sports, fashion, and the theater. Bibliography and Index.

2223. Time-Life. **This Fabulous Century: 1950-1960**. Rev. ed. Alexandria, VA: Time-Life, 1985. 288p. $24.95. ISBN 0-8094-5779-2. 7 up

Period photographs and illustrations accompany text describing American life from 1950 to 1960. Among the topics presented are the personalities of the era, fads, beat poets, politics and McCarthy, music, suburbia, culture, rebels, and the place of television. Bibliography and Index.

2224. Time-Life. **This Fabulous Century: 1960-1970**. Alexandria, VA: Time-Life, 1970. 288p. $24.95. ISBN 0-8094-5783-0. 7 up

Period photographs and illustrations accompany text describing American life from 1960 to 1970. Among the topics presented are the years of Kennedy and Camelot, the youth and love children, assassins, fashion, the older population, media, the emergence of Black society, celebrities, doves and hawks in war and antiwar arguments, athletes, singles, and science. Bibliography and Index.

2225. Time-Life. **Tribes of the Southern Woodlands**. Alexandria, VA: Time-Life, 1994. 176p. $18.95. ISBN 0-8094-9550-3. (The American Indians). 7 up

As early as 1500 BC, ancestors of powerful tribes such as the Choctaw, Chickasaw, Creek, Cherokee, and Seminole in the South built mounds from which to thank the gods. These have been covered by many for farms or other modern edifices, but some remain as a tribute to another time. The text looks at the lives of these people imperiled by the European settlers, their problems in the early eighteenth century in various wars, and their forced movement from Georgia toward Oklahoma in the early 1830s. Photo essays look at the monuments they built, the Seminole medicine man, the Trail of Tears, and corn production. Photographs, Illustrations, Bibliography, and Index.

2226.   Time-Life. **The Woman's Way**. Alexandria, VA: Time-Life, 1995. 192p. $18.95. ISBN 0-8094-9729-8. (The American Indians). 7 up

Throughout the history of Native American tribes, women have had positions of honor. They have held places of respect as mothers, healers, seers, economists, and policymakers. They have controlled the institutions of the tribes, including the rights to clan membership, tribal leadership, and the use of tribal lands. The text looks at the roles of sustainer, spiritualist, and keeper of the faith with photo essays covering similar concepts. Photographs, Bibliography, and Index.

2227.   Tingum, Janice. **E. B. White: The Elements of a Writer**. Minneapolis, MN: Lerner, 1995. 124p. $17.21. ISBN 0-8225-4922-0. 5 up

Elwyn Brooks White (1899-1985), known as Andy, loved to play with the animals in his farmyard when he was a boy. Their presence most likely led to the animals in *Charlotte's Web*, which he published in 1952. By the time he wrote the book, he had published in many other places but had worked continuously at the *New Yorker*, where he met his wife Katherine. As a writer, he also was concerned about style and vocabulary. Perhaps his most important other book is his revision of William Strunk's *The Elements of Style*. In it he continued the tradition of a love for good, correct writing. A private person, he was always devoted to his wife. Sources, Bibliography, and Index.

2228.   Tinling, Marion, ed. **With Women's Eyes: Visitors to the New World, 1775-1918**. Hamden, CT: Archon Books, 1993. 207p. $27.50. ISBN 0-208-02371-2. YA

At least 26 European women wrote about their visits to the New World between the American Revolution and World War I. Some were positive accounts, but others were horrified at the practice of slavery and the treatment of slaves, Native Americans, and women. Many of these women came alone and traveled with discomfort in their quests for the truth. Further Reading, Glossary, and Index.

2229.   Todd, Leonard. **Squaring Off**. New York: Viking, 1990. 150p. $13.95. ISBN 0-670-83377-0. 7-10

Willy, 13, wants to gain his widower father's approval and that of the stripper LuJane, whom his father brings to their Savannah, Georgia, home one night in the mid-1950s. LuJane befriends Willy. When his father embarrasses him by mentioning Willy's admiration of LuJane's physical attributes, LuJane decides to quit her job and establish a relationship with the father.

2230.   Toht, David W. **Sodbuster**. Richard Erickson, illustrator. Minneapolis, MN: Lerner, 1996. 48p. $14.96. ISBN 0-8225-2977-7. (American Pastfinder). 4-7

Between 1800 and 1850, many Americans went west because they wanted to own a farm of approximately 160 acres. With few tools and a team of oxen, they cleared land, raised barns, built fences, and started farms that began to thrive. Because breaking the prairie was the first job of these immigrants, they became known as "sodbusters." In two-page chapters the text looks at their efforts, their daily lives, home remedies, clothing, planting and harvesting, winter, going to market, celebrations, church, and school. Glossary and Index.

2231.   Tolbert-Rouchaleau, Jane. **James Weldon Johnson: Author**. New York: Chelsea House, 1988. 112p. $18.95; $7.95pa. ISBN 1-55546-596-X; 0-7910-0211-Xpa. (Black Americans of Achievement). 7 up

James Weldon Johnson (1871-1938) taught school and was admitted to the bar before writing "Lift Every Voice and Sing" in 1900. Then he formed a songwriting team. But he shifted to diplomacy, serving as consul to Venezuela and Nicaragua, and when he returned to the United States, fought for civil rights. He became an officer in the NAACP, organizing and directing the civil rights programs so that they became a political force. Through all, he continued to write. Photographs and reproductions enhance the text. Chronology, Further Reading, and Index.

2232.   Tomlinson, Michael. **Jonas Salk**. Vero Beach, FL: Rourke, 1993. 112p. $19.93. ISBN 0-86625-495-1. (Pioneers). 5-9

Jonas Salk (b. 1914) was the first person to find a vaccine for the polio virus, but he refused to patent it. He was a great humanitarian who, throughout his research years, was always looking for a way to improve the human condition. The text looks at his life and work. Photographs, Time Line, Glossary, Bibliography, Media Resources, and Index.

2233.   Tompkins, Nancy. **Roe v. Wade: The Fight over Life and Liberty**. New York: Franklin Watts, 1996. 144p. $22. ISBN 0-531-11286-1. (Historic Supreme Court Cases). 7 up

Among the chapter discussions in this version of *Roe v. Wade* are the topics of the events leading to the decision, the reactions within the pro-choice and antiabortion factions, the future of the decision, and the effect of RU-486. Most importantly, Tompkins focuses on the figures who were involved, including Justice Harry Blackmun, writer of the majority opinion in 1973; Sarah Weddington, the attorney arguing the case; and Norma McCorvey, the young woman who wanted an abortion when it was illegal in her home state of Texas.

2234. Toor, Rachel. **Eleanor Roosevelt**. New York: Chelsea House, 1989. 110p. $18.95. ISBN 1-55546-676-1. (American Women of Achievement). 5 up

Among the causes that Eleanor Roosevelt (1884-1962) espoused during her years in the public eye were feminism, labor reform, civil rights, and economic aid for the poor. After her husband died in 1945, she served two Presidents as a delegate to the United Nations. Hers was a strong voice in the twentieth century. Photographs highlight the text. Chronology, Further Reading, and Index.

2235. Topper, Frank, and Charles A. Wills. **A Historical Album of New Jersey**. Brookfield, CT: Millbrook Press, 1994. 64p. $16.40; $6.95pa. ISBN 1-56294-505-X; 1-56294-849-0pa. (Historical Album). 4-8

The text presents the land of New Jersey before it became a state, beginning with Native American civilizations and continuing through exploration and settlement. Early statehood developments and issues, and the role of large cities in the state's livelihood, lead to the present day. Prints, maps, and photographs illustrate the text. Gazetteer: Quick Facts, Key Events, Personalities, and Index.

2236. Townsend, Tom. **The Ghost Flyers**. Pat Finney, illustrator. Austin, TX: Eakin Press, 1993. 98p. $5.95pa. ISBN 0-89015-938-6pa. 6-8

Ghost flyers appeared in the night skies over the southwestern United States during 1896-1897. Harlin, 13, sees the ghost flyers while he shovels coal into the boiler of an engine.

2237. Toynton, Evelyn. **Growing Up in America**: **1830-1860**. Brookfield, CT: Millbrook Press, 1995. 96p. $16.90. ISBN 1-56294-453-3. 4-9

Toynton answers the question of what it was like to grow up in the years prior to the Civil War in the United States. Because children who lived in different parts of the country had different types of lives, she looks at children in New England, on the Plains, in the Sioux tribe, on the streets, and in bondage. Then she looks at the different activities they might have had at school, play, work, and reading. Further Reading, Bibliography, and Index. *Notable Children's Trade Books in the Field of Social Studies.*

2238. Tracy, Ann B. **What Do Cowboys Like?** Sag Harbor, NY: Permanent Press, 1994. 126p. $22. ISBN 1-877946-52-4. YA

In 1958, Louisa "Fish" Fisher is 16 and growing up in a small Maine town. Using first person, Fish tells about her first love, who happens to be an old friend. She attempts to handle her emotions by writing a novel in which her life is the subject. But in her senior year, tragedy occurs, and she rapidly transcends the innocence of first love to the experience of loss.

2239. Trimble, Stephen. **The People: Indians of the American Southwest**. Santa Fe, NM: School of American Research Press, 1993. $50; $29.95pa. ISBN 0-933452-36-5; 0-933452-37-3pa. 7 up

Although these interviews with contemporary tribal members reflect the present economic, social, and political status of the tribes, they are insights into the ways that the tribes have functioned through the centuries. Trimble describes traditional dances, ceremonies, and the arts from information collected on 50 reservations. They include the Plateau peoples of the Pueblos, Navajo, and Pai; the Upland peoples of the Yavapai, Apache, Ute, and Paiute; and the Desert peoples of the O'odham, Maricopa, Colorado River, and Yaqui. Annotated Chapter Bibliographies and Index.

2240. Trimble, Stephen. **Talking with the Clay: The Art of Pueblo Pottery**. Seattle, WA: University of Washington Press, 1987. 116p. $15.95pa. ISBN 0-295-96470-7pa. YA

In the text, Trimble defines "Pueblo" as a group of people who live in the southwestern area of the United States around Colorado, New Mexico, Arizona, and Utah. They see pottery as something with which they are born and with which they die. The pottery encompasses age-old traditions with modern designs (in some cases) or traditional. The clay; the mountain villages of Taos and Picuris; the red and black pottery of the Tewa Pueblos; the storytellers and birds of the Middle Rio Grande Pueblos; the Acoma, Laguna, and Zuni peoples; and the legacy of Sikyatki in the Hopi fill the text. Notes and Index.

2241. Truman, Margaret. **First Ladies**. New York: Random House, 1995. 368p. $25. ISBN 0-679-43439-9. New York: Fawcett, 1995. $12.95pa. ISBN 0-449-22323-Xpa. YA

In chapters covering topics such as "Woman of Mystery," "Partners in Love," "The Generals' Ladies," and "Pioneer Crusaders," the text looks at the roles of First Ladies. Because they are neither elected nor selected, First Ladies have always had a difficult role to fulfill. The public seems to want to define their roles rather than accept them for what they can add to the office of their husbands. Truman looks at how each one has coped with these difficulties. Index.

2242.   Trump, Fred. **Lincoln's Little Girl: A True Story**. Kit Wray, illustrator. Honesdale, PA: Boyds Mills Press, 1994. 184p. $19.95. ISBN 1-56397-375-8. 5-8

When Grace Bedell (b. 1848 or 1849) was 11 in 1860, she wrote Abraham Lincoln a letter. She suggested that he grow whiskers because they would increase his chances of becoming President. Although details of Lincoln's life after this time are almost public record, only the letters that Bedell wrote document her husband's service in the Civil War and their life homesteading in Kansas, fighting grasshopper plagues, tornadoes, prairie fires, and other disasters.

2243.   Tunbo, Frances G. **Stay Put, Robbie McAmis**. Charles Shaw, illustrator. Fort Worth, TX: Texas Christian University, 1988. 158p. $15.95. ISBN 0-87565-025-2. 4 up

In 1848, Robbie, 12, becomes separated from the rest of the wagons while crossing the Big Cypress River in East Texas. With him are an infant, three younger girls, a sickly boy of 10, and Grammie, a woman who seems to live in another world. He stays put, as his uncle told him to do, and the group begins surviving on the river's shore with their few provisions and the cow. Grammie regains her senses, and she and Robbie provide a loving environment for the children as they wait for a rescue. *Western Heritage Award*.

2244.   Tunnell, Michael O., and George W. Chilcoat. **The Children of Topaz: The Story of a Japanese-American Internment Camp Based on a Classroom Diary**. New York: Holiday House, 1996. 74p. $16.95. ISBN 0-8234-1239-3. 4-8.

A third grade teacher in the Topaz, Utah, internment camp recorded her students' responses to their situation in 1943. The authors use this diary as a basis for a discussion on the internment of Japanese Americans during World War II after the bombing of Pearl Harbor. They elaborate with information that clarifies the simple statements of the children. For Further Reading and Index.

2245.   Turner, Ann. **Shaker Hearts**. Wendell Minor, illustrator. New York: HarperCollins, 1997. Unpaged. $14.95. ISBN 0-06-025369-X. 3-8

Using Mother Ann Lee's phrase "hands to work; hearts to God," Turner creates a poetical look at the Shaker community, one of the most successful Utopian communities in America. The verses, which describe the daily activities, almost serve as short prayers with the illustrations revealing the life and the landscape of the Shaker people. An appendix discusses the contributions they made to society.

2246.   Turner, Ann. **Third Girl from the Left**. New York: Macmillan, 1986. 153p. $13.95. ISBN 0-02-789510-6. YA

Sarah, 18, hates the thought of staying in Maine, so she decides to go to Montana as a mail-order bride to marry a rancher. Her husband, 60, dies a month after she arrives, and she inherits the ranch. With the help of her Chinese cook, she keeps the ranch and learns how to manage it, happy to have the experience.

2247.   Turner, Glennette Tilley. **Lewis Howard Latimer**. Englewood Cliffs, NJ: Silver Burdett, 1990. 128p. $13.95. ISBN 0-382-09524-3. (Pioneers in Change). 5-9

Lewis Latimer (1848-1928), born to parents in Boston who had escaped from slavery and were almost returned to the South after the Fugitive Slave Act, fought for the Union in the Civil War. He began his experimenting and received a patent for water closets on trains. Then he made drawings for Alexander Graham Bell's first telephone. When Thomas Edison made an incandescent light bulb, the filament lasted only 40 hours. Two years later, Latimer invented the improved long-burning carbon filament. Then he worked on the "Maxim lamp," which was installed in large cities in the northeastern states. He also wrote the first book on electrical lighting called *Incandescent Electric Lighting*. He continued his work and tried to help immigrants and others in New York during his later life. He is remembered as a draftsman, inventor, technical writer, poet, essayist, musician, linguist, artist, family man, veteran, citizen, and civil rights activist. Important Dates, Bibliography, and Index.

2248.   Turner, Glennette Tilley. **Running for Our Lives**. Samuel Byrd, illustrator. New York: Holiday House, 1994. 198p. $15.95. ISBN 0-8234-1121-4. 4-8

In 1855, Luther and Carrie escape with their parents after their plantation owner leaves his Missouri home to fight abolitionists in Kansas. The family becomes separated by the Underground Railroad "conductor" when they are crossing the Mississippi, but they hope to reunite in Canada. Their difficult journey, with typical sibling arguments, leads them to an unknown aunt and, after four years, finally to their parents.

2249.   Turvey, Peter. **Inventions: Inventors and Ingenious Ideas**. New York: Franklin Watts, 1992. 48p. $13.95. ISBN 0-531-14308-2. (Timelines). 5-8

The text and illustrations combine to give the history of inventions, from the making of fire to the space stations of the future. Included are inventors and ingenious ideas during the classical period of the Greeks and Romans, the Middle Ages, the Renaissance, and the present. Chronology, Glossary, and Index.

2250. Twist, Clint. **Lewis and Clark: Exploring the Northwest**. Austin, TX: Raintree/Steck-Vaughn, 1994. 46p. $15.96. ISBN 0-8114-7255-8. (Beyond the Horizons). 5-8

Meriwether Lewis (1774-1809) and William Clark (1770-1838) led an expedition from 1804 to 1806 across the new land purchased by Thomas Jefferson. The text gives historical background, the preparation of the Corps of Discovery, the actual journey, the achievements of the expedition, information on Native North Americans, and what happened as a result of the expedition. Photographs, paintings, drawings, and maps augment the text. Glossary, Further Reading, and Index.

U

2251. Uchida, Yoshiko. **The Best Bad Thing**. New York: Atheneum, 1983. 136p. $15; $4.95pa. ISBN 0-689-50290-7; 0-689-71745-8pa. 3-7

The second book of the trilogy beginning with *A Jar of Dreams* and ending with *The Happiest Ending* sees Rinko's mother wanting Rinko to work with Mrs. Hatta for the summer. Rinko thinks that Mrs. Hatta is slightly crazy, but when she calls Rinko outside to see the lovely spider webs floating in the air, Rinko begins to change her mind. An old man living nearby also helps the summer become the "best bad thing" when he gives Rinko a kite and calls it an extension of the sky. *American Library Association Notable Books for Children* and *School Library Journal Best Book.*

2252. Uchida, Yoshiko. **The Happiest Ending**. New York: Macmillan, 1985. 120p. $15. ISBN 0-689-50326-1. 3-7

In the last book of the trilogy beginning with *A Jar of Dreams* and *The Best Bad Thing*, Rinko wants to be more American than Japanese, and she revolts against an arranged marriage between a young Japanese girl and an older man. When she sees the man's kindness and the appreciation that the girl has for this quality, she becomes more accepting of this traditional way to marry. *Bay Area Book Reviewers Association Award.*

2253. Uchida, Yoshiko. **The Invisible Thread**. 1991. New York: Beech Tree, 1992. 128p. $4.95pa. ISBN 0-688-13703-2pa. 5-8

Yoshiko Uchida (d. 1992) tells of her life growing up in America where her experiences included having to ask if someone cut "Japanese" hair and having another person complement her on her ability to speak English well while looking at her Japanese face. During World War II, when the Japanese bombed Pearl Harbor, she and her family were transported to Topaz, Utah, which she wrote about in *Journey to Topaz*. She eventually went to Smith College to graduate school and got a job teaching outside Philadelphia, where she could bring her parents from Topaz. Even with these indignities, Uchida managed to keep her integrity and her sense of humor as she created her award-winning books about the Japanese experience in America.

2254. Uchida, Yoshiko. **A Jar of Dreams**. New York: Atheneum, 1981. 144p. $14; $3.95pa. ISBN 0-689-50210-9; 0-689-71672-9pa. 3-7

The first book in a trilogy with *The Best Bad Thing* and *The Happiest Ending* presents Rinko, 11, and her family with all their dreams for their future as Japanese Americans in 1935. When an aunt comes to visit, she influences each person to start working toward one of their goals. Rinko's mother opens a laundry, her father starts his garage, and her brother returns to college. *Commonwealth Club of California Book Award* and *Friends of Children and Literature Award (FOCAL).*

2255. Uchida, Yoshiko. **Journey Home**. Charles Robinson, illustrator. New York: Macmillan, 1978. 144p. $15; $3.95pa. ISBN 0-689-50126-9; 0-689-71641-9pa. 5-9

In the sequel to *Journey to Topaz*, Yuki and her mother return from the internment camp to Berkeley, California, after World War II. They and the neighbors have to work together to restart their lives. They learn the meaning of forgiveness and acceptance when neighbors whose son was killed in Japan help them rebuild their firebombed store and invite them to celebrate Thanksgiving.

2256. Uchida, Yoshiko. **Journey to Topaz**. Donald Carrick, illustrator. 1971. Berkeley, CA: Creative Arts Books, 1985. 160p. $8.95pa. ISBN 0-916870-85-5pa. 4 up

Yuki Sakane, 11, born in America as a Nisei and therefore a citizen, looks forward to Christmas in 1941, but the Japanese bomb Pearl Harbor. The FBI comes and takes her father away, and then they take her, her mother, and brother to Topaz, Utah, to an internment camp. She makes new friends but faces hardships such as dust storms and a tragedy that disturbs everyone. Eventually the family reunites in Topaz, but their lives have been altered permanently. *American Library Association Notable Books for Children.*

2257. Uchida, Yoshiko. **Samurai of Gold Hill**. Ati Forberg, illustrator. 1972. Berkeley, CA: Creative Arts Books, 1985. 119p. $8.95pa. ISBN 0-916870-86-3pa. 4 up

Although he wants to be a samurai, Koichi must leave Japan when he is 12 in 1869 to sail to the United States because his clan and the Shogun are defeated. In Gold Hill, his father and partners in the Wakamatsu colony try to start a tea and silk farm, but miners destroy their work. When Koichi sees a Maidu Indian celebrate a ritual, he realizes that it looks very much like a Japanese ritual. He knows that people are not as different as they might seem.

2258.   Urban, Joan. **Richard Wright: Author**. New York: Chelsea House, 1989. 110p. $18.95. ISBN 1-55546-618-4. (Black Americans of Achievement). 7-10

   In 1947, Richard Wright (1908-1960) left America, after writing about it, for a self-imposed exile in emerging Third World nations. He had worked at menial jobs and vowed that he would become a writer. He worked during his twenties on a federally funded writer's project and then became a newspaper editor. A major literary prize helped him get a publishing contract. Two of his books, *Native Son* and *Black Boy*, give an honest look at the brutality of ghetto life and racial discrimination. Photographs enhance the text. Chronology, Further Reading, and Index.

2259.   Uschan, Michael V. **A Multicultural Portrait of World War I**. Freeport, NY: Marshall Cavendish, 1996. 80p. $18.95. ISBN 0-7614-0054-0. (Perspectives). 7 up

   The text gives the viewpoints of people of color, ethnic minorities, and the European American majority with quotations from primary sources. German Americans faced harsh discrimination, and southern African Americans migrated north to find work in the factories and the cities. The book looks at the origins of World War I and how the "melting pot" population of the country helped to fight it. It also traces Sarajevo from its place in starting the war to its current historical situation. Chronology, Further Reading, Glossary, and Index.

V

2260. Vail, John. **Thomas Paine**. New York: Chelsea House, 1990. 112p. $18.95. ISBN 1-55546-819-5. (World Leaders Past and Present). 5 up

Thomas Paine (1737-1809) grew up in an English Quaker family and did not come to America until he was almost 40. He worked as an editor in Pennsylvania and wrote numerous articles and political pamphlets arguing for independence from England. His writing inspired the colonists, and after the revolution, he helped found the new nation. In 1787, he went to France to help with that revolution. He rejected the idea of hereditary rule and became a proponent of popular rebellion. He was jailed for his views in France in 1793. Then he began to work on *The Age of Reason*, an attack on organized Christianity. He returned to America in 1802 at Thomas Jefferson's invitation, but he was out of favor because of his ideas. Photographs and engravings enhance the text. Chronology, Further Reading, and Index.

2261. Vail, John J. **World War II: The War in Europe**. San Diego, CA: Lucent, 1991. 128p. $16.95. ISBN 1-56006-407-2. (America's Wars). 7 up

The text examines the causes, effects, events, results, and long-term influences of World War II from the events leading to Germany's invasion of Poland to the death of Adolf Hitler in 1945. Details about persons, battles, and atrocities help the war become real. Maps, timelines, photographs, drawings, and paintings augment the text. Bibliography, Chronology, and Index.

2262. Van Der Linde, Laurel. **The Pony Express**. New York: New Discovery, 1993. 72p. $14.95. ISBN 0-02-759056-9. (Timestop). 6-9

The Pony Express began in 1860 and ran for only 18 months. During that time, it proved that mail could travel across the continent much faster than had been imagined. The text discusses the method of advertising for riders, the most famous riders (including Buffalo Bill Cody and Wild Bill Hickok), the Indian war in 1860, and other problems that riders had to overcome. Photographs and drawings enhance the text. Further Reading and Index.

2263. Van Dyck, Harry R. **Exercise of Conscience: A World War II Objector Remembers**. New York: Prometheus, 1990. 250p. $29.95. ISBN 0-87976-584-9. YA

Harry Van Dyck served as a conscientious objector in World War II. In this popular war, the public maligned and ridiculed those who objected. As a Mennonite, he refused to enter military service and worked instead in the Hawthornden State Mental Hospital near Cleveland. He and others like him lived in the CPS (Civilian Public Service) camp where their only commonality was a refusal to be in the military. His story gives a different view of World War II.

2264. Van Raven, Pieter. **Harpoon Island**. New York: Scribner's, 1989. 150p. $12.95. ISBN 0-684-19092-3. 7-10

Brady Barnes, 10, has come to Harpoon Island with his father before World War I. Mr. Barnes is a school-teacher, but Brady is underdeveloped in both speech and motor skills. Locals on the New England island spread rumors about Brady and about their German heritage. When Brady spots a German submarine off the coast, he saves their reputation. But his father leaves anyway, saying that such an act is insufficient to redeem two people.

2265. Van Raven, Pieter. **A Time of Troubles**. New York: Scribner's, 1990. 192p. $13.95. ISBN 0-684-19212-8. 7-10

In the 1930s during the Depression, Roy Purdy visits his father each Sunday in prison until his release, and they go from the East Coast to California. As they look for work, Roy's father continues to disappoint him with his dishonesty. Then they take opposite sides in the battle of migrant workers against growers, with Roy supporting the fruit pickers because he can no longer defend his father's lack of character.

2266. Van Steenwyk, Elizabeth. **The California Gold Rush: West with the Forty-Niners**. New York: Franklin Watts, 1991. 63p. $19.90. ISBN 0-531-20032-9. (First Books). 5-7

The California Gold Rush around 1846-1850 was an important event in the nineteenth century. It changed more people's lives than any other episode except the Civil War. It opened new routes of transportation and changed the face of California and the West. These topics and the lives of the miners before, during, and after the event appear in the text, which is enhanced with photographs and reproductions. Glossary, Further Reading, and Index.

2267. Van Steenwyk, Elizabeth. **Frontier Fever: The Scary, Superstitions—and Sometimes Sensible— Medicine of the Pioneers**. New York: Walker, 1995. 144p. $15.95. ISBN 0-8027-8401-1. 7 up

The U.S. Census Department declared that the American frontier no longer existed in 1890. During the days of the frontier, however, many had risked their lives, getting disease, broken bones, and gunshot wounds, for more freedom. Doctors in the frontier tried anything that might help heal. Some of the choices were chicken guts to treat appendicitis, bloodletting to relieve fever, firing guns in the air to stop epidemics, and other unscientific approaches. The text looks at some of these methods used and assesses what good they might have done other than having a placebo effect. Notes, Glossary, Bibliography, and Index. *Notable Children's Trade Books in the Field of Social Studies.*

2268. Van Steenwyk, Elizabeth. **Ida B. Wells-Barnett: Woman of Courage**. New York: Franklin Watts, 1992. 128p. $13.90. ISBN 0-531-13014-2. (Impact Biography). 7 up

Ida B. Wells-Barnett (1862-1931) was a civil rights advocate and a feminist. Born a slave in Mississippi, she became part owner of and a reporter for a newspaper in Memphis but had to leave when she upset the white citizens in town. She wrote about lynching and carried out crusades against it. The text looks at her courage and principles while giving pieces of historical information about the Civil War and the establishment of the NAACP. Notes and Index.

2269. Vare, Ethlie Ann, and Greg Ptacek. **Women Inventors and Their Discoveries**. Minneapolis, MN: Oliver Press, 1993. 160p. $14.95. ISBN 1-88150-806-4. 4-7

The text presents 10 women throughout American history who invented things. One of them, Fannie Farmer, wrote a modern cookbook using standardized measurements rather than a "pinch of this" and a "handful of that." Other inventions include Liquid Paper correction fluid, cosmetics and hair products for Black women, fiber for bulletproof vests, an indigo plant capable of producing a superior dye, and the Barbie doll. The women are mostly unknown, but their creations have made a mark on American society. Photographs, Bibliography, and Index.

2270. Veglahn, Nancy. **Women Scientists**. New York: Facts on File, 1991. 134p. $17.95. ISBN 0-8160-2482-0. 5 up

Many women scientists have not been sufficiently recognized for their achievements. The text looks at 11 women who have made major contributions to their scientific fields. They are Alice Eastwood, botanist (1859-1953); Nettie Maria Stevens, cytologist (1861-1912); Annie Jump Cannon, astronomer (1863-1941); Alice Hamilton, industrial medicine physician (1869-1970); Edith Quimby, radiation physicist (1891-1982); Gerty Cori, biochemist (1896-1957); Margaret Mead, anthropologist (1901-1978); Barbara McClintock, geneticist (b. 1902); Rachel Carson, environmentalist (1907-1964); Rosalyn Yalow, physiologist (b. 1921); and Mildred Dresselhaus, physicist (b. 1930). Index.

2271. Ventura, Piero, author/illustrator. **Clothing**. Boston: Houghton Mifflin, 1993. 64p. $16.95. ISBN 0-395-66791-7. 4-8

The text, with illustrations, gives a history of clothing. The periods and topics covered are prehistory, Egypt, the ancient East, tanning leather, Crete, Greek styles, Rome, classical society, Byzantium, the barbarians, from sheep to cloth, pyramidal societies, late Middle Ages, thirteenth and fourteenth centuries, merchants and tailors in the 1400s, end of the Middle Ages, society in the 1500s, sixteenth century, the early 1600s, the style of the Sun King, the early 1700s and getting dressed in the noble ranks, the French revolution, the early 1800s, nineteenth-century society, a tailor's shop in the early 1900s, and the mid-twentieth century. Glossary.

2272. Ventura, Piero, author/illustrator. **Food: Its Evolution Through the Ages**. Boston: Houghton Mifflin, 1994. 64p. $16.95. ISBN 0-395-66790-9. 4-8

Illustrations and text tell the story of food through the centuries. Included are hunting with pits and snares, bows and arrows, and traps; fishing; gatherers; agriculture in ancient Egypt and Rome; making bread; grain transportation; beekeeping, spices, and cured meats; animals and vegetables in the New World; harvesters; steam engines; freezing; canning; cattle raising and breed selection; pasteurization and sterilization; diet; factory ships; and new foods and products. Glossary.

2273. Ventura, Piero, author/illustrator. **1492: The Year of the New World**. New York: Putnam, 1992. 96p. $19.95. ISBN 0-399-22332-0. 4 up

Illustrations and text present what was happening in the Old World during 1492 in Germany, Flanders, England, France, the Ottoman Empire, Genoa, Portugal, and Spain. It looks at Columbus's voyage and those people found in this world: the Tainos, Aztecs, Maya, and Inca. Other important voyages of discovery after 1492 were to the Orient. Some Important Dates in European History 1493-1558, Important Dates in Italian Renaissance Art, Native North and South Americans, Five Hundred Years Later, and Index.

2274. Vick, Helen Hughes. **Tag Against Time**. Boulder, CO: Roberts Rinehart, 1996. $15.95; $9.95pa. ISBN 0-57140-006-0; 0-57140-007-9pa. 7 up

Tag traveled back in time with Walker, his Hopi friend, in the two books *Walker of Time* and *Walker's Journey Home*. He wonders how to return to his world as he comes out of the cave and watches Flagstaff, Arizona, as it changes from a tiny town into a trading center. He finds that the time is 1885, and he helps John Wesley Powell and James Stevenson prevent thieves from taking archaeological treasures. As he comes closer to the present, he aids in the stabilization of the ancient cliff-dwellers' homes in Walnut Canyon, outside Flagstaff, during World War II. He finds his way back home through his deeds.

2275. Vick, Helen Hughes. **Walker of Time**. Boulder, CO: Roberts Rinehart, 1993. $15.95; $9.95pa. ISBN 0-57140-000-1; 0-57140-001-Xpa. 7 up

Walker Talayesva, a Hopi of 15, and his friend Tag, 12, find themselves sent back in time by blue lightning. They enter a mysterious cave where soot from fires of AD 1250 and sacred Native American relics surprise them. They try to solve some of the problems facing the people they meet. *American Library Association Best Books for Young Adults.*

2276. Vick, Helen Hughes. **Walker's Journey Home**. Boulder, CO: Roberts Rinehart, 1995. $14.95; $9.95pa. ISBN 0-943173-84-1; 0-943173-80-9pa. 7 up

Walker Talayesva, 15, leads his Hopi people across the high desert from their cliff dwellings into the Hopi Mesas because they are dying from disease, failing crops, and lack of water. Walker wonders if he can complete the task for which his uncle sent him back to AD 1250: to save his people. *New York City School District Best Books for Teens.*

2277. Viola, Herman J. **Andrew Jackson**. New York: Chelsea House, 1986. 112p. $18.95. ISBN 0-87754-587-1. (World Leaders Past and Present). 5 up

Andrew Jackson (1767-1845) was born poor and rose to become President of the country. His charismatic personality and popularity helped him preserve the Union against secession threats from South Carolina, curtail the power in the Bank of the United States, and encourage territorial expansion. Citizens mourned him at his death, but some of his decisions involving minorities, especially Native Americans, must be questioned. Reproductions enhance the text. Chronology, Further Reading, and Index.

2278. Vlach, John Michael. **Back of the Big House**. Chapel Hill, NC: University of North Carolina Press, 1993. 258p. $37.50; $18.95pa. ISBN 0-8078-2085-7; 0-8078-4412-8pa. YA

With interviews from former slaves, photographs, and architectural drawings, the author analyzes how the slaves fit into the environment of the antebellum plantation houses in the South. He refutes the *Gone with the Wind* myth by showing the plantations as places dominated by the master but profoundly influenced by the slaves who worked there. Index.

2279. Vogt, Esther Loewen. **A Race for Land**. Scottdale, PA: Herald Press, 1992. 112p. $4.95pa. ISBN 0-8361-3575-Xpa. 4-7

Ben Martens, 12, and his family immigrate from Russia to Kansas in 1892. The next year they join the race for Cherokee land in Oklahoma Territory. Another man beats them to the claim that they especially wanted. But they find that other Mennonites live near their alternate claim, and a Cheyenne Indian helps Ben understand that God's love remains even when things seem hopeless.

2280. Voight, Cynthia. **David and Jonathan**. New York: Scholastic, 1992. 256p. $14.95. ISBN 0-590-45165-0. YA

In 1954, New Englander Henry is best friends with Jonathan and his extended Jewish family on Cape Cod in Massachusetts. Then Jon's cousin David, his only German relative to survive the Holocaust, comes to live with the family. His arrival changes the friendship. In 1967, they meet again when Henry, a surgeon, saves Jon from a severe Vietnam War injury, and they remember their past relationship.

2281. Voight, Cynthia. **Tree by Leaf**. New York: Atheneum, 1988. 192p. $13.95. ISBN 0-689-31403-5. 5-7

Clothilde, 12 in 1920, worries about her mother's difficulty with accepting responsibility; her older brother, who has run off to live with their paternal grandfather; and her father, when he returns from World War I and stays in the boathouse. Her father dreads the family's disgust when they see his disfigured face. Clothilde convinces him to come "home," and when he does, the family begins to look toward a more stable future.

2282. Volk, Toni. **Montana Women**. New York: Soho, 1992. 305p. $19.95; $12pa. ISBN 0-939149-60-5; 0-939149-89-3pa. YA

Etta and Pearl, sisters in their mid-twenties in 1944, both lose their fiancés in World War II. Each responds differently to her grief. Etta stays home, and Pearl meets someone, gets pregnant, and marries, only to have such a bad marriage that she and her daughter return to live with Etta in Montana.

2283. Von Ahnen, Katherine. **Heart of Naosaqua**. Paulette Livers Lambert, illustrator. Boulder, CO: Roberts Rinehart, 1996. 126p. $9.95pa. ISBN 1-57098-010-1pa. 4-8

Naosaqua, 12, lives with her grandmother in the Mesquakie village of Saukinek, on the Mississippi River in Missouri in 1823. When soldiers come one night and burn the village and the crops, the tribe must find a new place to live. They search and eventually settle on the Iowa River. Naosaqua vows to leave her true happiness in Saukinek and to one day return. She also worries about her father's absence, but when he returns, and Gray Beaver declares his love for her, she again has peace.

2284. Voss, Frederick S. **Reporting the War: The Journalistic Coverage of World War II**. Washington, DC: Smithsonian Institution Press, 1994. 217p. $39.95; $24.95pa. ISBN 1-56098-349-3; 1-56098-349-3pa. YA

More than 100 photographs and illustrations reveal real combat in World War II. Among those journals represented are Ernie Pyle, Edward R. Murrow, William Shirer, Margaret Bourke-White, Robert Capa, and Bill Mauldin. Topics include the role of censorship, combat artists, the difficulties of the Black press, war humor, and renegade correspondents. The collective information, based on an exhibition hung at the National Portrait Gallery, gives the flavor of life during this war. Index.

W

2285. Wade, Linda R. **James Carter: Thirty-Ninth President of the United States**. Chicago: Childrens Press, 1989. 110p. $17.26. ISBN 0-516-01372-6. (Encyclopedia of Presidents). 4-9

As the 39th President of the United States, James Carter (b. 1924) grew up in Plains, Georgia, and became the governor of Georgia. Carter served in the navy and was a businessman and civic leader before he became a politician and President. He served one term. Photographs, Chronology of American History, and Index.

2286. Wade, Linda R. **Warren G. Harding: Twenty-Ninth President of the United States**. Chicago: Childrens Press, 1989. 100p. $19.80. ISBN 0-516-01368-8. (Encyclopedia of Presidents). 4-9

Warren G. Harding (1865-1923) came to the presidency in 1921, after World War I. He wanted to return the country to "normalcy." He delegated power to his cabinet, among whom Herbert Hoover was Secretary of Commerce. Harding died in San Francisco while still serving as President. After his death, the revelations of corruption that occurred during his term tainted most of his successes. Photographs, Chronology of American History, and Index.

2287. Wadsworth, Ginger. **Rachel Carson: Voice for the Earth**. Minneapolis, MN: Lerner, 1992. 128p. $15.95. ISBN 0-8225-4907-7. 5-9

Portrayed as sensitive and passionate in this biography, Rachel Carson (1907-1964) grew up loving nature. She became a biologist whose literary success allowed her to leave her government job and devote her energy to research and see how humans were destroying the Earth. These findings propelled her to voice her concerns and become a leader of the environmental and conservation movement. Selections from her work pepper the text along with good black-and-white photographs. Bibliography and Index.

2288. Wadsworth, Ginger. **Susan Butcher: Sled Dog Racer**. Minneapolis, MN: Lerner, 1994. 63p. $15.95. ISBN 0-8225-2878-9. 4-9

Susan Butcher (b. 1954) won the Iditarod Race in Alaska four times. She and her training dogs, called "mushers," have completed the 1,049-mile trail by traveling 20 hours a day for more than 14 days straight. Her first win, in 1984, was an exciting moment in this grueling race. The texts tells about her life and the procedures for training dogs for such an ordeal. Statistics.

2289. Waggoner, Jeffrey. **The Assassination of President Kennedy: Opposing Viewpoints**. San Diego, CA: Greenhaven, 1990. 111p. $19.95. ISBN 0-89908-068-5. (Great Mysteries—Opposing Viewpoints). 7 up

John Fitzgerald Kennedy (1917-1963), 35th President of the United States, was assassinated by Lee Harvey Oswald on November 22, 1963. Questions about who decided to kill Kennedy have never been answered because Jack Ruby killed Oswald soon after. Evidence conflicts as to whether the assassination was the work of one man or a conspiracy. Black-and-white photographs highlight the text. Bibliography and Index.

2290. Wakin, Edward. **How TV Changed America's Mind**. William Cotton, illustrator. New York: Lothrup, Lee & Shepard, 1996. 248p. $15. ISBN 0-688-13482-3. 7-10

News and documentary reports have been a part of television offering since its beginning. Wakin looks at a history of these programs and their content in the decades since the 1950s by dividing them into confrontations, politics, wars, heroes and villains, and eye-openers. Among the events recalled are the Kennedy assassination, the Kefauver hearings, Rodney King's beating, and the Simpson trial. He shows the influence of this medium on American opinions for the last 50 years. Photographs, Further Reading, and Index.

2291. Wakin, Edward. **Photos That Made U.S. History, Volume 1: From the Civil War Era to the Atomic Age**. New York: Walker, 1993. 50p. $12.95. ISBN 0-8027-8230-2. 7-10

Wakin takes seven photographs and writes about their significance. He starts with Lincoln and the building of his presidential image. A photograph of Old Faithful at Yellowstone records its wonders. The faces of the poor show their needs. "Bits of Humanity" reveals the need to change injustice in the country. The Great Depression is clear in the face of Dorothea Lange's "Hungry and Desperate Mother." The flag rising on Iwo Jima tells about the patriotism engendered during World War II. And the mushroom cloud of an atomic bomb explosion shows what science can do. Index.

2292. Wakin, Edward. **Photos That Made U.S. History, Volume 2: From the Cold War Era to the Space Age**. New York: Walker, 1993. 45p. $12.95. ISBN 0-8027-8270-1. 7-10

In a series of photographs, Wakin recounts historical events and their importance. The photographs consist of Nixon as he puts a finger on Khrushchev's chest at the "kitchen debate"; the pictorial proof of the Russian missiles during the Cuban Missile Crisis; the attack of dogs on Blacks during the civil rights demonstrations; the shooting of a Viet Cong, which showed what was happening in Vietnam; the death of a student at Kent State in 1971; and the view of Earth from space as it rose out of the dark in 1968. Index.

2293. Waldman, Carl. **Word Dance: The Language of Native American Culture**. New York: Facts on File, 1994. 290p. $27.95; $15.95pa. ISBN 0-8160-2834-6; 0-8160-3494-Xpa. YA

Included in this text are words in the social sciences, science, religion, and the arts that relate to the language and culture of the American Indian, including slang and terms not used in English. Waldman gives the origin of the expressions "bury the hatchet," "happy hunting ground," "how," "resistance," and "Indian giver." He also covers the names of tribes and their legendary figures. He excludes battles, organizations, and peoples as they appear in other works. An appendix places the terms in categories such as archaeology, food production, tools, utensils, and weapons. Bibliography.

2294. Waldstreicher, David. **Emma Goldman**. New York: Chelsea House, 1990. 112p. $18.95. ISBN 1-55546-655-9. (American Women of Achievement). 7 up

Emma Goldman (1869-1940) spent her life advocating personal freedom for every individual. She fled a Jewish ghetto and immigrated to the United States in 1885. When the Haymarket Riot occurred in Chicago, during which four anarchists were hanged when they supported striking laborers, Goldman became active in the radical community of New York City. She spoke out against unemployment during the 1893 Depression and was imprisoned. People called her "Red Emma." She supported the rights of workers, women, and minorities. She lectured throughout the country and began an anarchist magazine named *Mother Earth*. She protested the military draft during World War I and was exiled to the Soviet Union. During the last 20 years of her life, she supported international causes like the antifascist movement in the Spanish Civil War. Photographs and reproductions enhance the text. Chronology, Further Reading, and Index.

2295. Walker, Lou Ann. **Hand, Heart, and Mind: The Story of the Education of America's Deaf People**. New York: Dial Press, 1994. 144p. $14.99. ISBN 0-8037-1225-1. 6-9

The text focuses on the history of education for the deaf by looking at the "oralists" and the "manualists." The oralists, led by Alexander Graham Bell, believed that the deaf should communicate with lip-reading and speech. The manualists, under Edward Gallaudet, felt that signing was important because it allowed the deaf to speak in their own language. The attitude toward these two sides reveals a cultural history and a civil rights issue as well as information about the nuances in signing. Twentieth-Century Deaf People of Achievement, Bibliography, and Index.

2296. Walker, Paul Robert. **Great Figures of the Wild West**. New York: Facts on File, 1992. 125p. $17.95. ISBN 0-8160-2576-2. (American Profiles). 7 up

The Wild West developed for a variety of reasons, one of them being that it was a place for people to go after the Civil War ended. Among those who gained fame in the Wild West were Sitting Bull (1834?-1890) who tried to protect the Sioux; Jesse James (1847-1882) and his outlaw gang; Buffalo Bill (1846-1917), first a scout and then a showman; Wyatt Earp (1848-1929), a lawman who skirted the law himself; Billy the Kid (1859-1881), an outlaw; Geronimo (1829-1909), the Apache who held out as long as he could; Belle Starr (1848-1889), legend more than fact; and Judge Roy Bean (1825?-1903), who enforced the law west of the Pecos. Index.

2297. Walker, Paul Robert. **Pride of Puerto Rico: The Life of Roberto Clemente**. San Diego, CA: Odyssey, Harcourt Brace, 1988. 157p. $4.95pa. ISBN 0-15-200562-5pa. 3-7

Roberto Clemente (1934-1972) was a right fielder for the Pittsburgh Pirates before he died in a plane crash while trying to help earthquake victims in Nicaragua. As a native of Puerto Rico, he made an enormous leap from the barrios of that area to the Baseball Hall of Fame soon after his untimely death. Bibliography and Roberto Clemente's Career Record.

2298. Walker, Paul Robert. **Spiritual Leaders**. New York: Facts on File, 1994. 144p. $17.95. ISBN 0-8160-2875-3. (American Indian Lives). 5 up

Religion has always been at the center of Native American life. The people in this collective biography were at the core of their tribes in trying to provide spiritual advice. They are Passaconaway, Son of the Bear (early sixteenth century); Popé, prophet of the Pueblo Revolt (late seventeenth century); Neolin, the Delaware prophet (mid-eighteenth century); Handsome Lake, prophet of the Good Word (late eighteenth century); Tenskwatawa, the Shawnee prophet (1775-1836); Kenekuk, the Kickapoo prophet (c. 1790-1852); Smohalla, the Washani prophet (d. 1895); John Slocum, the Shaker prophet (c. 1840-c. 1897); Zotom, warrior, artist, and missionary (1853-1913); Wovoka, Ghost Dance prophet (c. 1856-1932); Black Elk, Lakota holy man (1863-1950); Mountain Wolf Woman, Winnebago visionary (1884-1960); and Ruby Modesto, desert Cahuilla medicine woman (1913-1980). Annotated Bibliography and Index.

2299. Wallace, Anthony F. C. **The Long, Bitter Trail: Andrew Jackson and the Indians**. New York: Hill and Wang, 1993. 143p. $22.95. ISBN 0-8090-6631-9. YA

The Indian Removal Act of 1830 decreed that Native Americans must move from their homelands east of the Mississippi and relocate in Oklahoma. Among those removed were the Cherokees, Creeks, Choctaws,

Chickasaws, and Seminoles. President Andrew Jackson did not try to stop this migration because in his greed, he also wanted the land and profits that the migration would bring to whites. The text documents this sordid episode in American history. Bibliography and Index.

2300. Wallace, Bill. **Buffalo Gal**. New York: Holiday House, 1992. 185p. $15.95. ISBN 0-8234-0943-0. New York: Minstrel, 1993. 185p. $3.50pa. ISBN 0-671-79899-5pa. 5 up

In the summer of 1904, Amanda, nearly 16, looks forward to riding horseback with her boyfriend and to her coming-out party in San Francisco. Instead, her mother insists that she go with her to Texas to search for a herd of buffalo so she can help save them from extinction. Amanda hates the train journey but is more dismayed that the half-Comanche David Talltree will accompany them on their search. He goads her into a horseback race, and the two begin to respect each other as the summer continues. They fall in love, only to face separation while she returns home and he goes to Harvard Law School.

2301. Walter, Mildred Pitts. **Mississippi Challenge**. New York: Bradbury, 1992. 205p. $18.95. ISBN 0-02-792301-0. New York: Aladdin, 1996. 224p. $6.95pa. ISBN 0-689-80307-9pa. 7 up

Mississippi's history has long been a separate one for whites and Blacks. Prior to the Civil War, slave owners in other Southern states used to threaten to sell their slaves to someone in Mississippi because the plantation owners there had a reputation for treating their slaves cruelly. Through the years after the Civil War, Mississippi passed laws creating a poll tax, continued imposing subservience on Blacks with sharecropping, and ignored the proliferation of groups such as the Ku Klux Klan. In the mid-1960s, the Mississippi Freedom Democratic Society was formed, and federal marshals forced the University of Mississippi to integrate. The text covers these points and more in this honest account. Bibliography, Notes, and Index. *Coretta Scott King Honor Book.*

2302. Walter, Mildred Pitts. **Second Daughter: The Story of a Slave Girl**. New York: Scholastic 1996. 214p. $15.95. ISBN 0-590-48282-3. 6-9

Because her master's family likes her, Elizabeth Freeman, known as Mum Bet, hears the conversations that they have with their guests. She realizes that she can sue for cruel punishment in a court of law and possibly gain her freedom. Her sister Aissa (whom the family does not treat so favorably and who is fictional) tells the story of the court case in 1781. Her view of the American Revolution indicates that the men fight to preserve their property, including their slaves. To the astonishment of many, Mum Bet wins her case.

2303. Wangerin, Walter, Jr. **The Crying for a Vision**. New York: Simon & Schuster, 1994. 278p. $16; $3.95pa. ISBN 0-671-79911-8; 0-689-80650-7pa. 6-10

As a little boy, Moves Walking or *Waskn Mani*, a Lakota Sioux in the nineteenth century, has to live with his grandmother, the wise woman of the tribe, because he has no parents. When Fire Thunder returns from gathering horses, he cuts off the child's ear, but no one understands why until Moves Walking finds out that Fire Thunder had loved Moves Walking's mother, who abandoned him. As the years progress, Moves Walking's life becomes more involved with Fire Thunder, a man who seems to have no mercy. Then Fire Thunder begins to prove himself when he admits that he has tried to stay near his mentally retarded sister so he could help her. However, after she is raped and dies in childbirth, he fails again. Moves Walking takes the place of his grandmother with his wisdom. *Publishers Weekly Starred Review* and *School Library Journal Starred Review.*

2304. Waniek, Marilyn Nelson. **The Homeplace**. Baton Rouge, LA: Louisiana State University, 1990. 54p. $14.95. ISBN 0-8071-1640-8. YA

In this collection of poetry, Waniek presents her ancestors, starting with her mother's great-grandmother Diverne, who came to this country on a slave ship before the Civil War began and ended up in Kentucky. Diverne and a white slave owner's son, Pomp, bore children. Waniek's father, who served as one of the Tuskegee Airmen in World War II, is one of the grandchildren of their union. She gives a view of the history of an African American family in this country through different forms of poetry such as sonnet, ballad, and monologue.

2305. Warburton, Lois. **The Beginning of Writing**. San Diego, CA: Lucent, 1990. 128p. $16.95. ISBN 1-56006113-8. 6-10

Before people had writing, they had to communicate. The text looks at their attempts and how these cultures began to form alphabets in order to write. The text highlights the Egyptian, Mayan, Chinese, and American Indian societies. Photographs enhance the text. Bibliography, Glossary, and Index.

2306. Warburton, Lois. **The Chicago Fire**. Maurie Manning, illustrator. San Diego, CA: Lucent, 1990. 64p. $12.95. ISBN 1-56006-002-6. (World Disasters). 5-7

The text places the Chicago Fire of 1871 into a historical and social setting. This huge fire destroyed about four square miles of central Chicago (nearly one-third of the total area). Some people thought the city had died, and they left. However, others quickly rebuilt it, and the city continued its rapid growth. Facts and anecdotes tell the story of this disaster. Bibliography, Chronology, and Index.

2307. Warburton, Lois. **Chief Joseph**. San Diego, CA: Lucent, 1992. 111p. $16.95. ISBN 1-56006-030-1. (The Importance Of). 7-9

The titles of the chapters taken from Chief Joseph's writings give insight into his life (1840-1904). They are "I will tell you how the Indian sees things," "My father never sold our land," "My heart was hurt," "I would have taken my people to buffalo country without fighting," "We understood there was to be no more war," "I will fight no more forever," and "I have heard talk and talk." He led his people in the Nez Percé-American War in 1877 but did not want to fight the government army. Afterward, he continued to work for peace. For Further Reading, Works Consulted, and Index.

2308. Warburton, Lois. **Railroads: Bridging the Continents**. San Diego, CA: Lucent, 1991. 96p. $16.95. ISBN 1-56006-216-9. 6-9

In the text, period paintings, prints, and photographs from Library of Congress collections illustrate two-page spreads that present various topics. They include the major western trails, early railroads, and the inland and ocean waterways. The text examines the history, development, and technology of the steam engine and railroads; discusses the decline of rail transport in the United States; and describes the growth of railroads in Europe and Japan, focusing on their high-speed trains and magnetic levitation. Chronology and Index.

2309. Ward, Geoffrey C. **Closest Companion: The Unknown Story of the Intimate Friendship Between Franklin Roosevelt and Margaret Suckley**. Boston: Houghton Mifflin, 1995. 444p. $24.95. ISBN 0-395-66080-7. 11 up

After Franklin Roosevelt died, Margaret Lynch Suckley (known as Daisy), his sixth cousin and closest companion during World War II, told those who asked that she had nothing to add to the Roosevelt story. When she died in 1991 at 99, relatives found a black suitcase under her bed stuffed with thousands of pages of diaries that she had begun in 1933 when she started seeing the President. Also in the case were 38 letters, many very long, from him to her in his handwriting. The text looks at these papers and gives a different view of Roosevelt and the ever-present person that his staff considered to be mousy and a "mud hen." No one knew of the relationship of these two prior to Daisy's death. Index.

2310. Ward, Geoffrey C., and Ken Burns. **The Civil War: An Illustrated History**. New York: Knopf, 1990. 425p. $35pa. ISBN 0-679-74277-8pa. YA

The text, the companion volume to the PBS television series, looks at the Civil War with 475 images from libraries, museums, and newspapers. Those who lived during the time speak through their letters and diaries. The underlying theme of the text is that the Civil War is the defining event of American history. Additional essays by five professional historians give information about the causes of the war, the politics of both sides, the effect of emancipation, and the consequences of the war on people in the United States. Selected Bibliography and Index.

2311. Warner, J. F. **The U.S. Marine Corps**. Minneapolis, MN: Lerner, 1991. 88p. $22.95. ISBN 0-8225-1432-X. (Armed Services). 5-8

On November 10, 1775, the Marine Corps came into being. It fought its first battle on March 3, 1776, when Marines went ashore in the Bahamas and took the area from the British. In the twentieth century, large numbers of Marines fought in the wars. The text explains how to join the Marines and Marine life after boot camp. Photographs and drawings enhance the text. Index.

2312. Warner, John F. **Colonial American Homelife**. New York: Franklin Watts, 1993. 127p. $20.30. ISBN 0-531-12541-6. (Colonial America). 5 up

In looking at what the people in colonial America did every day, one sees their homes and furniture, their clothes and how they were made, their food, their schools and books, their games and leisure time, and how they got from one place to another. But some settlers did these things differently. The text looks at settlers from England, Sweden, Spain, and other countries as well as the Native Americans. Reproductions enhance the text. Glossary, Bibliography, and Index.

2313. Warren, Andrea. **Orphan Train Rider: One Boy's True Story**. Boston: Houghton Mifflin, 1996. 80p. $15.95. ISBN 0-395-69822-7. 4-7

The text alternates chapters that contain information about orphan trains with the actual experience of Lee Nailling, who rode the train west in 1926. Along the way, he experienced several rejections before he eventually had a positive family placement. His emotional turmoil reflects that of the many children who took the orphan train to a new life, which for some did not fulfill their hopes. Bibliography and Index. *Boston Globe-Horn Book Award* and *School Library Journal Best Book*.

2314. Warren, James A. **Cold War: The American Crusade Against the Soviet Union and World Communism, 1945-1990**. New York: Lothrop, Lee & Shepard, 1996. 288p. $16. ISBN 0-688-10596-3. 9 up

The text looks at America's attempt to contain the Soviet Union's expansionism during the 50 years of the Cold War. It discusses such topics as the Korean War, McCarthyism, the Hiss Case, the Rosenbergs, loyalty oaths, the Cuban Missle Crisis, the Berlin Wall, the Vietnam War, relationships with the Soviets and the Chinese, Reagan's actions in Latin America against Communism, and the fall of the Soviet Union. Warren argues that the Cold War dramatically increased military costs but that without American policy, the Soviet Union might not have disintegrated. Further Reading and Index.

2315. Warren, Scott, author/photographer. **Cities in the Sand: The Ancient Civilizations of the Southwest**. San Francisco: Chronicle Books, 1992. 64p. $10.95. ISBN 0-8118-0021-1. 4-7

The text looks at the history of three Native American cultures: the Anasazi, the Hohokam, and the Mogollon. The first segment looks at the archaeological digs and the physical settings that have identified artifacts dating back 11,000 years. Photographs of the sites give a sense of the places where the people lived, and discussions of artifacts tell something about their lifestyles. Glossary and Index.

2316. Washburne, Carolyn Knott. **A Multicultural Portrait of Colonial Life**. Freeport, NY: Marshall Cavendish, 1994. 80p. $18.95. ISBN 1-85435-657-7. (Perspectives). 7 up

Bartolomé de las Casas, one of the Spanish settlers who came to Cuba in the late 1400s, saw the settlers abuse the Indians, even cutting them to test the sharpness of their knives. He wrote of the natives' horror and tragedy. Thus Columbus's arrival must be questioned: Was it discovery or invasion? North Americans during the early 1600s governed themselves in various ways. The Native Americans had nearly 600 tribal groups organized into matrilineal clans or families. The Iroquois Confederacy of five, later six, tribes was governed through a democracy and interested Benjamin Franklin and George Washington as a model government for the 13 colonies. The European settlers eventually took over the rights of the Indians, refusing to let them have their separate governments. A comparison of family life, entertainment and leisure time, education, and religion among Native American, European colonizers, and African American slaves shows their differences. From these beginnings, the country established legacies, including some very biased policies that have been difficult to overcome, such as discrimination against racial minorities and women. Chronology, Glossary, Further Reading, and Index.

2317. Watkins, Tom H. **The Great Depression: America in the 1930s**. Boston: Little, Brown, 1993. 375p. $24.95; $12.95pa. ISBN 0-316-92453-9; 0-316-92454-7pa. YA

This companion to the PBS television series presents the story of the Great Depression in text and 150 poignant black-and-white photographs. It begins in 1929 with the collapse of the stock market and focuses on Franklin D. Roosevelt's administration and his New Deal social policies. By focusing on the people, Watkins captures the essence of the Depression and the deep chasm in the American cultural psyche that resulted. Annotated Bibliography and Index.

2318. Watson, Jude. **Audacious: Ivy's Story**. New York: Aladdin, 1995. 177p. $3.95pa. ISBN 0-689-80328-1pa. (Brides of Wildcat County). 7-10

Ivy Nesbitt, 18, leaves Maine in disgrace after her father is accused of embezzlement and dies from a heart attack and her fiancé rejects her. She goes to the California gold mining town of Last Chance, where she begins teaching. When her former fiancé finds her, he tells the secret that she wanted no one to know.

2319. Watson, Jude. **Dangerous: Savannah's Story**. New York: Aladdin, 1995. 179p. $3.95pa. ISBN 0-689-80326-5pa. (Brides of Wildcat County). 7-10

Shelby, 17 and known as Savannah, runs away from a forced marriage to a stranger and ends up in the California gold mining town of Last Chance. There she meets the youngest son of the gold mine owner and tries to begin her life anew.

2320. Watson, Jude. **Impetuous: Mattie's Story**. New York: Aladdin, 1996. 179p. $3.95pa. ISBN 0-689-80329-Xpa. (Brides of Wildcat County). 7-10

Mattie, 17, wants to escape her life of poverty, and she discovers that she can make her own way in the world if she disguises herself as a man. After she falls in love in the California gold mining town of Last Chance, she has to find out if the man who accepts her as a man will accept her as a woman.

2321. Watson, Jude. **Scandalous: Eden's Story**. New York: Aladdin, 1995. 179p. $3.95pa. ISBN 0-689-80327-3pa. (Brides of Wildcat County). 7-10

Eden's criminal background takes her to the California gold mining town of Last Chance at 17. She is a card shark who meets and falls in love with the oldest son of the richest man in town, but she is fearful that someone will come and reveal her past.

2322. Watson, Jude. **Tempestuous: Opal's Story**. New York: Aladdin, 1996. 179p. $5.99pa. ISBN 0-689-81023-7pa. (Brides of Wildcat County). 7-10

Opal Pollard, a free African American living in the California gold mining town of Last Chance, has a successful business and is happily engaged. But when someone comes to town who knows her past, she has to lose it all in order to keep her freedom.

2323.   Watson, Larry. **Justice**. Minneapolis, MN: Milkweed Press, 1995. 226p. $17.95. ISBN 1-57131-002-9. YA

In Montana at the turn of the century, Julian is the head of the Hayden family and a sheriff whose "justice" is clearly selfish. Julian's sons, one wild and without morals, the other kind and passive, continue to be loyal to him. The novel has two stories, one set in 1899 and the other in 1906. It is the prequel to *Montana 1948*, in which these boys have become men. This book gives insight about their youth.

2324.   Weaver, Will. **Farm Team**. New York: HarperCollins, 1995. 284p. $14.95. ISBN 0-06-023588-8. 8 up

Billy wants to play in the city league baseball game in the summer of 1971, but his father has to go to jail, and Billy realizes he must keep the family dairy farm going. Thus, he tells the coach he cannot play. But Billy and his mother devise a way to start a team on the farm so he will have a chance to do what he loves. A motley group shows up, but their passion for the game helps them win. *American Library Association Best Books for Young Adults*.

2325.   Weaver, Will. **Striking Out**. New York: HarperCollins, 1993. 272p. $15. ISBN 0-06-023346-X. 7 up

When Billy was 8, his 13-year-old brother died under the blades of a disk that lurched forward as Billy was driving the tractor. In 1970, Billy turns 13 and continues to try to help his hostile and bitter father on their Minnesota farm. A baseball coach discovers that Billy can pitch, and his mother starts to work in town. These two events cause them to reassess their lives during that year. *American Library Association Best Books for Young Adults, New York Public Library Books for the Teen Age,* and *American Booksellers Pick of the Lists*.

2326.   Weidhorn, Manfred. **Jackie Robinson**. New York: Atheneum, 1993. 207p. $15.95. ISBN 0-689-31644-5. 7 up

The day Jackie Robinson (1919-1972) started playing for the Dodgers begins this biography, and then it returns to his life in California after moving from Georgia. Robinson's athleticism, intelligence, leadership, and courage led baseball fans and others to cheer him throughout his life as the first Black to play major league baseball. He stayed calm even when he could not stay in the same hotel or eat at the same table with his teammates. From 1947 to 1956, he had a stunning career that qualified him for induction into the Baseball Hall of Fame. After retiring from baseball, he worked for civil rights.

2327.   Weidhorn, Manfred. **Robert E. Lee**. New York: Atheneum, 1988. 150p. $14.95. ISBN 0-689-31340-3. 7 up

Robert E. Lee (1807-1870) had to refuse Abraham Lincoln's request that he lead 100,000 Union soldiers to war against the South because he felt he should stick with his home state, Virginia. He fought for neither secession nor slavery but to defend his family, relatives, and friends against the invaders. He grew up in aristocratic poverty, graduated from West Point, and became a competent officer and then the military leader of the Confederates. Further Reading and Index.

2328.   Weiner, Eric. **The Civil War**. New York: Smithmark, 1992. 64p. $9.95. ISBN 0-831-72312-2. (Facts America). 4-8

The text presents an overview of the Civil War, its causes, major events from 1861 to 1865, and the aftermath. Illustrations enhance the text. Further Reading, Glossary, and Index.

2329.   Weintraub, Stanley. **The Last Great Victory: The End of World War II July/August 1945**. New York: Dutton, 1995. 730p. $35; $16.95pa. ISBN 0-525-93687-4; 0-452-27063-4pa. YA

The text reveals the intense racial hatred between the Japanese and Americans near the end of World War II and the barbarism of the fighting between them. By presenting the discussions of the American, Japanese, and Soviet governments day-by-day during July and August 1945, Weintraub shows how amazing the end of the war actually was because it neither destroyed Japan nor allowed the Soviets to occupy its northern part. The facts and the chronology speak loudly. He relates the estimates that the Battle of Tokyo would have cost 268,345 lives when extrapolated from the 82,000 casualties at Okinawa. The Japanese had more than 10 times as many military personnel on the home islands, and no one could estimate the effect of the kamikazes. Such figures support Truman's decision to drop the atomic bomb on Japan. Bibliography and Index.

2330.   Weisberg, Barbara. **Susan B. Anthony: Woman Suffragist**. New York: Chelsea House, 1988. 112p. $18.95; $7.95pa. ISBN 1-55546-639-7; 0-7910-0408-2pa. (American Women of Achievement). 5 up

Believing in the rights of all people, regardless of race or background, Susan B. Anthony (1820-1906) was one of the nineteenth century's greatest political crusaders. She grew up in a Quaker community and started her campaigns by condemning drunkenness and slavery. Over the next 50 years she fought for women's suffrage. Without her, the right of women to vote would most likely not have passed in 1920, 14 years after her death. Photographs and reproductions enhance the text. Glossary, Further Reading, and Index.

2331.   Weisbrot, Robert. **Father Divine: Religious Leader**. New York: Chelsea House, 1992. 120p. $18.95. ISBN 0-7910-1122-4. (Black Americans of Achievement). 5 up

George Baker (1879-1965) moved from Maryland to Harlem around 1915, where he began calling himself Major J. Divine. He launched his Peace Mission movement in 1930 to provide Sunday food for the poor. In 1940, his group gathered 250,000 signatures on an antilynching bill. Then he supported Freedom Rides and other civil rights campaigns from his new headquarters in Philadelphia. His second wife, Mother Divine, took over his work at his death. Photographs and reproductions enhance the text. Chronology, Further Reading, and Index.

2332.   Weisbrot, Robert. **Freedom Bound: A History of America's Civil Rights Movement**. New York: Norton, 1989. 350p. $21.95. ISBN 0-393-02704-X. YA

The text catalogs the Civil Rights movement from the late 1950s to the Reagan years in the presidency. It covers in detail the sit-ins, mass protests in the early 1960s, "Great Society" years in the mid-1960s, voting rights campaigns, Black nationalism, ghetto riots, and much more, giving an insight into the times from various perspectives. Annotated Bibliography and Index.

2333.   Weisbrot, Robert. **Marching Toward Freedom: 1957-1965**. New York: Chelsea House, 1994. 141p. $19.95; $7.95pa. ISBN 0-7910-2256-0; 0-7910-2682-5pa. (Milestones in Black American History). 6-9

The text relates the American Civil Rights movement with complementary photographs. The details reveal the various personalities involved in the struggle to change society. Glossary and Index.

2334.   Weitzman, David. **Great Lives: Human Culture**. New York: Scribner's, 1994. 294p. $22.95. ISBN 0-684-19438-4. (Great Lives). 5-9

Biographical profiles of 27 anthropologists and archaeologists describe their work and their motivations. They are Ruth Benedict (American, 1887-1948); Franz Boas (American, 1858-1942); James Henry Breasted (American, 1865-1935); Howard Carter (English, 1873-1939); Herbert, Fifth Earl of Carnarvon (English, 1866-1923); Jean-François Champollion (French, 1790-1832); Arthur Evans (English, 1851-1941); Alice Cunningham Fletcher (American, 1838-1923); Jane Goodall (English, b. 1934); Georg Fredrich Grotefend (German, 1775-1883); Zora Neale Hurston (American, 1891-1960); Alfred Kroeber (English, 1876-1960); Austen Henry Layard (French, 1817-1894); Louis S. B. Leakey (English, 1903-1972); Mary Nicol Leakey (English, b. 1913); Richard Leakey (Kenyan, b. 1944); Robert Harry Lowie (American, 1883-1957); Max Mallowan (English, 1904-1978); Margaret Mead (American, 1901-1978); Elsie Clews Parsons (American, 1875-1941); Hortense Powdermaker (American, 1900-1970); Mary Kawena Pukui (Hawaiian, 1895-1986); Heinrich Schliemann (German, 1822-1890); Michael Ventris (English, 1922-1956); Robert Eric Mortimer Wheeler (English, 1890-1976); Charles Leonard Woolley (English, 1880-1960); and Yigael Yadin (Israeli, 1917-1984). Further Reading and Index.

2335.   Weitzman, David. **Great Lives: Theater**. New York: Atheneum, 1996. 320p. $24. ISBN 0-689-80579-9. 9 up

Among the actors, actresses, and playwrights who have made important contributions to world theater are Sarah Bernhardt, Helen Hayes, Laurence Olivier, Paul Robeson, Henrik Ibsen, and George Bernard Shaw. The text looks at the times in which the artists lived, and the social, historical, and personal influences that affected their work. Bibliography and Index.

2336.   Weitzman, David, author/illustrator. **Thrashin' Time: Harvest Days in the Dakotas**. Boston: Godine, 1991. 80p. $24.95. ISBN 0-87923-910-7. 4-7

In 1912, Peter, 12, has his first encounter with a new steam engine thrasher. He and his father use the machine on their North Dakota farm and find that it finishes the job in much less time than their horses could do it.

2337.   Wekesser, Carol. **The Death Penalty: Opposing Viewpoints**. San Diego, CA: Greenhaven, 1991. 191p. $19.95. ISBN 0-89908-180-0. (Opposing Viewpoints). 8 up

The death penalty has been a subject of debate throughout the centuries. In the United States, it began with the creation of the democracy. The text presents pros and cons on several topics: whether the death penalty inhibits crime, whether it is just, if it is an effective punishment, if it discriminates against various cultural groups, and if certain crimes deserve it. Bibliography and Index.

2338.   Wekesser, Carol, ed. **Feminism: Opposing Viewpoints**. San Diego, CA: Greenhaven, 1995. 239p. $19.95. ISBN 1-56510-179-0. (Opposing Viewpoints). 9 up

Although many favor women's rights, many reject the negative connotations of being the kind of "feminist" that includes man-hater or lesbian, and they also dislike the sting of male backlash. Historical debates about women's roles have included voting rights, birth control, and the relative physical strength of women. In short essays both pro and con, written by public figures living during the fight for women's rights, the text examines different viewpoints. To see how feminism has affected women, one must look at pornography, women's legal rights, and the lawfulness of surrogate motherhood. Feminism affects society through inclusion or exclusion of its teachings, through ecofeminism (the concept of female traits in God or nature), and men's support of the movement. Some say feminism has ended; others disagree. If it has not, one must assess the goals of feminism in relation to capitalism, socialism, rights of the individual, economic quality, nurturing society, and abortion. For Further Discussion, Organizations to Contact, Bibliography of Books, and Index.

2339. Wert, Jeffrey D. **Custer: The Controversial Life of George Armstrong Custer**. New York: Simon & Schuster, 1996. 462p. $27.50. ISBN 0-684-81043-3. YA

George Armstrong Custer (1839-1876) was awarded an appointment to West Point so he would leave his Ohio town and the girl with whom he had been flirting. The most popular student in his class, Custer was also the worst, graduating last in 1861 with the most demerits. He loved fighting in the Civil War and became the army's youngest general; his troops thought he was the best cavalry officer. After the war, he was given the permanent rank of captain, served at various posts, and suffered suspension. When he announced the discovery of gold in the Black Hills, whites came into the area, and the government did not protect the Sioux's sacred lands. At Little Bighorn on June 25, 1876, Custer led 250 men against the Sioux while three others led seven companies. All of Custer's men died in this foolhardy battle. Bibliography and Index.

2340. Westerfeld, Scott. **The Berlin Airlift**. Englewood Cliffs, NJ: Silver Burdett, 1989. 64p. $16.98. ISBN 0-382-09833-1. (Turning Points). 5 up

Although the title indicates that the text covers the Berlin airlift in 1948 and 1949, it also discusses several other points important to the history of the time. It includes background on the Iron Curtain and on the Marshall Plan, with a biographical commentary on George Marshall, "Operation Vittles," and the rise of the Berlin Wall. Index and Suggested Reading.

2341. Wexler, Alan. **The Atlas of Westward Expansion**. Molly Braun, illustrator. New York: Facts on File, 1995. 240p. $40; $19.95pa. ISBN 0-8160-2660-2; 0-8160-3206-8pa. YA

The text and maps trace human immigration across the North American continent. People and their pioneer spirits, plus Manifest Destiny, President James K. Polk's rallying cry to settle the nation, shaped America's national identity. The chronological chapters cover the colonies looking westward (1754-1795), the extension of the empire (1796-1811), the crisis of settling the frontier (1812-1820), the expansion of the nation (1821-1845), the transcontinental republic (1846-1853), the wealth available in the West (1854-1860), the reshaping of the West (1861-1867), the end of the frontier with the growth of statehood (1868-1900), and an essay on the real significance of the frontier. The appendices include a profile of U.S. territorial expansion from 1783 to 1898 and a chronology of the expansion from 1750 to 1917. Bibliography and Index.

2342. Wheeler, Leslie, and Judith Peacock. **Events That Changed American History**. Austin, TX: Raintree/Steck-Vaughn, 1994. 48p. $15.96. ISBN 0-8114-4927-0. (20 Events Series). 6 up

With two-page spreads, the authors have given an overview of American history showing the pivotal points of change that have occurred since the founding of the Plymouth colony in 1620. Other events included are the introduction of slavery in 1619 to Jamestown, Virginia; the Declaration of Independence in 1776; the ratification of the Constitution in 1787; the 1800 election of Thomas Jefferson over Alexander Hamilton; the Louisiana Purchase in 1803; the Seneca Falls Convention in 1848; secession in 1860; the Emancipation Proclamation of 1863; the transcontinental railroad completion in 1869; the Pullman strike of 1894; the Spanish-American War in 1898; the Treaty of Versailles ending World War I in 1919; the National Origins Act of 1924, closing America's open door to immigrants; the Great Depression of the 1930s; the Japanese attack on Pearl Harbor, December 7, 1941; the Montgomery bus boycott, 1955-1956; the Cuban Missile Crisis in 1962; the Vietnam War from 1965 to 1973; and the Reagan election in 1980. Glossary, Suggested Readings, and Index.

2343. Wheeler, Richard. **Lee's Terrible Swift Sword: From Antietam to Chancellorsville: An Eyewitness History**. New York: HarperCollins, 1992. 430p. $30. ISBN 0-06-016650-9. YA

Using eyewitness accounts of the time, Wheeler presents the nine months of conflict, September 1862 to May 1863, during which the brutal battles of Antietam, Fredericksburg, and Chancellorsville occurred. McClellan stopped Lee's first attempt to invade the North at Antietam in September, but he was hesitant to win a decisive victory, so Lincoln relieved him of his command. His replacement, Ambrose Burnside, suffered 12,000 casualties at Fredericksburg against Lee, and "Fighting Joe" Hooker replaced him. In May 1863, Lee and Jackson used a brilliant flanking movement that routed Hooker. Unfortunately, Jackson died in the battle because of a mistake by his own troops. Lee's success made him confident that he could go north to Gettysburg and continue to win. Sources, References, and Index.

2344.   Wheeler, Richard. **On Fields of Fury: From the Wilderness to the Crater: An Eyewitness History**. New York: HarperCollins, 1991. 304p. $30. ISBN 0-06-016582-0. YA

Eyewitness accounts and regimental histories supply the information that Wheeler has woven into the story of May-July 1864, leading to the campaign of 1864 and its difficulty for the Army of Northern Virginia even though Robert E. Lee used the resources available to him as best as he could. Grant also excelled, and in the end, overcame. Maps, line drawings, and diagrams of battle plans show the strategy of each side. Bibliography and Index.

2345.   Wheeler, Richard. **A Rising Thunder: From Lincoln's Election to the Battle of Bull Run: An Eyewitness History**. New York: HarperCollins, 1994. 413p. $30. ISBN 0-06-016992-3. YA

Wheeler uses eyewitness accounts to tell the story of the Civil War. He begins with the election of Lincoln, follows with South Carolina's secession, the firing on Fort Sumter, other secessions, and the attempt to create armies after the Union lost at Norfolk. This book, covering the spring and summer of 1861, ends with the First Battle of Bull Run. Telling the story with the words of those who lived it gives the text an immediacy not otherwise possible. Illustrations, Maps, Bibliography, and Index.

2346.   Wheeler, Richard. **Sword over Richmond: An Eyewitness History of McClellan's Peninsula Campaign**. 1986. San Bernardino, CA: Borgo Press, 1991. 351p. $27. ISBN 0-8095-9038-7. YA

After the Union defeat at Bull Run in 1861, George B. McClellan became the commander of the Army of the Potomac. He planned carefully and preferred to go around an enemy rather than directly at it. He decided to take his army down the Potomac and Chesapeake in order to march up the Virginia peninsula and attack the Confederate capital from the east. He had an excellent opportunity, but he turned it into a major failure. Also included in these actions were the battle between the *Monitor* and *Merrimack* at sea, Stonewall Jackson in the Shenandoah Valley, and others. The text uses the words of civilian and military participants and observers. References, Supplementary Sources, and Index.

2347.   Wheeler, Richard. **Witness to Appomattox**. New York: HarperCollins, 1989. 255p. $19.95. ISBN 0-06-016078-0. YA

This "sequel" to *Witness to Gettysburg* incorporates accounts of those who observed the last days of the Civil War, including civilians and soldiers, some in letters and some in memoirs. They often asked about the apparent senselessness of fighting for so many years as they watched the events that took place. Bibliography and Index.

2348.   Wheeler, Richard. **Witness to Gettysburg**. New York: HarperCollins, 1987. 273p. $19.95. ISBN 0-06-015760-7. YA

Using eyewitness accounts of this major battle of the Civil War, Wheeler gives views from Gettysburg residents as well as those who were fighting in July 1863. One soldier pulled open his shirt to show his corporal the wound where a minnie ball had entered his chest and asked, "Colonel, won't you please write my folks that I died a soldier?" Another account tells of a young boy who knocked on a door after the battle, requesting to be hidden. He was from North Carolina, was tired of fighting, and never wanted to see another battle. The family gave him a suit of civilian clothes, and when Lee left the next morning, the boy stayed and settled in the area. Sources, References, and Index.

2349.   Whelan, Gloria. **Once on This Island**. New York: HarperCollins, 1995. 186p. $14.95; $4.50pa. ISBN 0-06-026248-6; 0-06-440619-9pa. 4-8

Mary O'Shea, 12, and her brother and sister try to look after their Mackinac, Michigan, farm when their father has to join the army in its 1812 fight against the British. In her first-person narrative, she is surprised to see the British flag fly over the captured fort and even more surprised that the friendly Indians have banded together to support the British cause. When her father returns after three years, he is greatly relieved to find that his children have succeeded at keeping their land in order.

2350.   Whelan, Gloria. **That Wild Berries Should Grow: The Diary of a Summer**. Grand Rapids, MI: William B. Eerdman, 1994. 122p. $13.99; $4.99pa. ISBN 0-8028-3754-9; 0-8028-5091-Xpa. 4-7

In 1933, the summer after Elsa, 12, gets sick, she leaves her Detroit home to stay with her grandparents at their "boring" Lake Huron summer home. With only the three of them on the land, she learns many things about the natural world around her, including how to eat tomatoes just picked from their vine. By the time her parents arrive to take her home, she knows she will return the next summer. *American Bookseller Pick of the Lists*.

2351.   White, Alana. **Come Next Spring**. New York: Clarion, 1990. 170p. $13.95. ISBN 0-395-52593-4. 4-8

In 1949, Salina, 12, dislikes the new girl Scooter. Scooter thinks that a highway through the farmland is okay, but Salina does not like change. The taffy-pulls and church socials throughout Salina's year stay the same, but she has to adjust to the "Outlanders," and develops a new friend as she loses an old one.

2352. White, Deborah Gray. **Let My People Go: African Americans 1804-1860**. New York: Oxford University Press, 1996. 141p. $21. ISBN 0-19-508769-0. (Young Oxford History of African Americans, 4). 6 up

In looking at the years from 1804 to 1860, the text tells the story of the active roles of both slaves and free Blacks in trying to abolish slavery. Simultaneously, slave owners spent much time and money trying to retain the profitable system. The book reveals the harshness of the times and dispels any ideas that slaves wanted to remain in bondage. Chronology, Further Reading, and Index.

2353. White, Ellen. **The Road Home**. New York: Scholastic, 1995. 469p. $15.95. ISBN 0-590-46737-9. 7 up

Rebecca Phillips, a triage nurse in Vietnam, faces the horrors of the war when they arrive in the emergency room. An injury returns her to her New England home, where she cannot overcome the emptiness she feels after having to kill a young enemy boy. She has great difficulty relating to her concerned parents and the casual attitude of people who do not understand the intensity of the war. She drinks to forget but eventually goes to Colorado to see an amputee who had rejected her in Vietnam. He too has little direction, and her unannounced arrival gives him a reason to live. They realize that much cannot be forgotten, but a future together, as she plans to go to medical school, may be productive for both. *American Library Association Best Books for Young Adults.*

2354. White, Richard. **Jordan Freeman Was My Friend**. New York: Four Walls Eight Windows, 1994. 223p. $18.95. ISBN 0-941423-73-5. YA

In 1781, Billy Latham, 11, becomes close friends with Jordan Freeman, an ex-slave who is servant to the militia colonel, William Ledyard, at Fort Griswold in Groton, Connecticut. Annoyed by the capture of a British ship, Benedict Arnold leads 900 mercenaries on a raid and kills many of the men trying to defend the fort, including Jordan. Billy and his father survive, and Billy has to cope with the horror he has watched while running gunpowder back and forth to the fighters.

2355. White, Ruth. **Belle Prater's Boy**. New York: Farrar, Straus & Giroux, 1996. 208p. $16. ISBN 0-374-30668-0. 5-8

During the 1950s, Beauty (Gypsy Arbutus Leemaster) has lovely golden curls, while her cousin Woodrow is cross-eyed and ill-dressed. Otherwise, they have things in common, such as one missing parent and deep pain. When Woodrow's mother, Belle Prater, deserts him, and his alcoholic father cannot look after him, he comes to live with his grandparents next door to Gypsy in Coal Station, Virginia, on the best street in town. Meanwhile, Gypsy has to come to terms with the knowledge that her father committed suicide. But Woodrow and Gypsy enjoy each other's jokes and stories as they cope with situations neither one wants to admit. *Boston Globe-Horn Book Award, School Library Journal Best Book,* and *Newbery Honor Book.*

2356. White, Ruth. **Sweet Creek Holler**. New York: Farrar, Straus, & Giroux, 1988. 215p. $13.95. ISBN 0-374-37360-4. 6-8

In the Appalachian community of Sweet Creek Holler, Ginny and her mother try to survive after Ginny's father is murdered when she is six. The people in the community all have difficult problems, some that they cannot overcome. The local gossip slanders the family, and Ginny's mother takes her to Pennsylvania and a new life by the time Ginny is 12. *American Library Association Notable Books for Children.*

2357. White, Ruth. **Weeping Willow**. New York: Farrar, Straus & Giroux, 1992. 246p. $16; $3.95pa. ISBN 0-374-38255-7; 0-374-48280-2pa. 8 up

Tiny spends her high school years in a rural Virginia mountain town. She is popular and musically talented. Her stepfather, however, attempts to abuse her, and does so with her younger sister. Tiny survives his cruelty and decides that she will escape by attending college.

2358. Whitelaw, Nancy. **Grace Hopper: Programming Pioneer**. Janet Hamlin, illustrator. New York: W. H. Freeman, 1996. 64p. $15.95; $5.95pa. ISBN 0-7167-6598-5; 0-7167-6599-3pa. (Science Superstars). 4-8

Grace Hopper served in the U.S. Navy, resigned, and returned to work on the first computer during World War II. She then rose to become an admiral. Her work on the ENIAC at Harvard helped to establish the computer. The text looks at her life and work. Further Reading, Glossary, and Index.

2359. Whitelaw, Nancy. **Margaret Sanger: "Every Child a Wanted Child."** New York: Dillon Press, 1994. 160p. $13.95. ISBN 0-87518-581-9. (People in Focus). 7 up

When she was 20, Margaret Sanger (1879-1966) watched her mother die from tuberculosis; she had been weakened by the birth of her 11 children. As a nurse, Sanger helped poor immigrant women deliver their children, including many more than they could cram in one or two rooms. Because birth control at the time was considered immoral, Sanger felt helpless as she watched these women have children they could not support. She decided to try to change the law, and she was scorned and jailed for her attempts. But by the time of her death, the public view of birth control had changed, and she took her place as a respected reformer. Selected Bibliography and Index.

2360. Whitelaw, Nancy. **Mr. Civil Rights: The Story of Thurgood Marshall**. Greensboro, NC: Morgan Reynolds, 1995. 121p. $17.95. ISBN 1-883846-10-2. (Notable Americans). 6-9

Thurgood Marshall (1908-1993) devoted himself early in life to ending racial injustice. After he attended college and law school, he began working as an attorney for the NAACP. He helped to argue the case that led to the Supreme Court decision ending school segregation. He later served as the first African American on the Supreme Court. The text begins with an incident when a man accused Marshall, 14, of being a "nigga" who pushed a white woman. Marshall had not even seen the woman, and he beat up the man. His boss freed him on bail, telling him that he had done a good job trying to deliver hats in boxes over which he could not see. Timeline, Glossary, Notes, Bibliography, and Index.

2361. Whitelaw, Nancy. **Theodore Roosevelt Takes Charge**. Morton Grove, IL: Albert Whitman, 1992. 192p. $14.95. ISBN 0-8075-7849-5. 6-12

Theodore Roosevelt (1858-1919) wanted his daughters to be wise and his sons to fight on the side of righteousness. He said to his children, "Don't flinch, don't foul, hit the line hard." For his own exercise, he boxed with an army officer and led his children on "obstacle walks" where they had to walk exactly behind him, even if he traveled over a haystack. Roosevelt became President when William McKinley was assassinated. Among his achievements was the signing of the Panama Canal Treaty. The text looks at his life. Books by Theodore Roosevelt, Chronology, Bibliography, and Index.

2362. Whitelaw, Nancy. **They Wrote Their Own Headlines: American Women Journalists**. Greensboro, NC: Morgan Reynolds, 1994. 144p. $17.95. ISBN 1-883846-06-4. 6-10

American women journalists historically have had few chances to excel, but some of them have done so in the twentieth century, and the text talks about these women. They are Ida M. Tarbell (1857-1944), activist; Dorothy Thompson (1893-1961), foreign correspondent; Margaret Bourke-White (1905-1971), photojournalist; Alice Dunnigan (1906-1983), African American White House correspondent; Ann Landers (1918-), advice columnist; Marguerite Higgins (1920-1963), war correspondent; and Charlayne Hunter-Gault (1942-), African American TV journalist. Bibliography and Index.

2363. Whitelaw, Nancy. **William Tecumseh Sherman: Defender and Destroyer**. Greensboro, NC: Morgan Reynolds, 1996. 111p. $18.95. ISBN 1-883846-12-9. (Notable Americans). 7-10

William Tecumseh Sherman (1820-1891) became a Union general during the Civil War. He gained fame for capturing Atlanta in 1864 and leading a destructive March to the Sea that cut the Confederacy into two parts. The text looks at his childhood, his graduation from West Point, and his undistinguished military career, from which he resigned. Then he became angry at the Southern states for seceding. He reenlisted and became a general. Although he was mentioned as presidential material several times, he said that he would not serve even if he was nominated and won. Bibliography, Chronology, Notes, and Index.

2364. Whitman, Sylvia. **Get Up and Go: The History of American Road Travel**. Minneapolis, MN: Lerner, 1996. 88p. $18.95. ISBN 0-8225-1735-3. (People's History). 5-9

Americans have always traveled, and the text looks at their history from Native Americans to the present. It covers the development of superhighways from paths through the woods; the progression of vehicles from wagons to steam engines; and bicycles, cars, and trucks. Historic photographs highlight the text. Selected Bibliography and Index.

2365. Whitman, Sylvia. **This Land Is Your Land: The American Conservation Movement**. Minneapolis, MN: Lerner, 1994. 88p. $18.95. ISBN 0-8225-1729-9. (People's History). 5-9

In 1872, Yellowstone National Park was founded. After that, Theodore Roosevelt met John Muir, who influenced Roosevelt's policy toward the national natural resources. Among those mentioned in the text as having important roles in saving the environment and conserving land are Rachel Carson and the Sierra Club. Photographs augment the text. Bibliography and Index.

2366. Whitman, Sylvia. **Uncle Sam Wants You! Military Men and Women of World War II**. Minneapolis, MN: Lerner, 1993. 80p. $18.95. ISBN 0-8225-1728-0. (People's History). 5-9

Both men and women made major contributions during World War II. The text looks at their experiences in the draft, at boot camp, in stateside duty, and during combat in Europe and the Pacific. It describes battlefield conditions with eyewitness accounts and focuses on the role of African Americans and women during the war. Both groups had to cope with prejudice, while all participants dealt with homesickness and periods of fear. Photographs, Bibliography, and Index. *New York Public Library Books for the Teen Age.*

2367.   Whitman, Sylvia. **V Is for Victory: The American Homefront During World War I**. Minneapolis, MN: Lerner, 1992. 80p. $18.95. ISBN 0-8225-1727-2. (People's History). 5-9

Containing photographs of ordinary people on farms, in factories, in homes, and in the streets, the text shows what life was like during World War II in America. The chapter topics include the important roles of women (Rosie the Riveter) and Black workers, rationing and drives for scrap, separation and waiting for soldiers to return, growth in the defense industry, race riots, and optimism at the end of the war. Bibliography and Index. *Notable Children's Trade Books in the Field of Social Studies.*

2368.   Whittaker, Dorothy. **Angels of the Swamp**. New York: Walker, 1991. 209p. $15.95. ISBN 0-8027-8129-2. 6-8

During the Depression in 1932, Taffy, 15; Jody, 12; and Jeff, 18, meet in a Florida swamp where Taffy and Jody have established a hideout on land that Jody's family owns. Both are orphans who are escaping from unpleasant situations. Jeff joins them because he has no money. As they establish bonds, they know that they will survive without Taffy having to go to a foster home or Jody back to his alcoholic uncle, because they can fish for a living.

2369.   Whyte, Edna Gardner, with Ann L. Cooper. **Rising Above It: An Autobiography**. New York: Orion, 1991. 257p. $20. ISBN 0-517-57685-6. YA

When Edna Gardner Whyte (b. 1902) wanted to fly, women could not even vote, so she had a difficult time realizing her goal. When she tested for her pilot's license in 1931, the inspector told her he did not want to give a woman a license. Her career became a crusade to show that women could perform as well as men. When denied the right to fly for the military, she taught military pilots. When commercial airlines would not hire her, she trained their pilots. Her fame came from daredevil solo racing that she began in 1933 and for which she earned more than 125 trophies. During her sixties, when she was denied a bank loan for an airport in Texas, she borrowed money from friends and began her business. She has received many of aviation's highest honors during more than 30,000 hours of flying. Bibliography and Index.

2370.   Wibberley, Leonard. **John Treegate's Musket**. 1959. Magnolia, MA: Peter Smith, 1993. 188p. $16.80. ISBN 0-8446-6655-6. New York: Farrar, Straus & Giroux, 1986. 188p. $3.95pa. ISBN 0-374-43788-2pa. 7 up

In 1769, Peter Treegate becomes an apprentice. He soon has to protect himself from another apprentice who commits murder. When Peter escapes from the murderer, he shipwrecks and washes ashore in South Carolina. There he meets Maclaren, a Scot exiled after Culloden in 1746. But Peter has amnesia and cannot tell Maclaren about his background. Six years later he returns to Boston and finds his identity and his father, John Treegate. *Southern California Council on Literature for Children and Young People's Awards: Excellence in a Series.*

2371.   Wibberley, Leonard. **The Last Battle**. New York: Farrar, Straus & Giroux, 1976. 198p. $7.95. ISBN 0-374-34349-7. 7 up

In 1812, Manly Treegate is captain of a ship sailing for New Orleans to help in the fight between the British and the French. His Uncle Peter is having problems in Spain. They eventually reunite in New Orleans after the British have been slaughtered unnecessarily.

2372.   Wibberley, Leonard. **Leopard's Prey**. New York: Farrar, Straus & Giroux, 1971. 184p. $4.50. ISBN 0-374-3-4378-0. 7 up

Peter Treegate's nephew Manly is 13 in 1807. One day he sails in the harbor near Norfolk, and a British ship captures him and impresses him into service. Because Peter has helped an escaped Haitian slave, he finds out from the slave how to rescue Manly and return him to Boston.

2373.   Wibberley, Leonard. **Peter Treegate's War**. New York: Farrar, Straus & Giroux, 1960. 156p. $4.50. ISBN 0-374-35874-5. 7 up

Peter, 16, decides to fight with Maclaren, the man he met in *John Treegate's Musket,* rather than his estranged father. Peter becomes imprisoned on a British warship, but he escapes. Later, at the home of a British soldier whom Peter forces to surrender, he sees a picture of Maclaren's clan tartan on the wall. He feels much closer to the man who helped him become independent than he does to his own father.

2374.   Wibberley, Leonard. **Red Pawns**. 1973. Magnolia, MA: Peter Smith, 1992. 183p. $22. ISBN 0-8446-6558-4. 7 up

In 1811, Manly Treegate, 18, hears his Uncle Peter warn that the Indian tribes will become "red pawns" in the battle to keep the American boundary east of the Ohio. Manly goes to the frontier and finds out how to defeat the Indians, but the government declares war anyway.

2375. Wibberley, Leonard. **Sea Captain from Salem**. New York: Farrar, Straus & Giroux, 1961. 186p. $4.50. ISBN 0-374-36435-4. 7 up

After Peace of God Manly sails to Paris, he tells Benjamin Franklin about the surrender at Saratoga. Then he tries to capture British ships in the English Channel. Instead, the British capture him, but he escapes, and his exploits impress the French. In 1778, the French decide to fight for the Americans against the British.

2376. Wibberley, Leonard. **Treegate's Raiders**. New York: Farrar, Straus & Giroux, 1962. 218p. $4.50. ISBN 0-374-37755-3. 7 up

By the time he is 21, Peter has washed ashore in *John Treegate's Musket* and survived battle in *Peter Treegate's War*. He meets George Washington in 1780. Washington, distressed at Benedict Arnold's treason, thinks the war will be won in the cities. Peter disagrees; he thinks that the American Revolution will be won on the frontier. Peter and his men fight on the frontier at King's Mountain, Tennessee. After the British capture Peter and the Americans rescue him, he travels to Yorktown for the British surrender.

2377. Wice, Paul B. **Miranda v. Arizona: You Have the Right to Remain Silent . . . .** New York: Franklin Watts, 1996. 158p. $22. ISBN 0-531-11250-0. (Historic Supreme Court Cases). 7 up

Ernest Miranda was accused of raping and kidnapping a young woman. The police told him that the victim had positively identified him, although she had not. Miranda confessed to the crime and was tried and convicted. The Supreme Court ruled that the police had not informed him of his right to remain silent and, therefore, his confession was invalid. This decision has affected law enforcement as a whole even though Miranda was tried again and convicted. The text looks at the situation and the decision. Further Reading and Index.

2378. Wilder, Laura Ingalls. **By the Shores of Silver Lake**. Garth Williams, illustrator. 1939. New York: HarperCollins, 1953. 292p. 15.95; $4.50pa. ISBN 0-06-026416-0; 0-06-440005-0pa. 3-7

In Dakota Territory, Laura's pa works on the railroad until he finds a homestead and files a claim. They all spend the winter 60 miles from anyone. Laura, 13, and Mary get to ride on a train, but a payroll robbery attempt surprises them. In the spring of 1880, more homesteaders come and build a new town. *Newbery Medal and American Library Association Notable Children's Books of 1940-1954.*

2379. Wilder, Laura Ingalls. **Farmer Boy**. Garth Williams, illustrator. 1933. New York: HarperCollins, 1953. 372p. $15.95; $4.50pa. ISBN 0-06-026425-X; 0-06-440003-4pa. 3-7

While Laura grows up in the West around 1875, Almanzo Wilder lives on a big farm in New York State. Although he goes to school when he can, he has much work to do. His best times are when the cobbler or the tin peddler visit or during the annual county fair. Almanzo also has a colt that his father gives him to break in when he is only 10. *American Library Association Notable Children's Books of 1940-1954.*

2380. Wilder, Laura Ingalls. **The First Four Years**. Garth Williams, illustrator. New York: HarperCollins, 1971. 137p. $15.95; $4.50pa. ISBN 0-06-026426-8; 0-06-440031-Xpa. 3-7

Laura and Almanzo Wilder begin their married life living on a small prairie homestead. Each year, however, brings disasters. Storms destroy their crops, they have sickness, and a fire damages their property. Although they have unpaid debts and worries, their little daughter Rose brings them much happiness. *Notable Children's Trade Books in the Field of Social Studies.*

2381. Wilder, Laura Ingalls. **Little House in the Big Woods**. Garth Williams, illustrator. 1932. New York: HarperCollins, 1953. 238p. $15.95; $4.50pa. ISBN 0-06-026430-6; 0-06-440001-8pa. 3-7

In 1872, Laura is five, and her family lives in the woods of Wisconsin. She loves the family togetherness of her father's stories and preparing meat, vegetables, and fruits for the long, snowy winter. But when spring comes, they enjoy the maple syrup rising from the trees and celebrate it with a dance. *American Library Association Notable Children's Books of 1940-1970, American Booksellers' Choices,* and *Lewis Carroll Shelf Award.*

2382. Wilder, Laura Ingalls. **Little House on the Prairie**. Garth Williams, illustrator. New York: Harper, 1953. 338p. $15.95; $4.50pa. ISBN 0-06-026445-4: 0-06-440002-6pa. 3-7

Laura, six, travels with her family to the Indian territory of Kansas on a covered wagon. They find a spot to build a log cabin, and the neighbors help them build it. The family has to plant their fields and plow them, hunt for their food, chop logs and find firewood, and gather grass to feed the cattle. A prairie fire burns too close, and they almost have an Indian uprising. Pa decides to leave when he hears that the U.S. government plans to move them. *American Library Association Notable Books for Children.*

2383. Wilder, Laura Ingalls. **Little Town on the Prairie**. Garth Williams, illustrator. New York: HarperCollins, 1953. 308p. $15.95; $4.50pa. ISBN 0-06-026450-0; 0-06-440007-7pa. 3-7

After the difficult winter in town, Laura enjoys the Fourth of July celebration and her first evening social. Life is good for the family because Laura wins a teaching certificate though she is only 15. She knows she can earn money to help send Mary to college in Iowa. And Almanzo Wilder asks to walk her home from church. *Newbery Honor Book* and *American Library Association Notable Children's Books of 1940-1954.*

2384. Wilder, Laura Ingalls. **The Long Winter**. Garth Williams, illustrator. 1940. New York: HarperCollins, 1953. 334p. $15.95; $4.50pa. ISBN 0-06-026460-8; 0-06-440006-9pa. 3-7

When the Indians warn that the winter of 1880-1881 will be difficult, Pa moves the family from the claim into town. Blizzards cut off all supplies to the outside world, and Mary and Laura are unable to go to school. When everyone needs food, Almanzo Wilder and another boy make a dangerous trip across the prairie for wheat. Not until May, when the train comes through, does the Ingalls family get their Christmas presents. *Newbery Honor Book* and *American Library Association Notable Children's Books of 1940-1954*.

2385. Wilder, Laura Ingalls. **On the Banks of Plum Creek**. Garth Williams, illustrator. 1937. New York: HarperCollins, 1953. 340p. $15.95; $4.50pa. ISBN 0-06-026471-3; 0-06-440004-2pa. 3-7

Laura, seven, and her family leave their Indian territory home and cross Kansas, Missouri, and Iowa, on their way to Minnesota, where they purchase land and move into a sod house beside Plum Creek. They eventually get a house with real windows, but grasshoppers destroy the wheat, and her father has to leave home to find work. *Newbery Honor Book* and *American Library Association Notable Children's Books of 1940-1954*.

2386. Wilder, Laura Ingalls. **On the Way Home**. New York: HarperCollins, 1976. 101p. $1.95pa. ISBN 0-06-440080-8pa. 4-7

In 1894, Laura Ingalls Wilder traveled with her husband, Almanzo Wilder, and their daughter, Rose, seven, from their drought-stricken farm in South Dakota to the Ozarks. She describes the towns they passed, the rivers they crossed, and the people they met along the way. Not for 40 years would she begin to write the "Little House" books, which told about her own childhood. Her journal gives a clear glimpse of the prairie while many were having difficulty surviving.

2387. Wilder, Laura Ingalls. **These Happy Golden Years**. 1943. Garth Williams, illustrator. New York: HarperCollins, 1971. 289p. $15.95; $4.50pa. ISBN 0-06-026480-2; 0-06-440008-5pa. 5-9

At 15, Laura Ingalls goes to teach school 12 miles from home. The students are taller than her, and she has to board with an unpleasant family. She is unhappy, but she needs the money to help her blind sister Mary go to school. Almanzo Wilder arrives every Friday and takes her home and then returns her on Sunday night. After three years, she decides to marry him. *Newbery Honor Book* and *American Library Association Notable Children's Books of 1940-1970*.

2388. Wilkes, Maria D. **Little House in Brookfield**. New York: HarperCollins, 1996. 298p. $14.95; $4.50pa. ISBN 0-06-026459-4; 0-06-440610-5pa. 3-7

Caroline, five in 1845, lives in Brookfield, Wisconsin, with her mother, grandmother, and five brothers and sisters after her father was lost at sea. She helps her mother as much as she can, and they struggle through the winter. Then in the summer, the garden grows, and the family has enough food. Best of all, she goes to school and finds that she might be able to learn rapidly along with her first best friend. This story is the first about the mother of Laura Ingalls Wilder, who wrote the *Little House* books.

2389. Wilkinson, Philip. **Building**. Dave King and Geoff Dann, illustrators. New York: Knopf, 1995. 61p. $16.95. ISBN 0-679-97256-0. (Eyewitness). 4-12

Photographs and drawings give clear pictures of the various aspects of building. Topics covered in two-page spreads are structural engineering, house construction, and building materials. These include wood, earth, bricks, stone, timber frames, the roof, thatching, columns and arches, vaults, staircases, fireplaces and chimneys, doors and doorways, windows, stained glass, balconies, and building on unusual topography. Index.

2390. Wilkinson, Philip, and Jacqueline Dineen. **People Who Changed the World**. Robert Ingpen, illustrator. New York: Chelsea House, 1994. 93p. $19.95. ISBN 0-7910-2764-3. (Turning Points in History). 5-10

Religious leaders, philosophers, and explorers have changed the world. Those presented in the text include Confucius (c. 551-479 BC), Gautama Buddha (c. 563-480 BC), Pericles (c. 495-429 BC), Jesus Christ (c. 6 BC-c. AD 30), Muhammad (c. AD 570-632), St. Benedict of Nursia (c. AD 480-550), Marco Polo (1215-1294), Lorenzo de Medici (1449-1492), Christopher Columbus (1451-1506), Martin Luther (1483-1546), Ferdinand Magellan (1480-1521), James Cook (1728-1779), Karl Marx (1818-1883), Henri Dunant (1828-1910), Sigmund Freud (1856-1939), Leopold II of Belgium (1835-1909) who colonized Africa, and Martin Luther King, Jr. (1929-1968). Events included are the Black Plague, the Irish Famine, and the Wall Street stock market crash. Further Reading and Index.

2391. Wilkinson, Philip, and Jacqueline Dineen. **Statesmen Who Changed the World**. Robert Ingpen, illustrator. New York: Chelsea House, 1994. 93p. $19.95. ISBN 0-7910-2762-7. (Turning Points in History). 5-10

Using the definition that a statesperson is someone who influences people around the world rather than only in their own country or neighborhood, the text looks at people who have had a vision of changes whether good or bad. Included are Asoka, the Buddhist emperor (270-232 BC); Shih Huang Ti, Emperor of China (259-210 BC);

Julius Caesar, Consul of Rome (100-44 BC); Constantine of Byzantium (AD 285-337); King John and the Magna Carta (1167-1216); Isabella of Castille (1451-1504) and Ferdinand II of Aragon (1452-1516); Cortés and the Aztec Empire (1485-1547); Ivan IV of Russia (1530-1584); the Manchu Empire of China under Prince Dorgon (1612-1650); Prague's Frederick V (1596-1632); the fall of the Bastille in 1789 under Louis XVI (1754-1793) and Marie Antoinette of Austria (1755-1793); Simón Bolívar (1783-1830) in South America; Emperor Meiji (1852-1912) opening up Japan; Palmerston (1784-1865) and the opening of India; Bismarck (1815-1898) and German unity; Lenin (1870-1924) and the Russian Revolution; Gandhi (1869-1948) and Indian independence; Mao (1893-1976) and the Chinese Long March; Eleanor Roosevelt (1884-1962) and the United Nations; and Gorbachev (b. 1931) and the Berlin Wall. Further Reading and Index.

2392.   Wilkinson, Philip, and Michael Pollard. **Generals Who Changed the World**. Robert Ingpen, illustrator. New York: Chelsea House, 1994. 93p. $19.95. ISBN 0-7910-2761-9. (Turning Points in History). 5-10
   Generals have changed the map of the Earth through the battles they have won or lost. The generals discussed in the text cover many centuries. They are Alexander of Macedonia (356-323 BC); the Vandals, Huns, and Visigoths under Alaric (c. AD 370-410); Viking raiders beginning in the eighth century; William I (c. 1027-1087) conquered England in 1066; Abu Bakr, leader of the Almoravids, who overcame Ghana in 1056; the first crusade in 1095 called by Urban II; Genghis Khan (c. 1162-1227) and the Mongols; Sultan Mehmet II (1432-1481) who overtook Byzantium; Babur (1483-1530), conqueror of India; the revolt of the Netherlands toward Spain under William the Silent (1533-1584); Drake and the defeat of the Spanish Armada in 1588 (1540-1596); John III Sobieski (1624-1696) saving Vienna from the Turks; James Wolfe (1727-1759) capturing Quebec; Washington (1732-1799) after Lexington; Napoleon (1769-1821) attacking Moscow; Robert E. Lee (1807-1870) and Sharpsburg; Paul Kruger's Boers (1825-1904) against Great Britain; the beginning of World War I under Kaiser Wilhelm II (1859-1941); Japan's bombing of Pearl Harbor with Hideki Tojo as prime minister (1884-1948); and Dwight Eisenhower (1890-1969) and D-Day. Further Reading and Index.

2393.   Wilkinson, Philip, and Michael Pollard. **Scientists Who Changed the World**. Robert R. Ingpen, illustrator. New York: Chelsea House, 1994. 93p. $19.95. ISBN 0-7910-2763-5. (Turning Points in History). 5-10
   People who have had an interest in why and how things happen have helped shape the world. Brief profiles of some of those scientists or groups appear in the text. They are Kaifung, Johannes Gutenburg (fifteenth century), Galileo Galilei (1564-1642), Isaac Newton (1642-1727), James Watt (1736-1819), Donkin and Hall (early nineteenth-century cannery), Louis Daguerre (1789-1851), Charles Darwin (1809-1882), Joseph Lister (1827-1912), Alexander Graham Bell (1847-1922), Marie Curie (1867-1934), the Wright brothers (early twentieth century), Henry Ford (1863-1947), Albert Einstein (1879-1955), John Logie Baird (1888-1946), Alan Turing (1912-1954), the Manhattan Project (early 1940s), Crick and Watson (twentieth century), Wilkins and Franklin (twentieth century), the launch of Sputnik I in 1957, and astronauts Aldrin, Armstrong, and Collins. Photographs enhance the text. Timeline and Index.

2394.   Williams, Brian. **Forts and Castles**. New York: Viking, 1994. 48p. $15.99. ISBN 0-670-85898-6. (See Through History). 6-9
   People began building forts and castles in prehistoric times when walled towns were important, and they continued through the Middle Ages. They helped kings control lands, protect their subjects, and impress their enemies. Armies tried to capture them and developed complex weapons to achieve their goals. See-through cutaways of a Mycenaean citadel in Greece, a besieged castle in the Middle Ages, the castle of a Japanese warlord, and a U.S. Army frontier fort highlight the text. Two-page topics cover information on Hattusas, Tiryns, the siege of Lachish, hill forts, the Great Wall of China, Roman forts, Masada, the Normans, Crusader castles, the Moors in Spain, the Renaissance, Japanese castles, Sacsayhuaman, Golconda, Vauban fortresses, cavalry fort, Fort Sumter, and the end of the age. Key Dates and Glossary and Index.

2395.   Williams, Brian, and Brenda Williams. **The Age of Discovery: From the Renaissance to American Independence**. James Field, illustrator. New York: Peter Bedrick, 1994. 64p. $18.95. ISBN 0-87226-311-8. (Timelink). 5-8
   The text presents history in 50-year segments and depicts discoveries from all cultures. Various aids such as comparative time charts, maps, charts, and graphs show the major historical events from 1491 to 1789 in the Americas, Asia, and Africa. Illustrations complement the text.

2396.   Williams, Jean Kinney. **The Amish**. New York: Franklin Watts, 1996. 111p. $20. ISBN 0-531-11275-6. (American Religious Experience). 7-10
   The text covers the background, development, culture, and current beliefs, including the selective use of technology, of the Amish. It is a balanced look at a group of people who choose not to enter the mainstream of America. Photographs and reproductions enhance the text. Further Reading, Notes, and Index.

2397. Williams, Jean Kinney. **The Mormons**. New York: Franklin Watts, 1996. 111p. $20. ISBN 0-531-11276-4. (American Religious Experience). 7-10

The text covers the background, development, culture, including the practice of polygamy, and current beliefs of the Mormons. It is a balanced look at a group of people who choose not to enter the mainstream of America. Photographs and reproductions enhance the text. Further Reading, Notes, and Index.

2398. Williams, Neva. **Patrick Desjarlait: Conversations with a Native American Artist**. Minneapolis, MN: Runestone Press, 1994. 56p. $21.50. ISBN 0-8225-3151-8. 6 up

Patrick Desjarlait (1921-1972) created vivid watercolor paintings of Chippewa (Ojibway or Anishinabe) life in northwestern Minnesota to preserve the culture. As he tells his story, he gives excellent information about growing up with tribal rituals and celebrations. He also discusses his role in the relocation camps for the Japanese in World War II. Glossary and Pronunciation Guide.

2399. Williamson, Penelope. **Heart of the West**. New York: Simon & Schuster, 1995. 591p. $22.50. ISBN 0-671-50822-9. New York: Bantam, 1996. 591p. $6.50pa. ISBN 0-440-22211-7pa. YA

Three women—Clementine Kennicutt from Boston, married to Gus McQueen; Hannah Yorke, the town prostitute; and Erlan Woo, a Chinese picture bride—become friends after being uprooted from their homes and resettled in Montana as pioneers in the nineteenth century. Their strong values unite them as they try to create civilization out of the land for their children.

2400. Willis, Patricia. **Out of the Storm**. New York: Clarion, 1995. 188p. $14.95. ISBN 0-395-68708-X. 5-7

Mandy's father does not return from World War II in 1945, and she, her mother, and brother have to move 40 miles away to live with an aunt where her mother can get a job to support them. Mandy, 12, hates the town but finds friends faster than she expected. When she saves sheep in a storm—more from guilt than from duty—she realizes that her father will not return and that staying in the town is okay.

2401. Willis, Patricia. **A Place to Claim as Home**. New York: Clarion, 1991. 166p. $13.95. ISBN 0-395-55395-4. 4-7

Pretending to be 15 during World War II, Henry, 13, gets a job helping Sarah on her farm for the summer. As an orphan, he loves the farm and soon begins to like the quiet and preoccupied Sarah. As families hear either good or bad news from relatives fighting in the war, they try to harvest their crops with the few men available. Henry hopes that Sarah's home will soon become his as well. *Friends of American Writers Juvenile Book Merit Award*.

2402. Wills, Charles. **The Battle of Little Bighorn**. Englewood Cliffs, NJ: Silver Burdett, 1990. 64p. $14.98; $7.95pa. ISBN 0-382-09952-4; 0-382-09948-6pa. (Turning Points in American History). 4-8

The text gives the background on the Battle of Little Bighorn and the shock when all of the U.S. soldiers were found dead on the ground. The relationship between whites and Native Americans becomes clear with additional information. Photographs highlight the text. Bibliography and Index.

2403. Wills, Charles. **A Historical Album of Alabama**. Brookfield, CT: Millbrook Press, 1994. 64p. $16.40; $6.95pa. ISBN 1-56294-591-2; 1-56294-854-7pa. (Historical Album). 4-8

The text presents the land of Alabama before it became a state, beginning with Native American civilizations and continuing through exploration and settlement. Early statehood developments and issues, and the role of large cities in the state's livelihood, lead to the present. Prints, maps, and photographs illustrate the text. Gazetteer: Quick Facts, Key Events, Personalities, and Index.

2404. Wills, Charles. **A Historical Album of California**. Brookfield, CT: Millbrook Press, 1994. 64p. $16.40; $6.95pa. ISBN 1-56294-479-7; 1-56294-759-1pa. (Historical Album). 4-8

Native Americans inhabited California for centuries before Columbus came to the New World in 1492. Disease, conflict, and loss of land when the settlers arrived destroyed life for these people. The Spanish came in the sixteenth century and settled in the eighteenth. In the early 1800s, Mexicans began to rule California. After the United States won the Mexican War, California became a territory in 1848, just as the gold rush started. Other information about California also appears in the text, which is complemented by photographs and reproductions. Gazetteer: Quick Facts, Key Events, Personalities, and Index.

2405. Wills, Charles. **A Historical Album of Connecticut**. Brookfield, CT: Millbrook Press, 1994. 64p. $16.40; $6.95pa. ISBN 1-56294-506-8; 1-56294-848-2pa. (Historical Album). 4-8

The text presents the land of Connecticut before it became a state, beginning with Native American civilizations and continuing through exploration and settlement. Early statehood developments and issues, and the role of large cities in the state's livelihood, lead to the present day. Prints, maps, and photographs illustrate the text. Gazetteer: Quick Facts, Key Events, Personalities, and Index.

2406. Wills, Charles. **A Historical Album of Florida**. Brookfield, CT: Millbrook Press, 1994. 64p. $16.40; $6.95pa. ISBN 1-56294-480-0; 1-56294-760-5pa. (Historical Album). 4-8

The text presents the land of Florida before it became a state, beginning with Native American civilizations and continuing through exploration and settlement. Early statehood developments, and issues and the role of large cities in the state's livelihood, lead to the present day. Prints, maps, and photographs illustrate the text. Gazetteer: Quick Facts, Key Events, Personalities, and Index.

2407. Wills, Charles. **A Historical Album of Illinois**. Brookfield, CT: Millbrook Press, 1994. 64p. $16.40; $6.95pa. ISBN 1-56294-482-7; 1-56294-761-3pa. (Historical Album). 4-8

The text presents the land of Illinois before it became a state, beginning with Native American civilizations and continuing through exploration and settlement. Early statehood developments and issues, and the role of large cities in the state's livelihood, lead to the present day. Prints, maps, and photographs illustrate the text. Gazetteer: Quick Facts, Key Events, Personalities, and Index.

2408. Wills, Charles. **A Historical Album of Nebraska**. Brookfield, CT: Millbrook Press, 1994. 64p. $16.40; $6.95pa. ISBN 1-56294-509-2; 1-56294-852-0pa. (Historical Album). 4-8

The text presents the land of Nebraska before it became a state, beginning with Native American civilizations and continuing through exploration and settlement. Early statehood developments and issues, and the role of large cities in the state's livelihood, lead to the present day. Prints, maps, and photographs illustrate the text. Gazetteer: Quick Facts, Key Events, Personalities, and Index.

2409. Wills, Charles. **A Historical Album of Oregon**. Brookfield, CT: Millbrook Press, 1994. 64p. $16.40; $6.95pa. ISBN 1-56294-594-7; 1-56294-855-5pa. (Historical Album). 4-8

The text presents the land of Oregon before it became a state, beginning with Native American civilizations and continuing through exploration and settlement. Early statehood developments and issues, and the role of large cities in the state's livelihood, lead to the present day. Prints, maps, and photographs illustrate the text. Gazetteer: Quick Facts, Key Events, Personalities, and Index.

2410. Wills, Charles. **A Historical Album of Texas**. Brookfield, CT: Millbrook Press, 1994. 64p. $16.40; $6.95pa. ISBN 1-56294-504-1; 1-56294-847-4pa. (Historical Album). 4-8

The text presents the land of Texas before it became a state, beginning with Native American civilizations and continuing through exploration and settlement. Early statehood developments and issues, and the role of large cities in the state's livelihood, lead to the present day. Prints, maps, and photographs illustrate the text. Gazetteer: Quick Facts, Key Events, Personalities, and Index.

2411. Wills, Garry. **Certain Trumpets: The Call of Leaders**. New York: Simon & Schuster, 1994. 336p. $23. ISBN 0-671-65702-X. New York: Touchstone, 1995. 336p. $14pa. ISBN 0-684-80138-8pa. YA

To examine leadership in people, Wills looks at Cesare Borgia (1476?-1507), Dorothy Day (1897-1980), King David (d. 961 BC), Mary Baker Eddy (1821-1910), Martha Graham (1893-1991), Martin Luther King, Jr. (1929-1968), Napoleon (1769-1821), Ross Perot (b. 1930), Franklin D. Roosevelt (1882-1945), Eleanor Roosevelt (1884-1962), Socrates (c. 47-0399 BC), Carl Stotz (1910?-1992), Harriet Tubman (c. 1820-1913), Andrew Young (b. 1932), and George Washington (1732-1799) . He analyzes what these people did, assesses their qualities to find what one should expect of a leader, and decides that good leaders concern themselves with the best situation for all, the "common good." Bibliography and Index.

2412. Wilson, Claire. **Quanah Parker: Comanche Chief**. New York: Chelsea House, 1991. 112p. $18.95. ISBN 0-7910-1702-8. (North American Indians of Achievement). 5 up

Quanah Parker (1854-1911) was the son of a Comanche war leader and Cynthia Ann Parker, a captured white settler. Parker became a respected warrior who led a band of Quahadi fighters in battle against intruders on Comanche lands. In 1875, after years of eluding the army, they were forced to surrender, and Parker led his people onto the reservation. He cooperated with his former enemies and used them to best advantage so that he made much money dealing with Texas cattlemen. He decided that his people had to bend, but not break, if they were to survive. Photographs enhance the text. Chronology, Further Reading, and Index.

2413. Wilson, Derek. **The Circumnavigators**. New York: Evans, 1989. 345p. $24.95. ISBN 0-87131-601-3. YA

People who have sailed around the world since Magellan in 1522 appear in these pages. Included in addition to Magellan are Drake, pirates, buccaneers, captains, sailors, and yachtsmen who recorded data later used by explorers. The first person to go around the world for pleasure was Annie Brassey in 1876; she gave dinner parties for 40 en route. Even today a trip around the world is an exciting adventure. Bibliography and Index.

2414. Wilson, Janet. **The Ingenious Mr. Peale: Painter, Patriot and Man of Science**. New York: Atheneum, 1996. 128p. $16. ISBN 0-689-31884-7. 5-9

Charles Willson Peale (1741-1827) is best known for his paintings and his interest in natural history. He found the bones of a mammoth and displayed them in his Philadelphia museum. But he became an artist because he owed money, and he painted portraits of Franklin and Washington. His other interests included revolutionary politics, inventing, farming, and the idea of motion pictures, and he unwillingly served in the military. The text looks at this man and notes his dilettantish approach to life. Bibliography and Index. *School Library Journal Best Book.*

2415. Wilson, Kate. **Earthquake! San Francisco, 1906**. Richard Courtney, illustrator. Austin, TX: Raintree/Steck-Vaughn, 1993. 54p. $22.83; $4.95pa. ISBN 0-8114-7216-7; 0-8114-8056-9pa. (Stories of America—Working Together). 5-9

After an earthquake struck San Francisco, California, in 1906, fires began to destroy many buildings, but the quake had wrecked water pipes throughout the city, and firefighters were helpless. George Lowe reported for the *San Francisco Chronicle,* and Helen Dare (on vacation) reported for the *Los Angeles Examiner.* They realized that they must get the news to the outside world, so they took the ferry across the bay to Oakland from where they could send their stories. Others also rapidly began orderly actions to overcome the devastation. One of these was General Funston, a man who had mapped Death Valley. He organized a militia for rebuilding; others collected mail in all forms (such as writing on sleeve cuffs) and sent it to worried relatives. Epilogue, Afterword, and Notes.

2416. Windle, Janice Woods. **True Women**. 1994. New York: Ivy, 1995. 464p. $6.99pa. ISBN 0-8041-1308-4pa. YA

The title of this novel about four generations of Texas women who were the author's ancestors comes from a report to the 1868 Texas state Constitutional Convention arguing that no "true woman" would want the right to vote. The women in the story, Euphemia, Georgia, and Bettie, were part of one of the earliest families to settle southwest Texas. From letters, photographs, family tales, documents, and interviews, their lives become three-dimensional. Euphemia, the first, who knows Sam Houston, the republic's first President, fights Indians and Mexicans and wants the right to vote. Bettie, the last one, stands up to the Ku Klux Klan. Other female relations—Black, American Indian, or white—of Windle also have roles in the story.

2417. Winslow, Mimi. **Loggers and Railroad Workers**. New York: Twenty-First Century Books, 1995. 96p. $16.98. ISBN 0-8050-2997-4. (Settling the West). 5-8

Two groups helped make settling in the West possible. Loggers cut the trees, and railroad workers helped build the rails that transported both people and goods. The text presents first-person views from loggers, who worried about being 200 feet up in a tree and the tree not falling exactly right, and from railroad workers, who had other concerns. Notes, Further Reading, and Index.

2418. Winter, Jeanette, author/illustrator. **The Christmas Tree Ship**. New York: Philomel, 1994. 32p. $14.95. ISBN 0-399-22693-1. 5-9

From 1887 until 1912, Captain Herman takes Christmas trees chopped in the Michigan woods on his schooner to the Clark Street Bridge in Chicago. In 1912, he encounters a fierce storm and sends a message in a bottle to his wife and daughters before he is lost at sea. The trees never arrive. The next year, after grieving for him, Captain Herman's wife and daughters know that they must take over the voyage so they can help the people waiting in Chicago have a happy Christmas season. *Bulletin Blue Ribbon Book.*

2419. Winter, Jeanette, author/illustrator **Klara's New World**. New York: Knopf, 1992. 41p. $15.99. ISBN 0-679-90626-6. 2-7

In 1852, Klara, eight, and her family have to leave Sweden during a famine. They go to America, where they hope to grow crops. They sail on an ocean, a river, and a lake as well as ride a train during the three months that they take to reach Minnesota.

2420. Wisler, G. Clifton. **The Drummer of Vicksburg**. New York: Lodestar, 1997. 144p. $15.99. ISBN 0-525-67537-X. 5-8

The life of Orion Howe, a Medal of Honor–winning drummer boy in the Civil War, is the basis for this story about a brave 14-year-old. Howe risked his life by running through enemy fire to tell General Sherman that the regiment for which he played the drum needed ammunition.

2421. Wisler, G. Clifton. **Jericho's Journey**. New York: Lodestar, 1993. 137p. $13.99; $3.99pa. ISBN 0-525-67428-4; 0-14-037065-Xpa. 4-8

Jericho, 11, wants to move to Texas because he has heard of Davy Crockett and Sam Houston as well as his Uncle Dan's tales after the battle of the Alamo. The reality of the journey to Texas does not include the ideal of his dreams, however, as the family, including his older brother, bossy sister, and two younger brothers, have encounters along the way. Wisler mentions in an afterword that some of the episodes come from entries in a frontier journal.

2422. Wisler, G. Clifton. **Mr. Lincoln's Drummer**. New York: Lodestar, 1995. 131p. $14.99. ISBN 0-525-67463-2. 4-8

Willie Johnson, 10 when the Civil War starts in 1861, plays the drum for a captain in town trying to get recruits. He makes enough money to help his family, and when his father joins for the salary, Willie decides that he will go with the Vermont group as the drummer boy. He is transferred to be a nurse, and his bravery wins him the Congressional Medal of Honor in 1863. The real Willie Johnson was the seventh soldier to receive that honor.

2423. Wisler, G. Clifton. **Mustang Flats**. New York: Lodestar, 1997. 144p. $14.99. ISBN 0-525-67544-2. 5-9

Alby Draper, 14, has to face a number of changes in his life when his father returns from the Civil War missing one leg. To lift the family from poverty, Alby and his father try to catch and tame wild mustangs and then sell them. During this process, they learn about each other, and Alby learns about himself.

2424. Wisler, G. Clifton. **Piper's Ferry**. New York: Dutton, 1990. 131p. $14.95. ISBN 0-525-67303-2. 6-8

Tim, 14, goes to see relatives in Texas, and while he is there, he decides to join the fight for freedom from Mexico in 1836. Although he is with family, he is lonely, and he talks to the family's bound servant, who was once a slave. Tim realizes that regardless of his emotional situation, he has the choice to remain or leave a place, unlike those who belong to someone else.

2425. Wisler, G. Clifton. **Red Cap**. New York: Dutton, 1991. 160p. $15. ISBN 0-525-67337-7. 5-9

Ransom J. Powell, 13 and four feet tall in 1862, runs away from his home in Frostburg, Maryland, to fight with the Union army in the Civil War. He becomes the drummer boy, but two years later, the Confederates capture him and take him to Camp Sumter, a prison in Andersonville, Georgia. He refuses to sign a parole that would release him from the stockade, and he again has the job of drummer boy, this time for the camp. This position and the kindness of a guard help him survive this terrible ordeal.

2426. Wisler, G. Clifton. **This New Land**. New York: Walker, 1987. 125p. $13.95. ISBN 0-8027-6727-3. (American History for Young People). 5-7

Richard, 12, leaves the Netherlands with his family after escaping from England and James I's religious tyranny in 1620. They travel first on the *Speedwell* and then on the *Mayflower* as they journey to the new colony in America. Richard's mother dies on board the *Mayflower*, and Richard goes with Miles Standish to meet the Native Americans Samoset and Squanto. Richard describes the cold, the number of pilgrims who die, and the relief of the settlers to have food and to celebrate their first year in their new land.

2427. Witcover, Paul. **Zora Neale Hurston**. New York: Chelsea House, 1990. 119p. $18.95; $7.95pa. ISBN 0-7910-1129-1; 0-7910-1154-2pa. (Black Americans of Achievement). 5 up

Zora Neale Hurston (1891-1960) began to support herself at 14 and eventually attended Howard University. She dreamed of becoming a writer throughout her youth, and in 1925 she won a major literary contest. In the same year, she entered Barnard College to study anthropology with a specialty in African American folklore. In the 1930s, she became well known for *Jonah's Gourd Vine*, *Mules and Men*, and *Their Eyes Were Watching God*. She also wrote an autobiography, *Dust Tracks on a Road*. Among her friends were Langston Hughes and Countee Cullen. Untrue and unsavory accusations in the press destroyed her reputation, but her work has recently resurfaced to positive critiques. She was original, intelligent, independent, and hardworking. Photographs and reproductions enhance the text. Chronology, Further Reading, and Index.

2428. Wolf, Sylvia. **Focus: Five Women Photographers: Julia Margaret Cameron, Margaret Bourke-White, Flor Garduño, Sandy Skoglund, Lorna Simpson**. Morton Grove, IL: Albert Whitman, 1994. 63p. $18.95. ISBN 0-8075-2531-6. 7 up

In addition to presenting a brief biography and summing up the ideas and work of each of the photographers spotlighted, the text also explains the photographic process and its history. Julia Margaret Cameron (British, 1815-1879) lived much of her life in India but did not begin making photographs until 1863, after she had returned to England and been given an old wooden camera. She found that portraits of people she knew were the most satisfying, and she photographed them with their clothes covered so that the focus would be on faces and not on the class in society their clothes revealed. Margaret Bourke-White (American, 1904-1971) became intrigued with buildings and industrial settings. She gave them prominence in her work and became a major figure in photojournalism, working for *Life* magazine. She also photographed such scenes as the liberation of the Nazi death camps in 1945 and India's Gandhi on his hunger strike. Flor Garduño (Mexican, b. 1957) creates stunning pictures documenting the timeless traditions of her Mexican culture as well as others. Sandy Skoglund (American, b. 1946) builds sets to photograph familiar scenes with startling changes such as a room with figures, two of them alive and covered in raisins. Lorna Simpson (American, b. 1960) wants her pictures to raise questions about how American society functions. Photo Credits and Selected Bibliography.

2429. Wolfe, Charles K. **Mahalia Jackson: Gospel Singer**. New York: Chelsea House, 1990. 103p. $18.95; $7.95pa. ISBN 1-55546-661-3; 0-7910-0440-6pa. (American Women of Achievement). 5 up

The drive of Mahalia Jackson (1912-1972) transformed gospel music by taking it from Black churches into the concert halls. She was orphaned at six but absorbed the music around her in New Orleans. At 15, her aunt sent her to Chicago to keep her away from the rowdy life. At 16, she started her career. She revolutionized gospel by adding blues inflections. Offstage, she had many friends in politics and knew Dr. Martin Luther King, Jr., and became involved in the Civil Rights movement. Photographs, Chronology, Further Reading, and Index.

2430. Wood, Frances M. **Becoming Rosemary**. New York: Bantam, 1997. 224p. $14.95. ISBN 0-385-32248-8. 5-9

Rosemary Weston expects to continue her daily tasks in North Carolina in 1790. But a cooper and his pregnant wife arrive, and his wife becomes Rosemary's friend. When rumors spread about witchcraft and evil regarding her friend, Rosemary realizes that she must take a stand.

2431. Wood, Marion. **Ancient America**. New York: Facts on File, 1990. 96p. $17.95. ISBN 0-8160-2210-0. (Cultural Atlas for Young People). 6-9

Wood covers the Americas, from the Inuit in the north to the Inca living in the empire that extended as far south as Chile. With as much information as possible, the text gives a picture of conditions in the Americas before the explorers came from Europe to change everything. Chronology, Glossary, Gazetteer, and Index. *New York Public Library Books for the Teen Age.*

2432. Wood, Ted. **A Boy Becomes a Man at Wounded Knee**. New York: Walker, 1992. 42p. $15.95; $6.95pa. ISBN 0-8027-8174-8; 0-8027-7446-6pa. 4-9

The text presents the events that led to the massacre of Lakota (Sioux) Indians at Wounded Knee in 1890. One hundred years later, Wanbli Numpa Afraid of Hawk, a young boy, rides with his people to commemorate this event, and he has a chance to understand what his people have suffered. Photographs and drawings enhance the text.

2433. Woods, Geraldine. **Affirmative Action**. New York: Franklin Watts, 1989. 128p. $19.14. ISBN 0-531-10657-8. (Impact). 7 up

Because affirmative action is a major force behind the rules of hiring today, knowing what it is and what it means gives a perspective on both the past and the present. The text looks at the history of discriminatory hiring in the United States before it presents the history of affirmative action. Various prior court cases and current cases against affirmative action that claim reverse discrimination are also included. Notes, Further Reading, and Index.

2434. Woog, Adam. **Duke Ellington**. San Diego, CA: Lucent, 1996. 112p. $16.95. ISBN 1-56006-073-5. (The Importance Of). 6 up

Duke Ellington (1899-1974) spent his childhood in Washington, D.C., and wrote his first composition at the age of 14. He taught himself music and received honors throughout the world. He blended popular and African American musical styles with European classical music. He did not like the term "jazz" and thought that it did not apply to his music. He created a big band because he felt that hearing one's music was important. His band could play his compositions on the morning after he finished them. The text presents his life with highlighting photographs. For Further Reading, Additional Works, and Index.

2435. Woog, Adam. **Harry Houdini**. San Diego, CA: Lucent, 1995. 112p. $16.95. ISBN 1-56006-053-0. (The Importance Of). 6 up

Harry Houdini (1874-1926) created mystery about himself by telling people that he had been born in Appleton, Wisconsin, when he had actually been born in Pest, Hungary, and immigrated to the United States when he was very young. After he started a career as a magician at 17, he gradually improved his abilities until he could escape from seemingly foolproof restraints. He gave his wife much of the credit for his success, but his personal charisma and knack for using the new media forms, radio and film, for publicity were also major factors. He earned the compliment of being called the "Great Escaper" and of being the best known of all magicians. Notes, For Further Reading, Additional Works Consulted, and Index.

2436. Woog, Adam. **Louis Armstrong**. San Diego, CA: Lucent, 1995. 112p. $16.95. ISBN 1-56006-059-X. (The Importance Of). 6 up

The text, with photographs to highlight, tells about Louis Armstrong's life (1900-1971). It also defines jazz and Armstrong's ability to play it. Nine chapters divide his life chronologically and look at his early life, stardom in New Orleans, the beginning of his fame after World War I, his life in Chicago and then on Broadway, his career, and his international fame. For Further Reading and Index.

2437. Wormser, Richard. **American Islam: Growing Up Muslim in America**. New York: Walker, 1994. 130p. $15.95. ISBN 0-8027-8343-0. 7 up

Currently, 4 to 6 million Muslims live in the United States. When females wear the *hejab* (scarf) as required by their religion, their affiliation becomes visible, and they are sometimes treated badly. The text includes the history of the origin and practice of Islam, beginning with Muhammad's birth in AD 570 in Mecca through Islam's first entry into America when African Americans brought it in the seventeenth century. Another brief history recounts the hostility of Christians toward Muslims, beginning with Pope Innocent's call for the first Crusade in 1095. These legacies affect contemporary beliefs. Wormser also contrasts traditional Islam with the Nation of Islam started by Elijah Muhammad and now led by Louis Farrakhan. The Nation of Islam does not pray five times a day; it practices separation from other races; and it rejects resurrection of the soul for a resurrection of the mind. Other names associated with the movement through history include Paul Cufee, Noble Drew Ali, and Marcus Garvey, but they are not Muslims who follow the specific teachings of Muhammad.

2438. Wormser, Richard. **Hoboes: Wandering in America 1870-1940**. New York: Walker, 1994. 136p. $17.95. ISBN 0-8027-8280-9. 7 up

Hoboes, scorned by mainstream American society, had their own communities between 1870 and 1940 as they were "flipping a freight" (jumping on trains) to ride across the country. They worked as transients but knew each other through their own sign language, slang, codes of law, and honor. In hobo colleges, founded in every major city (Chicago was the major capital), they discussed socialism, industrial law, political science, and economics and held as their intellectual and political heroes such people as Joe Hill, Emma Goldman, Gill Haywood, and Ben Reitman. Their era ended by 1940, but in the 1950s, people like Jack Kerouac, as recorded in *On the Road,* emulated their lifestyles.

2439. Wormser, Richard. **The Iron Horse: How the Railroads Changed America**. New York: Walker, 1993. 182p. $18.95. ISBN 0-8027-8221-3. 7 up

The first railroad opened in Baltimore, Maryland, in 1830, with a race between a gray mare and a steam locomotive called Tom Thumb. The horse finished first, but that was the last time a horse won. Topics include the barons who built the railroads, the effect of the railroad on the Civil War, the transcontinental railroad, railroad robbers, the thrill of the railroad, how railroads took lands from farmers and others, and safety laws subsequently enacted. Photographs and reproductions highlight the text. Glossary, Bibliography, and Index.

2440. Wormser, Richard. **Pinkerton: America's First Private Eye**. New York: Walker, 1990. 119p. $17.95. ISBN 0-8027-6964-0. 5-9

The most famous detective in the nineteenth century, Allan Pinkerton grew up in the worst slums of Glasgow, Scotland, and died on his American estate. He believed in upholding the law but broke it without hesitation during his fight against slavery. He fled Scotland because of his pro-labor activities, but in America he despised militant labor. He became a detective by accident, but when he began solving crimes, he changed from barrel making to police work and then opened his own agency. Further Reading and Index.

2441. Wormser, Richard L. **Three Faces of Vietnam**. New York: Franklin Watts, 1993. 157p. $13.90. ISBN 0-531-11142-3. 7 up

Starting in the 1950s when France occupied Vietnam, the text looks at the war until its end in 1975 through the eyes of three groups of people: the Vietnamese, American military personnel, and protesters at home. Personal anecdotes include the views of a Viet Cong sympathizer as well as many others collected from the aforementioned groups. Photographs, Maps, Notes, Further Reading, and Index.

2442. Worth, Richard. **Edith Wharton**. New York: Simon & Schuster, 1994. 154p. $14.95. ISBN 0-671-86615-X. (Classic American Writers). 9 up

Edith Wharton (1862-1937) grew up in New York. She and her wealthy family visited Paris and Newport, Rhode Island, regularly. She married, contributed her efforts to World War I, and was friendly with Henry James and other writers. The text looks at her life and how her writings reflect the society in which she lived as well as the disappointment that women often had in their relationships with the men in their elitist society. Chronology, Bibliography, and Index.

2443. Wright, David K. **Arthur Ashe: Breaking the Color Barrier in Tennis**. Springfield, NJ: Enslow, 1996. 128p. $18.95. ISBN 0-89490-689-5. 4-7

Arthur Ashe (1943-1993) rose from a Richmond, Virginia, neighborhood to become one of America's great tennis players, winning at Wimbledon. He always showed courage and discipline while trying to make tennis a color-blind sport. Even when he got heart disease and then AIDS from tainted blood, he kept his strength of character. Photographs, Further Reading, and Index.

2444.   Wright, David K. **John Lennon: The Beatles and Beyond**. Springfield, NJ: Enslow, 1996. 112p. $18.95. ISBN 0-89490-702-6. (People to Know). 7 up

The text looks at the complexities in Beatle John Lennon's background and how he developed as both a songwriter and a political activist. It also looks at the history of the Beatles as a musical group and Lennon's relationship to it. Photographs, Discography, Notes, and Index.

2445.   Wright, David K. **A Multicultural Portrait of the War in Vietnam**. Freeport, NY: Marshall Cavendish, 1996. 80p. $18.95. ISBN 0-7614-0052-4. (Perspectives). 7 up

Using the viewpoints of people of color, ethnic minorities, and European American majorities, the text presents a look at the Vietnam War with quotations from primary sources. It notes that these various groups were involved in the conflict both overseas and at home. During this time the nation, according to Wright, developed a concept of itself and its relationships to its various groups that it still holds. Chronology, Further Reading, Glossary, and Index.

2446.   Wright, David K. **A Multicultural Portrait of World War II**. Freeport, NY: Marshall Cavendish, 1994. 80p. $18.95. ISBN 1-85435-663-1. (Perspectives). 7 up

The text gives the viewpoints of people of color, ethnic minorities, and the European American majority about World War II with quotations from primary sources. It looks at the origins of the war and how the diverse racial and ethnic population of the country helped fight it, including Japanese American soldiers who fought for America. Chronology, Further Reading, Glossary, and Index.

2447.   Wright, Sarah. **A. Philip Randolph: Integration in the Workplace**. Englewood Cliffs, NJ: Silver Burdett, 1990. 130p. $12.95. ISBN 0-382-09922-2. (The History of the Civil Rights Movement). 7-9

A. Philip Randolph (1889-1979) organized the Brotherhood of Sleeping Car Porters and acted as a labor union officer for Pullman Car porters. In the 1940s, he organized two marches on Washington, but the laws were changed so that hiring practices became fair in the government and separation of races was banned in the military. In 1963, more than 250,000 came to Washington, D.C., to put pressure on Congress to pass the Civil Rights Bill. Randolph introduced Martin Luther King, Jr. at the gathering, and King delivered his "I Have a Dream" speech. Although the bill started with Kennedy, Lyndon Johnson gets credit for passing it. Timetable, Suggested Reading, Sources, and Index.

2448.   Wunderli, Stephen. **The Blue Between the Clouds**. New York: Henry Holt, 1992. 114p. $13.95. ISBN 0-8050-1772-0. 5 up

In Thistle, Utah, Matt, 11, plays with his friend Two Moons during the early 1940s. They help a pilot from World War I rebuild his old Fokker airplane and try to find excitement anywhere they can. When Two Moons has to leave, they have difficulty accepting the changes in their lives.

2449.   Wyman, Andrea. **Red Sky at Morning**. New York: Holiday House, 1991. 230p. $13.95. ISBN 0-8234-0903-1. 3-7

In 1909, Callie and her family remain in Indiana while her father travels to Oregon to buy a new farm for their family. While he is gone, her mother dies in childbirth; her sister has to leave home to find work; and she and her German grandfather must run the farm during a diphtheria epidemic. She also finds out things about her father that distress her, but when he returns, she adjusts, and all leave for Oregon.

2450.   Wyman, Carolyn. **Ella Fitzgerald: Jazz Singer Supreme**. New York: Franklin Watts, 1993. 128p. $22.10; $6.95pa. ISBN 0-531-13031-2; 0-531-15679-6pa. (Impact Biography). 7 up

Ella Fitzgerald (1918-1996) began her career as a 14-year-old at the Harlem Opera House, where she won a $25 prize. This was the first of her many honors, and she became known worldwide for her talent. But she had to face and overcome the difficulties of success during a time when she was denied entry into hotels and restaurants because she was Black. Her rise to fame coincided with the Civil Rights movement, and she helped break some of the barriers. Source Notes, Selected Discography, Bibliography, and Index.

2451.   Wyss, Thelma Hatch. **A Stranger Here**. 1993. New York: HarperCollins, 1996. 132p. $4.50pa. ISBN 0-06-447098-9pa. 7 up

During the summer of 1960, Jada spends the Idaho summer taking care of her Aunt May, but she has plenty of time to think about other things. When she goes into the attic one day, she plays an old record, and Starr appears, a soldier killed in World War II on the day she was born. He knows all about her, and through the summer, as he tells her about herself, she begins to understand her relationship with her parents and her aunt.

2452. Yagoda, Ben. **Will Rogers: A Biography**. New York: Knopf, 1993. 409p. $27.50. ISBN 0-394-58512-7. YA

Will Rogers (1879-1935) was the most popular man in the United States from the early 1920s until his death in an airplane crash in 1935. Forty million people read his newspaper column daily, and he entertained on the radio and as a lecturer, a movie star, and a sage. The text uses his letters and previously unpublished writings to show his responses to his life as a cowboy, as a traveler to such places as Argentina and South Africa, and as a human being. He was a decent man with common sense that came through in his performances. Notes and Index.

2453. Yannuzzi, Della. **Wilma Mankiller: Leader of the Cherokee Nation**. Springfield, NJ: Enslow, 1994. 104p. $17.95. ISBN 0-89490-498-1. (People to Know). 5-8

Wilma Pearl Mankiller (b. 1945) was sworn into office as the first female Principal Chief of the Cherokee Nation in 1985 after overcoming her own severe hardships and intense opposition. She has worked toward a financially independent and self-governing Cherokee Nation by reestablishing a Cherokee tribal judicial system. Chronology, Chapter Notes, Further Reading, and Index.

2454. Yannuzzi, Della A. **Zora Neale Hurston: Southern Storyteller**. Springfield, NJ: Enslow, 1996. 104p. $17.95. ISBN 0-89490-685-2. (African-American Biographies). 6-9

Zora Neale Hurston (1891-1960) was a complex and well-educated woman who was part of the Harlem Renaissance. The text looks at her life, with its hard work and belief in herself, as she pursued her writing and anthropological research. Photographs, Chronology, Further Reading, Notes, and Index.

2455. Yarbro, Chelsea Quinn. **Floating Illusions**. New York: HarperCollins, 1986. 215p. $12.95. ISBN 0-06-026643-0. 6-8

While Millicent, 14, crosses the Atlantic on an ocean liner in 1910, several people are murdered. Among the friends she makes during her investigation are a magician, a militant feminist, and Anton, a noble. When the magician's life is threatened, he can no longer be a suspect, and Millicent identifies the criminal.

2456. Yates, Diana. **Chief Joseph: Thunder Rolling down from the Mountains**. Staten Island, NY: Ward Hill Press, 1992. 137p. $14.95. ISBN 0-9623380-9-5. (Unsung Americans). 7 up

As the leader of the Nez Percé, Chief Joseph (1840-1904) wanted equal rights for men of all races, and he even continued to want peace as white settlers and the government drove his people from their lands. He urged reconciliation and mourned the deaths of all in the Nez Percé–American War in 1877. After that conflict, he continued to advocate self-determination for native peoples. Maps, Photographs, Notes, Bibliography, Chronology, and Index.

2457. Yates, Elizabeth. **Prudence Crandall: Woman of Courage**. Nora S. Unwin, illustrator. 1955. Honesdale, PA: Boyds Mills Press, 1996. 256p. $16.95. ISBN 1-56397-391-X. 7 up

Prudence Crandall opened a school for African American women in Canterbury, Connecticut. As a Quaker, she believed that all people were equal in the eyes of God and that these women deserved to have the same opportunities as others. Her school led people to accuse her of breaking the laws of man and God, but she refused to acquiesce, and for her stance she was tried and imprisoned.

2458. Yates, Janelle. **Woody Guthrie: American Balladeer**. Staten Island, NY: Ward Hill Press, 1995. 159p. $14.95; $10.95pa. ISBN 0-9623380-0-1; 1-9623380-5-2pa. (Unsung Americans). 7-10

Woody Guthrie (1912-1967) experienced the death of a sister when he was six, the poverty resulting from the dust storms of 1935, and the Great Depression. His family left Oklahoma for California and survived as migrant workers. Throughout all, he had his music, and he used it as a way to fight poverty and social injustice. His story is the history of twentieth-century folk music. In the end, he could not overcome Huntington's chorea. Epilogue, Notes, Bibliography, Chronology, and Index.

2459. Yep, Laurence. **Dragon's Gate**. New York: HarperCollins, 1993. 275p. $15; $4.95pa. ISBN 0-06-022972-1; 0-06-440489-7pa. 5 up

In this prequel to *Dragonwings*, in 1865, Otter arrives in the Sierra Mountains from Hwangtung Province in China, where he begins helping his adoptive father and uncle build the transcontinental railroad. Otter expects to see goldfields, but he only sees cleared trees and a vast cover of whiteness. His dream is to learn all that he can so that he can return to China and free it from the Manchu invaders. During the difficult work under hostile foremen, his uncle encourages him to have another dream, one in which he will be himself and do what he needs to do rather than what tradition has told him. After a strike for fewer hours and more pay with the other Chinese, and his uncle's death, Otter decides to take his advice. *Newbery Honor Book, New York Public Library Books for the Teen Age, American Booksellers Pick of the Lists, Commonwealth Club Silver Medal for Literature, John and Patricia Beatty Award,* and *American Library Association Notable Books for Children.*

2460.   Yep, Laurence. **Dragonwings**. New York: Harper, 1975. 256p. $14.89; $4.95pa. ISBN 0-06-026738-0; 0-06-440085-9pa. 7 up
    At eight in 1903, Moon Shadow sails from China to San Francisco to join his father Windrider, whom he has never met. He soon grows to love this laundryman who dreams of flying. His father begins to correspond with the Wright brothers about their machines, but because he must save money to bring his wife and other son to America, he has no money to spend on parts for his own experiments, and the Wright brothers get credit for the first airplane flight. Both Moon Shadow and his father endure the San Francisco earthquake in April 1906 and help the *demon* (white) woman for whom they work free other *demons* from their collapsed homes. *Newbery Honor Book, Friends of Children and Literature Award (FOCAL), Carter G. Woodson Book Award, IRA Children's Book Award, New York Public Library Books for the Teen Age, American Library Association Notable Children's Books of 1971-1975, Boston Globe-Horn Book Honor Book, Horn Book Fanfare Honor List, School Library Journal "Best of the Best" Children's Books 1966-1978, Notable Children's Trade Books in the Field of Social Studies, Lewis Carroll Shelf Award,* and *Phoenix Award.*

2461.   Yep, Laurence. **Mountain Light**. New York: HarperCollins, 1985. 282p. $12.89. ISBN 0-06-026759-3. 8 up
    During the 1850s, Squeaky, 19, has to escape the Chinese Manchu soldiers while trying to survive battles with fellow Chinese from different clans. He makes alliances, one of which is with Cassia. After her father's death, he goes to America to see her brother, who has been working in the goldfields.

2462.   Yep, Laurence. **The Star Fisher**. New York: Morrow, 1991. 150p. $12.95. ISBN 0-688-09365-5. 6-9
    Jean Lee, 15, has trouble making friends when her family moves from Ohio to West Virginia to open a laundry in 1927. The prejudice that she feels keeps her separate from others, but her younger siblings seem to have no trouble making friends. The landlady helps Jean Lee and her parents become more accepted through a variety of incidents that benefit both the town and the family. *Bulletin Blue Ribbon Book* and *Christopher Award.*

2463.   Yepsen, Roger. **City Trains: Moving Through America's Cities by Rail**. New York: Macmillan, 1993. 96p. $14.95. ISBN 0-02-793675-9. 5-8
    This history is illustrated with the various types of public transportation found in cities. They include horsecars, streetcars, trolleys, interurbans, cable cars, subways, light rails, and monorails. Bibliography and Index.

2464.   Yolen, Jane. **Briar Rose**. New York: Tor Books, 1992. 190p. $17.95; $5.99pa. ISBN 0-312-851359; 0-8125-5862-6pa. 8 up
    Becca's grandmother has adamantly declared that she is a princess, and Becca tells her before she dies that Becca will find the prince and the castle of the Briar Rose story that her grandmother told her. In the nursing home room are photographs, newspaper clippings, a ring, and a passport that her grandmother has kept in a box. Becca's investigation leads her to Fort Oswego, New York, a former World War II refugee camp, and to Chelmno, Poland, site of Nazi exterminations. She finds out that a partisan fighter had found her grandmother alive in a mass grave and revived her. They married, but after she became pregnant, Nazis murdered her husband. Such a story was not one that could be easily told.

2465.   Yolen, Jane. **The Devil's Arithmetic**. New York: Viking, 1988. 170p. $13. ISBN 0-670-81027-4. YA
    In this historical fantasy, Hannah becomes bored every year at the family Passover Seder. But when she is 13, she opens the door to symbolically welcome Elijah to the feast and finds herself in a Polish village *(shtetl)* during the 1940s, where everyone calls her "Chaya." She immediately forgets her past as she becomes involved in village life and its fear of the Nazis. When the Nazis take her family and her to a death camp, she only wants to survive. After she is returned to her former life, she understands the significance of the Seder and her history and knows that she will never forget. *National Jewish Awards, Sydney Taylor Book Award,* and *Association of Jewish Libraries Award.*

2466.   Youmans, Marly. **Catherwood**. New York: Farrar, Straus & Giroux, 1996. 165p. $20. ISBN 0-374-11972-4. YA
    Catherwood, a young mother from England, finds herself in New York in 1676. She loses her way home in her primitive community, and she and her child become lost in the wilderness where she and the infant survive for seven months. The story is based on an account from the Church Record of Westfield in the Massachusetts Colony.

2467.   Young, Carrie. **Nothing to Do but Stay: My Pioneer Mother**. Iowa City, IA: University of Iowa, 1991. 117p. $22.95. ISBN 0-87745-328-4. New York: Dell, 1993. 117p. $8.95pa. ISBN 0-385-31365-9pa. YA

In 1904, Young's mother, Carrine Gafkjen, came to North Dakota, where she began her own homestead. Before she married, she owned 320 acres. In the stories about her mother, Young discusses the everyday life that these settlers endured through blizzards, drought, and loneliness. They visit each other in this bilingual community, and they work together as families. That they survived seems miraculous.

2468.   Young, Ken. **Cy Young Award Winners**. New York: Walker, 1994. 147p. $14.95. ISBN 0-8027-8300-7. 5-8

Named after Denton True "Cy" Young, the Cy Young award goes to the best pitcher in the American and National Baseball Leagues at the end of each baseball season. The text tells the story behind Denny McLain (1968, 1969), Dwight Gooden (1985), Whitey Ford (1961), Sandy Koufax (1963, 1965, 1966), Bob Gibson (1968, 1970), Tom Seaver (1969, 1973, 1975), Steve Carlton (1972, 1977, 1980, 1982), Jim Palmer (1973, 1975), Fernando Valenzuela (1981), and Roger Clemens (1986, 1987, 1991). Appendix and Index.

2469.   Young, Mary, and Gerald Horne. **Testaments of Courage: Selections from Men's Slave Narratives**. New York: Franklin Watts, 1995. 128p. $20.60. ISBN 0-531-11205-5. (African-American Experience). 7 up

In chronological order, beginning with Louis Asa-Asa's 1831 account of his life as a slave and continuing through freedom, the text presents narratives from a variety of men who escaped from their situation. Among those included are Frederick Douglass, Solomon Northrup, William Wells Brown, and Nat Love, a black cowboy who gained fame in the West. Bibliography, Further Reading, and Index.

2470.   Young, Robert. **The Emancipation Proclamation: Why Lincoln Really Freed the Slaves**. New York: Dillon Press, 1995. 80p. $7.95pa. ISBN 0-382-24712-4pa. (Both Sides). 7-10

The text asks questions about the reasons behind Abraham Lincoln's decision to sign the Emancipation Proclamation on January 1, 1863. Did he sign it because he wanted slaves to be free, because he thought that all people were created equal, or because he thought it would be another maneuver to end the Civil War? An historical overview of slavery in the colonies precedes the debate showing the points made by each side. Time Line, Glossary, For Further Reading, and Index.

2471.   Young, Robert. **Hiroshima: Fifty Years of Debate**. New York: Dillon Press, 1994. 80p. $14.95; $7.95pa. ISBN 0-382-24713-2; 0-87518-610-6pa. (Both Sides). 7-10

After an introduction to the events of August 6, 1945, the text looks at the choices that the United States had when it decided to drop the atomic bomb on Hiroshima. Those who thought the bomb was necessary support their opinion with the points that the Allies would have had to invade Japan if the bomb had not dropped, that the United States needed to use the bomb after spending so much money on its development, that Japan was not trustworthy because militarists who thought that death was preferable to surrender controlled it, and that killing a large number of people with one bomb was no different than killing a few at a time for a long period. Those who were against the bomb said that Japan would not have enough strength to continue the war much longer, that it was making honest efforts at a peace agreement, that President Truman had perpetrated anti-Japanese sentiment in the United States, and that Truman was worried about Soviet expansion and the bomb would show U.S. strength. Timeline, Glossary, For Further Reading, and Index.

2472.   Young, Ronder Thomas. **Learning by Heart**. Boston: Houghton Mifflin, 1993. 172p. $3.99pa. ISBN 0-395-65369-X. 5-7

In the 1960s, Rachel, 10, must adjust to her family's move into a new house, a baby brother, and an African American housekeeper, Isabella. Isabella helps Rachel cope while she develops friendships with a Black girl and another girl whom her classmates consider "white trash." Although Rachel wants to accept people for themselves, she has to readjust her whole life when the family store is burned down and her parents can no longer pay for Isabella's help.

2473.   Yount, John. **Thief of Dreams**. New York: Viking, 1991. 227p. $18.95. ISBN 0-670-83802-0. Dallas, TX: Southern Methodist University Press, 1994. 227p. $10.95pa. ISBN 0-87074-375-9pa. YA

James, 13, moves in with his mother after his parents separate in 1948. In a fight during which a friend is badly beaten, James decides to leave home. His father searches for him and finds him in the woods almost frozen. The possibility of loss reunites the family.

2474.   Yount, Lisa. **Black Scientists**. New York: Facts on File, 1991. 111p. $17.95. ISBN 0-8160-2459-5. (American Profiles). 6-12

The Black scientists featured in this text are Daniel Hale Williams, first successful heart surgeon (1856-1931); George Washington Carver (c. 1865-1943), pure scientist who helped poor farmers; Ernest Everett Just (1883-1941), cytologist; Percy Lavon Julian (1899-1975), synthesizer of complex chemicals; Charles Richard

Drew (1904-1950) and the first programs to store blood and blood plasma; Jane Cooke Wright (b. 1919), chemotherapy researcher; Bertram O. Fraser-Reid (b. 1934), complex molecule analyzer; and John P. Moon (b. 1938), peripherals engineer working on computer storage and retrieval of data. Chronologies, Bibliographies, and Index.

2475.   Yount, Lisa. **Women Aviators**. New York: Facts on File, 1991. 144p. $17.95. ISBN 0-8160-3062-6. (American Profiles). 6-12

Less than seven years after the Wright brothers flew their first airplane, Blanche Stuart Scott became the first woman to take flying lessons. Other women followed her lead. Among them were Katherine Stinson (1891-1977), Bessie Coleman (1892-1926), Amelia Mary Earhart (1897-1937), Edna Gardner Whyte (1902-1993), Anne Morrow Lindbergh (b. 1906), Jacqueline Cochran (1906?-1980), Geraldine Fredritz Mock (b. 1925), Geraldyn Cobb (b. 1931), Bonnie Linda Tiburzi (b. 1948), Sally Kristin Ride (b. 1951), and Jeana L. Yeager (b. 1952). Chapter Bibliographies and Index.

Z

2476. Zall, P. M. **Becoming American: Young People in the American Revolution**. Hamden, CT: Linnet, Shoestring Press, 1993. 214p. $25. ISBN 0-208-02355-0. 7 up

Zall has compiled primary sources, including letters, journal entries, and court testimonies, from 23 people between 12 and 20 who lived during the American Revolution, 1767-1789. He introduces each by placing the individual in time and place. The recountings include a soldier at Bunker Hill, a girl who watched mobs destroy Quaker property, and Martha Jefferson writing from Paris about being aboard a ship crossing the Atlantic. Bibliography and Index.

2477. Zeinert, Karen, ed. **Captured by Indians: The Life of Mary Jemison**. Hamden, CT: Linnet, Shoe string Press, 1995. 104p. $17.50. ISBN 0-208-02368-2. 7 up

This book differs from James Seaver's book about Mary Jemison, published in 1824, because Zeinert has deleted references to Native Americans and other incidents that seem to be sensationalist. Zeinert uses the words of Mary Jemison (1742?-1833) to tell the story. When Jemison was 15 in 1758, Indians dragged her, her family, and friends from a Pennsylvania cabin. Only Mary and a neighbor boy survived the scalpings. From that point on, she was an Indian, adopted by the Senecas and married to a Delaware, a man whom she loved. She refused to leave the Indians. Her autobiography gives a clear picture of the Northeast frontier during the French and Indian War and the American Revolution. Glossary and Bibliography.

2478. Zeinert, Karen. **Elizabeth Van Lew: Southern Belle, Union Spy**. New York: Dillon Press, 1995. 160p. $13.95; $7.95pa. ISBN 0-87518-608-4; 0-382-24960-7pa. (People in Focus). 6-9

Elizabeth Van Lew spied for the North during the Civil War while she lived in Richmond, Virginia, and helped Union prisoners who managed to escape from their guards in Richmond. She had a secret room in her home to hide the soldiers. She also supplied escapees with weapons and directions that led them back to their regiments. Other courageous actions made her work important for the Union. Because of the stigma attached to her after the war by her neighbors, and losses that she incurred in trying to help former slaves, President Grant gave her the job of postmaster. Bibliography, For Further Reading, and Index.

2479. Zeinert, Karen, ed. **The Memoirs of Andrew Sherburne: Patriot and Privateer of the American Revolution**. Seymour Fleishman, illustrator. Hamden, CT: Linnet Books, Shoestring Press, 1993. 96p. $17.50. ISBN 0-208-02354-2. 5-8

At 13 in 1779, Andrew Sherburne went to sea against the British. He was taking a chance because he could come home rich, or he could be maimed, killed, diseased, or hung as a traitor because the British considered George Washington's navy to be no more than a bunch of pirates. Sherburne has many of the bad things happen to him. In his journal, he records his observations, which include colonial naval warfare, press gangs, smallpox, West Indian trade, British laws, and Americans breaking these laws. Glossary and For More Information.

2480. Zeinert, Karen. **The Salem Witchcraft Trials**. New York: Franklin Watts, 1989. 96p. $20.40. ISBN 0-531-10673-X. 5-10

Court records are the basis for this recounting of the Salem witchcraft trials held in Massachusetts. In 1692, a madness swept into Salem town. Many were arrested for witchcraft, and 19 suspected witnesses were hanged. The situation started with the claims of Betty Parris, age nine. The text presents a background of Puritan beliefs and then discusses the trials, beginning with the accusations and ending with the executions. Possible economic and psychological theories may explain these trials, but not until 1957 were the victims absolved of the charges against them. Bibliography and Index.

2481. Zeinert, Karen. **Those Incredible Women of World War II**. Brookfield, CT: Millbrook Press, 1996. 112p. $19.90. ISBN 1-56294-657-9. 5-8

Women struggled to take part in World War II by serving in the army, Navy, or Air Force. They became newspaper reporters and medical personnel. Leading 1,000 women flyers were the Woman's Air Force heads Genia Novak and Delphine Bohn. Olveta Culp Hobby directed the first American military organization for women, Women's Army Auxiliary Corps (WAAC). Jane Kendleigh served as the first Navy flight nurse on a battlefield, and Dr. Emily Barringer fought for women to join the medical corps. A major recorder of the effects of the war was Margaret Bourke-White, a photographer for *Life* magazine. Sigrid Schultz and Dorothy Thompson lived in Germany as journalists. Other correspondents included Ruth Cowan, Sonia Tomara, and Marguerite Higgins. At home, Frances Perkins served as the Secretary of Labor from 1933 until 1945. Afterword, Timeline, Notes, Bibliography, Further Reading, and Index. *New York Public Library Books for the Teen Age.*

2482.   Zelazny, Roger, and Gerald Hausman. **Wilderness**. New York: Tor Books, 1994. 304p. $21.95; $4.99pa. ISBN 0-312-85654-7; 0-8125-3534-0pa. YA

In the West during the early 1800s, John Colter and Hugh Glass had unsettling experiences. In alternating chapters, the authors tell their stories. In 1808, John Colter fled from Blackfeet Indians for 150 miles after they stripped him to a loincloth and gave him a head start. As the novel progresses, Colter admits to his fear of torture as the impetus that gives him strength. Hugh Glass, on the other hand, wanted revenge, but what he got was a mauling from a bear. Glass crawled to the nearest settlement, 100 miles away, for help. Nature and survival techniques fill the pages along with the stories of these courageous and determined mountain men.

2483.   Zell, Fran. **A Multicultural Portrait of the American Revolution**. New York: Benchmark, 1996. 80p. $18.95. ISBN 0-7614-0051-6. (Perspectives). 7 up

In the American Revolution, white European men fought for their own freedom while taking away the freedom of Native Americans who had been in the area for thousands of years. They also owned African American slaves and denied rights to women and poor European male settlers. The text looks at these ironies as it gives the viewpoints of people of color and the ethnic minorities who were also settlers. Chronology, Further Reading, Glossary, and Index.

2484.   Ziesk, Edra. **Margaret Mead**. New York: Chelsea House, 1990. 109p. $18.95. ISBN 1-55546-667-2. (American Women of Achievement). 5 up

Margaret Mead (1901-1978), an influential social scientist, changed the way many people see themselves and the society in which they live. Her first field trip as an anthropologist was to American Samoa in 1925, where she gathered the data for her book, *Coming of Age in Samoa*. Later she went to New Guinea, left, and returned to study sex roles. With her third husband, also an anthropologist, she made trips to Bali and New Guinea. For the last 40 years of her life, she was a curator at the New York American Museum of Natural History. Photographs enhance the text. Chronology, Further Reading, and Index.

2485.   Zimmer, Michael. **Cottonwood Station**. New York: Walker, 1993. 183p. $19.95. ISBN 0-8027-1273-8. YA

When the Cheyenne warriors under Medicine Wolf attack a stagecoach, Clint Dawson saves the passengers with his sniper's rifle and takes them to Cottonwood Station. He is unaware, however, that one of the passengers knows what Medicine Wolf wants, and that inside the Cottonwood Station walls is another villain, Rusty Cantrell, who has come with his gang. When Dawson discovers who wants what, he saves the victims in a final standoff.

2486.   Zimmer, Michael. **Dust and Glory**. New York: Walker, 1993. 183p. $18.95. ISBN 0-8027-4090-1. YA

When Gray Fletcher, a Texas Ranger, began to seek retaliation against Indians who killed his wife and one of their children, he learned that one event could change a life forever. His neighbor Jesse, 18, learns the same when he kills a Union soldier to protect his family. Jesse thought he could escape being hunted by joining others from Missouri as a member of Slaughter's Rangers, an underground group fighting the Union during the Civil War. He learns that one must often run, even when one wants to stay.

CD-ROMS: AN ANNOTATED BIBLIOGRAPHY

2487. **Air and Space Smithsonian Dreams of Flight**. CD-ROM. System requirements: IBM or compatible PC: 486/25 MHz or higher CPU, 4 MB RAM, 8 MB RAM recommended, Microsoft Windows 3.1 or later, CD-ROM drive, sound card, mouse, SVGA 256 color display, loudspeakers or headphones. Portland, OR: Creative Multimedia, 1995. $29.95. 5 up

The four areas to explore in this CD-ROM are Aviation Pioneers, Flying Machines, Milestones, and Culture. Each section includes multimedia resources, photographs, audio, personal interviews, and aerodynamic demonstrations. The disc includes the history of flight.

2488. **American History Explorer**. CD-ROM. System requirements: IBM or compatible PC: 386/16 MHz or higher CPU, 4 MB RAM, 8 MB RAM recommended, Microsoft Windows 3.1 or later, hard drive with 2 MB free, CD-ROM drive, sound card, mouse, SVGA 256 color display, loudspeakers or headphones. Hiawatha, IA: Parsons Technology, 1996. $49. 5-9

This multimedia presentation covers Native American settlement to 1875 in eight time periods beginning with Exploration and ending with Restoration. Presidents, election results, biographical facts, slide shows, songs, narrated slides, and captioned photographs are also available. The Map Studio includes 93 maps. Viewers can search media type, title, first words, matching words, or partial words.

2489. **Apollo Interactive: The Complete Insider's Guide**. CD-ROM. System requirements: IBM or compatible PC: 486/33 MHz or higher CPU, 8 MB RAM, Microsoft Windows 3.1 or later, CD-ROM drive, sound card, mouse, SVGA 256 color display, loudspeakers or headphones. Macintosh: 6 MB RAM, System 7.0, 13-inch monitor (256 colors), CD-ROM drive. Los Angeles: WizardWorks Group, 1995. $15. 5 up

The CD-ROM discusses each of the *Apollo* space voyages from 1967 to 1975. Drawings, animation, and historical video clips of each mission give a sense of its purpose and effect.

2490. **Beyond the Wall: Stories Behind Vietnan Wall**. CD-ROM. System requirements: IBM or compatible PC: 486/33 MHz or higher CPU, 8 MB RAM, Microsoft Windows 3.1 or later, CD-ROM drive, sound card, mouse, SVGA 256 color display, loudspeakers or headphones. Macintosh: 4 MB RAM, System 7.0, 13-inch monitor (256 colors), CD-ROM drive. Washington, D.C.: Magnet Interactive, 1995. $29.95. 7 up

This tour of the 492-foot wall memorializing those who died in Vietnam tells how it was created with Maya Lin submitting the winning design and gives a brief history of the war. The CD contains the names of the 58,196 soldiers who died or are missing in action by allowing the viewer to enter a name to search. The name and other information may be printed. Video clips re-create the construction of the wall, including name chiseling in the granite surface, and the war itself.

2491. **Campaigns, Candidates and the Presidency**. CD-ROM. System requirements: IBM or compatible PC: 386SX or higher CPU, 4 MB RAM, 8 MB RAM recommended, Microsoft Windows 3.1 or later, CD-ROM drive, sound card, mouse, SVGA 256 color display, loudspeakers or headphones. Carlsbad, CA: Compton's NewMedia, 1995. $39.95. 6 up

A biography, personal history, media, and tapes tells about each of the 42 Presidents from Washington to Clinton. Signed articles can be sorted by various themes such as policies and issues, historical events, and law and legal cases. Much information is available about the men who have led the United States since its beginning.

2492. **Critical Mass: America's Race to Build the Atomic Bomb**. CD-ROM. System requirements: IBM or compatible PC: 386SX or higher CPU, 4 MB RAM, Microsoft Windows 3.1 or later, CD-ROM drive, sound card, mouse, SVGA 256 color display, loudspeakers or headphones. Macintosh: 6 MB RAM, System 7.0, 13-inch monitor (256 colors), CD-ROM drive. Bellevue, WA: Corbis, 1996. $50. 7 up

Among the sections of this CD-ROM, which covers the Manhattan Project during World War II, are a graphical tour of Los Alamos, biographies of scientists involved in the project such as J. Robert Oppenheimer, newsreel films to re-create a sense of the period, and documentary segments that explain the engineering of these first atomic weapons. Government papers and personal letters are among the included documents available through hypertext.

2493.   **Daring to Fly! From Icarus to the Red Baron**. CD-ROM. System requirements: IBM or compatible PC: 386SX or higher CPU, 4 MB RAM, Microsoft Windows 3.1 or later, CD-ROM drive, sound card, mouse, SVGA 256 color display, loudspeakers or headphones. (Macintosh version available). Sausalito, CA: Arnowitz Studios, 1994. $59.95. 6-12

In the main menu of this CD-ROM, eight topic icons lead to exhibits such as "Science of Flight," "Lighter than Air," "Wings of War," and "Women Aloft" as it presents the history of flight from the dreams in myths through the post–World War I era of aviation.

2494.   **Events That Changed the World**. CD-ROM. System requirements: IBM or compatible PC: 486/33 MHz or higher CPU, 8 MB RAM, Microsoft Windows 3.1 or later, CD-ROM drive, sound card, mouse, SVGA 256 color display with 512K RAM, loudspeakers or headphones. Macintosh: 5 MB RAM, System 7.0, 13-inch monitor (256 colors), CD-ROM drive. New York: Integrated Communications and Entertainment, 1996. $29.95. 9 up

The topics featuring hundreds of people and places are "Rulers and Empires," "Religious Thought and Practice," "Conquest and War," "Revolution and Disaster," "Exploration," "Discovery and Creative Thought," and "Politics and Political Philosophy." Access to events occurs through a listing of people, the topics, or through several other methods. All help to create a comprehensive view of world history. Among the choices is Martin Luther King, Jr.'s "I Have a Dream" speech.

2495.   **Exploring the Titanic**. CD-ROM. System requirements: Macintosh LC or better: 4 MB RAM, System 7.0, color monitor (256 colors minimum), hard drive with 2.5 MB free, CD-ROM drive. New York: Scholastic, 1994. $149. 4-8

This CD-ROM is the interactive version of Robert D. Ballard's book, which details the sinking of the *Titanic* in 1912 and its recovery in 1985 from the submarine *Alvin*. A timeline references the event to other happenings in the world. Other avenues examine the ship, the technology used to locate it, and an exploration of the wreck itself. Twenty-nine synthesized voices give information. Pages from the book are printable as well as text and notes.

2496.   **Eyewitness Encyclopedia of Science**. CD-ROM. System requirements: IBM or compatible PC: 386/33 MHz or higher CPU, Microsoft Windows 3.1 or later, 4 MB RAM, CD-ROM drive, sound card, mouse, SVGA 256 colors, loudspeakers or headphones. (Macintosh version available). New York: Dorling Kindersley, 1994. $79.95. 5-8

Although the CD-ROM covers much more, it includes a "Who's Who" of scientists, their contributions, and information about their lives.

2497.   **Famous American Speeches: A Multimedia History, 1850 to the Present**. CD-ROM. System requirements: IBM or compatible PC: 386/33 MHz or higher CPU, 4 MB RAM, 8 MB recommended, Microsoft Windows 3.1 or later, CD-ROM drive, sound card, mouse, SVGA 256 color display, loudspeakers or headphones. Phoenix, AZ: Oryx Press, 1996. $129.95. 8 up

The speeches of influential people such as Presidents, government and military leaders, civil rights proponents, and others include such topics as civil rights, race relations, the Cold War, and women. Introductions and background place the speeches in context with pictures, audio, and video clips. The text can be searched in a variety of practical ways.

2498.   **Her Heritage: A Biographical Encyclopedia of American History**. CD-ROM. System requirements: Macintosh: 8 MB RAM, System 7.0 or higher, color monitor (256 colors minimum), CD-ROM drive. MS-DOS/MPC: 486SX/25 or higher CPU, 4 MB RAM, Microsoft Windows 3.1 or later, CD-ROM drive, sound card, mouse, SVGA 256 colors minimum, loudspeakers or headphones. Boston: Pilgrim New Media, 1994. $49.95. 4 up

Hundreds of American women listed in this program can be accessed alphabetically, by profession, or by topic. Biographical profiles; pseudonyms and pen names; awards, prizes, and fellowships; excerpts from diaries and memories; slides; and videos present these women. One may place bookmarks on specific women that permits a slide show of only those women who fit a particular topic. One may also make notes that will appear on the computer screen with a person. Video clips include a suffrage march at which Susan B. Anthony appeared.

2499.   **History Through Art: 20th Century**. CD-ROM. System requirements: IBM or compatible PC: 386/20 MHz or higher CPU, 4 MB RAM, 8 MB RAM recommended, Microsoft Windows 3.1 or later, CD-ROM drive, sound card, mouse, SVGA 256 color display, loudspeakers or headphones. Macintosh: 8 MB RAM, System 7.0, 13-inch monitor (256 colors), CD-ROM drive. Minneapolis, MN: Gareth Stevens, 1995. $75. 6 up

Urbanization changed artists' views in the twentieth century, and the development of photography reflects these changes. The modes available to study the art of the twentieth century on this CD-ROM are the Feature Presentation, Text, View, Index, Question, and Quiz.

2500.   **A House Divided: The Lincoln-Douglas Debates**. CD-ROM. System requirements: IBM or compatible PC: 486 or higher CPU, 8 MB RAM, Microsoft Windows 3.1 or later, CD-ROM drive, sound card, mouse, SVGA 256 color display, loudspeakers or headphones. Macintosh: 8 MB RAM, System 7.0 or later, 13-inch color monitor. San Mateo, CA: Grafica Multimedia, 1994. $49.95. 9-12

Video reenactments, photo essays, and artifacts are accessible to viewers through a replica of the historic home of William Reddick in Ottawa, Illinois. The "House Divided" speech and the debates are reenacted, and full-text scripts are printable. Also included are 29 songs and musical selections of the period along with an illustrated timeline, and comprehesive games.

2501.   **Ideas That Changed the World**. CD-ROM. System Requirements: IBM or compatible PC: 486/33 MHz or higher CPU, 8 MB RAM, Microsoft Windows 3.1 or later, CD-ROM drive, sound card, mouse, SVGA 256 color display with 512K RAM, loudspeakers or headphones. Macintosh: 5 MB RAM, System 7.0, 13-inch monitor (256 colors), CD-ROM drive. New York: Integrated Communications and Entertainment, 1996. $29.95. 9 up

Twenty-five video segments, thousands of illustrations and photographs, and animations discuss human inventions and discoveries. Hypertext links among biographies, timelines, ideas, and other topics give quick access to the almost limitless information in this program. Music and graphics complement the information. The general topics covered are "The First Inventions," "Improving Our Chance of Survival," "From Flint Tools to Production Lines," "Utilizing the Earth's Resources," "Using Natural and Artificial Materials," and "Shrinking the World." Inventions and architectural designs include such things as the wheel, computers, barrel vaulting, thatch, and myriad other items. Viewers can choose Who, What, and Where for information and for slide shows.

2502.   **Inside the White House**. CD-ROM. System requirements: IBM or compatible PC: 386SX or higher CPU, 4 MB RAM, CD-ROM drive, sound card, mouse, SVGA 256 color display, loudspeakers or headphones. New York: Chelsea House, 1995. $59.95. 3-12

Forty-one families have lived in the White House since the time of John Adams. This CD-ROM contains a virtual tour of the White House and of Air Force One in addition to biographies, photographs, and facts about families, pets, and other aspects of the presidency and of the people who lived in it.

2503.   **Landmark Documents in American History**. CD-ROM. System requirements: IBM or compatible PC: 486 or higher CPU, 8 MB RAM, Microsoft Windows 3.1 or later, CD-ROM drive, sound card, mouse, SVGA 256 color display, loudspeakers or headphones. New York: Facts on File, 1995. $295. 7 up

This database of primary source material contains Supreme Court case summaries, treaties, legislation, debates, and amendments. Supplementary materials include biographies, graphics, movies, and related documents. Keyword, subject, period, document type, people, country, and dates are some of the searches available.

2504.   **Lest We Forget: A History of the Holocaust**. CD-ROM. System requirements: IBM or compatible PC: 486/33 MHz or higher CPU, 8 MB RAM, Microsoft Windows 3.1 or later, CD-ROM drive, sound card, mouse, SVGA 256 color display, loudspeakers or headphones. Macintosh: 6 MB RAM, System 7.0, 13-inch monitor (256 colors), CD-ROM drive. Oak Harbor, WA: Logos Research, 1995. $59.95. 7 up

This view of Hitler's annihilation of European Jews uses video, audio, and animation. Sources include archival film footage, photographs, speeches, and text in four segments: "The Jewish People," "Hitler's Germany," "The Holocaust," and "The Aftermath."

2505.   **Life in Colonial America**. CD-ROM. System requirements: Macintosh: 2 MB RAM, System 7.0, 13-inch monitor (256 colors), CD-ROM drive. Fairfield, CT: Queue, 1996. $95. 9-12

The program contains four multimedia presentations with brief histories of the 13 colonies, a library of 34 primary documents, and maps and pictures. Among the focii are Jamestown, Plymouth, New York's New Amsterdam's manorial system, and Williamsburg. More than 30 maps supplement the information.

2506.   **Normandy: The Great Crusade**. CD-ROM. System requirements: IBM or compatible PC: 386SX or higher CPU, 4 MB RAM, CD-ROM drive, sound card, mouse, SVGA 256 color display, loudspeakers or headphones. Bethesda, MD: Discovery, 1994. $49.95. 10 up

Video, audio, radio clips, and still photographs describe the events of the Allied invasion of Normandy during World War II. Maps provide general reference, and supporting documents include profiles of war leaders, civilian letters, and diaries of enlisted men.

2507.   **One Tribe**. CD-ROM. System requirements: MS-DOS/MPC: 486/33 MHz or higher CPU, 4 MB RAM, Microsoft Windows 3.1 or later, CD-ROM drive, sound card, mouse, SVGA 256 colors minimum, loudspeakers or headphones. (Macintosh version available). Los Angeles: Virgin Sound and Vision, 1994. $24. 6-12

The video explores the diversity among humans. Twenty-five themed slide shows cover topics such as faces, rituals, and animals. Included is historical information about the evolution of humans in the areas of North America, Latin America, Europe, Asia, Australia, Africa, and the Arctic/Antarctic.

2508. **Our Times: The Multimedia Encyclopedia of the Twentieth Century**. CD-ROM. System requirements: IBM or compatible PC: 486/33 MHz or higher CPU, 4 MB RAM, Microsoft Windows 3.1 or later, CD-ROM drive, sound card, mouse, SVGA 256 color display, loudspeakers or headphones. Macintosh: 4 MB RAM, System 7.0, 13-inch monitor (256 colors), CD-ROM drive. Redwood City, CA: Vicarious, 1996. $69.95. 9 up

   With 52,000 articles, 2,500 images, and two hours of narration from James Earl Jones, the CD-ROM covers the people and events of the twentieth century. Special articles and commentary accompany the discussion on each decade.

2509. **Portraits of American Presidents**. CD-ROM. System requirements: MS-DOS/MPC: 486 or higher CPU, 4 MB RAM, Microsoft Windows 3.1 or later, hard drive with 3 MB free, CD-ROM drive, sound card, mouse, VGA or SVGA 256 colors minimum, loudspeakers or headphones. San Francisco: StarPress, $49.95. 5-12

   The Presidents are accessed through three chronological lists in categories A New Nation, National Struggle, and World Power. Each presidential entry includes general information about the man; subsequent screens highlight portions of the President's life.

2510. **Religions of the World**. CD-ROM. System requirements: IBM or compatible PC: 386SX or higher CPU, 4 MB RAM, Microsoft Windows 3.1 or later, CD-ROM drive, sound card, mouse, SVGA 256 color display, loudspeakers or headphones. Mississauga, Ontario, Canada: Mentorom Multimedia, 1996. $60. 7 up

   Eight major religions, their histories, and their beliefs compose this CD-ROM. The two key sections are "Aspects of Religion" and "Contemporary Issues." In "Aspects of Religion," the festivals, people, scriptures, worship, beliefs, artifacts, places, and communities of each religion appear. In "Contemporary Issues," the views of each faith on war, the environment, crime and punishment, social issues, and domestic issues such as race, marriage, abortion, and wealth can be compared. The eight religions are Buddhism, Christianity, Confucianism, Hinduism, Islam, Judaism, Shinto, and Sikhism. Photographs and text provide hypertext links among the topics presented.

2511. **Science Navigator**. CD-ROM. System requirements: IBM or compatible PC: 386 CPU, Microsoft Windows 3.0 or higher, 4 MB RAM, hard drive with 1.5 MB free, CD-ROM drive, VGA or SVGA. Macintosh: 4 MB RAM, System 7.0, CD-ROM drive, 13-inch monitor. New York: McGraw-Hill, 1995. $149.95. 7-12

   In addition to other searchable information, the CD-ROM includes biographical sketches from the *McGraw-Hill Dictionary of Scientic and Technical Terms*, 5th ed.

2512. **SkyTrip America**. CD-ROM. System requirements: IBM or compatible PC: 486/33 MHz or higher CPU, 8 MB RAM, Microsoft Windows 3.1 or later, CD-ROM drive, sound card, mouse, SVGA 256 color display, loudspeakers or headphones. New York: Discovery Channel Multimedia, 1996. $39.95. 4-8

   This CD-ROM approaches American history as historical fantasy by creating time-travel adventures. After choosing a vehicle in which to explore history, the viewer can write in a journal about places "visited" and create connections to video or other features of the program. Tours include Cultural Heritage, Democracy, A History of Immigration, Women in America, and Little Known Facts. Viewers can access information through a timeline and a glossary as well. Games include the Pony Express game, hangman trivia in a ghost town, and a Mining Maze game. Biographical profiles contain facts about such famous people as Jackie Robinson.

2513. **Stowaway! Stephen Biesty's Incredible Cross-Sections**. CD-ROM. System requirements: IBM or compatible PC: 386SX or higher CPU, 4 MB RAM, CD-ROM drive, sound card, mouse, SVGA 256 color display, loudspeakers or headphones. New York: Dorling Kindersley, 1994. $59.95. 6-12

   By clicking the mouse on any part of an eighteenth-century warship or one of its crew members, one gets information about the ship. After learning about many details of life on the ship, the viewer eventually finds the stowaway.

2514. **Time Almanac of the 20th Century**. CD-ROM. System requirements: MS-DOS/MPC: 386SX or higher CPU, 4 MB RAM, hard drive with 1.5 MB free, CD-ROM drive, sound card, mouse, SVGA 256 colors minimum, loudspeakers or headphones. Cambridge, MA: Softkey International, 1994. $29.95. 6-12

   Users can retrieve information from each decade from the first issue of *Time* magazine in the 1920s through 1993 using four different topics: Elections, Top Stories, Man of the Year, and Portraits. Events that occurred prior to *Time*'s publication are gleaned from other sources. Users can also gain information by keyword searches on medium and topic.

2515. **Total History**. 3 CD-ROMs. System requirements: IBM or compatible PC: 386SX or higher CPU, 4 MB RAM, CD-ROM drive, sound card, mouse, SVGA 256 color display, loudspeakers or headphones. New York: Bureau of Electronic Publishing–Chelsea House, 1995. $99.95. 4-12

   Multimedia U.S. History, *Multimedia World History* (same as *Teach Your Kids World History*), and *Multimedia World Factbook*, all available separately, comprise this package. *World History* provides information about books written throughout history by author or title, time periods, regions, and themes. There is a history of each day of the year as well as in other topics such as wars, technology, exploration, and maps. *U.S. History* presents American People, American Places, the Armed Forces, Exploring the Continent, General History, Science and Technology, Government, and Wars and Conflicts. Both programs provide slides and video clips. *World Factbook* allows access to facts in several ways such as searching topics, timelines, and glossaries. All keep a history of topics consulted during a session.

2516. **Voices of the 30s**. CD-ROM. System requirements: Macintosh: 4 MB RAM, System 7.0 or higher, color monitor, CD-ROM drive. Pleasantville, NY: Sunburst/Wings for Learning, 1994. $199. 5 up

This CD-ROM gives a strong and poignant view of the 1930s. The two categories of themes and resources include images and bibliography. A quotations menu has questions, comments about excerpts, and related topics from books. Six themes to examine are Government, Agriculture, Arts, Economics, History, and Ethics.

2517. **The War in Vietnam**. CD-ROM. System requirements: IBM or compatible PC: 486/33 MHz or higher CPU, 8 MB RAM, Microsoft Windows 3.1 or later, CD-ROM drive, sound card, mouse, SVGA 256 color display, loudspeakers or headphones. Macintosh: 6 MB RAM, System 7.0, 13-inch monitor (256 colors), CD-ROM drive. New York: Macmillan Digital, 1996. $49.99. 7 up

The CD begins with stories about the French in Indochina during the 1940s and concludes with the status of Vietnam in recent years. The articles, arranged chronologically, cover various time periods. Photographs, an hour of video, weapons, biographies, and much more information about this war give insight into its reasons for happening and the results of its unsettled ending.

2518. **The Way Things Work**. CD-ROM. System requirements: IBM or compatible PC: 386SX or higher CPU, 4 MB RAM, Microsoft Windows 3.1 or later, CD-ROM drive, sound card, mouse, SVGA 256 color display, loudspeakers or headphones. (Macintosh version available). New York: Dorling Kindersley, 1994. $79.95. 6-12

Animations containing a history timeline, brief biographies on inventors, specifications about the inventions, and scientific principles underlying them make this CD-ROM especially informative.

2519. **World War II, Global Conflict**. CD-ROM. System requirements: IBM or compatible PC: 386SX or higher CPU, 4 MB RAM, Microsoft Windows 3.1 or later, CD-ROM drive, sound card, mouse, SVGA 256 color display, loudspeakers or headphones. Mississauga, Ontario, Canada: Mentorom Multimedia, 1996. $60. 7 up

The CD-ROM presents the personalities and events of World War II through posters, cartoons, photographs, video, audio, and text-based documents from around the world. Two main areas are themes and case studies. The five main themes are African Americans, Propaganda, The Atom Bomb, D-Day, and The Holocaust. Each has a detailed analysis. Ten case studies look at battles, attitudes, and life at home through Pearl Harbor, GIs in Britain, the War in North Africa, The Blitz, Women at War, The Invasion of Normandy, Internment of Japanese Americans, Iwo Jima, Resistance, and The End of the War. Movement through the CD-ROM comes from a variety of hypertext links. *Best Educational CD-ROM International Emma Award* and *Nontheatrical Media Silver Apple*.

2520. **Wyatt Earp's Old West: A Multimedia Adventure in the Wild West**. CD-ROM. System requirements: IBM or compatible PC: 386SX required but 486/33 MHz or higher CPU recommended, 4 MB RAM, Microsoft Windows 3.1 or later, CD-ROM drive, sound card, mouse, SVGA 256 color display, loudspeakers or headphones. Macintosh: 4 MB RAM, System 7.0, 13-inch monitor (256 colors), CD-ROM drive. Danbury, CT: Grolier's Electronic Publishing, 1994. $49.95. 7-12

Video clips, computer graphics and animation, digitized photographs, and sound effects all contribute to a look at the American West around 1800. As George, a cowpoke, leads users through the town of Tombstone, Arizona, they may stop at the 48 locations around town and learn about life in each location.

VIDEOTAPES: AN ANNOTATED BIBLIOGRAPHY

2521. **Abigail Adams**. Videocassette. Color. 30 min. Schlessinger Video. Distr., Bala Cynwyd, PA: Library Video, 1995. $39.95. ISBN 1-57225-036-4. (American Women of Achievement). 7-12

The video asks why Abigail Adams (1744-1818) resisted conformity and if she could be considered a "rebel" as she helped shape the history and culture of the United States. Archival footage, sketches, photographs, recordings, interviews with historians, literary experts, and reenactments help to examine the impact of family; economic, social, and political circumstances; and her ability to empower herself.

2522. **Abraham Lincoln**. Videocassette. Color. 10 min. Princeton, NJ: Films for the Humanities and Sciences, 1989. $29.95. (Against the Odds). 4 up

Documentary footage, interviews, and animation help present this profile of Abraham Lincoln, the man who rose from clerking, rail splitting, and managing a mill to President of the United States.

2523. **Aces: A Story of the First Air War**. Videocassette. Color. 92 min. New York: National Film Board of Canada, 1994. $300. 9 up

The video tells the story of an airman during World War I using archival footage. *Cindy Silver Medal* and *Bronze Plaque, Columbus International Film & Video Festival.*

2524. **Across the Plains**. Videocassette. Color. 28 min. Princeton, NJ: Films for the Humanities and Sciences, 1992. $399 series; $109 ea. (The Oregon Trail). 5 up

Featuring oil paintings, black-and-white artwork, diary excerpts, and narration, this program traces the Oregon Trail from Independence, Missouri, to Fort Laramie, Wyoming. It also covers the problems of camping in the wilderness, the perils of accident, and encounters with Native Americans.

2525. **Act of War: The Overthrow of the Hawaiian Nation**. Videocassette. Color. 58 min. Honolulu, HI: Na Maka o ka Aina, 1993. $165. 9 up

In the 1890s, the United States acquired the Hawaiian Islands. The video intersperses commentary with readings, reenactments, photographs, and film footage to tell of the events that led to the invasion of Hawaii and its subsequent annexation. *Council on Nontheatrical Events, Golden Eagle; Bronze Plaque, Columbus International Film & Video Festival; Silver, Corporation for Public Broadcasting.*

2526. **Adelante Mujeres**. Videocassette. Color. 30 min. Windsor, CA: National Women's History Project, 1995. $125. 9 up

The video presents Mexican American Chicano women from the time of the Spanish conquest after Columbus's arrival into the 1990s.

2527. **African Americans**. Videocassette. Color. 30 min. Schlessinger Video. Distr., Bala Cynwyd, PA: Library Video, 1993. $39.95. (Multicultural Peoples of North America). 4-10

Based on the Chelsea House series Peoples of North America, the video highlights the African American culture. It gives reasons for African Americans being in America, explanations of customs and traditions, the history of their transition, and important leaders from the culture. Historians and sociologists discuss these aspects, and an African American family explains its cultural identity and shared memories.

2528. **African Americans Tell Their Story**. Videocassette. Color. 15 min. Chicago: Society for Visual Education, 1993. $89. 9 up

African Americans have had a major influence on this country's culture, history, and society. The program explores the roles of some of the leaders.

2529. **Airmen of World War II**. Videocassette. Color. 50 min. Bethesda, MD: Atlas Video, 1991. $99.95 set; $19.95 ea. (War Stories). 7 up
   On-camera interviews with veteran pilots of World War II allow them to tell about their perilous missions and what being a combat aviator was like.

2530. **Alexander Graham Bell: The Voice Heard Round the World**. Videocassette. Color. 25 min. Niles, IL: Aims Media, 1984. $49.95. (American Lifestyle). 4-9
   The video analyzes Bell's life and his achievements, including the invention of the telephone.

2531. **Alice Paul: We Were Arrested of Course!** Videocassette. Color. 25 min. Take One. Distr., New York: EPH, 1995. $79.95. 7 up
   Alice Paul and a group of women suffragists were thrown into prison, forcibly fed, and confined to a psychiatric ward when they picketed the White House in 1916. Reenactments and photographs show what the National Women's Party endured to force the President and the U.S. Congress to confront the issue of women's suffrage.

2532. **All Aboard for Philadelphia!** Videocassette. Color and B&W. 35 min. Philadelphia, PA: Historical Society of Pennsylvania, 1995. $21.95. 6 up
   The video gives a history of Philadelphia at the turn of the twentieth century by taking viewers on a trolley car with six stops. It shows the industrial area, the center city, industrial neighborhoods, streetcar and railroad suburbs, and the reform efforts to improve the inner city.

2533. **All the Unsung Heroes: The Story of the Vietnam Veterans Memorial**. Videocassette. Color. 30 min. Annandale, VA: Heritage America Group, 1992. $24.95. 7 up
   The Vietnam Memorial, often an emotional experience for its visitors, was a difficult memorial to erect. Maya Ying Lan's design caused controversy, but the structure has proven to be extraordinarily effective as people bring momentoes to place near the name of persons lost in Vietnam.

2534. **Amelia Earhart**. Videocassette. Color. 30 min. Schlessinger Video. Distr., Bala Cynwyd, PA: Library Video, 1995. $39.95. ISBN 1-57225-042-9. (American Women of Achievement). 7-12
   The video asks why Amelia Earhart (1897?-1937) resisted conformity and if she could be considered a "rebel" as she helped shape the history and culture of the United States. Archival footage, sketches, photographs, recordings, interviews with historians, literary experts, and reenactments help to examine the impact of family; economic, social, and political circumstances; and her ability to empower herself.

2535. **Amelia Earhart**. Videocassette. Color. 57 min. Alexandria, VA: PBS Video, 1993. $69.95. (The American Experience). 9 up
   Actress Kathy Bates narrates this video showing how Earhart (1897?-1937) and her husband, G. P. Putnam, tried to promote opportunities for her. Perhaps her mediocre flying skills and lack of concern about flight plans contributed to her failed last flight. *Young Adult Library Services Association Selected Film.*

2536. **America at War: The Undersea Stranglers**. Videocassette. Color. 23 min. Deerfield, IL: Coronet/MTI, 1990. $250. 9 up
   Submarines have been both tactical and strategic weapons since the Civil War, and actual battle footage of the world wars shows their effectiveness as well as their need for defense against antisubmarine warfare.

2537. **America in Asia**. Videocassette. Color. 60 min. Pacific Basin Institute. Distr., Washington, DC: Annenberg/CPB, 1992. $275 series; $29.95 ea. (Pacific Century). 11 up
   This series looks at 150 years of the Pacific regions' political and economic development with maps, charts, archival footage, and interviews with journalists and historians. It examines each country's relationship with the United States.

2538. **America in the Thirties: Depression and Optimism**. Videocassette. Color. 30 min. Princeton, NJ: Films for the Humanities and Sciences, 1990. $149. (World of the 30's). 9 up
   In the 1930s, America was both wonderful and horrible. The video contrasts the two sides through old movies, newsreels, photographs, and home movies. Events such as Hoovervilles, the Bonus Army, the Dust Bowl, trade union strikes, the collapse of the worldwide ecomony, and rearmament balance garden parties, music, fashion shows, prohibition, train travel, and new inventions show the times.

2539. **The American Constitution: The Ghosts of '87**. Videocassette. Color. 59 min. The Constitution Project. Chatsworth, CA: Aims Media, 1992. $395. 9 up

Actor Cliff Robertson portrays the personalities of several of the 55 delegates who met in Pennsylvania during 1787 to write the new Constitution of the United States as they grappled with the problems of representation, executive structure and election, slavery, and the Bill of Rights. The figures he represents in the video are George Washington, Alexander Hamilton, James Madison, Gouverneur Morris, Edmond Randolph, William Patterson, James Wilson, Benjamin Franklin, Roger Sherman, and George Mason.

2540. **American Constitution: The Road to Runnymede**. Videocassette. Color. 58 min. The Constitution Project. Chatsworth, CA: Aims Media, 1992. $395. 7 up

Actor Christopher Reeve presents the English roots of the U.S. Constitution with dramatic recreations about the six centuries from the Magna Carta in 1215 to the Philadelphia Convention in 1787. He discusses the Stuart kings, Parliament, Petition of Rights, John Locke, social contracts, English Bill of Rights, divine right, charters, Massachusetts Body of Liberties, French and Indian War, Virigina Stamp Act Resolves, George Mason, Patrick Henry, Bill of Rights, Articles of Confederation, and James Madison. *Columbus International Film & Video Festival, First Place Chris Award; Philadelphia International Film Festival, Silver Award; American Bar Association, Silver Gavel.*

2541. **American Consumerism (1890-1930)**. Videocassette. Color. 30 min. Schlessinger Video. Distr., Bala Cynwyd, PA: Library Video, 1995. $799 series; $39.95 ea. (United States History Video). 5-9

Dramatic readings and performances bring important events and historical figures together in this video that shows how Americans spent their money from 1890 to 1930.

2542. **The American Experience: Insanity on Trial**. Videocassette. Color. 58 min. WGBH, WNET, and KCET. Distr., Alexandria, VA: PBS Video, 1990. $59.95. 9 up

In 1880, James Garfield became a compromise candidate for President when Republicans could not agree between James G. Blaine, their most prominent leader, and Ulysses S. Grant, who was seeking a third term. The "Stalwarts," original supporters of Grant, finally nominated Garfield on the 36th ballot. Among the petitioners for public office was Gharles Guiteau, a lawyer from the Stalwart faction, who wanted to be in the French Consulate. He was denied, and when a non-Stalwart was appointed, Guiteau soon after, on July 2, shot Garfield twice. His trial lasted 72 days and raised the question of insanity as a legal defense. The video investigates this 72-day trial and the use of insanity as a legal defense since Guiteau said he heard either God or Satan's voice before he shot.

2543. **The American Experience: Lindbergh**. Videocassette. Color. 58 min. WGBH, WNET, and KCET. Distr., Alexandria, VA: PBS Video, 1990. $59.95. 9 up

The public made a hero out of Charles Lindbergh after he flew across the Atlantic alone in 1927, but he fell from grace because he approved of the Nazi Luftwaffe and America First activities. After the kidnapping and murder of his infant son, he left the country. Roosevelt writhdrew his military commission for World War II, but in his later years, as Lindbergh worked for conservation and the enviornment, he regained the admiration of the public.

2544. **The American Experience: The Iron Road**. Videocassette. Color. 59 min. WGBH, WNET, and KCET. Distr., Alexandria, VA: PBS Video, 1990. $59.95. 9 up

In its examination of the national dream for building the first transcontinental railroad, this video explains the startling difficulty of reaching that achievement in a country divided by the impending Civil War. Central to the achievement of the railroad were the contributions of Chinese and European immigrants and the relations with Native Americans.

2545. **American Fever**. Videocassette. Color. 15 min. Madison, WI: Her Own Words, 1994. $95. ISBN 1-877933-44-9. 6 up

A female narrator posing as Christie Vold prepares to emigrate from Norway to America in the nineteenth century. The photographs show her at home while packing garments, household items, and food. The video also records the mixed feelings that she has about leaving her home to join her fiancé, who has already left.

2546. **American Impressionists and Realists: In Search of the New**. Videocassette. Color. 22 min. Mayah Productions. Distr., Berkeley, CA: University of California Extension Center, 1995. $175. 6-12

Between the Civil War and World War I, the two groups of artists who influenced the art world were the Impressionists and the Realists. Archival film footage, photographs, and paintings document this period of American history.

2547. **American Independence 1776**. Videocassette. Color. 28 min. University of Warwick. Distr., Chicago: Encyclopaedia Britannica, 1990. $200. 7 up

Eighteenth-century art and buildings extant in Philadelphia illustrate the political influence of the city and two men, Thomas Jefferson and Thomas Paine. Jefferson saw the country as equal to any other country, and Paine saw humans as equal to each other; these complementary ideas strengthened the independence movement that the video so ably presents.

2548. **The American Republic**. Videocassettte. Color. 30 min. WGBH Educational Foundation. Distr., Washington, DC: Annenberg/CPB. 1989. $650 set; $29.95 ea. (The Western Tradition, Program 38). 11 up

The professor presenting this topic projects his excitement for history. He provides insight into the people, politics, thoughts, and events that have shaped western society. Resources from the Metropolitan Museum of Art illustrate the creation of the new government of the United States.

2549. **The American Revolution**. Videocassette. Color. 30 min. Schlessinger Video. Distr., Bala Cynwyd, PA: Library Video, 1995. $799 series; $39.95 ea. (United States History Video). 5-9

Dramatic readings and performances bring the important events and historical figures of the eighteenth century together in this video.

2550. **The American Revolution**. Videocassettte. Color. 30 min. WGBH Educational Foundation. Distr. Washington, DC: Annenberg/CPB. 1989. $650 set; $29.95 ea. (The Western Tradition, Program 37). 11 up

The professor presenting this topic projects his excitement for history. He provides insight into the people, politics, thoughts, and events that have shaped western society. Resources from the Metropolitan Museum of Art illustrate the beginnings of discontent and the battle over freedom from England.

2551. **America's Great Indian Leaders**. Videocassette. Color. 65 min. Media Process Group. Distr., Chicago: Questar Video, 1994. $29.95. ISBN 1-56855-028-6. 7 up

Crazy Horse of the Lakota Sioux, Chief Joseph of the Nez Percé, Geronimo of the Apache, and Quanah Parker, son of a white mother and her Indian captor, all made important contributions to their tribes. Live action, historic footage, photographs, and drawings place these men in their proper perspectives.

2552. **America's Great Indian Nations**. Videocassette. Color. 65 min. Media Process Group. Distr., Chicago: Questar, 1994. $29.95. ISBN 1-56855-058-8. 7 up

The history of America is inextricably tied to the history of the American Indian. The video looks at the achievements and heartbreaks of six Indian nations. These are the Iroquois in the Northeast, whose rules of governance influenced the writers of the Constitution; the Seminoles in Florida; the Shawnee of the Ohio River Valley led by Chief Tecumseh; the Navaho in the Southwest; the Cheyenne; and the Lakota, who defeated Custer at Little Big Horn.

2553. **America's Political Parties: The Democratic Party**. Videocassette. Color. 58 min. Manifold Productions. Chatsworth, CA: Aims Media, 1991. $129.95. 7 up

In clarifying what being "democratic" means, the video starts with the election of John F. Kennedy to the presidency. During the 1960s, the party wanted a world role for American policy, a strong economic system, and social values that extended liberty. By 1968, the party faced a fractious convention, the Vietnam War, and the antiwar movement. Jimmy Carter's presidency faced gas shortages, a hostage crisis, and inflation. In the 1980s, the Democrats gained the reputation of representing special interests rather than mainstream voters. Persons who comment on camera are Gary Hart, George McGovern, Tom Hayden, Jeanne Kirkpatrick, Eugene McCarthy, Walter Mondale, Geraldine Ferraro, and Michael Dukakis. *Houston International Film & Video Festival, Silver Award; American Film & Video Festival, Finalist.*

2554. **America's Political Parties: The Republican Party**. Videocassette. Color. 52 min. Manifold Productions. Distr., Chatsworth, CA: Aims Media, 1991. $129.95. 7 up

The development within the Republican Party between 1960 and 1988 led to the elections of Nixon, Reagan, and Bush to the presidency. A rivalry within the party existed between the Midwest (conservative) wing and the eastern (establishment) faction. The video reviews the behind-the-scene strategies at the National Conventions in 1960 for Nixon's nomination, 1964 with Barry Goldwater's nomination, 1968 with Nixon again, and on through 1988. Along with presidential highlights are interviews with Barry Goldwater, Newt Gingrich, William Bennett, and Lee Atwater. *International Film & Video Festival, Chris Plaque; Houston International Film & Video Festival, Bronze Award; International Film & TV Festival of New York, Finalist.*

2555. **America's Relations with Eastern Europe**. Videocassette. Color. 51 min. Washington, DC: Global View, 1990. $50. (Eastern Europe Breaking with the Past). 9 up

This video gives an overview of America's historical relationship with Eastern Europe. It contains Hungarian film that uses animation and archival footage to show what immigration was like to the United States, a Cold War documentary hosted by Ronald Reagan, and a satire of the Gorbachev-Reagan summit.

2556. **America's Transcontinental Railroad**. Videocassette. Color. 27 min. Entertainment Group. Distr., Irwindale, CA: Barr Media, 1994. $395. ISBN 0-7823-0562-8. 5-11

Dramatic reenactments, period photography, narrative, modern footage, and the music and art of the 1800s tell the story of the building of the transcontinental railway. At first thwarted by congressional debates, it succeeded with the toil of immigrants who connected the two coasts of the country on May 10, 1869, in Promontory, Utah. *Silver Apple, New England Film & Video Festival.*

2557. **America's Westward Expansion**. Videocassette. Color. 30 min. Madison, WI: Knowledge Unlimited, 1996. $59.95. ISBN 1-55933-197-6. 6 up

Contemporary and archival photographs, graphics, and other aspects help to show the development of the West. Among the topics covered in the brief presentation are the Northwest Ordinance, Lewis and Clark, Sacajawea, the Oregon Trail, Manifest Destiny, and the Mexican War. It begins in 1783 and continues to 1861 and the Civil War.

2558. **The Amish**. Videocassette. Color. 30 min. Schlessinger Video. Distr., Bala Cynwyd, PA: Library Video, 1993. $39.95. (Multicultural Peoples of North America). 4-10

Based on the Chelsea House series Peoples of North America, this video highlights the Amish culture. It gives reasons for the Amish immigration to America, explanations of customs and traditions, the history of their transition, and important leaders from the culture. Historians and sociologists discuss these aspects, and an Amish family explains its cultural identity, shared memories, and reasons for immigration.

2559. **Anzio and the Italian Campaign**. Videocassette. Color and B&W. 45 min. Bethesda, MD: Acorn Media, 1989. $19.95. (V for Victory). 7 up

Newsreel footage and stories from the homefront give information about World War II with features being a discussion of General Patton's successful campaign in Sicily and the bloody Anzio battle.

2560. **The Apache**. Videocassette. Color. 30 min. Schlessinger Video. Distr., Bala Cynwyd, PA: Library Video, 1993. $39.95. ISBN 1-879151-52-9. (Indians of North America). 4-10

Based on Chelsea House's Indians of North America series, the video tells the history and culture of the Apaches prior to the arrival of the Europeans and after the Spanish conquest. Interviews with leaders, historians, and teachers along with live-action footage show the real Apache tribe, located in the southwest United States and northern Mexico. *Finalist, Telly.*

2561. **Arab Americans**. Videocassette. Color. 30 min. Schlessinger Video. Distr., Bala Cynwyd, PA: Library Video, 1993. $39.95. (Multicultural Peoples of North America). 4-10

Based on the Chelsea House series Peoples of North America, the video highlights the Arab culture. It gives reasons for Arab immigration to America, explanations of customs and traditions, the history of their transition, and important leaders from the culture. Historians and sociologists discuss these aspects, and an Arab family explains its cultural identity, shared memories, and reasons for immigration.

2562. **Are We Winning Mommy? America and the Cold War**. Videocassette. Color. 87 min. Cine Information. New York: Cinema Guild, 1990. $395. 10 up

Although produced in 1986, the film gives a good overview of the undercurrents in the Cold War with news and film clips, historical footage, interviews, and debates. Six parts of the documentary trace the events during this period. They are "Grand Alliance," "Uneasy Peace," "Containing the Threat," "Red Menace," "Cold Warriors," and "No Place to Hide."

2563. **Arsenal of Democracy**. Videocassette. Color. 60 min. Blackside. Distr., Alexandria, VA: PBS Video, 1993. $79.95. ISBN 0-7936-1043-5. (The Great Depression). 8-12

When World War II broke out in Europe in 1939, it helped to end the Great Depression. In the United States, people still struggled. Although Franklin Delano Roosevelt's New Deal helped with the crisis, not until 1941, when the United States entered the war, did the Depression end. *Silver Apple, New England Film & Video Festival.*

2564. **As Seen By Both Sides: American and Vietnamese Artists Look at the War**. Videocassette. Color. 58 min. New York: Cinema Guild, 1995. $350. 10 up

By blending archival footage from the Vietnam War with artwork and interviews with people from different areas, the film's creators show the need to create beauty out of suffering. Words from artists and veterans on both sides of the war help to give a balanced view.

2565. **As the Wind Rocks the Wagon: An American Odyssey**. Videocassette. Color. 52 min. New York: APL Educational Video, 1990. $99.95. 7 up

Amy Warner performs a one-woman play in which she presents excerpts from the diaries of pioneer women. The scenes reveal details about the frontier life from 25 different diaries, covering the departure, the journey, and the arrival in Oregon or California.

2566. **At the River I Stand**. Videocassette. Color. 58 min. San Francisco: California Newsreel, 1994. $49. ISBN 1-57254-002-8. 9 up

Archival photographs and film transplant viewers to Memphis, Tennessee, in 1968, to the sanitation workers' strike where Martin Luther King, Jr. was assassinated. By telling both state and national events, the video attempts to draw a link between economics and the progress of the Civil Rights movement. *Council on Nontheatrical Events, Golden Eagle: Best Documentary, OAH.*

2567. **The Atlantic Coast of Winslow Homer**. Videocassette. Color. 10 min. Cos Cob, CT: Double Diamond, 1995. $29. 7 up

Winslow Homer painted pictures of the people who made their living by fishing the Atlantic Coast during the later half of the nineteenth century.

B

2568. **Balancing the Budget**. Videocassette. Color. 30 min. Toronto: TV Ontario, 1990. $499 series; $99 ea. (Ancient Civilizations). 6 up

Part of a series examining the origins of civilizations, the video investigates the human needs to search for food, to have security, and to be creative. This video looks at the discovery of agriculture and the domestication of animals as well as the rise of economics based on trade in Egypt.

2569. **Barnum's Big Top**. Videocassette. Color. 60 min. WGBH, WNET, and KCET. Distr., Alexandria, VA: PBS Video, 1992. $59.95. (The American Experience). 7 up

Archival film, photographs, journal entries, and interviews tell the story of P. T. Barnum, the founder of the "Greatest Show on Earth." This man converted the circus to its three-ring format in the early twentieth century. Additional discussion concerns the transient lives of circus performers.

2570. **The Battle of the Bulge and the Drive to the Rhine**. Videocassette. Color and B&W. 45 min. Bethesda, MD: Acorn Media, 1989. $19.95. (V for Victory). 7 up

In World War II, Hitler's last effort was a strike at the Allies in the Belgium forests. Newsreel footage and stories from the homefront present this attempt and the 101st Airborne at Bastogne as well as the seizure of the Remagan bridge.

2571. **The Battle of Yorktown: 1781**. Videocassette. Color. 34.49 min. Psthe-Cinema. Distr., Princeton, NJ: Films for the Humanities and Sciences, 1991. $149. 7 up

Live action reenactments, art reproductions, and contemporary film of historic places give an overview of the American Revolution rather than merely the last battle at Yorktown. Background information on settlers and the events leading to the declaration of war give a firm basis as to why the revolution occurred.

2572. **Beginnings**. Videocassette. Color. 29 min. Princeton, NJ: Films for the Humanities and Sciences, 1993. $399 series; $109 ea. (The Oregon Trail). 5 up

The history of the Oregon Trail shows how propaganda moved people to walk 2,000 miles into the unknown for a political agenda. Letters and notes from travelers enhance this first in a series of four on the Oregon Trail.

2573. **Bill of Rights Today: The 4th Amendment**. Videocassette. Color. 18 min. Focus. Distr., Irwindale, CA: Barr Media, 1992. $100. 9-12

The dramatization of a search and seizure followed by a court case allows a judge to tell the history of the Fourth Amendment and how recent court cases interpret its meaning.

2574. **Birth of a Community: Jews and the Gold Rush**. Videocassette. Color. 40 min. Magnes Museum Western Jewish History Center. Distr., Berkeley, CA: University of California Extension Center, 1995. $175. 4-12

Jewish pioneers came to California during the gold rush period around 1849. Archival photographs, vocal re-creations, old film footage, and historical commentary tell why they came and their way of life after they arrived.

2575. **Black Is My Color: The African American Experience**. Videocassette. Color. 15 min. Raleigh, NC: Rainbow Educational, 1991. $89. 4-8

Both Black and white children discuss the topics of slavery, abolitionism, Civil War, Reconstruction, segregation, and civil rights as they re-create the problems in America during the nineteenth and twentieth centuries.

2576. **The Black West**. Videocassette. Color. 24 min. Grand Rapids, MI: All Media Productions, 1992. $99. 5 up

Artwork and upbeat music provide background for information about the roles of Blacks in the settlement of the West. Among those presented who made a difference are a woman, a lawman, fur traders, explorers, cowboys, outlaws, and swindlers.

2577. **Blind Tom**. Videocassette. Color. 30 min. KCET and BEEM Foundation. Distr., Irwindale, CA: Barr Media, 1991. $75. 4-9

Born into slavery in 1849, Thomas Bethune, known as "Blind Tom," had an extraordinary ability at an early age to memorize music and play the piano. His music saved him from some of the unpleasantness of slave life, but it also unexpectedly bound him to his master after slaves were freed.

2578. **Blue Water: Great Naval Traditions**. Videocassette. Color. 50 min. Adler Video. Distr., Bethesda, MD: Acorn Media, 1994. $19.95. 11 up

Military rituals today may be used for show, but they have reasons for being. Colors paraded in front of soldiers each night reminded them of the flags they needed to follow in battle. The video includes the Ceremony of the Keys, the world's oldest ceremony continuously observed during which the Tower of London is locked for the night. Other rituals are the Royal Tournament, the Drumhead Services, and Trooping the Color.

2579. **Booker T. Washington**. Videocassette. Color. 30 min. Schlesinger Video. Distr., Bala Cynwyd, PA: Library Video, 1992. $39.95. (Black Americans of Achievement). 7 up

A complement to the Chelsea House series Black Americans of Achievement, the video introduces Booker T. Washington (1856-1915). Historians and other experts comment on his achievements using photos, old film footage, and modern live action for illustration.

2580. **Borderlines**. Videocassette. Color. 48 min. New York: Cinema Guild, 1994. $295. 9 up

A video drama of historical fiction presents Tennessee in the late 1930s when moonshine and borderline feuds regularly led to violence and murder. A teacher comes into the community, and although the situation appalls her, she can do nothing to break the cycle.

2581. **Breaking Barriers: A History of the Status of Women and the Role of the United Nations**. Videocassette. Color and B&W. 30 min. Red Bank, NJ: Lasch Media, 1994. $89.95. 9 up

With historical black-and-white film, the video examines the status of women according to political, religious, and economic perspectives, from ancient times to the present showing that a gender bias exists in all world religions.

2582. **Brother Minister: The Assassination of Malcolm X**. Videocassette. B&W. 115 min. Agoura Hills, CA: Millennium Entertainment, 1994. $89.95. 11 up

This documentary, divided into seven chapters, includes a review of Islam and Malcolm X's connection to it. Archival footage of Malcolm X and interviews with people he knew as well as a re-creation of his assassination highlight the film.

2583. **The Buffalo Soldiers**. Videocassette. Color. 47 min. Encino, CA: Bill Armstrong Productions, 1992. $19.95. 7 up

Rare photographs, historic film footage, narration, and interviews tell the story of the 9th and 10th regiments of Black soldiers who fought from 1867 to 1891 to bring order to the West and to Cuba.

2584. **Buffalo Soldiers: Black Soldiers in the Frontier Army**. Videocassette. Color. 30 min. Ft. Collins, CO: Old Army Press, 1996. $24.95. 9 up

Using the Colorado Historical Society's recent exhibit on the Buffalo Soldiers, Bill Gwaltney, a descendant of two of the soldiers, tells their story. As the video goes to each section of the exhibit, he describes its meaning with anecdotes and information.

2585. **Building the American Dream: Levittown, NY**. Videocassette. Color and B&W. 60 min. New York: Cinema Guild, 1994. $350. 9 up

From 1947 until 1951, William Levitt built more than 17,400 houses in Long Island and called the development Levittown. Each house helped people to reach their American dream of owning a house. This documentary, with interviews of and home movies about those who lived in Levitttown, begins at the end of World War II.

$$\boxed{C}$$

2586. **California Gold: Stories of Two Women**. Videocassette. Color. 20 min. Irwindale, CA: Barr Media, 1985. $75. 7 up

Two women remember California life when people hurried west in search of gold during the 1840s and 1850s.

2587. **Candlemaking**. Videocassette. Color. 11 min. Irwindale, CA: Barr Media, 1992. $60. (American History). 4-9

Live action, reenactments, maps, and graphics explain the pioneer process of candle making.

2588. **Causes of Revolt**. Videocassette. Color. 30 min. Schlessinger Video. Distr., Bala Cynwyd, PA: Library Video, 1995. $799 series; $39.95 ea. (United States History Video). 5-9

Dramatic readings and performances bring important events and historical figures together in this video about the beginnings of the American Revolution.

2589. **Causes of the Civil War**. Videocassette. Color. 30 min. Schlessinger Video. Distr., Bala Cynwyd, PA: Library Video, 1995. $799 series; $39.95 ea. (United States History Video). 5-9

Dramatic readings and performances bring important events and historical figures together in this video discussing the reasons behind the American Civil War.

2590. **Cesar Chavez**. Videocassette. Color. 30 min. Schlessinger Video. Distr., Bala Cynwyd, PA: Library Video, 1994. $39.95. (Hispanic and Latin American Heritage). 7-12

Biographical information and an overview of Cesar Chavez's (1927-1993) achievements show how important his commitment to the betterment of conditions for migrant workers has been in the twentieth century.

2591. **Changing Faces of Our Land: Once Upon a Time on the Farm**. Videocassette. Color. 28 min. Santa Monica, CA: Pyramid, 1993. $205. 7 up

A photo documentary, this video tells the story of farm life between 1945 and 1975, based on the book, *Successful Farming,* by Joe Monroe. Divided into segments on livestock, technology, and people, it shows a way of life that has almost disappeared since the farm population has dropped from almost 6 million to 2 million. *Council on Nontheatrical Events, Golden Eagle.*

2592. **Charles Garry: Street Fighter in the Courtroom**. Videocassette. Color. 58 min. San Diego, CA: Media Guild, 1992. $295. 5 up

Charles Garry grew up poor in California during the early 1900s where he faced prejudice as an Armenian immigrant. He became a lawyer, and his notable cases have included his defenses of the Chicago Seven and of Black Panthers Huey Newton and Bobby Seale.

2593. **Charles M. Russell, Artist of the Old West**. Videocassette. Color. 33 min. High Hopes. Distr., Chatsworth, CA: Aims Media, 1995. $195. ISBN 0-8068-8734-6. 7 up

After Charles Russell left St. Louis for Montana, he began to live his dream by becoming a cowboy. He preserved the life of the cowboy through his paintings and sculptures. The video includes commentary from historians, art experts, excerpts from Russell's letters, and his work. A background of Native American flute music helps to re-create the time and place in which he lived.

2594. **The Cherokee**. Videocassette. Color. 30 min. Schlessinger Video. Distr., Bala Cynwyd, PA: Library Video, 1993. $39.95. (Indians of North America). 4-10

This video, using photographs and film footage, focuses on the unique history of the Cherokee, who lived in the South and were relocated to Oklahoma during the early half of the nineteenth century. It also discusses the government, the spiritual, the mythical, and the role of women in this Native American tribe.

2595. **The Cheyenne**. Videocassette. Color. 30 min. Schlessinger Video. Distr., Bala Cynwyd, PA: Library Video, 1993. $39.95. (Indians of North America). 4-10

The video focuses on the unique history of the Cheyenne using photographs and film footage. It also discusses the government, the spiritual, the mythical, and the role of women.

2596. **The Chinook**. Videocassette. Color. 30 min. Schlessinger Video. Distr., Bala Cynwyd, PA: Library Video, 1994. $39.95. (Indians of North America). 4-10

The Chinook inhabited the Columbia River valley, where they traded widely throughout the Pacific Northwest. The video focuses on the unique history of the Chinook using photographs and film footage. It also discusses the government, the spiritual, the mythical, and the role of women.

2597. **Choosing a President**. 2 Videocassettes. Color. 17-25 min. ea. Madison, WI: Knowledge Unlimited, 1995. $59.99 ea. 6 up

The two cassettes are *Electing a President* and *The Presidency*. The first shows the process by which a person becomes President, including the electoral college, political parties, the voting process, campaigning, and the general election. The second discusses the roles of the President and the presidential powers granted in the Constitution.

2598. **The Chumash of California, A Docent's Story, Parts 1 & 2**. Videocassette. Color. 30 min. Derry, NH: Chip Taylor Communications, 1994. $199. 7 up

Filmed at the Native American Hall of the Natural History Museum in Los Angeles, California, this video presents docent and storyteller Sylvia Kahn's history of the Chumash people, which she illustrates using artifacts from the museum. She explains how they lived and the importance of nature in their lives.

2599. **The Civil War**. Videocassette. Color. 150 min. Alexandria, VA: PBS Video, 1994. $395. 9 up

The video uses archival photographs and witness accounts and covers five topics of importance in the war with the first one being slavery.

2600. **The Civil War, Episode 1: The Cause—1861**. Videocassette. Color. 99 min. Alexandria, VA: PBS Video, 1990. $79.95. 8 up

The first episode of the Ken Burns series focuses on the causes of the Civil War beginning with the election of Lincoln as President, then John Brown's raid on Harpers Ferry, and the choice to fire on Fort Sumter. *Emmy Nomination*.

2601. **The Civil War, Episode 2: A Very Bloody Affair—1862**. Videocassette. Color. 69 min. Alexandria, VA: PBS Video, 1990. $59.95. 8 up

This segment presents an overview of the staggering cost in human life of the War Between the States. *Emmy Nomination*.

2602. **The Civil War, Episode 3: Forever Free—1862**. Videocassette. Color. 76 min. Alexandria, VA: PBS Video, 1990. $59.95. 8 up

The third episode of the Civil War miniseries addresses Antietam. It also discusses the strategy planned for the Confederates by Robert E. Lee and Stonewall Jackson. Lincoln's decision to free the slaves complicates everything. *Emmy Nomination*.

2603. **The Civil War, Episode 4: Simply Murder—1863**. Videocassette. Color. 62 min. Alexandria,VA: PBS Video, 1990. $59.95. 8 up

The Union forces in this segment lose horribly at Fredericksburg, Virginia. But Lee loses Stonewall Jackson, a distressing situation for the Confederate army. *Emmy Nomination*.

2604. **The Civil War, Episode 5: The Universe of Battle—1863**. Videocassette. Color. 95 min. Alexandria, VA: PBS Video, 1990. $79.95. 8 up

Burns presents the battle at Gettysburg, Pennsylvania. During these three days in July 1863, more than 150,000 Americans lost their lives. *Emmy Nomination*.

2605. **The Civil War, Episode 6: Valley of the Shadow of Death—1864**. Videocassette. Color. 70 min. Alexandria, VA: PBS Video, 1990. $59.95. 8 up

Burns profiles the leaders in the War Between the States, Ulysses S. Grant and Robert E. Lee, and presents Sherman's assault on Atlanta. *Emmy Nomination*.

2606. **The Civil War, Episode 7: Most Hallowed Ground—1864**. Videocassette. Color. 72 min. Alexandria, VA: PBS Video, 1990. $59.95. 8 up

In 1864, Lincoln was reelected to the presidency. In this segment, the Union turns General Lee's mansion and grounds into the Arlington National Cemetery. *Emmy Nomination*.

2607. **The Civil War, Episode 8: War Is All Hell—1865**. Videocassette. Color. 69 min. Alexandria, VA: PBS Video, 1990. $59.95. 8 up

This segment shows Sherman's march to the sea from Atlanta and Lee's surrender to Grant, which finally stopped the destruction. *Emmy Nomination.*

2608. **The Civil War, Episode 9: The Better Angels of Our Nature—1865**. Videocassette. Color. 68 min. Alexandria, VA: PBS Video, 1990. $59.95. 8 up

The final episode of this Civil War miniseries examines Lincoln's assassination and reviews the character traits of the central participants in the devastation. *Emmy Nomination.*

2609. **Civil War Trains**. Videocassette. Color. 50 min. RPM Productions. Distr., Barrington, IL: Superior Productions, 1995. $29.95. 7 up

The United States Military Railroad played an important part in winning the Civil War.

2610. **Clara Barton**. Videocassette. Color. 30 min. Schlessinger Video. Distr., Bala Cynwyd, PA: Library Video, 1995. $39.95. ISBN 1-57225-040-2. (American Women of Achievement). 7-12

The video asks why Clara Barton (1821-1912) resisted conformity and if she could be considered a "rebel" as she helped shape the history and culture of the United States. Archival footage, sketches, photographs, recordings, interviews with historians, literary experts, and reenactments help to examine the impact of family; economic, social, and political circumstances; and her ability to empower herself.

2611. **The Cold War**. Videocassette. Color. 30 min. WGBH Educational Foundation. Distr., Washington, DC: Annenberg/CPB, 1989. $650 set; $29.95 ea. (The Western Tradition, Program 49). 11 up

The professor presenting this topic projects his excitement for history. He provides insight into the people, politics, thoughts, and events that have shaped western society. Resources from the Metropolitan Museum of Art illustrate the escalation of ill will between fascist and democratic countries.

2612. **The Cold War, (Part 3)**. Videocassette. Color. 30 min. Meridian Communications. Distr., Van Nuys, CA: Churchill Media, 1993. $250. ISBN 0-7932-3085-3. (The Torn Iron Curtain). 7 up

An overview of modern Russian history including the Revolution and the rise of Communism, the fall of Czar Nicholas II, World War I, World War II, Stalin, Krushchev, and Brezhnev leads to an explanation of how the Cold War developed and the interaction between the Soviet Union and the United States.

2613. **Colonial Williamsburg**. Videocassette. Color. 30 min. Glastonbury, CT: VideoTours, 1993. $24.95. 7 up

Archaeologists, curators, educators, and historians comment about the position of Williamsburg in American history. The major points of interest photographed in this living history museum are the Bruton Parish Church, the Capitol, William and Mary, the Courthouse, the Governor's Palace, and the Raleigh Tavern.

2614. **Colonization and Settlement (1585-1763)**. Videocassette. Color. 30 min. Schlessinger Video. Distr., Bala Cynwyd, PA: Library Video, 1995. $799 series; $39.95 ea. (United States History Video). 5-9

Dramatic readings and performances bring important events and historical figures together in this video.

2615. **Colonizing the American West**. Videocassette. Color. 38 min. Niles, IL: United Learning, 1995. $99. 7 up

Live-action video, reenactments, maps, and historic artwork help to tell the story of the struggles among Spain, England, Russia, and the United States to gain control of the Pacific Coast of North America. It shows a comparison between nineteenth-century life on a Spanish mission, a Russian colony, and an English fur-trading outpost.

2616. **Columbus: Gold, God and Glory**. Videocassette. Color. 58 min. Princeton, NJ: Films for the Humanities and Sciences, 1991. $149. 9 up

After 16 years of research, a Spanish professor set off from Cadiz in a sixteenth-century caravel with 16 inexperienced college students. The Columbus they discovered both before and after the voyage was a "hustler," rather than an explorer, who changed his nationality three times in order to get money for his expedition. He promised Queen Isabella new converts to Christianity, but he also wanted 10 percent of the booty collected in the New World. He kept a false journal of the voyage in case the Portuguese stopped him, and he was also an ineffectual governor.

2617. **Columbus and the Age of Discovery: The Crossing**. Videocassette. Color. 58 min. Princeton, NJ: Films for the Humanities and Sciences, 1993. $149. (WGBH Collection). 9 up

In this video, one of seven produced for the quincentennial of Columbus's voyage to the New World, modern-day sailors retrace the trip with replicas of the *Niña, Pinta,* and the *Santa Maria.* The difficulties of this undertaking become apparent as the sailors try to solve problems, and historians review the controversy about Columbus's abilities to lead.

2618. **The Comanche**. Videocassette. Color. 30 min. Schlessinger Video. Distr., Bala Cynwyd, PA: Library Video, 1993. $39.95. (Indians of North America). 4-10

The Comanche formerly lived on the southern Great Plains and in western Kansas, where they were nomadic buffalo hunters. This video focuses on the unique history of the Comanche using photographs and film footage. It additionally discusses the government, the spiritual, the mythical, and the role of women in the tribe.

2619. **The Constitution of the United States**. 2 Videocassettes. Color. 2 hrs. Las Vegas, NV: Library Distributors of America, 1993. $89.95 set. 9 up

An effective integration of graphics and text occur in this set of videos. Part I presents the historical developments from 1776 and the Declaration of Independence to 1787 and the Constitutional Convention. Part II examines each of the seven articles and 27 amendments to the Constitution of the United States.

2620. **Countdown to Independence: Causes of the American Revolution**. Videocassette. Color. 24 min. Raleigh, NC: Rainbow Educational, 1993. $89. 5-8

Among the causes of the Revolution outlined in the video, which uses full-motion footage, historical stills, and dramatized narration, are taxation without representation, the Boston Tea Party, the Quartering Acts, the Boston Massacre, and the Intolerable Acts. Questions that students answer as they go about their day at school transmit the information in a memorable way.

2621. **The Crash of 1929**. Videocassette. Color. 59 min. WGBH, WNET, and KCET. Distr., Alexandria, VA: PBS Video, 1991. $59.95. (The American Experience). 9 up

Newsreels and feature footage (some from movies about the era) explain what happened on Wall Street in October of 1929. What becomes clear is that those who had the money knew how to manipulate the market so that they made more while the small investors lost.

2622. **The Creek**. Videocassette. Color. 30 min. Schlessinger Video. Distr., Bala Cynwyd, PA: Library Video, 1994. $39.95. (Indians of North America). 4-10

The Creek originally lived in southwest Georgia but were relocated to central Oklahoma and southern Alabama in the nineteenth century. The video focuses on the unique history of the Creek through photographs and film footage. It additionally discusses the government, the spiritual, the mythical, and the role of women.

2623. **The Crow**. Videocassette. Color. 30 min. Schlessinger Video. Distr., Bala Cynwyd, PA: Library Video, 1994. $39.95. (Indians of North America). 4-10

The Crow once lived in the Great Plains, where they were nomadic buffalo hunters, before migrating into North Dakota. The video focuses on the unique history of the Crow using photographs and film footage. It additionally discusses the government, the spiritual, the mythical, and the role of women.

2624. **Custer at Little Bighorn**. Videocassette. Color. 54 min. Fort Collins, CO: Willoughby, 1992. $29.95. 9 up

The events that occurred between 1867 and 1876 when the Battle of Little Bighorn took place tell about conflicts between two different cultures, the Indians and the white settlers. The government wanted gold-bearing land that treaties had protected for the Indians while the Indians were losing buffalo as miners and settlers moved into the Black Hills and Dakota Territories. Reenactments of the battle lend immediacy to the thorough content of the program.

2625. **Custer's Last Trooper**. Videocassette. Color. 47 min. Encino, CA: Bill Armstrong, 1992. $24.95. 9 up

Graphics detail the military tactics of both the Indians and the Seventh Cavalry under Lt. Col. George A. Custer at the brief but bloody battle at Little Bighorn. Since an archaeological dig at the Reno/Benteen dump site discovered the remains of one of the troopers, the video also presents the methods used to identify and reconstruct these remains.

$$\boxed{\text{D}}$$

2626. **D-Day and the Battle for France**. Videocassette. Color and B&W. 45 min. Bethesda, MD: Atlas Video, 1989. $19.95. (V for Victory). 7 up

This program presents the landing on the 6th of June in 1944, which allowed the Allies to eventually win France and the war.

2627. **D-Day Omaha Beach**. Videocassette. Color. 50 min. Bethesda, MD: Atlas Video, 1991. $99.95 set; $19.95 ea. (War Stories). 7 up

On-camera interviews with veterans make this series on World War II especially human. In this video, soldiers who sailed across the English Channel to land on the Normandy beaches recall their mission.

2628. **D-Day + 50 . . . Normandy, Vol. 1**. Videocassette. Color and B&W. 106 min. Shreveport, LA: Destination Images, 1994. $35. (World War II). 10 up

Archival black-and-white footage from D-Day and computer-generated maps combined with contemporary footage of the invasion area gives insight into the invasion. Towns and battle areas featured include St. Mère Église, Utah Beach, and Pointe du Hoc.

2629. **The Dakota Conflict**. Videocassette. Color. 56 min. Bethesda, MD: Acorn Media, 1992. $19.95. 9 up

Using diaries, photographs, newspaper archives, and oral histories, the program recounts the story of the "The Great Sioux Uprising" in 1862, which began a 30-year fight for the Great Plains between white settlers and the Dakota Indians in Minnesota. The video dramatizes American history from Little Bighorn (1876) to Wounded Knee (1890).

2630. **Dakota Encounters**. Videocassette. Color. 135 min. Aberdeen, SD: Unity, 1993. $95. 7 up

Joseph Nicollet, a French astronomer, came to America in 1832 after losing his money, and the U.S. government hired him to map the region traveled by Lewis and Clark. His map of the Dakota Territories became the basis for other maps created of the American West when it was published in 1843 after his death.

2631. **Daley: The Last Boss**. Videocassette. Color. 112 min. PBS. Distr., Chicago: Public Media Home Video, 1995. $19.99. 10 up

Richard. J. Daley was mayor of Chicago for five terms from 1955 to 1975. Because interviews include his enemies as well as his family, this balanced picture of Daley shows the force of political bosses in American history. Film clips reveal not only Daley's life but the political and social history in America during his tenure.

2632. **Dancing in Moccasins: Keeping Native American Traditions Alive**. Videocassette. Color. 49 min. Princeton, NJ: Films for the Humanities and Sciences, 1994. $149. 7 up

Nearly 2 million Native Americans from 500 nations live on 278 reservations in the United States. The Indians' respect for the earth and the repeatedly broken treaties by the U.S. government become clear.

2633. **Daring to Dream**. Videocassette. Color. 24 min. Falls Church, VA: Landmark Media, 1993. $225. 7 up

This oral history presents the institutions and ideas that have been important to African Americans and how they helped the change from slavery to desegregation. Among them are religion, education, and vocational opportunity.

2634. **Dark Passages**. Videocassette. Color. 60 min. Alexandria, VA: PBS Video, 1995. $69.95. 11 up

The documentary tells about the Atlantic slave trade focusing on Goree Island off the coast of Dakar, Senegal. On that island, millions of Africans stayed until they were transported to the New World.

2635. **Dateline: 1943 Europe**. Videocassette. Color. 22.40 min. ABC News/Weintraub Prods. Distr., Deerfield, IL: Coronet/ MTI, 1989. $250. (The Eagle and the Bear). 9 up

This program traces the deterioration of relations between the United States and the Soviet Union as World War II came to an end. In addition to other information, it looks at the conferences at Tehran, Yalta, and Potsdam with the world leaders Joseph Stalin, Winston Churchill, and Franklin Roosevelt (Harry Truman at Potsdam) in attendance.

2636. **Democracy and Reform**. Videocassette. Color. 30 min. Schlessinger Video. Distr., Bala Cynwyd, PA: Library Video, 1995. $799 series; $39.95 ea. (United States History Video). 5-9

With the election of Andrew Jackson, the first President from the middle class, reform began. Dramatic readings and performances bring important events and historical figures together in this video.

2637. **Dineh Nation: The Navajo Story**. Videocassette. Color. 26 min. R & R Prods. New York: Filmakers Library, 1992. $195. 9 up

While battling the use of their lands by outsiders, the Dineh or Navajo Nation tries to keep its culture alive while living on the land in the traditional way. Photographs show the beautiful but difficult land of the nation in Arizona, New Mexico, and Utah.

2638.   Disobeying Orders: GI Resistance to the Vietnam War. Videocassette. Color. 29 min. New York: Filmakers Library, 1990. $295. 9 up

Vietnam veterans discuss their reaction to the war and how they felt when they saw the destruction and death while hearing from people at home who had no concept of what they were doing. Additional frustrations were their ethical questions about war and about obeying orders with which they did not agree, perceptions of race, and civil rights. These veterans have sincere reservations about their roles in the war. *National Educational Film & Video Festival, Bronze Apple.*

2639.   Dr. Ethel Allen: Minuses into Pluses. Videocassette. Color. 25 min. Take One. Distr., New York: EPH, 1995. $39.95. 7 up

Dr. Ethel Allen wanted to become a doctor when few women or Blacks were even admitted to medical school. After she graduated, she went to Philadelphia to practice. There she realized that the health needs of her patients were directly related to the community, and she decided to become a politican to lobby for them at half the salary.

2640.   Dr. Martin Luther King, Jr.: A Historical Perspective. Videocassette. Color. 60 min. Santa Monica, CA: Xenon, 1994. $29.95. 7 up

This program documents the life and spiritual, political, and civil rights work of Dr. King. It also provides a chronological account of the Civil Rights movement and highlights the important organizations and individuals. It also examines Dr. King's relationship with other leaders at the time. Newsreel footage, photographs, and recordings of Dr. King's speeches augment the narration.

2641.   Dreams of Equality. Videocassette. Color. 27 min. Dallas, TX: Media Projects, 1994. $99. 9 up

When Lucy Griswold was concerned about her daughter and her granddaughter's ability to support themselves, she wrote letters to her brother in which she told him about attending the first Convention for the Discussion of Rights of Women in 1838 in Seneca Falls, New York. Included are historical facts about Lucretia Mott and Elizabeth Cady Stanton and their efforts to change the laws for women.

E

2642.   The Eagle Triumphant. Videocassette. Color and B&W. 45 min. Bethesda, MD: Acorn Media, 1989. $19.95. (V for Victory). 7 up

This program presents the final victories of World War II in Europe and Asia through newsreel footage and stories from home.

2643.   The Early Colonists. 2 Videocassettes. Color. 30 min. Niles, IL: United Learning, 1992. $135. 5-8

The two videos, filmed at living museums in Maryland and Virginia, discuss what brought settlers to the colonies, how slavery was established, and living and survival skills the settlers needed. The two titles are *Forging a New World* and *Home Sweet Home: Daily Life in Early Colonial America.*

2644.   Edgar Allan Poe: Architect of Dreams. Videocassette. Color. 40 min. Viewfinders Films. Distr., Agoura Hills, CA: Monterey Home Video, 1995. $24.95. (About the Authors). 7 up

Edgar Allan Poe's short stories and poems received critical acclaim in nineteenth-century France before Americans recognized their value. The video explores his life.

2645.   Elijah Muhammad. Videocassette. Color. 30 min. Schlessinger Video. Distr., Bala Cynwyd, PA: Library Video, 1994. $39.95. (Black Americans of Achievement). 5 up

A complement to the Chelsea House series Black Americans of Achievement, the video introduces Elijah Muhammad (1897-1975). Historians and other experts comment on his achievements using photos, old film footage, and modern live-action film for illustration.

2646.   Elizabeth Cady Stanton and Susan B. Anthony. Videocassette. Color. 24 min. Princeton, NJ: Films for the Humanities and Sciences, 1988. $29.95. (Against the Odds). 4 up

Elizabeth Cady Stanton and Susan B. Anthony formed the National Women's Suffrage Association, leading to a national crusade to give the vote to women. Anthony was also among the first to support Black suffrage after the Civil War.

2647.   Emily Dickinson. Videocassette. Color. 30 min. Schlessinger Video. Distr., Bala Cynwyd, PA: Library Video, 1995. $39.95. ISBN 1-57225-041-0. (American Women of Achievement). 7-12

The video asks why Emily Dickinson (1830-1886) resisted conformity and if she could be considered a "rebel" as she helped shape the history and culture of the United States. Archival footage, sketches, photographs, recordings, interviews with historians, literary experts, and reenactments help to examine the impact of family; economic, social, and political circumstances; and her ability to empower herself.

2648. **Emily Dickinson: A Certain Slant of Light**. Videocassette. Color. 40 min. Viewfinders Films. Distr., Agoura Hills, CA: Monterey Home Video, 1995. $24.95. (About the Authors). 7 up

Emily Dickinson, a nineteenth-century poet, wrote in a style never used, and she created her own world inside her Amherst, Massachusetts, home while writing over 1,700 poems.

2649. **Equality: A History of the Women's Movement in America**. Videocassette. Color. 30 min. Wolfington. Distr., Bala Cynwyd, PA: Schlessinger Video, 1996. $39.95. 7 up

When Abigail Adams told her husband to "remember the ladies," she continued the concern for rights for women that inspired other women. Among these women were Elizabeth Cady Stanton, Lucretia Mott, Susan B. Anthony, Jane Addams, and Eleanor Roosevelt. Their work to improve conditions for immigrants and for women and children helped to change the lives of many.

2650. **The Era of Segregation: A Personal Perspective**. Videocassette. Color. 30 min. Madison, WI: Knowledge Unlimited, 1993. $69.95. ISBN 1-5593-3127-5. 6 up

Author Clifton L. Taulbert *(Once Upon a Time When We Were Colored)* looks at the history of segregation through historical footage and photographs. Having endured it himself, Taulbert gives an especially valuable insight to segregation. The video, divided into segments about legal segregation, family and community, the church, schools under segration, Civil Rights movement, and current issues, shows that problems still exist although much has changed. *1994 Council on Nontheatrical Events, Golden Eagle Award; Silver Medal, New York Festivals; Silver Apple, New England Film & Video Festival; Honorable Mention, Columbus International Film & Video Festival.*

2651. **Expansionism**. Videocassette. Color. 30 min. Schlessinger Video. Distr., Bala Cynwyd, PA: Library Video, 1995. $799 series; $39.95 ea. (United States History Video). 5-9

This video discusses the westward expansion in the early half of the nineteenth century. Dramatic readings and performances bring important events and historical figures together.

2652. **Eyes on the Prize II: A Nation of Law? (1968-1971)**. Videocassette. Color. 60 min. Blackside, Inc. Distr., Alexandria, VA: PBS Video, 1990. $59.95. 9 up

The U.S. government reacted to dissension in the late 1960s and early 1970s with the FBI trying to dismantle certain Black groups by using informants in the Black Panther Party in Chicago. The other event presented is the rebellion of the Attica Correctional Facility inmates in 1971.

2653. **Eyes on the Prize II: Ain't Gonna Shuffle No More (1964-1972)**. Videocassette. Color. 60 min. Blackside, Inc. Distr., Alexandria, VA: PBS Video, 1990. $59.95. 9 up

Three episodes of the early 1970s highlight the rise of Black identity. Muhammad Ali becomes a new Black hero, Howard University students take over buildings as they request a Black-focused curriculum, and the National Black Political Convention in Gary, Indiana, emphasizes the needs of the whole community.

2654. **Eyes on the Prize II: Back to the Movement (1979-mid 1980s)**. Videocassette. Color. 60 min. Blackside, Inc. Distr., Alexandria, VA: PBS Video, 1990. $59.95. 9 up

News videotape, photographs, film, and interviews with people contrast the events in Chicago and Miami. In Miami, the Black population was basically uprooted when the city built a freeway then a white jury acquitted a white man of the beating death of a Black man. In Chicago, more than 100,000 Black citizens registered to vote and helped Harold Washington beat a white man for the mayoral primary race.

2655. **Eyes on the Prize II: The Keys to the Kingdom (1974-1980)**. Videocassette. Color. 60 min. Blackside, Inc. Distr., Alexandria, VA: PBS Video, 1990. $59.95. 10 up

This video shows how communities, politicians, and courts helped with the efforts of the Civil Rights movement. The three parts are the Boston order for busing to integrate schools; Atlanta's mayor in the 1970s hiring minorities and women; and the Supreme Court's "reverse discrimination" ruling that Alan Bakke, a white man, should be admitted to medical school.

2656. **Eyes on the Prize II: Power! (1967-1968)**. Videocassette. Color. 60 min. Blackside 7, Inc. Distr., Alexandria, VA: PBS Video, 1990. $59.95. 9 up

News clips and interviews explore the importance of three situations in which communities tried to gain control of their lives. The video examines the Black Panther Party, Carl Stokes's successful campaign to become mayor of Cleveland, and the Ocean Hill–Brownsville section of Brooklyn's educational experiment.

2657.   **Eyes on the Prize II: The Promised Land (1967-1968)**. Videocassette. Color. 60 min. Blackside, Inc. Alexandria, VA: PBS Video, 1990. $59.95. 9 up

In 1967, Martin Luther King denounced the Vietnam War and tried to get the government to commit to reducing poverty. The events and ideas covered include King's political and financial difficulties resulting from his disapproval of the war, the Memphis garbage workers' strike, the urban riots, King's assassination, the Poor Peoples' Campaign, and Robert Kennedy's attempt to win the presidential nomination before his assassination.

2658.   **Eyes on the Prize II: The Time Has Come (1964-1966)**. Videocassette. Color. 59 min. Alexandria, VA: PBS Video, 1990. $59.95. 7 up

From 1964 to 1966, two Black leaders were rising against Martin Luther King's policy of nonviolence. Footage from the sixties and contemporary interviews show Stokely Carmichael and Malcolm X as they started a new era in the Civil Rights movement.

F

2659.   **The Fabulous Sixties**. 10 Videocassettes. Color and B&W. 45 min. ea. New York: Cinema Guild, 1993. $2,000 series; $250 ea. 9 up

This series of videos covers 1960 to 1969. Each video has a time code for the events so that the specific topics may be easily accessed. The series covers the decade from sociological, political, historical, and cultural points of view with Peter Jennings as the narrator.

2660.   **A Family Gathering**. Videocassette. Color. 58 min. WGBH, WNET, and KCET. Distr., Alexandria, VA: PBS Video, 1989. $59.95. (The American Experience). 9 up

One of the United States most shameful moments came at the beginning of World War II, when it decided to relocate Japanese Americans from the West Coast into internment camps. The program recreates emotion along with content in newsreels, home movie segments, brief interviews, and historical still pictures.

2661.   **Farming in America: A History**. Videocassette. Color. 20 min. Irwindale, CA: Barr Media, 1987. $75. 7 up

This video traces an industry that has almost disappeared but which helped to define American spirit and culture.

2662.   **Fateful Decade: From Little Rock to the Civil Rights Bill.** Videocassette. Color. 27 min. Princeton, NJ: Films for the Humanities and Sciences, 1990. $149. 9 up

Actual news footage of events during the 1950s and 1960s gives an immediacy to the Civil Rights movement. Scenes include Little Rock's Central High School and the National Guard; Martin Luther King, Jr. meeting with President Eisenhower; demonstrations and police clashes; the murder of Medgar Evars; the bombing of Birmingham Baptist Church; the Montgomery Freedom March; King's funeral; and his "I Have a Dream" speech.

2663.   **FDR**. 2 Videocassettes. Color. 4.5 hours. WGBH. Distr., Alexandria, VA: PBS Video, 1994. $125 set. (The American Experience). 10 up

Eyewitness accounts, archival footage, and commentary combine to present a detailed view of the life of Franklin Delano Roosevelt, the man who served longest as President of the United States. Part Two focuses on his presidency.

2664.   **The Fighting Marines**. Videocassette. Color. 50 min. Bethesda, MD: Atlas Video, 1991. $99.95 set; $19.95 ea. (War Stories). 7 up

On-camera interviews with veterans make this series on World War II especially human. In this video, five men describe their fears during island fighting at a close range, the agony of seeing their dead and wounded friends, and their personal feelings toward finding themselves alive.

2665.   **The Final Steps**. Videocassette. Color. 28 min. Princeton, NJ: Films for the Humanities and Sciences, 1992. $399 series; $109 ea. (The Oregon Trail). 5 up

Featuring oil paintings, black-and-white artwork, diary excerpts, and narration, this program traces the Oregon Trail as it winds to Willamette Valley, Oregon. It discusses the role of the British, the Forty-Niners rushing for gold on the trail, and the conflict with Native Americans during the later years of the trail.

2666. **Forever Activists: Stories from the Veterans of the Abraham Lincoln Brigade**. Videocassette. Color. 60 min. Clarity Educational Productions. Distr., Waltham, MA: National Center for Jewish Film, 1992. $295. 9 up

In 1986, members of the Abraham Lincoln Brigade were interviewd at their 50-year reunion. They retraced their intentions and concerns that led them to fight in the Spanish Civil War beginning in 1936.

2667. **Forever in Time: The Art of Edward S. Curtis**. Videocassette. Color. 50 min. New York: Cinema Guild, 1990. $295. 9 up

Edward S. Curtis (1868-1952) documented the life of the American Indian. Authentic footage and photographs give a biographical sketch of Curtis while tracing the role of the American Indian. Curtis knew Chief Seattle's daughter, Angeline, and he refused to believe the government story of Little Bighorn. His story proved to be true.

2668. **Fort McHenry: Preserving the Spirit of Liberty**. Videocassette. Color. 35 min. All American Video. Distr., Englewood, CO: SelectVideo, 1993. $19.95. 5 up

Fort McHenry, the national monument known as the "protector of Baltimore," is where the Americans won a battle in the War of 1812 that inspired Francis Scott Key to write "The Star Spangled Banner." This video covers the fort's history.

2669. **Frank Lloyd Wright: An American Original**. Videocassette. Color. 23 min. Greenwich, CT: Double Diamond, 1995. $89. 7 up

The video illustrates Frank Lloyd Wright's attempt to create unity with form and with purpose through his designs. It uses photographs, video, and architectural drawings of many of the buildings Wright designed.

2670. **Franklin D. Roosevelt**. Videocassette. Color. 38 min. Evanston, IL: Beacon Films, 1989. $195. (The Men of Our Time). 7 up

The video contains black-and-white film footage from the life of Franklin D. Roosevelt, which makes it a good review of Roosevelt's time and his presidency.

2671. **Frederick Douglass**. Videocassette. Color. 30 min. Schlessinger Video. Distr., Bala Cynwyd, PA: Library Video, 1992. $39.95. (Black Americans of Achievement). 7 up

A complement to the Chelsea House series Black Americans of Achievement, the video introduces Frederick Douglass (1817-1895). Historians and other experts comment on his achievements using photos, old film footage, and modern live action for illustration.

2672. **Frederick Douglass: When the Lion Wrote History**. Videocassette. Color. 90 min. WETA, Washington. Distr., Alexandria, VA: PBS Video, 1995. $89.95. 7 up

Among the list of achievements for Frederick Douglass (1817-1895) are civil rights advocate, public speaker, journalist, and diplomat. Historians analyze his motivations, and actors dramatize excerpts from his speeches during a comprehensive look at his life.

2673. **Freedom and Justice**. 4 Videocassettes. Color. 20-26:30 min. Cayce, SC: CQ Television Network, 1994. $149.95. 82-min. version on 1 video, $69.95. 7 up

Cecil J. Williams's photographs tell the struggle of South Carolina and its Civil Rights movement. Four chronological segments begin with activities in the 1940s and end with plans for the future. Student protests and Orangeburg events in the 1960s receive extra emphasis.

2674. **Freedom in Diversity**. Videocassette. 12 min. Video Dialog. Distr., San Diego, CA: Media Guild, 1991. $210. (Discovering History). 4-8

When students meet to decide who should be included in a discussion on great Americans, they review the roles of women since the 1700s; Black history from slavery to the present; and what Asians, Hispanics, and other ethnic groups have added to our American heritage.

2675. **Freedom Train**. Film. Color. 28 min. Kingberry and WDIV. Distr., New York: Filmakers Library, 1995. $295. 9 up

This film talks about the achievements of the National Negro Labor Council, formed in 1951, which helped to advance the cause of equal employment opportunities for African Americans. *National Educational Media, Bronze Apple*.

2676. **From an Eagle's Nest**. Videocassette. Color. 25 min. Eugene, OR: New Dimensions Media, 1994. $260. ISBN 1-56353-207-7. 7 up

This dramatization tells the story of an early colonial American midwife and lay healer whose medicinal herbal cures arouse suspicion and cause her great mental anguish. *Council on Nontheatrical Events, Golden Eagle*; *1st Place, Chicago International Film Festival*.

2677. **From Danger to Dignity: The Fight for Safe Abortion**. Videocassette. Color. 57 min. Concentric Media and KTEH. Distr., San Francisco: Concentric, 1995. $95. 11 up

This documentary film gives a history of the problems that women have had while getting illegal abortions. Archival footage shows women in hospitals suffering from failed abortions as well as women crossing into Mexico. This video shows how people risked their lives and careers to support a woman's right to make decisions about her body.

2678. **From East to West: The Asian-American Experience**. Videocassette. Color. 24 min. Video Dialog. Distr., Raleigh, NC: Rainbow Educational, 1993. $89. 5-8

The migrations to the United States from Asia began in 1850, with the Chinese coming to escape overpopulation in their own country. The Japanese wanted to avoid high taxes, and the Filipinos followed in an attempt to find homes and money. Their hard work made people fear them and led to the Chinese Exclusion Act of 1882. The second wave of Asian immigration occurred after the Vietnam War, and again, Asians proved to be hardworking citizens.

2679. **From the Bay of Pigs to the Brink**. Videocassette. Color. 16.5 min. Visnews. Distr., Princeton, NJ: Films for the Humanities and Sciences, 1991. $149. 7 up

In 1962, the Cuban Missile Crisis between the United States and the Soviet Union led the world to the brink of a nuclear conflict. Kennedy approved the Bay of Pigs invasion. When that failed, the Soviets brought missiles into Cuba. Negotiation and port blockades led the Soviets to remove the missiles, and after this incident, Moscow and Washington established a "hot line."

2680. **From the Home Front to the Front Lines**. Videocassette. Color and B&W. 45 min. Bethesda, MD: Acorn Media, 1989. $19.95. (V for Victory). 7 up

In this video using newsreel footage and stories from the homefront about World War II, the soldiers leave home for the front lines in Europe.

2681. **Frontier Buildings**. Videocassette. Color. 29 min. Irwindale, CA: Barr Media, 1992. $75. (American Frontier). 4-9

This video examines landmark structures on the western frontier.

2682. **Frontier Forts and the American Indian Wars in Texas**. Videocassette. Color. 60 min. Austin, TX: Forest Glen TV, 1993. $29.95. (Texas History Video). 6 up

Research by prominent historians help relate the daily lives of European, African, and Native Americans who battled for the Texas frontier. The video, divided into two segments on Forts and Indians Wars, uses contemporary reenactments to show the realities of frontier life. *Texas Historical Commission Award.*

2683. **Frontline: The Gulf War**. 2 Videocassettes. Color. 2 hours each. Distr., Alexandria, VA: PBS Video, 1995. $79.95 set. 11 up

This program, first presented on public television, talks about the Persian Gulf War from both the military and political perspectives. Interviews with leaders point out the irony of Saddam still being in power while those who supposedly bested him lost their positions in England and the United States. Graphics and live-action video cover all aspects of the conflict.

G

2684. **Gandy Dancers**. Videocassette. Color. 30 min. New York: Cinema Guild, 1994. $250. 7 up

Most of the workers who installed, repaired, and replaced the rail lines in the South from the late nineteenth century were African American. They used a caller to keep a steady synchronization so that they could do their work. Retired workers reenact the process supplemented by film clips and photographs.

2685. **Genbaku Shi: Killed by the Atomic Bomb**. Videocassette. Color. 57 min. Montreal, Canada: Casey G. Williams, 1993. $200. 7 up

Placing the long-term effect of World War II on the personal level, this documentary recounts the experiences of a member of one of the rescue teams who arrived after the truce between the United States and the Japanese. Vintage stills and narration mixed with interviews add to the video's effect.

2686. **General Douglas MacArthur**. Videocassette. Color. 50 min. ABC News and A&E Television. Distr., New York: New Video Group, 1996. $19.99. (Biography). 7 up

As a military man who attended West Point, Douglas MacArthur established his career and became known as "Father of the Modern Military Academy." He gained fame from his exploits on the Pacific front during World War II. The interviews with his friends and footage from the times give an insight into American history as well.

2687. **George Washington: The Man Who Wouldn't Be King**. Videocassette. Color. 60 min. Alexandria, VA: PBS Video, 1992. $59.95. (The American Experience). 9 up

Battle reenactments, interviews, and visits to historical sites help to dispell myths about George Washington. Both flaws and strengths make Washington, a general and a President, become a human being in this video.

2688. **George Washington Carver**. Videocassette. Color. 30 min. Schlessinger Video. Distr., Bala Cynwyd, PA: Library Video, 1992. $39.95. (Black Americans of Achievement). 7 up

A complement to the Chelsea House series Black Americans of Achievement, the video introduces George Washington Carver (1861-1943). Historians and other experts comment on his achievements using photos, old film footage, and modern live action for illustration.

2689. **George Washington Carver: A Man of Vision**. Videocassette. Color. 26 min. Niles, IL: United Learning, 1990. $89. 5 up

George Washington Carver, born a slave in the 1860s, developed an early interest in nature that he used to help him earn a master's degree in agriculture. His humanitarian and spiritual attributes show that one can unite religion and science to help others.

2690. **German Americans**. Videocassette. Color. 30 min. Schlessinger Video. Distr., Bala Cynwyd, PA: Library Video, 1993. $39.95. #6676. (Multicultural Peoples of North America). 4-10

Based on the Chelsea House series Peoples of North America, the video highlights the German culture. It gives reasons for the German immigration to America, explanations of customs and traditions, the history of their transition, and important leaders from the culture. Historians and sociologists discuss these aspects, and a German family explains its cultural identity, shared memories, and reasons for immigration.

2691. **Gettysburg**. Videocassette. Color. 40 min. Regency Home Video. Distr., Worcester, PA: Vision Video, 1994. $29.95. ISBN 1-56364-102-X. 6 up

Filmed on location with Civil War reenactors, the video is an authentic staging of the Gettysburg battle fought more than 130 years ago. The heavy equipment, the situations of the soldiers, and all other aspects of the battle become clear in this presentation.

2692. **Ghost Trains of the Old West**. 2 Videocassettes. Color. 60 min. ea. Agoura Hills, CA: Monterey Home Video, 1995. $19.95 ea. 7 up

These videos present the engines on the railroads that changed the United States.

2693. **Give Me Liberty: Patrick Henry—Voice of the Revolution**. Videocassette. Color. 23.5 min. Learning Corporation of America. Distr., Columbus, OH: Coronet/MTI, 1992. $250. (American Documents). 7 up

In live-action drama, Patrick Henry speaks and his contemporaries Thomas Jefferson and John Adams describe him. Henry defends Viriginia farmers and, later in his career, gives the famous speech "Give me liberty or give me death."

2694. **God Bless America and Poland Too**. Videocassette. Color. 58 min. WGBH, WNET, and KCET. Alexandria, VA: PBS Video, 1990. $59.95. (The American Experience). 9 up

The video documents the experiences of a man who immigrated to the United States from Poland in 1911. He becomes a barber and raises a family but never forgets his relatives. He sends them money and tries to sponsor nieces or nephews who either come to visit or to live in America. When he returns to Poland for a visit, his view of Poland is unlike that of most news programs.

2695. **Goin' to Chicago**. Videocassette. Color. 70 min. George King. San Francisco: California Newsreel, 1995. $69.95. 9 up

African Americans migrated to Chicago after World War II, especially those who had been Mississippi sharecroppers. The video looks at why and how they moved and the types of obstacles they faced in their new location. Commentary from a variety of people gives depth to the presentation.

2696. **The Great Age of Salmon**. Videocassette. Color. 30 min. Seattle, WA: John Sabella, 1995. $19.95. 7 up

Before salmon fishermen in the Northwest started to use technology, their industry was different. This video gives a glimpse of this past life.

2697. **Great Black Innovators**. Videocassette. Color. 35 min. Madison, WI: Knowledge Unlimited, 1995. $55. 4 up

A companion to James Michael Brodie's *Created Equal: The Lives and Ideas of Black American Innovators*, this video highlights various African Americans such as Benjamin Banneker and George Washington Carver as well as other inventors, scientists, and businesspeople. The video uses live footage, historic stills, and interviews.

2698. **Great Black Women**.Videocassette. Color. 45 min. Princeton, NJ: Films for the Humanities and Sciences, 1990. $149. 7 up

The video introduces 40 African American women who have contributed to contemporary culture. The best known include such entertainers as Natalie Cole and Tina Turner. But women from other fields including sports, civil rights, media, dance, acting, politics, education, modeling, literature, and business also appear.

2699. **The Great Campaigns of the Civil War**. 2 Videocassettes. Color. 2 hrs. Chicago: Questar Video, 1994. $39.95 set. ISBN 1-56855-038-3. 7 up

Reenactments, paintings, maps, photographs, and cinema footage describe the military engagements in the significant battles of the Civil War. Among the topics are the roles of women as nurses and caregivers, the youth of the soldiers, Lincoln's search for a general, low pay, inadequate weapons, and lack of sanitation.

2700. **The Great Depression and the New Deal**. Videocassette. Color. 30 min. Schlessinger Video. Distr., Bala Cynwyd, PA: Library Video, 1995. $799 series; $39.95 ea. (United States History Video). 5-9

Dramatic readings and performances bring important events and historical figures together in this video.

2701. **Great Ranches of the West**. Videocassette. Color. 60 min. Bethesda, MD: Acorn Media, 1992. $79.80 set; $19.95. (Great West Collection). 7 up

Exciting photography, good narration, and western music underlie this part of the series on cowboys in the American West. This video covers working ranches in New Mexico, Nevada, Hawaii, and Wyoming.

2702. **Greek Americans**. Videocassette. Color. 30 min. Schlessinger Video. Distr., Bala Cynwyd, PA: Library Video, 1993. $39.95. (Multicultural Peoples of North America). 4-10

Based on the Chelsea House series Peoples of North America, the video highlights the Greek culture. It gives reasons for Greek immigration to America, explanations of customs and traditions, the history of their transition, and important leaders from the culture. Historians and sociologists discuss these aspects, and a Greek family explains its cultural identity, shared memories, and reasons for immigration.

2703. **Guadalcanal and the Pacific Counterattack**. Videocassette. Color and B&W. 45 min. Bethesda, MD: Acorn Media, 1989. $19.95. (V for Victory). 7 up

During World War II, the United States fought the Japanese Pacific empire. The newsreel footage and stories from the home front here show jungle warfare on Guadalcanal, the naval combat off the Solomon Islands, and the fighting to control the Aleutian Islands.

2704. **Gulf War, Parts 1 and 2**. Videocassette. Color. Independent Television News. Distr., New York: Central Park Media, 1995. $29.95. 10 up

The two videos feature battle footage including General Norman Schwarzkopf taking command against Saddam Hussein, leader of Iraq.

H

2705. **Harriet Tubman**. Videocassette. Color. 30 min. Schlessinger Video. Distr., Bala Cynwyd, PA: Library Video, 1992. $39.95. (Black Americans of Achievement). 7 up

A complement to the Chelsea House series Black Americans of Achievement, the video introduces Harriet Tubman (1820?-1913). Historians and other experts comment on her achievements using photos, old film footage, and modern live action for illustration.

2706. **Harry S. Truman**. Videocassette. Color. 30 min. Yonkers, NY: Bennu, 1992. $49.95. 9-12

The biographical presentation of Harry S. Truman also looks at some of the decisions of his presidency, which include the bombing of the Japanese in 1945, the Marshall Plan to revive the economy of continental Europe, and the Truman Doctrine toward South America.

2707. **Heart of the Warrior**. Videocassette. Color. 54 min. Oakland, CA: Video Project, 1991. $150. 9 up

This video brings together an unlikely pair in a U.S. Army paratrooper who fought in Vietnam and a former paratrooper in the Soviet army who fought in Afghanistan. Both men lost a leg, and they find that their experiences of being wounded, facing unsympathetic people at home, and the teamwork required of soldiers is surprisingly similar. Photography of both war and peace complements the discussion.

2708. **Helen Keller**. Videocassette. Color. 30 min. Schlessinger Video. Distr., Bala Cynwyd, PA: Library Video, 1995. $39.95. ISBN 1-57225-043-7. (American Women of Achievement). 7-12

The video asks why Helen Keller (1880-1968) resisted conformity and if she could be considered a "rebel" as she helped shape the history and culture of the U.S. Archival footage, sketches, photographs, recordings, interviews with historians, literary experts, and reenactments help to examine the impact of family; economic, social, and political circumstances; and her ability to empower herself.

2709. **Heritage of the Black West**. Videocassette. Color. 25 min. Washington, DC: National Geographic, 1995. $110. 4-9

The video looks at today's cowboys while giving the history of African Americans in the development of the West. It also discusses the relationship of African Americans of both sexes to the Native Americans who were already in the West when the African Americans arrived.

2710. **Herman Melville: Consider the Sea**. Videocassette. Color. 40 min. Viewfinders Films. Distr., Agoura Hills, CA: Monterey Home Video, 1995. $24.95. (About the Authors). 7 up

Herman Melville's work describes the life of the sailor during the nineteenth century when the whaling industry flourished. The video uses excerpts from his writings to complement the biographical insights.

2711. **Hidden Heritage: The Roots of Black American Painting**. Videocassette. Color. 52 min. Falls Church, VA: Landmark Films, 1990. $250. 9 up

An African American artist, David Driscoll, uses information about his own life as a supplement to a historical perspective on the development of African American painting for more than 300 years in this country. Photographs, newsreels, and scenes from Hollywood movies help illustrate the horrors and the highlights of the times. He also presents well-known painters such as Johnston from the late eighteenth century, Tanner in the twentieth, and Motley, with others from his Harlem Renaissance peers.

2712. **Hiroshima: Why the Bomb Was Dropped**. Videocassette. Color. 70 min. ABC News. Washington, DC: Zenger Media, 1995. $89. 10 up

The video focuses on the controversy surrounding Harry Truman's decision to drop the bomb on Hiroshima in 1945. After a brief overview of the American reaction to World War II and the bombing of Pearl Harbor with an analysis of the Manhattan Project, the video presents the various opinions of those who were involved in the decision. It allows the viewer to think and to judge accordingly.

2713. **Hiroshima Maiden**. Videocassette. Color. 58 min. Arnold Shapiro. Distr., Chicago: Public Media Video, 1990. $29.95. (Wonderworks Family Movie). 5 up

In this professionally acted video, Miyeko, a Japanese girl badly scarred by the bombing of Hiroshima in 1945, comes to Connecticut to live with a family while she has plastic surgery. The son is fearful of her, and neighbors think she can cause radiation sickness in others. She and Johnny have to talk face-to-face before Johnny can understand her needs and respond to the misconceptions of his friends.

2714. **History in the Making: The 1980's Series**. 10 Videocassettes. Color. 30 min. ea. ABC News. Distr., Evanston, IL: Beacon Films, 1991. $149 ea. 7 up

Each of the 10 videos addresses one year of the 1980s. Each has the same divisions of one major news event, regular news, followed by other news events, entertainment, the arts, and sports. A list of trivia appears at the end of each video.

2715. **A History of Native Americans**. Videocassette. Color. 30 min. Schlessinger Video. Distr., Bala Cynwyd, PA: Library Video, 1994. $39.95. (Indians of North America). 4-10

This video examines the common histories of the tribes in the series, their relationships with the U.S. government, the role of nature and natural resources, and the roles of women within divergent groups.

2716. **A History of Slavery in America**. Videocassette. Color. 30 min. Schlessinger Video. Distr., Bala Cynwyd, PA: Library Video, 1994. $39.95. (Black Americans of Achievement). 7-12

Slavery became established at Jamestown in 1619 and did not end until 1865 in the United States. In interviews with historians and scholars, topics cover every aspect of slavery, including capture and transport of slaves, treatment of slaves, economic need for slaves, abolitionist movement, and the Underground Railroad. Individuals presented are Sojouner Truth, William Lloyd Garrison, Frederick Douglass, Harriet Tubman, Dred Scott, John Brown, and Abraham Lincoln.

2717. **A History of the Civil Rights Movement**. Videocassette. Color. 30 min. Schlessinger Video. Bala Cynwyd, PA: Library Video, 1993. $39.95. (Black Americans of Achievement). 7-12

Beginning with the Jim Crow laws of the 1800s, the video presents a chronology of slavery, emancipation, and these laws. The discussions include Plessy v. Ferguson, which reaffirmed segregation, the founding of the NAACP and SCLC, Brown v. Board of Education, the Montgomery bus boycott, the March on Washington, and the northern migration of southern Blacks. Figures presented are Booker T. Washington, W. E. B. Du Bois, Marcus Garvey, A. Philip Randolph, Rosa Parks, Martin Luther King, Jr., Malcolm X, and Jesse Jackson.

2718. **Home from the Eastern Sea**. Videocassette. Color. 58 min. New York: Filmakers Library, 1990. $445. 9 up

Looking at the history of the Chinese, Japanese, and Filipinos who came to Washington State gives an overview of the importance of these groups to the area's heritage. The first Chinese, denied citizenship until 1943, came without wives and left no written records, but they were instrumental in building the transcontinental railroad. The Japanese came from Hawaii to take jobs from which the Chinese were excluded. Then the Filipinos came in 1918 and worked as hard as the first two groups, but like the others, faced much discrimination in laws and attitudes. *Council on Nontheatrical Events, Golden Eagle; National Educational Film & Video Festival, Silver Apple.*

2719. **Homesteading: 70 Years on the Great Plains, 1862-1932**. Videocassette. Color. 18 min. Delphi. Distr., Niles, IL: United Learning, 1992. $89.95. 5 up

The 1862 Homestead Act offered 160 acres to anyone who would homestead in the Great Plains. The homesteading ended with the Dust Bowl in the 1930s. Those who went and stayed had to work hard to make a life from a piece of land with few trees and almost no water. Mechanical inventions toward the end of the nineteenth century helped, but the natural disaster of drought defeated many.

2720. **Houdini: The Great Escape**. Videocassette. Color. 50 min. ABC News and A&E Television. Distr., New York: New Video Group, 1996. $19.99. (Biography). 7 up

Ehrich Weiss transformed himself into Harry Houdini, from a Jewish immigrant to a magician. Old photographs and silent films showing his escapes along with period music recreate his abilities. Houdini's niece and contemporary magicians provide commentary.

2721. **Hull House: The House That Jane Built**. Videocassette. Color. 58 min. New York: Cinema Guild, 1993. $350. 9 up

Jane Addams opened Hull House in Chicago in 1889 to help the poor residents of their near West Side neighborhood. The filming, on location, shows how Hull House became a model for major social reform.

2722. **The Huron**. Videocassette. Color. 30 min. Schlessinger Video. Distr., Bala Cynwyd, PA: Library Video, 1994. $39.95. (Indians of North America). 4-10

The Huron lived in Ontario until a war with the Iroquois in the mid-seventeenth century destroyed much of the population. Remaining Huron live in northeast Oklahoma and are known as Wyandot. The video focuses on the unique history of the Huron using photographs and film footage. It also discusses the government, the spiritual, the mythical, and the role of women.

I

2723. **Ida B. Wells—A Passion for Justice**. Videocassette. Color. 58 min. WGBH, WNET, and KCET. Distr., Alexandria, VA: PBS Video, 1989. $59.95. (The American Experience). 9 up

Born into slavery, Ida B. Wells Barnett (1862-1931) spent her life crusading for better conditions for African Americans. She was a driving force in the early antilynching campaign and one of the NAACP organizers. The program includes readings from her writings (Toni Morrison is the reader), interviews with historians, authors, and her grandson. The video also gives a good view of post–Civil War life in the United States.

2724. **Immigration and Cultural Change**. Videocassette. Color. 30 min. Schlessinger Video. Distr., Bala Cynwyd, PA: Library Video, 1995. $799 series; $39.95 ea. (United States History Video). 5-9

In the second half of the nineteenth century, immigrants arrived to escape persecution and economic distress. Dramatic readings and performances bring important events and historical figures together in this video.

2725. **The Immigration Experience**. Videocassette. 12 min. Video Dialog. Distr., San Diego, CA: Media Guild, 1991. $210. (Discovering History). 4-8

Immigration began around 1850 in the United States, when people from countries such as Ireland, England, and Italy began arriving at Ellis Island. Portrayals of why they came and what they expected humanize this major evolution in America's history.

2726. **In the Blood of Man: The Sea of the Imagination**. Videocassette. Color. 26 min. Princeton, NJ: Films for the Humanities and Sciences, 1990. $149. (Blue Revolution). 9 up

The video looks at man's relationship to the sea during several historical periods. It covers Chinese, Japanese, people from the South Pacific, Arabians, Viking explorers, ancient Greeks, and Herman Melville's *Moby Dick*.

2727. **In the Land of Jim Crow: Fighting for Civil Rights**. Videocassette. Color. Deerfield, IL: Coronet/MTI, 1993. $250. 7 up

During a discussion with six black civil rights activists of the 1960s, the video looks at such topics as demonstrations, boycotts, sit-ins, and violence.

2728. **In Times Past: Radio Days**. Videocassette. Color and B&W. 71 min. Dayton, OH: GHI Media, 1992. $29.95. 7 up

Radio, born in the 1920s, created much static at first but soon became the focus of families gathered to listen to programs and music. The video gives a history of the 1930s as well as of the radio.

2729. **In Times Past: Traveling in Style**. 2 Videocassettes. Color. 70 min. ea. Dayton, OH: GHI Media, 1995. $34.95 set; $19.95 ea. 9 up

The videos look at the transportation modes in America's history, including trolleys, trains, riverboats, airplanes, and automobiles.

2730. **Indians of California**. Videocassette. Color. 22.5 min. Irwindale, CA: Barr Media, 1991. $125. (Native Americans). 4-8

A brief introduction to the origins of North American Indians comments that more than 100 different tribes that lived in the area that is now California. The largest group, the Yokuts, lived in the great central valley. A dramatization shares information about the daily lives of the Yokuts.

2731. **Indians of the Northwest**. Videocassette. Color. 20 min. Irwindale, CA: Barr Media, 1992. $125. (Native Americans). 3-8

The video, with live-action segments, maps, and drawings, focuses on the People of the Potlatch and shows the continuity of Native American culture.

2732. **Indians of the Plains**. Videocassette. Color. 16 min. Irwindale, CA: Barr Media, 1991. $125. (Native Americans). 3-8

The video, with live-action segments, maps, and drawings, focuses on the culture of the Plains Indians and their survival through buffalo hunting.

2733. **Indians of the Southeast**. Videocassette. Color. 20 min. Irwindale, CA: Barr Media, 1991. $125. (Native Americans). 3-8

Although focusing mainly on the Cherokee, the video, with live-action segments, maps, and drawings, includes interaction with the Europeans and how their arrival affected the Native Americans. The viewer sees the dependence of the Indian on the environment for all needs by recreating hunting, farming, and making weapons, baskets, and pottery.

2734. **Indians of the Southwest**. Videocassette. Color. 17 min. Irwindale, CA: Barr Media, 1992. $125. (Native Americans). 3-8

The Indians who have lived in the Southwest include the Navajo, Apache, Uma, and Pima. The video, with live action, maps, and drawings, shows the daily lives of these peoples as well as others.

2735. **Industrialization and Urbanization (1870-1910)**. Videocassette. Color. 30 min. Schlessinger Video. Distr., Bala Cynwyd, PA: Library Video, 1995. $799 series; $39.95 ea. (United States History Video). 5-9

Dramatic readings and performances bring important events and historical figures together in this video.

2736. **Irish Americans**. Videocassette. Color. 30 min. Schlessinger Video. Distr., Bala Cynwyd, PA: Library Video, 1993. $39.95. (Multicultural Peoples of North America). 4-10

Based on the Chelsea House series Peoples of North America, the video highlights the Irish culture. It gives reasons for the Irish immigration to America, explanations of customs and traditions, the history of their transition, and important leaders from the culture. Historians and sociologists discuss these aspects, and an Irish family explains its cultural identity, shared memories, and reasons for immigration.

2737. **The Iroquois**. Videocassette. Color. 30 min. Schlessinger Video. Distr., Bala Cynwyd, PA: Library Video, 1993. $39.95. ISBN 1-879151-57-X. (Indians of North America). 4-10

This video tells the history and culture of the Iroquois prior to the arrival of the Europeans. It focuses on the unique history of the Iroquois confederacy, composed of the Mohawk, Oneida, Onondaga, Cayuga, and Seneca peoples (Five Nations) in the eighteenth century, using photographs and film footage. It additionally discusses the government and its influence on the formation of the U.S. Constitution, the spiritual, the mythical, and the role of women.

2738. **Ishi, the Last Yahi**. Videocassette. Color. 57.20 min. Berkeley, CA: University of California Extension Center for Media & Independent Learning, 1992. $19.95. 7 up

This is the portrait of the last living member of an ancient tribe in California. He hid in the foothills for more than 40 years. *Cindy Gold Award; Western Heritage Awards Outstanding Documentary;* and *Red Earth American Indian Film & Video Festival Best Documentary.*

2739. **Italian Americans**. Videocassette. Color. 30 min. Schlessinger Video. Distr., Bala Cynwyd, PA: Library Video, 1993. $39.95. (Multicultural Peoples of North America). 4-10

Based on the Chelsea House series Peoples of North America, the video highlights the Italian culture. It gives reasons for the Italian immigration to America, explanations of customs and traditions, the history of their transition, and important leaders from the culture. Historians and sociologists discuss these aspects, and an Italian family explains its cultural identity, shared memories, and reasons for immigration.

2740. **Iwo Jima, Okinawa and the Push on Japan**. Videocassette. Color and B&W. 45 min. Bethesda, MD: Acorn Media, 1989. $19.95. (V for Victory). 7 up

After bitter island fighting on Iwo Jima during World War II, soldiers raised the flag on Mount Suribachi. Newsreel footage and stories from home aid this program about the fighting in the Pacific, including the devastating fire raids on Toyko and the suicidal Japanese kamikazes dive-bombing into American ships.

J

2741. **Jackie Robinson**. Videocassette. Color. 14 min. Princeton, NJ: Films for the Humanities and Sciences, 1989. $29.95. (Against the Odds). 4 up

Jackie Robinson (1919-1972) was modern major league baseball's first Black player, a skilled ambassador for his people, and a role model. He also was a record-breaker in several sports.

2742. **Jackie Robinson**. Videocassette. Color. 30 min. Schlessinger Video. Distr., Bala Cynwyd, PA: Library Video, 1992. $39.95. (Black Americans of Achievement). 7-12

A complement to the Chelsea House series Black Americans of Achievement, the video introduces Jackie Robinson (1919-1972). Historians and other experts comment on his achievements using photos, old film footage, and modern live action for illustration.

2743. **Jamestown**. Videocassette. Color. 18 min. Irwindale, CA: Barr Media, 1992. $75. (American Frontier). 4-9

This overview of the first major English settlement in America shows on-location footage and comments on the buildings.

2744. **Jamestown: The Beginning**. Videocassette. Color. 17 min. Eugene, OR: New Dimensions Media, 1992. $280. ISBN 1-56353-147-X. 5 up

This dramatic reenactment tells of the first English settlement in Virginia in 1607 from the point of view of John Leydon, one of the few settlers who survived the ordeal. *Council on Nontheatrical Events, Golden Eagle.*

2745. **Jane Addams**. Videocassette. Color. 30 min. Schlessinger Video. Distr., Bala Cynwyd, PA: Library Video, 1995. $39.95. ISBN 1-57225-037-2. (American Women of Achievement). 7-12

The video asks why Jane Addams (1860-1935) resisted conformity and if she could be considered a "rebel" as she helped shape the history and culture of the United States. Archival footage, sketches, photographs, recordings, interviews with historians, literary experts, and reenactments help to examine the impact of family; economic, social, and political circumstances; and her ability to empower herself.

2746. **Japanese Americans**. Videocassette. Color. 30 min. Schlessinger Video. Distr., Bala Cynwyd, PA: Library Video, 1993. $39.95. (Multicultural Peoples of North America). 4-10

Based on the Chelsea House series Peoples of North America, the video highlights the Japanese culture. It gives reasons for the Japanese immigration to America, explanations of customs and traditions, the history of their transition, and important leaders from the culture. Historians and sociologists discuss these aspects, and a Japanese family explains its cultural identity, shared memories, and reasons for immigration.

2747. **Jesse Owens**. Videocassette. Color. 30 min. Schlessinger Video. 1994. Distr., Bala Cynwyd, PA: Library Video, 1993. (Black Americans of Achievement). 5 up

A complement to the Chelsea House series Black Americans of Achievement, the video introduces Jesse Owens (1913-1981). Historians and other experts comment on his achievements using photos, old film footage, and modern live-action film for illustration.

2748. **Jewish Americans**. Videocassette. Color. 30 min. Schlessinger Video. Distr., Bala Cynwyd, PA: Library Video, 1993. $39.95. (Multicultural Peoples of North America). 4-10

Based on the Chelsea House series Peoples of North America, the video highlights the Jewish culture. It gives reasons for the Jewish immigration to America, explanations of customs and traditions, the history of their transition, and important leaders from the culture. Historians and sociologists discuss these aspects, and a Jewish family explains its cultural identity, shared memories, and reasons for immigration.

2749. **JFK: The Age of the Kennedy Presidency**. Videocassette. Color. 26 min. NBC. Chatsworth, CA: Aims Media, 1992. $99. (John F. Kennedy). 9 up

John F. Kennedy was inaugurated President of the United States in 1961 after winning the 1960 election. The video looks at the accomplishments he made as the 35th President.

2750. **JFK: The Day the Nation Cried**. Videocassette. Color. 52 min. New York: V.I.E.W. Video, 1989. $19.95. 7 up

The events of November 22, 1963, shocked the world, and this documentary emphasizes the psychological change that the assassination of John F. Kennedy caused. Black-and-white footage of national crises occurring during his presidency show the Bay of Pigs, the Berlin issue, the Cuban Missile Crisis, and the Nuclear Test Ban Treaty, which help to focus on his tenure in office.

2751. **JFK: The Death of a President.** Videocassette. Color. 27 min. NBC. Chatsworth, CA: Aims Media, 1992. $99. (John F. Kennedy). 9 up

On November 22, 1963, John F. Kennedy visited Dallas, Texas. There an assassin killed him. The program examines events both before and after the tragedy using news footage and commentary.

2752. **JFK: The Early Years**. Videocassette. Color. 25 min. NBC. Chatsworth, CA: Aims Media, 1992. $99. (John F. Kennedy). 9 up

This program examines the events and experiences that were part of John F. Kennedy's early youth and education and speculates how they influenced his ideas and his politics.

2753. **A Job at Ford's**. Videocassette. Color. 60 min. Blackside, Inc. Distr., Alexandria, VA: PBS Video, 1993. $79.95. ISBN 0-7936-1037-0. 8 up

In 1927, Henry Ford's automobile company was the most important business in the most important industry in America. But in 1929, with the fall of the stock market, its situation changed. *Council on Nontheatrical Events, Golden Eagle.*

2754. **John Fitzgerald Kennedy's Lost Pathway to Peace**. Videocassette. Color. 30 min. Goleta, CA: Riden International, 1991. $24.95. 9 up

The video emphasizes that more attention has been paid to President Kennedy's lifestyle than to his attempt to create worldwide peace. His speeches and historical footage intermingle to give a sense of his vision from which resulted a Nuclear Test Ban Treaty, a stronger United Nations, the creation of the U.S. Arms Control and Disarmament Agency, the Peace Corps, and other agencies.

2755. **Judaism: The Religion of the People**. Videocassette. Color. Delphi Productions. Distr., Niles, IL: United Learning, 1994. $95. ISBN 1-56007-396-9. 7 up

On location in Israel, Egypt, and the United States, the video traces the history, development, and practice of Judaism.

K

2756. **Kentucky Rifle**. Videocassette. Color. 11 min. Irwindale, CA: Barr Media, 1992. $60. (American History). 4-9

Live action, reenactments, maps, and graphics help tell the story of pioneer life. This video explains the care and use of rifles, one of their main tools.

2757. **Kontum Diary**. Videocassette. Color. 56 min. Oakland, CA: Video Project, 1995. $150. 9 up

After a battle during the Vietnam War, a 19-year-old American soldier found the diary of a North Vietnamese soldier. Later he had it translated, and what he found was poetry. The film chronicles the soldier, Paul Reed, when he returns to Vietnam with the diary and gives it to its owner. *Worldfest-Charleston Gold* and *New York Festivals*.

2758. **Korea/Vietnam**. Videocassette. Color. 80 min. Independent Television News. Distr., New York: Central Park Media, 1995. $29.95. (Wars in Peace). 10 up

The United States has been involved in two long wars since World War II. This program examines its role in those two wars through battle films, newsreels, and other documentary footage.

2759. **Korean Americans**. Videocassette. Color. 30 min. Schlessinger Video. Distr., Bala Cynwyd, PA: Library Video, 1993. $39.95. (Multicultural Peoples of North America). 4-10

Based on the Chelsea House series Peoples of North America, the video highlights the Korean culture. It gives reasons for the Korean immigration to America, explanations of customs and traditions, the history of their transition, and important leaders from the culture. Historians and sociologists discuss these aspects, and a Korean family explains its cultural identity, shared memories, and reasons for immigration.

L

2760. **Land and Landscape: Views of America's History and Culture**. Videocassette. Color. 28 min. National Museum of American Art/Smithsonian. Distr., Glenview IL: Crystal Productions, 1995. $85. (America Past and Present). 9 up

A view of America in the nineteenth and twentieth centuries appears through its landscape painting and photography.

2761. **Langston Hughes**. Videocassette. Color. 30 min. Schlessinger Video. 1994. Distr., Bala Cynwyd, PA: Library Video, 1993. $39.95. (Black Americans of Achievement). 7 up

A complement to the Chelsea House series Black Americans of Achievement, the video introduces Langston Hughes (1902-1967). Historians and other experts comment on his achievements using photos, old film footage, and modern live action for illustration.

2762. **The Last Cowboys**. Videocassette. Color. 60 min. Bethesda, MD: Acorn Media, 1992. $79.80 set; $19.95. (Great West Collection). 7 up

Exciting photography, good narration, and western music underlie this part of the series on cowboys in the American West. This video shows how cowboys have been depicted in art and photographs. It gives the history of the cowboy of yesterday by referring to the diary of a cowboy in the 1800s.

2763. **Last of the Mohicans**. Videocassette. Color. 28 min. Princeton, NJ: Films for the Humanities and Sciences, 1994. $149. 7 up

Interviews with historians and archaeologists, battle reenactments, and computer-generated maps of the region around Fort William Henry in upstate New York show that the French and Indian War (1754-1763) was a world conflict. Remains of soldiers show they were killed by the battle, by infectious disease, and by a massacre following a siege. Comparing the archaeological finds with James Fenimore Cooper's novel, *The Last of the Mohicans*, produces interesting results.

2764. **Last Stand at Little Big Horn**. Videocassette. Color. 60 min. Alexandria, VA: PBS Video, 1992. $59.95. 9 up

Although his scouts warned Custer that everyone would be killed in a battle against the Lakota and Cheyenne, he still decided to fight on June 25, 1867, because he disagreed with them and thought he could be a hero. Part of the discussion in the video focuses on the attitude that Native Americans were obstacles to be overcome as the country expanded to the west.

2765. **Latino Art and Culture in the United States**. Videocassette. Color. 28 min. National Museum of American Art/Smithsonian. Distr., Glenview, IL: Crystal Productions, 1995. $85. (America Past and Present). 6 up

This video traces the contributions of the peoples of Latin American heritage to the history and contemporary life of the United States.

2766. **Law and Outlaws of the West**. Videocassette. Color. 27 min. Irwindale, CA: Barr Media, 1992. $75. (American Frontier). 4-9

The program makes commentary about Joaquin Murietta, the O.K. Corral in Tombstone, Arizona, and other people and events.

2767. **Legacies**. Videocassette. Color. 30 min. Ontario, Canada: TVOntario, 1990. $499 series; $99 ea. (Ancient Civilizations). 6 up

Part of a series examining the origins of civilizations, the video investigates the human needs to search for food, to have security, and to be creative. This video looks at the debt owed to past civilizations, especially Rome. Architecture, law, government, language, drama, medicine, mathematics, and writing all come from the ancient world.

2768. **Legacy**. Videocassette. Color. 22 min. New York: Cinema Guild, 1994. $195. 9 up

The presentation questions the accepted Columbus myth by noting that the Tainos were not the unfriendly savages. Evidence from archaeological digs gives contrary views of the Columbus story.

2769. **Legacy of the Mound Builders**. Videocassette. Color. 17 min. Camera One. Distr., Eugene, OR: New Dimensions Media, 1995. $240. 5 up

The Mound Builders lived in North America and built an elaborate trade network that extended over half the continent more than 2,000 years ago. *Council on Nontheatrical Events, Golden Eagle.*

2770. **The Legacy of Thomas Jefferson**. Videocassette. Color. 26 min. Princeton, NJ: Films for the Humanities and Sciences, 1995. $89.95. 7 up

If Thomas Jefferson's principles had prevailed, they would have destroyed the United States, according to Judge Robert Bork. Bork and two historians discuss whether Jefferson was a champion of liberty or a dangerous radical.

2771. **The Lenape**. Videocassette. Color. 30 min. Schlessinger Video. Distr., Bala Cynwyd, PA: Library Video, 1994. $39.95. (Indians of North America). 4-10

The Lenape lost their land to white settlement in the seventeenth and eighteenth centuries (as the Delaware) and migrated into the Midwest. The video focuses on the unique history of the Lenape using photographs and film footage. It also discusses the government, the spiritual, the mythical, and the role of women.

2772. **The Lewis and Clark Trail**. Videocassette. Color. 20 min. Delphi. Distr., Niles, IL: United Learning, 1992. $89. 5-9

With reenactments, historical photographs, and lines from journals kept by the participants, the video examines the exploration of Lewis and Clark into the West from 1804 to 1806. Covered are the journey's objectives, scientific discoveries, historic importance, and survival methods. Especially striking is the photography of sites along the way and the acknowledgment of contributions that Native Americans like Sacagawea made to the success of the expedition.

2773. **The Life and Times of Abraham Lincoln**. Videocassette. Color. 14 min. Delphi. Distr., Niles, IL: United Learning, 1992. $79.95. 5-12

Reenactment footage, historical photographs, and illustrations present the places in Lincoln's life in the context of his times. Also included are recitations of excerpts from the Lincoln-Douglas debates, the Emancipation Proclamation, and the Gettysburg Address.

2774. **The Life and Times of George Washington**. Videocassette. Color. 14 min. Delphi. Distr., Niles, IL: United Learning, 1992. $79.95. 3-8

Historical art and live-action footage present a brief view of George Washington's life, with much information about Mount Vernon. Lifestyle and social expectations from 1732 to 1799 give a sense of the time.

2775. **The Life of George Washington**. Videocassette. Color. 30 min. Mt. Vernon Ladies Association. Distr., Whittier, CA: Finley-Holiday, 1989. $29.95. 6 up

In a straightforward manner, almost everything known about George Washington appears in the program. His exact words are featured as the video presents his early life, marriage, French and Indian War incidences, his work in Washington, and his final illness.

2776. **Lighthouses of New England**. Videocassette. Color. 30 min. Connecticut Public TV. Distr., Bethesda, MD: Acorn Media, 1993. $14.95. 7 up

The era of civilian lighthouse keepers ended in 1939 when the Coast Guard began to staff them. In 1990, all 450 lighthouses were automated. The history of these edifices gives a sense of another time in American history.

2777. **Lincoln: A Photobiography**. Videocassette. Color. 65 min. Miller-Brody. Distr., Chicago: American School Publishers, 1989. $98. 5-9

In a series of dissolving slides taken from Russell Freedman's Newbery Award–winning book and an actor portraying Lincoln, the program divides into four parts: "Backwoods Boy," "Law and Politics," "Emancipation," and "The Dreadful War."

2778. **Living Portraits of Historic Women: Of All the Nerve!** Videocassette. Color. 65 min. Seattle, WA: Paragon Media, 1996. $29.95. ISBN 1-57634-004-X. 9 up

In this video, seven women who were risk takers are presented. Among them are Lydia Pinkham (1819-1883) and her concern with women's health questions, Rosa Parks (b. 1913), Maria Montessori (1870-1952) and education, Eleanor of Aquitane (1122-1204) and her kings, Gertrude Stein (1874-1946) and her art, Theda Bara (1890-1955), an actress, and Eleanor Roosevelt (1884-1962).

2779. **The Loom**. Videocassette. Color. 11 min. Irwindale, CA: Barr Media, 1992. $60. (American History). 4-9

Live action, reenactments, maps, and graphics help tell the story of pioneer weaving and threading a loom.

2780. **Lost in Time**. Videocassette. Color. 60 min. Auburn TV. Distr., Evanston, IL: Wombat, 1990. $195. 7 up

A live-action production, the video covers the three major periods of development of Indian culture in the southeastern United States: the Paleo Hunters, the Archaic and Woodland Indians, and the Mississippian Indians from the Ice Age when people crossed the land bridge over the Bering Strait up to de Soto's exploration in 1540. The video shows what was happening in the Americas while civilizations were flourishing in the Fertile Crescent and Europe.

2781. **The Lottery: Who Fights Our Wars?** Videocassette. Color. 18 min. New York: Filmakers Library, 1995. $195. 9-12

Men have used a variety of methods to escape fighting wars since the 1860s when they could pay to get out of the draft or hire a substitute. Since then the Selective Service has tried to equalize who serves. After Vietnam, the army became an all-volunteer group although the Selective Service continues to rehearse the lottery. *National Educational Film & Video Festival, Bronze Apple; Council on Nontheatrical Events, Golden Eagle.*

2782. **The Lucky Ones: Allied Airmen and Buchenwald**. Videocassette. Color. 46 min. New York: National Film Board of Canada, 1994. $295. 9 up

In World War II, the Nazis captured 168 Allied airmen and held them at Buchenwald. They did not tell of the horrors they endured and witnessed until they had a reunion. As they walked around Buchenwald remembering, they decided to break the silence.

2783. **Lucretia Mott**. Videocassette. Color. 59 min. New York: EPH, 1994. $59.95. 7 up

In a dramatic presentation, the video shows the life of Lucretia Mott as she tried to defend women's rights, slaves, and Native Americans. Among the figures presented with Mott are Susan B. Anthony, Sojourner Truth, and William Lloyd Garrison. Reenactments of a Civil War battle and a Quaker meeting add interest.

2784. **Luisa Capetillo: Passion for Justice**. Videocassette. Color. 42 min. New York: Cinema Guild, 1994. $275. 7up

Luisa Capetillo, feminist and labor organizer, spent her life trying to stop the exploitation of tobacco and sugar workers in her native Puerto Rico during the early part of the twentieth century. Sepia-toned photographs, old film footage, and live action tell her story.

M

2785. **Madam C. J. Walker**. Videocassette. Color. 30 min. Schlessinger Video. Distr., Bala Cynwyd, PA: Library Video, 1992. $39.95. (Black Americans of Achievement). 7 up

A complement to the Chelsea House series Black Americans of Achievement, the video introduces Madam C. J. Walker (1867-1919). Historians and other experts comment on her achievements using photos, old film footage, and modern live action for illustration.

2786. **Making It Happen: Masters of Invention**. Videocassette. Color. 22 min. Bob Oliver Communications. Distr., Van Nuys, CA: Churchill Media, 1995. $99.95. 4 up

This video starts with the days of slavery and moves to the present as it profiles the Black inventors who have made major contributions to the progress of society. They include such men as inventor and astronomer Benjamin Bannecker, Edison's rival Louis Latimer, and Garrett Morgan, the inventor of the traffic signal.

2787. **Malcolm X**. Videocassette. Color. 15 min. Princeton, NJ: Films for the Humanities and Sciences, 1992. $34.95. 4 up

This program explores Malcolm X's philosophical evolution and examines the outside forces that helped him shape his beliefs. His father, a Baptist minister, was murdered; he became a Harlem hustler; and he took a pilgrimage to Mecca. For much of his life he struggled for African American equality.

2788. **Malcolm X**. Videocassette. Color. 30 min. Schlessinger Video. Distr., Bala Cynwyd, PA: Library Video, 1992. $39.95. (Black Americans of Achievement). 7-12

A complement to the Chelsea House series Black Americans of Achievement, the video introduces Malcolm X (1925-1965). Historians and other experts comment on his achievements using photos, old film footage, and modern live action for illustration.

2789. **Malcolm X: Make It Plain**. Videocassette. Color. 150 min. Blackside, Inc. and Roja. Distr., Alexandria, VA: PBS Video, 1994. $99. (The American Experience). 9 up

The video begins with historical black-and-white footage that traces Malcolm X's (1925-1965) stormy youth and continues to his life as an adult in this visual biography. *Council on Nontheatrical Events, Golden Eagle.*

2790. **Mansions of Newport**. Videocassette. Color. 33 min. Glastonbury, VT: VideoTours, 1990. $24.95. 7 up

In this tour of eight historical mansions built between 1748 and 1902, the program provides the historical, cultural, and economic significance of the social class who used these Newport, Rhode Island, houses only two to three months a year, especially between 1890 to 1914 and beyond.

2791. **Marcus Garvey**. Videocassette. Color. 30 min. Schlessinger Video. Distr., Bala Cynwyd, PA: Library Video, 1993. $39.95. (Black Americans of Achievement). 7 up

A complement to the Chelsea House series Black Americans of Achievement, the video introduces Marcus Garvey (1887-1940). Historians and other experts comment on his achievements using photos, old film footage, and modern live action for illustration.

2792. **Marian Anderson**. Videocassette. Color. 30 min. Schlessinger Video. Distr., Bala Cynwyd, PA: Library Video, 1995. $39.95. ISBN 1-57225-038-0. (American Women of Achievement). 7-12

The video asks why Marian Anderson (1897-1993) resisted conformity and if she could be considered a "rebel" as she helped shape the history and culture of the United States. Archival footage, sketches, photographs, recordings, interviews with historians, literary experts, and reenactments help to examine the impact of family; economic, social, and political circumstances; and her ability to empower herself.

2793. **Martin Luther King, Jr.** Videocassette. Color. 27 min. Princeton, NJ: Films for the Humanities and Sciences, 1996. $34.95. 4 up

Martin Luther King, Jr. was an ordained minister with a doctor's degree. He fought for freedom, justice, and equality, and his efforts were recognized in 1964 with a Nobel Peace Prize.

2794. **Martin Luther King, Jr.** Videocassette. Color. 30 min. Schlessinger Video. Distr., Bala Cynwyd, PA: Library Video, 1992. $39.95. (Black Americans of Achievement). 7-12

A complement to the Chelsea House series Black Americans of Achievement, the video introduces Martin Luther King, Jr. Historians and other experts comment on his achievements using photos, old film footage, and modern live action for illustration.

2795. **Martin Luther King, Jr. and the Civil Rights Movement**. Videocassette. Color. 20 min. Xenon. Distr., Chatsworth, CA: Aims Media, 1995. $99.95. 8 up

Dr. Martin Luther King, Jr. was a major force in the Civil Rights movement. This video chronicles his life and his leadership.

2796. **Mary McLeod Bethune**. Videocassette. Color. 30 min. Schlessinger Video. Distr., Bala Cynwyd, PA: Library Video, 1993. $39.95. (Black Americans of Achievement). 5 up

A complement to the Chelsea House series Black Americans of Achievement, the video introduces Mary McLeod Bethune (1875-1955). Historians and other experts comment on her achievements using photos, old film footage, and modern live action for illustration.

2797. **Matthew Henson**. Videocassette. Color. 30 min. Schlessinger Video. Distr., Bala Cynwyd, PA: Library Video, 1993. $39.95. (Black Americans of Achievement). 5 up

A complement to the Chelsea House series Black Americans of Achievement, the video introduces Matthew Henson (1866-1955). Historians and other experts comment on his achievements using photos, old film footage, and modern live action for illustration.

2798. **The Mayflower Pilgrims**. Videocassette. Color. 44 min. Distr., Harrington Park, NJ: Janson, 1996. $24.95. ISBN 1-56839-031-9. 7 up

This video, made in England, tells why the Pilgrims came to Massachusetts in 1620 from the British perspective. It sees the Pilgrims as a group of religious dissidents or nonconformists who refused to follow the Church of England based on William Brewster's account of his struggle for religious freedom.

2799. **Mean Things Happening**. Videocassette. Color. 60 min. Blackside, Inc. Distr., Alexandria, VA: PBS Video, 1993. $79.95. ISBN 0-7936-1041-9. (The Great Depression). 8 up

Working men and women during the 1930s battled landowners and factory managers for the right to join a union, even though they lived in a democracy—America. *Council on Nontheatrical Events, Golden Eagle.*

2800. **Men of the Frontier**. Videocassette. Color. 27 min. Irwindale, CA: Barr Media, 1992. $75. (American Frontier). 4-9

Some of the men on the frontier were writers. Among them were Mark Twain and Horace Greeley. Still others made contributions to the frontier way of life.

2801. **The Menominee**. Videocassette. Color. 30 min. Schlessinger Video. Distr., Bala Cynwyd, PA: Library Video, 1994. $39.95. (Indians of North America). 4-10

The video focuses on the unique history of the Menominee, who now live in northeast Wisconsin, using photographs and film footage. It also discusses the government, the spiritual, the mythical, and the role of women.

2802. **The Merchant Marine**. Videocassette. Color. 50 min. Bethesda, MD: Atlas Video, 1991. $99.95 set; $19.95 ea. (War Stories). 7 up

On-camera interviews with veterans make this series on World War II especially human. In this video, the merchant marines discuss their risks while defending themselves from the German U-boats and torpedo planes in their "Liberty Ships."

2803. **Mexican Americans**. Videocassette. Color. 30 min. Schlessinger Video. Distr., Bala Cynwyd, PA: Library Video, 1993. $39.95. (Multicultural Peoples of North America). 4-10

Based on the Chelsea House series Peoples of North America, the video highlights the Mexican culture. It gives reasons for the Mexican immigration to America, explanations of customs and traditions, history of their transition, and presents the important leaders from the culture. Historians and sociologists discuss these aspects, and a Mexican family explains its cultural identity, shared memories, and reasons for immigration.

2804. **Michigan Avenue: From Museums to the Magnificent Mile**. Videocassette. Color. 30 min. Wilmette IL: Perspectives, 1993. $34.95. ISBN 1-880005-05-0. (Skyline: Chicago). 7 up

The history of this Chicago street appears through the buildings that have been erected on it in the past centuries.

2805. **Midnight Ramble**. Videocassette. Color. 60 min. WGBH. Distr., Alexandria, VA: PBS Video, 1994. $69.95. (The American Experience). 10 up

Between 1910 and 1940, African Americans went to the movies late at night to see "race movies," movies created by Blacks about Blacks who were not stereotypes. Many scenes from movies, period music, and comments from actors who worked in the films in the context of newspaper clippings, photographs, and live-action film reveal this little-known part of history.

2806. **Mining Made the West**. Videocassette. Color. 34 min. Irwindale, CA: Barr Media, 1992. $75. (American Frontier). 4-9

The gold rush, beginning in 1849, brought many people to the West. Silver also had a role in the expansion of the United States.

2807. **Mission Life**. Videocassette. Color. 22 min. Irwindale, CA: Barr Media, 1992. $60. (American History). 4-9

Live action, reenactments, maps, and graphics help tell the story of the missions, based on priests' diaries.

2808. **Missions of California: Mission Santa Barbara**. Videocassette. Color. 10 min. Derry, NH: Chip Taylor Communications, 1989. $150. 4-8

The Franciscans founded Santa Barbara on December 4, 1786, and the mission has survived since its reconstruction in 1815 with six-foot walls. The program presents this mission and its importance during its 200-year history.

2809. **Mississippi America**. Videocassette. Color. 60 min. Carbondale, IL: Southern Illinois University, 1996. $19.95. 7 up

The documentary shows the 1964 Freedom Summer campaign to help Blacks in Mississippi register to vote. It focuses on the roles of the attorneys and the strategies that they used to outwit the local government authorities. Their work contributed to the 1965 passage of the Voting Rights Act. Ruby Dee and Ossie Davis narrate the presentation.

2810. **Mississippi Steamboats**. Videocassette. Color. 21 min. Irwindale, CA: Barr Media, 1993. $385. 4 up

Steamboats transported huge quantities of cotton from the plantations to the cities in the nineteenth century, and then they began transporting people. Archival film footage, period art, and photographs present some of the famous characters and events of the time when the steamboats paddled the Mississippi.

2811. **Monument Valley: Navajo Homeland**. Videocassette. Color. 30 min. Whittier, CA: Finley-Holiday, 1991. $24.95. 7 up

Monument Valley is home to more than 100,000 Navajos who farm and raise animals. Historic events important to the lives of the people include the Spanish introduction of the horse and sheep in the 1600s and the roles of trading posts in the early twentieth century.

2812. **A More Perfect Union: The Three Branches of the Federal Government**. 3 Videocassettes. Color. 45 min. Madison, WI: Knowledge Unlimited, 1991. $39.95 ea. 7-12

The three videos, *The Presidency, The Congress*, and *The Supreme Court*, examine the history, the powers, and the constitutional basis for each of the three branches of government. Incidents from the presidencies of F. D. Roosevelt, Harry Truman, and Richard Nixon illustrate the President's powers. How Congress makes bills into law becomes clearer as well as the importance of the Court's landmark cases.

2813. **More than Bows and Arrows**. Videocassette. Color. 60 min. Camera One. Distr., Los Angeles: Wood Knapp, 1992. $29.95. 7 up

Live action, historic film clips, and drawings illustrate the contributions of Native Americans from the Anasazi cliff dwellings to the mounds in the southeastern United States and their agricultural knowledge. M. Scott Momaday narrates about these and other accomplishments, including the Navajo code language, which helped to defeat the Japanese in World War II, mining, medicine, art, and entertainment.

2814. **Mount Vernon: Home of George Washington**. Videocassette. Color. 30 min. Whittier, CA: Finley-Holiday, 1989. $29.95. (American Heritage Series). 7 up

Washington (1732-1799) the man, as husband, gentleman farmer, businessman, host, and architect, comes through in this presentation of Washington and his home, Mount Vernon. Included are quotes from his writings, details from his personal life, and a sense of eighteenth-century Virginia.

2815. **Mountain Men**. Videocassette. Color. 16 min. Irwindale, CA: Barr Media, 1992. $60. (American History). 4-9

Live action, reenactments, maps, and graphics help tell the story of explorers and trappers in the early 1800s.

2816. **Mountain Wolf Woman: 1884-1960**. Videocassette. Color. 17 min. Madison, WI: Her Own Words, 1990. $95. 7 up

This story of a Winnebago Indian woman describes her childhood when she became excited over receiving a bicycle as well as her reluctance to go into an arranged marriage. Her granddaughter tells the story, showing how her grandmother adapted to many changes while remaining a strong and independent woman.

2817. **Mr. Jefferson and His University**. Videocassette. Color. 52 min. Princeton, NJ: Films for the Humanities and Sciences, 1993. $149. 7 up

Shot on location at Monticello, Williamsburg, and Charlottesville, the video shows the influence that Jefferson still has on the university that he founded in Virginia. His architecture and his moral beliefs led him to want to establish an environment for a new democratic "man" in the new American republic.

2818. **Mt. Clare: Cradle of the American Dream**. Videocassette. Color. 20 min. Parkton Media. Distr., Mountain View, CA: Hummingbird, 1989. $14.95. 7 up

In 1827, Baltimore, Maryland, businessmen needed to establish a link to the Ohio River. They conceived of building a railroad, a scheme that many viewed as impossible. They did, and they kept Baltimore's position as a trading route from being eroded by the Erie Canal. The video also discusses the railroad's contribution to the Civil War, World War I, and World War II.

2819. **Murder in Mississippi: The Price for Freedom**. Videocassette. Color. 52 min. Princeton, NJ: Films for the Humanities and Sciences, 1995. $149. 7 up

The Ku Klux Klan murdered three young men during "Freedom Summer" in Mississippi and shocked the nation; their actions changed the course of the Civil Rights movement.

2820. **My Heroes Have Always Been Cowboys**. Videocassette. Color. 60 min. Bethesda, MD: Acorn Media, 1992. $79.80 set; $19.95. (Great West Collection). 7 up

Exciting photography, good narration, and western music underlie this part of the series on cowboys in the American West. This video follows a two-week period during spring roundup at Old Six Ranch in west Texas showing what cowboys do and what roundup life is like.

N

2821. **The Narragansett**. Videocassette. Color. 30 min. Schlessinger Video. Distr., Bala Cynwyd, PA: Library Video, 1993. $39.95. (Indians of North America). 4-10

This video focuses on the unique history of the Narragansett using photographs and film footage. The tribe formerly inhabited Rhode Island, but King Philip's War in 1675-1676 nearly exterminated them. Some descendants remain in the area. The video also discusses the government, the spiritual, the mythical, and the role of women in the tribe.

2822. **A Nation in Turmoil**. Videocassette. Color. 30 min. Schlessinger Video. Distr., Bala Cynwyd, PA: Library Video, 1995. $799 series; $39.95 ea. (United States History Video). 5-9

Life began to change for American citizens in the late nineteenth century when people began to move to urban areas and shifted the population balance. Dramatic readings and performances bring important events and historical figures together in this video.

2823. **Native American Medicine**. Videocassette. Color. 55 min. Edwardsburg, MI: Meuninck's Media Methods, 1995. $29.95. 6-12

To ward off bad winds and let the healing spirits enter, Native Americans have used smudging, sweeping, dance, music, wild plants, massage, and the sweatlodge. Members of the Ottawa, Mixteca (Mexico), and Shawnee describe the traditional healing secrets of their ancestors.

2824. **Native Americans: People of the Desert**. Videocassette. Color. 24 min. Raleigh, NC: Rainbow Educational, 1992. $99. 4-7

Animated maps and historical reenactments portray the Native Americans who live in the desert. They include the Ute, Pima, Hopi, Navajo, and their ancestors, the Anasazi.

2825. **Native Americans: People of the Forest**. Videocassette. Color. 25 min. Peter Matulavich. Distr., Raleigh, NC: Rainbow Educational, 1994. $99. 4-8

A Chippewa family represents the typical life of an Eastern Woodland Indian. *Council on Nontheatrical Events, Golden Eagle; National Educational Media Gold Apple; Charleston International Film and Video Silver Plaque; Columbus International Film and Video Bronze Plaque;* and *Cindy Bronze Award.*

2826. **Native Americans: People of the Northwest Coast**. Videocassette. Color. 23 min. Raleigh, NC: Rainbow Educational, 1994. $99. 5-8

Filmed in 'Ksan, a recreated Gitksan village in British Columbia, the video shows life before the arrival of the Europeans in the seventeenth century, including theories about the migration over the Bering Sea land bridge.

2827. **Native Americans: People of the Plains**. Videocassette. Color. 24 min. Raleigh, NC: Rainbow Educational, 1993. $99. ISBN 1-56701-020-2. 4-8

In showing how the Native Americans hunted buffalo and used all its parts in the community, the video explains how the settlers destroyed the buffalo and, therefore, the livelihood of the Plains Indians. *Council on Nontheatrical Events, Golden Eagle; Gold Apple, New England Film & Video Festival.*

2828. **Native Americans: The History of a People**. Videocassette. Color. 25 min. Madison, WI: Knowledge Unlimited, 1992. $55. 4-12

In two parts, the video presents two groups of Native Americans who have lived on this continent, hunters and Mound Builders, whose way of life ended more than 600 years ago, probably with the Anasazi. The second part discusses the various ways that European settlers have taken away land privileges and tried to impose western culture on the Native Americans. Also included are Native Americans' recent attempts to have some of those wrongs righted.

2829. **The Navajo**. Videocassette. Color. 30 min. Schlessinger Video. Distr., Bala Cynwyd, PA: Library Video, 1993. $39.95. (Indians of North America). 4-10

This video focuses on the unique history of the Navajo, or *Diné*, using photographs and film footage. These people have lived in the Southwest and continue to inhabit the area of New Mexico, Arizona, and Utah. The video also discusses the government, the spiritual, the mythical, and the role of women in the tribe.

2830. **Navajo Code Talkers: The Epic Story**. Videocassette. Color. 57 min. N. Hollywood, CA: Tully Entertainment, 1995. $19.95. 7 up

The Navajo Indians played an important role as communicators for the U.S. Marine Corps during World War II. They used their language to create a code that the enemy could not break.

2831. **New Deal, New York**. Videocassette. Color. 60 min. Blackside, Inc. Distr., Alexandria, VA: PBS Video, 1993. $79.95. ISBN 0-7936-1039-7. (The Great Depression). 8 up

The relationship between Franklin D. Roosevelt and Fiorello LaGuardia, the mayor of New York City, changed New York and expanded the role of American government during the 1930s. Because discrimination occurred with New Deal programs, discrimination was outlawed when Roosevelt and Congress created the Works Progress Administration (WPA), and by 1936, New York City was beginning to recover from total poverty. *Council on Nontheatrical Events, Golden Eagle.*

2832. **A New Nation (1776-1815)**. Videocassette. Color. 30 min. Schlessinger Video. Distr., Bala Cynwyd, PA: Library Video, 1995. $799 series; $39.95 ea. (United States History Video). 5-9

Dramatic readings and performances bring important events and historical figures together in this video.

2833. **A New Public**. Videocassette. Color. 30 min. WGBH Educational Foundation. Distr., Washington, DC: Annenberg/CPB, 1989. $650 set; $29.95 ea. (The Western Tradition, Program 45). 11 up

The professor presenting this topic projects his excitement for history. He provides insight into the people, politics, thoughts, and events that have shaped western society. Resources from the Metropolitan Museum of Art illustrate the beliefs of the populace in the nineteenth century.

2834. **New York the Way It Was: The Old Neighborhood**. Videocassette. Color. 58 min. WIW21. Distr., Bethesda, MD: Acorn Media, 1995. $19.99. 9 up

Home movies, vintage photographs, and reminiscences reconstruct life in New York City during the 1940s and 1950s. It looks at the immigrant communities and the distinct neighborhoods that influenced the choices of those who lived there. Included are the brownstones, Police Athletic League teams, Grand Concourse, Madison Square Garden, Harlem, the Bronx, ethnic gangs, Prohibition's effect, trade unions, and community nursing efforts.

2835. **New York the Way It Was: Wish You Were Here**. Videocassette. Color. 58min. WIW21. Distr., Bethesda, MD: Acorn Media, 1995. $19.99. 9 up

Home movies, vintage photographs, and reminiscences reconstruct life in New York City during the 1940s and 1950s. It tells how the residents left daily cares to enjoy themselves in Coney Island, Steeplechase Park, Jones Beach, Montauk Point State Park, Hollywood Pavillion, and the Red Apple Restaurant as they drove to the Catskills. When they stayed in the city, they enjoyed roller skating, boccie, bowling, baseball, dancing, and drive-in movies on Saturday night. Education gave upward mobility to many.

2836. **Nightfighters**. Videocassette. Color. 55 min. Falls Church, VA: Landmark, 1994. $250. 9 up

Film clips, photographs, period music, and interviews with veterans tell the story of the Tuskegee airmen, the World War II air squadron composed of African Americans. Profiles included are Alfred "Chief" Anderson and Benjamin O. Davis, commanding officer.

2837. **Nikola Tesla: The Genius Who Lit the World**. Videocassette. Color. 42 min. Tesla Memorial Society. Distr., Valencia, CA: Tapeworm Video, 1995. $24.95. 9 up

Although Nikola Tesla's name is rarely associated with Thomas Edison, Tesla developed alternating current, which brought electricity to everyone, and designed the world's first hydroelectric power plant in 1895 at Niagara Falls. Rare news clips, photographs, and quotes from his writing tell the story of this little-known but important scientist.

2838. **1914-1918: World War I**. Videocassette. B&W. 25 min. Washington, DC: National Geographic, 1992. $110. 8 up

The video uses historical footage from World War I in describing the causes of the war. Intermingled with diplomatic information is the action of battle and pictures of some of the graves of the more than 10 million soldiers who died while fighting.

2839. **1929-1941: The Great Depression**. Videocassette. B&W. 25 min. Washington, DC: National Geographic, 1990. $99.95. 10 up

In 1929, a worldwide economic collapse began. It ended only with the onset of World War II and its need for full military and industrial production. The video explains the events and experiences of this time as well as the irregularities in the banking industry and the stock market. The archival film shows life during the 1920s and 1930s with the Dust Bowl, Hoovervilles, unemployment lines, and soup kitchens. Roosevelt's programs to combat the problem were the National Recovery Act, the Civilian Conservation Corps, the Works Progress Administration, the Wagner Act, the Securities Act, and the Social Security Act.

2840. **1945-1989: The Cold War**. Videocassette. Color. 25 min. Washington, DC: National Geographic, 1991. $110. 8 up

With newsreel footage, the history of the verbal conflict between the United States and the Soviet Union comes to life. The presentation of both obscure and well-known events helps to understand why this hostility occurred.

2841. **Nixon**. 3 Videocassettes. Color. 58 min. ea. WGBH, WNET, and KCET. Distr., Alexandria, VA: PBS Video, 1990. $150 set. (The American Experience). 9 up

The first of three tapes details Nixon's life until he was elected President of the United States in 1968. The second tape discusses the Nixon/Kissinger strategies for diplomacy with Vietnam, China, and the Soviet Union. Tape three gives an accurate and easily understandable assessment of "Watergate." The one thing that the series lacks is Nixon's cooperation, but everything included is public record.

2842. **Nixon—Man and President**. Videocassette. Color and B&W. 100 min. ABC News and A&E Television. Distr., New York: New Video Group, 1996. $19.95. ISBN 1-56501-742-0. (Biography). 11 up

Starting with Richard Nixon's birth in Yorba Linda, California, the video follows his life and his political career through his triumphs and his failures. Some of his biographers and his associates talk about his life and the inconsistencies in his presidency.

2843. **No Time for Tears—Vietnam: The Women Who Served**. Videocassette. Color. 60 min. New York: West End Films, 1994. $75. 9 up

Film footage, photos, and interviews with seven women who served in Vietnam show their experiences and problems there as well as the mental adjustments they made after returning home. *Critics Choice, Big Muddy Film Festival; Certificate of Merit, Chicago International Film Festival.*

2844. **North Africa and the Global War**. Videocassette. Color and B&W. 45 min. Bethesda, MD: Acorn Media, 1989. $19.95. (V for Victory). 7 up

General Dwight Eisenhower led the U.S. forces in Operation Torch in North Africa during World War II. Around the same time the Allied campaign in Burma, the battle for the Atlantic Ocean, and the air assault on Fortress Europe also occurred. They are presented here through newsreel footage and stories from the home front.

O

2845. **Old Sturbridge Village: Growing Up in New England**. Videocassette. Color. 30 min. VideoTours. Distr., Englewood, CO: SelectVideo, 1992. $24.95. 3-8

Set in 1835, this living history museum production tells the story of Sarah, 15, and her brother. The video presents a realistic look at life during that time.

2846. **One World, Many Worlds: Hispanic Diversity in the United States**. Videocassette. Color. 22 min. Raleigh, NC: Rainbow Educational, 1993. $89. 5-8

The program chronicles the history of Hispanic Americans, from the Spanish explorations and exploitations of the New World to the Mexican-American War and the struggles for independence throughout Central and South America. It also looks at the Hispanic influence on American culture.

2847. **The Oregon Trail**. Videocassette. Color. 25 min. Irwindale, CA: Barr Media, 1995. $395. 5-11

Reenactments and contemporary footage present one of the most important components of the westward movement over the United States in honor of its 150th anniversary.

2848. **Oregon's Historic Covered Bridges**. 3 Videocassettes. Color. 30 min. Sweet Home, OR: Hand Made Videos, 1995. $24.95 ea. 7 up

Still standing are 52 covered bridges in Oregon. They are featured in these three videos with historical background, including the information that coverings kept out much of the dampness and allowed the bridges to last almost five times as long as those uncovered.

2849. **Organizing America: The History of Trade Unions**. Videocassette. 40 min. Charleston, WV: Cambridge Educational, 1994. $89.95. 7 up

Using interviews, personal accounts, and archival footage, the video tells the story of trade unions and their accomplishments at getting minimum wages, improving health and safety conditions, stopping discrimination, increasing benefits, and assuring job security. *National Educational Media, Bronze Apple* and *U.S. International Film & Video Festival Silver Screen Award*.

2850. **The Orphan Trains**. Videocassette. Color. 60 min. Alexandria, VA: PBS Video, 1995. $59.95. (The American Experience). 9 up

Charles Loring Brace formed the Children's Aid Society to relocate homeless and orphaned children from New York City to the Midwest. More than 150,000 children went to 47 states by train where they went to strange homes. Some were treated like family, and others were abused. This segment of history from 1850 to 1930 reveals both the good and bad of American history.

2851. **Our Federal Government: The Legislative Branch**. Videocassette. Color. 28 min. Raleigh, NC: Rainbow Educational, 1993. $99. ISBN 1-56701-023-7. 5-8

Live action, historical prints, graphics, and documentary footage tell about the creation of the legislative branch and its function as part of the federal government. *Bronze Plaque, Columbus International Film & Video Festival*.

2852. **Our Federal Government: The Presidency**. Videocassette. Color. 23 min. Raleigh, NC: Rainbow Educational, 1993. $89. 5-8

This program gives an overview of the presidency, including its history, constitutional powers, and limitations. Documentary footage highlights the presidencies through that of Bill Clinton.

2853. **Our Federal Government: The Supreme Court**. Videocassette. Color. 22 min. Raleigh, NC: Rainbow Educational, 1993. $99. 5-8

The program gives a historical overview of the Supreme Court, beginning with its constitutional origin. The Court became influential under John Marshall, and the Marbury v. Madison case increased the Court's influence on American life. Other cases and information about the Court's decisions also appear.

P

2854. **Patrick Henry's Fight for Individual Rights**. Videocassette. Color. 29 min. Chicago: Encyclopaedia Britannica, 1990. $260. 4 up

Reenactments on location at historic sites throughout Virginia, along with historic photographs, show Patrick Henry from his birth in 1736 through his terms as governor of the state and his belief that Americans should have individual rights to protect them from a strong federal government.

2855. **Patton, A Genius for War**. Videocassette. Color. 100 min. ABC News and A&E Television. Distr., New York: New Video Group, 1995. $19.95. (Biography). 9 up

Patton and his men were responsible for liberating or capturing 81,000 square miles of enemy territory, capturing 1.25 million prisoners, and killing or wounding 500,000 of the enemy during World War II. Patton thought that he was a warrior from the past reincarnated, but the video also shows his faults as it looks at the man with narration and archival photos.

2856. **Paul Revere: The Midnight Rider**. Videocassette. Color. 50 min. ABC News and A&E Television. Distr., New York: New Video Group, 1996. $19.99. (Biography). 10 up

The real story of Paul Revere through the eyes of biographers and historians shows Revere's apprenticeship, his marriages, his membership in the Sons of Liberty, his political cartoons, and his activity in the revolutionary underground. Although not exciting, the video carefully traces Revere's life and his success after the war.

2857. **Pearl Harbor to Midway**. Videocassette. Color and B&W. 45 min. Bethesda, MD: Acorn Media, 1989. $19.95. (V for Victory). 7 up

Selected newsreels of the actual World War II battle begins with Japan's surprise attack on Pearl Harbor followed by the change from a peace time to a war time economy. The Flying Tigers and Doolittle's air raid precede the great naval battle off Midway Island.

2858. **The Peyote Road**. Videocassette. Color. 60 min. Kifaru, PeachDream, and The Native American Religious Freedom Project. Distr., San Francisco: Kifaru, 1993. $125. ISBN 1-880993-02-3. 9 up

This program documents the conflict of the U.S. Supreme Court with Native American Indian religious liberties. In 1990, the Court denied Native Americans the right to use peyote in sacred ceremonies. The Native Americans belief that this Europeanization of their faith is an attack on First Amendment rights for freedom of religion. *Council on Nontheatrical Events, Golden Eagle; Silver Apple, New England Film & Video Festival; Best of the Fest, Chicago International Film Festival.*

2859. **The Pilgrims' Story**. 2 Videocassettes. Color. 15.40-18.50 min. Huntsville, TX: Educational Video Network, 1995. $79.95 set; $49.95 ea. 6-12

The English Separatists first sought refuge in Holland and then in America, because they wanted freedom of worship. In the New World, they created a new life for themselves as they practiced their chosen religion.

2860. **Pirates: Passion and Plunder**. 2 Videocassettes. 2 hrs. New York: Questar, 1995. $39.95. ISBN 1-56855-065-0. 7 up

Two cassettes cover the *Pirates of the Old World: 400 BC-1575 AD* and *Pirates of the New World: 1575-1810 AD*. In the Old World, subjects include Greek myths and pirates; the first identifiable pirate, Queen Teuta of Yugoslavia; Ramses II of Egypt's attempts to stop piracy; Julius Caesar; the Vikings; the Barbary Corsairs; the Barbarosa brothers; Sir Francis Drake; Sir Walter Raleigh; Sir Henry Morgan; Pierre LeGrand; and Lolonais. Part II presents Captain William Kidd, Bloody Morgan, Spanish galleons, Blackbeard (Edward Teach), Mary Read, Anne Bonny, Calico Jack Rackham, Black Bart (Bartholomew Roberts), and Nathaniel Gordon. Some pirates were robbers while governments licensed others to "steal" for them.

2861. **Placer Gold**. Videocassette. Color. 11 min. Irwindale, CA: Barr Media, 1992. $60. (American History). 4-9

Live action, reenactments, maps, and graphics help tell the story of the life of miners during the California Gold Rush.

2862. **The Poet and the Rough Rider**. Videocassette. Color. 45 min. Walnut Creek, CA: SunWest Media, 1995. $19.95. 7 up

This is the dramatic creation of the three days that Teddy Roosevelt and John Muir spent in Yosemite National Park in California in 1903.

2863. **Polish Americans**. Videocassette. Color. 30 min. Schlessinger Video. Distr., Bala Cynwyd, PA: Library Video, 1993. $39.95. (Multicultural Peoples of North America). 4-10

Based on the Chelsea House series Peoples of North America, the video highlights the Polish culture. It gives reasons for the Polish immigration to America, explanations of customs and traditions, the history of their transition, and important leaders from the culture. Historians and sociologists discuss these aspects, and a Polish family explains its cultural identity, shared memories, and reasons for immigration.

2864. **Pony Express**. Videocassette. Color. 12 min. Irwindale, CA: Barr Media, 1992. $60. (American History). 4-9

Live action, reenactments, maps, and graphics explain the route of the riders on the Pony Express, the horses, and the equipment.

2865. **Post War U.S.A.** Videocassette. Color. 30 min. Schlessinger Video. Distr., Bala Cynwyd, PA: Library Video, 1995. $799 series; $39.95 ea. (United States History Video). 5-9

Dramatic readings and performances bring important events and historical figures together in this video.

2866. **The Potawatomi**. Videocassette. Color. 30 min. Schlessinger Video. Distr., Bala Cynwyd, PA: Library Video, 1994. $39.95. (Indians of North America). 4-10

The Potawatomi lived in the Midwest in the seventeenth and eighteenth centuries but migrated to Oklahoma, Kansas, Michigan, and Ontario. The video focuses on the unique history of the Potawatomi using photographs and film footage. The video also discusses the government, the spiritual, the mythical, and the role of women.

2867. **Prairie Cabin: A Norwegian Pioneer Woman's Story**. Videocassette. Color. 17 min. Madison, WI: Her Own Words, 1991. $95. 4-12

Color slides dissolving one into another enhance this first-person narrative. The video covers the life of a fictitious Norwegian woman who came to the American prairie in the mid-nineteenth century. Views of the cabin, household items, food, and the land, along with Norwegian Christmas customs transported to this New World, create an understanding of the immigrant's condition. The Norwegian singing in the background underscores the memories of home that the protagonist carries.

2868. **Prejudice: Monster Within**. Videocassette. Color. 30 min. Madison, WI: Knowledge Unlimited, 1995. $59.99. ISBN 1-55933-194-1. 5-9

The video examines prejudice against African Americans, Native Americans, and Japanese Americans during World War I, the Holocaust, and Bosnia. It uses news clips and insights that will help students to follow the topic.

2869. **Presenting Mr. Frederick Douglass**. Videocassette. Color. 60 min. Princeton, NJ: Films for the Humanities and Sciences, 1990. $149. (Against the Odds). 4 up

This theatrical performance features Fred Morsell as he dramatically recreates Douglass's famous speech on slavery and human rights. It was filmed in Washington, D.C., at the A.M.E. Church where Douglass delivered his last speech, "The Lesson of the Hour."

2870. **Pride & Prejudice: A History of Black Culture in America**. Videocassette. Color. 28 min. Madison, WI: Knowledge Unlimited, 1994. $55. ISBN 1-55933-150-X. 7 up

The video presents various problems and challenges that African Americans have faced in developing their own cultural practices throughout American history, especially with the rich diversity of views and artistic styles that African Americans demonstrate.

2871. **Progressive Movement**. Videocassette. Color. 30 min. Schlessinger Video. Distr., Bala Cynwyd, PA: Library Video, 1995. $799 series; $39.95 ea. (United States History Video). 5-9

In the second half of the nineteenth century, politics and economics began to change. Dramatic readings and performances bring important events and historical figures together in this video.

2872. **Public Sculpture: America's Legacy**. Videocassette. Color. 28.25 min. National Museum of American Art, Smithsonian. Distr., Glenview, IL: Crystal, 1994. $85. (America Past and Present). 7 up

In addition to the video, this package comes with slides and art repoductions. It is an interdisciplinary program combining American history with art by showing many American sculptures and commenting on their role in preserving and honoring our history. Included are men and women of several ethnic backgrounds.

2873. **Pueblo**. Videocassette. Color. 30 min. Schlessinger Video. Distr., Bala Cynwyd, PA: Library Video, 1994. $39.95. (Indians of North America). 4-10

The video focuses on the unique history of the Pueblo Indians using photographs and film footage. It also discusses the government, the spiritual, the mythical, and the role of women in the tribe.

2874. **Puerto Ricans**. Videocassette. Color. 30 min. Schlessinger Video. Distr., Bala Cynwyd, PA: Library Video, 1993. $39.95. (Multicultural Peoples of North America). 4-10

Based on the Chelsea House series Peoples of North America, the video highlights the Puerto Rican culture. It gives reasons for the Puerto Rican immigration to America, explanations of customs and traditions, the history of their transition, and important leaders from the culture. Historians and sociologists discuss these aspects, and a Puerto Rican family explains its cultural identity, shared memories, and reasons for immigration.

R

2875. **Race to Freedom: The Story of the Underground Railroad**. Videocassette. Color. 90 min. Grozvenor Park LII. Distr., Santa Monica, CA: Xenon Home Video, 1995. $79.95. 9 up

With the passage of the Fugitive Slave Act in 1850, slaves could no longer escape into "free states" to gain their freedom; they had to travel to Canada. This video drama tells of four slaves who escaped from North Carolina through the terror of capture with Harriet Tubman.

2876. **Railroads on the Frontier**. Videocassette. Color. 24 min. Irwindale, CA: Barr Media, 1992. $75. (American Frontier). 4-9

The railroads ran in the East and the West before they crossed the continent. They were important in the development of the frontier.

2877. **The Rails to Hell . . . and Back**. Videocassette. Color. 62 min. Remembrance Educational Media. Distr., Van Nuys, CA: Aims Media, 1990. $99.95. 7 up

This program features David Bergman, a survivor of the Holocaust. Bergman sits at a table with a male interviewer who asks him questions about his experience at 12 of being deported with his family to Czechoslovakia and being the only one of his family to survive. Supplemented with black-and-white photographs and Holocaust art, the experience becomes immediate for the viewer.

2878. **Raisin' Cane**. 2 Videocassettes. Color. 65 min ea. Del Valle, TX: Garfield Video, 1995. $24.95 ea. (Adventures in Archaeology). 7 up

The two videos, *Plantation Life in Early Texas* and *In Pursuit of the Past*, focus on the finds at the excavation of a major Texas antebellum site, the Abner Jackson sugar and cotton plantation. Interviews with historians, plantation descendants, anthropologists, and others help to recreate the time during which plantation life flourished.

2879. **Ranch Album**. Videocassette. Color. 60 min. Bethesda, MD: Acorn Media, 1992. $79.80 set; $19.95 ea. (Great West Collection). 7 up

Exciting photography, good narration, and western music underlie this part of the series on cowboys in the American West. This video follows the year on a ranch and presents the cowboys and their wives discussing what they do and what they think and feel about it.

2880. **Rancho Life**. Videocassette. Color. 21 min. Irwindale, CA: Barr Media, 1992. $60. (American History). 4-9

Live action, reenactments, maps, and graphics help tell the story of pioneer life for Spanish rancheros.

2881. **Reading Terminal Market**. Videocassette. Color. 28 min. Falls Church, VA: Landmark Media, 1993. $225. 6 up

This documentary tribute with personal narrative, vintage film, and photographs identifies Philadelphia's Reading Terminal Market and shows how it has contributed to the history of commerce in America.

2882. **The Real Stories of Al Capone, John Dillinger, Bonnie and Clyde**. Videocassette. Color. 75 min. Chicago: Questar Video, 1994. $29.95. ISBN 1-56855-030-8. 7 up

In the 1920s, several figures gained reputations that set them apart as notorious criminals. Rare photographs and black-and-white archival footage show the time as well as the people.

2883. **The Rebel Slave**. Videocassette. Color. 24 min. Princeton, NJ: Films for the Humanities and Sciences, 1989. $34.95. 3 up

A young slave during the Battle of Gettysburg has to free himself in many ways before he can be truly free. *Silver Award, Houston Film Festival.*

2884. **Reconstruction and Segregation (1870-1910)**. Videocassette. Color. 30 min. Schlessinger Video. Distr., Bala Cynwyd, PA: Library Video, 1995. $799 series; $39.95 ea. (United States History Video). 5-9

Dramatic readings and performances bring important events and historical figures together in this video.

2885. **The Reindeer Queen: The Story of Alaska's Sinrock Mary**. Videocassette. Color. 28 min. New York: Filmakers Library, 1992. $295. 9 up

Sinrock Mary, an Alaskan Eskimo, brought the first reindeer from Siberia to Alaska in the 1880s. She was a descendant of Sacagawea, the woman who accompanied Lewis and Clark on their western expedition. Old film footage and interviews with Mary's grandchildren tell about this noted businesswoman at the end of the nineteenth century. *National Educational Film & Video Festival, Gold Apple; Council on Nontheatrical Events, Golden Eagle; Athens International Film Festival, Best in Category; Margaret Mead Film Festival.*

2886. **Remembering Pearl Harbor**. Videocassette. Color. 50 min. Bethesda, MD: Atlas Video, 1991. $99.95 set; $19.95 ea. (War Stories). 7 up

On-camera interviews with veterans make this series on World War II especially human. In this video, one veteran remembers seeing the first Japanese planes and another heard the explosion of the *Arizona*.

2887. **The Revolutionary War Series**. 3 Videocassettes. Color. 90 min. Bethesda, MD: Discovery Channel Video, 1996. $49.95. ISBN 1-56331-348-0. 7 up

The three videos in this series are titled *Birth of a Nation*, *Victory or Death*, and *The Climactic Battle*. They give a clear analysis of the Revolutionary War with battle reenactments and historical detail. Primary sources such as newspapers, cartoons, and writings integrate into the video under the narration of Charles Kuralt.

2888. **Riding the Rails**. Videocassette. Color. 30 min. Skyfire. Distr., Barrington, IL: Superior Promotions, 1994. $19.95. 7 up

A brief history of steam engines and their use by the railroad industry provides an introduction to this video, which continues with information about oil and coal-fired engines. The program gives an insight into transportation across the United States between the 1930s and the 1950s.

2889. **Roberto Clemente**. Videocassette. Color. 30 min. Schlessinger Video. Distr., Bala Cynwyd, PA: Library Video, 1994. $39.95. ISBN 1-57225-028-3. (Hispanic and Latin American Heritage). 7-12

Biographical information and an overview of Roberto Clemente's achievements according to various experts help to establish the contributions he made as an Hispanic hero.

2890. **Roe v. Wade: The Debate Continues**. Videocassette. Color. 17 min. Educational Enrichment Materials. Distr., Chicago: American School Publishers, 1990. $57. 7 up

This video traces the history of the abortion issue in the United States. It discusses the relationship of the case with the birth control controversy early in the twentieth century and with the women's movement of the sixties and seventies. But it also presents the different public policies in other countries.

2891. **The Role of the First Lady**. Videocassette. Color. 26 min. Princeton, NJ: Films for the Humanities and Sciences, 1995. $89.95. 7 up

Presidents' wives have played varying roles, and the public has perceived these roles differently.

$$\boxed{\textbf{S}}$$

2892. **Sacajawea**. Videocassette. Color. 24 min. Princeton, NJ: Films for the Humanities and Sciences, 1989. $34.95. 3-8

Much of the success of Lewis and Clark's expedition to the Pacific Coast in 1805 rested with Sacajawea, their Indian guide. She translated for them and helped them get safe passage through several stretches of land. From her point of view, she tells of the group's challenges, their struggle to survive, the Missouri River crossing, wild animals, and other discoveries. *Emmy Award; Freedom Foundation Award; Council on Nontheatrical Events, Golden Eagle; Columbus International Film Festival Award.*

2893. **Samuel Morse: The Telegraph**. Videocassette. Color. 24 min. Irwindale, CA: Barr Media, 1989. $50. 7-9

This video gives an animated presentation on Samuel Morse and his inventions, including the telegraph.

2894. **The San Patricios: The Tragic Story of the St. Patrick's Battalion**. Videocassette. Color. 49 min. Day Productions. Distr., Alta Vista, CA: San Patricio, 1996. $79.95. 7 up

In the 1800s, some of the Irish immigrants in the U.S. Army deserted and joined the Mexican forces. The immigrants had come to escape the Potato Famine and have a chance to practice their own religion. They found prejudices in the U.S. Army, and they decided to join the Mexican Catholics, calling themselves the St. Patrick Battalion. Mexico and Ireland still treat them as heroes.

2895. **The Satellite Sky**. Videocassette. Color. 58 min. WGBH, WNET, and KCET. Distr., Alexandria,VA: PBS Video, 1991. $59.95. (The American Experience). 9 up

A historical view of all the satellites that have been sent into orbit since the space race began in the 1950s are discussed here. Interviews indicate the sense of fear that the Soviets would win such a race.

2896. **The Search for the First Americans**. Videocassette. Color. 60 min. BBC-TV and WBGH. Distr., Princeton, NJ: Films for the Humanities and Sciences, 1993. $149. (NOVA/WBGH Collection). 9 up

The first signs of humans in the Americas appeared 12,000 years ago, but researchers have discovered that although today's 50 million Native Americans speak more than 600 languages, they have a common ancestry with the Chinese and Japanese. Like the Asians, they have incisor tooth shapes that are scooped and shoveled rather than broad and flat, an outcome that is consistent with the theory that Native Americans came over the Bering Strait during the Ice Age more than 50,000 years ago.

2897. **The Second World War**. 2 Videocassettes. Color. 3 hrs. Repa Film. Distr., Ft. Lauderdale, FL: No-Bull, 1994. $89.95 set. 9 up

This unique view of World War II consists of film footage collected from combat photographers who represented the United States, Germany, Spain, Japan, England, Canada, the Soviet Union, and France. All of the main conflicts appear here with a balanced view of the action.

2898. **The Second World War**. Videocassette. Color. 30 min. WGBH Educational Foundation. Distr., Washington, DC: Annenberg/CPB, 1989. $650 set; $29.95 ea. (The Western Tradition, Program 48). 11 up

The professor presenting this topic projects his excitement for history. He provides insight into the people, politics, thoughts, and events that have shaped western society. Resources from the Metropolitan Museum of Art illustrate the prolongation of the First World War into a Second World War and more destruction.

2899. **Secrets of Little Bighorn**. Videocassette. Color. 28 min. Princeton, NJ: Films for the Humanities and Sciences, 1993. $149. 7 up

This intriguing film presents the findings of archaeologists who went to the battlefield at Little Bighorn; found artifacts including bullets, fragments of bone, and buttons; and had computers track the weapons. They rewrote the history of the battle and of Custer by showing that the battle was short with the Native Americans winning the entire time. Custer most likely was an opportunist who chose the wrong opportunity.

2900. **Seeds of Liberty: The Causes of the American Revolution**. Videocassette. Color. 22 min. Video Dialog. Distr., Raleigh, NC: Rainbow Educational, 1993. $89. 5-8

Giving special attention to the period between 1754 and 1767, the video discusses social, economic, and political changes. The topics presented include the French and Indian War, Pontiac, the Proclamation of 1763, the Sugar Act, Parliament, Sam Adams, the Quartering Act, the Stamp Act, Patrick Henry, Virginia Resolves, the Sons of Liberty, Lord North, the Boston Massacre, and Benjamin Franklin.

2901. **The Sellin' of Jamie Thomas**. 2 Videocassettes. Color. 24 min ea. Princeton, NJ: Films for the Humanities and Sciences, 1987. $34.95 ea. 3 up

Jamie Thomas, 11, and his parents are separated when the plantation owner sells all of his slaves. They manage to reunite and begin the flight to freedom. A farmer discovers them, and they struggle to adjust to life in a Quaker town. Jamie attends school for the first time, and his father works until a bounty hunter tries to take them. *Winner, Chicago International Film Festival.*

2902. **The Seminole**. Videocassette. Color. 30 min. Schlessinger Video. Distr., Bala Cynwyd, PA: Library Video, 1993. $39.95. (Indians of North America). 4-10

This video tells the history and culture of the Seminole prior to the arrival of the Europeans and the Spanish conquest. Using photographs and film footage, it focuses on the unique history of the Seminole, who kept the U.S. government from relocating them as they hid in the Florida Everglades. It also discusses the government, the spiritual, the mythical, and the role of women.

2903. **The Sensational Seventies**. 10 Videocassettes. Color. 48 min ea. New York: Cinema Guild, 1993. $2,000 series; $250 ea. 9 up

With a time code always on the screen, these 10 videos recount the events that occurred during the 1970s. The overview includes political, global, domestic, and sports events.

2904. **Settlers of the West**. Videocassette. Color. 26 min. Irwindale, CA: Barr Media, 1992. $75. (American Frontier). 4-9

Some of those who went west were able to establish a life. Others were not so fortunate. This video discusses Juan Cabrillo, the Spanish discoverer of California in 1542; the Donner party's difficulties on Donner Pass; and other settlers.

2905. **The Shakers**. Videocassette. Color. 47 min. Princeton, NJ: Films for the Humanities and Sciences, 1994. $149. 7 up

The Shaker movement originated in eighteenth-century France and England before its arrival in America in 1774. By 1826, 18 Shaker communities existed in eight eastern states. The Civil War and the decline of revivalism depleted the Shaker numbers, and very few remain. Another reason for the decline is that Shakers were celibate.

2906. **Sisters and Friends**. Videocassette. Color and B&W. 15 min. Madison, WI: Her Own Words, 1994. $95. ISBN 1-877933-46-5. 7 up

Although this video features contemporary women, the topic is ageless since the relationships among women have remained ones of strong friendship and respect for the traditions of their ancestors. Taped conversations along with old black-and-white photographs and color slides reveal childhood experiences, traditional songs, and changes in nature.

2907. **The Sky's the Limit**. Videocassette. Color. 13 min. Old Dog Productions. Distr., Niles, IL: United Learning, 1995. $95. 4-10

This program presents highlights of women in aviation, including Harriett Quimby, Bessie Coleman, and Amelia Earhart.

2908. **Slavery and Freedom**. Videocassette. Color. 30 min. Schlessinger Video. Distr., Bala Cynwyd, PA: Library Video, 1995. $799 series; $39.95 ea. (United States History Video). 5-9

Dramatic readings and performances bring important events and historical figures together in this video.

2909. **Slavery and the Road to Freedom**. Film. Color. 22 min. Advanced American Communication. Distr., Irwindale, CA: Barr Media, 1995. $395. 7 up

When an African American teenager begins to work on a history paper, the opinions about slavery from those who lived it makes the time become real. The teen realizes that similiar attitudes still exist. *Worldfest-Houston Gold.*

2910. **Smithsonian's Great Battles of the Civil War Vols. I-VII**. 7 Videocassettes. Color. 9 hrs. Smithsonian Institute and MasterVision. Distr., New York: Mastervision, 1993. $29.95 ea. 9 up

Live-action scenes show the major campaigns of the Civil War as well as lesser-known battles. Prominent historians explain the action while historic photographs, paintings, period music, artifacts, and maps illustrate their points in this thorough representation of the war.

2911. **Sojourner Truth**. Videocassette. Color. 30 min. Schlessinger Video. Distr., Bala Cynwyd, PA: Library Video, 1992. $39.95. (Black Americans of Achievement). 7 up

A complement to the Chelsea House series Black Americans of Achievement, the video introduces Sojourner Truth (1797-1883). Historians and other experts comment on her achievements using photos, old film footage, and modern live action for illustration.

2912. **Southern Justice: The Murder of Medgar Evers**. Videocassette. Color. 60 min. HBO. Distr., New York: Ambrose Video, 1995. $99.95. 12 up

This video tells about 30 years of civil rights history and the changes in Southern justice. It begins with the events that motivated Medgar Evers to take a leadership role in this movement and ends with Byron de la Beckwith's conviction three decades later for murdering Evers.

2913. **The Southwest of Georgia O'Keeffe**. Videocassette. Color. 10 min. Cos Cob, CT: Double Diamond, 1995. $29. 7 up

Georgia O'Keeffe spent much of her life in the Southwest and painted the landscapes and natural creations around her. This video looks at her life and her vision.

2914. **Spinning Wheel**. Videocassette. Color. 11 min. Irwindale, CA: Barr Media, 1992. $60. (American History). 4-9

Live action, reenactments, maps, and graphics explain the process of spinning from rough wool to smooth thread.

2915. **The Spirit of Pioneer Women**. Videocassette. Color. 27 min. Springfield, MO: Southwest Missouri State, 1994. $35. 7 up

Photographs help to underscore the difficult lives of women who were unprepared for the harsh pioneer life where washing clothes could take several days. They had no one to help them solve problems, but they survived.

2916. **Spy in the Sky: Story of U2 Spy Plane**. Videocassette. Color. 60 min. Alexandria, VA: PBS Video, 1996. $19.99. (American Experience). 9 up

In addition to the story of Francis Gary Powers is an account of the Cold War years between 1950 and 1960. The video describes the tensions between the United States and the Soviet Union, the development of the training of the CIA pilots, and the effect of *Sputnik*. Interviews with a variety of people closely associated with the situation, news reports, and other pertinent information show how serious the Cold War was during that period.

2917. **Stagecoach West**. Videocassette. Color. 13 min. Irwindale, CA: Barr Media, 1992. $60. (American History). 4-9

Live action, reenactments, maps, and graphics explain the life and times of stagecoach drivers and travelers.

2918. **Strangers in Their Own Land**. Videocassette. Color. 50 min. Gardena, CA: Professional Media Service, 1993. $79.95. 9 up

Narration, historic photographs, interviews, and live action all give an idea of what being a Native American means to a people whose past is inherent in its present. Filmed for the first time are a Kiowa black legging ceremony and a traditional wedding ceremony. Among those featured are a medicine man, a Kickapoo woman who speaks no English, Wilma Mankiller as chief of the Cherokee Nation, a physician practicing modern medicine, and a Persian Gulf War veteran honored as a warrior.

2919. **Submarine: Steel Boats, Iron Men**. Videocassette. Color. 58 min. West Long Branch, NJ: White Star 1989. $99.95. 9 up

An unusual look at a submarine comes when the film crew joins a submarine patrol and roams past the helm of the USS *Hyman G. Rickover*. Interspersed with the tour is footage from the World War I U-boats and interviews with retired navy officers about their roles in submarine warfare.

2920. **The Sunrise Dance**. Videocassette. Color. 28 min. New York: Filmakers Library, 1995. $295. 9-12

This documentary shows an ancient Apache coming-of-age ceremony not previously filmed. The ritual of the 13-year-old girl lasts three days and reaffirms her tribal identity and celebrates the role of women in the Apache society.

2921. **Super Chief: The Life and Legacy of Earl Warren**. Videocassette. Color. 33 min. Santa Monica, CA: Direct Cinema, 1990. $195. 7 up

In 1952, the governor of California, Earl Warren, made a deal with General Eisenhower that he would support his presidency if Eisenhower would appoint him to the Supreme Court. Warren became chief justice of a court that he had to mold into a cohesive body. He believed that every human should have a vote and that segregation kept people unequal. He also believed that the accused should have protection from police bullying with Miranda rights.

2922. **Surviving Columbus**. Videocassette. Color. 115 min. Alexandria, VA: PBS Video, 1993. $89.95. 11 up

The video, using footage shot in the American Southwest, recounts the history of the Pueblo Indian people showing how their lives, customs, and culture changed after the Spanish explorers conquered them during the Age of Discovery. Coronado left behind destruction when he met the Pueblo people and failed to find gold between 1539 and 1541. The Spanish colonized the Pueblo from 1598 to 1680.

2923. **Susan B. Anthony**. Videocassette. Color. 30 min. Schlessinger Video. Distr., Bala Cynwyd, PA: Library Video, 1995. $39.95. ISBN 1-57225-039-9. (American Women of Achievement). 7-12

The video asks why Susan B. Anthony (1820-1906) resisted conformity and if she could be considered a "rebel" as she helped shape the history and culture of the United States. Archival footage, sketches, photographs, recordings, interviews with historians, literary experts, and reenactments help to examine the impact of family; economic, social, and political circumstances; and her ability to empower herself.

2924. **The Susan B. Anthony Story: The Women's Suffrage Movement**. Videocassette. Color. 40 min. Richardson, TX: Grace Products, 1994. $89. (In Search of the Heroes). 5-12

Live-action footage of an encounter between a modern girl and Susan B. Anthony helps the girl see that if one dislikes the conditions in which one lives, one can refuse to live by the current rules and try to do something to change them. The historical footage about the suffragettes shows the girl that, because someone else struggled in the past, she has rights that she would not otherwise have had. *U.S. International Film & Video Festival Gold Camera; New York Festivals Finalist;* and *Telly Bronze Statuette.*

T

2925. **Tarawa and the Island War**. Videocassette. Color and B&W. 45 min. Bethesda, MD: Acorn Media, 1989. $19.95. (V for Victory). 7 up

Using newsreel footage and stories from the home front, this program on World War II presents the battles of Tarawa, Saipan, Guam, and Leyte Gulf in the Pacific area.

2926. **The Technological Revolution**. Videocassette. Color. 30 min. WGBH Educational Foundation. Distr., Washington, DC: Annenberg/CPB, 1989. $650 set; $29.95 ea. (The Western Tradition, Program 51). 11 up

The professor presenting this topic projects his excitement for history. He provides insight into the people, politics, thoughts, and events that have shaped western society. Resources from the Metropolitan Museum of Art illustrate the enormous change in life that computers and television created during the twentieth century.

2927. **Thieves of Time**. Videocassette. Color. 27 min. KAET. Distr., Alexandria, VA: PBS Video, 1993. $49.95. 9 up

The narration of Tony Hillerman underscores the shame in which America has engaged while digging up the remains of Native American burial sites and keeping the artifacts. The government underwrote grave robbing in the 1800s and displayed the artifacts in museums. Even Ford Motor Company advertisements encouraged this behavior. Finally, reparation laws require that the families of Native Americans should receive these skeletal remains of their ancestors.

2928. **This House of Power: A Tribute to the Role of the Church in African-American Experience**. Videocassette. Color. 50 min. Santa Monica, CA: Xenon, 1994. $29.95. 7 up

As part of the Black History series, this video explores how spiritualism, religion, and the Black church have helped to maintain spiritual traditions. It features Martin Luther King, Jr. and Marcus Garvey as church leaders who became political leaders.

2929. **This World Is Not Our Home**. Videocassette. Color. 13 min. Berkeley, CA: University of California Extension Center, 1995. $125. 4-12

A tribal elder of the Pomo tribe in California introduces the history, culture, and traditions of her people.

2930. **Thomas Alva Edison**. Videocassette. Color. 15 min. Princeton, NJ: Films for the Humanities and Sciences, 1988. $29.95. (Against the Odds). 4 up

Thomas Alva Edison (1847-1931) patented more than 1,000 inventions, including the carbon telephone transmitter, the microphone, the phonograph, the incandescent electric lamp, and the forerunner of the motion picture projector.

2931. **Thomas Edison: Electric Light**. Videocassette. Color. 24 min. Irwindale, CA: Barr Media, 1989. $50. 7-9

This animation tells the story of Thomas Edison's research as he tried to develop the electric light.

2932. **Thomas Jefferson: The Pursuit of Liberty**. Videocassette. Color. 40 min. Princeton, NJ: Films for the Humanities and Sciences, 1993. $29.95. 7 up

Modern footage of Monticello, Williamsburg, and Richmond along with period drawings and paintings present the highlights of Jefferson's career as founder of the University of Virginia and third President of the United States.

2933. **Three Worlds Meet (Origins—1620)**. Videocassette. Color. 30 min. Schlessinger Video. Distr., Bala Cynwyd, PA: Library Video, 1995. $799 series; $39.95 ea. (United States History Video). 5-9

Dramatic readings and performances bring important events and historical figures together in this video.

2934. **Through the Rockies**. Videocassette. Color. 28 min. Princeton, NJ: Films for the Humanities and Sciences, 1992. $399 series; $109 ea. (The Oregon Trail). 5 up

Featuring oil paintings, black-and-white artwork, diary excerpts, and narration, this program traces the Oregon Trail from Fort Laramie to Fort Hall, in Idaho. The video explains the problems of trail overcrowding, the dangers of disease such as cholera, various cutoffs and alternate routes, and Mormons on the trail.

2935. **Thurgood Marshall**. Videocassette. Color. 30 min. Schlessinger Video. Distr., Bala Cynwyd, PA: Library Video, 1992. $39.95. (Black Americans of Achievement). 7 up

A complement to the Chelsea House series Black Americans of Achievement, the video introduces Thurgood Marshall (1908-1993). Historians and other experts comment on his achievements using photos, old film footage, and modern live action for illustration.

2936. **A Time Remembered**. Videocassette. Color. 42 min. Van Nuys, CA: Churchill Media, 1994. $99.95. 7-12

After the Japanese bombed Pearl Harbor in 1941, the U.S. government interned more than 100,000 American citizens of Japanese ancestry. This video concentrates on a Japanese American community living on Terminal Island in Los Angeles harbor. Photographs document this sordid scene when people were removed, losing their businesses and their homes forever.

2937.   **The Times and Dreams of Martin Luther King, Jr.** Videocassette. Color. 30 min. N. Billerica, MA: Curriculum Associates, 1995. $69.95. 4-8

Julian Bond leads a discussion with students. He describes life in the segregated South in the 1950s and what it was like to be a friend of Dr. Martin Luther King, Jr. The discussion leads to how Dr. King's perseverance influenced other nations to promote human rights.

2938.   **To Be Somebody.** Videocassette. Color. 60 min. Blackside, Inc. Distr., Alexandria, VA: PBS Video, 1993. $79.95. ISBN 0-7936-1042-7. (The Great Depression). 8 up

Two very different people, heavyweight boxing champion Joe Louis and First Lady Eleanor Roosevelt, challenged America to live up to its promise of justice and opportunity for everybody regardless of race or faith. *Council on Nontheatrical Events, Golden Eagle; Gold Apple, NEFVF.*

2939.   **The Torch Has Been Passed: A History of the Early '60s.** Videocassette. Color. 21 min. Madison, WI: Knowledge Unlimited, 1994. $55. ISBN 1-55933-146-1. 8 up

Headlines, news footage, and archival stills show the events of 1960 to 1965. Among them were the Cuban Missile Crisis, the construction of the Berlin Wall, the Cold War, the Civil Rights movement, the Kennedy assassination, and the Vietnam War protests.

2940.   **Totem Poles: The Stories They Tell.** Videocassette. Color. 14 min. Cos Cob, CT: Double Diamond, 1993. $89. 6-9

The colors and designs in totem poles along the northwest Pacific Coast from Washington State to Alaska tell stories. The video explains some of the messages that the Tlingit, Haida, and Kwakiutl Indians tell in the poles.

2941.   **Touring America's Ghost Towns.** Videocassette. Color. 60 min. Media Process Group. Distr., Chicago: Questar Video, 1992. $29.95. 9 up

Shots of boomtowns as they appear today mixed with old photographs, scenes from old newsreels and movies, and reenactments present the history of these towns that appeared in Nevada, Colorado, Montana, Arizona, and New Mexico. Excesses of gambling, drinking, prostitution, and crimes always occurred as the boom moved from one place to another.

2942.   **Toward the Future.** Videocassette. Color. 30 min. WGBH Educational Foundation. Distr., Washington, DC: Annenberg/CPB, 1989. $650 set; $29.95 ea. (The Western Tradition, Program 52). 11 up

The professor presenting this topic projects his excitement for history. He provides insight into the people, politics, thoughts, and events that have shaped western society. Resources from the Metropolitan Museum of Art illustrate the concerns of the future in world relationships.

2943.   **Tragedy to Triumph: An Adventure with Helen Keller.** Videocassette. Color. 40 min. Richardson, TX: Grace Productions, 1995. $89. 5 up

A cast presents a play about Helen Keller and her achievements and tries to show the importance of understanding and accepting people with physical disabilities.

2944.   **Traveling in Style: Automobiles and Trolleys.** Videocassette. Color. 70 min. Dayton, OH: GHI Media, 1995. $34.95 set; $19.95 ea. (In Times Past). 7 up

In historic photographs and film footage as well as old movies, the history of transportation on trolleys, which allowed people to live further from the middle of cities, and in automobiles from Henry Ford's introduction of the Model T (Tin Lizzie) in 1908 intrigues the viewer.

2945.   **Traveling in Style: Trains, Riverboats, and Planes.** Videocassette. Color. 70 min. Dayton OH: GHI Media, 1995. $34.95 set; $19.95 ea. (In Times Past). 7 up

In historic photographs and film footage as well as old movies, the history of transportation on memorable trains, leisurely riverboats, and planes from the Wright brothers' flight in 1903 through World War I and Lindbergh's flight in 1927 across the Atlantic becomes apparent.

2946.   **Tsiolkovski: The Space Age.** Videocassette. Color. 24 min. Irwindale, CA: Barr Media, 1989. $50. 4-9

This animation explains how Tsiolkovski (1857-1935) conducted the crucial research that led him to the invention of the rocket in 1929.

2947.   **Tuskegee Airmen.** Videocassette. Color. 23 min. WCBS. New York: Carousel, 1992. $200. 7 up

Franklin D. Roosevelt established a training center for "black and brown" airmen in Tuskegee, Alabama. These men who served in World War II decided that they would be the best, and they never lost an escorted pilot in their assignment. After the war, they faced prejudice, but they kept their honor in their careers at home.

2948. **The 20's: From Illusion to Disillusion**. Videocassette. Color. 80 min. Princeton, NJ: Films for Humanities and Science, 1991. $149. 9 up

During the 1920s, from the end of World War I through the stock market crash and worldwide Depression in 1929, many events occurred that affected the political atmosphere of the world. Communism took control in Russia, Mussolini directed fascism in Italy, Germany and the Allies argued over reparations, Ghandhi founded the Indian peace movement, and civil war occurred in China. People began to get electricity in their homes, and the automobile went into mass production. Period films and newsreels relate this information.

U

2949. **Unearthing the Slave Trade**. Videocassette. Color. 26 min. Princeton, NJ: Films for the Humanities and Sciences, 1994. $149. 7 up

A large slave population helped to build New York City where the slaves' movements and freedoms were tightly controlled. Burials were a time when they could meet and practice rituals and customs brought from Africa. When builders unearthed a slave cemetery in New York City, archaeologists found enough to make this a historical landmark in 1993. Maps, newspapers, drawings, contemporary photographs, and footage of the excavation support the content.

2950. **The Unsinkable Delta Queen**. Videocassette. Color. 43 min. Delaney Communications. Distr., Cincinnati, OH: Sentimental, 1989. $24.95. 6 up

The *Delta Queen*, on the Mississippi River, is a working national historical landmark today. A tour of the boat shows its great paddlewheel, calliope, and elegant Victorian furnishings. During World War II, the boat performed duties for the U.S. government.

2951. **U.S. and the World (1865-1917)**. Videocassette. Color. 30 min. Schlessinger Video. Distr., Bala Cynwyd, PA: Library Video, 1995. $799 series; $39.95 ea. (United States History Video). 5-9

Dramatic readings and performances bring important events and historical figures together in this video.

2952. **The U.S.A. vs. "Tokyo Rose."** Videocassette. Color and B&W. 48 min. New York: Cinema Guild, 1995. $295. 9 up

Iva Toguri was visiting relatives in Japan when World War II broke out. She had been born in the United States and spoke perfect English, but she had to stay in Japan. She began using her skills to broadcast messages to Allied troops intended to break their morale. After the war, she was prosecuted for treason. She served six years in prison and President Gerald Ford pardoned her.

2953. **USS Arizona: The Life and Death of a Lady**. Videocassette. Color. 47 min. Encino, CA: Bill Armstrong, 1991. $19.95. 9 up

The video traces the life of the USS *Arizona* from its commissioning in June 1915, to its sinking in 1941 through to the 50th anniversary of Pearl Harbor in 1991. Two men meet for the film: the Japanese man who dropped the first bomb on the ship and an ensign who watched. Interviews with crew members and film clips recreate the scene of December 7, 1941.

V

2954. **Valley Forge: The Battle for Survival**. Videocassette. Color. 23 min. Princeton, NJ: Films for the Humanities and Sciences, 1991. $149. 7 up

In reenactments on location at Valley Forge Park in Pennsylvania, the situation that faced George Washington and his troops in 1777 becomes clear. Ten thousand troops suffered from hunger and cold with 20 percent dying, but they trained enough to defeat the British army. Also addressed are the roles of women and the daily life of the camp inhabitants.

2955. **Vietnam: A Case Study for Critical Thinking**. Videocassette. Color. 52 min. Charleston, WV: Cambridge Educational, 1988. $129.95. 7-12

Two historians offer opposing views on the involvement of the United States in Vietnam. One thinks the United States was wrong to interfere and the other supports the United States and claims that the war should have lasted until victory was declared.

2956. **Vietnam: After the Fire**. 2 Videocassettes. Color. 53 min ea. New York: Cinema Guild, 1989. $395 set; $250 ea. 9 up

More bombs dropped on Vietnam than on Europe during World War II. The program interviews Vietnamese survivors, although with physical and emotional scars, who seem to wonder why no one has helped them since the war's end.

2957. **Votes for Women?!: The 1913 U.S. Senate Testimony**. Videocassette. Color. 17 min. Madison, WI: Her Own Words, 1990. $95. 7 up

The video includes verbatim testimony from both sides as to why women should or should not have the vote. It shows pro- and anti-suffrage buttons, banners, and cartoons from the time.

W

2958. **W. E. B. Du Bois**. Videocassette. Color. 30 min. Schlessinger Video. Distr., Bala Cynwyd, PA: Library Video, 1993. $39.95. (Black Americans of Achievement). 7up

A complement to the Chelsea House series Black Americans of Achievement, the video introduces W. E. B. Du Bois (1868-1963). Historians and other experts comment on his achievements using photos, old film footage, and modern live action for illustration.

2959. **We Shall Overcome: The Song That Moved a Nation**. Videocassette. Color. 58 min. San Francisco: California Newsreel, 1989. $85. 9 up

Scenes in the video that show the social history of the Civil Rights movement include the 1945 Charleston tobacco strike, the 1963 March on Washington, sit-ins, voter registration drives, and other protest marches. This song became the anthem of the movement with folk singers of the sixties adding it to their performances.

2960. **West of Hester Street**. Videocassette. Color. 58 min. Dallas,TX: Media Projects, 1983. $39.95. 9 up

From 1907 to 1914, the influx of East European immigrants made Jewish leaders fearful that the United States would close its doors. They devised a plan for thousands to come through the port of Galveston in Texas. This dramatization shows a boy's journey from Russia into a new life in Texas. *Council on Nontheatrical Events, Golden Eagle.*

2961. **Western Europe: Our Legacy**. Videocassette. Color. 22 min. North Carolina State. Distr., Briarcliff Manor, NY: Benchmark Media, 1994. $395. (World Geography and History). 5-7

Western Europe remains the source for much of the social order and culture in the United States. The ancient Greeks had a democracy, good literature, and philosophy. The Romans had government administration, remnants of our partially Latin-based language, and Catholicism. The Renaissance provided a renewed interest in intellectual, artistic, and economic life. Other legacies were the Industrial Revolution and the influx of immigrants escaping religious and economic difficulties.

2962. **Westward Expansion: The Pioneer Challenge**. Videocassette. Color. 22 min. Raleigh, NC: Rainbow Educational, 1992. $89. 4-8

Live-action photography, maps, and nineteenth-century art enhance this presentation of the geographical influences that both helped and hindered the pioneers attempting to cross the mainland United States. The settlement of Hawaii and Alaska also included concerns about natural resources, natural boundaries, and climate.

2963. **Who Owns History?** Videocassette. Color. 26 min. Princeton, NJ: Films for the Humanities and Sciences, 1995. $89.95. 9 up

Every generation seems to rewrite history in order to make sense of the present. The video wonders if this will have an effect on future generations as they try to make sense of their present through the past.

2964. **Wilma Rudolph**. Videocassette. Color. 30 min. Schlessinger Video. Distr., Bala Cynwyd, PA: Library Video, 1995. $39.95. ISBN 1-57225-045-3. (American Women of Achievement). 7-12

The video asks why Wilma Rudolph (1940-1994) resisted conformity and if she could be considered a "rebel" as she helped shape the history and culture of the United States. Archival footage, sketches, photographs, recordings, interviews with historians, literary experts, and reenactments help to examine the impact of family; economic, social, and political circumstances; and her ability to empower herself.

2965. **Wiping the Tears of Seven Generations**. Videocassette. Color. 58 min. San Francisco: Kifaru, 1992. $29.95. 9 up

The program documents the Lakota Sioux's ceremony to bring its nation out of mourning for the sacred knowledge lost 100 years ago at the Battle of Wounded Knee. It also includes a history of the people through interviews, historical paintings, and photographs, with footage on location. *Silver Medal, New York Festivals.*

2966. **Women: First and Foremost Collector's Box Set**. 3 Videocassettes. Color. 60 min. ea. Monterey Movie. Distr., Agoura, VA: Monterey Home Video, 1995. $69.95 series; $24.95 ea. 9 up

These three videos present the American women who have defied their heritage to achieve a place at the forefront of history.

2967. **Women at War: From the Home Front to the Front Lines**. Videocassette. Color and B&W. 45 min. Bethesda, MD: Acorn Media, 1989. $19.95. (V for Victory). 7 up

With newsreels and stories from home, this program on World War II presents the contributions that women made. Overseas, women served in the WAVES, WACS, and nurse corps. At home, they worked in factories to keep the defense necessities ready.

2968. **Women in Rural America**. Videocassette. Color. 23 min. Niles, IL: United Learning, 1995. $95. 7 up

During the early part of the twentieth century, when more than 50 percent of Americans lived on farms, women helped to support their families and the nation. They canned, sewed, ironed, and cooked. Firsthand accounts and archival footage show these women at work through the post–World War I world when the number of farming families steadily decreased.

2969. **Women of the West**. Videocassette. Color. 28 min. Irwindale, CA: Barr Media, 1992. $75. (American Frontier). 4-9

Women helped keep the West going once people began to settle it. The video offers insights into the contributions of women in this uncivilized area.

2970. **Women of the West**. Videocassette. Color and B&W. 32 min. Chariot Productions. Distr., Niles, IL: United Learning, 1994. $95. ISBN 56007-244-X. 5-9

Women who went west gained freedom that they did not have if they remained at home. They became homesteaders, entertainers, imported brides, military wives, outlaws, militant feminists, and prostitutes. Old photography, live-action recreations, and first-person accounts show that the women came from Asian, African American, Native American, and European descent.

2971. **Women with Wings**. Videocassette. Color. 17 min. Oshkosh, WI: Experimental Aircraft, 1995. $12.95. 6 up

Eight women made contributions to aviation during the twentieth century. They include balloonist Sophie Blanchard, barnstormer Margie Hobbs, record-setter Louise Thalen, astronaut trainee Jerrie Cobb, military pilots Hanna Reitsch and Helen Richey, educator Louise Timken, and businesswoman Olive Ann Beech. The video gives a brief biography of each and her achievements.

2972. **Wonders of Man's Creation**. Videocassette. Color. 60 min. Reader's Digest and International Video Network. Distr., Pleasantville, NY: Reader's Digest, 1993. $25.95. (Great Wonders of the World). 9 up

This series uses live-action photography, archival documentary footage, and animation sequences to reveal some of the human creations that have become monuments of civilization. The featured ones are the Colosseum in Rome, Machu Picchu in Peru, the Great Wall of China, the Kremlin in Moscow, Versailles in France, the Statue of Liberty in New York, and in South Dakota, Mount Rushmore and the Chief Crazy Horse Monument.

2973. **Woodland Tribal Arts: Native American Arts**. Videocassette. Color. 23 min. Greenwich, CT: Double Diamond, 1995. $89. 5 up

By focusing on the artifacts of the Woodland Indian tribes such as the Iroquois and the Algonquin, the video tells their story. Among the artifacts are snowshoes, wampum, pottery, canoes, quill boxes, moccasins, longhouses, masks, and willow baskets. In these early settlements, development caused shifts from clay to iron cooking pots and stone to metal tools. The video gives a good sense of early Native American history.

2974. **The Working Cowboy**. Videocassette. Color. 60 min. Bethesda, MD: Acorn Media, 1992. $79.80 set; $19.95 ea. (Great West Collection). 7 up

Exciting photography, good narration, and western music underlie this part of the series on cowboys in the American West. This video shows a man in search of music who gets inspiration from his cowboy songs by going to ranches and joining cowboys in their work.

2975. **World War I**. Videocassette. Color. 30 min. Schlessinger Video. Distr., Bala Cynwyd, PA: Library Video, 1995. $799 series; $39.95 ea. (United States History Video). 5-9

Dramatic readings and performances bring important events and historical figures together in this video about World War I.

2976. **World War II**. Videocassette. Color. 30 min. Schlessinger Video. Distr., Bala Cynwyd, PA: Library Video, 1995. $799 series; $39.95 ea. (United States History Video). 5-9

Dramatic readings and performances bring the important events and historical figures together in this video about World War II.

2977. **World War Two**. Videocassette. B&W. 30 min. Princeton, NJ: Films for the Humanities and Sciences, 1990. $149. 9 up

All of the highlights of World War II on both the Atlantic and Pacific fronts are telescoped in this video through newsreel footage, from the invasion of Poland in 1939 to the signing of the peace treaty with Japan in 1945.

2978. **The Wright Brothers: How They Invented the Airplane**. Videocassette. Color. 40 min. Chicago: American School Publishers, 1992. $89. 7-9

Stills and vintage aviation footage document the careers and personal relationships of Wilbur and Orville as they worked on their airplane. The video uses Russell Freedman's *The Wright Brothers* as a source.

2979. **The Wright Stuff: Invention of Airplanes**. Videocassette. Color. 60 min. Alexandria, VA: PBS Video, 1996. $59.95. (American Experience). 9 up

This video uses family photographs, archival stills, letters, diaries, family members' comments, and historians' interpretations to tell the story of Orville and Wilbur Wright. Garrison Keillor narrates their story. They almost lost credit for their airplane by taking so long to get a patent for it in 1906.

2980. 2734. **The Yankton Sioux**. Videocassette. Color. 30 min. Schlessinger Video. Distr., Bala Cynwyd, PA: Library Video, 1993. $39.95. (Indians of North America). 4-10

The Yankton Sioux occupy a middle position between the Santee and Teton divisions of the Sioux in South Dakota. This video describes the history and culture of the Yankton Sioux prior to the arrival of the settlers. It focuses on the unique history of the tribe using photographs and film footage. It also discusses the government, the spiritual, the mythical, and the role of women in the tribe.

2981. **Ziveli: Medicine for the Heart**. Videocassette. Color. 51 min. El Cerrito, CA: Flower Films, 1988. $99.95. 7 up

The Serbian American communities began when the first immigrants arrived more than 100 years ago during California's Gold Rush. Much of the Serbian ethnic life appears, including the rituals of the Eastern Orthodox Church and the love of music. *Silver Award, Chicago International Film Festival.*

AUTHOR/ILLUSTRATOR INDEX

Reference is to entry numbers.

TITLE INDEX

Reference is to entry numbers.

SUBJECT INDEX

Reference is to entry numbers.

Abernathy, Ralph David, 1766
Abolitionists, 1818; Fiction, 381;
  African Americans, 2171;
  Time Travel, 1286. *See also*
  Allen, Richard; Brown,
  John; Cuffe, Paul; Douglass,
  Frederick; Terrell, Mary
  Church; Truth, Sojourner;
  Stowe, Harriett Beecher;
  Tubman, Harriet; *and*
  Turner, Nat
Abortion Rights, 828, 960, 2113,
  2233; Video, 2677
Abraham Lincoln Brigade; Video,
  2666
Abzug, Bella, 683
Adams, Abigail, 157, 232, 1613;
  Video, 2521
Adams, Ansel, 493
Adams, Grizzly, 1406
Adams, John, 270, 619, 633, 647,
  2090
  Family, 1865
Adams, John Quincy, 392, 647
Adams, Samuel, 658
Addams, Jane, 1020, 1180, 1397,
  1440, 1920; Video, 2721,
  2745
Adena, 2210
Affirmative Action, 2433
African American Heritage, 671;
  Fiction, 896
African American Women, 153,
  314, 1707; Fiction, 287, 302;
  Video, 2698
  Aviators. *See* Bragg, Janet
    Harmon; *and* Coleman,
    Bessie
  Athletes, 195, 197. *See also*
    Gibson, Althea; Hyman,
    Flo; *and* Rudolph, Wilma
  Authors, 718, 1618, 1771. *See*
    also Angelou, Maya;
    Brooks, Gwendolyn;
    Giovanni, Nikki;
    Hansberry, Lorraine;
    Hurston, Zora Neale;
    Morrison, Toni; *and*
    Wheatley, Phillis

  Musicians and Entertainers,
    1086. *See also* Carroll,
    Diahann; Fitzgerald,
    Ella; Franklin, Aretha;
    Holiday, Billie; Horn,
    Lena; Jackson, Mahalia;
    Price, Leontyne; *and*
    Smith, Bessie
African Americans, 21; Video,
  2527, 2528, 2575, 2633,
  2675
  Artists, 286; Video, 2711; *See*
    also Bearden, Romare;
    Johnson, William H.;
    and Pippin, Horace
  Astronauts, 312, 1683
  Athletes. *See* Ashe, Arthur;
    Louis, Joe; Owens,
    Jesse; Paige, Satchel;
    Robinson, Jackie; *and*
    Woods, Tiger
  Authors, 198. *See also*
    Baldwin, James;
    Chestnutt, Charles
    Waddell; Cullen,
    Countee; Dunbar, Paul
    Laurence; Ellison,
    Ralph; Hughes,
    Langston; *and* Wright,
    Richard
  Aviators and Astronauts, 936.
    See also Bluford, Guion
    S., Jr.; Bolden, Charles
    F., Jr.; Gregory,
    Frederick D; Jemison,
    Dr. Mae C.; and McNair,
    Ronald E.
  Canada, 1043
  Churches; Video, 2928
  Cinema; Video, 2805
  Educators. *See* Bethune, Mary
    McLeod; Du Bois, W. E.
    B.; Forten, Charlotte;
    Johnson, James Weldon;
    and Washington, Booker
    T.
  1804-1860, 2352
  1860-1880, 742
  Explorers, 935

  Family, 2304
  Firsts, 1717, 1769
  History, 905, 1442, 1451, 1541
  Innovators and Inventors;
    Video, 2697, 2786
  Leaders, 2203. *See also*
    Buffalo Soldiers; Davis,
    Benjamin O., Jr.;
    Flipper, Henry O.;
    James, Daniel Chappie;
    and Powell, Colin L.
  Literature and Art, 2139, 2140.
    See also Baldwin, James;
    Chestnutt, Charles
    Waddell; Cullen,
    Countee; Dunbar, Paul
    Laurence; Ellison,
    Ralph; Hughes,
    Langston; *and* Wright,
    Richard
  Music, 931. *See also*
    Armstrong, Louis; Basie,
    Count; Coltrane, John;
    Ellington, Duke;
    Gillespie, Dizzy; Parker,
    Charlie; and Robeson,
    Paul
  1964-1966; Video, 2658
  1964-1972; Video, 2653
  1967-1968; Video, 2656, 2657
  1968-1971; Video, 2652
  1974-1980; Video, 2655
  1979-mid 1980s; Video, 2654
  Scientists, 1773, 2474. *See also*
    Banneker, Benjamin;
    Beckwourth, James;
    Carver, George
    Washington; Chinn,
    May; Henson, Matthew;
    Just, Ernest Everett; *and*
    Latimer, Lewis
Agassiz, Louis, 1407
Ailey, Alvin, Jr., 670, 1296
Alabama, 2403
Alaska, 394; Fiction, 321, 925
Alcott, Louisa May, 308, 1213,
  1337, 1443, 1851
All-American Girls Professional
  Baseball League, 948, 1346